CORE C#
AND .NET

PRENTICE HALL
CORE SERIES

Core J2EE Patterns, Second Edition, Alur/Malks/Crupi

Core PHP Programming, Third Edition, Atkinson/Suraski

Core Lego Mindstorms, Bagnall

Core JSTL, Geary

Core JavaServer Faces, Geary/Horstmann

Core Web Programming, Second Edition, Hall/Brown

Core Servlets and JavaServer Pages, Second Edition,
Hall/Brown

Core Java™ 2, Volume I—Fundamentals,
Horstmann/Cornell

Core Java™ 2, Volume II—Advanced Features,
Horstmann/Cornell

Core C# and .NET, Perry

Core CSS, Second Edition, Schengili-Roberts

Core Security Patterns, Steel/Nagappan/Lai

Core Java Data Objects, Tyagi/Vorburger/
McCammon/Bobzin

***Core Web Application Development with PHP and
MySQL,*** Wandschneider

CORE C# AND .NET

Stephen C. Perry

PRENTICE
HALL
PTR   Prentice Hall Professional Technical Reference
Upper Saddle River, NJ • Boston • Indianapolis • San Francisco
New York • Toronto • Montreal • London • Munich • Paris • Madrid
Capetown • Sydney • Tokyo • Singapore • Mexico City

Many of the designations used by manufacturers and sellers to distinguish their products are claimed as trademarks. Where those designations appear in this book, and the publisher was aware of a trademark claim, the designations have been printed with initial capital letters or in all capitals.

The author and publisher have taken care in the preparation of this book, but make no expressed or implied warranty of any kind and assume no responsibility for errors or omissions. No liability is assumed for incidental or consequential damages in connection with or arising out of the use of the information or programs contained herein.

The publisher offers excellent discounts on this book when ordered in quantity for bulk purchases or special sales, which may include electronic versions and/or custom covers and content particular to your business, training goals, marketing focus, and branding interests. For more information, please contact:

U. S. Corporate and Government Sales
(800) 382-3419
corpsales@pearsontechgroup.com

For sales outside the U. S., please contact:

International Sales
international@pearsoned.com

Visit us on the Web: www.phptr.com

Library of Congress Cataloging-in-Publication Data

Perry, Stephen (Stephen C.)
  Core C# and .NET / Stephen Perry.
     p. cm.
  ISBN 0-13-147227-5
  1. C++ (Computer program language) 2. Microsoft .NET. I. Title.
  QA76.73.C153P468 2005
  005.13'3--dc22

                                        2005021301

ISBN 0-13-147227-5

Text printed in the United States on recycled paper at R. R. Donnelley in Crawfordsville, Indiana.

First printing, September 2005

Contents

ABOUT THE AUTHOR   XXIII
FOREWORD   XXV
PREFACE   XXVII
ACKNOWLEDGMENTS   XXX

PART I
FUNDAMENTALS OF C# PROGRAMMING AND INTRODUCTION TO .NET   2

CHAPTER 1
INTRODUCTION TO .NET AND C#   4

1.1   Overview of the .NET Framework   6

Microsoft .NET and the CLI Standards   7

1.2   Common Language Runtime   9

Compiling .NET Code   10

Common Type System   11

Assemblies   13

1.3   Framework Class Library   18

1.4 Working with the .NET Framework and SDK   22
   Updating the .NET Framework   23
   .NET Framework Tools   23
   Ildasm.exe   25
   wincv.exe   28
   Framework Configuration Tool   29
1.5 Understanding the C# Compiler   31
   Locating the Compiler   31
   Compiling from the Command Line   32
1.6 Summary   35
1.7 Test Your Understanding   36

CHAPTER 2
C# LANGUAGE FUNDAMENTALS   38
2.1 The Layout of a C# Program   40
   General C# Programming Notes   42
2.2 Primitives   45
   decimal   47
   bool   47
   char   48
   byte, sbyte   48
   short, int, long   48
   single, double   49
   Using Parse and TryParse to Convert a Numeric String   49
2.3 Operators: Arithmetic, Logical, and Conditional   50
   Arithmetic Operators   50
   Conditional and Relational Operators   51
   Control Flow Statements   52
   if-else   53
   switch   54
2.4 Loops   55
   while loop   55

do loop   56

for loop   56

foreach loop   57

Transferring Control Within a Loop   58

2.5   C# Preprocessing Directives   59

Conditional Compilation   60

Diagnostic Directives   60

Code Regions   61

2.6   Strings   61

String Literals   61

String Manipulation   63

2.7   Enumerated Types   66

Working with Enumerations   66

System.Enum Methods   68

Enums and Bit Flags   69

2.8   Arrays   69

Declaring and Creating an Array   70

Using System.Array Methods and Properties   71

2.9   Reference and Value Types   73

System.Object and System.ValueType   73

Memory Allocation for Reference and Value Types   74

Boxing   75

Summary of Value and Reference Type Differences   77

2.10   Summary   78

2.11   Test Your Understanding   78

CHAPTER 3
CLASS DESIGN IN C#   80

3.1   Introduction to a C# Class   82

3.2   Defining a Class   82

Attributes   83

Access Modifiers   85

Abstract, Sealed, and Static Modifiers   86

Class Identifier   86

Base Classes, Interfaces, and Inheritance   87

3.3   Overview of Class Members   88

Member Access Modifiers   89

3.4   Constants, Fields, and Properties   89

Constants   89

Fields   91

Properties   93

Indexers   95

3.5   Methods   97

Method Modifiers   98

Passing Parameters   103

3.6   Constructors   106

Instance Constructor   106

Private Constructor   110

Static Constructor   111

3.7   Delegates and Events   112

Delegates   113

Delegate-Based Event Handling   115

3.8   Operator Overloading   123

3.9   Interfaces   126

Creating and Using a Custom Interface   127

Working with Interfaces   129

3.10   Generics   131

3.11   Structures   134

Defining Structures   134

Using Methods and Properties with a Structure   136

3.12   Structure Versus Class   137

Structures Are Value Types and Classes Are Reference Types   138

Unlike a Class, a Structure Cannot Be Inherited   138

General Rules for Choosing Between a Structure and a Class   139

3.13　Summary　139

3.14　Test Your Understanding　140

CHAPTER 4
WORKING WITH OBJECTS IN C#　144

4.1　Object Creation　145

　　　Example: Creating Objects with Multiple Factories　148

4.2　Exception Handling　149

　　　System.Exception Class　150

　　　Writing Code to Handle Exceptions　151

　　　Example: Handling Common SystemException Exceptions　153

　　　How to Create a Custom Exception Class　155

　　　Unhandled Exceptions　157

　　　Exception Handling Guidelines　159

4.3　Implementing System.Object Methods in a Custom Class　160

　　　ToString() to Describe an Object　161

　　　Equals() to Compare Objects　163

　　　Cloning to Create a Copy of an Object　165

4.4　Working with .NET Collection Classes and Interfaces　167

　　　Collection Interfaces　168

　　　System.Collections Namespace　177

　　　Stack and Queue　177

　　　ArrayList　179

　　　Hashtable　181

　　　System.Collections.Generic Namespace　184

4.5　Object Serialization　187

　　　Binary Serialization　188

4.6　Object Life Cycle Management　192

　　　.NET Garbage Collection　192

4.7　Summary　198

4.8　Test Your Understanding　198

PART II
CREATING APPLICATIONS USING THE
.NET FRAMEWORK CLASS LIBRARY   200

CHAPTER 5
C# TEXT MANIPULATION AND FILE I/O   202

5.1   Characters and Unicode   204

    Unicode   204

    Working with Characters   205

5.2   The String Class   209

    Creating Strings   209

    Overview of String Operations   211

5.3   Comparing Strings   212

    Using String.Compare   213

    Using String.CompareOrdinal   215

5.4   Searching, Modifying, and Encoding a String's Content   216

    Searching the Contents of a String   216

    Searching a String That Contains Surrogates   217

    String Transformations   217

    String Encoding   219

5.5   StringBuilder   220

    StringBuilder Class Overview   221

    StringBuilder Versus String Concatenation   222

5.6   Formatting Numeric and DateTime Values   223

    Constructing a Format Item   224

    Formatting Numeric Values   225

    Formatting Dates and Time   227

5.7   Regular Expressions   232

    The Regex Class   232

    Creating Regular Expressions   237

    A Pattern Matching Example   239

Working with Groups   240

Examples of Using Regular Expressions   242

5.8   System.IO: Classes to Read and Write Streams of Data   244

The Stream Class   244

FileStreams   245

MemoryStreams   247

BufferedStreams   248

Using StreamReader and StreamWriter
to Read and Write Lines of Text   249

StringWriter and StringReader   251

Encryption with the CryptoStream Class   252

5.9   System.IO: Directories and Files   255

FileSystemInfo   256

Working with Directories Using the DirectoryInfo,
Directory, and Path Classes   256

Working with Files Using the FileInfo and File Classes   261

5.10   Summary   263

5.11   Test Your Understanding   264

CHAPTER 6
BUILDING WINDOWS FORMS APPLICATIONS   266

6.1   Programming a Windows Form   268

Building a Windows Forms Application by Hand   268

6.2   Windows.Forms Control Classes   271

The Control Class   272

Working with Controls   274

Control Events   279

6.3   The Form Class   285

Setting a Form's Appearance   286

Setting Form Location and Size   290

Displaying Forms   292

The Life Cycle of a Modeless Form   292

Forms Interaction—A Sample Application   294

Owner and Owned Forms   298

Message and Dialog Boxes   299

Multiple Document Interface Forms   301

6.4   Working with Menus   306

MenuItem Properties   306

Context Menus   307

6.5   Adding Help to a Form   308

ToolTips   309

Responding to F1 and the Help Button   311

The HelpProvider Component   312

6.6   Forms Inheritance   313

Building and Using a Forms Library   313

Using the Inherited Form   314

6.7   Summary   315

6.8   Test Your Understanding   316

CHAPTER 7
WINDOWS FORMS CONTROLS   318

7.1   A Survey of .NET Windows Forms Controls   319

7.2   Button Classes, Group Box, Panel, and Label   323

The Button Class   323

The CheckBox Class   324

The RadioButton Class   325

The GroupBox Class   327

The Panel Class   328

The Label Class   330

7.3   PictureBox and TextBox Controls   331

The PictureBox Class   331

The TextBox Class   333

7.4   ListBox, CheckedListBox, and ComboBox Classes   335

The ListBox Class   335

Other List Controls: the ComboBox and the CheckedListBox   341

7.5   The ListView and TreeView Classes   342

The ListView Class   342

The TreeView Class   349

7.6   The ProgressBar, Timer, and StatusStrip Classes   355

Building a StatusStrip   355

7.7   Building Custom Controls   358

Extending a Control   358

Building a Custom UserControl   359

A UserControl Example   359

Using the Custom User Control   361

Working with the User Control at Design Time   362

7.8   Using Drag and Drop with Controls   363

Overview of Drag and Drop   363

7.9   Using Resources   369

Working with Resource Files   369

Using Resource Files to Create Localized Forms   373

7.10   Summary   376

7.11   Test Your Understanding   376

CHAPTER 8
.NET GRAPHICS USING GDI+   378

8.1   GDI+ Overview   380

The Graphics Class   380

The Paint Event   384

8.2   Using the Graphics Object   388

Basic 2-D Graphics   388

Pens   393

Brushes   395

Colors   400

A Sample Project: Building a Color Viewer   402

8.3   Images   407

     Loading and Storing Images   408

     Manipulating Images   411

     Sample Project: Working with Images   414

     A Note on GDI and BitBlt for
     the Microsoft Windows Platform   421

8.4   Summary   423

8.5   Test Your Understanding   423

CHAPTER 9
FONTS, TEXT, AND PRINTING   426

9.1   Fonts   428

     Font Families   428

     The Font Class   430

9.2   Drawing Text Strings   433

     Drawing Multi-Line Text   434

     Formatting Strings with the StringFormat Class   435

     Using Tab Stops   436

     String Trimming, Alignment, and Wrapping   438

9.3   Printing   439

     Overview   439

     PrintDocument Class   441

     Printer Settings   442

     Page Settings   445

     PrintDocument Events   446

     PrintPage Event   448

     Previewing a Printed Report   449

     A Report Example   450

     Creating a Custom PrintDocument Class   454

9.4   Summary   457

9.5   Test Your Understanding   458

CHAPTER 10
WORKING WITH XML IN .NET 460

10.1 Working with XML 462

Using XML Serialization to Create XML Data 462

XML Schema Definition (XSD) 466

Using an XML Style Sheet 468

10.2 Techniques for Reading XML Data 472

XmlReader Class 472

XmlNodeReader Class 477

The XmlReaderSettings Class 479

Using an XML Schema to Validate XML Data 480

Options for Reading XML Data 481

10.3 Techniques for Writing XML Data 482

10.4 Using XPath to Search XML 485

Constructing XPath Queries 486

XmlDocument and XPath 489

XPathDocument and XPath 490

XmlDataDocument and XPath 491

10.5 Summary 493

10.6 Test Your Understanding 494

CHAPTER 11
ADO.NET 496

11.1 Overview of the ADO.NET Architecture 498

OLE DB Data Provider in .NET 498

.NET Data Provider 499

11.2 Data Access Models: Connected and Disconnected 502

Connected Model 502

Disconnected Model 504

11.3 ADO.NET Connected Model 506

Connection Classes 506

The Command Object   511

DataReader Object   516

11.4   DataSets, DataTables, and the Disconnected Model   518

The DataSet Class   518

DataTables   519

Loading Data into a DataSet   523

Using the DataAdapter to Update a Database   525

Defining Relationships Between Tables in a DataSet   530

Choosing Between the Connected and Disconnected Model   532

11.5   XML and ADO.NET   533

Using a DataSet to Create XML Data and Schema Files   534

Creating a DataSet Schema from XML   536

Reading XML Data into a DataSet   537

11.6   Summary   540

11.7   Test Your Understanding   541

CHAPTER 12
DATA BINDING WITH WINDOWS FORMS CONTROLS   544

12.1   Overview of Data Binding   546

Simple Data Binding   546

Complex Data Binding with List Controls   549

One-Way and Two-Way Data Binding   550

Using Binding Managers   552

12.2   Using Simple and Complex Data Binding in an Application   555

Binding to a DataTable   555

Binding Controls to an ArrayList   558

Adding an Item to the Data Source   560

Identifying Updates   561

Update Original Database with Changes   562

12.3   The DataGridView Class   563

Properties   564

Events   571

Setting Up Master-Detail DataGridViews   576

Virtual Mode   579

12.4 Summary   585

12.5 Test Your Understanding   585

PART III
ADVANCED USE OF C# AND THE .NET FRAMEWORK   588

CHAPTER 13
ASYNCHRONOUS PROGRAMMING
AND MULTITHREADING   590

13.1 What Is a Thread?   592

Multithreading   592

13.2 Asynchronous Programming   595

Asynchronous Delegates   596

Examples of Implementing Asynchronous Calls   599

13.3 Working Directly with Threads   609

Creating and Working with Threads   609

Multithreading in Action   613

Using the Thread Pool   617

Timers   618

13.4 Thread Synchronization   620

The Synchronization Attribute   622

The Monitor Class   623

The Mutex   625

The Semaphore   627

Avoiding Deadlock   628

Summary of Synchronization Techniques   630

13.5 Summary   631

13.6 Test Your Understanding   631

CHAPTER 14
CREATING DISTRIBUTED
APPLICATIONS WITH REMOTING   636

14.1   Application Domains   638

    Advantages of AppDomains   638

    Application Domains and Assemblies   639

    Working with the AppDomain Class   640

14.2   Remoting   643

    Remoting Architecture   644

    Types of Remoting   648

    Client-Activated Objects   650

    Server-Activated Objects   650

    Type Registration   652

    Remoting with a Server-Activated Object   654

    Remoting with a Client-Activated Object (CAO)   664

    Design Considerations in Creating a Distributed Application   670

14.3   Leasing and Sponsorship   671

    Leasing   672

    Sponsorship   675

14.4   Summary   678

14.5   Test Your Understanding   678

CHAPTER 15
CODE REFINEMENT, SECURITY, AND DEPLOYMENT   680

15.1   Following .NET Code Design Guidelines   682

    Using FxCop   683

15.2   Strongly Named Assemblies   686

    Creating a Strongly Named Assembly   687

    Delayed Signing   688

    Global Assembly Cache (GAC)   689

    Versioning   690

15.3 Security 692

Permissions and Permission Sets 693

Evidence 698

Security Policies 701

Configuring Security Policy 702

The .NET Framework Configuration Tool 704

Configuring Code Access Security with the
Configuration Tool—An Example 706

Requesting Permissions for an Assembly 711

Programmatic Security 715

15.4 Application Deployment Considerations 722

Microsoft Windows Deployment: XCOPY
Deployment Versus the Windows Installer 722

Deploying Assemblies in the Global Assembly Cache 723

Deploying Private Assemblies 724

Using CodeBase Configuration 725

Using a Configuration File to Manage
Multiple Versions of an Assembly 726

Assembly Version and Product Information 727

15.5 Summary 728

15.6 Test Your Understanding 728

PART IV
PROGRAMMING FOR THE INTERNET 730

CHAPTER 16
ASP.NET WEB FORMS AND CONTROLS 732

16.1 Client-Server Interaction over the Internet 734

Web Application Example: Implementing a BMI Calculator 735

Using ASP.NET to Implement a BMI Calculator 740

Inline Code Model 741

The Code-Behind Model   749

Code-Behind with Partial Classes   753

Page Class   754

16.2   Web Forms Controls   758

Web Controls Overview   759

Specifying the Appearance of a Web Control   760

Simple Controls   761

List Controls   766

The DataList Control   768

16.3   Data Binding and Data Source Controls   772

Binding to a DataReader   772

Binding to a DataSet   774

DataSource Controls   776

16.4   Validation Controls   784

Using Validation Controls   786

16.5   Master and Content Pages   789

Creating a Master Page   790

Creating a Content Page   791

Accessing the Master Page from a Content Page   792

16.6   Building and Using Custom Web Controls   793

A Custom Control Example   794

Using a Custom Control   796

Control State Management   797

Composite Controls   798

16.7   Selecting a Web Control to Display Data   801

16.8   Summary   802

16.9   Test Your Understanding   803

CHAPTER 17
THE ASP.NET APPLICATION ENVIRONMENT   806

17.1   HTTP Request and Response Classes   808

HttpRequest Object   808

HttpResponse Object   813

17.2   ASP.NET and Configuration Files   817

A Look Inside web.config   818

Adding a Custom Configuration Section   824

17.3   ASP.NET Application Security   827

Forms Authentication   827

An Example of Forms Authentication   830

17.4   Maintaining State   835

Application State   837

Session State   838

17.5   Caching   841

Page Output Caching   842

Data Caching   845

17.6   Creating a Web Client with WebRequest and WebResponse   848

WebRequest and WebResponse Classes   848

Web Client Example   848

17.7   HTTP Pipeline   851

Processing a Request in the Pipeline   851

HttpApplication Class   853

HTTP Modules   857

HTTP Handlers   862

17.8   Summary   866

17.9   Test Your Understanding   867

CHAPTER 18
XML WEB SERVICES   868

18.1   Introduction to Web Services   870

Discovering and Using a Web Service   871

18.2   Building an XML Web Service   875

Creating a Web Service by Hand   875

Creating a Web Service Using VS.NET   878

Extending the Web Service with the
WebService and WebMethod Attributes   880

18.3   Building an XML Web Service Client   884

Creating a Simple Client to Access the Web Service Class   884

Creating a Proxy with Visual Studio.NET   894

18.4   Understanding WSDL and SOAP   895

Web Services Description Language (WSDL)   895

Simple Object Access Protocol (SOAP)   898

18.5   Using Web Services with Complex Data Types   906

A Web Service to Return Images   907

Using Amazon Web Services   909

Creating a Proxy for the Amazon Web Services   911

Building a WinForms Web Service Client   913

18.6   Web Services Performance   916

Configuring the HTTP Connection   916

Working with Large Amounts of Data   917

18.7   Summary   918

18.8   Test Your Understanding   918

APPENDIX A
FEATURES SPECIFIC TO .NET 2.0 AND C# 2.0   920

APPENDIX B
DATAGRIDVIEW EVENTS AND DELEGATES   924

ANSWERS TO CHAPTER EXERCISES   938

INDEX   952

About the Author

Stephen Perry is a software architect specializing in the design and implementation of .NET applications. For the past three years he has designed and developed significant .NET-based solutions for clients in the textile, furniture, legal, and medical professions. Prior to that, he worked for more than 20 years in all phases of software development. With the extra 25 hours a week now available from the completion of the book, he'll have more time for triathlon training and watching "Seinfeld" reruns.

Foreword

Learning a new programming language, or even a new version of one, can be a lot like traveling to a foreign country. Some things will look familiar. Some things will look very odd. You can usually get by if you stick to the familiar; but, who wants to just "get by"? Often times, it's the odd things in a country, culture, or language where you can realize many interesting and valuable benefits.

To do it right, however, you'll need a proper guide or guide book. This is essential. Just as a good guide book will tell you what to see, when to see it, what to eat, what to avoid, and a few tips, so will a good programming book tell you what frameworks and classes to use, how to call their methods, what bad practices to avoid, and a few productivity tips and best practices.

This is exactly what Steve has provided you.

If you were to approach C# 2.0 from a 1.0 perspective, or from some other language background, you'd be missing out on all its new offerings. For example, I'm a seasoned developer and set in my ways. If you're like me, then you probably still write methods, loops, and other design patterns the same way you have for many years. You know it's not producing the most efficient code, but it's quick. It's easy to read and understand; and it works.

Steve has literally written the "Core" C# book here. He begins by introducing you to the important C# concepts and their interaction with the .NET Framework; but, then he deviates from the other C# reference books on the market and jumps right into the application of C#. These include most of the common, daily tasks that you could be asked to perform, such as working with text, files, databases, XML, Windows forms and controls, printing, ASP.NET Web applications, Web services, and remoting. Steve even provides you with asynchronous, multithreaded, security, and deployment topics as a bonus. You won't need another book on your shelf.

So, what are you waiting for? I think it's time to break a few of your familiar habits and experience some new culture!

Richard Hundhausen
Author, *Introducing Microsoft Visual Studio 2005 Team System*

Preface

"The process of preparing programs for a digital computer is especially attractive because it not only can be economically and scientifically rewarding, it can also be an aesthetic experience much like composing poetry or music."
— Donald Knuth, Preface to *Fundamental Algorithms* (1968)

Thirty-seven years later, programmers still experience the same creative satisfaction from developing a well-crafted program. It can be 10 lines of recursive code that pops into one's head at midnight, or it can be an entire production management system whose design requires a year of midnights. Then, as now, good programs still convey an impression of logic and naturalness—particularly to their users.

But the challenges have evolved. Software is required to be more malleable—it may be run from a LAN, the Internet, or a cellular phone. Security is also a much bigger issue, because the code may be accessible all over the world. This, in turn, raises issues of scalability and how to synchronize code for hundreds of concurrent users. More users bring more cultures, and the concomitant need to customize programs to meet the language and culture characteristics of a worldwide client base.

.NET—and the languages written for it—addresses these challenges as well as any unified development environment. This book is written for developers, software architects, and students who choose to work with the .NET Framework. All code in the book is written in C#, although only one chapter is specifically devoted to the syntactical structure of the C# language.

This book is not an introduction to programming—it assumes you are experienced in a computer language. This book is not an introduction to object-oriented programming (OOP)—although it will re-enforce the principles of encapsulation, polymorphism, and inheritance through numerous examples. Finally, this book is not an introduction to using Visual Studio.NET to develop C# programs. VS.NET is mentioned, but the emphasis is on developing and understanding C# and the .NET classes—independent of any IDE.

This book is intended for the experienced programmer who is moving to .NET and wants to get an overall feel for its capabilities. You may be a VB6 or C++ programmer seeking exposure to .NET; a VB.NET programmer expanding your repertoire into C#; or—and yes it does happen occasionally—a Java programmer investigating life on the far side. Here's what you'll find if you choose to journey through this book.

- **18 Chapters.** The first four chapters should be read in order. They provide an introduction to C# and a familiarity with using the .NET class libraries. The remaining chapters can be read selectively based on your interests. Chapters 6 and 7 describe how to develop Windows Forms applications. Chapters 8 and 9 deal with GDI+—the .NET graphics classes. Chapters 10 through 12 are about working with data. Both XML and ADO.NET are discussed. Chapters 13, 14, and 15 tackle the more advanced topics of threading, remoting, and code security, respectively. The final chapters form a Web trilogy: Chapter 16 discusses ASP.NET Web page development; Chapter 17 looks behind the scenes at how to manage state information and manage HTTP requests; the book closes with a look at Web Services in Chapter 18.
- **.NET 2.0.** The manuscript went to publication after the release of Beta 2.0. As such, it contains information based on that release. The 2.0 topics are integrated within the chapters, rather than placing them in a special 2.0 section. However, as a convenience, Appendix A contains a summary and separate index to the .NET 2.0 topics.
- **Coding examples.** Most of the code examples are short segments that emphasize a single construct or technique. The objective is to avoid filler code that does nothing but waste paper. Only when it is essential does a code example flow beyond a page in length. Note that all significant code examples are available as a download from `www.corecsharp.net` or indirectly at `www.phptr.com/title/` `0131472275`. To access the download area, enter the keyword **parsifal**.
- **Questions and answers.** Each chapter ends with a section of questions to test your knowledge. The answers are available in a single section at the end of the book.

- **Fact rather than opinion.** This book is not based on my opinion; it is based on the features inherent in .NET and C#. Core recommendations and notes are included with the intent of providing insight rather than opinion.

Although some will disagree, if you really want to learn C# and .NET, shut down your IDE, pull out your favorite text editor, and learn how to use the C# compiler from the command line. After you have mastered the fundamentals, you can switch to VS.NET and any other IDE for production programming.

Finally, a word about .NET and Microsoft: This book was developed using Microsoft .NET 1.x and Whidbey betas. It includes topics such as ADO.NET and ASP.NET that are very much Microsoft proprietary implementations. In fact, Microsoft has applied to patent these methodologies. However, all of C# and many of the .NET basic class libraries are based on a standard that enables them to be ported to other platforms. Now, and increasingly in the future, many of the techniques described in this book will be applicable to .NET like implementations (such as the Mono project, `http://www.mono-project.com/Main_Page`) on non-Windows platforms.

Acknowledgments

I have received assistance from a great number of people over the 21 months that went into the research and development of this book. I wish to thank first my wife, Rebecca, who tirelessly read through pages of unedited manuscripts, and used her systems programming background to add valuable recommendations. Next, I wish to thank the reviewers whose recommendations led to better chapter organization, fewer content and code errors, and a perspective on which topics to emphasize. Reviewers included Greg Beamer, James Edelen, Doug Holland, Curtiss Howard, Anand Narayanaswamy, and Gordon Weakliem. Special thanks go to Richard Hundhausen whose recommendations went well beyond the call of duty; and Cay Horstmann, who read every preliminary chapter and whose Java allegiance made him a wonderful and influential "Devil's Advocate." I also wish to thank Dr. Alan Tharp who encouraged the idea of writing a book on .NET and remains my most respected advisor in the computer profession.

Finally, it has been a pleasure working with the editors and staff at Prentice Hall PTR. I'm particularly grateful for the efforts of Stephane Nakib, Joan Murray, Ebony Haight, Jessica D'Amico, Kelli Brooks, and Vanessa Moore. This book would not exist without the efforts of my original editor Stephane Nakib. The idea for the book was hers, and her support for the project kept it moving in the early stages. My other editor, Joan Murray, took over midway through the project and provided the oversight, advice, and encouragement to complete the project. Production editor Vanessa Moore and copy editor Kelli Brooks performed the "dirty work" of turning the final manuscript—with its myriad inconsistencies and word misuse—into a presentable book. To them, I am especially grateful. Working with professionals such as these was of inestimable value on those days when writing was more Sisyphean than satisfying.

FUNDAMENTALS OF C# PROGRAMMING AND INTRODUCTION TO .NET

Part 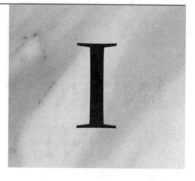 I

■ Chapter 1
Introduction to .NET and C# **4**

■ Chapter 2
C# Language Fundamentals **38**

■ Chapter 3
Class Design in C# **80**

■ Chapter 4
Working with Objects in C# **144**

INTRODUCTION TO .NET AND C#

Topics in This Chapter

- *Overview of the .NET Framework:* Architecture and features.

- *Common Language Runtime:* An overview of the tasks performed by the runtime portion of the .NET Framework: Just-in-Time (JIT) compiler, loading assemblies, and code verification.

- *Common Type System and Common Language Specifications:* Rules that govern Common Language Runtime (CLR) compatibility and language interoperability.

- *Assemblies:* A look at the structure of an assembly, the philosophy behind it, and the difference between private and shared assemblies.

- *Framework Class Library:* The Framework Library supplies hundreds of base classes grouped into logical namespaces.

- *Development Tools:* Several tools are provided with .NET to aid code development. These include Ildasm for disassembling code, WinCV to view the properties of a class, and the Framework Configuration tool.

- *Compiling and Running C# Programs:* Using the C# compiler from the command line and options for structuring an application.

Chapter

The effective use of a language requires a good deal more than learning the syntax and features of the language. In fact, the greater part of the learning curve for new technology is now concentrated in the programming environment. It is not enough to be proficient with the C# language; the successful developer and software architect must also be cognizant of the underlying class libraries and the tools available to probe these libraries, debug code, and check the efficiency of underlying code.

The purpose of this chapter is to provide an awareness of the .NET environment before you proceed to the syntax and semantics of the C# language. The emphasis is on how the environment, not the language, will affect the way you develop software. If you are new to .NET, it is necessary to embrace some new ideas. .NET changes the way you think of dealing with legacy code and version control; it changes the way program resources are disposed of; it permits code developed in one language to be used by another; it simplifies code deployment by eliminating a reliance on the system registry; and it creates a self-describing metalanguage that can be used to determine program logic at runtime. You will bump into all of these at some stage of the software development process, and they will influence how you design and deploy your applications.

To the programmer's eye, the .NET platform consists of a runtime environment coupled with a base class library. The layout of this chapter reflects that viewpoint. It contains separate sections on the Common Language Runtime (CLR) and the Framework Class Library (FCL). It then presents the basic tools that a developer may use to gain insight into the inner workings of the .NET Framework, as well as manage and distribute applications. As a prelude to Chapter 2, the final section introduces the C# compiler with examples of its use.

1.1 Overview of the .NET Framework

The .NET Framework is designed as an integrated environment for seamlessly developing and running applications on the Internet, on the desktop as Windows Forms, and even on mobile devices (with the Compact Framework). Its primary objectives are as follows:

- To provide a consistent object-oriented environment across the range of applications.
- To provide an environment that minimizes the versioning conflicts ("DLL Hell") that has bedeviled Windows (COM) programmers, and to simplify the code distribution/installation process.
- To provide a portable environment, based on certified standards, that can be hosted by any operating system. Already, C# and a major part of the .NET runtime, the Common Language Infrastructure (CLI), have been standardized by the ECMA.[1]
- To provide a managed environment in which code is easily verified for safe execution.

To achieve these broad objectives, the .NET Framework designers settled on an architecture that separates the framework into two parts: the Common Language Runtime (CLR) and the Framework Class Library (FCL). Figure 1-1 provides a stylized representation of this.

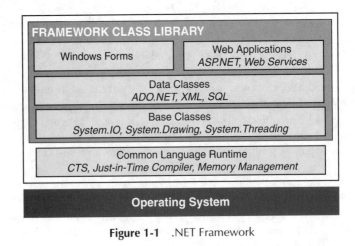

Figure 1-1   .NET Framework

---

1. ECMA International was formerly known as the European Computer Manufacturers Association and is referred to herein simply as the ECMA.

The CLR—which is Microsoft's implementation of the CLI standard—handles code execution and all of the tasks associated with it: compilation, memory management, security, thread management, and enforcement of type safety and use. Code that runs under the CLR is referred to as managed code. This is to distinguish it from unmanaged code that does not implement the requirements to run in the CLR—such as COM or Windows API based components.

The other major component, the Framework Class Library, is a reusable code library of types (classes, structures, and so on) available to applications running under .NET. As the figure shows, these include classes for database access, graphics, interoperating with unmanaged code, security, and both Web and Windows forms. All languages that target the .NET Framework use this common class library. Thus, after you gain experience using these types, you can apply that knowledge to any .NET language you may choose to program in.

Microsoft .NET and the CLI Standards

A natural concern for a developer that chooses to invest the time in learning C# and .NET is whether the acquired skill set can be transferred to other platforms. Specifically, is .NET a Microsoft product tethered only to the Windows operating system? Or is it a portable runtime and development platform that will be implemented on multiple operating systems? To answer the question, it is necessary to understand the relationship among Microsoft .NET, C#, and the Common Language Infrastructure (CLI) standards.

The CLI defines a platform-independent virtual code execution environment. It specifies no operating system, so it could just as easily be Linux as Windows. The centerpiece of the standard is the definition for a Common Intermediate Language (CIL) that must be produced by CLI compliant compilers and a type system that defines the data types supported by any compliant language. As described in the next section, this intermediate code is compiled into the native language of its host operating system.

The CLI also includes the standards for the C# language, which was developed and promoted by Microsoft. As such, it is the de facto standard language for .NET. However, other vendors have quickly adopted the CIL standard and produced—just to name a few—Python, Pascal, Fortran, Cobol, and Eiffel .NET compilers.

The .NET Framework, as depicted in Figure 1-1, is Microsoft's implementation of the CLI standards. The most important thing to note about this implementation is that it contains a great deal more features than are specified by the CLI architecture. To illustrate this, compare it to the CLI standards architecture shown in Figure 1-2.

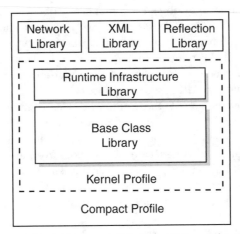

Figure 1-2   Architecture defined by CLI specifications

Briefly, the CLI defines two implementations: a minimal implementation known as a *Kernel Profile* and a more feature rich *Compact Profile*. The kernel contains the types and classes required by a compiler that is CLI compliant. The Base Class Library holds the basic data type classes, as well as classes that provide simple file access, define security attributes, and implement one-dimensional arrays. The Compact Profile adds three class libraries: an XML library that defines simple XML parsing, a Network library that provides HTTP support and access to ports, and a Reflection library that supports *reflection* (a way for a program to examine itself through metacode).

This book, which describes the Microsoft implementation, would be considerably shorter if it described only the CLI recommendations. There would be no chapters on ADO.NET (database classes), ASP.NET (Web classes), or Windows Forms—and the XML chapters would be greatly reduced. As you may guess, these libraries depend on the underlying Windows API for functionality. In addition, .NET permits a program to invoke the Win32 API using an *Interop* feature. This means that a .NET developer has access not only to the Win32 API but also legacy applications and components (COM).

By keeping this rather wide bridge to Windows, Microsoft's .NET implementation becomes more of a transparent than virtual environment—not that there's anything wrong with that. It gives developers making the transition to .NET the ability to create hybrid applications that combine .NET components with preexisting code. It also means that the .NET implementation code is not going to be ported to another operating system.

The good news for developers—and readers of this book—is that the additional Microsoft features are being adopted by CLI open source initiatives. Mono[2], one of the leading CLI projects, already includes major features such as ADO.NET, Windows Forms, full XML classes, and a rich set of Collections classes. This is particularly significant because it means the knowledge and skills obtained working with Microsoft .NET can be applied to implementations on Linux, BSD, and Solaris platforms. With that in mind, let's take an overview of the Microsoft CLI implementation.

1.2   Common Language Runtime

The Common Language Runtime manages the entire life cycle of an application: it locates code, compiles it, loads associated classes, manages its execution, and ensures automatic memory management. Moreover, it supports cross-language integration to permit code generated by different languages to interact seamlessly. This section peers into the inner workings of the Common Language Runtime to see how it accomplishes this. It is not an in-depth discussion, but is intended to make you comfortable with the terminology, appreciate the language-neutral architecture, and understand what's actually happening when you create and execute a program.

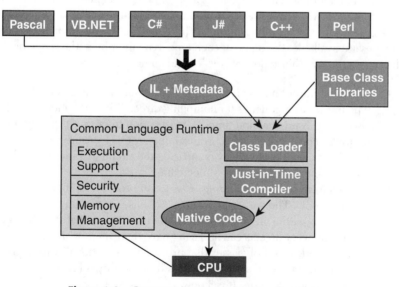

Figure 1-3   Common Language Runtime functions

2. http://www.mono-project.com/Main_Page

Compiling .NET Code

Compilers that are compliant with the CLR generate code that is targeted for the runtime, as opposed to a specific CPU. This code, known variously as Common Intermediate Language (CIL), Intermediate Language (IL), or Microsoft Intermediate Language (MSIL), is an assembler-type language that is packaged in an EXE or DLL file. Note that these are not standard executable files and require that the runtime's *Just-in-Time* (JIT) compiler convert the IL in them to a machine-specific code when an application actually runs. Because the Common Language Runtime is responsible for managing this IL, the code is known as *managed code*.

This intermediate code is one of the keys to meeting the .NET Framework's formal objective of language compatibility. As Figure 1-3 illustrates, the Common Language Runtime neither knows—nor needs to know—which language an application is created in. Its interaction is with the language-independent IL. Because applications communicate through their IL, output from one compiler can be integrated with code produced by a different compiler.

Another .NET goal, platform portability, is addressed by localizing the creation of machine code in the JIT compiler. This means that IL produced on one platform can be run on any other platform that has its own framework and a JIT compiler that emits its own machine code.

In addition to producing IL, compilers that target the CLR must emit *metadata* into every code module. The metadata is a set of tables that allows each code module to be self-descriptive. The tables contain information about the *assembly* containing the code, as well as a full description of the code itself. This information includes what types are available, the name of each type, type members, the scope or visibility of the type, and any other type features. Metadata has many uses:

- The most important use is by the JIT compiler, which gathers all the type information it needs for compiling directly from the metacode. It also uses this information for code verification to ensure the program performs correct operations. For example, the JIT ensures that a method is called correctly by comparing the calling parameters with those defined in the method's metadata.
- Metadata is used in the *Garbage Collection* process (memory management). The garbage collector (GC) uses metadata to know when fields within an object refer to other objects so that the GC can determine what objects can and can't have their memory reclaimed.
- .NET provides a set of classes that provide the functionality to read metadata from within a program. This functionality is known collectively as *reflection*. It is a powerful feature that permits a program to query the code at runtime and make decisions based on its discovery. As we will see later in the book, it is the key to working with custom *attributes*, which are a C#-supported construct for adding custom metadata to a program.

IL and metadata are crucial to providing language interoperability, but its real-world success hinges on all .NET compilers supporting a common set of data types and language specifications. For example, two languages cannot be compatible at the IL level if one language supports a 32-bit signed integer and the other does not. They may differ syntactically (for example, C# int versus a Visual Basic Integer), but there must be agreement of what base types each will support.

As discussed earlier, the CLI defines a formal specification, called the *Common Type System* (CTS), which is an integral part of the Common Language Runtime. It describes how types are defined and how they must behave in order to be supported by the Common Language Runtime.

Common Type System

The CTS provides a base set of data types for each language that runs on the .NET platform. In addition, it specifies how to declare and create custom types, and how to manage the lifetime of instances of these types. Figure 1-4 shows how .NET organizes the Common Type System.

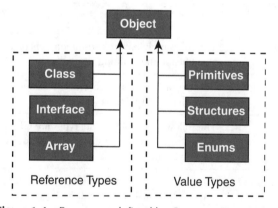

Figure 1-4 Base types defined by Common Type System

Two things stand out in this figure. The most obvious is that types are categorized as *reference* or *value* types. This taxonomy is based on how the types are stored and accessed in memory: reference types are accessed in a special memory area (called a *heap*) via pointers, whereas value types are referenced directly in a program stack. The other thing to note is that all types, both custom and .NET defined, must inherit from the predefined System.Object type. This ensures that all types support a basic set of inherited methods and properties.

Core Note

In .NET, "type" is a generic term that refers to a class, structure, enumeration, delegate, or interface.

A compiler that is compliant with the CTS specifications is guaranteed that its types can be hosted by the Common Language Runtime. This alone does not guarantee that the language can communicate with other languages. There is a more restrictive set of specifications, appropriately called the *Common Language Specification* (CLS), that provides the ultimate rules for language interoperability. These specifications define the minimal features that a compiler must include in order to target the CLR.

Table 1-1 contains some of the CLS rules to give you a flavor of the types of features that must be considered when creating CLS-compliant types (a complete list is included with the .NET SDK documentation).

Table 1-1   Selected Common Language Specification Features and Rules

Feature	Rule
Visibility (Scope)	The rules apply only to those members of a type that are available outside the defining assembly.
Characters and casing	For two variables to be considered distinct, they must differ by more than just their case.
Primitive types	The following primitive data types are CLS compliant: `Byte`, `Int16`, `Int32`, `Int64`, `Single`, `Double`, `Boolean`, `Char`, `Decimal`, `IntPtr`, and `String`.
Constructor invocation	A constructor must call the base class's constructor before it can access any of its instance data.
Array bounds	All dimensions of arrays must have a lower bound of zero (0).
Enumerations	The underlying type of an enumeration (enum) must be of the type `Byte`, `Int16`, `Int32`, or `Int64`.
Method signature	All return and parameter types used in a type or member signature must be CLS compliant.

These rules are both straightforward and specific. Let's look at a segment of C# code to see how they are applied:

```
public class Conversion
{
   public double Metric( double inches)
   { return (2.54 * inches); }
   public double metric( double miles)
   { return (miles / 0.62); }
}
```

Even if you are unfamiliar with C# code, you should still be able to detect where the code fails to comply with the CLS rules. The second rule in the table dictates that different names must differ by more than case. Obviously, `Metric` fails to meet this rule. This code runs fine in C#, but a program written in Visual Basic.NET—which ignores case sensitivity—would be unable to distinguish between the upper and lowercase references.

Assemblies

All of the managed code that runs in .NET must be contained in an assembly. Logically, the assembly is referenced as one EXE or DLL file. Physically, it may consist of a collection of one or more files that contain code or resources such as images or XML data.

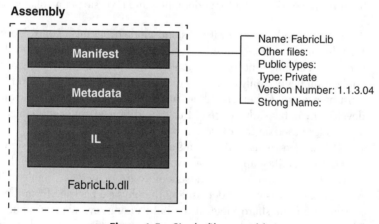

Figure 1-5   Single file assembly

An assembly is created when a .NET compatible compiler converts a file containing source code into a DLL or EXE file. As shown in Figure 1-5, an assembly contains a manifest, metadata, and the compiler-generated Intermediate Language (IL). Let's take a closer look at these:

Manifest. Each assembly must have one file that contains a *manifest*. The manifest is a set of tables containing metadata that lists the names of all files in the assembly, references to external assemblies, and information such as name and version that identify the assembly. *Strongly named assemblies* (discussed later) also include a unique digital signature. When an assembly is loaded, the CLR's first order of business is to open the file containing the manifest so it can identify the members of the assembly.

Metadata. In addition to the manifest tables just described, the C# compiler produces definition and reference tables. The definition tables provide a complete description of the types contained in the IL. For instance, there are tables defining types, methods, fields, parameters, and properties. The reference tables contain information on all references to types and other assemblies. The JIT compiler relies on these tables to convert the IL to native machine code.

IL. The role of Intermediate Language has already been discussed. Before the CLR can use IL, it must be packaged in an EXE or DLL assembly. The two are not identical: an EXE assembly must have an entry point that makes it executable; a DLL, on the other hand, is designed to function as a code library holding type definitions.

The assembly is more than just a logical way to package executable code. It forms the very heart of the .NET model for code deployment, version control, and security:

- All managed code, whether it is a stand-alone program, a control, or a DLL library containing reusable types, is packaged in an assembly. It is the most atomic unit that can be deployed on a system. When an application begins, only those assemblies required for initialization must be present. Other assemblies are loaded on demand. A judicious developer can take advantage of this to partition an application into assemblies based on their frequency of use.
- In .NET jargon, an assembly forms a *version boundary*. The version field in the manifest applies to all types and resources in the assembly. Thus, all the files comprising the assembly are treated as a single unit with the same version. By decoupling the physical package from the logical, .NET can share a logical attribute among several physical files. This is the fundamental characteristic that separates an assembly from a system based on the traditional DLLs.
- An assembly also forms a *security boundary* on which access permissions are based. C# uses *access modifiers* to control how types and type members in an assembly can be accessed. Two of these use the assembly as a boundary: `public` permits unrestricted access from any assembly; `internal` restricts access to types and members within the assembly.

As mentioned, an assembly may contain multiple files. These files are not restricted to code modules, but may be resource files such as graphic images and text files. A common use of these files is to permit resources that enable an application to provide a screen interface tailored to the country or language of the user. There is no limit to the number of files in the assembly. Figure 1-6 illustrates the layout of a multi-file assembly.

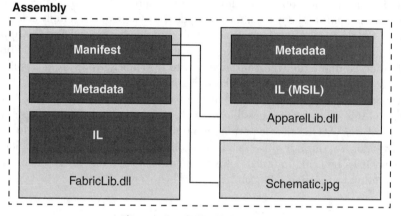

Figure 1-6   Multi-file assembly

In the multi-file assembly diagram, notice that the assembly's manifest contains the information that identifies all files in the assembly.

Although most assemblies consist of a single file, there are several cases where multi-file assemblies are advantageous:

- They allow you to combine modules created in different programming languages. A programming shop may rely on Visual Basic.NET for its Rapid Application Development (RAD) and C# for component or enterprise development. Code from both can coexist and interact in the .NET assembly.
- Code modules can be partitioned to optimize how code is loaded into the CLR. Related and frequently used code should be placed in one module; infrequently used code in another. The CLR does not load the modules until they are needed. If creating a class library, go a step further and group components with common life cycle, version, and security needs into separate assemblies.
- Resource files can be placed in their own module separate from IL modules. This makes it easier for multiple applications to share common resources.

Multi-file assemblies can be created by executing the C# compiler from the command line or using the Assembly Linker utility, `Al.exe`. An example using the C# compiler is provided in the last section of this chapter. Notably, Visual Studio.NET 2005 does not support the creation of multi-file assemblies.

Private and Shared Assemblies

Assemblies may be deployed in two ways: privately or globally. Assemblies that are located in an application's base directory or a subdirectory are called *privately deployed assemblies*. The installation and updating of a private assembly could not be simpler. It only requires copying the assembly into the directory, called the *AppBase*, where the application is located. No registry settings are needed. In addition, an application configuration file can be added to override settings in an application's manifest and permit an assembly's files to be moved within the AppBase.

A shared assembly is one installed in a global location, called the *Global Assembly Cache* (GAC), where it is accessible by multiple applications. The most significant feature of the GAC is that it permits multiple versions of an assembly to execute side-by-side. To support this, .NET overcomes the name conflict problem that plagues DLLs by using four attributes to identify an assembly: the file name, a culture identity, a version number, and a public key token.

Assembly Name △	Version	Culture	Public Key Token
Accessibility	2.0.3600.0		b03f5f7f11d50a3a
ADODB	7.0.3300.0		b03f5f7f11d50a3a
apphost	2.0.3600.0		b03f5f7f11d50a3a
AspNetMMCExt	2.0.3600.0		b03f5f7f11d50a3a
CRVsPackageLib	1.0.0.0		692fbea5521e1304
CrystalDecisions.CrystalReports.Engine	9.1.3300.0		692fbea5521e1304

Figure 1-7   Partial listing of Global Assembly Directory

Public assemblies are usually located in the `assembly` directory located beneath the system directory of the operating system (`WINNT\` on a Microsoft Windows 2000 operating system). As shown in Figure 1-7, the assemblies are listed in a special format that displays their four attributes (.NET Framework includes a DLL file that extends Windows Explorer to enable it to display the GAC contents). Let's take a quick look at these four attributes:

Assembly Name. Also referred to as the *friendly name*, this is the file name of the assembly minus the extension.

Version. Every assembly has a version number that applies to all files in the assembly. It consists of four numbers in the format

<major number>.<minor number>.<build>.<revision>

Typically, the major and minor version numbers are updated for changes that break backward compatibility. A version number can be assigned to an assembly by including an `AssemblyVersion` attribute in the assembly's source code.

Culture Setting. The contents of an assembly may be associated with a particular culture or language. This is designated by a two-letter code such as "en" for English or "fr" for French, and can be assigned with an `AssemblyCulture` attribute placed in source code:

```
[assembly: AssemblyCulture ("fr-CA")]
```

Public Key Token. To ensure that a shared assembly is unique and authentic, .NET requires that the creator mark the assembly with a *strong name*. This process, known as *signing*, requires the use of a public/private key pair. When the compiler builds the assembly, it uses the private key to generate a strong name. The public key is so large that a token is created by hashing the public key and taking its last eight bytes. This token is placed in the manifest of any client assembly that references a shared assembly and is used to identify the assembly during execution.

Core Note

An assembly that is signed with a public/private key is referred to as a strongly named assembly. All shared assemblies must have a strong name.

Precompiling an Assembly

After an assembly is loaded, the IL must be compiled to the machine's native code. If you are used to working with executables already in a machine code format, this should raise questions about performance and whether it's possible to create equivalent "executables" in .NET. The answer to the second part of the statement is yes; .NET does provide a way to precompile an assembly.

The .NET Framework includes a *Native Image Generator* (Ngen) tool that is used to compile an assembly into a "native image" that is stored in a native image cache— a reserved area of the GAC. Any time the CLR loads an assembly, it checks the cache to see if it has an associated native image available; if it does, it loads the precompiled code. On the surface, this seems a good idea to improve performance. However, in reality, there are several drawbacks.

Ngen creates an image for a hypothetical machine architecture, so that it will run, for example, on any machine with an x86 processor. In contrast, when the JIT in .NET runs, it is aware of the specific machine it is compiling for and can accordingly make optimizations. The result is that its output often outperforms that of the pre-compiled assembly. Another drawback to using a native image is that changes to a system's hardware configuration or operating system—such as a service pack update—often invalidate the precompiled assembly.

Core Recommendation

As a rule, a dynamically compiled assembly provides performance equal to, or better than, that of a precompiled executable created using Ngen.

Code Verification

As part of the JIT compile process, the Common Language Runtime performs two types of *verification*: IL verification and metadata validation. The purpose is to ensure that the code is verifiably *type-safe*. In practical terms, this means that param-eters in a calling and called method are checked to ensure they are the same type, or that a method returns only the type specified in its return type declaration. In short, the CLR searches through the IL and metadata to make sure that any value assigned to a variable is of a compatible type; if not, an exception occurs.

Core Note

By default, code produced by the C# compiler is verifiably type-safe. However, there is an `unsafe` *keyword that can be used to relax memory access restrictions within a C# program (such as referencing beyond an array boundary).*

A benefit of verified code is that the CLR can be certain that the code cannot affect another application by accessing memory outside of its allowable range. Con-sequently, the CLR is free to safely run multiple applications in a single process or address space, improving performance and reducing the use of OS resources.

1.3   Framework Class Library

The Framework Class Library (FCL) is a collection of classes and other types (enu-merations, structures, and interfaces) that are available to managed code written in any language that targets the CLR. This is significant, because it means that libraries are no longer tied to specific compilers. As a developer, you can familiarize yourself with the types in a library and be assured that you can use this knowledge with whatever .NET language you choose.

The resources within the FCL are organized into logical groupings called *namespaces*. For the most part, these groupings are by broad functionality. For example, types used for graphical operations are grouped into the `System.Drawing` and `System.Drawing.Drawing2D` namespaces; types required for file I/O are members of the `System.IO` namespace. Namespaces represent a logical concept, not a physical one.

The FCL comprises hundreds of assemblies (DLLs), and each assembly may contain multiple namespaces. In addition, a namespace may span multiple assemblies. To demonstrate, let's look inside an FCL assembly.

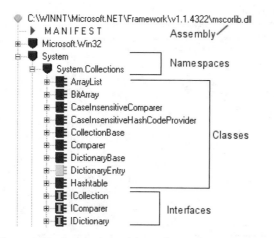

Figure 1-8　Output from Ildasm shows the namespaces and types that comprise an assembly

Figure 1-8 displays a portion of the output generated by using Ildasm.exe to examine the contents of the `mscorlib` assembly. Although this only a partial listing, you can see that `mscorlib` contains `System`, the preeminent namespace in .NET, which serves as a repository for the types that give .NET its basic functionality. The assembly is also home to the `System.Collections` namespace, which includes classes and interfaces used for manipulating collections of data.

Table 1-2 lists some of the most important namespaces in .NET. For reference, the last column in each row includes a chapter number in this book where you'll find the namespace(s) used.

Table 1-2   Selected FCL Namespaces

Namespace	Use	Chapter
`System`	Contains the basic data types used by all applications. It also contains exception classes, predefined attributes, a Math library, and classes for managing the application environment.	3, 18

`System.Collections`
`System.Collections.Specialized`
`System.Collections.Generic`
	Interfaces and classes used to manage collections of objects. These collections include the `ArrayList`, `Hashtable`, and `Stack`.	4

`System.Data`
`System.Data.OracleClient`
`System.Data.SqlClient`
`System.Data.OleDb`
`System.Data.Odbc`
	Classes used for database operations (ADO.NET). The client namespaces support Oracle and SQL Server, respectively; `OledDb` and `Odbc` define the data connection used.	11, 12

`System.Diagnostics`	Contains classes that can be used to trace program execution, debug, and work with system logs and performance counters.	13

`System.Drawing`
`System.Drawing.Drawing2D`
`System.Drawing.Printing`
`System.Drawing.Text`
	Provides graphics functionality for GDI+. These namespaces contain a class used for drawing as well as pens, brushes, geometric shapes, and fonts.	8, 9

`System.Globalization`	Contains classes that define culture-related information that affects the way dates, currency, and symbols are represented.	5
`System.IO`	Provides file and data stream I/O. These classes provide a way to access the underlying file systems of the host operating system.	5

Table 1-2   Selected FCL Namespaces *(continued)*

Namespace	Use	Chapter
`System.Net`	Classes that support network protocols and operations. Examples include WebRequest and WebResponse that request and fetch a Web page.	17
`System.Reflection` `System.Reflection.Emit`	Contains types that permit the runtime inspection of metadata. The `Emit` namespace allows a compiler or tool to generate metadata and IL dynamically.	7, 15, App. B
`System.Runtime.InterOpServices`	Provides interoperability between managed and unmanaged code such as legacy DLLs or COM.	8

`System.Security`
`System.Security.Permissions`
`System.Security.Cryptography`
	Classes used to manage .NET security. Defines classes that control access to operations and resources.	5, 15

`System.Text.RegularExpressions`	Classes that support .NET's regular expression engine.	5
`System.Threading` `System.Threading.Thread`	Manages threading activites: thread creation, synchronization, and thread pool access.	13

`System.Web`
`System.Web.Services`
`System.Web.UI`
`System.Web.UI.WebControls`
`System.Web.Security`
	The Internet-related classes referred to as ASP.NET. They manage browser-server communication requirements, manipulate cookies, and contain the controls that adorn a Web page.
	
	`Web.Services` includes those classes required for SOAP-based XML messaging.
	
	`Web.UI` includes classes and interfaces used for creating controls and pages that comprise Web forms.
		16, 17, 18

Table 1-2   Selected FCL Namespaces *(continued)*

Namespace	Use	Chapter
`System.Windows.Forms`	Classes used to build Windows desktop GUI applications. Controls including the `ListBox`, `TextBox`, `DataGrid`, and buttons are found here.	6, 7
`System.Xml`	Types for processing XML.	10

Namespaces provide a roadmap for navigating the FCL. For example, if your applications are Web based, you'll spend most of your time exploring the types in the `System.Web.*` namespaces. After you have learned the basics of .NET and gained proficiency with C#, you'll find that much of your time is spent familiarizing yourself with the built-in types contained in the Framework Class Library.

1.4   Working with the .NET Framework and SDK

The .NET Framework Software Development Kit (SDK) contains the tools, compilers, and documentation required to create software that will run on any machine that has the .NET Framework installed. It is available as a free download (100 megabytes) from Microsoft that can be installed on Windows XP, Windows 2000, Windows Server 2003, and subsequent Windows operating systems. If you have Visual Studio.NET installed, there is no need to download it because VS.NET automatically does it for you.

Clients using software developed with the SDK do not require the SDK on their machine; however, they do require a compatible version of the .NET Framework. This *.NET Framework Redistributable* is available as a free download[3] (20+ megabytes) and should be distributed to clients along with applications that require it. This redistributable can be installed on Windows 98 and ME, in addition to the ones listed for the SDK. With minor exceptions, .NET applications will run identically on all operating system platforms, because they are targeted for the Common Language Runtime and not the operating system. There are some system requirements such as a minimum Internet Explorer version of 5.01. These are listed at the download site.

---

3. `http://msdn.microsoft.com/netframework/downloads/updates/default.aspx`

Updating the .NET Framework

Unlike many development environments, installing a new version of the framework is almost effortless. The installation process places the updated version in a new directory having the name of the version. Most importantly, there is no file dependency between the new and older versions. Thus, all versions are functional on your system. Although it varies by operating system, the versions are usually in the path

```
\winnt\Microsoft.NET\Framework\v1.0.3705
\winnt\Microsoft.NET\Framework\v1.1.4322
\winnt\Microsoft.NET\Framework\v2.0.40607
```

The installation of any new software version raises the question of compatibility with applications developed using an older version. .NET makes it easy to run existing applications against any framework version. The key to this is the *application configuration file* (discussed in much greater detail in Chapter 15). This text file contains XML tags and elements that give the CLR instructions for executing an application. It can specify where external assemblies are located, which version to use, and, in this case, which versions of the .NET Framework an application or component supports. The configuration file can be created with any text editor, although it's preferable to rely on tools (such as the Framework Configuration tool) designed for the task. Your main use of the configuration file will be to test current applications against new framework releases. Although it can be done, it usually makes no sense to run an application against an earlier version than it was originally compiled against.

.NET Framework Tools

The .NET Framework automates as many tasks as possible and usually hides the details from the developer. However, there are times when manual intervention is required. These may be a need to better understand the details of an assembly or perform the housekeeping required to prepare an application for deployment. We have encountered several examples of such tasks throughout the chapter. These include the need to

- Add a file to an assembly
- View the contents of an assembly
- View the details of a specific class
- Generate a public/private key pair in order to create a strongly named assembly
- Edit configuration files

Many of these are better discussed within the context of later chapters. However, it is useful to be aware of which tools are available for performing these tasks; and a few, such as those for exploring classes and assemblies, should be mastered early in the .NET learning curve.

Table 1-3 lists some of the useful tools available to develop and distribute your applications. Three of these, Ildasm.exe, wincv.exe, and the .NET Framework Configuration tool, are the subject of further discussion.

Table 1-3   Selected .NET Framework Tools

Tool	Description
Al.exe Assembly Linker	Can be used for creating an assembly composed of modules from different compilers. It is also used to build resource-only (satellite) assemblies.
Fuslogvw.exe Assembly Binding Log Viewer	Used to troubleshoot the assembly loading process. It traces the steps followed while attempting to load an assembly.
Gacutil.exe Global Assembly Cache tool	Is used to install or delete an assembly in the Global Assembly Cache. It can also be used for listing the GAC's contents.
Ildasm.exe MSIL Disassembler	A tool for exploring an assembly, its IL, and metadata.
Mscorcfg.msc .NET Framework Configuration tool	A Microsoft Management Console (MMC) snap-in used to configure an assembly while avoiding direct manual changes to an application's configuration file. Designed primarily for administrators, a subset, Framework Wizards. Available for individual programmers.
Ngen.exe Native Image Generator	Compiles an assembly's IL into native machine code. This image is then placed in the native image cache.
Sn.exe Strong Name tool	Generates the keys that are used to create a strong—or signed—assembly.
wincv.exe Windows Forms Class Viewer	A visual interface to display searchable information about a class.
Wsdl.exe Web Services Description Language tool	Generates descriptive information about a Web Service that is used by a client to access the service.

Many of these tools are located in an SDK subdirectory:

```
c:\Program Files\Microsoft.NET\SDK\v2.0\Bin
```

To execute the tools at the command line (on a Windows operating system) while in any directory, it is first necessary to place the path to the utilities in the system `Path` variable. To do this, follow these steps:

1. Right click on the My Computer icon and select *Properties*.
2. Select Advanced – Environment Variables.
3. Choose the Path variable and add the SDK subdirectory path to it.

If you have Visual Studio installed, a simpler approach is to use the preconfigured Visual Studio command prompt. It automatically initializes the path information that enables you to access the command-line tools.

Ildasm.exe

The Intermediate Language Disassembler utility is supplied with the .NET Framework SDK and is usually located in the `Bin` subdirectory along the path where the SDK is installed. It is invaluable for investigating the .NET assembly environment and is one of the first tools you should become familiar with as you begin to work with .NET assemblies and code.

The easiest way to use the utility is to type in

```
C:\>Ildasm /adv
```

at a command-line prompt (the optional `/adv` switch makes advanced viewing options available). This invokes the GUI that provides a File menu you use to select the assembly to view. Note that it does not open files in the Global Assembly Cache.

Figure 1-9 shows an example of the output created when an assembly is opened in Ildasm. The contents are displayed in a readable, hierarchical format that contains the assembly name, `corecsharp1`, and all of its members.

This hierarchy can then be used to drill down to the underlying IL (or CIL) instructions for a specific member. As an example, let's consider the `Conversion` class. The figure shows that it consists of three methods: `Metric`, `conversion`, and `metric`. The original source code confirms this:

```
public class Conversion
{
    public double Metric( double inches)
    { return (2.54 * inches); }
    [CLSCompliantAttribute(false)]
    public double metric( double miles)
```

```
      { return (miles / 0.62); }
      public double conversion( double pounds)
      { return (pounds * 454);}
}
```

C:\Documents and Settings\Administrator\My Docum...
File View Help
C:\Documents and Settings\Administrator\My Documents\Visual Studio P
MANIFEST
corecsharp1
Assembly
<PrivateImplementationDetails>
Conversion
Class
.class public auto ansi beforefieldinit
.ctor : void()
Metric : float64(float64)
conversion : float64(float64)
metric : float64(float64)
Methods
DressShirtx
Fabrics
MyClass

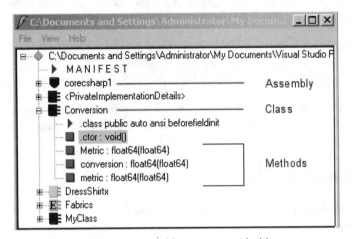

Figure 1-9 View assembly contents with Ildasm.exe

Double clicking on the `Metric` method brings up a screen that displays its IL (Figure 1-10).

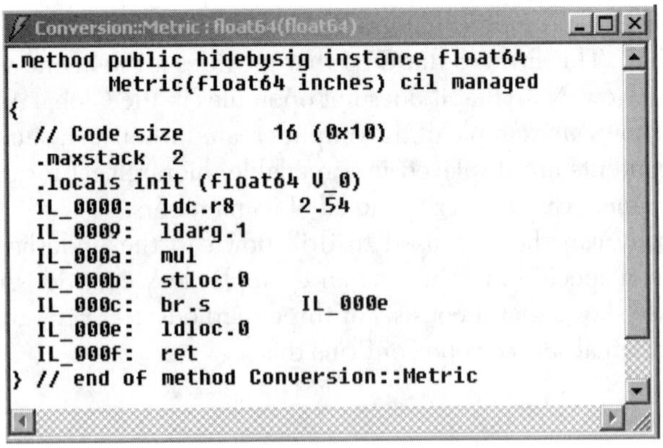

Conversion::Metric : float64(float64)
.method public hidebysig instance float64
Metric(float64 inches) cil managed
{
// Code size 16 (0x10)
.maxstack 2
.locals init (float64 V_0)
IL_0000: ldc.r8 2.54
IL_0009: ldarg.1
IL_000a: mul
IL_000b: stloc.0
IL_000c: br.s IL_000e
IL_000e: ldloc.0
IL_000f: ret
} // end of method Conversion::Metric

Figure 1-10 View of the IL

Ildasm can be used as a learning tool to solidify the concepts of IL and assemblies. It also has some practical uses. Suppose you have a third-party component (assembly) to work with for which there is no documentation. Ildasm provides a useful starting point in trying to uncover the interface details of the assembly.

Core Suggestion

Ildasm has a File – Dump *menu option that makes it useful for saving program documentation in a text file. Select* Dump Metainfo *to create a lengthy human-readable form of the assembly's metadata; select* Dump Statistics *to view a profile of the assembly that details how many bytes each part uses.*

Ildasm and Obfuscation

One of the natural concerns facing .NET developers is how to protect their code when a tool such as Ildasm—and other commercially available disassemblers—can be used to expose it. One solution is to use *obfuscation*—a technique that uses renaming and code manipulation sleight of hand to make the contents of an assembly unreadable by humans.

It is important to understand that obfuscation is not encryption. Encryption requires a decryption step so that the JIT compiler can process the code. Obfuscation transforms the IL code into a form that can be compiled using the tools of your development environment (see Figure 1-11).

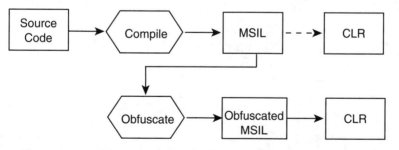

Figure 1-11   Obfuscation conceals the original Intermediate Language

The obfuscated code is functionally equivalent to the assembly's IL code and produces identical results when run by the CLR. How does it do this? The most common trick is to rename meaningful types and members with names that have no intrinsic meaning. If you look at obfuscated code, you'll see a lot of types named "a" or "b," for example. Of course, the obfuscation algorithm must be smart enough not to rename types that are used by outside assemblies that depend on the original name. Another common trick is to alter the control flow of the code without changing the logic. For example, a `while` statement may be replaced with a combination of `goto` and `if` statements.

An obfuscator is not included in the .NET SDK. Dotfuscator Community Edition, a limited-feature version of a commercial product, is available with Visual Studio.NET. Despite being a relatively unsophisticated product—and only available for the Microsoft environment—it is a good way to become familiar with the process. Several vendors now offer more advanced obfuscator products.

wincv.exe

WinCV is a class viewer analogous to the Visual Studio Object Viewer, for those not using Visual Studio. It is located in the `Program Files\Microsoft.Net\ SDK\V1.x\Bin` directory and can be run from the command prompt. When the window appears, type the name of the class you want to view into the Searching For box (see Figure 1-12).

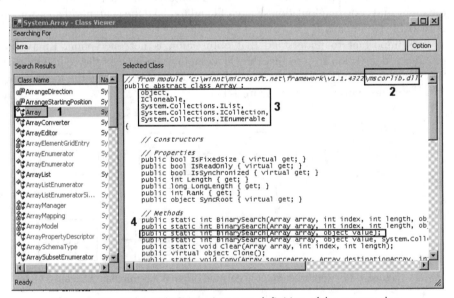

Figure 1-12   Using WinCV to view type definition of the `Array` class

WinCV provides a wealth of information about any type in the base class libraries. The four highlighted areas provide a sampling of what is available:

1. `System.Array` is the class that is being explored.
2. This class is located in the mscorlib.dll assembly. We have already mentioned that this assembly contains the .NET managed types.
3. This list contains the class, object, and interfaces that the `Array` class inherits from.
4. The definition of each method in the class is included. This definition, which includes accessibility, type, and parameters, is called the method's *signature*.

Framework Configuration Tool

This tool provides an easy way to manage and configure assemblies as well as set security policies for accessing code. This tool is packaged as a Microsoft Management Console (MMC) snap-in. To access it, select Administrative Tools from the Control Panel; then select the Microsoft .NET Framework Configuration tool. This tool is designed for administrators who need to do the following:

- **Manage assemblies.** Assemblies can be added to the GAC or deleted.
- **Configure assemblies.** When an assembly is updated, the publisher of the assembly is responsible for updating the *binding policy* of the assembly. This policy tells the CLR which version of an assembly to load when an application references an assembly. For example, if assembly version 1.1 replaces 1.0, the policy redirects version 1.0 to 1.1 so that it is loaded. This redirection information is contained in a configuration file.
- **View .NET Framework security and modify an assembly's security.** .NET security allows an assembly to be assigned certain permissions or rights. In addition, an assembly can require that other assemblies accessing it have certain permissions.
- **Manage how individual applications interact with an assembly or set of assemblies.** You can view a list of all assemblies an application uses and set the version that your application uses.

To illustrate a practical use of the configuration tool, let's look at how it can be used to address one of the most common problems that plagues the software development process: the need to drop back to a previous working version when a current application breaks. This can be a difficult task when server DLLs or assemblies are involved. .NET offers a rather clever solution to this problem: Each time an application runs, it logs the set of assemblies that are used by the program. If they are unchanged from the previous run, the CLR ignores them; if there are changes, however, a snapshot of the new set of assemblies is stored.

When an application fails, one option for the programmer is to revert to a previous version that ran successfully. The configuration tool can be used to redirect the application to an earlier assembly. However, there may be multiple assemblies involved. This is where the configuration tool comes in handy. It allows you to view previous assembly configurations and select the assemblies *en masse* to be used with the application.

To view and select previous configurations, select *Applications – Fix an Application* from the Configuration tool menu. Figure 1-13 combines the two dialog boxes that subsequently appear. The main window lists applications that have run and been recorded. The smaller window (a portion of a larger dialog) is displayed when you click on an application. This window lists the most recent (up to five) configurations associated with the application. You simply select the assembly configuration that you want the application to use.

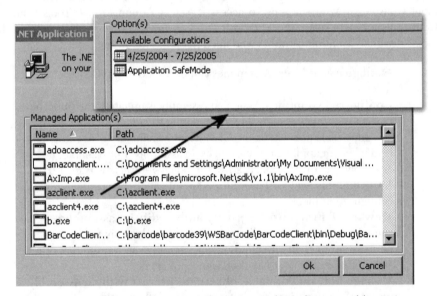

Figure 1-13   Using application configuration tool to select assembly version

This configuration tool is clearly targeted for administrators. Individual developers should rely on a subset of this tool that is packaged as three wizards: Adjust .NET Security, Trust An Assembly, and Fix An Application. Access these by selecting Framework Wizards from Administrative Tools.

1.5   Understanding the C# Compiler

Many developers writing nontrivial .NET applications rely on Visual Studio or some other Integrated Development Environment (IDE) to enter source code, link external assemblies, perform debugging, and create the final compiled output. If you fall into this category, it is not essential that you understand how to use the .NET SDK and raw C# compiler; however, it will increase your understanding of the .NET compilation process and give you a better feel for working with assemblies. As a byproduct, it will also acquaint you with the command line as a way to work with SDK programs. Many of the utilities presented in the previous section are invoked from the command line, and you will occasionally find it useful to perform compilation in that environment rather than firing up your IDE.

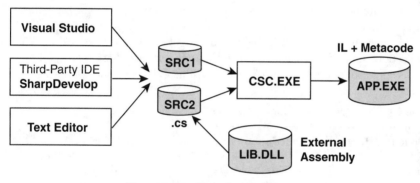

Figure 1-14   Compilation process

Figure 1-14 shows the basic steps that occur in converting source code to the final compiled output. The purpose of this section is to demonstrate how a text editor and the C# compiler can be used to build an application. Along the way, it will provide a detailed look at the many compiler options that are hidden by the IDE.

Locating the Compiler

The C# compiler, `csc.exe`, is located in the path where the .NET Framework is installed:

```
C:\winnt\Microsoft.NET\Framework\v2.0.40607
```

Of course, this may vary depending on your operating system and the version of Framework installed. To make the compiler available from the command line in any current directory, you must add this path to the system Path variable. Follow the steps described in the previous section for setting the path for the SDK utilities.

Type in the following statement at the command line to verify that the compiler can be accessed:

```
C:\>csc /help
```

Compiling from the Command Line

To compile the C# console application client.cs into the executable client.exe, enter either of the following statements at the command prompt:

```
C:\> csc client.cs
C:\> csc /t:exe client.cs
```

Both statements compile the source into an executable (.exe) file—the default output from the compiler. As shown in Table 1-4, the output type is specified using the /t: flag. To create a DLL file, set the target value to *library*. For a WinForms application, specify /t:winexe. Note that you can use /t:exe to create a WinForms application, but the console will be visible as background window.

Table 1-4   Selected Options for the C# Command-Line Compiler

Option	Description
/addmodule	Specifies a module that is to be included in the assembly created. This is an easy way to create a multi-file assembly.
/debug	Causes debug information to be produced.
/define	Preprocessor directive can be passed to compiler: /define:DEBUG.
/delaysign	Builds an assembly using *delayed signing* of the strong name. This is discussed in Chapter 15.
/doc	Used to specify that an output file containing XML documentation is to be produced.
/keyfile	Specifies the path to the .snk file containing the key pair used for strong signing (see Chapter 15).
/lib	Specifies where assemblies included in the /reference option are located.
/out	Name of the file containing compiled output. The default is the name of the input file with .exe suffix.

Table 1-4 Selected Options for the C# Command-Line Compiler *(continued)*

Option	Description
`/reference (/r)`	References an external assembly.
`/resource`	Used to embed resource files into the assembly that is created.
`/target (/t)`	Specifies the type of output file created:
	`/t:exe` builds a `*.exe` console application. This is the default output.
	`/t:library` builds a `*.dll` assembly.
	`/t:module` builds a module (Portable Executable file) that does not contain a manifest.
	`/t:winexe` builds a `*.exe` Windows Forms assembly.

The real value of working with the raw compiler is the ability to work with multiple files and assemblies. For demonstration purposes, create two simple C# source files: `client.cs` and `clientlib.cs`.

client.cs
```
using System;
public class MyApp
{
    static void Main(string[] args)
    {
        ShowName.ShowMe("Core C#");
    }
}
```

clientlib.cs
```
using System;
public class ShowName
{
    public static void ShowMe(string MyName)
    {
        Console.WriteLine(MyName);
    }
}
```

It's not important to understand the code details, only that the `client` routine calls a function in `clientlib` that writes a message to the console. Using the C# compiler, we can implement this relationship in a number of ways that not only demonstrate compiler options but also shed light on the use of assemblies.

Example 1: Compiling Multiple Files

The C# compiler accepts any number of input source files. It combines their output into a single file assembly:

```
csc /out:client.exe client.cs clientlib.cs
```

Example 2: Creating and Using a Code Library

The code in `clientlib` can be placed in a separate library that can be accessed by any client:

```
csc /t:library clientlib.cs
```

The output is an assembly named `clientlib.dll`. Now, compile the client code and reference this external assembly:

```
csc /r:clientlib.dll   client.cs
```

The output is an assembly named `client.exe`. If you examine this with Ildasm, you see that the manifest contains a reference to the `clientlib` assembly.

Example 3: Creating an Assembly with Multiple Files

Rather than existing as a separate assembly, `clientlib` can also be packaged as a separate file inside the `client.exe` assembly. Because only one file in an assembly may contain a manifest, it is first necessary to complile `clientlib.cs` into a Portable Executable[4] (PE) module. This is done by selecting *module* as the target output:

```
csc /t:module clientlib.cs
```

The output file is `clientfile.netmodule`. Now, it can be placed in the `client.exe` assembly by using the compiler's `addmodule` switch:

```
csc /addmodule:clientlib.netmodule client.cs
```

The resultant assembly consists of two files: `client.exe` and `clientlib.netmodule`.

These examples, shown in Figure 1-15, illustrate the fact that even a simple application presents the developer with multiple architectural choices for implementing an application.

---

4. The PE format defines the layout for executable files that run on 32- or 64-bit Windows systems.

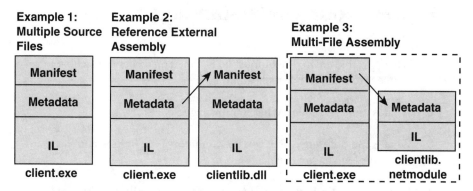

Figure 1-15 Options for deploying an application

1.6 Summary

The .NET Framework consists of the Common Language Runtime (CLR) and the Framework Class Library (FCL). The CLR manages all the tasks associated with code execution. It first ensures that code is CLR compliant based on the Common Language Specification (CLS) standard. It then loads an application and locates all dependent assemblies. Its Just-in-Time (JIT) compiler converts the IL contained in an application's assembly, the smallest deployable code unit in .NET, into native machine code. During the actual program execution, the CLR handles security, manages threads, allocates memory, and performs garbage collection for releasing unused memory.

All code must be packaged in an assembly in order for the CLR to use it. An assembly is either a single file or grouping of multiple physical files treated as a single unit. It may contain code modules as well as resource files.

The FCL provides a reusable set of classes and other types that are available to all CLR-compliant code. This eliminates the need for compiler-specific libraries. Although the FCL consists of several physical DLLs containing over a thousand types, it's made manageable by the use of namespaces that impose a logical hierarchy over all the types.

To assist the developer in debugging and deploying software, .NET includes a set of utilities that enables an administrator to perform such tasks as managing assemblies, precompiling assemblies, adding files to an assembly, and viewing class details. In addition, a wealth of open source .NET tools is becoming available to aid the development process.

1.7   Test Your Understanding

1. What portable environment must be installed on a client's machine to enable it to run a .NET application?

2. What is managed code? What is unmanaged code?

3. What is the difference between the Common Type System and the Common Language Specification?

4. How does the CLR allow code from different compilers to interact?

5. What is the role of the Global Assembly Cache?

6. What four components make up the identity of a strongly named assembly?

7. What is the relationship between a namespace and an assembly?

8. Describe what these commonly used acronyms stand for: CLR, GAC, FCL, IL.

C# Language
Fundamentals

Topics in This Chapter

- *Overview of a C# Program:* In addition to the basic elements that comprise a C# program, a developer needs to be aware of other .NET features such as commenting options and recommended naming conventions.

- *Primitives:* Primitives are the basic data types defined by the FCL to represent numbers, characters, and dates.

- *Operators:* C# uses traditional operator syntax to perform arithmetic and conditional operations.

- *Program Flow Statements:* Program flow can be controlled using `if` and `switch` statements for selection; and `while`, `do`, `for`, and `foreach` clauses for iteration.

- *String:* The `string` class supports the expected string operations: concatenation, extracting substrings, searching for instances of a character pattern, and both case sensitive and insensitive comparisons.

- *Enums:* An enumeration is a convenient way to assign descriptions that can be used to reference an underlying set of values.

- *Using Arrays:* Single- or multi-dimensional arrays of any type can be created in C#. After an array is created, the `System.Array` class can be used to sort and copy the array.

- *Reference and Value Types:* All types in .NET are either a value or reference type. It is important to understand the differences and how they can affect a program's performance.

Chapter 2

In September 2000, an ECMA[1] (international standardization group for information and communication systems) task group was established to define a Microsoft proposed standard for the C# programming language. Its stated design goal was to produce "a simple, modern, general-purpose, object-oriented programming language." The result, defined in a standard known as *ECMA-334*, is a satisfyingly clean language with a syntax that resembles Java, and clearly borrows from C++ and C. It's a language designed to promote software robustness with array bounds checking, strong type checking, and the prohibition of uninitialized variables.

This chapter introduces you to the fundamentals of the language: It illustrates the basic parts of a C# program; compares value and reference types; and describes the syntax for operators and statements used for looping and controlling program flow. As an experienced programmer, this should be familiar terrain through which you can move quickly. However, the section on *value* and *reference types* may demand a bit more attention. Understanding the differences in how .NET handles value and reference types can influence program design choices.

---

1. ECMA International was formerly known as European Computer Manufacturers Association and is referred to herein simply as ECMA.

2.1   The Layout of a C# Program

Figure 2-1 illustrates some of the basic features of a C# program.

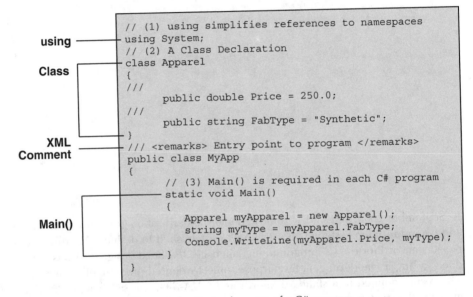

using

Class

XML Comment

Main()

```
// (1) using simplifies references to namespaces
using System;
// (2) A Class Declaration
class Apparel
{
///
    public double Price = 250.0;
///
    public string FabType = "Synthetic";
}
/// <remarks> Entry point to program </remarks>
public class MyApp
{
    // (3) Main() is required in each C# program
    static void Main()
    {
        Apparel myApparel = new Apparel();
        string myType = myApparel.FabType;
        Console.WriteLine(myApparel.Price, myType);
    }
}
```

Figure 2-1   Basic elements of a C# program

The code in Figure 2-1 consists of a class `MyApp` that contains the program logic and a class `Apparel` that contains the data. The program creates an instance of `Apparel` and assigns it to `myApparel`. This object is then used to print the values of the class members `FabType` and `Price` to the console. The important features to note include the following:

1. **The `using` statement specifies the namespace `System`.** Recall from Chapter 1, "Introduction to .NET and C#," that the .NET class libraries are organized into namespaces and that the `System` namespace contains all of the simple data types. The `using` statement tells the compiler to search this namespace when resolving references, making it unnecessary to use fully qualified names. For example, you can refer to `label` rather than `System.Web.UI.WebControls.Label`.

2. **All programming logic and data must be contained within a *type* definition.** All program logic and data must be embedded in a class, structure, enum, interface, or delegate. Unlike Visual Basic, for

instance, C# has no global variable that exists outside the scope of a type. Access to types and type members is strictly controlled by access modifiers. In this example, the access modifier `public` permits external classes—such as `MyApp`—to access the two members of the `Apparel` class.

3. **A `Main()` method is required for every executable C# application.** This method serves as the entry point to the application; it must always have the `static` modifier and the `M` must be capitalized. Overloaded forms of `Main()` define a return type and accept a parameter list as input.

Return an integer value:

```
static int Main()
{
    return 0; // must return an integer value
}
```

Receive a list of command-line arguments as a parameter and return an integer value:

```
static int Main(string[] args)
{
    // loop through arguments
    foreach(string myArg in args)
        Console.WriteLine(myArg);
    return 0;
}
```

The parameter is a string array containing the contents of the command line used to invoke the program. For example, this command line executes the program `MyApparel` and passes it two parameter values:

```
C:\> MyApparel 5 6
```

Core Note

The contents of the command line are passed as an argument to the `Main()` method. The `System.Environment.CommandLine` property also exposes the command line's contents.

General C# Programming Notes

Case Sensitivity

All variable and keywords are distinguished by case sensitivity. Replace `class` with `Class` in Figure 2-1 and the code will not compile.

Naming Conventions

The ECMA standard provides naming convention guidelines to be followed in your C# code. In addition to promoting consistency, following a strict naming policy can minimize errors related to case sensitivity that often result from undisciplined naming schemes. Table 2-1 summarizes some of the more important recommendations.

Note that the case of a name may be based on two capitalization schemes:

1. **Pascal.** The first character of each word is capitalized (for example, `MyClassAdder`).
2. **Camel.** The first character of each word, except the first, is capitalized (for example, `myClassAdder`).

Table 2-1   C# Naming Conventions

Type	Case	Notes and Examples
Class	Pascal	• Use noun or noun phrases. • Try to avoid starting with `I` because this is reserved for interfaces. • Do not use underscores.
Constant	Pascal	`public const double GramToPound = 454.0 ;`
Enum Type	Pascal	• Use Pascal case for the enum value names. • Use singular name for enums. `public enum WarmColor { Orange, Yellow, Brown}`
Event	Pascal	• The method that handles events should have the suffix `EventHandler`. • Event argument classes should have the suffix `EventArgs`.
Exception	Pascal	• Has suffix `Exception`.
Interface	Pascal	• Has prefix of `I`. `IDisposable`
Local Variable	Camel	• Variables with `public` access modifier use Pascal. `int myIndex`

Table 2-1   C# Naming Conventions *(continued)*

Type	Case	Notes and Examples
Method	Pascal	• Use verb or verb phrases for name.
Namespace	Pascal	• Do not have a namespace and class with the same name. • Use prefixes to avoid namespaces having the same name. For example, use a company name to categorize namespaces developed by that company. `Acme.GraphicsLib`
Property	Pascal	• Use noun or noun phrase.
Parameter	Camel	• Use meaningful names that describe the parameter's purpose.

The rule of thumb is to use Pascal capitalization everywhere except with parameters and local variables.

Commenting a C# Program

The C# compiler supports three types of embedded comments: an XML version and the two single-line (//) and multi-line (/* */) comments familiar to most programmers:

```
//    for a single line
/*    for one or more lines
                      */
/// <remarks> XML comment describing a class </remarks>
```

An XML comment begins with three slashes (///) and usually contains XML tags that document a particular aspect of the code such as a structure, a class, or class member. The C# parser can expand the XML tags to provide additional information and export them to an external file for further processing.

The <remarks> tag—shown in Figure 2-1—is used to describe a type (class). The C# compiler recognizes eight other primary tags that are associated with a particular program element (see Table 2-2). These tags are placed directly above the lines of code they refer to.

Table 2-2   XML Documentation Tags

Tag	Description
`<example>`	Text illustrating an example of using a particular program feature goes between the beginning and ending tags.
`<exception cref="Excep">`	cref attribute contains name of exception. `/// <exception cref="NoParmException"></exception>`
`<include file="myXML">`	file attribute is set to name of another XML file that is to be included in the XML documentation produced by this source code.
`<param name="parm1">`	name attribute contains the name of the parameter.
`<permission cref= "">`	Most of the time this is set to the following: `///<permission cref="System.Security.Permis-sionSet"> </permission>`
`<remarks>`	Provides additional information about a type not found in the `<summary>` section.
`<returns>`	Place a textual description of what is returned from a method or property between the beginning and ending tags.
`<seealso cref="price">`	The cref attribute is set to the name of an associated type, field, method, or other type member.
`<summary>`	Contains a class description; is used by IntelliSense in VisualStudio.NET.

The value of the XML comments lies in the fact that they can be exported to a separate XML file and then processed using standard XML parsing techniques. You must instruct the compiler to generate this file because it is not done by default.

The following line compiles the source code `consoleapp.cs` and creates an XML file `consoleXML`:

```
C:\> csc consoleapp.cs /doc:consoleXML.xml
```

If you compile the code in Figure 2-1, you'll find that the compiler generates warnings for all `public` members in your code:

```
Warning CS1591: Missing XML comment for publicly visible type ...
```

To suppress this, add the /nowarn:1591 option to the compile-line command. The option accepts multiple warning codes separated with a comma.

Core Note

Many documentation tools are available to transform and extend the C# XML documentation output. One of the most advanced is NDoc (ndoc.sourceforge.net), an open source tool that not only formats the XML but uses reflection to glean further information about an assembly.

2.2 Primitives

The next three sections of this chapter describe features that you'll find in most programming languages: variables and data types, operators, expressions, and statements that control the flow of operations. The discussion begins with *primitives*. As the name implies, these are the core C# data types used as building blocks for more complex class and structure types. Variables of this type contain a single value and always have the same predefined size. Table 2-3 provides a formal list of primitives, their corresponding core data types, and their sizes.

Table 2-3 C# Primitive Data Types

C# Primitive Type	FCL Data Type	Description
object	System.Object	Ultimate base type of all other types.
string	System.String	A sequence of Unicode characters.
decimal	System.Decimal	Precise decimal with 28 significant digits.
bool	System.Boolean	A value represented as true or false.
char	System.Char	A 16-bit Unicode character.
byte	System.Byte	8-bit unsigned integral type.
sbyte	System.SByte	8-bit signed integral type.
short	System.Int16	16-bit signed integral type.
int	System.Int32	32-bit signed integral type.

Table 2-3   C# Primitive Data Types *(continued)*

C# Primitive Type	FCL Data Type	Description
long	System.Int64	64-bit signed integral type.
ushort	System.UInt16	16-bit unsigned integral type.
uint	System.UInt32	32-bit unsigned integral type.
ulong	System.UIint64	64-bit unsigned integral type.
single (float)	System.Single	Single-precision floating-point type.
double	System.Double	Double-precision floating-point type.

As the table shows, primitives map directly to types in the base class library and can be used interchangeably. Consider these statements:

```
System.Int32 age = new System.Int32(17);
int age = 17;
System.Int32 age = 17;
```

They all generate exactly the same Intermediate Language (IL) code. The shorter version relies on C# providing the keyword int as an alias for the System.Int32 type. C# performs aliasing for all primitives.

Here are a few points to keep in mind when working with primitives:

- The keywords that identify the value type primitives (such as int) are actually aliases for an underlying structure (struct type in C#). Special members of these structures can be used to manipulate the primitives. For example, the Int32 structure has a field that returns the largest 32-bit integer and a method that converts a numeric string to an integer value:

  ```
  int iMax = int.MaxValue;    // Return largest integer
  int pVal = int.Parse("100"); // converts string to int
  ```

  The C# compiler supports implicit conversions if the conversion is a "safe" conversion that results in no loss of data. This occurs when the target of the conversion has a greater precision than the object being converted, and is called a *widening conversion*. In the case of a *narrowing conversion*, where the target has less precision, the conversion must have explicit *casting*. Casting is used to coerce, or convert, a value of one type into that of another. This is done syntactically by placing the target data type in parentheses in front of the value being converted: int i = (int)y;.

```
short i16 = 50;      // 16-bit integer
int i32 = i16;       // Okay: int has greater precision
i16 = i32;           // Fails: short is 16 bit, int is 32
i16 = (short) i32;   // Okay since casting used
```

• Literal values assigned to the types float, double, and decimal require that their value include a trailing letter: float requires F or f; double has an optional D or d; and decimal requires M or m.

```
decimal pct = .15M; // M is required for literal value
```

The remainder of this section offers an overview of the most useful primitives with the exception of string, which is discussed later in the chapter.

decimal

The decimal type is a 128-bit high-precision floating-point number. It provides 28 decimal digits of precision and is used in financial calculations where rounding cannot be tolerated. This example illustrates three of the many methods available to decimal type. Also observe that when assigning a literal value to a decimal type, the M suffix must be used.

```
decimal iRate = 3.9834M;          // decimal requires M
iRate = decimal.Round(iRate,2);   // Returns 3.98
decimal dividend = 512.0M;
decimal divisor = 51.0M;
decimal p = decimal.Parse("100.05");
// Next statement returns remainder = 2
decimal rem = decimal.Remainder(dividend,divisor);
```

bool

The only possible values of a bool type are true and false. It is not possible to cast a bool value to an integer—for example, convert true to a 1, or to cast a 1 or 0 to a bool.

```
bool bt = true;
string bStr = bt.ToString(); // returns "true"
bt = (bool) 1;               // fails
```

char

The char type represents a 16-bit Unicode character and is implemented as an unsigned integer. A char type accepts a variety of assignments: a character value placed between individual quote marks (' '); a casted numeric value; or an escape sequence. As the example illustrates, char also has a number of useful methods provided by the System.Char structure:

```
myChar =  'B';          // 'B' has an ASCII value of 66
myChar = (char) 66;     // Equivalent to 'B'
myChar = '\u0042';      // Unicode escape sequence
myChar = '\x0042';      // Hex escape sequence
myChar = '\t';          // Simple esc sequence:horizontal tab
bool bt;
string pattern = "123abcd?";
myChar = pattern[0];                    // '1'
bt = char.IsLetter(pattern,3);          // true    ('a')
bt = char.IsNumber(pattern,3);          // false
bt = char.IsLower(pattern,0);           // false   ('1')
bt = char.IsPunctuation(pattern,7);     // true    ('?')
bt = char.IsLetterOrDigit(pattern,1);   // true
bt = char.IsNumber(pattern,2);          // true    ('3')
string kstr="K";
char k = char.Parse(kstr);
```

byte, sbyte

A byte is an 8-bit unsigned integer with a value from 0 to 255. An sbyte is an 8-bit signed integer with a value from –128 to 127.

```
byte[] b = {0x00, 0x12, 0x34, 0x56, 0xAA, 0x55, 0xFF};
string s = b[4].ToString(); // returns 170
char myChar = (char) b[3];
```

short, int, long

These represent 16-, 32-, and 64-bit signed integer values, respectively. The unsigned versions are also available (ushort, uint, ulong).

```
short i16 = 200;
i16 = 0xC8 ;      // hex value for 200
int i32 = i16;    // no casting required
```

single, double

These are represented in 32-bit single-precision and 64-bit double-precision formats. In .NET 1.x, single is referred to as float.

- The single type has a value range of 1.5×10^{-45} to 3.4×10^{38} with 7-decimal digit precision.
- The double type has a value range of 5×10^{-324} to 1.7×10^{308} with 15- to 16-decimal digit precision.
- Floating-point operations return NaN *(Not a Number)* to signal that the result of the operation is undefined. For example, dividing 0.0 by 0.0 results in NaN.
- Use the System.Convert method when converting floating-point numbers to another type.

```
float xFloat = 24567.66F;
int xInt = Convert.ToInt32(xFloat);   // returns 24567
int xInt2 = (int) xFloat;
if(xInt == xInt2) {  }                // False
string xStr = Convert.ToString(xFloat);
single zero = 0;
if (Single.IsNaN(0 / zero)) {  }      // True
double xDouble = 124.56D;
```

Note that the F suffix is used when assigning a literal value to a single type, and D is optional for a double type.

Using Parse and TryParse to Convert a Numeric String

The primitive numeric types include Parse and TryParse methods that are used to convert a string of numbers to the specified numeric type. This code illustrates:

```
short shParse   = Int16.Parse("100");
int iParse      = Int32.Parse("100");
long lparse     = Int64.Parse("100");
decimal dParse = decimal.Parse("99.99");
float sParse    = float.Parse("99.99");
double dbParse = double.Parse("99.99");
```

TryParse, introduced in .NET 2.0, provides conditional parsing. It returns a boolean value indicating whether the parse is successful, which provides a way to avoid formal exception handling code. The following example uses an `Int32` type to demonstrate the two forms of `TryParse`:

```
int result;
// parse string and place result in result parameter
bool ok = Int32.TryParse("100", out result);
bool ok = Int32.TryParse("100", NumberStyles.Integer, null,
                          out result);
```

In the second form of this method, the first parameter is the text string being parsed, and the second parameter is a `NumberStyles` enumeration that describes what the input string may contain. The value is returned in the fourth parameter.

2.3   Operators: Arithmetic, Logical, and Conditional

The C# operators used for arithmetic operations, bit manipulation, and conditional program flow should be familiar to all programmers. This section presents an overview of these operators that is meant to serve as a syntactical reference.

Arithmetic Operators

Table 2-4 summarizes the basic numerical operators. The precedence in which these operators are applied during the evaluation of an expression is shown in parentheses, with 1 being the highest precedence.

Table 2-4   Numerical Operators

Operator		Description	Example
+ -	(3)	Addition Subtraction	`int x = y + 10;`

*
/
%
	(2)	Multiplication
		Division,
		Modulo
			`int x = 60;`
			`int y = 15;`
			`int z = x * y / 2;   // 450`
			`y = x % 29 ;   // remainder is 2`

++
--
	(1)	Prefix/postfix
		Increment/decrement
			`x = 5;`
			`Console.WriteLine(x++) // x = 5`
			`Console.WriteLine(++x) // x = 6`

~	(1)	Bitwise complement	`int x = ~127;    // returns -128`

Table 2-4 Numerical Operators *(continued)*

Operator		Description	Example

>>
<<
	(4)	Shift right
		Shift left
			`byte x = 10; // binary 10 is 01010`
			`int result = x << 1; // 20 = 10100`
			`result = x >> 2;     //  5 = 00101`
			Works with `byte, char, short, int,` and
			`long`

&
|
^
	(5-6-7)	Bitwise AND
		Bitwise OR
		Bitwise XOR
			`byte x = 12;          //    001100`
			`byte y = 11;          //    001011`
			`int result = x & y; //8 = 001000`
			`result = x ^ y;     //7 = 000111`

Core Note

C# does not provide an exponentiation operator. Instead, use the `Math.Pow()` *method to raise a number to a power, and* `Math.Exp()` *to raise e to a power.*

Conditional and Relational Operators

Relational operators are used to compare two values and determine their relationship. They are generally used in conjunction with conditional operators to form more complex decision constructs. Table 2-5 provides a summary of C# relational and conditional operators.

Table 2-5 Relational and Conditional Boolean Operators

Statement	Description	Example
== !=	Equality Inequality	`if (x == y) {...}`
< <= > >=	Numeric less than Less than or equal to Greater than Greater than or equal to	`if (x <= y) {...}`
&& ||	Logical AND Logical OR	`if  (x == y && y < 30) {...}` If first expression is false, second is not evaluated

Table 2-5 Relational and Conditional Boolean Operators *(continued)*

Statement	Description	Example
& |	Logical AND Logical OR	`if  (x== y | y < 30) {...}` Always evaluates second expression
!	Logical negation	`if !(x ==y && y < 30) {...}`

Note the two forms of the logical AND/OR operations. The `&&` and `||` operators do not evaluate the second expression if the first is false—a technique known as *short circuit evaluation*. The `&` and `|` operators always evaluate both expressions. They are used primarily when the expression values are returned from a method and you want to ensure that the methods are called.

In addition to the operators in Table 2-5, C# supports a `?:` operator for conditionally assigning a value to a variable. As this example shows, it is basically shorthand for using an `if-else` statement:

```
string pass;
int grade=74;
If(grade >= 70) pass="pass"; else pass="fail";
//      expression   ? op1  : op2
pass = (grade >= 70)  ? "pass" : "fail";
```

If the expression is `true`, the `?:` operator returns the first value; if it's `false`, the second is returned.

Control Flow Statements

The C# language provides `if` and `switch` conditional constructs that should be quite familiar to C++ and Java programmers. Table 2-6 provides a summary of these statements.

Table 2-6 Control Flow Statements

Conditional Statement	Example

`if (boolean expression) {`
`    // statements`
`} else {`
`    // statements`
`}`
	`if (bmi < 24.9) {`
	`    weight = "normal";`
	`    riskFactor = 2;`
	`} else {`
	`    weight = "over";`
	`    riskFactor=6;`
	`}`

Table 2-6 Control Flow Statements *(continued)*

Conditional Statement	Example
| ```c#
switch (expression)
{
    case constant expression:
        // statements;
        // break/goto/return()
    case constant expression:
        // statements;
        // break/goto/return()
    default:
        // statements;
        // break/goto/return()
}
``` | ```c#
switch (ndx)
{
    case 1:
        fabric = "cotton";
        blend = "100%";
        break;
    case 2:   // combine 2 & 3
    case 3:
        fabric = "cotton";
        blend = "60%";
        break;
    default:   // optional
        fabric = "cotton";
        blend = "50%";
        break;
}
``` |

- Constant expression may be an integer, enum value, or string.
- No "fall through" is permitted. Each case block must end with a statement that transfers control.

if-else

Syntax:

```c#
if ( boolean expression ) statement
if ( boolean expression ) statement1 else statement2
```

C# if statements behave as they do in other languages. The only issue you may encounter is how to format the statements when nesting multiple if-else clauses.

```c#
// Nested if statements
if (age > 16)
{
    if (sex == "M")
    {
        type = "Man";
    } else {
        type = "Woman" ;
    }
} else {
    type = "child";
}
```

```c#
if (age > 16)
    if (sex == "M")
        type = "Man";
    else
        type = "Woman" ;
else
    type = "child";
```

Both code segments are equivalent. The right-hand form takes advantage of the fact that curly braces are not required to surround single statements; and the subordinate if clause is regarded as a single statement, despite the fact that it takes several lines. The actual coding style selected is not as important as agreeing on a single style to be used.

switch

Syntax:

```
switch( expression ) {switch block}
```

The expression is one of the int types, a character, or a string. The switch block consists of case labels—and an optional default label—associated with a constant expression that must implicitly convert to the same type as the expression. Here is an example using a string expression:

```
// switch with string expression
using System;
public class MyApp
{
   static void Main(String[] args)
   {
      switch (args[0])
      {
         case "COTTON":    // is case sensitive
         case "cotton":
             Console.WriteLine("A good natural fiber.");
             goto case "natural";
         case "polyester":
             Console.WriteLine("A no-iron synthetic fiber.");
             break;
         case "natural":
             Console.WriteLine("A Natural Fiber. ");
             break;
         default:
             Console.WriteLine("Fiber is unknown.");
             break;
      }
   }
}
```

The most important things to observe in this example are as follows:

- C# does not permit execution to fall through one `case` block to the next. Each `case` block must end with a statement that transfers control. This will be a `break`, `goto`. or `return` statement.
- Multiple `case` labels may be associated with a single block of code.
- The `switch` statement is case sensitive; in the example, `"Cotton"` and `"COTTON"` represent two different values.

2.4 Loops

C# provides four iteration statements: `while`, `do`, `for`, and `foreach`. The first three are the same constructs you find in C, C++, and Java; the `foreach` statement is designed to loop through collections of data such as arrays.

while loop

Syntax:

```
while ( boolean expression ) { body }
```

The statement(s) in the loop body are executed until the boolean expression is `false`. The loop does not execute if the expression is initially `false`.

Example:

```
byte[] r = {0x00, 0x12, 0x34, 0x56, 0xAA, 0x55, 0xFF};
int ndx=0;
int totVal = 0;
while (ndx <=6)
{
    totVal +=      r[ndx];
    ndx += 1;
}
```

do loop

Syntax:

```
do { do-body } while ( boolean expression );
```

This is similar to the `while` statement except that the evaluation is performed at the end of the iteration. Consequently, this loop executes at least once.

Example:

```
byte[] r = {0x00, 0x12, 0x34, 0x56, 0xAA, 0x55, 0xFF};
int ndx=0;
int totVal = 0;
do
{
    totVal += r[ndx];
    ndx += 1;
}
while (ndx <= 6);
```

for loop

Syntax:

```
for ( [initialization]; [termination condition]; [iteration] )
    { for-body }
```

The `for` construct contains initialization, a termination condition, and the iteration statement to be used in the loop. All are optional. The initialization is executed once, and then the condition is checked; as long as it is `true`, the iteration update occurs after the body is executed. The iteration statement is usually a simple increment to the control variable, but may be any operation.

Example:

```
int[] r = {80, 88, 90, 72, 68, 94, 83};
int totVal = 0;
for (int ndx = 0; ndx <= 6; ndx++) {
    totVal += r[ndx];
}
```

If any of the clauses in the `for` statement are left out, they must be accounted for elsewhere in the code. This example illustrates how omission of the `for-iteration` clause is handled:

```
for   (ndx = 0; ndx < 6; )
{
    totVal += r[ndx];
    ndx++;            // increment here
}
```

You can also leave out all of the `for` clauses:

```
for (;;) { body   }   // equivalent to while(true) { body }
```

A `return`, `goto`, or `break` statement is required to exit this loop.

foreach loop

Syntax:

```
foreach ( type identifier in collection )   { body }
```

The *type* and *identifier* declare the *iteration variable*. This construct loops once for each element in the collection and sets the iteration variable to the value of the current collection element. The iteration variable is read-only, and a compile error occurs if the program attempts to set its value.

For demonstration purposes, we will use an array as the collection. Keep in mind, however, that it is not restricted to an array. There is a useful set of collection classes defined in .NET that work equally well with `foreach`. We look at those in Chapter 4, "Working with Objects in C#."

Example:

```
int totVal = 0;
foreach (int arrayVal in r)
{
    totVal += arrayVal;
}
```

In a one-dimensional array, iteration begins with index 0 and moves in ascending order. In a multi-dimensional array, iteration occurs through the rightmost index first. For example, in a two-dimensional array, iteration begins in the first column and moves across the row. When it reaches the end, it moves to the next row of the first column and iterates that row.

Transferring Control Within a Loop

It is often necessary to terminate a loop, or redirect the flow of statements within the loop body, based on conditions that arise during an iteration. For example, a while (true) loop obviously requires that the loop termination logic exists in the body. Table 2-7 summarizes the principal statements used to redirect the program flow.

Table 2-7   Statements to Exit a Loop or Redirect the Iteration

Statement	Description	Example
break	Redirects program control to the end point of a containing loop construct.	```while (true) { ndx+=1; if (ndx >10) break; }```
continue	Starts a new iteration of enclosing loop without executing remaining statements in loop.	```while (ndx <10) { ndx +=1; if(ndx %2 =1) continue; totVal += ndx; }```
goto *identifier*; goto case *exp*; goto default;	Directs program control to a label, a case statement within a switch block, or the default statement within a switch block. The goto may not transfer control into a nested scope—for example, a loop.	```public int FindMatch(string myColor) { string[] colorsAvail("blueaqua", "red", "green","navyblue"); int loc; int matches=0; foreach (colorType in colorsAvail) { loc = colortype.IndexOf(myColor); if (loc >=0) goto Found; continue; Found: matches += 1; } return(matches); }```
return [*expression*] ;	Returns program control to the method that called the current method. Returns no argument if the enclosing method has a void return type.	```public double Area(double w, double l) { return w * l; }```

There are few occasions where the use of a goto statement improves program logic. The goto default version may be useful in eliminating redundant code inside a switch block, but aside from that, avoid its use.

2.5 C# Preprocessing Directives

Preprocessing directives are statements read by the C# compiler during its lexical analysis phase. They can instruct the compiler to include/exclude code or even abort compilation based on the value of preprocessing directives.

A preprocessor directive is identified by the # character that must be the first non-blank character in the line. Blank spaces are permitted before and after the # symbol. Table 2-8 lists the directives that C# recognizes.

Table 2-8 Preprocessing Directives

C# Preprocessing Symbol	Description
#define #undef	Used to define and undefine a symbol. Defining a symbol makes it evaluate to true when used in a #if directive.
#if #elif #else #endif	Analogues to the C# if, else if, and else statements.
#line	Changes the line number sequence and can identify which file is the source for the line.
#region #endregion	Used to specify a block of code that you can expand or collapse when using the outlining feature of Visual Studio.NET.
#error #warning	#error causes the compiler to report a fatal error. #warning causes the compiler to report a warning and continue processing.

The three most common uses for preprocessing directives are to perform conditional compilation, add diagnostics to report errors and warnings, and define code regions.

Conditional Compilation

The #if related directives are used to selectively determine which code is included during compilation. Any code placed between the #if statement and #endif statement is included or excluded based on whether the #if condition is true or false. This is a powerful feature that is used most often for debug purposes. Here is an example that illustrates the concept:

```
#define DEBUG
using System;
public class MyApp
{
    public static void Main()
    {
        #if (DEBUG)
            Console.WriteLine("Debug Mode");
        #else
            Console.WriteLine("Release Mode");
        #endif
    }
}
```

Any #define directives must be placed at the beginning of the .cs file. A conditional compilation symbol has two states: *defined* or *undefined*. In this example, the DEBUG symbol is defined and the subsequent #if (DEBUG) statement evaluates to true. The explicit use of the #define directive permits you to control the debug state of each source file. Note that if you are using Visual Studio, you can specify a Debug build that results in the DEBUG symbol being automatically defined for each file in the project. No explicit #define directive is required.

You can also define a symbol on the C# compile command line using the /Define switch:

```
csc /Define:DEBUG myproject.cs
```

Compiling code with this statement is equivalent to including a #Define DEBUG statement in the source code.

Diagnostic Directives

Diagnostic directives issue warning and error messages that are treated just like any other compile-time errors and warnings. The #warning directive allows compilation to continue, whereas the #error terminates it.

```
#define CLIENT
#define DEBUG
using System;
public class MyApp
{
    public static void Main()
    {
        #if DEBUG && INHOUSE
            #warning Debug is on.
        #elif DEBUG && CLIENT
            #error Debug not allowed in Client Code.
        #endif
    // Rest of program follows here
```

In this example, compilation will terminate with an error message since DEBUG and CLIENT are defined.

Code Regions

The region directives are used to mark sections of code as regions. The region directive has no semantic meaning to the C# compiler, but is recognized by Visual Studio.NET, which uses it to hide or collapse code regions. Expect other third-party source management tools to take advantage of these directives.

```
#region
    // any C# statements
#endregion
```

2.6   Strings

The System.String, or string class, is a reference type that is represented internally by a sequence of 16-bit Unicode characters. Unlike other reference types, C# treats a string as a primitive type: It can be declared as a constant, and it can be assigned a literal string value.

String Literals

Literal values assigned to string variables take two forms: literals enclosed in quotation marks, and verbatim strings that begin with @" and end with a closing double quote ("). The difference between the two is how they handle escape characters. Regular literals respond to the meaning of escape characters, whereas verbatim strings treat them as regular text. Table 2-9 provides a summary of the escape characters that can be placed in strings.

Table 2-9   String Escape Characters

Escape Character	Description
\'	Inserts a single quote into a string
\"	Inserts a double quote
\\	Inserts a backslash; useful for file paths
\a	System alert
\b	Backspace
\f	Form feed
\n	Inserts a new line
\r	Carriage return
\t	Horizontal tab
\u	Unicode character
\v	Vertical tab
\0	Null character

A *verbatim string* serves the purpose its name implies: to include any character placed between the beginning and ending double quote. The following segment provides several examples of using literals:

```
string myQuote, path;
myQuote = @"The solution is in the problem.";
myQuote = "The solution\nis in the problem.";
myQuote = "The Unicode representation of f is \u0066";
// The next two statements assign the same value to myQuote.
myQuote = @"""The solution is in the problem. """;
myQuote = "\"The solution is in the problem. "";
// The next two statements assign the same value to path.
path    = @"c:\my documents\notes.txt";
path    = "c:\\my documents\\notes.txt";
path    = "c:\my documents\notes.txt";        // Fails
```

The regular literal string is normally your best choice because it supports the escape sequences. The verbatim is to be favored when the text contains backslashes. Its most common use is with file path values and *Regular Expression* matching patterns (discussed in Chapter 5, "C# Text Manipulation and File I/O").

String Manipulation

The System.String class contains a variety of string manipulation members. These include ways to determine a string's length, extract a substring, compare strings, and convert a string to upper- or lowercase. The following examples illustrate some of the more common operations.

Indexing Individual Characters in a String

The foreach and while loops offer the easiest way to iterate through the characters in a string. In both cases, the operations are read-only.

```
// Example 1 - using foreach statement
string myQuote = "The solution is in the problem.";
foreach (char cc in myQuote)
{
    Console.Write(cc.ToString());
}

// Example 2 - using while loop
int ndx = 0;
while (ndx < myQuote.Length)
{
    Console.Write(myQuote[ndx].ToString());
    ndx += 1;
}
```

Note that before an individual character can be displayed or assigned to a string, it must be converted to a string type.

String Concatenation

The + operator is used for concatenating two strings: s1 + s2 . Only one of these has to be a string type; the other can be any type, and its ToString method is called automatically to convert it.

```
string s1 = "My age = ";
int myAge = 28;
string cat = s1 + myAge;        // My age = 28
MyClass clStr = new MyClass;
Cat = "Class Name = " + clStr; // Class Name = MyClass
```

The concatenation operation is simple to use, but it is important to understand what is going on behind the scenes: During concatenation, the strings being joined are copied and a new combined string is allocated space. Each concatenation results in the allocation of more memory equal to the length of the new string. This is an acceptable use of resources as long as the number of concatenations is minimal. However, if concatenation occurs inside a long loop, an application's performance can suffer.

Consider an example where an HTML document is constructed by inserting the `<br>` tag between names in a list.

```
// assume names is an array containing 1000 names
string nameList = "";
foreach (string custName in names)
{
    // This is inefficient and should be avoided.
    nameList = nameList + custName+"<br>";
}
```

Each loop results in the creation of a new string consisting of the previous string plus the new appended name and tag. A better approach is to use the `String-Builder` class as a replacement for the concatenation operator. This class sets aside memory to operate on strings and thus avoids the copying and memory allocation drawbacks of the concatenation (+) operator. It includes methods to append, insert, delete, remove, and replace characters. `StringBuilder` is discussed in Chapter 5.

Extracting and Locating Substrings

The `Substring` method extracts selected portions of a string. Its two overloads are illustrated here:

```
string poem = "In Xanadu did Kubla Khan";
string poemSeg;
poemSeg = poem.Substring(10);      // did Kubla Khan
// second argument specifies length
poemSeg = poem.Substring(0,9);     // In Xanadu
```

The `IndexOf` method locates the next occurrence of a character pattern within a string. It searches for the occurrence from the beginning of the string or a specified location. Listing 2-1 illustrates this.

`IndexOf()` performs a case-sensitive search. To ensure both upper- and lower-case instances are counted, you could convert the original string to lowercase (`ToLower()`) before searching it. Note that there is also a `LastIndexOf` method that locates the last instance of a character pattern within a string.

Listing 2-1	Locating Text Occurrences in a String

```
// Method to count the occurrences of text in a given string
public static int CharCount(String strSource,String strToFind)
{
    int iCount=0;   // string type has index of 0
    int iPos=strSource.IndexOf(strToFind);
    while(iPos!=-1)
    {
        iCount++;
        iPos=strSource.IndexOf(strToFind, iPos+1);
    }
    return iCount;
}
public class MyApp
{
    static void Main()
    {
        string txt = "In Xanadu did Kubla Khan";
        int ct = CharCount(txt, "a"); // ct = 4
    }
}
```

Comparing Strings

This topic is more complex than one would expect. The first hint of this is when you look at the System.String members and discover that there are four comparison methods: Compare, CompareOrdinal, CompareTo, and Equals. The choice of a comparison method is based on factors such as whether the comparison should be case sensitive and whether it should take culture into account.

The .NET environment is designed to handle international character sets, currencies, and dates. To support this, the handling and representation of strings can be tailored to different countries and cultures. Consider, for example, how to compare the same date in U.S. and European format. The dates "12/19/04" and "19/12/04" are logically equal, but do not have the same code value. Only a comparison method that takes culture into consideration would consider them equal. Chapter 5 explains how the various comparison methods work and the factors to be considered in selecting one.

For the majority of applications, nothing more than the standard equality (==) operator is required. This code segment illustrates its use:

```
bool isMatch;
string title = "Ancient Mariner";
isMatch = (title          == "ANCIENT MARINER");    // false
```

```
isMatch = (title.ToUpper() == "ANCIENT MARINER");    // true
isMatch = (title            == "Ancient"+" Mariner"); // true
isMatch =  title.Equals("Ancient Mariner");          // true
```

Note that the == operator is just a syntactical shortcut for calling the Equals method; it is actually faster to call Equals() directly.

2.7   Enumerated Types

An enumerated type, or enum as it's called in C#, offers a convenient way to create a structured set of symbols to represent constant values.

Syntax:

```
[access modifiers] enum <identifier> [:enum-base] {enum body}
```

Example:

```
enum Fabric :short {
    Cotton = 1,
    Silk   = 2,
    Wool   = 4,
    Rayon  = 8,
    Other  = 128
}
```

Note: If the enum symbols are not set to a value, they are set automatically to the sequence 0, 1, 2, 3, and so on.

The access modifiers define the scope of the enum. The default is internal, which permits it to be accessed by any class in its assembly. Use public to make it available to any class in any assembly.

The optional enum-base defines the underlying type of the constants that correspond to the symbolic names. This must be an integral value of the type byte, sbyte, short, ushort, int, uint, long, or ulong. The default is int.

Working with Enumerations

Enumerated types not only improve program readability, but also minimize code changes when the underlying value changes. In such cases, all references to the value remain valid. Another advantage is that enumerated types are *strongly typed*. This means, for example, that when an enum type is passed as a parameter, the receiving method must have a matching parameter of the same type; otherwise, a compiler error occurs.

The code segment in Listing 2-2 illustrates these ideas using the `Fabric` enum from the preceding example.

Listing 2-2   Using an Enumerated Type

```
static double GetPrice(Fabric fab)
{
   switch(fab)
   {
      case Fabric.Cotton: return(3.55);
      case Fabric.Silk:   return(5.65);
      case Fabric.Wool:   return(4.05);
      case Fabric.Rayon:  return(3.20);
      case Fabric.Other:  return(2.50);
      default: return(0.0);
   }
}
static void Main()
{
   Fabric fab = Fabric.Cotton;
   int fabNum   = (int) fab;              // 1
   string fabType =  fab.ToString();      // "Cotton"
   string fabVal  =  fab.ToString("D");   // "1"
   double cost = GetPrice(fab);           // 3.55
}
```

Things to note:

- Casting is required to set the value of an enum to an integer variable:
  `fabNum = (int) fab;`
- The character value of the underlying constant value can be obtained using the `ToString()` method with the parameter `"D"`. `"D"` is a format character that converts a value to its decimal form.
- Passing an instance of the `Fabric` enum to `GetPrice` requires that the corresponding parameter in the `GetPrice` method is declared as the same type.

This example shows how easy it is to obtain the symbol name or constant value when the instance of an enum is known—that is, Cotton. But suppose there is a need to determine whether an enum contains a member with a specific symbol or constant value. You could use foreach to loop through the enum members, but there is a better solution. Enumerations implicitly inherit from System.Enum, and this class contains a set of methods that can be used to query an enumeration about its contents.

System.Enum Methods

Three of the more useful System.Enum methods are Enum.IsDefined, Enum.Parse, and Enum.GetName. The first two methods are often used together to determine if a value or symbol is a member of an enum, and then to create an instance of it. The easiest way to understand them is to see them in use. In this example, the enum Fabric is queried to determine if it contains a symbol matching a given string value. If so, an instance of the enum is created and the GetName method is used to print one of its values.

```
string fabStr = "Cotton";
// Determine if symbol Cotton exists in Fabric enum
if (Enum.IsDefined(typeof(Fabric),fabStr))
{
    // Create enum instance
    Fabric fab = (Fabric)Enum.Parse(
                 typeof(Fabric) , fabStr);
    // Output from the following statement is: "Silk"
    Console.WriteLine("Second value of Fabric Enum is: " +
                 Enum.GetName(typeof(Fabric), 2));
}
```

The IsDefined method takes two parameters: an enumeration type that the typeof operator returns and a string representing the symbol to be tested for. Another form of this method tests for a specified constant value if a numeric value is passed as the second parameter.

The Parse method takes the same arguments and creates an instance of an enumerated type. The variable fab created here is equivalent to the one created in Listing 2-2. It is important to ensure that the enum member exists before using the Parse method. If it does not, an exception is thrown.

The GetName method returns a string value of the enum whose value is passed as the second argument to the method. In this example, "Silk" is returned because its constant value is 2.

Enums and Bit Flags

It was not by accident that the values of the `Fabric` enum were set to powers of 2. Enum members are often used in logical operations where such values have obvious advantages in mapping to unique bit values. You may have code to identify a combination of values:

```
Fabric cotWool = Fabric.Cotton | Fabric.Wool;
Console.WriteLine(cotWool.ToString());   // Output: 5
```

It would be more meaningful if the output identified the variable as a combination of wool and cotton. This can be accomplished by adding the `[Flags]` attribute to the enum declaration:

```
[Flags]
enum Fabric :short {
```

The `ToString()` method checks an enum declaration to see if this attribute is present. If so, it treats the enum as a set of bitmapped flag elements. In this example, it cannot find a symbolic value equal to 5, so it uses the bit pattern "101" and prints the symbols having the bit patterns "001" and "100". The new output is a comma-delimited list: "Cotton, Wool".

2.8 Arrays

C#, like most programming languages, provides the array data structure as a way to collect and manipulate values of the same type. Unlike other languages, C# provides three types of arrays. One is implemented as an `ArrayList` object; another as a generic `List` object; and a third is derived from the `System.Array` class. The latter, which is discussed here, has the traditional characteristics most programmers associate with an array. The `ArrayList` is a more flexible object that includes special methods to insert and delete elements as well as dynamically resize itself. The `List` is a type-safe version of the `ArrayList` that was introduced with .NET 2.0 and may eventually replace the `ArrayList`. The `List` and `ArrayList` are discussed in Chapter 4, along with other `Collection` classes.

Before looking at the details of creating and using an array, you should be familiar with its general features:

- Each element in the array is of the type specified in the array declaration. Besides the usual primitive types, an array may contain structures, objects, enums, and even other arrays.

- Common Language Specification (CLS) compliance requires that all arrays be zero-based to ensure language interoperability (for example, an array reference in C# can be passed to code written in VB.NET). Although it is possible to create a non-zero–based array in C#, it is discouraged because array operations are optimized for zero-based dimensions.
- When an array is created, it is allocated space for a fixed number of elements. Its capacity cannot be dynamically increased. The `ArrayList/List` is usually a better choice when the number of elements the array must hold is unknown.

Declaring and Creating an Array

Syntax:

```
<type> identifier [ ] = new <type> [n]   [{ initializer list}]
```

Example:

```
int[] myRating;          // declares an array
myRating = new int[5];   // creates array and allocates memory
int[] myRating = new int[5] {3,4,7,2,8};
int[] myRating = {3,4,7,2,8};   // shorthand version

// Create array containing instances of an Apparel class.
Apparel myApparel = {new Apparel(), new Apparel(),
                 new Apparel()};

// Set to an enum
Fabric[] enumArray = new Fabric[2];
enumArray[0] = Fabric.Cotton;

// Create a 2-dimensional array with 3 rows and 2 columns
int[ , ] myRatings = {{3 , 7}, {4 , 9}, {2, 6}};
```

The size of the array is determined from the explicit dimensions or the number of elements in the optional initializer list. If a dimension and an initializer list are both included, the number of elements in the list must match the dimension(s). If no initialization values are specified, the array elements are initialized to 0 for numeric types or `null` for all others. The CLR enforces bounds checking—any attempt to reference an array index outside its dimensions results in an exception.

Using System.Array Methods and Properties

The `System.Array` class defines a number of properties and methods that are used
to query an array and manipulate its contents. Array operations include sorting, copying, searching for specific values, and clearing the contents. Table 2-10 summarizes
some of the more useful members of the `System.Array` class.

Table 2-10   Selected Members of `System.Array`

Member	Type	Description
Length	Instance property	Total number of elements in the array.
Rank	Instance property	Number of dimensions of the array.

CreateInstance	Static method	Creates an Array object.
		To create a single-dimensional array:
		`int[] rank1 =`
		`    (int[]) Array.CreateInstance(typeof(int),4);`

GetUpperBound(n)	Instance method	The upper bound of a specified dimension n. Returned value is *Length* − 1.
		`d0 = myArray.GetUpperBound(0);`
		`d1= myArray.GetUpperBound(1);`

Sort	Static method	Sorts the elements in an array or a section of an array.
Reverse	Static method	Reverses the elements in a one-dimensional array.
IndexOf, LastIndexOf	Static method	Returns the index of the first or last occurrence of a value in a one-dimensional array.
Clone	Instance method	Copies the contents of an array into a new array. The new array is a *shallow* copy of the original—that is, reference pointers, not values, are copied.
Copy	Static method	Copies a selected portion of one array to another.
Clear	Static method	Sets a specified range of elements in an array to zero or `null`.

The members are classified as *static* or *instance*. A static member is not associated with any particular array. It operates as a built-in function that takes any array as a parameter. The instance members, on the other hand, are associated with a specific instance of an array. The example shown in Listing 2-3 demonstrates how to use many of these class members.

Listing 2-3   Working with Arrays Using `System.Array` Members

```
class MyApp
{
   static void Main()
   {
      string[] artists = {"Rembrandt", "Velazquez",
            "Botticelli", "Goya", "Manet","El Greco"};
      // ..Sort array in ascending order
      Array.Sort(artists);
      // ..Invert the array
      Array.Reverse(artists);
      PrintArray(artists);  // call method to list array
      int ndx = Array.IndexOf(artists,"Goya");    // ndx = 3
      // ..Clone the array
      string[] artClone = (string[]) artists.Clone();
      // Do arrays point to same address?
      bool eq = Object.ReferenceEquals(
            artClone[0],artists[0]);  // true
      Array.Clear(artClone,0,artClone.Length);
      // ..Copy selected members of artists to artClone
      Array.Copy(artists,1,artClone,0,4);
      eq = Object.ReferenceEquals(
            artClone[0],artists[1]);  // true
   }
   // List contents of Array
   public static void PrintArray(string[] strArray)
   {
      for ( int i = 0; i<= strArray.GetUpperBound(0); i++ )
      {
         Console.WriteLine(strArray[i]);
      }
   }
}
```

Things to note:

- The Sort method has many overloaded forms. The simplest takes a single-dimensional array as a parameter and sorts it in place. Other forms permit arrays to be sorted using an interface defined by the programmer. This topic is examined in Chapter 4.
- The Clone method creates a copy of the artists array and assigns it to artClone. The cast (string[]) is required, because Clone returns an Object type. The Object.ReferenceEquals method is used to determine if the cloned array points to the same address as the original. Because string is a reference type, the clone merely copies pointers to the original array contents, rather than copying the contents. If the arrays had been value types, the actual contents would have been copied, and ReferenceEquals would have returned false.
- The Copy method copies a range of elements from one array to another and performs any casting as required. In this example, it takes the following parameters:

```
(source, source index, target, target index, # to copy)
```

2.9   Reference and Value Types

The Common Language Runtime (CLR) supports two kinds of types: *reference types* and *value types* (see Figure 2-2 on the following page). Reference types include classes, arrays, interfaces, and delegates. Value types include the primitive data types such as int, char, and byte as well as struct and enum types. Value and reference types are distinguished by their location in the .NET class hierarchy and the way in which .NET allocates memory for each. We'll look at both, beginning with the class inheritance hierarchy.

System.Object and System.ValueType

Both reference and value types inherit from the System.Object class. The difference is that almost all reference types inherit directly from it, whereas value types inherit further down the hierarchy—directly from the System.ValueType class.

As the base for all types, System.Object provides a set of methods that you can expect to find on all types. This set includes the ToString method used throughout this chapter, as well as methods to clone a type, create a unique hash code for a type, and compare type instances for equality. Chapter 4 discusses these methods in detail and describes how to implement them on custom classes.

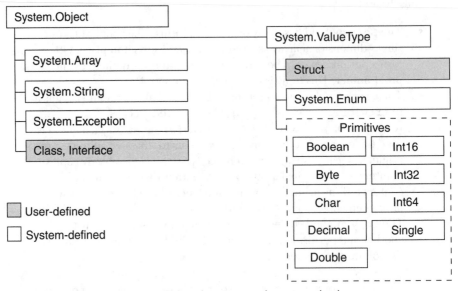

Figure 2-2   Hierarchy of common reference and value types

System.ValueType inherits from System.Object. It does not add any members, but does override some of the inherited methods to make them more suitable for value types. For example, Equals() is overridden to return true if the value of two objects' fields match. By definition, all value types implicitly inherit from the ValueType class.

Memory Allocation for Reference and Value Types

The primary difference between value and reference types is the way the CLR handles their memory requirements. Value types are allocated on a *runtime stack*, and reference types are placed on a *managed heap* that is referenced from the stack.

Figure 2-3 illustrates how the value and reference types from our example (refer to Figure 2-1) are represented in memory. Let's step through what happens when an instance of a reference type is created and is then assigned to a second variable:

```
Apparel myApparel  = new Apparel();
Apparel myApparel2 = myApparel;
```

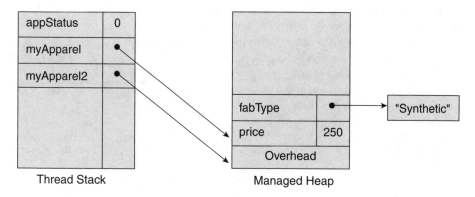

Figure 2-3 Memory layout for value and reference types

1. The CLR allocates memory for the object on the top of the managed heap.
2. Overhead information for the object is added to the heap. This information consists of a pointer to the object's method table and a `SyncBlockIndex` that is used to synchronize access to the object among multiple threads.
3. The `myApparel` object is created as an instance of the `Apparel` class, and its `Price` and `FabType` fields are placed on the heap.
4. The reference to `myApparel` is placed on the stack.
5. When a new reference variable `myApparel2` is created, it is placed on the stack and given a pointer to the existing object. Both reference variables—`myApparel` and `myApparel2`—now point to the same object.

Creating a reference object can be expensive in time and resources because of the multiple steps and required overhead. However, setting additional references to an existing object is quite efficient, because there is no need to make a physical copy of the object. The reverse is true for value types.

Boxing

.NET contains a special `object` type that accepts values of any data type. It provides a generic way to pass parameters and assign values when the type of the value being passed or assigned is not tied to a specific data type. Anything assigned to `object` must be treated as a reference type and stored on the heap. Consider the following statements:

```
int age = 17;
object refAge = age;
```

The first statement creates the variable age and places its value on the stack; the second assigns the value of age to a reference type. It places the value 17 on the heap, adds the overhead pointers described earlier, and adds a stack reference to it. This process of wrapping a value type so that it is treated as a reference type is known as *boxing*. Conversely, converting a reference type to a value type is known as *unboxing* and is performed by casting an object to its original type. Here, we unbox the object created in the preceding example:

```
int newAge = (int) refAge;
string newAge = (string) refAge;    // Fails. InvalidCastException
```

Note that the value being unboxed must be of the same type as the variable to which it is being cast.

In general, boxing can be ignored because the CLR handles the details transparently. However, it should be considered when designing code that stores large amounts of numeric data in memory. To illustrate, consider the System.Array and ArrayList classes mentioned earlier. Both are reference types, but they perform quite differently when used to store simple data values.

The ArrayList methods are designed to work on the generic object type. Consequently, the ArrayList stores all its items as reference types. If the data to be stored is a value type, it must be boxed before it can be stored. The array, on the other hand, can hold both value and reference types. It treats the reference types as the ArrayList does, but does not box value types.

The following code creates an array and an ArrayList of integer values. As shown in Figure 2-4, the values are stored quite differently in memory.

```
// Create array with four values
Int[] ages = {1,2,3,4};

// Place four values in ArrayList
ArrayList ages = new ArrayList();
For (int i=0; i<4; i++) {
   ages.add(i); // expects object parameter
}
```

The array stores the values as unboxed int values; the ArrayList boxes each value. It then adds overhead required by reference types. If your application stores large amounts of data in memory and does not require the special features of the ArrayList, the array is a more efficient implementation. If using .NET 2.0 or later, the List class is the best choice because it eliminates boxing and includes the more flexible ArrayList features.

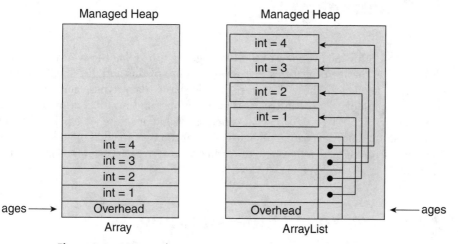

Figure 2-4   Memory layout comparison of `Array` and `ArrayList`

Summary of Value and Reference Type Differences

Memory Allocation

We have seen that memory allocation is the most significant difference between value and reference types. Reference types are allocated on the heap and value types on the thread or call stack. When a reference type is created, it is initialized to `null`, indicating it does not point to anything. A value type is initialized to zero (0).

Releasing Memory

Memory on the stack is freed when a variable goes out of scope. A garbage collection process that occurs when a system memory threshold is reached releases memory on the heap. Garbage collection is controlled by .NET and occurs automatically at unpredictable intervals. Chapter 4 discusses it in detail.

Variable Assignments

When a variable is set to a reference type, it receives a pointer to the original object—rather than the object value itself. When a variable is set to a value type, a field-by-field copy of the original variable is made and assigned to the new variable.

2.10 Summary

This chapter offers an overview of the C# language, providing the syntax and examples for using the list of features that form the core of this and just about any programming language. These features include basic data types, numerical and relational operators, loop constructs, strings, enums, and arrays. The final section stresses how all .NET types can be classified as a value or reference type. It explains the different memory allocation schemes used for the two. In addition, it looks at the concepts of boxing and unboxing: converting a value type to a reference type and converting a reference type back to a value type.

2.11 Test Your Understanding

1. Which method is required in each C# program, and what parameters does it take?

2. What are the three types of inline comments available in C#? Which can be exported?

3. What is a primitive?

4. What is printed by the following statements?

    ```
    int grade=78;
    bool pass = (grade >=70) ? true : false;
    Console.WriteLine(pass);
    ```

5. Which loop construct is executed at least once?

6. How do a break and a continue statement differ?

7. Given the following variables

    ```
    char c= 'c';
    double d= 120.0D;
    int i=10;
    string s="Rodin";
    ```

    which of the following fails to compile?

a. c = c+ i;
b. s += i;
c. c += s;
d. d += i;

8. Describe a potential drawback to using the + operator for concatenation. What is the recommended alternative?

9. Name the two base classes from which all value types inherit.

10. What prime value is printed by the final statement in this code?

```
int[] primes = new int[6] {1,3,5,7,11,13};
int[] primesClone = new int[6];
Array.Copy(primes,1,primesClone,1,5);
Console.WriteLine("Prime: "+primesClone[3]);
```

CLASS DESIGN
IN C#

Topics in This Chapter

- *Defining a Class:* The attributes and modifiers included in a class definition influence the behavior and accessibility of the class.

- *Constants:* A `const` type defines fixed values at compilation time.

- *Fields:* A field is typically used to maintain data inside a class.

- *Properties:* A property is the recommended way to expose a class's data.

- *Methods:* The functionality of a class is defined by its methods.

- *Inheritance:* By using inheritance, a class can take advantage of preexisting types.

- *Constructors:* This special purpose method is used to initialize a class.

- *Events and Delegates:* A program's actions are often triggered by events; delegates have the role of invoking methods to handle an event.

- *Operator Overloading:* Operators can be used to manipulate classes.

- *Interfaces:* An inherited interface defines the methods and properties that a `struct` or class must implement.

- *Generics:* By creating a generic class to store data, it is possible to eliminate casting, boxing, and ensure type safety.

- *Structures:* In some situations, a `struct` is a better choice than a class.

Chapter 3

This chapter provides an advanced introduction to using classes within the .NET environment. It is not a primer on object-oriented programming (OOP) and assumes you have some familiarity with the principles of encapsulation, inheritance, and polymorphism. C# is rich in object-oriented features, and the first challenge in working with classes is to understand the variety of syntactical contstructs. At the same time, it is necessary to appreciate the interaction between C# and .NET. Not only does the Framework Class Library (FCL) provide thousands of predefined classes, but it also provides a hierarchy of base classes from which all C# classes are derived.

The chapter presents topics in a progressive fashion—each section building on the previous. If you are new to C#, you should read from beginning to end; if you're familiar with the concepts and syntax, read sections selectively. The chapter begins by presenting the syntactical construct of a class and then breaks it down in detail. Attributes, modifiers, and members of the class body (constructors, properties, fields, and methods) are all explained. Sprinkled throughout are recommended .NET guidelines and best practices for designing and using custom classes. The objective is to show not only how to use classes, but also encourage good design practices that result in efficient code.

3.1   Introduction to a C# Class

Figure 3-1 displays a class declaration followed by a body containing typical class members: a constant, fields, a constructor containing initialization code, a property, and a method. Its purpose is to familiarize you with the syntax common to most C# classes and serve as a reference for later examples.

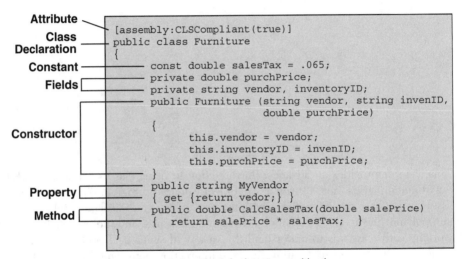

```
Attribute ─────        [assembly:CLSCompliant(true)]
    Class ──────       public class Furniture
Declaration                {
 Constant ───────          const double salesTax = .065;
   Fields [─────────       private double purchPrice;
           ─────────       private string vendor, inventoryID;
                           public Furniture (string vendor, string invenID,
                                             double purchPrice)
                           {
Constructor                    this.vendor = vendor;
                               this.inventoryID = invenID;
                               this.purchPrice = purchPrice;
                           }
                           public string MyVendor
 Property [──────────      { get {return vedor;} }
  Method [───────────      public double CalcSalesTax(double salePrice)
           ──────────      {  return salePrice * salesTax;  }
                       }
```

Figure 3-1   Class declaration and body

3.2   Defining a Class

A class definition consists of an optional attributes list, optional modifiers, the word `class` followed by the class identifier (name), and an optional list containing a base class or interfaces to be used for inheritance. Following this class declaration is the class body, consisting of the code and class members such as methods and properties.

Syntax for class definition:

```
[attributes] [modifiers] class  identifier [:baselist]
{class body} [;]
```

Classes—as do all .NET types—inherit from the `System.Object` class. This inheritance is implicit and is thus not specified as part of the class definition. As we'll see in the discussion of inheritance, this is important because a class can explicitly inherit from only one class.

Attributes

The optional attribute section consists of a pair of square brackets surrounding a comma-separated list of one or more attributes. An attribute consists of the attribute name followed by an optional list of positional or named arguments. The attribute may also contain an attribute target—that is, the entity to which the attribute applies.

Examples

The attribute section contains an attribute name only:

```
[ClassDesc]
```

Single attribute with named argument and positional argument (0):

```
[ClassDesc(Author="Knuth", 0)]
```

Multiple attributes can be defined within brackets.:

```
[ClassDesc(Author="Knuth"), ClassDesc(Author="James")]
```

Description

Attributes provide a way to associate additional information with a target entity. In our discussion, the target is a newly created class; but attributes may also be associated with methods, fields, properties, parameters, structures, assemblies, and modules. Their simple definition belies a truly innovative and powerful programming tool. Consider the following:

- An attribute is an instance of a public class. As such, it has fields and properties that can be used to provide rich descriptive information about a target or targets.
- All compilers that target the Common Language Runtime (CLR) recognize attributes and store information about them in the module's metadata. This is an elegant way to attach information to a program entity that can affect its behavior without modifying its implementation code. An application can then use `reflection` (a set of types for reading metadata) to read the metadata at runtime and make decisions based on its value.
- Hundreds of predefined attributes are included in the .NET Framework Class Library (FCL). They are used heavily in dealing with

interoperability issues such as accessing the Win32API or allowing .NET applications and COM objects to communicate. They also are used to control compiler operations. The [assembly:CLSCompliant-true)] attribute in Figure 3-1 tells the C# compiler to check the code for CLS compliance.

Core Note

Attributes provide a way to extend the metadata generated by the C# compiler with custom descriptive information about a class or class member.

.NET supports two types of attributes: *custom attributes* and *standard attributes*. Custom attributes are defined by the programmer. The compiler adds them to the metadata, but it's up to the programmer to write the reflection code that incorporates this metadata into the program. Standard attributes are part of the .NET Framework and recognized by the runtime and .NET compilers. The `Flags` attribute that was discussed in conjunction with enums in Chapter 2, "C# Language Fundamentals," is an example of this; another is the *conditional attribute*, described next.

Conditional Attribute

The conditional attribute is attached to methods only. Its purpose is to indicate whether the compiler should generate Intermediate Language (IL) code to call the method. The compiler makes this determination by evaluating the symbol that is part of the attribute. If the symbol is defined (using the `define` preprocessor directive), code that contains calls to the method is included in the IL. Here is an example to demonstrate this:

File: attribs.cs (attribs.dll)

```
#define DEBUG
using System;
using System.Diagnostics;    // Required for conditional attrib.
public class AttributeTest
{
   [Conditional("TRACE")]
   public static void ListTrace()
   { Console.WriteLine("Trace is On"); }
   [Conditional("DEBUG")]
   public static void ListDebug()
   { Console.WriteLine("Debug is On"); }
}
```

File: attribclient.cs (attribclient.exe)

```
#define TRACE
using System;
public class MyApp {
   static void Main()
   {
      Console.WriteLine("Testing Method Calls");
      AttributeTest.ListTrace();
      AttributeTest.ListDebug();
   }
}
```

Executing `attribclient` yields the following output:

```
Testing Method Calls
Trace is On
```

When `attribclient` is compiled, the compiler detects the existence of the TRACE symbol, so the call to `ListTrace` is included. Because `DEBUG` is not defined, the call to `ListDebug` is excluded. The compiler ignores the fact that `DEBUG` is defined in `attribs`; its action is based on the symbols defined in the file containing the method calls. Note that a conditional attribute can be used only with methods having a return type of void.

Access Modifiers

The primary role of modifiers is to designate the accessibility (also called scope or visibility) of types and type members. Specifically, a class access modifier indicates whether a class is accessible from other assemblies, the same assembly, a containing class, or classes derived from a containing class.

`public`	A class can be accessed from any assembly.
`protected`	Applies only to a nested class (class defined within another class). Access is limited to the container class or classes derived from the container class.
`internal`	Access is limited to classes in the same assembly. This is the default access.
`private`	Applies only to a nested class. Access is limited to the container class.
`protected internal`	The only case where multiple modifiers may be used. Access is limited to the current assembly or types derived from the containing class.

Core Note

A base class must be at least as accessible as its derived class. The following raises an error:

```
class  Furniture { }                // default access is internal
public class Sofa : Furniture { }   // error
```

The error occurs because the Furniture class (internal by default) is less accessible than the derived Sofa class. Errors such as this occur most frequently when a developer relies on a default modifer. This is one reason that modifiers should be included in a declaration.

Abstract, Sealed, and Static Modifiers

In addition to the access modifiers, C# provides a dozen or so other modifiers for use with types and type members. Of these, three can be used with classes: abstract, sealed, and static.

abstract   Indicates that a class is to be used only as a base class for other classes. This means that you cannot create an instance of the class directly. Any class derived from it must implement all of its abstract methods and accessors. Despite its name, an abstract class can possess nonabstract methods and properties.

sealed   Specifies that a class cannot be inherited (used as a base class). Note that .NET does not permit a class to be both abstract and sealed.

static   Specifies that a class contains only static members (.NET 2.0).

Class Identifier

This is the name assigned to the class. The ECMA standard recommends the following guidelines for naming the identifier:

- Use a noun or noun phrase.
- Use the *Pascal case* capitalization style: The first letter in the name and the first letter of each subsequent concatenated word are capitalized—for example, BinaryTree.
- Use abbreviations sparingly.
- Do not use a type prefix, such as C, to designate all classes—for example, BinaryTree, not CBinaryTree.
- Do not use the underscore character.

- By convention, interface names always begin with I; therefore, do not use I as the first character of a class name unless I is the first letter in an entire word—for example, `IntegralCalculator`.

Base Classes, Interfaces, and Inheritance

This optional list contains a previously defined class or interface(s) from which a class may derive its behavior and capabilities. The new class is referred to as the *derived class*, and the class or interface from which it inherits is the *base class* or *interface*. A base class must be listed before any interface(s).

Example

```
// .. FCL Interface and user-defined base class
public interface System.Icomparable
    {Int32 CompareTo(Object object); }
class Furniture {   }
// .. Derived Classes
class Sofa: Furniture { ... }   // Inherits from one base class
// Following inherits from one base class and one interface.
class Recliner: Furniture, IComparable {...}
```

The C# language does not permit multiple class inheritance, thus the base list can contain only one class. Because there is no limit on the number of inherited interfaces, this serves to increase the role of interfaces in the .NET world.

Core Note

- *Inheritance from a base class is referred to as* implementation inheritance. *The derived class inherits all of the members of the base class. However, the base class can prevent access to a member by defining it with the `private` modifier.*

- *Inheritance from an interface is referred to as* interface inheritance *because the interface does not provide implementation code. The derived class must provide the logic to implement any functions defined in the base interface(s).*

3.3   Overview of Class Members

Table 3-1 provides a summary of the types that comprise a .NET class. They can be classified broadly as members that hold data—constants, fields, and properties—and members that provide functionality—the constructor, method, and event. We'll look at each individually.

Table 3-1   Class Members

Member Type	Valid In	Description
Constant	Class, Structure	A symbol that represents an unchanging value. The compiler associates it with the class—not an instance of the class.
Field	Class, Structure	A variable that holds a data value. It may be read-only or read/write.
Property	Class, Structure	Provides access to a value in a class. It uses an *accessor* that specifies the code to be executed in order to read or write the value. The code to read or write to a property is implemented implicitly by .NET as two separate methods.
Constructor	Class, Structure	C# has three types of constructors: *Instance.* Initializes fields when an instance of a class is created. *Private.* Commonly used to prevent instances of a class from being created. *Static.* Initializes class before any instance is created.
Method	Class, Structure, Interface	A function associated with the class that defines an action or computation.
Events	Class, Structure, Interface	A way for a class or object to notify other classes or objects that its state has changed.
Types	Class, Structure, Interface	Classes, interfaces, structs, delegates.

Member Access Modifiers

The access modifiers used for a class declaration can also be applied to class members. They determine the classes and assemblies that have access to the class. Table 3-2 summarizes the scope of accessibility.

Table 3-2   Summary of Accessibility Provided by Access Modifiers

Class can be accessed by classes in:	Access Modifiers			
	public	protected	Internal	private
Another assembly	Yes	*	No	*
Same assembly	Yes	*	Yes	*
Containing class	Yes	Yes	Yes	Yes
Class derived from containing class	Yes	Yes	Yes	No

* Not applicable

3.4   Constants, Fields, and Properties

Constants, fields, and properties are the members of a class that maintain the content or state of the class. As a rule of thumb, use constants for values that will never change; use fields to maintain private data within a class; and use properties to control access to data in a class. Let's now look at the details of these three class members.

Constants

C# uses the const keyword to declare variables that have a fixed, unalterable value. Listing 3-1 provides an example of using constants. Although simple, the code illustrates several basic rules for defining and accessing constants.

Listing 3-1   Constants

```
using System;
class Conversions
{
   public const double Cm = 2.54;
   public const double Grams = 454.0 , km = .62 ;
   public const string ProjectName = "Metrics";
}
class ShowConversions
{
   static void Main()
   {
      double pounds, gramWeight;
      gramWeight = 1362;
      pounds = gramWeight / Conversions.Grams;
      Console.WriteLine(
         "{0} Grams= {1} Pounds", gramWeight,pounds);
      Console.WriteLine("Cm per inch {0}", Conversions.Cm);
      Conversions c= new Conversions();   // Create class
                                          // instance
      // This fails to compile. Cannot access const from object
      Console.WriteLine("Cm per inch {0}", c.Cm);
   }
}
```

- The const keyword can be used to declare multiple constants in one statement.
- A constant must be defined as a primitive type, such as string or double shown here (see Chapter 2 for a list of all C# primitives).
- Constants cannot be accessed from an instance of the class. Note that the ShowConversion class accesses the constants without instantiating the class.

The most important thing to recognize about a constant is that its value is determined at compile time. This can have important ramifications. For example, suppose the Furniture class in Figure 3-1 is contained in a DLL that is used by other assemblies as a source for the sales tax rate. If the rate changes, it would seem logical that assigning the new value to SalesTax and recompiling the DLL would then make the new value to external assemblies. However, the way .NET handles constants requires that all assemblies accessing the DLL must also be recompiled. The problem is that const types are evaluated at compile time.

When any calling routine is compiled against the DLL, the compiler locates all constant values in the DLL's metadata and hardcodes them in the executable code of the calling routine. This value is not changed until the calling routine is recompiled and reloads the value from the DLL. In cases such as tax, where a value is subject to change, it's preferable to define the value as a `readonly` field—sometimes referred to as a runtime constant.

Core Approach

It is often desirable to store a group of constants in a special utility or helper class. Declare them `public` to make them available to all classes. Because there is no need to create instances of the class, declare the class as `abstract`.

Fields

A field is also used to store data within a class. It differs from a `const` in two significant ways: Its value is determined at runtime, and its type is not restricted to primitives.

Field Modifiers

In addition to the access modifiers, fields have two additional modifiers: `static` and `readonly` (see Table 3-3).

Table 3-3   Field Modifiers

Modifier	Definition
static	The field is part of the class's state rather than any instances of the class. This means that it can be referenced directly (like a constant) by specifying `classname.fieldname` without creating an instance of the class.
readonly	The field can only be assigned a value in the declaration statement or class constructor. The net effect is to turn the field into a constant. An error results if code later attempts to change the value of the field.

As a rule of thumb, fields should be defined with the `private` attribute to ensure that the state of an object is safe from outside manipulation. Methods and properties should then be used to retrieve and set the private data if outside access is required.

Core Note

If a field is not initialized, it is set to the default value for its type: 0 for numbers, `null` for a reference type, single quotation marks (' ') for a string, and `false` for boolean.

There is one case where setting a field to `public` makes sense: when your program requires a global constant value. By declaring a field to be `public static readonly`, you can create a runtime constant. For example, this declaration in Figure 3-1:

```
const double salesTax = .065;
```

can be replaced with a field

```
public static readonly double SalesTax = .065;
```

A method then references this field as `Furniture.SalesTax`, and the `readonly` modifier ensures the value cannot be changed. Note that if you create an instance of this class, you cannot access `salesTax` as a member of that instance. An attempt to do so results in the compile error "static member cannot be accessed with an instance reference".

```
Furniture chair = new Furniture("Broyhill","12422",225.00);
double itemTax = chair.SalesTax;    // Raises an error
```

Using Static Read-Only Fields to Reference Class Instances

`Static readonly` fields can be used to represent groups of related constant data by declaring them a reference type such as a class instance or array. This is of use when the data can be represented by a limited number of objects with unchanging values.

This example presents the interesting concept of fields defined as instances of their containing class. The `static` modifier makes this possible, because it designates the field as part of the class and not its instances. Note that the `private` constructor prevents clients outside the scope of the class from creating new class instances. Thus, only those objects exposed by the fields are available outside the class.

The class also contains two instance fields, `yardPrice` and `deliveryWeeks`, that are declared as `private`. Access to them is controlled though a public method and property:

```
Upholstery.silk.FabCost(10);    // Value from method
Upholstery.silk.DeliveryTime;   // Value from property
```

Listing 3-2	Using Static Read-Only Fields as Reference Types

```
public class Upholstery
{
    // fields to contain price and delivery time for fabrics
    public static readonly Upholstery silk =
        new Upholstery(15.00, 8);
    public static readonly Upholstery wool =
        new Upholstery(12.00, 6);
    public static readonly Upholstery cotton =
        new Upholstery(9.00, 6);
    private double yardPrice;
    private int deliveryWeeks;
    // constructor - set price per yard and delivery time
    // private modifier prevents external class instantiation
    private Upholstery ( double yrPrice, int delWeeks)
    {
        yardPrice = yrPrice;
        deliveryWeeks = delWeeks;
    }
    // method to return total cost of fabric
    public double FabCost(double yards)
    {
        return yards * this.yardPrice;
    }
    // property to return delivery time
    public int DeliveryTime
        {get { return deliveryWeeks;}}
    // property to return price per yard
    public double PricePerYard
        {get {return yardPrice;}}
}
```

Properties

A property is used to control read and write access to values within a class. Java and C++ programmers create properties by writing an *accessor* method to retrieve field data and a *mutator* method to set it. Unlike these languages, the C# compiler actually recognizes a special property construct and provides a simplified syntax for creating and accessing data. In truth, the syntax is not a whole lot different than a comparable C++ implementation, but it does allow the compiler to generate more efficient code.

Syntax:
```
[attributes] <modifier>    <data type>   <property name>
```

```
{
    [access modifier] get
    {   ...
        return(propertyvalue)
    }
    [access modifier] set
    {   ...   Code to set a field to the keyword value   }
}
```

Note:

1. In addition to the four access modifiers, the property modifier may be
   static, abstract, new, virtual, or override. Abstract is used
   only in an abstract class; virtual is used in a base class and permits a subclass to override the property.
2. value is an implicit parameter containing the value passed when a
   property is called.
3. The get and set accessors may have different access modifiers.

Listing 3-3   Creating and Accessing a Property

```
public class  Upholstery
{
    private double yardPrice;
    // Property to return or set the price
    public double PricePerYard
    {
        get {return yardPrice;}    // Returns a property value
        set {                      // Sets a property value
            if ( value <= 0 )
                throw new ArgumentOutOfRangeException(
                "Price must be greater than 0.");
            yardPrice = value;
        }
    }
    ...
}
```

The syntax for accessing the property of a class instance is the same as for a field:

```
// fabObj is instance of Upholstery class
double fabricPrice = fabObj.PricePerYard;
fabObj.PricePerYard = 12.50D;
```

The `get` block of code serves as a traditional accessor method and the `set` block as a mutator method. Only one is required. Leave out the `get` block to make the property write-only or the `set` block to make it read-only.

All `return` statements in the body of a `get` block must specify an expression that is implicitly convertible to the property type.

In this example, the code in the `set` block checks to ensure that the property is set to a value greater than 0. This capability to check for invalid data is a major argument in favor of encapsulating data in a property.

If you were to examine the underlying code generated for this example, you would find that C# actually creates a method for each `get` or `set` block. These names are created by adding the prefix `get` or `set` to the property name—for example, `get_PricePerYard`. In the unlikely case you attempt to create a method with the same name as the internal one, you will receive a compile-time error.

The use of properties is not necessarily any less efficient than exposing fields directly. For a non-virtual property that contains only a small amount of code, the JIT (Just-in-Time) compiler may replace calls to the accessor methods with the actual code contained in the `get` or `set` block. This process, known as *inlining*, reduces the overhead of making calls at runtime. The result is code that is as efficient as that for fields, but much more flexible.

Indexers

An *indexer* is often referred to as a parameterized property. Like a property, it is declared within a class, and its body may contain `get` and `set` accessors that share the same syntax as property accessors. However, an indexer differs from a property in two significant ways: It accepts one or more parameters, and the keyword `this` is used as its name. Here is the formal syntax:

Syntax:

```
[attributes] <modifier><return type> this [parameter(s)]  {
```

Example:

```
public int this [int ndx] {
```

Note: The `static` modifier is not supported because indexers work only with instances.

In a nutshell, the indexer provides a way to access a collection of values maintained within a single class instance. The parameters passed to the indexer are used as a single- or multi-dimensional index to the collection. The example in Listing 3-4 should clarify the concept.

Listing 3-4   Using Indexer to Expose an Array of Objects

```
using System;
using System.Collections;   // Namespace containing ArrayList
public class  Upholstery
{
   // Class to represent upholstery fabric
   private double yardPrice;
   private int deliveryWeeks;
   private string fabName;
   // Constructor
   public Upholstery (double price, int delivery, string fabric)
   {
      this.yardPrice = price;
      this.deliveryWeeks = delivery;
      this.fabName = fabric;
   }
   // Three readonly properties to return Fabric information
   public int DeliveryTime
      {get {return deliveryWeeks;}}
   public double PricePerYard
      {get {return yardPrice;}}
   public string FabricName
      {get {return fabName;}}
}
public class Fabrics
{
   // Array to hold list of objects
   private ArrayList fabricArray = new ArrayList();
   // Indexer to add or return an object from the array
   public Upholstery this[int ndx]
   {
      get {
            if(!(ndx<0 || ndx > fabricArray.Count-1))
               return (Upholstery)fabricArray[ndx];
            // Return empty object
            else return(new Upholstery(0,0,""));
          }
            set { fabricArray.Insert(ndx, value);}
   }
}
public class IndexerApp
{
```

Listing 3-4	Using Indexer to Expose an Array of Objects *(continued)*

```
public static void Main()
{
    Fabrics sofaFabric = new Fabrics();
    // Use Indexer to create array of Objects
    sofaFabric[0] = new Upholstery(15.00, 8, "Silk");
    sofaFabric[1] = new Upholstery(12.00, 6, "Wool");
    sofaFabric[2] = new Upholstery(9.00, 6, "Cotton");
    // Next statement prints "Fabric: Silk"
    Console.WriteLine("Fabric: {0} ",
                        sofaFabric[0].FabricName);
}
}
```

The `Fabrics` class contains an indexer that uses the `get` and `set` accessors to control access to an internal array of `Upholstery` objects. A single instance of the `Fabrics` class is created and assigned to `sofaFabric`. The indexer allows the internal array to be directly accessed by an index parameter passed to the object:

```
Fabrics sofaFabric = new Fabrics();
// Use Indexer to create array of Objects
sofaFabric[0] = new Upholstery(15.00, 8, "Silk");
sofaFabric[1] = new Upholstery(12.00, 6, "Wool");
```

The advantage of using an indexer is that it hides the array handling details from the client, and it can also perform any validation checking or data modification before returning a value. Indexers are best used with objects whose properties can be represented as a collection, rather than a scalar value. In this example, the various fabrics available for sofas form a collection. We could also use the indexer to create a collection of fabrics used for curtains:

```
Fabrics curtainFabric = new Fabrics();
curtainFabric[0] = new Upholstery(11.00, 4, "Cotton");
curtainFabric[1] = new Upholstery(7.00, 5, "Rayon");
```

3.5 Methods

Methods are to classes as verbs are to sentences. They perform the actions that define the behavior of the class. A method is identified by its *signature*, which consists of the method name and the number and data type of each parameter. A signature is considered unique as long as no other method has the same name and matching parameter list. In addition to parameters, a method has a return type—void if nothing is returned—and a modifier list that determines its accessibility and polymorphic behavior.

For those who haven't recently boned up on Greek or object-oriented principles, polymorphism comes from the Greek *poly* (many) and *morphos* (shape). In programming terms, it refers to classes that share the same methods but implement them differently. Consider the `ToString` method implemented by all types. When used with an `int` type, it displays a numeric value as text; yet on a class instance, it displays the name of the underlying class—although this default should be overridden by a more meaningful implementation.

One of the challenges in using .NET methods is to understand the role that method modifiers play in defining the polymorphic behavior of an application. A base class uses them to signal that a method may be overridden or that an inheriting class must implement it. The inheriting class, in turn, uses modifiers to indicate whether it is overriding or hiding an inherited method. Let's look at how all this fits together.

Method Modifiers

In addition to the access modifiers, methods have seven additional modifiers shown in Table 3-4. Five of these—new, `virtual`, `override`, `sealed`, and `abstract`—provide a means for supporting polymorphism.

Table 3-4 Method Modifiers

Modifier	Description
static	The method is part of the class's state rather than any instances of the class. This means that it can be referenced directly by specifying `class-name.method (parameters)` without creating an instance of the class.
virtual	Designates that the method can be overridden in a subclass. This cannot be used with `static` or `private` access modifiers.
override	Specifies that the method overrides a method of the same name in a base class. This enables the method to define behavior unique to the subclass. The overriden method in the base class must be `virtual`.
new	Permits a method in an inherited class to "hide" a non-virtual method with a same name in the base class. It replaces the original method rather than overriding it.

Table 3-4   Method Modifiers *(continued)*

Modifier	Description
sealed	Prevents a derived class from overriding this method. • Is used in a derived class that will serve as the base for its own subclasses. • Must be used with the override modifier.
abstract	The method contains no implementation details and must be implemented by any subclass. Can only be used as a member of an abstract class.
extern	Indicates that the method is implemented externally. It is generally used with the DLLImport attribute that specifies a DLL to provide the implementation.

Static Modifier

As with other class members, the static modifier defines a member whose behavior is global to the class and not specific to an instance of a class. The modifier is most commonly used with *constructors* (described in the next section) and methods in helper classes that can be used without instantiation.

Listing 3-5   Static Method

```
using System;
class Conversions
{
   // class contains functions to provide metric conversions
   private static double cmPerInch = 2.54;
   private static double gmPerPound = 455;
   public static double inchesToMetric(double inches) {
      return(inches * cmPerInch);
   }
   public static double poundsToGrams(double pounds) {
      return(pounds * gmPerPound);
   }
}
class Test
{
   static void Main() {
      double cm, grams;
      cm = Conversions.inchesToMetric(28.5);
      grams = Conversions.poundsToGrams(984.4);
   }
}
```

In this example, the `Conversions` class contains methods that convert units from the English to metric system. There is no real reason to create an instance of the class, because the methods are invariant (the formulas never change) and can be conveniently accessed using the syntax `classname.method(parameter)`.

Method Inheritance with Virtual and Override Modifiers

Inheritance enables a program to create a new class that takes the form and functionality of an existing (base) class. The new class then adds code to distinguish its behavior from that of its base class. The capability of the subclass and base class to respond differently to the same message is classical polymorphism. In practical terms, this most often means that a base and derived class(es) provide different code for methods having the same signature.

By default, methods in the base class cannot be changed in the derived class. To overcome this, .NET provides the virtual modifier as a cue to the compiler that a method can be redefined in any class that inherits it. Similarly, the compiler requires that any derived class that alters a virtual method preface the method with the override modifier. Figure 3-2 and Listing 3-6 provide a simple illustration of this.

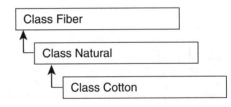

Figure 3-2   Relationship between base class and subclasses for Listing 3-6

| Listing 3-6 | Virtual Methods |

```
using System;
class Fiber
{
    public  virtual string ShowMe() { return("Base");}
}
class Natural:Fiber
{
    public override string ShowMe() { return("Natural");}
}
class Cotton:Natural
{
    public override string ShowMe() { return("Cotton");}
}
```

Listing 3-6	Virtual Methods *(continued)*

```
class Test
{
    static void Main ()
    {
        Fiber fib1 = new Natural();    // Instance of Natural
        Fiber fib2 = new Cotton();     // Instance of Cotton
        string fibVal;
        fibVal = fib1.ShowMe();        // Returns "Natural"
        fibVal = fib2.ShowMe();        // Returns "Cotton"
    }
}
```

In this example, Cotton is a subclass of Natural, which is itself a subclass of Fiber. Each subclass implements its own overriding code for the virtual method ShowMe.

```
fib1.ShowMe();      //returns   "Natural"
fib2.ShowMe();      //returns   "Cotton"
```

A subclass can inherit a virtual method without overriding it. If the Cotton class does not override ShowMe(), it uses the method defined in its base class Natural. In that case, the call to fib2.ShowMe() would return "Natural".

New Modifier and Versioning

There are situations where it is useful to hide inherited members of a base class. For example, your class may contain a method with the same signature as one in its base class. To notify the compiler that your subclass is creating its own version of the method, it should use the new modifier in the declaration.

ShowMe() is no longer virtual and cannot be overridden. For Natural to create its own version, it must use the new modifier in the method declaration to hide the inherited version. Observe the following:

- An instance of the Natural class that calls ShowMe() invokes the new method:

```
Natural myFiber = new Natural();
string fibTtype = myFiber.ShowMe();   // returns "Natural"
```

- Cotton inherits the new method from Natural:

```
Cotton myFiber = new Cotton();
string fibType = myFiber.ShowMe();    // returns "Natural"
```

- If ShowMe were declared as private rather than public in Natural, Cotton would inherit ShowMe from Fiber, because it cannot inherit a method that is out of scope.

Listing 3-7	Using the New Modifier for Versioning

```
public class Fiber
{
    public string ShowMe()        {return("Base");}
    public virtual string GetID() {return("BaseID");}
}
public class Natural:Fiber
{
    // Hide Inherited version of ShowMe
    new public string ShowMe()      {return("Natural");}
    public override string GetID() {return("NaturalID");}
    }
public class Cotton:Natural
{   // Inherits two methods: ShowMe() and GetID()
}
```

Sealed and Abstract Modifiers

A sealed modifier indicates that a method cannot be overridden in an inheriting class; an abstract modifier requires that the inheriting class implement it. In the latter case, the base class provides the method declaration but no implementation.

This code sample illustrates how an inheriting class uses the sealed modifier to prevent a method from being overridden further down the inheritance chain. Note that sealed is always paired with the override modifier.

```
class A {
    public virtual void PrintID{....}
}
class B: A {
    sealed override public void PrintID{...}
}
class C:B {
    // This is illegal because it is sealed in B.
    override public void PrintID{...}
}
```

An abstract method represents a function with a signature—but no implementation code—that must be defined by any non-abstract class inheriting it. This differs from a virtual method, which has implementation code, but may be redefined by an inheriting class. The following rules govern the use abstract methods:

- Abstract methods can only be declared in abstract classes; however, abstract classes may have non-abstract methods.
- The method body consists of a semicolon:

  ```
  public abstract void myMethod();
  ```

- Although implicitly virtual, abstract methods cannot have the virtual modifier.
- A virtual method can be overridden by an abstract method.

When facing the decision of whether to create an abstract class, a developer should also consider using an *interface*. The two are similar in that both create a blueprint for methods and properties without providing the implementation details. There are differences between the two, and a developer needs to be aware of these in order to make the better choice. The section on interfaces in this chapter offers a critical comparison.

Passing Parameters

By default, method parameters are passed by *value*, which means that a copy of the parameter's data—rather than the actual data—is passed to the method. Consequently, any change the target method makes to these copies does not affect the original parameters in the calling routine. If the parameter is a reference type, such as an instance of a class, a reference to the object is passed. This enables a called method to change or set a parameter value.

C# provides two modifiers that signify a parameter is being passed by reference: out and ref. Both of these keywords cause the address of the parameter to be passed to the target method. The one you use *depends on whether the parameter is initialized by the calling or called method*. Use ref when the calling method initializes the parameter value, and out when the called method assigns the initial value. By requiring these keywords, C# improves code readability by forcing the programmer to explicitly identify whether the called method is to modify or initialize the parameter.

The code in Listing 3-8 demonstrates the use of these modifiers.

Listing 3-8	Using the `ref` and `out` Parameter Modifiers

```
class TestParms
{
    public static void FillArray(out double[] prices)
    {
        prices = new double[4] {50.00,80.00,120.00,200.00};
    }
    public static void UpdateArray(ref double[] prices)
    {
        prices[0] = prices[0] * 1.50;
        prices[1] = prices[1] * 2.0;
    }
    public static double TaxVal(double ourPrice,
                               out double taxAmt)
    {
        double totVal = 1.10 * ourPrice;
        taxAmt = totVal - ourPrice;
        ourPrice = 0.0;  // Does not affect calling parameter
        return totVal;
    }
}
class MyApp
{
    public static void Main()
    {
        double[] priceArray;
        double taxAmt;
        //   (1) Call method to initialize array
        TestParms.FillArray(out priceArray);
        Console.WriteLine( priceArray[1].ToString());  // 80
        //   (2) Call method to update array
        TestParms.UpdateArray(ref priceArray);
        Console.WriteLine( priceArray[1].ToString());  // 160
        //   (3) Call method to calculate amount of tax.
        double ourPrice = 150.00;
        double newtax = TestParms.TaxVal(ourPrice, out taxAmt);
        Console.WriteLine( taxAmt.ToString());  // 15
        Console.WriteLine( ourPrice);           // 150.00
    }
}
```

In this example, the class `MyApp` is used to invoke three methods in the
`TestParms` class:

1. `FillArray` is invoked to initialize the array. This requires passing the
   array as a parameter with the `out` modifier.
2. The returned array is now passed to a second method that modifies
   two elements in the array. The `ref` modifier indicates the array can be
   modified.
3. `ourPrice` is passed to a method that calculates the amount of tax and
   assigns it to the parameter `taxAmt`. Although `ourPrice` is set to 0
   within the method, its value remains unchanged in the calling method
   because it is passed by value.

C# includes one other parameter modifier, `params`, which is used to pass a variable number of arguments to a method. Basically, the compiler maps the variable
number of arguments in the method invocation into a single parameter in the target
method. To illustrate, let's consider a method that calculates the average for a list of
numbers passed to it:

```
// Calculate average of variable number of arguments
public static double GetAvg(params double[] list)
{
    double tot = 0.0;
    for (int i = 0 ; i < list.Length; i++)
       tot += list[i];
    return tot / list.Length;
}
```

Except for the `params` modifier, the code for this method is no different than that
used to receive an array. Rather than sending an array, however, the invoking code
passes an actual list of arguments:

```
double avg;
avg = TestParms.GetAvg(12,15, 22, 5, 7 ,19);
avg = TestParms.GetAvg(100.50, 200, 300, 55,88,99,45);
```

When the compiler sees these method calls, it emits code that creates an array,
populates it with the arguments, and passes it to the method. The `params` modifier is
essentially a syntactical shortcut to avoid the explicit process of setting up and passing
an array.

Core Note

The params *keyword can only be used with the last parameter to a method.*

3.6   Constructors

The Common Language Runtime (CLR) requires that every class have a constructor—a special-purpose method that initializes a class or class instance the first time it is referenced. There are three basic types of constructors: instance, private (a special case of instance), and static.

Instance Constructor

Syntax:

```
[attributes] [modifiers]  <identifier> ( [parameter-list])
[:initializer] { constructor-body}
```

The syntax is the same as that of the method except that it does not have a return data type and adds an `initializer` option. There are a number of implementation and behavioral differences:

- The `identifier` (constructor name) must be the same as the class name.
- The `initializer` provides a way to invoke code prior to entering the `constructor-body`. It takes two forms:

  `base(argument list)`—Calls a base class
  `this(argument list)`—Calls another constructor in the same class

- If no explicit constructor is provided for a class, the compiler creates a default parameterless constructor.

The instance constructor is called as part of creating a class instance. Because a class may contain multiple constructors, the compiler calls the constructor whose signature matches that of the call:

```
Fiber fib1 = new Cotton();
Fiber fib1 = new Cotton("Egyptian");
```

.NET constructs an object by allocating memory, zeroing out the memory, and calling the instance constructor. The constructor sets the state of the object. Any fields in the class that are not explicitly initialized are set to zero or null, depending on the associated member type.

Inheritance and Constructors

Constructors, unlike methods, are not inherited. It is up to each class to define its own constructor(s) or use the default parameterless constructor. Each constructor must call a constructor in its base class before the first line of the calling constructor is executed. Because C# generates a call to the base class's default constructor automatically, the programmer typically does not bother with this. But there are exceptions. Consider this code in which the base class `Apparel` defines a constructor:

```
public class Apparel
{
    private string color;
    private decimal price;
    // constructor
    public Apparel(string c, decimal p, string b)
    {
        color = c;
        price = p;
    }
}
// class inheriting from Apparel
class Coat: Apparel
{
    private string length;
    public Coat(string c, decimal p, string b, string l)
    {
        length = l;
        // ... other code
    }
}
```

If you try to compile this, you'll get an error stating that "no overload for Apparel takes 0 arguments". Two factors conspire to cause this: first, because `Apparel` has an explicit constructor, the compiler does not add a default parameterless constructor to its class definition; and second, as part of compiling the constructor in the derived class, the compiler includes a call to the base class's default constructor—which in this case does not exist. The solution is either to add a parameterless constructor to `Apparel` or to include a call in the derived class to the explicit constructor. Let's look at how a constructor can explicitly call a constructor in a base class.

Using Initializers

The C# compiler provides the *base* initializer as a way for a constructor in an inherited class to invoke a constructor in its base class. This can be useful when several classes share common properties that are set by the base class constructor. Listing 3-9 demonstrates how a derived class, `Shirt`, uses a base initializer to call a constructor in `Apparel`.

Listing 3-9   A Constructor with a Base Initializer

```
using System;
public   class Apparel
{
   private string color;
   private decimal price;
   private string brand;
   // Constructor
   public Apparel(string c,decimal p,  string b)
   {
      color = c;
      price = p;
      brand = b;
   }

   public string ItemColor
   {
      get {return color;}
   }
   //   other properties and members go here
}

public class Shirt: Apparel
{
   private decimal mySleeve;
   private decimal myCollar;
   public Shirt (string c, decimal p,  string b,
      decimal sleeve, decimal collar)   : base(c,p,b)
   {
      mySleeve = sleeve;
      myCollar = collar;
   }
}
```

| Listing 3-9 | A Constructor with a Base Initializer *(continued)* |

```
public class TestClass
{
    static void Main()
    {
        Shirt shirtClass = new Shirt("white", 15.00m, "Arrow",
                                     32.0m, 15.5m);
        Console.WriteLine(shirtClass.ItemColor);  // "white"
    }
}
```

The compiler matches the signature of this initializer with the instance construc-tor in the base class that has a matching signature. Thus, when an instance of `Shirt` is created, it automatically calls the constructor in `Apparel` that has one parameter. This call is made before any code in `Shirt` is executed.

A second version of the initializer, one that uses the keyword `this` rather than `base`, also indicates which constructor is to be called when the class is instantiated. However, `this` refers to a constructor within the class instance, rather than the base class. This form of the initializer is useful for reducing the amount of compiler code generated in a class having multiple constructors and several fields to be initialized.

For example, if you examine the generated IL code for the following class, you would find that the fields `fiberType` and `color` are defined separately for each constructor.

```
public class Natural
{
    string fiberType = "Generic";
    string color = "white";
    // Constructors
    public Natural() { ... }
    public Natural(string cotton_type) { ... }
    public Natural(string cotton_type, string color) { ... }
}
```

For more efficient code, perform the field initialization in a single constructor and have the other constructors invoke it using the `this` initializer.

```
public Natural() {    // constructor initializes fields
    fiberType="Generic";
    color = "white";
}
// Following constructors use this() to call default
// constructor before constructor body is executed.
```

```
public Natural(string cotton_type): this() { ... }
public Natural(string cotton_type, string color):
   this() { ... }
```

Private Constructor

Recall that the `private` modifier makes a class member inaccessible outside its class. When applied to a class constructor, it prevents outside classes from creating instances of that class. Although somewhat non-intuitive (what good is a class that cannot be instantiated?), this turns out to be a surprisingly powerful feature.

Its most obvious use is with classes that provide functionality solely through static methods and fields. A classic example is the `System.Math` class found in the Framework Class Library.

It has two static fields, *pi* and the *e* (natural logarithmic base), as well as several methods that return trigonometric values. The methods behave as built-in functions, and there is no reason for a program to create an instance of the math class in order to use them.

In the earlier discussion of static methods, we presented a class (refer to Listing 3-5) that performs metric conversions. Listing 3-10 shows this class with the `private` constructor added.

Listing 3-10	Private Constructor Used with Class Containing Static Methods

```
using System;
class Conversions
{
    // class contains functions to provide metric conversions
    // static method can only work with static field.
    static cmPerInch = 2.54;
    private static double gmPerPound = 455;
    public static double inchesToMetric(double inches) {
        return(inches * cmPerInch);
    }
    public static double poundsToGrams(double pounds) {
        return(pounds*gmPerPound);
    }
    // Private constructor prevents creating class instance
    private Conversions()
    { ...    }
}
```

Although a simple example, this illustrates a class that does not require instantiation: The methods are static, and there is no state information that would be associated with an instance of the class.

A natural question that arises is whether it is better to use the `private` constructor or an `abstract` class to prevent instantiation. The answer lies in understanding the differences between the two. First, consider inheritance. Although an `abstract` class cannot be instantiated, its true purpose is to serve as a base for derived classes (that can be instantiated) to create their own implementation. A class employing a `private` constructor is not meant to be inherited, nor can it be. Secondly, recall that a `private` constructor only prevents outside classes from instantiating; it does not prevent an instance of the class from being created within the class itself.

The traits of the `private` constructor can also be applied to managing object creation. Although the `private` constructor prevents an outside method from instantiating its class, it does allow a `public` method in the class (sometimes called a *factory method*) to create an object. This means that a class can create instances of itself, control how the outside world accesses them, and control the number of instances created. This topic is discussed in Chapter 4, "Working with Objects in C#."

Static Constructor

Also known as a *class* or *type constructor*, the `static` constructor is executed after the type is loaded and before any one of the type members is accessed. Its primary purpose is to initialize static class members. This limited role results from the many restrictions that distinguish it from the `instance` constructor:

- It cannot have parameters and cannot be overloaded. Consequently, a class may have only one `static` constructor.
- It must have `private` access, which C# assigns automatically.
- It cannot call other constructors.
- It can only access static members.

Although it does not have a parameter, do not confuse it with a default base constructor, which must be an `instance` constructor. The following code illustrates the interplay between the `static` and `instance` constructors.

```
class BaseClass
{
    private static int callCounter;
    //   Static constructor
    static BaseClass(){
        Console.WriteLine("Static Constructor: "+callCounter);
    }
    //   Instance constructors
    public BaseClass()
```

```
    {
        callCounter+= 1;
        Console.WriteLine("Instance Constructor: "+callCounter);
    }
    // ... Other class operations
}
```

This class contains a `static` initializer, a `static` constructor, and an `instance` constructor. Let's look at the sequence of events that occur when the class is instantiated:

```
BaseClass myClass1 = new BaseClass();
BaseClass myClass2 = new BaseClass();
BaseClass myClass2 = new BaseClass();
```

Output:

```
Static Constructor: 0
Instance Constructor: 1
Instance Constructor: 2
Instance Constructor: 3
```

The compiler first emits code to initialize the static field to 0; it then executes the static constructor code that displays the initial value of `callCounter`. Next, the base constructor is executed. It increments the counter and displays its current value, which is now 1. Each time a new instance of `BaseClass` is created, the counter is incremented. Note that the static constructor is executed only once, no matter how many instances of the class are created.

3.7   Delegates and Events

Clicking a submit button, moving the mouse across a Form, pushing an `Enter` key, a character being received on an I/O port—each of these is an event that usually triggers a call to one or more special event handling routines within a program.

In the .NET world, events are bona fide class members—equal in status to properties and methods. Just about every class in the Framework Class Library has event members. A prime example is the `Control` class, which serves as a base class for all GUI components. Its events—including `Click`, `DoubleClick`, `KeyUp`, and `GotFocus`—are designed to recognize the most common actions that occur when a user interacts with a program. But an event is only one side of the coin. On the other side is a method that responds to, or handles, the event. Thus, if you look at the `Control` class methods, you'll find `OnClick`, `OnDoubleClick`, `OnKeyUp`, and the other methods that correspond to their events.

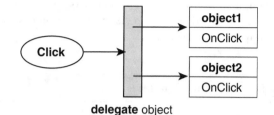

delegate object

Figure 3-3   Event handling relationships

Figure 3-3 illustrates the fundamental relationship between events and event handlers that is described in this section. You'll often see this relationship referred to in terms of *publisher/subscriber*, where the object setting off the event is the publisher and the method handling it is the subscriber.

Delegates

Connecting an event to the handling method(s) is a `delegate` object. This object maintains a list of methods that it calls when an event occurs. Its role is similar to that of the *callback* functions that Windows API programmers are used to, but it represents a considerable improvement in safeguarding code.

In Microsoft Windows programming, a callback occurs when a function calls another function using a function pointer it receives. The calling function has no way of knowing whether the address actually refers to a valid function. As a result, program errors and crashes often occur due to bad memory references. The .NET `delegate` eliminates this problem. The C# compiler performs type checking to ensure that a delegate only calls methods that have a signature and return type matching that specified in the delegate declaration. As an example, consider this `delegate` declaration:

```
public delegate void MyString (string msg);
```

When the delegate is declared, the C# compiler creates a `sealed` class having the name of the delegate identifier (`MyString`). This class defines a constructor that accepts the name of a method—static or instance—as one of its parameters. It also contains methods that enable the delegate to maintain a list of target methods. This means that—unlike the callback approach—a single delegate can call multiple event handling methods.

A method must be *registered* with a delegate for it to be called by that delegate. Only methods that return no value and accept a single `string` parameter can be registered with this delegate; otherwise, a compilation error occurs. Listing 3-11 shows how to declare the `MyString` delegate and register multiple methods with it. When the delegate is called, it loops through its internal invocation list and calls all the registered methods in the order they were registered. The process of calling multiple methods is referred to as *multicasting*.

Listing 3-11	Multicasting Delegate

```
// file: delegate.cs
using System;
using System.Threading;
class DelegateSample
{
    public delegate void MyString(string s);
    public static void PrintLower(string s){
        Console.WriteLine(s.ToLower());
    }

    public static void PrintUpper(string s){
        Console.WriteLine(s.ToUpper());
    }

    public static void Main()
    {
        MyString myDel;
        // register method to be called by delegate
        myDel =  new MyString(PrintLower);
        // register second method
        myDel += new MyString(PrintUpper);
        // call delegate
        myDel("My Name is Violetta.");
        // Output: my name is violetta.
        //         MY NAME IS VIOLETTA.
    }
}
```

Note that the += operator is used to add a method to the invocation list. Conversely, a method can be removed using the -= operator:

```
myDel += new MyString(PrintUpper); // register for callback
myDel -= new MyString(PrintUpper); // remove method from list
```

In the preceding example, the delegate calls each method *synchronously*, which means that each succeeding method is called only after the preceding method has completed operation. There are two potential problems with this: a method could "hang up" and never return control, or a method could simply take a long time to process—blocking the entire application. To remedy this, .NET allows delegates to make *asynchronous calls* to methods. When this occurs, the called method runs on a separate thread than the calling method. The calling method can then determine when the invoked method has completed its task by polling it, or having it call back a method when it is completed. Asynchronous calls are discussed in Chapter 13, "Asynchronous Programming and Multithreading."

Delegate-Based Event Handling

In abstract terms, the .NET event model is based on the *Observer* Design Pattern. This pattern is defined as "a one-to-many dependency between objects so that when one object changes state, all its dependents are notified and updated automatically."[1] We can modify this definition to describe the .NET event handling model depicted in Figure 3-3: "when an event occurs, all the delegate's registered methods are notified and executed automatically." An understanding of how events and delegates work together is the key to handling events properly in .NET.

To illustrate, let's look at two examples. We'll begin with built-in events that have a predefined delegate. Then, we'll examine how to create events and delegates for a custom class.

Working with Built-In Events

The example in Listing 3-12 displays a form and permits a user to draw a line on the form by pushing a mouse key down, dragging the mouse, and then raising the mouse key. To get the endpoints of the line, it is necessary to recognize the MouseDown and MouseUp events. When a MouseUp occurs, the line is drawn.

The delegate, MouseEventHandler, and the event, MouseDown, are predefined in the Framework Class Library. The developer's task is reduced to implementing the event handler code and registering it with the delegate. The += operator is used to register methods associated with an event.

```
this.MouseDown += new MouseEventHandler(OnMouseDown);
```

The underlying construct of this statement is

```
this.event += new delegate(event handler method);
```

---

1. *Design Patterns* by Erich Gamma, Richard Helm, Ralph Johnson, and John Vlissides; Addison-Wesley, 1995.

To implement an event handler you must provide the signature defined by the delegate. You can find this in documentation that describes the declaration of the MouseEventHandler delegate:

```
public delegate void MouseEventHandler(
   object sender,
   MouseEventArgs e)
```

Listing 3-12   Event Handler Example

```
using System;
using System.Windows.Forms;
using System.Drawing;
class DrawingForm:Form
{
   private int lastX;
   private int lastY;
   private Pen myPen= Pens.Black; // defines color of drawn line
   public DrawingForm() {
      this.Text = "Drawing Pad";
      // Create delegates to call MouseUp and MouseDown
      this.MouseDown += new MouseEventHandler(OnMouseDown);
      this.MouseUp   += new MouseEventHandler(OnMouseUp);
   }
   private void OnMouseDown(object sender, MouseEventArgs e)
   {
      lastX = e.X;
      lastY = e.Y;
   }
   private void OnMouseUp(object sender, MouseEventArgs e)
   {
      // The next two statements draw a line on the form
      Graphics g = this.CreateGraphics();
      if (lastX >0 ){
         g.DrawLine(myPen,  lastX,lastY,e.X,e.Y);
      }
      lastX = e.X;
      lastY = e.Y;
   }
   static void Main() {
      Application.Run(new DrawingForm());
   }
}
```

Using Anonymous Methods with Delegates

.NET 2.0 introduced a language construct known as *anonymous methods* that eliminates the need for a separate event handler method; instead, the event handling code is encapsulated within the delegate. For example, we can replace the following statement from Listing 3-12:

```
this.MouseDown += new MouseEventHandler(OnMouseDown);
```

with this code that creates a delegate and includes the code to be executed when the delegate is invoked:

```
this.MouseDown += delegate(object sender, EventArgs e)
{
    lastX = e.X;
    lastY = e.Y;
}
```

The code block, which replaces `OnMouseDown`, requires no method name and is thus referred to as an anonymous method. Let's look at its formal syntax:

delegate [(parameter-list)] {anonymous-method-block}

- The `delegate` keyword is placed in front of the code that is executed when the delegate is invoked.
- An optional parameter list may be used to pass data to the code block. These parameters should match those declared by the delegate. In this example, the parameters correspond to those required by the predefined delegate `MouseEventHandler`.
- When the C# compiler encounters the anonymous code block, it creates a new class and constructs a method inside it to contain the code block. This method is called when the delegate is invoked.

To further clarify the use of anonymous methods, let's use them to simplify the example shown earlier in Listing 3-11. In the original version, a custom delegate is declared, and two callback methods are implemented and registered with the delegate. In the new version, the two callback methods are replaced with anonymous code blocks:

```
// delegate declaration
public delegate void MyString(string s);

// Register two anonymous methods with the delegate
MyString myDel;
myDel =  delegate(string s) { Console.WriteLine(s.ToLower()); };
```

```
myDel += delegate(string s) { Console.WriteLine(s.ToUpper()); };
// invoke delegate
myDel("My name is Violetta");
```

When the delegate is called, it executes the code provided in the two anonymous methods, which results in the input string being printed in all lower- and uppercase letters, respectively.

Defining Custom Events

When writing your own classes, it is often necessary to define custom events that signal when some change of state has occurred. For example, you may have a component running that monitors an I/O port and notifies another program about the status of data being received. You could use raw delegates to manage the event notification; but allowing direct access to a delegate means that any method can fire the event by simply invoking the delegate. A better approach—and that used by classes in the Framework Class Library—is to use the event keyword to specify a delegate that will be called when the event occurs.

The syntax for declaring an event is

```
public event  <delegate name>  <event name>
```

Let's look at a simple example that illustrates the interaction of an event and delegate:

```
public class IOMonitor
{
    // Declare delegate
    public delegate void IODelegate(String s);
    // Define event variable
    public event IODelegate DataReceived ;
    // Fire the event
    public void FireReceivedEvent (string msg)
    {
        if (DataReceived != null)   // Always check for null
        {
            DataReceived(msg);       // Invoke callbacks
        }
    }
}
```

This code declares the event DataReceived and uses it in the FireReceived-Event method to fire the event. For demonstration purposes, FireReceivedEvent is assigned a public access modifier; in most cases, it would be private to ensure that the event could only be fired within the IOMonitor class. Note that it is good practice to always check the event delegate for `null` before publishing the event. Otherwise, an exception is thrown if the delegate's invocation list is empty (no client has subscribed to the event).

Only a few lines of code are required to register a method with the delegate and then invoke the event:

```
IOMonitor monitor = new IOMonitor();
// You must provide a method that handles the callback
monitor.DataReceived += new IODelegate(callback method);
monitor.FireReceivedEvent("Buffer Full");   // Fire event
```

Defining a Delegate to Work with Events

In the preceding example, the event delegate defines a method signature that takes a single `string` parameter. This helps simplify the example, but in practice, the signature should conform to that used by all built-in .NET delegates. The `EventHandler` delegate provides an example of the signature that should be used:

```
public delegate void EventHandler(object sender,
                                  EventArgs eventArgs);
```

The delegate signature should define a `void` return type, and have an `object` and `EventArgs` type parameter. The `sender` parameter identifies the publisher of the event; this enables a client to use a single method to handle and identify an event that may originate from multiple sources.

The second parameter contains the data associated with the event. .NET provides the `EventArgs` class as a generic container to hold a list of arguments. This offers several advantages, the most important being that it decouples the event handler method from the event publisher. For example, new arguments can be added later to the `EventArgs` container without affecting existing subscribers.

Creating an `EventArgs` type to be used as a parameter requires defining a new class that inherits from `EventArgs`. Here is an example that contains a single `string` property. The value of this property is set prior to firing the event in which it is included as a parameter.

```
public class IOEventArgs: EventArgs
{
    public IOEventArgs(string msg){
        this.eventMsg = msg;
    }
    public string Msg{
        get {return eventMsg;}
    }
    private string eventMsg;
}
```

`IOEventArgs` illustrates the guidelines to follow when defining an `EventArgs` class:

- It must inherit from the `EventArgs` class.
- Its name should end with `EventArgs`.
- Define the arguments as `readonly` fields or properties.
- Use a constructor to initialize the values.

If an event does not generate data, there is no need to create a class to serve as the `EventArgs` parameter. Instead, simply pass `EventArgs.Empty`.

Core Note

If your delegate uses the `EventHandler` signature, you can use `EventHandler` as your delegate instead of creating your own. Because it is part of the .NET Framework Class Library, there is no need to declare it.

An Event Handling Example

Let's bring these aforementioned ideas into play with an event-based stock trading example. For brevity, the code in Listing 3-13 includes only an event to indicate when shares of a stock are sold. A stock purchase event can be added using similar logic.

Listing 3-13   Implementing a Custom Event-Based Application

```
//File: stocktrader.cs
using System;
// (1) Declare delegate
public delegate void TraderDelegate(object sender,
                                    EventArgs e);
// (2) A class to define the arguments passed to the delegate
public class TraderEventArgs: EventArgs
{
    public TraderEventArgs(int shs, decimal prc, string msg,
                           string sym){
        this.tradeMsg   = msg;
        this.tradeprice = prc;
        this.tradeshs   = shs;
        this.tradesym   = sym;
    }
```

<table>
<tr><td>**Listing 3-13**</td><td>Implementing a Custom Event-Based Application (continued)</td></tr>
</table>

```csharp
   public string Desc{
      get {return tradeMsg;}
   }
   public decimal SalesPrice{
      get {return tradeprice;}
   }
   public int Shares{
      get {return tradeshs;}
   }
   public string Symbol{
      get {return tradesym;}
   }

   private string  tradeMsg;
   private decimal tradeprice;
   private int tradeshs;
   private string tradesym;
}
// (3) class defining event handling methods
public class EventHandlerClass
{
   public void HandleStockSale(object sender,EventArgs e)
   {
      // do housekeeping for stock purchase
      TraderEventArgs ev = (TraderEventArgs) e;
      decimal totSale = (decimal)(ev.Shares * ev.SalesPrice);
      Console.WriteLine(ev.Desc);
   }
   public void LogTransaction(object sender,EventArgs e)
   {
      TraderEventArgs ev = (TraderEventArgs) e;
      Console.WriteLine(ev.Symbol+" "+ev.Shares.ToString()
                     +" "+ev.SalesPrice.ToString("###.##"));
   }
}
// (4) Class to sell stock and publish stock sold event
public class Seller
{
   // Define event indicating a stock sale
   public event TraderDelegate StockSold;
   public void StartUp(string sym, int shs, decimal curr)
```

Listing 3-13	Implementing a Custom Event-Based Application *(continued)*

```
        {
            decimal salePrice= GetSalePrice(curr);
            TraderEventArgs t = new TraderEventArgs(shs,salePrice,
                    sym+" Sold at "+salePrice.ToString("###.##"), sym);
            FireSellEvent(t);   // Fire event
        }
        // method to return price at which stock is sold
        // this simulates a random price movement from current price
        private decimal GetSalePrice(decimal curr)
        {
            Random rNum = new Random();
            // returns random number between 0 and 1
            decimal rndSale = (decimal)rNum.NextDouble() * 4;
            decimal salePrice= curr - 2 + rndSale;
            return salePrice;
        }
        private void FireSellEvent(EventArgs e)
        {
            if (StockSold != null)  // Publish defensively
            {
                StockSold(this, e);  // Invoke callbacks by delegate
            }
        }
    }

    class MyApp
    {
        public static void Main()
        {
            EventHandlerClass eClass= new EventHandlerClass();
            Seller sell = new Seller();
            // Register two event handlers for stocksold event
            sell.StockSold += new TraderDelegate(
                        eClass.HandleStockSale);
            sell.StockSold += new TraderDelegate(
                        eClass.LogTransaction);
            // Invoke method to sell stock(symbol, curr price,
                                              sell price)
            sell.StartUp("HPQ",100, 26);
        }
    }
```

The class `Seller` is at the heart of the application. It performs the stock transaction and signals it by publishing a `StockSold` event. The client requesting the transaction registers two event handlers, `HandleStockSale` and `LogTransaction`, to be notified when the event occurs. Note also how the `TraderEvents` class exposes the transaction details to the event handlers.

3.8   Operator Overloading

Built-in operators such as + and - are used so instinctively that one rarely thinks of them as a predefined implementation for manipulating intrinsic types. In C#, for example, the + operator is used for addition or concatenation depending on the data types involved. Clearly, each must be supported by different underlying code. Because the compiler knows what a numeric and string type represent, it is quite capable of doing this. It makes sense then that these operators cannot be applied to custom classes or structures of which the compiler has no knowledge.

It turns out that C# provides a mechanism referred to as *operator overloading* that enables a class to implement code that determines how the class responds to the operator. The code for overloading an operator is syntactically similar to that of a method:

```
public static <return type> operator <op> ( parameter list)
{ implementation code}
```

Several rules govern its usage:

- The `public` and `static` modifiers are required.
- The return type is the class type when working with classes. It can never be void.
- op is a binary, unary, or relational operator. Both equals (==) and not equals (!=) must be implemented in a relational pair.
- Binary operators require two arguments; unary operators require one argument.

Operator overloading with classes does not have to be limited to geometric or spatial objects. The example shown in Listing 3-14 demonstrates how to use the concept to maintain stocks in a portfolio. It contains two classes: one that represents a stock (defined by its price, number of shares, and risk factor) and one that represents the portfolio of stocks. Two overloaded operators (+ and -) add and remove stocks from the portfolio.

Listing 3-14   Operator Overloading for Classes

```csharp
using System;
class Portfolio
{
   public decimal risk;
   public decimal totValue;
   // Overloaded operator to add stock to Portfolio
   public static Portfolio operator + (Portfolio p,Stock s)
   {
      decimal currVal  = p.totValue;
      decimal currRisk = p.risk;
      p.totValue = p.totValue + s.StockVal;
      p.risk = (currVal/p.totValue)*p.risk +
         (s.StockVal/p.totValue)* s.BetaVal;
      return p;
   }
   // Overloaded operator to remove stock from Portfolio
   public static Portfolio operator - (Portfolio p,Stock s)
   {
      p.totValue = p.totValue - s.StockVal;
      p.risk = p.risk - ((s.BetaVal-p.risk)
                      *(s.StockVal/p.totValue));
      return p;
   }
}
class Stock
{
   private decimal value;
   private decimal beta; // risk increases with value
   public  Stock(decimal myBeta, decimal myValue,
                 int shares)
   {
      value = (decimal) myValue * shares;
      beta = myBeta;
   }
   public decimal StockVal
      { get {return value; } }

   public decimal BetaVal
      { get {return beta; } }
}
class MyApp
{
```

Listing 3-14	Operator Overloading for Classes *(continued)*

```
public static void Main()
{
    Portfolio p = new Portfolio();
    // 200 shs of HPQ at $25, 100 shs of IBM @ $95
    Stock hpq  = new Stock(1.1M, 25M, 200);
    Stock ibm  = new Stock(1.05M, 95.0M, 100);
    p += hpq;    // Add hpq
    p += ibm;    // Add ibm
    Console.Write("value:{0} ",p.totValue.ToString());
    Console.WriteLine(" risk: {0}",
                        p.risk.ToString("#.00"));
    // value = 14,500 and risk = 1.07
    p -= ibm;    // Remove ibm from portfolio
    Console.Write("value:{0} ",p.totValue.ToString());
    Console.Write(" risk: {0}",p.risk.ToString("#.00"));
    // value = 5000 and risk = 1.10
}
}
```

The addition or deletion of a stock causes the portfolio total value and weighted risk factor to be adjusted. For example, when both stocks are added to the portfolio, the risk is 1.07. Remove ibm and the risk is 1.10, the risk of hpq alone.

When choosing to implement operator overloading, be aware that .NET languages are not required to support it. The easiest way to provide interoperability for those languages (such as Visual Basic.NET) lacking this feature is to include an additional class member that performs the same function:

```
public static Portfolio AddStocks ( Portfolio p, Stock s)
{ return p + s; }
```

In this case, the code exposes a public method whose implementation calls the overloaded method.

Another approach is to take advantage of the fact that language interaction occurs at the Intermediate Language level and that each operator is represented in the IL by a hidden method. Thus, if a language knows how to invoke this method, it can access the operator.

The ECMA standard provides a list of method names that correspond to each operator. For example, the + and & used in the preceding code are represented by op_Addition and op_BitwiseAnd, respectively. A language would access the overloaded + operator with its own syntactic variation of the following code:

```
newPortfolio = P.op_Addition(P, s)
```

Either approach works, but relying on assembly language is probably less appealing than providing a custom public method.

Although the discussion has been on classes, operator overloading also can be applied to simple data types. For example, you could define your own exponentiation operator for integers.

3.9   Interfaces

Syntax:

```
[attributes] [modifiers] interface  identifier [:baselist]
{interface body} [;]
```

The syntax of the interface declaration is identical to that of a class except that the keyword `interface` replaces `class`. This should not be surprising, because an interface is basically a class that declares, but does not implement, its members. An instance of it cannot be created, and classes that inherit from it must implement all of its methods.

This sounds similar to an `abstract` class, which also cannot be instantiated and requires derived classes to implement its abstract methods. The difference is that an abstract class has many more capabilities: It may be inherited by subclasses, and it may contain state data and concrete methods.

One rule of thumb when deciding whether to use a class or interface type is the relationship between the type and its inheriting classes. An interface defines a behavior for a class—something it "can do." The built-in .NET `ICloneable` interface, which permits an object to create a copy of itself, is an example of this. Classes, on the other hand, should be used when the inheriting class is a "type of" the base class. For example, you could create a shape as a base class, a circle as a subclass of shape, and the capability to change the size of the shape as an interface method.

Aside from their differing roles, there are numerous implementation and usage differences between a class and an interface:

- An interface cannot inherit from a class.
- An interface can inherit from multiple interfaces.
- A class can inherit from multiple interfaces, but only one class.
- Interface members must be methods, properties, events, or indexers.
- All interface members must have `public` access (the default).
- By convention, an interface name should begin with an uppercase I.

Creating and Using a Custom Interface

Listing 3-15 demonstrates how to define, implement, and program against a simple custom interface:

Listing 3-15	Interface Basics

```
public interface IShapeFunction
{
    double GetArea();      //  public abstract method
}

class Circle : IShapeFunction    // Inherit Interface
{
    private double radius;
    public circle( double rad)
    {
        radius = rad;
    }
    public double GetArea()
    {
        return ( Math.PI*radius * radius);
    }
    public string ShowMe()
    {
        return ("Circle");
    }
}

class Rectangle: IShapeFunction        // Inherit interface
{
    private double width, height;
    public rectangle( double myWidth, double myHeight)
    {
        width= myWidth;
        height= myHeight;
    }
    public double GetArea()
    {
        return (width * height);
    }
}
```

Listing 3-15   Interface Basics (continued)

```
class MyApp
{
    public static void Main()
    {
        Circle myCircle = new Circle(4);
        // Interface variable that references a circle object.
        IShapeFunction myICircle = myCircle;
        Rectangle myRectangle = new Rectangle(4,8);
        // Place shape instances in an array
        IShapeFunction[] myShapes = {myCircle, myRectangle};
        // The next two statements print the same results
        MessageBox.Show(myCircle.GetArea().ToString());
        MessageBox.Show(myShapes[0].GetArea().ToString());
        MessageBox.Show(myCircle.ShowMe());    // class method
        MessageBox.Show(myICircle.GetArea().ToString());
        // The following will not compile because myICircle can
        // access only members of the IShapeFunction interface.
        MessageBox.Show(myICircle.ShowMe());
    }
}
```

The declaration of the interface and implementation of the classes is straightforward: A Circle and Rectangle class inherit the IShapeFunction interface and implement its GetArea method.

Conceptually, it is useful to think of a class that implements one or more interfaces as having multiple types. It has its own innate type, but it also can be viewed as having the type of each interface it implements. Consider this code in the MyApp class:

```
Circle myCircle = new Circle(4);
IShapeFunction myICircle = myCircle;
```

The first statement creates an instance of the Circle class. The second statement creates a variable that refers to this circle object. However, because it is specified as an IShapeFunction type, it can only access members of that interface. This is why an attempt to reference the ShowMe method fails. By using the interface type, you effectively create a filter that restricts access to members of the interface only.

One of the most valuable aspects of working with interfaces is that a programmer can treat disparate classes in a similar manner, as long at they implement the same interface.

```
IShapeFunction[] myShapes = {myCircle, myRectangle};
MessageBox.Show(myShapes[0].GetArea().ToString());
```

This code creates an array that can contain any class that implements the IShape-Function interface. Its only interest is in using the GetArea method, and it neither has nor requires any knowledge of other class members. We can easily extend this example to create a class to work with this array that has no knowledge of the Circle or Rectangle class.

```
public class ShapeUtil
{
    public static double SumAreas
        (IShapeFunction[] funArray)
    {
        double tot = 0.0;
        for (int i = 0; i < funArray.Length; i++)
            { tot += funArray[i].GetArea();   }
        return tot;
    }
}
// Access this method with ShapeUtil.SumAreas(myShapes);
```

The code in this class can be used with any concrete class that implements the IShapeFunction interface.

Core Approach

For maximum program flexibility, consider using interface types, rather than class types, when defining method parameters. This ensures there is no limit on the types of classes that can be passed to the method, as long as they implement the required interface.

Working with Interfaces

Determining Which Interface Members Are Available

You may not always know at compile time whether a class implements a specific interface. This is often the case when working with a collection that contains a number of types. To perform this check at runtime, use the as or is keyword in your code.

```
// (1)  as keyword to determine if interface is implemented
Circle myCircle = new Circle(5.0);
IShapeFunction myICircle;
myICircle = myCircle as IShapeFunction;
If (myICircle !=null) //interface is implemented

// (2)  is keyword to determine if interface is implemented
Circle myCircle = new Circle(5.0);
If (myCircle is IShapeFunction) // True if interface implemented
```

Accessing Interface Methods

Because a class may inherit methods from a base class and/or multiple interfaces, there is the possibility that inherited methods will have the same name. To avoid this ambiguity, specify an interface method declaration in the derived class with the interface and method name:

```
double IShapeFunction.GetArea() {   // <interface>.<method>
```

This not only permits a class to implement multiple methods, but has the added effect of limiting access to this method to interface references only. For example, the following would result in an error:

```
Circle myCircle = new Circle(5.0);
// cannot reference explicit method
double myArea = myCircle.GetArea();
```

Interfaces Versus Abstract Classes

In the overall design of a system, the real issue is not whether to use a class or interface, but how to best mix the two. The C# restriction on multiple implementation inheritance assures an expanded role for interfaces. It is just too burdensome to try to load all the needed functionality into one base class or a hierarchy of base classes.

A better solution is to define a base class and then expand its capabilities by adding corresponding interfaces. This permits developers to use the class directly without regard to whether the methods are interface implementations. Yet, it also permits the developer to make use of the interface and ignore the other class members.

Of course, you must consider the drawbacks to using interfaces. A well-designed base class reduces the burden on the inherited class to implement everything by promoting code reuse. Also, a non-abstract class can add a member without breaking any existing derived class; adding a member to an interface would break any class implementing the interface.

3.10 Generics

To understand and appreciate the concept of generics, consider the need to create a class that will manage a collection of objects. The objects may be of any type and are specified at compile time by a parameter passed to the class. Moreover, the collection class must be type-safe—meaning that it will accept only objects of the specified type.

In the 1.x versions of .NET, there is no way to create such a class. Your best option is to create a class that contains an array (or other container type) that treats everything as an object. As shown here, casting, or an as operator, is then required to access the actual object type. It is also necessary to include code that verifies the stored object is the correct type.

```
Object[] myStack = new object[50];
myStack[0] = new Circle(5.0);    // place Circle object in array
myStack[1] = "Circle";           // place string in array
Circle c1 = myStack[0] as Circle;
if( c1!=null) {                  // circle object obtained
Circle c2 = (Circle) myStack[1]; // invalid case exception
```

Generics, introduced with .NET 2.0, offer an elegant solution that eliminates the casting, explicit type checking, and boxing that occurs for value type objects. The primary challenge of working with generics is getting used to the syntax, which can be used with a class, interface, or structure.

The best way to approach the syntax is to think of it as a way to pass the data type you'll be working with as a parameter to the generic class. Here is the declaration for a generic class:

```
public class myCollection<T>
{
    T[] myStack = new T[50];
}
```

The *type parameter* T is placed in brackets and serves as a placeholder for the actual type. The compiler recognizes any reference to T within the body of the class and replaces it with the actual type requested. As this statement shows, creating an instance of a generic class is straightforward:

```
myCollection <string> = new myCollection<string>;
```

In this case, string is a *type argument* and specifies that the class is to work with string types only. Note that more than one type parameter may be used, and that the type parameter can be any name, although Microsoft uses (and recommends) single characters in its generic classes.

Although a class may be generic, it can restrict the types that it will accept. This is done by including an optional list of constraints for each type parameter. To declare a constraint, add the where keyword followed by a list of parameter/requirement pairs. The following declaration requires that the type parameter implement the ISerializable and IComparable interfaces:

```
public class myCollection<T> where
   T:ISerializable,
   T:IComparable
```

A parameter may have multiple interface constraints and a single class restraint. In addition, there are three special constraints to be aware of:

class—Parameter must be reference type.
struct—Parameter must be value type.
new()—Type parameter must have a parameterless constructor.

An example of a generic class is provided in Listing 3-16. The class implements an array that manages objects of the type specified in the type parameter. It includes methods to add items to the array, compare items, and return an item count. It includes one constraint that restricts the type parameter to a reference type.

Listing 3-16   A Generic Class to Hold Data

```
using System.Collections.Generic
public class GenStack<T>
   where T:class     // constraint restricts access to ref types
{
   private T[] stackCollection;
   private int count = 0;
   // Constructor
   public GenStack(int size)
   {
      stackCollection = new T[size];
   }
   public void Add(T item)
   {
      stackCollection[count] = item;
      count += 1;
   }
```

Listing 3-16	A Generic Class to Hold Data *(continued)*

```
    // Indexer to expose elements in internal array
    public T this[int ndx]
    {
        get
        {
            if (!(ndx < 0 || ndx > count - 1))
                return stackCollection[ndx];
            // Return empty object
            else return (default(T));
        }
    }
    public int ItemCount
    {
        get {return count;}
    }
    public int Compare<C>(T value1, T value2)
    {
        // Case-sensitive comparison: -1, 0(match), 1
        return Comparer<T>.Default.Compare(value1, value2);
    }
}
```

The following code demonstrates how a client could access the generic class described in Listing 3-16:

```
// Create instance to hold 10 items of type string
GenStack<string> myStack = new GenStack<string>(10);
myStack.Add("Leslie");
myStack.Add("Joanna");
Console.WriteLine(myStack.ItemCount);   // 2
Console.WriteLine(myStack[1]);          // Joanna
int rel = myStack.Compare<string>("Joanna", "joanna");  // -1
Console.WriteLine(rel.ToString());
```

Generics and the .NET generic collection classes are discussed further in Chapter 4.

3.11 Structures

A .NET structure—struct in C# syntax—is often described as a lightweight class. It is similar to a class in that its members include fields, methods, properties, events, and constructors; and it can inherit from interfaces. But there are also implementation differences and restrictions that limit its capabilities vis-à-vis a class:

- A struct is a value type. It implicitly inherits from the System.ValueType.
- A struct cannot inherit from classes, nor can it be inherited.
- An explicitly declared constructor must have at least one parameter.
- struct members cannot have initializers. The field members must be initialized by the constructor or the client code that creates the constructor.

Because a struct is a value type, it is stored on the stack where a program works directly with its contents. This generally provides quicker access than indirectly accessing data through a pointer to the heap. On the downside, structs can slow things down when passed back and forth as parameters. Rather than passing a reference, the CLR copies a struct and sends the copy to the receiving method. Also, a struct faces the boxing and unboxing issue of value types.

When deciding whether to use a struct to represent your data, consider the fact that types that naturally have *value semantics* (objects that directly contain their value as opposed to a reference to a value) are often implemented underneath as a struct. Examples include the primitives discussed in Chapter 2, the color structure whose properties (red, aqua, and so on) define colors in .NET, the DateTime structure used for date-related operations, and various graphics structures used to represent objects such as points and rectangles.

Defining Structures

Syntax:

```
[attribute] [modifier] struct identifier [:interfaces]
{struct-body}
```

Example:

```
public struct DressShirt
{
    public float CollarSz;
    public int SleeveLn;
```

```
   // constructor
   public DressShirt(float collar, int sleeve)
   {
      this.CollarSz = collar;
      this.SleeveLn = sleeve;
   }
}
```

The syntax clearly resembles a class. In fact, replace `struct` with `class` and the code compiles. It has a `public` modifier that permits access from any assembly. The default modifier is `internal`, which restricts access to the containing assembly. No interfaces are specified—although a `struct` can inherit from an interface—so the `struct` is not required to implement any specific methods.

Core Note

It is possible to specify the layout of a `struct`'s fields in memory using the `StructLayout` attribute. This is most commonly used when the `struct` is to be accessed by unmanaged code that expects a specific physical layout of the data. By default, the fields in a `struct` are stored in sequential memory locations.

An instance of the structure can be created in two ways:

```
DressShirt dShirt = new DressShirt(16, 33);
DressShirt myShirt = new DressShirt();
myShirt.CollarSz = 16.5F;
myShirt.SleeveLn = 33;
```

The first statement creates an instance that relies on the user-defined constructor to initialize the field values. When designing such a constructor, be aware that *you must initialize all fields* within the constructor; otherwise, the compiler will issue an error.

The second statement also creates an instance of the `struct` by calling the default constructor, which initializes the fields to default values of zero (0). Note the difference here between a `struct` and a class: A `struct` always has a default parameterless constructor; a class has the default parameterless constructor only if there are no explicitly defined constructors.

Using Methods and Properties with a Structure

Methods and properties are usually associated with classes, but they play an equally important role in the use of structures. In fact, a client accessing a method has no syntactical clue as to whether the method or property is associated with a class or struct. Listing 3-17 extends the original example to add two properties and a method.

Listing 3-17	Basic Elements of a Struct

```
public struct DressShirt
{
    private float CollarSz;
    private int SleeveLn;
    public DressShirt(float collar, int sleeve)
    {
        this.CollarSz = collar;
        this.SleeveLn = sleeve;
    }

    // Properties to return sleeve and collar values
    public int Sleeve
    {
        get {return (SleeveLn);}
        set {SleeveLn = value;}
    }
    public float Collar
    {
        get {return (CollarSz); }
        // "value" is an implicit parameter
        set {CollarSz = value;    }
    }

    // Method to convert size to different scale
    public string ShirtSize()
    {
        string mySize = "S";
        if (CollarSz > 14.5) mySize = "M";
        if (CollarSz > 15.5) mySize = "L";
        if (CollarSz > 16.5) mySize = "XL";
        return (mySize);
    }
}
```

The most important thing to note about this code is that it could be cut and pasted into a class and run with no changes. Although a `struct` doesn't support all of the features of a class, the ones it does are implemented using identical syntax.

3.12 Structure Versus Class

Many developers instinctively select a class to represent data and the operations performed on it. However, there are cases where a `struct` is a better choice, as evidenced by its use in the Framework Class Library to represent simple data types. This section compares the two and offers general guidelines to consider when choosing between the two.

Table 3-5 Comparison of Structure and Class

	Structure	Class
Default access level of the type	Internal	Internal
Default access level for data members	Public	Private
Default access level for properties and methods	Private	Private
Value or reference type	Value	Reference
Can be a base for new types	No	Yes
Implement interfaces	Yes	Yes
Raise and handle events	Yes	Yes
Scope of members	Structure	Class
Instance initialization	Constructor—with or without parameters. A `struct` cannot contain a custom parameterless constructor.	Constructor—with or without parameters.
Can be nested	Yes	Yes
Has a destructor	No	Yes (Finalizer)

It is clear from the table that structures possess many of the features and capabilities of classes. Consequently, a developer may have difficulty deciding which is the better choice. The answer lies in understanding the few—but significant—differences between the two.

Structures Are Value Types and Classes Are Reference Types

As mentioned, classes are allocated space from the managed heap when the object or class instance is created. The address of the object (on the heap) is returned to the variable representing the object. In contrast, a variable set to a `struct` type contains the structure's actual data—not a pointer. The ramifications of this are most pronounced when passing arguments to functions. Reference types simply require that a pointer be passed, whereas structures require that a copy of all fields be made and passed to the function.

The structure does have some advantages with regard to memory allocation and Garbage Collection. Structure instances are allocated in a thread's stack rather than the managed heap, thus avoiding the associated overhead of managing pointers. Memory management is also simpler. When a copy of a structure is no longer reachable, its memory is collected and made available. In contrast, classes often require special code to handle unmanaged resources or invoke the system's garbage collection routine. Garbage Collection is covered in the next chapter.

Unlike a Class, a Structure Cannot Be Inherited

This is a departure from C++ conventions that permit a class to use an existing structure as a base class and permit a structure to use a class as a base. Is the .NET lack of support for this a step backward? Not really. It better delineates the role of the structure versus the class—making the structure less of a pseudo-class and more of a data structure. In addition, it provides for a more efficient implementation of the structure. The restriction enables the compiler to minimize the amount of administrative code that would be required to support inheritance. For example, because the compiler knows that a structure's methods cannot be overridden by subclasses, it can optimize the method invocation by expanding the method code inline rather than executing a method call.

General Rules for Choosing Between a Structure and a Class

The easiest way to make the choice is to compare the features of the type that you are designing with the following checklist. *If any of these are true, you should use a class.*

- The type needs to serve as a base for deriving other types.
- The type needs to inherit from another class. Note that although a structure cannot explicitly specify a base class, it does implicitly inherit from the System.ValueType and may override the inherited methods.
- The type is frequently passed as a method parameter. Performance degrades as copies of the structure are created with each call. An exception to this is when the structure exists inside an array. Because an array is a reference type, only a pointer to the array is passed.
- The type is used as the return type of methods. In the case where the return type is a structure, the system must copy the structure from the called function to the calling program.

3.13 Summary

The goal of the C# language architects was to create a "component-oriented" language based on the traditional object-oriented principles of encapsulation, inheritance, and polymorphism. Toward this end, they included language features that make properties, events, and attributes first-class language constructs. Properties now have their own get and set syntax; events can be created with the event keyword and linked to delegates that call registered methods when the event occurs; custom or built-in attributes can be attached to a class or selected class members to add descriptive information to an assembly's metacode.

C# provides several forms of method declarations: a virtual method permits a derived class to implement its own version of the method; sealed prevents a derived class from overriding it; and abstract requires a derived class to implement its own version of the method.

In some cases, a structure or interface provides a better programming solution than a class. The C# struct is an efficient, simple way to represent self-contained data types that don't require the overhead of classes. An interface is a practical way to define a behavior that can be passed on to inheriting classes. In .NET, its value is enhanced because a class (or struct) can inherit from any number of interfaces—but from only one class.

3.14 Test Your Understanding

1. What type of class cannot be inherited?

2. How many classes can a class directly inherit? How many interfaces?

3. Referring to the following class, answer the questions below:

    ```
    public class ShowName {
        public static void ShowMe(string MyName)
        { Console.WriteLine(MyName); }
    }
    ```

    a. Can the method ShowName be referenced from s?

    ```
    ShowName s = new ShowName();
    s.ShowMe("Giacomo");
    ```

    b. Write a code sample that will print "My Name is Ishmael".

4. Can an abstract class have non-abstract methods?

5. What keyword must a derived class use to replace a non-virtual inherited method?

6. What are the results from running the following code?

    ```
    public class ParmTest
    {
        public static void GetCoordinates(ref int x, int y)
        {
            x= x+y;
            y= y+x;
        }
    }
    // calling method
    int x=20;
    int y=40;
    ParmTest.GetCoordinates(ref x, y);
    Console.WriteLine("x="+x+" y="+y);
    ```

    a. x=60 y=40
    b. x=20 y=60
    c. x=20 y=40
    d. x=60 y=60

7. What is the best way to ensure that languages that do not recognize operator overloading can access C# code containing this feature?

8. Name two ways that you can prevent a class from being instantiated.

9. Your application contains a class StoreSales that fires an event when an item is sold. The event provides the saleprice (decimal), date (DateTime), and the itemnum (int) to its subscribers. Create an event handler that processes the ItemSold event by extracting and printing the sales data.

```
public delegate void SaleDelegate(object sender,
                                   SaleEvArgs e);
public event SaleDelegate ItemSold;
StoreSales mysale= new StoreSale();
mySale.ItemSold += new SaleDelegate(PrintSale);
```

10. What happens if you attempt to compile and run the following code?

```
using System;
public class Base
{
    public void aMethod(int i, String s)
    {
        Console.WriteLine("Base Method");
    }
    public Base()
    {
        Console.WriteLine("Base Constructor");
    }
}

public class Child: Base
{
    string parm="Hello";
    public static void Main(String[] argv)
    {
        Child c = new Child();
        c.aMethod();
    }
    void aMethod(int i, string Parm)
    {
        Console.WriteLine(Parm);
    }
    public void aMethod()
    { }
}
```

a. Error during compilation.
b. "Base Constructor" is printed.
c. "Base Constructor" and "Base Method" are printed.
d. "Base Constructor" and "Hello" are printed.

Working with Objects in C#

Topics in This Chapter

- *Creating Objects:* Learn how to use a factory design pattern to create objects.

- *Exception Handling:* Effective exception handling requires an understanding of how exceptions are *thrown* and *caught* in .NET. Along with an overview of exception handling, this section looks at how to create custom exception objects.

- *Using System.Object Methods:* Familiarity with the `System.Object` methods is necessary if you want to create custom collection classes that implement the standard features found in classes contained in the Framework Class Library.

- *Collection Classes and Interfaces:* .NET offers a variety of collection classes for managing multiple objects. This section looks at arrays, hash tables, and stacks, among others. Of particular interest are the 2.0 classes that support generics.

- *Object Serialization:* Objects can be converted (serialized) into a binary stream or an XML formatted stream. An example using the binary serializer is presented.

- *Object Life Cycle Management:* .NET Garbage Collection automatically removes unreferenced objects. This can produce unwanted results unless measures are taken to ensure that objects are destroyed properly.

Chapter 4

The purpose of this chapter is to consider what happens to a class when it becomes an object. This metamorphosis raises some interesting questions: What is the best way to create an object? How do you ensure that an object handles errors gracefully? How do you prevent an object from wasting resources (the dreaded memory leak)? What is the best way to work with groups of objects? How do you dispose of an object? Although these questions are unlikely to keep a developer awake at night, their consideration should lead to a keener insight into class design.

In an attempt to answer these questions, a variety of topics are presented. These include how to create objects using established *design patterns*; how to implement the `System.Object` methods on custom classes; how to implement exception handling; how to persist objects using serialization; and how to use collection classes and interfaces to manage groups of objects. The chapter concludes with a look at how to design an object so that it shuts down properly when subject to .NET Garbage Collection.

4.1   Object Creation

The subject of creating objects typically receives less attention than that of designing classes; but it is important enough that a formal body of techniques known as *creational patterns* has been developed to provide object creation models. A popular approach—used throughout the Framework Class Library (FCL)—is to implement the *factory* creational pattern. As the name implies, the factory is an object whose sole purpose is to create other objects—much like a real-world factory. Its advantage is that it handles all the details of object creation; a client instructs the factory which object to create and is generally unaffected by any implementation changes that may occur.

There are a number of ways to implement the factory pattern. This section presents two logical approaches—illustrated in Figures 4-1 and 4-2.

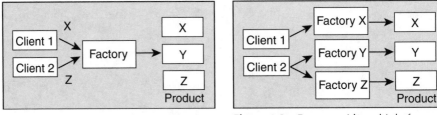

Figure 4-1   Factory with one factory class   **Figure 4-2**   Factory with multiple factory classes

Figure 4-1 represents the case where one factory is used to produce all of the related products (objects). In Figure 4-2, each product has its own factory, and the client sends the request to the factory that produces the desired object. We'll look at examples of both, beginning with code for the single factory implementation (see Listing 4-1).

Listing 4-1	Using a Class Factory to Create Objects—Single Factory

```
public interface IApparel     // Interface representing product
{
    string ShowMe();
    bool Knit         // Property to indicate if Knit
    { get; }
}
public class SportsShirt : IApparel
{
    public string ShowMe()
    {
        return("Sports Shirt");
    }
    public bool Knit
    { get {return true;} }
```

Listing 4-1	Using a Class Factory to Create Objects—Single Factory *(continued)*

```
}
public class DressShirt : IApparel
{
    public string ShowMe()
    {
        return("Dress Shirt");
    }
    public bool Knit
    { get {return false;} }
}
// Factory to return instances of apparel classes
public class ApparelFactory
{
    public IApparel CreateApparel( string apptype)
    {
        switch (apptype)
        {
          case "MDRSHIRT":
              return new DressShirt();
          case "MSPSHIRT":
              return new SportsShirt();
        }
        return null;
    }
}
```

In this example, the class factory implements a method named `CreateApparel` that returns objects. The most important thing to note is that this method is declared with `IApparel` as its return type, which enables it to return an instance of any class that implements that interface.

```
public IApparel CreateApparel( string apptype)
```

The same effect could be achieved by replacing the interface with an *abstract* class. This could yield better code reuse in situations where objects share common behavior, but should be weighed against other factors that were discussed in Chapter 3, "Class Design in C#."

With the factory and product classes defined, all the hard work has been done. It's a simple matter for clients to create objects:

```
ApparelFactory factory= new ApparelFactory();
IApparel ob1 = factory.CreateApparel("MDRSHIRT");
IApparel ob2 = factory.CreateApparel("MSPSHIRT");
string shirtType = ob1.ShowMe(); // Returns "Dress Shirt"
```

If the application needs to add any more products, the factory is supplied with the new code, but no changes are required on the client side. It only needs to be aware of how to request all available products.

Example: Creating Objects with Multiple Factories

This solution adds an abstract class (we could use an interface) for the factory and two concrete subclasses that implement it to produce specific apparel objects:

```
// abstract
public abstract class AppFactory
{
    public  abstract IApparel CreateApparel();
}
// Concrete factory classes
public class DressShirtFactory:AppFactory
{
    public override IApparel CreateApparel( )
    { return new DressShirt(); }
}
public class SportShirtFactory : AppFactory
{
    public override IApparel CreateApparel( )
    { return new SportsShirt(); }
}
```

We have created the abstract class so that its subclasses can be passed to a new `ApparelCollector` class that serves as an intermediary between the clients and the factories. Specifically, the client passes the factory to this class, and it is responsible for calling the appropriate factory.

```
public class ApparelCollector
{
    public void CollectApparel(AppFactory factory)
    {
        IApparel apparel = factory.CreateApparel();
    }
}
```

The code to use the new class is analogous to that in the first example:

```
AppFactory factory = new DressShirtFactory();
IApparel obj2 = new ApparelCollector().CollectApparel(factory);
```

For a simple example like this, the first approach using one factory is easier to implement. However, there are cases where it's preferable to have multiple factories. The objects may be grouped into families of products (a shirt factory and a dress factory, for example), or you may have a distributed application where it makes sense for different developers to provide their own factory classes.

4.2 Exception Handling

One of the most important aspects of managing an object is to ensure that its behavior and interaction with the system does not result in a program terminating in error. This means that an application must deal gracefully with any runtime errors that occur, whether they originate from faulty application code, the Framework Class Library, or hardware faults.

.NET provides developers with a technique called structured exception handling (SEH) to deal with error conditions. The basic idea is that when an exception occurs, an exception object is created and passed along with program control to a specially designated section of code. In .NET terms, the exception object is *thrown* from one section of code to another section that *catches* it.

Compared to error handling techniques that rely on error codes and setting bit values, SEH offers significant advantages:

- The exception is passed to the application as an object whose properties include a description of the exception, the assembly that threw the exception, and a stack trace that shows the sequence of calls leading to the exception.
- If an exception is thrown and an application does not catch it, the Common Language Runtime (CLR) terminates the application. This forces the developer to take error handling seriously.
- The exception handling and detection code does not have to be located where the errors occur. This means, for example, that exception handling code could be placed in a special class devoted to that purpose.
- Exceptions are used exclusively and consistently at both the application and system level. All methods in the .NET Framework throw exceptions when an error occurs.

Before looking at the actual mechanics of implementing exception handling, let's examine the exception itself. As previously mentioned, an exception is a class instance. All .NET exceptions derive from the `System.Exception` class. So, an understanding of this class is essential to working with exceptions.

System.Exception Class

As shown in Figure 4-3, `System.Exception` is the base class for two generic subclasses—`SystemException` and `ApplicationException`—from which all exception objects directly inherit. .NET Framework exceptions (such as `IOException` and `ArithmeticException`) derive directly from `IOException`, whereas custom application exceptions should inherit from `ApplicationException`. The sole purpose of these classes is to categorize exceptions, because they do not add any properties or methods to the base `System.Exception` class.

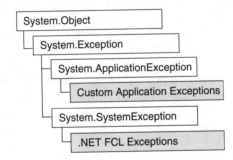

Figure 4-3   .NET exception classes hierarchy

The `System.Exception` class contains relatively few members. Table 4-1 summarizes the members discussed in this section.

Table 4-1   `System.Exception` Class Properties

Property	Type	Description
HelpLink	string	Contains a URL that points to help documentation.
InnerException	Exception	Is set to `null` unless the exception occurs while a previous exception is being handled. A `GetBaseException` method can be used to list a chain of previous inner exceptions.
Message	string	The text describing the exception.

Table 4-1   `System.Exception` Class Properties *(continued)*

Property	Type	Description
Source	string	Name of the assembly that generated the exception.
StackTrace	string	Contains the sequence of method names and signatures that were called prior to the exception. It is invaluable for debugging.
TargetSite	MethodBase	Provides details about the method that threw the exception. The property is an object of type `Method-Base`. It returns the name of the method in which the exception occurred. It also has a `DeclaringType` property that returns the name of the class containing the method.
HResult	Int32	This is a protected property used when interoperating with COM code. When an exception is thrown to a COM client, this value is converted to an `HRESULT` in the COM world of unmanaged code.

Writing Code to Handle Exceptions

C# uses a `try/catch/finally` construct to implement exception handling (see Figure 4-4). When an exception occurs, the system searches for a `catch` block that can handle the current type of exception. It begins its search in the current method, working down the list of `catch` blocks sequentially. If none is found, it then searches the `catch` blocks in the calling method associated with the relevant `try` block. If the search yields no matching `catch` block, an *unhandled exception* occurs. As discussed later, the application is responsible for defining a policy to deal with this. Let's look at the details of using these three blocks.

The **try** Block

The code inside the `try` block is referred to as a *guarded region* because it has associated `catch` or `finally` blocks to handle possible exceptions or cleanup duties. Each `try` block must have at least one accompanying `catch` or `finally` block.

The **catch** Block

A `catch` block consists of the keyword `catch` followed by an expression in parentheses called the *exception filter* that indicates the type of exception to which it responds. Following this is the code body that implements the response.

```
try {
    // Code that may cause an exception.
    // It may consist of multiple lines of code.
}
// May contain any number of catch blocks.
catch(exception name) {
    // Place code here that handles the exception.
    // Catch block may contain a throw statement.
}
catch(exception name) {
    // Place code here that handles the exception.
}

finally {
    // This code is always executed whether or not an
    // exception occurs.
}
```

Figure 4-4 Code blocks used for exception handling

The exception filter identifies the exception it handles and also serves as a parameter when an exception is thrown to it. Consider the following statement:

```
catch (DivideByZeroException ex)  {  ... }
```

The filter will be invoked if a `System.DivideByZeroException` occurs. The variable ex references the exception and provides access to its properties, such as `ex.Message` and `ex.StackTrace` .

When using multiple `catch` blocks, ordering is important. They should be listed hierarchically, beginning with the most specific exceptions and ending with the more general ones. In fact, the compiler generates an error if you do not order them correctly.

```
catch (DivideByZeroException ex)  {  ... }
catch (IndexOutOfRangeException ex) { ... }
catch (Exception ex)  {  ... }
```

This codes first looks for specific exceptions such as a division by zero or an index out of range. The final exception filter, `Exception`, catches any exception derived from `System.Exception`. When an exception is caught, the code in the block is executed and all other `catch` blocks are skipped. Control then flows to the `finally` block—if one exists.

Note that the `catch` block may include a `throw` statement to pass the exception further up the call stack to the previous caller. The `throw` statement has an optional parameter placed in parentheses that can be used to identify the type of exception being thrown. If `throw` is used without a parameter, it throws the exception caught by the current block. You typically throw an exception when the calling method is better suited to handle it.

The **finally** Block

Regarded as the "cleanup" block, the `finally` block is executed whether or not an exception occurs and is a convenient place to perform any cleanup operations such as closing files or database connections. This block must be included if there are no `catch` blocks; otherwise, it is optional.

Example: Handling Common SystemException Exceptions

Listing 4-2 illustrates the use of the `try/catch/finally` blocks in dealing with an exception generated by the CLR.

Listing 4-2	Handling Exceptions Generated by the CLR

```
using System;
// Class to illustrate results of division by zero
public class TestExcep
{
    public static int Calc(int j)
    {
        return (100 / j);
    }
}
class MyApp
{
    public static void Main()
    {
        TestExcep exTest = new TestExcep();
        try
        {
            // Create divide by zero in called method
            int dZero = TestExcep.Calc(0);
            // This statement is not executed
            Console.WriteLine("Result: {0}",dZero);
        }
```

| Listing 4-2 | Handling Exceptions Generated by the CLR *(continued)* |

```
         catch(DivideByZeroException ex)
         {
            Console.WriteLine("{0}\n{1}\n", ex.Message, ex.Source);
            Console.WriteLine(ex.TargetSite.ToString());
            Console.WriteLine(ex.StackTrace);
         }
         catch (Exception ex)
         {
            Console.WriteLine("General "+ex.Message);
         }
         finally
         {
            Console.WriteLine("Cleanup occurs here.");
         }
      }
}
```

In this example, `TestExcep.Calc` throws a division by zero exception when `MyApp` calls it with a zero value. Because `Calc` has no code to handle the exception, the exception is thrown back automatically to `MyApp` at the point where `Calc` was called. From there, control passes to the block provided to handle `DivideByZeroException` exceptions. For demonstration purposes, the statements in the `catch` block display the following information provided by the exception object:

Property	Value Printed
ex.Message	Attempted to divide by zero
ex.Source	zeroexcept *(assembly name)*
ex.TargetSite	Void Main()
ex.StackTrace	at MyApp.Main()

Core Recommendation

`StackTrace` displays only those methods on the call stack to the level where the exception is first handled—not where it occurs. Although you may be tempted to catch exceptions at the point where they occur in order to view the full call stack, this is discouraged. It may improve diagnostics; however, it takes time and space to throw an exception and its entire call stack. Usually, the lower on a call stack that an exception occurs, the more likely it is that the conditions causing it can be avoided by improved coding logic.

How to Create a Custom Exception Class

Custom exception classes are useful when you need to describe errors in terms of the class that issues the error. For example, you may want the exception to describe the specific behavior causing the error or to indicate a problem with a parameter that does not meet some required criteria. In general, first look to the most specific system exception available; if that is inadequate, consider creating your own.

In Listing 4-3, a method throws a custom exception if the object it receives does not implement the two required interfaces. The exception, NoDescException, returns a message describing the error and the name of the object causing the failure.

Listing 4-3	Building a Custom Exception Class

```
// Custom Exception Class
[Serializable]
public class NoDescException : ApplicationException
{  // Three constructors should be implemented
   public NoDescException(){}
   public NoDescException(string message):base(message){}
   public NoDescException(string message, Exception innerEx)
        :base(message, innerEx){ }
}

// Interfaces that shape objects are to implement
public interface IShapeFunction
   { double GetArea(); }
public interface IShapeDescription
   { string ShowMe();}

// Circle and Rectangle classes are defined
class Circle : IShapeFunction
{
   private double radius;
   public Circle (double rad)
   {
      radius= rad;
   }
   // Methods to implement both interfaces
   public double GetArea()
   {  return (3.14*radius*radius);   }
}
```

Listing 4-3   Building a Custom Exception Class *(continued)*

```
class Rectangle : IShapeFunction, IShapeDescription
{
   private int width, height;
   public Rectangle(int w, int h)
   {
      width= w;
      height=h;
   }
   // Methods to implement both interfaces
   public double GetArea()
   { return (height*width);   }
   public string ShowMe()
   { return("rectangle");      }
}

public class ObjAreas
{
   public static void ShowAreas(object ObjShape)
   {
      // Check to see if interfaces are implemented
      if (!(ObjShape is IShapeDescription &&
         ObjShape is IShapeFunction) )
      {
         // Throw custom exception
         string objName = ObjShape.ToString();
         throw new NoDescException
            ("Interface not implemented for "+objName);
      }
      // Continue processing since interfaces exist
      IShapeFunction myShape    = (IShapeFunction)ObjShape;
      IShapeDescription myDesc = (IShapeDescription) ObjShape;
      string desc = myDesc.ShowMe();
      Console.WriteLine(desc+" Area= "+
                     myShape.GetArea().ToString());
   }
}
```

To view the custom exception in action, let's create two shape objects and pass them via calls to the static ObjAreas.ShowAreas method.

```
Circle myCircle = new Circle(4.0);
Rectangle myRect = new Rectangle(5,2);
try
```

```
{
    ObjAreas.ShowAreas(myRect);
    ObjAreas.ShowAreas(myCircle);
}
catch (NoDescException ex)
{
    Console.WriteLine(ex.Message);
}
```

The `ShowAreas` method checks to ensure the object it has received implements the two interfaces. If not, it throws an instance of `NoDescException` and control passes to the calling code. In this example, the `Circle` object implements only one interface, resulting in an exception.

Pay particular attention to the design of `NoDescException`. It is a useful model that illustrates the rules to be followed in implementing a custom exception type:

- The class should be derived from `ApplicationException`.
- By convention, the exception name should end in `Exception`. The `Exception` base class defines three public constructors that should be included:

  1. A parameterless constructor to serve as the default.
  2. A constructor with one string parameter—usually the message.
  3. A constructor with a string parameter and an `Exception` object parameter that is used when an exception occurs while a previous exception is being handled.

- Use the `base` initializer to call the base class to take care of the actual object creation. If you choose to add fields or properties, add a new constructor to initialize these values.
- The `Serializable` attribute specifies that the exception can be *serialized*, which means it can be represented as XML for purposes of storing it or transmitting it. Typically, you can ignore this attribute, because it's only required if an exception object is being thrown from code in one *application domain* to another. Application domains are discussed Chapter 15, "Code Refinement, Security, and Deployment"; for now, think of them as logical partitions that .NET uses to isolate code segments.

Unhandled Exceptions

Unhandled exceptions occur when the CLR is unable to find a `catch` filter to handle the exception. The default result is that the CLR will handle it with its own methods. Although this provides a warning to a user or developer, it is not a recommended way to deal with it. The solution is in the problem: Take advantage of .NET's unhandled exception event handlers to funnel all of the exceptions to your own custom exception handling class.

The custom class provides a convenient way to establish a policy for dealing with unhandled exceptions. The code can be implemented to recognize whether it is dealing with a debug or release version, and respond accordingly. For example, in debug version, your main concern is to start the debugger; in a release version, you should log the error and provide a meaningful screen that allows the user to end the program.

Unfortunately, there is no single approach that applies to all C# programming needs. Your actual solution depends on whether you are working with a Console, Windows Form, Web Forms, or Web Services application. In this section, we will look at how to implement a Windows Forms solution, which is conceptually the same as for a Console application. Web Forms and Web Services are addressed in the Web Applications chapters, Chapters 16–18.

Unhandled Exceptions in a Windows Forms Application

Event handling was discussed in the previous chapter along with the important role of delegates. We can now use those techniques to register our own callback method that processes any unhandled exceptions thrown in the Windows application.

When an exception occurs in Windows, the application's `OnThreadException` method is ultimately called. It displays a dialog box describing the unhandled exception. You can override this by creating and registering your own method that matches the signature of the `System.Threading.ThreadExceptionEventHandler` delegate. Listing 4-4 shows one way this can be implemented.

`MyUnhandledMethod` is defined to handle the exception and must be registered to receive the callback. The following code registers the method for the `Thread-Exception` event using the `ThreadExceptionEventHandler` delegate and runs the application:

```
static void Main()
{
   Application.ThreadException += new
      ThreadExceptionEventHandler(UnForgiven.MyUnhandledMethod);
   Application.Run(new Form1());
}
```

The implementation code in the method is straightforward. The most interesting aspect is the use of preprocessor directives (`#if DEBUG`) to execute code based on whether the application is in release or debug mode.

Listing 4-4	Unhandled Exceptions in a Windows Form

```
// Class to receive callback to process unhandled exceptions
using System.Diagnostics;
using System.Windows.Forms;
using System.Threading;
public class UnForgiven
{
    // Class signature matches ThreadExceptionEventHandler
    public static void MyUnhandledMethod
        (object sender, ThreadExceptionEventArgs e)
    {
#if DEBUG
    // Statements for debug mode
    // Display trace and start the Debugger
    MessageBox.Show("Debug: "+e.ToString());
#else
    // Statements for release mode
    // Provide output to user and log errors
    MessageBox.Show("Release: "+e.ToString());
#endif
    }
}
```

For a Console application, the same approach is used except that the delegate and event names are different. You would register the method with the following:

```
Thread.GetDomain().UnhandledException += new
    UnhandledExceptionEventHandler(
        UnForgiven.MyUnhandledMethodAp);
```

Also, the method's EventArgs parameter changes to UnhandledException-EventArgs.

Exception Handling Guidelines

The use of exception handling is the key to implementing code that performs in a stable manner when unexpected conditions occur. But successful exception handling requires more than surrounding code with try and catch blocks. Thought must be given to which exceptions should be caught and what to do with a caught exception. Included here are some general rules to consider. For a more extensive list, consult online "best practices" information.

Only catch exceptions when you have a specific need to do the following:

- Perform a recovery
- Perform a cleanup, particularly to release resources
- Log information
- Provide extra debug information

Use exceptions to handle unexpected events, not as a way to implement logic.

Distinguish between error handling and exception handling. Incorrectly formatted credit card numbers or incorrect passwords, for example, are all occurrences that should be anticipated and handled by the logic of your code. An unavailable database table or hardware failure requires an exception.

Don't catch or throw base exception types.

The base exception type System.Exception is a catch-all exception that can be used to catch any exception this is not specifically identified and caught. Much like "fools gold," its intuitive appeal is deceptive. The objective of exception handling is to identify specific exceptions and handle with code appropriate for them; catching each exception prevents the unexpected ones from being identified. As a rule, catch specific exceptions and allow unidentified ones to propagate up the call stack.

Make liberal use of finally blocks.

The purpose of a finally block is to perform any housekeeping chores before a method is exited. It is implemented as part of both try/catch/finally and try/finally constructs. Because code should be more liberal in its use of throws than catches, an application should contain more try/finally constructs than try/catch constructs.

The inclusion of thorough, intelligent exception handling code in an application is one of the hallmarks of well-written code. Although you'll find code segments in this book where exception handling is ignored or used sparingly, understand that this is done only in the interest of simplifying code examples. In real-world programming, there are no excuses for leaving it out.

4.3   Implementing System.Object Methods in a Custom Class

When creating a custom class, particularly one that will be available to other developers, it is important to ensure that it observes the proper rules of object etiquette. It should be CLS compliant, provide adequate exception handling, and adhere to OOP principles of encapsulation and inheritance when providing member accessibility. A class should also implement the features that .NET developers are accustomed to when working with Framework classes. These features include a custom implementation of the `System.Object` methods that all classes inherit:

- `ToString()`. By default, this method returns the name of the class. It should be overridden to display contents of the object that distinguish it from other instances of the class.
- `Equals()`. This is used to compare instances of a class to determine if they are equal. It's up to the class to define what equality means. This could mean that two objects have matching field values or that two objects reference the same memory location.
- `MemberwiseClone()`. This method returns a copy of an object that contains the object's value fields only—referred to as a *shallow copy*. A custom class can use this method to return a copy of itself or implement its own clone method to return a *deep copy* that also includes reference type values.

The remainder of this section provides examples of overriding or using these methods in custom classes. Note that `System.Object.Finalize`—a method to perform cleanup duties before an object is claimed by garbage collection—is discussed in Section 4.6, "Object Life Cycle Management."

ToString() to Describe an Object

This method is most commonly used with primitive types to convert numbers to a string format that can be displayed or printed. When used with objects, the default is to return the fully qualified name of the object: `<namespace>.<classname>`. It's common to override this and return a string containing selected values from members of the object. A good example of this is the exception object from the previous section (refer to Figure 4-3) that returns the `Message` and `StackTrace` values:

```
ex.ToString()    // Output:
                 //   Attempted to divide by zero
                 //   at TestExcep.Calc(Int32 j)
                 //   at MyApp.Main()
```

The code shown in Listing 4-5 demonstrates how easy it is to implement `ToString` in your own class.

The `StringBuilder` class is used to create the text string returned by the method. It provides an efficient way of handling strings and is described in Chapter 5, "C# Text Manipulation and File I/O."

| Listing 4-5 | Overriding ToString() |

```
using System.Text;
using System;
public class Chair
{
    private double myPrice;
    private string myVendor, myID;
    public Upholstery myUpholstery;
    public  Chair(double price, string vendor, string sku)
    {  myPrice = price;
       myVendor = vendor;
       myID = sku;
    }
    // Override System.Object ToString()
    public override string ToString()
    {
        StringBuilder chairSB = new StringBuilder();
        chairSB.AppendFormat("ITEM = Chair");
        chairSB.AppendFormat(" VENDOR = {0}", this.myVendor);
        chairSB.AppendFormat(" PRICE = {0}",
                             this.myPrice.ToString());
        return chairSB.ToString();
    }
    public string MyVen
    {
        get {return myVendor;}
    }
    //... other properties to expose myPrice, myID
}
public class Upholstery
{
    public string Fabric ;
    public Upholstery( string fab)
    { Fabric = fab; }
}
```

The following statements create an instance of the object and set desc to the more meaningful value returned by ToString():

```
Chair myChair = new Chair(120.0, "Broyhill", "60-1222");
string desc = myChair.ToString());
// Returns ITEM = Chair VENDOR = Broyhill PRICE = 120.0
```

Equals() to Compare Objects

When comparing two reference types, `Equals` returns true only if they point to the same object in memory. To compare objects based on their value (value equality rather than referential equality), you must override the default method. An example of this is the `String` class—a reference type that implements `Equals` to perform a value comparison based on the characters in the strings.

The code in Listing 4-6 illustrates how to override `Equals` in the `Chair` class to compare objects using value semantics. It also overrides the `GetHashCode` method—always recommended when overriding `Equals`.

Listing 4-6   Overriding `Equals()`

```
public override bool Equals(Object obj)
{
   // Include the following two statements if this class
   // derives from a class that overrides Equals()
   //if (!base.Equals(obj))
   //   return false;
   // (1) Null objects cannot be compared
   if (obj == null) return false;
   // (2) Check object types
   if (this.GetType() != obj.GetType()) return false;
   // (3) Cast object so we can access its fields
   Chair otherObj = (Chair) obj;
   // (4) Compare reference fields
   if (!Object.Equals(myUpholstery,
             otherObj.myUpholstery)) return false;
   // (5) Compare Value Type members
   if (!myVendor.Equals(otherObj.myVendor)) return false;
   if (!myPrice.Equals(otherObj.myPrice))   return false;
   if (!myID.Equals(otherObj.myID))         return false;
   return true;
}
// Override GetHashCode - Required if Equals overridden
public override int GetHashCode()
{
   return myID.GetHashCode();
}
```

This method compares an instance of the current object with the one passed to it. The first step is to ensure that the received object is not null. Next, following the steps in Figure 4-5, the types of the two objects are compared to make sure they match.

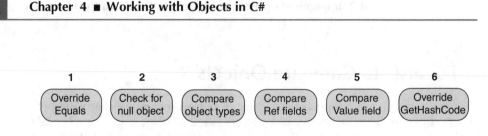

Figure 4-5   Steps in overriding `Equals()`

The heart of the method consists of comparing the field values of the two objects. To compare reference fields, it uses the static `Object.Equals` method, which takes two objects as arguments. It returns `true` if the two objects reference the same instance, if both objects are null, or if the object's `Equals` comparison returns `true`. Value types are compared using the field's `Equals` method:

```
if (!myID.Equals(otherObj.myID))
return false;
```

Here is an example that demonstrates the new `Equals` method. It creates two `Chair` objects, sets their fields to the same value, and performs a comparison:

```
Chair myChair = new Chair(150.0, "Lane", "78-0988");
myChair.myUpholstery = new Upholstery("Silk");
Chair newChair = new Chair(150.0, "Lane", "78-0988");
newChair.myUpholstery= new Upholstery("Silk");
// Next statement returns false. Why?
bool eq = ( myChair.Equals(newChair));
```

Although the two objects have identical field values, the comparison fails—which is probably not what you want. The reason is that the objects point to two different `myUpholstery` instances, causing their reference comparison to fail. The solution is to override the `Equals` method in the `Upholstery` class, so that it performs a value comparison of the `Fabric` fields. To do so, place this code inside its `Equals` method, in addition to the other overhead code shown in Listing 4-6:

```
Upholstery otherObj = (Upholstery) obj;
if (!Fabric.Equals(otherObj.Fabric)) return false;
```

Overriding GetHashCode

The `GetHashCode` method generates an `Int32` hash code value for any object. This value serves as an identifier that can be used to place any object in a hash table collection. The Framework designers decreed that any two objects that are equal must have the same hash code. As a result, any new `Equals` method must be paired with a `GetHashCode` method to ensure that identical objects generate the same hash code value.

Ideally, the hash code values generated over the range of objects represent a wide distribution. This example used a simple algorithm that calls the base type's Get-HashCode method to return a value based on the item's ID. This is a good choice because the IDs are unique for each item, the ID is an instance field, and the ID field value is immutable—being set only in the constructor.

Determining If References Point to the Same Object

After you override the original Equals method to compare object values, your application may still need to determine if reference variables refer to the same object. System.Object has a static method called ReferenceEquals for this purpose. It is used here with our Chair class:

```
Chair chair1 = new Chair(120.0, "Broyhill", "66-9888") )
Chair chair2 = new Chair(120.0, "Broyhill", "66-9933") )
Chair chair3 = chair1;
if (Object.ReferenceEquals(chair1, chair3) )
   { MessageBox.Show("Same object");}
else
   { MessageBox.Show("Different objects");}
```

The method returns true because chair1 and chair3 reference the same instance.

Cloning to Create a Copy of an Object

The usual way to create an object is by using the new operator to invoke a constructor. An alternative approach is to make a copy or clone of an existing object. The object being cloned may be a class instance, an array, a string, or any reference type; primitives cannot be cloned. For a class to be cloneable, it must implement the ICloneable interface. This is a simple interface defined as

```
public interface ICloneable
{
    Object Clone();
}
```

It consists of a single method, Clone, that is implemented to create a copy of the object. The cloned object may represent a shallow copy or a deep copy of the object's fields. A shallow copy creates a new instance of the original object type, and then copies the non-static fields from the original object to the new object. For a reference type, only a pointer to the value is copied. Thus, the clone points to the same reference object as the original. A deep copy duplicates everything. It creates a copy of reference objects and provides a reference to them in the copy.

Figure 4-6 depicts a shallow and deep copy for this instance of the Chair class:

```
Chair myChair = new Chair(150.0, "Lane", "78-0988");
Upholstery myFabric = new Upholstery("Silk");
myChair.myUpholstery = myFabric;
```

In both cases, the clone of the myChair object contains its own copy of the value type fields. However, the shallow copy points to the same instance of myUpholstery as the original; in the deep copy, it references a duplicate object.

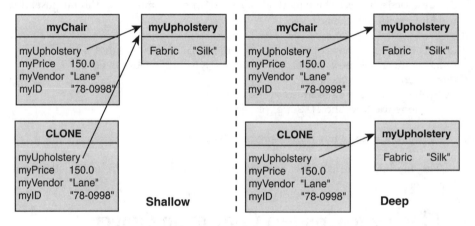

Figure 4-6   Comparison of shallow and deep copy

Let's now look at how to implement shallow cloning on a custom object. Deep cloning (not discussed) is specific to each class, and it essentially requires creating an instance of the object to be cloned and copying all field values to the clone. Any reference objects must also be created and assigned values from the original referenced objects.

How to Create a Shallow Copy

A shallow copy is sufficient when the object to be copied contains no reference type fields needed by the copy. The easiest way to implement shallow copying is to use the System.Object.MemberwiseClone method, a protected, non-virtual method that makes a shallow copy of the object it is associated with. We use this to enable the Chair class to clone itself:

```
public class Chair: ICloneable
{
   //... other code from Listing 4-5
```

```
public Object Clone()
{
    return MemberwiseClone(); // from System.Object
}
```

The only requirements are that the class inherit the `ICloneable` interface and implement the `Clone` method using `MemberwiseClone`. To demonstrate, let's use this code segment to create a shallow copy clone of `myChair` by calling its `Clone` method:

```
// Make clone of myChair
Chair chairClone = (Chair)myChair.Clone();
bool isEqual;
// (1) Following evaluates to false
isEqual = Object.ReferenceEquals(myChair,chairClone);
// (2) Following evaluates to true
isEqual = Object.ReferenceEquals(
        myChair.myUpholstery,chairClone.myUpholstery);
```

The results confirm this is a shallow copy: The reference comparison of `myChair` and its clone fails because `chairClone` is created as a copy of the original object; on the other hand, the comparison of the reference field `myUpholstery` succeeds because the original and clone objects point to the same instance of the `myUphol-stery` class.

4.4 Working with .NET Collection Classes and Interfaces

In .NET, *collection* is a general term that applies to the set of classes that represent the classic data structures used to group related types of data. These classes include stacks, queues, hash tables, arrays, and dictionaries. All are contained in one of two namespaces: `System.Collections` or `System.Collections.Generic`. In .NET versions 1.0 and 1.1, `System.Collections` was home to all collection classes. In the .NET 2.0 release, these original classes were revised to support *generics*—a way to make collections type-safe.

The .NET developers left the original namespace in for backward compatibility and added the `System.Collections.Generic` namespace to contain the generic classes. With the exception of the generics features, the classes in the two namespaces offer the same functionality—although there are a few name changes. To avoid confusion, much of this section refers to the `System.Collections` namespace. The details of generics are presented at the end of the section.

To best work with container classes such as the `ArrayList` and `Hashtable`, a developer should be familiar with the interfaces they implement. Interfaces not only provide a uniform way of managing and accessing the contents of a collection, but they are the key to creating a custom collection. We'll begin the section by looking at the most useful interfaces and the behavior they impart to the collection classes. Then, we'll examine selected collection classes.

Collection Interfaces

Interfaces play a major role in the implementation of the concrete collection classes. All collections inherit from the `ICollection` interface, and most inherit from the `IEnumerable` interface. This means that a developer can use common code semantics to work with the different collections. For example, the `foreach` statement is used to traverse the elements of a collection whether it is a `Hashtable`, a `Sorted-List`, or a custom collection. The only requirement is that the class implements the `IEnumerable` interface.

Table 4-2 summarizes the most important interfaces inherited by the collection classes. `IComparer` provides a uniform way of comparing elements for the purpose of sorting; `IDictionary` defines the special members required by the `Hashtable` and `Dictionary` objects; similarly, `IList` is the base interface for the `ArrayList` collection.

Table 4-2 `System.Collections`

Interface	Description
ICollection	The base interface for the collection classes. It contains properties to provide the number of elements in the collection and whether it is thread-safe. It also contains a method that copies elements of the collection into an array.
IComparer	Exposes a method that is used to compare two objects and plays a vital role in allowing objects in a collection to be sorted.
IDictionary	Allows an object to represent its data as a collection of key-and-value pairs.
IDictionaryEnumerator	Permits iteration through the contents of an object that implements the `IDictionary` interface.
IEnumerator IEnumerable	Supports a simple iteration through a collection. The iteration only supports reading of data in the collection.
IHashCodeProvider	Supplies a hash code for an object. It contains one method: `GetHashCode(object obj)`
IList	The base interface of all lists. It controls whether the elements in the list can be modified, added, or deleted.

The UML-like diagram in Figure 4-7 shows how these interfaces are related. Recall that interfaces may inherit from multiple interfaces. Here, for example, IDictionary and IList inherit from IEnumerable and ICollection. Also of special interest is the GetEnumerator method that is used by interfaces to return the IEnumerator interface.

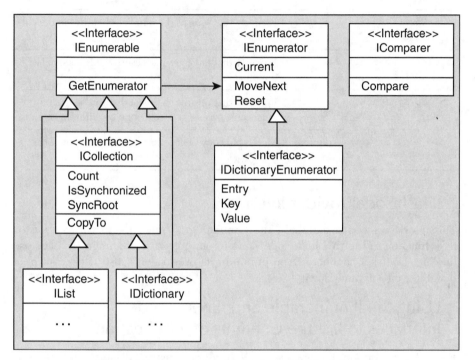

Figure 4-7 System.Collections Interface diagram

Of these interfaces, IDictionary and IList are the most important when considering the built-in collections provided by the FCL. For this reason, we'll discuss them later in the context of the collection classes.

ICollection Interface

This interface provides the minimal information that a collection must implement. All classes in the System.Collections namespace inherit it (see Table 4-3).

The IsSynchronized and SyncRoot properties require explanation if you are not yet familiar with *threading* (discussed in Chapter 13, "Asynchronous Programming and Multithreading"). Briefly, their purpose is to ensure the integrity of data in a collection while it is being accessed by multiple clients. It's analogous to locking records in a database to prevent conflicting updates by multiple users.

Table 4-3   `ICollection` Members

Member	Description
`int Count`	Property that returns the number of entries in the collection.
`bool IsSynchronized`	Property that indicates if access to the collection is thread-safe.
`object SyncRoot`	Property that returns an object that can be used to synchronize access to a collection by different threads.
`void CopyTo( array, index)`	Method to copy the contents of the collection to an array.

IHashCodeProvider Interface

This interface has one member—the `GetHashCode` method—that uses a custom hash function to return a hash code value for an object. The `Hashtable` class uses this interface as a parameter type in one of its overloaded constructors, but other than that you will rarely see it.

Using the IEnumerable and IEnumerator Interfaces to List the Contents of a Collection

For a class to support iteration using the `foreach` construct, it must implement the `IEnumerable` and `IEnumerator` interfaces. `IEnumerator` defines the methods and properties used to implement the enumerator pattern; `IEnumerable` serves only to return an `IEnumerator` object. Table 4-4 summarizes the member(s) provided by each interface.

These members are implemented in a custom collection class as a way to enable users to traverse the objects in the collection. To understand how to use these members, let's look at the underlying code that implements the `foreach` construct.

The `foreach` loop offers a simple syntax:

```
foreach ( ElementType element in collection)
{
    Console.WriteLine(element.Name);
}
```

Table 4-4 `IEnumerable` and `IEnumerator`

Member	Description
`IEnumerable.GetEnumerator()`	Returns an `IEnumerator` object that is used to iterate through collection.
`IEnumerator.Current`	Property that returns the current value in a collection.
`IEnumerator.MoveNext()`	Advances the enumerator to the next item in the collection. Returns `bool`.
`IEnumerator.Reset()`	Sets the enumerator to its beginning position in the collection. This method is not included in the `Generic` namespace.

The compiler expands the `foreach` construct into a `while` loop that employs `IEnumerable` and `IEnumerator` members:

```
// Get enumerator object using collection's GetEnumerator method
IEnumerator enumerator =
        ((IEnumerable) (collection)).GetEnumerator();
try
{
   while (enumerator.MoveNext())
   {
      ElementType element = (ElementType)enumerator.Current;
      Console.WriteLine(element.Name);
   }
}
finally
//  Determine if enumerator implements IDisposable interface
//  If so, execute Dispose method to release resources
{
   IDisposable disposable = enumerator as System.IDisposable;
   If( disposable !=null) disposable.Dispose();
}
```

When a client wants to iterate across the members of a collection (enumerable), it obtains an enumerator object using the `IEnumerable.GetEnumerator` method. The client then uses the members of the enumerator to traverse the collection: `MoveNext()` moves to the next element in the collection, and the `Current` property returns the object referenced by the current index of the enumerator. Formally, this is an implementation of the *iteration* design pattern.

Core Note

Enumerating through a collection is intrinsically not a thread-safe procedure. If another client (thread) modifies the collection during the enumeration, an exception is thrown. To guarantee thread safety, lock the collection prior to traversing it:

```
lock( myCollection.SyncRoot )
{
    foreach ( Object item in myCollection )
    {
        // Insert your code here
    }
}
```

Iterators

The foreach construct provides a simple and uniform way to iterate across members of a collection. For this reason, it is a good practice—almost a *de facto* requirement—that any custom collection support foreach. Because this requires that the collection class support the IEnumerable and IEnumerator interfaces, the traditional approach is to explicitly implement each member of these interfaces inside the collection class. Referencing Table 4-4, this means writing code to support the GetEnumerator method of the IEnumerable interface, and the MoveNext, Current, and Reset members of IEnumerator. In essence, it is necessary to build a state machine that keeps track of the most recently accessed item in a collection and knows how to move to the next item.

C# 2.0 introduced a new syntax referred to as *iterators* that greatly simplifies the task of implementing an iterator pattern. It includes a yield return (also a yield break) statement that causes the compiler to automatically generate code to implement the IEnumerable and IEnumerator interfaces. To illustrate, let's add iterators to the GenStack collection class that was introduced in the generics discussion in Chapter 3. (Note that iterators work identically in a non-generics collection.)

Listing 4-7 shows part of the original GenStack class with two new members that implement iterators: a GetEnumerator method that returns an enumerator to traverse the collection in the order items are stored, and a Reverse property that returns an enumerator to traverse the collection in reverse order. Both use yield return to generate the underlying code that supports foreach iteration.

Listing 4-7	Using Iterators to Implement Enumeration

```
using System;
using System.Collections.Generic;
public class GenStack<T>: IEnumerable<T>
{
   // Use generics type parameter to specify array type
   private T[] stackCollection;
   private int count = 0;
   // Constructor
   public GenStack(int size)
   {
      stackCollection = new T[size];
   }
   // (1) Iterator
   public IEnumerator<T> GetEnumerator()
   {
      for (int i = 0; i < count; i++)
      {
         yield return stackCollection[i];
      }
   }
   // (2) Property to return the collection in reverse order
   public IEnumerable<T> Reverse
   {
      get
      {
         for (int i = count - 1; i >= 0; i--)
         {
            yield return stackCollection[i];
         }
      }
   }
   public void Add(T item)
   {
      stackCollection[count] = item;
      count += 1;
   }
   // other class methods go here ...
```

This code should raise some obvious questions about iterators: Where is the implementation of IEnumerator? And how can a method with an IEnumerator return type or a property with an IEnumerable return type seemingly return a string value?

The answer to these questions is that the compiler generates the code to take care of the details. If the member containing the `yield return` statement is an `IEnumerable` type, the compiler implements the necessary generics or non-generics version of both `IEnumerable` and `IEnumerator`; if the member is an `IEnumerator` type, it implements only the two enumerator interfaces. The developer's responsibility is limited to providing the logic that defines how the collection is traversed and what items are returned. The compiler uses this logic to implement the `IEnumerator.MoveNext` method.

The client code to access the `GenStack` collection is straightforward. An instance of the `GenStack` class is created to hold ten `string` elements. Three items are added to the collection and are then displayed in original and reverse sequence.

```
GenStack<string> myStack = new GenStack<string>(10);
myStack.Add("Aida");
myStack.Add("La Boheme");
myStack.Add("Carmen");
// uses enumerator from GetEnumerator()
foreach (string s in myStack)
   Console.WriteLine(s);
// uses enumerator from Reverse property
foreach (string s in myStack.Reverse)
   Console.WriteLine(s);
```

The `Reverse` property demonstrates how easy it is to create multiple iterators for a collection. You simply implement a property that traverses the collection in some order and uses the `yield return` statement(s) to return an item in the collection.

Core Note

In order to stop iteration before an entire collection is traversed, use the `yield break` keywords. This causes `MoveNext()` to return `false`.

There are some restrictions on using `yield return` or `yield break`:

* It can only be used inside a method, property (get accessor), or operator.
* It cannot be used inside a `finally` block, an anonymous method, or a method that has `ref` or `out` arguments.
* The method or property containing yield return must have a return type of `Collections.IEnumerable`, `Collections.Generic.IEnumerable<>`, `Collections.IEnumerator`, or `Collections.Generic.IEnumerator<>`.

Using the IComparable and IComparer Interfaces to Perform Sorting

Chapter 2, "C# Language Fundamentals," included a discussion of the `System.Array` object and its associated `Sort` method. That method is designed for primitive types such as strings and numeric values. However, it can be extended to work with more complex objects by implementing the `IComparable` and `IComparer` interfaces on the objects to be sorted.

IComparable

Unlike the other interfaces in this section, `IComparable` is a member of the *System* namespace. It has only one member, the method `CompareTo`:

```
int CompareTo(Object obj)
```

Returned Value	Condition
Less than 0	Current instance < obj
0	Current instance = obj
Greater than 0	Current instance > obj

The object in parentheses is compared to the current instance of the object implementing `CompareTo`, and the returned value indicates the results of the comparison. Let's use this method to extend the `Chair` class so that it can be sorted on its `myPrice` field. This requires adding the `IComparable` inheritance and implementing the `CompareTo` method.

```
public class Chair : ICloneable, IComparable
{
    private double myPrice;
    private string myVendor, myID;
    public Upholstery myUpholstery;
    //… Constructor and other code
    // Add implementation of CompareTo to sort in ascending
    int IComparable.CompareTo(Object obj)
    {
        if (obj is Chair) {
            Chair castObj = (Chair)obj;
            if (this.myPrice > castObj.myPrice)
                    return 1;
            if (this.myPrice < castObj.myPrice)
                    return -1;
            else return 0;
```

```
          // Reverse 1 and -1 to sort in descending order
      }
    throw new ArgumentException("object in not a Chair");
    }
```

The code to sort an array of `Chair` objects is straightforward because all the work is done inside the `Chair` class:

```
Chair[]chairsOrdered = new Chair[4];
chairsOrdered[0] = new Chair(150.0, "Lane","99-88");
chairsOrdered[1] = new Chair(250.0, "Lane","99-00");
chairsOrdered[2] = new Chair(100.0, "Lane","98-88");
chairsOrdered[3] = new Chair(120.0, "Harris","93-9");
Array.Sort(chairsOrdered);
// Lists in ascending order of price
foreach(Chair c in chairsOrdered)
    MessageBox.Show(c.ToString());
```

IComparer

The previous example allows you to sort items on one field. A more flexible and realistic approach is to permit sorting on multiple fields. This can be done using an overloaded form of `Array.Sort` that takes an object that implements `IComparer` as its second parameter.

`IComparer` is similar to `IComparable` in that it exposes only one member, `Compare`, that receives two objects. It returns a value of –1, 0, or 1 based on whether the first object is less than, equal to, or greater than the second. The first object is usually the array to be sorted, and the second object is a class implementing a custom `Compare` method for a specific object field. This class can be implemented as a separate helper class or as a nested class within the class you are trying to sort (`Chair`).

This code creates a helper class that sorts the `Chair` objects by the `myVendor` field:

```
public class CompareByVen : IComparer
{
    public CompareByVen() { }
    int IComparer.Compare(object obj1, object obj2)
    {
        // obj1 contains array being sorted
        // obj2 is instance of helper sort class
        Chair castObj1 = (Chair)obj1;
        Chair castObj2 = (Chair)obj2;
        return String.Compare
            (castObj1.myVendor,castObj2.myVendor);
    }
}
```

If you refer back to the Chair class definition (refer to Figure 4-6 on page 166), you will notice that there is a problem with this code: myVendor is a private member and not accessible in this outside class. To make the example work, change it to public. A better solution, of course, is to add a property to expose the value of the field.

In order to sort, pass both the array to be sorted and an instance of the helper class to Sort:

```
Array.Sort(chairsOrdered,new CompareByVen());
```

In summary, sorting by more than one field is accomplished by adding classes that implement Compare for each sortable field.

System.Collections Namespace

The classes in this namespace provide a variety of data containers for managing collections of data. As shown in Figure 4-8, it is useful to categorize them based on the *primary* interface they implement: ICollection, IList, or IDictionary.

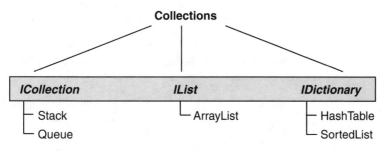

Figure 4-8   Selected classes in System.Collections

The purpose of interfaces is to provide a common set of behaviors for classes. Thus, rather than look at the details of all the classes, we will look at the interfaces themselves as well as some representative classes that illustrate how the members of the interfaces are implemented. We've already looked at ICollection, so let's begin with two basic collections that inherit from it.

Stack and Queue

The Stack and the Queue are the simplest of the collection classes. Because they do not inherit from IList or IDictionary, they do not provide indexed or keyed access. The order of insertion controls how objects are retrieved from them. In a Stack, all insertions and deletions occur at one end of the list; in a Queue, insertions are made at one end and deletions at the other. Table 4-5 compares the two.

Table 4-5   Stack and Queue—Selected Members and Features

Description	Stack	Queue
Method of maintaining data	Last-in, first-out (LIFO)	First-in, first-out (FIFO)
Add an item	`Push()`	`EnQueue()`
Remove an item	`Pop()`	`DeQueue()`
Return the current item without removing it	`Peek()`	`Peek()`
Determine whether an item is in the collection	`Includes()`	`Includes()`

Constructors	`Stack()`
	• Empty stack with default capacity
	`Stack(ICollection)`
	• Stack is filled with received collection
	`Stack(int)`
	• Set stack to initial int capacity
		`Queue()`
		• Default capacity and growth factor
		`Queue(ICollection)`
		• Filled with received collection
		`Queue(int)`
		• Set queue to initial int capacity
		`Queue(int, float)`
		• Set initial capacity and growth factor

Stacks play a useful role for an application that needs to maintain state information in order to hold tasks to be "performed later." The call stack associated with exception handling is a classic example; stacks are also used widely in text parsing operations. Listing 4-8 provides an example of some of the basic stack operations.

Listing 4-8   Using the Stack Container

```
public class ShowStack  {
   public static void Main()
   {
      Stack myStack = new Stack();
      myStack.Push(new Chair(250.0, "Adams Bros.", "87-00" ));
      myStack.Push(new Chair(100.0, "Broyhill","87-04"  ));
      myStack.Push(new Chair(100.0, "Lane","86-09"  ));
      PrintValues( myStack );          // Adams - Broyhill - Lane
```

Listing 4-8	Using the Stack Container *(continued)*

```
        // Pop top object and push a new one on stack
        myStack.Pop();
        myStack.Push(new Chair(300.0, "American Chair"));
        Console.WriteLine(myStack.Peek().ToString()); // American
    }
    public static void PrintValues( IEnumerable myCollection )
    {
        System.Collections.IEnumerator myEnumerator =
            myCollection.GetEnumerator();
        while ( myEnumerator.MoveNext() )
            Consle.WriteLine(myEnumerator.Current.ToString());
            // Could list specific chair fields with
            // myChair = (Chair) myEnumerator.Current;
    }
}
```

Three objects are added to the stack. `PrintValues` enumerates the stack and lists the objects in the reverse order they were added. The `Pop` method removes "Lane" from the top of the stack. A new object is pushed onto the stack and the `Peek` method lists it. Note that the `foreach` statement could also be used to list the contents of the `Stack`.

ArrayList

The `ArrayList` includes all the features of the `System.Array`, but also extends it to include dynamic sizing and insertion/deletion of items at a specific location in the list. These additional features are defined by the `IList` interface from which `ArrayList` inherits.

IList Interface

This interface, whose members are listed in Table 4-6, is used to retrieve the contents of a collection via a zero-based numeric index. This permits insertion and removal at random location within the list.

The most important thing to observe about this interface is that it operates on `object` types. This means that an `ArrayList`—or any collection implementing `IList`—may contain types of any kind. However, this flexibility comes at a cost: Casting must be widely used in order to access the object's contents, and value types must be converted to objects (*boxed*) in order to be stored in the collection. As we see shortly, C# 2.0 offers a new feature—called *generics*—that addresses both issues. However, the basic functionality of the `ArrayList`, as illustrated in this code segment, remains the same.

```
ArrayList chairList = new ArrayList( );
// alternative: ArrayList chairList = new ArrayList(5);
chairList.Add(new Chair(350.0, "Adams", "88-00"));
chairList.Add(new Chair(380.0, "Lane", "99-33"));
chairList.Add(new Chair(250.0, "Broyhill", "89-01"));
PrintValues(chairList);  // Adams - Lane - Broyhill
//
chairList.Insert(1,new Chair(100,"Kincaid"));
chairList.RemoveAt(2);
Console.WriteLine("Object Count: {0}",chairList.Count);
//
PrintValues(chairList); // Adams - Kincaid - Broyhill
// Copy objects to an array
Object chairArray = chairList.ToArray();
PrintValues((IEnumerable) chairArray);
```

Table 4-6   IList Members

Interface	Description
bool IsFixedSize	Indicates whether the collection has a fixed size. A fixed size prevents the addition or removal of items after the collection is created.
bool IsReadOnly	Items in a collection can be read but not modified.
int IndexOf(object)	Determines the index of a specific item in the collection.
int Add(object)	Adds an item to the end of a list. It returns the value of the index where the item was added.
void Insert (index, object) void RemoveAt (index) void Remove (object)	Methods to insert a value at a specific index; delete the value at a specific index; and remove the first occurrence of an item having the specified value.
void Clear()	Remove all items from a collection.
bool Contains(object)	Returns true if a collection contains an item with a specified value.

This parameterless declaration of ArrayList causes a default amount of memory to be initially allocated. You can control the initial allocation by passing a size parameter to the constructor that specifies the number of elements you expect it to hold. In both cases, the allocated space is automatically doubled if the capacity is exceeded.

Hashtable

The Hashtable is a .NET version of a dictionary for storing key-value pairs. It associates data with a key and uses the key (a transformation algorithm is applied) to determine a location where the data is stored in the table. When data is requested, the same steps are followed except that the calculated memory location is used to retrieve data rather than store it.

Syntax:

```
public class Hashtable : IDictionary, ICollection, IEnumerable,
    ISerializable, IDeserializationCallback, ICloneable
```

As shown here, the Hashtable inherits from many interfaces; of these, IDictionary is of the most interest because it provides the properties and methods used to store and retrieve data.

IDictionary Interface

Collections implementing the IDictionary interface contain items that can be retrieved by an associated key value. Table 4-7 summarizes the most important members for working with such a collection.

Table 4-7   IDictionary Member

Member	Description
bool IsFixedSize	Indicates whether IDictionary has a fixed size. A fixed size prevents the addition or removal of items after the collection is created.
bool IsReadOnly	Elements in a collection can be read but not modified.
ICollection Keys ICollection Values	Properties that return the keys and values of the collection.
void Add (key, value) void Clear () void Remove (key)	Methods to add a key-value pair to a collection, remove a specific key, and remove all items (clear) from the collection.
bool Contains	Returns true if a collection contains an element with a specified key.
IDictionaryEnumerator GetEnumerator ()	Returns an instance of the IDictionaryEnumerator type that is required for enumerating through a dictionary.

IDictionaryEnumerator Interface

As shown in Figure 4-7 on page 169, `IDictionaryEnumerator` inherits from `IEnumerator`. It adds properties to enumerate through a dictionary by retrieving keys, values, or both.

Table 4-8   `IDictionaryEnumerator` Members

Member	Description
`DictionaryEntry  Entry`	The variable `Entry` is used to retrieve both the key and value when iterating through a collection.
`object Key` `object Value`	Properties that return the keys and values of the current collection entry.

All classes derived from `IDictionary` maintain two internal lists of data: one for keys and one for the associated value, which may be an object. The values are stored in a location based on the hash code of the key. This code is provided by the key's `System.Object.GetHashCode` method, although it is possible to override this with your own hash algorithm.

This structure is efficient for searching, but less so for insertion. Because keys may generate the same hash code, a collision occurs that requires the code be recalculated until a free bucket is found. For this reason, the `Hashtable` is recommended for situations where a large amount of relatively static data is to be searched by key values.

Create a Hashtable

A parameterless constructor creates a `Hashtable` with a default number of buckets allocated and an implicit *load factor* of 1. The load factor is the ratio of values to buckets the storage should maintain. For example, a load factor of .5 means that a hash table should maintain twice as many buckets as there are values in the table. The alternate syntax to specify the initial number of buckets and load factor is

```
Hashtable chairHash = new Hashtable(1000, .6)
```

The following code creates a hash table and adds objects to it:

```
// Create HashTable
Hashtable chairHash = new Hashtable();
// Add key - value pair to Hashtable
chairHash.Add ("88-00", new Chair(350.0, "Adams", "88-00");
chairHash.Add ("99-03", new Chair(380.0, "Lane", "99-03");
```

```
// or this syntax
chairHash["89-01"] = new Chair(250.0, "Broyhill", "89-01");
```

There are many ways to add values to a `Hashtable`, including loading them from another collection. The preceding example shows the most straightforward approach. Note that a `System.Argument` exception is thrown if you attempt to add a value using a key that already exists in the table. To check for a key, use the `ContainsKey` method:

```
// Check for existence of a key
bool keyFound;
if (chairHash.ContainsKey("88-00"))
   { keyFound = true;}
else
   {keyFound = false;}
```

List Keys in a Hashtable

The following iterates through the `Keys` property collection:

```
// List Keys
foreach (string invenKey in chairHash.Keys)
   { MessageBox.Show(invenKey); }
```

List Values in a Hashtable

These statements iterate through the `Values` in a hash table:

```
// List Values
foreach (Chair chairVal in chairHash.Values)
   { MessageBox.Show(chairVal.myVendor);}
```

List Keys and Values in a Hashtable

This code lists the keys and values in a hash table:

```
foreach ( DictionaryEntry deChair in chairHash)
{
   Chair obj = (Chair) deChair.Value;
   MessageBox.Show(deChair.Key+" "+ obj.myVendor);
}
```

The entry in a Hashtable is stored as a DictionaryEntry type. It has a Value and Key property that expose the actual value and key. Note that the value is returned as an object that must be cast to a Chair type in order to access its fields.

Core Note

According to .NET documentation (1.x), a synchronized version of a Hashtable *that is supposed to be thread-safe for a single writer and concurrent readers can be created using the* Synchronized *method:*

Hashtable safeHT = Hashtable.Synchronized(newHashtable());

Unfortunately, the .NET 1.x versions of the Hashtable *have been proven not to be thread-safe for reading. Later versions may correct this flaw.*

This section has given you a flavor of working with System.Collections interfaces and classes. The classes presented are designed to meet most general-purpose programming needs. There are numerous other useful classes in the namespace as well as in the System.Collections.Specialized namespace. You should have little trouble working with either, because all of their classes inherit from the same interfaces presented in this section.

System.Collections.Generic Namespace

Recall from Chapter 3 that generics are used to implement type-safe classes, structures, and interfaces. The declaration of a generic type includes one (or more) *type parameters* in brackets (<>) that serve(s) as a placeholder for the actual type to be used. When an instance of this type is created, the client uses these parameters to pass the specific type of data to be used in the generic type. Thus, a single generic class can handle multiple types of data in a type-specific manner.

No classes benefit more from generics than the collections classes, which stored any type of data as an object in .NET 1.x. The effect of this was to place the burden of casting and type verification on the developer. Without such verification, a single ArrayList instance could be used to store a string, an integer, or a custom object. Only at runtime would the error be detected.

The System.Collections.Generic namespace provides the generic versions of the classes in the System.Collections namespace. If you are familiar with the non-generic classes, switching to the generic type is straightforward. For example, this code segment using the ArrayList:

```
ArrayList primes = new ArrayList();
primes.Add(1);
primes.Add(3);
int pSum = (int)primes[0] + (int)primes[1];
primes.Add("test");
```

can be replaced with the generics version:

```
List<int> primes = new List<int>();
primes.Add(1);
primes.Add(3);
int pSum = primes[0] + primes[1];
primes.Add("text");    // will not compile
```

The declaration of `List` includes a type parameter that tells the compiler what type of data the object may contain—`int` in this case. The compiler then generates code that expects the specified type. For the developer, this eliminates the need for casting and type verification at runtime. From a memory usage and efficiency standpoint, it also eliminates *boxing* (conversion to objects) when primitives are stored in the collection.

Comparison of System.Collections and System.Collections.Generic Namespaces

As the following side-by-side comparison shows, the classes in the two namespaces share the same name with three exceptions: `Hashtable` becomes `Dictionary<>`, `ArrayList` becomes `List<>`, and `SortedList` is renamed `SortedDictionary<>`.

System.Collections	System.Collections.Generic
Comparer	Comparer<T>
Hashtable	Dictionary<K,T>
ArrayList	List<T>
Queue	Queue<T>
SortedList	SortedDictionary<K,T>
Stack	Stack<T>
ICollection	ICollection<T>
IComparable	IComparable<T>
IComparer	IComparer<T>
IDictionary	IDictionary<K,T>
IEnumerable	IEnumerable<T>
IEnumerator	IEnumerator<T>
IKeyComparer	IKeyComparer<T>
IList	IList<T>
(not applicable)	LinkedList<T>

The only other points to note regard IEnumerator. Unlike the original version, the generics version inherits from IDisposable and does not support the Reset method.

An Example Using a Generics Collections Class

Switching to the generics versions of the collection classes is primarily a matter of getting used to a new syntax, because the functionality provided by the generics and non-generics classes is virtually identical. To demonstrate, here are two examples. The first uses the Hashtable to store and retrieve instances of the Chair class (defined in Listing 4-5); the second example performs the same functions but uses the Dictionary class—the generics version of the Hashtable.

This segment consists of a Hashtable declaration and two methods: one to store a Chair object in the table and the other to retrieve an object based on a given key value.

```
// Example 1: Using Hashtable
public Hashtable ht = new Hashtable();
// Store Chair object in table using a unique product identifier
private void saveHT(double price, string ven, string sku)
{
    if (!ht.ContainsKey(sku))
    {
        ht.Add(sku, new Chair(price,ven,sku));
    }
}
// Display vendor and price for a product identifier
private void showChairHT(string sku)
{
    if (ht.ContainsKey(key))
    {
        if (ht[key] is Chair)  // Prevent casting exception
        {
            Chair ch = (Chair)ht[sku];
            Console.WriteLine(ch.MyVen + " " + ch.MyPr);
        }
        else
        { Console.WriteLine("Invalid Type: " +
                            (ht[key].GetType().ToString()));
        }
    }
}
```

Observe how data is retrieved from the Hashtable. Because data is stored as an object, verification is required to ensure that the object being retrieved is a Chair type; casting is then used to access the members of the object. These steps are unnecessary when the type-safe Dictionary class is used in place of the Hashtable.

The Dictionary<K,V> class accepts two type parameters that allow it to be strongly typed: K is the key type and V is the type of the value stored in the collection. In this example, the key is a string representing the unique product identifier, and the value stored in the Dictionary is a Chair type.

```
// Example 2: Using Generics Dictionary to replace Hashtable
//    Dictionary accepts string as key and Chair as data type
Dictionary<string,Chair> htgen = new Dictionary<string,Chair>();
//
private void saveGen(double price, string ven, string sku)
{
   if (!htgen.ContainsKey(sku))
   {
      htgen.Add(sku, new Chair(price,ven,sku));
   }
}

private void showChairGen(string sku)
{
   if (htgen.ContainsKey(key))
   {
      Chair ch = htgen[sku];    // No casting required
      Console.WriteLine(ch.MyVen + " " + ch.MyPr);
   }
}
```

The important advantage of generics is illustrated in the showChairGen method. It has no need to check the type of the stored object or perform casting.

In the long run, the new generic collection classes will render the classes in the System.Collections namespace obsolete. For that reason, new code development should use the generic classes where possible.

4.5   Object Serialization

In .NET, serialization refers to the process of converting an object or collection of objects into a format suitable for streaming across a network—a Web Service, for example—or storing in memory, a file, or a database. Deserialization is the reverse process that takes the serialized stream and converts it back into its original object(s).

.NET support three primary types of serialization:

- **Binary.** Uses the `BinaryFormatter` class to serialize a type into a binary stream.
- **SOAP.** Uses the `SoapFormatter` class to serialize a type into XML formatted according to SOAP (Simple Object Access Protocol) standards.
- **XML.** Uses the `XmlSerializer` class to serialize a type into basic XML (described in Chapter 10, "Working with XML in .NET"). Web Services uses this type of serialization.

Serialization is used primarily for two tasks: to implement Web Services and to store (persist) collections of objects to a medium from which they can be later resurrected. Web Services and their use of XML serialization are discussed in Chapter 18, "XML Web Services." This section focuses on how to use binary serialization to store and retrieve objects. The examples use File I/O (see Chapter 5) methods to read and write to a file, which should be easily understood within the context of their usage.

Binary Serialization

The `BinaryFormatter` object that performs binary serialization is found in the `System.Runtime.Serialization.Formatters.Binary` namespace. It performs serialization and deserialization using the `Serialize` and `Deserialize` methods, respectively, which it inherits from the `IFormatter` interface.

Listing 4-9 provides an example of binary serialization using simple class members. A hash table is created and populated with two `Chair` objects. Next, a `FileStream` object is instantiated that points to a file on the local drive where the serialized output is stored. A `BinaryFormatter` is then created, and its `Serialize` method is used to serialize the hash table's contents to a file. To confirm the process, the hash table is cleared and the `BinaryFormatter` object is used to deserialize the contents of the file into the hash table. Finally, one of the members from a restored object in the hash table is printed—verifying that the original contents have been restored.

Listing 4-9	Serialization of a Hashtable

```
using System;
using System.Runtime.Serialization;
using System.Runtime.Serialization.Formatters.Binary;
using System.IO;
```

Listing 4-9	Serialization of a Hashtable *(continued)*

```
// Store Chair objects in a Hashtable
Hashtable ht = new Hashtable();
// Chair and Upholstery must have [Serializable] attribute
Chair ch = new Chair(100.00D, "Broyhill", "10-09");
ch.myUpholstery = new Upholstery("Cotton");
ht.Add("10-09", ch);
// Add second item to table
ch = new Chair(200.00D, "Lane", "11-19");
ch.myUpholstery = new Upholstery("Silk");
ht.Add("11-19", ch);
// (1) Serialize
// Create a new file; if file exits it is overwritten
FileStream fs= new  FileStream("c:\\chairs.dat",
                                   FileMode.Create);
BinaryFormatter bf= new BinaryFormatter();
bf.Serialize(fs,ht);
fs.Close();
// (2) Deserialize binary file into a Hashtable of objects
ht.Clear();   // Clear hash table.
fs = new FileStream("c:\\chairs.dat", FileMode.Open);
ht =   (Hashtable) bf.Deserialize(fs);
// Confirm objects properly recreated
ch = (Chair)ht["11-19"];
Console.WriteLine(ch.myUpholstery.Fabric);   // "Silk"
fs.Close();
```

Observe the following key points:

- The serialization and IO namespaces should be declared.
- The Chair and Upholstery classes must have the [Serializable]
  attribute; otherwise, a runtime error occurs when Serialize() is
  executed.
- Serialization creates an object graph that includes references from one
  object to another. The result is a deep copy of the objects. In this
  example, the myUpholstery field of Chair is set to an instance of the
  Upholstery class before it is serialized. Serialization stores a copy of
  the object—rather than a reference. When deserialization occurs, the
  Upholstery object is restored.

Excluding Class Members from Serialization

You can selectively exclude class members from being serialized by attaching the [NonSerialized] attribute to them. For example, you can prevent the myUphol-stery field of the Chair class from being serialized by including this:

```
[NonSerialized]
public Upholstery myUpholstery;
```

The primary reason for marking a field NonSerialized is that it may have no meaning where it is serialized. Because an object graph may be loaded onto a machine different from the one on which it was stored, types that are tied to system operations are the most likely candidates to be excluded. These include delegates, events, file handles, and threads.

Core Note

A class cannot inherit the Serializable attribute from a base class; it must explicitly include the attribute. On the other hand, a derived class can be made serializable only if its base class is serializable.

Binary Serialization Events

.NET 2.0 introduced support for four binary serialization and deserialization events, as summarized in Table 4-9.

Table 4-9   Serialization and Deserialization Events

Event	Attribute	Description
OnSerializing	[Serializing]	Occurs before objects are serialized. Event handler is called for each object to be serialized.
OnSerialized	[Serialized]	Occurs after objects are serialized. Event handler is called once for each object serialized.
OnDeserializing	[Deserializing]	Occurs before objects are deserialized. Event handler is called once for each object to be deserialized.
OnDeserialized	[Deserialized]	Occurs after objects have been deserialized. Event handler is called for each deserialized object.

An event handler for these events is implemented in the object being serialized and must satisfy two requirements: the attribute associated with the event must be attached to the method, and the method must have this signature:

```
void <event name>(StreamingContext context)
```

To illustrate, here is a method called after all objects have been deserialized. The binary formatter iterates the list of objects in the order they were deserialized and calls each object's OnDeserialized method. This example uses the event handler to selectively update a field in the object. A more common use is to assign values to fields that were not serialized.

```
public class Chair
    {
        // other code here
    [OnDeserialized]
    void OnDeserialized(StreamingContext context)
    {
        // Edit vendor name after object is created
        if (MyVen == "Lane") MyVen = "Lane Bros.";
    }
}
```

Note that more than one method can have the same event attribute, and that more than one attribute can be assigned to a method—although the latter is rarely practical.

Handling Version Changes to a Serialized Object

Suppose the Chair class from the preceding examples is redesigned. A field could be added or deleted, for example. What happens if one then attempts to deserialize objects in the old format to the new format? It's not an uncommon problem, and .NET offers some solutions.

If a field is deleted, the binary formatter simply ignores the extra data in the deserialized stream. However, if the formatter detects a new field in the target object, it throws an exception. To prevent this, an [OptionalField] attribute can be attached to the new field(s). Continuing the previous example, let's add a field to Chair that designates the type of wood finish:

```
[OptionalField]
private string finish;
```

The presence of the attribute causes the formatter to assign a default null value to the finish field, and no exception is thrown. The application may also take advantage of the deserialized event to assign a value to the new field:

```
void OnDeserialized(StreamingContext context)
{
    if (MyVen == "Lane") finish = "Oak"; else finish = "Cherry";
}
```

4.6   Object Life Cycle Management

Memory allocation and deallocation have always been the bane of developers. Even the most experienced C++ and COM programmer is faced with memory leaks and attempts to access nonexistent objects that either never existed or have already been destroyed. In an effort to remove these responsibilities from the programmer, .NET implements a memory management system that features a *managed heap* and automatic *Garbage Collection.*

Recall from Chapter 2, "C# Language Fundamentals," that the managed heap is a pre-allocated area of memory that .NET uses to store reference types and data. Each time an instance of a class is created, it receives memory from the heap. This is a faster and cleaner solution than programming environments that rely on the operating system to handle memory allocation.

Allocating memory from the stack is straightforward: A pointer keeps track of the next free memory address and allocates memory from the top of the heap. The important thing to note about the allocated memory is that it is always contiguous. There is no fragmentation or complex overhead to keep track of free memory blocks. Of course, at some point the heap is exhausted and unused space must be recovered. This is where the .NET automatic Garbage Collection comes into play.

.NET Garbage Collection

Each time a managed object is created, .NET keeps track of it in a tree-like graph of nodes that associates each object with the object that created or uses it. In addition, each time another client references an object or a reference is assigned to a variable, the graph is updated. At the top of this graph is a list of *roots*, or parts of the application that exist as long at the program is running (see Figure 4-9). These include static variables, CPU registers, and any local or parameter variables that refer to objects on the managed heap. These serve as the starting point from which the .NET Framework uses a *reference-tracing* technique to remove objects from the heap and reclaim memory.

The Garbage Collection process begins when some memory threshold is reached. At this point, the Garbage Collector (GC) searches through the graph of objects and marks those that are "reachable." These are kept alive while the unreachable ones are considered to be garbage. The next step is to remove the unreferenced objects (garbage) and compact the heap memory. This is a complicated process because the collector must deal with the twin tasks of updating all old references to the new object addresses and ensuring that the state of the heap is not altered as Garbage Collection takes place.

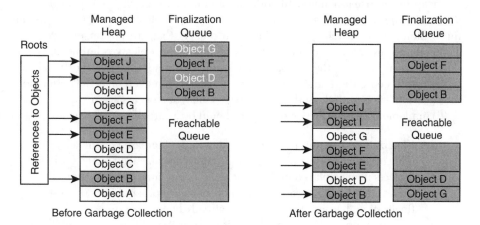

Figure 4-9 .NET Garbage Collection process

The details of Garbage Collection are not as important to the programmer as the fact that it is a nondeterministic (occurs unpredictably) event that deals with managed resources only. This leaves the programmer facing two problems: how to dispose of unmanaged resources such as files or network connections, and how to dispose of them in a timely manner. The solution to the first problem is to implement a method named `Finalize` that manages object cleanup; the second is solved by adding a `Dispose` method that can be called to release resources before Garbage Collection occurs. As we will see, these two methods do not operate autonomously. Proper object termination requires a solution that coordinates the actions of both methods.

Core Note

Garbage Collection typically occurs when the CLR detects that some memory threshold has been reached. However, there is a static method `GC.Collect` that can be called to trigger Garbage Collection. It can be useful under controlled conditions while debugging and testing, but should not be used as part of an application.

Object Finalization

Objects that contain a `Finalize` method are treated differently during both object creation and Garbage Collection than those that do not contain a `Finalize` method. When an object implementing a `Finalize` method is created, space is allocated on the heap in the usual manner. In addition, a pointer to the object is placed in the *finalization queue* (see Figure 4-9). During Garbage Collection, the GC scans the finalization queue searching for pointers to objects that are no longer reachable. Those found are moved to the *freachable queue*. The objects referenced in this queue remain alive, so that a special background thread can scan the freachable queue and execute the `Finalize` method on each referenced object. The memory for these objects is not released until Garbage Collection occurs again.

To implement `Finalize` correctly, you should be aware of several issues:

- Finalization degrades performance due to the increased overhead. Only use it when the object holds resources not managed by the CLR.
- Objects may be placed in the freachable queue in any order. Therefore, your `Finalize` code should not reference other objects that use finalization, because they may have already been processed.
- Call the base `Finalize` method within your `Finalize` method so it can perform any cleanup: `base.Finalize()`.
- Finalization code that fails to complete execution prevents the background thread from executing the `Finalize` method of any other objects in the queue. Infinite loops or synchronization locks with infinite timeouts are always to be avoided, but are particularly deleterious when part of the cleanup code.

It turns out that you do not have to implement `Finalize` directly. Instead, you can create a *destructor* and place the finalization code in it. The compiler converts the destructor code into a `Finalize` method that provides exception handling, includes a call to the base class `Finalize`, and contains the code entered into the destructor:

```
Public class Chair
{
   public Chair() { }
   ~Chair()   // Destructor
   { // finalization code  }
}
```

Note that an attempt to code both a destructor and `Finalize` method results in a compiler error.

As it stands, this finalization approach suffers from its dependency on the GC to implement the `Finalize` method whenever it chooses. Performance and scalability are adversely affected when expensive resources cannot be released when they are no longer needed. Fortunately, the CLR provides a way to notify an object to perform cleanup operations and make itself unavailable. This *deterministic finalization* relies on a public Dispose method that a client is responsible for calling.

IDisposable.Dispose()

Although the Dispose method can be implemented independently, the recommended convention is to use it as a member of the IDisposable interface. This allows a client to take advantage of the fact that an object can be tested for the existence of an interface. Only if it detects IDisposable does it attempt to call the Dispose method. Listing 4-10 presents a general pattern for calling the Dispose method.

Listing 4-10	Pattern for Calling Dispose()

```
public class MyConnections: IDisposable
{
    public void Dispose()
    {
        // code to dispose of resources
        base.Dispose(); // include call to base Dispose()
    }
    public void UseResources() { }
}
// Client code to call Dispose()
class MyApp
{
    public static void Main()
    {
        MyConnections connObj;
        connObj = new MyConnections();
        try
        {
            connObj.UseResources();
        }
        finally   // Call dispose() if it exists
        {
            IDisposable testDisp;
            testDisp = connObj as IDisposable;
            if(testDisp != null)
                { testDisp.Dispose(); }
        }
    }
}
```

This code takes advantage of the finally block to ensure that Dispose is called even if an exception occurs. Note that you can shorten this code by replacing the try/finally block with a using construct that generates the equivalent code:

```
Using(connObj)
{ connObj.UseResources() }
```

Using Dispose and Finalize

When Dispose is executed, the object's unmanaged resources are released and the object is effectively disposed of. This raises a couple of questions: First, what happens if Dispose is called after the resources are released? And second, if Finalize is implemented, how do we prevent the GC from executing it since cleanup has already occurred?

The easiest way to handle calls to a disposed object's Dispose method is to raise an exception. In fact, the ObjectDisposedException exception is available for this purpose. To implement this, add a boolean property that is set to true when Dispose is first called. On subsequent calls, the object checks this value and throws an exception if it is true.

Because there is no guarantee that a client will call Dispose, Finalize should also be implemented when resource cleanup is required. Typically, the same cleanup method is used by both, so there is no need for the GC to perform finalization if Dispose has already been called. The solution is to execute the SuppressFinalize method when Dispose is called. This static method, which takes an object as a parameter, notifies the GC not to place the object on the freachable queue.

Listing 4-11 shows how these ideas are incorporated in actual code.

Listing 4-11	Pattern for Implementing Dispose() and Finalize()

```
public class MyConnections: IDisposable
{
    private bool isDisposed = false;
    protected bool Disposed
    {
        get{ return isDisposed; }
    }
    public void Dispose()
    {
        if (isDisposed == false)
        {
```

Listing 4-11	Pattern for Implementing `Dispose()` and `Finalize()` (continued)

```
         CleanUp();
         IsDisposed = true;
         GC.SuppressFinalize(this);
      }
   }
   protected virtual void CleanUp()
   {
      // cleanup code here
   }
   ~MyConnections()    // Destructor that creates Finalize()
   { CleanUp(); }
   public void UseResources()
   {
      // code to perform actions
      if(Disposed)
      {
         throw new ObjectDisposedException
            ("Object has been disposed of");
      }
   }
}
// Inheriting class that implements its own cleanup
public class DBConnections: MyConnections
{
   protected override void CleanUp()
   {
      // implement cleanup here
      base.CleanUp();
   }
}
```

The key features of this code include the following:

- A common method, CleanUp, has been introduced and is called from both Dispose and Finalize . It is defined as protected and virtual, and contains no concrete code.
- Classes that inherit from the base class MyConnections are responsible for implementing the CleanUp. As part of this, they must be sure to call the Cleanup method of the base class. This ensures that cleanup code runs on all levels of the class hierarchy.

- The read-only property `Disposed` has been added and is checked before methods in the base class are executed.

In summary, the .NET Garbage Collection scheme is designed to allow programmers to focus on their application logic and not deal with details of memory allocation and deallocation. It works well as long as the objects are dealing with managed resources. However, when there are valuable unmanaged resources at stake, a deterministic method of freeing them is required. This section has shown how the `Dispose` and `Finalize` methods can be used in concert to manage this aspect of an object's life cycle.

4.7   Summary

This chapter has discussed how to work with objects. We've seen how to create them, manipulate them, clone them, group them in collections, and destroy them. The chapter began with a description of how to use a factory design pattern to create objects. It closed with a look at how object resources are released through automatic Garbage Collection and how this process can be enhanced programmatically through the use of the `Dispose` and `Finalize` methods. In between, the chapter examined how to make applications more robust with the use of intelligent exception handling, how to customize the `System.Object` methods such as `Equals` and `ToString` to work with your own objects, how cloning can be used to make deep or shallow copies, and how to use the built-in classes available in the `System.Collections` and `System.Collections.Generic` namespaces.

As a by-product of this chapter, you should now have a much greater appreciation of the important role that *interfaces* play in application design. They represent the base product when constructing a class factory, and they allow you to clone (`ICloneable`), sort (`IComparer`), or enumerate (`IEnumerable`) custom classes. Knowing that an object implements a particular interface gives you an immediate insight into the capabilities of the object.

4.8   Test Your Understanding

1. What are the advantages of using a class factory to create objects?

2. Which class should custom exceptions inherit from? Which constructors should be included?

3. How does the default `System.Object.Equals` method determine if two objects are equal?

4. Which interface(s) must a class implement in order to support the `foreach` statement?

5. What is the main advantage of using generics?

6. What is the purpose of implementing `IDisposable` on a class?

7. Refer to the following code:

```
public class test: ICloneable
{
    public int Age;
    public string Name;
    public test(string myname)
    { Name = myname;      }
    public Object Clone()
    { return MemberwiseClone(); }
}
// Create instances of class
test myTest = new test("Joanna");
myTest.Age = 36;
test clone1 = (test) mytest.Clone();
test clone2 = myTest;
```

Indicate whether the following statements evaluate to `true` or `false`:

a. `Object.ReferenceEquals(myTest.Name, clone1.Name)`
b. `Object.ReferenceEquals(myTest.Age, clone1.Age)`
c. `myTest.Name = "Julie";`
   `Object.ReferenceEquals(myTest.Name, clone1.Name)`
d. `Object.ReferenceEquals(myTest.Name, clone2.Name)`

8. How does implementing `Finalize` on an object affect its Garbage Collection?

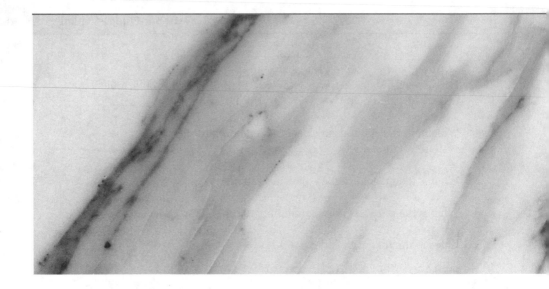

CREATING
APPLICATIONS
USING THE
.NET FRAMEWORK
CLASS LIBRARY

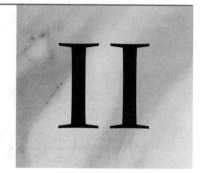

Part II

- Chapter 5
  C# Text Manipulation and File I/O   **202**

- Chapter 6
  Building Windows Forms Applications   **266**

- Chapter 7
  Windows Forms Controls   **318**

- Chapter 8
  .NET Graphics Using GDI+   **378**

- Chapter 9
  Fonts, Text, and Printing   **426**

- Chapter 10
  Working with XML in .NET   **460**

- Chapter 11
  ADO.NET   **496**

- Chapter 12
  Data Binding with Windows Forms Controls   **544**

C# Text
Manipulation
and File I/O

Topics in This Chapter

- *Characters and Unicode:* By default, .NET stores a character as a 16-bit Unicode character. This enables an application to support international character sets—a technique referred to as localization.

- *String Overview:* In .NET, strings are immutable. To use strings efficiently, it is necessary to understand what this means and how immutability affects string operations.

- *String Operations:* In addition to basic string operations, .NET supports advanced formatting techniques for numbers and dates.

- *StringBuilder:* The `StringBuilder` class offers an efficient alternative to concatenation for constructing screens.

- *Regular Expressions:* The .NET `Regex` class provides an engine that uses regular expressions to parse, match, and extract values in a string.

- *Text Streams:* Stream classes permit data to be read and written as a stream of bytes that can be encrypted and buffered.

- *Text Reading and Writing:* The `StreamReader` and `StreamWriter` classes make it easy to read from and write to physical files.

- *System.IO:* Classes in this namespace enable an application to work with underlying directory structure of the host operating system.

Chapter

This chapter introduces the string handling capabilities provided by the .NET classes. Topics include how to use the basic String methods for extracting and manipulating string content; the use of the String.Format method to display numbers and dates in special formats; and the use of regular expressions (regexes) to perform advanced pattern matching. Also included is a look at the underlying features of .NET that influence how an application works with text. Topics include how the Just-In-Time (JIT) compiler optimizes the use of literal strings; the importance of Unicode as the cornerstone of character and string representations in .NET; and the built-in *localization* features that permit applications to automatically take into account the culture-specific characteristics of languages and countries.

This chapter is divided into two major topics. The first topic focuses on how to create, represent, and manipulate strings using the System.Char, System.String, and Regex classes; the second takes up a related topic of how to store and retrieve string data. It begins by looking at the Stream class and how to use it to process raw bytes of data as streams that can be stored in files or transmitted across a network. The discussion then moves to using the TextReader/TextWriter classes to read and write strings as lines of text. The chapter concludes with examples of how members of the System.IO namespace are used to access the Microsoft Windows directory and file structure.

5.1 Characters and Unicode

One of the watershed events in computing was the introduction of the ASCII 7-bit character set in 1968 as a standardized encoding scheme to uniquely identify alphanumeric characters and other common symbols. It was largely based on the Latin alphabet and contained 128 characters. The subsequent ANSI standard doubled the number of characters—primarily to include symbols for European alphabets and currencies. However, because it was still based on Latin characters, a number of incompatible encoding schemes sprang up to represent non-Latin alphabets such as the Greek and Arabic languages.

Recognizing the need for a universal encoding scheme, an international consortium devised the Unicode specification. It is now a standard, accepted worldwide, that defines a unique number for every character "no matter what the platform, no matter what the program, no matter what the language."[1]

Unicode

NET fully supports the Unicode standard. Its internal representation of a character is an unsigned 16-bit number that conforms to the Unicode encoding scheme. Two bytes enable a character to represent up to 65,536 values. Figure 5-1 illustrates why two bytes are needed.

The uppercase character on the left is a member of the Basic Latin character set that consists of the original 128 ASCII characters. Its decimal value of 75 can be depicted in 8 bits; the unneeded bits are set to zero. However, the other three characters have values that range from 310 (0x0136) to 56,609 (0xDB05), which can be represented by no less than two bytes.

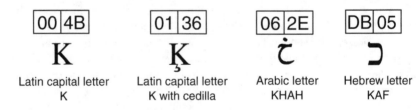

00 4B	01 36	06 2E	DB 05
K	Ķ	خ	כ
Latin capital letter K	Latin capital letter K with cedilla	Arabic letter KHAH	Hebrew letter KAF

Figure 5-1   Unicode memory layout of a character

---

1. Unicode Consortium—www.unicode.org.

Unicode characters have a unique identifier made up of a name and value, referred to as a *code point*. The current version 4.0 defines identifiers for 96,382 characters. These characters are grouped in over 130 character sets that include language scripts, symbols for math, music, OCR, geometric shapes, Braille, and many other uses.

Because 16 bits cannot represent the nearly 100,000 characters supported worldwide, more bytes are required for some character sets. The Unicode solution is a mechanism by which two sets of 16-bit units define a character. This pair of code units is known as a *surrogate pair*. Together, this *high surrogate* and *low surrogate* represent a single 32-bit *abstract* character into which characters are mapped. This approach supports over 1,000,000 characters. The surrogates are constructed from values that reside in a reserved area at the high end of the Unicode code space so that they are not mistaken for actual characters.

As a developer, you can pretty much ignore the details of whether a character requires 16 or 32 bits because the .NET API and classes handle the underlying details of representing Unicode characters. One exception to this—discussed later in this section—occurs if you parse individual bytes in a stream and need to recognize the surrogates. For this, .NET provides a special object to iterate through the bytes.

Core Note

Unicode characters can only be displayed if your computer has a font supporting them. On a Windows operating system, you can install a font extension (`ttfext.exe`) that displays the supported Unicode ranges for a `.ttf` font. To use it, right-click the `.ttf` font name and select Properties. Console applications cannot print Unicode characters because console output always displays in a non-proportional typeface.

Working with Characters

A single character is represented in .NET as a `char` (or `Char`) structure. The `char` structure defines a small set of members (see `char` in Chapter 2, "C# Language Fundamentals") that can be used to inspect and transform its value. Here is a brief review of some standard character operations.

Assigning a Value to a Char Type

The most obvious way to assign a value to a `char` variable is with a literal value. However, because a `char` value is represented internally as a number, you can also assign it a numeric value. Here are examples of each:

```
string klm = "KLM";
byte    b = 75;
char k;
// Different ways to assign 'K' to variable K
k = 'K';
k = klm[0];              // Assign "K" from first value in klm
k = (char) 75;           // Cast decimal
k = (char) b;            // cast byte
k = Convert.ToChar(75);  // Converts value to a char
```

Converting a Char Value to a Numeric Value

When a character is converted to a number, the result is the underlying Unicode (ordinal) value of the character. Casting is the most efficient way to do this, although Convert methods can also be used. In the special case where the char is a digit and you want to assign the linguistic value—rather than the Unicode value—use the static GetNumericValue method.

```
// '7' has Unicode value of 55
char k = '7';
int n = (int) k;               // n = 55
n = (int) char.GetNumericValue(k);    // n = 7
```

Characters and Localization

One of the most important features of .NET is the capability to automatically recognize and incorporate culture-specific rules of a language or country into an application. This process, known as localization, may affect how a date or number is formatted, which currency symbol appears in a report, or how string comparisons are carried out. In practical terms, localization means a single application would display the date May 9, 2004 as 9/5/2004 to a user in Paris, France and as 5/9/2004 to a user in Paris, Texas. The Common Language Runtime (CLR) automatically recognizes the local computer's culture and makes the adjustments.

The .NET Framework provides more than a hundred *culture names* and identifiers that are used with the CultureInfo class to designate the language/country to be used with culture sensitive operations in a program. Although localization has a greater impact when working with strings, the Char.ToUpper method in this example is a useful way to demonstrate the concept.

```
// Include the System.Globalization namespace
// Using CultureInfo - Azerbaijan
char i = 'i';
// Second parameter is false to use default culture settings
// associated with selected culture
CultureInfo myCI = new CultureInfo("az", false );
i = Char.ToUpper(i,myCI);
```

An overload of ToUpper() accepts a CultureInfo object that specifies the culture (language and country) to be used in executing the method. In this case, az stands for the Azeri language of the country Azerbaijan (more about this follows). When the Common Language Runtime sees the CultureInfo parameter, it takes into account any aspects of the culture that might affect the operation. When no parameter is provided, the CLR uses the system's default culture.

Core Note

On a Windows operating system, the .NET Framework obtains its default culture information from the system's country and language settings. It assigns these values to the Thread.CurrentThread.CurrentCulture *property. You can set these options by choosing Regional Options in the Control Panel.*

So why choose Azerbaijan, a small nation on the Caspian Sea, to demonstrate localization? Among all the countries in the world that use the Latin character set, only Azerbaijan and Turkey capitalize the letter i not with I (U+0049), but with an I that has a dot above it (U+0130). To ensure that ToUpper() performs this operation correctly, we must create an instance of the CultureInfo class with the Azeri culture name—represented by az—and pass it to the method. This results in the correct Unicode character—and a satisfied population of 8.3 million Azerbaijani.

Characters and Their Unicode Categories

The Unicode Standard classifies Unicode characters into one of 30 categories. .NET provides a UnicodeCategory enumeration that represents each of these categories and a Char.GetUnicodecategory() method to return a character's category. Here is an example:

```
Char k  = 'K';
int iCat = (int) char.GetUnicodeCategory(k);   // 0
Console.WriteLine(char.GetUnicodeCategory(k)); // UppercaseLetter
char cr = (Char)13;
iCat = (int) char.GetUnicodeCategory(cr);      // 14
Console.WriteLine(char.GetUnicodeCategory(cr)); // Control
```

The method correctly identifies K as an UppercaseLetter and the carriage return as a Control character. As an alternative to the unwieldy GetUnicodeCategory, char includes a set of static methods as a shortcut for identifying a character's Unicode category. They are nothing more than wrappers that return a true or false value based on an internal call to GetUnicodeCategory. Table 5-1 lists these methods.

Table 5-1   Char Methods That Verify Unicode Categories

Method	Unicode Category	Description
IsControl	4	Control code whose Unicode value is U+007F, or in the range U+0000 through U+001F, or U+0080 through U+009F.
IsDigit	8	Is in the range 0–9.
IsLetter	0, 1, 2, 4	Letter.
IsLetterorDigit	0, 1, 8,	Union of letters and digits.
IsLower	1	Lowercase letter.
IsUpper	0	Uppercase letter.
IsPunctuation	18, 19, 20, 21, 22, 23, 24	Punctuation symbol—for example, DashPunctuation(19) or OpenPunctuation(20), OtherPunctuation(24).
IsSeparator	11, 12, 13	Space separator, line separator, paragraph separator.
IsSurrogate	16	Value is a high or low surrogate.
IsSymbol	25, 26, 28	Symbol.
IsWhiteSpace	11	Whitespace can be any of these characters: space (0x20), carriage return (0x0D), horizontal tab (0x09), line feed (0x0A), form feed (0x0C), or vertical tab (0x0B).

Using these methods is straightforward. The main point of interest is that they have overloads that accept a single char parameter, or two parameters specifying a string and index to the character within the string.

```
Console.WriteLine(Char.IsSymbol('+'));            // true
Console.WriteLine(Char.IsPunctuation('+')):       // false
string str = "black magic";
Console.WriteLine(Char.IsWhiteSpace(str, 5));     // true
char p = '.';
Console.WriteLine(Char.IsPunctuation(p));         // true
Int iCat = (int) char.GetUnicodeCategory(p);      // 24
Char p = '(';
Console.WriteLine(Char.IsPunctuation(p));         // true
int iCat = (int) char.GetUnicodeCategory(p);      // 20
```

5.2   The String Class

The `System.String` class was introduced in Chapter 2. This section expands that discussion to include a more detailed look at creating, comparing, and formatting strings. Before proceeding to these operations, let's first review the salient points from Chapter 2:

- The `System.String` class is a reference type having value semantics. This means that unlike most reference types, string comparisons are based on the value of the strings and not their location.
- A string is a sequence of `Char` types. Any reference to a character within a string is treated as a `char`.
- Strings are *immutable*. This means that after a string is created, it cannot be changed at its current memory location: You cannot shorten it, append to it, or change a character within it. The string value can be changed, of course, but the modified string is stored in a new memory location. The original string remains until the Garbage Collector removes it.
- The `System.Text.StringBuilder` class provides a set of methods to construct and manipulate strings within a buffer. When the operations are completed, the contents are converted to a string. `String-Builder` should be used when an application makes extensive use of concatenation and string modifications.

Creating Strings

A string is created by declaring a variable as a `string` type and assigning a value to it. The value may be a literal string or dynamically created using concatenation. This is often a perfunctory process and not an area that most programmers consider when trying to improve code efficiency. In .NET, however, an understanding of how literal strings are handled can help a developer improve program performance.

String Interning

One of the points of emphasis in Chapter 1, "Introduction to .NET and C#," was to distinguish how value and reference types are stored in memory. Recall that value types are stored on a stack, whereas reference types are placed on a managed heap. It turns out that that the CLR also sets aside a third area in memory called the *intern pool*, where it stores all the string literals during compilation. The purpose of this pool is to eliminate duplicate string values from being stored.

Consider the following code:

```
string poem1 = "Kubla Khan";
string poem2 = "Kubla Khan";
string poem3 = String.Copy(poem2); // Create new string object
string poem4 = "Christabel";
```

Figure 5-2 shows a simplified view of how the strings and their values are stored in memory.

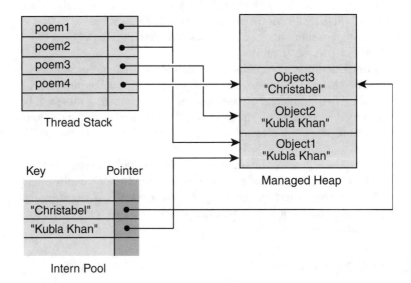

Figure 5-2   String interning

The intern pool is implemented as a hash table. The hash table *key* is the actual string and its *pointer* references the associated string object on the managed heap. When the JITcompiler compiles the preceding code, it places the first instance of "Kubla Khan" (poem1) in the pool and creates a reference to the string object on the managed heap. When it encounters the second string reference to "Kubla Khan" (poem2), the CLR sees that the string already exists in memory and, instead of creating a new string, simply assigns poem2 to the same object as poem1. This process is known as string interning. Continuing with the example, the String.Copy method creates a new string poem3 and creates an object for it in the managed heap. Finally, the string literal associated with poem4 is added to the pool.

To examine the practical effects of string interning, let's extend the previous example. We add code that uses the equivalence (==) operator to compare string values and the Object.ReferenceEquals method to compare their addresses.

```
Console.WriteLine(poem1 == poem2);                      // true
Console.WriteLine(poem1 == poem3);                      // true
Console.WriteLine(ReferenceEquals(poem1, poem3)); // false
Console.WriteLine(ReferenceEquals(poem1,
                  "Kubla Khan"));                       // true
```

The first two statements compare the value of the variables and—as expected—return a `true` value. The third statement compares the memory location of the variables `poem3` and `poem2`. Because they reference different objects in the heap, a value of `false` is returned.

The .NET designers decided to exclude dynamically created values from the intern pool because checking the intern pool each time a string was created would hamper performance. However, they did include the `String.Intern` method as a way to selectively add dynamically created strings to the literal pool.

```
string khan = " Khan";
string poem5 = "Kubla" + khan;
Console.WriteLine(ReferenceEquals(poem5, poem1)); // false
// Place the contents of poem5 in the intern pool—if not there
poem5 = String.Intern(poem5);
Console.WriteLine(ReferenceEquals(poem5, poem1)); // true
```

The `String.Intern` method searches for the value of `poem5` (`"Kubla Khan"`) in the intern pool; because it is already in the pool, there is no need to add it. The method returns a reference to the already existing object (`Object1`) and assigns it to `poem5`. Because `poem5` and `poem1` now point to the same object, the comparison in the final statement is `true`. Note that the original object created for `poem5` is released and swept up during the next Garbage Collection.

Core Recommendation

Use the `string.Intern` method to allow a string variable to take advantage of comparison by reference, but only if it is involved in numerous comparisons.

Overview of String Operations

The `System.String` class provides a large number of static and instance methods, most of which have several overload forms. For discussion purposes, they can be grouped into four major categories based on their primary function:

- **String Comparisons.** The `String.Equals`, `String.Compare`, and `String.CompareOrdinal` methods offer different ways to compare string values. The choice depends on whether an ordinal or lexical comparison is needed, and whether case or culture should influence the operation.
- **Indexing and Searching.** A string is an array of Unicode characters that may be searched by iterating through it as an array or by using special index methods to locate string values.
- **String Transformations.** This is a catchall category that includes methods for inserting, padding, removing, replacing, trimming, and splitting character strings.
- **Formatting.** NET provides format specifiers that are used in conjunction with `String.Format` to represent numeric and `DateTime` values in a number of standard and custom formats.

Many of the string methods—particularly for formatting and comparisons—are culture dependent. Where applicable, we look at how culture affects the behavior of a method.

5.3 Comparing Strings

The most efficient way to determine if two string variables are equal is to see if they refer to the same memory address. We did this earlier using the `ReferenceEquals` method. If two variables do not share the same memory address, it is necessary to perform a character-by-character comparison of the respective values to determine their equality. This takes longer than comparing addresses, but is often unavoidable.

.NET attempts to optimize the process by providing the `String.Equals` method that performs both reference and value comparisons automatically. We can describe its operation in the following pseudo-code:

```
If string1 and string2 reference the same memory location
   Then strings must be equal
Else
   Compare strings character by character to determine equality
```

This code segment demonstrates the static and reference forms of the `Equals` method:

```
string poem1 = "Kubla Khan";
string poem2 = "Kubla Khan";
string poem3 = String.Copy(poem2);
string poem4 = "kubla khan";
```

```
//
Console.WriteLine(String.Equals(poem1,poem2));   // true
Console.WriteLine(poem1.Equals(poem3));           // true
Console.WriteLine(poem1 == poem3);       // equivalent to Equals
Console.WriteLine(poem1 == poem4);       // false - case differs
```

Note that the == operator, which calls the Equals method underneath, is a more convenient way of expressing the comparison.

Although the Equals method satisfies most comparison needs, it contains no overloads that allow it to take case sensitivity and culture into account. To address this shortcoming, the string class includes the Compare method.

Using String.Compare

String.Compare is a flexible comparison method that is used when culture or case must be taken into account. Its many overloads accept culture and case-sensitive parameters, as well as supporting substring comparisons.

Syntax:

```
int Compare (string str1, string str2)
Compare (string str1, string str2, bool IgnoreCase)
Compare (string str1, string str2, bool IgnoreCase,
        CultureInfo ci)
Compare (string str1, int index1, string str2, int index2,
        int len)
```

Parameters:

str1 and str2	Specify strings to be compared.
IgnoreCase	Set true to make comparison case-insensitive (default is false).
index1 and index2	Starting position in str1 and str2.
ci	A CultureInfo object indicating the culture to be used.

Compare returns an integer value that indicates the results of the comparison. If the two strings are equal, a value of 0 is returned; if the first string is less than the second, a value less than zero is returned; if the first string is greater than the second, a value greater than zero is returned.

The following segment shows how to use Compare to make case-insensitive and case-sensitive comparisons:

```
int result;
string stringUpper = "AUTUMN";
```

```
string stringLower = "autumn";
// (1) Lexical comparison: "A" is greater than "a"
result = string.Compare(stringUpper,stringLower);        // 1
// (2) IgnoreCase set to false
result = string.Compare(stringUpper,stringLower,false); // 1
// (3)Perform case-insensitive comparison
result = string.Compare(stringUpper,stringLower,true);   // 0
```

Perhaps even more important than case is the potential effect of culture information on a comparison operation. .NET contains a list of comparison rules for each culture that it supports. When the Compare method is executed, the CLR checks the culture associated with it and applies the rules. The result is that two strings may compare differently on a computer with a US culture vis-à-vis one with a Japanese culture. There are cases where it may be important to override the current culture to ensure that the program behaves the same for all users. For example, it may be crucial that a sort operation order items exactly the same no matter where the application is run.

By default, the Compare method uses culture information based on the Thread.CurrentThread.CurrentCulture property. To override the default, supply a CultureInfo object as a parameter to the method. This statement shows how to create an object to represent the German language and country:

```
CultureInfo ci = new CultureInfo("de-DE");  // German culture
```

To explicitly specify a default culture or no culture, the CultureInfo class has two properties that can be passed as parameters—CurrentCulture, which tells a method to use the culture of the current thread, and InvariantCulture, which tells a method to ignore any culture.

Let's look at a concrete example of how culture differences affect the results of a Compare() operation.

```
using System.Globalization;    // Required for CultureInfo

// Perform case-sensitive comparison for Czech culture
string s1 = "circle";
string s2 = "chair";
result = string.Compare(s1, s2,
        true, CultureInfo.CurrentCulture));        // 1
result = string.Compare(s1, s2,
        true, CultureInfo.InvariantCulture));      // 1
// Use the Czech culture
result = string.Compare(s1, s2,
        true, new CultureInfo("cs-CZ"));           // -1
```

The string values "circle" and "chair" are compared using the US culture, no culture, and the Czech culture. The first two comparisons return a value indicating that "circle" > "chair", which is what you expect. However, the result using the Czech culture is the opposite of that obtained from the other comparisons. This is because one of the rules of the Czech language specifies that "ch" is to be treated as a single character that lexically appears after "c".

Core Recommendation

When writing an application that takes culture into account, it is good practice to include an explicit CultureInfo parameter in those methods that accept such a parameter. This provides a measure of self-documentation that clarifies whether the specific method is subject to culture variation.

Using String.CompareOrdinal

To perform a comparison that is based strictly on the ordinal value of characters, use String.CompareOrdinal. Its simple algorithm compares the Unicode value of two strings and returns a value less than zero if the first string is less than the second; a value of zero if the strings are equal; and a value greater than zero if the first string is greater than the second. This code shows the difference between it and the Compare method:

```
string stringUpper = "AUTUMN";
string stringLower = "autumn";
//
result = string.Compare(stringUpper,stringLower,
        false, CultureInfo.InvariantCulture);          // 1
result = string.CompareOrdinal(stringUpper,stringLower);  // -32
```

Compare performs a lexical comparison that regards the uppercase string to be greater than the lowercase. CompareOrdinal examines the underlying Unicode values. Because A (U+0041) is less than a (U+0061), the first string is less than the second.

5.4   Searching, Modifying, and Encoding a String's Content

This section describes `string` methods that are used to perform diverse but familiar tasks such as locating a substring within a string, changing the case of a string, replacing or removing text, splitting a string into delimited substrings, and trimming leading and trailing spaces.

Searching the Contents of a String

A string is an implicit zero-based array of chars that can be searched using the array syntax `string[n]`, where n is a character position within the string. For locating a substring of one or more characters in a string, the `string` class offers the `IndexOf` and `IndexOfAny` methods. Table 5-2 summarizes these.

Table 5-2   Ways to Examine Characters Within a String

String Member	Description

`[ n ]`	Indexes a 16-bit character located at position n within a string.
	
	 ```int ndx= 0;```
	```while (ndx < poem.Length)```
	```{```
	``` Console.Write(poem[ndx]); //Kubla Khan```
	``` ndx += 1;```
	```}```

`IndexOf/LastIndexOf`
 	
 `(string, [int start],`
 `[int count])`
 	
 count. Number of chars to examine.
	Returns the index of the first/last occurrence of a specified string within an instance. Returns –1 if no match.
	
	 ```string poem = "Kubla Khan";```
	```int n = poem.IndexOf("la"); // 3```
	```n = poem.IndexOf('K'); // 0```
	```n = poem.IndexOf('K',4); // 6```

`IndexOfAny/LastIndexOfAny`	Returns the index of the first/last character in an array of Unicode characters.
	
	 ```string poem = "Kubla Khan";```
	```char[] vowels = new char[5]```
	``` {'a', 'e', 'i', 'o', 'u'};```
	```n = poem.IndexOfAny(vowels); // 1```
	```n = poem.LastIndexOfAny(vowels); // 8```
	```n = poem.IndexOfAny(vowels,2); // 4```

Searching a String That Contains Surrogates

All of these techniques assume that a string consists of a sequence of 16-bit characters. Suppose, however, that your application must work with a Far Eastern character set of 32-bit characters. These are represented in storage as a *surrogate pair* consisting of a high and low 16-bit value. Clearly, this presents a problem for an expression such as poem[ndx], which would return only half of a surrogate pair.

For applications that must work with surrogates, .NET provides the StringInfo class that treats all characters as *text elements* and can automatically detect whether a character is 16 bits or a surrogate. Its most important member is the GetTextElementEnumerator method, which returns an enumerator that can be used to iterate through text elements in a string.

```
TextElementEnumerator tEnum =
        StringInfo.GetTextElementEnumerator(poem) ;
while (tEnum.MoveNext())  // Step through the string
{
   Console.WriteLine(tEnum.Current);  // Print current char
}
```

Recall from the discussion of enumerators in Chapter 4, "Working with Objects in C#," that MoveNext() and Current are members implemented by all enumerators.

String Transformations

Table 5-3 summarizes the most important string class methods for modifying a string. Because the original string is immutable, any string constructed by these methods is actually a new string with its own allocated memory.

Table 5-3 Methods for Manipulating and Transforming Strings

Tag	Description

Insert (int, string)	Inserts a string at the specified position.
	
	```string mariner = "and he stoppeth three";```
	```string verse = mariner.Insert(```
	``` mariner.IndexOf(" three")," one of");```
	```// verse --> "and he stoppeth one of three"```

PadRight/PadLeft	Pads a string with a given character until it is a specified width. If no character is specified, whitespace is used.
	
	```string rem = "and so on";```
	```rem = rem.PadRight(rem.Length+3,'.');```
	```// rem --> "and so on..."```

Table 5-3 Methods for Manipulating and Transforming Strings *(continued)*

Tag	Description

`Remove(p , n)`	Removes n characters beginning at position p.
	
	```string verse = "It is an Ancient Mariner";```
	```string newverse = (verse.Remove(0,9));```
	```// newverse --> "Ancient Mariner"```

`Replace (A , B)`	Replaces all occurrences of A with B, where A and B are chars or strings.
	
	```string aString = "nap ace sap path";```
	```string iString = aString.Replace('a','i');```
	```// iString --> "nip ice sip pith"```

`Split( char[])`	The char array contains delimiters that are used to break a string into substrings that are returned as elements in a string array.
	
	```string words = "red,blue orange ";```
	```string [] split = words.Split(new Char []```
	``` {' ', ','});```
	```Console.WriteLine(split[2]); // orange```

`ToUpper()`
`ToUpper(CultureInfo)`
`ToLower()`
`ToLower(CultureInfo)`
	Returns an upper- or lowercase copy of the string.
	
	```string poem2="Kubla Khan";```
	```poem2= poem2.ToUpper(```
	``` CultureInfo.InvariantCulture);```

`Trim()`
`Trim(params char[])`
	Removes all leading and trailing whitespaces. If a char array is provided, all leading and trailing characters in the array are removed.
	
	```string name = " Samuel Coleridge";```
	```name = name.Trim(); // "Samuel Coleridge"```

`TrimEnd (params char[])`
`TrimStart(params char[])`
	Removes all leading or trailing characters specified in a char array. If null is specified, whitespaces are removed.
	
	```string name = " Samuel Coleridge";```
	```trimName = name.TrimStart(null);```
	```shortname = name.TrimEnd('e','g','i');```
	```// shortName --> "Samuel Colerid"```

`Substring(n)`
`Substring(n, 1)`
	Extracts the string beginning at a specified position (n) and of length l, if specified.
	
	```string title="Kubla Khan";```
	```Console.WriteLine(title.Substring(2,3));```
	```//bla```

Table 5-3   Methods for Manipulating and Transforming Strings *(continued)*

Tag	Description
`ToCharArray()` `ToCharArray(n, 1)`	Extracts characters from a string and places in an array of Unicode characters.

	``
	string myVowels = "aeiou";
	char[] vowelArr;
	vowelArr = myVowels.ToCharArray();
	Console.WriteLine(vowelArr[1]); // "e"
	``

Most of these methods have analogues in other languages and behave as you would expect. Somewhat surprisingly, as we see in the next section, most of these methods are not available in the `StringBuilder` class. Only `Replace`, `Remove`, and `Insert` are included.

String Encoding

Encoding comes into play when you need to convert between strings and bytes for operations such as writing a string to a file or streaming it across a network. Character encoding and decoding offer two major benefits: efficiency and interoperability. Most strings read in English consist of characters that can be represented by 8 bits. Encoding can be used to strip an extra byte (from the 16-bit Unicode memory representation) for transmission and storage. The flexibility of encoding is also important in allowing an application to interoperate with legacy data or third-party data encoded in different formats.

The .NET Framework supports many forms of character encoding and decoding. The most frequently used include the following:

- **UTF-8.** Each character is encoded as a sequence of 1 to 4 bytes, based on its underlying value. ASCII compatible characters are stored in 1 byte; characters between 0x0080 and 0x07ff are stored in 2 bytes; and characters having a value greater than or equal to 0x0800 are converted to 3 bytes. Surrogates are written as 4 bytes. UTF-8 (which stands for UCS Transformation Format, 8-bit form) is usually the default for .NET classes when no encoding is specified.
- **UTF-16.** Each character is encoded as 2 bytes (except surrogates), which is how characters are represented internally in .NET. This is also referred to as Unicode encoding.
- **ASCII.** Encodes each character as an 8-bit ASCII character. This should be used when all characters are in the ASCII range (0x00 to 0x7F). Attempting to encode a character outside of the ACII range yields whatever value is in the character's low byte.

Encoding and decoding are performed using the `Encoding` class found in the `System.Text` namespace. This abstract class has several static properties that return an object used to implement a specific encoding technique. These properties include `ASCII`, `UTF8`, and `Unicode`. The latter is used for UTF-16 encoding.

An encoding object offers several methods—each having several overloads—for converting between characters and bytes. Here is an example that illustrates two of the most useful methods: `GetBytes`, which converts a text string to bytes, and `GetString`, which reverses the process and converts a byte array to a string.

```
string text= "In Xanadu did Kubla Khan";
Encoding UTF8Encoder = Encoding.UTF8;
byte[] textChars = UTF8Encoder.GetBytes(text);
Console.WriteLine(textChars.Length);          // 24
// Store using UTF-16
textChars = Encoding.Unicode.GetBytes(text);
Console.WriteLine(textChars.Length);          // 48
// Treat characters as two bytes
string decodedText = Encoding.Unicode.GetString(textChars);
Console.WriteLine(decodedText); // "In Xanadu did ...   "
```

You can also instantiate the encoding objects directly. In this example, the UTF-8 object could be created with

```
UTF8Encoding UTF8Encoder = new UTF8Encoding();
```

With the exception of `ASCIIEncoding`, the constructor for these classes defines parameters that allow more control over the encoding process. For example, you can specify whether an exception is thrown when invalid encoding is detected.

5.5 StringBuilder

The primary drawback of strings is that memory must be allocated each time the contents of a string variable are changed. Suppose we create a loop that iterates 100 times and concatenates one character to a string during each iteration. We could end up with a hundred strings in memory, each differing from its preceding one by a single character.

The `StringBuilder` class addresses this problem by allocating a work area (buffer) where its methods can be applied to the string. These methods include ways to append, insert, delete, remove, and replace characters. After the operations are complete, the `ToString` method is called to convert the buffer to a string that can be assigned to a string variable. Listing 5-1 introduces some of the `StringBuilder` methods in an example that creates a comma delimited list.

Listing 5-1 Introduction to `StringBuilder`

```
using System;
using System.Text;
public class MyApp
{
    static void Main()
    {
        // Create comma delimited string with quotes around names
        string namesF = "Jan Donna Kim ";
        string namesM = "Rob James";
        StringBuilder sbCSV = new StringBuilder();
        sbCSV.Append(namesF).Append(namesM);
        sbCSV.Replace(" ","'","'");
        // Insert quote at beginning and end of string
        sbCSV.Insert(0,"'").Append("'");
        string csv = sbCSV.ToString();
        // csv = 'Jan','Donna','Kim','Rob','James'
    }
}
```

All operations occur in a single buffer and require no memory allocation until the final assignment to csv. Let's take a formal look at the class and its members.

StringBuilder Class Overview

Constructors for the `StringBuilder` class accept an initial string value as well as integer values that specify the initial space allocated to the buffer (in characters) and the maximum space allowed.

```
// Stringbuilder(initial value)
StringBuilder sb1 = new StringBuilder("abc");
// StringBuilder(initial value, initial capacity)
StringBuilder sb2 = new StringBuilder("abc", 16);
// StringBuiler(Initial Capacity, maximum capacity)
StringBuilder sb3 = new StringBuilder(32,128);
```

The idea behind `StringBuilder` is to use it as a buffer in which string operations are performed. Here is a sample of how its `Append`, `Insert`, `Replace`, and `Remove` methods work:

```
int i = 4;
char[] ch = {'w','h','i','t','e'};
string myColor = " orange";
```

```
StringBuilder sb = new StringBuilder("red blue green");
sb.Insert(0, ch);              // whitered blue green
sb.Insert(5," ");              // white red blue green
sb.Insert(0,i);                // 4white red blue green
sb.Remove(1,5);                // 4 red blue green
sb.Append(myColor);            // 4 red blue green orange
sb.Replace("blue","violet");   // 4 red violet green orange
string colors = sb.ToString();
```

StringBuilder Versus String Concatenation

Listing 5-2 tests the performance of StringBuilder versus the concatenation operator. The first part of this program uses the + operator to concatenate the letter a to a string in each of a loop's 50,000 iterations. The second half does the same, but uses the StringBuilder.Append method. The Environment.TickCount provides the beginning and ending time in milliseconds.

Listing 5-2	Comparison of StringBuilder and Regular Concatenation

```
using System;
using System.Text;
public class MyApp
{
    static void Main()
    {
        Console.WriteLine("String routine");
        string a = "a";
        string str = string.Empty;
        int istart, istop;
        istart = Environment.TickCount;
        Console.WriteLine("Start: "+istart);
        // Use regular C# concatenation operator
        for(int i=0; i<50000; i++)
        {
            str += a;
        }
        istop = Environment.TickCount;
        Console.WriteLine("Stop: "+istop);
        Console.WriteLine("Difference: " + (istop-istart));
        // Perform concatenation with StringBuilder
```

Listing 5-2	Comparison of `StringBuilder` and Regular Concatenation *(continued)*

```
    Console.WriteLine("StringBuilder routine");
    StringBuilder builder = new StringBuilder();
    istart = Environment.TickCount;
    Console.WriteLine("Start: "+istart);
    for(int i=0; i<50000; i++)
    {
        builder.Append(a);
    }
    istop = Environment.TickCount;
    str = builder.ToString();
    Console.WriteLine("Stop: "+Environment.TickCount);
    Console.WriteLine("Difference: "+ (istop-istart));
  }
}
```

Executing this program results in the following output:

```
String routine
Start: 1422091687
Stop: 1422100046
Difference: 9359
StringBuilder routine
Start: 1422100046
Stop: 1422100062
Difference: 16
```

The results clearly indicate the improved performance `StringBuilder` provides: The standard concatenation requires 9,359 milliseconds versus 16 milliseconds for `StringBuilder`. When tested with loops of 1,000 iterations, `StringBuilder` shows no significant advantage. Unless your application involves extensive text manipulation, the standard concatenation operator should be used.

5.6   Formatting Numeric and DateTime Values

The `String.Format` method is the primary means of formatting date and numeric data for display. It accepts a string composed of text and embedded format items followed by one or more data arguments. Each format item references a data argument and specifies how it is to be formatted. The CLR creates the output string by converting each data value to a string (using `ToString`), formatting it according to its corresponding format item, and then replacing the format item with the formatted data value. Here is a simple example:

```
String s= String.Format("The square root of {0} is {1}.",64,8);
// output: The square root of 64 is 8.
```

The method has several overloads, but this is the most common and illustrates two features common to all: a format string and a list of data arguments. Note that `Console.WriteLine` accepts the same parameters and can be used in place of `String.Format` for console output.

Constructing a Format Item

Figure 5-3 breaks down a `String.Format` example into its basic elements. The most interesting of these is the format item, which defines the way data is displayed.

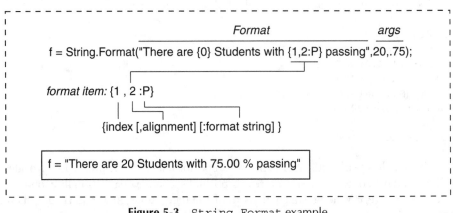

Figure 5-3   `String.Format` example

As we can see, each format item consists of an index and an optional alignment and format string. All are enclosed in brace characters:

1. The *index* is a zero-based integer that indicates the argument to which it is to be applied. The index can be repeated to refer to the same argument more than once.

2. The optional *alignment* is an integer that indicates the minimum width of the area that contains the formatted value. If alignment value

is positive, the argument value is right justified; if the value is negative, it is left justified.

3. The optional *format string* contains the formatting codes to be applied to the argument value. If it is not specified, the output of the argument's `ToString` method is used. .NET provides several standard format codes to be used with numbers and dates as well as codes that are used to create custom format strings.

Formatting Numeric Values

Nine characters, or format specifiers, are available to format numbers into currency, scientific, hexadecimal, and other representations. Each character can have an integer appended to it that specifies a precision particular to that format—usually this indicates the number of decimal places. C# recognizes the standard format specifiers[2] shown in Table 5-4.

Table 5-4   Formatting Numeric Values with Standard Numeric Format Strings

Format Specifier	Description	Pattern	Output
C or c	Currency. Number is represented as a currency amount. The precision specifies the number of decimal places.	{0:C2}, 1458.75	$ 1,458.75
D or d	Decimal. Applies to integral values. The precision indicates the total number of spaces the number occupies; is padded with zeros on left if necessary.	{0:D5}, 455 {0:D5}, -455	00455 -00455
E or e	Scientific. The number is converted to a scientific notation: ddddE+nnn. The precision specifies the number of digits after the decimal point.	{0,10:E2}, 3298.78 {0,10:E4}, -54783.4	3.30+E003 -5.4783+E004
F or f	Fixed Point. The number is converted to format of: ddd.ddd. The precision indicates the number of decimal places.	{0,10:F0}, 162.57 {0,10:F2}, 8162.57	162 8162.57

---

2. Microsoft Windows users can set formats using the Control Panel – Regional Options settings.

Table 5-4 Formatting Numeric Values with Standard Numeric Format Strings *(continued)*

Format Specifier	Description	Pattern	Output
G or g	General. The number is converted to fixed point or scientific notation based on the precision and type of number. Scientific is used if the exponent is greater than or equal to the specified precision or less than –4.	{0,10:G}, .0000099 {0,10:G2}, 455.89 {0,10:G3}, 455.89 {0,10:G}, 783229.34	9.9E-06 4.6E+02 456 783229.34
N or n	Number. Converts to a string that uses commas as thousands separators. The precision specifies the number of decimal places.	{0,10:N}, 1045.78 {0,10:N1}, 45.98	1,045.78 45.9
P or p	Percent. Number is multiplied by 100 and presented as percent with number of decimal places specified by precision.	{0,10:P}, 0.78 {0,10:P3}, 0.7865	78.00 % 78.650 %
R or r	Round-trip. Converts to a string that retains all decimal place accuracy. Then number to be converted must be floating point.	{0,10:R}, 1.62736	1.62736
X or x	Hexadecimal. Converts the number to its hex representation. The precision indicates the minimum number of digits shown. Number is padded with zeros if needed.	{0,10:X}, 25 {0,10:X4}, 25 {0,10:x4}, 31	19 0019 001f

The patterns in this table can also be used directly with `Console.Write` and `Console.WriteLine`:

```
Console.WriteLine("The Hex value of {0} is {0:X} ",31); //1F
```

The format specifiers can be used alone to enhance output from the `ToString` method:

```
decimal pct = .758M;
Console.Write("The percent is "+pct.ToString("P2")); // 75.80 %
```

.NET also provides special formatting characters that can be used to create custom numeric formats. The most useful characters are pound sign (#), zero (0), comma (,), period (.), percent sign (%), and semi-colon (;). The following code demonstrates their use:

```
decimal dVal = 2145.88M;    // decimal values require M suffix
string myFormat;
myFormat = dVal.ToString("#####");         //  2146
myFormat = dVal.ToString("#,###.00");      //  2,145.88
myFormat = String.Format("Value is {0:#,###.00;
(#,###.00)}",-4567);
// semicolon specifies alternate formats. (4,567.00)
myFormat = String.Format("Value is {0:$#,###.00}", 4567);
                                           //  $4,567.00
Console.WriteLine("{0:##.00%}",.18);       //  18.00 %
```

The role of these characters should be self-explanatory except for the semicolon (;), which deserves further explanation. It separates the format into two groups: the first is applied to positive values and the second to negative. Two semicolons can be used to create three groups for positive, negative, and zero values, respectively.

Formatting Dates and Time

Date formatting requires a `DateTime` object. As with numbers, this object has its own set of standard format specifiers. Table 5-5 summarizes these.

Table 5-5 Formatting Dates with Standard Characters

Format Specifier	Description	Example—English	Example—German
d	Short date pattern	1/19/2004	19.1.2004
D	Long date pattern	Monday, January 19, 2004	Montag, 19 Januar, 2004
f	Full date/time pattern (short time)	Monday, January 19, 2004 4:05 PM	Montag, 19 Januar, 2004 16:05
F	Full date/time pattern (full time)	Monday, January 19, 2004 4:05:20 PM	Montag, 19 Januar, 2004 16:05:20
g	General date/time pattern (short time)	1/19/2004 4:05 PM	19/1/2004 16:05
G	General date/time pattern (long time)	1/19/2004 4:05:20 PM	19/1/2004 16:05:20

Table 5-5 Formatting Dates with Standard Characters *(continued)*

Format Specifier	Description	Example—English	Example—German
M, m	Month day pattern	January 19	19 Januar
Y, y	Year month pattern	January, 2004	Januar, 2004
t	Short time pattern	4:05 PM	16:05
T	Long time pattern	4:05:20 PM	16:05:20
s	Universal Sortable Date-Time pattern. Conforms to ISO 8601. Uses local time.	2004-01-19T16:05:20	2004-01-19T16:05:20
u	Universal Sortable Date-Time pattern	2004-01-19 16:05:20Z	2004-01-19 16:05:20Z
U	Universal Sortable Date-Time pattern. Uses universal time.	Monday, January 19, 2004 21:05:20 PM	Montag, 19. Januar, 2004 21:05:20

Here are some concrete examples that demonstrate date formatting. In each case, an instance of a `DateTime` object is passed an argument to a format string.

```
DateTime curDate = DateTime.Now;  // Get Current Date
Console.Writeline("Date: {0:d} ", curDate);   // 1/19/2004
// f: --> Monday, January 19, 2004 5:05 PM
Console.Writeline("Date: {0:f} ", curDate);
// g: --> 1/19/2004 5:05 PM
Console.Writeline("Date: {0:g} ", curDate);
```

If none of the standard format specifiers meet your need, you can construct a custom format from a set of character sequences designed for that purpose. Table 5-6 lists some of the more useful ones for formatting dates.

Table 5-6 Character Patterns for Custom Date Formatting

Format	Description	Example
d	Day of month. No leading zero.	5
dd	Day of month. Always has two digits.	05

Table 5-6   Character Patterns for Custom Date Formatting *(continued)*

Format	Description	Example
ddd	Day of week with three-character abbreviation.	Mon
dddd	Day of week full name.	Monday
M	Month number. No leading zero.	1
MM	Month number with leading zero if needed.	01
MMM	Month name with three-character abbreviation.	Jan
MMMM	Full name of month.	January
y	Year. Last one or two digits.	5
yy	Year. Last one or two digits with leading zero if needed.	05
yyyy	Four-digit year.	2004
HH	Hour in 24-hour format.	15
mm	Minutes with leading zero if needed.	20

Here are some examples of custom date formats:

```
DateTime curDate = DateTime.Now;
f = String.Format("{0:dddd} {0:MMM} {0:dd}", curDate);
// output: Monday Jan 19

f = currDate.ToString("dd MMM yyyy")
// output: 19 Jan 2004

// The standard short date format (d) is equivalent to this:
Console.WriteLine(currDate.ToString("M/d/yyyy"));   // 1/19/2004
Console.WriteLine(currDate.ToString("d"));          // 1/19/2004

CultureInfo ci = new CultureInfo("de-DE");           // German
f = currDate.ToString("dd-MMMM-yyyy HH:mm", ci)
// output: 19-Januar-2004 23:07
```

ToString is recommended over String.Format for custom date formatting. It has a more convenient syntax for embedding blanks and special separators between the date elements; in addition, its second parameter is a culture indicator that makes it easy to test different cultures.

Dates and Culture

Dates are represented differently throughout the world, and the ability to add culture as a determinant in formatting dates shifts the burden to .NET from the developer. For example, if the culture on your system is German, dates are automatically formatted to reflect a European format: the day precedes the month; the day, month, and year are separated by periods (.) rather than slashes (/); and the phrase Monday, January 19 becomes Montag, 19. Januar. Here is an example that uses ToString with a German CultureInfo parameter:

```
CultureInfo ci = new CultureInfo("de-DE");        // German
Console.WriteLine(curDate.ToString("D",ci));
// output ---> Montag, 19. Januar 2004
Console.WriteLine(curDate.ToString("dddd",ci));   // -->Montag
```

The last statement uses the special custom format "dddd" to print the day of the week. This is favored over the DateTime.DayofWeek enum property that returns only an English value.

NumberFormatInfo and DateTimeFormatInfo Classes

These two classes govern how the previously described format patterns are applied to dates and numbers. For example, the NumberFormatInfo class includes properties that specify the character to be used as a currency symbol, the character to be used as a decimal separator, and the number of decimal digits to use when displaying a currency value. Similarly, DateTimeFormatInfo defines properties that correspond to virtually all of the standard format specifiers for dates. One example is the FullDateTimePattern property that defines the pattern returned when the character F is used to format a date.

NumberFormatInfo and DateTimeFormatInfo are associated with specific cultures, and their properties are the means for creating the unique formats required by different cultures. .NET provides a predefined set of property values for each culture, but they can be overridden.

Their properties are accessed in different ways depending on whether the current or non-current culture is being referenced (current culture is the culture associated with the current thread). The following statements reference the current culture:

```
NumberFormatInfo.CurrentInfo.<property>
CultureInfo.CurrentCulture.NumberFormat.<property>
```

The first statement uses the static property CurrentInfo and implicitly uses the current culture. The second statement specifies a culture explicitly (CurrentCulture) and is suited for accessing properties associated with a non-current CultureInfo instance.

```
CultureInfo ci = new CultureInfo("de-DE");
string f = ci.NumberFormat.CurrencySymbol;
```

`NumberFormatInfo` and `DateTimeFormatInfo` properties associated with a non-current culture can be changed; those associated with the current thread are read-only. Listing 5-3 offers a sampling of how to work with these classes.

Listing 5-3	Using `NumberFormatInfo` and `DateTimeFormatInfo`

```
using System
using System.Globalization
Class MyApp
{
   // NumberFormatInfo
   string curSym = NumberFormatInfo.CurrentInfo.CurrencySymbol;
   int dd  = NumberFormatInfo.CurrentInfo.CurrencyDecimalDigits;
   int pdd = NumberFormatInfo.CurrentInfo.PercentDecimalDigits;
   // --> curSym = "$"   dd = 2  pdd = 2
   // DateTimeFormatInfo
   string ldp= DateTimeFormatInfo.CurrentInfo.LongDatePattern;
   // --> ldp = "dddd, MMMM, dd, yyyy"
   string enDay = DateTimeFormatInfo.CurrentInfo.DayNames[1];
   string month = DateTimeFormatInfo.CurrentInfo.MonthNames[1];
   CultureInfo ci = new CultureInfo("de-DE");
   string deDay = ci.DateTimeFormat.DayNames[1];
   // --> enDay = "Monday"  month = February  deDay = "Montag"
   // Change the default number of decimal places
   // in a percentage
   decimal passRate = .840M;
   Console.Write(passRate.ToString("p",ci));  // 84,00%
   ci.NumberFormat.PercentDecimalDigits = 1;
   Console.Write(passRate.ToString("p",ci));  // 84,0%
}
```

In summary, .NET offers a variety of standard patterns that satisfy most needs to format dates and numbers. Behind the scenes, there are two classes, `NumberFormatInfo` and `DateTimeFormatInfo`, that define the symbols and rules used for formatting. .NET provides each culture with its own set of properties associated with an instance of these classes.

5.7   Regular Expressions

The use of strings and expressions to perform pattern matching dates from the earliest programming languages. In the mid-1960s SNOBOL was designed for the express purpose of text and string manipulation. It influenced the subsequent development of the *grep* tool in the Unix environment that makes extensive use of regular expressions. Those who have worked with grep or Perl or other scripting languages will recognize the similarity in the .NET implementation of regular expressions.

Pattern matching is based on the simple concept of applying a special pattern string to some text source in order to match an instance or instances of that pattern within the text. The pattern applied against the text is referred to as a regular expression, or *regex*, for short.

Entire books have been devoted to the topic of regular expressions. This section is intended to provide the essential knowledge required to get you started using regular expressions in the .NET world. The focus is on using the Regex class, and creating regular expressions from the set of characters and symbols available for that purpose.

The Regex Class

You can think of the Regex class as the engine that evaluates regular expressions and applies them to target strings. It provides both static and instance methods that use regexes for text searching, extraction, and replacement. The Regex class and all related classes are found in the System.Text.RegularExpressions namespace.

Syntax:

```
Regex( string pattern )
Regex( string pattern, RegexOptions)
```

Parameters:

pattern	Regular expression used for pattern matching.
RegexOptions	An enum whose values control how the regex is applied. Values include:

CultureInvariant—Ignore culture.

IgnoreCase—Ignore upper- or lowercase.

RightToLeft—Process string right to left.

Example:

```
Regex r1 = new Regex(" ");    // Regular expression is a blank
String words[] = r1.Split("red blue orange yellow");
// Regular expression matches upper- or lowercase "at"
Regex r2 = new Regex("at", RegexOptions.IgnoreCase);
```

As the example shows, creating a `Regex` object is quite simple. The first parameter to its constructor is a regular expression. The optional second parameter is one or more (separated by |) `RegexOptions` enum values that control how the regex is applied.

Regex Methods

The `Regex` class contains a number of methods for pattern matching and text manipulation. These include `IsMatch`, `Replace`, `Split`, `Match`, and `Matches`. All have instance and static overloads that are similar, but not identical.

Core Recommendation

If you plan to use a regular expression repeatedly, it is more efficient to create a Regex object. When the object is created, it compiles the expression into a form that can be used as long as the object exists. In contrast, static methods recompile the expression each time they are used.

Let's now examine some of the more important `Regex` methods. We'll keep the regular expressions simple for now because the emphasis at this stage is on understanding the methods—not regular expressions.

IsMatch()

This method matches the regular expression against an input string and returns a boolean value indicating whether a match is found.

```
string searchStr = "He went that a way";
Regex myRegex = new Regex("at");
// instance methods
bool match = myRegex.IsMatch(searchStr);            // true
// Begin search at position 12 in the string
match = myRegex.IsMatch(searchStr,12);              // false
// Static Methods - both return true
match = Regex.IsMatch(searchStr,"at");
match = Regex.IsMatch(searchStr,"AT",RegexOptions.IgnoreCase);
```

Replace()

This method returns a string that replaces occurrences of a matched pattern with a specified replacement string. This method has several overloads that permit you to specify a start position for the search or control how many replacements are made.

Syntax:

```
static Replace (string input, string pattern, string replacement
                [,RegexOptions])

Replace(string input, string replacement)
Replace(string input, string replacement, int count)
Replace(string input, string replacement, int count, int startat)
```

The count parameter denotes the maximum number of matches; startat indicates where in the string to begin the matching process. There are also versions of this method—which you may want to explore further—that accept a MatchEvaluator delegate parameter. This delegate is called each time a match is found and can be used to customize the replacement process.

Here is a code segment that illustrates the static and instance forms of the method:

```
string newStr;
newStr = Regex.Replace("soft rose","o","i");   // sift rise
// instance method
Regex myRegex = new Regex("o");                 // regex = "o"
// Now specify that only one replacement may occur
newStr = myRegex.Replace("soft rose","i",1);    // sift rose
```

Split()

This method splits a string at each point a match occurs and places that matching occurrence in an array. It is similar to the String.Split method, except that the match is based on a regular expression rather than a character or character string.

Syntax:

```
String[] Split(string input)
String[] Split(string input, int count)
String[] Split(string input, int count, int startat)
Static String[] Split(string input, string pattern)
```

Parameters:

input   The string to split.

count   The maximum number of array elements to return. A count value of 0 results in as many matches as possible. If the number of matches is greater than count, the last match consists of the remainder of the string.

startat   The character position in *input* where the search begins.

pattern   The regex pattern to be matched against the input string.

This short example parses a string consisting of a list of artists' last names and places them in an array. A comma followed by zero or more blanks separates the names. The regular expression to match this delimiter string is: ", [ ]*". You will see how to construct this later in the section.

```
string impressionists = "Manet,Monet, Degas, Pissarro,Sisley";
// Regex to match a comma followed by 0 or more spaces
string patt = @",[ ]*";
// Static method
string[] artists = Regex.Split(impressionists, patt);
// Instance method is used to accept maximum of four matches
Regex myRegex = new Regex(patt);
string[] artists4 = myRegex.Split(impressionists, 4);
foreach (string master in artists4)
    Console.Write(master);
// Output --> "Manet" "Monet" "Degas" "Pissarro,Sisley"
```

Match() and Matches()

These related methods search an input string for a match to the regular expression. `Match()` returns a single `Match` object and `Matches()` returns the object `Match-Collection`, a collection of all matches.

Syntax:

```
Match Match(string input)
Match Match(string input, int startat)
Match Match(string input, int startat, int numchars)
static Match(string input, string pattern, [RegexOptions])
```

The `Matches` method has similar overloads but returns a `MatchCollection` object.

`Match` and `Matches` are the most useful `Regex` methods. The `Match` object they return is rich in properties that expose the matched string, its length, and its location within the target string. It also includes a `Groups` property that allows the matched string to be further broken down into matching substrings. Table 5-7 shows selected members of the `Match` class.

The following code demonstrates the use of these class members. Note that the dot (.) in the regular expression functions as a wildcard character that matches any single character.

```
string verse = "In Xanadu did Kubla Khan";
string patt = ".an...";        // "." matches any character
Match verseMatch = Regex.Match(verse, patt);
Console.WriteLine(verseMatch.Value);   // Xanadu
```

```
Console.WriteLine(verseMatch.Index);    // 3
//
string newPatt = "K(..)";                    //contains group(..)
Match kMatch = Regex.Match(verse, newPatt);
while (kMatch.Success) {
    Console.Write(kMatch.Value);        // -->Kub  -->Kha
    Console.Write(kMatch.Groups[1]);    // -->ub   -->ha
    kMatch = kMatch.NextMatch();
}
```

This example uses NextMatch to iterate through the target string and assign each match to kMatch (if NextMatch is left out, an infinite loop results). The parentheses surrounding the two dots in newPatt break the pattern into *groups* without affecting the actual pattern matching. In this example, the two characters after K are assigned to group objects that are accessed in the Groups collection.

Table 5-7   Selected Members of the Match Class

Member	Description
Index	Property returning the position in the string where the first character of the match is found.
Groups	A collection of groups within the class. Groups are created by placing sections of the regex with parentheses. The text that matches the pattern in parentheses is placed in the Groups collection.
Length	Length of the matched string.
Success	True or False depending on whether a match was found.
Value	Returns the matching substring.
NextMatch()	Returns a new Match with the results from the next match operation, beginning with the character after the previous match, if any.

Sometimes, an application may need to collect all of the matches before processing them—which is the purpose of the MatchCollection class. This class is just a container for holding Match objects and is created using the Regex.Matches method discussed earlier. Its most useful properties are Count, which returns the number of captures, and Item, which returns an individual member of the collection. Here is how the NextMatch loop in the previous example could be rewritten:

```
string verse = "In Xanadu did Kubla Khan";
String newpatt = "K(..)";
foreach (Match kMatch in Regex.Matches(verse, newpatt))
```

```
Console.Write(kMatch.Value);   // -->Kub  -->Kha
// Could also create explicit collection and work with it.
MatchCollection mc = Regex.Matches(verse, newpatt);
Console.WriteLine(mc.Count);       // 2
```

Creating Regular Expressions

The examples used to illustrate the Regex methods have employed only rudimentary regular expressions. Now, let's explore how to create regular expressions that are genuinely useful. If you are new to the subject, you will discover that designing Regex patterns tends to be a trial-and-error process; and the endeavor can yield a solution of simple elegance—or maddening complexity. Fortunately, almost all of the commonly used patterns can be found on one of the Web sites that maintain a searchable library of Regex patterns (www.regexlib.com is one such site).

A regular expression can be broken down into four different types of metacharacters that have their own role in the matching process:

- **Matching characters.** These match a specific type of character—for example, \d matches any digit from 0 to 9.
- **Repetition characters.** Used to prevent having to repeat a matching character or item—for example, \d{3} can be used instead of \d\d\d to match three digits.
- **Positional characters.** Designate the location in the target string where a match must occur—for example, ^\d{3} requires that the match occur at the beginning of the string.
- **Escape sequences.** Use the backslash (\) in front of characters that otherwise have special meaning—for example, \} permits the right brace to be matched.

Table 5-8 summarizes the most frequently used patterns.

Table 5-8   Regular Expression Patterns

Pattern	Matching Criterion	Example
+	Match one or more occurrences of the previous item.	to+ matches too and tooo. It does not match t.
*	Match zero or more occurrences of the previous item.	to* matches t or too or tooo.
?	Match zero or one occurrence of the previous item. Performs "non-greedy" matching.	te?n matches ten or tn. It does not match teen.

Table 5-8   Regular Expression Patterns *(continued)*

Pattern	Matching Criterion	Example
{n}	Match exactly n occurrences of the previous character.	te{2}n matches teen. It does not match ten or teeen.
{n,}	Match at least n occurrences of the previous character.	te{1,}n matches ten and teen. It does not match tn.
{n,m}	Match at least n and no more than m occurrences of the previous character.	te{1,2}n matches ten and teen.
\	Treat the next character literally. Used to match characters that have special meaning such as the patterns +, *, and ?.	A\+B matches A+B. The slash (\) is required because + has special meaning.
\d \D	Match any digit (\d) or non-digit (\D). This is equivalent to [0-9] or [^0-9], respectively.	\d\d matches 55. \D\D matches xx.
\w \W	Match any word plus underscore (\w) or non-word (\W) character. \w is equivalent to [a-zA-Z0-9_]. \W is equivalent to [^a-zA-Z0-9_].	\w\w\w\w matches A_19 . \W\W\W matches ($).
\n \r \t \v \f	Match newline, carriage return, tab, vertical tab, or form feed, respectively.	N/A
\s \S	Match any whitespace (\s) or non-whitespace (\S). A whitespace is usually a space or tab character.	\w\s\w\s\w matches A B C.
. (dot)	Matches any single character. Does not match a newline.	a.c matches abc. It does not match abcc.
|	Logical OR.	"in|en" matches enquiry.
[. . .]	Match any single character between the brackets. Hyphens may be used to indicate a range.	[aeiou] matches u. [\d\D] matches a single digit or non-digit.
[^. . .]	All characters except those in the brackets.	[^aeiou] matches x.

A Pattern Matching Example

Let's apply these character patterns to create a regular expression that matches a Social Security Number (SSN):

```
bool iMatch = Regex.IsMatch("245-09-8444",
                    @"\d\d\d-\d\d-\d\d\d\d");
```

This is the most straightforward approach: Each character in the Social Security Number matches a corresponding pattern in the regular expression. It's easy to see, however, that simply repeating symbols can become unwieldy if a long string is to be matched. Repetition characters improve this:

```
bool iMatch = Regex.IsMatch("245-09-8444",
                    @"\d{3}-\d{2}-\d{4}");
```

Another consideration in matching the Social Security Number may be to restrict where it exists in the text. You may want to ensure it is on a line by itself, or at the beginning or end of a line. This requires using *position characters* at the beginning or end of the matching sequence.

Let's alter the pattern so that it matches only if the Social Security Number exists by itself on the line. To do this, we need two characters: one to ensure the match is at the beginning of the line, and one to ensure that it is also at the end. According to Table 5-9, ^ and $ can be placed around the expression to meet these criteria. The new string is

```
@"^\d{3}-\d{2}-\d{4}$"
```

These positional characters do not take up any space in the expression—that is, they indicate where matching may occur but are not involved in the actual matching process.

Table 5-9 Characters That Specify Where a Match Must Occur

Position Character	Description
^	Following pattern must be at the start of a string or line.
$	Preceding pattern must be at end of a string or line.
\A	Preceding pattern must be at the start of a string.
\b \B	Move to a word boundary (\b), where a word character and non-word character meet, or a non-word boundary.
\z \Z	Pattern must be at the end of a string (\z) or at the end of a string before a newline.

As a final refinement to the SSN pattern, let's break it into *groups* so that the three sets of numbers separated by dashes can be easily examined. To create a group, place parentheses around the parts of the expression that you want to examine independently. Here is a simple code example that uses the revised pattern:

```
string ssn = "245-09-8444";
string ssnPatt = @"^(\d{3})-(\d{2})-(\d{4})$";
Match ssnMatch = Regex.Match(ssn, ssnPatt);
if (ssnMatch.Success){
    Console.WriteLine(ssnMatch.Value);          // 245-09-8444
    Console.WriteLine(ssnMatch.Groups.Count);   // 4
    // Count is 4 since Groups[0] is set to entire SSN
    Console.Write(ssnMatch.Groups[1]);          // 245
    Console.Write(ssnMatch.Groups[2]);          // 09
    Console.Write(ssnMatch.Groups[3]);          // 8444
}
```

We now have a useful pattern that incorporates position, repetition, and group characters. The approach that was used to create this pattern—started with an obvious pattern and refined it through multiple stages—is a useful way to create complex regular expressions (see Figure 5-4).

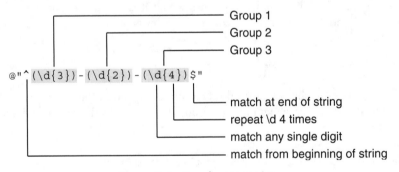

Figure 5-4   Regular expression

Working with Groups

As we saw in the preceding example, the text resulting from a match can be automatically partitioned into substrings or groups by enclosing sections of the regular expression in parentheses. The text that matches the enclosed pattern becomes a member of the `Match.Groups[]` collection. This collection can be indexed as a zero-based array: the 0 element is the entire match, element 1 is the first group, element 2 the second, and so on.

Groups can be named to make them easier to work with. The name designator is placed adjacent to the opening parenthesis using the syntax ?<name>. To demonstrate the use of groups, let's suppose we need to parse a string containing the forecasted temperatures for the week (for brevity, only two days are included):

```
string txt ="Monday Hi:88 Lo:56 Tuesday Hi:91 Lo:61";
```

The regex to match this includes two groups: day and temps. The following code creates a collection of matches and then iterates through the collection, printing the content of each group:

```
string rgPatt =
@"(?<day>[a-zA-Z]+)\s*(?<temps>Hi:\d+\s*Lo:\d+)";
MatchCollection mc = Regex.Matches(txt, rgPatt); //Get matches
foreach(Match m in mc)
{
    Console.WriteLine("{0} {1}",
                    m.Groups["day"],m.Groups["temps"]);
}
//Output:    Monday Hi:88 Lo:56
//           Tuesday Hi:91 Lo:61
```

Core Note

There are times when you do not want the presence of parentheses to designate a group that captures a match. A common example is the use of parentheses to create an OR expression—for example, (an|in|on). To make this a non-capturing group, place ?: inside the parentheses—for example, (?:an|in|on).

Backreferencing a Group

It is often useful to create a regular expression that includes matching logic based on the results of previous matches within the expression. For example, during a grammatical check, word processors flag any word that is a repeat of the preceding word(s). We can create a regular expression to perform the same operation. The secret is to define a group that matches a word and then uses the matched value as part of the pattern. To illustrate, consider the following code:

```
string speech = "Four score and and seven years";
patt = @"(\b[a-zA-Z]+\b)\s\1";            // Match repeated words
MatchCollection mc = Regex.Matches(speech, patt);
```

```
foreach(Match m in mc) {
     Console.WriteLine(m.Groups[1]);    // --> and
}
```

This code matches only the repeated words. Let's examine the regular expression:

Text/Pattern	Description
and and @"(\b[a-zA-Z]+\b)\s	Matches a word bounded on each side by a word boundary (\b) and followed by a whitespace.
and **and** \1	The backreference indicator. Any group can be referenced with a slash (\) followed by the group number. The effect is to insert the group's matched value into the expression.

A group can also be referenced by name rather than number. The syntax for this backreference is \k followed by the group name enclosed in <>:

```
patt = @"(?<word>\b[a-zA-Z]+\b)\s\k<word>";
```

Examples of Using Regular Expressions

This section closes with a quick look at some patterns that can be used to handle common pattern matching challenges. Two things should be clear from these examples: There are virtually unlimited ways to create expressions to solve a single problem, and many pattern matching problems involve nuances that are not immediately obvious.

Using Replace to Reverse Words

```
string userName = "Claudel, Camille";
userName = Regex.Replace( userName, @"(\w+),\s*(\w+)", "$2 $1" );
Console.WriteLine(userName);    // Camille Claudel
```

The regular expression assigns the last and first name to groups 1 and 2. The third parameter in the Replace method allows these groups to be referenced by placing $ in front of the group number. In this case, the effect is to replace the entire matched name with the match from group 2 (first name) followed by the match from group 1 (last name).

Parsing Numbers

```
String myText = "98, 98.0, +98.0, +98";
string numPatt = @"\d+";                      // Integer
numPatt = @"(\d+\.?\d*)|(\.\d+)";             // Allow decimal
numPatt = @"([+-]?\d+\.?\d*)|([+-]?\.\d+)";   // Allow + or -
```

Note the use of the OR (|) symbol in the third line of code to offer alternate patterns. In this case, it permits an optional number before the decimal.

The following code uses the ^ character to anchor the pattern to the beginning of the line. The regular expression contains a group that matches four bytes at a time. The * character causes the group to be repeated until there is nothing to match. Each time the group is applied, it captures a 4-digit hex number that is placed in the CaptureCollection object.

```
string hex = "00AA001CFF0C";
string hexPatt =  @"^(?<hex4>[a-fA-F\d]{4})*";
Match hexMatch = Regex.Match(hex,hexPatt);
Console.WriteLine(hexMatch.Value); // --> 00AA001CFF0C
CaptureCollection cc = hexMatch.Groups["hex4"].Captures;
foreach (Capture c in cc)
   Console.Write(c.Value); // --> 00AA 001C FF0C
```

Figure 5-5 shows the hierarchical relationship among the Match, GroupCollection, and CaptureCollection classes.

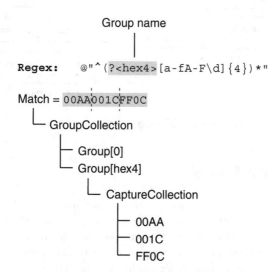

Figure 5-5   Hex numbers captured by regular expression

5.8   System.IO: Classes to Read and Write Streams of Data

The System.IO namespace contains the primary classes used to move and process streams of data. The data source may be in the form of text strings, as discussed in this chapter, or raw bytes of data coming from a network or device on an I/O port. Classes derived from the Stream class work with raw bytes; those derived from the TextReader and TextWriter classes operate with characters and text strings (see Figure 5-6). We'll begin the discussion with the Stream class and look at how its derived classes are used to manipulate byte streams of data. Then, we'll examine how data in a more structured text format is handled using the TextReader and Text-Writer classes.

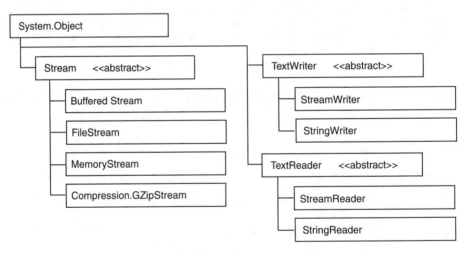

Figure 5-6   Selected System.IO classes

The Stream Class

This class defines the generic members for working with raw byte streams. Its purpose is to abstract data into a stream of bytes independent of any underlying data devices. This frees the programmer to focus on the data stream rather than device characteristics. The class members support three fundamental areas of operation: reading, writing, and seeking (identifying the current byte position within a stream).

Table 5-10 summarizes some of its important members. Not included are methods for asynchronous I/O, a topic covered in Chapter 13, "Asynchronous Programming and Multithreading."

Table 5-10   Selected `Stream` Members

Member	Description
CanRead CanSeek CanWrite	Indicates whether the stream supports reading, seeking, or writing.
Length	Length of stream in bytes; returns long type.
Position	Gets or sets the position within the current stream; has long type.
Close()	Closes the current stream and releases resources associated with it.
Flush()	Flushes data in buffers to the underlying device—for example, a file.
Read(byte array, offset, count) ReadByte()	Reads a sequence of bytes from the stream and advances the position within the stream to the number of bytes read. `ReadByte` reads one byte. `Read` returns number of bytes read; `ReadByte` returns –1 if at end of the stream.
SetLength()	Sets the length of the current stream. It can be used to extend or truncate a stream.
Seek()	Sets the position within the current stream.
Write(byte array, offset, count) WriteByte()	Writes a sequence of bytes (`Write`) or one byte (`WriteByte`) to the current stream. Neither has a return value.

These methods and properties provide the bulk of the functionality for the `FileStream`, `MemoryStream`, and `BufferedStream` classes, which we examine next.

FileStreams

A `FileStream` object is created to process a stream of bytes associated with a *backing store*—a term used to refer to any storage medium such as disk or memory. The following code segment demonstrates how it is used for reading and writing bytes:

```
try
{
    // Create FileStream object
    FileStream fs = new FileStream(@"c:\artists\log.txt",
            FileMode.OpenOrCreate, FileAccess.ReadWrite);
    byte[] alpha = new byte[6] {65,66,67,68,69,70}; //ABCDEF
    // Write array of bytes to a file
    // Equivalent to: fs.Write(alpha,0, alpha.Length);
    foreach (byte b in alpha) {
        fs.WriteByte(b);}
    // Read bytes from file
    fs.Position = 0;            // Move to beginning of file
    for (int i = 0; i< fs.Length; i++)
        Console.Write((char) fs.ReadByte()); //ABCDEF
    fs.Close();
catch(Exception ex)
{
    Console.Write(ex.Message);
}
```

As this example illustrates, a stream is essentially a byte array with an internal pointer that marks a current location in the stream. The ReadByte and WriteByte methods process stream bytes in sequence. The Position property moves the internal pointer to any position in the stream. By opening the FileStream for Read-Write, the program can intermix reading and writing without closing the file.

Creating a FileStream

The FileStream class has several constructors. The most useful ones accept the path of the file being associated with the object and optional parameters that define file mode, access rights, and sharing rights. The possible values for these parameters are shown in Figure 5-7.

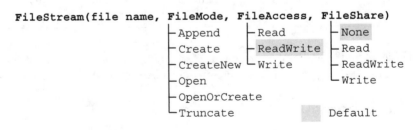

Figure 5-7 Options for FileStream constructors

The `FileMode` enumeration designates how the operating system is to open the file and where to position the file pointer for subsequent reading or writing. Table 5-11 is worth noting because you will see the enumeration used by several classes in the `System.IO` namespace.

Table 5-11   `FileMode` Enumeration Values

Value	Description
Append	Opens an existing file or creates a new one. Writing begins at the end of the file.
Create	Creates a new file. An existing file is overwritten.
CreateNew	Creates a new file. An exception is thrown if the file already exists.
Open	Opens an existing file.
OpenOrCreate	Opens a file if it exists; otherwise, creates a new one.
Truncate	Opens an existing file, removes its contents, and positions the file pointer to the beginning of the file.

The `FileAccess` enumeration defines how the current `FileStream` may access the file; `FileShare` defines how file streams in other processes may access it. For example, `FileShare.Read` permits multiple file streams to be created that can simultaneously read the same file.

MemoryStreams

As the name suggests, this class is used to stream bytes to and from memory as a substitute for a temporary external physical store. To demonstrate, here is an example that copies a file. It reads the original file into a memory stream and then writes this to a `FileStream` using the `WriteTo` method:

```
FileStream fsIn = new FileStream(@"c:\manet.bmp",
            FileMode.Open, FileAccess.Read);
FileStream fsOut = new FileStream(@"c:\manetcopy.bmp",
            FileMode.OpenOrCreate, FileAccess.Write);
MemoryStream ms = new MemoryStream();
// Input image byte-by-byte and store in memory stream
int imgByte;
while ((imgByte = fsIn.ReadByte())!=-1){
   ms.WriteByte((byte)imgByte);
}
```

```
ms.WriteTo(fsOut);                 // Copy image from memory to disk
byte[] imgArray = ms.ToArray(); // Convert to array of bytes
fsIn.Close();
fsOut.Close();
ms.Close();
```

BufferedStreams

One way to improve I/O performance is to limit the number of reads and writes to an external device—particularly when small amounts of data are involved. Buffers have long offered a solution for collecting small amounts of data into larger amounts that could then be sent more efficiently to a device. The BufferedStream object contains a buffer that performs this role for an underlying stream. You create the object by passing an existing stream object to its constructor. The BufferedStream then performs the I/O operations, and when the buffer is full or closed, its contents are flushed to the underlying stream. By default, the BufferedStream maintains a buffer size of 4096 bytes, but passing a size parameter to the constructor can change this.

Buffers are commonly used to improve performance when reading bytes from an I/O port or network. Here is an example that associates a BufferedStream with an underlying FileStream. The heart of the code consists of a loop in which Fill-Bytes (simulating an I/O device) is called to return an array of bytes. These bytes are written to a buffer rather than directly to the file. When fileBuffer is closed, any remaining bytes are flushed to the FileStream fsOut1. A write operation to the physical device then occurs.

```
private void SaveStream() {
   Stream fsOut1 = new FileStream(@"c:\captured.txt",
      FileMode.OpenOrCreate, FileAccess.Write);
   BufferedStream fileBuffer = new BufferedStream(fsOut1);
   byte[] buff;              // Array to hold bytes written to buffer
   bool readMore=true;
   while(readMore) {
      buff = FillBytes();            // Get array of bytes
      for (int j = 0;j<buff[16];j++){
         fileBuffer.WriteByte(buff[j]);    // Store bytes in buffer
      }
      if(buff[16]< 16) readMore=false;   // Indicates no more data
   }
   fileBuffer.Close();  // Flushes all remaining buffer content
   fsOut1.Close();      // Must close after bufferedstream
}
// Method to simulate I/O device receiving data
private static byte[] FillBytes() {
```

```
Random rand = new Random();
byte[] r = new Byte[17];
// Store random numbers to return in array
for (int j=0;j<16;j++) {
    r[j]= (byte) rand.Next();
    if(r[j]==171)            // Arbitrary end of stream value
    {
        r[16]=(byte)(j);   // Number of bytes in array
        return r;
    }
}
System.Threading.Thread.Sleep(500);   // Delay 500ms
return r;
}
```

Using StreamReader and StreamWriter to Read and Write Lines of Text

Unlike the `Stream` derived classes, `StreamWriter` and `StreamReader` are designed to work with text rather than raw bytes. The abstract `TextWriter` and `TextReader` classes from which they derive define methods for reading and writing text as lines of characters. Keep in mind that these methods rely on a `FileStream` object underneath to perform the actual data transfer.

Writing to a Text File

`StreamWriter` writes text using its `Write` and `WriteLine` methods. Note their differences:

- `WriteLine` works only with strings and automatically appends a newline (carriage return\linefeed).
- `Write` does not append a newline character and can write strings as well as the textual representation of any basic data type (`int32`, `single`, and so on) to the text stream.

The `StreamWriter` object is created using one of several constructors:

Syntax (partial list):

```
public StreamWriter(string path)
public StreamWriter(stream s)
public StreamWriter(string path, bool append)
public StreamWriter(string path, bool append, Encoding encoding)
```

Parameters:

path	Path and name of file to be opened.
s	Previously created Stream object—typically a `FileStream`.
append	Set to true to append data to file; false overwrites.
encoding	Specifies how characters are encoded as they are written to a file. The default is UTF-8 (UCS Transformation Format) that stores characters in the minimum number of bytes required.

This example creates a `StreamWriter` object from a `FileStream` and writes two lines of text to the associated file:

```
string filePath = @"c:\cup.txt";
// Could use: StreamWriter sw = new StreamWriter(filePath);
// Use FileStream to create StreamWriter
FileStream fs = new FileStream(filePath, FileMode.OpenOrCreate,
                   FileAccess.ReadWrite);
StreamWriter sw2 = new StreamWriter(fs);
// Now that it is created, write to the file
sw2.WriteLine("The world is a cup");
sw2.WriteLine("brimming\nwith water.");
sw2.Close();  // Free resources
```

Reading from a Text File

A `StreamReader` object is used to read text from a file. Much like `StreamWriter`, an instance of it can be created from an underlying `Stream` object, and it can include an encoding specification parameter. When it is created, it has several methods for reading and viewing character data (see Table 5-12).

Table 5-12   Selected `StreamReader` Methods

Member	Description
`Peek()`	Returns the next available character without moving the position of the reader. Returns an int value of the character or –1 if none exists.
`Read()` `Read(char buff, int ndx, int count)`	Reads next character (`Read()`) from a stream or reads next count characters into a character array beginning at ndx.
`ReadLine()`	Returns a string comprising one line of text.
`ReadToEnd()`	Reads all characters from the current position to the end of the `TextReader`. Useful for downloading a small text file over a network stream.

This code creates a `StreamReader` object by passing an explicit `FileStream` object to the constructor. The `FileStream` is used later to reposition the reader to the beginning of the file.

```
String path= @"c:\cup.txt";
if(File.Exists(path))
{
    FileStream fs = new FileStream(path,
            FileMode.OpenOrCreate, FileAccess.ReadWrite);
    StreamReader reader = new StreamReader(fs);
    // or StreamReader reader = new StreamReader(path);
    // (1) Read first line
    string line = reader.ReadLine();
    // (2) Read four bytes on next line
    char[] buff  = new char[4];
    int count = reader.Read(buff,0,buff.Length);
    // (3) Read to end of file
    string cup = reader.ReadToEnd();
    // (4) Reposition to beginning of file
    //     Could also use reader.BaseStream.Position = 0;
    fs.Position = 0;
    // (5) Read from first line to end of file
    line = null;
    while ((line = reader.ReadLine()) != null){
        Console.WriteLine(line);
    }
    reader.Close();
}
```

Core Note

A `StreamReader` *has an underlying* `FileStream` *even if it is not created with an explicit one. It is accessed by the* `BaseStream` *property and can be used to reposition the reader within the stream using its* `Seek` *method. This example moves the reader to the beginning of a file:*

`reader.BaseStream.Seek(0, SeekOrigin.Begin);`

StringWriter and StringReader

These two classes do not require a lot of discussion, because they are so similar in practice to the `StreamWriter` and `StreamReader`. The main difference is that these streams are stored in memory, rather than in a file. The following example should be self-explanatory:

```
StringWriter writer = new StringWriter();
writer.WriteLine("Today I have returned,");
writer.WriteLine("after long months ");
writer.Write("that seemed like centuries");
writer.Write(writer.NewLine);
writer.Close();
// Read String just written from memory
string myString = writer.ToString();
StringReader reader = new StringReader(myString);
string line = null;
while ((line = reader.ReadLine()) !=null) {
   Console.WriteLine(line);
}
reader.Close();
```

The most interesting aspect of the StringWriter is that it is implemented underneath as a StringBuilder object. In fact, StringWriter has a GetString-Builder method that can be used to retrieve it:

```
StringWriter writer = new StringWriter();
writer.WriteLine("Today I have returned,");
// Get underlying StringBuilder
StringBuilder sb = writer.GetStringBuilder();
sb.Append("after long months ");
Console.WriteLine(sb.ToString());
writer.Close();
```

Core Recommendation

Use the StringWriter and StringBuilder classes to work with large strings in memory. A typical approach is to use the StreamReader.ReadToEnd method to load a text file into memory where it can be written to the StringWriter and manipulated by the StringBuilder.

Encryption with the CryptoStream Class

An advantage of using streams is the ability to layer them to add functionality. We saw earlier how the BufferedStream class performs I/O on top of an underlying FileStream. Another class that can be layered on a base stream is the Crypto-Stream class that enables data in the underlying stream to be encrypted and decrypted. This section describes how to use this class in conjunction with the

`StreamWriter` and `StreamReader` classes to read and write encrypted text in a `FileStream`. Figure 5-8 shows how each class is composed from the underlying class.

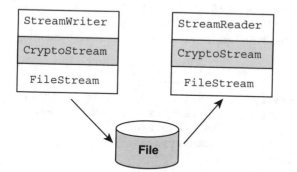

Figure 5-8 Layering streams for encryption/decryption

`CryptoStream` is located in the `System.Security.Cryptography` namespace. It is quite simple to use, requiring only a couple of lines of code to apply it to a stream. The .NET Framework provides multiple cryptography algorithms that can be used with this class. Later, you may want to investigate the merits of these algorithms, but for now, our interest is in how to use them with the `CryptoStream` class.

Two techniques are used to encrypt data: assymmetric (or *public key*) and symmetric (or *private key*). Public key is referred to as asymmetric because a public key is used to decrypt data, while a different private key is used to encrypt it. Symmetric uses the same private key for both purposes. In our example, we are going to use a private key algorithm. The .NET Framework Class Library contains four classes that implement symmetric algorithms:

- `DESCryptoServiceProvider`—Digital Encryption Standard (DES) algorithm
- `RC2CryptoServiceProvider`—RC2 algorithm
- `RijndaelManaged`—Rijndael algorithm
- `TrippleDESCryptoServiceProvider`—TrippleDES algorithm

We use the DES algorithm in our example, but we could have chosen any of the others because implementation details are identical. First, an instance of the class is created. Then, its `key` and `IV` (Initialization Vector) properties are set to the same key value. DES requires these to be 8 bytes; other algorithms require different lengths. Of course, the key is used to encrypt and decrypt data. The IV ensures that repeated text is not encrypted identically. After the DES object is created, it is passed as an argument to the constructor of the CryptoStream class. The CryptoStream object simply treats the object encapsulating the algorithm as a black box.

The example shown here includes two methods: one to encrypt and write data to a file stream, and the other to decrypt the same data while reading it back. The encryption is performed by WriteEncrypt, which receives a FileStream object parameter encapsulating the output file and a second parameter containing the message to be encrypted; ReadEncrypt receives a FileStream representing the file to be read.

```
fs = new FileStream("C:\\test.txt", FileMode.Create,
                    FileAccess.Write);
MyApp.WriteEncrypt(fs, "Selected site is in Italy.");
fs= new FileStream("C:\\test.txt",FileMode.Open,
                    FileAccess.Read);
string msg = MyApp.ReadEncrypt(fs);
Console.WriteLine(msg);
fs.Close();
```

WriteEncrypt encrypts the message and writes it to the file stream using a StreamWriter object that serves as a wrapper for a CrytpoStream object. CryptoStream has a lone constructor that accepts the file stream, an object encapsulating the DES algorithm logic, and an enumeration specifying its mode.

```
// Encrypt FileStream
private static void WriteEncrypt(FileStream fs, string msg) {
    // (1) Create Data Encryption Standard (DES) object
    DESCryptoServiceProvider crypt = new
            DESCryptoServiceProvider();
    // (2) Create a key and Initialization Vector -
    // requires 8 bytes
    crypt.Key = new byte[] {71,72,83,84,85,96,97,78};
    crypt.IV  = new byte[] {71,72,83,84,85,96,97,78};
    // (3) Create CryptoStream stream object
    CryptoStream cs = new CryptoStream(fs,
        crypt.CreateEncryptor(),CryptoStreamMode.Write);
    // (4) Create StreamWriter using CryptoStream
    StreamWriter sw = new StreamWriter(cs);
    sw.Write(msg);
    sw.Close();
    cs.Close();
}
```

ReadEncrypt reverses the actions of WriteEncrypt. It decodes the data in the file stream and returns the data as a string object. To do this, it layers a CryptoStream stream on top of the FileStream to perform decryption. It then creates a StreamReader from the CryptoStream stream that actually reads the data from the stream.

```
// Read and decrypt a file stream.
private static string ReadEncrypt(FileStream fs) {
    // (1) Create Data Encryption Standard (DES) object
    DESCryptoServiceProvider crypt =
            new DESCryptoServiceProvider();
    // (2) Create a key and Initialization Vector
    crypt.Key = new byte[] {71,72,83,84,85,96,97,78};
    crypt.IV  = new byte[] {71,72,83,84,85,96,97,78};
    // (3) Create CryptoStream stream object
    CryptoStream cs = new CryptoStream(fs,
            crypt.CreateDecryptor(),CryptoStreamMode.Read);
    // (4) Create StreamReader using CryptoStream
    StreamReader sr = new StreamReader(cs);
    string msg = sr.ReadToEnd();
    sr.Close();
    cs.Close();
    return msg;
}
```

5.9   System.IO: Directories and Files

The System.IO namespace includes a set of system-related classes that are used to manage files and directories. Figure 5-9 shows a hierarchy of the most useful classes. Directory and DirectoryInfo contain members to create, delete, and query directories. The only significant difference in the two is that you use Directory with static methods, whereas a DirectoryInfo object must be created to use instance methods. In a parallel manner, File and FileInfo provide static and instance methods for working with files.

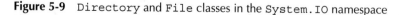

Figure 5-9   Directory and File classes in the System.IO namespace

FileSystemInfo

The `FileSystemInfo` class is a base class for `DirectoryInfo` and `FileInfo`. It defines a range of members that are used primarily to provide information about a file or directory. The abstract `FileSystemInfo` class takes advantage of the fact that files and directories share common features. Its properties include `CreationTime`, `LastAccessTime`, `LastWriteTime`, `Name`, and `FullName`. It also includes two important methods: `Delete` to delete a file or directory and `Refresh` that updates the latest file and directory information.

Here is a quick look at some of the `FileSystemInfo` members using `Directory-Info` and `FileInfo` objects. Note the use of the `Refresh` method before checking the directory and file attributes.

```
// DirectoryInfo
string dir  = @"c:\artists";
DirectoryInfo di = new DirectoryInfo(dir);
di.Refresh();
DateTime IODate = di.CreationTime;
Console.WriteLine("{0:d}",IODate)           // 10/9/2001
// FileInfo
string file = @"C:\artists\manet.jpg";
FileInfo fi = new FileInfo(file);
if (fi.Exists) {
    fi.Refresh();
    IODate = fi.CreationTime;
    Console.WriteLine("{0:d}",IODate);      // 5/15/2004
    Console.WriteLine(fi.Name);             // monet.txt
    Console.WriteLine(fi.Extension);        // .txt
    FileAttributes attrib = fi.Attributes;
    Console.WriteLine((int) attrib);        // 32
    Console.WriteLine(attrib);              // Archive
}
```

Working with Directories Using the DirectoryInfo, Directory, and Path Classes

When working with directories, you usually have a choice between using the instance methods of `DirectoryInfo` or the corresponding static methods of `Directory`. As a rule, if you are going to refer to a directory in several operations, use an instance of `DirectoryInfo`. Table 5-13 provides a comparison summary of the available methods.

Table 5-13 Comparison of Selected `DirectoryInfo` and `Directory` Members

`DirectoryInfo`		`Directory`	
Member	**Description**	**Member**	**Description**
`Create()` `CreateSubdirectory()`	Create a directory or subdirectory.	`CreateDirectory()`	Pass the string path to the method. Failure results in an exception.
`Delete()`	Delete a directory.	`Delete(string)` `Delete(string, bool)`	First version deletes an empty directory. Second version deletes a directory and all subdirectories if boolean value is true.
`GetDirectories()`	Returns an array of `DirectoryInfo` type containing all subdirectories in the current directory.	`GetDirectories(string)` `GetDirectories(string, string filter)`	Returns a string array containing the names of directories in the path. A filter may be used to specify directory names.
`GetFiles()`	Returns an array of `FileInfo` types containing all files in the directory.	`GetFiles(string)` `GetFiles(string, filter)`	Returns string array of files in directory. A filter may be used to match against file names. The filter may contain wildcard characters ? or * to match a single character or zero or more characters.
`Parent`	Retrieves parent directory of current path.	`GetParent()`	Retrieves parent directory of specified path.
N/A		`GetLogicalDrives()`	Returns string containing logical drives on system. Format: `<drive>:\`

Let's look at some examples using both static and instance methods to manipulate and list directory members. The sample code assumes the directory structure shown in Figure 5-10.

```
C:\
    \artists
    \impressionists
        monet.txt
        monet.htm
        sisley.txt
    \expressionists
        scheile.txt
        wollheim.txt
```

Figure 5-10 Directory structure used in `Directory` examples

Create a Subdirectory

This code adds a subdirectory named `cubists` below `expressionists`:

```
// Directory static method to create directory
string newPath =
     @"c:\artists\expressionists\cubists";
if (!Directory.Exists(newPath))
   Directory.CreateDirectory(newPath);

// DirectoryInfo
string curPath= @"c:\artists\expressionists";
di = new DirectoryInfo(curPath);
if (di.Exists) di.CreateSubdirectory(newPath);
```

Delete a Subdirectory

This code deletes the `cubists` subdirectory just created:

```
string newPath = @"c:\artists\expressionists\cubists";
// Directory
if (Directory.Exists(newPath)) Directory.Delete(newPath);
// The following fails because the directory still contains files
Directory.Delete(@"c:\artists\expressionists");
// The following succeeds because true is passed to the method
Directory.Delete(@"c:\artists\expressionists",true);

// DirectoryInfo
DirectoryInfo di = new DirectoryInfo(newPath);
If (di.Exists) di.Delete();
```

List Directories and Files

This code defines a method that recursively loops through and lists the subdirectories and selected files on the `C:\artists` path. It uses the static `Directory` methods `GetDirectories` and `GetFiles`. Both of these return string values.

```
static readonly int Depth=4; // Specify directory level to search
ShowDir (@"c:\artists\", 0); // Call method to list files
// Display directories and files using recursion
public static void ShowDir(string sourceDir, int recursionLvl)
{
   if (recursionLvl<= Depth) // Limit subdirectory search depth
   {
      // Process the list of files found in the directory
      Console.WriteLine(sourceDir);
      foreach( string fileName in
              Directory.GetFiles(sourceDir,"s*.*"))
      {
         Console.WriteLine("  "+Path.GetFileName(fileName));

      // Use recursion to process subdirectories
      foreach(string subDir in
              Directory.GetDirectories(sourceDir))
         ShowDir(subDir,recursionLvl+1);  // Recursive call
   }
}
```

`GetFiles` returns a full path name. The static `Path.GetFileName` method is used to extract the file name and extension from the path. For demonstration purposes, a filter has been added to the `GetFiles` method to have it return only the path of files that begins with s.

Here is the same operation using the `DirectoryInfo` class. Its `GetDirectories` and `GetFiles` methods behave differently than the `Directory` versions: They return objects rather than strings, and they return the immediate directory or file name rather than the entire path.

```
// DirectoryInfo
public static void ShowDir(DirectoryInfo sourceDir,
                           int recursionLvl)
{
   if (recursionLvl<= Depth)  // Limit subdirectory search depth
   {
      // Process the list of files found in the directory
      Console.WriteLine(sourceDir.FullName);
      foreach( FileInfo fileName in
```

```
        sourceDir.GetFiles("s*.*"))
    Console.WriteLine("  "+fileName);
    // Use recursion to process subdirectories
    foreach(DirectoryInfo subDir in sourceDir.GetDirectories())
        ShowDir2(subDir,recursionLvl+1);  // Recursive call
    }
}
```

The method is called with two parameters: a `DirectoryInfo` object that encapsulates the path and an initial depth of 0.

```
DirectoryInfo dirInfo = new DirectoryInfo(@"c:\artists\");
ShowDir(dirInfo, 0);
```

Using the Path Class to Operate on Path Names

To eliminate the need for developers to create code that manipulates a path string, .NET provides a `Path` class that consists of static methods designed to operate on a path string. The methods—a shortcut for Regex patterns—extract selected parts of a path or return a boolean value indicating whether the path satisfies some criterion. Note that because the format of a path is platform dependent (a Linux path is specified differently than a Windows path), the .NET implementation of this class is tailored to the platform on which it runs.

To illustrate the static `Path` methods, let's look at the results of applying selected methods to this path:

```
string fullPath = @"c:\artists\impressionists\monet.htm";
```

Method	Returns
`Path.GetDirectoryName(fullPath)`	`c:\artists\impressionists`
`Path.GetExtension(fullPath)`	`.htm`
`GetFileName(fullPath)`	`monet.htm`
`GetFullPath(fullPath)`	`c:\artists\impressionists\monet.htm`
`GetPathRoot(fullPath)`	`c:\`
`Path.HasExtension(fullPath)`	`true`

Working with Files Using the FileInfo and File Classes

The `FileInfo` and `File` classes are used for two purposes: to provide descriptive information about a file and to perform basic file operations. The classes include methods to copy, move, and delete files, as well as open files for reading and writing. This short segment uses a `FileInfo` object to display a file's properties, and the static `File.Copy` method to copy a file:

```
string fname= @"c:\artists\impressionists\degas.txt";
// Using the FileInfo class to print file information
FileInfo fi = new FileInfo(fname);  // Create FileInfo object
if (fi.Exists)
{
    Console.Write("Length: {0}\nName: {1}\nDirectory: {2}",
    fi.Length, fi.Name, fi.DirectoryName);
    // output: --> 488  degas.txt  c:\artists\impressionists
}
// Use File class to copy a file to another directory
if (File.Exists(fname))
{
    try
    {
        // Exception is thrown if file exists in target directory
        // (source, destination, overwrite=false)
        File.Copy(fname,@"c:\artists\19thcentury\degas.txt",false);
    }
    catch(Exception ex)
    {
        Console.Write(ex.Message);
    }
}
```

Using FileInfo and File to Open Files

The `File` and `FileInfo` classes offer an alternative to creating `FileStream`, `StreamWriter`, and `StreamReader` objects directly. Table 5-14 summarizes the `FileInfo` methods used to open a file. The static `File` methods are identical except that their first parameter is always a string containing the name or path of the file to open.

Table 5-14   Selected `FileInfo` Methods for Opening a File

Member	Returns	Description

`Open(mode)`
`Open(mode,access)`
`Open(mode,access,share)`
	`FileStream`	Opens a file with access and sharing privileges. The three overloads take `File-Mode`, `FileAccess`, and `FileShare` enumerations.

`Create()`	`FileStream`	Creates a file and returns a `FileStream` object. If file exists, returns reference to it.
`OpenRead()`	`FileStream`	Opens the file in read mode.
`OpenWrite()`	`FileStream`	Opens a file in write mode.
`AppendText()`	`StreamWriter`	Opens the file in append mode. If file does not exist, it is created. Equivalent to `StreamWriter(string, true)`.
`CreateText()`	`StreamWriter`	Opens a file for writing. If the file exists, its contents are overwritten. Equivalent to `StreamWriter(string, false)`.
`OpenText()`	`StreamReader`	Opens the file in read mode. Equivalent to `StreamReader(string)`.

The `FileInfo.Open` method is the generic and most flexible way to open a file:

```
public FileStream Open(FileMode mode, FileAccess access,
                       FileShare share)
```

`Create`, `OpenRead`, and `OpenWrite` are specific cases of `Open` that offer an easy-to-use method that returns a `FileStream` object and requires no parameters. Similarly, the `OpenText`, `AppendText`, and `CreateText` methods return a `Stream-Reader` or `StreamWriter` object.

The decision to create a `FileStream` (or `StreamReader/StreamWriter`) using `FileInfo` or the `FileStream` constructor should be based on how the underlying file is used in the application. If the file is being opened for a single purpose, such as for input by a `StreamReader`, creating a `FileStream` directly is the best approach. If multiple operations are required on the file, a `FileInfo` object is better. This example illustrates the advantages of using `FileInfo`. First, it creates a `FileStream` that is used for writing to a file; then, another `FileStream` is created to read the file's contents; finally, `FileInfo.Delete` is used to delete the file.

```
FileInfo    fi = new FileInfo(@"c:\temp.txt");
FileStream  fs = fi.Create();          // Create file
StreamWriter sw= new StreamWriter(fs);  // Create StreamWriter
sw.Write("With my crossbow\nI shot the Albatross. ");
sw.Close();                            // Close StreamWriter
// Now use fi to create a StreamReader
fs = fi.OpenRead();                    // Open for reading
StreamReader sr = new StreamReader(fs);
while(( string l = sr.ReadLine())!= null)
{
    Console.WriteLine(l);        // --> With my crossbow
}                                // --> I shot the Albatross.
sr.Close();
fs.Close();
fi.Delete();                     // Delete temporary file
```

5.10 Summary

The demands of working with text have increased considerably from the days when it meant dealing with 7-bit ASCII or ANSII characters. Today, the Unicode standard defines the representation of more than 90,000 characters comprising the world's alphabets. We've seen that .NET fully embraces this standard with its 16-bit characters. In addition, it supports the concept of localization, which ensures that a machine's local culture information is taken into account when manipulating and representing data strings.

String handling is facilitated by a rich set of methods available through the String and StringBuilder classes. A variety of string comparison methods are available with options to include case and culture in the comparisons. The String.Format method is of particular note with its capacity to display dates and numbers in a wide range of standard and custom formats. String manipulation and concatenation can result in an inefficient use of memory. We saw how the StringBuilder class is an efficient alternative for basic string operations. Applications that require sophisticated pattern matching, parsing, and string extraction can use regular expressions in conjunction with the Regex class.

The System.IO namespace provides a number of classes for reading and writing data: The FileStream class is used to process raw bytes of data; MemoryStream and BufferedStream allow bytes to be written to memory or buffered; the StreamReader and StreamWriter classes support the more traditional line-oriented I/O. Operations related to managing files and directories are available as methods on the File, FileInfo, Directory, and DirectoryInfo classes. These are used to create, copy, delete, and list files and directories.

5.11 Test Your Understanding

1. Which class encapsulates information about a specific culture?

2. Name two ways to access the default culture within an application.

3. Match each regular expression:

    1. `@"(\b[^\Wa-z0-9_][^\WA-Z0-9_]*\b)"`
    2. `@"(\b[^\Wa-z0-9_]+\b)"`
    3. `@"(\b[^\WA-Z0-9_]+\b)"`

    with the function it performs:

    a. Find all capitalized words.
    b. Find all lowercase words.
    c. Find all words with the initial letter capitalized.

4. When is it more advantageous to use the instance methods of `Regex` rather than the static ones?

5. Which string comparison method(s) is (are) used to implement this statement:

    ```
    if (myString == "Monday") bool sw = true;
    ```

6. Match each statement:

    1. `curdt.ToString("D")`
    2. `curdt.ToString("M")`
    3. `curdt.ToString("ddd MMM dd")`

    with its output:

    a. March 9
    b. Tuesday, March 9, 2004
    c. Tue Mar 09

7. Which of these objects is not created from an existing `FileStream`?

    a. `FileInfo`
    b. `StreamReader`
    c. `BufferedStream`

8. You can create a `FileStream` object with this statement:

```
FileStream fs = new FileStream(fname,
                   FileMode.OpenOrCreate,
                   FileAccess.Write,FileShare.None);
```

   Which one of the following statements creates an identical
   `FileStream` using an existing `FileInfo` object, `fi`?

   a. `fs = fi.OpenWrite();`
   b. `fs = fi.Create();`
   c. `fs = fi.CreateText();`

9. Indicate whether the following comparisons are true or false:

   a. `(string.Compare("Alpha","alpha") >0)`
   b. `(string.Compare("Alpha","alpha",true) ==0)`
   c. `(string.CompareOrdinal("Alpha","alpha")>0)`
   d. `(string.Equals("alpha","Alpha"))`

BUILDING WINDOWS FORMS APPLICATIONS

Topics in This Chapter

- *Introduction:* With just a few lines of code, you can build a Windows Forms (WinForms) application that demonstrates the basics of event handling and creating child forms.

- *Using Form Controls:* All controls inherit from the base `Control` class. The members of this class provide a uniform way of positioning, sizing, and modifying a control's appearance.

- *The Form Class:* The `Form` class includes custom properties that affect its appearance, and enable it to work with menus and manage child forms.

- *Message and Dialog Boxes:* A pop-up window to provide user interaction or information can be created as a message or dialog box.

- *MDI Forms:* A Multiple Document Interface (MDI) is a container that holds child forms. A main menu permits the forms to be organized, accessed, and manipulated.

- *Working with Menus:* .NET supports two types of menus: a main form menu and a context menu that can be associated with individual controls.

- *Adding Help to a Form:* Help buttons, ToolTips, and HTML Help are options for adding help to a form.

- *Form Inheritance:* Visual inheritance enables a form to be created quickly, by inheriting the interface elements and functionality from another form.

Chapter

This chapter is aimed at developers responsible for creating Graphical User Interface (GUI) applications for the desktop—as opposed to applications that run on a Web server or mobile device. The distinction is important because .NET provides separate class libraries for each type of application and groups them into distinct namespaces:

- `System.Windows.Forms`. Windows Forms (WinForms).
- `System.Web.UIWebControls`. Web Forms.
- `System.Web.UIMobileControls`. Mobile Forms for hand-held and pocket devices.

Although this chapter focuses on Windows Forms, it is important to recognize that modern applications increasingly have to support multiple environments. Acknowledging this, .NET strives to present a uniform "look and feel" for applications developed in each. The forms and controls in all three namespaces provide similar, but not identical, functionality. The knowledge you acquire in this chapter will shorten the learning curve required to develop .NET applications for the Web and mobile devices.

Developers usually rely on an Integrated Development Environment (IDE), such as Visual Studio, to develop GUI applications. This makes it easy to overlook the fact that a form is a class that inherits from other classes and has its own properties and methods. To provide a true understanding of forms, this chapter peers beneath the IDE surface at the class members and how their implementation defines and affects the behavior of the form. The discussion includes how to display forms, resize them, make them scrollable or transparent, create inherited forms, and have them react to mouse and keyboard actions.

This is not a chapter about the principles of GUI design, but it does demonstrate how adding amenities, such as Help files and a tab order among controls, improves form usability. Controls, by the way, are discussed only in a generic sense. A detailed look at specific controls is left to Chapter 7, "Windows Forms Controls."

6.1   Programming a Windows Form

All Windows Forms programs begin execution at a designated main window. This window is actually a `Form` object that inherits from the `System.Windows.Forms.Form` class. The initial window is displayed by passing an instance of it to the static `Application.Run` method.

The challenge for the developer is to craft an interface that meets the basic rule of design—*form follows function*. This means that a form's design should support its functionality to the greatest extent possible. To achieve this, a developer must understand the properties, methods, and events of the `Form` class, as well as those of the individual controls that are placed on the form.

Building a Windows Forms Application by Hand

Let's create a simple Windows application using a text editor and the C# compiler from the command line. This application, shown in Listing 6-1, consists of a single window with a button that pops up a message when the button is clicked. The simple exercise demonstrates how to create a form, add a control to it, and set up an event handler to respond to an event fired by the control.

Listing 6-1	Basic Windows Forms Application Built by Hand

```
using System;
using System.Windows.Forms;
using System.Drawing;
class MyWinApp
{
    static void Main()
    {
    // (1) Create form and invoke it
    Form mainForm = new SimpleForm();
    Application.Run(mainForm);
    }
}
```

Listing 6-1	Basic Windows Forms Application Built by Hand *(continued)*

```
// User Form derived from base class Form
class SimpleForm:Form
{
    private Button button1;
    public SimpleForm() {
        this.Text = "Hand Made Form";
        // (2) Create a button control and set some attributes
        button1 = new Button();
        button1.Location = new Point(96,112);
        button1.Size = new Size(72,24);
        button1.Text= "Status";
        this.Controls.Add(button1);
        // (3) Create delegate to call routine when click occurs
        button1.Click += new EventHandler(button1_Click);
    }
    void button1_Click(object sender, EventArgs e) {
        MessageBox.Show("Up and Running");
    }
}
```

Recall from Chapter 1, "Introduction to .NET and C#," that command-line compilation requires providing a target output file and a reference to any required assemblies. In this case, we include the System.Windows.Forms assembly that contains the necessary WinForms classes. To compile, save the preceding source code as winform.cs and enter the following statement at the command prompt:

```
csc /t:winform.exe /r:System.Windows.Forms.dll winform.cs
```

After it compiles, run the program by typing winform; the screen shown in Figure 6-1 should appear. The output consists of a parent form and a second form created by clicking the button. An important point to note is that the parent form cannot be accessed as long as the second window is open. This is an example of a *modal form*, where only the last form opened can be accessed. The alternative is a *modeless form*, in which a parent window spawns a child window and the user can access either the parent or child window(s). Both of these are discussed later.

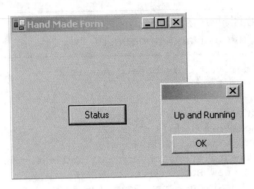

Figure 6-1   Introductory Windows application

The code breaks logically into three sections:

1. **Form Creation.**
   The parent form is an instance of the class `SimpleForm`, which inherits from `Form` and defines the form's custom features. The form—and program—is invoked by passing the instance to the `Application.Run` method.

2. **Create Button Control.**
   A control is placed on a form by creating an instance of the control and adding it to the form. Each form has a `Controls` property that returns a `Control.Collection` type that represents the collection of controls contained on a form. In this example, the `Controls.Add` method is used to add a button to the form. Note that a corresponding `Remove` method is also available to dynamically remove a control from its containing form. An IDE uses this same `Add` method when you drag a control onto a form at design time. However, if you want to add or delete controls at runtime, you will be responsible for the coding.

   Controls have a number of properties that govern their appearance. The two most basic ones are `Size` and `Location`. They are implemented as:

   ```
   button1.Size = new Size(72,24);    // width, height
   button1.Location = new Point(96,112); //x,y
   ```

   The struct `Size` has a constructor that takes the width and height as parameters; the constructor for `Point` accepts the x and y coordinates of the button within the container.

3. **Handle Button Click Event.**
   Event handling requires providing a method to respond to the event and creating a delegate that invokes the method when the event occurs (refer to Chapter 3, "Class Design in C#," for details of event handling). In this example, `button1_Click` is the method that processes the event. The delegate associated with the `Click` event is created with the following statement:

   ```
   button1.Click += new EventHandler(button1_Click);
   ```

   This statement creates an instance of the built-in delegate `EventHandler` and registers the method `button1_Click` with it.

Core Note

.NET 2.0 adds a feature known as Partial Types, which permits a class to be physically separated into different files. To create a partial class, place the keyword `partial` *in front of* `class` *in each file containing a segment of the class. Note that only one class declaration should specify* `Forms` *inheritance. The compilation process combines all the files into one class—identical to a single physical class. For Windows applications, partial classes seem something of a solution in search of a problem. However, for Web applications, they serve a genuine need, as is discussed in Chapter 16, "ASP.NET Web Forms and Controls."*

This exercise should emphasize the fact that working with forms is like working with any other classes in .NET. It requires gaining a familiarity with the class members and using standard C# programming techniques to access them.

6.2 Windows.Forms Control Classes

The previous examples have demonstrated how a custom form is derived from the `Windows.Forms.Form` class. Now, let's take a broader look at the class hierarchy from which the form derives and the functionality that each class offers (see Figure 6-2).

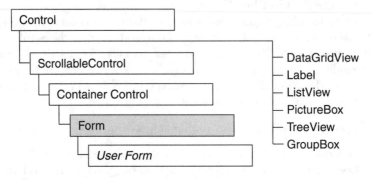

Figure 6-2   Windows Forms class hierarchy

The Control Class

It may seem counterintuitive that the Form class is below the Control class on the hierarchical chain, because a form typically contains controls. But the hierarchy represents inheritance, not containment. A Form is a container control, and the generic members of the Control class can be applied to it just as they are to a simple Label or TextBox.

System.Windows.Forms.dll contains more than fifty controls that are available for use on a Windows Form. A few that inherit directly from Control are listed in Figure 6-2. All controls share a core set of inherited properties, methods, and events. These members allow you to size and position the control; adorn it with text, colors, and style features; and respond to keyboard and mouse events. This chapter examines the properties that are common to all inheriting controls; Chapter 7 offers a detailed look at the individual controls and how to use their distinct features in applications.

Control Properties

Table 6-1 defines some of the properties common to most types that inherit from Control.

Table 6-1   Common Control Properties

Category	Property	Description
Size and position	Size	A Size object that exposes the width and height.
	Location	Location is a Point object that specifies the x and y coordinates of the top left of the control.

Table 6-1   Common Control Properties *(continued)*

Category	Property	Description
Size and position *(continued)*	`Width, Height, Top, Left, Right`	These `int` values are derived from the size and location of the object. For example, `Right` is equal to `Left + Width`; `Bottom` is equal to `Top + Height`.

	`Bounds`	`Bounds` is a rectangle that defines a control's position and size:
		`Button.Bounds =`
		    `new Rectangle (10,10,50,60)`

	`ClientRectangle`	`ClientRectangle` is a rectangle that represents the client area of the control—that is, the area excluding scroll bars, titles, and so on.
	`Anchor`	Specifies which edges of the container the control is anchored to. This is useful when the container is resized.
	`Dock`	Controls which edge of the container the control docks to.
Color and appearance	`BackColor, ForeColor`	Specifies the background and foreground color for the control. Color is specified as a static property of the `Color` structure.
	`BackGroundImage`	`BackGroundImage` specifies an image to be used in the background of the control.
Text	`Text`	`Text` associated with the control.
	`Font`	`Font` describes the characteristics of the text font: typeface, size, bold, and so on.
Focus	`TabIndex`	`int` value that indicates the tab order of this control within its container.
	`TabStop`	Boolean value that indicates whether this control can receive focus from the Tab key.
	`Focused`	Boolean value indicating whether a control has input focus.
	`Visible`	Boolean value indicating whether the control is displayed.
Keyboard and mouse	`MouseButtons`	Returns the current state of the mouse buttons (left, right, and middle).

Table 6-1   Common Control Properties *(continued)*

Category	Property	Description
Keyboard and mouse *(continued)*	MousePosition	Returns a Point type that specifies the cursor position.
	ModifierKeys	Indicates which of the modifier keys (Shift, Ctrl, Alt) is pressed.
	Cursor	Specifies the shape of the mouse pointer when it is over the control. Assigned value is a static property of the Cursors class. These include: .Hand .Cross UpArrow Default .Beam .Arrow WaitCursor
Runtime status	Handle	int value representing the handle of Windows control.
	Focused	bool value indicating whether the control has focus.

Working with Controls

When you drag a control onto a form, position it, and size it, VisualStudio.NET (VS.NET) automatically generates code that translates the visual design to the underlying property values. There are times, however, when a program needs to modify controls at runtime to hide them, move them, and even resize them. In fact, size and position are often based on the user's screen size, which can only be detected at runtime. An IDE cannot do this, so it is necessary that a programmer understand how these properties are used to design an effective control layout.

Size and Position

As we saw in the earlier example, the size of a control is determined by the Size object, which is a member of the System.Drawing namespace:

```
button1.Size = new Size(80,40);   // (width, height)
button2.Size = button1.Size;      // Assign size to second button
```

A control can be resized during runtime by assigning a new Size object to it. This code snippet demonstrates how the Click event handler method can be used to change the size of the button when it is clicked:

```
private void button1_Click(object sender, System.EventArgs e)
{
    MessageBox.Show("Up and Running");
    Button button1 = (Button) sender;   //Cast object to Button
    button1.Size = new Size(90,20);     //Dynamically resize
```

The `System.Drawing.Point` object can be used to assign a control's location. Its arguments set the x and y coordinates—in pixels—of the upper-left corner of a control. The x coordinate is the number of pixels from the left side of the container. The y coordinate is the number of pixels from the top of the container.

```
button1.Location = new Point(20,40);   // (x,y) coordinates
```

It is important to recognize that this location is relative to the control's container. Thus, if a button is inside a `GroupBox`, the button's location is relative to it and not the form itself. A control's `Location` also can be changed at runtime by assigning a new `Point` object.

Another approach is to set the size and location in one statement using the `Bounds` property:

```
button1.Bounds = new Rectangle(20,40, 100,80);
```

A `Rectangle` object is created with its upper-left corner at the x,y coordinates (20,40) and its lower-right coordinates at (100,80). This corresponds to a width of 80 pixels and a height of 40 pixels.

How to Anchor and Dock a Control

The `Dock` property is used to attach a control to one of the edges of its container. By default, most controls have docking set to `none`; some exceptions are the `StatusStrip/StatusBar` that is set to `Bottom` and the `ToolStrip/ToolBar` that is set to `Top`. The options, which are members of the `DockStyle` enumeration, are `Top`, `Bottom`, `Left`, `Right`, and `Fill`. The `Fill` option attaches the control to all four corners and resizes it as the container is resized. To attach a `TextBox` to the top of a form, use

```
TextBox1.Dock = DockStyle.Top;
```

Figure 6-3 illustrates how docking affects a control's size and position as the form is resized. This example shows four text boxes docked, as indicated.

Resizing the form does not affect the size of controls docked on the left or right. However, controls docked to the top and bottom are stretched or shrunk horizontally so that they take all the space available to them.

Core Note

The `Form` class and all other container controls have a `DockPadding` property that can be set to control the amount of space (in pixels) between the container's edge and the docked control.

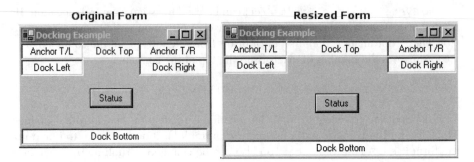

Figure 6-3   Control resizing and positioning using the Dock property

The Anchor property allows a control to be placed in a fixed position relative to a combination of the top, left, right, or bottom edge of its container. Figure 6-4 illustrates the effects of anchoring.

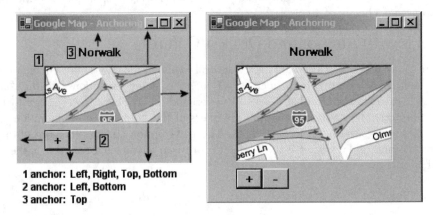

Figure 6-4   How anchoring affects the resizing and positioning of controls

The distance between the controls' anchored edges remains unchanged as the form is stretched. The PictureBox (1) is stretched horizontally and vertically so that it remains the same distance from all edges; the Panel (2) control maintains a constant distance from the left and bottom edge; and the Label (3), which is anchored only to the top, retains its distance from the top, left, and right edges of the form.

The code to define a control's anchor position sets the Anchor property to values of the AnchorStyles enumeration (Bottom, Left, None, Right, Top). Multiple values are combined using the OR (|) operator:

```
btnPanel.Anchor = (AnchorStyles.Bottom | AnchorStyles.Left);
```

Tab Order and Focus

Tab order defines the sequence in which the input focus is given to controls when the Tab key is pressed. The default sequence is the order in which the controls are added to the container.

The tab order should anticipate the logical sequence in which users expect to input data and thus guide them through the process. The form in Figure 6-5 represents such a design: The user can tab from the first field down to subsequent fields and finally to the button that invokes the final action.

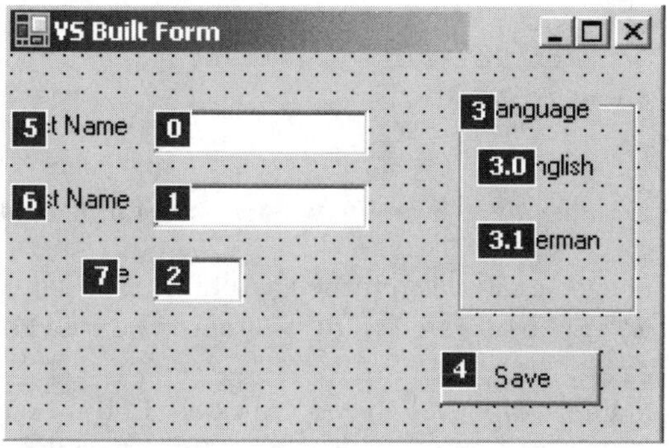

Figure 6-5 Tab order for controls on a form

Observe two things in the figure: First, even though labels have a tab order, they are ignored and never gain focus; and second, controls in a container have a tab order that is relative to the container—not the form.

A control's tab order is determined by the value of its `TabIndex` property:

```
TextBox1.TabIndex = 0;   //First item in tab sequence
```

In VS.NET, you can set this property directly with the Property Manager, or by selecting ViewTabOrder and clicking the boxes over each control to set the value. If you do not want a control to be included in the tab order, set its `TabStop` value to `false`. This does not, however, prevent it from receiving focus from a mouse click.

When a form is loaded, the input focus is on the control (that accepts mouse or keyboard input) with the lowest `TabIndex` value. During execution, the focus can be given to a selected control using the `Focus` method:

```
if(textBox1.CanFocus)
{ textBox1.Focus(); }
```

Iterating Through Controls on a Form

All controls on a form are contained in a `Controls` collection. By enumerating through this collection, it is possible to examine each control, identify it by name and type, and modify properties as needed. One common use is to clear the value of selected fields on a form in a refresh operation. This short example examines each control in Figure 6-5 and displays its name and type:

```
int ctrlCt = this.Controls.Count;    //  8
foreach (Control ct in this.Controls)
{
   object ob = ct.GetType();
   MessageBox.Show(ob.ToString());   //Displays type as string
   MessageBox.Show(ct.Name);
}
```

There are several things to be aware of when enumerating control objects:

- The type of each control is returned as a fully qualified name. For example, a `TextBox` is referred to as `System.Forms.Form.TextBox`.
- Only a container's top-level objects are listed. In this example, the `Controls.Count` value is 8 rather than 10 because the `GroupBox` is counted as one control and its child controls are excluded.
- You can use a control's `HasChildren` property to determine if it is a container. Listing 6-2 uses recursion to list all child controls.

Listing 6-2	Enumerate All Controls on a Form Recursively

```
void IterateThroughControls(Control parent)
{
   foreach (Control c in parent.Controls)
   {
      MessageBox.Show(c.ToString());
      if(c.HasChildren)
      {
         IterateThroughControls(c);
      }
   }
}
```

Applying this code to Figure 6-5 results in all controls on the main form being listed hierarchically. A control is listed followed by any child it may have.

Control Events

When you push a key on the keyboard or click the mouse, the control that is the target of this action fires an event to indicate the specific action that has occurred. A registered event handling routine then responds to the event and formulates what action to take.

The first step in handling an event is to identify the delegate associated with the event. You must then register the event handling method with it, and make sure the method's signature matches the parameters specified by the delegate. Table 6-2 summarizes the information required to work with mouse and keyboard triggered events.

Table 6-2   Control Events

Event	Built-In Delegate/ Parameters	Description
Click, DoubleClick, MouseEnter, MouseLeave, MouseHover, MouseWheel	EventHandler (object sender, EventArgs e)	Events triggered by clicking, double clicking, or moving the mouse.
MouseDown, MouseUp, MouseMove	MouseEventHandler (object sender, MouseEventArgs)	Events triggered by mouse and mouse button motions. Note that this event is not triggered if the mouse action occurs within a control in the current container.
KeyUp, KeyDown	KeyEventHandler (object sender, KeyEventArgs e)	Events triggered by key being raised or lowered.
KeyPress	KeyPressEventHandler (object sender, KeyPressEventArgs e)	Event triggered by pressing any key.

Handling Mouse Events

In addition to the familiar Click and DoubleClick events, all Windows Forms controls inherit the MouseHover, MouseEnter, and MouseLeave events. The latter two are fired when the mouse enters and leaves the confines of a control. They are useful for creating a MouseOver effect that is so common to Web pages.

To illustrate this, let's consider an example that changes the background color on a text box when a mouse passes over it. The following code sets up delegates to call OnMouseEnter and OnMouseLeave to perform the background coloring:

```
TextBox userID = new TextBox();
userID.MouseEnter += new EventHandler(OnMouseEnter);
userID.MouseLeave += new EventHandler(OnMouseLeave);
```

The event handler methods match the signature of the EventHandler delegate and cast the sender parameter to a Control type to access its properties.

```
private void OnMouseEnter(object sender, System.EventArgs e){
    Control ctrl = (Control) sender;
    ctrl.BackColor= Color.Bisque;
}
private void OnMouseLeave(object sender, System.EventArgs e){
    Control ctrl = (Control) sender;
    ctrl.BackColor= Color.White;
}
```

Core Note

It is possible to handle events by overriding the default event handlers of the base Control class. These methods are named using the pattern Oneventname—for example, OnMouseDown, OnMouseMove, and so on. To be consistent with .NET, the delegate approach is recommended over this. It permits a control to specify multiple event handlers for an event, and it also permits a single event handler to process multiple events.

The delegates for the MouseDown, MouseUp, and MouseMove events take a second argument of the MouseEventArgs type rather than the generic EventArgs type. This type reveals additional status information about a mouse via the properties shown in Table 6-3.

The properties in this table are particularly useful for applications that must track mouse movement across a form. Prime examples are graphics programs that rely on mouse location and button selection to control onscreen drawing. To illustrate, Listing 6-3 is a simple drawing program that draws a line on a form's surface, beginning at the point where the mouse key is pressed and ending where it is raised. To make it a bit more interesting, the application draws the line in black if the left button is dragged, and in red if the right button is dragged.

Table 6-3 Properties of `MouseEventArgs`

Property	Description
`Button`	Indicates which mouse button was pressed. The attribute value is defined by the `MouseButtons` enumeration: `Left`, `Middle`, `None`, `Right`
`Clicks`	Number of clicks since last event.
`Delta`	Number of detents the mouse wheel rotates. A positive number means it's moving forward; a negative number shows backward motion.
`X, Y`	Mouse coordinates relative to the container's upper-left corner. This is equivalent to the control's `MousePosition` property.

Listing 6-3   Using Mouse Events to Draw on a Form

```
using System;
using System.Windows.Forms;
using System.Drawing;
class MyWinApp
{
   static void Main() {
   Form mainForm = new DrawingForm();
   Application.Run(mainForm);
   }
}
// User Form derived from base class Form
class DrawingForm:Form
{
   Point lastPoint = Point.Empty; // Save coordinates
   public Pen myPen;       //Defines color of line
   public DrawingForm()
   {
      this.Text = "Drawing Pad";
      // reate delegates to call MouseUp and MouseDown
      this.MouseDown += new MouseEventHandler(OnMouseDown);
      this.MouseUp   += new MouseEventHandler(OnMouseUp);
   }
```

Listing 6-3   Using Mouse Events to Draw on a Form *(continued)*

```
    private void OnMouseDown(object sender, MouseEventArgs e)
    {
       myPen = (e.Button==MouseButtons.Right)? Pens.Red:
             Pens.Black;
       lastPoint.X = e.X;
       lastPoint.Y = e.Y;
    }

    private void OnMouseUp(object sender, MouseEventArgs e)
    {
       // Create graphics object
       Graphics g = this.CreateGraphics();
       if (lastPoint != Point.Empty)
          g.DrawLine(myPen, lastPoint.X,lastPoint.Y,e.X,e.Y);
       lastPoint.X = e.X;
       lastPoint.Y = e.Y;
       g.Dispose();
    }
}
```

Even without an understanding of .NET graphics, the role of the graphics-related classes should be self-evident. A `Graphics` object is created to do the actual drawing using its `DrawLine` method. The parameters for this method are the `Pen` object that defines the color and the coordinates of the line to be drawn. When a button is pressed, the program saves the coordinate and sets `myPen` based on which button is pressed: a red pen for the right button and black for the left. When the mouse button is raised, the line is drawn from the previous coordinate to the current location. The `MouseEventArgs` object provides all the information required to do this.

Handling Keyboard Events

Keyboard events are also handled by defining a delegate to call a custom event handling method. Two arguments are passed to the event handler: the `sender` argument identifies the object that raised the event and the second argument contains fields describing the event. For the `KeyPress` event, this second argument is of the `Key-PressEventArgs` type. This type contains a `Handled` field that is set to `true` by the event handling routine to indicate it has processed the event. Its other property is `KeyChar`, which identifies the key that is pressed.

`KeyChar` is useful for restricting the input that a field accepts. This code segment demonstrates how easy it is to limit a field's input to digits. When a non-digit is entered, `Handled` is set to `true`, which prevents the form engine from displaying the character. Otherwise, the event handling routine does nothing and the character is displayed.

```
private void OnKeyPress(object sender,  KeyPressEventArgs e)
{
   if (! char.IsDigit(e.KeyChar)) e.Handled = true;
}
```

The `KeyPress` event is only fired for printable character keys; it ignores non-character keys such as Alt or Shift. To recognize all keystrokes, it is necessary to turn to the `KeyDown` and `KeyUp` events. Their event handlers receive a `KeyEvent-Args` type parameter that identifies a single keystroke or combination of keystrokes. Table 6-4 lists the important properties provided by `KeyEventArgs`.

Table 6-4   `KeyEventArgs` Properties

Member	Description
Alt, Control, Shift	Boolean value that indicates whether the Alt, Control, or Shift key was pressed.
Handled	Boolean value that indicates whether an event was handled.
KeyCode	Returns the key code for the event. This code is of the `Keys` enumeration type.
KeyData	Returns the key data for the event. This is also of the `Keys` enumeration type, but differs from the `KeyCode` in that it recognizes multiple keys.
Modifiers	Indicates which combination of modifier keys (Alt, Ctrl, and Shift) was pressed.

A few things to note:

- The `Alt`, `Control`, and `Shift` properties are simply shortcuts for comparing the `KeyCode` value with the `Alt`, `Control`, or `Shift` member of the `Keys` enumeration.
- `KeyCode` represents a single key value; `KeyData` contains a value for a single key or combination of keys pressed.
- The `Keys` enumeration is the secret to key recognition because its members represent all keys. If using Visual Studio.NET, Intellisense lists all of its members when the enum is used in a comparison; otherwise, you need to refer to online documentation for the exact member name because the names are not always what you expect. For example, digits are designated by `D1`, `D2`, and so on.

The preceding code segment showed how to use `KeyPress` to ensure a user presses only number keys (0–9). However, it does not prevent one from pasting non-numeric data using the Ctrl-V key combination. A solution is to use the `KeyDown` event to detect this key sequence and set a flag notifying the `KeyPress` event handler to ignore the attempt to paste.

In this example, two event handlers are registered to be called when a user attempts to enter data into a text box using the keyboard. `KeyDown` is invoked first, and it sets paste to `true` if the user is pushing the Ctrl-V key combination. The `KeyPress` event handler uses this flag to determine whether to accept the key strokes.

```
private bool paste;

//Register event handlers for TextBox t.
//They should be registered in this order,
//because the last registered is the
//first executed
t.KeyPress += new KeyPressEventHandler(OnKeyPress);
t.KeyDown  += new KeyEventHandler(OnKeyDown);

private void OnKeyDown(object sender, KeyEventArgs e)
{
if (e.Modifiers == Keys.Control  && e.KeyCode == Keys.V)
{
   paste=true; //Flag indicating paste attempt
   string msg = string.Format("Modifier: {0} \nKeyCode: {1}
      \nKeyData: {2}", e.Modifiers.ToString(),
        e.KeyCode.ToString(), e.KeyData.ToString());
   MessageBox.Show(msg);       //Display property values
}

private void OnKeyPress(object sender, KeyPressEventArgs e)
{
   if (paste==true)  e.Handled = true;
}
```

This program displays the following values for the selected `KeyEventArgs` properties when Ctrl-V is pressed:

```
Modifier:  Control
KeyCode:   V
KeyData:   Control, V
```

6.3   The Form Class

The Form object inherits all the members of the Control class as well as the ScrollableControl class, which provides properties that enable scrolling. To this it adds a large number of properties that enable it to control its appearance, work with child forms, create modal forms, display menus, and interact with the desktop via tool and status bars. Table 6-5 shows a selected list of these properties.

Table 6-5   Selected Form Properties

Category	Property	Description
Appearance	FormBorderStyle	Gets or sets the border style of the form. It is defined by the FormBorderStyle enumeration: Fixed3D None FixedSingle Sizable FixedDialog
	ControlBox	Boolean value that determines whether the menu icon in the left corner of a form and the close button on the upper right are shown.
	MaximizeBox MinimizeBox	Boolean value that indicates whether these buttons are displayed on the form.
	Opacity	Gets or sets the opacity of the form and all of its controls. The maximum value (least transparent) is 1.0. Does not work with Windows 95/98.
	TransparencyKey	A color that represents transparent areas on the form. Any control or portion of the form that has a back color equal to this color is not displayed. Clicking this transparent area sends the event to any form below it.
Size and position	AutoScale	Indicates whether the form adjusts its size to accommodate the size of the font used.
	ClientSize	Size of the form excluding borders and the title bar.
	DesktopLocation	A Point type that indicates where the form is located on the desktop window.

Table 6-5   Selected Form Properties *(continued)*

Category	Property	Description
Size and position *(continued)*	StartPosition	Specifies the initial position of a form. It takes a FormStartPosition enum value: CenterParent—Centered within bounds of parent form. CenterScreen—Centered within the display. Manual—Use the DeskTopLocation value. Windows DefaultLocation—Windows sets value.
	MinimumSize MaximumSize	A Size object that designates the maximum and minimum size for the form. A value of (0,0) indicates no minimum or maximum.
	ShowInTaskBar	Boolean value specifying whether application is represented in Windows task bar. Default is true.
	TopLevel TopMost	Indicates whether to display the form as a TopLevel window or TopMost window. A top-level window has no parent; top-most form is always displayed on top of all other non-TopMost forms.
	WindowState	Indicates how the form is displayed on startup. It takes a value from the FormWindowState enumeration: Maximized, Minimized, or Normal.
Owner forms	Owner	The form designated as the owner of the form.
	OwnedForms	A Form array containing the forms owned by a form.

Setting a Form's Appearance

The four properties shown in Figure 6-6 control which buttons and icon are present on the top border of a form. The Icon property specifies the .ico file to be used as the icon in the left corner; the ControlBox value determines whether the icon and close button are displayed (true) or not displayed (false); similarly, the Maximize-Box and MinimizeBox determine whether their associated buttons appear.

The purpose of these properties is to govern functionality more than appearance. For example, it often makes sense to suppress the minimize and maximize buttons on modal forms in order to prevent a user from maximizing the form and hiding the underlying parent form.

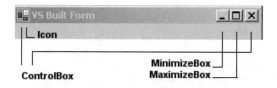

Figure 6-6   Properties to control what appears on the title bar

Form Opacity

A form's opacity property determines its level of transparency. Values ranges from 0 to 1.0, where anything less than 1.0 results in partial transparency that allows elements beneath the form to be viewed. Most forms work best with a value of 1.0, but adjusting opacity can be an effective way to display child or TopMost forms that hide an underlying form. A common approach is to set the opacity of such a form to 1.0 when it has focus, and reduce the opacity when it loses focus. This technique is often used with search windows that float on top of the document they are searching.

Let's look at how to set up a form that sets its opacity to 1 when it is active and to .8 when it is not the active form. To do this, we take advantage of the Deactivate and Activated events that are triggered when a form loses or gains focus. We first set up the delegates to call the event handling routines:

```
this.Deactivate += new System.EventHandler(Form_Deactivate);
this.Activated  += new System.EventHandler(Form_Activate);
```

The code for the corresponding event handlers is trivial:

```
void Form_Deactivate(object sender, EventArgs e)
{    this.Opacity= .8;    }

void Form_Activate(object sender, EventArgs e)
{    this.Opacity= 1;    }
```

Form Transparency

Opacity affects the transparency of an entire form. There is another property, TransparencyKey, which can be used to make only selected areas of a form totally transparent. This property designates a pixel color that is rendered as transparent when the form is drawn. The effect is to create a hole in the form that makes any area below the form visible. In fact, if you click a transparent area, the event is recognized by the form below.

The most popular use of transparency is to create non-rectangular forms. When used in conjunction with a border style of FormBorderStyle.None to remove the title bar, a form of just about any geometric shape can be created. The next example illustrates how to create and use the cross-shaped form in Figure 6-7.

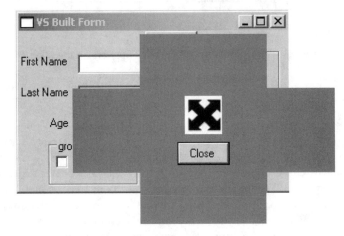

Figure 6-7   Form using transparency to create irregular appearance

The only requirement in creating the shape of the form is to lay out the transparent areas in the same color as the transparency key color. Be certain to select a color that will not be used elsewhere on the form. A standard approach is to set the back color of the form to the transparency key color, and draw an image in a different color that it will appear as the visible form.

To create the form in Figure 6-7, place `Panel` controls in each corner of a standard form and set their `BackColor` property to `Color.Red`. The form is created and displayed using this code:

```
CustomForm myForm = new CustomForm();
myForm.TransparencyKey = Color.Red;
myForm.FormBorderStyle= FormBorderStyle.None;
myForm.Show();
```

This achieves the effect of making the panel areas transparent and removing the title bar. With the title bar gone, it is necessary to provide a way for the user to move the form. This is where the mouse event handling discussed earlier comes to the rescue.

At the center of the form is a multiple arrow image displayed in a `PictureBox` that the user can click and use to drag the form. Listing 6-4 shows how the `Mouse-Down`, `MouseUp`, and `MouseMove` events are used to implement form movement.

Listing 6-4	Using Form Transparency to Create a Non-Rectangular Form

```csharp
using System;
using System.Drawing;
using System.Collections;
using System.ComponentModel;
using System.Windows.Forms;
public class CustomForm : Form
{
   private Point lastPoint = Point.Empty;   //Save mousedown
   public CustomForm()
   {
      InitializeComponent();   // set up form
      //Associate mouse events with pictureBox
      pictureBox1.MouseDown += new MouseEventHandler(
            OnMouseDown);
      pictureBox1.MouseUp   += new MouseEventHandler(OnMouseUp);
      pictureBox1.MouseMove += new MouseEventHandler(
            OnMouseMove);
   }
   private void OnMouseDown(object sender, MouseEventArgs e)
   {
      lastPoint.X = e.X;
      lastPoint.Y = e.Y;
   }

   private void OnMouseUp(object sender, MouseEventArgs e)
   {
      lastPoint = Point.Empty;
   }

   //Move the form in response to the mouse being dragged
   private void OnMouseMove(object sender, MouseEventArgs e)
   {
      if (lastPoint != Point.Empty)
      {
         //Move form in response to mouse movement
         int xInc = e.X - lastPoint.X;
         int yInc = e.Y - lastPoint.Y;
         this.Location = new Point(this.Left + xInc,
                     this.Top+yInc);
      }
   }
```

Listing 6-4	Using Form Transparency to Create a Non-Rectangular Form (continued)

```
    // Close Window
    private void button1_Click(object sender, System.EventArgs e)
    {
        this.Close();
    }
}
```

The logic is straightforward. When the user clicks the PictureBox, the coordinates are recorded as lastPoint. As the user moves the mouse, the Location property of the form is adjusted to reflect the difference between the new coordinates and the original saved location. When the mouse button is raised, lastPoint is cleared. Note that a complete implementation should also include code to handle form resizing.

Setting Form Location and Size

The initial location of a form is determined directly or indirectly by its StartPosition property. As described in Table 6-6, it takes its value from the FormStartPosition enumeration. These values allow it to be placed in the center of the screen, in the center of a parent form, at a Windows default location, or at an arbitrarily selected location. Manual offers the greatest flexibility because it allows the program to set the location.

The initial location is normally set in the Form.Load event handler. This example loads the form 200 pixels to the right of the upper-left corner of the screen:

```
private void opaque_Load(object sender, System.EventArgs e)
{
    this.DesktopLocation = new Point(200,0);
}
```

The form's initial location can also be set by the form that creates and displays the form object:

```
opaque opForm = new opaque();
opForm.Opacity = 1;
opForm.TopMost = true;    //Always display form on top
opForm.StartPosition = FormStartPosition.Manual;
opForm.DesktopLocation = new Point(10,10);
opForm.Show();
```

This code creates an instance of the form opaque and sets its TopMost property so that the form is always displayed on top of other forms in the same application. The DeskTopLocation property sets the form's initial location. For it to work, however, the StartPostion property must first be set to FormStartPosition.Manual.

Core Note

The DesktopLocation property sets coordinates within a screen's working area, which is the area not occupied by a task bar. The Location property of the Control class sets the coordinates relative to the upper-left edge of the control's container.

A form's size can be set using either its Size or ClientSize property. The latter is usually preferred because it specifies the workable area of the form—the area that excludes the title bar, scrollbars, and any edges. This property is set to an instance of a Size object:

```
this.ClientSize = new System.Drawing.Size(208, 133);
```

It is often desirable to position or size a form relative to the primary (.NET supports multiple screens for an application) screen size. The screen size is available through the Screen.PrimaryScreen.WorkingArea property. This returns a rectangle that represents the size of the screen excluding task bars, docked toolbars, and docked windows. Here is an example that uses the screen size to set a form's width and height:

```
int w = Screen.PrimaryScreen.WorkingArea.Width;
int h = Screen.PrimaryScreen.WorkingArea.Height;
this.ClientSize = new Size(w/4,h/4);
```

After a form is active, you may want to control how it can be resized. The aptly named MinimumSize and MaximumSize properties take care of this. In the following example, the maximum form size is set to one-half the width and height of the working screen area:

```
//w and h are the screen's width and height
this.MaximumSize = new Size(w/2,h/2);
this.MinimumSize = new Size(200, 150);
```

Setting both width and height to zero removes any size restrictions.

Displaying Forms

After a main form is up and running, it can create instances of new forms and display them in two ways: using the `Form.ShowDialog` method or the `Form.Show` method inherited from the `Control` class. `Form.ShowDialog` displays a form as a modal dialog box. When activated, this type of form does not relinquish control to other forms in the application until it is closed. Dialog boxes are discussed at the end of this section.

`Form.Show` displays a modeless form, which means that the form has no relationship with the creating form, and the user is free to select the new or original form. If the creating form is not the main form, it can be closed without affecting the new form; closing the main form automatically closes all forms in an application.

The Life Cycle of a Modeless Form

A form is subject to a finite number of activities during its lifetime: It is created, displayed, loses and gains focus, and finally is closed. Most of these activities are accompanied by one or more events that enable the program to perform necessary tasks associated with the event. Table 6-6 summarizes these actions and events.

Table 6-6   The Life Cycle of a Modeless Form

Action	Events Triggered	Description
Form object created		The form's constructor is called. In Visual Studio, the `InitializeComponent` method is called to initialize the form.
Form displayed: `Form.Show()`	`Form.Load` `Form.Activated`	The `Load` event is called first, followed by the `Activated` event.
Form activated	`Form.Activated`	This occurs when the user selects the form. This becomes an "active" form.
Form deactivated	`Form.Deactivate`	Form is deactivated when it loses focus.
Form closed	`Form.Deactivate` `Form.Closing` `Form.Closed`	Form is closed by executing `Form.Close` or clicking on the form's close button.

Let's look at some of the code associated with these events.

Creating and Displaying a Form

When one form creates another form, there are coding requirements on both sides. The created form must set up code in its constructor to perform initialization and create controls. In addition, delegates should be set up to call event handling routines. If using Visual Studio.NET, any user initialization code should be placed after the call to InitializeComponent.

For the class that creates the new form object, the most obvious task is the creation and display of the object. A less obvious task may be to ensure that only one instance of the class is created because you may not want a new object popping up each time a button on the original form is clicked. One way to manage this is to take advantage of the Closed event that occurs when a created form is closed (another way, using OwnedForms, is discussed shortly). If the form has not been closed, a new instance is not created. The code that follows illustrates this.

An EventHandler delegate is set up to notify a method when the new form, opForm, is closed. A flag controls what action occurs when the button to create or display the form is pushed. If an instance of the form does not exist, it is created and displayed; if it does exist, the Form.Activate method is used to give it focus.

```
//Next statement is at beginning of form's code
public opaque opForm;
bool closed = true;    //Flag to indicate if opForm exists
//Create new form or give focus to existing one
private void button1_Click(object sender, System.EventArgs e)
{
    if (closed)
    {
        closed = false;
        opForm = new opaque();
        //Call OnOpClose when new form closes
        opForm.Closed += new EventHandler(OnOpClose);
        opForm.Show();       //Display new form object
    } else {
        opForm.Activate();   //Give focus to form
    }
}
//Event handler called when child form is closed
private void OnOpClose(object sender, System.EventArgs e)
{
    closed = true;    //Flag indicating form is closed
}
```

Form Activation and Deactivation

A form becomes active when it is first shown or later, when the user clicks on it or moves to it using an Alt-Tab key to iterate through the task bar. This fires the form's `Activated` event. Conversely, when the form loses focus—through closing or dese-lection—the `Deactivate` event occurs. In the next code segment, the `Deactivate` event handler changes the text on a button to Resume and disables the button; the `Activated` event handler re-enables the button.

```
this.Deactivate += new System.EventHandler(Form_Deactivate);
this.Activated  += new System.EventHandler(Form_Activate);
//
void Form_Deactivate(object sender, EventArgs e)
{   button1.Enabled = false;
    button1.Text = "Resume";         }
void Form_Activate(object sender, EventArgs e)
{   button1.Enabled = true;    }
```

Closing a Form

The `Closing` event occurs as a form is being closed and provides the last opportunity to perform some cleanup duties or prevent the form from closing. This event uses the `CancelEventHandler` delegate to invoke event handling methods. The delegate defines a `CancelEventArgs` parameter that contains a `Cancel` property, which is set to `true` to cancel the closing. In this example, the user is given a final prompt before the form closes:

```
this.Closing += new CancelEventHandler(Form_Closing);
void Form_Closing(object sender, CancelEventArgs e)
{
   if(MessageBox.Show("Are you sure you want to Exit?", "",
      MessageBoxButtons.YesNo) == DialogResult.No)
   {
      //Cancel the closing of the form
      e.Cancel = true;
   }
}
```

Forms Interaction—A Sample Application

When multiple form objects have been created, there must be a way for one form to access the state and contents of controls on another form. It's primarily a matter of setting the proper access modifiers to expose fields and properties on each form. To illustrate, let's build an application that consists of two modeless forms (see Figure 6-8). The main form contains two controls: a `Textbox` that holds the document being processed and a Search button that, when clicked, passes control to a search form. The search form has a `Textbox` that accepts text to be searched for in the main form's document. By default, the search phrase is any highlighted text in the document; it can also be entered directly by the user.

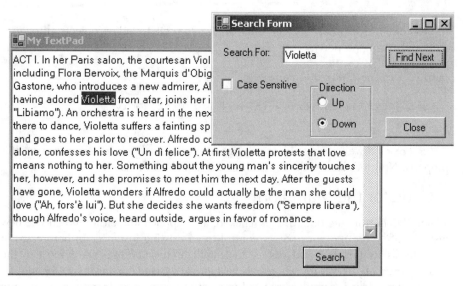

Figure 6-8   Text search application using multiple forms

When the Find Next button is pushed, the application searches for the next occurrence of the search string in the main document. If an occurrence is located, it is highlighted. To make it more interesting, the form includes options to search forward or backward and perform a case-sensitive or case-insensitive search.

The main challenge in developing this application is to determine how each form makes the content of its controls available to the other form. `DocForm`, the main form, must expose the contents of `documentText` so that the search form can search the text in it and highlight an occurrence of matching text. The search form, `SearchForm`, must expose the contents of `txtSearch`, the `TextBox` containing the search phrase, so that the main form can set it to the value of any highlighted text before passing control to the form.

`DocForm` shares the contents of `documentText` through a text box field `myText` that is assigned the value of `documentText` when the form loads. Setting `myText` to `public static` enables the search form to access the text box properties by simply qualifying them with `DocForm.myText`.

```
public static TextBox myText;    //Declare public variable

private void docForm_Load(object sender, System.EventArgs e)
{
    myText = documentText;
}
```

SearchForm exposes the contents of txtSearch to other objects through a write-only string property.

```
public String SearchPhrase
{
    set { txtSearch.Text = value;}    //Write Only
}
```

DocForm, as well as any object creating an instance of SearchForm, can set this property. Now let's look at the remaining code details of the two forms.

Code for the Main Form

When the button on DocForm is clicked, the application either creates a new instance of SearchForm or passes control to an existing instance. In both cases, it first checks its text box and passes any highlighted text (SelectedText) to the SearchForm object via its SearchPhrase property (see Listing 6-5). Techniques described in earlier examples are used to create the object and set up a delegate to notify the DocForm object when the search form object closes.

Listing 6-5	Method to Pass Control to Search Form Instance

```
private void btnSearch_Click(object sender, System.EventArgs e)
{
    //Create instance of search form if it does not exist
    if (closed)
    {
        closed= false;
        searchForm = new SearchForm();    //Create instance
        searchForm.TopMost = true;
        searchForm.Closed += new EventHandler(onSearchClosed);
        searchForm.StartPosition = FormStartPosition.Manual;
        searchForm.DesktopLocation = new Point(this.Right-200,
                this.Top-20);
        searchForm.SearchPhrase = documentText.SelectedText;
        searchForm.Show();
```

Listing 6-5	Method to Pass Control to Search Form Instance *(continued)*

```
    } else {
        searchForm.SearchPhrase = documentText.SelectedText;
        searchForm.Activate();
    }
}
private void onSearchClosed(object sender, System.EventArgs e)
{    closed= true;    }
```

Code for the Search Form

Listing 6-6 displays the code executed when the Find Next button is clicked. The search for the next occurrence of the search string can proceed up the document using the LastIndexOf method or down the document using IndexOf. Logic is also included to ignore or recognize case sensitivity.

Listing 6-6	Search for Matching Text on Another Form

```
private void btnFind_Click(object sender, System.EventArgs e)
{
    int ib;        //Index to indicate position of match
    string myBuff = DocForm.myText.Text; //Text box contents
    string searchText= this.txtSearch.Text;   //Search string
    int ln = searchText.Length;          //Length of search string
    if (ln>0)
    {
        //Get current location of selected text
        int selStart = DocForm.myText.SelectionStart;
        if (selStart >= DocForm.myText.Text.Length)
        {
            ib = 0;
        } else {
            ib = selStart + ln;
        }
        if (!this.chkCase.Checked) //Case-insensitive search
        {
            searchText = searchText.ToUpper();
            myBuff = myBuff.ToUpper();
        }
```

| Listing 6-6 | Search for Matching Text on Another Form *(continued)* |

```
      if (this.radDown.Checked)ib =
          myBuff.IndexOf(searchText,ib);
      if (this.radUp.Checked && ib>ln-1)ib =
              myBuff.LastIndexOf(searchText,ib-2,ib-1);
      if (ib >= 0)           //Highlight text on main form
      {
        DocForm.myText.SelectionStart = ib;
        DocForm.myText.SelectionLength = txtSearch.Text.Length;
      }
   }
}
```

Owner and Owned Forms

When a form displays an instance of a modeless form, it does not by default create an explicit relationship between itself and the new form. The forms operate autonomously: They either can be closed (except for a main form, which causes all forms to be closed) or minimized without affecting the other; and the creator form has no easy way to distinguish among instances of the forms it has launched.

Often, however, one form does have a dependency on the other. In the preceding example, the floating search window exists only as a companion to a document that it searches. Its relationship to the form that created it is referred to as an owner-owned relationship. In .NET, this can be more than just a logical relationship. A form has an Owner property that can be set to the instance of the form that "owns" it. After this relationship is formally established, the behavior of the owner and owned form(s) is linked. For example, the owned form is always visually on top of its owner form. This eliminates the need to make SearchForm a TopMost form in our preceding example.

An owner-owned relationship is easily established by setting the Owner property of a newly created form to the form that is creating it.

```
opaque opForm = new opaque();
opForm.Owner = this;    //Current form now owns new form
opForm.Show();
```

This relationship affects the user's interaction with the form in three ways: The owned form is always on top of the owner form even if the owner is active; closing the owner form also closes the owned form; and minimizing the owner form minimizes all owned forms and results in only one icon in the task bar.

Another advantage of the owner-owned relationship is that an owner form has an OwnedForms collection that contains all the owned forms it creates. The following example demonstrates how an owner form creates two owned forms, opForm and opForm2, and then enumerates the collection to set the caption of each form before displaying it:

```
opaque opForm = new opaque();
opForm.Owner = this;  //Set current form to owner form
opaque opForm2 = new opaque();
opForm2.Owner = this; //Set current form to owner form
for (int ndx=0; ndx<this.OwnedForms.Length; ndx++)
{
   myForms.Text = "Owner: Form1 - Form"+ndx.ToString();
   myForms.Show();
}
```

Note that although modal forms exhibit the features of an owned form, the Owner property must be set to establish an explicit relationship.

Message and Dialog Boxes

.NET provides a set of classes and enumerations that make it easy to create a message or dialog window to interact with a user. The simplest approach is to use the MessageBox class and its versatile Show method. The other approach is to create a custom form and invoke it with the form's ShowDialog method. Both of these methods create modal forms.

MessageBox

The MessageBox class uses its Show method to display a message box that may contain text, buttons, and even an icon. The Show method includes these overloads:

Syntax:

```
static DialogResult Show(string msg)
static DialogResult Show(string msg, string caption)
static DialogResult Show(string msg, string caption,
      MessageBoxButtons buttons)
static DialogResult Show(string msg, string caption,
      MessageBoxButtons buttons, MessageBoxIcon icon,
      MessageBoxDefaultButton defBtn)
```

DialogResult. The method returns one of the enum members Abort, Cancel, Ignore, No, None, OK, Retry, and Yes.

MessageBoxIcon. This enumeration places an icon on the message box. Members include Asterisk, Error, Exclamation, Hand, Information, None, Question, Stop, and Warning.

MessageBoxButtons. This is an enumeration with values that determine which buttons are displayed in the message box. Its members are AbortRetryIgnore, OK, OKCancel, RetryCancel, YesNo, and YesNoCancel. The buttons correspond to the text in the member name. For example, YesNo results in a form with a Yes and No button.

MessageBoxDefaultButton. This an enumeration that defines the default button on the screen. Its members are Button1, Button2, and Button3.

Figure 6-9, which is created with the following statement, provides a visual summary of these parameter options:

```
MessageBox.Show("OK to Close", "Game Status",
        MessageBoxButtons.YesNoCancel,MessageBoxIcon.Question,
        MessageBoxDefaultButton.Button2 );
```

Figure 6-9 MessageBox.Show example

Clicking one of the three buttons returns a value of DialogResult.Yes, DialogResult.No, or DialogResult.Cancel, respectively.

ShowDialog

The ShowDialog method permits you to create a custom form that is displayed in modal mode. It is useful when you need a dialog form to display a few custom fields of information. Like the MessageBox, it uses buttons to communicate with the user.

The form used as the dialog box is a standard form containing any controls you want to place on it. Although not required, the form's buttons are usually implemented to return a DialogResult enum value. The following code handles the Click event for the two buttons shown on the form in Figure 6-10:

```
private void buttonOK_Click(object sender, System.EventArgs e)
{ this.DialogResult = DialogResult.OK; }
private void buttonCancel_Click(object sender, System.EventArgs e)
{ this.DialogResult = DialogResult.Cancel; }
```

To complete the form, we also need to set a default button and provide a way for the form to be cancelled if the user presses the Esc key. This is done by setting the form's `AcceptButton` and `CancelButton` properties in the form's constructor.

```
AcceptButton = buttonOK;        //Button to receive default focus
CancelButton = buttonCancel;    //Fires when Esc pushed
```

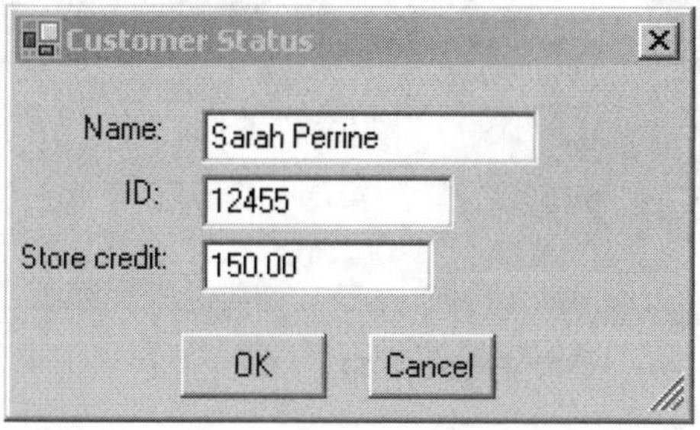

Figure 6-10   Creating a menu with VS.NET

The code that creates and displays the form is similar to previous examples. The only difference is that the new form instance calls its `ShowDialog` method and returns a `DialogResult` type result.

```
customer cust = new customer();
cust.MinimizeBox = false;
cust.MaximizeBox = false;
if (cust.ShowDialog() == DialogResult.OK)
{   MessageBox.Show("Returns OK"); }
else
{   MessageBox.Show("Returns Cancel"); }
```

Multiple Document Interface Forms

A Multiple Document Interface (MDI) application is characterized by one application window and several document windows. Structurally, a single container is used to hold multiple documents. To manage the collection of documents, the MDI application includes a menu system with options to open, save, and close a document; switch between documents; and arrange the documents in various visual layouts.

No special classes are required to create an MDI application. The only requirement is that one form be designated the container by setting its `IsMdiContainer`
property to `true`. Child forms are designated by setting their `MdiParent` property to
the container form.

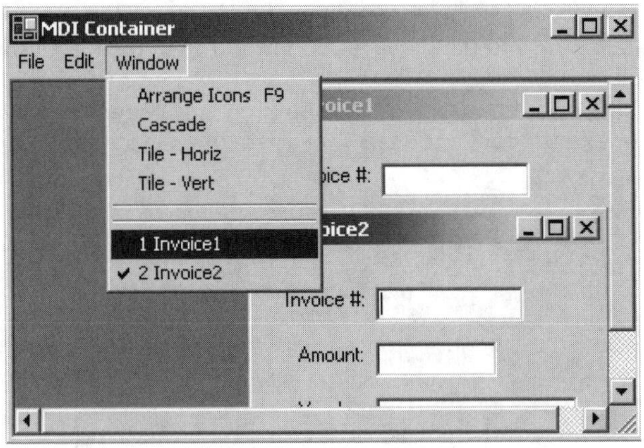

Figure 6-11   MDI form

The MDI form in Figure 6-11 shows the three elements that comprise an MDI
form: the parent container; the child form(s); and a menu to manage the creation,
selection, and arrangement of the child forms.

The container form is created by including this statement in its constructor:

```
this.IsMdiContainer = true;
```

By tradition, child forms are created by selecting an option on the File menu such
as File-New or File-Open. The supporting code creates an instance of the child form
and sets its `MdiParent` property.

```
invForm myForm = new invForm();
myForm.MdiParent = this;
mdiCt += mdiCt;    //Count number of forms created
myForm.Text= "Invoice" + mdiCt.ToString();
myForm.Show();
```

A variable that counts the number of forms created is appended to each form's
`Text` property to uniquely identify it.

Creating a Menu and MDI Form

A discussion of MDI forms is incomplete without considering the requirements for a menu to manage the windows within the container. Minimally, an MDI parent menu should contain a File section for creating and retrieving forms and a Windows section that lists all child forms and permits form selection.

A basic menu is constructed from two classes: the `MainMenu` class that acts as a container for the whole menu structure and the `MenuItem` class that represents the menu items in the menu. Both of these classes expose a `MenuItems` collection property that is used to create the menu hierarchy by adding subitems to each class that represent the menu options. After the menu items are in place, the next step is to tie them to appropriate event handling routines using the familiar delegate approach. Let's step through an example that demonstrates how to create the menu system shown in Figure 6-12. Afterwards, we'll look at creating the menu in Visual Studio.NET. It is certainly much quicker and easier to use VS.NET, but it is less flexible if you need to create menus at runtime.

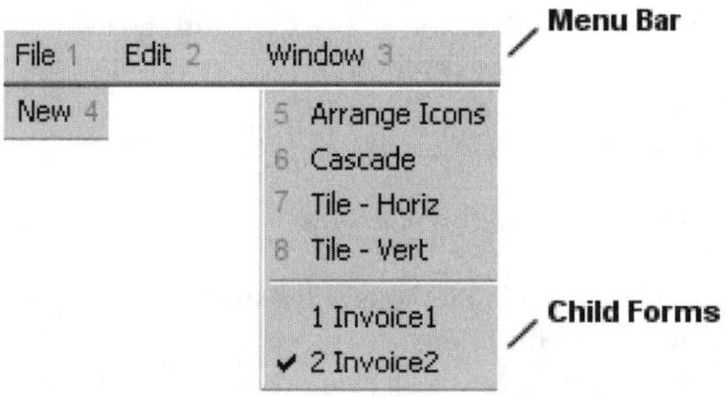

Figure 6-12   MDI Form menu

The first step is to declare the main menu object and the menu items as class variables. (To avoid repetition, code for all menu items is not shown.)

```
private MainMenu mainMenu1;
private MenuItem menuItem1;    //File
private MenuItem menuItem2;    //Edit
private MenuItem menuItem3;    //Window
private MenuItem menuItem4;    //File - New
```

The main menu and menu items are created inside the class constructor:

```
this.mainMenu1 = new System.Windows.Forms.MainMenu();
this.menuItem1 = new System.Windows.Forms.MenuItem("File");
```

```
this.menuItem2 = new System.Windows.Forms.MenuItem("Edit");
this.menuItem3 = new System.Windows.Forms.MenuItem("Window");
this.menuItem4 = new System.Windows.Forms.MenuItem("New");
```

Next, the menu hierarchy is established by adding menu items to the main menu object to create the menu bar. The menu bar items then have menu items added to their MenuItems collection, which creates the drop-down menu.

```
//Add menu items to main menu object
this.mainMenu1.MenuItems.AddRange(new
     System.Windows.Forms.MenuItem[] {
         this.menuItem1,
         this.menuItem2,
         this.menuItem3});
//Add menu item below File
this.menuItem1.MenuItems.Add(this.menuItem4);
//Add menu items to Window menu item
this.menuItem3.MdiList = true;    //Causes child forms to display
this.menuItem3.MenuItems.AddRange(new
System.Windows.Forms.MenuItem[] {this.menuItem5,
     this.menuItem6, this.menuItem7, this.menuItem8});
//Set menu on form
this.Menu = this.mainMenu1;
```

The main points to observe in this code are:

- The Add and AddRange methods add a single or multiple menu items to the MenuItems collection.
- Setting a menu item's MdiList property to true causes a list of child forms to appear in the menu below that menu item (Invoice1 and Invoice2 are listed in Figure 6-12).
- To place a menu on a form, set the form's Menu property to the Main-Menu object.

The final step is to set up event handling code that provides logic to support the menu operations. Here is the code to define a delegate and method to support an event fired by clicking the File–New menu item. The code creates a new instance of invForm each time this menu item is clicked.

```
//Following is defined in constructor
MenuItem4.Click += new System.EventHandler(menuItem4_Click);

private void menuItem4_Click(object sender, System.EventArgs e)
{
   invForm myForm = new invForm();
```

```
    myForm.MdiParent = this;
    mdiCt += mdiCt;    //Count number of forms created
    myForm.Text= "Invoice" + mdiCt.ToString();
    myForm.Show();
}
```

The `Window` option on the menu bar has submenu items that let you rearrange the child forms within the MDI container. The `LayoutMdi` method of a form makes implementing this almost trivial. After setting up delegates in the usual manner, create the event handling routines:

```
private void menuItem6_Click(object sender, System.EventArgs e){
    this.LayoutMdi(MdiLayout.ArrangeIcons);
}

private void menuItem6_Click(object sender, System.EventArgs e){
    this.LayoutMdi(MdiLayout.Cascade);
}

private void menuItem7_Click(object sender, System.EventArgs e){
    this.LayoutMdi(MdiLayout.TileHorizontal);
}

private void menuItem8_Click(object sender, System.EventArgs e){
    this.LayoutMdi(MdiLayout.TileVertical);
}
```

The methods reorder the window by passing the appropriate `MdiLayout` enumeration value to the `LayoutMdi` method.

Creating an MDI Menu Using VisualStudio.NET

With the Form Designer open, double click the MainMenu icon in the Toolbox window. Two things happen: An icon appears in the component tray at the bottom and a menu template appears docked to the top of the form. Type the menu item titles into the cells that appear (see Figure 6-13). The top horizontal row of cells represents the menu bar; by moving vertically, you create drop-down menu items below the top-level items. After typing in the item name, double click the cell to create a `Click` event for the menu item. VS.NET creates the delegate and method stub automatically.

Use the Property Window (press F4), which displays properties of the active cell, to change the default names assigned to menu items and set any other values.

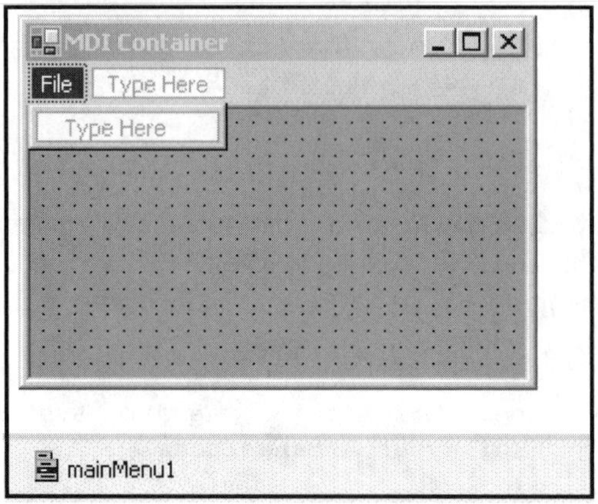

Figure 6-13   Creating a menu with VS.NET

6.4   Working with Menus

The previous section provided a solid introduction to menus. This section adds a checklist of `MenuItem` properties that affect an item's appearance and describes how to use the `ContextMenu` class.

MenuItem Properties

The .NET menu system is designed with the utilitarian philosophy that the value of a thing depends on its utility. Its menu item is not a thing of beauty, but it works. Here are some of its more useful properties:

`Enabled`. Setting this to `false`, grays out the button and makes it unavailable.

`Checked`. Places a checkmark beside the menu item text.

`RadioCheck`. Places a radio button beside the menu item text; `Checked` must also be `true`.

`BreakBar` or `Break`. Setting this to `true` places the menu item in a new column.

`Shortcut`. Defines a shortcut key from one of the `Shortcut` enum members. These members represent a key or key combination (such as `Shortcut.AltF10`) that causes the menu item to be selected when the keys are pressed. On a related matter, note that you can also place an & in front of a letter in the menu item text to produce a *hot key* that causes the item to be selected by pressing Alt-*letter*.

Context Menus

In addition to the `MainMenu` and `MenuItem` classes that have been discussed, there is a `ContextMenu` class that also inherits from the `Menu` class. This `ContextMenu` class is associated with individual controls and is used most often to provide a context-sensitive pop-up menu when the user right-clicks on a control.

The statements to construct a menu based on `ContextMenu` are the same as with a `MainMenu`. The only difference is that visually there is no top-level menu bar, and the menu is displayed near the control where it is invoked.

A menu can be associated with multiple controls, or each control can have its own menu. Typically, one menu is used for each control type. For example, you might have a context menu for all

`TextBox` controls, and another for buttons. To illustrate, let's create a menu that colors the background of a `TextBox` control (see Figure 6-14).

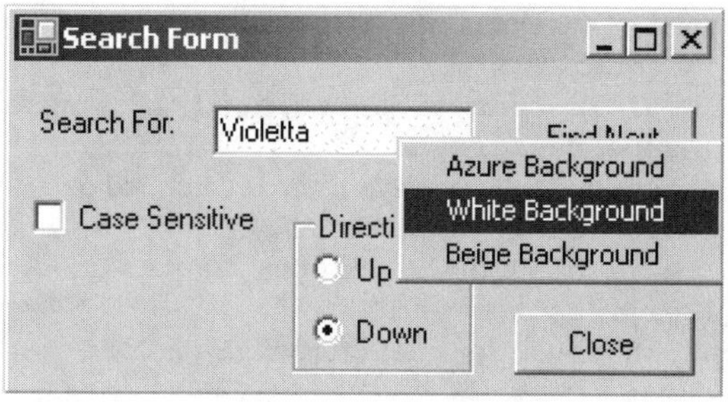

Figure 6-14   Context menu

Constructing a Context Menu

Creating a context menu is similar to creating a `MainMenu`. If using VS.NET, you drag the `ContextMenu` control to the form and visually add menu items. If coding by hand, you create an instance of the `ContextMenu` class and add menu items using the `MenuItems.Add` method. Following is a sampling of the code used to create the menu. Note that a single method handles the `Click` event on each menu item.

```
private ContextMenu contextMenu1;   //Context menu
private TextBox txtSearch;           //Text box that will use menu
// Following is in constructor
contextMenu1 = new ContextMenu();
// Add menu items and event handler using Add method
contextMenu1.MenuItems.Add("Azure Background",
     new System.EventHandler(this.menuItem_Click));
```

```
contextMenu1.MenuItems.Add("White Background",
    new System.EventHandler(this.menuItem_Click));
contextMenu1.MenuItems.Add("Beige Background",
    new System.EventHandler(this.menuItem_Click));
```

The completed menu is attached to a control by setting the control's Context-Menu property to the context menu:

```
//Associate text box with a context menu
this.txtSearch.ContextMenu = this.contextMenu1;
```

A right-click on txtSearch causes the menu to pop up. Click one of the menu items and this event handling routine is called:

```
private void menuItem_Click(object sender, System.EventArgs e)
{
    //Sender identifies specific menu item selected
    MenuItem conMi = (MenuItem) sender;
    string txt = conMi.Text;
    //SourceControl is control associated with this event
    if(txt == "Azure Background")
        this.contextMenu1.SourceControl.BackColor = Color.Azure;
    if(txt == "White Background")
        this.contextMenu1.SourceControl.BackColor = Color.White;
    if(txt == "Beige Background")
        this.contextMenu1.SourceControl.BackColor = Color.Beige;
}
```

The two most important things to note in this example are that the argument sender identifies the selected menu item and that the context menu property SourceControl identifies the control associated with the event. This capability to identify the control and the menu item enables one method to handle events from any control on the form or any menu item in the context menu.

6.5 Adding Help to a Form

The majority of software users do not read documentation, except as a last resort. Users expect a program to be intuitive and provide context-sensitive documentation where it is needed. In addition to the Help option on the main menu bar, a polished program should provide assistance down to the individual controls on the form.

.NET offers multiple ways to configure an integrated help system:

- Easy-to-use ToolTips that are displayed when the mouse moves over a control. These are specified as a control property provided by the `ToolTip` component.
- The *HelpProvider* component is an "extender" that adds properties to existing controls. These properties enable the control to reference Microsoft HTML Help (.chm) files.
- A custom event handler can be written to implement code that explicitly handles the `Control.HelpRequested` event that is fired by pressing the F1 key or using a Help button.

ToolTips

This component adds mouseover capabilities to controls. If using VS.NET, you simply select the `ToolTip` control from the tool box and add it to your form. The effect of this is to add a `string` property (`ToolTip on toolTip1`) to each control, whose value is displayed when the mouse hovers over the control.

Of more interest is using ToolTips within a program to dynamically provide annotation for objects on a screen. Maps, which can be created dynamically in response to user requests, offer a prime example. They typically contain points of interest implemented as labels or picture boxes. As an example, consider the display in Figure 6-15, which shows a constellation and labels for its most important stars. When a user passes the cursor over the label, tool tip text describing the star is shown.

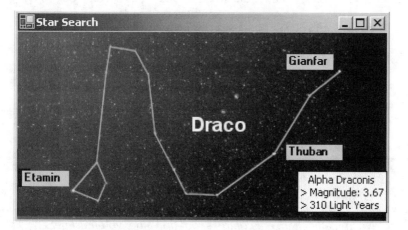

Figure 6-15   ToolTip information is displayed when mouse passes over name

Listing 6-7 shows a portion of the code that creates the form displayed in the figure. The form's BackGroundImage property is set to the image representing the constellation. Labels are placed on top of this that correspond to the position of three stars (code for only one star is shown). The Tag property of each label is set to the description of the star, and a ToolTip associates this information with the label using the SetToolTip method.

Listing 6-7	Using ToolTips to Annotate an Image

```
public class StarMap:Form
{
   public StarMap()
   {
     this.Text = "Star Search";
     this.Width=400;
     this.Height=220;
     // Place image of constellation on form
     this.BackgroundImage= new Bitmap(@"c:\dracoblack.gif");
     // Add name of star on Label
     Label star1 = new Label();
     Star1.Location = new Point(285,115);
     Star1.Size = new Size(60,16);
     star1.Text = "Thuban";
     star1.Tag = "   Alpha Draconis\n> Magnitude: 3.67\n>"+
                 " 310 Light Years";
     star1.Font = new Font(star.Font, star.Font.Style |
                           FontStyle.Bold);
     this.Controls.Add(star1);
     ToolTip toolTip1 = new ToolTip();
     toolTip1.AutoPopDelay= 1500;  // Tool tip displays
                                   // for 1.5 secs.
     // Tool tip text comes from Tag property of Label
     toolTip1.SetToolTip(star1, star1.Tag.ToString());
     // Add labels for other stars Etamin and Gianfar here ...
   }
}
```

Core Note

To dynamically change a control's tool tip value, you must get an instance of the control's ToolTip, execute its RemoveAll method, and then use SetToolTip to reset the value of the tool tip string.

Responding to F1 and the Help Button

Many users regard the F1 key as a de facto way to invoke help. .NET provides built-in F1 support by causing a `Control.HelpRequested` event to fire when the user presses the F1 key. This event also fires when a user clicks the context-sensitive Help button at the top of a form and then clicks on a control using the Help cursor. See Figure 6-16.

Figure 6-16   The Help button

The Help button is displayed by setting these form properties:

- Set `MinimizeBox` and `MaxmizeBox` to `false`.
- Set `HelpButton` to `true`.

A recommended approach is to create one event handler routine and have each control invoke it. As an example, the following code defines delegates for two text boxes that notify the `ShowHelp` method when the `HelpRequested` event occurs. This method uses either a `Tag` property associated with each control or the control's name to specify help germane to that control.

```
this.date.HelpRequested  += new HelpEventHandler(ShowHelp);
this.ssn.HelpRequested   += new HelpEventHandler(ShowHelp);
this.ssn.Tag    = "Enter as: nnn-nn-nnnn";
this.date.Tag   = "Enter as: mm/dd/yyyy";

private void ShowHelp(object sender, HelpEventArgs e)
{
    Control reqControl = (Control)sender;
    // Technique 1: Use tag associated with control
    MessageBox.Show(reqControl.Tag.ToString());
    // Technique 2: Link to specific text within a CHM file
    string anchor = "#"+reqControl.Name;
    // ShowHelp invokes a compiled Help file
    Help.ShowHelp(reqControl,@"c:\ctest.chm",HelpNavigator.Topic,
                "customers.htm"+anchor);
    e.Handled = true;  // Always set this
}
```

The event handler receives two arguments: the familiar `sender` that identifies the control that has focus when the event occurs and `HelpEventArgs`, which has `Handled` and `MousePos` as its only two properties. `Handled` is set to indicate the event has been handled. `MousePos` is a `Point` type that specifies the location of the cursor on the form.

The method provides context-sensitive help by identifying the active control and using this knowledge to select the Help text to be displayed. In this example, the first technique displays the `tag` property of a control as the Help message. The second—and more interesting technique—uses `Help.ShowHelp` to display a section of an HTML file that uses the control's name as an anchor tag. Specifically, it looks inside `ctest.chm` for the `customers.htm` page. Then, it searches that page for a named anchor tag such as `<a name=ssn>`. If found, it displays the HTML at that location.

`ShowHelp` is the most useful method of the `Help` class. It includes several overloads to show compiled Help files (`.chm`) or HTML files in an HTML Help format.

```
// URL may be .chm file or html file
public static void ShowHelp(Control parent, string url);

// HelpNavigator defines the type of .chm file to be displayed
public static void ShowHelp(Control parent, string url,
                        HelpNavigator navigator);

// Displays contents of Help file for a specified keyword
public static void ShowHelp(Control parent, string url,
                        string keyword);

// param is used with HelpNavigator.Topic to refine selection
public static void ShowHelp(Control parent, string url,
                        HelpNavigator navigator, object param);
```

The `HelpNavigator` enumeration specifies which part of a `.chm` file is displayed. It's values include `TableofContents`, `Find`, `Index`, and `Topic`. If you are unfamiliar with them, compiled Help files package multiple HTML files along with an optional table of contents and keyword indexes. The downloadable Microsoft HTML Help Workshop is the easiest way to learn how to use and create these files.

The HelpProvider Component

This component is a wrapper that is used primarily with Visual Studio.NET. Its main value is that it eliminates the need to explicitly handle the `HelpRequested` event. It is an extender that adds several properties to each control. These properties essentially correspond to the parameters in the `ShowHelp` method, which it calls underneath.

Add the `HelpProvider` to a form by selecting it from the tool box. Then, set its `HelpNameSpace` property to the name of the HTML or `.chm` file that the underlying `ShowHelp` method should reference (this corresponds to the URL parameter).

Each control on the form adds four extended properties:

1. `ShowHelp`. Set to `true` to make activate Help feature.
2. `HelpNavigator`. Takes the `HelpNavigator` enumeration value.
3. `HelpKeyword`. Corresponds to the `param` or `keyword` parameter in `ShowHelp`.
4. `HelpString`. This contains a message that is displayed when the Help button is used to click a control.

Help is not enabled on a control that has `ShowHelp` set to `false`. If it is set to `true`, but the other properties are not set, the file referenced in `HelpNameSpace` is displayed. A popular Help configuration is to set only the `HelpString` value so that the Help button brings up a short specific message and F1 brings up an HTML page.

6.6 Forms Inheritance

Just as a class inherits from a base class, a GUI form—which is also a class—can inherit the settings, properties, and control layout of a preexisting form. This means that you can create forms with standard features to serve as templates for derived forms. Before looking at the details of inheritance, let's first examine how to store a set of base forms in a code library and organize them by namespace.

Building and Using a Forms Library

Each form consists of a physical `.cs` file. A library of multiple forms is created by compiling each `.cs` file into a common `.dll` file. After this is done, the forms can be accessed by any compliant language—not just the one they are written in.

As an example, let's use the compiler from the command line to compile two forms into a single `.dll` file:

```
csc /t:library product.cs customer.cs  /out:ADCFormLib.dll
```

A base form must provide a namespace for the derived form to reference it. The following code defines a `Products` namespace for our example:

```
namespace Products
{
    public class ProductForm : System.Windows.Forms.Form
    {
```

To inherit this form, a class uses the standard inheritance syntax and designates the base class by its namespace and class name:

```
// User Form derived from base class Form
class NewProductForm: Products.ProductForm
{
```

As a final step, the compiler must be given a reference to the external assembly ADCFormLib so that the base class can be located. If using VS.NET, you use the Project-AddReference menu option to specify the assembly; from the command line, the reference flag is used.

```
csc /t:winexe /r:ADCFormLib.dll myApp.cs
```

Using the Inherited Form

If the derived form provides no additional code, it generates a form identical to its base form when executed. Of course, the derived form is free to add controls and supporting code. The only restriction is that menu items cannot be added to an existing menu; however, an entire menu can be added to the form and even replace an existing one on the base form.

The properties of inherited controls can be changed, but their default access modifier of private must first be changed to protected, and the base form then recompiled. The derived form is then free to make modifications: It may reposition the control or even set its Visible property to false to keep it from being displayed.

Overriding Events

Suppose the base form contains a button that responds to a click by calling event handler code to close the form. However, in your derived form, you want to add some data verification checks before the form closes. One's instinct is to add a delegate and event handler method to respond to the button Click event in the derived form. However, this does not override the original event handler in the base form, and both event handling routines get called. The solution is to restructure the original event handler to call a virtual method that can be overridden in the derived form. Here is sample code for the base form:

```
private void btn1_Clicked(object sender, System.EventArgs e)
{
    ButtonClicks();    // Have virtual method do actual work
}
protected virtual void ButtonClicks()
{
    this.Close();
}
```

The derived form simply overrides the virtual method and includes its own code to handle the event:

```
protected override void ButtonClicks() {
    // Code to perform any data validation
    this.Close();
}
```

Creating Inherited Forms with Visual Studio.NET

To create an inherited form using Visual Studio, open a project containing the form to serve as the base and compile it. Then, select Project-Add Inherited Form from the menu. Give the new form a name and open it. Next, an Inheritance Picker dialog box appears that lists the eligible base forms. Use the Browse feature to display forms that are in external libraries.

Select a base form and the new inherited form appears in the designer window. All of the controls on the form are marked with a plus (+), and you will find that only properties on the form itself are exposed. At this point, you can add controls or modify existing ones using the techniques just described.

6.7   Summary

Despite the migration of applications to the Internet, there is still a compelling need for Windows Forms programming. Windows Forms provide features and functionality superior to those of Web Forms. Moreover, the majority of real-world applications continue to run on local area networks. The .NET Framework Class Library provides a rich set of classes to support forms programming. The Control class at the top of the hierarchy provides the basic properties, methods, and events that allow controls to be positioned and manipulated on a form. Keyboard and mouse events enable a program to recognize any keys or mouse buttons that are clicked, as well as cursor position.

The Form class inherits all of the Control class members and adds to it properties that specify form appearance, position, and relationship with other forms. A form created by another form may be modal, which means it does not relinquish focus until it is closed, or modeless, in which case focus can be given to either form. In a multiple document interface (MDI) application, one form serves as a container to hold child forms. The container usually provides a menu for selecting or rearranging its child forms.

.NET includes a HelpRequested event that is fired when a user pushes the F1 key. This can be combined with the Help.ShowHelp method, which supports compiled HTML (.chm) files, to enable a developer to provide context-sensitive help on a form.

6.8   Test Your Understanding

1. From which class must a Windows Forms application inherit?

2. Describe the difference between anchoring and docking.

3. What MouseEventArgs properties are used to identify the mouse coordinates and button clicked?

4. Which Form property is used to create an irregular shaped form?

5. What is the primary difference between a modal and modeless form?

6. How does creating an owner-owned form relationship affect the behavior of the related forms?

7. What form properties must be set in order to display a Help button?

8. Compare using a Help button and a ToolTip.

9. Describe how a base form can structure its event handling code so that an inherited form can override an event.

WINDOWS FORMS CONTROLS

Topics in This Chapter

- *Introduction:* A class hierarchy diagram offers a natural way to group Windows Forms controls by their functionality.

- *Button Controls:* The `Button`, `CheckBox`, and `RadioButton` controls are designed to permit users to make one or more selections on a form.

- *PictureBox and TextBoxt Controls:* The `PictureBox` control is used to display and scale images; the `TextBox` control can be used to easily display and edit single or multiple lines of text.

- *List Controls:* The `ListBox`, `ComboBox`, and `CheckListBox` offer different interfaces for displaying and manipulating data in a list format.

- *ListView and TreeView Controls:* The `ListView` offers multiple views for displaying data items and their associated icons. The `TreeView` presents hierarchical information in an easy-to-navigate tree structure.

- *Timer and Progress Bar Controls:* A timer can be used to control when an event is invoked, a `ProgressBar` to visually monitor the progress of an operation.

- *Building a User Control:* When no control meets an application's needs, a custom one can be crafted by combining multiple controls or adding features to an existing one.

- *Moving Data Between Controls:* Drag and drop provides an easy way for users to copy or move an item from one control to another. .NET offers a variety of classes and events required to implement this feature.

- *Using Resources:* Resources required by a program, such as title, descriptive labels, and images, can be embedded within an application's assembly or stored in a *satellite* assembly. This is particularly useful for developing international applications.

Chapter 7

The previous chapter introduced the `Control` class and the methods, properties, and events it defines for all controls. This chapter moves beyond that to examine the specific features of individual controls. It begins with a survey of the more important .NET controls, before taking an in-depth look at how to implement controls such as the `TextBox`, `ListBox`, `TreeView`, and `ListView`. Also included is a discussion of the .NET drag-and-drop features that are used to move or copy data from one control to another.

Windows Forms (WinForms) are not restricted to using the standard built-in controls. Custom GUI controls can be created by extending an existing control, building a totally new control, or fashioning a user control from a set of related widgets. Examples illustrate how to extend a control and construct a user control. The chapter concludes with a look at resource files and how they are used to create GUI applications that support users from multiple countries and cultures.

7.1 A Survey of .NET Windows Forms Controls

The `System.Windows.Forms` namespace contains a large family of controls that add both form and function to a Windows-based user interface. Each control inherits a common set of members from the `Control` class. To these, it adds the methods, properties, and events that give the control its own distinctive behavior and appearance.

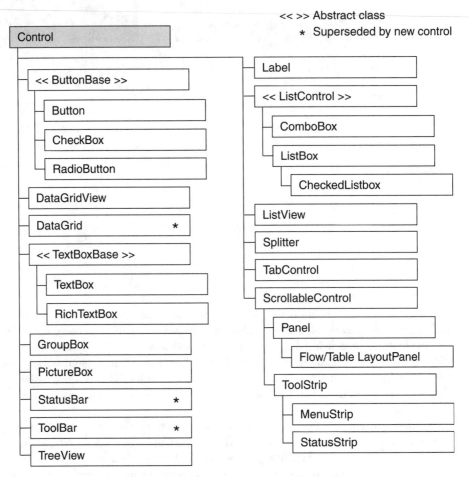

Figure 7-1   Windows Forms control hierarchy

Figure 7-1 shows the inheritance hierarchy of the Windows Forms controls. The controls marked by an asterisk (*) exist primarily to provide backward compatibility between .NET 2.0 and .NET 1.x. Specifically, the DataGrid has been superseded by the DataGridView, the StatusBar by the StatusStrip, and the ToolBar by the ToolStrip. Table 7-1 provides a summary of the more frequently used controls in this hierarchy.

Table 7-1   Selected Windows Forms Controls

Control	Use	Description
Button	Fires an event when a mouse click occurs or the Enter or Esc key is pressed.	Represents a button on a form. Its text property determines the caption displayed on the button's surface.
CheckBox	Permits a user to select one or more options.	Consists of a check box with text or an image beside it. The check box can also be represented as a button by setting: checkBox1.Appearance = Appearance.Button
CheckedListBox	Displays list of items.	ListBox with checkbox preceding each item in list.
ComboBox	Provides TextBox and ListBox functionality.	Hybrid control that consists of a text-box and a drop-down list. It combines properties from both the TextBox and the ListBox.
DataGridView GridView	Manipulates data in a grid format.	The DataGridView is the foremost control to represent relational data. It supports binding to a database. The DataGridView was introduced in .NET 2.0 and supersedes the DataGrid.
GroupBox	Groups controls.	Use primarily to group radio buttons; it places a border around the controls it contains.
ImageList	Manages a collection of images.	Container control that holds a collection of images used by other controls such as the ToolStrip, ListView, and TreeView.
Label	Adds descriptive information to a form.	Text that describes the contents of a control or instructions for using a control or form.
ListBox	Displays a list of items— one or more of which may be selected.	May contain simple text or objects. Its methods, properties, and events allow items to be selected, modified, added, and sorted.

Table 7-1   Selected Windows Forms Controls *(continued)*

Control	Use	Description
ListView	Displays items and subitems.	May take a grid format where each row represents a different item and subitems. It also permits items to be displayed as icons.
MenuStrip	Adds a menu to a form.	Provides a menu and submenu system for a form. It supersedes the `Main-Menu` control.
Panel FlowPanelLayout TablePanelLayout	Groups controls.	A visible or invisible container that groups controls. Can be made scrollable. `FlowPanelLayout` automatically aligns controls vertically or horizontally. `TablePanelLayout` aligns controls in a grid.
PictureBox	Contains a graphic.	Used to hold images in a variety of standard formats. Properties enable images to be positioned and sized within control's borders.
ProgressBar	Depicts an application's progress.	Displays the familiar progress bar that gives a user feedback regarding the progress of some event such as file copying.
RadioButton	Permits user to make one choice among a group of options.	Represents a Windows radio button.
StatusStrip	Provides a set of panels that indicate program status.	Provides a status bar that is used to provide contextual status information about current form activities.
TextBox	Accepts user input.	Can be designed to accept single- or multi-line input. Properties allow it to mask input for passwords, scroll, set letter casing automatically, and limit contents to read-only.
TreeView	Displays data as nodes in a tree.	Features include the ability to collapse or expand, add, remove, and copy nodes in a tree.

This chapter lacks the space to provide a detailed look at each control. Instead, it takes a selective approach that attempts to provide a flavor of the controls and features that most benefit the GUI developer. Notable omissions are the `DataGrid-View` control, which is included in the discussion of data binding in Chapter 12, "Data Binding with Windows Forms Controls," and the menu controls that were discussed in Chapter 6, "Building Windows Forms Applications."

7.2   Button Classes, Group Box, Panel, and Label

The Button Class

A button is the most popular way to enable a user to initiate some program action. Typically, the button responds to a mouse click or keystroke by firing a `Click` event that is handled by an event handler method that implements the desired response.

constructor: `public Button()`

The constructor creates a button instance with no label. The button's `Text` property sets its caption and can be used to define an access key (see *Handling Button Events* section); its `Image` property is used to place an image on the button's background.

Setting a Button's Appearance

Button styles in .NET are limited to placing text and an image on a button, making it flat or three-dimensional, and setting the background/foreground color to any available color. The following properties are used to define the appearance of buttons, check boxes, and radio buttons:

FlatStyle	This can take four values: `FlatStyle.Flat`, `FlatStyle.Popup`, `FlatStyle.Standard`, and `FlatStyle.System`. `Standard` is the usual three-dimensional button. `Flat` creates a flat button. `Popup` creates flat button that becomes three-dimensional on a mouse-over. `System` results in a button drawn to suit the style of the operating system.
Image	Specifies the image to be placed on the button. The `Image.From-File` method is used to create the image object from a specified file:

```
button1.Image = Image.FromFile("c:\\book.gif");
```

ImageAlign	Specifies the position of the image on the button. It is set to a value of the ContentAlignment enum:
	button1.ImageAlign = ContentAlignment.MiddleRight;
TextAlign	Specifies the position of text on the image using the ContentAlignment value.

Handling Button Events

A button's Click event can be triggered in several ways: by a mouse click of the button, by pressing the Enter key or space bar, or by pressing the Alt key in combination with an access key. An access key is created by placing an & in front of one of the characters in the control's Text property value.

The following code segment declares a button, sets its access key to C, and registers an event handler to be called when the Click event is triggered:

```
Button btnClose = new Button();
btnClose.Text= "&Close";  // Pushing ALT + C triggers event
btnClose.Click += new EventHandler(btnClose_Clicked);
// Handle Mouse Click, ENTER key, or Space Bar
private void btnClose_Clicked(object sender, System.EventArgs e)
{ this.Close();  }
```

Note that a button's Click event can also occur in cases when the button does not have focus. The AcceptButton and CancelButton form properties can specify a button whose Click event is triggered by pushing the Enter or Esc keys, respectively.

Core Suggestion

Set a form's CancelButton property to a button whose Click event handler closes the form. This provides a convenient way for users to close a window by pushing the Esc key.

The CheckBox Class

The CheckBox control allows a user to select a combination of options on a form—in contrast to the RadioButton, which allows only one selection from a group.

constructor: public CheckBox()

The constructor creates an unchecked check box with no label. The Text and Image properties allow the placement of an optional text description or image beside the box.

Setting a CheckBox's Appearance

Check boxes can be displayed in two styles: as a traditional check box followed by text (or an image) or as a toggle button that is raised when unchecked and flat when checked. The appearance is selected by setting the `Appearance` property to `Appearance.Normal` or `Appearance.Button`. The following code creates the two check boxes shown in Figure 7-2.

```
// Create traditional check box
this.checkBox1 = new CheckBox();
this.checkBox1.Location =
        new System.Drawing.Point(10,120);
this.checkBox1.Text = "La Traviata";
this.checkBox1.Checked = true;
// Create Button style check box
this.checkBox2 = new CheckBox();
this.checkBox2.Location =
        new System.Drawing.Point(10,150);
this.checkBox2.Text = "Parsifal";
this.checkBox2.Appearance = Appearance.Button;
this.checkBox2.Checked = true;
this.checkBox2.TextAlign = ContentAlignment.MiddleCenter;
```

Figure 7-2   CheckBox styles

The RadioButton Class

The `RadioButton` is a selection control that functions the same as a check box except that only one radio button within a group can be selected. A group consists of multiple controls located within the same immediate container.

constructor: `public RadioButton()`

The constructor creates an unchecked `RadioButton` with no associated text. The `Text` and `Image` properties allow the placement of an optional text description or image beside the box. A radio button's appearance is defined by the same properties used with the check box and button: `Appearance` and `FlatStyle`.

Placing Radio Buttons in a Group

Radio buttons are placed in groups that allow only one item in the group to be selected. For example, a 10-question multiple choice form would require 10 groups of radio buttons. Aside from the functional need, groups also provide an opportunity to create an aesthetically appealing layout.

The frequently used `GroupBox` and `Panel` container controls support background images and styles that can enhance a form's appearance. Figure 7-3 shows the striking effect (even more so in color) that can be achieved by placing radio buttons on top of a `GroupBox` that has a background image.

Figure 7-3   Radio buttons in a `GroupBox` that has a background image

Listing 7-1 presents a sample of the code that is used to place the radio buttons on the `GroupBox` control and make them transparent so as to reveal the background image.

Listing 7-1   Placing Radio Buttons in a `GroupBox`

```
using System.Drawing;
using System.Windows.Forms;
public class OperaForm : Form
{
    private RadioButton radioButton1;
    private RadioButton radioButton2;
    private RadioButton radioButton3;
    private GroupBox groupBox1;
    public OperaForm()
    {
        this.groupBox1 = new GroupBox();
        this.radioButton3 = new RadioButton();
        this.radioButton2 = new RadioButton();
```

Listing 7-1 Placing Radio Buttons in a GroupBox *(continued)*

```
    this.radioButton1 = new RadioButton();
    // All three radio buttons are created like this
    // For brevity only code for one button is included
    this.radioButton3.BackColor = Color.Transparent;
    this.radioButton3.Font = new Font("Microsoft Sans Serif",
                              8.25F, FontStyle.Bold);
    this.radioButton3.ForeColor =
        SystemColors.ActiveCaptionText;
    this.radioButton3.Location = new Point(16, 80);
    this.radioButton3.Name = "radioButton3";
    this.radioButton3.Text = "Parsifal";
    // Group Box
    this.groupBox1 = new GroupBox();
    this.groupBox1.BackgroundImage =
        Image.FromFile("C:\\opera.jpg");
    this.groupBox1.Size = new Size(120, 112);
    // Add radio buttons to groupbox
    groupBox1.Add( new Control[]{radioButton1,radiobutton2,
                       radioButton3});
  }
}
```

Note that the BackColor property of the radio button is set to Color.Transparent. This allows the background image of groupBox1 to be displayed. By default, BackColor is an *ambient* property, which means that it takes the color of its parent control. If no color is assigned to the radio button, it takes the BackColor of groupBox1 and hides the image.

The GroupBox Class

A GroupBox is a container control that places a border around its collection of controls. As demonstrated in the preceding example, it is often used to group radio buttons; but it is also a convenient way to organize and manage any related controls on a form. For example, setting the Enabled property of a group box to false disables all controls in the group box.

constructor: public GroupBox()

The constructor creates an untitled GroupBox having a default width of 200 pixels and a default height of 100 pixels.

The Panel Class

The `Panel` control is a container used to group a collection of controls. It's closely related to the `GroupBox` control, but as a descendent of the `ScrollableControl` class, it adds a scrolling capability.

constructor: `public Panel()`

Its single constructor creates a borderless container area that has scrolling disabled. By default, a `Panel` takes the background color of its container, which makes it invisible on a form.

Because the `GroupBox` and `Panel` serve the same purpose, the programmer is often faced with the choice of which to use. Here are the factors to consider in selecting one:

- A `GroupBox` may have a visible caption, whereas the `Panel` does not.
- A `GroupBox` always displays a border; a `Panel`'s border is determined by its `BorderStyle` property. It may be set to `BorderStyle.None`, `BorderStyle.Single`, or `BorderStyle.Fixed3D`.
- A `GroupBox` does not support scrolling; a `Panel` enables automatic scrolling when its `AutoScroll` property is set to `true`.

A `Panel` offers no features to assist in positioning or aligning the controls it contains. For this reason, it is best used when the control layout is known at design time. But this is not always possible. Many applications populate a form with controls based on criteria known only at runtime. To support the dynamic creation of controls, .NET offers two layout containers that inherit from `Panel` and automatically position controls within the container: the `FlowLayoutPanel` and the `TableLayoutPanel`.

The FlowLayoutPanel Control

Figure 7-4 shows the layout of controls using a `FlowLayoutPanel`.

Figure 7-4   `FlowLayoutPanel`

This "no-frills" control has a single parameterless constructor and two properties worth noting: a `FlowDirection` property that specifies the direction in which controls are to be added to the container, and a `WrapControls` property that indicates whether child controls are rendered on another row or truncated.

The following code creates a `FlowLayoutPanel` and adds controls to its collection:

```
FlowLayoutPanel flp = new FlowLayoutPanel();
flp.FlowDirection = FlowDirection.LefttoRight;
// Controls are automatically positioned left to right
flp.Controls.Add(Button1);
flp.Controls.Add(Button2);
flp.Controls.Add(TextBox1);
flp.Controls.Add(Button3);
this.Controls.Add(flp);        // Add container to form
```

The `FlowDirection` enumerator members are `BottomUp`, `LeftToRight`, `RighttoLeft`, and `TopDown`. `LefttoRight` is the default.

TableLayoutPanel Control

Figure 7-5 shows the grid layout that results from using a `TableLayoutPanel` container.

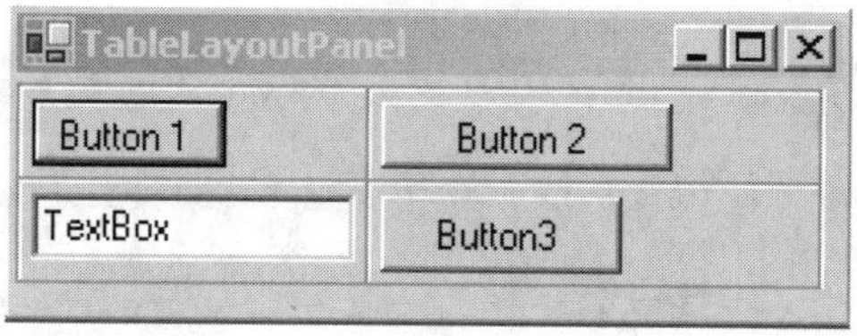

Figure 7-5   `TableLayoutPanel` organizes controls in a grid

This code segment creates a `TableLayoutPanel` and adds the same four controls used in the previous example. Container properties are set to define a layout grid that has two rows, two columns, and uses an `Inset` border style around each cell. Controls are always added to the container moving left-to-right, top-to-bottom.

```
TableLayoutPanel tlp = new TableLayoutPanel();
// Causes the inset around each cell
tlp.CellBorderStyle = TableLayoutPanelCellBorderStyle.Inset;
tlp.ColumnCount = 2;       // Grid has two columns
tlp.RowCount    = 2;       // Grid has two rows
// If grid is full add extra cells by adding column
tlp.GrowStyle = TableLayoutPanelGrowStyle.AddColumns;
// Padding (pixels)within each cell (left, top, right, bottom)
```

```
tlp.Padding = new Padding(1,1,4,5);
tlp.Controls.Add(Button1);
tlp.Controls.Add(Button2);
// Other controls added here
```

The GrowStyle property is worth noting. It specifies how controls are added to the container when all of its rows and columns are filled. In this example, AddColumns specifies that a column be added to accommodate new controls. The other options are AddRows and None; the latter causes an exception to be thrown if an attempt is made to add a control when the panel is filled.

The Label Class

The Label class is used to add descriptive information to a form.

constructor: public Label()

The constructor creates an instance of a label having no caption. Use the Text property to assign a value to the label. The Image, BorderStyle, and TextAlign properties can be used to define and embellish the label's appearance.

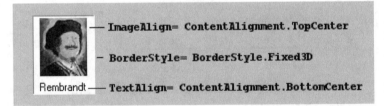

Figure 7-6   Label containing an image and text

The following code creates the label shown in Figure 7-6:

```
Label imgLabel = new Label();
imgLabel.BackColor= Color.White;
Image img = Image.FromFile("c:\\rembrandt.jpg");
imgLabel.Image= img;
imgLabel.ImageAlign= ContentAlignment.TopCenter;
imgLabel.Text="Rembrandt";
imgLabel.TextAlign= ContentAlignment.BottomCenter;
imgLabel.BorderStyle= BorderStyle.Fixed3D;
imgLabel.Size = new Size(img.Width+10, img.Height+25);
```

One of its less familiar properties is UseMnemonic. By setting it to true and placing a mnemonic (& followed by a character) in the label's text, you can create an access key. For example, if a label has a value of &Sum, pressing Alt-S shifts the focus to the control (based on tab order) following the label.

7.3   PictureBox and TextBox Controls

The PictureBox Class

The PictureBox control is used to display images having a bitmap, icon, metafile, JPEG, GIF, or PNG format. It is a dynamic control that allows images to be selected at design time or runtime, and permits them to be resized and repositioned within the control.

constructor: public PictureBox()

The constructor creates an empty (Image = null) picture box that has its Size-Mode property set so that any images are displayed in the upper-left corner of the box.

The two properties to be familiar with are Image and SizeMode. Image, of course, specifies the graphic to be displayed in the PictureBox. SizeMode specifies how the image is rendered within the PictureBox. It can be assigned one of four values from the PictureBoxSizeMode enumeration:

1. AutoSize. PictureBox is sized to equal the image.
2. CenterImage. Image is centered in box and clipped if necessary.
3. Normal. Image is place in upper-left corner and clipped if necessary.
4. StretchImage. Image is stretched or reduced to fit in box.

Figure 7-7 illustrates some of the features of the PictureBox control. It consists of a form with three small picture boxes to hold thumbnail images and a larger picture box to display a full-sized image. The large image is displayed when the user double-clicks on a thumbnail image.

The code, given in Listing 7-2, is straightforward. The event handler ShowPic responds to each DoubleClick event by setting the Image property of the large PictureBox (bigPicture) to the image contained in the thumbnail. Note that the original images are the size of bigPicture and are automatically reduced (by setting SizeMode) to fit within the thumbnail picture boxes.

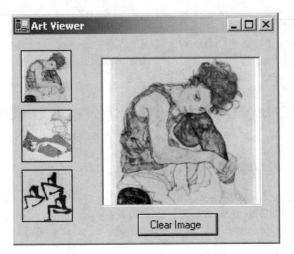

Figure 7-7   Thumbnail images in small picture boxes are displayed at full size in a larger viewing window

| Listing 7-2 | Working with Picture Boxes |

```
using System;
using System.Drawing;
using System.Windows.Forms;
public class ArtForm : Form
{
   private PictureBox bigPicture;
   private PictureBox tn1;
   private PictureBox tn2;
   private PictureBox tn3;
   private Button btnClear;
   public ArtForm()
   {
      bigPicture = new PictureBox();
      tn1 = new PictureBox();
      tn2 = new PictureBox();
      tn3 = new PictureBox();
      btnClear = new Button();
      bigPicture.Location = new Point(90, 30);
      bigPicture.Name = "bigPicture";
      bigPicture.Size = new Size(160, 160);
      this.Controls.Add(bigPicture);
```

Listing 7-2   Working with Picture Boxes *(continued)*

```
       // Define picturebox to hold first thumbnail image
       tn1.BorderStyle = BorderStyle.FixedSingle;
       tn1.Cursor = Cursors.Hand;
       tn1.Image = Image.FromFile("C:\\schiele1.jpg");
       tn1.Location = new Point(8, 16);
       tn1.Name = "tn1";
       tn1.Size = new Size(56, 56);
       tn1.SizeMode = PictureBoxSizeMode.StretchImage;
       this.Controls.Add(tn1);
       // Code for other thumbnails would go here
       // Button to clear picture box
       btnClear.Location = new Point(136, 192);
       btnClear.Name = "btnClear";
       btnClear.Size = new Size(88, 24);
       btnClear.Text = "Clear Image";
       this.Controls.Add(btnClear);
       btnClear.Click += new EventHandler(this.btnClear_Click);
       // Set up event handlers for double click events
       tn1.DoubleClick += new EventHandler(ShowPic);
       tn2.DoubleClick += new EventHandler(ShowPic);
       tn3.DoubleClick += new EventHandler(ShowPic);
   }
   static void Main()
   {
       Application.Run(new ArtForm());
   }
   private void btnClear_Click(object sender, EventArgs e)
   {
       bigPicture.Image = null;    // Clear image
   }
   private void ShowPic (object sender, EventArgs e)
   {
       // Sender is thumbnail image that is double clicked
       bigPicture.Image = ((PictureBox) sender).Image;
   }
}
```

The TextBox Class

The familiar TextBox is an easy-to-use control that has several properties that affect its appearance, but few that control its content. This leaves the developer with the task of setting up event handlers and data verification routines to control what is entered in the box.

constructor: `public TextBox()`

The constructor creates a `TextBox` that accepts one line of text and uses the color and font assigned to its container. From such humble origins, the control is easily transformed into a multi-line text handling box that accepts a specific number of characters and formats them to the left, right, or center. Figure 7-8 illustrates some of the properties used to do this.

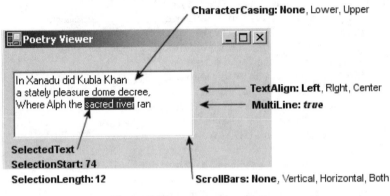

Figure 7-8   `TextBox` properties

The text is placed in the box using the `Text` property and `AppendText` method:

```
txtPoetry.Text =
  "In Xanadu did Kubla Khan\r\na stately pleasure dome decree,";
txtPoetry.AppendText("\r\nWhere Alph the sacred river ran");
```

A couple of other `TextBox` properties to note are `ReadOnly`, which prevents text from being modified, and `PasswordChar`, which is set to a character used to mask characters entered—usually a password.

TextBoxes and Carriage Returns

When storing data from a `TextBox` into a database, you want to make sure there are no special characters embedded in the text, such as a carriage return. If you look at the `TextBox` properties, you'll find `AcceptsReturn`, which looks like a simple solution. Setting it to `false` should cause a `TextBox` to ignore the user pressing an Enter key. However, the name of this property is somewhat misleading. It only works when the form's `AcceptButton` property is set to a button on the form. Recall that this property causes the associated button's `Click` handler to be executed when the Enter key is pressed. If `AcceptButton` is not set (and the `MultiLine` property of the text box is set to `true`), the `TextBox` receives a newline (`\r\n`) when the Enter key is pushed.

This leaves the developer with the task of handling unwanted carriage returns. Two approaches are available: capture the keystrokes as they are entered or extract the characters before storing the text. The first approach uses a keyboard event handler, which you should be familiar with from the previous chapter.

```
// Set up event handler in constructor for TextBox txtPoetry
txtPoetry.KeyPress += new KeyPressEventHandler(onKeyPress);

private void onKeyPress( object sender, KeyPressEventArgs e)
{
    if(e.KeyChar == (char)13) e.Handled = true;
}
```

Setting Handled to true prevents the carriage return/linefeed from being added to the text box. This works fine for keyboard entry but has no effect on a cut-and-paste operation. To cover this occurrence, you can use the keyboard handling events described in Chapter 6 to prevent pasting, or you can perform a final verification step that replaces any returns with a blank or any character of your choice.

```
txtPoetry.Text = txtPoetry.Text.Replace(Environment.NewLine," ");
```

Core Note

Two common approaches for entering a carriage return/linefeed programmatically into a TextBox are

```
txtPoetry.Text = "Line 1\r\nLine 2";
txtPoetry.Text = "Line 1"+Environment.NewLine+"Line 2";
```

7.4   ListBox, CheckedListBox, and ComboBox Classes

The ListBox Class

The ListBox control is used to provide a list of items from which the user may select one or more items. This list is typically text but can also include images and objects. Other features of the ListBox include methods to perform text-based searches, sorting, multi-column display, horizontal and vertical scroll bars, and an easy way to override the default appearance and create owner-drawn ListBox items.

```
constructor: public ListBox()
```

The constructor creates an empty ListBox. The code to populate a ListBox is typically placed in the containing form's constructor or Form.Load event handler. If the ListBox.Sorted property is set to true, ListBox items are sorted alphabetically in ascending order. Also, vertical scroll bars are added automatically if the control is not long enough to display all items.

Adding Items to a ListBox

A ListBox has an Items collection that contains all elements of the list. Elements can be added by binding the ListBox to a data source (described in Chapter 11, "ADO.NET") or manually by using the Add method. If the Sorted property is false, the items are listed in the order they are entered. There is also an Insert method that places an item at a specified location.

```
lstArtists.Items.Add("Monet");
lstArtists.Items.Add("Rembrandt");
lstArtists.Items.Add("Manet");
lstArtists.Items.Insert(0, "Botticelli"); //Place at top
```

Core Note

To prevent a ListBox from repainting itself each time an item is added, execute the ListBox.BeginUpdate method prior to adding and ListBox.EndUpdate after the last item is added.

List boxes may also contain objects. Because an object may have many members, this raises the question of what is displayed in the TextBox list. Because by default a ListBox displays the results of an item's ToString method, it is necessary to override this System.Object method to return the string you want displayed. The following class is used to create ListBox items:

```
// Instances of this class will be placed in a ListBox
public class Artist
{
   public string BDate, DDate, Country;
   private string firstname;
   private string lastname;
   public Artist(string birth, string death, string fname,
                 string lname, string ctry)
   {
      BDate = birth;
```

```
       DDate = death;
       Country = ctry;
       firstname = fname;
       lastname = lname;
    }
  public override string ToString() {
       return (lastname+" , "+firstname);
    }
  public string GetLName      {
       get{ return lastname;}
    }
  public string GetFName      {
       get{ return firstname;}
    }
}
```

ToString has been overridden to return the artist's last and first names, which are displayed in the ListBox. The ListBox (Figure 7-9) is populated using these statements:

```
lstArtists.Items.Add
    (new Artist("1832", "1883", "Edouard", "Manet","Fr" ));
lstArtists.Items.Add
    (new Artist("1840", "1926", "Claude", "Monet","Fr"));
lstArtists.Items.Add
    (new Artist("1606", "1669", "Von Rijn", "Rembrandt","Ne"));
lstArtists.Items.Add
    (new Artist("1445", "1510", "Sandre", "Botticelli","It"));
```

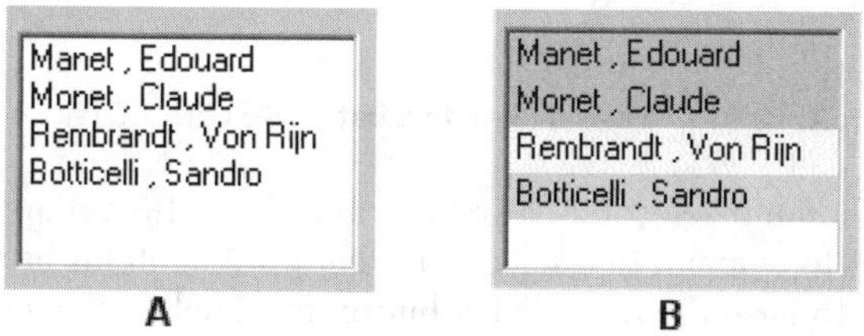

          A   **B**

Figure 7-9   ListBox items: (A) Default and (B) Custom drawn

Selecting and Searching for Items in a ListBox

The `SelectionMode` property determines the number of items a `ListBox` allows to be selected at one time. It takes four values from the `SelectionMode` enumeration: `None`, `Single`, `MultiSingle`, and `MultiExtended`. `MultiSingle` allows selection by clicking an item or pressing the space bar; `MultiExtended` permits the use of the Shift and Ctrl keys.

The `SelectedIndexChanged` event provides an easy way to detect when an item in a `ListBox` is selected. It is fired when the user clicks on an item or uses the arrow keys to traverse a list. A common use is to display further information about the selection in other controls on the form. Here is code that displays an artist's dates of birth and death when the artist's name is selected from the `ListBox` in Figure 7-9:

```
// Set up event handler in constructor
lstArtists.SelectedIndexChanged += new EventHandler(ShowArtist);
//
private void ShowArtist(object sender, EventArgs e)
{
   // Cast to artist object in order to access properties
   Artist myArtist = lstArtists.SelectedItem as Artist;
   if (myArtist != null) {
      txtBirth.Text = myArtist.Dob; // Place dates in text boxes
      txtDeath.Text = myArtist.Dod;
   }
}
```

The `SelectedItem` property returns the item selected in the `ListBox`. This object is assigned to `myArtist` using the as operator, which ensures the object is an `Artist` type. The `SelectedIndex` property can also be used to reference the selected item:

```
myArtist = lstArtists.Items[lstArtists.SelectedIndex] as Artist;
```

Working with a multi-selection `ListBox` requires a different approach. You typically do not want to respond to a selection event until all items have been selected. One approach is to have the user click a button to signal that all choices have been made and the next action is required. All selections are exposed as part of the `SelectedItems` collection, so it is an easy matter to enumerate the items:

```
foreach (Artist a in lstArtists.SelectedItems)
   MessageBox.Show(a.GetLName);
```

The `SetSelected` method provides a way to programatically select an item or items in a `ListBox`. It highlights the item(s) and fires the `SelectedIndexChanged` event. In this example, `SetSelected` is used to highlight all artists who were born in France:

```
lstArtists.ClearSelected();    // Clear selected items
for (int ndx =0; ndx < lstArtists.Items.Count-1; ndx ++)
{
    Artist a = lstArtists.Items[ndx] as Artist;
    if (a.country == "Fr") lstArtists.SetSelected(ndx,true);
}
```

Customizing the Appearance of a ListBox

The `ListBox`, along with the `ComboBox`, `MenuItem`, and `TabControl` controls, is an *owner-drawn* control. This means that by setting a control property, you can have it fire an event when the control's contents need to be drawn. A custom event handler takes care of the actual drawing.

To enable owner drawing of the `ListBox`, the `DrawMode` property must be set to one of two `DrawMode` enumeration values: `OwnerDrawFixed` or `OwnerDrawVariable`. The former draws each item a fixed size; the latter permits variable-sized items. Both of these cause the `DrawItem` event to be fired and rely on its event handler to perform the drawing.

Using the `ListBox` from the previous example, we can use the constructor to set `DrawMode` and register an event handler for the `DrawItem` event:

```
lstArtists.DrawMode = DrawMode.OwnerDrawFixed;
lstArtists.ItemHeight = 16;    // Height (pixels) of item
lstArtists.DrawItem += new DrawItemEventHandler(DrawList);
```

The `DrawItemEventHandler` delegate has two parameters: the familiar `sender` object and the `DrawItemEventArgs` object. The latter is of more interest. It contains properties related to the control's appearance and state as well as a couple of useful drawing methods. Table 7-2 summarizes these.

Table 7-2 `DrawItemEventArgs` Properties

Member	Description
BackColor	Background color assigned to the control.
Bounds	Defines the coordinates of the item to be drawn as a `Rectangle` object.
Font	Returns the font assigned to the item being drawn.
ForeColor	Foreground color of the control. This is the color of the text displayed.
Graphics	Represents the surface (as a `Graphics` object) on which the drawing occurs.

Table 7-2 `DrawItemEventArgs` Properties *(continued)*

Member	Description
`Index`	The index in the control where the item is being drawn.
`State`	The state of the item being drawn. This value is a `DrawItem-State` enumeration. For a `ListBox`, its value is `Selected` (1) or `None(0)`.
`DrawBackground()`	Draws the default background.
`DrawFocusRectangle()`	Draws the focus rectangle around the item if it has focus.

`Index` is used to locate the item. `Font`, `BackColor`, and `ForeColor` return the current preferences for each. `Bounds` defines the rectangular area circumscribing the item and is used to indicate where drawing should occur. `State` is useful for making drawing decisions based on whether the item is selected. This is particularly useful when the `ListBox` supports multiple selections. We looked at the `Graphics` object briefly in the last chapter when demonstrating how to draw on a form. Here, it is used to draw in the `Bounds` area. Finally, the two methods, `DrawBackground` and `DrawFocusRectangle`, are used as their name implies.

The event handler to draw items in the `ListBox` is shown in Listing 7-3. Its behavior is determined by the operation being performed: If an item has been selected, a black border is drawn in the background to highlight the selection; if an item is added, the background is filled with a color corresponding to the artist's country, and the first and last names of the artist are displayed.

The routine does require knowledge of some GDI+ concepts (see Chapter 8, ".NET Graphics Using GDI+"). However, the purpose of the methods should be clear from their name and context: `FillRectangle` fills a rectangular area defined by the `Rectangle` object, and `DrawString` draws text to the `Graphics` object using a font color defined by the `Brush` object. Figure 7-9(B) shows the output.

Listing 7-3	Event Handler to Draw Items in a `ListBox`

```
private void DrawList(object sender, DrawItemEventArgs e)
{
    // Draw ListBox Items
    string ctry;
    Rectangle rect = e.Bounds;
    Artist a = lstArtists.Items[e.Index] as Artist;
    string artistName = a.ToString();
    if ( (e.State & DrawItemState.Selected) ==
                DrawItemState.Selected )
    {
```

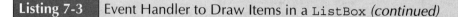

| Listing 7-3 | Event Handler to Draw Items in a `ListBox` *(continued)* |

```
    // Draw Black border around the selected item
    e.Graphics.DrawRectangle(Pens.Black,rect);
  } else {
    ctry = a.Country;
    Brush b;    // Object used to define backcolor
    // Each country will have a different backcolor
    b = Brushes.LightYellow;       // Netherlands
    if (ctry == "Fr")  b = Brushes.LightGreen;
    if (ctry == "It")  b = Brushes.Yellow;
    e.Graphics.FillRectangle(b,rect);}
    e.Graphics.DrawString(artistName,e.Font,
                      Brushes.Black,rect);
  }
}
```

Other List Controls: the ComboBox and the CheckedListBox

The `ComboBox` control is a hybrid control combining a `ListBox` with a `TextBox` (see Figure 7-10). Like the `ListBox`, it derives from the `ListControl` and thus possesses most of the same properties.

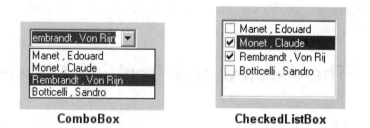

ComboBox   **CheckedListBox**

Figure 7-10   `ComboBox` and `CheckedListBox` controls are variations on `ListBox`

Visually, the `ComboBox` control consists of a text box whose contents are available through its `Text` property and a drop-down list from which a selected item is available through the `SelectedItem` property. When an item is selected, its textual representation is displayed in the text box window. A `ComboBox` can be useful in constructing questionnaires where the user selects an item from the drop-down list or, optionally, types in his own answer. Its construction is similar to the `ListBox`:

```
ComboBox cbArtists = new ComboBox();
cbArtists.Size = new System.Drawing.Size(120, 21);
cbArtists.MaxDropDownItems= 4;   // Max number of items to display
cbArtists.DropDownWidth = 140;   // Width of drop-down portion
cbArtists.Items.Add(new Artist("1832", "1883",
                               "Edouard", "Manet","Fr" ));
// Add other items here...
```

The `CheckedListBox` is a variation on the `ListBox` control that adds a check box to each item in the list. The default behavior of the control is to select an item on the first click, and check or uncheck it on the second click. To toggle the check on and off with a single click, set the `CheckOnClick` property to `true`.

Although it does not support multiple selections, the `CheckedListBox` does allow multiple items to be checked and includes them in a `CheckedItems` collection. The code here loops through a collection of `Artist` objects that have been checked on the control:

```
// List all items with checked box.
foreach (Artist a in clBox.CheckedItems)
   MessageBox.Show(a.ToString()); //    -> Monet, Claude
```

You can also iterate through the collection and explicitly determine the checked state:

```
For (int i=0; I< clBox.Items.Count; i++)
{
   if(clBox.GetItemCheckState(i) == CheckState.Checked)
   { Do something }  else {do something if not checked }
}
```

7.5   The ListView and TreeView Classes

The ListView Class

`ListView` is another control that displays lists of information. It represents data relationally as items and subitems. The data can be represented in a variety of formats that include a multi-column grid and large or small icons to represent item data. Also, images and check boxes can adorn the control.

Figure 7-11 illustrates the basic properties and methods used to lay out a Details view of the control—a format obviously tailored to displaying database tables. The first column contains text for an *item*—as well as a picture—the remaining columns contain *subitems* for the parent item.

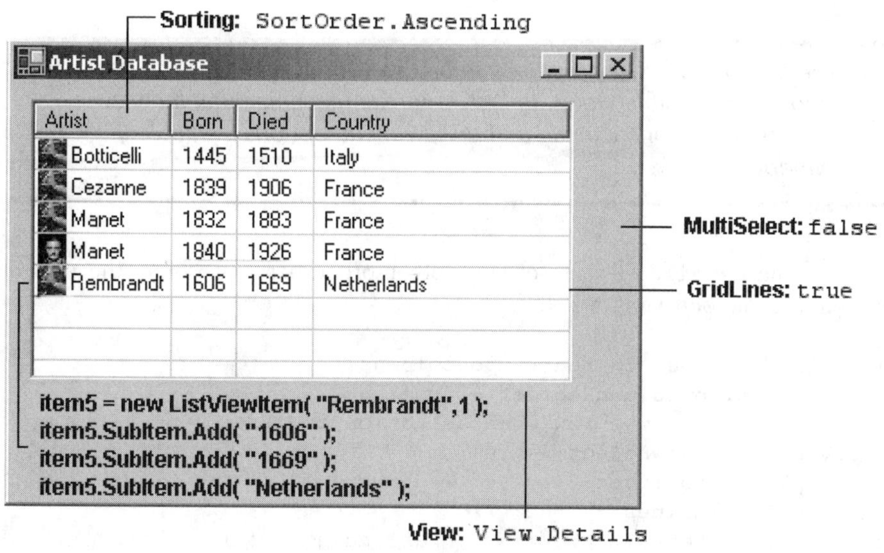

Sorting: SortOrder.Ascending

Artist	Born	Died	Country
Botticelli	1445	1510	Italy
Cezanne	1839	1906	France
Manet	1832	1883	France
Manet	1840	1926	France
Rembrandt	1606	1669	Netherlands

MultiSelect: false

GridLines: true

```
item5 = new ListViewItem( "Rembrandt",1 );
item5.SubItem.Add( "1606" );
item5.SubItem.Add( "1669" );
item5.SubItem.Add( "Netherlands" );
```

View: View.Details

Figure 7-11 ListView control

Let's look at how this style of the ListView is constructed.

Creating a ListView Object

The ListView is created with a parameterless constructor:

```
ListView listView1 = new ListView();
```

Define Appearance of ListView Object

```
// Set the view to show details
listView1.View = View.Details;
```

The View property specifies one of five layouts for the control:

- Details. An icon and item's text are displayed in column one. Sub-items are displayed in the remaining columns.
- LargeIcon. A large icon is shown for each item with a label below the icon.
- List. Each item is displayed as a small icon with a label to its right. The icons are arranged in columns across the control.
- SmallIcon. Each item appears in a single column as a small icon with a label to its right.
- *Tile. Each item appears as a full-size icon with the label and sub-item details to the right of it. Only available for Windows XP and 2003.

Core Note

The `ListView.View` *property can be changed at runtime to switch among the possible views. In fact, you may recognize that the view options correspond exactly to the View menu options available in Windows Explorer.*

After the `Details` view is selected, other properties that define the control's appearance and behavior are set:

```
// Allow the user to rearrange columns
listView1.AllowColumnReorder = true;
// Select the entire row when selection is made
listView1.FullRowSelect = true;
// Display grid lines
listView1.GridLines = true;
// Sort the items in the list in ascending order
listView1.Sorting = SortOrder.Ascending;
```

These properties automatically sort the items, permit the user to drag columns around to rearrange their order, and cause a whole row to be highlighted when the user selects an item.

Set Column Headers

In a `Details` view, data is not displayed until at least one column is added to the control. Add columns using the `Columns.Add` method. Its simplest form is

```
ListView.Columns.Add(caption, width, textAlign)
```

`Caption` is the text to be displayed. `Width` specifies the column's width in pixels. It is set to –1 to size automatically to the largest item in the column, or –2 to size to the width of the header.

```
// Create column headers for the items and subitems
    listView1.Columns.Add("Artist", -2, HorizontalAlignment.Left);
    listView1.Columns.Add("Born", -2, HorizontalAlignment.Left);
    listView1.Columns.Add("Died", -2, HorizontalAlignment.Left);
    listView1.Columns.Add("Country", -2, HorizontalAlignment.Left);
```

The `Add` method creates and adds a `ColumnHeader` type to the `ListView`'s Columns collection. The method also has an overload that adds a `ColumnHeader` object directly:

```
ColumnHeader cHeader:
cHeader.Text = "Artist";
cHeader.Width = -2;
cHeader.TextAlign = HorizontalAlignment.Left;
ListView.Columns.Add(ColumnHeader cHeader);
```

Create ListView Items

Several overloaded forms of the ListView constructor are available. They can be used to create a single item or a single item and its subitems. There are also options to specify the icon associated with the item and set the foreground and background colors.

Constructors:

```
public ListViewItem(string text);
public ListViewItem(string[] items );
public ListViewItem(string text,int imageIndex );
public ListViewItem(string[] items,int imageIndex );
public ListViewItem(string[] items,int imageIndex,
          Color foreColor,Color backColor,Font font);
```

The following code demonstrates how different overloads can be used to create the items and subitems shown earlier in Figure 7-8:

```
// Create item and three subitems
ListViewItem item1 = new ListViewItem("Manet",2);
item1.SubItems.Add("1832");
item1.SubItems.Add("1883");
item1.SubItems.Add("France");
// Create item and subitems using a constructor only
ListViewItem item2 = new ListViewItem
        (new string[] {"Monet","1840","1926","France"}, 3);
// Create item and subitems with blue background color
ListViewItem item3 = new ListViewItem
        (new string[] {"Cezanne","1839","1906","France"}, 1,
        Color.Empty, Color.LightBlue, null);
```

To display the items, add them to the Items collection of the ListView control:

```
// Add the items to the ListView
   listView1.Items.AddRange(
      new ListViewItem[]{item1,item2,item3,item4,item5});
```

Specifying Icons

Two collections of images can be associated with a ListView control as ImageList properties: LargeImageList, which contains images used in the LargeIcon view;

and SmallImageList, which contains images used in all other views. Think of these as zero-based arrays of images that are associated with a ListViewItem by the imageIndex parameter in the ListViewItem constructor. Even though they are referred to as icons, the images may be of any standard graphics format.

The following code creates two ImageList objects, adds images to them, and assigns them to the LargeImageList and SmallImageList properties:

```
// Create two ImageList objects
   ImageList imageListSmall = new ImageList();
   ImageList imageListLarge = new ImageList();
   imageListLarge.ImageSize = new Size(50,50); // Set image size
   // Initialize the ImageList objects
   // Can use same images in both collections since they're resized
   imageListSmall.Images.Add(Bitmap.FromFile("C:\\botti.gif"));
   imageListSmall.Images.Add(Bitmap.FromFile("C:\\cezanne.gif"));
   imageListLarge.Images.Add(Bitmap.FromFile("C:\\botti.gif"));
   imageListLarge.Images.Add(Bitmap.FromFile("C:\\cezanne.gif"));
   // Add other images here
   // Assign the ImageList objects to the ListView.
   listView1.LargeImageList = imageListLarge;
   listView1.SmallImageList = imageListSmall;
   ListViewItem lvItem1 = new ListViewItem("Cezanne",1);
```

An index of 1 selects the cezanne.gif images as the large and small icons. Specifying an index not in the ImageList results in the icon at index 0 being displayed. If neither ImageList is defined, no icon is displayed. Figure 7-12 shows the ListView from Figure 7-11 with its view set to View.LargeIcon:

```
listView1.View = View.LargeIcon;
```

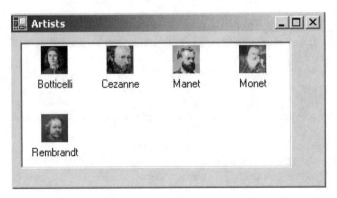

Figure 7-12   LargeIcon view

Working with the ListView Control

Common tasks associated with the `ListView` control include iterating over the contents of the control, iterating over selected items only, detecting the item that has focus, and—when in `Details` view—sorting the items by any column. Following are some code segments to perform these tasks.

Iterating over All Items or Selected Items

You can use `foreach` to create nested loops that select an item and then iterate through the collection of subitems for the item in the outside loop:

```
foreach (ListViewItem lvi in listView1.Items)
{
    string row = "";
    foreach(ListViewItem.ListViewSubItem sub in lvi.SubItems)
    {
        row += " " + sub.Text;
    }
    MessageBox.Show(row); // List concatenated subitems
}
```

There are a couple of things to be aware of when working with these collections. First, the first subitem (index 0) element actually contains the text for the item—not a subitem. Second, the ordering of subitems is not affected by rearranging columns in the `ListView` control. This changes the appearance but does not affect the underlying ordering of subitems.

The same logic is used to list only selected items (`MultiSelect` = true permits multiple items to be selected). The only difference is that the iteration occurs over the `ListView.SelectedItems` collection:

```
foreach (ListViewItem lvisel in listView1.SelectedItems)
```

Detecting the Currently Selected Item

In addition to the basic control events such as `Click` and `DoubleClick`, the `List-View` control adds a `SelectedIndexChanged` event to indicate when focus is shifted from one item to another. The following code implements an event handler that uses the `FocusedItem` property to identify the current item:

```
// Set this in the constructor
listView1.SelectedIndexChanged +=
        new EventHandler(lv_IndexChanged);
// Handle SelectedIndexChanged Event
private void lv_IndexChanged(object sender, System.EventArgs e)
```

```
{
    string ItemText = listView1.FocusedItem.Text;
}
```

Note that this code can also be used with the Click events because they also use the EventHandler delegate. The MouseDown and MouseUp events can also be used to detect the current item. Here is a sample MouseDown event handler:

```
private void listView1_MouseDown(object sender, MouseEventArgs e)
{
    ListViewItem selection = listView1.GetItemAt(e.X, e.Y);
    if (selection != null)
    {
        MessageBox.Show("Item Selected: "+selection.Text);
    }
}
```

The ListView.GetItemAt method returns an item at the coordinates where the mouse button is pressed. If the mouse is not over an item, null is returned.

Sorting Items on a ListView Control

Sorting items in a ListView control by column values is a surprisingly simple feature to implement. The secret to its simplicity is the ListViewItemSorter property that specifies the object to sort the items anytime the ListView.Sort method is called. Implementation requires three steps:

1. Set up a delegate to connect a ColumnClick event with an event handler.
2. Create an event handler method that sets the ListViewItemSorter property to an instance of the class that performs the sorting comparison.
3. Create a class to compare column values. It must inherit the IComparer interface and implement the IComparer.Compare method.

The following code implements the logic: When a column is clicked, the event handler creates an instance of the ListViewItemComparer class by passing it the column that was clicked. This object is assigned to the ListViewItemSorter property, which causes sorting to occur. Sorting with the IComparer interface is discussed in Chapter 4, "Working with Objects in C#").

```
// Connect the ColumnClick event to its event handler
listView1.ColumnClick +=new ColumnClickEventHandler(ColumnClick);
// ColumnClick event handler
private void ColumnClick(object o, ColumnClickEventArgs e)
```

```
{
    // Setting this property immediately sorts the
    // ListView using the ListViewItemComparer object
    this.listView1.ListViewItemSorter =
        new ListViewItemComparer(e.Column);
}
// Class to implement the sorting of items by columns
class ListViewItemComparer : IComparer
{
    private int col;
    public ListViewItemComparer()
    {
        col = 0;    // Use as default column
    }
    public ListViewItemComparer(int column)
        {
        col = column;
    }
    // Implement IComparer.Compare method
    public int Compare(object x, object y)
    {
        string xText = ((ListViewItem)x).SubItems[col].Text;
        string yText = ((ListViewItem)y).SubItems[col].Text;
        return String.Compare(xText, yText);
    }
}
}
```

The TreeView Class

As the name implies, the TreeView control provides a tree-like view of hierarchical data as its user interface. Underneath, its programming model is based on the familiar tree structure consisting of parent nodes and child nodes. Each node is implemented as a TreeNode object that can in turn have its own Nodes collection. Figure 7-13 shows a TreeView control that is used in conjunction with a ListView to display enum members of a selected assembly. (We'll look at the application that creates it shortly.)

The TreeNode Class

Each item in a tree is represented by an instance of the TreeNode class. Data is associated with each node using the TreeNode's Text, Tag, or ImageIndex properties. The Text property holds the node's label that is displayed in the TreeView control. Tag is an object type, which means that any type of data can be associated with the node by assigning a custom class object to it. ImageIndex is an index to an Image-List associated with the containing TreeView control. It specifies the image to be displayed next to the node.

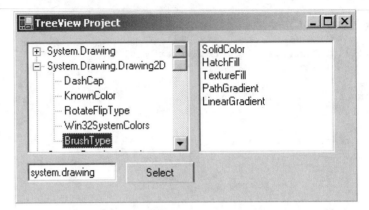

Figure 7-13 Using TreeView control (left) and ListView (right) to list enum values

In addition to these basic properties, the TreeNode class provides numerous other members that are used to add and remove nodes, modify a node's appearance, and navigate the collection of nodes in a node tree (see Table 7-3).

Table 7-3 Selected Members of the TreeNode Class

Use	Member	Description
Appearance	BackColor, ForeColor	Sets the background color and text color of the node.
	Expand(), Collapse()	Expands the node to display child nodes or collapses the tree so no child nodes are shown.
Navigation	FirstNode, LastNode, NextNode, PrevNode	Returns the first or last node in the collection. Returns the next or previous node (sibling) relative to the current node.
	Index	The index of the current node in the collection.
	Parent	Returns the current node's parent.
Node Manipulation	Nodes.Add(), Nodes.Remove(), Nodes.Insert(), Nodes.Clear()	Adds or removes a node to a Nodes collection. Insert adds a node at an indexed location, and Clear removes all tree nodes from the collection.
	Clone()	Copies a tree node and entire subtree.

Let's look at how `TreeView` and `TreeNode` members are used to perform fundamental `TreeView` operations.

Adding and Removing Nodes

The following code creates the tree in Figure 7-14 using a combination of `Add`, `Insert`, and `Clone` methods. The methods are performed on a preexisting `treeView1` control.

```
TreeNode tNode;
// Add parent node to treeView1 control
tNode = treeView1.Nodes.Add("A");
// Add child node: two overloads available
tNode.Nodes.Add(new TreeNode("C"));
tNode.Nodes.Add("D"));
// Insert node after C
tNode.Nodes.Insert(1,new TreeNode("E"));
// Add parent node to treeView1 control
tNode = treeView1.Nodes.Add("B");
```

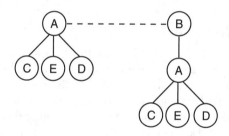

Figure 7-14   `TreeView` node representation

At this point, we still need to add a copy of node A and its subtree to the parent node B. This is done by cloning the A subtree and adding it to node B. Node A is referenced as `treeView1.Nodes[0]` because it is the first node in the control's collection. Note that the `Add` method appends nodes to a collection, and they can be referenced by their zero-based position within the collection:

```
// Clone first parent node and add to node B
TreeNode clNode = (TreeNode) treeView1.Nodes[0].Clone();
tNode.Nodes.Add(clNode);
// Add and remove node for demonstration purposes
tNode.Nodes.Add("G");
tNode.Nodes.Remove(tNode.LastNode);
```

Iterating Through the Nodes in a TreeView

As with any collection, the foreach statement provides the easiest way to loop through the collection's members. The following statements display all the top-level nodes in a control:

```
foreach (TreeNode tn in treeView1.Nodes)
{
   MessageBox.Show(tn.Text);
   // If (tn.IsVisible) true if node is visible
   // If (tn.IsSelected) true if node is currently selected
}
```

An alternate approach is to move through the collection using the Tree-Node.NextNode property:

```
tNode = treeView1.Nodes[0];
while (tNode != null) {
   MessageBox.Show(tNode.Text);
   tNode = tNode.NextNode;
}
```

Detecting a Selected Node

When a node is selected, the TreeView control fires an AfterSelect event that passes a TreeViewEventArgs parameter to the event handling code. This parameter identifies the action causing the selection and the node selected. The TreeView example that follows illustrates how to handle this event.

You can also handle the MouseDown event and detect the node using the Get-NodeAt method that returns the node—if any—at the current mouse coordinates.

```
private void treeView1_MouseDown(object sender, MouseEventArgs e)
{
   TreeNode tn = treeView1.GetNodeAt(e.X, e.Y);
   // You might want to remove the node:  tn.Remove()
}
```

A TreeView Example That Uses Reflection

This example demonstrates how to create a simple object browser (refer to Figure 7-13) that uses a TreeView to display enumeration types for a specified assembly. When a node on the tree is clicked, the members for the selected enumeration are displayed in a ListView control.

Information about an assembly is stored in its metadata, and .NET provides classes in the System.Reflection namespace for exposing this metadata. The code in Listing 7-4 iterates across the types in an assembly to build the TreeView. The parent nodes consist of unique namespace names, and the child nodes are the types contained in the namespaces. To include only enum types, a check is made to ensure that the type inherits from `System.Enum`.

Listing 7-4	Using a `TreeView` and Reflection to List Enums in an Assembly

```
using System.Reflection;
//
private void GetEnums()
{
    TreeNode tNode=null;
    Assembly refAssembly ;
    Hashtable ht= new Hashtable();   // Keep track of namespaces
    string assem = AssemName.Text;   // Textbox with assembly name
    tvEnum.Nodes.Clear();            // Remove all nodes from tree
    // Load assembly to be probed
    refAssembly = Assembly.Load(assem);
    foreach (Type t in refAssembly.GetTypes())
    {
        // Get only types that inherit from System.Enum
        if(t.BaseType!=null && t.BaseType.FullName=="System.Enum")
        {
            string myEnum  = t.FullName;
            string  nSpace =
                    myEnum.Substring(0,myEnum.LastIndexOf("."));
            myEnum= myEnum.Substring(myEnum.LastIndexOf(".")+1) ;
            // Determine if namespace in hashtable
            if( ht.Contains(nSpace))
            {
                // Find parent node representing this namespace
                foreach (TreeNode tp in tvEnum.Nodes)
                {
                    if(tp.Text == myEnum) { tNode=tp; break;}
                }
            }
            else
            {
                // Add parent node to display namespace
                tNode = tvEnum.Nodes.Add(nSpace);
                ht.Add(nSpace,nSpace);
            }
```

Listing 7-4 Using a `TreeView` and Reflection to List Enums in an Assembly *(continued)*

```
            // Add Child - name of enumeration
            TreeNode cNode = new TreeNode();
            cNode.Text= myEnum;
            cNode.Tag = t;      // Contains specific enumeration
            tNode.Nodes.Add(cNode);
         }
      }
   }
```

Notice how reflection is used. The static `Assembly.Load` method is used to create an `Assembly` type. The `Assembly.GetTypes` is then used to return a `Type` array containing all types in the designated assembly.

```
refAssembly = Assembly.Load(assem);
foreach (Type t in refAssembly.GetTypes())
```

The `Type.FullName` property returns the name of the type, which includes the namespace. This is used to extract the enum name and the namespace name. The `Type` is stored in the `Tag` field of the child nodes and is used later to retrieve the members of the enum.

After the `TreeView` is built, the final task is to display the field members of an enumeration when its node is clicked. This requires registering an event handler to be notified when an `AfterSelect` event occurs:

```
tvEnum.AfterSelect += new
   TreeViewEventHandler(tvEnum_AfterSelect);
```

The event handler identifies the selected node from the `TreeViewEvent-Args.Node` property. It casts the node's `Tag` field to a `Type` class (an enumerator in this case) and uses the `GetMembers` method to retrieve the type's members as `MemberInfo` types. The name of each field member—exposed by the `MemberInfo.Name` property—is displayed in the `ListView`:

```
// ListView lView;
// lView.View = View.List;
private void tvEnum_AfterSelect(Object sender,
                                TreeViewEventArgs e)
{
   TreeNode tn = e.Node;    // Node selected
   ListViewItem lvItem;
```

```
if(tn.Parent !=null)     // Exclude parent nodes
{
   lView.Items.Clear(); // Clear ListView before adding items
   Type cNode = (Type) tn.Tag;
   // Use Reflection to iterate members in a Type
   foreach (MemberInfo mi in cNode.GetMembers())
   {
      if(mi.MemberType==MemberTypes.Field &&
                   mi.Name != "value__" )  // skip this
      {
         lView.Items.Add(mi.Name);
      }
   }
}
}
```

7.6   The ProgressBar, Timer, and StatusStrip Classes

The ProgressBar and Timer are lightweight controls that have complementary roles in an application: The Timer initiates action and the ProgressBar reflects the status of an operation or action. In fact, the Timer is not a control, but a component that inherits from the ComponentModel.Component class. It is used most often in processes to regulate some background activity. This may be a periodic update to a log file or a scheduled backup of data. A ProgressBar, on the other hand, provides visual feedback regarding the progress of an operation—such as file copying or steps in an installation.

The third class discussed in this section is the StatusStrip, which is often used in conjunction with a timer and ProgressBar. It's rendered on a form as a strip divided into one or more sections or panes that provide status information. Each section is implemented as a control that is added to the StatusStrip container. For a control to be included in the StatusStrip, it must inherit from the ToolStrip-Item class.

Building a StatusStrip

Let's now build a form that includes a multi-pane StatusStrip. As shown in Figure 7-15, the strip consists of a label, progress bar, and panel controls. The label (Tool-StripLabel) provides textual information describing the overall status of the application. The progress bar is implemented as a ToolStripProgressBar object. It is functionally equivalent to a ProgressBar, but inherits from ToolStripItem. A

StatusStripPanel shows the elapsed time since the form was launched. An event handler that is triggered by a timer updates both the progress bar and clock panel every five seconds.

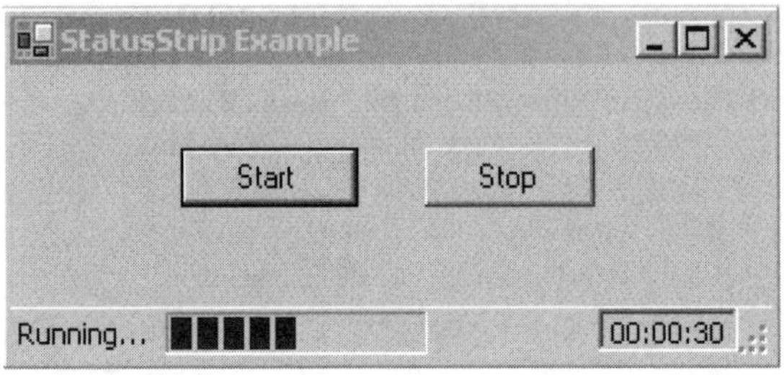

Figure 7-15   StatusStrip with Label, ProgressBar, and Panel

Listing 7-5 contains the code to create the StatusStrip. The left and right ends of the progress bar are set to represent the values 0 and 120, respectively. The bar is set to increase in a step size of 10 units each time the PerformStep method is executed. It recycles every minute.

The Timer controls when the bar is incremented and when the elapsed time is updated. Its Interval property is set to a value that controls how frequently its Tick event is fired. In this example, the event is fired every 5 seconds, which results in the progress bar being incremented by 10 units and the elapsed time by 5 seconds.

Listing 7-5   StatusStrip That Uses a ProgressBar and Timer

```
// These variables have class scope
Timer currTimer;
StatusStrip statusStrip1;
StatusStripPanel panel1;
ToolStripProgressBar pb;
DateTime startDate = DateTime.Now;

private void BuildStrip()
{
   currTimer = new Timer();
   currTimer.Enabled = true;
   currTimer.Interval = 5000; // Fire tick event every 5 seconds
   currTimer.Tick += new EventHandler(timer_Tick);
   // Panel to contain elapsed time
```

Listing 7-5	StatusStrip That Uses a ProgressBar and Timer (continued)

```
panel1 = new StatusStripPanel();
panel1.BorderStyle = Border3DStyle.Sunken;
panel1.Text = "00:00:00";
panel1.Padding = new Padding(2);
panel1.Name = "clock";
panel1.Alignment = ToolStripItemAlignment.Tail; //Right align
// Label to display application status
ToolStripLabel ts = new ToolStripLabel();
ts.Text = "Running...";
// ProgressBar to show time elapsing
pb = new ToolStripProgressBar();
pb.Step    = 10;        // Size of each step or increment
pb.Minimum = 0;
pb.Maximum = 120;       // Allow 12 steps
// Status strip to contain components
statusStrip1 = new StatusStrip();
statusStrip1.Height = 20;
statusStrip1.AutoSize = true;
// Add components to strip
statusStrip1.Items.AddRange(new ToolStripItem[] {
    ts, pb, panel1 } );
this.Controls.Add(statusStrip1);
}
private void timer_Tick(object sender, EventArgs e)
{
    // Get difference between current datetime
    // and form startup time
    TimeSpan ts = DateTime.Now.Subtract(startDate);
    string elapsed = ts.Hours.ToString("00") + ":" +
        ts.Minutes.ToString("00") +
        ":" + ts.Seconds.ToString("00");
    ((StatusStripPanel)statusStrip1.Items[
        "clock"]).Text= elapsed;
    // Advance progress bar
    if (pb.Value == pb.Maximum) pb.Value = 0;
    pb.PerformStep();    // Increment progress bar
}
```

The StatusStripPanel that displays the elapsed time has several properties that control its appearance and location. In addition to those shown here, it has an Image property that allows it to display an image. The StatusStripPanel class inherits from the `ToolStripLabel` class that is used in the first pane. Both can be used to display text, but the panel includes a `BorderStyle` property that `ToolStripLabel` lacks.

7.7   Building Custom Controls

At some point, you will face a programming task for which a standard WinForms control does not provide the functionality you need. For example, you may want to extend a `TextBox` control so that its background color changes according to its content, group a frequently used set of radio buttons into a single control, or create a new control that shows a digital clock face with the date underneath. These needs correspond to the three principal types of custom controls:

1. A control that derives from an existing control and extends its functionality.
2. A control that can serve as container to allow multiple controls to interact. This type of control is referred to as a *user control*. It derives directly from `System.Windows.Forms.UserControl` rather than `Control`, as do standard controls.
3. A control that derives directly from the `Control` class. This type of control is built "from scratch," and it is the developer's responsibility to draw its GUI interface and implement the methods and properties that allow it to be manipulated by code.

Let's now look at how to extend an existing control and create a user control.

Extending a Control

The easiest way to create a custom control is to extend an existing one. To demonstrate this, let's derive a `TextBox` that accepts only digits. The code is quite simple. Create a new class `NumericTextBox` with `TextBox` as its base class. The only code required is an event handler to process the `KeyPress` event and accept only a digit.

```
class NumericTextBox: TextBox
{
   public NumericTextBox()
   {
      this.KeyPress += new KeyPressEventHandler(TextBoxKeyPress);
   }
   protected void TextBoxKeyPress(object sender,
                                  KeyPressEventArgs e)
```

```
    {
        if (! char.IsDigit(e.KeyChar)) e.Handled = true;
    }
}
```

After the extended control is compiled into a DLL file, it can be added to any form.

Building a Custom UserControl

Think of a user control as a subform. Like a form, it provides a container surface on which related widgets are placed. When compiled, the entire set of controls is treated as a single user control. Of course, users still can interact directly with any of the member controls. Programmatic and design-time access to control members is available through methods and properties defined on the user control.

The easiest way to design a control is with an IDE such as Visual Studio.NET (VS.NET), which makes it easy to position and size controls. The usual way to create a user control in VS.NET is to open a project as a *Windows Control Library* type. This immediately brings up a control designer window. The design window can also be accessed in a Windows Application by selecting Project – Add User Control from the top menu bar or right-clicking on the Solution Explorer and selecting Add – Add User Control. Although VS.NET can speed up the process of creating a control, it does not generate any proprietary code that cannot be duplicated using a text editor.

A UserControl Example

As an example, let's create a control that can be used to create a questionnaire. The control consists of a label whose value represents the question, and three radio buttons contained on a panel control that represent the user's choice of answers. The control exposes three properties: one that assigns the question to the label, one to set the background color of the panel control, and another that identifies the radio button associated with the user's answer.

Figure 7-16 shows the layout of the user control and the names assigned to each contained control.

Here is how the members are represented as fields within the `UserControl1` class:

```
public class UserControl1 : System.Windows.Forms.UserControl
{
    private Panel panel1;
    private RadioButton radAgree;
    private RadioButton radDisagree;
    private RadioButton radUn;
    private Label qLabel;
```

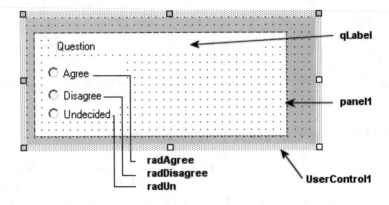

Figure 7-16   Layout of a custom user control

Listing 7-6 contains the code for three properties: SetQ that sets the label's text property to the question, PanelColor that sets the color of the panel, and Choice, which returns the answer selected by the user as a Choices enum type.

Listing 7-6	Implementing Properties for a Custom User Control

```
public enum Choices
{
    Agree      = 1,
    DisAgree   = 2,
    Undecided    = 3,
}
public string SetQ
{
    set {qLabel.Text = value;}
    get {return(qLabel.Text);}
}
public Color PanelColor
{
    set {panel1.BackColor= value;}
    get {return(panel1.BackColor);}
}
public Choices Choice
{
    get
    {
```

Listing 7-6	Implementing Properties for a Custom User Control *(continued)*

```
        Choices usel;
        usel = Choices.Undecided;
        if (radDisagree.Checked) usel= Choices.DisAgree;
        if (radAgree.Checked) usel = Choices.Agree;
        return(usel);}
    }
}
```

Using the Custom User Control

If the user control is developed as part of a VS.NET Windows Application project, it is automatically added to the tool box under the Windows Forms tab. Simply select it and drop it onto the form. Otherwise, you have to right-click on a tool box tab, select Customize ToolBox, browse for the control, and add it to the tool box.

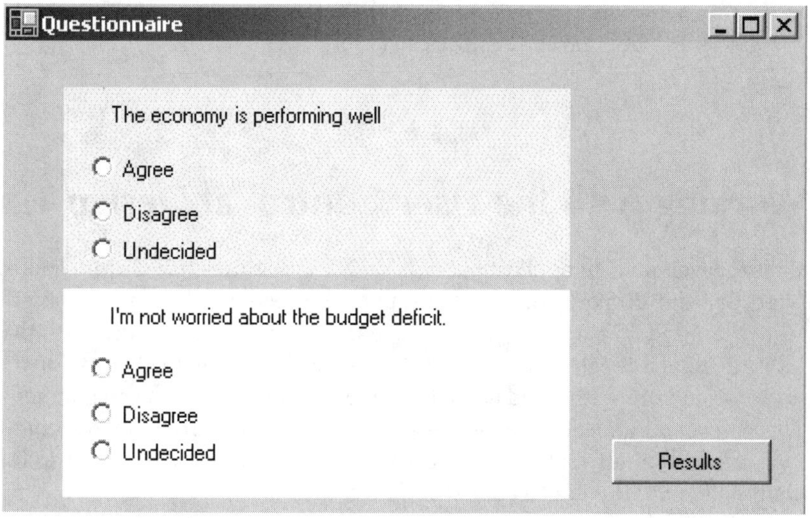

Figure 7-17   Custom user controls on a form

Figure 7-17 provides an example of using this new control. In this example, we place two control instances on the form and name them Q1 and Q2:

```
private usercontrol.UserControl1 Q1;
private usercontrol.UserControl1 Q2;
```

The properties can be set in the constructor or at runtime in the `Form.Load` event handler. If using VS.NET, the properties can be set at design time using the Property Browser.

```
Q1.SetQ = "The economy is performing well";
Q2.SetQ = "I'm not worried about the budget deficit.";
Q1.PanelColor = Color.Beige;
```

The final step in the application is to do something with the results after the questionnaire has been completed. The following code iterates through the controls on the form when the button is clicked. When a `UserControl1` type is encountered, its `Choice` property is used to return the user's selection.

```
private void button1_Click(object sender, System.EventArgs e)
{
   foreach (Control ct in this.Controls)
   {
      if (ct is usercontrol.UserControl1)
      {
         UserControl1 uc = (UserControl1)ct;
         // Display control name and user's answer
         MessageBox.Show(ct.Name+" "+
             uc.Choice.ToString());
      }
   }
}
```

Working with the User Control at Design Time

If you are developing an application with VS.NET that uses this custom control, you will find that the Property Browser lists all of the read/write properties. By default, they are placed in a Misc category and have no description associated with them. To add a professional touch to your control, you should create a category for the control's events and properties and add a textual description for each category member.

The categories and descriptions available in the Property Browser come from metadata based on attributes attached to a type's members. Here is an example of attributes added to the `PanelColor` property:

```
[Browsable(true),
Category("QControl"),
Description("Color of panel behind question block")]
public Color PanelColor
{
   set {panel1.BackColor = value;}
   get {return (panel1.BackColor);}
}
```

The `Browsable` attribute indicates whether the property is to be displayed in the browser. The default is `true`. The other two attributes specify the category under which the property is displayed and the text that appears below the Property Browser when the property is selected.

Always keep in mind that the motive for creating custom user controls is reusability. There is no point in spending time creating elaborate controls that are used only once. As this example illustrates, they are most effective when they solve a problem that occurs repeatedly.

7.8 Using Drag and Drop with Controls

The ability to drag data from one control and drop it onto another has long been a familiar feature of GUI programming. .NET supports this feature with several classes and enumerations that enable a control to be the target and/or source of the drag-and-drop operation.

Overview of Drag and Drop

The operation requires a source control that contains the data to be moved or copied, and a target control that receives the dragged data. The source initiates the action in response to an event—usually a `MouseDown` event. The source control's event handler begins the actual operation by invoking its `DoDragDrop` method. This method has two parameters: the data being dragged and a `DragDropEffects` enum type parameter that specifies the effects or actions the source control supports (see Table 7-4).

Table 7-4 `DragDropEffects` Enumeration

Member	Description
`All`	The data is moved to the target control, and scrolling occurs in the target control to display the newly positioned data.
`Copy`	Data is copied from target to source.
`Link`	Data from the source is linked to the target.
`Move`	The data is moved from the source to the target control.
`None`	The target control refuses to accept data.
`Scroll`	Scrolling occurs or will occur on the target control.

As the mouse moves across the form, the DoDragDrop method determines the control under the current cursor location. If this control has its AllowDrop property set to true, it is a valid drop target and its DragEnter event is raised. The DragEnter event handler has two tasks: to verify that the data being dragged is an acceptable type and to ensure the requested action (Effect) is acceptable. When the actual drop occurs, the destination control raises a DragDrop event. This event handler is responsible for placing the data in the target control (see Figure 7-18).

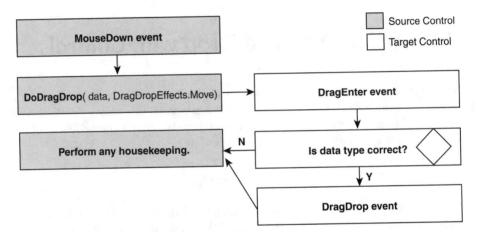

Figure 7-18   Sequence of events in drag-and-drop operation

After the DragDrop event handler finishes, the source control performs any cleanup operations. For example, if the operation involves moving data—as opposed to copying—the data must be removed from the source control.

To demonstrate these ideas, let's create an application that assigns players to a team from a roster of available players (see Figure 7-19). Team A is created by dragging names from the Available Players to the Team A list. Both lists are implemented with list boxes, and the Available Players list is set for single selection.

A name is selected by pressing the right mouse button and dragging the name to the target list. To add some interest, holding the Ctrl key copies a name rather than moving it.

After the form and controls are created, the first step is to set up the source control (lstPlayers) to respond to the MouseDown event and the target control (lstTeamA) to handle the DragEnter and DragDrop events:

```
lstPlayers.MouseDown +=
        new MouseEventHandler(Players_MouseDown);
lstTeamA.DragEnter    += new DragEventHandler(TeamA_DragEnter);
lstTeamA.DragDrop     += new DragEventHandler(TeamA_Drop);
```

The next step is to code the event handlers on the source and target control(s) that implement the drag-and-drop operation.

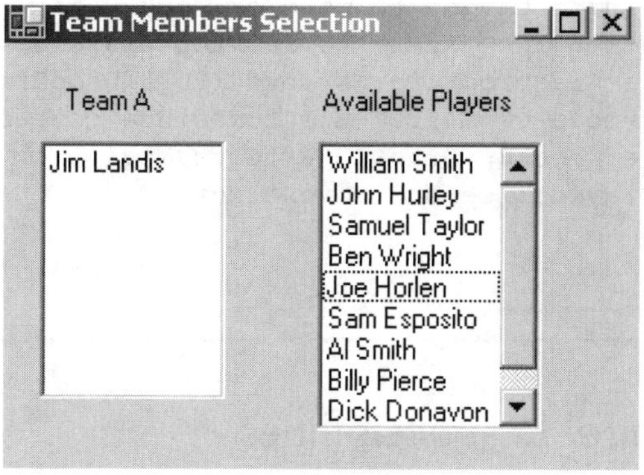

Figure 7-19   Drag-and-drop example

Source Control Responsibilities

The MouseDown event handler for the source ListBox first checks to ensure that an item has been selected. It then calls DoDragDrop, passing it the value of the selected item as well as the acceptable effects: Move and Copy. The DragDropEffects enumeration has a FlagsAttribute attribute, which means that any bitwise combination of its values can be passed. The value returned from this method is the effect that is actually used by the target. The event handler uses this information to perform any operations required to implement the effect. In this example, a move operation means that the dragged value must be removed from the source control.

Listing 7-7	Initiating a Drag-and-Drop Operation from the Source Control

```
private void Players_MouseDown(object sender, MouseEventArgs e)
{
   if ( lstPlayers.SelectedIndex >=0)
   {
      string players;
      int ndx = lstPlayers.SelectedIndex;
      DragDropEffects effect;
      players = lstPlayers.Items[ndx].ToString();
      if(players != "")
      {
```

Listing 7-7	Initiating a Drag-and-Drop Operation from the Source Control *(continued)*

```
      // Permit target to move or copy data
      effect = lstPlayers.DoDragDrop(players,
            DragDropEffects.Move | DragDropEffects.Copy);
      // Remove item from ListBox since move occurred
      if (effect == DragDropEffects.Move)
      lstPlayers.Items.RemoveAt(ndx);
   }
 }
}
```

Target Control Responsibilities

The destination control must implement the event handlers for the DragEnter and DragDrop events. Both of these events receive a DragEventArgs type parameter (see Table 7-5) that contains the information required to process the drag-and-drop event.

Table 7-5   DragEventArgs Properties

Member	Description
AllowedEffect	The effects that are supported by the source control. Example to determine if Move is supported: `if ((e.AllowedEffect & DragDropEffects.Move) == DragDropEffects.Move)`
Data	Returns the IDataObject that contains data associated with this operation. This object implements methods that return information about the data. These include GetData, which fetches the data, and GetDataPresent, which checks the data type.
Effect	Gets or sets the target drop effect.
KeyState	Returns the state of the Alt key, Ctrl key, Shift key, and mouse buttons as an integer: 1—Left mouse button 8—Ctrl key 2—Right mouse button 16—Middle mouse button 4—Shift key 32—Alt key
X, Y	x and y coordinates of the mouse pointer.

The `Data`, `Effect`, and `KeyState` members are used as follows:

- `Data.GetDataPresent` is used by the `DragEnter` event handler to ensure that the data is a type the target control can process.
- The `DragDrop` event handler uses `Data.GetData` to access the data being dragged to it. The parameter to this method is usually a static field of the `DataFormats` class that specifies the format of the returned data.
- The `DragEnter` event handler uses `KeyState` to determine the status of the mouse and keys in order to determine the effect it will use to process the data. Recall that in this example, pressing the Ctrl key signals that data is to copied rather than moved.
- `Effect` is set by the `DragEnter` event handler to notify the source as to how—or if—it processed the data. A setting of `DragDrop-Effects.None` prevents the `DragDrop` event from firing.

Listing 7-8 shows the code for the two event handlers.

Listing 7-8	Handling the `DragEnter` and `DragDrop` Events

```
[FlagsAttribute]
enum KeyPushed
{
    // Corresponds to DragEventArgs.KeyState values
    LeftMouse    = 1,
    RightMouse   = 2,
    ShiftKey     = 4,
    CtrlKey      = 8,
    MiddleMouse  = 16,
    AltKey       = 32,
}
private void TeamA_DragEnter(object sender, DragEventArgs e)
{
    KeyPushed kp = (KeyPushed) e.KeyState;
    // Make sure data type is string
    if (e.Data.GetDataPresent(typeof(string)))
    {
        // Only accept drag with left mouse key
        if ( (kp & KeyPushed.LeftMouse) == KeyPushed.LeftMouse)
        {
            if ((kp & KeyPushed.CtrlKey) == KeyPushed.CtrlKey)
            {
                e.Effect = DragDropEffects.Copy;    // Copy
```

Listing 7-8	Handling the DragEnter and DragDrop Events *(continued)*

```
            }
            else
            {
                e.Effect = DragDropEffects.Move;   // Move
            }
        }
        else   // Is not left mouse key
        {
            e.Effect = DragDropEffects.None;
        }
    } else    // Is not a string
    {
        e.Effect = DragDropEffects.None;
    }
}
// Handle DragDrop event
private void TeamA_Drop(object sender, DragEventArgs e)
{
    // Add dropped data to TextBox
    lstTeamA.Items.Add(
        (string) e.Data.GetData(DataFormats.Text));
}
```

An enum is created with the FlagsAttributes attribute to make checking the KeyState value easier and more readable. The logical "anding" of KeyState with the value of the CtrlKey (8) returns a value equal to the value of the CtrlKey if the Ctrl key is pressed.

A control can serve as source and target in the same application. You could make this example more flexible by having the list boxes assume both roles. This would allow you to return a player from lstTeamA back to the lstPlayers ListBox. All that is required is to add the appropriate event handlers.

Core Note

Drag and drop is not just for text. The DataFormats class predefines the formats that can be accepted as static fields. These include Bitmap, PenData, WaveAudio, and numerous others.

7.9 Using Resources

Figure 7-7, shown earlier in the chapter, illustrates the use of `PictureBox` controls to enlarge and display a selected thumbnail image. Each thumbnail image is loaded into the application from a local file:

```
tn1 = new PictureBox();
tn1.Image = Image.FromFile("c:\\schiele1.jpg");
```

This code works fine as long as the file `schiele1.jpg` exists in the root directory of the user's computer. However, relying on the directory path to locate this file has two obvious disadvantages: The file could be deleted or renamed by the user, and it's an external resource that has to be handled separately from the code during installation. Both problems can be solved by embedding the image in the assembly rather than treating it as an external resource.

Consider a GUI application that is to be used in multiple countries with different languages. The challenge is to adapt the screens to each country. At a minimum, this requires including text in the native language, and may also require changing images and the location of controls on the form. The ideal solution separates the logic of the program from the user interface. Such a solution treats the GUI for each country as an interchangeable resource that is loaded based on the culture settings (the country and language) of the computer.

The common denominator in these two examples is the need to bind an external *resource* to an application. .NET provides special resource files that can be used to hold just about any nonexecutable data such as strings, images, and persisted data. These resource files can be included in an assembly—obviating the need for external files—or compiled into *satellite assemblies* that can be accessed on demand by an application's main assembly.

Let's now look at the basics of working with resource files and how to embed them in assemblies; then, we will look at the role of satellite assemblies in *localized* applications.

Working with Resource Files

Resource files come in three formats: `*.txt` files in name/value format, `*.resx` files in an XML format, and `*.resources` files in a binary format. Why three? The text format provides an easy way to add string resources, the XML version supports both strings and other objects such as images, and the binary version is the binary equivalent of the XML file. It is the only format that can be embedded in an assembly—the other formats must be converted into a `.resources` file before they can be linked to an assembly. Figure 7-20 illustrates the approaches that can be used to create a `.resources` file.

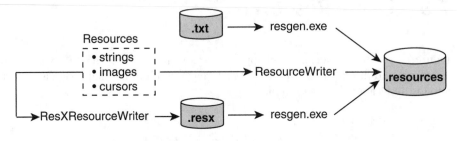

Figure 7-20   A `.resources` file can be created from a text file, resources, or a `.resx` file

The `System.Resources` namespace contains the types required to manipulate resource files. It includes classes to read from and write to both resource file formats, as well as load resources from an assembly into a program.

Creating Resource Strings from a Text File

Resource files containing string values are useful when it is necessary for a single application to present an interface that must be customized for the environment in which it runs. A resource file eliminates the need to code multiple versions of an application; instead, a developer creates a single application and multiple resource files that contain the interface captions, text, messages, and titles. For example, an English version of an application would have the English resource file embedded in its assembly; a German version would embed the German resource file. Creating resource strings and accessing them in an application requires four steps:

1. Create a text file with the name/value strings to be used in the application. The file takes this format:

   ```
   ;German version    (this is a comment)
   Language=German
   Select=Wählen Sie aus
   Page=Seite
   Previous=Vorherig
   Next=Nächst
   ```

2. Convert the text file to a `.resources` file using the Resource File Generator utility `resgen.exe`:

   ```
   > resgen german.txt  german.resources
   ```

   Note that the text editor used to create the text file should save it using UTF-8 encoding, which `resgen` expects by default.

3. Use the `System.Resources.ResourceManager` class to read the strings from the resource file. As shown here, the `ResourceManager` class accepts two arguments: the name of the resource file and the assembly containing it. The `Assembly` class is part of the `System.Reflection` namespace and is used in this case to return the current assembly. After the resource manager is created, its `GetString` method is used by the application to retrieve strings from the resource file by their string name:

```
// new ResourceManager(resource file, assembly)
ResourceManager rm = new ResourceManager(
      "german",Assembly.GetExecutingAssembly());
nxtButton.Text= rm.GetString("Next");
```

4. For this preceding code to work, of course, the resource file must be part of the application's assembly. It's bound to the assembly during compilation:

```
csc /t:exe /resource:german.resources myApp.cs
```

Using the ResourceWriter Class to Create a .resources File

The preceding solution works well for adding strings to a resource file. However, a resource file can also contain other objects such as images and cursor shapes. To place these in a `.resources` file, .NET offers the `System.Resources.Resource-Writer` class. The following code, which would be placed in a utility or helper file, shows how to create a `ResourceWriter` object and use its `AddResource` method to store a string and image in a resource file:

```
IResourceWriter writer = new ResourceWriter(
      "myResources.resources");  // .Resources output file
Image img = Image.FromFile(@"c:\schiele1.jpg");
rw.AddResource("Page","Seite");    // Add string
rw.AddResource("artistwife",img);  // Add image
rw.Close();                        // Flush resources to the file
```

Using the ResourceManager Class to Access Resources

As we did with string resources, we use the `ResourceManager` class to access object resources from within the application. To illustrate, let's return to the code presented at the beginning of this section:

```
tn1.Image = Image.FromFile("C:\\schiele1.jpg");
```

The `ResourceManager` allows us to replace the reference to an external file, with a reference to this same image that is now part of the assembly. The `GetString` method from the earlier example is replaced by the `GetObject` method:

```
ResourceManager rm = new
     ResourceManager("myresources",
                     Assembly.GetExecutingAssembly());
// Extract image from resources in assembly
tn1.Image = (Bitmap) rm.GetObject("artistwife");
```

Using the ResXResourceWriter Class to Create a .resx File

The `ResXResourceWriter` class is similar to the `ResourceWriter` class except that it is used to add resources to a `.resx` file, which represents resources in an intermediate XML format. This format is useful when creating utility programs to read, manage, and edit resources—a difficult task to perform with the binary `.resources` file.

```
ResXResourceWriter rwx = new
     ResXResourceWriter(@"c:\myresources.resx");
Image img = Image.FromFile(@"c:\schiele1.jpg");
rwx.AddResource("artistwife",img);  // Add image
rwx.Generate();   // Flush all added resources to the file
```

The resultant file contains XML header information followed by name/value tags for each resource entry. The actual data—an image in this case—is stored between the value tags. Here is a section of the file `myresources.resx` when viewed in a text editor:

```
<data name="face" type="System.Drawing.Bitmap, System.Drawing,
   Version=1.0.3300.0,Culture=neutral,
   PublicKeyToken=b03f5f7f11d50a3a" mimetype="application/x-
   microsoft.net.object.bytearray.base64">
<value>        ----    Actual Image bytes go here ----
</value>
```

Note that although this example stores only one image in the file, a `.resx` file can contain multiple resource types.

Using the ResXResourceReader Class to Read a .resx file

The `ResXResourceReader` class provides an `IDictionaryEnumerator` (see Chapter 4) that is used to iterate through the tag(s) in a `.resx` file. This code segment lists the contents of a resource file:

```
ResXResourceReader rrx = new
        ResXResourceReader("c:\\myresources.resx");
// Enumerate the collection of tags
foreach (DictionaryEntry de in rrx)
{
    MessageBox.Show("Name: "+de.Key.ToString()+"\nValue: " +
                    de.Value.ToString());
    // Output --> Name:    artistwife
    //         --> Value: System.Drawing.Bitmap
}
rrx.Close();
```

Converting a .resx File to a .resources File

The `.resx` file is converted to a `.resources` file using `resgen.exe`:

```
resgen myresources.resx   myresources.resources
```

If the second parameter is not included, the output file will have the same base name as the source file. Also, note that this utility can be used to create a `.resources` file from a `.resx` file. The syntax is the same as in the preceding example—just reverse the parameters.

VS.NET and Resources

Visual Studio.NET automatically creates a `.resx` file for each form in a project and updates them as more resources are added to the project. You can see the resource file(s) by selecting the Show All Files icon in the Solution Explorer.

When a build occurs, `.resources` files are created from the `.resx` files. In the code itself, a `ResourceManager` object is created to provide runtime access to the resources:

```
ResourceManager resources = new ResourceManager(typeof(Form1));
```

Using Resource Files to Create Localized Forms

In .NET vernacular, a *localized* application is one that provides multi-language support. This typically means providing user interfaces that display text and images customized for individual countries or cultures. The .NET resource files are designed to support such applications.

In a nutshell, resource files can be set up for each culture being supported. For example, one file may have all the control labels and text on its interface in German; another may have the same controls with French text. When the application runs, it looks at the culture settings of the computer it is running on and pulls in the appropriate resources. This little bit of magic is accomplished by associating resource files with the `CultureInfo` class that designates a language, or language and culture. The resource files are packaged as *satellite assemblies*, which are resource files stored as DLLs.

Resource Localization Using Visual Studio.NET

To make a form localized, you must set its `Localizable` property to `true`. This has the effect of turning each control on a form into a resource that has its properties stored in the form's `.resx` file. This sets the stage for creating separate `.resx` files for each culture a form supports.

Recall from Chapter 5, "C# Text Manipulation and File I/O," that a culture is specified by a two-character language code followed by an optional two-character country code. For example, the code for English in the United States is `en-US`. The terms *neutral culture* and *specific culture* are terms to describe a culture. A specific culture has both the language and country specified; a neutral culture has only the language. Consult the MSDN documentation on the `CultureInfo` class for a complete list of culture names.

To associate other cultures with a form, set the form's `Language` property to another locale from the drop-down list in the Properties window. This causes a `.resx` file to be created for the new culture. You can now customize the form for this culture by changing text, resizing controls, or moving controls around. This new property information is stored in the `.resx` file for this culture only—leaving the `.resx` files for other cultures unaffected.

The resource files are stored in folders, as shown in Figure 7-21. When the project is built, a *satellite assembly* is created to contain the resources for each culture, as shown in Figure 7-22. This DLL file has the same name in each folder.

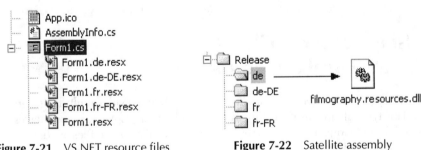

Figure 7-21   VS.NET resource files for multiple cultures

Figure 7-22   Satellite assembly

Determining Localization Resources at Runtime

By default, an application's thread has its `CurrentThread.CurrentUICulture` property set to the culture setting of the machine it is running on. Instances of the `ResourceManager`, in turn, use this value to determine which resources to load. They do this by searching for the satellite assembly in the folder associated with the culture—a reason why the naming and location of resource folders and files is important. If no culture-specific resources are found, the resources in the main assembly are used.

Core Note

The easiest way to test an application with other culture settings is to set the `CurrentUICulture` to the desired culture. The following statement, for example, is placed before `InitializeComponent()` in VS.NET to set the specific culture to German:

```
System.Threading.Thread.CurrentThread.CurrentUICulture =
    new System.Globalization.CultureInfo("de-DE");
```

Creating a Satellite Assembly Without VS.NET

One of the advantages of using satellite assemblies is that they can be added to an application, or modified, without recompiling the application. The only requirements are that a folder be set up along the proper path, and that the folder and satellite assembly have the proper name.

Suppose you have a `.resx` file that has been converted by your translator to French Canadian. You can manually create and add a satellite assembly to the application in three steps:

1. Convert the `.resx` file to a `.resources` file:

   ```
   filmography.Form1.fr-CA.resources
   ```

2. Convert the .resources file to a satellite assembly using the Assembly Linker (`Al.exe`):

   ```
   Al.exe
           /t:lib
           /embed:filmography.Form1.fr-CA.resources
           /culture:fr-CA
           /out:filmography.resources.dll
   ```

3. Create the `fr-CA` folder beneath `Release` folder and copy the new assembly file into it.

Placing the satellite assembly in the proper folder makes it immediately available to the executable and does not require compiling the application.

7.10 Summary

There are more than 50 GUI controls available in the .NET Framework Class Library. This chapter has taken a selective look at some of the more important ones. They all derive from the `System.Windows.Forms.Control` class that provides the inherited properties and methods that all the controls have in common.

Although each control is functionally unique, it is possible to create a taxonomy of controls based on similar characteristics and behavior. The button types, which are used to intitiate an action or make a selection, include the simple `Button`, `CheckBox`, and `RadioButton`. These are often grouped using a `GroupBox` or `Panel` control. The `TextBox` can be used to hold a single line of text or an entire document. Numerous methods are available to search the box and identify selected text within it. The `PictureBox` is available to hold images and has a `SizeMode` property that is used to position and size an image within the box.

Several controls are available for presenting lists of data. The `ListBox` and `ComboBox` display data in a simple text format. However, the underlying data may be a class object with multiple properties. The `TreeView` and `ListView` are useful for displaying data with a hierarchical relationship. The `ListView` can display data in multiple views that include a grid layout and icon representation of data. The `TreeView` presents a tree metaphor to the developer, with data represented as parent and child nodes.

Most of the controls support the drag-and-drop operation that makes it easy to move or copy data from one control to another. The source control initiates the action by calling a `DoDragDrop` method that passes the data and permissible effects to the target control.

For applications that require nonstandard controls, .NET lets you create custom controls. They may be created from scratch, derived from an existing control, or created as a combination of controls in a user control container.

7.11 Test Your Understanding

1. Why is a container control such as a `GroupBox` used with radio buttons?

2. What is the `SizeMode` property set to in order to automatically resize and fill an image in a `PictureBox`?

3. Suppose you place objects in a `ListBox` that have these properties:

   `string Vendor, string ProductID, int Quantity`

   How do you have the `ListBox` display the `ProductID` and `Quantity`?

4. What event is fired when an item in a `ListBox` is selected? What `ListBox` properties are used to identify the selected item?

5. What property and value are set on a `ListView` to display its full contents in a grid layout?

6. Which `TreeNode` property can be used to store object data in a `TreeView` node?

7. Which two events must the destination control in a drag-and-drop operation support?

8. The Property Browser in VS.NET uses metadata to categorize a control's properties and events and assign default values. How do you generate this information for the properties in a custom control?

9. What class is used to read text from a text resource file embedded in an assembly? What method is used to read values from the file?

.NET Graphics Using GDI+

Topics in This Chapter

- *Graphics Overview:* The first step in working with GDI+ is to understand how to create and use a `Graphics` object. This section looks at how this object is created and used to handle the `Paint` event.

- *Using the Graphics Object to Create Shapes:* .NET offers a variety of standard geometric shapes that can be drawn in outline form or filled in. The `GraphicsPath` class serves as a container that enables geometric shapes to be connected.

- *Using Pens and Brushes:* Pens are used to draw shapes in outline form in different colors and widths; a brush is used to fill in shapes and create solid and gradient patterns.

- *Color:* Colors may be defined according to red/green/blue (RGB) values or hue/saturation/brightness (HSB) values. Our project example illustrates RGB and HSB color spaces. By representing a color as an object, .NET permits it to be transformed by changing property values.

- *Images:* .NET includes methods to load, display, and transform images. The most useful of these is the `Graphics.DrawImage` method that allows images to be magnified, reduced, and rotated.

Chapter 8

Very few programmers are artists, and only a minority of developers is involved in the world of gaming where graphics have an obvious justification. Yet, there is something compelling about writing an application that draws on a computer screen. For one thing, it's not difficult. An array of built-in functions makes it easy to create geometric objects, color them, and even animate them. In this regard, .NET should satisfy the would-be artist that resides in many programmers.

To understand the .NET graphics model, it is useful to look at its predecessor—the Win32 Graphical Device Interface (GDI). This API introduced a large set of drawing objects that could be used to create device independent graphics. The idea was to draw to a logical coordinate system rather than a device specific coordinate system—freeing the developer to concentrate on the program logic and not device details. .NET essentially takes this API, wraps it up in classes that make it easier to work with, and adds a wealth of new features.

The graphics classes are collectively called GDI+. This chapter looks at the underlying principles that govern the use of the GDI+, and then examines the classes and the functionality they provide. Several programming examples are included that should provide the tools you will need to further explore the .NET graphics namespaces.

Keep in mind that GDI+ is not restricted to `WinForms` applications. Its members are also available to applications that need to create images dynamically for the Internet (Web Forms and Web Services). You should also recognize that GDI+ is useful for more than just games or graphics applications. Knowledge of its classes is essential if you want to design your own controls or modify the appearance of existing ones.

8.1 GDI+ Overview

The types that make up GDI+ are contained in the `gdiplus.dll` file. .NET neatly separates the classes and enumerations into logically named namespaces that reflect their use. As Figure 8-1 shows, the GDI+ functions fall into three broad categories: two-dimensional vector graphics, image manipulation, and typography (the combining of fonts and text strings to produce text output).

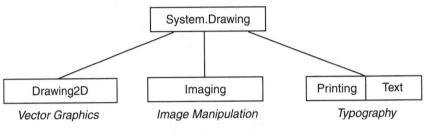

Figure 8-1 GDI+ namespaces

This figure does not depict inheritance, but a general hierarchical relationship between the GDI+ namespaces. `System.Drawing` is placed at the top of the chart because it contains the basic objects required for any graphic output: `Pen`, `Brush`, `Color`, and `Font`. But most importantly, it contains the `Graphics` class. This class is an abstract representation of the surface or canvas on which you draw. The first requirement for any drawing operation is to get an instance of this class, so the `Graphics` object is clearly a fruitful place to begin the discussion of .NET graphics.

The Graphics Class

Drawing requires a surface to draw on, a coordinate system for positioning and aligning shapes, and a tool to perform the drawing. GDI+ encapsulates this functionality in the `System.Drawing.Graphics` class. Its static methods allow a `Graphics` object to be created for images and controls; and its instance methods support the drawing of various shapes such as circles, triangles, and text. If you are familiar with using the Win32 API for graphics, you will recognize that this corresponds closely to a *device context* in GDI. But the `Graphics` object is of a simpler design. A device context is a structure that maintains state information about a drawing and is passed as an argument to drawing functions. The `Graphics` object represents the drawing surface and provides methods for drawing on it.

Let's see how code gains access to a `Graphics` object. Your application most likely will work with a `Graphics` object inside the scope of an event handler, where the object is passed as a member of an EventArgs parameter. The Paint event, which occurs each time a control is drawn, is by far the most common source of Graphics objects. Other events that have a Graphics object sent to their event handler include PaintValue, BeginPrint, EndPrint, and PrintDocument.PrintPage. The latter three are crucial to printing and are discussed in the next chapter.

Although you cannot directly instantiate an object from the Graphics class, you can use methods provided by the Graphics and Control classes to create an object. The most frequently used is Control.CreateGraphics—an instance method that returns a graphics object for the control calling the method. The Graphics class includes the FromHwnd method that relies on passing a control's Handle to obtain a Graphics object related to the control. Let's look at both approaches.

How to Obtain a Graphics Object from a Control Using CreateGraphics

The easiest way to create a Graphics object for a control is to use its CreateGraphics method. This method requires no parameters and is inherited from the Control class by all controls. To demonstrate, let's create an example that draws on a Panel control when the top button is clicked and refreshes all or part of the panel in response to another button click. The user interface to this program is shown in Figure 8-2 and will be used in subsequent examples.

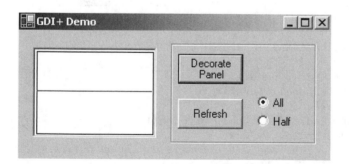

Figure 8-2 Interface to demonstrate using Graphics object to draw on a control

Listing 8-1 contains the code for the Click event handlers associated with each button. When the Decorate Panel button (btnDecor) is clicked, a Graphics object is created and used to draw a rectangle around the edge of the panel as well as a horizontal line through the middle. When the Refresh button (btnRefresh) is clicked, the panel's Invalidate method is called to redraw all or half of the panel. (More on the Invalidate command is coming shortly.)

Listing 8-1	Using `Control.CreateGraphics` to Obtain a Graphics Object

```csharp
using System.Drawing;
//
private void btnDecor_Click(object sender, System.EventArgs e)
{
    // Create a graphics object to draw on panel1
    Graphics cg = this.panel1.CreateGraphics();
    try {
        int pWidth  = panel1.ClientRectangle.Width;
        int pHeight = panel1.ClientRectangle.Height;
        // Draw a rectangle around border
        cg.DrawRectangle(Pens.Black,2,2,pWidth-4, pHeight-4);
        // Draw a horizontal line through the middle
        cg.DrawLine(Pens.Red,2,(pHeight-4)/2,pWidth-4,
                    (pHeight-4)/2);
    }
    finally {
        cg.Dispose();   // You should always dispose of object
    }
}
private void btnRefresh_Click(object sender,
                              System.EventArgs e)
{
// Invokes Invalidate to repaint the panel control
    if (this.radAll.Checked)    // Radio button - All
    {
        // Redraw panel1
        this.panel1.Invalidate();
        } else {
        // Redraw left half of panel1
        Rectangle r = new
            Rectangle(0,0,panel1.ClientRectangle.Width/2,
            ClientRectangle.Height);
        this.panel1.Invalidate(r); // Repaint area r
        this.panel1.Update();      // Force Paint event
    }
}
```

The btnDecor_Click event handler uses the DrawRectangle and DrawLine methods to adorn panel1. Their parameters—the coordinates that define the shapes—are derived from the dimensions of the containing panel control. When the drawing is completed, the Dispose method is used to clean up system resources held by the object. (Refer to Chapter 4, "Working with Objects in C#," for a discussion of the IDisposable interface.) You should always dispose of the Graphics object when finished with it. The try-finally construct ensures that Dispose is called even if an interrupt occurs. As shown in the next example, a using statement provides an equivalent alternative to try-finally.

The btnRefresh Click event handler is presented as a way to provide insight into how forms and controls are drawn and refreshed in a WinForms environment. A form and its child controls are drawn (displayed) in response to a Paint event. Each control has an associated method that is responsible for drawing the control when the event occurs. The Paint event is triggered when a form or control is uncovered, resized, or minimized and restored.

How to Obtain a Graphics Object Using Graphics Methods

The Graphics class has three static methods that provide a way to obtain a Graphics object:

- Graphics.FromHdc. Creates the Graphics object from a specified handle to a Win32 device context. This is used primarily for interoperating with GDI.
- Graphics.FromImage. Creates a Graphics object from an instance of a .NET graphic object such as a Bitmap or Image. It is often used in ASP.NET (Internet) applications to dynamically create images and graphs that can be served to a Web browser. This is done by creating an empty Bitmap object, obtaining a Graphics object using FromImage, drawing to the Bitmap, and then saving the Bitmap in one of the standard image formats.
- Graphics.FromHwnd. Creates the Graphics object from a handle to a Window, Form, or control. This is similar to GDI programming that requires a handle to a device context in order to display output to a specific device.

Each control inherits the Handle property from the Control class. This property can be used with the FromHwnd method as an alternative to the Control.CreateGraphics method. The following routine uses this approach to draw lines on panel1 when a MouseDown event occurs on the panel (see Figure 8-3).

Note that the Graphics object is created inside a using statement. This statement generates the same code as a try-finally construct that includes a g.Dispose() statement in the finally block.

```
private void panel1OnMouseDown(object sender, MouseEventArgs e)
{
```

```
// The using statement automatically calls g.Dispose()
using( Graphics g= Graphics.FromHwnd(panel1.Handle))
{
    g.DrawLine(Pens.Red,e.X,e.Y,20,20);
}
}
```

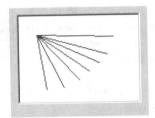

Figure 8-3   Output for MouseDown example

The Paint Event

A `Paint` event is triggered in a WinForms application when a form or control needs to be partially or fully redrawn. This normally occurs during the natural use of a GUI application as the window is moved, resized, and hidden behind other windows. Importantly, a `Paint` event can also be triggered programatically by a call to a control's `Invalidate` method.

Using Invalidate() to Request a Paint Event

The `Control.Invalidate` method triggers a `Paint` event request. The `btnRefresh_Click` event handler in Listing 8-1 showed two overloads of the method. The parameterless version requests that the entire panel control be redrawn; the second specifies that only the portion of the control's region specified by a rectangle be redrawn.

Here are some of the overloads for this method:

```
public void Invalidate()
public void Invalidate(bool invalidatechildren)
public void Invalidate(Rectangle rc)
public void Invalidate(Rectangle rc, bool invalidatechildren)
```

Note: Passing a `true` value for the `invalidatechildren` parameter causes all child controls to be redrawn.

`Invalidate` requests a `Paint` event, but does not force one. It permits the operating system to take care of more important events before invoking the `Paint` event.

To force immediate action on the paint request, follow the `Invalidate` statement with a call to `Control.Update`.

Let's look at what happens on `panel1` after a `Paint` event occurs. Figure 8-4 shows the consequences of repainting the left half of the control. The results are probably not what you desire: half of the rectangle and line are now gone. This is because the control's paint event handler knows only how to redraw the control. It has no knowledge of any drawing that may occur outside of its scope. An easy solution in this case is to call a method to redraw the rectangle and line after calling `Invalidate`. But what happens if Windows invokes the `Paint` event because half of the form is covered and uncovered by another window? This clears the control and our code is unaware it needs to redraw the rectangle and line. The solution is to handle the drawing within the `Paint` event handler.

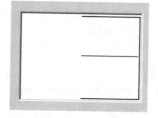

Figure 8-4   Effects of invalidating a region

Core Note

When a form is resized, regions within the original area are not redrawn. To force all of a control or form to be redrawn, pass the following arguments to its `SetStyle` method. Only use this when necessary, because it slows down the paint process.

```
this.SetStyle(ControlStyles.ResizeRedraw, true);
```

Implementing a Paint Event Handler

After the `Paint` event occurs, a data class `PaintEventArgs` is passed as a parameter to the Paint event handler. This class provides access to the `Graphics` object and to a rectangle `ClipRectangle` that defines the area where drawing may occur. Together, these properties make it a simple task to perform all the painting within the scope of the event handler.

Let's see how to rectify the problem in the preceding example, where our drawing on `panel1` disappears each time the paint event occurs. The solution, of course, is to perform the drawing inside the paint event handler. To do this, first register our event handler with the `PaintEventHandler` delegate:

```
this.panel1.Paint += new PaintEventHandler(paint_Panel);
```

Next, set up the event handler with the code to draw a rectangle and horizontal line on the panel. The `Graphics` object is made available through the `PaintEventArgs` parameter.

```
private void paint_Panel( object sender, PaintEventArgs e)
{
    Graphics cg = e.Graphics;
    int pWidth  = panel1.ClientRectangle.Width;
    int pHeight = panel1.ClientRectangle.Height;
    cg.DrawRectangle(Pens.Black,2,2,pWidth-4, pHeight-4);
    cg.DrawLine(Pens.Red,2,(pHeight-4)/2,pWidth-4,
                (pHeight-4)/2);
    base.OnPaint(e);    // Call base class implementation
}
```

The `Control.OnPaint` method is called when a `Paint` event occurs. Its role is not to implement any functionality, but to invoke the delegates registered for the event. To ensure these delegates are called, you should normally invoke the `OnPaint` method within the event handler. The exception to this rule is: To avoid screen flickering, do not call this method if painting the entire surface of a control.

Painting is a slow and expensive operation. For this reason, `PaintEventArgs` provides the `ClipRectangle` property to define the area that is displayed when drawing occurs. Any drawing outside this area is automatically clipped. However, it is important to realize that clipping affects what is displayed—it does not prevent the drawing code from being executed. Thus, if you have a time-consuming custom paint routine, the entire painting process will occur each time the routine is called, unless you include logic to paint only what is needed.

The following example illustrates how to draw selectively. It paints a pattern of semi-randomly colored rectangles onto a form's panel (see Figure 8-5). Before each rectangle is drawn, a check is made to confirm that the rectangle is in the clipping area.

```
private void paint_Panel( object sender,  PaintEventArgs e)
{
    Graphics g = e.Graphics;
    for (int i = 0; i< this.panel1.Width;i+=20)
    {
        for (int j=0; j< his.panel1.Height;j+=20)
        {
            Rectangle r= new Rectangle(i,j,20,20);
            if (r.IntersectsWith(e.ClipRectangle))
```

```
    {
        // FromArgb is discussed in Color section
        Brush b = new SolidBrush(Color.FromArgb((i*j)%255,
            (i+j)%255, ((i+j)*j)%255));
        g.FillRectangle(b,r);
        g.DrawRectangle(Pens.White,r);
    }
  }
 }
}
```

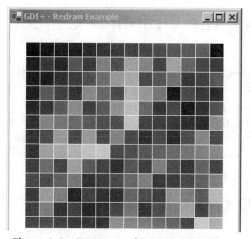

Figure 8-5   Pattern used in paint example

The key to this code is the `Rectangle.IntersectsWith` method that checks for the intersection of two rectangles. In this case, it tests for overlap between the rectangle to be drawn and the clip area. If the rectangle intersects the clip area, it needs to be drawn. Thus, the method can be used to limit the portion of the screen that has to be repainted. To test the effects, this code was run with and without the `IntersectsWith` method. When included, the event handler required 0 to 17 milliseconds—depending on the size of the area to be repainted. When run without `IntersectsWith`, the event handler required 17 milliseconds to redraw all the rectangles.

Another approach to providing custom painting for a form or control is to create a subclass that overrides the base class's `OnPaint` method. In this example, `myPanel` is derived from the `Panel` class and overrides the `OnPaint` method to draw a custom diagonal line through the center of the panel.

```
// New class myPanel inherits from base class Panel
public class myPanel: Panel
{
```

```
protected override void OnPaint(PaintEventArgs e)
{
    Graphics g = e.Graphics;
    g.DrawLine(Pens.Aqua,0,0,this.Width,this.Height);
    base.OnPaint(e);
}
}
```

Unless the new subclass is added to a class library for use in other applications, it is simpler to write an event handler to provide custom painting.

8.2   Using the Graphics Object

Let's look at the details of actually drawing with the Graphics object. The Graphics class contains several methods for rendering basic geometric patterns. In addition to the DrawLine method used in previous examples, there are methods for drawing rectangles, polygons, ellipses, curves, and other basic shapes. In general, each shape can be drawn as an outline using the Pen class, or filled in using the Brush class. The DrawEllipse and FillEllipse methods are examples of this. Let's look at some examples.

Basic 2-D Graphics

Figure 8-6 demonstrates some of the basic shapes that can be drawn with the Graphics methods. The shapes vary, but the syntax for each method is quite similar. Each accepts a drawing object—either a pen or brush—to use for rendering the shape, and the coordinates that determine the size and positions of the shape. A Rectangle object is often used to provide a shape's boundary.

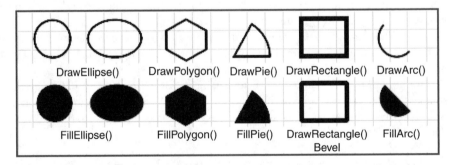

Figure 8-6   Basic 2-D shapes

The following code segments draw the shapes shown in Figure 8-6. To keep things simple, the variables x and y are used to specify the location where the shape is drawn. These are set to the coordinates of the upper-left corner of a shape.

```
Pen blkPen = new Pen(Brushes.Black,2 );  // width=2
// Set this to draw smooth lines
g.SmoothingMode =
      System.Drawing.Drawing2D.SmoothingMode.AntiAlias;
// (1) Draw Circle and Draw Filled Circle
Rectangle r = new Rectangle(new Point(x,y),new Size(40,40));
g.DrawEllipse(blkPen, r);
g.FillEllipse(Brushes.Black,x,y+60,40,40);
// (2) Draw Ellipse and Filled Ellipse
int w = 60;
int h= 40;
Rectangle r = new Rectangle(new Point(x,y),new Size(w,h));
g.DrawEllipse(blkPen, r);
r = new Rectangle(new Point(x,y+60), new Size(w,h));
g.FillEllipse(Brushes.Red, r);
// (3) Draw Polygon
Point pt1 = new Point(x, y);
Point pt2 = new Point(x+22, y+12);
Point pt3 = new Point(x+22, y+32);
Point pt4 = new Point(x, y+44);
Point pt5 = new Point(x-22, y+32);
Point pt6 = new Point(x-22, y+12);
Point[] myPoints = {pt1, pt2, pt3, pt4, pt5, pt6};
g.DrawPolygon(blkPen, myPoints);
// Points would be changed so as not to draw over
// original polygon
g.FillPolygon(Brushes.Black, myPoints);
// (4)Draw Pie Shape and filled pie
Rectangle r = new Rectangle( new Point(x,y),new Size(80,80));
// Create start and sweep angles
int startAngle =  0;     // Clockwise from x-axis
int sweepAngle = -60;    // Clockwise from start angle
g.DrawPie(blkPen, r, startAngle, sweepAngle);
g.FillPie(Brushes.Black, x,y+60,80,80,startAngle, sweepAngle);
// (5) Draw Rectangle and Rectangle with beveled edges
blkPen.Width=5;    // make pen thicker to show bevel
g.DrawRectangle(blkPen,x,y,50,40);
blkPen.LineJoin = LineJoin.Bevel;
g.DrawRectangle(blkPen,x,y+60,50,40);
// (6) Draw Arc and Filled Pie
startAngle=45;
sweepAngle=180;
g.DrawArc(blkPen, x,y,40,40,startAngle, sweepAngle);
g.FillPie(Brushes.Black, x,y+60,40,40,startAngle,sweepAngle);
```

These code segments illustrate how easy it is to create simple shapes with a minimum of code. .NET also makes it easy to create more complex shapes by combining primitive shapes using the GraphicsPath class.

Creating Shapes with the GraphicsPath Class

The GraphicsPath class, which is a member of the System.Drawing.Drawing2D namespace, is used to create a container for a collection of primitive shapes. Succinctly, it permits you to add basic shapes to its collection and then to treat the collection as a single entity for the purpose of drawing and filling the overall shape. Before looking at a code example, you should be aware of some of the basic features of the GraphicsPath class:

- It automatically connects the last point of a line or arc to the first point of a succeeding line or arc.
- Its CloseFigure method can be used to automatically close open shapes, such as an arc. The first and last points of the shape are connected.
- Its StartFigure method prevents the previous line from being automatically connected to the next line.
- Its Dispose method should always be called when the object is no longer in use.

The following code creates and displays the Infinity Cross shown in Figure 8-7. It is constructed by adding five polygons to the GraphicsPath container object. The Graphics object then draws the outline and fills in the cross.

```
// g is the Graphics object
g.SmoothingMode = SmoothingMode.AntiAlias;
// Define five polygons
Point[] ptsT= {new Point(120,20),new Point(160,20),
     new Point(140,50)};
Point[] ptsL= {new Point(90,50),new Point(90,90),
     new Point(120,70)};
Point[] ptsB= {new Point(120,120),new Point(160,120),
     new Point(140,90)};
Point[] ptsR= {new Point(190,90), new Point(190,50),
     new Point(160, 70)};
Point[] ptsCenter = {new Point(140,50), new Point(120,70),
     new Point(140,90), new Point(160,70)};
// Create the GraphicsPath object and add the polygons to it
GraphicsPath gp = new GraphicsPath();
gp.AddPolygon(ptsT);    // Add top polygon
gp.AddPolygon(ptsL);    // Add left polygon
gp.AddPolygon(ptsB);    // Add bottom polygon
```

```
gp.AddPolygon(ptsR);    // Add right polygon
gp.AddPolygon(ptsCenter);
g.DrawPath(new Pen(Color.Red,2),gp); // Draw GraphicsPath
g.FillPath(Brushes.Gold,gp); // Fill the polygons
```

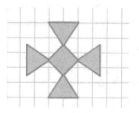

Figure 8-7 Infinity Cross

Instead of drawing and filling each polygon separately, we use a single `DrawPath` and `FillPath` statement to do the job.

The `GraphicsPath` class has several methods worth exploring—`AddCircle`, `AddArc`, `AddEllipse`, `AddString`, `Warp`, and others—for applications that require the complex manipulation of shapes. One of the more interesting is the `Transform` method that can be used to rotate or shift the coordinates of a `DrawPath` object. This following code segment offers a taste of how it works. A transformation matrix is created with values that shift the x coordinates by 50 units and leave the y coordinates unchanged. This `Transform` method applies the matrix to the `DrawPath` and shifts the coordinates; the shape is then drawn 50 units to the right of the first shape.

```
Matrix translateMatrix = new Matrix();
translateMatrix.Translate(50, 0);   // Offset x coordinate by 50
gp.Transform(translateMatrix);      // Transform path
g.DrawPath(Pens.Orange,gp);         // Display at new location
```

Hit Testing with Shapes

One of the reasons for placing shapes on a form is to permit a user to trigger an action by clicking a shape—as if she had clicked a button. Unlike a control, you cannot associate an event with a shape. Instead, you associate a `MouseDown` event with the container that holds the shape(s). Recall that a `MouseDown` event handler receives the x and y coordinates where the event occurs. After it has these, it is a simple process to use the rectangle and `GraphicsPath` methods to verify whether a point falls within their area:

```
bool Rectangle.Contains(Point(x,y))
bool GraphicsPath.IsVisible(Point(x,y))
```

To illustrate, consider an application that displays a map of US states and responds to a click on a state by displaying the name of the state capital. The map image is placed in a `PictureBox`, and rectangles and polygons are drawn on the states to set up the *hit areas* that respond to a `MouseDown` event. Figure 8-8 shows how the picture box's paint handler routine draws rectangles on three states and a polygon on Florida. (Of course, the shapes would not be visible in the actual application.) To respond to a pressed mouse key, set up a delegate to call an event handler when the `MouseDown` event occurs:

```
this.pictureBox1.MouseDown += new
      MouseEventHandler(down_Picture);
```

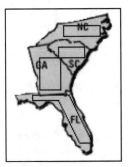

Figure 8-8   Hit test example

The following code implements event handler logic to determine if the mouse down occurs within the boundary of any shape.

```
private void down_Picture( object sender, MouseEventArgs e)
{
   // Rectangles and GraphicsPath gp are defined
   // as class variables
   if (rectNC.Contains(e.X,e.Y) )
   { MessageBox.Show("Capital: Raleigh"); }
   else if(rectSC.Contains(e.X,e.Y))
   { MessageBox.Show("Capital: Columbia");}
   else if(rectGA.Contains(e.X,e.Y))
   { MessageBox.Show("Capital: Atlanta");}
   else if(gp.IsVisible(e.X,e.Y))
   {MessageBox.Show("Capital: Tallahassee");}
}
```

After you have a basic understanding of how to create and use shapes, the next step is to enhance these shapes with eye catching graphical effects such as gradients, textured colors, and different line styles and widths. This requires an understanding of the System.Drawing classes: Pen, Brush, and Color.

Pens

The Graphics object must receive an instance of the Pen class to draw a shape's outline. Our examples thus far have used a static property of the Pens class—Pens.Blue, for example—to create a Pen object that is passed to the Graphics object. This is convenient, but in many cases you will want to create your own Pen object in order to use non-standard colors and take advantage of the Pen properties.

Constructors:

```
public Pen (Color color);
public Pen (Color color, single width);
public Pen (Brush brush);
public Pen (Brush brush, single width);
```

Example:

```
Pen p1 = new Pen(Color.Red, 5);
Pen p2 = new Pen(Color.Red); // Default width of 1
```

The constructors allow you to create a Pen object of a specified color and width. You can also set its attributes based on a Brush object, which we cover later in this section. Note that the Pen class inherits the IDisposable interface, which means that you should always call the Pen object's Dispose method when finished with it.

Besides color and width, the Pen class offers a variety of properties that allow you to control the appearance of the lines and curves the Pen object draws. Table 8-1 contains a partial list of these properties.

Table 8-1   Selected Pen Properties

Member	Description
Alignment	Determines how a line is drawn for closed shapes. Specifically, it specifies whether the line is drawn on the bounding perimeter or inside it.
Color	Color used to draw the shape or text.

Table 8-1   Selected Pen Properties *(continued)*

Member	Description
DashCap	The cap style used at the beginning and end of dashes in a dashed line. A cap style is a graphic shape such as an arrow.
DashOffset	Distance from start of a line to the beginning of its dash pattern.
DashStyle	The type of dashed lines used. This is based on the DashStyle enumeration.
PenType	Specifies how a line is filled—for example, textured, solid, or gradient. It is determined by the Brush property of the Pen.
StartCap EndCap	The cap style used at the beginning and end of lines. This comes from the LineCap enumeration that includes arrows, diamonds, and squares—for example, LineCap.Square.
Width	Floating point value used to set width of Pen.

Let's look at some of the more interesting properties in detail.

DashStyle

This property defines the line style, which can be Solid, Dash, Dot, DashDot, DashDotDot, or Custom (see Figure 8-9). The property's value comes from the DashStyle enumeration.

```
Pen p1 = new Pen(Color.Black, 3);
p1.DashStyle = DashStyle.Dash;
g.DrawLine(p1,20,20,180,20);
```

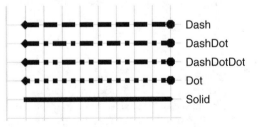

Figure 8-9   DashStyles and LineCaps

StartCap and EndCap

These properties define the shape used to begin and end a line. The value comes from the LineCap enumeration, which includes ArrowAnchor, DiamondAnchor, Round, RoundAnchor, Square, SquareAnchor, and Triangle. Examples of the DiamondAnchor and RoundAnchor are shown in Figure 8-9. The following code is used to create the lines in the figure:

```
Graphics g = pictureBox1.CreateGraphics();
Pen p1 = new Pen(Color.Black, 5);
p1.StartCap = LineCap.DiamondAnchor;
p1.EndCap   = LineCap.RoundAnchor;
int yLine = 20;
foreach(string ds in Enum.GetNames(typeof(DashStyle)))
{
   if (ds != "Custom") // Ignore Custom DashStyle type
   {
      // Parse creates an enum type from a string
      p1.DashStyle = (DashStyle)Enum.Parse(
                     typeof(DashStyle), ds);
      g.DrawLine(p1,20,yLine,120,yLine);
      g.DrawString(ds,new Font("Arial",10),Brushes.Black,
                   140,yLine-8);
      yLine += 20;
   }
}
```

The code loops through the DashStyle enumeration and draws a line for each enum value except Custom. It also uses the DrawString method to display the name of the enumeration values. This method is discussed in Chapter 9.

Brushes

Brush objects are used by these Graphics methods to create filled geometric shapes:

FillClosedCurve	FillEllipse	FillPath	FillPie
FillPolygon	FillRectangle	FillRectangles	FillRegion

All of these receive a Brush object as their first argument. As with the Pen class, the easiest way to provide a brush is to use a predefined object that represents one of the standard colors—for example, Brushes.AntiqueWhite. To create more interesting effects, such as fills with patterns and gradients, it is necessary to instantiate your own Brush type. Unlike the Pen class, you cannot create an instance of the abstract Brush class; instead, you use one of its inheriting classes summarized in Table 8-2.

Table 8-2 Brush Types That Derive from the `Brush` Class

Brush Type	Description
SolidBrush	Defines a brush of a single color. It has a single constructor: `Brush b = new SolidBrush(Color.Red);`

TextureBrush	Uses a preexisting image (`*.gif`, `*.bmp`, or `*.jpg`) to fill a shape.
	`Image img = Image.FromFile("c:\\flower.jpg");`
	`Brush b = new TextureBrush(img);`

HatchBrush	Defines a rectangular brush with a foreground color, background color, and hatch style. Located in the `System.Drawing.Drawing2D` namespace.
LinearGradientBrush	Supports either a two-color or multi-color gradient. All linear gradients occur along a line defined by two points or a rectangle. Located in the `Drawing2D` namespace.
PathGradientBrush	Fills the interior of a `GraphicsPath` object with a gradient. Located in the `Drawing2D` namespace.

Note that all `Brush` classes have a `Dispose` method that should be called to destroy the `Brush` object when it is no longer needed.

The two most popular of these classes are `HatchBrush`, which is handy for creating charts, and `LinearGradientBrush`, for customizing the background of controls. Let's take a closer look at both of these.

The HatchBrush Class

As the name implies, this class fills the interior of a shape with a hatched appearance.

Constructors:

```
public HatchBrush(HatchStyle hStyle, Color forecolor)
public HatchBrush(HatchStyle hstyle, Color forecolor,
                  Color backcolor)
```

Parameters:

hStyle   `HatchStyle` enumeration that specifies the hatch pattern.

forecolor   The color of the lines that are drawn.

backcolor   Color of the space between the lines (black is default).

The predefined HatchStyle patterns make it a simple process to create elaborate, multi-color fill patterns. The following code is used to create the DarkVertical and DottedDiamond rectangles at the top of each column in Figure 8-10.

```
Graphics g = pictureBox1.CreateGraphics();
// Fill Rectangle with DarkVertical pattern
Brush b = new HatchBrush(HatchStyle.DarkVertical,
                    Color.Blue,Color.LightGray);
g.FillRectangle(b,20,20,80,60);
// Fill Rectangle with DottedDiamond pattern
b = new HatchBrush(HatchStyle.DottedDiamond,
                    Color.Blue,Color.LightGray);
g.FillRectangle(b,120,20,80,60);
```

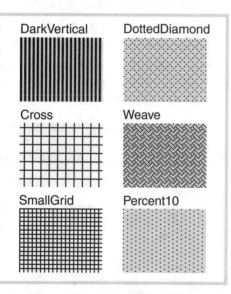

Figure 8-10   Using HatchBrush with some of the available hatch styles

The LinearGradientBrush Class

In its simplest form, this class creates a transition that takes one color and gradually blends it into a second color. The direction of the transition can be set to horizontal, vertical, or any specified angle. The location where the transition begins can be set to a focal point other than the beginning of the area to be filled in. In cases where the gradient must be tiled to completely fill an area, options are available to control how each repeat is displayed. These options can be confusing, so let's begin with how to

create a gradient brush and then work with examples that demonstrate the more useful properties and methods of the LinearGradientBrush class.

Constructors:

```
public LinearGradientBrush(Rectangle rect, Color color1,
    Color color2, LinearGradientMode linearGradientMode)

public LinearGradientBrush(Rectangle rect, Color color1,
    Color color2, float angle)
```

Parameters:

rect	Rectangle specifying the bounds of the gradient.
color1	The start color in the gradient.
color2	The end color in the gradient.
angle	The angle in degrees moving clockwise from the x axis.
LinearGradientMode	A LinearGradientMode enum value: Horizontal, Vertical, BackwardDiagonal, ForwardDiagonal

There is no substitute for experimentation when it comes to understanding graphics related concepts. Figure 8-11 shows the output from filling a rectangle with various configurations of a LinearGradientBrush object. Here is the code that creates
these examples:

```
// Draw rectangles filled with gradient in a pictureBox
Graphics g = pictureBox1.CreateGraphics();
Size sz = new Size(100,80);
Rectangle rb = new Rectangle(new Point(20,20),sz);
// (1) Vertical Gradient (90 degrees)
LinearGradientBrush b = new
      LinearGradientBrush(rb,Color.DarkBlue,Color.LightBlue,90);
g.FillRectangle(b,rb);
rb.X=140;
// (2) Horizontal Gradient
b = new LinearGradientBrush(rb,Color.DarkBlue,
                            Color.LightBlue,0);
g.FillRectangle(b,rb);
rb.Y = 120;
rb.X = 20;
// (3) Horizontal with center focal point
b = new LinearGradientBrush(rb,Color.DarkBlue,
                            Color.LightBlue,0);
// Place end color at position (0-1) within brush
```

```
b.SetBlendTriangularShape(.5f);
g.FillRectangle(b,rb);
```

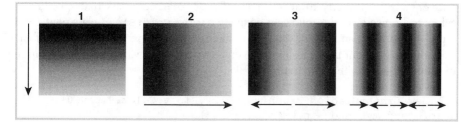

Figure 8-11   LinearGradientBrush examples:
(1) Vertical, (2) Horizontal, (3) Focus Point, (4) Tiling

The main point of interest in this code is the use of the SetBlendTriangular-Shape method to create the blending effect shown in the third rectangle in Figure 8-11. This method takes an argument between 0 and 1.0 that specifies a relative focus point where the end color is displayed. The gradient then "falls off" on either side of this point to the start color.

The fourth rectangle in the figure is created by repeating the original brush pattern. The following code defines a small gradient brush that is used to fill a larger rectangle:

```
// Tiling Example - create small rectangle for gradient brush
Rectangle rb1 = new Rectangle(new Point(0,0),new Size(20,20));
b = new LinearGradientBrush(rb,Color.DarkBlue,
                            Color.LightBlue,0);
b.WrapMode = WrapMode.TileFlipX;
// Fill larger rectangle with repeats of small gradient rectangle
g.FillRectangle(b,rb);
```

Notice how the light and dark colors are reversed horizontally before each repeat occurs: [light-dark][dark-light]. The WrapMode property determines how the repeated gradient is displayed. In this example, it is set to the WrapMode enum value of Tile-FlipX, which causes the gradient to be reversed horizontally before repeating. The most useful enum values include the following:

Tile	Repeats the gradient.
TileFlipX	Reverses the gradient horizontally before repeating.
TileFlipXY	Reverses the gradient horizontally and vertically before repeating.
TileFlipY	Reverses the gradient vertically before repeating.

Creating a Multi-Color Gradient

It takes only a few lines of code to create a `LinearGradientBrush` object that creates a multi-color gradient. The key is to set the `LinearGradientBrush.Interpo-lationColors` property to an instance of a `ColorBlend` class that specifies the colors to be used. As the following code shows, the `ColorBlend` class contains an array of colors and an array of values that indicate the relative position (0–1) of each color on the gradient line. This example creates a gradient with a transition from red to white to blue—with white in the middle.

```
b = new LinearGradientBrush(rb,Color.Empty,Color.Empty,0);
ColorBlend myBlend = new ColorBlend();
// Specify colors to include in gradient
myBlend.Colors = new Color[]
        {Color.Red, Color.White, Color.Blue,};
// Position of colors in gradient
myBlend.Positions = new float[] {0f, .5f, 1f};
b.InterpolationColors = myBlend;  // Overrides constructor colors
```

Colors

.NET implements the `Color` object as a structure that includes a large number of colors predefined as `static` properties. For example, when a reference is made to `Color.Indigo`, the returned value is simply the `Indigo` property. However, there is more to the structure than just a list of color properties. Other properties and methods permit you to deconstruct a color value into its internal byte representation or build a color from numeric values. To appreciate this, let's look at how colors are represented.

Computers—as opposed to the world of printing—use the RGB (red/green/blue) color system to create a 32-bit unsigned integer value that represents a color. Think of RGB as a three-dimensional space with the red, green, and blue values along each axis. Any point within that space represents a unique RGB coordinate value. Throw in a fourth component, the *alpha* value—that specifies the color's transparency—and you have the 4-byte *AlphaRGB* (ARGB) value that defines a color. For example, Indigo has RGB values of 75, 0, 130, and an alpha value of 255 (no transparency). This is represented by the hex value 4B0082FF.

Colors can also be represented by the HSL (hue/saturation/luminosity) and HSB (hue/saturation/brightness) color spaces. While RGB values follow no easily discernible pattern, HSL and HSB are based on the standard *color wheel* (see Figure 8-12) that presents colors in an orderly progression that makes it easy to visualize the sequence. Hue is represented as an angle going counterclockwise around the wheel. The saturation is the distance from the center of the wheel toward the outer edge. Colors on the outer edge have full saturation. Brightness measures the intensity of a color. Colors shown on the wheel have 100% brightness, which decreases as they are darkened (black has 0% brightness). There is no standard for assigning HSB/HSL values. Programs often use values between 0 and 255 to correspond to the RGB numbering scheme. As we will see, .NET assigns the actual angle to the hue, and values between 0 and 1 to the saturation and brightness.

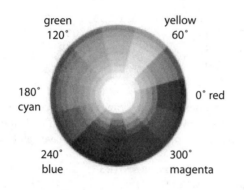

Figure 8-12   Color wheel

How to Create a Color Object

The `Color` structure provides three static methods for creating a `Color` object: `FromName`, `FromKnownColor`, and `FromArgb`. `FromName` takes the name of a color as a string argument and creates a new struct: `Color magenta = Color.FromName("Magenta")`. The name must match one in the `KnownColor` enumeration values, which is an enumeration of all the colors represented as properties in the `Color` and `SystemColor` structures.

`FromKnownColor` takes a `KnownColor` enumeration value as its argument and produces a struct for that color:

```
Color magenta = Color.FromKnownColor(KnownColor.Magenta);
```

`FromArgb` allows you to specify a color by RGB and alpha values, which makes it easy to change the transparency of an existing color. Here are some of its overloads:

```
// (r, g, b)
Color slate1 = Color.FromArgb (112, 128, 144);
// (alpha, r, g, b)
Color slate2 = Color.FromArgb (255, 112, 128, 144);
// (alpha, Color)
Color lightslate = Color.FromArgb(50, slate2 );
```

Examining the Characteristics of a Color Object

The Color structure has four properties that return the ARGB values of a color: Color.A, Color.R, Color.G, and Color.B. All of these properties have a value in the range 0 to 255.

```
Color slateGray = Color.FromArgb(255,112,128,144);
byte a = slateGray.A;                 // 255
byte r = slateGray.R;                 // 112
byte g = slateGray.G;                 // 128
byte b = slateGray.B;                 // 144
```

The individual HSB values of a color can be extracted using the Color.GetHue, GetSaturation, and GetBrightness methods. The hue is measured in degrees as a value from 0.0 to 360.0. Saturation and brightness have values between 0 and 1.

```
Color slateGray = Color.FromArgb(255,112,128,144);
float hue = slateGray.GetHue();            //  210 degrees
float sat = slateGray.GetSaturation();     // .125
float brt = slateGray.GetBrightness();     // .501
```

Observe in Figure 8-12 that the hue of 210 degrees (moving clockwise from 0) falls between cyan and blue on the circle—which is where you would expect to find a slate gray color.

A Sample Project: Building a Color Viewer

The best way to grasp how the color spaces relate to actual .NET colors is to visually associate the colors with their RGB and HSB values. .NET offers a ColorDialog class that can be used to display available colors; however, it does not identify colors by the system-defined names that most developers work with. So, let's build a simple color viewer that displays colors by name and at the same time demonstrates how to use the GDI+ types discussed in this section.

Figure 8-13 shows the user interface for this application. It consists of a Tree-View on the right that contains all the colors in the KnownColor enumeration organized into 12 color groups. These groups correspond to the primary, secondary, and tertiary[1] colors of the color wheel. In terms of hues, each section is 30 degrees on the circle. The interface also contains two panels, a larger one in which a selected color is displayed, and a smaller one that displays a brightness gradient for the selected color. This is created using a multi-color gradient comprising black and white at each end, and the color at a focus point determined by its Brightness value. The remainder

---

1. Tertiary colors are red-orange, yellow-orange, yellow-green, blue-green, blue-violet, and red-violet.

of the screen displays RGB and HSB values obtained using the properties and methods discussed earlier.

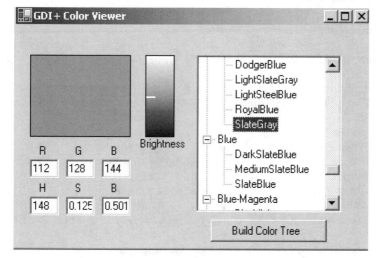

Figure 8-13   Example: Color viewer demonstrates working with colors and gradients

The code for this application is shown in Listings 8-2 and 8-3. The former contains code to populate the `TreeNode` structure with the color nodes; Listing 8-3 shows the methods used to display the selected color and its color space values. The routine code for laying out controls on a form is excluded.

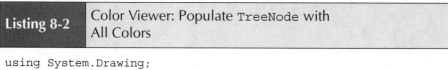

Listing 8-2	Color Viewer: Populate `TreeNode` with All Colors

```
using System.Drawing;
using System.Windows.Forms;
using System.Drawing.Drawing2D;
public class Form1 : Form
{
    public Form1()
    {
        InitializeComponent();  // Lay out controls on Form1
        // Set up event handler to be fired when node is selected
        colorTree.AfterSelect += new
            TreeViewEventHandler(ColorTree_AfterSelect);
        BuildWheel();   // Create Parent Nodes for 12 categories
    }
```

Listing 8-2   Color Viewer: Populate TreeNode with All Colors (continued)

```
[STAThread]
static void Main()
{
    Application.Run(new Form1());
}
// Parent Nodes in TreeView for each segment of color wheel
private void BuildWheel()
{
    TreeNode tNode;
    tNode = colorTree.Nodes.Add("Red");
    tNode = colorTree.Nodes.Add("Orange");
    tNode = colorTree.Nodes.Add("Yellow");
    // Remainder of nodes are added here ....
}
private void button1_Click(object sender, System.EventArgs e)
{
    // Add Colors to TreeNode Structure
    // Loop through KnownColor enum values
    Array objColor = Enum.GetValues(typeof(KnownColor));
    for (int i=0; i < objColor.Length; i++)
    {
        KnownColor kc = (KnownColor) objColor.GetValue(i);
        Color c = Color.FromKnownColor(kc);
        if (!c.IsSystemColor) // Exclude System UI colors
        {
            InsertColor(c, c.GetHue());
        }
    }
}
private void InsertColor(Color myColor, float hue)
{
    TreeNode tNode;
    TreeNode cNode = new TreeNode();
    // Offset is used to start color categories at 345 degrees
    float hueOffset = hue + 15;
    if (hueOffset >360) hueOffset -= 360;
    // Get one of 12 color categories
    int colorCat = (int)(hueOffset -.1)/30;
    tNode = colorTree.Nodes[colorCat];  // Get parent node
    // Add HSB values to node's Tag
    HSB nodeHSB = new HSB(hue, myColor.GetSaturation(),
            myColor.GetBrightness());
```

Listing 8-2	Color Viewer: Populate TreeNode with All Colors (continued)

```
    cNode.Tag  = nodeHSB;        // Tag contains HSB values
    cNode.Text = myColor.Name;
    int nodeCt = tNode.Nodes.Count;
    bool insert=false;
    // Insert colors in ascending hue value
    for (int i=0; i< nodeCt && insert==false ;i++)
    {
        nodeHSB = (HSB)tNode.Nodes[i].Tag;
        if (hue < nodeHSB.Hue)
        {
            tNode.Nodes.Insert(i,cNode);
            insert = true;
        }
    }
    if (!insert) tNode.Nodes.Add(cNode);
}
public struct HSB
{
    public float Hue;
    public float Saturation;
    public float Brightness;
    public HSB(float H, float S, float B)
    {
        Hue = H;
        Saturation = S;
        Brightness = B;
    }
}
// ---> Methods to Display Colors go here
}
```

When the application is executed, the form's constructor calls BuildWheel to create the tree structure of parent nodes that represent the 12 color categories. Then, when the Build Color Tree button is clicked, the Click event handler loops through the KnownColor enum value (excluding system colors) and calls InsertColor to insert the color under the correct parent node. The Tag field of the added node (color) is set to an HSB struct that contains the hue, saturation, and brightness for the color. Nodes are stored in ascending order of Hue value. (See Chapter 7, "Windows Forms Controls," for a discussion of the TreeNode control.)

Listing 8-3 contains the code for both the node selection event handler and for ShowColor, the method that displays the color, draws the brightness scale, and fills all the text boxes with RGB and HSB values.

Listing 8-3	Color Viewer: Display Selected Color and Values

```
private void ColorTree_AfterSelect(Object sender,
      TreeViewEventArgs e)
// Event handler for AfterSelect event
{
   // Call method to display color and info
   if (e.Node.Parent != null) ShowColor(e.Node);
}
private void ShowColor(TreeNode viewNode)
{
   Graphics g  = panel1.CreateGraphics();  // Color panel
   Graphics g2 = panel2.CreateGraphics();  // Brightness panel
   try
   {
      // Convert node's text value to Color object
      Color myColor = Color.FromName(viewNode.Text);
      Brush b = new SolidBrush(myColor);
      // Display selected color
      g.FillRectangle(b, 0,0,panel1.Width,panel1.Height);
      HSB hsbVal= (HSB) viewNode.Tag;
      // Convert hue to value between 0 and 255 for displaying
      int huescaled = (int) (hsbVal.Hue / 360 * 255);
      hText.Text = huescaled.ToString();
      sText.Text = hsbVal.Saturation.ToString();
      lText.Text = hsbVal.Brightness.ToString();
      rText.Text = myColor.R.ToString();
      gText.Text = myColor.G.ToString();
      bText.Text = myColor.B.ToString();
      // Draw Brightness scale
      Rectangle rect = new Rectangle(new Point(0,0),
            new Size(panel2.Width, panel2.Height));
      // Create multi-color brush gradient for brightness scale
      LinearGradientBrush bg = new LinearGradientBrush(rect,
            Color.Empty, Color.Empty,90);
      ColorBlend myBlend = new ColorBlend();
      myBlend.Colors = new Color[] {Color.White, myColor,
            Color.Black};
      myBlend.Positions = new float[]{0f,
            1-hsbVal.Brightness,1f};
```

Listing 8-3	Color Viewer: Display Selected Color and Values *(continued)*

```
        bg.InterpolationColors = myBlend;
        g2.FillRectangle(bg, rect);
        // Draw marker on brightness scale showing current color
        int colorPt = (int)((1-hsbVal.Brightness)* panel1.Height);
        g2.FillRectangle(Brushes.White,0,colorPt,10,2);
        b.Dispose();
        bg.Dispose();
    }
    finally
    {
        g.Dispose();
        g2.Dispose();
    }
}
```

The code incorporates several of the concepts already discussed in this section. Its main purpose is to demonstrate how `Color`, `Graphics`, and `Brush` objects work together. A `SolidBrush` is used to fill `panel1` with a color sample, a gradient brush creates the brightness scale, and `Color` properties provide the RGB values displayed on the screen.

8.3   Images

GDI+ provides a wide range of functionality for working with images in a runtime environment. It includes support for the following:

- The standard image formats such as GIF and JPG files.
- Creating images dynamically in memory that can then be displayed in a WinForms environment or served up as images on a Web server or Web Service.
- Using images as a surface to draw on.

The two most important classes for handling images are the `Image` and `Bitmap` class. `Image` is an abstract class that serves as a base class for the derived `Bitmap` class. It provides useful methods for loading and storing images, as well as gleaning information about an image, such as its height and width. But for the most part, working with images requires the creation of objects that represent raster images. This responsibility devolves to the `Bitmap` class, and we use it exclusively in this section.

Tasks associated with using images in applications fall into three general categories:

- **Loading and storing images.** Images can be retrieved from files, from a stream of bytes, from the system clipboard, or from resource files. After you have loaded or created an image, it is easily saved into a specified image format using the `Save` method of the `Image` or `Bitmap` class.
- **Displaying an image.** Images are dynamically displayed by writing them to the surface area of a form or control encapsulated by a `Graphics` object.
- **Manipulating an image.** An image is represented by an array of bits in memory. These bits can be manipulated in an unlimited number of ways to transform the image. Traditional image operations include resizing, cropping, rotating, and skewing. GDI+ also supports changing an image's overall transparency or resolution and altering individual bits within an image.

Loading and Storing Images

The easiest way to bring an image into memory is to pass the name of the file to a `Bitmap` constructor. Alternatively, you can use the `FromFile` method inherited from the `Image` class.

```
string fname = "c:\\globe.gif";
Bitmap bmp = new Bitmap(fname);
bmp = (Bitmap)Bitmap.FromFile(fname); // Cast to convert Image
```

In both cases, the image stored in `bmp` is the same size as the image in the file. Another `Bitmap` constructor can be used to scale the image as it is loaded. This code loads and scales an image to half its size:

```
int w = Image.FromFile(fname).Width;
int h = Image.FromFile(fname).Height;
Size sz= new Size(w/2,h/2);
bmp = new Bitmap(Image.FromFile(fname), sz); //Scales
```

GDI+ support images in several standard formats: bitmaps (BMP), Graphics Interchange Format (GIF), Joint Photographic Experts Group (JPEG), Portable Network Graphics (PNG), and the Tag Image File Format (TIFF). These are used for both loading and storing images and, in fact, make it quite simple to convert one format to another. Here is an example that loads a GIF file and stores it in JPEG format:

```
string fname = "c:\\globe.gif";
bmp = new Bitmap(Image.FromFile(fname));
bmp.Save("c:\\globe.jpg",
         System.Drawing.Imaging.ImageFormat.Jpeg);
// Compare size of old and new file
FileInfo fi= new FileInfo(fname);
int old = (int) fi.Length;
fi = new FileInfo("c:\\globe.jpg");
string msg = String.Format("Original: {0} New:
{1}",old,fi.Length);
MessageBox.Show(msg);  // ---> Original: 28996 New: 6736
```

The Save method has five overloads; its simplest forms take the name of the file to be written to as its first parameter and an optional ImageFormat type as its second. The ImageFormat class has several properties that specify the format of the image output file. If you have any experience with image files, you already know that the format plays a key role in the size of the file. In this example, the new JPEG file is less than one-fourth the size of the original GIF file.

To support multiple file formats, GDI+ uses encoders to save images to a file and decoders to load images. These are referred to generically as *codecs* (*code-dec*ode). An advantage of using codecs is that new image formats can be supported by writing a decoder and encoder for them.

.NET provides the ImageCodecInfo class to provide information about installed image codecs. Most applications allow GDI+ to control all aspects of loading and storing image files, and have no need for the codecs information. However, you may want to use it to discover what codecs are available on your machine. The following code loops through and displays the list of installed encoders (see Figure 8-14):

```
// Using System.Drawing.Imaging
string myList="";
foreach(ImageCodecInfo co in ImageCodecInfo.GetImageEncoders())
    myList = myList +"\n"+co.CodecName;
Console.WriteLine(myList);
```

Figure 8-14   Codecs

The `DrawImage` method of the `Graphics` object is used to display an image on the `Graphics` object's surface. These two statements load an image and draw it full size at the upper-left corner of the graphics surface (0,0). If the `Graphics` object surface is smaller than the image, the image is cropped (see the first figure in the following example).

```
Bitmap bmp = new Bitmap("C:\\globe.gif");
g.DrawImage(bmp,0,0);      // Draw at coordinates 0,0
```

`DrawImage` has some 30 overloaded versions that give you a range of control over sizing, placement, and image selection. Many of these include a destination rectangle, which forces the source image to be resized to fit the rectangle. Other variations include a source rectangle that permits you to specify a portion of the source image to be displayed; and some include both a destination and source rectangle.

The following examples capture most of the basic effects that can be achieved. Note that the source image is 192×160 pixels for all examples, and the destination panel is 96×80 pixels.

1. The source image is drawn at its full size on the target surface. Cropping occurs because the destination panel is smaller than the source image.

```
Graphics g = panel1.CreateGraphics();
g.DrawImage(bmp,0,0);
```

2. The source image is scaled to fit the destination rectangle.

```
Rectangle dRect = new
    Rectangle(new Point(0,0),
    new Size(panel1.Width,panel1.Height));
g.DrawImage(bmp, dRect);
//Or panel1.ClientRectangle
```

3. Part of the source rectangle (`left corner = 100,0`) is selected.

```
Rectangle sRect = new
    Rectangle(new Point(100,0),
    new Size(192,160));
g.DrawImage(bmp,0,0,sRect,GraphicsUnit.Pixel);
```

4. Combines examples 2 and 3: A portion of the source rectangle is scaled to fit dimensions of destination rectangle.

```
g.DrawImage(bmp,dRect,sRect,
               GraphicsUnit.Pixel);
```

5. The destination points specify where the upper-left, upper-right, and lower-left point of the original are placed. The fourth point is determined automatically in order to create a parallelogram.

```
Point[]dp = {new Point(10,0),new Point(80,10),
     new Point(0,70)};    // ul, ur, ll
g.DrawImage(bmp,dp);
```

The `DrawImage` variations shown here illustrate many familiar image effects: zoom in and zoom out are achieved by defining a destination rectangle larger (zoom in) or smaller (zoom out) than the source image; image skewing and rotation are products of mapping the corners of the original image to three destination points, as shown in the figure to the left of Example 5.

A Note on Displaying Icons

Icons (`.ico` files) do not inherit from the `Image` class and cannot be rendered by the `DrawImage` method; instead, they use the `Graphics.DrawIcon` method. To display one, create an `Icon` object and pass the file name or `Stream` object containing the image to the constructor. Then, use `DrawIcon` to display the image at a desired location.

```
Icon icon = new Icon("c:\\clock.ico");
g.DrawIcon(icon,120,220);   // Display at x=120, y=220
icon.Dispose();             // Always dispose of object
g.Dispose();
```

Manipulating Images

.NET also supports some more advanced image manipulation techniques that allow an application to rotate, mirror, flip, and change individual pixels in an image. We'll look at these techniques and also examine the advantage of building an image in memory before displaying it to a physical device.

Rotating and Mirroring

Operations that rotate or skew an image normally rely on the `DrawImage` overload that maps three corners of the original image to destination points that define a parallelogram.

```
void DrawImage(Image image, Point destPoints[])
```

Recall from an earlier example that the destination points are the new coordinates of the upper-left, upper-right, and lower-left corners of the source image. Figure 8-15 illustrates the effects that can be achieved by altering the destination points.

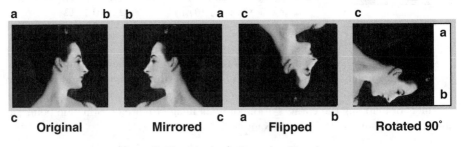

Figure 8-15   Manipulation using DrawImage

The following code is used to create a mirrored image from the original image. Think of the image as a page that has been turned over from left to right: points a and b are switched, and point c is now the lower-right edge.

```
Bitmap bmp = new Bitmap(fname);                    // Get image
// Mirror Image
Point ptA = new Point(bmp.Width,0);                // Upper left
Point ptB = new Point(0,0);                        // Upper right
Point ptC = new Point(bmp.Width, bmp.Height);      // Lower left
Point[]dp = {ptA,ptB,ptC};
g.DrawImage(bmp,dp);
```

Many of these same effects can be achieved using the `Bitmap.RotateFlip` method, which has this signature:

```
Public void RotateFlip(RotateFlipType rft)
```

`RotateFlipType` is an enumeration that indicates how many degrees to rotate the image and whether to "flip" it after rotating (available rotations are 90, 180, and 270 degrees). Here are a couple of examples:

```
// Rotate 90 degrees
bmp.RotateFlip(RotateFlipType.Rotate90FlipNone);
// Rotate 90 degrees and flip along the vertical axis
bmp.RotateFlip(RotateFlipType.Rotate90FlipY);
// Flip horizontally (mirror)
bmp.RotateFlip(RotateFlipType.RotateNoneFlipX);
```

The most important thing to recognize about this method is that it changes the actual image in memory—as opposed to DrawImage, which simply changes it on the drawing surface. For example, if you rotate an image 90 degrees and then rotate it 90 degrees again, the image will be rotated a total of 180 degrees in memory.

Working with a Buffered Image

All of the preceding examples are based on drawing directly to a visible panel control on a form. It is also possible to load an image into, or draw your own image onto, an internal Bitmap object before displaying it. This can offer several advantages:

- It permits you to create images such as graphs dynamically and display them in the application or load them into Web pages for display.
- It improves performance by permitting the application to respond to a Paint event by redrawing a stored image, rather than having to reconstruct the image from scratch.
- It permits you to keep the current "state" of the image. As long as all transformations, such as rotating or changing colors, are made first to the Bitmap object in memory, it will always represent the current state of the image.

To demonstrate, let's input a two-color image, place it in memory, change pixels in it, and write it to a panel. Figure 8-16 shows the initial image and the final image after pixels are swapped.

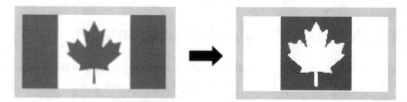

Figure 8-16   Use GetPixel() and SetPixel() to swap pixels

The following code creates a Bitmap object bmpMem that serves as a buffer where the pixels are swapped on the flag before it is displayed. We use the Graphics.From-

Image method to obtain a Graphics object that can write to the image in memory. Other new features to note are the use of GetPixel and SetPixel to read and write pixels on the image.

```
Graphics g = pan.CreateGraphics();   // Create from a panel
Bitmap bmp = new Bitmap("c:\\flag.gif");
g.DrawImage(bmp,0,0);                 // Draw flag to panel
Bitmap bmpMem = new Bitmap(bmp.Width,bmp.Height);
Graphics gMem = Graphics.FromImage(bmpMem);
gMem.DrawImage(bmp,0,0);              // Draw flag to memory
// Define a color object for the red pixels
Color cnRed = Color.FromArgb(255,214,41,33);   // a,r,g,b
// Loop through all pixels in image and swap them
for (int y=0; y<bmpMem.Height; y++)
{
    for (int x=0; x<bmpMem.Width; x++)
    {
        Color px = bmpMem.GetPixel(x,y);
        if(px.G > 240)
            bmpMem.SetPixel(x,y, cnRed);         // Set white to red
        else  bmpMem.SetPixel(x,y,Color.White); // Set red to white
    }
}
g.DrawImage(bmpMem,0,0);              // Display reversed flag on panel
gMem.Dispose();
g.Dispose();
```

Core Note

Applications that dynamically create images for display should draw them offscreen onto a Bitmap and then render them to the screen when completed.

Sample Project: Working with Images

This application brings together many of the concepts presented in this chapter: handling the Paint event; using Invalidation to clear portions of a screen; and using DrawImage to rotate, flip, and zoom in and out on an image.

The screen for the program is shown in Figure 8-17. It consists of a menu with three main selections: File is used to load an image; Image has options to mirror, flip, or copy an image; and Screen refreshes the screen. The panel control on the left serves as the main viewing window into which an image is loaded. The Image menu options are applied to this panel. The smaller panel is where part of the main image is copied. The + and – buttons zoom in and out, respectively.

The copying process is the most interesting part of the application. A user selects a rectangular area of the image by pressing the mouse button and dragging the mouse over the image. When the mouse button is raised, the selected area can be copied to the smaller panel by choosing Image-Copy from the menu.

Figure 8-17   User interface for Image Viewer [Source: Lourve, Paris]

The code for this project is presented in three sections: the menu operations, drawing the selection rectangle, and the functions associated with the small panel (panel2).

Implementing Menu Operations

The following fields are defined at the form level to make them available for menu operations:

```
private Bitmap bmp;          // Holds original loaded image
private Bitmap newbmp;        // Holds latest version of image
private bool imageStatus = false; // Indicates image is loaded
private int resizeLevel;      // Level image magnified/reduced
```

Listing 8-4 contains the code for the menu options to load an image into the viewing panel, flip an image, mirror an image, and refresh the viewing panel. The Image-Copy option is discussed in the code related to manipulating the image on panel2.

| Listing 8-4 | Image Viewer: Menu Items |

```
Private void menuItem6_Click(object sender, System.EventArgs e)
{
    // Load image from file
    OpenFileDialog fd = new OpenFileDialog();
    fd.InitialDirectory = "c:\\" ;
    fd.Filter = "Image Files | *.JPG;*.GIF";
    if (fd.ShowDialog() == DialogResult.OK)
    {
        string fname= fd.FileName;
        using(Graphics g = panel1.CreateGraphics())
        {
            bmp = new Bitmap(fname); // Load image from file
            newBmp = bmp;               // Save copy of image
            // Clear main panel before drawing to it
            g.FillRectangle(Brushes.White,0,0,
                    panel1.Width,panel1.Height );
            Rectangle r = new Rectangle(0,0,bmp.Width,
                    bmp.Height);
            g.DrawImage(bmp,r);         // Draw image on panel
            ImageStatus = true;         // Indicates image exists
            // Clear small panel
            Graphics gClear= panel2.CreateGraphics();
            g.FillRectangle(Brushes.White,0,0,
                    panel2.Width,panel2.Height );
            gClear.Dispose();
        }
    }
}
private void menuItem4_Click(object sender, System.EventArgs e)
{
    // Mirror image
    Graphics g= panel1.CreateGraphics();
    int h = newBmp.Height;
    int w = newBmp.Width;
    Point[] destPts = {
                new Point(w,0),
                new Point(0,0),
                new Point(w,h) };
    Bitmap tempBmp = new Bitmap(w,h);
    Graphics gr= Graphics.FromImage(tempBmp);
    gr.DrawImage(newBmp, destPts); // Mirror temporary image
    g.DrawImage(tempBmp,0,0);       // Draw image on panel
    newBmp = tempBmp;               // Set to mirrored image
```

Listing 8-4	Image Viewer: Menu Items *(continued)*

```
    g.Dispose();
    gr.Dispose();
}
private void menuItem3_Click(object sender, System.EventArgs e)
{
    // Flip image vertically
    newBmp.RotateFlip(RotateFlipType.RotateNoneFlipY);
    Graphics g = panel1.CreateGraphics();
    g.DrawImage(newBmp,0,0);
    g.Dispose();
}
private void menuItem9_Click(object sender, System.EventArgs e)
{
    // Refresh Screen
    panel1.Invalidate();     // Redraw entire panel
    panel1.Update();
    selectStatus = false;    // Refreshing removes selected area
}
```

The file loading routine displays a dialog box for the user to enter the image file name. If this image file exists, it is opened and displayed in `panel1`. If the image is larger than the panel, it is cropped.

The method that mirrors an image first creates a temporary `Bitmap` and uses `DrawImage`, as described earlier, to mirror the image to its surface. The mirrored image is displayed in the panel and saved in `newBmp`. Flipping could be done in a similar way, but for demonstration purposes, we use the `RotateFlip` method to directly transform `newBmp` before it is displayed.

The screen refresh routine simply calls `Invalidate` and `Update` to redraw the image on `panel1`. The main effect of this is to remove any selection rectangle (discussed next) that has been drawn on the image.

Drawing a Selection Rectangle on the Image

Listing 8-5 contains event handlers for `Paint`, `MouseDown`, `MouseUp`, and `Mouse-Move`. These routines permit the user to select a rectangular area on the image that can then be copied to `panel2`. The event handling routines are associated with the events using this code in the constructor:

```
panel1.MouseDown += new MouseEventHandler(Mouse_Down);
panel1.MouseUp   += new MouseEventHandler(Mouse_Up);
panel1.MouseMove += new MouseEventHandler(Mouse_Move);
panel1.Paint     += new PaintEventHandler(RePaint);
```

The following fields, defined at the form level, are used to keep status information:

```
private Point lastPoint = Point.Empty; // Tracks mouse movement
private Point origPoint = Point.Empty; // Mouse down coordinates
private Rectangle rectSel;             // Selected area
private bool selectStatus = false;     // True if area selected
```

When a MouseDown occurs, origPoint is set to the x,y coordinates and serves as the origin of the rectangle that is to be drawn. Dragging the mouse results in a rectangle being displayed that tracks the mouse movement. The MouseMove event handler must draw the rectangle at the new position and erase the previous rectangle. It uses lastPoint and origPoint to determine the part of the image to redraw in order to erase the previous rectangle. The new rectangle is determined by the current mouse coordinates and origPoint. When the MouseUp event occurs, rectSel is set to the final rectangle.

Listing 8-5	Image Viewer: Select Area of Image to Copy

```
private void RePaint(object sender, PaintEventArgs e)
{
   Graphics g = e.Graphics;
   // Redraw part of current image to panel
   if (ImageStatus) g.DrawImage(newBmp,
       e.ClipRectangle,e.ClipRectangle, GraphicsUnit.Pixel);
   base.OnPaint(e);
}
private void Mouse_Down(object sender, MouseEventArgs e)
{
   if (lastPoint != Point.Empty)
   {
      panel1.Invalidate(rectSel); // Clear previous rect.
      panel1.Update();
   }
   lastPoint.X= e.X;
   lastPoint.Y= e.Y;
   origPoint = lastPoint;    // Save origin of selected area
   selectStatus=true;
}
private void Mouse_Up(object sender, MouseEventArgs e)
{
   // Selected area complete. Define it as a rectangle.
   rectSel.X = e.X;
   if (e.X > origPoint.X) rectSel.X = origPoint.X;
   rectSel.Y = origPoint.Y;
```

| Listing 8-5 | Image Viewer: Select Area of Image to Copy *(continued)* |

```
    rectSel.Width = Math.Abs(e.X- origPoint.X)+1;
    rectSel.Height= Math.Abs(e.Y - origPoint.Y)+1;
    origPoint = Point.Empty;
    if (rectSel.Width < 2) selectStatus=false;
}
private void Mouse_Move(object sender, MouseEventArgs e)
{
    // Tracks mouse movement to draw bounding rectangle
    if (origPoint != Point.Empty)
    {
        Rectangle r;
        Rectangle rd;
        // Get rectangle area to invalidate
        int xop = origPoint.X;
            if (xop > lastPoint.X) xop= lastPoint.X;
            int w = Math.Abs(origPoint.X - lastPoint.X)+1;
            int h = lastPoint.Y - origPoint.Y+1;
            r = new Rectangle(xop,origPoint.Y,w,h);
            // Get rectangle area to draw
            xop = e.X >= origPoint.X ? origPoint.X:e.X;
            w = Math.Abs(origPoint.X - e.X);
            h = e.Y - origPoint.Y;
            rd = new Rectangle(xop, origPoint.Y,w,h);
            Graphics g = panel1.CreateGraphics();
            // Redraw image over previous rectangle
            g.DrawImage(newBmp,r,r);
            // Draw rectangle around selected area
            g.DrawRectangle(Pens.Red,rd);
            g.Dispose();
            lastPoint.X= e.X;
            lastPoint.Y= e.Y;
    }
}
```

The logic for creating the rectangles is based on establishing a point of origin where the first MouseDown occurs. The subsequent rectangles then attempt to use that point's coordinates for the upper left corner. However, if the mouse is moved to the left of the origin, the upper left corner must be based on this x value. This is why the MouseUp and MouseMove routines check to see if the current x coordinate e.x is less than that of the origin.

Copying and Manipulating the Image on the Small Panel

The following code is executed when Image – Copy is selected from the menu. The selected area is defined by the rectangle rectSel. The image bounded by this rectangle is drawn to a temporary Bitmap, which is then drawn to panel2. A copy of the contents of panel2 is always maintained in the Bitmap smallBmp.

```
if (selectStatus)
{
   Graphics g = panel2.CreateGraphics();
   g.FillRectangle(Brushes.White,panel2.ClientRectangle);
   Rectangle rd = new
         Rectangle(0,0,rectSel.Width,rectSel.Height);
   Bitmap temp = new Bitmap(rectSel.Width,rectSel.Height);
   Graphics gi = Graphics.FromImage(temp);
   // Draw selected portion of image onto temp
   gi.DrawImage(newBmp,rd,rectSel,GraphicsUnit.Pixel);
   smallBmp = temp;    // save image displayed on panel2
   // Draw image onto panel2
   g.DrawImage(smallBmp,rd);
   g.Dispose();
    resizeLevel = 0;   // Keeps track of magnification/reduction
}
```

The plus (+) and minus (–) buttons are used to enlarge or reduce the image on panel2. The actual enlargement or reduction is performed in memory on small-Bmp, which holds the original copied image. This is then drawn to the small panel. As shown in the code here, the magnification algorithm is quite simple: The width and height of the original image are increased in increments of .25 and used as the dimensions of the target rectangle.

```
// Enlarge image
Graphics g = panel2.CreateGraphics();
if (smallBmp != null)
{
   resizeLevel= resizeLevel+1;
   float fac= (float) (1.0+(resizeLevel*.25));
   int w = (int)(smallBmp.Width*fac);
   int h = (int)(smallBmp.Height*fac);
   Rectangle rd= new Rectangle(0,0,w,h);  // Destination rect.
   Bitmap tempBmp = new Bitmap(w,h);
   Graphics gi = Graphics.FromImage(tempBmp);
   // Draw enlarged image to tempBmp Bitmap
```

```
    gi.DrawImage(smallBmp,rd);
    g.DrawImage(tempBmp,rd);    // Display enlarged image
    gi.Dispose();
}
g.Dispose();
```

The code to reduce the image is similar, except that the width and height of the target rectangle are decremented by a factor of .25:

```
resizeLevel= (resizeLevel>-3)?resizeLevel-1:resizeLevel;
float fac= (float) (1.0+(resizeLevel*.25));
int w = (int)(smallBmp.Width*fac);
int h =(int) (smallBmp.Height*fac);
```

A Note on GDI and BitBlt for the Microsoft Windows Platform

As we have seen in the preceding examples, `Graphics.DrawImage` is an easy-to-use method for drawing to a visible external device or to a `Bitmap` object in memory. As a rule, it meets the graphics demands of most programs. However, there are situations where a more flexible or faster method is required. One of the more common graphics requirements is to perform a screen capture of an entire display or a portion of a form used as a drawing area. Unfortunately, GDI+ does not provide a direct way to copy bits from the screen memory. You may also have a graphics-intensive application that requires the constant redrawing of complex images. In both cases, the solution may well be to use GDI—specifically the `BitBlt` function.

If you have worked with the Win32 API, you are undoubtedly familiar with `BitBlt`. If not, `BitBlt`, which is short for Bit Block Transfer, is a very fast method for copying bits to and from a screen's memory, usually with the support of the graphics card. In fact, the `DrawImage` method uses `BitBlt` underneath to perform its operations.

Even though it is part of the Win32 API, .NET makes it easy to use the `BitBlt` function. The first step is to use the `System.Runtime.InteropServices` namespace to provide the `DllImportAttribute` for the function. This attribute makes the Win32 API available to managed code.

```
[System.Runtime.InteropServices.DllImportAttribute("gdi32.dll")]
private static extern int BitBlt(
    IntPtr hDestDC,      // Handle to target device context
    int xDest,           // x coordinate of destination
    int yDest,           // y coordinate of destination
    int nWidth,          // Width of memory being copied
    int nHeight,         // Height of memory being copied
    IntPtr hSrcDC,       // Handle to source device context
```

```
   int xSrc,              // x coordinate of image source
   int ySrc,              // y coordinate of image source
   System.Int32 dwRop     // Copy is specified by 0x00CC0020
);
```

This function copies a rectangular bitmap from a source to a destination. The source and destination are designated by handles to their *device context*. (In Windows, a device context is a data structure that describes the object's drawing surface and where to locate it in memory.) The type of bit transfer performed is determined by the value of the dwRop parameter. A simple copy takes the value shown in the declaration. By changing this value, you can specify that the source and target bits be combined by AND, OR, XOR, and other logical operators.

Using bitBlt is straightforward. In this example, the contents of a panel are copied to a Bitmap object in memory. Creating the Graphics object for the panel and Bitmap should be familiar territory. Next, use the Graphics object's GetHdc method to obtain a handle for the device context for the panel and Bitmap. These are then passed to the bitBlt function along with a ropType argument that tells the function to perform a straight copy operation.

```
// Draw an image on to a panel
Graphics g = panel1.CreateGraphics();
g.DrawLine(Pens.Black,10,10,50,50);
g.DrawEllipse(Pens.Blue,0,30,40,30);
// Create a memory Bitmap object to be the destination
Bitmap fxMem = new Bitmap(panel1.Width,panel1.Height);
Graphics gfxMem = Graphics.FromImage(fxMem);
int ropType= 0x00CC0020;    // perform a copy operation
// Get references to the device context for the source and target
IntPtr HDCSrc= g.GetHdc();
IntPtr HDCMem= gfxMem.GetHdc();
// Copy a rectangular area from the panel of size 100 x 100
bitBlt(HDCMem,0,0,100,100,HDCSrc,0,0,ropType);
// Release resources when finished
g.ReleaseHdc(HDCSrc);
gfxMem.ReleaseHdc(HDCMem);
g.Dispose();
gfxMem.Dispose();
```

Always pair each GetHdc with a ReleaseHdc, and only place calls to GDI functions within their scope. GDI+ operations between the statements are ignored.

8.4 Summary

GDI+ supports a wide range of graphics-related operations ranging from drawing to image manipulation. All require use of the Graphics object that encapsulates the drawing surface and provides methods for drawing geometric shapes and images to the abstract surface. The graphic is typically rendered to a form or control on the form to be displayed in a user interface.

The task of drawing is simplified by the availability of methods to create predefined geometric shapes such as lines, ellipses, and rectangles. These shapes are outlined using a Pen object that can take virtually any color or width, and can be drawn as a solid line or broken into a series of dashes, dots, and combinations of these. The shapes are filled with special brush objects such as SolidBrush, TextureBrush, LinearGradientBrush, and HatchBrush.

The Image and Bitmap classes are used in .NET to represent raster-based images. Most of the standard image formats—BMP, GIF, JPG, and PNG—are supported. After an image is loaded or drawn, the Graphics.DrawImage method may be used to rotate, skew, mirror, resize, and crop images as it displays them to the Graphics object's surface.

When custom graphics are included in a form or control, it is necessary to respond to the Paint event, to redraw all or part of the graphics on demand. A program can force this event for a control by invoking the Control.Invalidate method.

8.5 Test Your Understanding

1. What two properties does PaintEventArgs provide a Paint handler routine? Describe the role of each.

2. What method is called to trigger a Paint event for a control?

3. Which image is drawn by the following code?

    ```
    GraphicsPath gp = new GraphicsPath();
    gp.AddLine(0,0,60,0);
    gp.AddLine(0,20,60,20);
    g.DrawPath(new Pen(Color.Black,2),gp);
    ```

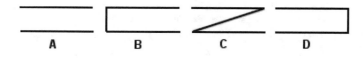

A   B   C   D

4. Which of these statements will cause a compile-time error?

   a. `Brush sb = new SolidBrush(Color.Chartreuse);`
   b. `Brush b = new Brush(Color.Red);`
   c. `Brush h = new HatchBrush(HatchStyle.DottedDiamond,`
      `                         Color.Blue,Color.Red);`

5. Which of these colors is more transparent?

   ```
   Color a = FromArgb(255,112,128,144);
   Color b = FromArgb(200,212,128,200);
   ```

6. You are drawing an image that is 200×200 pixels onto a panel that is 100×100 pixels. The image is contained in the `Bitmap bmp`, and the following statement is used:

   ```
   g.DrawImage(bmp, panel1.ClientRectangle);
   ```

   What percent of the image is displayed?

   a. 25%
   b. 50%
   c. 100%

7. The Russian artist Wassily Kandinsky translated the dance movements of Gret Palucca into a series of schematic diagrams consisting of simple geometric shapes. The following is a computer generated schematic (approximating Kandinsky's) that corresponds to the accompanying dance position. The schematic is created with a `GraphicsPath` object and the statements that follow. However, the statements have been rearranged, and your task is to place them in a sequence to draw the schematic. Recall that a `GraphicsPath` object automatically connects objects.

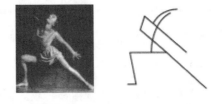

```
Graphics g = panel1.CreateGraphics();
g.SmoothingMode = SmoothingMode.AntiAlias;
GraphicsPath gp = new GraphicsPath();
gp.AddLine(10,170,30,170);
gp.AddLine(40,50,50,20);
```

```
gp.StartFigure();
gp.AddLine(16,100,100,100);
gp.AddLine(50,20,145,100);
gp.AddLine(100,100,190,180);
gp.StartFigure();
gp.AddArc(65,10,120,180,180,80);
g.DrawPath(new Pen(Color.Black,2),gp);
gp.StartFigure();
gp.AddArc(65,5,120,100,200,70);
```

8. The following statements are applied to the original image A:

```
Point ptA = new Point(bmp.Height,0);
Point ptB = new Point(bmp.Height,bmp.Width);
Point ptC = new Point(0,0);
Point[] dp = {ptA,ptB,ptC};
g.DrawImage(bmp,dp);
```

Which image is drawn by the last statement?

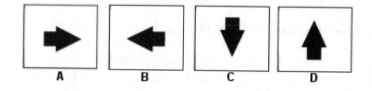

A   B   C   D

FONTS, TEXT, AND PRINTING

Topics in This Chapter

- *Fonts:* .NET classes support the creation of individual font objects and font families. Treating a font as an object allows an application to set a font's style and size through properties.

- *Text:* The `Graphics.DrawString` method and `StringFormat` class are used together to draw and format text on a drawing surface.

- *Printing:* The `PrintDocument` class provides the methods, properties, and events used to control .NET printing. It exposes properties that allow printer selection, page setup, and choice of pages to be printed.

- *Creating a Custom PrintDocument Class:* A custom `PrintDocument` class provides an application greater control over the printing process and can be used to ensure a consistent format for reports.

Chapter

Chapter 8, ".NET Graphics Using GDI+," focused on the use of GDI+ for creating graphics and working with images. This chapter continues the exploration of GDI+ with the focus shifting to its use for "drawing text." One typically thinks of text as being printed—rather than drawn. In the .NET world, however, the display and rendering of text relies on techniques similar to those required to display any graphic: a `Graphics` object must be created, and its methods used to position and render text strings—the shape of which is determined by the font used.

This chapter begins with a look at fonts and an explanation of the relationship between fonts, font families, and typefaces. It then looks at the classes used to create fonts and the options for sizing them and selecting font styles. The `Graphics.Draw-String` method is the primary tool for rendering text and has several overloads that support a number of formatting features: text alignment, text wrapping, the creation of columnar text, and trimming, to name a few.

The chapter concludes with a detailed look at printing. An incremental approach is taken. A simple example that illustrates the basic classes is presented. Building on these fundamentals, a more complex and realistic multi-page report with headers, multiple columns, and end-of-page handling is presented. Throughout, the emphasis is on understanding the GDI+ classes that support printer selection, page layout, and page creation.

9.1   Fonts

GDI+ supports only OpenType and TrueType fonts. Both of these font types are defined by mathematical representations that allow them to be scaled and rotated easily. This is in contrast to raster fonts that represent characters by a bitmap of a predetermined size. Although prevalent a few years ago, these font types are now only a historical footnote in the .NET world.

The term *font* is often used as a catchall term to describe what are in fact typefaces and font families. In .NET, it is important to have a precise definition for these terms because both Font and FontFamily are .NET classes. Before discussing how to implement these classes, let's look at the proper definition of these terms.

- A *font family* is at the top of the hierarchy and consists of a group of typefaces that may be of any style, but share the same basic appearance. *Tahoma* is a font family.
- A *typeface* is one step up the hierarchy and refers to a set of fonts that share the same family and style but can be any size. *Tahoma bold* is a typeface.
- A *font* defines how a character is represented in terms of font family, style, and size. For example (see Figure 9-1), *Tahoma Regular10* describes a font in the Tahoma font family having a regular style—as opposed to bold or italic—and a size of 10 points.

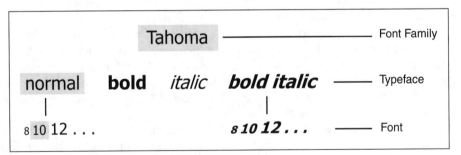

Figure 9-1   Relationship of fonts, typefaces, and font families

Font Families

The FontFamily class has two primary purposes: to create a FontFamily object that is later used to create an instance of a Font, or to provide the names of all font families available on the user's computer system.

Creating a FontFamily Object

Constructors:

```
public FontFamily (string name);
public FontFamily (GenericFontFamilies genfamilies);
```

Parameters:

name A font family name such as Arial or Tahoma.

```
FontFamily ff = new FontFamily("Arial");  // Arial family
```

GenericFontFamilies An enumeration (in the System.Drawing.Text namespace) that has three values: Monospace, Serif, and SansSerif. This constructor is useful when you are interested in a generic font family rather than a specific one. The following constructor specifies a font family in which each character takes an equal amount of space horizontally. (Courier New is a common monospace family.)

```
FontFamily ff = new FontFamily(GenericFontFamilies.Monospace);
```

As a rule, the more specific you are about the font family, the more control you have over the appearance of the application, which makes the first constructor preferable in most cases. However, use a generic font family if you are unsure about the availability of a specific font on a user's computer.

Listing Font Families

The FontFamily.Families property returns an array of available font families. This is useful for allowing a program to select a font internally to use for displaying fonts to users, so they can select one. The following code enumerates the array of font families and displays the name of the family using the Name property; it also uses the IsStyleAvailable method to determine if the family supports a bold style font.

```
string txt = "";
foreach (FontFamily ff in FontFamily.Families)
{
    txt += ff.Name;
    if (ff.IsStyleAvailable(FontStyle.Bold))txt= += " (B)";
    txt += "\r\n"; // Line feed
}
textBox1.Text = txt;    // Place font family names in textbox
```

The Font Class

Although several constructors are available for creating fonts, they fall into two categories based on whether their first parameter is a FontFamily type or a string containing the name of a FontFamily. Other parameters specify the size of the font, its style, and the units to be used for sizing. Here are the most commonly used constructors:

Constructors:

```
public Font(FontFamily ff, Float emSize);
public Font(FontFamily ff, Float emSize, FontStyle style);
public Font(FontFamily ff, Float emSize, GraphicsUnit unit);
public Font(FontFamily ff, Float emSize, FontStyle style,
            GraphicsUnit unit);

public Font(String famname, Float emSize);
public Font(String famname, Float emSize, FontStyle style);
public Font(String famname, Float emSize, GraphicsUnit unit);
public Font(String famname, Float emSize, FontStyle style,
            GraphicsUnit unit);
```

Parameters:

emSize   The size of the font in terms of the GraphicsUnit. The default GraphicsUnit is Point.

style   A FontStyle enumeration value: Bold, Italic, Regular, Strikeout, or Underline. All font families do not support all styles.

unit   The units in which the font is measured. This is one of the Graphics-Unit enumeration values:

     Point—1/72nd inch   *Inch*
     Display—1/96th inch   *Millimeter*
     Document—1/300th inch   *Pixel* (based on device resolution)

GraphicsUnits and sizing are discussed later in this section.

Creating a Font

Creating fonts is easy; the difficulty lies in deciding which of the many constructors to use. If you have already created a font family, the simplest constructor is

```
FontFamily ff = new FontFamily("Arial");
Font normFont = new Font(ff,10);       // Arial Regular 10 pt.
```

The simplest approach, without using a font family, is to pass the typeface name and size to a constructor:

```
Font normFont = new Font("Arial",10)   // Arial Regular 10 point
```

By default, a Regular font style is provided. To override this, pass a `FontStyle` enumeration value to the constructor:

```
Font boldFont = new Font("Arial",10,FontStyle.Bold);
Font bldItFont = new Font("Arial",10,
        FontStyle.Bold | FontStyle.Italic); // Arial bold italic 10
```

The second example illustrates how to combine styles. Note that if a style is specified that is not supported by the font family, an exception will occur.

The `Font` class implements the `IDisposable` interface, which means that a font's `Dispose` method should be called when the font is no longer needed. As we did in the previous chapter with the `Graphics` object, we can create the `Font` object inside a `using` construct, to ensure the font resources are freed even if an exception occurs.

```
using (Font normFont = new Font("Arial",12)) {
```

Using Font Metrics to Determine Font Height

The term *font metrics* refers to the characteristics that define the height of a font family. .NET provides both `Font` and `FontClass` methods to expose these values. To best understand them, it is useful to look at the legacy of typesetting and the terms that have been carried forward from the days of Gutenberg's printing press to the .NET Framework Class Library.

In typography, the square grid (imagine graph paper) used to lay out the outline (glyph) of a font is referred to as the *em square*. It consists of thousands of cells—each measured as one *design unit*. The outline of each character is created in an em square and consists of three parts: a *descent*, which is the part of the character below the established baseline for all characters; the *ascent*, which is the part above the baseline; and the *leading*, which provides the vertical spacing between characters on adjacent lines (see Figure 9-2).

Figure 9-2   Font metrics: the components of a font

Table 9-1 lists the methods and properties used to retrieve the metrics associated with the em height, descent, ascent, and total line space for a font family. Most of the values are returned as design units, which are quite easy to convert to a `Graphics-Unit`. The key is to remember that the total number of design units in the em is equivalent to the base size argument passed to the `Font` constructor. Here is an example of retrieving metrics for an Arial 20-point font:

```
FontFamily ff = new FontFamily("Arial");
Font myFont   = new Font(ff,20);    // Height is 20 points
int emHeight  = ff.GetEmHeight(FontStyle.Regular);      // 2048
int ascHeight = ff.GetCellAscent(FontStyle.Regular);    // 1854
int desHeight = ff.GetCellDescent(FontStyle.Regular);   // 434
int lineSpace = ff.GetLineSpacing(FontStyle.Regular);   // 2355
// Get Line Height in Points (20 x (2355/2048))
float guHeight = myFont.Size * (lineSpace / emHeight); // 22.99
float guHeight2 = myFont.GetHeight(); // 30.66 pixels
```

The primary value of this exercise is to establish familiarity with the terms and units used to express font metrics. Most applications that print or display lines of text are interested primarily in the height of a line. This value is returned by the `Font.GetHeight` method and is also available through the `Graphics.Measure-String` method described in the next section.

Table 9-1   Using `Font` and `FontFamily` to Obtain Font Metrics

Member	Units	Description
FontFamily.GetEmHeight	Design units	The height of the em square used to design the font family. TrueType fonts usually have a value of 2,048.
FontFamily.GetCellAscent	Design units	The height of a character above the base line.
FontFamily.GetCellDescent	Design units	The height of a character below the base line.
FontFamily.GetLineSpacing	Design units	The total height reserved for a character plus line spacing. The sum of `CellAscent`, `CellDescent`, and `Leading` (see Figure 9-2). This value is usually 12 to 15 percent greater than the em height.
Font.Size	Graphics unit	The base size (size passed to constructor).

Table 9-1   Using Font and Font Family to Obtain Font Metrics *(continued)*

Member	Units	Description
Font.SizeInPoints	Points	The base size in points.
Font.GetHeight	Pixels	The total height of a line. Calculated by converting LineSpacing value to pixels.

Definitions:

cell height   = ascent + descent

em height   = cell height − internal leading

line spacing = cell height + external leading

9.2   Drawing Text Strings

The Graphics.DrawString method is the most straightforward way to place text on a drawing surface. All of its overloaded forms take a string to be printed, a font to represent the text, and a brush object to paint the text. The location where the text is to be printed is specified by a Point object, x and y coordinates, or a Rectangle object. The most interesting parameter is an optional StringFormat object that provides the formatting attributes for the DrawString method. We'll examine it in detail in the discussion on formatting.

Here are the overloads for DrawString. Note that StringFormat is optional in each.

Overloads:

```
public DrawString(string, font, brush, PointF
    [,StringFormat]);
public DrawString(string, font, brush, float, float
    [,StringFormat]);
public DrawString(string, font, brush, RectangleF
    [,StringFormat]);
```

Example:

```
Font regFont = new Font("Tahoma",12);
String s = "ice mast high came floating by as green as emerald.";
// Draw text beginning at coordinates  (20,5)
g.DrawString(s, regFont, Brushes.Black, 20,5);
regFont.Dispose();
```

In this example, the upper-left corner of the text string is located at the x,y coordinate 20 pixels from the left edge and 5 pixels from the top of the drawing surface. If the printed text extends beyond the boundary of the drawing surface, the text is truncated. You may want this in some cases, but more often you'll prefer that long lines be broken and printed as multiple lines.

Drawing Multi-Line Text

Several Drawstring overloads receive a rectangle to define where the output string is drawn. Text drawn into these rectangular areas is automatically wrapped to the next line if it reaches beyond the rectangle's boundary. The following code displays the fragment of poetry in an area 200 pixels wide and 50 pixels high.

```
String s = "and ice mast high came floating by as green
    as emerald."
// All units in pixels
RectangleF rf = new RectangleF(20,5,200,50);
// Fit text in rectangle
g.Drawstring(s,regFont,Brushes.Black, rf);
```

Word wrapping is often preferable to line truncation, but raises the problem of determining how many lines of text must be accommodated. If there are more lines of text than can fit into the rectangle, they are truncated. To avoid truncation, you could calculate the height of the required rectangle by taking into account the font (f), total string length(s), and rectangle width (w). It turns out that .NET Graphics.MeasureString method performs this exact operation. One of its overloads takes the string, font, and desired line width as arguments, and returns a SizeF object whose Width and Height properties provide pixel values that define the required rectangle.

```
SizeF sf = g.MeasureString(String s, Font f, int w);
```

Using this method, the preceding code can be rewritten to handle the dynamic creation of the bounding rectangle:

```
Font regFont = new Font("Tahoma",12);
String s = "and ice mast high came floating by as green
    as emerald."
int lineWidth = 200;
SizeF sf = g.MeasureString(s, regFont, lineWidth);
// Create rectangular drawing area based on return
// height and width
RectangleF rf = new RectangleF(20,5,sf.Width, sf.Height);
// Draw text in rectangle
```

```
g.Drawstring(s,regFont,Brushes.Black, rf);
// Draw rectangle around text
g.DrawRectangle(Pens.Red,20F,5F,rf.Width, rf.Height);
```

Note that `DrawString` recognizes newline (`\r\n`) characters and creates a line break when one is encountered.

Formatting Strings with the StringFormat Class

When passed as an argument to the `DrawString` method, a `StringFormat` object can provide a number of formatting effects. It can be used to define tab positions, set column widths, apply right or left justification, and control text wrapping and truncation. As we will see in the next section, it is the primary tool for creating formatted reports. The members that we will make heaviest use of are shown in Table 9-2.

Table 9-2   Important `StringFormat` Members

Member	Description
Alignment	A `StringAlignment` enumeration value:
	`StringAlignment.Center`—Text is centered in layout rectangle.
	`StringAlignment.Far`—Text is aligned to the right for left-to-right text.
	`StringAlignment.Near`—Text is aligned to the left for left-to-right text.
Trimming	A `StringTrimming` enumeration value that specifies how to trim characters that do not completely fit in the layout rectangle:
	`StringTrimming.Character`—Text is trimmed to the nearest character.
	`StringTrimming.EllipsisCharacter`—Text is trimmed to the nearest character and an ellipsis (...) is placed at the end of the line.
	`StringTrimming.Word`—Text is trimmed to the nearest word.
SetTabStops	Takes two parameters: `SetTabStops(firstTabOffset, tabStops)`
	`FirstTabOffset`—Number of spaces between beginning of line and first tab stop.
	`TabStops`—Array of distances between tab stops.
FormatFlags	This bit-coded property provides a variety of options for controlling print layout when printing within a rectangle.
	`StringFormatFlags.DirectionVertical`—Draws text from top-to-bottom.
	`StringFormatFlags.LineLimit`—Only entire lines are displayed within the rectangle.
	`StringFormatFlags.NoWrap`—Disables text wrapping. The result is that text is printed on one line only, irrespective of the rectangle's height.

Using Tab Stops

Tab stops provide a way to align proportionate-spaced font characters into columns. To set up tab stops, you create a `StringFormat` object, use its `SetTabStops` method to define an array of tab positions, and then pass this object to the `Draw-String` method along with the text string containing tab characters (`\t`).

Core Note

If no tab stops are specified, default tab stops are set up at intervals equal to four times the size of the font. A 10-point font would have default tabs every 40 points.

As shown in Table 9-2, the `SetTabStops` method takes two arguments: the offset from the beginning of the line and an array of floating point values that specify the distance between tab stops. Here is an example that demonstrates various ways to define tab stops:

```
float[] tStops = {50f, 100f, 100f};  //Stops at: 50, 150, and 250
float[] tStops = {50f};         // Stops at: 50, 100, 150
```

You can see that it is not necessary to specify a tab stop for every tab. If a string contains a tab for which there is no corresponding tab stop, the last tab stop in the array is repeated. Listing 9-1 demonstrates using tabs to set column headers.

Listing 9-1	Using Tab Stops to Display Columns of Data

```
private void RePaint(object sender, PaintEventArgs e)
{
    Graphics g = e.Graphics;
    Font hdrFont = new Font("Arial", 10,FontStyle.Bold);
    Font bdyFont = new Font("Arial", 10);
    // (1) Create StringFormat Object
    StringFormat strFmt = new StringFormat();
    // (2) Define Tab stops
    float[] ts = {140,60,40};
    strFmt.SetTabStops(0, ts);
    // (3) Define column header text to be printed with tabs
    string header = "Artist\tCountry\tBorn\tDied";
```

Listing 9-1	Using Tab Stops to Display Columns of Data *(continued)*

```
// (4) Print column headers
g.DrawString(header, hdrFont, Brushes.Black,10,10,strFmt);
// Print one line below header
string artist = "Edouard Manet\tEngland\t1832\t1892";
g.DrawString(artist,bdyFont,Brushes.Black,10,
            10 + bdyFont.GetHeight(), strFmt);
bdyFont.Dispose();
hdrFont.Dispose();
}
```

Figure 9-3 shows the four-column output from this code. Note that the second column begins at the x coordinate 150, which is the first tab stop (140) plus the x coordinate (10) specified in DrawString.

Figure 9-3 Printing with tab stops

The unit of measurement in this example is a pixel. This unit of measurement is determined by the Graphics.PageUnit property. To override the default (pixels), set the property to a GraphicsUnit enumeration value—for example, g.PageUnit = GraphicsUnit.Inch. Be aware that all subsequent drawing done with the Graphics object will use these units.

Core Note

The use of tab spaces only supports left justification for proportionate fonts. If you need right justification—a virtual necessity for displaying financial data—pass a rectangle that has the appropriate coordinates to the DrawString method. Then, set the Alignment property of StringFormat to StringAlignment.Far.

String Trimming, Alignment, and Wrapping

The StringFormat Trimming and Alignment properties dictate how text is placed within a RectangleF object. Alignment works as you would expect, allowing you to center, right justify, or left justify a string. Trimming specifies how to truncate a string that extends beyond the boundaries of a rectangle when wrapping is not in effect. The basic options are to truncate on a word or character.

The following code segments demonstrate some of the common ways these properties can be used to format text strings.

Example 1: Printing Without a StringFormat Object

```
Font fnt = new Font("Tahoma",10,FontStyle.Bold);
RectangleF r = new RectangleF(5,5,220,60);
string txt = "dew drops are the gems of morning";
g.DrawString(txt,fnt,Brushes.Black,r);
g.DrawRectangle(Pens.Red,r.X,r.Y,r.Width,r.Height);
```

> **dew drops are the gems of
> morning**

Example 2: Printing with NoWrap Option

```
StringFormat strFmt = new StringFormat();
strFmt.FormatFlags = StringFormatFlags.NoWrap;
g.DrawString(txt,fnt,Brushes.Black,r,strFmt);
```

> **dew drops are the gems of mor**

Example 3: Printing with NoWrap and Clipping on a Word

```
StringFormat strFmt = new StringFormat();
strFmt.FormatFlags = StringFormatFlags.NoWrap;
strFmt.Trimming = StringTrimming.Word;
g.DrawString(txt,fnt,Brushes.Black,r,strFmt);
```

> **dew drops are the gems of**

Example 4: Printing with NoWrap, Clipping on Word, and Right Justification

```
StringFormat strFmt = new StringFormat();
strFmt.FormatFlags = StringFormatFlags.NoWrap;
strFmt.Trimming = StringTrimming.Word;
strFmt.Alignment = StringAlignment.Far;
g.DrawString(txt,fnt,Brushes.Black,r,strFmt);
```

> **dew drops are the gems of**
> **morning**

`StringFormat` also has a `LineAlignment` property that permits a text string to be centered vertically within a rectangle. To demonstrate, let's add two statements to Example 4:

```
strFmt.Alignment = StringAlignment.Center;
strFmt.LineAlignment = StringAlignment.Center;
```

> **dew drops are the gems of**
> **morning**

9.3 Printing

The techniques discussed in Sections 9.1 and 9.2 are device independent, which means they can be used for drawing to a printer as well as a screen. This section deals specifically with the task of creating reports intended for output to a printer. For complex reporting needs, you may well turn to Crystal Reports—which has special support in Visual Studio.NET—or SQL Server Reports. However, standard reports can be handled quite nicely using the native .NET classes available. Moreover, this approach enables you to understand the fundamentals of .NET printing and apply your knowledge of event handling and inheritance to customize the printing process.

Overview

The `PrintDocument` class—a member of the `System.Drawing.Printing` namespace—provides the methods, properties, and events that control the print process. Consequently, the first step in setting up a program that sends output to a printer is to create a `PrintDocument` object.

```
PrintDocument pd = new PrintDocument();
```

The printing process in initiated when the `PrintDocument.Print` method is invoked. As shown in Figure 9-4, this triggers the `BeginPrint` and `PrintPage` events of the `PrintDocument` class.

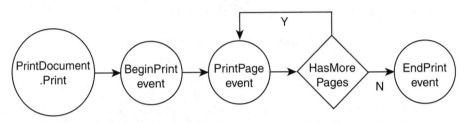

Figure 9-4   `PrintDocument` events that occur during the printing process

An event handler wired to the `PrintPage` event contains the logic and statements that produce the output. This routine typically determines how many lines can be printed—based on the page size—and contains the `DrawString` statements that generate the output. It is also responsible for notifying the underlying print controller whether there are more pages to print. It does this by setting the `HasMorePages` property, which is passed as an argument to the event handler, to `true` or `false`.

The basic `PrintDocument` events can be integrated with print dialog boxes that enable a user to preview output, select a printer, and specify page options. Listing 9-2 displays a simple model for printing that incorporates the essential elements required. Printing is initiated when `btnPrint` is clicked.

Listing 9-2   Basic Steps in Printing

```
using System.Drawing;
using System.Drawing.Printing;
using System.Windows.Forms;
// Code for Form class goes here
   // Respond to button click
   private void btnPrint_Click(object sender,
                                 System.EventArgs e)
   { PrintReport();    }
   // Set up overhead for printing
   private void PrintReport()
   {
```

Listing 9-2	Basic Steps in Printing *(continued)*

```
        // (1) Create PrintDocument object
        PrintDocument pd = new PrintDocument();
        // (2) Create PrintDialog
        PrintDialog pDialog = new PrintDialog();
        pDialog.Document = pd;
        // (3) Create PrintPreviewDialog
        PrintPreviewDialog prevDialog = new PrintPreviewDialog();
        prevDialog.Document = pd;
        // (4) Tie event handler to PrintPage event
        pd.PrintPage += new PrintPageEventHandler(Inven_Report);
        // (5) Display Print Dialog and print if OK received
        if (pDialog.ShowDialog()== DialogResult.OK)
        {
            pd.Print(); // Invoke PrintPage event
        }
    }
    private void Inven_Report(object sender,
                                PrintPageEventArgs e)
    {
        Graphics g = e.Graphics;
        Font myFont = new Font("Arial",10);
        g.DrawString("Sample Output",myFont,Brushes.Black,10,10);
        myFont.Dispose();
    }
}
```

This simple example illustrates the rudiments of printing, but does not address issues such as handling multiple pages or fitting multiple lines within the boundaries of a page. To extend the code to handle these real-world issues, we need to take a closer look at the PrintDocument class.

PrintDocument Class

Figure 9-5 should make it clear that the PrintDocument object is involved in just about all aspects of printing: It provides access to paper size, orientation, and document margins through the DefaultPageSettings class; PrinterSettings allows selection of a printer as well as the number of copies and range of pages to be printed; and event handlers associated with the PrintDocument events take care of initialization and cleanup chores related to the printing process. The PrintController class works at a level closer to the printer. It is used behind the scenes to control the print preview process and tell the printer exactly how to print a document.

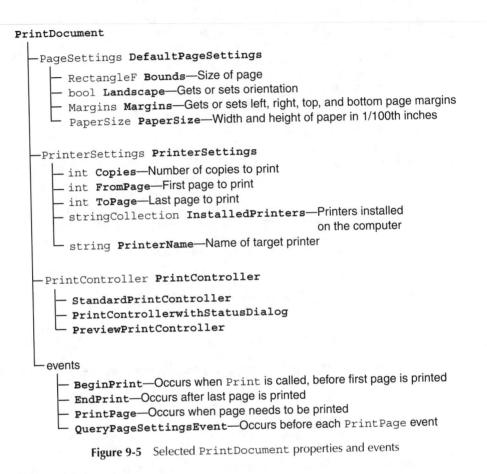

Figure 9-5   Selected PrintDocument properties and events

An understanding of these classes and events is essential to implementing a robust and flexible printing application that provides users full access to printing options.

Printer Settings

The PrinterSettings object maintains properties that specify the printer to be used and how the document is to be printed—page range, number of copies, and whether collating or duplexing is used. These values can be set programmatically or by allowing the user to select them from the Windows PrintDialog component. Note that when a user selects an option on the PrintDialog dialog box, he is actually setting a property on the underlying PrinterSettings object.

Selecting a Printer

The simplest approach is to display the `PrintDialog` window that contains a drop-down list of printers:

```
PrintDocument pd = new PrintDocument();
PrintDialog pDialog = new PrintDialog();
pDialog.Document = pd;
if (pDialog.ShowDialog()== DialogResult.OK)
{
   pd.Print(); // Invoke PrintPage event
}
```

You can also create your own printer selection list by enumerating the `InstalledPrinters` collection:

```
// Place names of printer in printerList ListBox
foreach(string pName in PrinterSettings.InstalledPrinters)
printerList.Items.Add(pName);
```

After the printer is selected, it is assigned to the `PrinterName` property:

```
string printer=
      printerList.Items[printerList.SelectedIndex].ToString();
pd.PrinterSettings.PrinterName = printer;
```

Selecting Pages to Print

The `PrinterSettings.PrintRange` property indicates the range of pages to be printed. Its value is a `PrintRange` enumeration value—`AllPages`, `Selection`, or `SomePages`—that corresponds to the All, Pages, and Selection print range options on the PrintDialog form. If Pages is selected, the `PrinterSettings.FromPage` and `ToPage` properties specify the first and last page to print. There are several things to take into consideration when working with a print range:

- To make the Selection and Pages radio buttons available on the PrintDialog form, set `PrintDialog.AllowSomePages` and `PrintDialog.AllowSelection` to true.
- The program must set the `FromPage` and `ToPage` values before displaying the Print dialog box. In addition, it's a good practice to set the `MinimumPage` and `MaximumPage` values to ensure the user does not enter an invalid page number.
- Keep in mind that the values entered on a `PrintDialog` form do nothing more than provide parameters that are available to the application. It is the responsibility of the `PrintPage` event handler to implement the logic that ensures the selected pages are printed.

The following segment includes logic to recognize a page range selection:

```
pDialog.AllowSomePages = true;
pd.PrinterSettings.FromPage =1;
pd.PrinterSettings.ToPage = maxPg;
pd.PrinterSettings.MinimumPage=1;
pd.PrinterSettings.MaximumPage= maxPg;
if (pDialog.ShowDialog()== DialogResult.OK)
{
   maxPg = 5;    // Last page to print
   currPg= 1;    // Current page to print
   if (pDialog.PrinterSettings.PrintRange ==
       PrintRange.SomePages)
   {
       currPg = pd.PrinterSettings.FromPage;
       maxPg  = pd.PrinterSettings.ToPage;
   }
   pd.Print(); // Invoke PrintPage event
}
```

This code assigns the first and last page to be printed to `currPg` and `maxPg`. These both have class-wide scope and are used by the `PrintPage` event handler to determine which pages to print.

Setting Printer Resolution

The `PrinterSettings` class exposes all of the print resolutions available to the printer through its `PrinterResolutions` collection. You can loop through this collection and list or select a resolution by examining the `Kind` property of the contained `PrinterResolution` objects. This property takes one of five `PrinterResolution-Kind` enumeration values: `Custom`, `Draft`, `High`, `Low`, or `Medium`. The following code searches the `PrinterResolutions` collection for a `High` resolution and assigns that as a `PrinterSettings` value:

```
foreach (PrinterResolution pr in
        pd.PrinterSettings.PrinterResolutions)
{
   if (pr.Kind == PrinterResolutionKind.High)
   {
      pd.PageSettings.PrinterResolution = pr;
      break;
   }
}
```

Page Settings

The properties of the `PageSettings` class define the layout and orientation of the page being printed to. Just as the `PrinterSettings` properties correspond to the `PrintDialog`, the `PageSettings` properties reflect the values of the `PageSetup-Dialog`.

```
PageSetupDialog ps = new PageSetupDialog();
ps.Document = pd;    // Assign reference to PrinterDocument
ps.ShowDialog();
```

This dialog box lets the user set all the margins, choose landscape or portrait orientation, select a paper type, and set printer resolution. These values are exposed through the `DefaultPageSettings` properties listed in Figure 9-5. As we will see, they are also made available to the `PrintPage` event handler through the `PrintPageEventArgs` parameter and to the `QueryPageSettingsEvent` through its `QueryPageSettingsEventArgs` parameter. The latter can update the values, whereas `PrintPage` has read-only access.

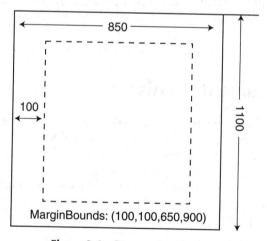

Figure 9-6 Page settings layout

Figure 9-6 illustrates the layout of a page that has the following `DefaultPage-Settings` values:

```
Bounds.X = 0;
Bounds.Y = 0;
Bounds.Width = 850;
```

```
Bounds.Height = 1100;
PaperSize.PaperName = "Letter";
PaperSize.Height = 1100;
PaperSize.Width = 850;
Margins.Left = 100;
Margins.Right = 100;
Margins.Top = 100;
Margins.Bottom = 100;
```

All measurements are in hundredths of an inch. The `MarginBounds` rectangle shown in the figure represents the area inside the margins. It is not a `PrinterSettings` property and is made available only to the `PrintPage` event handler.

Core Note

Many printers preserve an edge around a form where printing cannot occur. On many laser printers, for example, this is one-quarter of an inch. In practical terms, this means that all horizontal coordinates used for printing are shifted; thus, if `DrawString` is passed an x coordinate of 100, it actually prints at 125. It is particularly important to be aware of this when printing on preprinted forms where measurements must be exact.

PrintDocument Events

Four `PrintDocument` events are triggered during the printing process: `BeginPrint`, `QueryPageSettingsEvent`, `PrintPage`, and `EndPrint`. As we've already seen, `PrintPage` is the most important of these from the standpoint of code development because it contains the logic and statements used to generate the printed output. It is not necessary to handle the other three events, but they do provide a handy way to deal with the overhead of initialization and disposing of resources when the printing is complete.

BeginPrint Event

This event occurs when the `PrintDocument.Print` method is called and is a useful place to create font objects and open data connections. The `PrintEventHandler` delegate is used to register the event handler routine for the event:

```
pd.BeginPrint += new PrintEventHandler(Rpt_BeginPrint);
```

This simple event handler creates the font to be used in the report. The font must be declared to have scope throughout the class.

```
private void Rpt_BeginPrint(object sender, PrintEventArgs e)
{
   rptFont = new Font("Arial",10);
   lineHeight= (int)rptFont.GetHeight();  // Line height
}
```

EndPrint Event

This event occurs after all printing is completed and can be used to destroy resources no longer needed. Associate an event handler with the event using

```
pd.EndPrint += new PrintEventHandler(Rpt_EndPrint);
```

This simple event handler disposes of the font created in the `BeginPrint` handler:

```
private void Rpt_EndPrint(object sender, PrintEventArgs e)
{
   rptFont.Dispose();
}
```

QueryPageSettingsEvent Event

This event occurs before each page is printed and provides an opportunity to adjust the page settings on a page-by-page basis. Its event handler is associated with the event using the following code:

```
pd.QueryPageSettings += new
      QueryPageSettingsEventHandler(Rpt_Query);
```

The second argument to this event handler exposes a `PageSettings` object and a `Cancel` property that can be set to `true` to cancel printing. This is the last opportunity before printing to set any `PageSettings` properties, because they are read-only in the `PrintPage` event. This code sets special margins for the first page of the report:

```
private void Rpt_Query(object sender,
                         QueryPageSettingsEventArgs e)
{
   // This is the last chance to change page settings
   // If first page, change margins for title
   if (currPg ==1) e.PageSettings.Margins =
                     new Margins(200,200,200,200);
   else e.PageSettings.Margins = new Margins(100,100,100,100);
}
```

This event handler should be implemented only if there is a need to change page settings for specific pages in a report. Otherwise, the `DefaultPageSettings` properties will prevail throughout.

PrintPage Event

The steps required to create and print a report fall into two categories: setting up the print environment and actually printing the report. The `PrinterSettings` and `PageSettings` classes that have been discussed are central to defining how the report will look. After their values are set, it's the responsibility of the `PrintPage` event handler to print the report to the selected printer, while being cognizant of the paper type, margins, and page orientation.

Figure 9-7 lists some of the generic tasks that an event handler must deal with in generating a report. Although the specific implementation of each task varies by application, it's a useful outline to follow in designing the event handler code. We will see an example shortly that uses this outline to implement a simple report application.

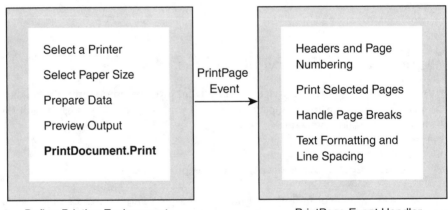

Figure 9-7   Tasks required to print a report

Defining the PrintPage Event Handler

The event handler method matches the signature of the `PrintPageEventHandler` delegate (refer to Listing 9-2):

```
public delegate void PrintPageEventHandler(
        object sender, PrintPageEventArgs e);
```

The `PrintPageEventArgs` argument provides the system data necessary for printing. As shown in Table 9-3, its properties include the `Graphics` object, `Page-Settings` object, and a `MarginBounds` rectangle—mentioned earlier—that defines the area within the margins. These properties, along with variables defined at a class level, provide all the information used for printing.

Table 9-3   `PrintPageEventArgs` Members

Property	Description
Cancel	Boolean value that can be set to `true` to cancel the printing.
Graphics	The `Graphics` object used to write to printer.
HasMorePages	Boolean value indicating whether more pages are to be printed. Default is `false`.
MarginBounds	Rectangular area representing the area within the margins.
PageBounds	Rectangular area representing the entire page.
PageSettings	Page settings for the page to be printed.

Previewing a Printed Report

The capability to preview a report onscreen prior to printing—or as a substitute for printing—is a powerful feature. It is particularly useful during the development process where a screen preview can reduce debugging time, as well as your investment in print cartridges.

To preview the printer output, you must set up a `PrintPreviewDialog` object and set its `Document` property to an instance of the `PrintDocument`:

```
PrintPreviewDialog prevDialog = new PrintPreviewDialog();
    prevDialog.Document = pd;
```

The preview process is invoked by calling the `ShowDialog` method:

```
prevDialog.ShowDialog();
```

After this method is called, the same steps are followed as in actually printing the document. The difference is that the output is displayed in a special preview window (see Figure 9-8). This provides the obvious advantage of using the same code for both previewing and printing.

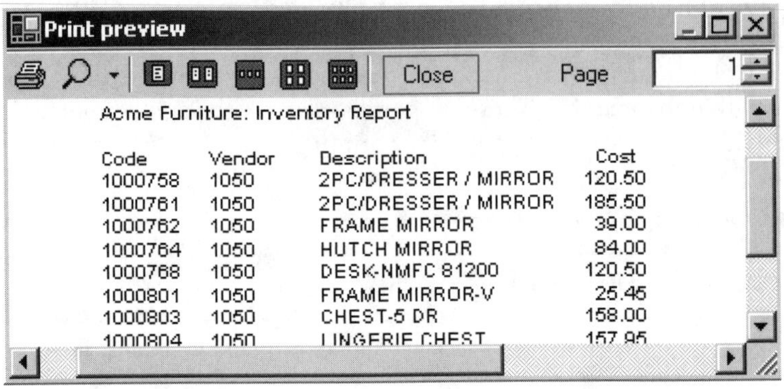

Figure 9-8   Report can be previewed before printing

A Report Example

This example is intended to illustrate the basic elements of printing a multi-page report. It includes a data source that provides an unknown number of records, a title and column header for each page, and detailed rows of data consisting of left-justified text and right-justified numeric data.

Data Source for the Report

The data in a report can come from a variety of sources, although it most often comes from a database. Because database access is not discussed until Chapter 11, "ADO.NET," let's use a text file containing comma-delimited inventory records as the data source. Each record consists of a product ID, vendor ID, description, and price:

```
1000761,1050,2PC/DRESSER/MIRROR,185.50
```

A `StreamReader` object is used to load the data and is declared to have class-wide scope so it is available to the `PrintPage` event handler:

```
// Using System.IO namespace is required
// StreamReader sr; is set up in class declaration
sr = new StreamReader("c:\\inventory.txt");
```

The `PrintPage` event handler uses the `StreamReader` to input each inventory record from the text file as a string. The string is split into separate fields that are stored in the `prtLine` array. The event handler also contains logic to recognize page breaks and perform any column totaling desired.

Code for the Application

Listing 9-3 contains the code for the `PrintDocument` event handlers implemented in the application. Because you cannot pass your own arguments to an event handler, the code must rely on variables declared at the class level to maintain state information. These include the following:

```
StreamReader sr;    // StreamReader to read inventor from file
string[]prtLine;    // Array containing fields for one record
Font rptFont;       // Font for report body
Font hdrFont;       // Font for header
string title= "Acme Furniture: Inventory Report";
float lineHeight;   // Height of a line (100ths inches)
```

The fonts and `StreamReader` are initialized in the `BeginPrint` event handler. The corresponding `EndPrint` event handler then disposes of the two fonts and closes the `StreamReader`.

Listing 9-3	Creating a Report

```
// pd.PrintPage  += new PrintPageEventHandler(Inven_Report);
// pd.BeginPrint += new PrintEventHandler(Rpt_BeginPrint);
// pd.EndPrint   += new PrintEventHandler(Rpt_EndPrint);
//
// BeginPrint event handler
private void Rpt_BeginPrint(object sender, PrintEventArgs e)
{
   // Create fonts to be used and get line spacing.
   rptFont = new Font("Arial",10);
   hdrFont = new Font(rptFont,FontStyle.Bold);
   // insert code here to set up Data Source...
}
// EndPrint event Handler
private void Rpt_EndPrint(object sender, PrintEventArgs e)
{
   // Remove Font resources
   rptFont.Dispose();
   hdrFont.Dispose();
   sr.Close();         // Close StreamReader
}
// PrintPage event Handler
private void Inven_Report(object sender, PrintPageEventArgs e)
{
```

Listing 9-3   Creating a Report *(continued)*

```
Graphics g = e.Graphics;
int xpos= e.MarginBounds.Left;
int lineCt = 0;
// Next line returns 15.97 for Arial-10
lineHeight = hdrFont.GetHeight(g);
// Calculate maximum number of lines per page
int linesPerPage = int((e.MarginBounds.Bottom -
        e.MarginBounds.Top)/lineHeight -2);
float yPos = 2* lineHeight+ e.MarginBounds.Top;
int hdrPos = e.MarginBounds.Top;
// Call method to print title and column headers
PrintHdr(g,hdrPos, e.MarginBounds.Left);
string prod;
char[]delim=  {','};
while(( prod =sr.ReadLine())!=null)
{
   prtLine= prod.Split(delim,4);
   yPos += lineHeight;   // Get y coordinate of line
   PrintDetail(g,yPos);  // Print inventory record
   if(lineCt > linesPerPage)
   {
      e.HasMorePages= true;
      break;
   }
}
}
private void PrintHdr( Graphics g, int yPos, int xPos)
{
   // Draw Report Title
   g.DrawString(title,hdrFont,Brushes.Black,xPos,yPos);
   // Draw Column Header
   float[] ts = {80, 80,200};
   StringFormat strFmt = new StringFormat();
   strFmt.SetTabStops(0,ts);
   g.DrawString("Code\tVendor\tDescription\tCost",
      hdrFont,Brushes.Black,xPos,yPos+2*lineHeight,strFmt);
}
private void PrintDetail(Graphics g, float yPos)
{
   int xPos = 100;
   StringFormat strFmt = new StringFormat();
   strFmt.Trimming = StringTrimming.EllipsisCharacter;
   strFmt.FormatFlags = StringFormatFlags.NoWrap;
   RectangleF r = new RectangleF(xPos+160,yPos,
                              200,lineHeight);
```

| Listing 9-3 | Creating a Report *(continued)* |

```
// Get data fields from array
string invenid = prtLine[0];
string vendor  = prtLine[1];
string desc    = prtLine[2];
decimal price  = decimal.Parse(prtLine[3]);
g.DrawString(invenid, rptFont,Brushes.Black,xPos, yPos);
g.DrawString(vendor, rptFont,Brushes.Black,xPos+80, yPos);
// Print description within a rectangle
g.DrawString(desc, rptFont,Brushes.Black,r,strFmt);
// Print cost right justified
strFmt.Alignment = StringAlignment.Far;  // Right justify
strFmt.Trimming= StringTrimming.None;
g.DrawString(price.ToString("#,###.00"),
     rptFont,Brushes.Black, xPos+400,yPos,strFmt);
}
```

The PrintPage event handler Inven_Report directs the printing process by calling PrintHdr to print the title and column header on each page and PrintDetail to print each line of inventory data. Its responsibilities include the following:

- Using the MarginBounds rectangle to set the x and y coordinates of the title at the upper-left corner of the page within the margins.
- Calculating the maximum number of lines to be printed on a page. This is derived by dividing the distance between the top and bottom margin by the height of a line. It then subtracts 2 from this to take the header into account.
- Setting the HasMorePages property to indicate whether more pages remain to be printed.

The PrintHdr routine is straightforward. It prints the title at the coordinates passed to it, and then uses tabs to print the column headers. The PrintDetail method is a bit more interesting, as it demonstrates some of the classes discussed earlier in the chapter. It prints the inventory description in a rectangle and uses the StringFormat class to prevent wrapping and specify truncation on a character. StringFormat is also used to right justify the price of an item in the last column.

Figure 9-9 shows an example of output from this application. Measured from the left margin, the first three columns have an x coordinate of 0, 80, and 160, respectively. Note that the fourth column is right justified, which means that its x coordinate of 400 specifies where the right edge of the string is positioned. Vertical spacing is determined by the lineHeight variable that is calculated as

```
float lineHeight = hdrFont.GetHeight(g);
```

This form of the GetHeight method returns a value based on the GraphicsUnit of the Graphics object passed to it. By default, the Graphics object passed to the BeginPrint event handler has a GraphicsUnit of 100 dpi. The margin values and all coordinates in the example are in hundredths of an inch. .NET takes care of automatically scaling these units to match the printer's resolution.

Acme Furniture: Inventory Report

Code	Vendor	Description	Cost
1000758	1050	2PC/DRESSER/MIRROR	120.50
1000761	1050	2PC/DRESSER/MIRROR	185.50
1000762	1050	FRAME MIRROR	39.00
1000764	1050	HUTCH MIRROR	84.00
1000768	1050	DESK-NMFC 81200	120.50

Figure 9-9   Output from the report example

Creating a Custom PrintDocument Class

The generic PrintDocument class is easy to use, but has shortcomings with regard to data encapsulation. In the preceding example, it is necessary to declare variables that have class-wide scope—such as the StreamReader—to make them available to the various methods that handle PrintDocument events. A better solution is to derive a custom PrintDocument class that accepts parameters and uses properties and private fields to encapsulate information about line height, fonts, and the data source. Listing 9-4 shows the code from the preceding example rewritten to support a derived PrintDocument class.

Creating a custom PrintDocument class turns out to be a simple and straightforward procedure. The first step is to create a class that inherits from PrintDocument. Then, private variables are defined that support the fonts and title that are now exposed as properties. Finally, the derived class overrides the OnBeginPrint, OnEndPrint, and OnPrintPage methods of the base PrintDocument class.

The overhead required before printing the report is reduced to creating the new ReportPrintDocument object and assigning property values.

```
string myTitle = "Acme Furniture: Inventory Report";
ReportPrintDocument rpd = new ReportPrintDocument(myTitle);
rpd.TitleFont = new Font("Arial",10, FontStyle.Bold);
rpd.ReportFont = new Font("Arial",10);
PrintPreviewDialog prevDialog = new PrintPreviewDialog();
```

```
prevDialog.Document = rpd;
prevDialog.ShowDialog();    // Preview Report
// Show Print Dialog and print report
PrintDialog pDialog = new PrintDialog();
pDialog.Document = rpd;
if (pDialog.ShowDialog() == DialogResult.OK)
{
   rpd.Print();
}
```

The preceding code takes advantage of the new constructor to pass in the title when the object is created. It also sets the two fonts used in the report.

Listing 9-4 Creating a Custom `PrintDocument` Class

```
// Derived Print Document Class
public class ReportPrintDocument: PrintDocument
{
   private Font hdrFont;
   private Font rptFont;
   private string title;
   private StreamReader sr;
   private float lineHeight;
   // Constructors
   public ReportPrintDocument()
   {}
   public ReportPrintDocument(string myTitle)
   {
      title = myTitle;
   }
   // Property to contain report title
   public string ReportTitle
   {
      get {return title;}
      set {title = value;}
   }
   // Fonts are exposed as properties
   public Font TitleFont
   {
      get {return hdrFont;}
      set {hdrFont = value;}
   }
```

Listing 9-4   Creating a Custom `PrintDocument` Class *(continued)*

```
public Font ReportFont
{
   get {return rptFont;}
   set {rptFont = value;}
}
// BeginPrint event handler
protected override void OnBeginPrint(PrintEventArgs e)
{
   base.OnBeginPrint(e);
   // Assign Default Fonts if none selected
   if (TitleFont == null)
   {
      TitleFont =
          new Font("Arial",10,FontStyle.Bold);
      ReportFont = new Font("Arial",10);
   }
   / Code to create StreamReader or other data source
   // goes here ...
   sr = new StreamReader(inputFile);
}
protected override void OnEndPrint(PrintEventArgs e)
{
   base.OnEndPrint(e);
   TitleFont.Dispose();
   ReportFont.Dispose();
   sr.Close();
}
// Print Page event handler
protected override void OnPrintPage(PrintPageEventArgs e)
{
   base.OnPrintPage(e);
   // Remainder of code for this class is same as in
   // Listing 9-3 for Inven_Report, PrintDetail, and
   // PrintHdr
}
}
```

This example is easily extended to include page numbering and footers. For frequent reporting needs, it may be worth the effort to create a generic report generator that includes user selectable data source, column headers, and column totaling options.

9.4   Summary

This chapter has focused on using the GDI+ library to display and print text. The first section explained how to create and use font families and font classes. The emphasis was on how to construct fonts and understand the elements that comprise a font by looking at font metrics.

After a font has been created, the `Graphics.DrawString` method is used to draw a text string to a display or printer. Its many overloads permit text to be drawn at specific coordinates or within a rectangular area. By default, text printed in a rectangle is left justified and wrapped to the next line when it hits the bounds of the rectangle. This default formatting can be overridden by passing a `StringFormat` object to the `DrawString` method. The `StringFormat` class is the key to .NET text formatting. It is used to justify text, specify how text is truncated, and set tab stops for creating columnar output.

GDI+ provides several classes designed to support printing to a printer. These include the following:

- `PrintDocument`. Sends output to the printer. Its `Print` method initiates the printing process and triggers the `BeginPrint`, `QueryPage-SettingsEvent`, `PrintPage`, and `EndPrint` events. The event handler for the `PrintPage` event contains the logic for performing the actual printing.
- `PrintPreviewDialog`. Enables output to be previewed before printing.
- `PrinterSettings`. Has properties that specify the page range to be printed, the list of available printers, and the name of the target printer. These values correspond to those a user can select on the `PrintDialog` dialog box.
- `DefaultPageSettings`. Has properties that set the bounds of a page, the orientation (landscape or portrait), the margins, and the paper size. These values correspond to those selected on the `PageSetupDialog` dialog box.

An example for printing a columnar report demonstrated how these classes can be combined to create an application that provides basic report writing. As a final example, we illustrated how the shortcomings of the `PrintDocument` class can be overcome by creating a custom `PrintDocument` class that preserves data encapsulation.

9.5 Test Your Understanding

1. Does *Arial Bold* refer to a font family, typeface, or font?

2. What is the default unit of measurement for a font? What size is it (in inches)?

3. Which method and enumeration are used to right justify an output string?

4. When the following code is executed, what is the x coordinate where the third column begins?

```
float[] tStops = {50f, 60f, 200f, 40f};
StringFormat sf = new StringFormat();
sf.SetTabStops(0,tStops);
string hdr = "Col1\tCol2\tCol3\tCol4";
g.DrawString(hdr, myFont, Brushes.Black, 10,10,sf);
```

5. Which `PrintDocument` event is called after `PrintDocument.Print` is executed?

6. Which class available to the `PrintPage` event handler defines the margins for a page?

7. What three steps must be included to permit a document to be previewed before printing?

WORKING WITH XML IN .NET

Topics in This Chapter

- *Introduction to Using XML:* Introduces some of the basic concepts of working with XML. These include the XML validation and the use of an XML style sheet.

- *Reading XML Data:* Explains how to use the .NET XML stack to access XML data. The `XmlReader`, `XmlNodeReader`, `XmlTextReader` are examined.

- *Writing XML Data:* The easiest way to create XML data is to use the .NET `XmlSerializer` to serialize data into the XML format. When the data is not in a format that can be serialized, an alternative is the `XmlWriter` class.

- *Searching and Updating XML Documents:* XPath is a query language to search XML documents. Examples illustrate how to use it to search an `XmlDocument`, `XmlDataDocument`, and `XPathDocument`.

Chapter

Extensible Markup Language (XML) plays a key role in the .NET universe. Configuration files that govern an application or Web page's behavior are deployed in XML; objects are stored or streamed across the Internet by serializing them into an XML representation; Web Services intercommunication is based on XML; and as we see in Chapter 11, "ADO.NET," .NET methods support the interchange of data between an XML and relational data table format.

XML describes data as a combination of markup language and content that is analogous to the way HTML describes a Web page. Its flexibility permits it to easily represent flat, relational, or hierarchical data. To support one of its design goals—that it "should be human-legible and reasonably clear"[1]—it is represented in a text-only format. This gives it the significant advantage of being platform independent, which has made it the de facto standard for transmitting data over the Internet.

This chapter focuses on pure XML and the classes that reside in the `System.Xml` namespace hierarchy. It begins with basic background information on XML: how schemas are used to validate XML data and how style sheets are used to alter the way XML is displayed. The remaining sections present the .NET classes that are used to read, write, update, and search XML documents. If you are unfamiliar with .NET XML, you may surprised how quickly you become comfortable with reading and searching XML data. Extracting information from even a complex XML structure is

---

1. W3C Extensible Markup Language (XML), 1.0 (Third Edition),
   `http://www.w3.org/TR/REC-xml/`

refreshingly easy with the XPath query language—and far less tedious than the original search techniques that required traversing each node of an XML tree. In many ways, it is now as easy to work with XML as it is to work with relational data.

10.1 Working with XML

Being literate in one's spoken language is defined as having the basic ability to read and write that language. In XML, functional literacy embraces more than reading and writing XML data. In addition to the XML data document, there is an XML Schema document (`.xsd`) that is used to validate the content and structure of an XML document. If the XML data is to be displayed or transformed, one or more XML style sheets (`.xsl`) can be used to define the transformation. Thus, we can define our own form of XML literacy as the ability to do five things:

1. Create an XML file.
2. Read and query an XML file.
3. Create an XML Schema document.
4. Use an XML Schema document to validate XML data.
5. Create and use an XML style sheet to transform XML data.

The purpose of this section is to introduce XML concepts and terminology, as well as some .NET techniques for performing the preceding tasks. Of the five tasks, all are covered in this section, with the exception of reading and querying XML data, which is presented in later sections.

Using XML Serialization to Create XML Data

As discussed in Chapter 4, "Working with Objects in C#," serialization is a convenient way to store objects so they can later be deserialized into the original objects. If the natural state of your data allows it to be represented as objects, or if your application already has it represented as objects, XML serialization often offers a good choice for converting it into an XML format. However, there are some restrictions to keep in mind when applying XML serialization to a class:

- The class must contain a `public` default (parameterless) constructor.
- Only a `public` property or field can be serialized.
- A read-only property cannot be serialized.
- To serialize the objects in a custom collection class, the class must derive from the `System.Collections.CollectionBase` class and include an indexer. The easiest way to serialize multiple objects is usually to place them in a strongly typed array.

An Example Using the XmlSerializer Class

Listing 10-1 shows the XML file that we're going to use for further examples in this section. It was created by serializing instances of the class shown in Listing 10-2.

Listing 10-1   Sample XML File

```xml
<?xml version="1.0" standalone="yes"?>
   <films>
      <movies>
         <movie_ID>5</movie_ID>
         <movie_Title>Citizen Kane </movie_Title>
         <movie_Year>1941</movie_Year>
         <movie_DirectorID>Orson Welles</movie_DirectorID>
         <bestPicture>Y</bestPicture>
         <AFIRank>1</AFIRank>
      </movies>
      <movies>
         <movie_ID>6</movie_ID>
         <movie_Title>Casablanca </movie_Title>
         <movie_Year>1942</movie_Year>
         <movie_Director>Michael Curtiz</movie_Director>
         <bestPicture>Y</bestPicture>
         <AFIRank>1</AFIRank>
      </movies>
   </films>
```

In comparing Listings 10-1 and 10-2, it should be obvious that the XML elements are a direct rendering of the public properties defined for the `movies` class. The only exceptional feature in the code is the `XmlElement` attribute, which will be discussed shortly.

Listing 10-2   Using XmlSerializer to Create an XML File

```csharp
using System.Xml;
using System.Xml.Serialization;
// other code here ...
public class movies
{
   public movies()   // Parameterless constructor is required
   {  }
   public movies(int ID, string title, string dir,string pic,
               int yr, int movierank)
   {
```

Listing 10-2 Using `XmlSerializer` to Create an XML File *(continued)*

```
    movieID = ID;
    movie_Director = dir;
    bestPicture = pic;
    rank = movierank;
    movie_Title = title;
    movie_Year = yr;
}
// Public properties that are serialized
public int movieID
{
    get { return mID; }
    set { mID = value; }
}
public string movie_Title
{
    get { return mTitle; }
    set { mTitle = value; }
}
public int movie_Year
{
    get { return mYear; }
    set { mYear = value; }
}
public string movie_Director
{
    get { return mDirector; }
    set { mDirector = value; }
}
public string bestPicture
{
    get { return mbestPicture; }
    set { mbestPicture = value; }
}
[XmlElement("AFIRank")]
public int rank
{
    get { return mAFIRank; }
    set { mAFIRank = value; }
}
private int mID;
private string mTitle;
private int mYear;
private string mDirector;
private string mbestPicture;
private int mAFIRank;
}
```

To transform the class in Listing 10-2 to the XML in Listing 10-1, we follow the three steps shown in the code that follows. First, the objects to be serialized are created and stored in an array. Second, an XmlSerializer object is created. Its constructor (one of many constructor overloads) takes the object type it is serializing as the first parameter and an attribute as the second. The attribute enables us to assign "films" as the name of the root element in the XML output. The final step is to execute the XmlSerializer.Serialize method to send the serialized output to a selected stream—a file in this case.

```
// (1) Create array of objects to be serialized
movies[] films = {new movies(5,"Citizen Kane","Orson Welles",
                         "Y", 1941,1 ),
               new movies(6,"Casablanca","Michael Curtiz",
                         "Y", 1942,2)};
// (2) Create serializer
//      This attribute is used to assign name to XML root element
XmlRootAttribute xRoot = new XmlRootAttribute();
    xRoot.ElementName = "films";
    xRoot.Namespace = "http://www.corecsharp.net";
    xRoot.IsNullable = true;
// Specify that an array of movies types is to be serialized
XmlSerializer xSerial = new XmlSerializer(typeof(movies[]),
                                      xRoot);
string filename=@"c:\oscarwinners.xml";
// (3) Stream to write XML into
TextWriter writer = new StreamWriter(filename);
xSerial.Serialize(writer,films);
```

Serialization Attributes

By default, the elements created from a class take the name of the property they represent. For example, the movie_Title property is serialized as a <movie_Title> element. However, there is a set of serialization attributes that can be used to override the default serialization results. Listing 10-2 includes an XmlElement attribute whose purpose is to assign a name to the XML element that is different than that of the corresponding property or field. In this case, the rank property name is replaced with AFIRank in the XML.

There are more than a dozen serialization attributes. Here are some other commonly used ones:

XmlAttribute   Is attached to a property or field and causes it to be rendered as an attribute within an element.

Example: XmlAttribute("movieID")]

Result: <movies movieID="5">

XmlIgnore	Causes the field or property to be excluded from the XML.
XmlText	Causes the value of the field or property to be rendered as text. No elements are created for the member name.

Example: [XmlText]
            public string movie_Title{

Result: <movies movieID="5">Citizen Kane

XML Schema Definition (XSD)

The XML Schema Definition document is an XML file that is used to validate the contents of another XML document. The schema is essentially a template that defines in detail what is permitted in an associated XML document. Its role is similar to that of the BNF (Backus-Naur Form) notation that defines a language's syntax for a compiler.

.NET provides several ways (others are included in Chapter 11, "ADO.NET") to create a schema from an XML data document. One of the easiest ways is to use the XML Schema Definition tool (Xsd.exe). Simply run it from a command line and specify the XML file for which it is to produce a schema:

```
C:/ xsd.exe  oscarwinners.xml
```

The output, oscarwinners.xsd, is shown in Listing 10-3.

Listing 10-3	XML Schema to Apply Against XML in Listing 10-1

```
<xs:schema id="films" xmlns=""
        xmlns:xs=http://www.w3.org/2001/XMLSchema
        xmlns:msdata="urn:schemas-microsoft-com:xml-msdata">
    <xs:element name="films" msdata:IsDataSet="true">
      <xs:complexType>
        <xs:choice minOccurs="0" maxOccurs="unbounded">
          <xs:element name="movies">
            <xs:complexType>
              <xs:sequence>
                <xs:element name="movie_ID" type="xs:int"
                      minOccurs="0" />
                <xs:element name="movie_Title" type="xs:string"
                      minOccurs="0" />
                <xs:element name="movie_Year" type="xs:int"
                      minOccurs="0" />
```

Listing 10-3	XML Schema to Apply Against XML in Listing 10-1 (continued)

```
        <xs:element name="movie_Director" type="xs:string"
                minOccurs="0" />
        <xs:element name="bestPicture" type="xs:string"
                minOccurs="0" />
        <xs:element name="AFIRank" type="xs:int"
                minOccurs="0"
        />
      </xs:sequence>
    </xs:complexType>
  </xs:element>
  </xs:choice>
  </xs:complexType>
 </xs:element>
</xs:schema>
```

As should be evident from this small sample, the XML Schema language has a rather complex syntax. Those interested in all of its details can find them at the URL shown in the first line of the schema. For those with a more casual interest, the most important thing to note is that the heart of the document is a description of the valid types that may be contained in the XML data that the schema describes. In addition to the `string` and `int` types shown here, other supported types include `boolean`, `double`, `float`, `dateTime`, and `hexBinary`.

The types specified in the schema are designated as simple or complex. The `complextype` element defines any node that has children or an attribute; the `simpletype` has no attribute or child. You'll encounter many schemas where the simple types are defined at the beginning of the schema, and complex types are later defined as a combination of simple types.

XML Schema Validation

A schema is used by a validator to check an XML document for conformance to the layout and content defined by the schema. .NET implements validation as a read and check process. As a class iterates through each node in an XML tree, the node is validated. Listing 10-4 illustrates how the `XmlValidatingReader` class performs this operation.

First, an `XmlTextReader` is created to stream through the nodes in the data document. It is passed as an argument to the constructor for the `XmlValidating-Reader`. Then, the `ValidationType` property is set to indicate a schema will be used for validation. This property can also be set to XDR or DTD to support older validation schemas.

The next step is to add the schema that will be used for validating to the reader's schema collection. Finally, the `XmlValidatingReader` is used to read the stream of XML nodes. Exception handling is used to display any validation error that occurs.

Listing 10-4	XML Schema Validation

```
private static bool ValidateSchema(string xml, string xsd)
{
   // Parameters: XML document and schemas
   // (1) Create a validating reader
   XmlTextReader tr = new XmlTextReader(xml);
   XmlValidatingReader xvr = new XmlValidatingReader(tr);
   // (2) Indicate schema validation
   xvr.ValidationType= ValidationType.Schema;
   // (3) Add schema to be used for validation
   xvr.Schemas.Add(null, xsd);
   try
   {
      Console.WriteLine("Validating: ");
      // Loop through all elements in XML document
      while(xvr.Read())
      {
         Console.Write(".");
      }
   }catch (Exception ex)
   { Console.WriteLine( "\n{0}",ex.Message); return false;}
   return true;
}
```

Note that the `XmlValidatingReader` class implements the `XmlReader` class underneath. We'll demonstrate using `XmlReader` to perform validation in the next section. In fact, in most cases, `XmlReader` (.NET 2.0 implmentation) now makes `XmlValidatingReader` obsolete.

Using an XML Style Sheet

A style sheet is a document that describes how to transform raw XML data into a different format. The mechanism that performs the transformation is referred to as an XSLT (Extensible Style Language Transformation) processor. Figure 10-1 illustrates the process: The XSLT processor takes as input the XML document to be transformed and the XSL document that defines the transformation to be applied. This approach permits output to be generated dynamically in a variety of formats. These include XML, HTML or ASPX for a Web page, and a PDF document.

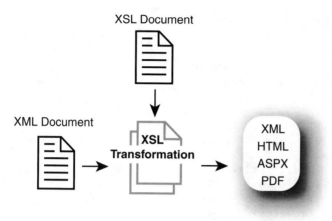

Figure 10-1   Publishing documents with XSLT

The XslTransform Class

The .NET version of the XSLT processor is the XslTransform class found in the System.Xml.Xsl namespace. To demonstrate its use, we'll transform our XML movie data into an HTML file for display by a browser (see Figure 10-2).

Movie Title	Movie Year	AFI Rank	Director
Casablanca	1942	2	Michael Curtiz
Citizen Kane	1941	1	Orson Welles

Figure 10-2   XML data is transformed into this HTML output

Before the XslTransform class can be applied, an XSLT style sheet that describes the transformation must be created. Listing 10-5 contains the style sheet that will be used. As you can see, it is a mixture of HTML markup, XSL elements, and XSL commands that displays rows of movie information with three columns. The XSL elements and functions are the key to the transformation. When the XSL style sheet is processed, the XSL elements are replaced with the data from the original XML document.

Listing 10-5	XML Style Sheet to Create HTML Output

```
<?xml version="1.0"?>
<xsl:stylesheet version="1.0"
    xmlns:xsl="http://www.w3.org/1999/XSL/Transform">
  <xsl:template match="/">
   <HTML>
     <TITLE>Movies</TITLE>
     <Table border="0" padding="0" cellspacing="1">
     <THEAD>
       <TH>Movie Title</TH>
       <TH>Movie Year </TH>
       <TH>AFI Rank   </TH>
       <TH>Director   </TH>
     </THEAD>
     <xsl:for-each select="//movies">
        <xsl:sort select="movie_Title" />
       <tr>
         <td><xsl:value-of select="movie_Title"/> </td>
         <td align="center"><xsl:value-of select=
              "movie_Year"/></td>
         <td align="center"><xsl:value-of select=
              "AFIRank" /></td>
      <td><xsl:value-of select="movie_Director" /></td>
        </tr>
        </xsl:for-each>
        </Table>
      </HTML>
   </xsl:template>
 </xsl:stylesheet>
```

Some points of interest:

- The URL in the namespace of the `<xsl:stylesheet>` element must be exactly as shown here.
- The `match` attribute is set to an XPath query that indicates which elements in the XML file are to be converted. Setting `match="/"` selects all elements.
- The `for-each` construct loops through a group of selected nodes specified by an XPath expression following the `select` attribute. XPath is discussed in Section 10.4, "Using XPath to Search XML."
- The `value-of` function extracts a selected value from the XML document and inserts it into the output.

- The `<xsl:sort>` element is used to sort the incoming data and is used in conjunction with the `for-each` construct. Here is its syntax:

```
select = XPath expression
order = {"ascending" | "descending"}
data-type = {"text" | "number"}
case-order = {"upper-first" | "lower-first"}
```

After a style sheet is created, using it to transform a document is a breeze. As shown by the following code, applying the `XslTransform` class is straightforward. After creating an instance of it, you use its `Load` method to specify the file containing the style sheet. The `XslTransform.Transform` method performs the transformation. This method has several overloads. The version used here requires an `Xpath-Document` object that represents the XML document, as a parameter, and an `XmlWriter` parameter that designates where the output is written—an HTML file in this case.

```
// Transform XML into HTML and store in movies.htm
XmlWriter writer = new
        XmlTextWriter("c:\\movies.htm",Encoding.UTF8);
XslTransform xslt = new XslTransform();
XPathDocument xpd = new
        XPathDocument("c:\\oscarwinners.xml");
xslt.Load("movies.xsl");
xslt.Transform(xpd, null, writer,null);
```

Core Note

You can link a style sheet to an XML document by placing an `href` statement in the XML document on the line preceding the root element definition:

```
<?xml:stylesheet type="text/xsl" href="movies.xsl" ?>
```

If a document is linked to a style sheet that converts XML to HTML, most browsers automatically perform the transformation and display the HTML. This can be a quick way to perform trial-and-error testing when developing a style sheet.

It takes only a small leap from this simple XSLT example to appreciate the potential of being able to transform XML documents dynamically. It is a natural area of growth for Web Services and Web pages that now on demand accept input in one format, transform it, and serve the output up in a different format.

10.2 Techniques for Reading XML Data

XML can be represented in two basic ways: as the familiar external document containing embedded data, or as an in-memory tree structure know as a Document Object
Model (DOM). In the former case, XML can be read in a forward-only manner as a
stream of tokens representing the file's content. The object that performs the reading
stays connected to the data source during the read operations. The XmlReader and
XmlTextReader shown in Figure 10-3 operate in this manner.

   More options are available for processing the DOM because it is stored in memory and can be traversed randomly. For simply reading a tree, the XmlNodeReader
class offers an efficient way to traverse a tree in a forward, read-only manner. Other
more sophisticated approaches that also permit tree modification are covered later in
this section.

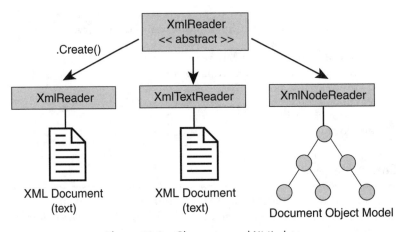

Figure 10-3   Classes to read XML data

XmlReader Class

XmlReader is an abstract class possessing methods and properties that enable an application to pull data from an XML file one node at a time in a forward-only, read-only
manner. A depth-first search is performed, beginning with the root node in the document. Nodes are inspected using the Name, NodeType, and Value properties.

   XmlReader serves as a base class for the concrete classes XmlTextReader and
XmlNodeReader. As an abstract class, XmlReader cannot be directly instantiated;
however, it has a static Create method that can return an instance of the XmlReader
class. This feature became available with the release of .NET Framework 2.0 and is
recommended over the XmlTextReader class for reading XML streams.

Listing 10-6 illustrates how to create an `XmlReader` object and use it to read the contents of a short XML document file. The code is also useful for illustrating how .NET converts the content of the file into a stream of node objects. It's important to understand the concept of nodes because an XML or HTML document is defined (by the official W3C Document Object Model (DOM) specification[2]) as a hierarchy of node objects.

Listing 10-6	Using `XmlReader` to Read an XML Document

```
// Include these namespaces:
// using System.Xml;
// using System.Xml.XPath;
public void ShowNodes()
{
    //(1) Settings object enables/disables features on XmlReader
    XmlReaderSettings settings = new XmlReaderSettings();
    settings.ConformanceLevel = ConformanceLevel.Fragment;
    settings.IgnoreWhitespace = true;
    try
    {
        //(2) Create XmlReader object
        XmlReader rdr = XmlReader.Create("c:\\oscarsshort.xml",
                                        settings);
        while (rdr.Read())
        {
            Format(rdr);
        }
        rdr.Close();
    }
    catch (Exception e)
    {
        Console.WriteLine ("Exception: {0}", e.ToString());
    }
}
private static void Format(XmlTextReader reader)
{
    //(3) Print Current node properties
    Console.Write( reader.NodeType+ "<" + reader.Name + ">" +
                reader.Value);
    Console.WriteLine();
}
```

---

2. W3C Document Object Model (DOM) Level 3 Core Specification, April, 2004, http://www.w3.org/TR/2004/REC-DOM-Level-3-Core-20040407/core.html

Before creating the XmlReader, the code first creates an XmlReaderSettings object. This object sets features that define how the XmlReader object processes the input stream. For example, the ConformanceLevel property specifies how the input is checked. The statement

```
settings.ConformanceLevel = ConformanceLevel.Fragment;
```

specifies that the input must conform to the standards that define an XML 1.0 *document fragment*—an XML document that does not necessarily have a root node.

This object and the name of the XML document file are then passed to the Create method that returns an XmlReader instance:

```
XmlReader rdr = XmlReader.Create("c:\\oscarsshort.xml,settings);
```

The file's content is read in a node at a time by the XmlReader.Read method, which prints the NodeType, Name, and Value of each node. Listing 10-7 shows the input file and a portion of the generated output. Line numbers have been added so that an input line and its corresponding node information can be compared.

Listing 10-7	XML Input and Corresponding Nodes

Input File: oscarsshort.xml

```
(1)  <?xml version="1.0" standalone="yes"?>
(2)  <films>
(3)   <movies>
(4)     <!-- Selected by AFI as best movie -->
(5)     <movie_ID>5</movie_ID>
(6)     <![CDATA[<a href="http://www.imdb.com/tt0467/">Kane</a>]]>
(7)     <movie_Title>Citizen Kane </movie_Title>
(8)     <movie_Year>1941</movie_Year>
(9)     <movie_Director>Orson Welles</movie_Director>
(10)    <bestPicture>Y</bestPicture>
(11)  </movies>
(12)</films>
```

Program Output (NodeType, <Name>, Value):

```
(1)  XmlDeclaration<xml>version="1.0" standalone="yes"
(2)  Element<films>
(3)  Element<movies>
(4)  Comment<> Selected by AFI as best movie
```

Listing 10-7	XML Input and Corresponding Nodes *(continued)*

```
(5) Element<movie_ID>
       Text<>5
    EndElement<movie_ID>
(6) CDATA<><a href="http://www.imdb.com/tt0467/">Kane</a>
(7) Element<movie_Title>
       Text<>Citizen Kane
    EndElement<movie_Title>
       ...
(12) EndElement<films>
```

Programs that use XmlReader typically implement a logic pattern that consists of an outer loop that reads nodes and an inner switch statement that identifies the node using an XMLNodeType enumeration. The logic to process the node information is handled in the case blocks:

```
while (reader.Read())
{
    switch (reader.NodeType)
    {
        case XmlNodeType.Element:
        // Attributes are contained in elements
            while(reader.MoveToNextAttribute())
            {
                Console.WriteLine(reader.Name+reader.Value);
            }
        break;
        case XmlNodeType.Text:
        // Process ..
        break;
        case XmlNodeType.EndElement
        // Process ..
        break;
    }
}
```

The Element, Text, and Attribute nodes mark most of the data content in an XML document. Note that the Attribute node is regarded as metadata attached to an element and is the only one not exposed directly by the XmlReader.Read method. As shown in the preceding code segment, the attributes in an Element can be accessed using the MoveToNextAttribute method.

Table 10-1 summarizes the node types. It is worth noting that these types are not an arbitrary .NET implementation. With the exception of `Whitespace` and `Xml-Declaration`, they conform to the DOM Structure Model recommendation.

Table 10-1 `XmlNodeType` Enumeration

Option	Description and Use

Attribute	An attribute or value contained within an element. Example:
	
	`<movie_title genre="comedy">The Lady Eve`
	`</movie_title>`
	
	Attribute is `genre="comedy"`. Attributes must be located within an element.
	
	`if(reader.NodeType==XmlNodeType.Element){`
	`   while(reader.MoveToNextAttribute())`
	`     {`
	`       Console.WriteLine(reader.Name+reader.Value);`
	`     }`

CData	Designates that the element is not to be parsed. Markup characters are treated as text:
	
	`![CDATA[<ELEMENT>`
	`<a href="http://www.imdb.com">movies</a>`
	`</ELEMENT>]]>`

Comment	To make a comment:
	
	`<!-- comment -->`
	
	To have comments ignored:
	
	`XmlReaderSettings.IgnoreComment = true;`

Document	A document root object that provides access to the entire XML document.
DocumentFragment	A document fragment. This is a node or subtree with a document. It provides a way to work with part of a document.
DocumentType	Document type declaration indicated by `<!DOCTYPE ... >`. Can refer to an external Document Type Definition (DTD) file or be an inline block containing `Entity` and `Notation` declarations.
Element	An XML element. Designated by the `< >` brackets: `<movie_Title>`
EndElement	An XML end element tag. Marks the end of an element: `</movie_Title>`

Table 10-1 XmlNodeType Enumeration *(continued)*

Option	Description and Use
EndEntity	End of an Entity declaration.
| Entity | Defines text or a resource to replace the entity name in the XML. An entity is defined as a child of a document type node: <br><br>```
<!DOCTYPE movies[
   <!ENTITY leadingactress "stanwyck">
]>
```<br><br>XML would then reference this as:<br><br>```
<actress>&leadingactress;</actress>
``` |
| EntityReference | A reference to the entity. In the preceding example, `&leadingactress;` is an EntityReference. |
| Notation | A notation that is declared within a DocumentType declaration. Primary use is to pass information to the XML processor. Example:<br><br>```
<!NOTATION homepage="www.sci.com" !>
``` |
| ProcessingInstruction | Useful for providing information about how the data was generated or how to process it.<br>Example:<br><br>```
<?pi1 Requires IE 5.0 and above ?>
``` |
| Text | The text content of a node. |
| Whitespace | Whitespace refers to formatting characters such as tabs, line feeds, returns, and spaces that exist between the markup and affect the layout of a document. |
| XmlDeclaration | The first node in the document. It provides version information.<br><br>```
<?xml version="1.0" standalone="yes"?>
``` |

XmlNodeReader Class

The XmlNodeReader is another forward-only reader that processes XML as a stream of nodes. It differs from the XmlReader class in two significant ways:

- It processes nodes from an in-memory DOM tree structure rather than a text file.
- It can begin reading at any subtree node in the structure—not just at the root node (beginning of the document).
```

In Listing 10-8, an `XmlNodeReader` object is used to list the movie title and year from the XML-formatted movies database. The code contains an interesting twist: The `XmlNodeReader` object is not used directly, but instead is passed as a parameter to the constructor of an `XmlReader` object. The object serves as a wrapper that performs the actual reading. This approach has the advantage of allowing the `XmlSettings` values to be assigned to the reader.

Listing 10-8   Using `XmlNodeReader` to Read an XML Document

```
private void ListMovies()
{
    // (1) Specify XML file to be loaded as a DOM
    XmlDocument doc = new XmlDocument();
    doc.Load("c:\\oscarwinners.xml");
    // (2) Settings for use with XmlNodeReader object
    XmlReaderSettings settings = new XmlReaderSettings();
    settings.ConformanceLevel = ConformanceLevel.Fragment;
    settings.IgnoreWhitespace = true;
    settings.IgnoreComments = true;
    // (3) Create a nodereader object
    XmlNodeReader noderdr = new XmlNodeReader(doc);
    // (4) Create an XmlReader as a wrapper around node reader
    XmlReader reader = XmlReader.Create(noderdr, settings);
    while (reader.Read())
    {
        if(reader.NodeType==XmlNodeType.Element){
            if (reader.Name == "movie_Title")
            {
                reader.Read();  // next node is text for title
                Console.Write(reader.Value);    // Movie Title
            }
            if (reader.Name == "movie_Year")
            {
                reader.Read();  // next node is text for year
                Console.WriteLine(reader.Value); // year
            }
        }
    }
}
```

The parameter passed to the `XmlNodeReader` constructor determines the first node in the tree to be read. When the entire document is passed—as in this example—reading begins with the top node in the tree. To select a specific node, use the `XmlDocument.SelectSingleNode` method as illustrated in this segment:

```
XmlDocument doc = new XmlDocument();
doc.Load("c:\\oscarwinners.xml");  // Build tree in memory
XmlNodeReader noderdr = new
      XmlNodeReader(doc.SelectSingleNode("films/movies[2]"));
```

Refer to Listing 10-1 and you can see that this selects the second `movies` element group, which contains information on *Casablanca*.

If your application requires read-only access to XML data and the capability to read selected subtrees, the `XmlNodeReader` is an efficient solution. When updating, writing, and searching become requirements, a more sophisticated approach is required; we'll look at those techniques later in this section.

The XmlReaderSettings Class

A significant advantage of using an `XmlReader` object—directly or as a wrapper—is the presence of the `XmlReaderSettings` class as a way to define the behavior of the `XmlReader` object. Its most useful properties specify which node types in the input stream are ignored and whether XML validation is performed. Table 10-2 lists the `XmlReaderSettings` properties.

Table 10-2   Properties of the `XmlReaderSettings` Class

Property	Default Value	Description
CheckCharacters	true	Indicates whether characters and XML names are checked for illegal XML characters. An exception is thrown if one is encountered.
CloseInput	false	An `XmlReader` object may be created by passing a stream to it. This property indicates whether the stream is closed when the reader object is closed.
ConformanceLevel	Document	Indicates whether the XML should conform to the standards for a `Document` or `DocumentFragment`.

Table 10-2   Properties of the `XmlReaderSettings` Class *(continued)*

Property	Default Value	Description
`DtdValidate`	false	Indicates whether to perform DTD validation.
`IgnoreComments` `IgnoreInlineSchema` `IgnoreProcessingInstructions` `IgnoreSchemaLocation` `IgnoreValidationWarnings` `IgnoreWhitespace`	false true false true true false	Specify whether a particular node type is processed or ignored by the `XmlReader.Read` method.
`LineNumberOffset` `LinePositionOffset`	0 0	`XmlReader` numbers lines in the XML document beginning with 0. Set this property to change the beginning line number and line position values.
`Schemas`	is empty	Contains the `XmlSchemaSet` to be used for XML Schema Definition Language (XSD) validation.
`XsdValidate`	false	Indicates whether XSD validation is performed.

Using an XML Schema to Validate XML Data

The final two properties listed in Table 10-2—`Schemas` and `XsdValidate`—are used to validate XML data against a schema. Recall that a schema is a template that describes the permissible content in an XML file or stream. Validation can be (should be) used to ensure that data being read conforms to the rules of the schema. To request validation, you must add the validating schema to the `XmlSchemaSet` collection of the `Schemas` property; next, set `XsdValidate` to `true`; and finally, define an event handler to be called if a validation error occurs. The following code fragment shows the code used with the schema and XML data in Listings 10-1 and 10-3:

```
XmlReaderSettings settings = new XmlReaderSettings();
// (1) Specify schema to be used for validation
settings.Schemas.Add(null,"c:\\oscarwinners.xsd");
// (2) Must set this to true
settings.XsdValidate = true;
// (3) Delegate to handle validation error event
settings.ValidationEventHandler += new
    System.Xml.Schema.ValidationEventHandler(SchemaValidation);
```

```
// (4) Create reader and pass settings to it
XmlReader rdr = XmlReader.Create("c:\\oscarwinners.xml",
      settings);
// process XML data ...
...
// Method to handle errors detected during schema validation
private void SchemaValidation(object sender,
System.Xml.Schema.ValidationEventArgs e)
{
   MessageBox.Show(e.Message);
}
```

Note that a detected error does not stop processing. This means that all the XML data can be checked in one pass without restarting the program.

Options for Reading XML Data

All the preceding examples that read XML data share two characteristics: data is read a node at a time, and a node's value is extracted as a string using the `Xml-Reader.Value` property. This keeps things simple, but ignores the underlying XML data. For example, XML often contains numeric data or data that is the product of serializing a class. Both cases can be handled more efficiently using other `Xml-Reader` methods.

`XmlReader` has a suite of `ReadValueAsxxx` methods that can read the contents of a node in its native form. These include `ReadValueAsBoolean`, `ReadValueAs-DateTime`, `ReadValueAsDecimal`, `ReadValueAsDouble`, `ReadValueAsInt32`, `ReadValueAsInt64`, and `ReadValueAsSingle`. Here's an example:

```
int age;
if(reader.Name == "Age") age= reader.ReadValueAsInt32();
```

XML that corresponds to the public properties or fields of a class can be read directly into an instance of the class with the `ReadAsObject` method. This fragment reads the XML data shown in Listing 10-1 into an instance of the `movies` class. Note that the name of the field or property must match an element name in the XML data.

```
// Deserialize XML into a movies object
if (rdr.NodeType == XmlNodeType.Element && rdr.Name == "movies")
{
   movies m = (movies)rdr.ReadAsObject(typeof(movies));
   // Do something with object
}
// XML data is read directly into this class
public class movies
```

```
{
    public int movie_ID;
    public string movie_Title;
    public string movie_Year;
    private string director;
    public string bestPicture;
    public string movie_Director
    {
        set { director = value; }
        get { return (director); }
    }
}
```

10.3 Techniques for Writing XML Data

In many cases, the easiest way to present data in an XML format is to use .NET serialization. As demonstrated in Section 10.1, if the data is in a collection class, it can be serialized using the `XmlSerializer` class; as we see in the next chapter, if it's in a `DataSet`, the `DataSet.WriteXml` method can be applied. The advantages of serialization are that it is easy to use, generates well-formed XML, and is symmetrical—the XML that is written can be read back to create the original data objects.

For cases where serialization is not an option—a comma delimited file, for instance—or where more control over the XML layout is needed, the `XmlWriter` class is the best .NET solution.

Writing XML with the XmlWriter Class

The `XmlWriter` class offers precise control over each character written to an XML stream or file. However, this flexibility does require a general knowledge of XML and can be tedious to code, because a distinct `Writexxx` method is used to generate each node type. On the positive side, it offers several compliance checking features, and the ability to write CLR typed data directly to the XML stream:

- `XmlWriterSettings.CheckCharacters` property configures the `XmlWriter` to check for illegal characters in text nodes and XML names, as well as check the validity of XML names. An exception is thrown if an invalid character is detected.
- `XmlWriterSettings.ConformanceLevel` property configures the `XmlWriter` to guarantee that the stream complies with the conformance level that is specified. For example, the XML may be set to conform to a document or document fragment.

- `XmlWriter.WriteValue` method is used to write data to the XML stream as a CLR type (`int`, `double`, and so on) without having to first convert it to a string.

Listing 10-9 illustrates the basic principles involved in using the `XmlWriter` class. Not surprisingly, there are a lot of similarities to the closely related `XmlReader` class. Both use the `Create` method to create an object instance, and both have constructor overloads that accept a settings object—`XmlWriterSettings`, in this case—to define the behavior of the reader or writer. The most important of these setting properties is the conformance level that specifies either document or fragment (a subtree) conformance.

A series of self-describing methods, which support all the node types listed in Table 10-1, generate the XML. Note that exception handling should always be enabled to trap any attempt to write an invalid name or character.

Listing 10-9	Write XML Using `XmlWriter` Class

```
private void WriteMovie()
{
    string[,] movieList = { { "Annie Hall", "Woody Allen" },
                            { "Lawrence of Arabia", "David Lean" } };
    // (1) Define settings to govern writer actions
    XmlWriterSettings settings = new XmlWriterSettings();
    settings.Indent = true;
    settings.IndentChars = ("    ");
    settings.ConformanceLevel = ConformanceLevel.Document;
    settings.CloseOutput = false;
    settings.OmitXmlDeclaration = false;
    // (2) Create XmlWriter object
    XmlWriter writer = XmlWriter.Create("c:\\mymovies.xml",
                                        settings);
    writer.WriteStartDocument();
    writer.WriteComment("Output from xmlwriter class");
    writer.WriteStartElement("films");
    for (int i = 0; i <= movieList.GetUpperBound(0) ; i++)
    {
        try
        {
            writer.WriteStartElement("movie");
            writer.WriteElementString("Title", movieList[i, 0]);
            writer.WriteElementString("Director", movieList[i, 1]);
            writer.WriteStartElement("Movie_ID");
            writer.WriteValue(i); // No need to convert to string
```

Listing 10-9   Write XML Using `XmlWriter` Class *(continued)*

```
                writer.WriteEndElement();
                writer.WriteEndElement();
        }
        catch (Exception ex)
        {
                MessageBox.Show(ex.Message);
        }
}
writer.WriteEndElement();
writer.Flush();  // Flush any remaining content to XML stream
writer.Close();
/*
    Output:
    <?xml version="1.0" encoding="utf-8"?>
    <!--Output from xmlwriter class-->
    <films>
        <movie>
            <Title>Annie Hall</Title>
            <Director>Woody Allen</Director>
            <Movie_ID>0</Movie_ID>
        </movie>
        <movie>
            <Title>Lawrence of Arabia</Title>
            <Director>David Lean</Director>
            <Movie_ID>1</Movie_ID>
        </movie>
    </films>
*/
}
```

Before leaving the topic of XML writing, note that .NET also provides `XmlTextWriter` and `XmlNodeWriter` classes as concrete implementations of the abstract `XmlWriter` class. The former does not offer any significant advantages over the `XmlWriter`. The node writer is a bit more useful. It creates a DOM tree in memory that can be processed using the many classes and methods designed for that task. Refer to .NET documentation for `XmlNodeWriter` details.

10.4 Using XPath to Search XML

A significant benefit of representing XML in a tree model—as opposed to a data stream—is the capability to query and locate the tree's content using XML Path Language (XPath). This technique is similar to using a SQL command on relational data. An XPath expression (query) is created and passed to an engine that evaluates it. The expression is parsed and executed against a data store. The returned value(s) may be a set of nodes or a scalar value.

XPath is a formal query language defined by the XML Path Language 2.0 specification (www.w3.org/TR/xpath). Syntactically, its most commonly used expressions resemble a file system path and may represent either the absolute or relative position of nodes in the tree.

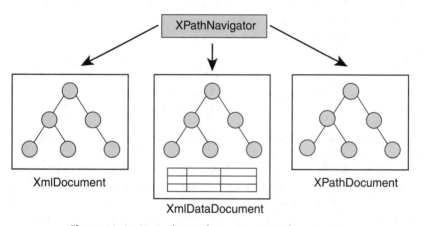

Figure 10-4   XML classes that support XPath navigation

In the .NET Framework, XPath evaluation is exposed through the XPathNavigator abstract class. The navigator is an XPath processor that works on top of any XML data source that exposes the IXPathNavigable interface. The most important member of this interface is the CreateNavigator method, which returns an XPathNavigator object. Figure 10-4 shows three classes that implement this interface. Of these, XmlDocument and XmlDataDocument are members of the System.Xml namespace; XPathDocument (as well as the XmlNavigator class) resides in the System.Xml.XPath namespace.

- XmlDocument. Implements the W3C Document Object Model (DOM) and supports XPath queries, navigation, and editing.

- `XmlDataDocument`. In addition to the features it inherits from `Xml-Document`, it provides the capability to map XML data to a `DataSet`. Any changes to the `DataSet` are reflected in the XML tree and vice versa.
- `XPathDocument`. This class is optimized to perform XPath queries and represents XML in a tree of read-only nodes that is more streamlined than the DOM.

Constructing XPath Queries

Queries can be executed against each of these classes using either an `XPathNavigator` object or the `SelectNodes` method implemented by each class. Generic code looks like this:

```
// XPATHEXPRESSION is the XPath query applied to the data
// (1) Return a list of nodes
XmlDocument doc = new XmlDocument();
doc.Load("movies.xml");
XmlNodeList selection = doc.SelectNodes(XPATHEXPRESSION);
// (2) Create a navigator and execute the query
XPathNavigator nav = doc.CreateNavigator();
XPathNodeIterator iterator = nav.Select(XPATHEXPRESSION);
```

The `XpathNodeIterator` class encapsulates a list of nodes and provides a way to iterate over the list.

As with regular expressions (refer to Chapter 5, "C# Text Manipulation and File I/O"), an XPath query has its own syntax and operators that must be mastered in order to efficiently query an XML document. To demonstrate some of the fundamental XPath operators, we'll create queries against the data in Listing 10-10.

Listing 10-10	XML Representation of Directors/Movies Relationship

```
<films>
  <directors>
    <director_id>54</director_id>
    <first_name>Martin</first_name>
    <last_name>Scorsese</last_name>
    <movies>
      <movie_ID>30</movie_ID>
      <movie_Title>Taxi Driver</movie_Title>
      <movie_DirectorID>54</movie_DirectorID>
      <movie_Year>1976</movie_Year>
```

Listing 10-10	XML Representation of Directors/Movies Relationship *(continued)*

```
    </movies>
    <movies>
      <movie_ID>28</movie_ID>
      <movie_Title>Raging Bull </movie_Title>
      <movie_DirectorID>54</movie_DirectorID>
      <movie_Year>1980</movie_Year>
    </movies>
  </directors>
</films>
```

Table 10-3 summarizes commonly used XPath operators and provides an example of using each.

Table 10-3 XPath Operators

Operator	Description
Child operator (/)	References the root of the XML document, where the expression begins searching. The following expression returns the last_name node for each director in the table: `/films/directors/last_name`

Recursive descendant operator (//)	This operator indicates that the search should include descendants along the specified path. The following all return the same set of last_name nodes. The difference is that the first begins searching at the root, and second at each directors node:
	
	`//last_name`
	`//directors//last_name`

Wildcard operator (*)	Returns all nodes below the specified path location. The following returns all nodes that are descendants of the movies node: `//movies/*`
Current operator (.)	Refers to the currently selected node in the tree, when navigating through a tree node-by-node. It effectively becomes the root node when the operator is applied. In this example, if the current node is a directors node, this will find any last_name child nodes: `.//last_name`

Table 10-3   XPath Operators *(continued)*

Operator	Description
Parent operator (`..`)	Used to represent the node that is the parent of the current node. If the current node were a `movies` node, this would use the `directors` node as the start of the path: `../last_name`
Attribute operator (`@`)	Returns any attributes specified. The following example would return the movie's runtime assuming there were attributes such as `<movie_ID time="98">` included in the XML. `//movies//@time`

Filter operator (`[ ]`)	Allows nodes to be filtered based on a matching criteria. The following example is used to retrieve all movie titles directed by Martin Scorsese:
	
	`//directors[last_name='Scorsese']`
	`    /movies/movie_Title`

Collection operator (`[ ]`)	Uses brackets just as the filter, but specifies a node based on an ordinal value. Is used to distinguish among nodes with the same name. This example returns the node for the second movie, *Raging Bull*: `//movies[2]` (Index is not 0 based.)
Union operator (`|`)	Returns the union of nodes found on specified paths. This example returns the first and last name of each director: `//last_name | //first_name`

Note that the filter operator permits nodes to be selected by their content. There are a number of functions and operators that can be used to specify the matching criteria. Table 10-4 lists some of these.

Table 10-4   Functions and Operators used to Create an XPath Filter

Function/Operator	Description
`and, or`	Logical operators.
Example: `"directors[last_name= 'Scorsese' and first_name= 'Martin']"`	
`position( )`	Selects node(s) at specified position.
Example: `"//movies[position()=2]"`	

Table 10-4 Functions and Operators used to Create an XPath Filter *(continued)*

Function/Operator	Description
`contains(node,string)`	Matches if node value contains specified string.
Example: `"//movies[contains(movie_Title,'Tax')]"`	
`starts-with(node,string)`	Matches if node value begins with specified string.
Example: `"//movies[starts-with(movie_Title,'A')]"`	
`substring-after(string,string)`	Extracts substring from the first string that follows occurrence of second string.
Example: `"//movies[substring-after('The Graduate','The ')='Graduate']"`	
`substring(string, pos,length)`	Extracts substring from node value.
Example: `"//movies[substring(movie_Title,2,1)='a']"`	

Refer to the XPath standard (`http://www.w3.org/TR/xpath`) for a comprehensive list of operators and functions.

Let's now look at examples of using XPath queries to search, delete, and add data to an XML tree. Our source XML file is shown in Listing 10-10. For demonstration purposes, examples are included that represent the XML data as an `XmlDocument`, `XPathDocument`, and `XmlDataDocument`.

XmlDocument and XPath

The expression in this example extracts the set of `last_name` nodes. It then prints the associated text. Note that underneath, `SelectNodes` uses a navigator to evaluate the expression.

```
string exp = "/films/directors/last_name";
XmlDocument doc = new XmlDocument();
doc.Load("directormovies.xml");   // Build DOM tree
XmlNodeList directors = doc.SelectNodes(exp);
foreach(XmlNode n in directors)
    Console.WriteLine(n.InnerText);   // Last name or director
```

The `XmlNode.InnerText` property concatenates the values of child nodes and displays them as a text string. This is a convenient way to display tree contents during application testing.

XPathDocument and XPath

For applications that only need to query an XML document, the XPathDocument is the recommended class. It is free of the overhead required for updating a tree and runs 20 to 30 percent faster than XmlDocument. In addition, it can be created using an XmlReader to load all or part of a document into it. This is done by creating the reader, positioning it to a desired subtree, and then passing it to the XPathDocument constructor. In this example, the XmlReader is positioned at the root node, so the entire tree is read in:

```
string exp = "/films/directors/last_name";
// Create method was added with .NET 2.0
XmlReader rdr = XmlReader.Create("c:\\directormovies.xml");
// Pass XmlReader to the constructor
xDoc = new XPathDocument(rdr);
XPathNavigator nav= xDoc.CreateNavigator();
XPathNodeIterator iterator;
iterator = nav.Select(exp);
// List last name of each director
while (iterator.MoveNext())
    Console.WriteLine(iterator.Current.Value);
// Now, list only movies for Martin Scorsese
string exp2 =
    "//directors[last_name='Scorsese']/movies/movie_Title";
iterator = nav.Select(exp2);
while (iterator.MoveNext())
    Console.WriteLine(iterator.Current.Value);
```

Core Note

Unlike the SelectNodes *method, the navigator's* Select *method accepts XPath expressions as both plain text and precompiled objects. The following statements demonstrate how a compiled expression could be used in the preceding example:*

```
string exp = "/films/directors/last_name";
// use XmlNavigator to create XPathExpression object
XPathExpression compExp = nav.Compile(exp);
iterator = nav.Select(compExp);
```

Compiling an expression improves performance when the expression (query) is used more than once.

XmlDataDocument and XPath

The XmlDataDocument class allows you to take a DataSet (an object containing rows of data) and create a replica of it as a tree structure. The tree not only represents the DatSet, but is synchronized with it. This means that changes made to the DOM or DataSet are automatically reflected in the other.

Because XmlDataDocument is derived from XmlDocument, it supports the basic methods and properties used to manipulate XML data. To these, it adds methods specifically related to working with a DataSet. The most interesting of these is the GetRowFromElement method that takes an XmlElement and converts it to a corresponding DataRow.

A short example illustrates how XPath is used to retrieve the set of nodes representing the movies associated with a selected director. The nodes are then converted to a DataRow, which is used to print data from a column in the row.

```
// Create document by passing in associated DataSet
XmlDataDocument xmlDoc = new XmlDataDocument(ds);
string exp = "//directors[last_name='Scorsese']/movies";
XmlNodeList nodeList =
      xmlDoc.DocumentElement.SelectNodes(exp);
DataRow myRow;
foreach (XmlNode myNode in nodeList)
{
   myRow = xmlDoc.GetRowFromElement((XmlElement)myNode);
   if (myRow != null){
      // Print Movie Title from a DataRow
      Console.WriteLine(myRow["movie_Title"].ToString());
   }
}
```

This class should be used only when its hybrid features add value to an application. Otherwise, use XmlDocument if updates are required or XPathDocument if the data is read-only.

Adding and Removing Nodes on a Tree

Besides locating and reading data, many applications need to add, edit, and delete information in an XML document tree. This is done using methods that edit the content of a node and add or delete nodes. After the changes have been made to the tree, the updated DOM is saved to a file.

To demonstrate how to add and remove nodes, we'll operate on the subtree presented as text in Listing 10-10 and as a graphical tree in Figure 10-5.

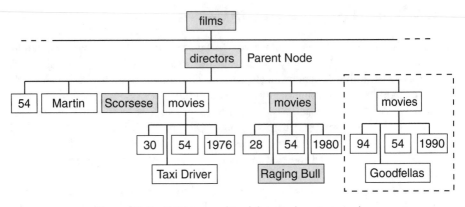

Figure 10-5   Subtree used to delete and remove nodes

This example uses the `XmlDocument` class to represent the tree for which we will remove one `movies` element and add another one. XPath is used to locate the `movies` node for `Raging Bull` along the path containing `Scorsese` as the director:

```
"//directors[last_name='Scorsese']/movies[movie_Title=
    'Raging Bull']"
```

This node is deleted by locating its parent node, which is on the level directly above it, and executing its `RemoveChild` method.

Listing 10-11	Using `XmlDocument` and `XPath` to Add and Remove Nodes

```
Public void UseXPath()
{
   XmlDocument doc = new XmlDocument();
   doc.Load("c:\\directormovies.xml");
   // (1) Locate movie to remove
   string exp = "//directors[last_name='Scorsese']/
        movies[movie_Title='Raging Bull']";
   XmlNode movieNode = doc.SelectSingleNode(exp);
   // (2) Delete node and child nodes for movie
   XmlNode directorNode = movieNode.ParentNode;
   directorNode.RemoveChild(movieNode);
   // (3) Add new movie for this director
   //      First, get and save director's ID
```

Listing 10-11	Using XmlDocument and XPath to Add and Remove Nodes *(continued)*

```
    string directorID =
        directorNode.SelectSingleNode("director_id").InnerText;
    // XmlElement is dervied from XmlNode and adds members
    XmlElement movieEl = doc.CreateElement("movies");
    directorNode.AppendChild(movieEl);
    // (4) Add Movie Description
    AppendChildElement(movieEl, "movie_ID", "94");
    AppendChildElement(movieEl, "movie_Title", "Goodfellas");
    AppendChildElement(movieEl, "movie_Year", "1990");
    AppendChildElement(movieEl, "movie_DirectorID",
                                directorID);
    // (5) Save updated XML Document
    doc.Save("c:\\directormovies2.xml");
}
// Create node and append to parent
public void AppendChildElement(XmlNode parent, string elName,
                                string elValue)
{
    XmlElement newEl =
        parent.OwnerDocument.CreateElement(elName);
    newEl.InnerText = elValue;
    parent.AppendChild(newEl);
}
```

Adding a node requires first locating the node that will be used to attach the new node. Then, the document's Create*xxx* method is used to generate an XmlNode or XmlNode-derived object that will be added to the tree. The node is attached using the current node's AppendChild, InsertAfter, or InsertBefore method to position the new node in the tree. In this example, we add a movies element that contains information for the movie *Goodfellas*.

10.5 Summary

To work with XML, a basic understanding of the XML document, schema, and style sheet is required. An XML document, which is a representation of information based on XML guidelines, can be created in numerous ways. The XmlSerializer class can be used when the data takes the form of an object or objects within a program. After the XML document is created, a schema can be derived from it using the XML

Schema Definition (XSD) tool. Several classes use the schema to provide automatic document validation. The usefulness of XML data is extended by the capability to transform it into virtually any other format using an XML style sheet. The style sheet defines a set of rules that are applied during XML Style Sheet Transformation (XSLT).

XML data can be processed as a stream of nodes or an in-memory tree known as a Document Object Model (DOM). The `XmlReader` and `XmlNodeReader` classes provide an efficient way to process XML as a read-only, forward-only stream. The `XmlReader`, `XPathDocument`, and `XmlDataReader` classes offer methods for processing nodes in the tree structure.

In many cases, data extraction from an XML tree can be best achieved using a query, rather than traversing the tree nodes. The XPath expression presents a rich, standardized syntax that is easily used to specify criteria for extracting a node, or multiple nodes, from an XML tree.

10.6 Test Your Understanding

1. `XmlReader` is an abstract class. How do you create an instance of it to read an XML document?

2. What is the purpose of the `XmlReaderSettings` class?

3. Which of these classes cannot be used to update an XML document?

    a.   `XmlDocument`
    b.   `XmlDataDocument`
    c.   `XmlPathDocument`

4. Using the XML data from Listing 10-10, show the node values returned by the following XPath expressions:

    a.   `//movies[substring( movie_Title,2,1)='a']`
    b.   `//movies[2]`
    c.   `//movies[movie_Year >= 1978]`
    d.   `//directors[last_name='Scorsese']`
           `/movies/movie_Title`

5. Describe two ways to perform schema validation on an XML document.

ADO.NET

Topics in This Chapter

- *ADO.NET Architecture:* ADO.NET provides access to data using custom or generic data providers. This section looks at the classes a provider must supply that enable an application to connect to a data source and interact with it using SQL commands.

- *Introduction to Using ADO.NET:* ADO.NET supports data access using a connected or disconnected connectivity model. An introduction and comparison of the two architectures is provided.

- *The Connected Model:* Use of the connected model requires an understanding of the role that Connection and Command classes have in retrieving data. Examples illustrate how to create a connection and use the Command class to issue SQL commands, invoke stored procedures, and manage multi-command transactions.

- *The Disconnected Model:* Disconnected data is stored in an in-memory DataTable or DataSet. The latter is usually made up of multiple DataTables that serve as a local relational data store for an application. A DataAdapter is typically used to load this data and then apply updates to the original data source. Techniques are introduced for handling synchronization issues that arise when updating disconnected data.

- *XML Data Access:* Although it does not provide intrinsic XML classes, ADO.NET supports XML integration through properties and methods of the DataSet class. Examples show how to use WriteXml and ReadXml to create an XML file from a DataSet and populate a DataSet from an XML file, respectively.

Chapter

ADO.NET is based on a flexible set of classes that allow data to be accessed from within the managed environment of .NET. These classes are used to access a variety of data sources including relational databases, XML files, spreadsheets, and text files. Data access is through an API, known as a managed data provider. This provider may be written specifically for a database, or may be a more generic provider such as OLE DB or ODBC (Open DataBase Connectivity). Provider classes expose a connection object that binds an application to a data source, and a command object that supports the use of standard SQL commands to fetch, add, update, or delete data.

ADO.NET supports two broad models for accessing data: disconnected and connected. The disconnected model downloads data to a client's machine where it is encapsulated as an in-memory `DataSet` that can be accessed like a local relational database. The connected model relies on record-by-record access that requires an open and sustained connection to the data source. Recognizing the most appropriate model to use in an application is at the heart of understanding ADO.NET. This chapter examines both models—offering code examples that demonstrate the classes used to implement each.

11.1 Overview of the ADO.NET Architecture

The ADO.NET architecture is designed to make life easier for both the application developer and the database provider. To the developer, it presents a set of abstract classes that define a common set of methods and properties that can be used to access any data source. The data source is treated as an abstract entity, much like a drawing surface is to the GDI+ classes. Figure 11-1 depicts this concept.

For database providers, ADO.NET serves as a blueprint that describes the base API classes and interface specifications providers must supply with their product. Beneath the surface, the vendor implements the custom code for connecting to their database, processing SQL commands, and returning the results. Many database products, such as MySQL and Oracle, have custom .NET data provider implementations available. In addition, they have generic OLE DB versions. The .NET data provider should always be the first choice because it offers better performance and often supports added custom features. Let's look at both the OLE DB and native .NET data providers

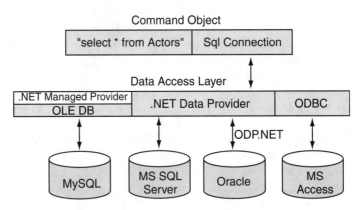

Figure 11-1   ADO.NET data access options

OLE DB Data Provider in .NET

An OLE DB provider is the code that sits between the data consumer and the native API of a data source. It maps the generic OLE DB API to the data source's native APIs. It is a COM-based solution in which the data consumer and provider are COM objects that communicate through COM interfaces. Database vendors and third parties have written OLE DB providers for just about every significant data source. In contrast, far fewer .NET data providers exist. To provide a bridge to these preexisting OLE DB interfaces, .NET includes an OleDB data provider that functions as a thin wrapper to route calls into the native OLE DB. Because interoperability with COM requires switching between managed and unmanaged code, performance can be severely degraded.[1]

As we see in the next section, writing code to use OLE DB is essentially the same as working with a .NET data provider. In fact, new .NET classes provide a "factory" that can dynamically produce code for a selected provider. Consequently, responding to a vendor's upgrade from OLE DB to a custom provider should have no appreciable effect on program logic.

.NET Data Provider

The .NET data provider provides the same basic service to the client as the OLE DB provider: exposing a data source's API to a client. Its advantage is that it can directly access the native API of the data source, rather than relying on an intermediate data access bridge. Native providers may also include additional features to manipulate data types native to the data source and improve performance. For example, the Oracle provider, ODP.NET, includes adjustable settings to control connection pooling, the number of rows to be pre-fetched, and the size of non-scalar data being fetched.

Data Provider Objects for Accessing Data

A managed data provider exposes four classes that enable a data consumer to access the provider's data source. Although these classes are specific to the provider, they derive from abstract ADO.NET classes:

- DbConnection. Establishes a connection to the data source.
- DbCommand. Used to query or send a command to the data source.
- DbDataReader. Provides read-only and forward-only access to the data source.
- DBDataAdapter. Serves as a channel through which a DataSet connects to a provider.

Because these are abstract classes, the developer is responsible for specifying the vendor's specific implementation within the code. As we see next, the object names can be hard coded or provided generically by a provider factory class.

---

1. Test results for .NET 1.1 have shown the SQL Client provider to be up to 10 times faster than OLE DB.

Provider Factories

Each data provider registers a `ProviderFactory` class and a provider string in the `machine.config` file. The available providers can be listed using the static `GetFactoryClasses` method of the `DbProviderFactories` class. As this code shows, the method returns a `DataTable` containing four columns of information about the provider.

```
DataTable tb = DbProviderFactories.GetFactoryClasses();
foreach (DataRow drow in tb.Rows )
{
   StringBuilder sb = new StringBuilder("");
   for (int i=0; i<tb.Columns.Count; i++)
   {
      sb.Append((i+1).ToString()).Append(drow[i].ToString());
      sb.Append("\n");
   }
   Console.WriteLine(sb.ToString());
}
```

Running this code for ADO.NET 2.0 lists four Microsoft written providers: `Odbc`, `OleDb`, `OracleClient`, and `SqlClient`. Figure 11-2 shows output for the `SqlClient` provider.

```
1 SqlClient Data Provider
2 .Net Framework Data Provider for SqlServer
3 System.Data.SqlClient
4 System.Data.SqlClient.SqlClientFactory, System.Data,
   Version=2.0.3600.0, Culture=neutral,
   PublicKeyToken=b77a5c561934e089
```

Figure 11-2   Data provider information returned by GetFactoryClasses()

To use these providers, your code must create objects specific to the provider. For example, the connection object for each would be an `OdbcConnection`, `OleDbConnection`, `OracleConnection`, or `SqlConnection` type. You can create the objects supplied by the providers directly:

```
SqlConnection conn = new SqlConnection();
SqlCommand cmd     = new SqlCommand();
SqlDataReader dr   = cmd.ExecuteReader();
```

However, suppose your application has to support multiple data sources. A switch/case construct could be used, but a better—and more flexible—approach is to use a class factory to create these objects dynamically based on the provider selected. ADO.NET provides just that—a DbProviderFactory class that is used to return objects required by a specific data provider. It works quite simply. A string containing the provider name is passed to the GetFactory method of the DbProviderFactories class. The method returns a factory object that is used to create the specific objects required by the provider. Listing 11-1 demonstrates using a factory.

Listing 11-1   Using the DbProviderFactory Class

```
// System.Data.Common namespace is required
DbProviderFactory factory ;
string provider = "System.Data.SqlClient";  // data provider
string connstr = "Data Source=MYSERVER;Initial Catalog=films;
          User Id=filmsadmin;Password=bogart;";
// Get factory object for SQL Server
factory = DbProviderFactories.GetFactory(provider);
// Get connection object. using ensures connection is closed.
using (DbConnection   conn = factory.CreateConnection())
{
    conn.ConnectionString = connstr;
    try
    {
        conn.Open();
        DbCommand cmd = factory.CreateCommand(); // Command object
        cmd.CommandText = "SELECT * FROM movies WHERE movie_ID=8" ;
        cmd.Connection = conn;
        DbDataReader dr;
        dr = cmd.ExecuteReader();
        dr.Read();
        MessageBox.Show((string)dr["movie_Title"]);
        conn.Close();
    }
    catch (DbException ex)
    { MessageBox.Show(ex.ToString()); }
    catch (Exception ex)
    { MessageBox.Show(ex.ToString()); }
    finally { conn.Close(); }
}
```

This approach requires only that a provider and connection string be provided. For example, we can easily switch this to an ODBC provider by changing two statements:

```
string provider= "System.Data.Odbc";
// The DSN (Data Source Name) is defined using an ODBC utility
string connstr = "DSN=movies;Database=films";
```

Note that the factory class provides a series of `Create` methods that returns the objects specific to the data provider. These methods include `CreateCommand`, `CreateConnection`, and `CreateDataAdapter`.

11.2 Data Access Models: Connected and Disconnected

This section offers an overview of using ADO.NET to access data stored in relational tables. Through simple examples, it presents the classes and concepts that distinguish the connected and disconnected access models.

All examples in this section—as well as the entire chapter—use data from the `Films` database defined in Figure 11-3. It consists of a `movies` table containing the top 100 movies as selected by the American Film Institute (AFI) in 1996, an `actors` table that lists the principal actors who performed in the movies, and an `actor-movie` helper table that links the two. The data is downloadable as a Microsoft Access (.mdb) file and an XML text (.xml) file.

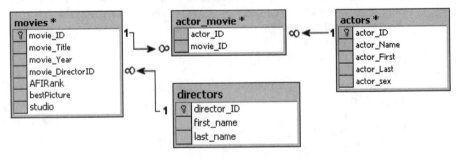

Figure 11-3   Films database tables

Connected Model

In the ADO.NET connected mode, an active connection is maintained between an application's `DataReader` object and a data source. A row of data is returned from the data source each time the object's `Read` method is executed. The most important characteristic of the connected model is that it reads data from a resultset (records returned by a SQL command) one record at a time in a forward-only, read-only manner. It provides no direct way to update or add data. Figure 11-4 depicts the relationship between the DataReader, Command, and Connection classes that comprise the connected model.

Figure 11-4 DataReader is used in ADO.NET connected mode

Working with the DataReader typically involves four steps:

1. The connection object is created by passing a connection string to its constructor.
2. A string variable is assigned the SQL command that specifies the data to fetch.
3. A command object is created. Its overloads accept a connection object, a query string, and a transaction object (for executing a group of commands).
4. The DataReader object is created by executing the Command.ExecuteReader() method. This object is then used to read the query results one line at a time over the active data connection.

The following code segment illustrates these steps with a SqlClient data provider. The code reads movie titles from the database and displays them in a ListBox control. Note that the DataReader, Command, and Connection objects are described in detail later in this chapter.

```
//System.Data.SqlClient namespace is required
// (1) Create Connection
SqlConnection conn = new SqlConnection(connstr);
conn.Open();
// (2) Query string
string sql = "SELECT movie_Title FROM movies ORDER BY
movie_Year";
// (3) Create Command object
SqlCommand cmd = new SqlCommand(sql, conn);
DbDataReader rdr;
```

```
// (4) Create DataReader
rdr = cmd.ExecuteReader(CommandBehavior.CloseConnection);
while (rdr.Read())
{
    listBox1.Items.Add(rdr["movie_Title"]);   // Fill ListBox
}
rdr.Close();   // Always close datareader
```

The parameter to `ExecuteReader` specifies that the connection is closed when the data reader object is closed.

Disconnected Model

The concept behind the disconnected model is quite simple: Data is loaded—using a SQL command—from an external source into a memory cache on the client's machine; the resultset is manipulated on the local machine; and any updates are passed from data in memory back to the data source.

The model is "disconnected" because the connection is only open long enough to read data from the source and make updates. By placing data on the client's machine, server resources—data connections, memory, processing time—are freed that would otherwise be required to manipulate the data. The drawback is the time required to load the resultset, and the memory used to store it.

As Figure 11-5 illustrates, the key components of the disconnected model are the `DataApdapter` and `DataSet`. The `DataAdapter` serves as a bridge between the data source and the `DataSet`, retrieving data into the tables that comprise the `DataSet` and pushing changes back to the data source. A `DataSet` object functions as an in-memory relational database that contains one or more `DataTables`, along with optional relationships that bind the tables. A `DataTable` contains rows and columns of data that usually derive from a table in the source database.

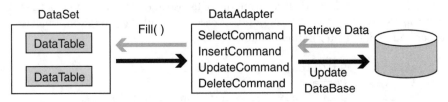

Figure 11-5   `DataAdapter` is used in ADO.NET disconnected mode

Among the numerous methods and properties exposed by the `DataAdapter` class, the `Fill` and `Update` methods are the two most important. `Fill` passes a query to a database and stores the returned set of data in a selected `DataTable`;

Update performs a deletion, insertion, or update operation based on changes within the DataSet. The actual update commands are exposed as DataAdapter properties. The DataAdapter is presented in much more detail in Section 11.4, "DataSets, DataTables, and the Disconnected Model."

Core Note

Each data provider supplies its own data adapter. Thus, if you look through the System.Data child namespaces (SqlClient, OracleClient, Oledb), you'll find a SqlDataAdapter, OracleDataAdapter, and OleDbDataAdapter, among others. An easy way to acquire the desired adapter in your application is to call the DbProviderFactory.CreateDataAdapter method to return an instance of it.

As a simple introduction to how a DataAdapter and DataSet work together, Listing 11-2 shows how to create a DataTable, fill it with data from a database, and add it to a DataSet.

Listing 11-2	Using a DataAdapter to Load Data from a Database

```
string sql = "SELECT movie_Title, movie_Year FROM movies";
string connStr = " Data Source=MYSERVER;Initial Catalog=films;
                   User Id=filmsadmin;Password=bogart;";
// (1) Create data adapter object
SqlDataAdapter da = new SqlDataAdapter(sql,connStr);
// (2) Create dataset
DataSet ds = new DataSet();
// (3) Create table in dataset and fill with data
da.Fill(ds, "movies");   // Fill table with query results
DataTable dt = ds.Tables["movies"];
// (4) Add movie titles to list box
for (int i=0; i< dt.Rows.Count;i++)
{
   DataRow row = dt.Rows[i];
   listBox1.Items.Add(row["movie_Title"]);
}
```

The first step is to create an instance of a SqlDataAdapter by passing the select command and the connection string to its constructor. The data adapter takes care of creating the Connection object and opening and closing the connection as needed.

After an empty `DataSet` is created, the `DataAdapter`'s `Fill` method creates a table `movies` in the `DataSet` and fills it with rows of data returned by the SQL command. Each column of the table corresponds to a column in the source data table. Behind the scenes, the data transfer is performed by creating a `SqlDataReader` that is closed after the transfer is complete.

The data in the table is then used to populate a list box by looping through the rows of the table. As we see in the next chapter, we could achieve the same effect by binding the list control to the table—a mechanism for automatically filling a control with data from a bound source.

11.3 ADO.NET Connected Model

As described earlier, the connected model is based on establishing a connection to a database and then using commands to update, delete, or read data on the connected source. The distinguishing characteristic of this model is that commands are issued directly to the data source over a live connection—which remains open until the operations are complete. Whether working with a connected or disconnected model, the first step in accessing a data source is to create a connection object to serve as a communications pathway between the application and database.

Connection Classes

There are multiple connection classes in ADO.NET—each specific to a data provider. These include `SqlConnection`, `OracleConnection`, `OleDBConnection`, and `OdbcConnection`. Although each may include custom features, ADO.NET compatibility requires that a connector class implement the `IDbConnection` interface. Table 11-1 summarizes the members defined by this interface.

Table 11-1   Members of the `IDbConnection` Interface

Category	Name	Description
Property	`ConnectionString`	Gets or sets the string used to connect to a data source.
Property	`ConnectionTimeout`	The number of seconds to wait while trying to establish a connection to a data source before timing out.
Property	`Database`	Name of the database associated with the current connection.

Table 11-1 Members of the `IDbConnection` Interface *(continued)*

Category	Name	Description
Property	`State`	Current state of the connection. Returns a `Connec-tionState` enumeration name: `Broken`, `Closed`, `Connecting`, `Executing`, `Fetching`, or `Open`.
Method	`Open` `Close`	Opens a connection. Rolls back any pending operations and closes the connection—returning it to a connection pool, if one is used.
Method	`BeginTransaction`	Initiates a database transaction.
Method	`ChangeDatabase`	Changes the current database for an open connection. The new database name is passed as string to the method.
Method	`CreateCommand`	Creates a command object to be associated with connection.

Core Note

Even though connection classes implement the `IDbConnection` interface, they do not necessarily have to provide meaningful functionality. For example, the `OracleConnection` class does not support the `ConnectionTimeOut`, `Database`, or `ChangeDatabase` members.

Connection String

The connection string specifies the data source and necessary information required to access the data source, such as password and ID. In addition to this basic information, the string can include values for fields specific to a data provider. For example, a SQL Server connection string can include values for `Connection Timeout` and `Packet Size` (size of network packet).

Table 11-2 offers a representative list of commonly used connection strings.

The connection string is used to create the connection object. This is typically done by passing the string to the constructor of the connection object.

```
string cn= "Data Source=MYSERVER;Initial Catalog=films;
           User Id=filmsadmin;Password=bogart;";
SqlConnection conn = new SqlConnection(cn);
conn.Open();   // Open connection
```

Table 11-2 Connection String Examples

Connection Type	Description and Use

SqlConnection
Using SQL Server authentication.
	`"server=MYSERVER;`
	`uid=filmsadmin;`
	`pwd=bogart;`
	`database=films;"`
	
	Or
	
	`"Data Source=MYSERVER;User ID=filmsadmin;`
	`password=bogart;Initial Catalog=films;"`

SqlConnection
Using Windows authentication.
	`"server=MYSERVER;`
	`database=films;`
	`Trusted_Connection=yes"`

OleDbConnection
Connects to a Microsoft Access
database.
	`"Provider=Microsoft.Jet.OLEDB.4.0;`
	`Data Source=c:\\movies.mdb;"`
	
	For Internet applications, you may not be able to specify a physical path. Use MapPath to convert a virtual path into a physical path:
	
	`string path=`
	`    Server.MapPath("/data/movies.mdb");`
	`Data Source="+path+";"`

ODBC (DSN)	`"DSN=movies;".`

A connection string can also be built using a safer, object-oriented manner using one of the ConnectionStringBuilder classes supplied by a managed data provider.[2] As this code demonstrates, the values comprising the connection string are assigned to properties of this class. Internally, the object constructs a string from these properties and exposes it as a ConnectionString property.

```
SqlConnectionStringBuilder sqlBldr = new
      SqlConnectionStringBuilder();
scb.DataSource    = "MYSERVER";
// Or scp["Data Source"] = "MYSERVER";
sqlBldr.Password  = "bogart";
sqlBldr.UserID    = "filmsadmin";
sqlBldr.InitialCatalog = "films";
SqlConnection conn = new
SqlConnection(sqlBldr.ConnectionString);
conn.Open();
```

---

2. SqlClient, Oracle, OleDB, and ODBC implementations are available with ADO.NET 2.0.

The `ConnectionStringBuilder` object is also useful for applications that input the connection string from a configuration file or other source. Setting the `Connec-tionString` property to the connection string value exposes members that control the behavior of the connection. Table 11-3 lists selected properties of the `SqlCon-nectionStringBuilder` class.

Table 11-3   Selected Properties of the `SqlConnectionStringBuilder` Class

Method	Description
`Asynchronous-Processing`	Boolean value that indicates whether asynchronous process is permitted on the connection. The command object is responsible for making asynchronous requests.
`ConnectionTimeout`	Corresponds to the `ConnectionTimeout` property of the `Connection` object.
`DataSource`	Name or address of the SQL Server to connect to.
`MaxPoolSize` `MinPoolSize`	Sets or returns the maximum and minimum number of connections in the connection pool for a specific connection string.
`Password`	Password for accessing SQL Server account.
`Pooling`	A boolean value that indicates whether connection pooling is used.
`UserID`	User ID required to access a SQL Server account.

Core Note

For demonstration purposes, the connection strings in these examples are shown as cleartext within the application's code. In reality, a connection string should be stored outside of an application's assembly. For Web applications, the `Web.Config` file is often a reasonable choice. As described in Chapter 17, "The ASP.NET Application Environment," .NET includes a special configuration section to hold connection strings and supports techniques to encrypt the configuration information.

Desktop applications that access a central database can store the information on the client's machine (in the registry or a configuration file) or have it downloaded as part of an application's startup. The latter approach provides better scalability and security, particularly if the server returns a connection object rather than the string.

Connection Pooling

Creating a connection is a time-consuming process—in some cases taking longer than the subsequent commands take to execute. To eliminate this overhead, ADO.NET creates a pool of identical connections for each unique connection string request it receives. This enables future requests with that connection string to be satisfied from the pool, rather than by reconnecting to the server and performing the overhead to validate the connection.

There are several rules governing connection pooling that you should be aware of:

- Connection pooling is turned on by default. It can be disabled for a SqlConnection by including "Pooling=false" in the connection string; an OleDbConnection requires "OLE DB Services=-4".
- Each connection pool is associated with a distinct connection string. When a connection is requested, the pool handler compares the connection string with those of existing pools. If it matches, a connection is allocated from the pool.
- If all connections in a pool are in use when a request is made, the request is queued until a connection becomes free. Connections are freed when the Close or Dispose method on a connection is called.
- The connection pool is closed when all connections in it are released by their owners and have timed out.

Under SQL Server, you control the behavior of connection pooling by including key-value pairs in the connection string. These keywords can be used to set minimum and maximum numbers of connections in the pool, and to specify whether a connection is reset when it is taken from the pool. Of particular note is the Lifetime keyword that specifies how long a connection may live until it is destroyed. This value is checked when a connection is returned to the pool. If the connection has been open longer than its Lifetime value, it is destroyed.

This code fragment demonstrates the use of these keywords for SqlClient:

```
cnString = "Server=MYSERVER;Trusted_Connection=yes;
        database=films;"              +
        "connection reset=false;" +
        "connection Lifetime=60;" +   // Seconds
        "min pool size=1;"            +
        "max pool size=50";                // Default=100
SqlConnection conn = new SqlConnection(cnString);
```

The Command Object

After a connection object is created, the next step in accessing a database—for the connected model—is to create a command object that submits a query or action command to a data source. Command classes are made available by data providers and must implement the IDbCommand interface.

Creating a Command Object

You can use one of its several constructors to create a command object directly, or use the ProviderFactory approach mentioned in Section 11.1.

This segment demonstrates how to create a command object and explicitly set its properties:

```
SqlConnection conn = new SqlConnection(connstr);
Conn.open();
string sql = "insert into movies(movie_Title,movie_Year,
        movie_Director) values(@title,@yr,@bestpicture)";
SqlCommand cmd = new SqlCommand();
// Assign connection object and sql query to command object
cmd.Connection = conn;
cmd.commandText = sql;
// Fill in parameter values in query
// This is recommended over concatenation in a query string
cmd.Parameters.AddWithValue ("@title", "Schindler's List");
cmd.Parameters.AddWithValue ("@yr", "1993");
cmd.Parameters.AddWithValue ("@bestpic", "Y");
```

In situations where multiple data providers may be used, a provider factory provides a more flexible approach. The factory is created by passing its constructor a string containing the data provider. The factory's CreateCommand method is used to return a command object.

```
string provider = "System.Data.SqlClient";
DBProviderFactory factory =
   DbProviderFactories.GetFactory(provider);
DbCommand cmd    = factory.CreateCommand();
cmd.CommandText = sql;       // Query or command
cmd.Connection  = conn;      // Connection object
```

Note that DbCommand is an abstract class that implements the IDbCommand interface. It assumes the role of a generic command object. This can eliminate the need to cast the returned command object to a specific provider's command object such as

`SqlCommand`. However, casting is required if you need to access custom features of a provider's command class—for example, only `SqlCommand` has an `ExecuteXml-Reader` method.

Executing a Command

The SQL command assigned to the `CommandText` property is executed using one of the four command methods in Table 11-4.

Table 11-4   Command `Executexxx` Methods

Method	Description

ExecuteNonQuery	Executes an action query and returns the number of rows affected:
	
	`cmd.CommandText = "DELETE movies WHERE movie_ID=220";`
	`int ct = cmd.ExecuteNonQuery();`

ExecuteReader	Executes a query and returns a `DataReader` object that provides access to the query's resultset. This method accepts an optional `CommandBehavior` object that can improve execution efficiency.
	
	`cmd.CommandText="SELECT * FROM movies`
	`    WHERE movie_year > '1945';`
	`SqlDataReader rdr= cmd.ExecuteReader();`

ExecuteScalar	Executes a query and returns the value of the first column in the first row of the resultset as a scalar value.
	
	`cmd.CommandText="SELECT COUNT(movie_title)`
	`    FROM movies";`
	`int movieCt = (int) cmd.ExecuteScalar();`

ExecuteXmlReader	Available for SQL Server data provider only. Returns an `XmlReader` object that is used to access the resultset. `XmlReader` is discussed in Chapter 10, "Working with XML in .NET."

The `ExecuteReader` method is the most important of these methods. It returns a `DataReader` object that exposes the rows returned by the query. The behavior of this method can be modified by using its overload that accepts a `CommandBehavior` type parameter. As an example, the following statement specifies that a single row of data is to be returned:

```
rdr = cmd.ExecuteReader(sql, CommandBehavior.SingleResult);
```

Some data providers take advantage of this parameter to optimize query execution. The list of values for the `CommandBehavior` enumeration includes the following:

- `SingleRow`. Indicates that the query should return one row. Default behavior is to return multiple resultsets.
- `SingleResult`. The query is expected to return a single scalar value.
- `KeyInfo`. Returns column and primary key information. It is used with a data reader's `GetSchema` method to fetch column schema information.
- `SchemaOnly`. Used to retrieve column names for the resultset. Example:

```
dr=cmd.ExecuteReader(CommandBehavior.SchemaOnly);
string col1= dr.GetName(0);   // First column name
```

- `SequentialAccess`. Permits data in the returned row to be accessed sequentially by column. This is used with large binary (BLOB) or text fields.
- `CloseConnection`. Close connection when reader is closed.

Executing Stored Procedures with the Command Object

A stored procedure is a set of SQL code stored in a database that can be executed as a script. It's a powerful feature that enables logic to be encapsulated, shared, and reused among applications. ADO.NET supports the execution of stored procedures for `OleDb`, `SqlClient`, `ODBC`, and `OracleClient` data providers.

Executing a stored procedure is quite simple: set the `SqlCommand.CommandText` property to the name of the procedure; set the `CommandType` property to the enumeration `CommandType.StoredProcedure`; and then call the `ExecuteNonQuery` method.

```
cmd.CommandText = "SP_AddMovie";  // Stored procedure name
cmd.CommandType = CommandType.StoredProcedure;
cmd.ExecuteNonQuery();
```

When a stored procedure contains input or output parameters, they must be added to the command object's `Parameters` collection before the procedure is executed. To demonstrate, let's execute the stored procedure shown in Listing 11-3. This procedure allows records to be fetched from the `movies` table as pages containing 10 rows of data. Input to the procedure is the desired page; the output parameter is the total number of pages available. This code fragment illustrates how parameters are set and how the procedure is invoked to return the first page:

```
SqlCommand cmd  = new SqlCommand();
cmd.CommandText = "SPMOVIES_LIST";  // Stored procedure name
cmd.CommandType = CommandType.StoredProcedure;
cmd.Parameters.Add(@PageRequest", SqlDbType.Int);
```

```
cmd.Parameters.Add(@TotalPages", SqlDbType.Int);
cmd.Parameters[0].Direction= ParameterDirection.Input;
cmd.Parameters[0].Value= 1;            // Retrieve first page
cmd.Parameters[1].Direction=ParameterDirection.Output;
cmd.CommandTimeout=10;   // Give command 10 seconds to execute
SqlDataReader rdr = cmd.ExecuteReader();
while (rdr.Read()){
//    do something with results
}
rdr.Close();   // Must close before reading parameters
int totpages=  cmd.Parameters[1].Value;
```

This example uses the `SqlClient` data provider. With a couple of changes, `OleDb` can be used just as easily. The primary difference is in the way they handle parameters. `SqlClient` requires that the parameter names match the names in the stored procedure; `OleDb` passes parameters based on position, so the name is irrelevant. If the procedure sends back a return code, `OleDB` must designate the first parameter in the list to handle it. `SqlClient` simply adds a parameter—the name is unimportant—that has its direction set to `ReturnValue`.

Listing 11-3	Stored SQL Server Procedure to Return a Page of Records

```
CREATE PROCEDURE SPMOVIES_LIST
    @PageRequest int,
    @TotalPages int output
AS
    /*
        Procedure to return a resultset of movies ordered
        by title.
        Resultset contains 10 movies for the specified page.
    */
    SET NOCOUNT ON
    select @TotalPages = CEILING(COUNT(*)/10) from movies
    if @PageRequest = 1 or @PageRequest <1
    begin
        select top 10 * from movies order by movie_Title
        set @PageRequest = 1
        return 0
    end
    begin
        if @PageRequest > @TotalPages
            set @PageRequest = @TotalPages
        declare @RowCount int
        set @RowCount = (@PageRequest * 10)
```

Listing 11-3	Stored SQL Server Procedure to Return a Page of Records *(continued)*

```
      exec ('SELECT * FROM
      (SELECT TOP 10 a.* FROM
      (SELECT TOP ' + @RowCount + ' * FROM movies ORDER BY
          movie_Title) a
       ORDER BY movie_Title desc) b
       ORDER BY Movie_Title')

      return 0
   end
```

Using Parameterized Commands Without Stored Procedures

An earlier example (see "Creating a Command Object" on page 511) used this statement to create a SQL command to store a movie in the `Films` database:

```
string sql = "insert into movies(movie_Title,movie_Year,
      bestpicture) values(@title,@yr,@bestpic)";
// Parameters set values to be stored
cmd.Parameters.AddWithValue ("@title", "Schindler's List");
cmd.Parameters.AddWithValue ("@yr", "1993");
cmd.Parameters.AddWithValue ("@bestpic", "Y");
```

The alternative, which uses concatenation, looks like this:

```
string title = "Schindler''s List";  // Two single quotes needed
string yr = "1993";
string pic = "Y";
sql = "insert into movies(movie_Title,movie_Year,
      bestpicture) values";
sql += "('"+title+"',"+yr+",'"+pic+"') ";
```

Not only is the parameterized version more readable and less prone to syntactical error, but it also provides a significant benefit: It automatically handles the problem of placing double single quotes (' ') in a SQL command. This problem occurs when attempting to store a value such as O'Quinn, which has an embedded quote that conflicts with SQL syntax. Parameters eliminate the usual approach to search each string and replace an embedded single quote with a pair of single quotes.

DataReader Object

As we have seen in several examples, a `DataReader` exposes the rows and columns of data returned as the result of executing a query. Row access is defined by the `IDataReader` interface that each `DataReader` must implement; column access is defined by the `IDataRecord` interface. We'll look at the most important members defined by these interfaces as well as some custom features added by data providers.

Accessing Rows with DataReader

A `DataReader` returns a single row from a resultset each time its `Read` method is executed. If no rows remain, the method returns `false`. The reader should be closed after row processing is completed in order to free system resources. You can check the `DataReader.IsClosed` property to determine if a reader is closed.

Although a `DataReader` is associated with a single command, the command may contain multiple queries that return multiple resultsets. This code fragment demonstrates how a `DataReader` processes the rows returned by two queries.

```
string q1 = "SELECT * FROM movies WHERE movie_Year < 1940";
string q2 = "SELECT * FROM movies WHERE movie_Year > 1980";
cmd.CommandText = q1 + ";" + q2;
DbDataReader rdr = cmd.ExecuteReader();
bool readNext = true;
while (readNext)
{
    while (rdr.Read())
    {
        MessageBox.Show(rdr.GetString(1));
    }
    readNext = rdr.NextResult(); // Another resultset?
}
rdr.Close();
conn.Close();
```

The two things to note are the construction of the `CommandString` with multiple queries and the use of the `NextResult` method to determine if results from another query are present.

Core Note

The `DataReader` has no property or method that provides the number of rows returned in its resultset. Because data is received one row at a time, the resultset could be altered by additions and deletions to the database as records are read. However, there is a `HasRows` property that returns `true` if the data reader contains one or more rows.

Accessing Column Values with DataReader

There are numerous ways to access data contained in the columns of the current `DataReader` row: as an array with column number (zero-based) or name used as an index; using the `GetValue` method by passing it a column number; and using one of the strongly typed `Getxxx` methods that include `GetString`, `GetInt32`, `GetDateTime`, and `GetDouble`. The following code segment contains an example of each technique:

```
cmd.CommandText="SELECT movie_ID, movie_Title FROM movies";
rdr = cmd.ExecuteReader();
rdr.Read();
string title;
// Multiple ways to access data in a column
title = rdr.GetString(1);
title = (string)rdr.GetSqlString(1); // SqlClient provider
title = (string)rdr.GetValue(1);
title = (string)rdr["movie_Title"];  // Implicit item
title = (string)rdr[1];              // Implicit item
```

The `GetString` method has the advantage of mapping the database contents to a native .NET data type. The other approaches return object types that require casting. For this reason, use of the `Get` methods is recommended. Note that although `GetString` does not require casting, it does not perform any conversion; thus, if the data is not of the type expected, an exception is thrown.

Many applications rely on a separate data access layer to provide a `DataReader`. In such cases, the application may require metadata to identify column names, data types, and other columnar information. Column names, which are useful for generating report headings, are readily available through the `GetName` method:

```
// List column names for a DataReader
DbDataReader rdr = GetReader();          // Get a DataReader
for (int k = 0; k < rdr.FieldCount; k++)
{
    Console.WriteLine(rdr.GetName(k));   // Column name
}
rdr.Close();
```

Complete column schema information is available through the `GetSchemaTable` method. It returns a `DataTable` in which there is one row for each field (column) in the resultset. The columns in the table represent schema information. This code segment demonstrates how to access all the column information for a resultset. For brevity, only three of the 24 columns of information are shown:

```
DataTable schemaTable = rdr.GetSchemaTable();
int ict = 0;
foreach (DataRow r in schemaTable.Rows)
{
    foreach (DataColumn c in schemaTable.Columns){
        Console.WriteLine(ict.ToString()+"
                        "+c.ColumnName + ": "+r[c]);
        ict++;
    }
}
// Selected Output:
//        0 ColumnName: movie_ID
//        1 ColumnOrdinal: 0
//        12 DataType: System.Int32
```

11.4 DataSets, DataTables, and the Disconnected Model

The ADO.NET disconnected model is based on using a DataSet object as an in-memory cache. A DataAdapter serves as the intermediary between the DataSet and the data source that loads the cache with data. After it has completed its task, the DataAdapter returns the connection object to the pool, thus disconnecting the data from the data source. Interestingly, the DataAdapter is actually a wrapper around a data provider's DataReader, which performs the actual data loading.

The DataSet Class

In many ways, a DataSet object plays the role of an in-memory database. Its Tables property exposes a collection of DataTables that contain data and a data schema describing the data. The Relations property returns a collection of DataRelation objects that define how tables are interrelated. In addition, DataSet methods are available to Copy, Merge, and Clear the contents of the DataSet.

Keep in mind that the DataSet and DataTable are core parts of ADO.NET and—unlike the Connection, DataReader, and DataAdapter—they are not tied to a specific data provider. An application can create, define, and populate a DataSet with data from any source.

Besides tables and their relations, a DataSet can also contain custom information defined by the application. A look at Figure 11-6 shows the major collection classes in the DataSet hierarchy. Among these is PropertyCollection, which is a set of custom properties stored in a hash table and exposed through the DataSet.Extended-Properties property. It is often used to hold a time stamp or descriptive information such as column validation requirements for tables in the data set.

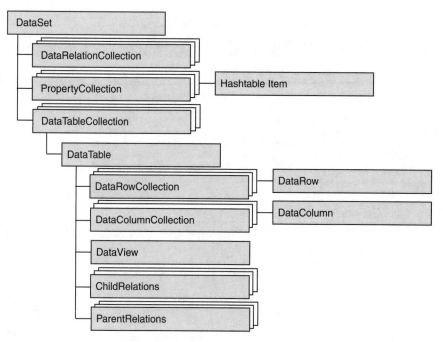

Figure 11-6   DataSet class hierarchy

The discussion of the DataSet class begins with its most important member—the DataTable collection.

DataTables

One step below the DataSet in the disconnected model hierarchy is the DataTable collection. This collection—accessed through the DataSet.Tables property—stores data in a row-column format that mimics tables in a relational database. The DataTable class has a rich set of properties and methods that make it useful as a stand-alone data source or as part of a table collection in a DataSet. The most important of these are the Columns and Rows properties, which define the layout and content of a table.

DataColumns

The DataTable.Columns property exposes a collection of DataColumn objects that represent each data field in the DataTable. Taken together, the column properties produce the data schema for the table. Table 11-5 summarizes the most important properties.

Table 11-5 Properties of the `DataColumn` Class

Method	Description
`ColumnName`	Name of the column.
`DataType`	Type of data contained in this column.
	Example: `col1.DataType = System.Type.GetType("System.String")`
`MaxLength`	Maximum length of a text column. `-1` if there is no maximum length.
`ReadOnly`	Indicates whether the values in the column can be modified.
`AllowDBNull`	Boolean value that indicates whether the column may contain null values.
`Unique`	Boolean value that indicates whether the column may contain duplicate values.
`Expression`	An expression defining how the value of a column is calculated.
	Example: `colTax.Expression = "colSales * .085";`
`Caption`	The caption displayed in the user interface.
`DataTable`	The name of the `DataTable` containing this column.

`DataTable` columns are created automatically when the table is filled with the results of a database query or from reading an XML file. However, for applications that fill a table dynamically—such as from user input or real-time data acquisition—it may be necessary to write the code that defines the table structure. It's a worthwhile exercise in its own right that enhances a developer's understanding of the `DataSet` hierarchy.

The following segment creates a `DataTable` object, creates `DataColumn` objects, assigns property values to the columns, and adds them to the `DataTable`. To make things interesting, a calculated column is included.

```
DataTable tb = new DataTable("Order");
DataColumn dCol = new DataColumn("ID",
      Type.GetType("System.Int16"));
dCol.Unique = true;  // ID must be unique for each data row
dCol.AllowDBNull = false;
tb.Columns.Add(dCol);
dCol= new DataColumn("Price", Type.GetType("System.Decimal"));
tb.Columns.Add(dCol);
dCol=new DataColumn("Quan",Type.GetType("System.Int16"));
tb.Columns.Add(dCol);
```

```
dCol= new DataColumn("Total",Type.GetType("System.Decimal"));
dCol.Expression= "Price * Quan";
tb.Columns.Add(dCol);
// List column names and data type
foreach (DataColumn dc in tb.Columns)
{
    Console.WriteLine(dc.ColumnName);
    Console.WriteLine(dc.DataType.ToString());
}
```

Note that the ID column is defined to contain unique values. This constraint qualifies the column to be used as a key field in establishing a parent-child relationship with another table in a DataSet. To qualify, the key must be unique—as in this case—or defined as a *primary key* for the table. You assign a primary key to a table by setting its PrimaryKey field to the value of an array containing the column(s) to be used as the key. Here is an example that specifies the ID field a primary key:

```
DataColumn[] col = {tb.Columns["ID"]};
tb.PrimaryKey = col;
```

We'll see how to use a primary key to create table relationships and merge data later in this section.

Core Note

If a primary key consists of more than one column—such as a first and last name—you can enforce a unique constraint on these columns in three steps: by creating an array to hold the columns, creating a UniqueConstraint object by passing the array to its constructor; and adding the constraint to the data table's Constraints collection:

```
DataColumn[] cols = {tb.Columns["fname"]
                     tb.Columns["lname"]};
tb.Constraints.Add(new UniqueConstraint("nameKey", cols));
```

DataRows

Data is added to a table by creating a new DataRow object, filling it with column data, and adding the row to the table's DataRow collection. Here is an example that places data in the table created in the preceding example.

```
DataRow row;
row = tb.NewRow();      // Create DataRow
row["Title"] = "Casablanca";
```

```
row["Price"] = 22.95;
row["Quan"] = 2;
row["ID"] = 12001;
tb.Rows.Add(row);         // Add row to Rows collection
Console.WriteLine(tb.Rows[0]["Total"].ToString()); // 45.90
```

A `DataTable` has methods that allow it to commit and roll back changes made to the table. In order to do this, it keeps the status of each row in the `DataRow.Row-State` property. This property is set to one of five `DataRowState` enumeration values: `Added`, `Deleted`, `Detached`, `Modifed`, or `Unchanged`. Let's extend the preceding example to demonstrate how these values are set:

```
tb.Rows.Add(row);                        // Added
tb.AcceptChanges();                      // ...Commit changes
Console.Write(row.RowState);             // Unchanged
tb.Rows[0].Delete();                     // Deleted
// Undo deletion
tb.RejectChanges();                      // ...Roll back
Console.Write(tb.Rows[0].RowState);      // Unchanged
DataRow myRow;
MyRow = tb.NewRow();                     // Detached
```

The two `DataTable` methods `AcceptChanges` and `RejectChanges` are equivalent to the commit and rollback operations in a database. These apply to all changes made from the time the table was loaded or since `AcceptChanges` was previously invoked. In this example, we are able to restore a deleted row because the deletion is not committed before `RejectChanges` is called. Note that the changes are to the data table—not the original data source.

For each column value in a row, ADO.NET maintains a current and original value. When `RejectChanges` is called, the current values are set to the original values. The opposite occurs if `AcceptChanges` is called. The two sets of values can be accessed concurrently through the `DataRowVersion` enumerations `Current` and `Original`:

```
DataRow r = tb.Rows[0];
r["Price"]= 14.95;
r.AcceptChanges();
r["Price"]= 16.95;
Console.WriteLine("Current: {0} Original: {1} ",
      r["Price",DataRowVersion.Current],
      r["Price",DataRowVersion.Original]);
// output:  Current: 16.95  Original: 14.95
```

Keeping track of table row changes takes on added importance when the purpose is to update an underlying data source. We'll see later in this section how the `Data-Adapter` updates database tables with changes made to `DataTable` rows.

Loading Data into a DataSet

Now that we have seen how to construct a `DataTable` and punch data into it row-by-row, let's look at how data and a data schema can be automatically loaded from a relational database into tables in a `DataSet`. For details on loading XML data, refer to Section 11.5, "XML and ADO.NET," on page 533.

Using the DataReader to Load Data into a DataSet

A `DataReader` object can be used in conjunction with a `DataSet` or `DataTable` to fill a table with the rows generated by a query. This requires creating a `DataReader` object and passing it as a parameter to the `DataTable.Load` method:

```
cmd.CommandText = "SELECT * FROM movies WHERE movie_Year < 1945";
DBDataReader rdr =
      cmd.ExecuteReader(CommandBehavior.CloseConnection);
DataTable dt = new DataTable("movies");
dt.Load(rdr);    // Load data and schema into table
Console.WriteLine(rdr.IsClosed);    // True
```

The `DataReader` is closed automatically after all of the rows have been loaded. The `CloseConnection` parameter ensures that the connection is also closed.

If the table already contains data, the `Load` method merges the new data with the existing rows of data. Merging occurs only if rows share a primary key. If no primary key is defined, rows are appended. An overloaded version of `Load` takes a second parameter that defines how rows are combined. This parameter is a `LoadOption` enumeration type having one of three values: `OverwriteRow`, `PreserveCurrent-Values`, or `UpdateCurrentValues`. These options specify whether the merge operation overwrites the entire row, original values only, or current values only. This code segment illustrates how data is merged with existing rows to overwrite the current column values:

```
cmd.CommandText = "SELECT * FROM movies WHERE movie_Year < 1945";
DBDataReader rdr = cmd.ExecuteReader( );
DataTable dt = new DataTable("movies");
dt.Load(rdr);                         // Load rows into table
Console.Write(dt.Rows[0]["movie_Title"]);  // Casablanca

// Assign primary key so rows can be merged
DataColumn[] col = new DataColumn[1];
```

```
col[0] = dt.Columns["movie_ID"];
dt.PrimaryKey = col;
DataRow r = dt.Rows[0];                // Get first row of data
r["movie_Title"] = "new title";        // Change current column value
// Since reader is closed, must fill reader again
rdr = cmd.ExecuteReader(CommandBehavior.CloseConnection);
// Merge data with current rows. Overwrites current values
dt.Load(rdr, LoadOption.UpdateCurrentValues );
// Updated value has been overwritten
Console.Write(dt.Rows[0]["movie_Title"]);  // Casablanca
```

Using the DataAdapter to Load Data into a DataSet

A `DataAdapter` object can be used to fill an existing table, or create and fill a new table, with the results from a query. The first step in this process is to create an instance of the `DataAdapter` for a specific data provider. As the following code shows, several constructor overloads are available:

```
// (1) The easiest: a query and connection string as arguments
String sql = "SELECT * FROM movies";
SqlDataAdapter da = new SqlDataAdapter(sql, connStr);

// (2) Assign a command object to the SelectCommand property
SqlDataAdapter da = new SqlDataAdapter();
SqlConnection conn = new SqlConnection(connStr);
da.SelectCommand = new SqlCommand(sql,conn);

// (3) Pass in a query string and connection object
SqlConnection conn = new SqlConnection(connStr);
SqlDataAdapter da = new SqlDataAdapter(sql, conn);
```

Of these, the first version is the simplest. It accepts two strings containing the query and connection. From these, it constructs a `SqlCommand` object that is assigned internally to its `SelectCommand` property. Unlike the other constructors, there is no need to write code that explicitly creates a `SqlCommand` or `SqlConnection` object.

In the overloads that accept a connection object as a parameter, the opening and closing of the connection is left to the `DataAdapter`. If you add a statement to explicitly open the connection, you must also include code to close it. Otherwise, the `DataAdapter` leaves it open, which locks the data in the database.

After the `DataAdapter` object is created, its `Fill` method is executed to load data into a new or existing table. In this example, a new table is created and assigned the default name `Table`:

```
DataSet ds = new DataSet();
// Create DataTable, load data, and add to DataSet
// Could use da.Fill(ds,"movies") to specify table name.
int numrecs = da.Fill(ds);  // Returns number of records loaded
```

For an existing table, the behavior of the `Fill` command depends on whether the table has a primary key. If it does, those rows having a key that matches the key of the incoming data are replaced. Incoming rows that do not match an existing row are appended to the `DataTable`.

Using the DataAdapter to Update a Database

After a `DataAdapter` has loaded data into a table, the underlying connection is closed, and subsequent changes made to the data are reflected only in the `DataSet`—not the underlying data source. To apply changes to the data source, a `DataAdapter` is used to restore the connection and send the changed rows to the database. The same `DataAdapter` used to fill the `DataSet` can be used to perform this task.

The `DataAdapter` has three properties—`InsertCommand`, `DeleteCommand`, and `UpdateCommand`—that are assigned the actual SQL commands to perform the tasks that correspond to the property name. These commands are executed when the `Upate` method of the `DataAdapter` is invoked. The challenge lies in creating the SQL commands that post the changes and assigning them to the appropriate `Data-Adapter` properties. Fortunately, each data provider implements a `Command-Builder` class that can be used to handle this task automatically.

The CommandBuilder Object

A `CommandBuilder` object generates the commands necessary to update a data source with changes made to a `DataSet`. It's amazingly self-sufficient. You create an instance of it by passing the related `DataAdapter` object to its constructor; then, when the `DataAdapter.Update` method is called, the SQL commands are generated and executed. The following segment shows how changes to a `DataTable` are flushed to the database associated with the `DataAdapter`:

```
DataTable dt= ds.Tables["movies"]; // Shortcut to reference table

// (1) Use command builder to generate update commands
SqlCommandBuilder sb = new SqlCommandBuilder(da);

// (2) Add movie to table
DataRow drow = dt.NewRow();
drow["movie_Title"] = "Taxi Driver";
drow["movie_Year"] = "1976";
```

```
dt.Rows.Add(drow);

// (3) Delete row from table
dt.Rows[4].Delete();

// (4) Edit Column value
dt.Rows[5]["movie_Year"] = "1944";

// (5) Update underlying Sql Server table
int updates = da.Update(ds, "movies");
MessageBox.Show("Rows Changed: " +updates.ToString());   // 3
```

There are a couple of restrictions to be aware of when using the Command-
Builder: The Select command associated with the DataAdapter must refer to a
single table, and the source table in the database must include a primary key or a column that contains unique values. This column (or columns) must be included in the
original Select command.

Core Note

You can create your own update commands without using a
CommandBuilder. Although it can be a lengthy process, it can also yield
more efficient commands. For applications that require considerable
database updates, you may want to consult an ADO.NET book for
details on coding update logic directly.

Synchronizing the DataSet and the DataBase

As demonstrated in this example, the use of a DataAdapter simplifies and automates the process of updating a database—or any data store. However, there is a rock
in this snowball: the problem of multi-user updates. The disconnected model is
based on *optimistic concurrency*, an approach in which the rows of the underlying
data source are not locked between the time they are read and the time updates are
applied to the data source. During this interval, another user may update the data
source. Fortunately, the Update method recognizes if changes have occurred since
the previous read and fails to apply changes to a row that has been altered.

There are two basic strategies for dealing with a concurrency error when multiple updates are being applied: roll back all changes if a violation occurs, or apply
the updates that do not cause an error and identify the ones that do so they can be
reprocessed.

Using Transactions to Roll Back Multiple Updates

When the DataAdapter.ContinueUpdateonErrors property is set to false, an exception is thrown when a row update cannot be completed. This prevents subsequent updates from being attempted, but does not affect updates that occurred prior to the exception. Because updates may be interdependent, applications often require an all-or-none strategy. The easiest way to implement this strategy is to create a .NET transaction in which all of the update commands execute. To do so, create a SqlTransaction object and associate it with the SqlDataAdapter.SelectCommand by passing it to its constructor. If an exception occurs, the transaction's Rollback method is used to undo any changes; if no exceptions occur, the Commit method is executed to apply all the update commands. Listing 11-4 is an example that wraps the updates inside a transaction.

Listing 11-4	Using Transaction to Roll Back Database Updates

```
SqlDataAdapter da = new SqlDataAdapter();
SqlCommandBuilder sb = new SqlCommandBuilder(da);
SqlTransaction tran;
SqlConnection conn = new SqlConnection(connStr);
conn.Open();        // Must open to use with transaction
// (1) Create a transaction
SqlTransaction tran = conn.BeginTransaction();
// (2) Associate the SelectCommand with the transaction
da.SelectCommand = new SqlCommand(sql, conn, tran);
DataSet ds = new DataSet();
da.Fill(ds, "movies");
//
// Code in this section makes updates to DataSet rows
try
{
   int updates = da.Update(ds, "movies");
   MessageBox.Show("Updates: "+updates.ToString());
}
// (3) If exception occurs, roll back all updates in transaction
catch (Exception ex)
{
   MessageBox.Show(ex.Message);    // Error updating
   if (tran != null)
   {
      tran.Rollback();        // Roll back any updates
      tran = null;
      MessageBox.Show("All updates rolled back.");
   }
}
```

Listing 11-4	Using Transaction to Roll Back Database Updates (continued)

```
finally
{
// (4) If no errors, commit all updates
   if (tran != null)
   {
       tran.Commit();
       MessageBox.Show("All updates successful. ");
       tran = null;
   }
}
conn.Close();
```

Identifying Rows That Cause Update Errors

When `DataAdapter.ContinueUpdateonErrors` is set to `true`, processing does not halt if a row cannot be updated. Instead, the `DataAdapter` updates all rows that do not cause an error. It is then up to the programmer to identify the rows that failed and determine how to reprocess them.

Rows that fail to update are easily identified by their `DataRowState` property (discussed earlier in the description of `DataRows`). Rows whose update succeeds have a value of `Unchanged`; rows that fail have their original `Added`, `Deleted`, or `Modified` value. A simple code segment demonstrates how to loop through the rows and identify those that are not updated (see Listing 11-5).

Listing 11-5	Identify Attempts to Update a Database That Fails

```
// SqlDataAdapter da loads movies table
da.ContinueUpdateOnError = true;
DataSet ds = new DataSet();
try
{
   da.Fill(ds, "movies");
   DataTable dt = ds.Tables["movies"];
   SqlCommandBuilder sb = new SqlCommandBuilder(da);
   // ... Sample Update operations
   dt.Rows[29].Delete();                        // Delete
   dt.Rows[30]["movie_Year"] = "1933";          // Update
   dt.Rows[30]["movie_Title"] = "King Kong";    // Update
```

```
dt.Rows[31]["movie_Title"] = "Fantasia";    // Update
DataRow drow = dt.NewRow();
drow["movie_Title"] = "M*A*S*H";
drow["movie_Year"] = "1970";
dt.Rows.Add(drow);                          // insert
// Submit updates
int updates = da.Update(ds, "movies");
// Following is true if any update failed
if (ds.HasChanges())
{
    // Load rows that failed into a DataSet
    DataSet failures = ds.GetChanges();
    int rowsFailed = failures.Rows.Count;
    Console.WriteLine("Update Failures: "+rowsFailed);
    foreach (DataRow r in failures.Tables[0].Rows )
    {
        string state = r.RowState.ToString());
        // Have to reject changes to show deleted row
        if (r.RowState == DataRowState.Deleted)
            r.RejectChanges();
        string ID= ((int)r["movie_ID"]).ToString();
        string msg= state + " Movie ID: "+ID;
        Console.WriteLine(msg);
    }
}
```

Note that even though the delete occurs first, it does not affect the other operations. The SQL statement that deletes or updates a row is based on a row's primary key value—not relative position. Also, be aware that updates on the same row are combined and counted as a single row update by the Update method. In this example, updates to row 30 count as one update.

Handling concurrency issues is not a simple task. After you identify the failures, the next step—how to respond to the failures—is less clear, and depends on the application. Often times, it is necessary to re-read the rows from the database and compare them with the rows that failed in order to determine how to respond. The ability to recognize RowState and the current and original values of rows is the key to developing code that resolves update conflicts.

Defining Relationships Between Tables in a DataSet

A `DataRelation` is a parent/child relationship between two `DataTables`. It is defined on matching columns in the two tables. The columns must be the same `DataType`, and the column in the parent table must have unique values. The syntax for its constructor is

```
public DataRelation(
    string relationName,
    DataColumn parentColumn,
    DataColumn childColumn)
```

A `DataSet` has a `Relations` property that provides access to the collection of `DataRelations` defined for tables contained in the `DataSet`. Use the `Relations.Add` method to place relations in the collection. Listing 11-6 illustrates these ideas. It contains code to set up a parent/child relationship between the `directors` and `movies` tables in order to list movies by each director.

Listing 11-6	Create a Relationship Between the Directors and Movies Tables

```
DataSet ds = new DataSet();
// (1) Fill table with movies
string sql = "SELECT movie_ID,movie_Title,movie_DirectorID,
        movie_Year FROM movies";
SqlConnection conn = new SqlConnection(connStr);
SqlCommand cmd = new SqlCommand();
SqlDataAdapter da = new SqlDataAdapter(sql, conn);
da.Fill(ds, "movies");
// (2) Fill table with directors
sql = "SELECT director_id,(first_name + ' '+ last_name) AS
        fullname FROM directors";
da.SelectCommand.CommandText = sql;
da.Fill(ds, "directors");
// (3) Define relationship between directors and movies
DataTable parent = ds.Tables["directors"];
DataTable child = ds.Tables["movies"];
DataRelation relation = new DataRelation("directormovies",
        parent.Columns["director_ID"],
        child.Columns["movie_DirectorID"]);
```

Listing 11-6	Create a Relationship Between the Directors and Movies Tables *(continued)*

```
// (4) Add relation to DataSet
ds.Relations.Add(relation);
// (5) List each director and his or her movies
foreach (DataRow r in parent.Rows)
{
    Console.WriteLine(r["fullname"];      // Director name
    foreach (DataRow rc in
      r.GetChildRows("directormovies"))
    {
      Console.WriteLine("  "+rc["movie_title"]);
    }
}
/*
    Sample Output:
      David Lean
          Lawrence of Arabia
          Bridge on the River Kwai, The
      Victor Fleming
          Gone with the Wind
          Wizard of Oz, The
*/
```

Relations and Constraints

When a relationship is defined between two tables, it has the effect of adding a `ForeignKeyConstraint` to the `Constraints` collections of the child `DataTable`. This constraint determines how the child table is affected when rows in a parent table are changed or deleted. In practical terms, this means that if you delete a row in the parent table, you can have the related child row(s) deleted—or optionally, have their key value set to `null`. Similarly, if a key value is changed in the parent table, the related rows in the child can have their key value changed or set to `null`.

The rule in effect is determined by the value of the `DeleteRule` and `UpdateRule` properties of the constraint. These can take one of four `Rule` enumeration values:

- `Cascade`. Deletes or updates related rows in child table. This is the default.
- `None`. Takes no action.
- `SetDefault`. Sets key values in child rows to column's default value.
- `SetNull`. Sets key values in child rows to `null`.

This code segment illustrates how constraints affect the capability to add a row to a child table and delete or change a row in the parent table. The tables from the preceding example are used.

```
// (1) Try to add row with new key to child table
DataRow row = child.NewRow();
row["movie_directorID"] = 999;
child.Rows.Add(row);    // Fails - 999 does not exist in parent
// (2) Delete row in parent table
row = parent.Rows[0];
row.Delete();           // Deletes rows in child having this key
// (3) Relax constraints and retry adding row
ds.EnforceConstraints = false;
row["movie_directorID"] = 999;
child.Rows.Add(row);    // Succeeds
ds.EnforceConstraints = true;      // Turn back on
// (4) Change constraint to set rows to null if parent changed
((ForeignKeyConstraint)child.Constraints[0]).DeleteRule =
        Rule.SetNull ;
```

Note that setting the `EnforceConstraints` property to `false` turns off all constraints—which in database terms eliminates the check for *referential integrity*.[3] This allows a movie to be added even though its `movie_DirectorID` column (foreign key) does not have a corresponding row in the `directors` table. It also permits a director to be deleted even though a movie by that director exists in the `movies` table. This clearly compromises the integrity of the database and should be used only when testing or populating individual tables in a database.

Choosing Between the Connected and Disconnected Model

The `DataReader` and `DataSet` offer different approaches to processing data—each with its advantages and disadvantages. The `DataReader` provides forward-only, read-only access to data. By processing a row at a time, it minimizes memory requirements. A `DataSet`, on the other hand, offers read/write access to data, but requires enough memory to hold a copy of the data fetched from a data source. From this, you can derive a couple of general rules: If the application does not require the capability to update the data source and is used merely for display and selection purposes, a `DataReader` should be the first consideration; if the application requires updating data, a `DataSet` should be considered.

---

3. The foreign key in any referencing table must always refer to a valid row in the referenced table.

Of course, the general rules have to be weighed against other factors. If the data source contains a large number of records, a `DataSet` may require too many resources; or if the data requires only a few updates, the combination of `Data-Reader` and `Command` object to execute updates may make more sense. Despite the gray areas, there are many situations where one is clearly preferable to the other.

A `DataSet` is a good choice when the following apply:

- Data need to be serialized and/or sent over the wire using HTTP.
- Multiple read-only controls on a Windows Form are bound to the data source.
- A Windows Form control such as a `GridView` or `DataView` is bound to an updatable data source.
- A desktop application must edit, add, and delete rows of data.

A `DataReader` is a good choice when the following apply:

- A large number of records must be handled so that the memory requirements and time to load make a `DataSet` impracticable.
- The data is read-only and bound to a Windows or Web Form list control.
- The database is highly volatile, and the contents of a `DataSet` might be updated often.

11.5 XML and ADO.NET

Just as relational data has a schema that defines its tables, columns, and relationships, XML uses a Schema Definition language (XSD) to define the layout of an XML document. Its main use is to validate the content of XML data. See Section 10.1, "Working with XML," for a discussion of XML Schema.

The XML classes reside in the `System.Xml` namespace hierarchy and are not part of ADO.NET. However, the ADO.NET `DataSet` class provides a bridge between the two with a set of methods that interacts with XML data and schemas:

- `ReadXML`. Loads XML data into a `DatSet`.
- `WriteXml` and `GetXml`. Writes the `DataSet`'s contents to an XML formatted stream.
- `WriteXmlSchema` and `GetXmlSchema`. Generates an XML Schema from the `DataSet` schema.
- `ReadXmlSchema`. Reads an XML Schema file and creates a database schema.
- `InferXmlSchema`. Creates a `DataSet` schema from XML data.

- `GetXml` and `GetXmlSchema`, Returns a string containing the XML representation of the data or the XSD schema for XML representation.

We'll first look at examples that show how to write XML from a `DataSet`. This XML output is then used as input in subsequent examples that create a `DataSet` from XML.

Using a DataSet to Create XML Data and Schema Files

When working with XML, the `DataSet` is used as an intermediary to convert between XML and relational data. For this to work, the XML data should be structured so that it can be represented by the relationships and row-column layout that characterizes relational data.

The following code segment illustrates how easy it is to create an XML data file and schema from a `DataSet`'s contents. A `DataAdapter` is used to populate a `DataSet` with a subset of the `movies` table. The `WriteXml` and `WriteXmlSchema` methods are then used to translate this to XML output.

```
DataSet ds = new DataSet("films");
DataTable dt = ds.Tables.Add("movies");
string sql = "SELECT * FROM movies WHERE bestPicture='Y'";
SqlDataAdapter da = new SqlDataAdapter(sql, conn);
da.Fill(dt);
// Write Schema representing DataTable to a file
ds.WriteXmlSchema("c:\\oscars.xsd");   // create schema
// Write Table data to an XML file
ds.WriteXml("c:\\oscarwinners.xml");   // data in xml format
/* To place schema inline with XML data in same file:
   ds.WriteXml(("c:\\oscarwinners.xml",
            XmlWriteMode.WriteSchema);
*/
```

The schema output shown in Listing 11-7 defines the permissible content of an XML document (file). If you compare this with Figure 11-3 on page 502, you can get a general feel for how it works. For example, each field in the `movies` table is represented by an element containing the permissible field name and type.

Listing 11-7	XML Schema from Movies Table—`oscars.xsd`

```xml
<?xml version="1.0" encoding="utf-16"?>
<xs:schema id="films" xmlns=""
xmlns:xs="http://www.w3.org/2001/XMLSchema"
xmlns:msdata="urn:schemas-microsoft-com:xml-msdata">
  <xs:element name="films" msdata:IsDataSet="true">
    <xs:complexType>
      <xs:choice minOccurs="0" maxOccurs="unbounded">
        <xs:element name="movies">
          <xs:complexType>
            <xs:sequence>
              <xs:element name="movie_ID" type="xs:int"
                    minOccurs="0" />
              <xs:element name="movie_Title" type="xs:string"
                    minOccurs="0" />
              <xs:element name="movie_Year" type="xs:int"
                    minOccurs="0" />
              <xs:element name="movie_DirectorID" type="xs:int"
                    minOccurs="0" />
              <xs:element name="AFIRank" type="xs:int"
                    minOccurs="0" />
              <xs:element name="bestPicture" type="xs:string"
                    minOccurs="0" />
            </xs:sequence>
          </xs:complexType>
        </xs:element>
      </xs:choice>
    </xs:complexType>
  </xs:element>
</xs:schema>
```

Listing 11-8 displays an abridged listing of the XML version of the relational data. The name of the `DataSet` is the root element. Each row in the table is represented by a child element (`movies`) containing elements that correspond to the columns in the data table.

Listing 11-8	Movies Data as an XML Document— `oscarwinners.xml`

```xml
<?xml version="1.0" encoding="utf-16"?>
<?xml version="1.0" standalone="yes"?>
<films>
  <movies>
    <movie_ID>5</movie_ID>
    <movie_Title>Citizen Kane </movie_Title>
    <movie_Year>1941</movie_Year>
    <movie_DirectorID>1</movie_Director>
    <AFIRank>1</AFIRank>
    <bestPicture>Y</bestPicture>
  </movies>
  <movies>
    <movie_ID>6</movie_ID>
    <movie_Title>Casablanca </movie_Title>
    <movie_Year>1942</movie_Year>
    <movie_DirectorID>2</movie_Director>
    <AFIRank>2</AFIRank>
    <bestPicture>Y</bestPicture>
  </movies>
  ...
</films>
```

Creating a DataSet Schema from XML

Each ADO.NET `DataSet` has a schema that defines the tables, table columns, and table relationships that comprise the `DataSet`. As we saw in the preceding example, this schema can be translated into an XML schema using the `WriteXmlSchema` method. `ReadXmlSchema` mirrors the process—adding tables and relationships to a `DataSet`. In this example, the XML schema for the `movies` table (refer to Listing 11-7) is used to create a `DataSet` schema:

```
DataSet ds = new DataSet();
ds.ReadXmlSchema("c:\\oscars.xsd");
DataTable tb = ds.Tables[0];
// List Columns for table
string colList = tb.TableName +": ";
for (int i = 0; i < tb.Columns.Count; i++)
   { colList += tb.Columns[i].Caption + "   "; }
Console.WriteLine(colList);
```

```
/* output is:
movies: movie_ID  movie_Title  movie_Year movie_DirectorID
        bestpicture AFIRank
*/
```

It is also possible to create a schema by inferring its structure from the XML data or using a `DataAdapter` to configure the schema:

```
// (1) Create schema by inferring it from XML data
ds.Tables.Clear();    // Remove tables from DataSet
ds.InferXmlSchema("c:\\oscarwinners.xml",null);

// (2) Create schema using Data Adapter
ds.Tables.Clear();
string sql = "SELECT * FROM movies";
SqlDataAdapter da = new SqlDataAdapter(sql, connStr);
// Creates DataTable named "movies"
da.FillSchema(ds, SchemaType.Source, "movies");
```

Core Note

By creating the `DataSet` schema(s) in a separate step from reading in XML data, you can control the data that is read from the source XML file. Only data for the columns defined by the schema are read in. Conversely, if the schema defines more columns than are in the XML file, these columns are empty in the `DataSet`.

Reading XML Data into a DataSet

The `DataSet.ReadXml` method provides a way to read either data only or both the data and schema into a `DataSet`. The method has several overloads that determine whether a schema is also created. The two overloads used with files are

```
XmlReadMode ReadXml(string XMLfilename);
XmlReadMode ReadXml(string XMLfilename, XmlReadMode mode);
```

Parameters:

XMLfilename   Name of file (.xml) containing XML data.

mode   One of the `XmlReadMode` enumeration values.

The `XmlReadMode` parameter merits special attention. Its value specifies how a schema is derived for the table(s) in a `DataSet`. It can specify three sources for the schema: from a schema contained (inline) in the XML file, from the schema already associated with the DataSet, or by inferring a schema from the contents of the XML file. Table 11-6 summarizes how selected enumeration members specify the schema source. The numbers in the table indicate the order in which a schema is selected. For example, ReadSchema specifies that the inline schema is the first choice; if it does not exist, the schema associated with the DataSet is used; if neither exists, a data table is not built.

Table 11-6   XmlReadMode Values Determine How a Schema Is Derived for a DataSet

XmlReadMode	Schema Source			Comment
	Inline	DataSet	Infer	
Auto	1	2	3	The default when no XmlReadMode is provided.
IgnoreSchema		1		Uses only the DataSet's schema. Data in the file that is not in the schema is ignored.
InferSchema			1	Ignores inline schema, and builds tables by inference from XML file. Error occurs if DataSet already contains conflicting schema.
ReadSchema	1	2		If tables created from inline schema already exist in DataSet, an exception is thrown.

The code segment in Listing 11-9 loads an XML file into a DataSet and then calls a method to display the contents of each row in the table created. Because the DataSet does not have a predefined schema, and the file does not include an inline schema, ReadXml infers it from the contents of the file.

Listing 11-9	Using ReadXml to Load XML Data into a DataSet

```
//  Load XML data into dataset and create schema if one does
//  not exist
DataSet ds = new DataSet();
ds.ReadXml("c:\\oscarwinners.xml");
```

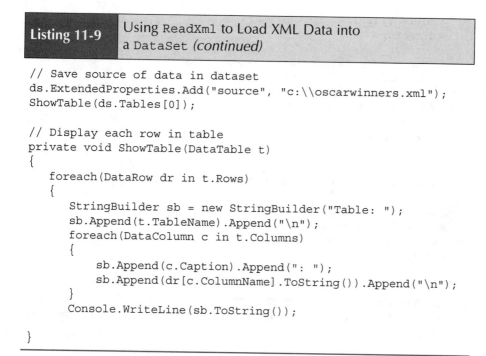

Listing 11-9	Using `ReadXml` to Load XML Data into a `DataSet` *(continued)*

```
// Save source of data in dataset
ds.ExtendedProperties.Add("source", "c:\\oscarwinners.xml");
ShowTable(ds.Tables[0]);

// Display each row in table
private void ShowTable(DataTable t)
{
    foreach(DataRow dr in t.Rows)
    {
        StringBuilder sb = new StringBuilder("Table: ");
        sb.Append(t.TableName).Append("\n");
        foreach(DataColumn c in t.Columns)
        {
            sb.Append(c.Caption).Append(": ");
            sb.Append(dr[c.ColumnName].ToString()).Append("\n");
        }
        Console.WriteLine(sb.ToString());
    }
}
```

Note the use of `ExtendedProperties` to store the name of the data source in the data set. Because this collection of custom properties is implemented as a `Hash-table`, it is accessed using that syntax:

```
string src = (string)ds.ExtendedProperties["source"];
ds.ExtendedProperties.Clear(); // clear hash table
```

Using ReadXml with Nested XML Data

The XML file used in the preceding example has a simple structure that is easily transformed into a single table: The `<movies>` tag (refer to Listing 11-8) represents a row in a table, and the elements contained within it become column values. Most XML is more complex than this example and requires multiple tables to represent it. Although `ReadXml` has limitations (it cannot handle attributes), it can recognize nested XML and render multiple tables from it. As an example, let's alter the `oscar-winners.xml` file to include a `<director>` tag within each `<movies>` block.

```
<films>
  <movies>
    <movie_ID>5</movie_ID>
    <movie_Title>Citizen Kane </movie_Title>
```

```
    <movie_Year>1941</movie_Year>
    <director>
      <first_name>Orson</first_name>
      <last_name>Welles</last_name>
    </director>
    <bestPicture>Y</bestPicture>
    <AFIRank>1</AFIRank>
  </movies>
  ... more movies here
</films>
```

Next, run this code to display the contents of the table(s) created:

```
DataSet ds = new DataSet();
ds.ReadXml("c:\\oscarwinnersv2.xml");
foreach (DataTable dt in ds.Tables)
   ShowTable(dt);
```

Figure 11-7 depicts the DataSet tables created from reading the XML file. It creates two tables, automatically generates a movies_ID key for each table, and assigns values to this key, which link a row in the movies table to an associated row in the director table.

DataTable

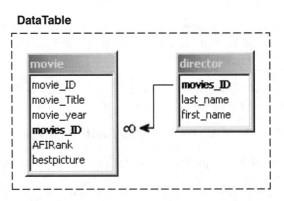

Figure 11-7   DataSet tables and relationship created from XML

11.6 Summary

ADO.NET supports two database connectivity models: connected and disconnected. The connected model remains connected to the underlying database while traversing a resultset in a forward-only read-only manner; the disconnected model can retrieve a resultset into an in-memory cache and disconnect itself from the source data. Two distinctly separate data storage objects are available for implementing these models: the `DataReader` and the `DataSet`. The `DataReader` serves up data a row at a time; the `DataSet` functions as an in-memory relational database. Changes to the contents of the `DataSet` can be posted back to the original data source using the `DataAdapter` object. This object includes properties and methods designed to address synchronization issues that arise when disconnected data is used to update a database.

Although XML classes are not part of the ADO.NET namespaces, a level of interaction between relational and XML data is provided through the ADO.NET `DataSet` class. This class includes `WriteXmlSchema` and `WriteXml` methods that are used to create an XML schema and document. The versatile `DataSet.ReadXml` method has several overloads that are used to construct a `DataSet` from an XML data file or schema.

11.7 Test Your Understanding

1. What four classes must a .NET data provider supply?

2. Given the following code:

```
SqlCommand cmd = new SqlCommand();
cmd.Connection = conn;
string s = "insert into movies(movie_title, movie_year,
            bestpicture)values(&p1,&p2,&p3); "
cmd.CommandText= s;
```

which of the following code segments completes the SQL query string to insert the movie row?

a.
```
string p1="Star Wars";
int p2 = 1977;
string p3= "N";
```
b.
```
cmd.Parameters.AddWithValue ("@p1","Star Wars");
cmd.Parameters.AddWithValue ("@p2", "1977");
cmd.Parameters.AddWithValue ("@p3", "N");
```
c.
```
cmd.Parameters.Add("@p1", SqlDbType.NVarChar, 100);
cmd.Parameters.Add("@p2", SqlDbType.NVarChar, 4);
cmd.Parameters.Add("@p3", SqlDbType.NVarChar, 1);
p1.Value = "Star Wars";
p2.Value = "1977";
p3.Value = "N";
```

3. Describe the purpose of these three command object methods:

```
ExecuteNonQuery
ExecuteReader
ExecuteScalar
```

4. Compare the role of the `DataReader` and the `DataAdapter`.

5. What is the difference between a `DataSet` and a `DataTable`?

6. The `DataRowState` property maintains the status of a row. Which of these is not a valid `DataRowState` value?

   a. `Added`
   b. `Deleted`
   c. `Rejected`
   d. `Changed`

7. You have an XML file and want to create a `DataSet` that has rows and columns that match the layout of the XML file. The XML file does not have a schema (`.xsd`) file associated with it. What `DataSet` method is used to create the `DataSet` schema?

DATA BINDING WITH WINDOWS FORMS CONTROLS

Topics in This Chapter

- *DataBinding Overview:* Associating data with a control is easy on the surface; however, it is important to understand what's going on underneath. This section provides an overview of simple and complex data binding, one-way and two-way data binding, and the role of the `Binding` and `BindingManagerBase` classes.

- *A Data Binding Application:* A Windows Forms application illustrates how to bind data in a `DataSet` and `DataTable` to simple and complex controls.

- *The DataGridView:* The `DataGridView` introduced with .NET 2.0 has a rich set of features that enable it to display and manipulate relational data. Examples illustrate how to create a master-detail grid and a virtual mode grid.

Chapter

Chapter 11, "ADO.NET," discussed how to access data using ADO.NET. This chapter extends the discussion to describe the techniques by which data is "bound" to the Windows Forms controls that display data. Because all controls derive their data binding capabilities from the base `Control` class, knowledge of its properties and methods can be applied to all controls. Although many of the same concepts apply to Web controls, data binding for them is discussed separately in Chapter 16, "ASP.NET Web Forms and Controls."

Data binding comes in two flavors: simple and complex. Controls that contain one value, such as a label or `Textbox`, rely on simple binding. Controls populated with rows of data, such as a `ListBox`, `DataGrid`, or `DataGridView`, require complex binding. We'll look at how both are implemented.

Of the Windows Forms controls that bind to data, the `DataGridView` is the most complex and useful. Its layout maps directly to the rows and columns of a relational database or similarly structured XML document. This chapter takes a detailed look at the properties and methods of this control, and provides examples of how this control can be used to implement common database applications.

12.1 Overview of Data Binding

Data binding provides a way to link the contents of a control with an underlying data source. The advantage to this linkage or "binding" is that changes to the immediate data source can be reflected automatically in data controls bound to it, and changes in the data control are posted automatically to the intermediate data source. The term *intermediate data source* is used to distinguish it from the original data source, which may be an external database. The controls cannot be bound directly to a data source over an active connection. Binding is restricted to the in-memory representation of the data. Figure 12-1 shows the basic components of the binding model: the original data source, the intermediate storage, and the Form controls that are bound to values in the local storage through a `binding` object. Let's examine the model in more detail.

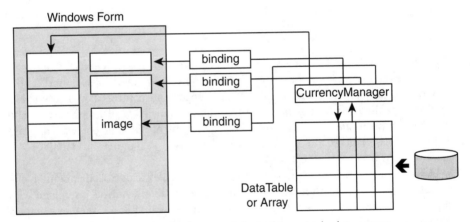

Figure 12-1   Multiple controls bound to a single data source

Simple Data Binding

Simple data binding, which is available to all controls, links a data source to one or more properties of a control. A good example is the `Textbox` control that exposes easily recognizable properties such as `Text`, `Width`, and `BackColor`. An application can set these dynamically by binding them to a data source. Here is a code segment that creates an object whose public properties are mapped to the properties on the `TextBox`.

```
// Create object (width, text, color)
TextParms tp = new TextParms(200, "Casablanca", Color.Beige);
// Bind text and BackColor properties of control
txtMovie.DataBindings.Add("Text", tp, "Tb_Text");
txtMovie.DataBindings.Add("BackColor", tp, "Tb_Background");

// Or create binding and then add in two steps
Binding binding = new Binding("Width", tp, "Tb_Width");
txtMovie.DataBindings.Add(binding);
```

The DataBindings.Add method creates a collection of bindings that links the data source to the control's properties. The method's syntax is

```
DataBindings.Add( control property, data source, data member)
```

control property	Property on the control that is being bound.
data source	Object that contains data being bound to control.
data member	Data member on the data source that is being used. Set this to null if the data source's ToString() method provides the value.

A control may have multiple bindings associated with it, but only one per property. This means that the code used to create a binding can be executed only once; a second attempt would generate an exception. To avoid this, each call to add a binding should be preceded with code that checks to see if a binding already exists; if there is a binding, it should be removed.

```
if (txtMovie.DataBindings["Text"] != null)
    txtMovie.DataBindings.Remove(txtMovie.DataBindings["Text"]);
txtMovie.DataBindings.Add("Text", tp, "Tb_Text");
```

Binding to a List

The true value of data binding becomes obvious when the data source contains multiple items to be displayed. In the preceding example, the control was bound to a single object. Let's now create an array of these objects—each representing a different movie. Instead of binding to a single object, the control is bound to the array (see Figure 12-2). The control can still only display a single movie title at a time, but we can scroll through the array and display a different title that corresponds to the current array item selected. This scrolling is accomplished using a *binding manager*, which is discussed shortly.

This example creates an ArrayList of objects that are used to set the TextBox properties on the fly.

```
ArrayList tbList = new ArrayList();
// Beige color indicated movie won oscar as best picture
tbList.Add(new TextParms(200,"Casablanca",Color.Beige));
tbList.Add(new TextParms(200, "Citizen Kane", Color.White));
tbList.Add(new TextParms(200, "King Kong", Color.White));
// Bind to properties on the Textbox
txtMovie.DataBindings.Add("Text", tbList, "Tb_Text");
txtMovie.DataBindings.Add("BackColor", tbList,
                              "Tb_Background");
txtMovie.DataBindings.Add("Width", tbList, "Tb_Width");
```

The one difference in the bindings from the preceding example is that the data source now refers to the ArrayList. By default, the TextBox takes the values associated with the first item in the array. When the index of the array points to the second row, the displayed value changes to "Citizen Kane".

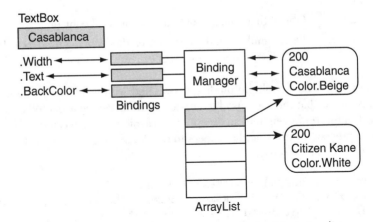

Figure 12-2   Binding TextBox properties to objects in a list

Simple Binding with ADO.NET

Binding to a table in a DataSet is basically the same as binding to a list. In this example, the Text property of the control is bound to the movie_Year column in a DataTable.

```
ds = new DataSet("films");
string sql = "select * from movies order by movie_Year";
da = new SqlDataAdapter(sql, conn);
da.Fill(ds,"movies");       // create datatable "movies"
// Bind text property to movie_Year column in movies table
txtYr.DataBindings.Add("Text", ds,"movies.movie_Year");
```

Although the control could be bound directly to a `DataTable`, the recommended approach is to bind the property to a `DataSet` and use the `DataTable` name as a qualifier to specify the column that provides the data. This makes it clear which table the value is coming from.

Complex Data Binding with List Controls

Complex binding is only available on controls that include properties to specify a data source and data members on the data source. This select group of controls is limited to the `ListBox`, `CheckedListBox`, `ComboBox`, `DataGrid`, and `DataGridView`. Complex binding allows each control to bind to a collection of data—the data source must support the `IList` interface—and display multiple items at once. Because the `DataGridView` is discussed at length in the last half of this chapter, let's look at how complex binding is implemented on the `ListBox` control. The details also apply to other `List` controls.

Binding a list control to a data source requires setting a minimum of two properties: `DataSource`, which specifies the source, and `DisplayMember`, which describes the member—usually a data column or property—in the data source that is displayed in the control. This code segment illustrates how a `ListBox` bound to a `DataSet` displays movie titles:

```
da.Fill(ds,"movies");
DataTable dt = ds.Tables[0];
// Minimum properties to bind listbox to a DataTable
listBox1.DataSource = ds;
listBox1.DisplayMember = "movies.movie_Title";

// Optional property that assigns a value to each item row
listBox1.ValueMember = "movies.movie_ID";
```

After these values are set, the list box is automatically filled. The `DataSource` property can be changed programmatically to fill the control with a different set of data, or it can be set to `null` to clear the control's content. Note also that although no `Binding` object is explicitly created, a `DataBindings` collection is created underneath and is accessible through code.

The bound list box control is often grouped with other controls, such as a text box or label, in order to display multiple values from a row of data. When the controls are bound to the same data source, scrolling through the list box causes each control to display a value from the same data row. To illustrate, let's add the following simple bindings to the preceding code:

```
txtStudio.DataBindings.Add("Text", ds,"movies.studio");
txtYear.DataBindings.Add("Text", ds,"movies.movie_Year");
```

These text boxes display the studio name and year of the movie currently selected in the list box (see Figure 12-3).

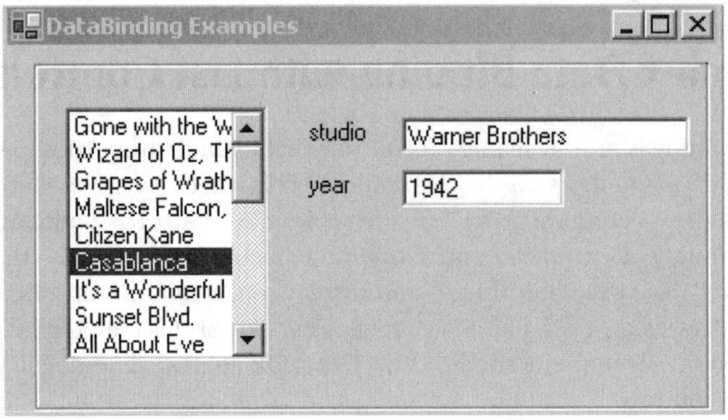

Figure 12-3   Using data binding to populate controls on a form

One-Way and Two-Way Data Binding

The data bound to a control can be changed in two ways: by updating the underlying data source, such as adding a row to a table, or by modifying the visible contents of the control. In both cases, the changes should be reflected in the associated control or data source—a process referred to as two-way data binding. In general, that is what happens. However, a control may be bound to a data source in read-only mode when its only purpose is to present data. To understand how these techniques are implemented, let's look at how updating occurs—from the perspective of the control and the data source.

Effects on the Data Source of Updating a Control Value

By default, changes made to data in a control are also made to the underlying in-memory data source. If the `year` value in Figure 12-3 is changed, the value in the corresponding row and column of the `DataTable` is also changed. Note that if the year is represented as an integer in the table, the value entered in the control must be an integer value. Data binding automatically checks types and rejects values (keeps the same value in the control) that do not match the type of the underlying data.

In the case where a control is bound to a property on an object, the property must provide write support in order for its value to be updated. For example, if the year and studio list boxes in the preceding example were bound to the following properties, respectively, only year could be updated; changes made to the studio control would be ignored and it would revert to its original value.

```
public int Movie_Year { set { myYear = value;     }
                        get { return myYear;      } }

// Read only property. Control cannot update this.
public string Studio   { get { return myStudio; } }
```

Note that changes in a control are not propagated to the data source until the user moves to another item in the GUI control. Underneath, this changes the current position within the binding manager—firing an event that causes the data to be updated.

Effects on a Control of Updating the Data Source

When a `DataSet` is used as the data source for controls, any additions, deletions, or changes made to the data are automatically reflected in the associated bound control(s). Custom data sources require some programming assistance to accomplish this.

If a control is bound to an object property, a change to the value of that property is not automatically sent to the control. Instead, the binding manager looks for an event named *property*Changed on the data source. If found, it provides a handler for this event to receive notice when that property's value changes. To enable the binding manager to handle a changed value, you must define a *property*Changed event on the data source class, and fire the event when a change occurs. To illustrate, let's extend the previous example to add the event to the class containing the `Movie_Year` property, and add code to fire the event when the property changes.

```
// Event to notify bound control that value has changed
public event EventHandler Movie_YearChanged;

// Property control is bound to year value
public int Movie_Year {
    set {
            myYear = value;
            // Notify bound control(s) of change
            if (Movie_YearChanged != null)
                Movie_YearChanged(this, EventArgs.Empty);
    }
    get { return myYear; }
}
```

The other situation to handle is when a data item is deleted from or added to the data source. Controls that are bound to the source using simple binding are updated automatically; controls using complex binding are not. In the latter case, the update can be forced by executing the `Refresh` method of a `CurrencyManager` object. As we see next, the `CurrencyManager` is a binding manager especially designed for list data sources.

Using Binding Managers

As illustrated in Figure 12-4, each data source has a binding manager that keeps track of all connections to it. When the data source is updated, the binding manager is responsible for synchronizing the values in all controls bound to the data. Conversely, if a value is changed on one of the bound controls, the manager updates the source data accordingly. A binding manager is associated with only one data source. Thus, if an application has controls bound to multiple data sources, each will have its own manager.

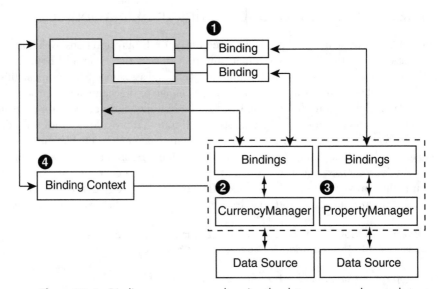

Figure 12-4   Binding managers synchronize the data source and controls

Binding requires the interaction of several objects to coordinate the two-way flow of data between a data source and control. Let's look at the four most important objects, which are denoted by numbers in Figure 12-4.

1. `Binding`. Maintains a simple binding between a property on a control and a property on a single object. The following statements demonstrate how to create a binding and gain access to it:

```
txtYr.DataBindings.Add("Text", ds,
                       "movies.movie_Year");
Binding binding = txtYr.DataBindings["Text"];
// "txtYr"
MessageBox.Show(binding.Control.ToString());
```

```
// Create a binding manager object
BindingManagerBase mgr= binding.BindingManagerBase;
```

2. CurrencyManager. This class derives from the abstract Binding-
    ManagerBase class and serves as a binding manager for list data
    sources such as a DataTable or Array. This object provides five
    members that an application can use to manage the relationship
    between a data source and control:

    *   Bindings. Returns the collection of bindings being managed.
    *   Count. The number of rows in the list that is being managed.
    *   Current. Returns the current item (such as a row) in the data
        source as an object.
    *   Position. Gets/sets the position in the data source currently
        indexed by the control.
    *   PositionChanged. Fires when the Position in the list changes.
    *   CurrentChanged. Is triggered when the bound value changes.

3. PropertyManager. This class, which also derives from BindingMan-
    agerBase, maps the properties on an object to properties on a bound
    control.

4. BindingContext. Observe in Figure 12-4 that the BindingContext
    is linked to a form and a collection of BindingManagerBase objects.
    Its job is to manage a collection of binding managers for a specific
    control—in this case, a Form. The control could just as well be a
    Panel or GroupBox on a form. A program's main interest in the
    BindingContext is to use it to gain access to the binding manager
    for a data source. These statements, for example, return the manager
    for the table movies.

```
BindingManagerBase mgr = this.BindingContext[ds,"movies"];
// Or use casting to get specific manager.
CurrencyManager mgr= (CurrencyManager)
                     this.BindingContext[ds,"movies"];
```

Using the BindingManagerBase to Navigate a List

Let's now look at how the members of the BindingManagerBase class are used to
move through the items in a source data list and simultaneously update the contents
of controls bound to the list. The example binds a list box and text box to the familiar
movies data table.

```
// Bind listbox to a dataset.datatable
listBox1.DataSource = ds;
listBox1.DisplayMember = "movies.movie_Title";
```

```
// Bind to TextBox
txtStudio.DataBindings.Add("text", ds, "movies.studio");
// BindingManagerBase bmb has class-wide scope
bmb = this.BindingContext[ds, "movies"];
// Create delegate pointing to event handler
bmb.PositionChanged += new
        EventHandler(bmb_PositionChanged);
```

The following method moves to the next item in the data source list when a button is clicked. It would typically be paired with a method to move backward in the list.

```
// This method moves to the next row in the table.
// If at the end of the table it moves to the beginning.
private void Forward_Click (object sender, EventArgs e)
{
    if (listBox1.Items.Count > 0)
    {
        bmb.Position = bmb.Position >= bmb.Count - 1 ? 0 :
                ++bmb.Position;
    }
}
```

The PositionChanged event is fired each time the binding manager moves to a new position in the list. This could be triggered programmatically or by the user clicking a row in the list box control.

```
private void bmb_PositionChanged(object sender,
                                    EventArgs e)
{
    BindingManagerBase bmb = (BindingManagerBase)sender;
    // Item should be a DataRowView if from a table
    object ob = bmb.Current.GetType();
    if (ob == typeof(System.Data.DataRowView))
    {
        DataRowView view = (DataRowView)bmb.Current;
        // Could access: ((string)view["movie_Title"]);
    }
}
```

Note that the Current property is used to return an object representing the current item. The data source in this example is a data table, but the object returned is not the expected DataRow—it is a DataRowView object. It is up to the code to provide the proper casting to access properties in the selected item.

12.2 Using Simple and Complex Data Binding in an Application

Several concepts were introduced in the first section. Let's bring them together in an application that relies on data binding to display and update information from the Films database. Figure 12-5 shows a screen shot of the application's user interface.

Each control on the Windows Form—except buttons—is bound to a data source. A ListBox and ComboBox illustrate complex binding; two text boxes, a CheckBox, and a PictureBox, are bound using simple binding. The controls can be bound dynamically to either a data table or an array that contains custom objects. The Scroll button moves down the list box by internally using a binding manager to advance to the next item in the data source list. Let's dissect the program by looking at code associated with the buttons. Much of the code should be familiar from code segments in the previous section and does not require further explanation.

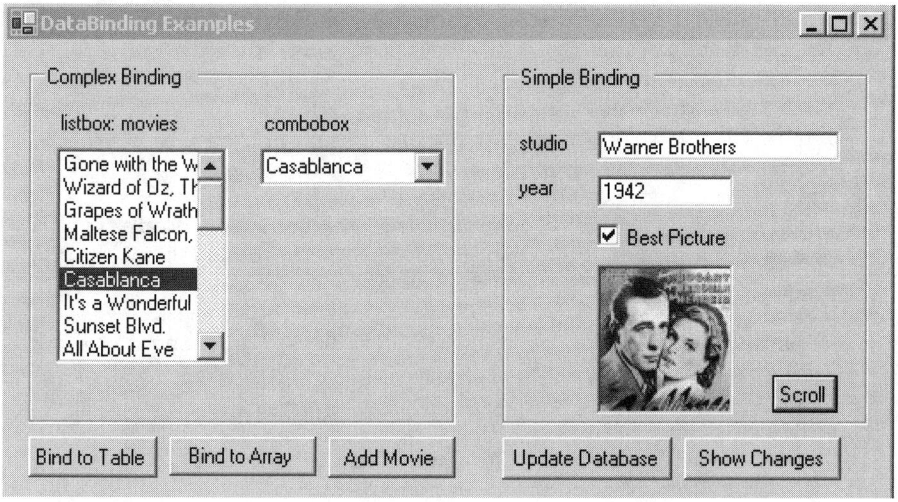

Figure 12-5   Application combining complex and simple binding

Binding to a DataTable

The code in Listing 12-1 is executed when the Bind to Table button is clicked. It loads the necessary data from the Films database into a table and binds the controls on the form to it. This populates the ListBox and ComboBox with a list of movie titles. The value in the other controls is derived from the content of the current row (highlighted in the list box). The most interesting of these is the `PictureBox`, which has its `BackgroundImage` property bound to a column in the table containing images. Because the database does not contain images, the program adds this column to the data table and fills it with images for the movie in each row.

Listing 12-1	Binding Controls to a `DataSet`

```
// Bind control to data from a database
private void btnTableBind_Click(object sender, EventArgs e)
{
    SqlConnection conn = new SqlConnection(GetString());
    conn.Open();
    ds = new DataSet("films");
    string sql = "SELECT movie_ID, movie_title, movie_year,
        studio, afi_rank, CASE WHEN bestpicture ='Y'
        THEN 1 ELSE 0 END as BestPicture FROM movies ORDER BY
        movie_Year";
    da = new SqlDataAdapter(sql, conn);
    // Command builder keeps track of changes to data
    SqlCommandBuilder sb = new SqlCommandBuilder(da);
    da.Fill(ds,"movies");
    DataTable dt = ds.Tables[0];
    Data Column dCol = new DataColumn("movie_Image",
        Type.GetType("System.Object"));
    dt.Columns.Add(dCol);
    // Place image in new column. Name is based on movie ranking.
    Image defaultImage = Image.FromFile(@"c:\defaultimg.jpg");
    foreach (DataRow dRow in dt.Rows)
    {
        string rank = ((int)dRow["afi_rank"]).ToString();
        string imgFile = "c:\\afi" + rank + ".gif";
        try
        {
            Image imgObject = Image.FromFile(imgFile);
            dRow["movie_Image"] = imgObject;
        }
        catch (Exception ex)
        {
            dRow["movie_Image"] = defaultImage;
        }
    }
    // Nothing to this point should be considered a change
    dt.AcceptChanges();
```

Listing 12-1   Binding Controls to a `DataSet` *(continued)*

```
// Bind listbox and combobox to datasource
listBox1.DataSource = ds;
listBox1.DisplayMember = "movies.movie_Title";
listBox1.ValueMember = "movies.movie_ID";
comboBox1.DataSource = ds;
comboBox1.DisplayMember = "movies.movie_Title";
// Binding manager has global scope
bmb = this.BindingContext[ds, "movies"];
bmb.PositionChanged += new
      EventHandler(bmb_PositionChanged);
try
{
   // TextBox.Text  - binds to studio name
   if(txtStudio.DataBindings["text"] != null)
        txtStudio.DataBindings.Remove(
            txtStudio.DataBindings["Text"]);
   txtStudio.DataBindings.Add("text", ds, "movies.studio");

   // TextBox.Text - binds to year movie released
   if(txtYear.DataBindings["text"] != null)
        txtYear.DataBindings.Remove(
             txtYear.DataBindings["Text"]);
   txtYear.DataBindings.Add("text", ds,
                         "movies.movie_year");

   // CheckBox.Checked - binds to best picture value (0 or 1)
   if (checkBox1.DataBindings["Checked"] != null)
        checkBox1.DataBindings.Remove(
           checkBox1.DataBindings["Checked"]);
   checkBox1.DataBindings.Add("Checked", ds,
        "movies.BestPicture");

   // PictureBox.BackgroundImage - Binds to image
   if (pictureBox1.DataBindings["BackgroundImage"] != null)
        pictureBox1.DataBindings.Remove(
           pictureBox1.DataBindings["BackgroundImage"]);
   pictureBox1.DataBindings.Add("BackgroundImage", ds,
        "movies.movie_Image");
}
catch (Exception ex)
{
   MessageBox.Show(ex.Message);
}
}
```

Binding Controls to an ArrayList

Clicking the Bind to Array button, binds the controls to an `ArrayList` that is filled with instances of the custom class `MyMovie` (see Listing 12-2). After the data source is created, the binding process is identical to that followed with the data set.

Listing 12-2	Binding Controls to an Array of Objects

```
// Bind control to array populated with instances of custom
class
private void BindToArray()
{
   movieList = new ArrayList();
   Image movieImg = Image.FromFile(@"c:\defaultimg.jpg");
   // Create objects and add to array
   movieList.Add(new MyMovie("2","Casablanca",1942,
         "Warner Bros.",true, Image.FromFile("c:\afi2.gif")));
   movieList.Add(new MyMovie("1","Citizen Kane", 1941,
         "RKO", false,
         Image.FromFile("c:\afi1.gif")));
   movieList.Add(new MyMovie("4","Gone with the Wind", 1941,
         "Selznick International", true,
         Image.FromFile("c:\afi4.gif")));
   //
   listBox1.DataSource = movieList;
   listBox1.DisplayMember = "Movie_Title";
   //
   comboBox1.DataSource = movieList;
   comboBox1.DisplayMember = "Movie_Title";
   bmb = this.BindingContext[movieList]; ;
   bmb.PositionChanged += new
         EventHandler(bmb_PositionChanged);
   if (txtStudio.DataBindings["Text"] != null)
         txtStudio.DataBindings.Remove(
               txtStudio.DataBindings["Text"]);
   txtStudio.DataBindings.Add("Text", movieList, "Studio");
   //
   if (txtYear.DataBindings["Text"] != null)
         txtYear.DataBindings.Remove(
               txtYear.DataBindings["Text"]);
   txtYear.DataBindings.Add("Text", movieList, "Movie_Year");
```

Listing 12-2   Binding Controls to an Array of Objects *(continued)*

```
//
if (checkBox1.DataBindings["Checked"] != null)
      checkBox1.DataBindings.Remove(
         checkBox1.DataBindings["Checked"]);
checkBox1.DataBindings.Add("Checked", movieList,
                        "BestPicture");
//
if (pictureBox1.DataBindings["BackgroundImage"] != null)
      pictureBox1.DataBindings.Remove(
         pictureBox1.DataBindings["BackgroundImage"]);
pictureBox1.DataBindings.Add("BackgroundImage", movieList,
      "Movie_Image");
}
```

When designing a custom class to be used as a data source, the primary consideration is whether the bindable properties provide read-only or read/write access. If they are read-only, the only requirement is that they be `public`. For properties that can be updated, the class must expose and fire an event to which the binding can subscribe. Recall that the name of this event is *propertyname*`Changed`. This event is fired in the `Set` block of the property (see Listing 12-3).

Listing 12-3   Custom Data Source Class

```
// Bind control to array populated with instances of
// custom class
public class MyMovie
{
   private string myID;
   private string myTitle;
   private int myYear;
   private string myStudio;
   private bool myBestPicture;
   private Image myImage;
   //
   public event EventHandler Movie_YearChanged;
   public event EventHandler StudioChanged;
   public MyMovie(string id, string title, int year,
                  string studio,
         bool bp, Image img)
```

Listing 12-3	Custom Data Source Class *(continued)*

```
{
    myTitle = title;
    myYear = year;
    myStudio = studio;
    myBestPicture = bp;
    myImage = img;
    myID = id;
}
// Only public properties can be bound to control
public string Movie_Title  { get { return myTitle; } }
// Make read/write so update can occur
public int Movie_Year {
    get { return myYear; }
    set {
        myYear = value;
        if (Movie_YearChanged != null)
            Movie_YearChanged(this, EventArgs.Empty);
    }
}

public string Studio {
    get { return myStudio; }
    set {
        myStudio = value;
        if (StudioChanged != null) StudioChanged(this,
            EventArgs.Empty);
    }
}
public Image   Movie_Image  { get { return myImage; } }
public bool    BestPicture  { get { return myBestPicture; } }
}
```

Adding an Item to the Data Source

Clicking the Add Movie button causes information about a single movie to be added to the data source (see Listing 12-4). If the source is a table, a row is added; if an array, an object is created and inserted. An addition to a data table is automatically pushed to the control and made visible. When a custom object is added, the Refresh method of the CurrencyManager must be executed to synchronize the control. Note that Refresh is specific to the CurrencyManager class and not available on BindingManagerBase.

Listing 12-4	Add an Item to a Data Source

```
// Test effects of adding a new item to the data source
private void button2_Click(object sender, EventArgs e)
{
    if (ds != null)
    {
        // Add a row to the table
        DataTable dt = ds.Tables[0];
        DataRow dRow = dt.NewRow();
        dRow["movie_ID"] = 99;
        dRow["movie_Title"] = "Rear Window";
        dRow["movie_Year"] = "1954";
        dRow["studio"] = "Paramount";
        dRow["BestPicture"] = 0;
        dRow["afi_rank"] = 42;
        Image defaultImage = Image.FromFile(@"c:\afi42.gif");
        dRow["movie_Image"] = defaultImage;
        dt.Rows.Add(dRow);
    }
    else
    {
        Image movieImg = Image.FromFile(@"c:\afi42.gif");
        movieList.Add(new MyMovie("42", "Rear Window", 1954,
                "Paramount", false, movieImg));
        // Refresh() is needed to display item in ListBox/ComboBox
        CurrencyManager cm =
                (CurrencyManager)this.BindingContext[movieList];
        cm.Refresh();
    }
}
```

Identifying Updates

The rows in a table have a `RowState` property that can be used to determine if a value in the row has been changed (discussed in Chapter 11). This method checks the value of that property for each row in the data source table. If the value is `DataRowState.Modified`, each column in the row is checked to determine which values have changed (see Listing 12-5). This routine can be used to determine whether an update to the original database is necessary. Observe that the method checks only for data changes. You can easily extend it to check for deletions and additions.

Listing 12-5	Check Data Source for Any Updates

```
// Checks status of each row in data table to identify any
// changes. This works only when data source is a Data Table.
private bool DataIsDirty(DataTable dt){
    bool result = false;
    foreach(DataRow drw in dt.Rows){
        // Check all rows in the table for a modified state
        if(drw.RowState == DataRowState.Modified)
        {
            string msg = (string)drw["movie_Title"]+":";
            string curr;
            string orig;
            // Examine each column in the row for a change
            foreach(DataColumn col in dt.Columns)
            {
                curr= drw[col,
                    DataRowVersion.Current].ToString().Trim();
                orig= drw[col,
                    DataRowVersion.Original].ToString().Trim();
                if(!curr.Equals(orig) || curr != orig ||
                    string.CompareOrdinal(curr,orig) !=0)
                {
                    msg += "\r\n" + orig + " " + curr;
                    result=true;
                }
            }
            MessageBox.Show(msg);    // Display changes in a row
        }
    }
    return result;
}
```

Update Original Database with Changes

When the modifiable data source is a data table, the Update method of its associated DataAdapter can be used to flush changes to the database. This topic is discussed in detail in Section 11.4, "DataSets, DataTables, and the Disconnected Model."

```
try
{
    int updates = da.Update(ds, "movies");
    MessageBox.Show("Updates: "+updates.ToString());
}
```

```
catch (Exception ex)
{
   MessageBox.Show(ex.Message);
}
```

12.3 The DataGridView Class

The DataGridView control, introduced with .NET 2.0, supersedes the DataGrid—which now exists primarily for legacy purposes. With more than a hundred properties and methods, the DataGridView is by far the most complex Windows Forms control for displaying data. Accordingly, it is also the most flexible. Styles that govern appearance can be applied on a cell-by-cell basis, by rows, by columns, or across all cells in the grid. Cells are not limited to text. They may contain a TextBox, Image, CheckBox, Link, or Button control.

Data binding is supported by the DataSource property, just as with the controls defined in the previous section. In addition, the DataGridView provides a unique *virtual* mode that permits it to handle more than 100,000 rows of data. DataGridView methods, events, and properties allow an application to easily manage the mapping between virtual and physical storage.

All of these features are discussed in this section. We'll look at selected properties and events along with code examples that illustrate their use.

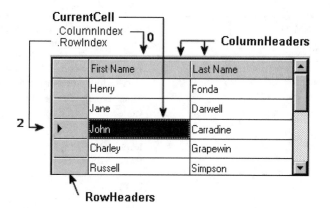

Figure 12-6   Basic DataGridView elements

Properties

Despite its myriad features, the `DataGridView` has an elegantly simple structure. As shown in Figure 12-6, in its most elemental form, it consists of column headers, row headers, and cells. To these, we can add the `Columns` and `Rows` collections that allow an application to access the grid by indexing a row or column. That is the foundation. Each property and event discussed in this section relates to one of these five classes.

The `DataGridView` class inherits many of its properties from the `Control` class; to these, it adds properties required to support its own special characteristics and behavior. The properties listed in Table 12-1 are primarily in this latter category. The list is not meant to be exhaustive; instead, it presents those properties you'll refer to most frequently when implementing a grid.

Table 12-1   Selected Properties of the `DataGridView` Class

Category	Property Name	Description
User functionality	`AllowUserToAddRows` `AllowUserToDeleteRows`	Indicates whether a user may add/delete rows. Default: `true`.
	`AllowUserToOrderColumns`	Indicates whether user can rearrange columns.
	`ColumnHeadersHeight-Resizable`	Indicates whether the user can change the height of the column headers. Default: `true`.
	`MultiSelect`	Indicates whether user may select one or more rows at a time.

	`SelectionMode`	Indicates the cells selected when clicking any individual or header cell. enum `DataGridViewSelectionMode` values:
		
		`ColumnHeaderSelect`
		`RowHeaderSelect`
		`FullColumnSelect`
		`FullRowSelect`
		`CellSelect`

	`ReadOnly`	Indicates whether user can modify data in cells. Values: `true` or `false`.
Appearance	`AlternatingRowsDefault-CellStyle`	Gets or sets the default cell style applied to the odd numbered rows in the grid.
	`BackColor`	The background color of the grid.

Table 12-1   Selected Properties of the `DataGridView` Class *(continued)*

Category	Property Name	Description
Appearance *(continued)*	`BackgroundColor`	Gets or sets the background color for the area of the grid not containing data cells or column/row headers.

	`BorderStyle`	Gets or sets the border style for the `DataGridView`.
		enum `BorderStyle` values:
		
		`BorderStyle.Fixed3D`
		`BorderStyle.FixedSingle`
		`BorderStyle.None`

	`CellBorderStyle`	Gets or sets the border style used for cells in the grid.
		enum `DataGridViewCellBorderStyle` values:
		
		(to draw between rows)
		`SingleHorizontal`
		`SunkenHorizontal`
		`RaisedHorizontal`
		
		(to draw between columns)
		`SingleVertical`
		`SunkenVertical`
		`RaisedVertical`
		
		(to place a border between rows and columns)
		`SingleSunken`
		`Raised`

	`ColumnCount`	Gets or sets the number of columns in the `DataGridView`.

	`ColumnHeadersBorderStyle`
	`RowHeadersBorderStyle`
		Border style applied to to column/row headers.
		enum `DataGridViewHeaderBorder-Style` values:
		
		`Custom` `Raised` `Sunk`
		`None` `Single`

	`ColumnHeadersVisible` `RowHeadersVisible`	Displays or suppresses headers. Values: `true` or `false`.
	`ColumnHeaderDefaultCell-Style`	Defines cell style properties for column header cells.

Table 12-1   Selected Properties of the `DataGridView` Class *(continued)*

Category	Property Name	Description
Appearance *(continued)*	`DefaultCellStyle`	`DataGridViewCellStyle` object that defines the default cell style properties for cells. Note that this includes column header cells.
	`FirstDisplayedCell`	The first cell displayed in the grid, usually upper-left corner.
	`GridColor`	The color of the lines separating the cells.
Collections	`Columns`	Collection of all grid columns. Individual columns are accessed by an index: `Columns[iI]`.
	`Rows`	Collection of all grid rows. Individual rows are accessed by an index: `Rows[i]`.
	`SelectedColumns`	Collection of columns selected.
	`SelectedRows`	Collection of rows selected.
	`SelectedCells`	Collection of cells selected.

Constructing a DataGridView

Listing 12-6 shows how to define columns for a `DataGridView`, set properties to define its appearance and behavior, and add rows of data. (We'll see in the succeeding example how to use the more common approach of loading data from a database.)

Note that the column header cells and data cells have different styles. If a style is not set for the header, it uses the same `DefaultCellStyle` as the data cells.

Listing 12-6   Setting `DataGridView` Properties and Adding Rows of Data

```
// Set properties of a DataGridView and fill with data
private void CreateGrid()
{
   // (1) Define column headers
   dataGridView1.ColumnCount = 3;
   dataGridView1.Columns[0].HeaderText = "Movie Title";
   dataGridView1.Columns[1].HeaderText = "Year";
```

Listing 12-6 Setting `DataGridView` Properties and Adding Rows of Data *(continued)*

```
dataGridView1.Columns[2].HeaderText = "Director";
dataGridView1.Columns[1].Name  = "Year";
dataGridView1.Columns[0].Width = 150;
dataGridView1.Columns[1].Width = 40;
dataGridView1.Columns[2].Width = 110;
// (2) Define style for data cells
DataGridViewCellStyle style = new DataGridViewCellStyle();
style.BackColor = Color.Bisque;
style.Font = new Font("Arial", 8, FontStyle.Bold);
style.ForeColor = Color.Navy;
//                      (left,top,right,bottom)
style.Padding = new Padding(5, 2, 5, 5);
style.SelectionBackColor = Color.LightBlue;
dataGridView1.DefaultCellStyle = style;
// (3) Define style for column headers
DataGridViewCellStyle styleHdr = new
       DataGridViewCellStyle();
styleHdr.Padding = new Padding(1, 1, 1, 1);
styleHdr.BackColor = Color.OldLace;
styleHdr.ForeColor = Color.Black;
dataGridView1.ColumnHeadersDefaultCellStyle = styleHdr;
// (4) Define user capabilities
dataGridView1.AllowUserToAddRows       = false;
dataGridView1.AllowUserToOrderColumns = false;
dataGridView1.AllowUserToDeleteRows   = false;
// (5) Place data in grid manually (datasource is better)
object[] row1 = {"Casablanca", "1942","Michael Curtiz"};
dataGridView1.Rows.Add(row1);
object[] row2 = {"Raging Bull","1980","Martin Scorsese"};
dataGridView1.Rows.Add(row2);
object[] row3 = {"On the Waterfront","1954","Elia Kazan"};
dataGridView1.Rows.Add(row3);
object[] row4 = {"Some Like it Hot","1959","Billy Wilder"};
dataGridView1.Rows.Add(row4);
}
```

Figure 12-7 shows the `DataGridView` created by this code.

Movie Title	Year	Director
Casablanca	1942	Michael Curtiz
Raging Bull	1980	Martin Scorsese
On the Waterfront	1954	Elia Kazan
Some Like it Hot	1959	Billy Wilder

Figure 12-7   `DataGridView` built from code in Listing 12-6

DataBinding with a DataGridView

A `DataGridView` is bound to a data source using complex binding. As in our list box example, the `DataSource` property specifies the data source. The similarity ends there, however, because a `DataGridView` must display multiple data values. To do so, the `DataMember` property is set to the name of a table within the data source. The data to be displayed in each column is specified by setting the column's `DataPropertyName` property to the name of the underlying data table column.

```
// Turn this off so column names do not come from data source
dataGridView1.AutoGenerateColumns = false;
// Specify table as data source
dataGridView1.DataSource = ds;         // Dataset
dataGridView1.DataMember = "movies";   // Table in dataset
// Tie the columns in the grid to column names in the data table
dataGridView1.Columns[0].DataPropertyName = "Title";
dataGridView1.Columns[1].DataPropertyName = "Year";
dataGridView1.Columns[2].DataPropertyName = "director";
```

The `DataGridView` supports two-way data binding for ADO.NET data sources: Changes made to the grid are reflected in the underlying table, and changes made to the table are reflected in the grid. For example, this code responds to a button click by adding a new row to the grid's data source. The addition is immediately reflected in the control. However, if we try to add a row directly to the `DataGridView`, an exception occurs because adding directly to a bound control is not permitted.

```
private void buttonAdd_Click(object sender, EventArgs e)
{
   // Adding to underlying table is okay
   r[0] = "TAXI";
```

```
        r[1] = "1976";
        r[2] = "Martin Scorsese";
        dt.Rows.Add(r);
        // Adding directly to DataGridView does not work
        object[] row = {"The Third Man", "1949", "Orson Welles"};
        DataRow r = dt.NewRow();
        DataGridView1.Rows.Add(row4);   // Fails!
}
```

Updating the original database from which a grid is loaded can be done by issuing individual SQL commands or using a `DataAdapter`. The discussion in the previous section applies.

Core Note

A `DataGridView` may have a mixture of bound and non-bound columns. Thus, columns can be added to a bound control, but rows cannot.

Setting the Row Height

The default height of rows in a `DataGridView` is based on accommodating a single line of text. If the row contains large sized fonts or images, they are truncated. It is usually better to force the grid to take the size of each cell in the row into account and base the overall height on the tallest cell. That's the role of the grid's `AutoSizeRows` method. Its simplest overloaded version takes a single parameter—a `DataGridViewAutoSizeRowsMode` enumeration value—that indicates the criterion used for setting row height. The two most useful enumeration members are `ColumnAllRows`, which bases the row height on all columns in the row, and `ColumnsDisplayedRows`, which applies the same criterion, but to visible rows only.

```
dataGridView1.AutoSizeRows(
        DataGridViewAutoSizeRowsMode.ColumnsAllRows);
```

The `AutoSizeRows` method sets the row size when it is executed. If subsequent updates cause the height of cells in a row to change, the row height does not adjust to the changes. Also, if a row is sortable, clicking a column header to sort the grid causes all rows to revert to the default row height. Fortunately, the `DataGridView` has an `AutoSizeRowsMode` property that causes row heights to automatically adjust to changes in grid content.

```
dataGridView1.AutoSizeRowsMode =
        DataGridViewAutoSizeRowsMode.HeaderAndColumnsAllRows;
```

Note that this statement does not take effect until the `AutoSizeRows` method is executed, and that it prevents users from manually resizing rows.

Working with Columns and Column Types

The `DataGridView` is not a full-blown spreadsheet, but it does offer some features a user expects from a spreadsheet. These include the following:

- **Frozen Column(s).** For a grid that requires horizontal scrolling, it is often useful to "freeze" columns so that they always remain on the screen. Setting a column's `Frozen` property to `true` has the effect of freezing it and all columns to its left.

  ```
  dataGridView1.Columns[0].Frozen = true;
  ```

- **ReadOnly Columns.** Selected column can be made read-only.

  ```
  dataGridView1.Columns[2].ReadOnly = true;
  ```

- **Minimum Width.** By default, a user can widen and narrow columns in a grid. The minimum size permitted for a column can be controlled by setting the `MinimumWidth` property to a value in pixels:

  ```
  dataGridView1.Columns[0].MinimumWidth=100;
  ```

- **Sorting.** By default, clicking a column header sorts the rows based on values in that column—if the column contains sortable values. It's `SortMode` property can be used to disable sorting:

  ```
  dataGridView1.Columns[0].SortMode =
            DataGridViewColumnSortMode.NotSortable;
  ```

- **Multiple Column Types.** Six predefined column classes are available that can be used to represent information in a grid, using the familiar formats of the `TextBox`, `CheckBox`, `Image`, `Button`, `ComboBox`, and `Link`. The name for each of these controls follows the format `Data-GridViewControlnameColumn`.

  This code segment adds a column of buttons to a grid. The first step is to create an instance of the column class. Its characteristics and data values—if any—are then set. Finally, the `Columns.Add` method is used to add the column to the grid's column collection.

  ```
  // (1) Create instance of column type
  DataGridViewButtonColumn buttons = new
        DataGridViewButtonColumn();
  // Text to place in column header
  buttons.HeaderText = "Delete";
  ```

```
// (2) Set characteristics of control
buttons.Text = "Delete";    // Default text for button
buttons.FlatStyle = FlatStyle.Standard;
// Create a datagridview cell to use as a template to set
// all buttons in the column to the same style.
buttons.CellTemplate = new DataGridViewButtonCell();
buttons.CellTemplate.Style.BackColor = Color.Yellow ;
buttons.CellTemplate.Style.Font = new Font("Arial", 8);
// Specify column position on grid
buttons.DisplayIndex = 1;
// (3) Add column to grid
dataGridView.Columns.Add(buttons);
```

Any of the column types may be bound to a data source. Although a button is usually set manually, it can be bound to a property in the grid's data source in two ways:

```
// Use the DataGridviewButtonColumn class
buttons.DataPropertyName = "Title";
// Use the Columns class (button is in column 1 of the grid)
dataGridView3.Columns[1].DataPropertyName = "Title";
```

Buttons provide a convenient way for a user to select a grid row and trigger an action such as a pop-up form that displays further information related to the row. Buttons located in grid cells, however, have no direct event, such as a `Click`, associated with them. Instead, events are associated with an action on the overall grid or specific cells on the grid. By identifying a cell for instance, an event handler can determine which button is clicked.

Events

Just about every mouse and cursor movement that can occur over a `DataGridView` can be detected by one of its events. In addition, events signify when data is changed, added, or deleted. Table 12-2 provides a summary of the most useful events. Accompanying the table is a list of the delegate used to implement these events. (See Appendix B for a complete list of events.)

Table 12-2   Selected `DataGridView` Events

Category	Event (Delegate)	Description
Cell actions	CellValueChanged (1)	Occurs when the value of a cell changes.
	CurrentCellChanged (3)	Occurs when the value of the current cell changes

Table 12-2   Selected `DataGridView` Events *(continued)*

Category	Event (Delegate)	Description
Cell actions *(continued)*	`CellClick` (1)	Occurs when any part of the cell is clicked. This includes cell borders and padding.
	`CellContentClick` (1)	Occurs only if the cell content is clicked.
	`CellEnter` (1) `CellLeave` (1)	Occurs when cell receives/loses input focus.
	`CellFormatting` (5)	Occurs prior to formatting a cell for display.
	`CellMouseClick` (2) `CellMouseDoubleClick` (2)	Occurs whenever a mouse clicks/double clicks anywhere on a cell.
	`CellMouseDown` (2) `CellMouseUp` (2)	Occurs when a mouse button is pressed/raised while it is over a cell.
	`CellMouseEnter` (1) `CellMouseLeave` (1)	Occurs when the mouse pointer enters or leaves a cell's area.
	`CellPainting` (6)	Raised when a cell is to be painted.
Column actions	`ColumnHeaderMouseClick` (2) `ColumnHeaderMouseDouble-Click` (2)	Occurs when a column header is clicked/double clicked.
Row actions	`RowEnter` (1) `RowLeave` (1)	Occurs when a row receives/loses the input focus.
	`RowHeaderMouseClick` (2) `RowHeaderDoubleMouse-Click` (2)	Occurs when a user clicks/double clicks a row header.
	`UserAddedRow` (4) `UserDeletedRow` (4)	Occurs when a user adds/deletes a row in the grid.
Data error	`DataError` (7)	Occurs when an external data parsing or validation operations fails. Typically occurs due to an attempt to load invalid data into a data grid cell.

The following are delegates associated with events in Table 12-2:

(1) ```
public sealed delegate void DataGridViewCellEventHandler(
    object sender, DataGridViewCellEventArgs e)
```

(2) ```
public sealed delegate void DataGridViewCellMouseEventHandler(
    object sender, DataGridViewCellMouseEventArgs e)
```

(3) ```
public sealed delegate void EventHandler(
    object sender, EventHandlerArgs e)
```

(4) ```
public sealed delegate void DataGridViewRowEventHandler (
    object sender, DataGridViewRowEventArgs e)
```

(5) ```
public sealed delegate void
    DataGridViewCellFormattingEventHandler(
        object sender, DataGridViewCellFormattingEventArgs e)
```

(6) ```
public sealed delegate void
    DataGridViewCellPaintingEventHandler(
        object sender, DataGridViewCellPaintingEventArgs e)
```

(7) ```
public sealed delegate void
    DataGridViewDataErrorEventHandler(
        object sender, DataGridViewDataErrorEventArgs e)
```

Let's look at some common uses for these events.

## Cell Formatting

The CellFormatting event gives you the opportunity to format a cell before it is rendered. This comes in handy if you want to distinguish a subset of cells by some criteria. For example, the grid in Figure 12-7 contains a column indicating the year a movie was released. Let's change the background color of cells in that column to red if the year is less than 1950.

```
// Set cells in year column to red if year is less than 1950
private void Grid3_CellFormatting(object sender,
    DataGridViewCellFormattingEventArgs e)
{
    if (this.dataGridView3.Columns[e.ColumnIndex].Name == "Year")
    {
        string yr = (string)e.Value;
        if (Int32.Parse(yr) < 1950)
        {
            e.CellStyle.ForeColor = Color.Red;
```
```

```
            e.CellStyle.SelectionForeColor = Color.Red;
            // Indicate that event was handled
            e.FormattingApplied = true;
         }
      }
}
```

The `ColumnIndex` property of the `EventArgs` parameter is used to determine if the year column is being formatted. If so, the code checks the year and formats the cell accordingly. Note that the `FormattingApplied` property must be set if custom formatting is performed.

Recognizing Selected Rows, Columns, and Cells

As shown in Table 12-2, selecting a cell in a grid can trigger any number of events that can be used to indicate the current cell or the cell just left. Some of the events are almost over-engineered. For example, there seems little to distinguish `CellContentClick` and `CellClick`. Others exist to recognize grid navigation using both the mouse and keyboard: The `CellClick` is not triggered by arrow keys; however, the `CellEnter` event is fired no matter how a cell is selected. All of these cell-related events have a consistent event handler signature. The `EventArgs` parameter provides column and row index properties to identify the cell. Here is an example:

```
private void Grid1_CellEnter(object sender,
      DataGridViewCellEventArgs e)
{
   // Both of these display the column index of the selected cell
   MessageBox.Show("enter "+e.ColumnIndex.ToString());
   MessageBox.Show(
         DataGridView1.CurrentCell.ColumnIndex.ToString());
}
```

Core Note

Although row and column header cells cannot become "current cells," they are assigned a column and row index value. Row headers always have a column index of –1, and column headers have row index of –1.

The cell events can be used to recognize a single row and column selection. However, a grid may also permit multiple row, column, and cell selections. In these cases, it is necessary to use the `SelectedRows`, `SelectedColumns`, and `SelectedCells` collections to access the selected grid values.

Multiple row selection is made available on a `DataGridView` by setting its `MultiSelect` property to `true`—which is the default value. A row is selected by clicking its row header. It can also be selected by clicking any cell in the row if the grid's `SelectionMode` property is set to `DataGridViewSelectionMode.FullRowSelect`. The property can also be set to `FullColumnSelect`, which causes a cell's column to be selected. Note that column and row selection are mutually exclusive: only one can be in effect at a time.

This segment illustrates how to iterate through the collection of selected rows. The same approach is used for columns and cells.

```
// Display selected row numbers and content of its column 1
if (dataGridView1.SelectedRows.Count > 0)
{
    StringBuilder sb = new StringBuilder();
    for (int i = 0; i < dataGridView1.SelectedRows.Count; i++)
    {
        sb.Append("Row: ");
        sb.Append(
            dataGridView1.SelectedRows[i].Index.ToString() );
        sb.Append( dataGridView1.SelectedRows[i].Cells[1].Value);
        sb.Append(Environment.NewLine);
    }
    MessageBox.Show (sb.ToString(), "Selected Rows");
}
```

Data Error Handling

The `DataError` event fires when a problem occurs loading data into a grid or posting data from the grid to the underlying data store. The error is quite easy to detect: compare the value of the `Context` property of the `ErrorEventArgs` parameter with the `DataGridViewDataErrorContext` enumeration values. Here is an example:

```
// Define event handler
DataGridView1.DataError += new
    DataGridViewDataErrorEventHandler(DataGridView1_DataError);

// DataError Event Handler
private void dataGridView1_DataError(object sender,
    DataGridViewDataErrorEventArgs dgError)
{
    // Context provides information about the grid when the
    // error occurred.
    MessageBox.Show("Error: " + dgError.Context.ToString());
    // Problem committing grid data to underlying data source
    if (dgError.Context == DataGridViewDataErrorContext.Commit)
    {
```

```
        MessageBox.Show("Commit error");
    }
    // Occurs when selection cursor moves to another cell
    if (dgError.Context ==
            DataGridViewDataErrorContext.CurrentCellChange)
    {
        MessageBox.Show("Cell change");
    }
    if (dgError.Context ==
            DataGridViewDataErrorContext.Parsing)
    {
        MessageBox.Show("parsing error");
    }
    // Could not format data coming from/going to data source
    if (dgError.Context ==
            DataGridViewDataErrorContext.Formatting)
    {
        MessageBox.Show("formatting error");
    }
}
```

Setting Up Master-Detail DataGridViews

One of the more common relationships between tables in a database is that of the master-detail relationship, where the records in the master table have multiple associated records in the detail table. DataGridViews provide a natural way of displaying this relationship. To illustrate, let's create an application based on the Films database that displays a master grid containing a list of movies and a detail grid that display actors who played in the movie selected in the first grid. To make it interesting, we'll include an image column in the movie grid that contains a picture of the Oscar statuette for movies that won for best picture.

The master grid is bound to the movies table; the details grid is bound to the actors table. Both tables, as shown in Figure 12-8, contain the columns that are bound to their respective DataGridView columns. In addition, they contain a movieID column that links the two in the master-detail relationship.

The tables and their relationships are created using the techniques described in Chapter 11:

```
ds = new DataSet();
DataTable dt = new DataTable("movies");   // Master
DataTable da = new DataTable("actors");   // Detail
da.Columns.Add("movieID");
da.Columns.Add("firstname");
da.Columns.Add("lastname");
```

```
//
dt.Columns.Add("movieID");
dt.Columns.Add("Title");
dt.Columns.Add("Year");
dt.Columns.Add("picture", typeof(Bitmap));   // To hold image
ds.Tables.Add(dt);
ds.Tables.Add(da);
// Define master-detail relationship
DataRelation rel = new DataRelation("movieactor",
      dt.Columns["movieID"], da.Columns["movieID"]);
ds.Relations.Add(rel);
```

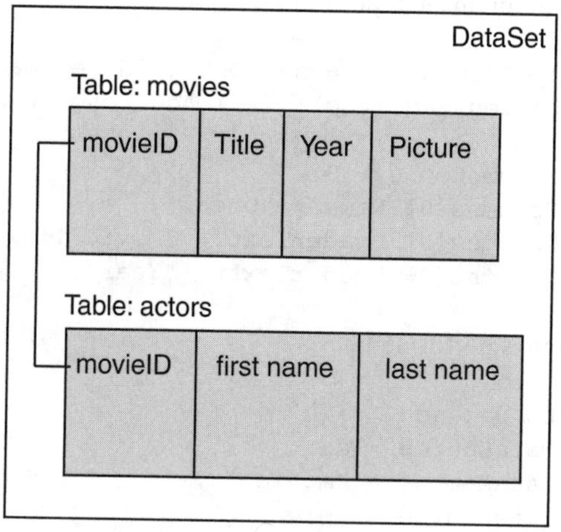

Figure 12-8   Master-detail tables

After defining the table schemas, they are populated from the database using a `DataReader` object. Because the database does not contain an image—although it could—the image is inserted based on the value of the `bestPicture` field.

```
Bitmap oscar   = new Bitmap(@"c:\oscar.gif");    // Oscar image
Bitmap nooscar = new Bitmap(@"c:\nooscar.gif"); // Blank image
// Populate movies table from datareader
while (dr.Read())
{
   DataRow drow = dt.NewRow();
   drow["Title"] = (string)(dr["movie_Title"]);
   drow["Year"]  = ((int)dr["movie_Year"]).ToString();
   drow["movieID"] = (int)dr["movie_ID"];
```

```
    if ((string)dr["bestPicture"] == "Y") drow["picture"] =
        oscar; else drow["picture"] = nooscar;
   dt.Rows.Add(drow);
}
```

The `actors` table is filled with the results of the query:

```
sql = "SELECT am.movie_ID, actor_first,actor_last FROM actors a
    JOIN actor_movie am ON a.actor_ID = am.actor_ID";
```

After the tables are created and populated, the final steps are to define the grids and bind their columns to the tables. This segment adds three columns to the master grid—one of which is an image type column.

```
DataGridViewImageColumn vic = new DataGridViewImageColumn();
dataGridView1.Columns.Add(vic);    // Add image type column
//
dataGridView1.ColumnCount = 3;
dataGridView1.Columns[0].Name = "Oscar";
dataGridView1.Columns[1].HeaderText = "Movie Title";
dataGridView1.Columns[2].HeaderText = "Year";
```

Then, the binding is performed:

```
// Bind grids to dataset
dataGridView1.DataSource = ds;
dataGridView1.DataMember = "movies";
dataGridView2.DataSource = ds;
// ***Set to DataRelation for detail
dataGridView2.DataMember = dt.TableName+".movieactor";
// Bind grid columns to table columns
dataGridView1.Columns[0].DataPropertyName = "picture";
dataGridView1.Columns[1].DataPropertyName = "Title";
dataGridView1.Columns[2].DataPropertyName = "Year";
dataGridView1.Columns[3].DataPropertyName = "director";
dataGridView2.Columns[0].DataPropertyName = "firstname";
dataGridView2.Columns[1].DataPropertyName = "lastname";
```

Pay close attention to the binding of `dataGridView2`. It is bound to the relationship defined between the tables, rather than directly to the `actors` table. This binding causes the names of the movie's cast to be displayed in the grid when a movie is selected.

Figure 12-9 shows a sample screen. Much of the excluded code in this example deals with setting grid styles and capabilities. A full code listing is available in the book's code download. (See the Preface for the download URL addresses and instructions.)

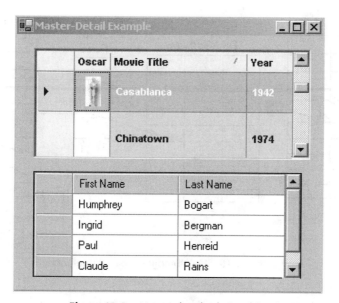

Figure 12-9   Master-detail relationship

Virtual Mode

When a `DataGridView` is bound to a data source, the entire data source must exist
in memory. This enables quick refreshing of the control's cells as a user navigates
from row to row. The downside is that a large data store may have prohibitive memory requirements. To handle excessive memory requirements, a `DataGridView` can
be run in virtual mode by setting its `VirtualMode` property to `true`. In this mode,
the application takes responsibility for maintaining an underlying data cache to handle the population, editing, and deletion of `DataGridView` cells based on actions of
the user. The cache contains data for a selected portion of the grid. If a row in the
grid cannot be satisfied from cache, the application must load the cache with the necessary data from the original data source. Figure 12-10 compares virtual storage with
binding to a `DataTable`.

Virtual mode implementation requires that an application handle two special
virtual mode events: `CellValueNeeded`, which occurs when a cell value must be
displayed; and `CellValuePushed`, which occurs when a cell's value is edited.
Other events are also required to manage the data cache. These are summarized in
Table 12-3.

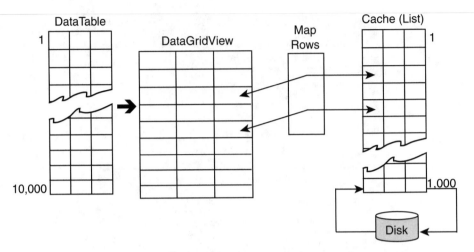

Figure 12-10   Data binding versus virtual mode

Table 12-3   `DataGridView` Events Used to Implement Virtual Mode

Event	Description
NewRowsNeeded	Virtual mode event. Occurs when a row is appended to the `Data-GridView`.
CellValueNeeded	Virtual mode event. Occurs when cell in grid needs to be displayed.
CellValuePushed	Virtual mode event. Occurs when a cell value is edited by the user.
RowValidated	Occurs when another row is selected.
UserDeletingRow	Occurs when a row is selected and the Delete key is pressed.

To illustrate the fundamentals of implementing a `DataGridView` in virtual mode, let's look at the code used to create the `DataGridView` shown in Figure 12-11.

The variables having class scope are shown here. Note that the data cache is implemented as a generics `List` object that holds instances of the `movie` class. The movie class exposes three properties that are displayed on the grid: `Title`, `Movie_Year`, and `Director`.

```
DataGridView dgv;
List<movie> movieList = new List<movie>(20);  // cache
bool rowNeeded;    // True when new row appended to grid
int storeRow = 0;
int currRow = -1; // Set to row being added
movie currMovie;  // Holds movie object for current row
```

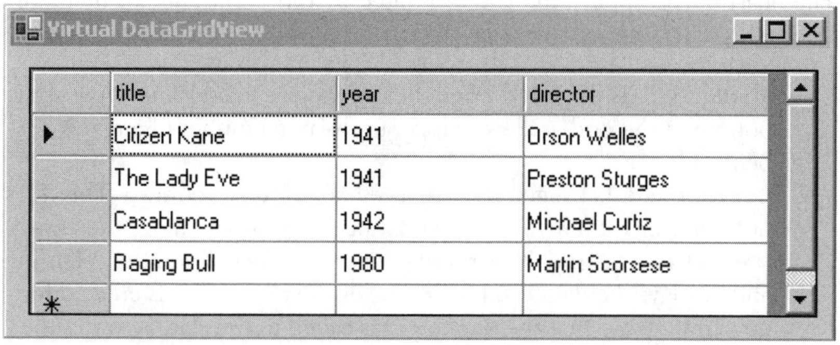

Figure 12-11 `DataGridView` using virtual mode

Listing 12-7 shows the overhead code to initialize the `DataGridView`, register the event handlers, and populate the data cache (this would usually come from a database).

Listing 12-7 Virtual `DataGridView`: Initialization

```
// Set properties of a DataGridView and fill with data
dgv = new DataGridView();
// Event handlers for virtual mode events
dgv.CellValueNeeded += new
    DataGridViewCellValueEventHandler(CellNeeded);
dgv.CellValuePushed += new
    DataGridViewCellValueEventHandler(CellPushed);
dgv.NewRowNeeded += new
    DataGridViewRowEventHandler(RowNeeded);
// Event handlers always available for DataGridView
dgv.UserDeletingRow += new
    DataGridViewRowCancelEventHandler (RowDeleting);
dgv.RowValidated += new
    DataGridViewCellEventHandler( RowValidated);
dgv.VirtualMode = true;
dgv.RowCount = 5;
dgv.ColumnCount = 3;
// Headers for columns
dgv.Columns[0].HeaderText = "title";
dgv.Columns[1].HeaderText = "year";
dgv.Columns[2].HeaderText = "director";
// Fill cache. In production, this would come from database.
movieList.Add(new movie("Citizen Kane",1941,"Orson Welles"));
movieList.Add(new movie("The Lady Eve",1941,"
                    "Preston Sturges"));
// ... Add other movies here
```

The heart of the application is represented by the event handler methods shown in Listing 12-8. To summarize them:

- RowNeeded. Is triggered when the user begins to add a new row at the bottom of the grid. currRow is set to the row number of any row being added.
- CellNeeded. Is triggered when a cell needs to be redrawn. This does not require that a row be selected, but occurs as you move the cursor over cells in the grid. This routine identifies the column the cell is in and displays the data from the cache or the object that is created for new rows. Note that the MapRow() is called to translate a row in the grid to its corresponding row in the cache. In this simple example, there is always a one-to-one relationship because the cache and grid contain the same number of rows. In a production application, row 5000 in a grid might map to row 1 in the cache.
- CellPushed. Called when a cell value is edited. This routine updates a movie object that represents the selected row with the new value.
- RowValidated. Signals that a different row has been selected and is used to update the previous row. If the row exists in the cache, it is updated; a new row is added to the cache.
- RowDeleting. Called when user selects a row to delete. If the row exists in the cache, it is removed.

Listing 12-8   Virtual `DataGridView`: Event Handlers

```
// Called when a new row is appended to grid
private void RowNeeded(object sender,
                       DataGridViewRowEventArgs e)
{
   rowNeeded = true;
   currRow = dgv.Rows.Count - 1;
}

// Called when a cell must be displayed/refreshed
private void CellNeeded(object sender,
                        DataGridViewCellValueEventArgs e)
{
   if (rowNeeded)
   {
      rowNeeded = false;
      currMovie = new movie();
      return;
   }
```

Listing 12-8 Virtual `DataGridView`: Event Handlers *(continued)*

```
    storeRow = MapRow(e.RowIndex);
    if(storeRow >=0 && currRow ==-1)
        currMovie = movieList[storeRow];
    string colName = dgv.Columns[e.ColumnIndex].HeaderText;
    if(storeRow>=0)  // Refresh cell from cache
    {
        if (colName == "title")e.Value =
            movieList[storeRow].Title;
        if (colName == "year") e.Value =
            movieList[storeRow].Movie_Year.ToString();
        if (colName == "director") e.Value =
            movieList[storeRow].Director;
    } else           // refresh cell from object for new row
    {
        if (colName == "title")e.Value = currMovie.Title;
        if (colName == "year")e.Value =
            currMovie.Movie_Year.ToString();
        if (colName == "director") e.Value = currMovie.Director;
    }
}
// Cell has been updated
private void CellPushed(object sender,
                        DataGridViewCellValueEventArgs e)
{
    // Update property on movie object for this row
    storeRow = MapRow(e.RowIndex);
    string colName = dgv.Columns[e.ColumnIndex].HeaderText;
    if (colName == "title") currMovie.Title = (string)e.Value;
    if (colName == "year")
    {
        int retval;
        if(int.TryParse((string)e.Value,out retval))
            currMovie.Movie_Year = retval;
    }
    if (colName == "director") currMovie.Director =
        (string)e.Value;
}
// Occurs when user changes current row
// Update previous row in cache when this occurs
private void RowValidated(object sender,
                        DataGridViewCellEventArgs e)
```

Listing 12-8	Virtual `DataGridView`: Event Handlers *(continued)*

```
{
    storeRow = MapRow(e.RowIndex);
    if (storeRow < 0) storeRow = movieList.Count;
    currRow = -1;
    if (currMovie != null)
    {
        // Save the modified Customer object in the data store.
        storeRow = MapRow(e.RowIndex);
        if (storeRow >= 0)
            movieList[storeRow] = currMovie;
        else movieList.Add(currMovie);
            currMovie = null;
    }
}
// Row selected and Del key pushed
private void RowDeleting(object sender,
                         DataGridViewRowCancelEventArgs e)
{
    if (MapRow(e.Row.Index)>=0)
    { movieList.RemoveAt(e.Row.Index); }
    if (e.Row.Index == currRow)
    {
        currRow = -1;
        currMovie = null;
    }
}
// Maps grid row to row in cache. More logic would be added
// for application that refreshes cache from database.
private int MapRow(int dgvRow)
{
    if (dgvRow < movieList.Count)return dgvRow;
        else return -1;
}
```

This example provides only the basic details for implementing a virtual `Data-GridView`. The next step is to extend it to include a virtual memory manager that reloads the cache when data must be fetched from disk to display a cell.

12.4 Summary

Data binding is used to link the data displayed in a control with an underlying data source. In many cases, it can eliminate the manual code required to populate controls. There are two basic types of binding: simple and complex. Simple is used with controls that display only one value; complex is used to display multiple data values in selected controls such as a list box or data grid.

Each data source has a binding manager that keeps track of all connections to it. This manager is responsible for synchronizing values in the data store and controls bound to it. For list data sources such as an array or data table, the binding manager is a `CurrencyManager` object; for a property on an object, the binding manager is a `PropertyManger` object. Both of these objects expose methods that allow them to be used to navigate through their data source.

Of the data bound controls, the `DataGridView` offers the richest interface. It permits data to be displayed and manipulated in a grid format. Style classes and appearance properties enable almost all of its features to be customized. Its event members allow virtually any action involving the grid to be detected—from a click on a cell to the addition of a row. It also permits control types such as a `button`, `image`, or `ComboBox` to be inserted into any of its cells. Although data binding is typically used to populate a `DataGridView`, the control also supports a virtual mode that allows an application to manage the grid's content using a custom data cache.

12.5 Test Your Understanding

1. Indicate whether the following are true or false:
    a. A `TextBox` supports complex binding.
    b. The width of a control can be bound to a data source.
    c. All controls support simple binding.
    d. A data source can only be bound to one control at a time.
    e. A data source may have multiple binding managers.
    f. Changes made to the value of a control are always propagated to the data source.
    g. Controls can be bound to custom data objects.
    h. The `PropertyManager` class inherits from the `CurrencyManager` class.
    i. Only `public` properties may be bound to a control.

2. What is the difference between simple and complex binding? One-way and two-way binding?

3. Describe how to allow a custom data source to support two-way binding.

4. Which property and enumeration cause the entire row in a Data-GridView to be highlighted when a single cell in the row is selected?

5. Which of these cannot be included in a DataGridView cell?

   a.   TextBox
   b.   ListBox
   c.   Button
   d.   ComboBox

6. How do you ensure that a column in a DataGridView is always displayed on the screen?

ADVANCED USE OF C# AND THE .NET FRAMEWORK

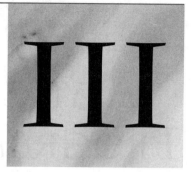

Part **III**

■ Chapter 13
Asynchronous Programming and
Multithreading **590**

■ Chapter 14
Creating Distributed Applications
with Remoting **636**

■ Chapter 15
Code Refinement, Security,
and Deployment **680**

ASYNCHRONOUS PROGRAMMING AND MULTITHREADING

Topics in This Chapter

- *Asynchronous Programming:* Unlike synchronous programming, in which a task can begin only when the preceding one completes, asynchronous programming permits multiple tasks to be performed simultaneously.

- *Multithreading:* Multiple threads can enhance the performance of an application that can separate its tasks into operations that can run on separate threads. This section describes how a program can implement multithreading, the factors that affect thread scheduling, and when it's useful to create multiple threads.

- *Thread Synchronization:* The use of multiple threads in an application raises several synchronization issues regarding how to create thread-safe code. Several .NET manual synchronization techniques are presented, including the `Monitor` class, the `Mutex` class, and the use of semaphores.

Chapter

An application or component can be designed to operate in a synchronous or asynchronous manner. In the synchronous model, tasks are performed in sequence—as in a relay race, one runner (task) must complete his segment before the next one can start. In contrast, asynchronous programming permits an application to be broken into subtasks that perform concurrently. This approach (sometimes referred to as *send and forget*) allows one method to call another method and then continue processing without waiting for the called method to finish.

The key to asynchronous programming is the use of threads. A *thread* is essentially a code sequence that runs independently. This permits a program to work on multiple tasks in a parallel manner. For example, an application may use one thread to accept user input to a form, while a second thread concurrently processes a print request. When used judiciously, threads can greatly improve a program's performance and responsiveness; when used incorrectly, they can cause programs to hang or terminate without properly completing a task.

A thread is created and run by the operating system—not by .NET. What .NET does is create a wrapper around a thread so that it obeys the rules of the .NET managed environment. An asynchronous application may work indirectly or directly with threads. In the former case, delegates are used to automatically allocate and handle threads; in the latter case, a program explicitly creates instances of the Thread class and takes responsibility for synchronizing thread behavior.

The chapter begins with an overview of threads and then looks at asynchronous programming using both delegates and explicit thread creation. The final section examines the synchronization issues that arise when multiple threads are running, and introduces several synchronization techniques that can be used to enable threads to share resources.

13.1 What Is a Thread?

When an assembly (.exe file) begins execution, a *primary thread* is created that serves as the entry point to the application—in C#, this is an application's `Main()` method. The thread is the unit or agent responsible for executing code.

.NET does not physically create threads—that is the responsibility of the operating system. Instead, it provides a `Thread` class that serves as a *managed version* of the unmanaged physical thread. The `Thread` class, located in the `System.Threading` namespace, exposes properties and methods that allow a program to perform thread-related operations. These class members allow an application to create a thread, set its priority, suspend, activate or kill it, and have it run in the background or foreground.

Figure 13-1 is a simplified representation of the relationship between a process, applications, and threads. Physically, a thread consists of CPU registers, a call stack (memory used for maintaining parameter data and method calls), and a container known as *Thread Local Storage* (TLS) that holds the state information for a thread.

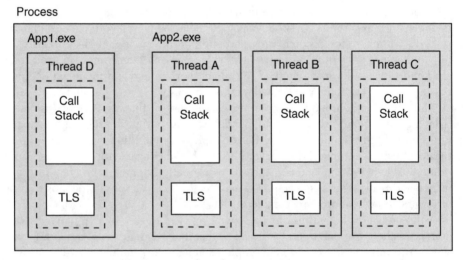

Figure 13-1   Threads contained in a process

Multithreading

In a single CPU system, only one thread can execute at a time. The order in which threads run is based on their priority. When a thread reaches the top of the priority queue, its code stream is executed for a fixed amount of time known as a *time slice*. If the thread does not complete execution, its state information must be stored so that the thread can later resume execution at the point it is interrupted. The state information includes registers, stack pointers, and a program counter that tells the thread which instruction is executed next. All of this information is stored in the area of memory allocated to Thread Local Storage.

Core Note

.NET provides support for multiple processor systems by permitting a process to be assigned to a processor. This is set using the ProcessAffinity *property of the* System.Diagnostics.Process *class.*

Thread Priority

As mentioned, the order in which a thread runs is based strictly on its priority. If a thread is running and a thread with a higher priority becomes available to run, the running thread is preempted to allow the higher priority thread to run. If more than one thread has the same priority, the operating system executes them in a round-robin fashion.

In .NET, a thread's Priority property is used to get or set its priority level. It may have one of five values based on the ThreadPriority enum: Lowest, BelowNormal, Normal, AboveNormal, and Highest. The default is ThreadPriority.Normal.

You should override thread priorities only in situations where a task has a clearly defined need to execute with a low or high priority. Using thread priorities to fine-tune an algorithm can be self-defeating for several reasons:

- Even threads with the highest priority are subject to blocking by other threads.
- Raising the priority of a thread can place it into competition with the operating system's threads, which can affect overall system performance.
- An operating system keeps track of when a thread runs. If a thread has not run for a while, its priority is increased to enable it to be executed.

Foreground and Background Threads

.NET classifies each thread as either a background or foreground thread. The difference in these two types is quite simple: An application ends when all foreground threads stop; and any background threads still running are stopped as part of the shutdown process.

By default, a new thread is set to run as a foreground thread. It can be changed to background by setting its `IsBackground` property to `true`. Clearly, you only want to set this for noncritical tasks that can logically and safely end when the program does. Note that even though .NET attempts to notify all background threads when the program shuts down, it's good practice to explicitly manage thread termination.

Thread State

During its lifetime, a thread may exist in several states: It begins life in an `Unstarted` state; after it is started and the CPU begins executing it, it is in `Running` mode; when its slice of execution time ends, the operating system may suspend it; or if it has completed running, it moves into `Stopped` mode. `Running`, `Stopped`, and `Suspended` are somewhat deterministic states that occur naturally as the operating system manages thread execution. Another state, known as `WaitSleepJoin`, occurs when a thread must wait for resources or for another thread to complete its execution. After this blocking ends, the thread is then eligible to move into `Running` mode.

Figure 13-2 illustrates the states that a thread may assume and the methods that invoke these states. It is not a complete state diagram, because it does not depict the events that can lead to a thread being placed in an inconsistent state. For example, you cannot start a running thread nor can you abort a suspended thread. Such attempts cause an interrupt to be thrown.

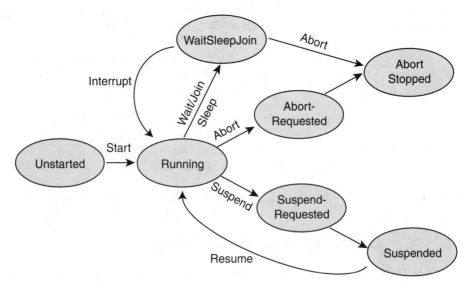

Figure 13-2   Thread states

A thread's current state is available through a read-only property named `Thread-State`. This property's value is based on the `ThreadState` enum that defines 10 states:

```
Aborted          = 256    StopRequested    = 1
AbortRequested = 128      Suspended        = 64
Background       = 4      SuspendRequested = 2
Running          = 0      Unstarted        = 8
Stopped          = 16     WaitSleepJoin    = 32
```

If a program is not interested in a specific state, but does need to know if a thread has been terminated, the Boolean `Thread.IsAlive` property should be used.

13.2 Asynchronous Programming

In a synchronous (single-threaded) application, program execution follows a single path; in an asynchronous (multithreaded) version, operations occur in parallel on multiple paths of execution. This advantage of this latter approach is that slow applications, such as file I/O, can be performed on a separate thread while the main thread continues execution.

Figure 13-3 provides an abstract representation of the two techniques. In the synchronous version, each method is executed in sequence; in the asynchronous version, method B runs at the same time as A and C. This prospect of two or more tasks running (nearly) simultaneously raises a set of questions not present in a single-threaded program:

- What type of communication between the main thread and worker thread is required? The code on the worker thread can be invoked and forgotten, or it may be necessary for the main thread to know when the task is completed.
- How does the main thread know when the worker thread is completed? Two approaches are available: the *callback* technique, in which the worker thread returns control to the main thread when it is finished; or a polling approach, in which the main thread calls a method that returns the results of the worker thread execution.
- How to synchronize thread requests for the same resources? The issues here are similar to those faced when synchronizing access to a database. The integrity of the data must be maintained and *deadlock* situations must be avoided.
- How to shutdown an application while worker threads are still executing? Several choices are available: They can be terminated; the main application can continue to run until all threads finish; or the main application can end and allow the threads to continue running.

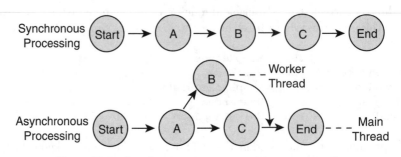

Figure 13-3 Synchronous versus asynchronous execution

Before tackling these issues, let's first look at the basics of how to write code that provides asynchronous code execution. As we see in the next section, threads can be explicitly created and used for parallel code execution. An easier approach is to use a delegate to allocate a worker thread and call a method to execute on the thread—a process referred to as *asynchronous delegate invocation*. Delegates can also be used to specify the callback method that a worker thread calls when it finishes execution.

Although a discussion of creating threads is deferred until later in this chapter, it's worth noting now that the threads allocated for asynchronous methods come from a pre-allocated *thread pool*. This eliminates the overhead of dynamically creating threads and also means they can be reused. At the same time, indiscriminate use of asynchronous calls can exhaust the thread pool—causing operations to wait until new threads are available. We'll discuss remedies for this in the section on threads.

Asynchronous Delegates

Delegates—which were introduced in Chapter 4, "Working with Objects in C#"— provide a way to notify one or more subscribing methods when an event occurs. In the earlier examples, all calls were synchronous (to methods on the same thread). But delegates can also be used to make an asynchronous call that invokes a method on a separate worker thread. Before looking at the details of this, let's review what a delegate is and how it's used.

The following code segment illustrates the basic steps involved in declaring a delegate and using it to invoke a subscribing method. The key points to note are that the callback method(s) must have the same signature as the delegate's declaration, and that multiple methods can be placed on the delegate's invocation chain (list of methods to call). In this example, the delegate is defined to accept a string parameter and return no value. ShowUpper and ShowMessage have the same signature.

```
//(1) Declare delegate. Declare anywhere a class can be declared.
public delegate void myDelegate(string msg);
```

```
private void TestDelegate()
{
   // (2) Create instance of delegate and pass method to it
   myDelegate msgDelegate= new myDelegate(ShowMessage);
   //      Second method is placed on delegate invocation chain
   msgDelegate+= new myDelegate(ShowUpper);
   // (3) Invoke delegate
   msgDelegate("Delegate Called.");
}
// First method called by delegate
private void ShowMessage(string msg)
{
   MessageBox.Show(msg);
}
// Second method called by delegate
private void ShowUpper(string msg)
{
   msg = msg.ToUpper();    // Make uppercase before displaying
   MessageBox.Show(msg);
}
```

Understanding the Delegate Class

When a delegate is defined, .NET automatically creates a class to represent the delegate. Here is the code generated for the delegate in the preceding example:

```
// Class created from delegate declaration
public class myDelegate : MulticastDelegate
{
   // Constructor
   public myDelegate(Object target, Int32 methodPtr);
   public void virtual Invoke(string msg);
   // Used for asynchronous invocation
   public virtual IAsyncResult BeginInvoke(
          string msg, AsyncCallback callback,
          Object state);
   // Used to get results from called method
   public virtual void EndInvoke(IAsyncResult result);
   // Other members are not shown
}
```

A close look at the code reveals how delegates support both synchronous and asynchronous calls.

Constructor

Takes two parameters. The important thing to note here is that when your program creates an instance of the delegate, it passes a method name to the constructor—not two parameters. The compiler takes care of the details of generating the parameters from the method name.

Invoke

The compiler generates a call to this method by default when a delegate is invoked. This causes all methods in the invocation list to be called synchronously. Execution on the caller's thread is blocked until all of the methods in the list have executed.

BeginInvoke

This is the method that enables a delegate to support asynchronous calls. Invoking it causes the delegate to call its registered method on a separate worker thread. BeginInvoke has two required parameters: the first is an AsyncCallback delegate that specifies the method to be called when the asynchronous method has completed its work; the second contains a value that is passed to the delegate when the method finishes executing. Both of these values are set to null if no callback is required. Any parameters defined in the delegate's signature precede these required parameters.

Let's look at the simplest form of BeginInvoke first, where no callback delegate is provided. Here is the code to invoke the delegate defined in the preceding example asynchronously:

```
IAsyncResult IAsync =
     msgDelegate.BeginInvoke("Delegate Called.",null,null)
```

There is one small problem, however—this delegate has two methods registered with it and delegates invoked asynchronously can have only one. An attempt to compile this fails. The solution is to register only ShowMessage or ShowUpper with the delegate.

Note that BeginInvoke returns an object that implements the IAsyncResult interface. As we see later, this object has two important purposes: It is used to retrieve the output generated by the asynchronous method; and its IsCompleted property can be used to monitor the status of the asynchronous operation.

You can also pass an AsyncCallBack delegate as a parameter to BeginInvoke that specifies a callback method the asynchronous method invokes when its execution ends. This enables the calling thread to continue its tasks without continually polling the worker thread to determine if it has finished. In this code segment, myCallBack is called when ShowMessage finishes.

```
private delegate void myDelegate(string msg);
myDelegate d= new myDelegate(ShowMessage);
d.BeginInvoke("OK",new AsyncCallback(myCallBack),null);
```

It is important to be aware that myCallBack is run on a thread from the thread pool rather than the application's main thread. As we will see, this affects the design of UI (user interface) applications.

EndInvoke

Is called to retrieve the results returned by the asynchronous method. The method is called by passing it an object that implements the IAsyncResult interface—the same object returned when BeginInvoke is called. These two statements illustrate this approach:

```
// Save the interface returned
IAsyncResult IAsync = GetStatus.BeginInvoke(null,null);
// ... Do some work here; then get returned value
int status = GetStatus.EndInvoke(IAsync);
```

EndInvoke should be called even if the asynchronous method returns no value. It can be used to detect exceptions that may be thrown by the asynchronous method; and more importantly, it notifies the Common Language Runtime (CLR) to clean up resources that were used in creating the asynchronous call.

Examples of Implementing Asynchronous Calls

The challenge in using BeginInvoke is to determine when the called asynchronous method finishes executing. As touched on earlier, the .NET Framework offers several options:

- **EndInvoke.** After BeginInvoke is called, the main thread can continue working and then call this method. The call to EndInvoke blocks process on the main thread until the asynchronous worker thread completes its execution. This should never be used on a thread that services a user interface because it will lock up the interface.
- **Use a WaitHandle Synchronization object.** The IAsyncResult object returned by BeginInvoke has a WaitHandle property that contains a synchronization object. The calling thread can use this object (or objects) to wait until one or more asynchronous tasks complete execution.
- **CallBack Method.** As mentioned earlier, one of the parameters to BeginInvoke can be a delegate that specifies a method to be called when the asynchronous method finishes. Because the callback method is run on a new thread from the thread pool, this technique is useful only when the original calling thread does not need to process the results of the asynchronous method.

- **Polling.** The IAsyncResult object has an IsCompleted property that is set to true when the method called by BeginInvoke finishes executing. Polling is achieved by periodically checking this value.

Figure 13-4 illustrates the four options.

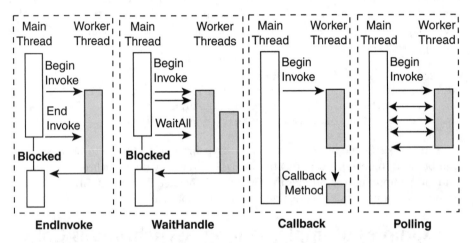

Figure 13-4   Options for detecting the completion of an asynchronous task

Using Polling and Synchronization Objects

Table 13-1 lists the IAsyncResult properties that are instrumental in implementing the various asynchronous models. The class is in the System.Runtime.Remoting.Messaging namespace.

Table 13-1   Selected IAsyncResult Properties

Property	Description
AsyncState	The object that is passed as the last parameter to the Begin-Invoke method.
AsyncWaitHandle	Returns a WaitHandle type object that is used to wait for access to resources. Access is indicated by a "signal" that the asynchronous task has completed. Its methods allow for various synchronization schemes based on one or multiple active threads: WaitOne. Blocks thread until WaitHandle receives signal. WaitAny. Waits for any thread to send a signal (static). WaitAll. Waits for all threads to send a signal (static).

Table 13-1   Selected `IAsyncResult` Properties *(continued)*

Property	Description
AsyncDelegate	Returns the delegate used for the asynchronous call.
IsCompleted	Boolean value that returns the status of the asynchronous call.

The `WaitHandle` and `IsCompleted` properties are often used together to implement polling logic that checks whether a method has finished running. Listing 13-1
illustrates this cooperation. A polling loop is set up that runs until `IsCompleted` is
true. Inside the loop, some work is performed and the `WaitHandle.WaitOne`
method is called to detect if the asynchronous method is done. `WaitOne` blocks processing until it receives a signal or its specified wait time (20 milliseconds in this
example) expires.

Listing 13-1   Asynchronous Invocation Using Polling to Check Status

```
// Code to return a Body Mass Index Value
private delegate decimal bmiDelegate(decimal ht, decimal wt);
decimal ht_in = 72;
decimal wt_lbs=168;
// (1) Invoke delegate asynchronously
bmiDelegate bd= new bmiDelegate(CalcBMI);
IAsyncResult asRes= bd.BeginInvoke(ht_in, wt_lbs,null,null);
int numPolls=0;
while(!asRes.IsCompleted)
{
   //     Do some work here
   // (2) Wait 20 milliseconds for method to signal completion
   asRes.AsyncWaitHandle.WaitOne(20,false);
   numPolls+=1;
}
// (3) Get result now that asynchronous method has finished
decimal myBMI = bd.EndInvoke(asRes);
Console.WriteLine("Polls: {0}  BMI: {1:##.00}",
      numPolls, myBMI);         // --> Polls: 3  BMI: 22.78
// Calculate BMI
private decimal CalcBMI(decimal ht, decimal wt)
{
   Thread.Sleep(200);           // Simulate a delay of 200 ms
   Console.WriteLine("Thread:{0}",
        Thread.CurrentThread.GetHash());
   return((wt * 703 *10/(ht*ht))/10);
}
```

For demonstration purposes, this example includes a 200-millisecond delay in the asynchronous method CalcBMI. This causes WaitOne, which blocks for up to 20 milliseconds, to execute seven times (occasionally eight) before the loop ends. Because EndInvoke is not reached until the asynchronous calculation has ended, it causes no blocking.

A more interesting use of the WaitHandle methods is to manage multiple asynchronous tasks running concurrently. In this example, the static WaitAll method is used to ensure that three asynchronous tasks have completed before the results are retrieved. The method is executed by passing it an array that contains the wait handle created by each call to BeginInvoke. As a side note, this point where threads must rendezvous before execution can proceed is referred to as a *barrier*.

```
int istart= Environment.TickCount;   // Start Time
bmiDelegate bd1     = new bmiDelegate(Form1.CalcBMI);
IAsyncResult asRes1 = bd1.BeginInvoke(72, 168,null,null);
//
bmiDelegate bd2     = new bmiDelegate(CalcBMI);
IAsyncResult asRes2 = bd2.BeginInvoke(62, 124,null,null);
//
bmiDelegate bd3     = new bmiDelegate(CalcBMI);
IAsyncResult asRes3 = bd3.BeginInvoke(67, 132,null,null);
// Set up array of wait handles as required by WaitAll method
WaitHandle[] bmiHandles = {asRes1.AsyncWaitHandle,
                           asRes2.AsyncWaitHandle,
                           asRes3.AsyncWaitHandle);
// Block execution until all threads finish at this barrier point
WaitHandle.WaitAll(bmiHandles);
int iend = Environment.TickCount;
// Print time required to execute all asynchronous tasks
Console.WriteLine("Elapsed Time: {0}", iend - istart);
// Get results
decimal myBMI1 = bd1.EndInvoke(asRes1);
decimal myBMI2 = bd2.EndInvoke(asRes2);
decimal myBMI3 = bd3.EndInvoke(asRes3);
```

To test performance, the method containing this code was executed multiple times during a single session. The results showed that execution time was more than 700 milliseconds for the first execution and declined to 203 for the fourth and subsequent ones when three different threads were allocated.

Execution:	1	2	3	4	5
Thread:	75	75	80	75	75
Thread:	75	80	12	80	80
Thread:	80	75	80	12	12
Time(ms):	750	578	406	203	203

For comparison, the code was then run to execute the three tasks with each `BeginInvoke` followed by an `EndInvoke`. It ran at a consistent 610 ms, which is what would be expected given the 200 ms block by each `EndInvoke`—and is equivalent to using synchronous code. The lesson to a developer is that asynchronous code should be used when a method will be executed frequently; otherwise the overhead to set up multithreading negates the benefits.

Core Note

Applications that need to host ActiveX controls or interact with the clipboard must apply the STAThread (single-threaded apartment) attribute to their `Main()` method. Unfortunately, you cannot use `WaitAll()` in applications that have this attribute due to conflicts between COM and the Win32 method that `WaitAll` wraps. Visual Studio users should be aware of this because C# under VS.NET adds the attribute by default.

Using Callbacks

Callbacks provide a way for a calling method to launch an asynchronous task and have it call a specified method when it is done. This is not only an intuitively appealing model, but is usually the most efficient asynchronous model—permitting the calling thread to focus on its own processing rather than waiting for an activity to end. As a rule, the callback approach is preferred when the program is event driven; polling and waiting are better suited for applications that operate in a more algorithmic, deterministic manner.

The next-to-last parameter passed to `BeginInvoke` is an optional delegate of type `AsyncCallback`. The method name passed to this delegate is the callback method that an asynchronous task calls when it finishes executing a method. The example in Listing 13-2 should clarify these details.

Listing 13-2	Using a Callback Method with Asynchronous Calls

```
using System.Runtime.Remoting.Messaging ;
// Delegate is defined globally for class
public delegate decimal bmiDelegate(decimal wt, decimal ht);

public class BMIExample
{
```

Listing 13-2	Using a Callback Method with Asynchronous Calls *(continued)*

```
public void BMICaller(decimal ht, decimal wt, string name)
{
    bmiDelegate bd= new bmiDelegate(CalcBMI);
    // Pass callback method and state value
    bd.BeginInvoke(ht,wt,new AsyncCallback(OnCallBack),name);
}
// This method is invoked when CalcBMI ends
private void OnCallBack(IAsyncResult asResult)
{
    // Need AsyncResult so we can get original delegate
    AsyncResult asyncObj = (AsyncResult)asResult;
    // Get state value
    string name= (string)asyncObj.AsyncState ;
    // Get original delegate so EndInvoke can be called
    bmiDelegate bd= (bmiDelegate)asyncObj.AsyncDelegate;
    // Always include exception handling
    try {
        decimal bmi = bd.EndInvoke(asResult);
        Console.WriteLine("BMI for {0}: {1:##.00}",name,bmi);
    } catch (Exception ex)
    {
        Console.WriteLine(ex.Message);
    }
}
private decimal CalcBMI(decimal ht, decimal wt)
{
    Console.WriteLine("Thread:{0}",
        Thread.CurrentThread.GetHashCode());
    return((wt * 703 *10/(ht*ht))/10);
}
}
```

Things to note:

- The `BeginInvoke` signature includes optional data parameters as well as a delegate containing the callback method and a state object:

  ```
  bd.BeginInvoke(ht,wt,new AsyncCallback(OnCallBack),name);
  ```

- The final parameter can be information of any type that is useful to the code that receives control after the asynchronous method completes. In this example, we pass the name of the person whose BMI is calculated.

- The callback method must have the signature defined by the `Async-Callback` delegate.

  ```
  public delegate void AsyncCallback(IAsyncResult
      asyncResult);
  ```

- The callback method must cast its parameter to an `AsyncResult` type in order to access the original delegate and call `EndInvoke`.

  ```
  AsyncResult asyncObj = (AsyncResult)asResult;
  // Get the original delegate
  bmiDelegate bd= (bmiDelegate)asyncObj.AsyncDelegate;
  decimal bmi = bd.EndInvoke(asResult);
  ```

- The call to `EndInvoke` should always be inside an exception handling block. When an exception occurs on an asynchronous method, .NET catches the exception and later rethrows it when `EndInvoke` is called.
- The `BMICaller` method is invoked from an instance of `BMIExample` using the following code. Note that the main thread is put to sleep so it does not end before the result is calculated.

  ```
  BMIExample bmi = new BMIExample();
  bmi.BMICaller(68,122, "Diana");
  Thread.Sleep(500);  // Give it time to complete
  ```

Multiple Threads and User Interface Controls

When working with Windows Forms and user interfaces in general, it is important to understand that all controls on a form belong to the same thread and should be accessed only by code running on that thread. If multiple threads are running, a control should not be accessed—even though it's technically accessible—by any code not running on the same thread as the control. This is a .NET commandment; and as is the nature of commandments, it can be broken—but with unpredictable results. Suppose our application wants to use the callback method in the preceding example to display the calculated BMI value on a label control. One's instinct might be to assign the value directly to the control:

```
private void OnCallBack(IAsyncResult asResult)
{
    // ... Initialization code goes here
    decimal bmi = bd.EndInvoke(asResult);
    Label.Text= bmi.ToText();  // Set label on UI to BMI value
}
```

This may work temporarily, but should be avoided. As an alternative, .NET permits a limited number of methods on the `Control` class to be called from other threads: `Invoke`, `BeginInvoke`, `EndInvoke`, and `CreateGraphics`. Calling a control's Invoke or BeginInvoke method causes the method specified in the dele-gate parameter to be *executed on the UI thread of that control*. The method can then work directly with the control.

To illustrate, let's replace the assignment to Label.Text with a call to a method DisplayBMI that sets the label value:

```
DisplayBMI(bmi);
```

We also add a new delegate, which is passed to Invoke, that has a parameter to hold the calculated value.

```
// Delegate to pass BMI value to method
private delegate void labelDelegate(decimal bmi);

private void DisplayBMI(decimal bmi)
{
    // Determines if the current thread is the same thread
    // the Form was created on.
    if(this.InvokeRequired == false)
    {
        labelthread.Text= bmi.ToString("##.00");
    }
    else
    {
        // The Form's Invoke method is executed, which
        // causes DisplayBMI to run on the UI thread.
        // bmiObj is array of arguments to pass to method.
        object[] bmiObj= {bmi};
        this.Invoke(new labelDelegate(DisplayBMI),bmiObj);
    }
}
```

This code segment illustrates an important point about threads and code: The same code can be run on multiple threads. The first time this method is called, it runs on the same thread as OnCallBack. The InvokeRequired property is used to determine if the current thread can access the form. If not, the Invoke method is executed with a delegate that calls back DisplayBMI on the UI thread—permitting it to now interact with the UI controls. To make this an asynchronous call, you only need replace Invoke with BeginInvoke.

Using MethodInvoker to Create a Thread

In situations where your code needs to create a new thread but does not require passing arguments or receiving a return value, the system-defined MethodInvoker delegate should be considered. It is the simplest possible delegate—it takes no parameters and returns no value. It is created by passing the name of a method to be called to its constructor. It may then be invoked synchronously (Invoke) or asynchronously (BeginInvoke):

```
// NewThread is method called by delegate
MethodInvoker mi = new MethodInvoker(NewThread);
// Note that parameters do not have to be null
mi.BeginInvoke(null,null); // Asynchronous call
mi();                      // Synchronous call
```

The advantage of using the built-in delegate is that you do not have to design your own, and it runs more efficiently than an equivalent custom delegate.

Using Asynchronous Calls to Perform I/O

Asynchronous operations are not new; they were originally implemented in operating systems via hardware and software as a way to balance the slow I/O (Input/Output) process against the much faster CPU operations. To encourage asynchronous I/O, the .NET Framework includes methods on its major I/O classes that can be used to implement the asynchronous model without explicitly creating delegates or threads. These classes include FileStream, HttpWebRequest, Socket, and Network-Stream. Let's look at an example using the FileStream class that was introduced in Chapter 5, "C# Text Manipulation and File I/O."

FileStream inherits from the System.IO.Stream class an abstract class that supports asynchronous operations with its BeginRead, BeginWrite, EndRead, and EndWrite methods. The Beginxxx methods are analogous to BeginInvoke and include callback and status parameters; the Endxxx methods provide blocking until a corresponding Beginxxx method finishes.

The code in Listing 13-3 uses BeginRead to create a thread that reads a file and passes control to a callback method that compresses the file content and writes it as a .gz file. The basic callback method operations are similar to those in Listing 13-2. Note how the file name is retrieved from the AsyncState property. The compression technique—based on the GZipStream class—is available only in .NET 2.0 and above.

Listing 13-3   Using Aysnchronous I/O to Compress a File

```
// Special namespaces required:
using System.IO.Compression;
using System.Runtime.Remoting.Messaging;
//
// Variables with class scope
Byte[] buffer;
FileStream infile;
```

Listing 13-3   Using Aysnchronous I/O to Compress a File *(continued)*

```
// Compress a specified file using GZip compression
private void Compress_File(string fileName)
{
   bool useAsync = true;  // Specifies asynchronous I/O
   infile = new FileStream(fileName, FileMode.Open,
         FileAccess.Read, FileShare.Read, 2000, useAsync);
   buffer = new byte[infile.Length];
   int ln = buffer.Length;
   // Read file and let callback method handle compression
   IAsyncResult ar = infile.BeginRead(buffer, 0, ln,
         new AsyncCallback(Zip_Completed), fileName);
   //
}
// Callback method that compresses raw data and stores in file
private void Zip_Completed(IAsyncResult asResult)
{
   // Retrieve file name from state object
   string filename = (string)asResult.AsyncState;
   infile.EndRead(asResult);    // Wrap up asynchronous read
   infile.Close();
   //
   MemoryStream ms = new MemoryStream();
   // Memory stream will hold compressed data
   GZipStream zipStream = new GZipStream(ms,
         CompressionMode.Compress, true);
   // Write raw data in compressed form to memory stream
   zipStream.Write(buffer, 0, buffer.Length);
   zipStream.Close();
   // Store compressed data in a file
   FileStream fs = new FileStream(filename+".gz",
         FileMode.OpenOrCreate,FileAccess.Write,FileShare.Read);
   byte[] compressedData = ms.ToArray();
   fs.Write(compressedData, 0, compressedData.Length);
   fs.Close();
}
```

As a rule, asynchronous techniques are not required for file I/O. In fact, for read and write operations of less than 64KB, .NET uses synchronous I/O even if asynchronous is specified. Also, note that if you specify asynchronous operation in the FileStream constructor (by setting the useAsync parameter to true), and then use synchronous methods, performance may slow dramatically. As we demonstrate in later chapters, asynchronous techniques provide a greater performance boost to networking and Web Services applications than to file I/O.

13.3 Working Directly with Threads

The asynchronous techniques discussed in the previous section work best when an application or component's operations can be run on independent threads that contain all the data and methods they need for execution—and when the threads have no interest in the state of other concurrently running threads. The asynchronous techniques do not work as well for applications running concurrent threads that do have to share resources and be aware of the activities of other threads.

The challenge is no longer to determine when a thread finishes executing, but how to synchronize the activities of multiple threads so they do not corrupt each other's work. It's not an easy thing to do, but it can greatly improve a program's performance and a component's usability. In this section, we'll look at how to create and manage threads running concurrently. This serves as a background for the final section that focuses on synchronization techniques used to ensure thread safety.

Creating and Working with Threads

An application can create a thread, identify it, set its priority, set it to run in the background or foreground, coordinate its activities with other threads, and abort it. Let's look at the details.

The Current Thread

All code runs on either the primary thread or a worker thread that is accessible through the `CurrentThread` property of the `Thread` class. We can use this thread to illustrate some of the selected `Thread` properties and methods that provide information about a thread:

```
Thread currThread = Thread.CurrentThread;
Console.WriteLine(currThread.GetHashCode());
Console.WriteLine(currThread.CurrentCulture);        // en-US
Console.WriteLine(currThread.Priority);              // normal
Console.WriteLine(currThread.IsBackground);          // false
Console.WriteLine(AppDomain.GetCurrentThreadId());   // 3008
```

`Thread.GetHashCode` overrides the `Object.GetHashCode` method to return a thread ID. The thread ID is not the same as the physical thread ID assigned by the operating system. That ID, which .NET uses internally to recognize threads, is obtained by calling the `AppDomain.GetCurrentThreadID` method.

Creating Threads

To create a thread, pass its constructor a delegate that references the method to be called when the thread is started. The delegate parameter may be an instance of the ThreadStart or ParameterizedTheadStart delegate. The difference in the two is their signature: ThreadStart accepts no parameters and returns no value; ParameterizedThreadStart accepts an object as a parameter, which provides a convenient way to pass data to thread.

After the thread is created, its Start method is invoked to launch the thread. This segment illustrates how the two delegates are used to create a thread:

```
Thread newThread  = new Thread(new ThreadStart(GetBMI));
newThread.Start();        // Launch thread asynchronously

Thread newThread  = new Thread(new
     ParameterizedThreadStart(GetBMI));
newThread.Start(40);      // Pass data to the thread
```

To demonstrate thread usage, let's modify the method to calculate a BMI value (see Listing 13-2) to execute on a worker thread (Listing 13-4). The weight and height values are passed in an array object and extracted using casting. The calculated value is exposed as a property of the BMI class.

Listing 13-4	Passing Parameters to a Thread's Method

```
// Create instance of class and set properties
BMI b = new BMI();
decimal[] bmiParms = { 168M, 73M };  // Weight and height
// Thread will execute method in class instance
Thread newThread  = new Thread(
     new ParameterizedThreadStart(b.GetBMI));
newThread.Start(bmiParms);          // Pass parameter to thread
Console.WriteLine(newThread.ThreadState);  // Unstarted
Console.WriteLine(b.Bmi); // Use property to display result
// Rest of main class ...
}
public class BMI
{
   private decimal bmival;
   public void GetBMI(object obj)
   {
      decimal[] parms= (decimal[])obj;
      decimal weight = parms[0];
      decimal height = parms[1] ;
```

Listing 13-4	Passing Parameters to a Thread's Method *(continued)*

```
        // Simulate delay to do some work
        Thread.Sleep(1000);   // Build in a delay of one second
        bmival = (weight * 703 * 10/(height*height))/10 ;
    }
    // Property to return BMI value
    public decimal Bmi
    { get {return bmival; }}
}
```

In reality, the method GetBMI does not do enough work to justify running on a separate thread; to simulate work, the Sleep method is called to block the thread for a second before it performs the calculation. At the same time, the main thread continues executing. It displays the worker thread state and then displays the calculated value. However, this logic creates a *race condition* in which the calling thread needs the worker thread to complete the calculation before the result is displayed. Because of the delay we've included in GetBMI, that is unlikely—and at best unpredictable.

One solution is to use the Thread.Join method, which allows one thread to wait for another to finish. In the code shown here, the Join method blocks processing on the main thread until the thread running the GetBMI code ends execution:

```
newThread.Start();
Console.WriteLine(newThread.ThreadState);
newThread.Join();         // Block until thread finishes
Console.WriteLine(b.bmi);
```

Note that the most common use of Join is as a safeguard to ensure that worker threads have terminated before an application is shut down.

Aborting a Thread

Any started thread that is not in a suspended state can be requested to terminate using the Thread.Abort method. Invoking this method causes a ThreadAbortException to be raised on its associated thread; thus, the code running the thread must implement the proper exception handling code. Listing 13-5 shows the code to implement both the call and the exception handling.

The calling method creates a thread, sleeps for a second, and then issues an Abort on the worker thread. The parameter to this command is a string that can be displayed when the subsequent exception occurs. The Join command is then used to wait for the return after the thread has terminated.

The method running on the worker thread loops until it is aborted. It is structured to catch the `ThreadAbortException` raised by the `Abort` command and print the message exposed by the exception's `ExceptionState` property.

Listing 13-5	How to Abort a Thread

```csharp
using System;
using System.Threading;
class TestAbort
{
   public static void Main()
   {
      Thread newThread = new Thread(new ThreadStart(TestMethod));
      newThread.Start();
      Thread.Sleep(1000);
      if(newThread.IsAlive)
      {
         Console.WriteLine("Aborting thread.");
         // (1) Call abort and send message to Exception handler
         newThread.Abort("Need to close all threads.");
         // (2) Wait for the thread to terminate
         newThread.Join();
         Console.WriteLine("Shutting down.");
      }
   }

   static void TestMethod()
   {
      try
      {
         bool iloop=true;
         while(iloop)
         {
            Console.WriteLine("Worker thread running.");
            Thread.Sleep(500);
            // Include next statement to prevent abort
            // iloop=false;
         }
      }
      catch(ThreadAbortException abortException)
      {
        // (3) Display message sent with abort command
        Console.WriteLine((string)abortException.ExceptionState);
      }
   }
}
```

The `Abort` command should not be regarded as a standard way to terminate threads, any more than emergency brakes should be regarded as a normal way to stop a car. If the thread does not have adequate exception handling, it will fail to perform any necessary cleanup actions—leading to unpredictable results. Alternate approaches to terminating a thread are presented in the section on thread synchronization.

Multithreading in Action

To gain insight into thread scheduling and performance issues, let's set up an application to create multiple threads that request the same resources. Figure 13-5 illustrates our test model. The server is a class that loads images from its disk storage on request and returns them as a stream of bytes to a client. The client spins seven threads with each thread requesting five images. To make things interesting, the threads are given one of two different priorities. Parenthetically, this client can be used for stress testing because the number of threads and images requested can be set to any value.

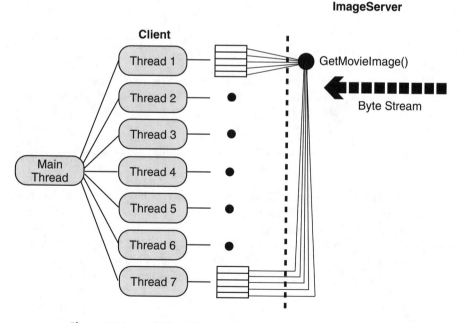

Figure 13-5 Multithreading used to return images as a byte array

The ImageServer class shown in Listing 13-6 uses the Stream class to input the requested image file, write it into a memory stream, and convert this stream to an array of bytes that is returned to the client. Note that any exceptions thrown in the server are handled by the client code.

Listing 13-6	Class to Return Images

```
public class ImageServer
{
    public static byte[] GetMovieImage(string imageName,
                                       int threadNum )
    {
        // Returns requested image to client as a series of bytes,

        // and displays thread number of calling thread.
        int imgByte;
        imageName= "c:\\images\\"+imageName;
        // If file not available exception is thrown and caught by
        // client.
        FileStream s = File.OpenRead(imageName);
        MemoryStream ms = new MemoryStream();
        while((imgByte =s.ReadByte())!=-1)
        {
            ms.WriteByte(((byte)imgByte));
        }
        // Display order in which threads are processed
        Console.WriteLine("Processing on Thread: {0}",threadNum);
        return ms.ToArray();
    }
}
```

The code shown in Listing 13-7 uses the techniques described earlier to create seven threads that call the static FetchImage method on the ImageServer class. The threads are alternately assigned a priority of Lowest or AboveNormal, so that we can observe how their scheduling is affected by priority. Each thread makes five requests for an image from the server by calling its GetMovieImage method. These calls are inside an exception handling block that displays any exception message originating at the server.

Listing 13-7   Using Multithreading to Retrieve Images

```
using System;
using System.Collections;
using System.Threading;
namespace ThreadExample
{
   class SimpleClient
   {
      static void Main(string[] args)
      {
         Threader t=new Threader();
      }
   }
   class Threader
   {
      ImageServer server;
      public Threader(){
         server = new ImageServer(); Object used to fetch images
         StartThreader();
      }
      public void StartThreader()
      {
         // Create seven threads to retrieve images
         for (int i=0; i<7; i++)
         {
            // (1) Create delegate
           ThreadStart threadStart = new ThreadStart(FetchImage);
            // (2) Create thread
            Thread workerThread = new Thread(threadStart);
            // (3) Set two priorities for comparison testing
            if( i % 2 == 1)
              workerThread.Priority = ThreadPriority.Lowest;
            else
              workerThread.Priority = ThreadPriority.AboveNormal;
            // (4) Launch Thread
            workerThread.Start();
         }
      }
      public void FetchImage()
      {
         // Display Thread ID
         Console.WriteLine(
              "Spinning: "+Thread.CurrentThread.GetHashCode());
```

Listing 13-7   Using Multithreading to Retrieve Images *(continued)*

```
string[] posters = {"afi1.gif","afi2.gif",
                        "afi4.gif", "afi7.gif","afi89gif"};
// Retrieve five images on each thread
try
{
    for (int i=0;i<5;i++)
    {
        byte[] imgArray = server.GetMovieImage(
            posters[i],
            Thread.CurrentThread.GetHashCode());
        MemoryStream ms = new MemoryStream(imgArray);
        Bitmap bmp = new Bitmap(ms);
    }
}
catch (Exception ex)
{
    Console.WriteLine(ex.Message);
}
} // FetchImage
} // Threader
// ImageServer class goes here...
} // ThreadExample
```

Because GetMovieImage prints the hash code associated with each image it
returns, we can determine the order in which thread requests are fulfilled. Figure
13-6 shows the results of running this application. The even-numbered threads have
the higher priority and are processed first in round-robin sequence. The lower priority threads are then processed with no interleaved execution among the threads.

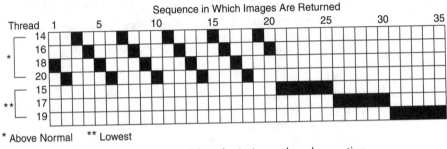

Figure 13-6   Effect of thread priority on thread execution

The program was run several times to test the effects of varying the number of images requested. In general, the same scheduling pattern shown here prevails, although as more images are requested the lower priority threads tend to run in an interleaved fashion.

Using the Thread Pool

Creating threads can be a relatively expensive process, and for this reason, .NET maintains a collection of predefined threads known as a *thread pool*. Threads in this pool can be acquired by an application and then returned for reuse when they have finished running. Recall from Section 13.2 that when a program uses asynchronous delegate invocation to create a thread, the thread actually comes from the thread pool. An application can also access this pool directly by following two simple steps.

The first step is to create a `WaitCallback` delegate that points to the method to be executed by the thread. This method must, of course, match the signature of the delegate, which takes one `object` parameter and returns no value. Next, the `QueueUserWorkItem` static method of the `ThreadPool` class is called. The first parameter to this method is the delegate; it also takes an optional second parameter that can be used to pass information to the method called by the delegate.

To illustrate, let's alter the previous example to acquire threads from a pool rather than creating them explicitly. An object parameter must be added to `FetchImage` so that it matches the delegate signature. Then, replace the code to create threads with these two statements:

```
WaitCallback callBack = new WaitCallback(FetchImage);
ThreadPool.QueueUserWorkItem(callBack, "image returned");
```

This places a request on the thread pool queue for the next available thread. The first time this runs, the pool must create a thread, which points out an important fact about the thread pool. It contains no threads when it is created, and handles all thread requests by either creating a thread or activating one already in the pool. The pool has a limit (25) on the number of threads it can hold, and if these are all used, a request must wait for a thread to be returned. You can get some information about the status of the thread pool using the `GetAvailableThreads` method:

```
int workerThreads;
int asyncThreads;
ThreadPool.GetAvailableThreads(out workerThreads, out
asyncThreads);
```

This method returns two values: the difference between the maximum number of worker and asynchronous threads the pool supports, and the number of each currently active. Thus, if three worker threads are being used, the `workerThreads` argument has a value of 22.

The thread pool is most useful for applications that repeatedly require threads for a short duration. For an application that requires only a few threads that run simultaneously, the thread pool offers little advantage. In fact, the time required to create a thread and place it in the thread pool exceeds that of explicitly creating a new thread.

Core Note

Threads exist in the thread pool in a suspended state. If a thread is not used in a given time interval, it destroys itself—freeing its resources.

Timers

Many applications have a need to perform polling periodically to collect information or check the status of devices attached to a port. Conceptually, this could be implemented by coupling a timer with a delegate: The delegate handles the call to a specified method, while the timer invokes the delegate to place the calls at a specified interval. In .NET, it is not necessary to write your own code to do this; instead, you can use its prepackaged `Timer` classes. Let's look at a couple of the most useful ones: `System.Timers.Timer` and `Windows.Forms.Timer`. The former is for general use, whereas the latter is designed for Windows Forms applications.

System.Timers.Timer Class

To use the `Timer` class, simply register an event handling method or methods with the class's `Elapsed` event. The signature of the method(s) must match that of the `ElapsedEventHandler` delegate associated with the event:

```
public delegate void ElapsedEventHandler(object sender,
                                         ElapsedEventArgs e);
```

The `Elapsed` event occurs at an interval specified by the `Timer.Interval` property. A thread from the thread pool is used to make the call into the event handler(s). This code segment demonstrates how the `Timer` causes a method to be called every second:

```
using System;
using System.Timers;
```

```
public class TimerTest
{
   public static void Main()
   {
      SetTimer t = new SetTimer();
      t.StartTimer();
   }
}
class SetTimer
{
   int istart;
   public void StartTimer()
   {
      istart= Environment.TickCount; //Time when execution begins
         Timer myTimer = new myTimer();
         myTimer.Elapsed+=new ElapsedEventHandler(OnTimedEvent);
      myTimer.Interval=1000;                 // 1000 milliseconds
      myTimer.Enabled=true;
      Console.WriteLine("Press any key to end program.");
      Console.Read();
      myTimer.Stop();
   }
   // Timer event handler
   private void OnTimedEvent(object source, ElapsedEventArgs e)
   {
      Console.WriteLine("Elapsed Time: {0}",
                     Environment.TickCount-istart);
   }
}
```

System.Windows.Forms.Timer Class

We can dispense with a code example of this class, because its implementation parallels that of the Timers.Timer class, with two differences: It uses a Tick exception rather than Elapsed, and it uses the familiar EventHandler as its delegate. However, the feature that distinguishes it from the other Timer class is that it does not use a thread from the thread pool to call a method. Instead, it places calls on a queue to be handled by the main UI thread. Except for situations where the time required by the invoked method may make the form unresponsive, a timer is preferable to using threading. It eliminates the need to deal with concurrent threads and also enables the event handler to directly update the form's controls—something that cannot be done by code on another thread.

13.4 Thread Synchronization

Thread synchronization refers to the techniques employed to share resources among concurrent threads in an efficient and orderly manner. The specific objective of these techniques is to ensure *thread safety*. A class (or its members) is thread-safe when it can be accessed by multiple threads without having its state corrupted. The potential corruption arises from the nature of thread scheduling. Recall from the previous section that a thread executes in time slices. If it does not finish its task, its state is preserved and later restored when the thread resumes execution. However, while suspended, another thread may have executed the same method and altered some global variables or database values that invalidate the results of the original thread. As an example, consider the pseudo-code in Figure 13-7 that describes how concurrent threads execute the same code segment.

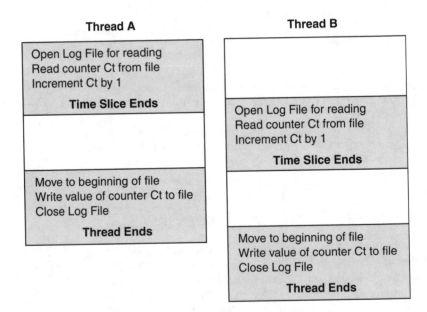

Figure 13-7   Execution path that requires synchronization

Because the first thread is suspended before it updates the log file, both threads update the file with the same value. Because server applications may have hundreds of active threads, there is clear need for a mechanism to control access to shared resources.

The implementation of the pseudo-code is presented in Listing 13-8. Executing this code multiple times produces inconsistent results, which is the pitfall of using code that is not thread-safe. About half the time, the counter is incremented correctly by 2; other times, the first thread is preempted and the second thread gets in before the first finishes updating. In this case, the counter is incorrectly incremented by 1.

Listing 13-8	Example of Class That Requires Synchronization

```
using System;
using System.Threading;
using System.IO;
public class MyApp
{
    public static void Main()
    {
        CallerClass cc = new CallerClass();
        Thread worker1 =
                new Thread(new ThreadStart(cc.CallUpdate));
        Thread worker2 =
                new Thread(new ThreadStart(cc.CallUpdate));
        worker1.Start();
        worker2.Start();
    }
}
public class CallerClass
{
    WorkClass wc;
    public CallerClass()
    {
        wc= new WorkClass();   // create object to update log
    }
    public void CallUpdate()
    {
        wc.UpdateLog();
    }
}
public class WorkClass
{
    public void UpdateLog()
    {
```

Listing 13-8	Example of Class That Requires Synchronization *(continued)*

```
    // Open stream for reading and writing
    try
    {
        FileStream fs = new
        FileStream(@"c:\log.txt",FileMode.OpenOrCreate,
            FileAccess.ReadWrite, FileShare.ReadWrite);
        StreamReader sr = new StreamReader(fs);
        // Read current counter
        string ctr = sr.ReadLine();
        if(ctr==null) ctr="0";
        int oldCt = int.Parse(ctr) + 1;
        // If the thread's time slice ends here, the counter
        // is not updated.
        fs.Seek(0,SeekOrigin.Begin);
        StreamWriter sw= new StreamWriter(fs);
        sw.WriteLine(oldCt.ToString());
        Console.WriteLine(oldCt);
        sw.Close();
        sr.Close();
    } catch(Exception ex)
        {
            Console.WriteLine(ex.Message);
        }
    }
}    // WorkClass
```

A solution is to ensure that after a thread invokes UpdateLog, no other thread can access it until the method completes execution. That is essentially how synchronization works: permitting only one thread to have ownership of a resource at a given time. Only when the owner voluntarily relinquishes ownership of the code or resource is it made available to another thread. Let's examine the different synchronization techniques available to implement this strategy.

The Synchronization Attribute

The developers of .NET recognized that the overhead required to make all classes thread-safe by default would result in unacceptable performance. Their solution was to create a .NET architecture that naturally supports the ability to lock code segments, but leaves the choice and technique up to the developer. An example of this is the optional Synchronization attribute. When attached to a class, it instructs

.NET to give a thread exclusive access to an object's code until the thread completes execution. Here is the code that implements this type of synchronization in the log update example:

```
[Synchronization]
public class WorkClass: ContextBoundObject
```

The class to which the [Synchronization] attribute is applied should derive from the ContextBoundObject class. When .NET sees this is a base class, it places the object in a *context* and applies the synchronization to the context. This is referred to as *context-bound synchronization*. For this to make sense, let's look at the .NET architecture to understand what a context is.

When an application starts, the operating system runs it inside a process. The .NET runtime is then loaded and creates one or more application domains (App-Domains) inside the process. As we will see in the next chapter, these are essentially logical processes that provide the managed environment demanded by .NET applications. Just as a process may contain multiple AppDomains, an AppDomain may contain multiple contexts.

A context can be defined as a logical grouping of components (objects) that share the same .NET *component services*. Think of a context as a layer that .NET wraps around an object so that it can apply a service to it. When a call is made to this object, it is intercepted by .NET and the requested service is applied before the call is routed to the object. Synchronization is one type of component service. In our example, .NET intercepts the call to UpdateLog and blocks the calling thread if another thread has ownership of the context containing this method. Another component service of interest—*call authorization*—enables .NET to check the calling thread to ensure it has the proper credentials to access the object.

The [Synchronization] attribute is the easiest way to control thread access to a class—only two statements are changed in our preceding example. The drawback to this approach is that it must be applied to the entire class—even if only a small section of the class contains critical code that requires thread synchronization. The manual synchronization approaches we look at next permit a more granular implementation.

The Monitor Class

The Monitor class allows a single thread to place a lock on an object. Its methods are used to control thread access to an entire object or selected sections of code in an object. Enter and Exit are its most commonly used methods. Enter assigns ownership of the lock to the calling thread and prevents any other thread from acquiring it as long as the thread owns it. Exit releases the lock. Let's look at these methods in action.

Using Monitor to Lock an Object

`Monitor.Enter` takes an object as a parameter and attempts to grant the current thread exclusive access to the object. If another thread owns the object, the requesting thread is blocked until the object is free. The object is freed by executing the complementary `Monitor.Exit`.

To illustrate the use of a monitor, let's return to the example in Listing 13-8 in which two threads compete to read and update a log file. The read and write operations are performed by calling the `UpdateLog` method on a `WorkClass` object. To ensure these operations are not interrupted, we can use a monitor to lock the object until the method completes executing. As shown here, it requires adding only two statements:

```
public void CallUpdate()
{
    Monitor.Enter(wc);     // wc is WorkClass object
    wc.UpdateLog();
    Monitor.Exit(wc);
```

In addition to `Monitor.Enter`, there is a `Monitor.TryEnter` method that attempts to acquire an exclusive lock and return a `true` or `false` value indicating whether it succeeds. Its overloads include one that accepts a parameter specifying the number of millseconds to wait for the lock:

```
if (!Monitor.TryEnter(obj) return; // Return if lock unavailable
if (!Monitor.TryEnter(obj, 500) return; // Wait 500 ms for lock
```

Encapsulating a Monitor

A problem with the preceding approach is that it relies on clients to use the monitor for locking; however, there is nothing to prevent them from executing `UpdateLog` without first applying the lock. To avoid this, a better design approach is to encapsulate the lock(s) in the code that accesses the shared resource(s). As shown here, by placing `Monitor.Enter` inside `UpdateLog`, the thread that gains access to this lock has exclusive control of the code within the scope of the monitor (to the point where `Monitor.Exit` is executed).

```
public void UpdateLog()
{
    Monitor.Enter(this);    // Acquire a lock
    try
    {
        // Code to be synchronized
    }
    finally   // Always executed
```

```
{
    Monitor.Exit(this);    // Relinquish lock
}
```

Note the use of `finally` to ensure that `Monitor.Exit` executes. This is critical, because if it does not execute, other threads calling this code are indefinitely blocked. To make it easier to construct the monitor code, C# includes the `lock` statement as a shortcut to the `try/finally` block. For example, the previous statements can be replaced with the following:

```
lock(this)
{
    // Code to be synchronized
}
```

`Monitor` and `lock` can also be used with static methods and properties. To do so, pass the type of object as a command parameter rather than the object itself:

```
Monitor.Enter(typeof(WorkClass));
// Synchronized code ...
Monitor.Exit(typeof(WorkClass));
```

Core Recommendation

Be wary of using synchronization in static methods. Deadlocks can result when a static method in class A calls static methods in class B, and vice versa. Even if a deadlock does not occur, performance is likely to suffer.

The Mutex

To understand the `Mutex` class, it is first necessary to have some familiarity with the `WaitHandle` class from which it is derived. This abstract class defines "wait" methods that are used by a thread to gain ownership of a `WaitHandle` object, such as a mutex. We saw earlier in the chapter (refer to Table 13-1) how asynchronous calls use the `WaitOne` method to block a thread until the asynchronous operation is completed. There is also a `WaitAll` method that can be used to block a thread until a set of `WaitHandle` objects—or the resources they protect—are available.

An application can create an instance of the `Mutex` class using one of several constructors. The most useful are

```
public Mutex();
public Mutex(bool initiallyOwned);
public Mutex(bool initiallyOwned, string name);
```

The two optional parameters are important. The *initiallyOwned* parameter indicates whether the thread creating the object wants to have immediate ownership of it. This is usually set to `false` when the mutex is created within a class whose resources it is protecting. The *name* parameter permits a name or identifier to be assigned to the mutex. This permits a specific mutex to be referenced across App-Domains and even processes. Because thread safety usually relies on encapsulating the locking techniques within an object, exposing them by name to outside methods is not recommended.

Using a mutex to provide thread-safe code is a straightforward process. A mutex object is created, and calls to its wait methods are placed strategically in the code where single thread access is necessary. The wait method serves as a request for ownership of the mutex. If another thread owns it, the requesting thread is blocked and placed on a wait queue. The thread remains blocked until the mutex receives a signal from its owner that it has been released. An owner thread releases a mutex in two ways: by calling the object's `ReleaseMutex` method or when the thread is terminated. Here is an example of how the log update application is altered to use a mutex to provide thread safety:

```
public class WorkClass
{
   Mutex logMutex;
   public WorkClass()
   {
      logMutex = new Mutex(false);
   }

   public void UpdateLog()
   {
      logMutex.WaitOne();   // Wait for mutex to become available
        // Code to be synchronized
      logMutex.ReleaseMutex();
   }
}
```

As part of creating an instance of `WorkClass`, the constructor creates an instance of the `Mutex` class. The Boolean `false` parameter passed to its constructor indicates that it is not owned (the parameterless constructor also sets ownership to `false`). The first thread that executes `UpdateLog` then gains access to the mutex through the `WaitOne` call; when the second thread executes this statement, it is blocked until the first thread releases the mutex.

The Semaphore

The Semaphore class is another WaitHandle derived class. It functions as a shared counter and—like a mutex—uses a wait call to control thread access to a code section or resource. Unlike a mutex, it permits multiple threads to concurrently access a resource. The number of threads is limited only by the specified maximum value of the semaphore.

When a thread issues a semaphore wait call, the thread is not blocked if the semaphore value is greater than 0. It is given access to the code and the semaphore value is decremented by 1. The semaphore value is incremented when the thread calls the semaphore's Release method. These characteristics make the semaphore a useful tool for managing a limited number of resources such as connections or windows that can be opened in an application.

The Semaphore class has several overloaded constructor formats, but all require the two parameters shown in this version:

```
public Semaphore(int initialCount, int maximumCount );
```

The *maximumCount* parameter specifies the maximum number of concurrent thread requests the semaphore can handle; *initialCount* is the initial number of requests the semaphore can handle. Here is an example:

```
Semaphore s = new Semaphore(5,10);
```

This semaphore permits a maximum of 10 concurrent threads to access a resource. When it is first created, only 5 are permitted. To increase this number, execute the Semaphore.Release(n) command—where n is the number used to increment the count permitted. The intended purpose of this command is to free resources when a thread completes executing and wants to exit a semaphore. However, the command can be issued even if the thread has never requested the semaphore.

Now let's see how the Semaphore class can be used to provide synchronization for the log update example. As a WaitHandle derived class, its implementation is almost identical to the mutex. In this example, the semaphore is created with its initial and maximum values set to 1—thus restricting access to one thread at a time.

```
public class WorkClass
{
    private Semaphore s;
    public WorkClass()
    {
        // Permit one thread to have access to the semaphore
        s  = new Semaphore(1, 1);
    }
```

```
public void UpdateLog(object obj)
{
    try {
        s.WaitOne();    // Blocks current thread
    // code to update log ...
    } finally
    {
        s.Release();
    }
}
}
```

Avoiding Deadlock

When concurrent threads compete for resources, there is always the possibility that a thread may be blocked from accessing a resource (*starvation*) or that a set of threads may be blocked while waiting for a condition that cannot be resolved. This *deadlock* situation most often arises when thread A, which owns a resource, also needs a resource owned by thread B; meanwhile, thread B needs the resource owned by thread A. When thread A makes its request, it is put in suspended mode until the resource owned by B is available. This, of course, prevents thread B from accessing A's resource. Figure 13-8 depicts this situation.

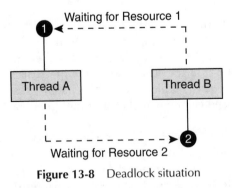

Figure 13-8   Deadlock situation

Most deadlocks can be traced to code that allows resources to be locked in an inconsistent manner. As an example, consider an application that transfers money from one bank account to another using the method shown here:

```
public void Transfer(Account acctFrom,
                     Account acctTo, decimal amt)
{
```

```
    Monitor.Enter(acctFrom);   // Acquire lock on from account
    Monitor.Enter(acctTo);     // Acquire lock on to account
    // Perform transfer ...
    Monitor.Exit(acctFrom);    // Release lock
    Monitor.Exit(acctTo);      // Release lock
}
```

As you would expect, the method locks both account objects so that it has exclusive control before performing the transaction. Now, suppose two threads are running and simultaneously call this method to perform a funds transfer:

```
Thread A:   Transfer(Acct1000, Acct1500, 500.00);
Thread B:   Transfer(Acct1500, Acct1000, 300.00);
```

The problem is that the two threads are attempting to acquire the same resources (accounts) in a different order and run the risk of creating a deadlock if one is preempted before acquiring both locks. There are a couple of solutions. First, we could lock the code segment being executed to prevent a thread from being preempted until both resources are acquired:

```
lock(this)
{
    ... Monitor statements
}
```

Unfortunately, this can produce a performance bottleneck. Suppose another method is working with one of the account objects required for the current transaction. The thread executing the method is blocked as well as all other threads waiting to perform a funds transfer.

A second solution—recommended for multithreading in general—is to *impose some order on the condition variables that determine how locking can occur.* In this example, we can impose a lock sequence based on the objects' account numbers. Specifically, a lock must be acquired on the account with the lower account number before the second lock can be obtained.

```
If(acctFrom < acctTo)
{
    Monitor.Enter(acctFrom);
    Monitor.Enter(acctTo);
}else
{
    Monitor.Enter(acctTo);
    Monitor.Enter(acctFrom);
}
```

As this example should demonstrate, a deadlock is not caused by thread synchronization per se, but by poorly designed thread synchronization. To avoid this, code should be designed to guarantee that threads acquire resource locks in a consistent order.

Summary of Synchronization Techniques

Table 13-2 provides an overview of the synchronization techniques discussed in this chapter and provides general advice on selecting the one to best suit your application's needs.

Table 13-2   Overview of Selected Thread Synchronization Techniques

Technique	Description	When to Use
Synchronization attribute	An attribute that can be used with classes that inherit from the `ContextBoundObject` class.	To limit thread access to an entire object. If you need to protect only a small section of code while permitting access to other class members, choose another technique.
Monitor/lock	Locks selected code segments that are encased between a `Monitor.Enter` and `Monitor.Exit` statement. Lock provides equivalent code with built-in event handling.	To provide single thread access to selected code segments in an object. To synchronize access to value types, use a mutex.
Mutex	Uses wait methods inherited from the `WaitHandle` class to manage thread access to resources.	To permit a thread to request exclusive access to one or more resources. Requests can be made across AppDomains and processes.
Semaphore	Uses wait methods inherited from the `WaitHandle` class to manage multiple concurrent thread access to resources.	To make a limited number of resources available concurrently to more than one thread.

In addition to these, .NET offers specialized synchronization classes that are designed for narrowly defined tasks. These include `Interlocked`, which is used to increment and exchange values, and `ReaderWriterLock`, which locks the writing operation on a file but leaves reading open to all threads. Refer to online documentation (such as MSDN) for details on using these.

13.5 Summary

Designing an application to perform tasks concurrently can result in an application that provides better responsiveness to a user and manages system resources more efficiently. This requires replacing the traditional synchronous approach to code execution with an asynchronous approach that uses threads. A thread is a path of execution. Each program begins running on a main thread that may create worker threads to perform tasks concurrent to its own processing.

One way to create a thread that executes a specified method is to make an *asynchronous delegate invocation*. This is done by creating a delegate and passing it the name of the method to be called. The delegate is then invoked with its `BeginInvoke` method. This causes the delegate's method to be executed on a thread that is fetched from a *thread pool* managed by .NET. An optional parameter to `BeginInvoke` is a callback method that is called when the worker thread ends. Unlike synchronous processing, in which a call to a method blocks processing in the calling method, asynchronous invocation returns control to the calling method so that it can continue processing.

Applications that require more control over a thread can create their own by passing a `ThreadStart` or `ParameterizedThreadStart` delegate to the `Thread` constructor. A thread is executed by calling its `Start` method.

After the decision is made to use threads, the problem of *thread-safe* code must be considered. An operating system executes threads in time slices. When a thread's time expires, it is swapped out and another thread begins executing. The effects of a thread being interrupted in the middle of a task can produce unpredictable results. Thread synchronization is used to ensure that one thread has exclusive access to a code path until it completes processing. .NET provides several approaches to synchronization: an automatic approach that uses the `Synchronization` attribute to lock an object until a thread has finished using it; and the `Mutex`, `Monitor`, and `Semaphore` classes that provide a manual—but more granular—approach to implementing thread safety.

13.6 Test Your Understanding

1. An asynchronous delegate must have a void return value.

   a. True
   b. False

2. Given this delegate

    ```
    private delegate void myDelegate(string msg);
    myDelegate d = new myDelegate(PrintMessage);
    ```

    identify the role of ia, p1, p2, and p3 in this BeginInvoke call:

    ```
    ia = d.BeginInvoke(p1, p2, p3);
    ```

3. What is thread local storage used for?

4. What is the default maximum number of threads that a thread pool can hold?

5. What two delegates are used to create a thread directly, and how do they differ?

6. Describe a syntactically simpler way to generate the following code:

    ```
    Monitor.Enter(obj);
    {
        // Code to synchronize
    } finally {
        Monitor.Exit(obj);
    }
    ```

7. How many times does the following code print the console message?

    ```
    private static s;
    public static void Main()
    {
        s = new Semaphore(0, 3);
        // Create and start five numbered threads
        for(int i = 1; i <= 5; i++)
        {
            Thread t = new Thread(new ThreadStart(Worker));
            t.Start();
        }
    }
    private static void Worker(object num)
    {
        s.WaitOne();
        Console.WriteLine("Thread enters semaphore  ");
        Thread.Sleep(100);
        s.Release();
    }
    ```

    a. 0
    b. 1
    c. 3
    d. 5

8. What happens when you attempt to run this code?

```
class UseMutex
{
    public void ThreadStart()
    {
        Mutex mutex = new Mutex(false, "MyMutex");
        mutex.WaitOne();
        Console.WriteLine("Worker Thread");
    }

    static void Main()
    {
        UseMutex obj = new UseMutex();
        Thread thread = new Thread(
                new ThreadStart(obj.ThreadStart));
        Mutex mutex = new Mutex(true, "MyMutex");
        thread.Start();
        Thread.Sleep(1000);
        Console.WriteLine("Primary Thread");
        mutex.ReleaseMutex();
    }
}
```

    a. It prints: Worker Thread
                       Primary Thread
    b. It prints: Primary Thread
                       Worker Thread
    c. The program deadlocks and there is no output.

9. To illustrate deadlocking, Edsger Dijkstra introduced a "Dining Philosopher" metaphor that has become a classical way of introducing resource allocation and deadlocking. The metaphor (with variations) goes like this:

Five philosophers, who spend their lives alternately thinking and eating, are sitting around a table. In the center of the round table is an infinite supply of food. Before each philosopher is a plate, and between each pair of plates is a single chopstick. Once a philosopher quits thinking, he or she attempts to eat. In order to eat, a philosopher must have possession of the chopstick to the left and right of the plate.

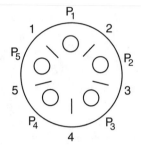

Your challenge is to design a program that creates five threads—one to represent each philosopher—that continually perform the tasks of thinking and eating. The program should implement a synchronization scheme that allows each thread to periodically acquire two chopsticks so that it can eat for a fixed or random (your choice) amount of time. After eating, a philosopher should release its chopsticks and think for a while before trying to eat again.

Hint: Use `Monitor.Wait()` to try to acquire chopsticks, and `Monitor.PulseAll()` to notify all threads that chopsticks are being released.

CREATING DISTRIBUTED APPLICATIONS WITH REMOTING

Topics in This Chapter

- *Application Domains:* The logical partition within which a .NET application runs is called an application domain (or AppDomain). In this chapter, we examine how applications communicate and access resources across AppDomain boundaries.

- *Remoting:* An application may call a method that resides in another AppDomain, another process, or on another machine. This process, known as remoting, requires creating a client and server that agree to communicate across these boundaries. This chapter looks at the options available to implement remoting.

- *Leasing and Sponsorship:* Garbage Collection in .NET does not recognize remote references when removing objects. To prevent a remote object from being destroyed, .NET provides a `Lease` object that is used to reference a remote object so that it avoids Garbage Collection.

Chapter 14

This chapter introduces the .NET way of developing distributed applications. The emphasis is on how a technique known as *remoting* permits client computers to access resources on other local or remote computers. Remoting is typically designed for intranet applications, although it does support the HTTP protocol for communicating over the Internet. In some cases, it may be regarded as an alternative to Web Services and a Web browser. We'll see in this chapter that remoting offers more flexibility and a richer set of features than these standard Web-based solutions.

To fully appreciate remoting technology, it is necessary to understand the relationship among processes, application domains, and assemblies. Toward that end, the first section explains the role of the application domain in the .NET architecture. We'll see that the security and code isolation it offers requires that objects in separate AppDomains agree upon the port number, protocol, and type of message formatting before they can communicate.

The second section forms the heart of the chapter. It provides both a conceptual and hands-on approach to remoting. Code examples illustrate how to select and implement the remoting options that best fit a distributed application. The section describes how to create client- and server-activated objects, select formatting and protocol options, deploy assemblies for a distributed application, and use leases to manage the lifetime of an object.

You may want to follow up this chapter by reading the chapter on Web Services, which presents a second .NET technique for implementing a distributed application. Although there are conceptual similarities between remoting and Web Services, there are also distinct differences in performance, interoperability, and implementation complexity that an architect must understand. A reading of these chapters should provide the know-how to select the approach that best meets the requirements of your distributed application.

14.1 Application Domains

When you install .NET on a machine, you create a virtual, managed environment in which applications can run. This environment is designed to insulate applications from the demands and vagaries of the host operating system. The AppDomain is one of the key architectural features supporting the managed environment.

Most operating systems see the world in terms of processes that provide the resources, such as memory and tables required by applications. Because a .NET application cannot run directly in the unmanaged process, .NET partitions a process into one or more logical areas in which assemblies execute. These logical areas are AppDomains. As shown in Figure 14-1, a process may contain more than one App-Domain and an AppDomain may contain one or more assemblies. A default AppDo-main is created when the Common Language Runtime (CLR) initializes, and additional ones are created by the CLR as needed. An application may also instruct the CLR to create a new AppDomain.

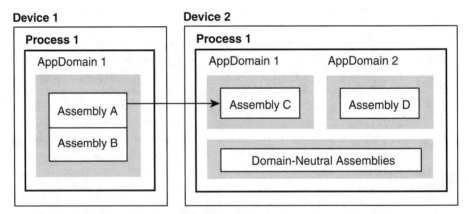

Figure 14-1   Multiple application domains may reside in a single process

Advantages of AppDomains

Aside from the need for a managed environment, the use of AppDomains provides several advantages over the traditional process-based architecture:

- **Code Isolation.** AppDomains institute a level of fault isolation that prevents a code failure in one AppDomain from causing another App-Domain to crash. .NET achieves this code separation in two ways: by preventing an AppDomain from directly referencing objects in another

AppDomain, and by having each AppDomain load and maintain its own copy of key assemblies that allow it to run independently. As a by-product of this, an AppDomain can be selectively debugged and unloaded without directly affecting other AppDomains in the process.

- **Performance.** Implementing an application to run in multiple App-Domains can produce better performance than a comparable design that relies on multiple processes. This efficiency derives from several factors: A physical process requires more memory and resources than AppDomains, which share the resources of a single process; creating and disposing of processes is much more time consuming than comparable operations on AppDomains; and making a call between processes is slower and requires more overhead than making a call between AppDomains residing in the same process.

- **Security.** By its very nature, an AppDomain presents a security boundary between its contained resources and assemblies attempting to access them. To cross this boundary, an outside assembly must rely on *remoting*, which requires cooperation between the AppDomains. In addition, an AppDomain has its own security policy that it can impose upon assemblies to restrict their permissible operations. This "sandbox" security model allows AppDomains to ensure that assemblies are well behaved. In Chapter 15, "Code Refinement, Security, and Deployment," we'll look at examples of using AppDomains to enforce code security.

Application Domains and Assemblies

When an application runs, it may reference code in several assemblies. By default, the CLR loads these referenced assemblies into the AppDomain of the calling assembly. This means that if a process contains multiple AppDomains that reference the same assembly, a copy of that assembly is placed in each domain. However, it is possible to override the default and share a single assembly among multiple domains. Assemblies used in this manner are referred to as *domain-neutral assemblies*.

Some crucial assemblies required by all applications are automatically loaded as domain-neutral. The most prominent of these is `mscorlib.dll`, an assembly that contains the native types integral to the .NET Framework. However, a developer can also specify that a custom assembly be made domain-neutral so that domains can share it.

The use of a domain-neutral assembly saves memory. However, there is a trade-off in terms of performance and flexibility in assigning permissions to assemblies. Even shared assemblies require that their static data and methods be copied into the App-Domains that reference them. The overhead to manage this can slow performance. Only one set of permissions, defining what operations an assembly can perform, can be assigned to domain-neutral assemblies. Thus, if an AppDomain requires a different set of permissions, it must have its own copy of the assembly.

Working with the AppDomain Class

The `System.AppDomain` class exposes methods and properties that enable an application to create an AppDomain, remove an AppDomain from a process, enumerate the assemblies it contains, and identify itself by name or internal ID. The majority of applications do not require programming at the AppDomain level; however, applications with a need to isolate a custom type library, or include special security features, will find direct interaction with the class a necessity.

In this section, we'll look at an example that illustrates some of the basic techniques used to manipulate an AppDomain. Working though this code should not only make you familiar with the basic class members, but also further clarify the relationship that exists among a process, an AppDomain, and an assembly.

The example defines two classes: `RemoteClass`, which is compiled into a DLL file, and `AppDomainClient`, which is compiled into `AppdTestClient.exe`. `RemoteClass` is packaged as an assembly that does nothing more than display the name of the domain in which it is running. It uses the static `AppDomain.Current-Domain` property to retrieve the current domain, and displays its name using the `FriendlyName` property.

Note that `RemoteClass` derives from `MarshalByRefObject`. As we see in the next section on remoting, this is required if an object is to be accessed from an App-Domain other than its own.

```
// AppdTestClass.dll assembly
using System;
using System.Diagnostics;
namespace AppDomainTest
{
    public class RemoteClass: MarshalByRefObject
    {
        public void ShowDomain()
        {
            AppDomain currentAppDomain = AppDomain.CurrentDomain;
            Console.WriteLine("Domain:{0}",
                    currentAppDomain.FriendlyName);
        }
    }
}
```

`AppDomainClient`, shown in Listing 14-1, illustrates how to use several `AppDomain` class members. It begins by creating an instance of `RemoteClass` using the following statement:

```
(RemoteClass)currentAppDomain.CreateInstanceAndUnwrap(
              "appdtestclass", "AppDomainTest.RemoteClass");
```

The first parameter is the name of the assembly, and the second is the name of the type being instantiated. This statement returns an object that is cast to an instance of RemoteClass. The object's ShowDomain method is then executed to display the domain it is running in. In this case, the console output is appdtestclient.exe, the default name given to the AppDomain when the assembly is executed. The remainder of the code displays the assemblies in the AppDomain, creates a new AppDomain, and repeats these operations for it.

Listing 14-1	Working with Application Domains

```
// AppdTestClient.exe assembly
using System;
using System.Reflection;
using AppDomainTest;
public class AppDomainClient
{
    static void Main()
    {
        AppDomain currentAppDomain;
        currentAppDomain = AppDomain.CurrentDomain;
        RemoteClass rc;
        // (1) Create instance of RemoteClass
        rc=(RemoteClass)currentAppDomain.CreateInstanceAndUnwrap(
                "appdtestclass", "AppDomainTest.RemoteClass");
        // (2) Execute method on RemoteClass
        rc.ShowDomain();
        // (3) Show assemblies in this appdomain
        Assembly[] currAssemblies =
               currentAppDomain.GetAssemblies();
        ShowAssemblies (currAssemblies);
        // (4) Create a new AppDomain
        AppDomain myAppDomain =
               AppDomain.CreateDomain("New Domain");
        rc=(RemoteClass)myAppDomain.CreateInstanceAndUnwrap(
               "appdtestclass", "AppDomainTest.RemoteClass");
        rc.ShowDomain();
        // (5) Show assemblies in new appdomain
        currAssemblies = myAppDomain.GetAssemblies();
        ShowAssemblies(currAssemblies);
        // (6) The domain a thread runs in can be displayed
        Console.Write(
               System.Threading.Thread.GetDomain().FriendlyName);
```

Listing 14-1   Working with Application Domains *(continued)*

```
    // (7) Unload the new appdomain from the process
    AppDomain.Unload(myAppDomain);
}

    private static void ShowAssemblies(
        Assembly[] currAssemblies)
    {
        foreach(Assembly a in currAssemblies)
        {
            Console.WriteLine(
                " Assembly Name: {0}",a.GetName().Name);
        }
    }
}
```

Figure 14-2 shows the three assemblies that exist in the default AppDomain: mscor-lib, appdtestclient, and appdtestclass. Mscorlib is automatically loaded by .NET because it contains the System namespace required by the application.

Note that the process also includes a second domain that holds two assemblies. This AppDomain is created using the static CreateDomain method:

```
AppDomain myAppDomain = AppDomain.CreateDomain("New Domain");
```

The two assemblies are loaded when AppDomainClient creates an instance of RemoteClass. As you would expect, executing ShowDomain causes the console to display "New Domain" as the name of the current domain.

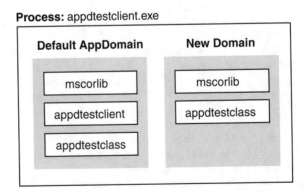

Figure 14-2   AppDomains and assemblies created from code in Listing 14-1

The final step in the example is to unload the new domain from the process. Note that .NET does not permit an individual assembly to be unloaded from an AppDomain.

14.2 Remoting

At its core, remoting is as a way to permit applications in separate AppDomains to communicate and exchange data. This is usually characterized as a client-server relationship in which the client accesses resources or objects on a remote server that agrees to provide access. The way in which this agreement between client and server is implemented is what remoting is all about. The physical proximity of the App-Domains does not matter: They may be in the same process, in different processes, or on different machines on different continents.

Remoting is often portrayed as a concept that is difficult to understand and implement—particularly when compared to Web Services. This sentiment is misleading and simply not true for many applications.

Consider the steps required to enable a client to access an object on a remote server:

- Create a TCP or HTTP connection between the client and server.
- Select how the messages sent between server and client are formatted.
- Register the type that is to be accessed remotely.
- Create the remote object and activate it from the server or the client.

.NET takes care of all the details. You don't have to understand the underlying details of TCP, HTTP, or ports—just specify that you want a connection and what port to use. If HTTP is selected, communications use a Simple Object Access Protocol (SOAP) format; for TCP, binary is used. The registration process occurs on both the server and client. The client selects a registration method and passes it a couple of parameters that specify the address of the server and the type (class) to be accessed. The server registers the types and ports that it wants to make available to clients, and how it will make them available. For example, it may implement the object as a singleton that is created once and handles calls from all clients; or it may choose to create a new object to handle each call.

Figure 14-3 depicts the learning curve that developers new to remoting can expect to encounter. By hiding much of the underlying communications details, .NET enables a developer to quickly develop functioning applications that can access remote objects. The complexity often associated with remoting comes into play as you move further up the learning curve to take advantage of advanced remoting techniques such as creating sink providers and custom transport channels. Knowledge of these advanced techniques enables one to customize the way distributed applications communicate. For information on these topics, refer to a book on advanced .NET remoting, such as *Advanced .NET Remoting* by Ingo Rammer.[1]

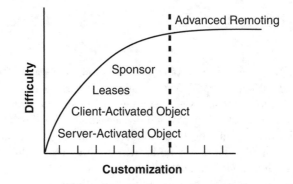

Figure 14-3   The learning curve for developing remoting applications

This chapter focuses on topics to the left of the advanced remoting line. You'll learn how to design applications that permit remote objects to be created by either the server or the client, how to control the lifetime of these objects, and how to design and deploy assemblies that best take advantage of the remoting architecture. There are quite a few code examples whose purpose is to present prototypes that you can use to implement a wide range of remoting applications. Included are examples of a server that streams requested images to clients, and a message server that both receives messages and sends them to the targeted recipient upon request.

Remoting Architecture

When a client attempts to invoke a method on a remote object, its call passes through several layers on the client side. The first of these is a *proxy*—an abstract class that has the same interface as the remote object it represents. It verifies that the number and type of arguments in the call are correct, packages the request into a message, and passes it to the client *channel*. The channel is responsible for transporting the request to the remote object. At a minimum, the channel consists of a *formatter sink* that serializes the request into a stream and a client *transport sink* that actually transmits the request to a port on the server. The sinks within a channel are referred to as a *sink chain*. Aside from the two standard sinks, the channel may also contain custom sinks that operate on the request stream.

---

1. *Advanced .NET Remoting*, Second Edition, by Ingo Rammer and Mario Szpuszta; Apress, 2005.

On the server side, the process is reversed, as the server transport sink receives the message and sends it up the chain. After the formatter rebuilds the request from the stream, .NET creates the object on the server and executes the requested method.

Figure 14-4 illustrates the client-server roles in a remoting architecture. Let's examine its three key components: proxies, formatter classes, and channel classes.

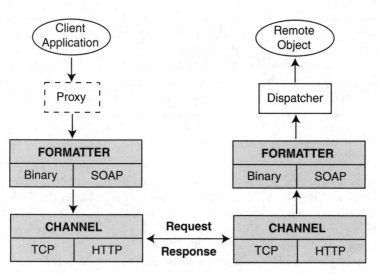

Figure 14-4   High-level view of .NET remoting architecture

Proxies

When a client attempts to communicate with a remote object, its reference to the object is actually handled by an intermediary known as a *proxy*. For .NET remoting, there are two types of proxies: a *transparent proxy* that the client communicates with directly, and a *real proxy* that takes the client request and forwards it to the remote object.

The transparent proxy is created by the CLR to present an interface to the client that is identical to the remote class. This enables the CLR to verify that all client calls match the signature of the target method—that is, the type and number of parameters match. Although the CLR takes care of constructing the transparent proxy, the developer is responsible for ensuring that the CLR has the metadata that defines the remote class available at compile time and runtime. The easiest way is to provide the client with a copy of the server assembly that contains the class. But, as we discuss later, there are better alternatives.

After the transparent proxy verifies the call, it packages the request into a message object—a class that implements the IMessage interface. The message object is passed as a parameter to the real proxy's Invoke method, which passes it into a channel. There, a formatter object serializes the message and passes it to a channel object that physically sends the message to the remote object.

Core Note

The real proxy that is responsible for sending a message to a remote object is an implementation of the RealProxy class that is generated automatically by the CLR. Although this meets the needs of most remoting applications, a developer has the option of creating a custom implementation.

Formatters

Two formatters are included as part of the .NET Remoting classes: a binary formatter and a SOAP formatter. SOAP, which is discussed in detail in the Web Services chapter, serializes messages into an XML format. Binary produces a much smaller message stream than SOAP, because it sends the message as a raw byte stream.

By default, SOAP is used when the HTTP protocol is selected and binary is used with the TCP protocol. However, you can also choose to send SOAP over TCP and binary over HTTP. Although not as efficient as the binary format, the combination of SOAP and HTTP has become a de facto standard for transmitting data through firewalls whether using remoting or Web Services. The binary format is recommended for cases where firewalls are not an issue.

Channels

Channel objects are created from classes that implement the IChannel interface. .NET comes with two that handle most needs: HttpChannel and TcpChannel. It is the responsibility of the remote host to register the channel over which it is willing to provide access; similarly, the client registers the channel it wants to issue its calls on.

In its simplest form, registration on the host consists of creating an instance of the channel object and registering it by passing it as a parameter to the static Register-Channel method of the ChannelServices class. This example registers an HTTP channel on port 3200:

```
// Channel Registration
HttpChannel c = new HttpChannel(3200);  // Port 3200
ChannelServices.RegisterChannel(c);
```

The only difference in registering on the client side is that the port number does not have to be specified:

```
HttpChannel c = new HttpChannel();
ChannelServices.RegisterChannel(c);
```

There are some rules to keep in mind when registering channels on the client and server:

- Both the host and client can register multiple channels; however, the client must register a channel that matches one the host has registered.
- Multiple channels cannot use the same port.
- By default, HTTP and TCP channels are given the names http and tcp, respectively. If you attempt to register multiple HTTP or TCP channels using the default name, you will receive an exception. The way around this is to create the channels using a constructor (described shortly) that accepts a channel name parameter.

As an alternative to embedding the channel and protocol information within code, .NET permits it to be specified in configuration files associated with the client and host assemblies. For example, if the host assembly is named MessageHost.exe, we could have a configuration file name MessageHost.exe.config containing the following port and formatting specification.

```
<application>
   <channels>
      <channel ref="http" port="3200"/>
   </channels>
</application>
```

A program uses this file by passing the file name to the static Configure method of the RemotingConfiguration class:

```
RemotingConfiguration.Configure("MessageHost.exe.config");
```

The configuration file must be in the same directory as the assembly referencing it.

Assigning a Name to a Channel

To open multiple channels using the same protocol, a host must assign a name to each channel. To do so, it must use this form of the HttpChannel constructor:

```
HttpChannel(IDictionary properties,
            IClientChannelSinkProvider csp,
            IserverChannelSinkProvicer ssp )
```

Only the first parameter is of interest for naming purposes. The second or third can be used to specify the formatter used on the client or server side:

```
IDictionary chProps = new Hashtable();
chProps["name"] = "Httpchannel01";
chProps["port"] = "3202";
ChannelServices.RegisterChannel(new HttpChannel(chProps,
                                    null, null));
```

Types of Remoting

Recall that the parameters in a C# method may be passed by *value* or by *reference*. Remoting uses the same concept to permit a client to access objects—although the terminology is a bit different. When a client gets an actual copy of the object, it is referred to as *marshaling by value (MBV)*; when the client gets only a reference to the remote object, it is referred to as *marshaling by reference (MBR)*. The term marshaling simply refers to the transfer of the object or request between the client and server.

Marshaling by Value

When an object is marshaled by value, the client receives a copy of the object in its own application domain. It can then work with the object locally and has no need for a proxy. This approach is much less popular than marshaling by reference where all calls are made on a remote object. However, for objects that are designed to run on a client as easily as on a server, and are called frequently, this can reduce the overhead of calls to the server.

As an example, consider an object that calculates body mass index (BMI). Instead of having the server implement the class and return BMI values, it can be designed to return the BMI object itself. The client can then use the object locally and avoid further calls to the server. Let's see how to implement this.

For an object to be marshaled by value, it must be serializable. This means that the class must either implement the `ISerializable` interface or—the easier approach—have the `[Serializable]` attribute. Here is the code for the class on the server:

```
[Serializable]
public class BMICalculator
{
    // Calculate body mass index
    public decimal inches;
    public decimal pounds;
    public decimal GetBMI()
    {
        return ((pounds*703* 10/(inches*inches))/10);
    }
}
```

The `HealthTools` class that is marshaled by reference returns an instance of `BMICalculator`:

```
public class HealthTools: MarshalByRefObject
{
    // Return objects to calculate BMI
    public BMICalculator GetBMIObj(){
        return new BMICalculator();
    }
```

The client creates an instance of `HealthTools` and calls the `GetBMIObj` method to return the calculator object:

```
HealthMonitor remoteObj = new HealthMonitor();
BMICalculator calc= remoteObj.GetBMIObj();
calc.pounds= 168M;
calc.inches= 73M;
Console.WriteLine(calc.GetBMI());
```

It is important to understand that this example uses both marshaling by value and marshaling by reference: an MBR type (`HealthTools`) implements a method (`GetBMIObj`) that returns an MBV type (`BMICalculator`). You should recognize this as a form of the factory design pattern discussed in Chapter 4, "Working with Objects in C#."

Marshaling by Reference

Marshaling by reference (MBR) occurs when a client makes a call on an object running on a remote server. The call is marshaled to the server by the proxy, and the results of the call are then marshaled back to the client.

Objects accessed using MBR must inherit from the `MarshalbyRefObject` class. Its most important members, `InitializeLiIfetimeServices` and `GetLife-TimeServices`, create and retrieve objects that are used to control how long a remoting object is kept alive on the server. Managing the lifetime of an object is a key feature of remoting and is discussed later in this section.

`MarshalByRefObjects` come in two flavors: *client-activated objects* (CAO) and *server-activated objects* (SAO)—also commonly referred to as *well-known objects* (WKO). Server-activated objects are further separated into *single call* and *singleton* types. A server may implement both client-activated and server-activated objects. It's up to the client to choose which one to use. If the client selects SAO, the server makes the determination as to whether to use server-activated single call or server-activated singleton objects.

The choice of activation mode profoundly affects the overall design, performance, and scalability of a remoting application. It determines when objects are created, how many objects are created, how their lifecycle is managed, and whether objects maintain state information. Let's look at the details.

Client-Activated Objects

The use and behavior of a client-activated object (CAO) resembles that of a locally created object. Both can be created using the new operator; both may have parameterized constructors in addition to their default constructor; and both maintain state information in properties or fields. As shown in Figure 14-5, they differ in that the CAO runs on a host in a separate application domain and is called by a proxy.

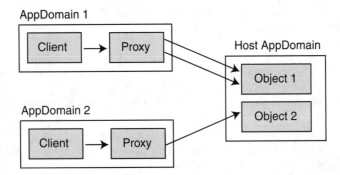

Figure 14-5   Client-activated objects: client retains control of object

The fact that the object resides in another AppDomain means that it is subject to Garbage Collection there and can be destroyed even though the remote client is still using it. .NET handles this potential problem by assigning a *lease* to each object that can be used to keep it alive. Leases are discussed in detail later in this chapter.

Server-Activated Objects

A server-activated object (SAO) may be implemented as a singleton or single call object. The former is best suited for sharing a single resource or collaborative operation among multiple users. Examples include a chat server and class factory. Single call mode is used when clients need to execute a relatively short operation on the server that does not require maintaining state information from one call to the next. This approach is the most scalable solution and has the added advantage of working well in an environment that uses load balancing to direct calls to multiple servers.

Server-Activated Singleton

Figure 14-6 illustrates how a single object is used to handle all calls in single-ton-based design. The server creates the object when the first client attempts to access it—not when it tries to create it. Because the object is created only once, efforts by other clients to create an instance of it are ignored; instead, they are all given a reference to the same singleton object. Each time a client invokes the object, the CLR allocates a new thread from the thread pool. For this reason, it is the responsibility of the developer to ensure the server code is thread-safe. This also limits scalability because there is usually only a finite number of threads available.

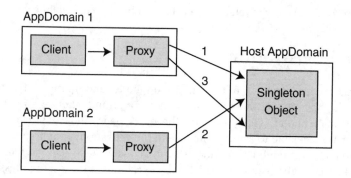

Figure 14-6   Server-activated singleton object: one object handles all calls

Server-Activated Single Call

In single call activation mode, the server creates a new object each time a call is made on an object. After the call has been handled, the object is deactivated. Figure 14-7 illustrates how multiple calls are handled: The first call has been completed and the object created for it destroyed; at this point, the proxy of the client that made this call references a null value. The second call comes from another client and results in the creation of the second server object. Finally, the first client makes its second call and a third object is created.

The advantage of single call activation is that resources are made available as soon as a call is completed. This is in contrast to the client-activated call where the client holds on to the resources until it has finished using the object. The disadvantage of the single call is that it does not inherently maintain state information between calls. If you do want to take advantage of single call scalability, but require that information about previous calls be maintained, you can design the server to maintain its own state information in a file or database.

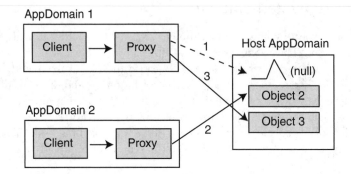

Figure 14-7   Server-activated single call: one object is created for each request

Type Registration

An application may support multiple activation modes and multiple objects. A client indicates the object(s) it wants to access on a server and whether to use client- or server-activation mode. The server, on the other hand, indicates which objects it wants to make available to remote clients and the activation mode that is required to access them. This is done using a mechanism known as *type registration*. As a complement to channel registration, which tells .NET how to transport messages, type registration specifies the objects that can be remotely accessed and the activation mode to use. It's the final part of the agreement that permits a client in one AppDomain to access objects on a host in another AppDomain.

Registering Server-Activated Objects

A host assembly uses the `RegisterWellKnowServiceType` method of the `RemotingConfiguration` class to register a type. The method has three parameters: the type of the object, a string representing the object's URI (universal resource identifier), and a `WellKnownObjectMode` enum that indicates whether the object is implemented as a singleton or single call object. This code segment registers a `MessageManager` object to execute as a singleton.

```
// Server Registration: Server-Activated Objects
Type ServerType = typeof(SimpleServer.MessageManager);
RemotingConfiguration.RegisterWellKnownServiceType(
     ServerType,                        // Type of Object
     "MyObject",                        // Arbitrary name
     WellKnownObjectMode.Singleton );
```

Replace `Singleton` with `SingleCall` to register the object to run in single call mode.

To access an SAO, a client uses the `RegisterWellKnownClientType` method. It takes two parameters: the object type and a string containing the URL where the object can be located. Note that the client does not have any say in whether it uses a singleton or single call object—it uses whichever the server provides.

```
// Client Registration: Server-Activated Objects
Type ServerType = typeof(SimpleServer.MessageManager);
string url= "http://localhost:3200/MyObject";
// Register type for Server Activation Mode
RemotingConfiguration.RegisterWellKnownClientType(
      ServerType,
      url);
MessageManager mm = new MessageManager();
```

When the client uses new to create an instance of the object, .NET recognizes that the object is registered and uses its URL to locate it.

Registering Client-Activated Objects

A host uses the `RegisterActivatedServiceType` method to register a CAO. It requires only one parameter—the object type:

```
// Server Registration: Client-ativated Objects
Type ServerType = typeof(ImageServer);   // ImageServer class
RemotingConfiguration.RegisterActivatedServiceType(
      ServerType);
```

The client registration is almost as easy. It invokes the `RegisterActivatedClientType` method and passes it the object type and URL where the object can be located:

```
// Client Registration: Client-ativated Objects
Type ServerType = typeof(ImageServer);
RemotingConfiguration.RegisterActivatedClientType(
      ServerType,
      "tcp://localhost:3201");
```

Type Registration Using a Configuration File

As with channels, the type registration instructions can be placed in an assembly's configuration file. These two code segments illustrate how to register the SAO from the preceding example on the server and client:

```
//Server: Register MessageManager object as a singleton
<application >
   <service>
```

```
      <wellknown
       mode="Singleton"
       type="SimpleServer.MessageManager, msgserver"
       objectUri="MyObject"/>
   </service>
</application>

//Client: Register MessageManager object on port 3200
<application >
   <client >
      <wellknown
       type="SimpleServer.MessageManager, msgserver"
       url="http://localhost:3200/MyObject" />
   </client>
</application>
```

Observe that the registration information is represented as attributes in the <wellknown> tag, and that the type attribute denotes the object by its namespace and name as well as the assembly containing it.

Client-activated registration uses an <activated> tag to specify the remote object in both the server and client configuration file.

```
//Server: Register ImageServer to be client-activated
<application >
   <service >
      <activated type="ImageServer,caoimageserver"/>
   </service>
</application>
```

The client also includes a url attribute to provide the address of the remote object:

```
//Client: Register ImageServer to be client-activated
<application >
   <client url="tcp://localhost:3201" >
      <activated type="ImageServer,caoimageserver"/>
   </client>
</application>
```

Remoting with a Server-Activated Object

With an understanding of how to register channels and types, you're ready to implement a remoting application. Our first example builds an application that permits users to post and retrieve messages from other users. It's based on SAO, and we'll look at two ways to design it. Our second example uses CAO to retrieve images from an image server.

A Message Server Example

The minimum requirements for a remoting application are an assembly containing the client code, and an assembly that runs as a server and provides the implementation code for the remoting objects. As Figure 14-8 shows, the more common model uses three assemblies: a client, a host that performs channel and type registration, and a server that contains code for the objects. This is the model used for our initial message server project.

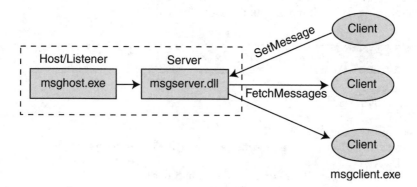

Figure 14-8   Three assemblies are used in message server remoting example

Before examining the code, we need to clarify the terminology used to describe the assemblies. In this chapter, *server* refers to an assembly that declares and implements the remote classes; *host* or *listener* refers to an assembly that contains the code to perform type and channel registration. If the host and server functions are combined, the assembly is referred to as a server or host/server. In the world of remoting literature, you'll find that some authors reverse this meaning of host and server, whereas others refer to the host as *general* assembly.

Our message server application consists of three source files that are compiled into the msgserver.dll, msghost.exe, and msgclient.exe assemblies:

```
csc /t:library       msgserver.cs
csc /r:msgserver.dll msghost.cs
csc /r:msgserver.dll msgclient.cs
```

Note that the server code is packaged as a library (DLL) and must be referenced by both the host and client during compilation.

Server Assembly

Listing 14-2 contains the code for a `MessageManager` class that is made available to clients as a server-activated singleton. Aside from the required `MarshalByRefObject` inheritance, the class is indistinguishable from a non-remoting class. It exposes two methods, `SetMessage` and `FetchMessages`, which are used to post and retrieve messages, respectively. A call to `SetMessage` contains the ID of the sender and recipient along with the message. This information is packaged into an instance of the `Envelope` class and stored in an array. Clients retrieve messages by invoking `FetchMessages` with their client ID. The method searches the array of messages and returns a string containing all messages for that ID.

Listing 14-2	Remoting Server

```
// msgserver.cs   (DLL)
using System;
using System.Collections;
namespace SimpleServer{
   public class MessageManager: MarshalByRefObject
   {
      ArrayList Messages = new ArrayList();

      public MessageManager()
      {
         Console.WriteLine("Message Object Created.");
      }
      // Concatenate all messages and return string to client
      public string FetchMessages(string clientID)
      {
         string msgList= "";
         for (int i=Messages.Count-1;i>=0;i--)
         {
            Envelope env= (Envelope)Messages[i];
            if(env.RecipientID== clientID)
            {
               msgList+= env.SenderID+": "+env.Message+"\n";
               Messages.RemoveAt(i);   // Remove message
            }
         }
         Console.WriteLine("Sending:\n {0}",msgList);
         return(msgList);
      }
      // Accept message from client and store in memory
      public void SetMessage(string msg, string sender,
                        string recipient)
```

Listing 14-2   Remoting Server (continued)

```
        {
            // Save Message received from client as object
            // in an array
            Envelope env= new Envelope();
            env.Message= msg;
            env.SenderID= sender;
            env.RecipientID= recipient;
            Messages.Add(env);            // add message to array
            Console.WriteLine("Received:\n{0}", msg);
        }
    }
    // Messages are stored as instances of Envelope
    public class Envelope
    {
        public string Message;
        public string SenderID;
        public string RecipientID;
    }
}
```

Host Assembly

The host assembly, shown in Listing 14-3, performs channel and type registration. The channel is configured to use HTTP over port 3200; and the `MessageManager` object is designated to run as a singleton. Keep in mind that the port number, which is essentially an address associated with the application, should be greater than 1024 so as not to conflict with reserved port IDs.

Listing 14-3   Remoting Host/Listener

```
// msghost.cs  (exe)
using System;
using System.Runtime.Remoting;
using System.Runtime.Remoting.Channels;
using System.Runtime.Remoting.Channels.Http;
using SimpleServer;                        // Namespace of server
namespace SimpleHost
{
    public class MessageHost
    {
```

Listing 14-3   Remoting Host/Listener *(continued)*

```
static void Main()
{
    Console.WriteLine("Host Started.");
    // Channel Registration
    HttpChannel c = new HttpChannel(3200);
    ChannelServices.RegisterChannel(c);
    // Type Registration-Use server-activated object (SAO)
    // Type is specified as (namespace.class)
    Type ServerType = typeof(SimpleServer.MessageManager);
    RemotingConfiguration.RegisterWellKnownServiceType(
        ServerType,                    // Type of Object
        "MyObject",                    // Arbitrary name
        WellKnownObjectMode.Singleton );
    Console.Read();   // Keep host running
    }
  }
}
```

After registration is completed, this assembly continues running and monitors port 3200 for calls to MessageManager. Any messages received are passed on to the object.

Client Assembly

The code for the client class is shown in Listing 14-4. It is run from the command line and takes an optional parameter that is used as the client ID:

```
> msgclient 005
```

The client first registers the type and channel. The latter must specify the same port (3200) as registered by the host assembly. Following registration, an instance of MessageManager is created using the new operator. When the user types an R, the object retrieves messages; to send a message, an S is entered at one prompt and the recipient ID and message at the next prompt.

Listing 14-4   Remoting Client

```
// msgclient.cs   (exe)
using System;
using System.Runtime.Remoting;
using System.Runtime.Remoting.Channels;
```

Listing 14-4   Remoting Client *(continued)*

```csharp
using System.Runtime.Remoting.Channels.Http;
using System.Collections;
using SimpleServer;    // Namespace of server
namespace SimpleClient
{
   public class MessageClient
   {
      static void Main(string[] args)
      {
         string myID;
         // Client ID is passed as command line argument
         if(args.Length>0) myID= args[0]; else myID="001";
         Console.WriteLine("Client Started.");
         // (1) Channel Registration
         HttpChannel c = new HttpChannel();
         ChannelServices.RegisterChannel(c);
         // (2) Type Registration: SAO using port 3200
         Type ServerType = typeof(SimpleServer.MessageManager);
         string url= "http://localhost:3200/MyObject";
         // Register type for Server Activation Mode
         RemotingConfiguration.RegisterWellKnownClientType(
               ServerType,url);
         // (3) Create instance of Remote Object
         MessageManager mm = new MessageManager();
         string msg;
         string oper="";
         // Allow user to send or receive a message
         while(oper !="Q")
         {
            Console.WriteLine("(S)end, (R)eceive, (Q)uit");
            oper= Console.ReadLine();
            oper = oper.ToUpper();
            if(oper=="S"){
              Console.WriteLine("enter Recipient ID: messsage");
               msg= Console.ReadLine();
               // : Separates ID and message
               int ndx= msg.IndexOf(":");
               if(ndx>0) {
                 string recipientID=msg.Substring(0,ndx).Trim();
                  msg= msg.Substring(ndx+1);
                  mm.SetMessage(msg, myID, recipientID);
               }
            } else
```

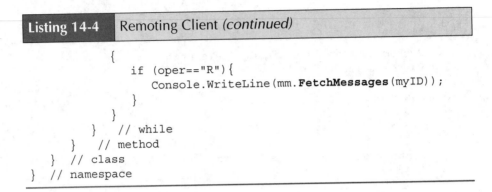

```
          {
              if (oper=="R"){
                  Console.WriteLine(mm.FetchMessages(myID));
              }
          }
      }   // while
   }   // method
}   // class
}   // namespace
```

Figure 14-9 shows the interactive dialog on the client screen and the correspond-ing output on the server/host screen. Observe that Message Object Created, which is inside the constructor, occurs when the first call is made to the remote object—not when the host begins executing. Also, the constructor is only executed once because this is a singleton object.

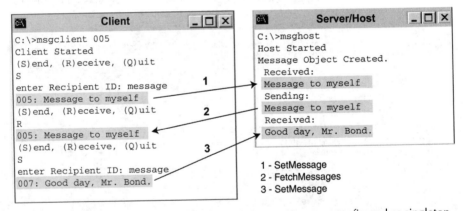

Figure 14-9   Client interacting with remote `MessageServer` configured as singleton

MessageServer Configuration Files

Both `msghost` and `msgclient` contain code to perform explicit channel and type registration. As mentioned previously in this section, an alternative is to place chan-nel and/or type registration information in an assembly's configuration file. The in-line registration code is then replaced with a call to a static `Configure` method that reads the configuration file and performs the registration:

```
RemotingConfiguration.Configure("MsgHost.exe.config");
```

Here is how the configuration for `msghost.exe` is expressed in XML:

```
//msghost.exe.config
<configuration>
   <system.runtime.remoting>
      <application name = "SimpleHost">
         <service>
           <wellknown
            mode="Singleton"
            type="SimpleServer.MessageManager, msgserver"
            objectUri="MyObject"/>
         </service>
         <channels>
                    <channel ref="http" port="3200"/>
         </channels>
      </application>
   </system.runtime.remoting>
</configuration>
```

If you compare this with the source code, it's obvious that information in the `wellknown` tag corresponds to the parameters in the `RegisterWellKnownServiceType` method; and the `channel` tag provides information encapsulated in the `HttpChannel` object. The client configuration file shows a similar correspondence between these tags and source code:

```
//msgclient.exe.config
<configuration>
   <system.runtime.remoting>
      <application name = "SimpleClient">
         <client >
           <wellknown
            type="SimpleServer.MessageManager, msgserver"
            url="http://localhost:3200/MyObject" />
         </client>
         <channels>
              <channel ref="http"/>
         </channels>
      </application>
   </system.runtime.remoting>
</configuration>
```

Note that the file contains no tag to specify the type of formatting to be used—so the default applies. You can specify a different formatter by extending the channel block:

```
<channel ref="http">
   <clientProviders>
      <formatter ref="Binary" />
   </clientProviders>
</channel>
```

Using an Interface Assembly with Server-Activated Objects

In the preceding example, the `msgserver` assembly is packaged as a DLL and must be deployed on both the host and client machine. On the server, it provides the actual code that is executed when a call to the remote object occurs. The client requires the assembly's metadata to compile and build a proxy at runtime, but has no use for the Intermediate Language (IL). Rather than placing this code on each client's machine—exposing it to anyone with a disassembler—the application can be redesigned to use an interface assembly to provide the metadata required by the client.

To do this, we'll combine the code in the `msghost` and `msgserver` file to create an assembly that both implements the object and performs registration. The third assembly, now called `msggeneral`, contains an interface that defines the methods supported by the `MessageServer` class (see Figure 14-10). The client then gets its metadata from this lightweight assembly rather than the full server assembly.

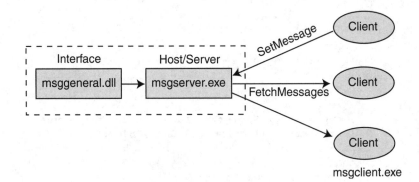

Figure 14-10 `MessageServer` redesigned to use an interface to provide remote object metadata

The simple interface shown here defines the signature of the two methods exposed by the remote class.

```
// msggeneral.cs  (DLL)
namespace SimpleServer
{
```

```
// Define an interface to provide method descriptions
// used by client and implemented by server.
public interface IMessageManager
{
    string FetchMessages(string clientID);
    void    SetMessage(string message, string sender,
                       string recipient);
}
}
```

The server assembly contains the same object implementation code as in the first example. However, it now inherits from the newly defined `IMessageManager` interface and includes the registration code from the host/listener assembly. This code is contained in a new class `StartServer` that provides an entry point to the assembly so that it can be compiled into an `.exe` file.

```
// msgserverv2.cs (exe)
public class MessageManager: MarshalByRefObject, IMessageManager
// Code for MessageManager and Envelope class goes here ...
// Class to provide entry point to assembly and perform
// registration
class StartServer
{
    static void Main()
    {
        Console.WriteLine("Host Started.");
        // Channel Registration
        HttpChannel c = new HttpChannel(3200);
        ChannelServices.RegisterChannel(c);
        // Type Registration
        Type ServerType = typeof(SimpleServer.MessageManager);
        RemotingConfiguration.RegisterWellKnownServiceType(
            ServerType,      // Type of Object
            "MyObject",      // Arbitrary name
            WellKnownObjectMode.Singleton);
        Console.Read();
    }
}
```

Changes are required in the client code to account for the fact that the description of the remote object now comes from an interface; and because it's not possible to directly instantiate an interface, another way must be found to gain a reference to the remote object. The solution is to use `Activator.GetObject` to return an instance of the interface. This is an important point: .NET returns interface information to the client but creates the actual object on the server where it runs as a server-activated object. As this code segment illustrates, `Activator.GetObject` performs registration and returns an object in one step:

```
Type ServerType = typeof(IMessageManager);
// Activate Remote Object and perform registration
object remoteObj = Activator.GetObject(
     ServerType,
     "http://localhost:3200/MyObject");
IMessageManager mm = (IMessageManager) remoteObj;
```

No other changes are required in the `msgclient.cs` code.

The three source files are compiled into the `msgserver.exe`, `msggeneral.dll`, and `msgclient.exe` assemblies:

```
csc /t:library        msggeneral.cs
csc /r:msggeneral.dll /out:msgserver.exe msgserverv2.cs
csc /r:msggeneral.dll msgclient.cs
```

Remoting with a Client-Activated Object (CAO)

In the preceding server-activated singleton example, each call to the remote object is handled by the same object. In the client-activated model, each client creates its own object and can make multiple calls to that object (refer to Figure 14-5 on page 650). The model does not scale particularly well because a large number of concurrent client-created objects can deplete system resources. However, when the expected number of users is small and there is a need to maintain state information between calls, this model should be considered.

An Image Server Example

This project implements a remote server that serves up images to clients upon request. It loads the requested file from local storage and delivers it as a byte stream to the client. After being received by the client, the bytes are then reassembled into the original image.[2]

Prior to examining the code, let's consider the rationale behind implementing the server using client activation, rather than one of the server-activation modes. A singleton can be ruled out; because each client's request is independent of any other client's request, there is no need to maintain state information. The choice between single call activation and client activation is less clear-cut and depends on expected client behavior. If a large number of clients requesting a single image are expected,

---

2. For comparison, this image server is implemented in Chapter 18, "XML Web Services," as a Web Service.

single call is preferable because it manages resources better by discarding the server object as soon as the request is completed. If a client is expected to make several image requests during a session, client activation is preferred. It allows a client to create and reuse one object for several calls—obviating the need to build and tear down objects with each request.

Host Assembly

The host/listener assembly has the familiar task of registering the channel(s) and type. Because this application revolves around streaming raw bytes of data, binary formatting is selected over SOAP. This does not have to be specified directly, because the choice of the TCP protocol assigns binary formatting by default.

The other noteworthy change from the server-activated example is that `Regis-terActivatedServiceTypeCode` is used for type registration instead of `Regis-terWellKnownServiceType`.

```
using System.Runtime.Remoting.Channels.Tcp;

// Channel Registration for TCP
TcpChannel c = new TcpChannel(3201);
ChannelServices.RegisterChannel(c);
// Type Registration for CAO
Type ServerType = typeof(ImageServer);
RemotingConfiguration.RegisterActivatedServiceType(
        ServerType);
```

Server Assembly

Listing 14-5 provides the implementation of the `ImageServer` class, which exposes two methods: `GetFiles` and `GetMovieImage`. The former returns an array containing the name of all available image files. `GetMovieImage` is the heart of the system. It receives a string containing the name of a requested image, opens the corresponding file as a memory stream, and converts it to an array of bytes that is returned to the client. (See Chapter 5, "C# Text Manipulation and File I/O," for a refresher on memory streams.)

Listing 14-5	Using Remoting to Implement an Image Server

```
// caoimageserver.cs   (DLL)
using System;
using System.Runtime.Remoting;
using System.Collections;
using System.Drawing;
using System.IO;
```

Listing 14-5	Using Remoting to Implement an Image Server (continued)

```
public class ImageServer: MarshalByRefObject
{
    // Return list of available images as a string array
    public ArrayList GetFiles()
    {
        ArrayList a = new ArrayList();
        string dir=@"c:\images\";
        foreach(string fileName in Directory.GetFiles(dir))
        {
            // Strip path from file name
            int ndx= fileName.LastIndexOf("\\");
            string imgName = fileName.Substring(ndx+1);
            a.Add(imgName);
        }
        return a;
    }
    // Return requested image as byte stream
    public byte[] GetMovieImage(string imageName)
    {
        int imgByte;
        imageName= "c:\\images\\"+imageName;
        FileStream s = File.OpenRead(imageName);
        MemoryStream ms = new MemoryStream();
        while((imgByte =s.ReadByte())!=-1)
        {
            ms.WriteByte(((byte)imgByte));
        }
        return ms.ToArray();
    }
}
```

Client Assembly

The registration steps in Listing 14-6 enable the client to communicate with the host using TCP on port 3201. The call to RegisterActivatedClientType, which registers the ImageServer type, corresponds to the RegisterActivatedServiceType call on the host. After registration, the new operator is used to give the client a reference to the remote object (via a proxy).

Listing 14-6   Using a Client-Activated Object to Access
`ImageServer`

```csharp
// caoimageclient.cs   (.exe)
using System;
using System.Runtime.Remoting;
using System.Runtime.Remoting.Channels;
using System.Runtime.Remoting.Channels.Tcp;
using System.Collections;
using System.Drawing;
using System.IO;
namespace SimpleImageClient
{
    class ImageClient
    {
        static void Main(string[] args)
        {
            // (1) Register channel for TCP/Binary
            TcpChannel c = new TcpChannel();
            ChannelServices.RegisterChannel(c);
            // (2) Register remote type for CAO
            Type ServerType = typeof(ImageServer);
            RemotingConfiguration.RegisterActivatedClientType(
                    ServerType,
                    "tcp://localhost:3201");
            ImageServer imgMgr=null;
            bool serverOK=true;    // Indicates whether server is up
            // (3) Create instance of remote object
            try{
                imgMgr = new ImageServer();
            } catch (Exception ex) {
                Console.WriteLine(ex.Message);
                serverOK=false;
            }
            if(serverOK)
            {
                string oper="";
                while(oper !="Q")
                {
                    Console.WriteLine(
                            "(L)ist files, (R)etrieve, (Q)uit");
                    oper= Console.ReadLine();
                    oper = oper.ToUpper();
                    if(oper=="R"){
```

Listing 14-6	Using a Client-Activated Object to Access ImageServer *(continued)*

```
                    Console.WriteLine(
                         "Enter image name to retrieve:");
                    string fname= Console.ReadLine();
                 // Exception is handled if image cannot be found
                    try
                    {
                       // Request image from server
                       byte[] image = imgMgr.GetMovieImage(fname);
                       MemoryStream memStream = new
                             MemoryStream(image);
                       Console.WriteLine("Image Size: {0}",
                                         memStream.Length);
                       // Convert memory stream to a Bitmap object
                       Bitmap bm = new Bitmap(memStream);
                       // Save image on local system
                       bm.Save("c:\\cs\\"+fname,
                          System.Drawing.Imaging.ImageFormat.Jpeg);
                    } catch (Exception ex) {
                       Console.WriteLine(ex.Message);
                    }
                 }
                 else
                 {
                    if (oper=="L")    // List image file names
                    {
                       try
                       {
                          ArrayList images = imgMgr.GetFiles();
                          for (int i=0;i<images.Count;i++)
                          {
                             Console.WriteLine(images[i]);
                          }
                       } catch (Exception ex) {
                          Console.WriteLine(ex.Message);
                       }
                    }
                 }
              }   // while
           }   // serverok
        }   // Main
     }   // class
  }   // namespace
```

The code implementation is based on a simple command-line menu. When L is entered, a list of available images is displayed on the console; when R is entered, the program prompts for the name of a file to be downloaded. This image name is sent to the server, which returns the image—if it exists—as an array of bytes. A `Bitmap` object is created and its `Save` method is used to store the image on the client's disk.

Deploying the CAO Application

Use the C# compiler to create `caoimagelistener.exe`, `caoimageserver.dll`, and `caoimageclient.exe`:

```
csc /t:library             caoimageserver.cs
csc /r:caoimageserver.dll  caoimagelistener.cs
csc /r:caoimageserver.dll  caoimageclient.cs
```

Note that this implementation requires packaging `caoimageserver.dll` with `caoimageclient.exe` on the client's machine. As discussed earlier, this exposes the server code on the client machine. For the SAO application described earlier, using an interface implementation solved this problem. A similar approach can be used with client-activated objects, but requires creating a "factory" that returns an interface for the server object. Another solution is to use the .NET *SoapSuds* utility to extract metadata from the server assembly into a DLL that can be deployed instead of the server assembly. This utility is executed at the command-line prompt:

```
soapsuds -ia:caoimageserver -oa:serverstub.dll -nowp
```

```
-ia:   specifies the input assembly; do not include .dll or .exe
-oa:   specifies the output assembly that will contain the metadata.
-nowp specifies that a nonwrapped proxy is to be created. A wrapped
      proxy can be used only with SOAP channels and is designed
      for working with Web Services.
```

The output assembly, `serverstub.dll`, is now referenced as the client is compiled and is deployed on the client's machine along with the client assembly.

```
csc /r:serverstub.dll caoimageclient.cs
```

You now have two approaches that can be used to avoid deploying an entire server implementation assembly on the client's machine: an interface assembly or an assembly created from SoapSuds generated metadata. Which is better? In general, the interface approach is recommended. SoapSuds works well, but doesn't work for all cases. For example, if an assembly contains a class that implements `ISerializable` or has the `[Serializable]` attribute, it does not generate metadata for any of the class's properties. However, if you have a relatively simple server assembly as in the preceding example, SoapSuds can be used effectively.

Design Considerations in Creating a Distributed Application

One of the first decisions required in designing a remoting application is whether to use server- or client-activated objects. Here are some general guidelines:

- If the application requires that the server maintain state information—as was the case in our message server example—an SAO singleton is the obvious choice. If the application does not require a singleton, do not use it. Scalability and synchronization can be a problem when accommodating a large number of users.
- If each call to a remote object is independent of other calls, an SAO single call model is the best choice. This is also the most scalable solution because it does not maintain state information and is destroyed as soon as it's no longer needed.
- The third choice—the client-activated object—allows the client to create the object and maintain state information in instance variables between calls. One drawback is that the model does not support the use of a shared interface assembly to provide the metadata required to create a proxy. Instead, a class-factory approach or SoapSuds must be used.

Configuring Assemblies

After the remoting model has been chosen, there remains the choice of how to design the assemblies required on the client and server side of the application. As discussed earlier, the client side of the application requires the client application, plus an assembly, to provide the necessary information for .NET to construct a proxy. The server implementation assembly is not a good choice because it includes code. Alternatives are a metadata assembly provided by the SoapSuds utility or an assembly that includes only an interface for the server class. Figure 14-11 summarizes the most common design choices.

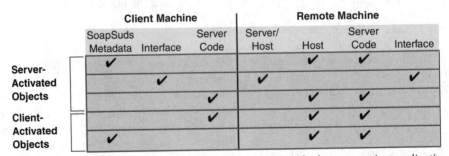

	Client Machine			Remote Machine			
	SoapSuds Metadata	Interface	Server Code	Server/ Host	Host	Server Code	Interface
Server- Activated Objects	✔				✔	✔	
		✔		✔			✔
			✔		✔	✔	
Client- Activated Objects			✔		✔	✔	
	✔				✔	✔	

Figure 14-11   Assembly combinations that can be used to deploy a remoting application

Assembly Definitions:

SoapSuds Metadata	An assembly created by running SoapSuds against a server assembly.
Interface	An assembly containing an interface that defines the server class.
Server Code	A DLL containing the implementation of the remote class.
Server/Host	An .exe file containing code to implement the remote class and perform type and channel registration.
Host	An .exe file that performs type and channel registration.

Each row shown in Figure 14-11 indicates the type of assemblies to be used in an application. For example, the second row shows a possible configuration for a server-activated object design. A DLL containing an interface inherited by the remote class is deployed on the client along with the client's executable assembly; the server side shares the same interface assembly and contains the interface implementation, as well as the registration code in a single server/host assembly.

This figure represents only a starting point in the design process, because many remoting applications are hybrids that may combine both SAO and CAO. However, an understanding of these core design techniques provides the foundation needed to implement and deploy more complex applications.

14.3 Leasing and Sponsorship

One of the signature features of .NET is its use of Garbage Collection to remove unused objects. As was discussed in Chapter 4, .NET maintains a graph to keep track of all references to objects in the managed heap. When Garbage Collection occurs, those objects for which references cannot be found are destroyed. Because .NET only recognizes references within a process, objects referenced by remote clients would be subject to Garbage Collection leaving the remote client(s) with no host object to call.

The rather clever .NET solution is to assign a *lease* object to each client-activated object or server-activated singleton when they are created. (Server-activated single call objects are not affected because they only exist for the duration of a call.) The lease provides a reference to the object that keeps the object from being made available for Garbage Collection as long as the lease exists—which is based on the lease time assigned to the lease. The time associated with the lease is referred to as the object's time-to-live (TTL).

As we see next, a lease may be renewed programatically by calling methods on the lease object to increase its lease time. If the lease does expire, .NET looks for an object associated with the lease, known as a *sponsor*, and gives it a chance to renew the lease. Let's look at the details.

Leasing

A lease is an object created internally by .NET that implements the `ILease` interface. This interface, located in the `System.Runtime.Remoting.Lifetime` namespace, defines the members that are used to govern a lease's behavior. These include properties to get or set the initial time of the lease (the default is 5 minutes), obtain the time remaining on the lease, and specify the time a lease is renewed for when its associated object is invoked. Table 14-1 summarizes the `ILease` members.

Table 14-1   `ILease` Interface Members

Member	Description
`CurrentLeaseTime`	Amount of time remaining before the object is made available for Garbage Collection. If it is invoked, the lease time is reset.
`CurrentState`	Returns the current state of the lease, defined by a `LeaseState` enumeration: `Active`, `Expired`, `Initial`, `Null`, or `Renewing`.
`InitialLeaseTime`	Gets or sets the initial amount of time-to-live that a lease assigns to an object. Default is 5 minutes.
`RenewOnCallTime`	Gets or sets the amount of time—specified using `TimeSpan`—that a call to an object increases the `CurrentLeaseTime`. Default is 2 minutes.
`SponsorshipTimeout`	Gets or sets the amount of time available for a sponsor to provide a new lease renewal time. Default is 2 minutes.
`Register()`	Registers a sponsor for the lease.
`Renew()`	Renews a lease for a specified amount of time.
`UnRegister()`	Removes a sponsor from an object's list of sponsors.

Setting Initial Lease Values for Objects in an Application

You can override the default values assigned to lease properties in an application's configuration file. For example, to set the lease values for all objects in our image server example, insert the following into the `caoimagehost.exe.config` file:

```
<application >
  <lifetime
    leaseTime = "8M"
```

```
        renewOnCallTime = "6M"
    />
    ...
</application>
```

In this example, the time is specified in minutes (M), but it may also be specified as days (D), hours (H), seconds (S), or milliseconds (MS).

The same effect can be achieved inside a program by setting static properties on the LifetimeServices class:

```
LifetimeServices.LeaseTime = System.TimeSpan.FromMinutes(8);
LifetimeServices.RenewOnCallTime =
        System.TimeSpan.FromMinutes(6);
```

Setting the Lease Values for an Individual Object

Both of the aforementioned techniques for setting initial lease values apply to all objects hosted by the server. To set lease values on an object-by-object basis, a different approach is required. Recall that for a class to implement remoting it must inherit the MarshalByRefObject class. This class includes an InitializeLifeTimeService method that is responsible for returning lease objects. It is a simple matter to override this method in a program to assign your own initial values to the lease object.

```
using System.Runtime.Remoting.Lifetime;  // Contains ILease
public class MessageManager: MarshalByRefObject, IMessageManager
{
// Override this method to set lease initialization values
public override object InitializeLifetimeService()
{
    ILease msgLease = (ILease)base.InitializeLifetimeService();
    msgLease.InitialLeaseTime = TimeSpan.FromMinutes(8);
    msgLease.RenewOnCallTime  = TimeSpan.FromMinutes(6);
    return msgLease;
}
}
```

Note that implementation of this method overrides any values in the configuration file. This means that a configuration file can be used to set default values for all objects, and this method override approach can be used to set non-default values for selected objects.

After a lease is in an active state, the only property on the lease that can be changed is its CurrentLeaseTime. This value can be renewed by a sponsor (described later) or by having the client or object explicitly invoke the lease's Renew method.

```
// Client
(ILease) lease=(ILease)RemotingServices.GetLifetimeServices(ob)
// Object on server
(ILease) lease=(ILease)RemotingServices.GetLifetimeSer-
vices(this)
if(lease.CurrentLeaseTime.TotalMinutes < 1.0)
     lease.Renew(TimeSpan.FromMinutes(5));
```

If the current lease time is greater than this renewal time, the lease is not reset.

The Lease Manager

Running in the background of each AppDomain is a *lease manager* that keeps track of each server object and its associated lease. The primary function of the manager is to periodically examine the leases for time expiration and invoke a sponsor if the lease has expired.

The lease manager uses a timer to control how frequently it checks for lease expirations. By default, this is set to 10 seconds. To override the default, add this setting in the configuration file:

```
<application >
   <lifetime
      LeaseManagerPollTime"5S"
   />
```

The value can also be set programmatically using the `LifetimeServices` class:

```
LifetimeServices.LeaseManagerPollTime =
     System.TimeSpan.FromSeconds(5);
```

The Lifetime of a Lease

It should be clear from the discussion thus far that a lease has a nondeterministic lifetime whose actual length is determined by calls on the associated object, direct invocation of the lease's Renew method, and any renewal coming from a lease's sponsor(s). The state diagram in Figure 14-12 illustrates the relationship between these actions and the current state of a lease. Note that a lease may be in one of four states—Initial, Active, Renewing, or Expired.

When a remote object is created, .NET creates a corresponding lease and sets its InitialLeaseTime—in descending order of priority—to either a value set programmatically, a value in the configuration file, or a default value of 5 minutes. The lease moves into an active state, and its time begins to tick away. When a call is made on the object, the remaining lease time is compared with the `renewOnCallTime` value. The lease time is set to the greater of the two values. For example, if 4 minutes remain, and the renew time is 6 minutes, the value is set 6 minutes; if 7 minutes remain, the value is not altered. When the TTL value goes to 0, the lease manager checks to see if the lease has a sponsor that will assign a new lease time; if not, the object is deactivated and made available for Garbage Collection. Calls made on an object whose lease has expired throw an exception indicating that "no receiver could be found" or the "object has been disconnected." For this reason, it is important to surround all calls on a remote object with exception handling code.

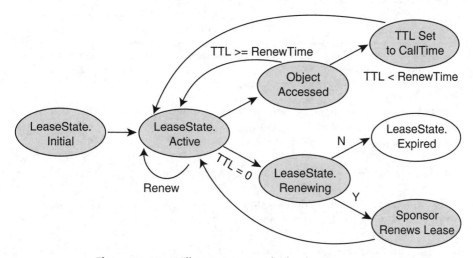

Figure 14-12   Different states in which a lease may exist

Sponsorship

A program's final opportunity to renew a lease is when the lease's `CurrentLease-Time` value winds down to 0. At this point, the lease enters a `LeaseState.Renewing` state (see Figure 14-12), and the lease manager checks to see if any sponsor has been registered with the object (a lease may have sponsors created by multiple clients). If a sponsor is found, it is called and given the opportunity to renew the lease by returning a `TimeSpan` value that becomes the new TTL for the object.

This sponsorship model, based on registration and callbacks, closely resembles the .NET event handling model. In fact, a sponsor can be viewed as an event handler that is called when the lease time approaches 0. Table 14-2 spells out the similarities.

Table 14-2   Similarities Between an Event Handler and a Sponsor

Event Handler	Sponsor
Registers with a delegate to handle an object's event.	Registers with an object's lease when an object is created.
An event handler may be registered for multiple events.	A sponsor may register with multiple leases.
Implements a method that is called to take some action when the event occurs.	Implements a class that contains a method, `Renewal`, that is called when the `TTL=0` event occurs. The method then takes action to extend or end the lease.
Signature of event handling method must match that of the delegate.	Renewal must always have this signature: `Timespan Renewal(ILease lease)`

Although an event handler is a method, a sponsor is a class that meets two requirements: It inherits from `MarshalByRefObject`, and it implements the `ISponsor` interface:

```
public class ImageSponsor: MarshalByRefObject, ISponsor
```

The `ISponsor` interface defines only one member—a method, `Renewal`—that returns the new TTL value for the object as a `TimeSpan` type:

```
public TimeSpan Renewal(ILease lease)
```

A sponsor can be implemented on the server, client, or in a third-party assembly. The only requirement is that the lease manager can locate it. In reality, a sponsor should be defined where the application can best assess the factors that determine how or if an object's lease is extended. For an SAO singleton, this is on the server/host; for a CAO, the code should be on the client, because only the client knows how it's going to be using the object.

To demonstrate the details of implementing a sponsor, let's add one to the client code (see Listing 14-6) used in the image server example. It can be done in four steps:

1. Add namespaces that define an HTTP channel to be used to receive the callback from the lease manager, and the `ILease` and `ISponsor` interfaces:

    ```
    using System.Runtime.Remoting.Channels.Http;
    // Contains ILease and ISponsor
    using System.Runtime.Remoting.Lifetime;
    ```

2. Register the channel to be used for the callback from the lease manager. Setting the port to 0 instructs .NET to automatically use any available port:

```
// Register channel for callback from lease manager
HttpChannel c2 = new HttpChannel(0);
ChannelServices.RegisterChannel(c2);
```

This could also be done in a client configuration file:

```
<channels>
   <channel ref="http" port="0">
</channels>
```

3. Register a sponsor for the lease. First, use GetLifetimeService to get a reference to the lease. Then, pass an instance of the sponsor to the ILease.Register method:

```
// Register sponsor
ISponsor currSponsor = new ImageSponsor();
ILease lease =
        (ILease)RemotingServices.GetLifetimeService(imgMgr);
lease.Register(currSponsor);
```

4. Define the sponsor class. It must have the proper inheritance and must provide an implementation of the ISponsor method Renewal.

```
// Implement Sponsor
public class ImageSponsor: MarshalByRefObject, ISponsor
{
    public TimeSpan Renewal(ILease lease)
    {
        Console.WriteLine(lease.CurrentLeaseTime);
        // Set object's time to live to 10 minutes
        return TimeSpan.FromMinutes(10);
    }
}
```

In this example, the sponsor renews the lease for 10 more minutes. Because this sponsor is called each time the TTL approaches 0, the object associated with the lease exists as long as the client is running. A more sophisticated implementation would include logic that decides whether to renew the lease. To indicate no renewal, the sponsor returns TimeSpan.Zero.

Core Note

A client-based sponsor works only if the server can access the client. This technique cannot be used for a client situated behind a firewall that blocks access.

14.4 Summary

To run code in a managed environment, .NET creates partitions called application domains for the assemblies to execute in. The AppDomain, which runs inside of a physical process, has the advantage of providing more secure code through code isolation and security boundaries. The boundaries prevent an object in one AppDomain from directly accessing an object in another AppDomain. For them to communicate, .NET provides a set of classes that support *remoting*—a technique that enables objects to communicate across AppDomain boundaries.

Remoting provides a way to implement client-server or peer-to-peer distributed applications. It's designed to conceal the underlying details of how messages are transported and permit the developer to focus on higher level tasks such as selecting a protocol or the way the transported message is formatted. A key component of the remoting architecture is the use of a proxy on the client side that serves as a surrogate for the remote object. It interacts with the client by presenting the same interface as on the remote object and encapsulates the information required to translate client calls into actual calls on the remote object.

The remote objects can be implemented in several ways: as a *singleton* that services all requests, as a server-activated *single call* object that is created each time the object is invoked, or as a client-activated object that persists as long as the client keeps it alive. The three offer a variety of different characteristics that enable a developer to select one most suited for an application.

14.5 Test Your Understanding

1. True or False?

   a. A process may contain multiple AppDomains.
   b. An AppDomain may contain multiple assemblies.
   c. An AppDomain can contain both EXE and DLL assemblies.
   d. An AppDomain can be unloaded from memory.

2. What are the three types of object activation modes, and which protocols can be used with each?

3. Which activation mode creates a new object each time a client invokes a method on the object? Which mode creates a new object only the first time a client invokes a method?

4. Explain the difference between `CurrentLeaseTime`, `Initial-LeaseTime`, and `RenewalOncallTime`.

5. What determines how often the lease manager checks for lease expirations?

6. Which activation modes support the use of leases?

7. When is a server-activated singleton object created?

   a. When the host begins running.
   b. When the client uses the `new` operator to create an instance of the object.
   c. When the client first calls a method on the object.
   d. When the object type is registered by the host.

8. Compare channel registration and type registration.

9. What is the reason to use SoapSuds or an interface when designing a remoting application? How is SoapSuds used?

CODE REFINEMENT, SECURITY, AND DEPLOYMENT

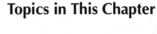

Topics in This Chapter

- *Code Refinement:* .NET provides a tool, FxCop, which analyzes code by checking it against a set of best practice rules and recommendations. This tool is designed for building components, but most applications can benefit from it as way to amend and refine how code is implemented. An example demonstrates how to analyze code using this tool's command-line interface.

- *Strongly Named Assemblies:* One aspect of code security is being able to verify an application's origin and version. .NET provides a way to mark an assembly with a key that identifies it, and supports an assembly versioning scheme that distinguishes between code versions—allowing multiple versions of a component to coexist.

- *Application Security:* The .NET Code Access Security model is based on a simple principle: allow code to access system resources and perform operations only when it has permission to do so. Before an assembly can access resources such as files, sockets, or the registry, it is checked for *evidence* to determine the *permissions* that it can be given. This chapter explains the overall security model and looks at how it is applied administratively and within code.

- *Application Deployment:* One of the touted benefits of .NET is the ability to install an application using XCOPY deployment—simple file copying. However, many applications require a more sophisticated approach that takes into account security policies and resource management. This chapter presents a checklist of issues to be considered.

Chapter 15

In the earliest days of programming, computers were used primarily to perform calculations and tedious tabulations. The measure of a program's correctness was whether it produced accurate results for a given set of input values. Modern software development now relies more on component-based solutions. The components often come from multiple sources, and it's not always possible to know the origin or trustworthiness of the components. As a result, code security and the ease of deploying and updating an application are now important metrics against which an application's success is judged.

This chapter looks at the issues and steps involved in producing a deliverable .NET software product. It breaks the process down into the three categories shown in Figure 15-1: code refinement, which looks at how code is tested against best practice rules; code security, which ensures that code is accessed only by other code that has permission to do so; and code deployment, which looks at how an application or component is packaged and made available for deployment.

The first section shows how to use FxCop as a tool to analyze an assembly and generate code change recommendations based on a predefined set of coding standards. The second section looks at the details of how to create a *strongly named* assembly and the security benefits that accrue from doing so.

The next section—which forms the heart of the chapter—explores the topic of Code Access Security (CAS). It explains how an administrator uses .NET tools to define a multi-level security policy for a computing environment and how security features are embedded in code. It also stresses understanding the interrelated security roles of *evidence, policy,* and *permissions.*

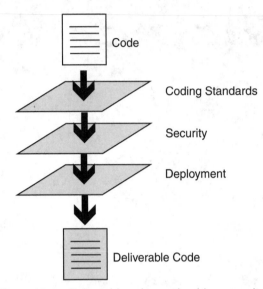

Figure 15-1   Deliverable software should meet coding standards, be secure, and be easily deployed

The chapter concludes with a look at the issues to be considered in deploying an application to users or customers. The advantages and disadvantages of using XCOPY or an installer to physically distribute an application are discussed.

15.1 Following .NET Code Design Guidelines

The developers of .NET included a set of rules[1] that are intended to serve as a guide for writing code that runs on the .NET platform. Although the rules are written with component developers in mind (Microsoft uses them for its managed code libraries), any application can benefit from them.

To help a developer incorporate these rules and best practices in their code, .NET includes the FxCop tool that analyzes code against these rules. Some of the rules may be stricter than your development environment requires; or they may simply conflict with your own standards—you may prefer non-Microsoft naming conventions, for

---

1. http://msdn.microsoft.com/library/default.asp?url=/library/en-us/
   cpgenref/html/cpconnetframeworkdesignguidelines.asp

instance. To accommodate your own coding standards, the tool permits you to disable rules and add custom ones. Figure 15-2 shows how rules are displayed with check boxes that make it easy to enable or disable them.

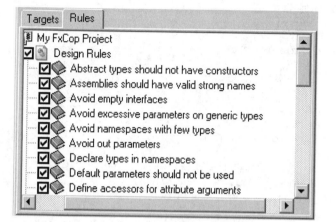

Figure 15-2   FxCop allows rules to be enabled or disabled by clicking a check box

FxCop is available as both a GUI (`fxcop.exe`) and command line (`fxcopcmd.exe`) application. Downloads of the latest version and documentation are free and available at several Web locations. The download also includes an SDK that can be used to create custom rules—a topic beyond the scope of this section.

Using FxCop

The purpose of FxCop is to analyze an assembly and produce output that pinpoints code features that violate the set of recommended best practices. To illustrate how it works, let's create an assembly from the code in Listing 15-1 and run it through FxCop. The program is a simple console application that accepts an input string, reverses it, and prints it. A simple menu permits the user to specify whether she wants to reverse a string or quit.

To test with FxCop, compile the program and pass the assembly to FxCop:

```
C:/> csc fxtest.cs
C:/> fxcopcmd  /file:fxtest.exe  /out:fxoutput.txt
```

Due to the length of the output, it's better to direct it to a file rather than display it.

| Listing 15-1 | Code to Be Analyzed by FxCop |

```
//fxtest.cs
using System;
using System.Text;
namespace FxTesting
{
    public class TestApp
    {
        static void Main()
        {
            string msg;
            string oper="";
            while(oper !="Q")
            {
                Console.WriteLine("(R)everse, (Q)uit");
                oper= Console.ReadLine();
                oper = oper.ToUpper();
                if(oper=="R"){
                    Console.WriteLine("Enter phrase to reverse:");
                    msg= Console.ReadLine();
                    if(msg.Length>1) msg= Reverse(msg);
                    Console.WriteLine(msg);
                }
            }
        }
        // Function to reverse a string
        public static String Reverse(String stringParameter)
        {
            if(stringParameter.Length==1)
            {
                return stringParameter;
            }
            else
            {
                return Reverse(stringParameter.Substring(1)) +
                            stringParameter.Substring(0,1);
            }
        }
    }
}
```

The output is serialized as XML that contains Message tags, describing each occurrence where the code does not conform to the recommended practices. Here is an example of the raw code comprising one message:

```
<Message TypeName="AssembliesShouldHaveValidStrongNames"
    Category="Microsoft.Design" CheckId="CA2210" Status="Active"
    Created="2005-01-12 02:41:07Z" FixCategory="NonBreaking">
    <Issue Name="NoStrongName" Certainty="95"
        Level="CriticalError">Sign 'fxtest' with a strong name key.
    </Issue>
</Message>
```

Let's look at the analysis FxCop produces for the `fxtest` assembly. For brevity, only the `TypeName` values from the XML are listed. Beneath each is a description of the code changes that will eliminate the message:

(1) `"AssembliesShouldDeclareMinimumSecurity"`
Requires adding a permission attribute that specifies the permissions required by this assembly. This is explained in Section 15.3 of this chapter.

(2) `"AssembliesShouldHaveValidStrongNames"`
Assembly should be assigned a *strong name*, which is a key that identifies the assembly. Assigning strong names is described in Section 15.2 of this chapter.

(3) `"MarkAssembliesWithAssemblyVersion"`
Add version attribute: `[assembly: AssemblyVersion("1.0.0.0")]`.

(4) `"MarkAssembliesWithClsCompliant"`
Add compliant attribute: `[System.CLSCompliant(true)]`.

(5) `"MarkAssembliesWithComVisible"`
Add `ComVisible` attribute: `[ComVisible(true)]`.
This exposes public managed assemblies and types to COM. By default, they are not visible to COM.

(6) `"StaticHolderTypesShouldNotHaveConstructors"`
Because the class `TestApp` has only static members, it should not have a public constructor. In this case, the public constructor is the default parameterless constructor. To override this, add: `private TestApp() {}`.

(7) `"AvoidUnnecessaryStringCreation"`
To avoid allocating memory for strings, string operations should be avoided. The solution is to eliminate `oper = oper.ToUpper();` and to use case-insensitive comparisons in the code, such as `if(string.Compare(oper, "R", true)==0)`.

(8) `"AvoidTypeNamesInParameters"`
Naming rules recommend that type names not be included as part of a parameter name. In this case, it objects to the parameter name `stringParameter`.

A review of the output shows that the assembly recommendations (1 through 5) are oriented toward components that will be stored in libraries and used by other code. As one would expect, the emphasis is on how component code interacts with other code. In general, security and type visibility is of more importance here than in general application development. Recommendations 6 and 7 promote more efficient code, whereas rule 8 is a subjective naming convention.

Many of the rules are overly restrictive for most programming environments, and you'll want to disable them. However, it is beneficial to be aware of them. They represent a set of best practices that have evolved with .NET. Even if you do not incorporate them in your code, understanding the reasoning behind them will deepen your knowledge of .NET.

15.2 Strongly Named Assemblies

The software development process relies increasingly on integrating code with components from multiple vendors. The vendor may be well known and trusted, or the component may be Internet freeware from an unknown developer. In both cases, security concerns demand a way to identify and authenticate the software. The most reliable solution is to sign the software with some unique digital signature that guarantees its origin and trustworthiness. The certificates that identify the publisher of downloadable software on the Internet are an example of this.

One of the integral parts of .NET security is the use of signing to create a uniquely identifiable assembly. .NET refers to such an assembly as *strongly named*. A strongly named assembly uses four attributes to uniquely identify itself: its file or *simple* name, a version number, a culture identity, and a public key token (discussed later). Together, these four are referred to as the "name" of the assembly. In addition, the assembly has the digital signature created by signing it. All of this is stored in the assembly's manifest.[2]

Although an assembly does need to be strongly named, doing so offers several advantages:

- It enables version control. Although you can add a version number to an assembly, the Common Language Runtime (CLR) ignores the version information unless the assembly is strongly named. As we will see later, having versioning in effect permits multiple versions of a component to run and ensures compatibility between assemblies sharing a version number.

---

2. The manifest is a set of tables containing metadata that describes the files in the assembly.

- It permits an assembly to be placed in the Global Assembly Cache (GAC) where it can be shared among calling assemblies.
- The .NET Code Access Policy can be used to grant or restrict permissions to assemblies based on their strong name. In addition, the strong name can also be used programmatically to control access to resources.
- It allows assemblies to have the same name, because the assemblies are identified by their unique information—not their name.

Creating a Strongly Named Assembly

The first step in creating a strong name is to create a pair of public and private encryption keys. During compilation, the private key is used to encrypt the hashed contents of the files contained in the assembly. The encrypted string that is produced is the digital signature that "signs" the assembly. It is stored in the manifest, along with the public key. Here are the steps to create and use a strongly named assembly:

1. A strong name is generated using asymmetric public key cryptography. This scheme relies on a private key that is used for encryption and a public key that decrypts. To create a file containing this key pair, use the *Strong Name* command-line utility as shown here:

   ```
   SN -k <keyfilename>
   SN -k  KeyLib.snk
   ```

2. Because the public key that is created is so large, .NET creates a more manageable *public key token* that is a 64-bit hash of the public key. When a client assembly is built that references a strongly named assembly, the public key token of the referenced assembly is stored in the manifest of the client assembly as a way to reference the target assembly.

3. After you have the file containing the public/private key pair, creating the strongly named assembly is simple: just place the `AssemblyKey-File` attribute (located in the `System.Refection` namespace) in your code at the assembly level:

   ```
   [assembly: AssemblyKeyFile("KeyLib.snk")]
   ```

4. This statement causes the compiler to extract the private key from the specified file and use it to sign the assembly. At the same time, the public key is placed in the assembly's manifest. Note that if you invoke the C# compiler from the command line, you can leave out the `AssemblyKeyFile` attribute and use the `/keyfile` flag to specify the path to the `.snk` file.

5. When the runtime loads this assembly, it essentially reverses the sign-ing process: It decrypts the signature using the public key found in the manifest. Then, it performs a hash of the assembly's contents and compares this with the decrypted hash. If they do not match, the assembly is not allowed to run.

Figure 15-3 summarizes the overall process. Note how decryption works. The decrypted signature yields a hash that should match the output when a new hash is performed on the assembly. If the two match, you can be sure that the private key associated with the public key was used for the original signing, and that the assem-bly has not been tampered with—changing even one bit will result in a different hash.

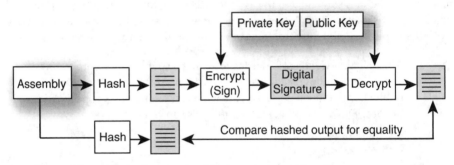

Figure 15-3   Using private and public keys to sign and verify a strong assembly

Core Note

A digital signature is not the same thing as a digital certificate. The digital signature in a strongly named assembly tells you nothing about who created the assembly, whereas a certificate contains the identity information that is used to authenticate the certificate publisher. Refer to documentation on Authenticode to learn how to obtain and use a certificate with an assembly.

Delayed Signing

It is imperative that the private key generated using Sn.exe (or some other process) not be compromised, because it is how an organization uniquely signs its software. If another party has access to the key, consumers cannot trust the ownership of the assembly.

One measure to secure the key is to limit its availability to developers, or withhold it altogether. During the development stage, developers are given only the public key. Use of the private key is delayed until it is necessary to sign the final software version. Delayed signing requires different steps than are used for creating a strongly named assembly:

1. Sn.exe is used to create a file containing the public/private key pair. This should be the task of the security administrator.

2. Sn.exe is run again to extract the public key into a separate file. The command uses the –p switch, and specifies the original file and the file to contain the public key:

   ```
   SN -p  KeyLib.snk  PubKeyLib.snk
   ```

3. The public key file is distributed to developers who must add two attributes to their assemblies to perform partial signing and have the public key stored in the assembly's manifest.

   ```
   [assembly: AssemblyKeyFile("PubKeyLib.snk")]
   [assembly: AssemblyDelaySign(true)]
   ```

4. If you follow these preceding steps to create an assembly, you'll find that an exception occurs ("strong name validation failed") when you try to load it. This is because the assembly does not have a valid signature. To instruct the runtime to skip signature verification, run Sn.exe with the –Vr switch and specify the delay-signed assembly:

   ```
   SN -Vr <delay-signed assembly>
   ```

5. Prior to deployment, the assembly should be officially signed. Use SN with the –R switch to sign it:

   ```
   SN -R <delay-signed assembly>
   ```

   To reinstate signature verification for the assembly, run

   ```
   SN -Vu <assembly>
   ```

Because an assembly references another strongly named assembly using its public key, there is no need to rebuild assemblies dependent on this one.

Global Assembly Cache (GAC)

The Global Assembly Cache is a special directory set aside where strongly named assemblies can be stored and located by the CLR. As part of resolving references at load time, the CLR automatically looks in the GAC for the requested assembly. The obvious advantage of storing assemblies in the GAC is that they are located in a central, well known location where they can be located and shared by multiple applications. A less obvious advantage is that the strong name signatures for assemblies in the GAC are verified only when installed in the GAC. This improves the performance of applications referencing these assemblies, because no verification is required when loading the assembly.

Physically, the GAC is a Microsoft Windows directory located on the following path:

```
C:\winnt\assembly
```

You can view its contents using a shell extension (ShFusion.dll) that is added to Windows Explorer as part of the .NET Framework installation. Each entry displays an assembly's name, type, version number, and public key token. By clicking an assembly entry, you can bring up a context menu that permits you to display the assembly's properties or delete it.

The easiest way to install a strongly named assembly into the GAC (or uninstall one) is to use GACUtil.exe, a command-line utility that ships with .NET SDK. Here is the syntax for performing selected operations:

>gacutil /i <assembly>	Installs assembly in GAC.
>gacutil /u <assembly>	Uninstalls an assembly from the GAC.
>gacutil /if <assembly>	Installs assembly in GAC; if an assembly with that name already exists, it is overwritten.
>gacutil /l	Lists contents of GAC.

There are a couple of drawbacks to storing an assembly in the GAC. First, it is difficult to reference during compilation due to the verbose GAC subdirectory naming conventions. An alternative is to compile referencing a local copy of the assembly. Then, remove the local assembly after compilation is completed.

Another possible drawback stems from the fact that an assembly cannot be copied into the GAC. If your application requires an assembly in the GAC, it eliminates deploying an application by simply copying files to a client's machine. Deployment issues are discussed in the last section of this chapter.

Versioning

A major benefit of using strongly named assemblies is that the CLR uses the assembly's version information to bind assemblies that are dependent on each other. When such an assembly is loaded, the CLR checks the version number of referenced assemblies to ensure they have the same version numbers as recorded in the calling assembly's manifest. If the version fails to match (usually because a new version has been created), an exception is thrown.

Assigning a Version Number to an Assembly

Every assembly has a version number. A default value is used if one is not explicitly defined. The version can be assigned using the Assembly Linker (Al.exe) tool, but is usually declared within the code using an AssemblyVersion attribute:

```
[assembly: AssemblyVersion("1.0.0.0")]
```

The version number has four parts:

```
<major version>.<minor version>.<build number>.<revision>
```

You can specify all the values or you can accept the default build number, revision number, or both by using an asterisk (*). For example:

```
[assembly:AssemblyVersion("2.3.")]     yields 2.3.0.0
[assembly:AssemblyVersion("2.3.*")]    yields 2.3.1830,4000
```

When an asterisk (*) is specified for the build number, a default build number is calculated by taking the number of days since January 1, 2000. The default revision number is the number of seconds past midnight divided by two.

You can use reflection to view an assembly's version along with the other parts of its identity. To illustrate, add the following attributes to the code in Listing 15-1 to create a custom version number and strong name:

```
[assembly: AssemblyKeyFile("Keylb.snk")]
[assembly: AssemblyVersion("1.0.*")]
```

Compile the code and use the Assembly.GetName method to display the assembly's identification.

```
Console.WriteLine(Assembly.GetExecutingAssembly().GetName());
```

This method returns an instance of the AssemblyName class that contains the assembly's simple name, culture, public key or public key token, and version.

```
fxtest, Version=1.0.1839.24546, Culture=neutral,
    PublicKeyToken=1f081c4ba0eeb6db
```

15.3 Security

The centerpiece of .NET security is the *Code Access Security* model. As the name implies, it is based on code access—not user access. Conceptually, the model is quite simple. Before an assembly or component within an assembly may access system resources (files, the registry, event log, and others), the CLR checks to ensure that it has permission to do so. It does this by collecting *evidence* about the assembly—where is it located and its content. Based on this evidence, it grants the assembly certain *permissions* to access resources and perform operations. Figure 15-4 illustrates the key elements in this process and introduces the terms that you must know in order to administer security.

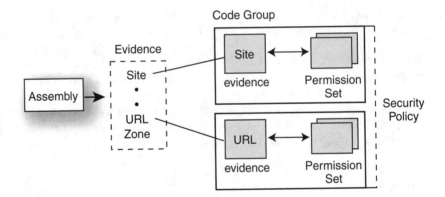

Figure 15-4   An assembly is matched with code groups whose evidence it satisfies

When an assembly is loaded, the CLR gathers its evidence and attempts to match it with *code groups* whose evidence it satisfies. A code group is a binding between a set of permissions and a single type of evidence. For example, a code group may be defined so that only assemblies from a particular application directory are allowed to have Web access. If an assembly's *site evidence* indicates it is from that directory, it is part of the code group and has Web access. An assembly can be a member of multiple code groups, and, consequently, can have multiple permissions.

.NET provides predefined evidence, permissions, code groups, and security policies—a collection of code groups. Although code can be used to hook into and modify some aspects of security, an administrator performs the bulk of security configuration and management using .NET tools. In most cases, the predefined elements are all that an administrator needs. However, the security model is flexible, and permits an administrator to create security policies from custom evidence, permissions, and code groups.

This abstract representation of .NET security shown in Figure 15-4 is implemented in concrete types: The `Evidence` class is a collection that holds evidence objects; permission classes grant access to a resource or the right to perform some action; and a `PermissionSet` is a collection class that groups permissions and contains methods to manipulate them. The following sections take a close look at evidence, permissions, and how they are related. You'll then see how to implement a security policy, both as an administrator and by accessing the permission classes through code.

Permissions and Permission Sets

A permission is the right to access a resource or perform some action. An assembly is assigned a permission when its evidence matches the evidence requirements for a permission set. Figure 15-5 illustrates how permissions come into play when an assembly attempts to access a resource. In this case, assembly A calls assembly B, which creates a `FileStream` object and attempts to use its `Write` method. The code in the .NET Framework Class Library that implements this method demands that the calling assembly have permission to perform file I/O. Moreover, it requires that all assemblies further up the call stack also have this permission. This check—known as *walking the call stack*—ensures that an assembly that does not have a required permission cannot use one that does to illegally perform an operation.

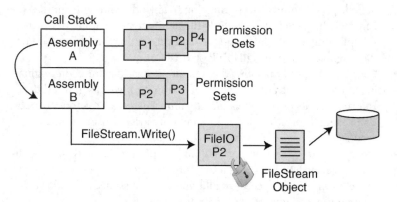

Figure 15-5   An assembly must have permission to perform file I/O

Because both Assembly B and Assembly A possess the `FileIO` permission, the write operation is permitted. An exception of type `System.Security.Security-Exception` is thrown if either assembly does not have the requisite permission.

Permissions are often interrelated: for example, the permission to write to a file requires an accompanying permission to access the directory containing the file. To avoid having to grant and deny all permissions on an individual basis, .NET includes a `PermissionSet` class that allows a collection of permissions to be treated as a single entity for the purpose of denying or granting permissions.

As we shall see, permission sets can be created and applied programmatically by creating and adding individual permission objects to a `PermissionSet` collection. An alternate approach is to use the .NET Configuration tool to create permission sets and assign them to code groups. To encourage this approach, .NET includes predefined permission sets.

Named Permission Sets

.NET provides seven built-in or *named permission* sets. They range from the most restrictive `Nothing`, which prevents an assembly from loading, to the least restrictive `Full-Trust`, which permits unrestricted access to all of the permissions listed in Table 15-1. Here they are in ascending order of trust:

- `Nothing`. Prevents an assembly from being loaded. This is used primarily when the code is deemed untrustworthy because its origin cannot be determined.
- `Execution`. Permits code to load and run, but little else. It cannot access external resources. Such code is useful only for making calculations.
- `Internet`. Allows code to display and implement a user interface. By default, .NET grants this permission to all code coming from the Internet. Its permissions include the ability to open a file, perform safe printing, create safe top-level and subwindows, and connect to the originating site using HTTP or HTTPS.
- `LocalIntranet`. Specifies the default permissions for code originating in the local intranet. In addition to the permissions granted the Internet set, its permissions include unrestricted access to `FileDialogs`, default printing privileges, and unrestricted user interface access.
- `Everything`. Grants all permissions except permission to skip verification, because this is needed to verify the code is type-safe.
- `FullTrust`. Grants access to all built-in permissions. All code running on the local machine is given this by default.

Figure 15-6 lists the most interesting permission sets along with the individual permissions they contain. These sets cannot be modified; however, they can be copied and used as a base set for creating a custom permission set.

Permission	Internet	Local-Intranet	Everything	Full-Trust
Environment Variables		Read USERNAME	Unrestricted	Unrestricted
File Dialog	File Open	Unrestricted		
File IO				
Isolated Storage File	Domain isolation by user	Assembly isolation		
Reflection		Member and Type		
Registry				
Security	Execution	Execution/Assert		
User Interface	Top-Level Windows	Unrestricted		
KeyContainerPermission				
DNS		Unrestricted		
WebBrowserPermission				
Printing	Safe printing	Default		
Socket Access				
Web Access				
Event Log		Local machine		
Performance Counter				
OLE DB				
SQL Client				
StorePermission				

Figure 15-6   Permissions associated with selected named permission sets

Permission Set Attributes

The built-in permission sets provide a convenient way to request permission for more than one permission type at a time. This code segment shows the syntax to request permission for the LocalIntranet permission set. It attaches a PermissionSetAttribute with a Name value set to the name of the desired permission set:

```
[PermissionSet(SecurityAction.Demand,Name="LocalIntranet")]
public string GetTitle()   // Requires LocalIntranet
{}
```

Note that all named permission sets except Everything can be applied as an attribute.

.NET Built-in Security Permissions

The individual permissions shown in Figure 15-5 are implemented in .NET as built-in permission classes. In addition to being accessed by the security configuration tools, they can also be accessed by code to implement a finer-grained security than can be configured using administrative tools.

Table 15-1 summarizes the more important built-in permission classes.

Table 15-1   Built-in Permission Classes

Namespace	Class Name	Controls Permission To:
System.Security.Permissions	Environment	Access user and OS environment variables
	FileDialog	Access files or folders using a file dialog box.
	FileIO	Access files or folders.
	IsolatedStorage	Configure isolated storage and set quota on size of user's store.
	KeyContainer	Access key containers. A key container is an area within a key database that contains key pairs used for cryptography.
	Reflection	Access metadata using Reflection commands.
	Registry	Access system registry.
	Security	Access security permissions.
	Store	Stores containing X.509 certificates. X.509 is a standard for public key certificates. Most commonly used for securing transmission of data over Internet.
	UI	User interfaces and the clipboard.
System.Net	Dns	Domain name servers.
	Socket	Connect or accept connects at a specified socket. A socket is an address designated by a port # and IP address.
	Web	Connect to or from a Web host.
System.Drawing	Printing	Access printers.
System.Data.Common	DBData	Access data using a data provider.

Table 15-1   Built-in Permission Classes *(continued)*

Namespace	Class Name	Controls Permission To:
System.Data.SqlClient	SqlClient	Use SQL Server data provider.
System	EventLog	Write to or browse a machine's event log.
System.ServiceProcess	ServiceController	Access to control or browse a machine's services.
System.Messaging	MessageQueue	Access the message queue.

All permission classes inherit and implement the interfaces shown in Figure 15-7. Of these, IPermission and IStackWalk are the most useful. IPermission defines a Demand method that triggers the stack walk mentioned earlier; IStack-Walk contains methods that permit a program to modify how the stack walk is performed. This proves to be a handy way to ensure that a called component does not perform an action outside of those that are requested. We'll look at these interfaces in more detail in the discussion of programmatic security.

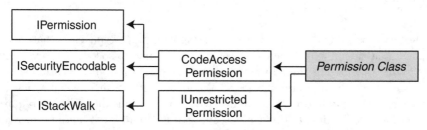

Figure 15-7   Interfaces inherited by permission classes

Identity Permissions

Recall that when the CLR loads an assembly, it matches the assembly's evidence against that required by code groups and grants permissions from the code groups whose criteria it meets. These code group derived permissions are either custom permissions or built-in permissions as described in Table 15-1.

The CLR also grants another set of permissions that correspond directly to the identity evidence provided by the assembly. For example, there are ZoneIdentity-Permission and StrongNamedIdentityPermission classes that demand an assembly originate from a specific zone or have a specific strong name identity. Table 15-2 lists the origin-based identity classes.

Table 15-2   Identity Permission Classes

Class	Identity Represented
`PublisherIdentityPermission`	The digital signature of the assembly's publisher.
`SiteIdentityPermission`	Web site where the code comes from.
`StrongNamedIdentityPermission`	Strong name of the assembly.
`URLIdentityPermission`	URL where the code comes from. This includes the protocols HTTP, HTTPS, and FTP.
`ZoneIdentityPermission`	Zone where the code originates: `Internet`, `Intranet`, `MyComputer`, `NoZone`, `Trusted`, `Untrusted`.

Unlike the built-in permissions described earlier, these classes cannot be administered using configuration tools. Instead, a program creates an instance of an identity permission class and uses its methods to demand that an assembly provide a specified identity to perform some action. This programmatic use of permission classes is referred to as *imperative security*.

Permission Attributes

All security permission classes have a corresponding *attribute* class that can be applied as an attribute to an assembly, class, and method to specify security equivalent to that provided by the permission class. This is referred to as *declarative security*, and serves two useful purposes: When applied at the assembly level, a permission attribute informs the runtime which permissions the assembly requires, and enables the runtime to throw an exception if it cannot grant these permissions; when applied to classes and methods within the code, the attribute specifies which permissions any calling assemblies must have to use this assembly. Examples using declarative security are provided later in the chapter.

Evidence

To qualify as a member of a code group and assume its privileges, an assembly must provide evidence that matches the evidence membership requirements of the code group. This evidence is based on either the assembly's origin or its signature. The origin identification includes `Site`, `Url`, and `Zone` evidence; the signature refers to an assembly's strong name, its digitally signed certificate (such as X.509), or a hash of the assembly's content. The Common Language Runtime provides seven predefined types of evidence. They are referred to by names used in the security administrative tools:

- `Strong Name`. An assembly with a `Strong Name` has a public key that can be used to identify the assembly. A class or method can be configured to accept calls only from an assembly having a specified public key value. The most common use for this is to identify third-party components that share the same public key. A `Strong Name` has two other properties, `Version` and `Name`, that also can be required as evidence by a host assembly.
- `Publisher`. This evidence indicates that an assembly has been digitally signed with a certificate such as X.509. Certificates are provided by a trusted certificate authority and are most commonly used for secure Internet transactions. When a signed assembly is loaded, the CLR recognizes the certificate and adds a Publisher object to the assembly.
- `Hash`. By applying a computational algorithm to an assembly, a unique identifier known as a hash is created. This hash evidence is automatically added to each assembly and serves to identify particular builds of the assembly. Any change in the compiled code yields a different hash value—even if the version is unchanged.
- `Application Directory`. This evidence is used to grant a permission set to all assemblies that are located in a specified directory or in a subdirectory of the running application.
- `Site`. `Site` evidence is the top-level portion of a URL that excludes the format and any subdirectory identifiers. For example, `www.corecsharp.net` is extracted as site evidence from `http://www.corecsharp.net/code`.
- URL. This evidence consists of the entire URL identifying where an assembly comes from. In the preceding example, `http://www.corecsharp.net/code` is provided as URL evidence.
- `Zone`. The `System.Security.SecurityZone` enumeration defines five security zones: `MyComputer`, `Intranet`, `Internet`, `Trusted`, and `Untrusted`. An assembly's zone evidence is the zone from which it comes.
  - `MyComputer`. Code coming from the local machine.
  - `Intranet`. Code coming from computers on the same local area network.
  - `Internet`. Code coming from the Internet that is identified by an HTTP or IP address. If the local machine is identified as `http://localhost/`, it is part of the `Internet` zone.
  - `Trusted`. Identifies Internet sites that are trusted. These sites are specified using Microsoft Internet Explorer (IE).
  - `Untrusted`. Sites specified in IE as being malicious or untrustworthy.

In addition to these, there is also a blank evidence known as All Code evidence that is used by an administrator to create a code group that matches all assemblies.

The CLR maintains evidence in an instance of the Evidence collection class. This object contains two evidence collections: one for the built-in host evidence and another for user-defined evidence. This evidence is made available to security policy, which then determines the permissions available to the assembly. You can use reflection to view evidence programmatically. In this example, we view the evidence for an assembly, movieclient.exe, which is located on the local machine (the assembly's source code is presented later in this section):

```
using System;
using System.Reflection;
using System.Security.Policy;
class ClassEvidence
{
    public static void Main()
    {
        Assembly ClientAssembly;
        // (1)Load object to reference movieclient assembly
        ClientAssembly = Assembly.Load("movieclient");
        // (2) Evidence is available through Evidence property
        Evidence ev = ClientAssembly.Evidence;
        // (3) Display each evidence object
        foreach (object ob in ev)
        {
            Console.WriteLine(ob.ToString());
        }
    }
}
```

Output from the program reveals the Zone, Url, Strong Name, and Hash evidence associated with the assembly. No Site evidence is present because the assembly's Url origin is defined by a file:// rather than an http:// format. Application Directory evidence is also missing because it comes from the host application, not the assembly's metadata.

```
<System.Security.Policy.Zone version="1">
    <Zone>MyComputer</Zone>
</System.Security.Policy.Zone>

<System.Security.Policy.Url version="1">
    <Url>file://C:/movieclient.EXE</Url>
</System.Security.Policy.Url>

<StrongName version="1"
```

```
              Key="002400... 8D2"
              Name="movieclient"
              Version="0.0.0.0"/>

<System.Security.Policy.Hash version="1">
  <RawData>4D5A90000300000004000000FFFF0000B80
  </RawData>
</System.Security.Policy.Hash>
```

Security Policies

A .NET *security policy* defines how assembly evidence is evaluated to determine the permissions that are granted to the assembly. .NET recognizes four policy levels: Enterprise, Machine, User, and Application Domain. The policy-level names describe their recommended usage. Enterprise is intended to define security policy across all machines in the enterprise; Machine defines security for a single machine; User defines security policy for individual users; and Application Domain security is applied to code running in a specific AppDomain. Enterprise, Machine, and User policies are configured by an administrator. AppDomain policy, which is implemented only programmatically and used for special cases, is not discussed.

Despite their names, policies can be configured in any way an administrator chooses. The User policy could be set up to define enterprise security and the Machine policy to define user security. However, an administrator should take advantage of the names and use them to apply security to their intended target. As you will see in the discussion of the .NET Framework Configuration Tool (see "The .NET Framework Configuration Tool" on page 704), the security policy is granular enough to allow custom security policies on individual machines and users.

How .NET Applies Security Policies

Each security policy level is made up of one or more code sets. Each code set, in turn, contains a set of permissions that are mapped to a specific evidence type. Figure 15-8 illustrates how code sets and policy levels are combined to yield a permission set for an assembly.

The .NET security manager is responsible for evaluating evidence and policy to determine the permissions granted. It begins at the enterprise level and determines the permissions in it that can be granted to the assembly. In this example, enterprise contains three code groups—two of which the assembly's evidence satisfies. The logical union of these permissions produces the permission set at this level. The other two policy levels are evaluated in the same way, yielding their associated permission set. The logical intersection of the three permission sets produces the permission set that is assigned to the assembly. In this case, the final set consists of permissions 2 and 5—the only permissions present on each level.

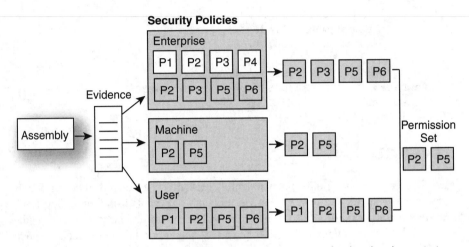

Figure 15-8   A permission set is created from the intersection of policy level permissions

Configuring Security Policy

Physically, each policy level is stored as a configurable XML file that defines a hierarchy of code groups for the policy. The Enterprise policy file, `enterprisec.con-fig`, and the Machine policy file, `security.config`[3], are stored in the same folder on a Microsoft Windows system:

```
<Windows Directory>\Microsoft.NET\Framework\<Version>\config\
```

The User policy file is named `security.config` and is located on the path

```
<Documents and Settings>\<User Name>\Application Data\Microsoft\
     CLR Security Config\<Version>\
```

Listing 15-2 contains an extract from the Machine policy file that illustrates the file layout. It comprises four major sections:

`<SecurityClasses>`	Defines all individual permissions.
`<NamedPermissionSets>`	Defines named permission sets.
`<CodeGroup>`	Provides a name and permission set for code group.
`<FullTrustAssemblies>`	List of trusted assemblies.

---

3. Not to be confused with the `machine.config` file that holds machine-wide configuration data.

The code group section is structured as a multi-level hierarchy, with the conditions for granting permissions becoming more restrictive at each lower level.

Listing 15-2	Extracts from the Machine Policy File `Security.Config`

```
<SecurityClasses>
   <SecurityClass Name="WebPermission"
         Description="System.Net.WebPermission, System,
         Version=2.0.3600.0, Culture=neutral,
         PublicKeyToken=b77a5c561934e089"/>
   <SecurityClass Name="EventLogPermission"
         Description="System.Diagnostics.EventLogPermission,
         System, Version=2.0.3600.0, Culture=neutral,
         PublicKeyToken=b77a5c561934e089"/>
   ...
</SecurityClasses>
<NamedPermissionSets>
   <PermissionSet class="NamedPermissionSet"
         version="1"
         Name="LocalIntranet"
         Description="Default rights given to applications on
         the local intranet">
      <IPermission class="EnvironmentPermission"
         version="1" Read="USERNAME"/>
      <IPermission class="FileDialogPermission"
         version="1" Unrestricted="true"/>
   ...
</PermissionSet>
...
</NamedPermissionSets>
<CodeGroup class="UnionCodeGroup"
         version="1"
         PermissionSetName="Nothing"
         Name="All_Code"
         Description="Code group grants no ...">
      <IMembershipCondition class="AllMembershipCondition"
         version="1"/>
   <CodeGroup class="UnionCodeGroup"
         version="1"
         PermissionSetName="FullTrust"
         Name="My_Computer_Zone"
         Description="Code group grants ...">
      ...
   </CodeGroup>
```

Listing 15-2	Extracts from the Machine Policy File Security.Config (continued)

```
    ... additional code groups here
</CodeGroup>
<FullTrustAssemblies>
    <IMembershipCondition class="StrongNameMembershipCondition"
            version="1"
            PublicKeyBlob="00000000000000000400000000000000"
            Name="mscorlib.resources"
            AssemblyVersion="Version=2.0.3600.0"/>
    <IMembershipCondition class="StrongNameMembershipCondition"
            version="1"
            PublicKeyBlob="00000000000000000400000000000000"
            Name="System"
            AssemblyVersion="Version=2.0.3600.0"/>
    ...
</FullTrustAssemblies>
```

.NET provides two ways to work with these policy files: a command-line Code Access Security Policy (caspol) and a graphical Configuration tool (MSCorCfg.msc). Both can be used to modify the default configuration, create custom code groups, create custom permission sets, and export policies to be deployed with an application. We'll look at both tools in this section, with an emphasis on the Configuration tool because its visual interface makes it more popular and easier to learn than the command-line approach.

The .NET Framework Configuration Tool

On a Microsoft Windows system, you start the Configuration tool by selecting Microsoft .NET Framework Configuration from the Administrative Tools folder or by selecting Run and typing **MSCORCFG.MSC**. The program interface consists of a window divided into two panes. As shown in Figure 15-9, the left side contains a tree structure comprising multiple folders. Of these, the Runtime Security Policy folder expands to display a hierarchy of security information.

At the top level of the hierarchy are the three folders representing the Enterprise, Machine, and User policies. Beneath each of these are folders that contain code groups, permission sets, and policy assemblies. This hierarchy is, of course, simply a visual representation of the underlying XML policy files. You can observe this by comparing the raw XML tags in Listing 15-2 with the items displayed under the Machine policy.

```
□─🖳 Runtime Security Policy
 ⊞─🖳 Enterprise
 □─💻 Machine
    □─🖳 Code Groups
       □─◆ All_Code
          □─◆ My_Computer_Zone ──────────────
              ◆ Microsoft_Strong_Name
              ◆ ECMA_Strong_Name
          □─◆ LocalIntranet_Zone ────────────
              ◇ Intranet_Same_Site_Access
              ◇ Intranet_Same_Directory_Access
          □─◆ Internet_Zone ─────────────────
              ◇ Internet_Same_Site_Access
            ◆ Restricted_Zone
          □─◆ Trusted_Zone ──────────────────
              ◇ Trusted_Same_Site_Access
          □─◇ Application_Security_Manager ───
              ◇ Intranet_Same_Site_Access
              ◇ Intranet_Same_Directory_Access
            ◆ My_Computer_Url
```

[Child Code Groups]

Microsoft_Strong_Name
ECMA_Strong_Name

Intranet_Same_Site_Access
Intranet_Same_Directory_Access

Internet_Same_Site_Access

Trusted_Same_Site_Access

Intranet_Same_Site_Access
Intranet_Same_Directory_Access

Figure 15-9   Interface for the .NET Framework Configuration tool

The Default Configuration Policies

The `Enterprise` and `User` policies contain a single default code group named `All_Code`. If you click it, you'll see this description in the right panel:

"Code group grants *all code full trust* and forms the root of the code group tree."

Specifically, this code group binds `All Code` evidence with the `FullTrust` permission set. Recall that all assemblies qualify as members of code groups that use `All Code` evidence and that the `FullTrust` permission set offers unrestricted permissions. The net effect of binding these two is to create `Enterprise` and `User` policies that offer unlimited permissions to all assemblies. In other words, these two policies offer no security at all by default.

Core Note

The code groups provided by .NET are named after the evidence they represent. Because no two code groups may have the same name, custom code groups must use a modified naming convention.

The `Machine` security policy is far more interesting and instructive. At its root is the `All_Code` code group. Unlike the other two policies, it binds `All   Code` evidence to the `Nothing` permission set, which means the code group grants no permissions. To find the permissions, you must look to the code groups nested beneath this root. The first level contains six groups: `My_Computer_Zone`, `LocalIntranet_Zone`, `Internet_Zone`, `Restricted_Zone`, `Trusted_Zone`, and `Application_Security_Manager`. All except `Restricted_Zone` have one or more child code groups. Let's look at how default permissions are granted for two of these: `My_Computer_Zone` and `LocalIntranet_Zone`. To view details about the other code groups, simply right-click their name to bring up a properties window.

My_Computer_Zone Code Group

This code group grants the `FullTrust` permission set to assemblies that satisfy the `My Computer` zone evidence. Its two child code groups grant `FullTrust` to assemblies that have `Strong Name` evidence containing either the Microsoft public key or the ECMA public key, also known as the Standard Public Key.[4] It is important to understand that an assembly can satisfy the `Strong Name` evidence without satisfying the `My Computer` zone evidence. This is because .NET evaluates child code groups even if the conditions for the parent group are not satisfied. Conversely, a code group's properties can be set to instruct .NET not to evaluate child groups if the conditions of the parent code group are satisfied.

LocalIntranet_Zone Code Group

This code group grants the `LocalIntranet` permission set to assemblies that satisfy the `Local Intranet` zone evidence—any computers on the same local area network as the machine on which the host code runs. This code group has two child code groups: `Intranet_Same_Site_Access` and `Intranet_Same_Directory_Access`. The former permits code to access the site of its origin; the latter permits code to access its original install directory. The practical effect of these permissions is to permit code to perform I/O on its local storage.

Configuring Code Access Security with the Configuration Tool—An Example

To illustrate how to use the Configuration tool, we'll create a new permission set and assign it the `Reflection` and `Execution` permissions. Next, we'll create a code

---

4. Assemblies based on the European Computer Manufacturers Association (ECMA) specifications for the Common Language Infrastructure (CLI) contain an ECMA public key. These include `system.dll` and `mscorlib.dll`. The key is actually a placeholder that is mapped to a key pair provided by the particular CLR installation.

group that maps the new permission set to `Url` evidence that specifies a directory on the local machine. The effect is to grant the `Reflection` permission to any assembly that runs from this directory.

For testing, we'll create a simple application that uses reflection to access a private field in this assembly's class:

```
// (movieclass.dll) Will use reflection to access this class
using System;
public class Movies
{
    private int ID;
    private string Director;
    public string title;
    public string year;
}
```

Listing 15-3 contains the code that accesses the private `Director` field. This is done by calling the `Type.GetField` method and passing as arguments the field name and flags that request access to a private field in a class instance.

Listing 15-3	Assembly Requiring Reflection Permission

```
// configtest.cs
using System;
using System.Reflection;
class ClassEvidence
{
    public static void Main()
    {
        Assembly ClientAssembly;
        ClientAssembly = Assembly.Load("movieclass");
        // Get the desired Type in the Assembly
        Type myType = ClientAssembly.GetType("Movies");
        // Get the FieldInfo for private field "Director".
        // Specify nonpublic field and instance class.
        // Accessing private members requires Reflection
        // Permission.
        FieldInfo myFieldInfo = myType.GetField("Director",
                BindingFlags.NonPublic | BindingFlags.Instance);
        if (myFieldInfo !=null)
            Console.WriteLine("Field: {0} Type: {1}",
                            myFieldInfo.Name,
                            myFieldInfo.FieldType);
```

Listing 15-3	Assembly Requiring Reflection Permission *(continued)*

```
    {
        // output: Field: Director   Type: System.String
    } else {
        Console.WriteLine("Could not access field.");
    }
  }
}
```

Creating a Permission Set

Follow these steps to create the permission set:

1. Right-click the Permission Sets folder under Machine policy and select New.
2. Enter **Reflection** as the name of the set and provide a description.
3. On the next screen, select Security from the Available Permissions. Check Enable Assembly Execution and Allow Evidence Control from the permission settings window.
4. Select Reflection from the Available Permissions. Check Grant Assemblies Unrestricted Permission to Discover Information About Other Assemblies.
5. Click Finish and the permission set named Reflection appears in the left pane.

You now have a permission set that allows an assembly the rights associated with the Reflection permission.

Creating a Code Group

Follow these steps to create the code group:

1. Right-click the All_Code node—under Machine-Code Groups—and select New.
2. Enter **My_Computer_Url** as the name of the group and provide a description.
3. For the Condition Type, choose URL.
4. For the URL, enter **file://c:/cas/***. This specifies the folder from which an assembly must originate in order to satisfy the Url evidence.
5. Next, assign the new Reflection permission set to the code group and click Finish.

6. Click the new code group in the left pane and select Edit Code Group Properties. Check the option This Policy Level Will Only Have the Permissions from the Permission Set Associated with the Code Group.

The final step is necessary to make this example work. Setting this *Exclusive* option tells .NET to assign only the permissions of the new code group to any code found in the specified directory path. If this option is not set, the code is evaluated against all Machine level code groups and receives permissions from all whose evidence it matches. Also, note that code not located in the specified subdirectory is unaffected by the new code group and receives the default Machine policy permissions.

Testing the New Code Group

To demonstrate the effects of this new code group, compile the program and store a copy of configtest.exe in C:\ and C:\CAS\. Run both copies from the command line, and they should succeed. Now, use the Configuration tool to change the permission set for the My_Computer_Url code group from Reflection to Internet. When you now run the program from the CAS subdirectory, it fails because the Internet permission set does not include the Reflection permission. The program still runs fine from C:\, because its permissions come from the other code groups in the Machine policy.

This is a simple example, but it illustrates the core principle behind Code Access Security of assigning permissions to an assembly based on an analysis of its evidence. In this case, identical assemblies receive different permissions based on the directory in which the code resides. The evidence is a Url specified directory, but could just as easily be an Internet site, the assembly's Strong Name, or its security zone.

Determining the Permissions Granted to an Assembly

It is not easy to empirically determine the permissions that are granted to a given assembly. You must gather the evidence for the assembly, determine the security policies in effect from the XML policy files, and evaluate the evidence in light of the policies. Fortunately, the .NET Configuration tool and Caspol utility can perform this evaluation for you.

To use the Configuration tool, right-click the Runtime Security Policy folder and select Evaluate Assembly from the context menu. Use the Browse button to locate the assembly in the file directory. Select View Permissions Granted to Assembly, and click the Next button to display the individual permissions. For c:\cas\configtest.exe from the preceding example, Security and Reflection are listed. For c:\configtest.exe, Unrestricted is listed.

`Caspol` is run from the command line. Among its numerous options is `-rsp`, which resolves permissions for an assembly. To determine permissions for the `con-figtest` assembly, enter this command:

```
C:\>caspol -rsp c:\cas\configtest.exe
```

Output is in an XML format and correctly includes `Security` and `Reflection`, as well as two identity permissions: `UrlIdentity` and `ZoneIdentity` (`MyCom-puter`). The identity permissions can be ignored because specific permissions are provided.

You can also use `caspol` to understand why an assembly qualifies for its permissions by identifying the code groups that the assembly belongs to. Enter the previous command, except replace the `-rsp` option with the `-rsg` (resolve code group) option:

```
C:\>caspol -rsg c:\cas\configtest.exe
```

This output shows that a code group uses `Url` evidence to grant its permission set (`Reflection`) exclusively to any assembly in the specified directory. Because our assembly is in that directory, the `Security` and `Reflection` permissions must come from this code group:

```
Level = Enterprise
Code Groups:
1.  All code: FullTrust

Level = Machine
Code Groups:
1.  All code: Nothing
    1.1.  Zone - MyComputer: FullTrust
    1.6.  Url - file://C:/cas/*: Reflection (Exclusive)

Level = User
Code Groups:
1.  All code: FullTrust
```

Note that you can view the contents of the `Reflection` permission set by executing

```
C:\>caspol -m -lp
```

The serialized XML output lists the permissions associated with all permission sets at the machine policy level—including the `Reflection` permission set.

Determining the Permissions Required by an Assembly

One of the objectives of designing an effective security policy is to grant an assembly only those permissions it requires, and no more. The ease of using predefined permission sets should be resisted when it allows an assembly to access resources that it does not require. In the preceding example, the `configtest` assembly required only the capability to execute and access members of the `Reflection` namespace. To satisfy these narrow requirements, we created a custom permission set containing the `Security` and `Reflection` permissions. This custom permission set was clearly a better choice than the unrestricted permissions offered by `Everything` and `FullTrust`—the only predefined permission sets granting the `Reflection` permission.

Given the obvious advantage of using customized permission sets, the question becomes how an administrator identifies the minimum permissions required by an assembly. .NET offers two utilities for this purpose: *PermView* and *PermCalc*. PermView, which is discussed in the next section, displays the permissions explicitly requested—using attributes—by an application; PermCalc evaluates an assembly and produces serialized XML output of the required permission classes. It is run from the command line, as shown here:

```
C:\>permcalc c:\cas\configtest.exe
```

Evaluating an assembly to determine its required permissions is a difficult task and not always guaranteed to provide accurate results. In fact, when the utility is run against `configtest`, it displays `FileIOPermission`—but not `Reflection`—as a required permission. However, if we add an attribute (described next) to the code requesting the `Reflection` permission, the utility correctly displays this as a required permission. As a rule, the only way to be certain which permissions an assembly requires is to declare them in the code—our next topic.

Requesting Permissions for an Assembly

Including permission attributes in code is referred to as *declarative security*, and it serves two primary purposes: When applied at the assembly level, the attribute serves to inform the runtime which permissions the assembly requires—or does not require—to function; when applied at the class or method levels, it protects resources by demanding that callers possess specific permissions to access a resource through the current assembly. Attributes used for this latter purpose trigger or modify a *stack walk* that verifies all assemblies in the call chain can access the called assembly. We'll examine this in "Programmatic Security" on page 715. For now, the focus is on how to use assembly-level attributes to adjust security within a program.

Although the term *request* is broadly used to describe the use of permission attributes, it's better described as a way for an assembly to publish (in metadata) its permission requirements. The effectiveness of including permission attributes in code is governed by three rules:

- An assembly cannot receive any more permissions than are defined by the security policy rules—no matter what it "requests."
- Although requests cannot cause code to receive extra permissions to which it is not entitled, it can influence the runtime to deny permissions.
- An assembly receives permissions whether it requests them or not. The example shown in Listing 15-3 does not include a permission attribute, but it receives all the permissions that it qualifies for based in the evidence it provides the runtime.

Despite the fact that you do not have to include permission requests in your code, there are important reasons for doing so:

- It allows PermView to display the permissions required by an assembly and also improves the reliability of PermCalc. This provides a quick way for administrators to collect assembly requirements and design an appropriate security policy.
- Permission attribute information is stored in the assembly's manifest where it is evaluated by the CLR when loading the assembly. This permits the runtime to prevent an assembly from executing if it does not have the requested permissions. In most cases, this is preferable to having the program begin execution and then shut down unexpectedly because it has inadequate permissions.
- It enables code to specify only those permissions it needs. So why are extra permissions a problem if you don't use them? Because the code may have a bug, or exploitable feature, that malicious calling code can use to take advantage of the "extra" permissions.

For a full trust environment where code has unrestricted permissions—typically in-house applications—security is not a significant factor, and it may not be necessary to apply security attributes. However, if you operate in a security-conscious environment or are creating components for use by other software, you should include security attributes as a means of providing self-documenting security.

How to Apply a Permission Attribute

Because the permission attribute is to have assembly scope, it is declared in the first line of code following the using statement(s):

```
[assembly : PermissionAttribute(
            SecurityAction.membername,
            PermissionAttribute property)
]
```

Let's examine its construction:

Assembly   Indicates the attribute has assembly scope.

*Permission*Attribute   The permission class being requested.

SecurityAction   An enumeration describing the type of permission
                            request. Three values can be assigned to the assembly
                            scope:

                            RequestMinimum—The minimum permissions required
                            to run.

                            RequestOptional—Permissions the code can use but
                            does not require. This implicitly refuses all other permis-
                            sions not requested. Be careful with this, because it is not
                            obvious that a request for one permission causes all other
                            non-requested permissions to be denied.

                            RequestRefuse—Permissions that should not be
                            assigned to the assembly even if it qualifies for them.

The final argument to the constructor sets a property of the permission attribute class to a value that describes the specific permission requested. The following example should clarify this.

Testing a Permission Attribute

To demonstrate the effects of applying a permission attribute, let's add this statement to the source for `configtest`, shown in Listing 15-3:

```
//place on line preceding: class ClassEvidence
 [assembly : ReflectionPermission(
             SecurityAction.RequestMinimum,
             Flags=ReflectionPermissionFlag.TypeInformation)
]
```

The `ReflectionPermission` attribute class is used to request the minimum permissions required to run. The second parameter, `TypeInformation`, is an enumeration property of the class that permits reflection on nonvisible members of a class. (Recall that the sole purpose of this code is to use reflection in order to access a private field on a class.)

Compile and run the code from the C:\ root directory. Because applications run on the local machine have unrestricted permissions, the program runs successfully. Let's see what happens if the second parameter does not specify a permission that enables access to a private field. To test this, change the enumeration value to ReflectionEmit—an arbitrary property that only permits the assembly to emit metacode. When run with this parameter, the assembly again succeeds because it continues to receive unrestricted permissions on the local machine. As a final test, change the first parameter to SecurityAction.RequestOptional. This causes the assembly to fail, because only the requested ReflectionEmit permission is granted to it. Table 15-3 summarizes how content of the permission attribute affects the assembly's operation.

Table 15-3   Effect of Changing Permission Attribute on Assembly

Attribute Parameters	Result	Explanation
SecurityAction.RequestMinimum Flags = ReflectionPermission- Flag.TypeInformation	Succeeds	RequestMinimum ensures that assembly is granted all permissions determined by security policy. Includes Reflection. TypeInformation permits reflection on members that are not visible.
SecurityAction.RequestMinimum Flags = ReflectionPermission- Flag.ReflectionEmit	Succeeds	RequestMinimum ensures that assembly is granted all permissions determined by security policy. Includes Reflection. ReflectionEmit parameter does not specify the permission required by the assembly.
SecurityActionRequestOptional Flags = ReflectionPermission- Flag.ReflectionEmit	Fails	RequestOptional causes all non-requested permissions to be denied. Because ReflectionEmit does not provide permission to access a non-public field, the assembly fails.

Programmatic Security

The .NET Configuration tool provides a broad stroke approach to defining security for a computing environment. In most cases, this is satisfactory. If two assemblies come from the same security zone, it usually makes sense to grant them the same permissions. However, suppose you are developing components for clients with an unknown security policy, or you are using third-party components whose trustworthiness is unknown. In both cases, programmatic security offers a way to enforce security specifically for these components.

Programmatic security is implemented by using .NET permission classes to control and enforce security on a calling assembly or a called assembly. This is an important point: The calling assembly can override permissions granted by the CAS and prevent the assembly from accessing a resource; conversely, a called assembly can refuse to perform an operation unless the calling assembly—or assemblies—has permissions it requires. The key to implementing programmatic security is a mechanism known as a *stack walk*.

Stack Walk

As mentioned earlier in the chapter, a stack walk refers to steps the CLR follows to verify that all methods in a call stack have permission to perform an operation or access a system resource. This ensures that an immediate client with the proper permissions is not called by malicious code further up the stack that does not have permission.

As shown in Figure 15-10, a stack walk is triggered when code invokes a permission's Demand method. This method is inherited from the IPermission interface (refer to Figure 15-7), which includes other methods such as Intersect and Union that allow permission objects to be logically combined.

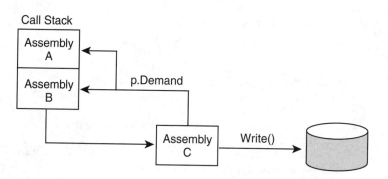

Figure 15-10   Invoking the Permission.Demand method triggers a stack walk

The Demand method is used extensively throughout the .NET Framework to ensure that applications requesting operations such as file I/O or database access have the proper permissions. Although most calls to the Framework Class Library (FCL) are protected in this way, it can still be useful to demand a stack walk within your code. You may want to apply even stricter permission requirements than the FCL demands, or you may want to ensure that a lengthy operation has all the required permissions before it is launched.

To provide a simple illustration, let's create a component that returns information about a requested movie from our Films database (see Chapter 11). Listings 15-4 and 15-5 contain the component and client code, respectively. For brevity, the ADO.NET code is excluded, but is available as downloadable code.

Because the SqlClient permission is required to access a SQL Server database, the component includes the following code to ensure that the calling assembly has this permission:

```
SqlClientPermission sqlPerm=
     new SqlClientPermission(PermissionState.Unrestricted);
sqlPerm.Demand();  // Trigger stack walk
```

The code simply creates an instance of the desired permission class and calls its Demand method. There is no limit on the number of permission objects that can be created and used to demand a stack walk. However, it is an expensive process and should be used judiciously.

Listing 15-4	Component to Illustrate Code Access Security

```
// filmcomponent.cs   (.dll)
using System.Data.SqlClient;
using System;
namespace moviecomponents
{
   public class MovieData
   {
     // Return MovieProfile object
     public static MovieProfile GetMovie(string movietitle)
     {
        // Return null if movie not found
        MovieProfile mp = null;
        // Demand SqlClient permission from methods on call stack
        SqlClientPermission sqlPerm= new
              SqlClientPermission(PermissionState.Unrestricted);
        sqlPerm.Demand();
```

| Listing 15-4 | Component to Illustrate Code Access Security *(continued)* |

```
      //*** Code here to query database for movie information
      //*** Requires SqlClient permission
      return mp;
   }
}
public  class MovieProfile
{
   private string pTitle;
   private int pYear;
   private int pRank;
   private string pOscar;
   public MovieProfile(string title, int year,
                       int afiRank, string bestFilm)
   {
      pTitle= title;
      pYear = year;
      pRank = afiRank;
      pOscar = bestFilm;
   }
   // Readonly properties
   public string Title
   {
      get{return pTitle;}
   }
   public int Year
   {
      get{return pYear;}
   }
   public int Ranking
   {
      get{return pRank;}
   }
   public string BestPicture
   {
      get{return pOscar;}
   }
}     // class
}      // namespace
```

Listing 15-5	Assembly to Access Film Component

```
// movieclient.cs   (.exe)
using System;
using moviecomponents;
namespace MovieClient
{
    class MovieMgr
    {
        static void Main(string[] args)
        {
            string myMovie;
            if(args.Length>0)
            {
                myMovie= args[0];
                // Call component to fetch movie data
                MovieProfile mp = MovieData.GetMovie(myMovie);
                if(mp==null)
                {
                    Console.WriteLine("Movie not found");
                }
                else
                {
                    Console.WriteLine("Year:{0} AFI Rank: {1}",
                                      mp.Year, mp.Ranking);
                }
            }
        }
    }    // class
}        // namespace
```

This code can be tested from the command line. Compile both the component and client. Then, run the client by passing it the movie name as a parameter:

```
C:\>csc /t:library filmcomponent.cs
C:\>csc /r:filmcomponent.dll movieclient.cs
C:\>movieclient casablanca
Year: 1942  AFI Rank:2
```

Because code running on a local machine has unrestricted permissions (by default), the stack walk verifies that movieclient has the necessary permission. To make the example more interesting, let's run the client when it does not have the SqlClient permission. The easiest way to remove this permission is by adding an assembly-level permission attribute that explicitly refuses the permission. You do this by passing the `SecurityAction.RequestRefuse` enumeration to the constructor of the permission attribute you do not want granted to the assembly. To refuse the `SqlClient` permission, place this statement before the namespace statement in the client code:

```
[assembly : SqlClientPermission(SecurityAction.RequestRefuse)]
```

Building and running the modified `SqlClient` results in a security exception being thrown.

Stack Walk Modifiers

Just as a called assembly has the rights to initiate a stack walk, the objects on the call stack have the right to modify the behavior of the stack walk. For example, they can cause the walk to fail, or stop the walk at the current object so that it does not check objects further up the stack. These capabilities have significant security implications: inducing a stack walk failure is a way for a client to restrict what actions a called assembly may perform; and terminating a stack early can improve performance by eliminating unnecessary steps in a repeated stack walk.

The ability to modify a stack walk is provided by methods in the `IStackWalk` interface (refer to Figure 15-7) that all permissions must implement. This interface defines the `Demand` method that initiates a stack walk, and three other methods, `Assert`, `Deny`, and `PermitOnly`, that modify a stack walk's normal operation. `Assert` stops the stack walk at the current stack frame; `Deny` causes the walk to fail; and `PermitOnly` specifies the only permission that an object will allow a stack walk to verify.

To demonstrate these methods, let's modify the code in Listing 15-5 to implement each method. First, we add namespaces so that we can access `IStackWalk` and the permission:

```
using System.Security;
using System.Data.SqlClient;
using System.Security.Permissions;
```

Then, the code is changed to create an `IStackWalk` object that is set to the permission being checked by the stack walk—in this case, `SqlClientPermission`:

```
myMovie= args[0];
//
IStackWalk stackWalker;
stackWalker = new
      SqlClientPermission(PermissionState.Unrestricted);
stackWalker.Deny();         // Deny use of SqlClient by GetMovie
// Call component to fetch movie data
try{
   MovieProfile mp = MovieData.GetMovie(myMovie);
```

In our first example, we call the permission's Deny() method that causes the stack walk's verification of the SqlClient permission to fail. Filmcomponent cannot access the database and throws an exception.

Now, replace the call to Deny with a call to Assert. Assert prevents the stack walk from continuing further up the code stack—unnecessary in this case because there is no other object on the stack. The stack walk succeeds because movieclient has the required permission, and database access is permitted.

Core Note

On the surface, the use of Assert seems to undermine the reason for a stack walk—to ensure that all objects on the call stack have a required permission. To make sure the method is not used to hide potentially malicious code on the call chain, .NET requires that the asserting code have a special security permission before it can assert; then, as added protection, it triggers a stack walk when code makes an assertion that verifies that all code above it has the asserted permission.

The final way to modify the stack walk is by using the PermitOnly method to indicate specific permissions that the code is willing to let the called assembly use. In the current example, the calling assembly has unrestricted permissions; the component filmcomponent has need for only the SqlClient permission. By using PermitOnly to specify this permission, movieclient thwarts any stack walks that attempt to verify other permissions.

An assembly may be required to call multiple components, each with its own permission requirements. You may need to permit SQL access for one and file I/O for another. If you call PermitOnly a second time to override the first call, an exception is thrown. Instead, you must clear the effects of the first call by calling CodeAccessPermission's static RevertPeritOnly method; then, you call PermitOnly with a new permission. The following segment could be added to our code to remove SqlClient as the only allowed permission, and replace it with the Reflection permission.

```
// Remove effects of previous PermitOnly call
CodeAccessPermission.RevertPermitOnly();
stackWalker = new ReflectionPermission(
     ReflectionPermissionFlag.TypeInformation);
// Allow stack walk to verify Reflection permission only
stackWalker.PermitOnly();
// Now call a method that requires Reflection
```

Declarative Security Using Permission Attributes

The security technique just described that explicitly calls a permission's Demand method to invoke a stack walk is referred to as *imperative security*. An alternative form of security that uses attributes to achieve the same effect is known as *declarative security*. We looked at one version of this in the earlier discussion of how to use permission attributes to request permissions. In this section, we'll see how the other form of declarative security is used to attach attributes to classes or methods to verify that clients have the necessary permissions to use current code.

The easiest way to explain declarative security is to compare it with its imperative counterpart. Here are the statements from Listing 15-4 that trigger a stack walk. Below it is an equivalent attribute declaration that results in the same stack walk.

```
// Imperative Security
SqlClientPermission sqlPerm= new
      SqlClientPermission(PermissionState.Unrestricted);
sqlPerm.Demand();

// Declarative Security
[SqlClientPermission(SecurityAction.Demand)]
public static MovieProfile GetMovie(string movietitle){
```

The syntax for the attribute constructor is straightforward. It consists of the permission attribute class name with a parameter specifying a SecurityAction enumeration member. Depending on the permission type, there may also be a second parameter that specifies a property value for the permission class.

The most interesting feature of the attribute declaration is its SecurityAction parameter that specifies the action caused by the attribute. Its three most important members and their uses are the following:

- Demand. Triggers a stack walk at runtime that requires all callers on the call stack to have a specified permission or identity.
- LinkDemand. Only the immediate caller is required to have a specified permission or identity. This check occurs during loading and eliminates the performance penalty of using a stack walk. However, because all objects on the call stack are not checked, this should only be used when you are certain the call stack is secure.
- InheritanceDemand. Requires that any subclass inheriting from the current code has required security permissions. Without this check, malicious code could use inheritance or the capability of overriding protected methods, for its own purposes. This check occurs during loading.

The final two enumeration members result in checks that occur during loading and have no comparable statements that can be executed at runtime. However, the use of demand security to trigger a stack walk is common to both and leaves the developer with the decision of which to use. In where the component knows which permissions it needs at compile time, declarative security is recommended. Its syntax is simpler, and it provides a form of self-documentation. Also, declarative security information is placed in an assembly's manifest where it is available to the CLR during loading. As a rule, the sooner the CLR has information about code, the more efficiently it can operate.

Imperative security is recommended when variables that affect security are unknown at compile time. It's also easier to use when more granular security is required: attributes usually apply to a class or method, whereas demand statements can be placed anywhere in code.

15.4 Application Deployment Considerations

The purpose of this section is to take a broad look at the issues that should be considered when deciding on a strategy for installing your application. Much of the discussion centers on practical issues such as how deployment is affected by the use of public or private assemblies, how configuration files are used to tell the CLR where to search for an assembly, and how configuration files ease the problems of distributing new versions of an assembly.

Microsoft Windows Deployment: XCOPY Deployment Versus the Windows Installer

Almost always included in the list of the top .NET features is the promise of using XCOPY deployment to install your application on client machines. The idea is to create a simple script that uses the XCOPY utility to copy your assemblies and resource files to the specified directories on the client's machine. It is a terrific idea and works—if you have an application with only a few assembly files that can be stored in a local directory. However, there are a lot of installation scenarios where XCOPY does not work: It cannot be used to register a COM component in your application, and it cannot be used to store an assembly in the GAC. In addition, for a professional application, XCOPY does not provide the well-designed interface that customers expect.

The most popular alternative to XCOPY is the Microsoft Windows Installer that ships with most of its operating systems and is also available as a separate download.

The installer is an installation service that processes files having a special format (.msi) and performs install operations based on their content. An .msi file is referred to as a Windows Installer Package, and an install can contain more than one of these files.

The easiest way to create an MSI file for your application is using Visual Studio .NET. It has a wizard that steps you through the process. If your application requires special Code Access Security policies, use the Configuration tool to create an install package. To do so, right-click the Runtime Security Policy node and select Create a Deployment Package. The ensuing wizard steps you through the process. You can also create a custom installer by creating a class that inherits from the System.Configuration.Install.Installer class and overrides its Install and Uninstall methods.

Core Note

.NET 2.0 and Visual Studio 2005 introduce a ClickOnce technology that is designed to simplify the installation and update of Windows applications. The idea is to create the application and use VS.NET to "publish" it to a File or Web Server. The location is provided as a URL to users who link to a Web page that provides install instructions. Included with the application is a manifest that describes the assembly and files that comprise the application. This information is used to determine whether an update is available for the application. The update process can be set up to automatically check for updates each time the application is run, or only run when requested.

ClickOnce works for straightforward installations that do not need to access the registry or install assemblies in the GAC. It is also targeted for the Microsoft Windows environment, as it contains shortcuts and an uninstall feature used by Windows. Although VS.NET is the easiest way to publish an application for installation, it can be done manually.

Deploying Assemblies in the Global Assembly Cache

.NET supports two assembly deployment models: private and shared. A private assembly is identified by its file name—without the extension—and is stored locally with other assemblies that it references or that reference it. Shared assemblies are stored in the Global Assembly Cache. Although this is a convenient way to make an assembly available to multiple applications, it does present an installation problem. Recall from the earlier discussion that an assembly cannot be copied into the GAC;

instead, a special tool is required to install or "register" it. During code development, the GACUtil.exe utility is used for this purpose. However, this tool is not included with the end-user version of the .NET Framework redistributable package, so there is no assurance that it will exist on the user's machine. Instead, use the Windows Installer.

Deploying Private Assemblies

The easiest way to deploy an application with multiple private assemblies is to place all of the assemblies in the same directory. This home directory, referred to as the application's *base directory*, is the first place the CLR looks when trying to locate an assembly. However, using a single directory prevents assemblies from being grouped into folders that logically describe their purpose. For example, an application may have a set of assemblies dedicated to graphics and another dedicated to database access. Placing these in \Graphics and \Data subfolders represents a more logical and easier-to-maintain code deployment.

To see how to set up a meaningful directory structure for an application, let's first look at how the CLR locates private assemblies. This discovery process, called *probing*, begins with the application's base directory. If the assembly is not located there, it searches for an immediate subdirectory having the same name as the target assembly. For example, if the assembly is myClass, it looks first for the directory myClass.dll and then myClass.exe. The CLR loads the assembly from the first directory in which it locates it.

In our case, we want to use a directory structure that is not based on the name of the assemblies. To force the CLR to extend its probe into other folders, we must add a special <probing> element to the application's configuration file. For an application named myApp.exe, we create a configuration file named myApp.exe.config and store it in the application's base directory. Included in the file is a <probing> tag with a privatePath attribute that specifies the subdirectories (below the base directory) for the CLR to search.

```
<configuration>
   <runtime>
      <assemblyBinding xmlns="urn:schemas-microsoft-com:asm.v1">
         <probing privatePath="\graphics;\data" />
      </assemblyBinding>
   </runtime>
</configuration>
```

By default, the specified search paths are relative to the application's base directory. You can also specify an absolute path, but the path must specify a folder below the application's base directory.

The application configuration file in this example is rather simple, and you may choose to build it manually. However, because the file often contains other configuration elements, manual manipulation can quickly become an unwieldy task. As an alternative, you can use the same Configuration tool described in the CAS discussion. It has an `Applications` folder that can be opened and will lead you through the steps to create a configuration file for a selected assembly. One of its more useful and instructive features is an option to view a list of other assemblies that the selected assembly depends on.

Using CodeBase Configuration

A `<codebase>` element provides another way to specify the location of an assembly. It differs from the `<probing>` element in that it can specify any directory on the machine, as well as a location on a file or Web server across a network. The CLR uses the URI information provided by this element to download an assembly the first time it is requested by an application. Notice how `<codebase>` is used in the following sample configuration file.

The `<codebase>` element, along with a companion `<assemblyIdentity>` element, is placed inside the `<dependentAssembly>` block. The `<assemblyIdentity>` element provides information about the assembly the CLR is attempting to locate: its simple name, public key token, and culture. The `<codebase>` element provides the assembly's version number and location where it can be found. If the assembly is not strongly named, the version information is ignored.

```
<configuration>
  <runtime>
    <assemblyBinding xmlns="urn:schemas-microsoft-com:asm.v1">
      <dependentAssembly>
        <assemblyIdentity name="movieclass"
          publicKeyToken="1F081C4BA0EEB6DB"
            culture="neutral" />
        <codeBase version="1.0.0.0"
                  href="http://localhost/scp/movieclass.dll" />
      </dependentAssembly>
    </assemblyBinding>
  </runtime>
</configuration>
```

The `href` can also refer to the local file system:

```
<codeBase version="1.0.0.0"
                  href="file:///e:\movieclass.dll"  />
```

Using a Configuration File to Manage Multiple Versions of an Assembly

One of the advantages of using a strongly named assembly is the version binding feature it offers. When Assembly A is compiled against Assembly B, A is bound to the specific version of B used during the compilation. If Assembly B is replaced with a new version, the CLR recognizes this at load time and throws an exception. It is a good security feature, but can make updates to B more time-consuming because all assemblies dependent on it must be recompiled.

A configuration file can be used to override version binding by instructing the runtime to load a different version of the assembly than was originally bound to the calling assembly. This redirection is achieved by adding a `<bindingRedirect>` element that specifies the original version and the new version to be used in place of it. Here is how the previous configuration file is altered to have a newer version of the `movieclass` assembly loaded:

```
<configuration>
  <runtime>
    <assemblyBinding xmlns="urn:schemas-microsoft-com:asm.v1">
      <dependentAssembly>
        <assemblyIdentity name="movieclass"
          publicKeyToken="1F081C4BA0EEB6DB"
              culture="neutral" />
        <bindingRedirect oldVersion="1.0.0.0"
                         newVersion="2.0.0.0"/>

        <codeBase version="2.0.0.0"
                  href="http://localhost/scp/movieclass.dll" />

      </dependentAssembly>
    </assemblyBinding>
  </runtime>
</configuration>
```

Use of the `<bindingRedirect>` element inside an application configuration file offers a flexible and practical approach to matching applications with new or older versions of a component. For example, both versions of the component can run side by side on the same machine. One application can continue to use the older version, whereas the configuration file of a second application is modified to direct it to the newer component. Moreover, if the second application encounters problems with the new component, the `<bindingRedirect>` element can be removed and the application will revert to using the original component.

Assembly Version and Product Information

As a final note on deployment, it is good practice to include assembly-level attributes to your assembly to provide useful information to clients that want to examine the properties of your .exe or .dll file. As an example, the attributes in the following code yield the properties shown in Figure 15-11:

```
using System;
using System.Reflection;
[assembly:AssemblyVersion("2.0.0.0")]
[assembly:AssemblyCompany("Acme Software")]
[assembly:AssemblyCopyright("Copyright (c) 2005 Stephen Perry")]
[assembly:AssemblyTrademark("")]
// Set the version ProductName & ProductVersion fields
[assembly:AssemblyProduct("Core C# Examples")]
[assembly:AssemblyInformationalVersion("2.0.0.0")]
[assembly:AssemblyTitle("Core C# movieclass.dll")]
[assembly:AssemblyDescription("This is a sample C# class")]
//
public class Movies
{
// ... Remainder of code
```

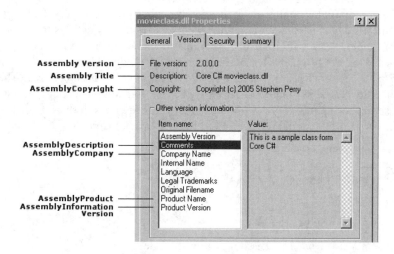

Figure 15-11 Attributes provide information identifying an assembly

15.5 Summary

There is more to developing an application or component than simply implementing code to handle a specific task or set of tasks. Ancillary issues such as code correctness, adherence to code standards, code efficiency, security, and code deployment must be addressed. This chapter has presented an overview of tools and approaches available to handle these issues in .NET.

A useful tool for determining how your code meets .NET coding standards is FxCop. It's included with the .NET SDK and evaluates an assembly against a set of rules that define good coding practice. You can add custom rules and disable rules that don't apply.

To secure an application, .NET employs a concept known as Code Access Security. Unlike role- or user-based security—which .NET also supports—CAS restricts what resources code can access. When an assembly loads, .NET gathers information about its identity known as *evidence*. It evaluates the evidence against security policies and maps it into a set of permissions that are granted to the assembly. A security administrator typically configures the security policy using the .NET Configuration tool, although a command-line utility is also available. Security can also be implemented in code. Permissions are nothing more than classes, and can be used by developers to request permissions for an assembly and demand that calling assemblies have the necessary permissions to access a secure resource.

The final step in developing an application is settling on a deployment strategy. In .NET, this can be as easy as creating an install based on copying files to a machine (XCOPY deployment); alternatively, MSI files can be created for use with the Microsoft Windows Installer. One of the key install decisions is how to deploy assemblies. Private assemblies are placed together in a common directory path; shared assemblies are stored in the Global Assembly Cache. In addition, a configuration file can be set up to instruct the runtime to search for assemblies in directories on the local computer or a remote Web server located across a network.

15.6 Test Your Understanding

1. Indicate whether the following are true or false:

    a. A strongly named assembly must be stored in the GAC.
    b. When compiling an application, the CLR automatically searches the GAC for a referenced assembly.
    c. When loading an assembly, the CLR automatically searches the GAC for a referenced assembly.
    d. A public key token must exist in the manifest of an assembly referencing a strongly named assembly.

2. You are developing a component for a class library and want to follow good coding practices. Evaluate the assembly with FxCop. The output includes the following message. What is missing from your code?

```
TypeName= "AssembliesShouldDeclareMinimumSecurity"
```

3. What are the four parts of an assembly's strong name?

4. How do you assign a version number to an assembly? How are default values for the *build number* and *revision* determined?

5. What three methods are used to modify a stack walk? Describe the role of each.

6. What is delayed signing, and why is it used?

7. Identify each of the following: predefined permission, named permission set, and security zone.

8. Indicate whether the following statements about assembly deployment are true or false:

    a. Only a strongly named assembly can be placed in the GAC.
    b. The `<probing>` element must specify a directory below the application's base directory.
    c. The `<codeBase>` element is used to redirect the CLR to use a newer version of an assembly.
    d. XCOPY deployment can be used to install shared assemblies.

9. What element or elements need to be added to this application configuration file so that the application will access the new version 2.0.0.0 of this component, rather than the previous 1.0.0.0 version? Both the application and component reside in `c:\data\`.

```
<dependentAssembly>
    <assemblyIdentity name="movieclass"
        publicKeyToken="1F081C4BA0EEB6DB"
                culture="neutral" />

    ---> Insert code here
</dependentAssembly>
```

PROGRAMMING
FOR THE
INTERNET

 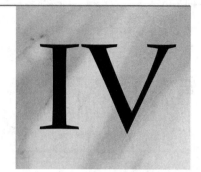

Part **IV**

■ *Chapter 16*
  ASP.NET Web Forms and Controls   **732**

■ *Chapter 17*
  The ASP.NET Application Environment   **806**

■ *Chapter 18*
  XML Web Services   **868**

ASP.NET WEB FORMS AND CONTROLS

Topics in This Chapter

- *Web Client-Server Communications:* Web page requests and responses rely on HTML to represent content, and HTTP to define the protocol that governs client-server interaction. JavaScript, ASP, and ASP.NET are compared as ways to develop an application.

- *Structure of an .aspx Page:* An .aspx Web page is compiled as a class. It contains a variety of directives that control the page's behavior and can link it to external code. This section looks at the basic elements that comprise an .aspx file, including how Viewstate is used to maintain state information for the form.

- *Inline and Code-Behind Pages:* ASP.NET offers three models for designing a Web application: inline code, code-behind, and code-behind with partial classes. The latter two permit the page interface to be separated from the program logic. The implementation code is placed in a code-behind file that is referenced by an .aspx page.

- *HTML Server-Side Controls and Web Controls:* ASP.NET provides controls that correspond to HTML tags and are accessed as classes in the server-side code. It also provides a number of native "Web" controls that include features not found on standard HTML controls. These include validation controls, data source controls, and sophisticated data display controls such as the DataList, GridView, and TreeView.

- *Master and Content Pages:* ASP.NET supports the creation of a master Web page that serves as a template for other "content" pages that visually inherit from it. This chapter explains how to create master pages containing special "place holder" controls that define where derived content pages may insert their custom content.

Chapter 16

Developing applications to run on the Internet is a broad topic, and this book devotes its last three chapters to the subject. This chapter introduces key features of ASP.NET and focuses on using controls to create Web pages; Chapter 17, "The ASP.NET Application Environment," looks at application development issues such as managing sessions and configuring ASP.NET control files; and the book's final chapter discusses Web Services.

ASP.NET is technically regarded as the next generation of ASP. There are syntactic similarities and compatibilities, but the differences are even greater. Thus, this chapter makes no attempt to explain ASP.NET in terms of ASP. There are some comparisons, but no prior knowledge of ASP is assumed. You will also find traces of JavaScript sprinkled in a couple of applications, but the code is easily understood within the context of the examples.

The first section provides a tour of client-server Web interaction. It begins with a simple JavaScript application that demonstrates the fundamental techniques used to transfer information between a client and Web server. It then shows how the ASP.NET model encapsulates these principles and adds an object-oriented approach to Web page design and implementation. Subsequent sections survey the array of Web presentation and validation controls. Special attention is given to the `DataList` and `GridView` controls.

One note: IIS (Microsoft Internet Information Server) is conspicuous by its absence in our discussion. Although all of the applications were tested in an IIS environment, and the preponderance of ASP.NET applications will run on this Web server, they are not bound to it. Microsoft has created an open-source HTTP server named *Cassini* that is written in C#. It's fully HTTP/1.1 compliant, supports directory browsing, as well as many of the standard MIME types, and most importantly, supports ASP.NET. It has been tested on Apache servers and is clearly geared toward making ASP.NET the Web development tool of choice for multiple Web platforms.

16.1 Client-Server Interaction over the Internet

At its core, the Internet consists of resources and users who want to access Web-based resources. Three mechanisms are required to enable this access: a naming scheme (URI) to locate the resources, a protocol (HTTP) defining how the request/response process works, and a language (HTML) for publishing information and providing a means to navigate to the resources. This environment is quite different than that facing the Windows Forms programmer and presents the Web application developer with three major challenges:

- **HTML.** The developer must be familiar with the Hypertext Markup Language in order to create Web Forms. Certainly, HTML generators are a useful accessory, but at some point, the developer has to understand the raw HTML.
- **HTTP.** The primary task of a Web application is to respond to HTTP requests. These requests may be sent by either an HTTP GET or POST method and may contain headers in addition to the main message body. The language used by the Web developer must provide access to the full HTTP message. For example, to process a received form, a Web application must be able to extract data from fields on the form. Header information can be equally important. It can be used to control caching, identify the source of the request, and pass cookies between the client and server.
- **State.** There is no intrinsic feature in HTML or HTTP that maintains the state of variables during the request/response operation. Figure 16-1 illustrates this. The client receives an empty survey form, fills it out, and posts it back to the server. The server detects an error and returns the same Web page—which is blank again. Preserving data (state) over the round trip(s) between client and server is, perhaps, the biggest challenge facing the Web programmer.

One of the best ways to understand and appreciate a technology is to compare it with other technologies that perform a similar task. With that in mind, this section takes a simple Web application and implements it in JavaScript, ASP, and ASP.NET. The objectives are twofold: to understand the problems associated with implementing a Web Forms application, and to illustrate the evolutionary approach that ASP.NET uses to meet these challenges. You do not need experience with ASP or JavaScript to understand the examples, but it helps. Their function is to demonstrate how the HTTP GET and POST methods send data to a server and maintain state information. The examples could just as easily use Perl or PHP scripting.

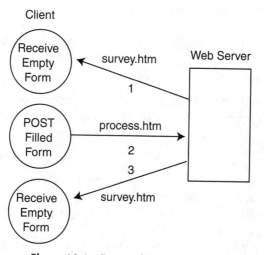

Figure 16-1 Request/response process

Web Application Example: Implementing a BMI Calculator

This application calculates the Body Mass Index (BMI) for a given height and weight. The user enters this information (see Figure 16-2) into a form and then clicks Submit Form to send the request to a server. The server calculates the BMI and returns a Web page that includes the BMI and original data entered.

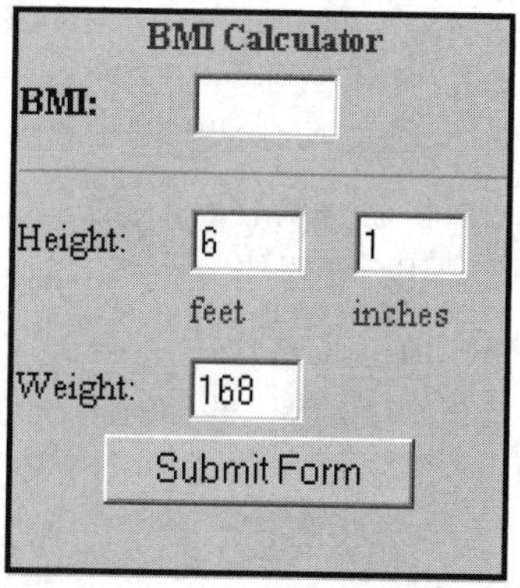

Figure 16-2 BMI Web calculator

Realistically, the calculation could be done using JavaScript on the client's page without requiring a trip to the server. But let's suppose that we also want to record each time the calculator is used. For that, a trip to the server is necessary.

A JavaScript BMI Calculator

JavaScript remains the primary language used for client-side coding on a Web application. It is platform and browser independent (although there are a few exceptions). As we will see later, ASP.NET automatically generates JavaScript for its client-side processing.

The first example uses JavaScript on both the client and server side. Listing 16-1 contains the HTML and JavaScript that comprise the client-side page. For brevity, some of the less important code is excluded.

The HTML in the <body> defines the fields and buttons on a form bmi_input. This form defines GET as the HTML method for delivering the contents of the form to the server. When the button is clicked, control passes to the JavaScript function post that verifies the content of the form and sends it to the server. We'll get to the other JavaScript code after we look at the server side.

Listing 16-1	JavaScript/HTML to Display a BMI Calculator— bmi.htm

```
<HTML>
<HEAD><TITLE>BMI Calculator</TITLE>
<SCRIPT LANGUAGE="Javascript" TYPE="text/javascript">
<!--
// hrefstr is set to querystring values—if any
var hrefstr= location.search.substring(1,
     location.search.length);
function showbmi(){
   if (hrefstr )   // display values in form fields
   {
      var parms    = hrefstr.split('&');
      var f = self.document.forms[0];
      f.bmi.value = eval(parms[0]);
      f.hti.value = eval(parms[2]);
      f.wt.value  = eval(parms[3]);
      f.htf.value = eval(parms[1]);
   }
}
// -->Code for Verify goes here.
// Post Form to Web Host
function post() {
   if (verify()) //Call function to verify values in form fields
```

Listing 16-1	JavaScript/HTML to Display a BMI Calculator— bmi.htm *(continued)*

```
    {
        var f = self.document.forms[0];
        f.bmi.value=0;
        f.submit();  // Use HTTP GET to send form to server
    }
}
//-->
</script>
</HEAD>
<BODY bgcolor=#ffffff>
<FORM NAME="bmi_input" method=GET action=bmicalculator.htm>
    <table border=0 cellpadding=2 cellspacing=0 width=180
        bgcolor=#cccccc>
    <tr><td colspan=3 align=center><font size=2 color=#33333>
        <b>BMI Calculator</b> </td></tr>
    <tr><td><font size=2 ><b>BMI:</b></td>
        <td colspan=2 ><input type=text size=5 name=bmi>
    </td></tr>
    <tr><td colspan=3><hr size=1></td></tr>
    <tr><td><font size=2 >Height:</td>
        <td><input type=text size=3 name=htf maxlength=1></td>
        <td><input type=text size=3 name=hti maxlength=2></td>
    </tr>
    <tr><td> </td><td valign=top><font size=2>feet</td>
        <td valign=top><font size=2>inches</td>
    </tr>
    <tr><td><font size=2 >Weight:</td>
        <td colspan=2><input type=text size=3 name=wt
            maxlength=3></td>
    </tr>
    <tr><td colspan=3 align=center>
    <INPUT TYPE="button" VALUE="Submit Form" ONCLICK=
            "self.post()";>
    </td></tr>
    <tr><td colspan=3> </td></tr>
    </table>
</FORM>
<SCRIPT LANGUAGE="Javascript" TYPE="text/javascript">
<!--
    showbmi();    // Fills form with values if they exist
//-->
</script>
</body>
</html>
```

Using the GET method causes the form's data to be sent to the server as part of the URL. This string of data, referred to as a *query string*, contains name-value pairs that correspond to the name of the fields on the form, followed by their value. Figure 16-3 shows how form data is passed to the Web page `bmicalculator.htm` that calculates the BMI.

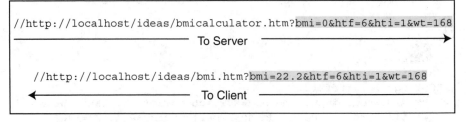

Figure 16-3   Passing data in a query string

Data is returned to the client in the same manner—by appending it to the URL of the page containing the original form. Note that `bmi` is now set to the calculated value. Here is the server-side code that creates this response:

```
<html><head></head>
<body >
<script language="javascript">
<!-
    // Use location.search to access the query string
    var hrefstr = location.search.substring(1,
          location.search.length);
    var parms   = hrefstr.split('&');
       feet     =  parms[1];
       inch     =  parms[2];
       pounds   =  parms[3];
       totinches = eval(feet)*12 + eval(inch);
       // ..... Calculate BMI
       var h2 = totinches * totinches;
       bmi = Math.round(eval(pounds) * 703 * 10/ h2)/10;
       // --> Place code here to maintain count of visits.
       //... Return value and original parameters as a query string
       ndx = hrefstr.indexOf('htf');
       self.location = 'bmi.htm?bmi=
             '+bmi+"&"+hrefstr.substring(ndx);
    //-->
</script>
</body></html>
```

This code grabs the values from the query string using `location.search`, parses them, calculates the BMI, and then creates a URL for the page to be returned. The final step is for the client browser to display the calculated BMI value.

At the bottom of the code in Listing 16-1 is a call to the JavaScript function `showbmi()`. This function operates much like the preceding server code. It extracts the data from the query string and displays it in the appropriate fields on the form. Note that the function `first` confirms that the query string is not empty, as will be the case the first time the form is loaded.

The use of a query string is popular for applications that transfer small amounts of data. However, it becomes a problem with large forms because the query string is limited by the 2K maximum string length imposed by some browsers (IE). In addition, it raises obvious security concerns by exposing data in a URL line that can be altered by the user. Query string encryption can mitigate this problem and should be considered where it makes sense. A more robust solution is to use the HTTP POST method in place of GET.

An ASP (Active Server Pages) BMI Calculator

JavaScript is intended primarily for client-side scripting and cannot process data sent by a POST method. This example replaces the JavaScript server code with an ASP file that handles the POST request. We change one statement in the client code to indicate that POST is being used and to provide the name of the ASP server page:

```
<FORM NAME="bmi_input" method=POST action=bmicalculator.asp>
```

The code for the ASP server file is quite simple. It accesses the data passed from the client by referencing a `request` object. The data is passed to a VBScript function that calculates the BMI. A URL is then constructed that contains the query string with the BMI value and other parameters. The `response.redirect` method sends the form to the client's browser.

```
<script language="VBScript" runat="server">
function getBMI(inch,feet,pounds)
   totinches = feet*12 + inch
   h2 = totinches * totinches
   getBMI= (pounds * 703 * 10/ h2)/10
end function
</script>
<%
   ' ... POST data is available in request object
   inch    = request("hti")
   feet    = request("htf")
   pounds  = request("wt")
   bmi= left(cstr(getBMI(inch,feet,pounds)),4)
```

```
'  ... return value and original parameters as a query string
hrefstr = "&htf=" +cstr(feet) + "&hti=" + cstr(inch) +
          "&wt="&cstr(pounds)
response.redirect ("bmi3.htm?bmi="+bmi+hrefstr)
%>
```

This solution illustrates the fundamental ASP approach of using VBScript to interact with HTTP response and request objects. In addition, HTML and JavaScript can
be intermixed with the ASP code to create Web Forms. Although this offers a degree
of flexibility, it often results in a babel of code and inconsistent coding techniques.

Using ASP.NET to Implement a BMI Calculator

Before building an ASP.NET solution for the calculator, let's first take a general look
at the features of ASP.NET and how they affect Web Forms programming. One way
to understand the Web Forms model is to look at the requirements faced by the
ASP.NET designers—and how they met them.

- **Integration with the .NET environment.** Web Forms are built on
  the Common Language Runtime (CLR) and have access to all types in
  the Framework Class Library, as well as special namespaces, such as
  `System.Web` and `System.Web.UI` that support Web applications. An
  important aspect of .NET integration is that it is required only on the
  server side; users are not required to install the .NET Framework on
  their computers. The emphasis is on rendering code that runs unaided
  on a browser. In fact, the emitted code is tailored to recognize the
  browser it is running on, so it can take full advantage of its features.
- **Linking client-side HTML controls with server-side controls.** All
  controls in ASP.NET are classes. Controls that appear on a browser window are renderings based on HTML tags. To reconcile this differing
  technology, ASP.NET includes server-side controls that map directly to
  HTML tags. For example, the `<input type = text>` tags we saw in
  the earlier examples are represented by the `HtmlInputText` class
  found in the `System.Web.UI.HtmlControls` namespace. When
  information on a Web page is sent to a server, all HTML tags designated
  to run on the server are converted into their corresponding .NET class
  and compiled as members of the Web page. We'll see how HTML tags
  are mapped to server controls in the next example.
- **Compiled rather than interpreted Web pages.** Traditionally, Web
  pages have been rendered by JavaScript, VBScript, Perl, and other
  scripting interpreters. In contrast, an ASP.NET Web page consists of a
  user interface defined by HTML, and interface logic written in a
  .NET language such as C# or VB.NET. The first request for an ASP

page (.aspx file) results in the page being compiled into a .NET class. Further requests are then handled by the assembly created by compilation. For the user, it means faster Web access; for the developer, it means applications are developed using the same .NET tools available for desktop and component applications.

ASP.NET offers three models for implementing a Web application:

- **Inline code.** The HTML markup code and application code (C#) coexist in a single .aspx file.
- **Code-behind.** The markup code and application code are placed in separate files. The markup is in an .aspx file and the logic code resides in a .cs or dll file.
- **Partial classes.** This is a variation of the code-behind model that places the markup and code in separate files. The difference is that the code-behind file is implemented using *partial classes*. It is stored as a .cs file and is compiled along with the markup file. This model is available only with ASP.NET versions 2.0 and later.

None of the models offers a performance advantage over the others. This leaves the choice of model up to one's preference—or need—for code separation. Let's now examine the models by using each to implement the BMI application.

Inline Code Model

The code for the BMI Web Form application is shown in Listing 16-2. Although it resembles an HTML page, an .aspx page is actually an XML-formatted page. It is processed on the server and used to generate a mixture of HTML and JavaScript that is sent to the browser.

Notice that this example contains actual C# code—between the `<script>` `</script>` tags—that calculates the BMI value. This method is executed on the server and is not visible as source code to the client.

Listing 16-2	ASP.NET Inline Code Implementation of a BMI Calculator

```
<%@ Page Language="C#"  %>
<HTML>
<HEAD><TITLE>BMI Calculator</TITLE>
<script  runat="Server">
   // Calculate BMI from values on form
```

Listing 16-2	ASP.NET Inline Code Implementation of a BMI Calculator *(continued)*

```
    private void getBMI(object sender, System.EventArgs e)
    {
       try
       {
          decimal f =  Convert.ToDecimal(htf.Value);
          decimal inch = Convert.ToDecimal(hti.Value);
          decimal w = Convert.ToDecimal(wt.Value);
          decimal totinches = f * 12 + inch;
          decimal h2 = totinches * totinches;
          decimal massIndex = (w * 703 * 10/ h2)/10;
          bmi.Value = massIndex.ToString("##.##");
       }catch (Exception ex)
          { bmi.Value=" "; }
    }
</script>
</HEAD>
<BODY bgcolor=#ffffff>
<FORM NAME="bmi_input" runat=server>
    <table border=0 cellpadding=2 cellspacing=0 width= 180
        bgcolor=#cccccc>
    <tr><td colspan=3 align=center><font size=2>
        <b>BMI Calculator</b>
        </td></tr>
    <tr><td><font size=2 ><b>BMI:</b></td>
        <td colspan=2 ><input type=text size=5 id=bmi
                runat=server></td></tr>
    <tr><td colspan=3><hr size=1></td>
    </tr>
    <tr><td><font size=2 >Height:</td>
        <td><input type=text size=3 id=htf maxlength=1
                runat=server></td>
        <td><input type=text size=3 id=hti maxlength=2
                runat=server></td>
    </tr>
    <tr><td> </td><td valign=top><font size=2>feet</td>
        <td valign=top><font size=2>inches</td>
    </tr>
    <tr><td><font size=2 >Weight:</td>
        <td colspan=2><input type=text size=3 id=wt maxlength=3
                runat=server></td>
    </tr>
    <tr><td colspan=3 align=center>
```

Listing 16-2	ASP.NET Inline Code Implementation of a BMI Calculator *(continued)*

```
<INPUT TYPE="button" VALUE="Submit Form"
        OnServerClick="getBMI"
        id=bmiButton runat=server>
    </td>
</tr>
<tr><td colspan=3> </td>
</tr>
</table>
</FORM>
</body>
</html>
```

To understand the differences between standard HTML and ASP.NET code, let's compare how controls are specified in Listing 16-1 versus Listing 16-2.

- The most obvious difference is the addition of the `runat=server` attribute in the `<Form>` and `<Input>` tags. This designation converts any HTML elements to HTML server controls that can be processed by the server-side code prior to sending them to the browser. The following code illustrates how an `<input>` tag is transformed before it emitted to the client's browser:

  ASP.NET statement:
  ```
  <input type=text size=3 id=wt maxlength=3 runat=server>
  ```
  HTML statement emitted:
  ```
  <input name="wt" id="wt" type="text" size="3"
      maxlength="3" value="168" />
  ```

- The `<Form>` tag does not include the method or action attribute. By default, the POST method is used. As the following code shows, the page is self-referencing, which means the page sends the form to itself.

  ASP.NET statement:
  ```
  <FORM NAME="bmi_input" runat=server>
  ```
  HTML statement emitted:
  ```
  <form name="_ctl0" method="post" action="bmi.aspx"
      id="_ctl0">
  ```

- The `<button>` tag contains an `OnServerClick` event delegate. This indicates that a method on the server will handle the event. The resulting HTML references a JavaScript function that has been added to post the form when the button is clicked.

HTML statement emitted:
```
<input language="javascript" onclick =
    "__doPostBack('_ctl1','')" name="_ctl1"
    type="button" value="Submit Form" />
```

ASP.NET also adds three hidden fields to the HTML page it returns to the browser:

```
<input type="hidden" name="__EVENTTARGET" value="" />
<input type="hidden" name="__EVENTARGUMENT" value="" />
<input type="hidden" name="__VIEWSTATE"
    value="dDwxMzc5NjU4NTAwOzs+iIczTTLHA74jT/02tIwU9FRx5uc=" />
```

The first field, __EVENTTARGET, specifies the control that invoked the request (known as a *postback*) to the server; the second, __EVENTARGUMENT, contains any parameters required by the event. The __VIEWSTATE field is by far the most interesting.

View State

View state is the feature in ASP.NET that automatically maintains the state of server-side controls (controls declared with runat=server) as a form makes the round trip between the client and the server. In other words, it allows a page to place data in a control such as a ListBox or GridView one time—usually when the page is first loaded—and ensures the data is retained as subsequent postbacks occur. Here is how it works.

When a page is posted back to the server, the data in the hidden __VIEWSTATE field is deserialized and used to set the state of controls and the overall Web page. Data received in the HTTP request as part of a POST operation is used to set the values of those related controls (note that for controls whose contents are posted—TextBox, CheckBox, RadioButtons—the posted data overwrites the view state data). The __VIEWSTATE field is then updated before it is passed back to the client. The returned view state value plays no role on the client other than to represent a snapshot of control values at the time the page is received by the browser.

Because the view state string can be viewed in a source listing, questions about security become a legitimate issue. However, unlike the query string, the value is not represented as clear text.

```
value="dDwxMzc5NjU4NTAwOzs+iIczTTLHA74jT/02tIwU9FRx5uc="
```

By default, a machine-specific authentication code is calculated on the data and appended to the view state string. The full string is then Base64 encoded. It is possible to decode the string, but the difficulty in doing so will thwart most casual efforts. Tampering with the string can also be detected by the server and results in a security exception being thrown. As always, use Secure Sockets Layer (SSL) to ensure absolute security for Internet communications.

Core Note

Maintaining view state data within a Web page makes the page independent of the server. This means that a Web page request can be sent to any server in a Web farm—rather than restricting it to a single server.

Performance is another issue that must be considered when working with the view state value. By default, it maintains data for all server-side controls on the form. The control information is not limited to only the data value associated with the control. For example, when a `DataGrid` is used, the view state includes not only the data in each cell, but also column and row headers, and related style attributes. The view state data can easily add several thousand bytes to a Web page and slow performance.

To improve performance, you may want to disable view state for the Web page and apply it only to selected controls. Set the `EnableViewState` attribute in the `@Page` directive to disable it at the page level:

```
<%@ Page Language="C#" EnableViewState="False" %>
```

Then, to enable view state for an individual control, apply the attribute as shown in the following code:

```
<input type=text size=3 id=wt maxlength=3 EnableViewState=true
    runat=server >
```

Of course, you can also take the opposite tact and leave view state on for the page and turn it off for selective controls.

The decision to enable or disable view state is one of the key decisions in designing a Web page that displays large amounts of data in a server-side control. The easiest approach is to allow `ViewState` to take care of the details. However, this can result in a large HTML payload being transferred repeatedly between browser and server. An alternative is to design the code to reload the data into the controls on each postback. The data may be fetched from the original source—usually a database—or it may be stored on the server in session state or a cache. These last two options are described in Chapter 17, "The ASP.NET Application Environment."

Core Note

ViewState maintains not only a control's data but also its state. For example, it keeps track of the last item(s) selected in a ListBox and permits the ListBox to be redisplayed in its most recent state. The drawback of manually repopulating a control, rather than using ViewState, is that this state information is lost.

The @Page Directive

The last element to discuss in Listing 16-2 is the @Page directive. An .aspx file can contain only one @Page directive, and it is typically—although not required—the first statement in the file. The purpose of this directive is to assign attribute values that control the overall behavior of the Web page, as well as specify how the page is assembled and compiled on the server. Table 16-1 lists selected attributes for the @Page directive.

Table 16-1   Attributes for the @Page Directive

Attribute/Value	Description
EnableSessionState = value	Specifies the type of access the page has to the session state information. Sessions are discussed in Chapter 17.
EnableViewState = bool	Enables or disables view state for the page. Individual controls can override this value.
EnableViewStateMac = bool	Is used to make the view state more secure by adding a validator hash string to the view state string that enables the page to detect any possible attempt at corrupting original data.
SmartNavigation = bool	Setting this to true can improve the rendering of pages for users of Internet Explorer 5.0 and later. Its improvements include • Eliminating flickering when a page loads. • Retaining the input focus on the field last having it. • Preserving the scroll position on pages longer than one screen.
ErrorPage = url	Specifies the URL of a Web page that is called when an unhandled exception occurs.

Table 16-1   Attributes for the `@Page` Directive *(continued)*

Attribute/Value	Description
`Culture = string`	A culture setting for the page based on the `Culture-Info` class. This attribute affects how culture-dependent functions, such as numbers and dates, are displayed. The following setting causes a `DateTime` object to be displayed in a European format using German months and days: `Culture="de-DE"`. These settings can also be set in the `Web.config` file as described in the next chapter.
`UICulture = id`	Specifies the user interface culture for this page. Example: `UICulture="de"`
`Trace = bool`	Turns tracing on or off for the page. Default is `false`. When tracing is on, diagnostic information about a single request for an `.aspx` page is collected. The results of the trace are available programmatically and are appended as a series of tables at the bottom of the browser output. Tracing is discussed in Chapter 17.
`Inherits = class name`	Specifies the base class used to generate a class from the `.aspx` file. The default is `System.Web.UI.Page`. If code-behind is used, the class name from this code is used.
`MasterPageFile = master page`	Specifies the "master page" from which the current page visually inherits its layout. Introduced with 2.0.
`theme = theme name`	Specifies the subdirectory containing the `.skin` file (specifies the appearance of controls) and any other images and style sheets that define the look and style (theme) of a page. The theme file is stored in the `/app_themes` subdirectory. Introduced with 2.0.
`Language = language`	Specifies the language for inline code.
`Codebehind = *.dll`	Specifies the name of a compiled code-behind file. This file must be in the `\bin` subdirectory of the application.
`Codefile = *.cs`	Specifies a code-behind file containing a partial class. Introduced with 2.0.
`Src = path`	Specifies a code-behind file containing source code.

The `Codebehind`, `Codefile`, and `Src` attributes specify the assembly or source file containing the business logic code for the page. Instead of placing code between `<script></script>` tags as we did in Listing 16-2, the code is placed in a separate code-behind file that is referenced by these attributes. Before discussing code-behind, let's look at some additional directives that are frequently used in `.aspx` pages.

Other Directives

@Import Directive

This directive is used to import a namespace in an `.aspx` page. It serves the same purpose as the C# `using` statement.

```
<%@ Import namespace="System.Net" %>
```

Several namespaces are automatically imported in a page, making this directive unnecessary in most cases. These namespaces include

- `System, System.IO`
- `System.Web.UI, System.Web.UI.HtmlControls,`
  `System.Web.UI.WebControls`
- `System.Web, System.Web.SessionState, System.Web.Caching`
- `System.Text, System.Text.RegularExpressions`

@Assembly Directive

This directive links an assembly to the current page while the page is being compiled. This provides the page with access to all types in the assembly. It takes two forms:

```
<%@ Assembly Name="webfunctions" %>
<%@ Assembly Src="webfunctions.cs" %>
```

The first version references an assembly that may be private or deployed in the Global Assembly Cache; the second statement causes the source to be dynamically compiled into an assembly that is linked to the Web page. Note that assemblies in the application's `\bin` subdirectory are automatically linked to a page and do not need to be referenced.

@Register Directive

This directive associates alias names with namespaces and classes. Its purpose is to provide a convenient syntax for adding custom controls to a Web page. The directive takes two forms:

Syntax:

```
<%@ Register Tagprefix="tagprefix" Namespace="namespace"
    Assembly="assembly" %>
<%@ Register Tagprefix="tagprefix" Tagname="tagname"
    Src="pathname" %>
```

Attributes:

Tagprefix	Alias for a namespace.
Namespace	The namespace to associate with `Tagprefix`.
Assembly	Assembly in which namespace resides.
Tagname	Alias to associate with a class.
Src	The file containing the user control

The first form of the directive is used to add an ASP.NET server control to a page; the second form is used with a custom control contained in a source file. In the latter case, the `TagPrefix` and `TagName` are always used together as a colon-separated pair. Here is a code segment that places a user control defined in the file `hdr.ascx` on a Web page. The `@Register` directive defines the alias pair that is used to declare the control on the Web page.

```
<%@ Register TagPrefix="ucl" TagName="hdr" Src="hdr.ascx" %>

<form id="Form1" method="post" runat="server">
    <ucl:hdr id="Hdr1" runat="server"></ucl:hdr>
</form>
```

We'll make use of this directive in Section 16.4, which provides examples of how to create and use custom controls. Note that `@Register` directive information also can be stored in the `Web.config` file (see Chapter 17), eliminating the need to place it in a Web page.

The Code-Behind Model

The example in Listing 16-2 contains both C# to implement program logic and HTML to render the user interface. A Web page can also be configured as an `.aspx` file, containing only the interface code and a separate code-behind file that contains the program logic and serves as the base class for compiling the `.aspx` file (see Figure 16-4). This code-behind file takes the `.cs` extension.

The code-behind page is linked to the `.aspx` file as an assembly or source file using the `Codebehind` or `Src` attributes of the `@Page` directive. If the `Codebehind` attribute is used, the assembly must be stored in the `\bin` directory of the application.

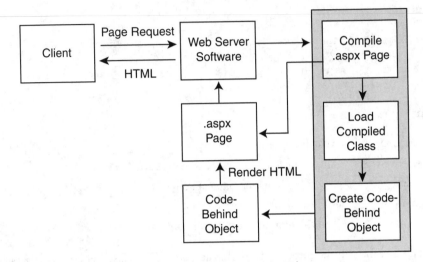

Figure 16-4   How ASP.NET responds to a Web page request

Let's now look at how the code in Listing 16-2 can be changed to use a code-behind file. We create a code-behind file named `bmicb.cs` (see Listing 16-3) to replace the code currently between the `<script/>` tags. The `@Page` directive links this file to the `.aspx` file:

```
<%@ Page Language="C#" Src="bmicb.cs" Inherits="BMI" %>
```

The code-behind page is always structured as a class whose name must be specified by an `Inherits` attribute. This class is shown in Listing 16-3. Let's take a close look at it, because knowledge of how the code-behind file and the `.aspx` file interact on the server is essential to understanding the ASP.NET Web page model.

Listing 16-3	Code-Behind File for BMI Calculator— `bmicb.cs`

```
using System;
using System.Web.UI.HtmlControls;
public class BMI : System.Web.UI.Page
{
    //      <input type=text id=htf runat=server>
    protected HtmlInputText htf;
    //      <input type=text id=hti runat=server>
    protected HtmlInputText hti;
    //      <input type=text id=wt runat=server>
    protected HtmlInputText wt;
```

Listing 16-3	Code-Behind File for BMI Calculator—bmicb.cs *(continued)*

```
//      <input type=text id=bmi runat=server>
protected HtmlInputText bmi;
//      <input type="button" VALUE="Submit Form" id=bmiButton
//      runat=server>
protected HtmlInputButton bmiButton;

override protected void OnInit(EventArgs e)
{
    // Delegate to handle button click on client
    bmiButton.ServerClick += new EventHandler(getBMI);
}
protected void getBMI(object sender, System.EventArgs e)
{
    decimal f =  Convert.ToDecimal(htf.Value);
    decimal inch = Convert.ToDecimal(hti.Value);
    decimal w = Convert.ToDecimal(wt.Value);
    decimal totinches = f * 12 + inch;
    decimal h2 = totinches * totinches;
    decimal massIndex = (w * 703 * 10/ h2)/10;
    bmi.Value = massIndex.ToString("##.##");
}
}
```

The first thing to observe from this listing is that it consists of one class—BMI—that derives from the System.Web.UI.Page class. The Page class is to Web Forms what the Form class is to Windows Forms. Like the Form, it has a sequence of events that are fired when it is initialized and loaded. It also has several properties that control its behavior—many of which correspond to the @Page directive attributes already discussed. We'll look at the Page class later in this section.

One of the trickiest aspects of learning ASP.NET is grasping how server-side controls work—specifically, how the content and action of controls displayed on a browser are managed on the server. Figure 16-5 illustrates the relationship. Each server control is declared as a field in the BMI class. When the values of the controls are posted to the server, they are assigned as field values. In this example, all of the controls are HTML controls—that is, standard HTML controls with the runat=server attribute.

The id value in the tag must match the field name identically. The field types are defined in the System.Web.UI.HtmlControls namespace. Each HTML control has a one-to-one mapping with an HTML tag, as shown in Table 16-2.

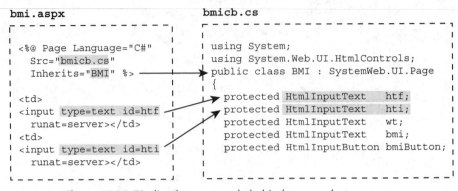

Figure 16-5   Binding between code-behind page and `.aspx` page

Table 16-2   HTML Controls and Their Tags

Control	HTML Tag
HtmlAnchor	`<a>`
HtmlSelect	`<select>`
HtmlTextArea	`<textarea>`
HtmlButton	`<input type=button>` `<input type=submit>`
HtmlCheckBox	`<input type=checkbox>`
HtmlRadio	`<input type=radio>`
HtmlHidden	`<input type=hidden>`
HtmlInputText	`<input type=text>`
HtmlInputFile	`<input type=file>`
HtmlForm	`<form>`
HtmlImage	`<img>`
HtmlTable	`<table>`
HtmlTableRow HtmlTableCell	`<tr>` `<td>`
HtmlGenericControl	All other unmapped tags such as `<div>` and `<p>`

Handling Events on the Server

In our example, clicking the Submit button sends a request to the server to calculate and return a BMI value based on the form's content. The `.aspx` code for the button looks like this:

```
<INPUT TYPE="button" VALUE="Submit Form"
    id=bmiButton runat=server>
```

Compare this with the tag defining the button in Listing 16-2:

```
<INPUT TYPE="button" VALUE="Submit Form" OnServerClick="getBMI"
    id=bmiButton runat=server>
```

This earlier code defines a method (`getBMI`) to be called when the click event occurs. Because our current example has the method placed in a code-behind file, there is no reference to it in the `.aspx` file. Instead, the server-side code handles the event using a standard delegate-based event handling approach. An event handler method (`getBMI`) is defined that matches the signature of the `EventHandler` delegate. Then, using the button's `id` value, we create a delegate instance that registers the method for the `ServerClick` event of the `bmiButton` control:

```
bmiButton.ServerClick += new EventHandler(getBMI);
```

When the button is clicked on the browser, the contents of the form are posted to the server, which recognizes the button click event and calls the appropriate event handler. This raises one obvious question: Because a form can contain any number of buttons, how does the server determine the event that triggered the post-back? The answer is that the name of the control causing the event is passed to the server in the __EVENTTARGET hidden field that was discussed earlier. This is handled automatically by ASP.NET; the developer's responsibility is to create the delegate and server-side control event handler.

Code-Behind with Partial Classes

The problem with the preceding code-behind model is that each control in the markup page must be explicitly mapped to a protected member in the code page. Changes to the markup page require that the code page members be kept in sync. The use of a *partial class* in the code-behind page eliminates the need for the protected class member. The partial class is compiled with the markup page, which permits the markup and code sections to directly access each other's members. The effect is the same as using the inline model. To demonstrate this, extract the `getBMI` method from the inline code (refer to Listing 16-2) and place it in its own file inside a partial class. The result is a code-behind partial class as shown in Listing 16-4.

Listing 16-4	Code-Behind Partial Class File for BMI Calculator

```
//file: bmi.aspx.cs
using System;
partial class BMICalc: System.Web.UI.Page{}
{
   void getBMI (Object sender, EventArgs e)
   {
      try
      {
         decimal f =  Convert.ToDecimal(htf.Value);
         decimal inch = Convert.ToDecimal(hti.Value);
         decimal w = Convert.ToDecimal(wt.Value);
         decimal totinches = f * 12 + inch;
         decimal h2 = totinches * totinches;
         decimal massIndex = (w * 703 * 10/ h2)/10;
         bmi.Value = massIndex.ToString("##.##");
      } catch (Exception ex)
         { bmi.Value=" "; }
   }
}
```

The client markup page links to this code by specifying the file name and the partial class name in its @Page declaration:

```
<%@ Page codefile="bmi.aspx.cs" inherits="BMICalc" %>
```

ASP.NET 2.0 continues to support the original code-behind model, but it should be used only for preexisting code. New development should employ the inline or partial class model.

Page Class

The first time an ASP.NET page is accessed, it is parsed and compiled into an assembly. This is a relatively slow process that results in the delay one notices the first time the .aspx page is called. Subsequent requests receive much faster responses because the assembly handles them. This assembly consists of a single class that contains all of the server-side code, as well as static HTML code.

The compiled class derives either directly from the System.Web.UI.Page class or indirectly via an intermediate code-behind class. It is important to understand the members of the Page class. Its methods and properties define much of the functionality the .aspx code relies on for handling requests, and its events define junctures at which the code must perform initialization and housekeeping tasks.

Table 16-3 summarizes some of the important properties of the `Page` class.

Table 16-3   Selected Properties of the `Page` Class

Control	HTML Tag
Application	Returns the `HttpApplicationState` object that contains information about the executing application.
EnableViewState	Boolean value that indicates whether controls retain their values between requests. Default is `true`.
IsPostBack	Boolean value indicating whether the page is being loaded and accessed for the first time or in response to a postback.
PreviousPage	Provides a reference to the page originating the call. Information on the calling page is available when the page is reached by cross-page posting or is invoked by `HttpUtilityServer.Transfer()`.
Request	Gets the `HttpRequest` object that provides access to data contained in the current request.
Response	Gets the `HttpResponse` object that is used to programmatically send HTTP responses to the client.
Server	Gets the `HttpServerUtility` object provided by the HTTP runtime.
Session	Gets the `HttpSessionState` object, which provides information about the state of the current session.

The `Application` and `Session` properties provide state information for a Web application and are discussed in the next chapter.

HttpRequest and HttpResponse Objects

The `Request` and `Response` properties expose underlying objects (`HttpRequest` and `HttpResponse`) that are used to interact with the incoming HTTP request and the outgoing HTTP response. These classes include properties and methods to read cookies from the client's machine, receive uploaded files, identify the browser, get the IP address of the client, and insert custom content into the outgoing HTTP body. Chapter 17 discusses these in detail, but as an introduction, let's look a simple code example that illustrates the fundamentals of accessing these objects within an `.aspx` page.

The next code segment uses the `Response.Output.Write` method to write information into the HTTP content returned to a browser. The information comes from `Request.Browser` properties that indicate the type of client. Note that by using `<% %>` tags in an `.aspx` file, we can intersperse these statements with the HTML code. Do this judiciously. An `.aspx` file is much easier to read when the C# code is segregated between `<script>` tags, as shown in Listing 16-2, or placed in a code-behind file.

```
<table border=0 cellpadding=0 cellspacing=0>
    <%
        Response.Output.Write(@"<tr><td>Browser Version: {0}
            </td></tr>", Request.Browser.Type); //    IE6
    %>
</table>
```

Using IsPostBack

This useful property enables a Web application to distinguish between a postback and the first time a Web page is invoked. It lets the program know when to initialize values that only need to be set once. A typical example is a `ListBox` that contains unchanging values, such as all of the states in the United States. When assigned, these values are subsequently maintained in the `__VIEWSTATE` hidden field and do not need to be re-initialized.

To demonstrate, let's extend our BMI inline code example to display the date and time when the user first requests the Web page. When displayed, this date and time remain unchanged no matter how many times the BMI calculation is subsequently requested.

The date and time are displayed using a `<span/>` tag, which is added beneath the opening `<FORM>` tag (refer to Figure 16-2) in the `bmi.aspx` file. (This is equivalent to a Web control `Label`.)

```
<FORM NAME="bmi_input" runat=server>
<span id=sessionstart runat=server/><br>
```

In the code section, we must assign the date and time to the inner contents of the `<span>` tag the first time that the page is called. Here is the code to do this:

```
void Page_Load(object sender, EventArgs e)
{
    if(!this.IsPostBack) sessionstart.InnerText =
        DateTime.Now.ToString();
}
```

Recall that the code on the server is compiled into a class that inherits from the `Page` class. This class includes several events—discussed in the following section—that are triggered when a request is sent to the Web page. The most useful is the `Page_Load` event that is raised each time the page is loaded. Applications typically include an event hander for it that checks `IsPostBack` and performs initialization if the call is not a postback. In this example, the `InnerText` field of the `<span>` tags is set to the date and time the first time the page is loaded.

Page Events

The preceding example demonstrates how the `Page_Load` event handler provides a convenient place to initialize variables. The `Load` event is only one of four events defined by the `System.Web.UI.Page` class. The others are `Init`, `PreRender`, and `UnLoad`. These occur in a fixed sequence as shown in Figure 16-6.

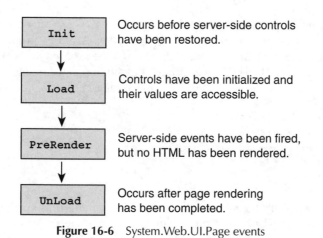

Figure 16-6 System.Web.UI.Page events

To best understand the role of each, let's look at what happens when a form is posted to a server:

1. The temporary class for the page is generated, compiled, and loaded. The ASP.NET runtime begins processing the page and fires the `Page.Init` event.
2. The state of the page object and its controls are set from data in the POST variables and the __VIEWSTATE field. The `Page.Load` event is fired. Typically, the `OnLoad` event handler is overridden to initialize control values and establish database connections.
3. Events related to all controls are fired. The last event that occurs is the one that caused the postback. After all server-side control events have been processed, the `Page.PreRender` event occurs.
4. The page enters its rendering phase. The class that represents the page calls the Render method on all the individual controls included in the page.
5. The `HTTPResponse` is issued, sending the rendered HTML to the client. The `Page.Unload` event completes the process. This event should be used to release resources by closing files and database connections.

Although Web Forms provide an event-based model that is similar to the Windows Forms model, the key difference is that the events do not actually fire until control returns to the server. There they must occur in the fixed order described in this section. Your code interacts with these events by overriding or replacing the event handlers for the events described in Figure 16-6.

Cross-Page Posting

A Web page in .NET 1.x could only post to itself. In 2.0, you can designate a target page, other than the current page, by setting the PostBackUrl property of a Button, ImageButton, or LinkButton to the address of the target page. Posting occurs when the button is clicked. To demonstrate, the button defined in this code posts the contents of the current form to nextstep.aspx when the button is clicked.

```
<asp:button id="postBtn"
   text="redirect"
   postbackurl="nextstep.aspx"
   runat="Server">
</asp:button>
```

The page to which a form is posted can view the contents of the calling form using the PreviousPage property. In this example, nextstep.aspx uses PreviousPage to get the text value of the button that initiated the post. Of course, this technique would be used more often to gather data from text boxes on the posted form.

```
if(!this.IsPostBack)
{
   // Sets text to the value of the Text property of the button
   // from the calling form having the id postBtn: "redirect"
   string text =
        ((Button)PreviousPage.FindControl("postBtn")).Text;
}
```

16.2 Web Forms Controls

The designer of an ASP.NET Web page can choose from three types of controls for the GUI design: client-side HTML controls, HTML server controls, and Web Forms controls. Client-side controls are the traditional controls defined by HTML tags (<table>, <button>, <input>, and others). These controls are still useful for client-side form validation and creating hyperlinks.

HTML server controls are server-side versions of the standard HTML controls (see Listing 16-2). As we have seen, they're created by adding a runat = server attribute to the HTML tag. The main reason they are included in .NET is to ease the transition from legacy HTML files to ASP.NET. However, except for incurring less overhead, there is no real advantage in using HTML server controls. Web controls— a much more powerful alternative—are nearly as easy to implement and unlock the full capabilities of ASP.NET.

Web controls are native ASP.NET controls that extend the features of the HTML server controls and add non-HTML controls, such as a calendar and data grid. They are actual classes in the .NET Framework and expose properties that enable the developer to exert much more control over their appearance and behavior than is possible with server controls. With the exception of the `Table`—the HTML table is easier to work with for general use—Web controls should be the control of choice for ASP.NET pages.

Web Controls Overview

Web controls behave much like the HTML server controls: Each has a corresponding class; those with a user interface render themselves in HTML understandable by a browser; and most expose events that are handled on the server. A significant difference from the HTML controls is that Web controls provide a richer object model. From the `WebControl` class, they inherit properties that affect their appearance: `ForeColor`, `BackColor`, `BorderColor`, `BorderStyle`, `Height`, and `Width`. In addition, many can be bound to a data source that provides their content.

A Web control is declared using the `asp:` prefix. For example, a `TextBox` and `Button` are declared as

```
<asp:TextBox id="First Name" type="text" runat="server" />
<asp:Button  id="Save" Text="Save Data" runat="server"
      OnClick="SaveBtn_Click" />
```

ASP.NET Web controls are defined in the `System.Web.UI.WebControls` namespace. There are a lot of them—more than 70 with the release of ASP.NET 2.0. They naturally fall into functional categories that provide a convenient way to present them (see Figure 16-7):

- **Simple controls.** Enhanced alternatives to the HTML Server controls and standard HTML tags.
- **List controls.** These inherit directly from the `System.Web.UI.Web-Controls.ListControl` class and are populated by `ListItem` objects.
- **Data Display controls.** These complex controls are designed to display multiple rows of data (`GridView`, `DataList`, `Repeater`) or multiple fields for a single row of data (`FormView`, `DetailsView`).

- **Data Source controls.** Introduced with ADO.NET 2.0, these controls serve as source of data for other controls—primarily the data display controls—that bind to them. As their names imply, these controls provide data from a variety of sources.
- **Validation controls.** These helper controls perform predefined and custom data validation on other controls.
- **Login controls.** A set of controls designed to control the login process by managing and authenticating users.

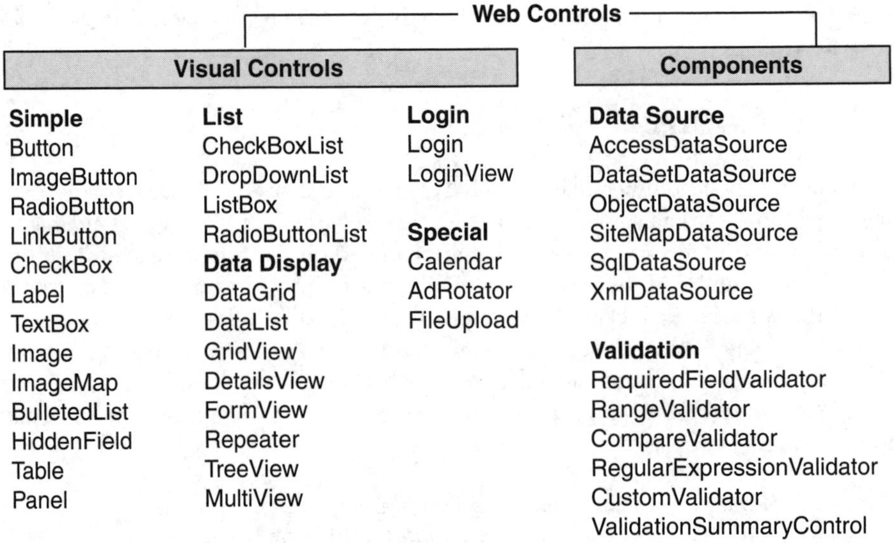

```
                              ┌──── Web Controls ────┐
        ┌─────────────────────────┐      ┌──────────────────────┐
        │     Visual Controls     │      │      Components       │
        └─────────────────────────┘      └──────────────────────┘
```

Simple	List	Login	Data Source
Button	CheckBoxList	Login	AccessDataSource
ImageButton	DropDownList	LoginView	DataSetDataSource
RadioButton	ListBox		ObjectDataSource
LinkButton	RadioButtonList	**Special**	SiteMapDataSource
CheckBox	**Data Display**	Calendar	SqlDataSource
Label	DataGrid	AdRotator	XmlDataSource
TextBox	DataList	FileUpload	
Image	GridView		**Validation**
ImageMap	DetailsView		RequiredFieldValidator
BulletedList	FormView		RangeValidator
HiddenField	Repeater		CompareValidator
Table	TreeView		RegularExpressionValidator
Panel	MultiView		CustomValidator
			ValidationSummaryControl

Figure 16-7   ASP.NET Web controls

In addition to these, there are a few of highly specialized controls: Calendar, AdRotator, and FileUpload. This section provides examples of commonly used visual controls, as well Validation controls and the new (.NET 2.0) Data Source controls. Before examining specific controls, let's look at the properties shared by all Web controls that govern their appearance.

Specifying the Appearance of a Web Control

All Web controls inherit numerous properties from the base WebControl class that can be used to set their appearance and behavior. The properties are most effective when used to decorate simple controls where their effect is more pronounced than with complex controls. Table 16-4 demonstrates how these properties can be used to alter the appearance of a simple Button control.

Table 16-4 Properties That Affect the Appearance of a Web Control

Property	Button1	Button2	Button3
Width	80	100	100
Height	20	20	24
BackColor	#ffffff	#efefe4	#cccccc
BorderStyle	Double	Dotted	None
BorderWidth	1	1	1
BorderColor	Red	Black	Black
Font-Names	Sans-Serif	Sans-Serif	Courier
Font-Size	8pt	10pt	11pt
Font-Bold	true	true	true
Button Displayed	Upload File	Upload File	Upload File

Other useful properties include `Enabled`, `Visible`, and `TabIndex`. The latter indicates the tab order of a control. Note that browsers may render these properties differently or ignore some of them altogether. For example, Firefox and Netscape tend to ignore the `Width` property.

Simple Controls

The simple controls are typically used in combination to create an interface for users to enter data or make selections. The easiest way to present and manage controls that are related by function and style is to place them in a common container. In traditional HTML, the `<DIV>` element is used for this purpose; in ASP.NET, the `panel` control serves as a generic container (and is often rendered in browsers as a `<DIV>` element). There are many advantages to using a panel to layout controls:

- It eliminates the need for multiple Web pages. Because ASP.NET is designed around posting back to the calling Web page, it's an easy way for a single Web page to present multiple interfaces by simply toggling panels' visibility on or off.
- Controls on a panel maintain data that can be referenced even if the panel is not visible. This eliminates the use of multiple hidden fields.

- It serves to unify the appearance of grouped controls by providing a common background or border. A screen is easily sectioned into multiple panels.

The screens in Figure 16-8 are created using a combination of button, label, text box, and panel controls. The page consists of a form that accepts name and address information. Controls to accept name fields are contained on one panel, whereas address fields are on another. Clicking the Name and Address buttons toggles the visibility property of the two panels. The effect is to reuse the same display space for both types of data—obviating the need for a long scrolling form or multiple Web pages.

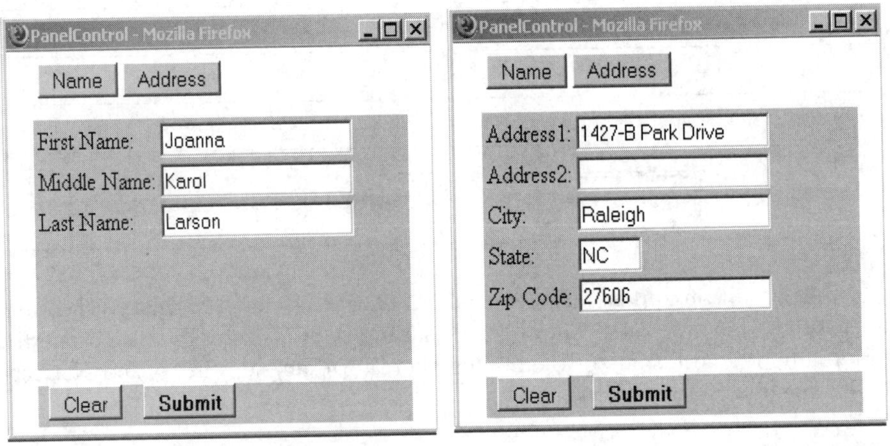

Figure 16-8   Using panels to manage simple controls

A look at the underlying code reveals the syntax and mechanics of working with Web controls. We'll look at the three most interesting areas of the code: the Page_Load event handler, the button declarations and event handlers, and the layout of the panels.

Using the Page_Load Event to Initialize the Screen

When the page is loaded for the first time, the panel that accepts name fields, pnlName, is made visible, whereas pnlAddress has its visibility turned off.

```
<script  runat="Server">
   void Page_Load(object sender, EventArgs e)
{
   if(!this.IsPostBack) {
```

```
        pnlName.Visible = true;
        pnlAddress.Visible = false;
    }
}
```

Buttons

The two menu buttons across the top of the form are declared as

```
<asp:Button ID="btnName" CommandName="name"
    OnCommand="Button_Command" text="Name" Runat="server" />
<asp:Button ID="btnAddress" CommandName="address"
    OnCommand="Button_Command" text="Address" Runat="server" />
```

The buttons specify Button_Command as an event handler to be called when each button is clicked. As shown in the event handler code, the buttons' CommandName property identifies the button raising the event. This enables a single method to handle multiple button clicks, which is a useful way to group code performing similar tasks. It's most commonly used with buttons that control column sorting in a grid.

```
void  Button_Command(Object sender, CommandEventArgs e) {
    // CommandName identifies control invoking event
    switch(e.CommandName)
    {
        case "address":
            pnlName.Visible = false;
            pnlAddress.Visible = true;
            break;
        case "name":
            pnlAddress.Visible= false;
            pnlName.Visible = true;
            break;
        default:
            break;
    }
}
```

The Clear and Submit buttons use the OnClick property—rather than OnCommand—to specify their Click event handlers as separate methods:

```
<asp:Panel id="pnlBottom"
    style="Z-INDEX:103; LEFT:20px;POSITION:absolute; TOP: 240px"
        runat="server"
        BackColor=#cccccc
        Height="26px"
        Width="278px">
```

```
 
<asp:Button id="btnClear" Text="Clear"  OnClick="clear_Form"
    runat="server"  />
  
<asp:Button ID="btnSubmit" Text="Submit" Font-Bold="true"
      OnClick="store_Form" runat="server" />
</asp:Panel>
```

The most important thing to note about the event handlers is their signature. The Click event requires an EventArgs type as the second parameter; the Command event requires a CommandEventArgs type.

```
private void clear_Form(object sender, System.EventArgs e)
{
   if(pnlName.Visible)
   {
      txtFirstName.Text  ="";
      txtLastName.Text   ="";
      txtMiddleName.Text ="";
   } else
   {
      // Clear fields on pnlAddress
   }
}
private void store_Form(object sender, System.EventArgs e)
{
   // Code to verify and store Form
}
```

Core Note

ASP.NET 2.0 adds an OnClientClick property to the Button, ImageButton, and LinkButton controls, which can be used to execute client-side script. The following code causes a JavaScript function to be executed when the button is clicked.

```
<asp:Button id=btn text="Client Click" OnClientClick="popup()"
    runat="server" />
```

Using Panels

The panel declaration specifies its location, size, and appearance attributes such as background color. Controls are placed on the panel by declaring them within the <asp:Panel /> tags. In this example, the text box and label controls are members of the panel's control collection:

```
<asp:Panel id="pnlName" runat="server"
   style="Z-INDEX: 101; LEFT: 20px;
   POSITION: absolute; TOP: 64px"
   BackColor = "LightGreen" Height="160px" Width="278px">
<TABLE>
   <TR>
      <TD><asp:Label id="lblFirstName" Runat="server"
             text="First Name:"></asp:Label></TD>
      <TD><asp:TextBox id="txtFirstName" MaxLength=30
             Runat="server"></asp:TextBox></TD></TR>
   <TR>
      <TD><asp:Label id="lblMiddleName" Runat="server"
             text="Middle Name:"></asp:Label></TD>
      <TD><asp:TextBox id="txtMiddleName" MaxLength=30
             Runat="server"></asp:TextBox></TD></TR>
   <TR>
      <TD><asp:Label id="lblLastName" Runat="server"
             text="Last Name:"></asp:Label></TD>
      <TD><asp:TextBox id="txtLastName" MaxLength=30
             Runat="server"></asp:TextBox></TD></TR>
</TABLE>
</asp:Panel>
```

It is interesting to note how ASP.NET tailors the HTML code to capabilities of the client browser. The HTML returned to Internet Explorer renders the panel as a <div> element.

```
<div id="pnlName" style="background-color:LightGreen;
     height:160px;width:278px;Z-INDEX: 103; LEFT: 20px;
     POSITION: absolute; TOP: 64px">
```

The Firefox and Netscape browsers receive HTML in which the panel is rendered as a table:

```
<table id="pnlName" cellpadding="0" cellspacing="0" border="0"
     bgcolor="LightGreen" height="160" width="278"
     style="Z-INDEX: 101; LEFT: 20px; POSITION: absolute;
     TOP: 64px"><tr><td>
```

Core Note

ASP.NET 2.0 adds a ScrollBars property to the panel control. It can be set to Vertical, Horizontal, or Both. Beware that not all browsers support this feature.

Text Box

With the exception of the MaxLength property that limits the amount of text entered in the control, the text box controls in this example rely on default property values. However, they can be customized easily to present a more meaningful interface. The most useful properties include Width and Column, which both specify the width of the control (Column is the better choice since all browsers recognize it); ReadOnly, which can be used to prevent the user from changing the content; Rows, which specifies the number of rows in a multi-line text box; and TextMode, which indicates whether the text box is SingleLine, MultiLine, or contains a Password. In the latter case, text entered into the text box is masked.

The text box also supports an OnTextChanged property that specifies an event handler method to call when text in the box is changed. However, this is a *delayed* event that is not processed on the server until a *round-trip* event occurs. You can prevent the event from being delayed by adding the AutoPostBack = true property to the control's declaration. However, for best performance, the program should be designed to process all control content in one trip.

List Controls

The four ASP.NET list controls—DropDownBox, ListBox, CheckBoxList, and RadioButtonList—provide alternative ways of representing a collection of data. All are data-bound controls that provide a visual interface for an underlying ListItemCollection; and all are derived from the System.Web.UI.WebControls.ListControl class that contributes the properties and methods used to populate the controls with data and detect selected control items (see Figure 16-9).

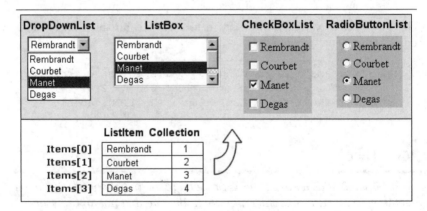

Figure 16-9   List control display data from underlying ListItem collection

Filling the Control with Data

Individual data items within a list control are represented as a ListItem control. There are several ways to specify the text displayed for an item in the list control. The most common method is by placing text between the opening and closing tags of the ListItem control—referred to as the *inner HTML content*. You can also use the Text property to specify the text displayed in the list control for the item.

```
<asp:RadioButtonList id="RadioButtonList" BackColor="LightBlue"
      RepeatColumns=1 RepeatDirection="Vertical" runat="server">
  <asp:ListItem Value="1">Rembrandt />
  <asp:ListItem Value="2">Courbet />
  <asp:ListItem Value="3" Text="Manet" />
  <asp:ListItem Value="4">Degas />
</asp:RadioButtonList>
```

The ListItem control also exposes a Value property that allows you to associate a value with the item in the list control, in addition to the text displayed in the control. This is often used as a key when retrieving data related to the selected item from a database table.

As mentioned, list controls are data bound, which means they expose a DataSource property that can be set to reference a collection of data. The control's DataBind method is called to load the data from the source into the control. It is possible to bind to many kinds of data sources, such as database tables, hash tables, XML files, and even other controls.

As an example, let's declare a ListBox that will be bound to an array:

```
<asp:ListBox id="ListBox" runat="server" Rows=4 Width=150px>
</asp:ListBox>
```

In the script section of the .aspx page, we define an array and bind its contents to the ListBox. The DataBind method copies the data from the array into the control, creating a ListItem collection (see Figure 16-9).

```
<script runat="Server">
void Page_Load(object sender, EventArgs e) {
   string[] artists = new string[4] {"Rembrandt","Courbet",
                 "Manet","Degas"};
   //
   if( !this.IsPostBack) {
      // Bind the first time the page is loaded
      ListBox.DataSource = artists;
      ListBox.DataBind();
   }
}
```

Note that the binding occurs only when the page is loaded the first time. View-State is used to populate the control on subsequent postbacks.

Selecting an Item

When an item in a list control is selected, the SelectedIndexChanged event occurs. A postback to the server occurs only if the control specifies an event handler to be called, and sets the AutoPostBack attribute to true.

```
<asp:ListBox id="ListBox" runat="server"
   SelectionMode="Multiple" Rows=4
   AutoPostBack="true"
   OnSelectedIndexChanged="ShowSelections"
   Width=150px>
</asp:ListBox>
```

The event handler declaration has the familiar parameters of the EventHandler delegate declaration.

```
public void ShowSelections(Object sender, EventArgs e) {
   Label1.Text="";
   foreach (ListItem item in ListBox.Items)
   {
      if(item.Selected)
      {
         Label1.Text += item.Text + "<br>";
      }
   }
}
```

The event handler iterates through the items in the ListBox and displays those that are selected. By default, the ListBox permits only one item to be selected, but this can be overridden by setting SelectionMode to Multiple.

A single selected item is available through three properties: SelectedIndex returns the index of a selected item in the list; SelectedItem returns the entire item; and SelectedValue returns the value of the selected item. If there are multiple selected items, these properties return information on the selected item having the lowest index.

The DataList Control

The DataList control makes it easy to display data in a repeating pattern. The idea is to create a template that defines the layout for items it contains. Each "item" is defined as a mixture of visual Web controls and HTML. Item content comes from one or more fields in a data source. When an instance of the DataList control is set to a data source, such as a `DataReader`, each row of the data source is represented as an item in the `DataList`. The `DataList` is processed much like a `ListBox` control: `Items.Count` provides the number of items in the control, and the `SelectedIndex` and `SelectedItem` properties reference a specific item.

To illustrate the use of this control, let's create a Web page that lists DVDs for sale. The items for sale are displayed in two-column rows as shown in Figure 16-10. The row/column layout is specified in the `DataList` declaration:

```
<ASP:DataList id="MyDataList" RepeatColumns="2"
   RepeatDirection="Horizontal" OnItemCommand="Item_Command"
   runat="server">
```

The `RepeatColumns` property specifies the number of columns displayed, and `RepeatDirection` indicates the direction in which items are displayed. `OnItem-Command` specifies the method to be called when a button in the `DataList` control is clicked. In this example, the `ItemCommand` event fires when the user adds an item to the cart. Here is an example of the code to handle this event:

```
private void Item_Command(object source,
      System.Web.UI.WebControls.DataListCommandEventArgs e)
{
   // (1) Crucial: select an item in the DataList
   MyDataList.SelectedIndex = e.Item.ItemIndex;
   // (2) Get the value of a control in the selected item
   string id= ((Label)
      MyDataList.SelectedItem.FindControl("movID")).Text;
}
```

An item selected in the `DataList` is indexed by the `SelectedIndex` property. After an item is selected, the `FindControl` method can be used to obtain a reference to any control in the item definition. In this case, the value of the `Label` containing the movie's ID is assigned to a variable.

The `ItemTemplate` shown in Listing 16-5 describes the appearance of each item. The most important thing to note in this code is the use of `DataBinder.Eval` to bind to a property or column in the data source. As shown here, the method has two overloads, one of which takes a formatting parameter.

```
<%# DataBinder.Eval(Container.DataItem, "movie_ID") %>
<%# DataBinder.Eval(Container.DataItem,"r_price", " {0:c2}") %>
```

Note that ASP.NET 2.0 offers a simpler, but equivalent version:

```
<%# Eval("movie_ID") %>
```

Either construct is replaced by the corresponding data from the data source. It can be displayed directly in the HTML stream or assigned to a control's property.

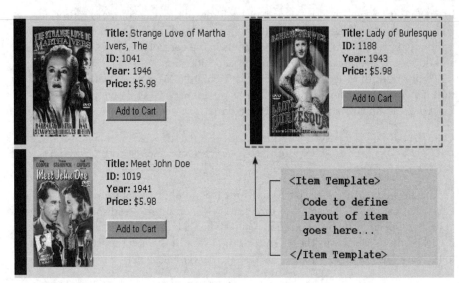

Figure 16-10   DataList control is used to display items in repeated format

| Listing 16-5 | Defining an ItemTemplate for a DataList Control |

```
<ItemTemplate>
   <table cellpadding=10 style="font: 10pt verdana" width=380>
      <tr>
         <td width=1 bgcolor="00000"/>
         <td valign="top">
         <a href=showdvd.aspx?id=<%# DataBinder.Eval(
            Container.DataItem, "movie_ID") %>>
         <img align="top" border=0
            src='./images/<%# DataBinder.Eval(
            Container.DataItem, "movie_ImgID") %>' ></a>
         </td>
         <td valign="top">
         <b>Title: </b><%# DataBinder.Eval(
            Container.DataItem, "movie_title") %><br>
         <b>ID: </b>
            <asp:Label id="movID"
               Text=<%# DataBinder.Eval(Container.DataItem,
                  "movie_ID") %>
               runat="server" >
            </asp:Label></b><br>
```

Listing 16-5	Defining an ItemTemplate for a `DataList` Control *(continued)*

```
        <b>Year:   </b><%# DataBinder.Eval(
            Container.DataItem, "movie_Year") %><br>
        <b>Price: </b><%# DataBinder.Eval(Container.DataItem,
            "r_price", " {0:c2}") %><br>
        <%# DataBinder.Eval(Container.DataItem,
            "movie_shortdesc") %> <br>
        <asp:Button  Value="Select"  Text="Add to Cart"
            BackColor="#bda563"
            CommandName="cart"
            runat=server>
        </asp:Button> <br>
        </td>
    </tr>
    </table>
</ItemTemplate>
```

The easiest part of working with a `DataList` is binding it to a data source. In this example, we use a `DataReader` to load rows from a database. To display these rows as items in the control, set the `DataSource` to the reader and then bind it:

```
rdr= cmd.ExecuteReader();
MyDataList.DataSource= rdr;
MyDataList.DataBind();
```

The contents of the `DataList` can be changed at any time by reassigning and binding a new data source.

Core Note

`DataBinder.Eval` and `Eval` use reflection to perform late-bound evaluation. The advantage of this approach is that it can determine the data type (making casting unnecessary) and has a simple formatting syntax. The disadvantage is that it is much slower than an early-bound approach. As an alternative—particularly when formatting is not needed—consider this early-bound syntax:

```
<%# ((IDataRecord)Container.DataItem)["movie_ID"] %>
```

`IDataRecord` casting is used when a `DataReader` is the data source. Cast with `DataRowView` when the data source is a `DataSet`.

In summary, the DataList acts as composite control that can be configured to display data in just about any format. In addition to the ItemTemplate, it supports header, footer, edit, and select templates that can be used to expand its capabilities beyond those described in this section.

16.3 Data Binding and Data Source Controls

Data binding enables the contents of a control to be populated by data from a designated data source. Technically speaking, the data source is any collection of data that implements the IEnumerable interface. In simple cases, the source may be an object such as an Array, ArrayList, Hashtable, or SortedList. More often, the data comes from an ADO.NET DataTable, DataSet, or IDataReader object. The control may bind directly to one of these objects, or indirectly, using the special data source controls introduced with ASP.NET 2.0.

Binding to a DataReader

The data reader provides a forward-only, read-only resultset that is the most efficient way to present data. It is generated by issuing the ExecuteReader method of the IDbCommand object. A control binds to the results by setting its DataSource property to the data reader object and executing its DataBind method.

The example in Listing 16-6 illustrates how a data reader is used to populate a ListBox with movie titles from the Films database (described in Chapter 10). The values displayed in the ListBox are based on the value assigned to the DataText-Field property—in this case, the Movie_Title column in the movies table. The DataValueField property specifies an additional column value that is assigned to each item in the ListBox. When an item is selected, this latter value is returned by the SelectedValue property.

Listing 16-6	Data Binding a List Box to a Data Reader

```
<%@ Page Language="C#" %>
<%@Import namespace="System.Data.SqlClient" %>
<%@Import namespace="System.Data" %>
<html>
<body>
<head><TITLE>Bind Films data to a ListBox</TITLE>
```

Listing 16-6 Data Binding a List Box to a Data Reader *(continued)*

```
<script runat="Server">
   void Page_Load(object sender, EventArgs e) {
      if(!this.IsPostBack) {
         getMovies();
      }
   }
   private void getMovies()
   {
      string cnstr=GetConnString(); // Get a connection string
      SqlConnection conn = new SqlConnection(cnstr);
      IDataReader rdr=null;
      IDbCommand cmd = new SqlCommand();
      cmd.Connection= conn;
      conn.Open();
      cmd.Connection=conn;
      cmd.CommandText="SELECT movie_id, movie_title FROM movies
         ORDER BY AFIRank";
      conn.Open();
      rdr = cmd.ExecuteReader();
      // Bind DataReader to ListBox
      ListBoxMovie.DataSource = rdr;
      ListBoxMovie.DataBind();
      conn.Close();
      rdr.Close();
   }
   </script>
   </head>
   <FORM NAME="FORM1" runat=server>
   <asp:ListBox
      id="ListBoxMovie"
      dataValueField = "movie_ID"
      dataTextField  = "movie_title"
      AppendDataBoundItems=true
      Rows="10"
      BackColor=#efefe4
      font-size=9pt
      runat="server" >
    <asp:ListItem Value=-1 Text="Select Movie" />
   </asp:ListBox>
</FORM>
</body>
</html>
```

Observe the presence of the `AppendDataBoundItems` property in the `ListBox` declaration. This property, a new feature added by ASP.NET 2.0, provides a way to specify whether data binding should overwrite any preexisting items in a list control. This is particularly useful for placing an entry in a list that precedes the actual data. In the preceding example, the `ListBox` declaration includes a `ListItem` that causes `Select Movie` to be placed in it first row.

Binding to a DataSet

It is often preferable to bind a server control to a data reader, rather than to a `DataSet`. To understand why, let's compare the two (see Figure 16-11). The data reader connects to a table and streams data into the control when the `DataBind` method is called. A data set, on the other hand, is a cache in memory that is filled with the resultset when the `DataAdapter.Fill` method is invoked. Its contents are then copied into the control when the control's `DataBind` method is called. In a WinForms application, the data set remains available to the application until it is closed; in a Web application, the data set disappears after a reply is sent to the browser. As we discuss in the next chapter, it can be saved as a `Session` variable, but this requires memory and can lead to scalability problems.

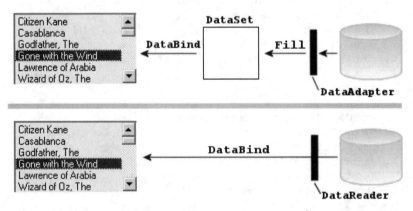

Figure 16-11   `DataReader` versus `DataSet` as a control's `DataSource`

There are a couple of situations in which using a `DataSet` makes sense. One is when multiple controls are bound to the contents of a `DataSet`. In this code segment, a data set is built that contains a list of all the movies in a table. Two `ListBox` controls are then populated with different views of the data. One `ListBox` contains movies produced prior to 1951, and the other contains those produced on or after that year. The advantage of the `DataSet` in this case is that only one query is applied against the database.

```
string sql ="SELECT movie_id, movie_title,movie_year FROM movies
      ORDER BY movie_year";
SqlDataAdapter da = new SqlDataAdapter(sql,conn);
DataSet ds = new DataSet();
da.Fill(ds,"Movies");  // DataSet and DataTable
DataView dview = new DataView(ds.Tables["Movies"]);
dview.RowFilter = "movie_year < 1951";
// List box containing movies before 1951
ListBoxMovie.DataSource= dview;
ListBoxMovie.DataBind();
// List box containing movies produced after 1950
dview.RowFilter = "vendor_name > 1950";
ListBoxMovie2.DataSource= dview;
ListBoxMovie2.DataBind();
```

A DataSet is also useful when the Web application is designed as a three-tier
Web site in which the presentation layer accesses a database through an intermediate
data access layer. The data access layer contains a method or methods that return a
DataSet in response to the call.

Let's look at how the .aspx file in Listing 16-6 can be converted from its current
two-tier structure to a three-tier design. The first step is to remove the getMovies
method and place it in a separate assembly. In the following code, the method is part
of the DataMethods class and rewritten to return a data set containing the vendor
data. This code is compiled into a DLL file and placed in the bin subdirectory below
the Web page.

```
// datalayer.dll - place in \bin subdirectory below application
using System.Data.SqlClient;
using System.Data;
namespace myUtil{
   public class DataMethods{
      public DataSet getMovies(){
         string cnstr= GetConnString(); // Get a connection string
         SqlConnection conn = new SqlConnection(cnstr);
         IDbCommand cmd = new SqlCommand();
         cmd.Connection= conn;
         string sql="SELECT movie_id, movie_title FROM
               movies ORDER BY AFIRank";
         SqlDataAdapter da = new SqlDataAdapter(sql,conn);
         DataSet ds = new DataSet();
         da.Fill(ds,"Movies");
         return (ds);
      }
   }
}
```

The code changes in the .aspx file are minimal. An @Import directive is added so that the namespace in datalayer.dll can be accessed.

```
<%@Import namespace="myUtil" %>
```

The getMovies call is replaced with the following:

```
if(!this.IsPostBack) {
   DataMethods dm = new DataMethods();
   DataSet ds = dm.getMovies();
   ListBoxMovie.DataSource = ds;
   ListBoxMovie.DataBind();
}
```

The use of a data presentation layer promotes code reusability, hides the messy ADO.NET connection details, and results in cleaner code.

DataSource Controls

As we have seen, ASP.NET makes it easy to bind a control to data by simply setting the control's DataSource property to the collection of data it is to display. However, it is still up to the developer to assemble the collection of data. For example, using the data reader as a data source requires the following pattern of operations:

1. Create a data connection.
2. Create a Command object.
3. Build a query and use the Command object to retrieve data into a data reader.

Data source controls encapsulate the functionality required to perform these operations—eliminating the need for coding by the developer. The data-bound control is no longer bound to the data collection, but to a data source control. To illustrate, Figure 16-12 shows how a grid can be populated by binding it to a data reader or a SqlDataSource control.

Data controls are not limited to database access. In fact, ASP.NET 2.0 supports data source controls that attach to six types of data:

- AccessDataSource. Binds to a Microsoft Access database.
- DataSetDataSource. Binds to non-hierarchical XML data.
- ObjectDataSource. Binds to data through custom classes implemented in a data access layer.
- SiteMapdataSource. Binds to XML site maps.
- SqlDataSource. Binds to a SQL database.
- XmlDataSource. Binds to XML documents.

We'll look at the SqlDataSource, ObjectDataSource, and XmlDataSource controls in this section.

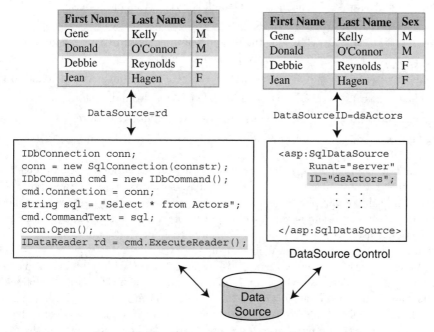

Figure 16-12 Comparison of data binding using ADO.NET code versus DataSource control

SqlDataSource Control

This control represents a connection to a relational data store, such as SQL Server, DB2, or Oracle. It requires a .NET managed data provider with the capability to return a SQL resultset.

The SqlDataSource control is declared using standard Web control syntax.

Control Declaration:

```
<asp:sqldatasource  runat="server" id="controlID"
```

Properties:

ConnectionString   Connection string to access database.

ProviderName   Managed provider. Default is SqlClient.

`DataSourceMode`	Controls how the select command retrieves data. Is a `SqlDataSourceMode` enumeration: `DataSet` or `DataReader`. Default is `DataSet`.
`EnableCaching`	True or false. Default is `false`. Can only be used if `DataSourceMode` is `DataSet`.
`CacheDuration`	How long the contents of the data source are maintained in memory. Value is in seconds.
`SelectCommand`	SQL statement that retrieves data from associated data store.
`DeleteCommand`	SQL statement to delete row(s) from data store.
`InsertCommand`	SQL statement to insert row(s) into data store.
`UpdateCommand`	SQL statement to update row(s) in data store.

The four command properties are strings that contain either a SQL command or the name of a stored procedure (if the database supports it) to be executed. Each command can contain parameters whose values are defined by an associated collection of parameters. In an upcoming example, we'll see how the `SelectParameters` collection is used with `SelectCommand`. Before that, let's look at how the `SqlData-Control` is used to populate a Web control.

As in our earlier example, Listing 16-7 fills a `ListBox` with the name of movies from the `Films` database. However, in place of raw ADO.NET coding, it defines a data source control and assigns to its `SelectCommand` property a SQL select string that retrieves a list of movies from the database. A `ListBox` control is declared with its `DataSourceID` property set to the ID of the data source control. When the page is loaded, the list control is populated with the resultset.

Listing 16-7	Binding a `ListBox` to a `SqlDataSource` Control

```
<%@ Page Language="C#"  %>
<%@Import namespace="System.Data.SqlClient" %>
<%@Import namespace="System.Data" %>
<HTML>
<HEAD><TITLE>Using a DataSource Control</TITLE>
</HEAD>
<body>
<form id="Form1" runat="server">
   <asp:sqldatasource runat="server" id="SqlDataSource1"
      connectionstring="SERVER=(local);DATABASE=FILMS;
      Integrated Security=SSPI; "
      providername = "System.Data.SqlClient"
```

Listing 16-7	Binding a `ListBox` to a `SqlDataSource` Control *(continued)*

```
        selectCommand= "SELECT movie_ID, movie_Title FROM movies
                        ORDER BY AFIRank" >
    </asp:sqldatasource>
    <table border=0>
    <tr><td>
    <asp:ListBox runat="server" id="ListBoxMovie"
        dataSourceid    = "SqlDataSource1"
        dataValueField  = "movie_ID"
        dataTtextField  = "movie_Title" />
    </td></tr>
    </table>
</form>
</body>
</html>
```

Let's extend this example so that when a movie is selected from the list, its cast members are displayed. To do this, we add a `GridView`, as shown in Figure 16-13.

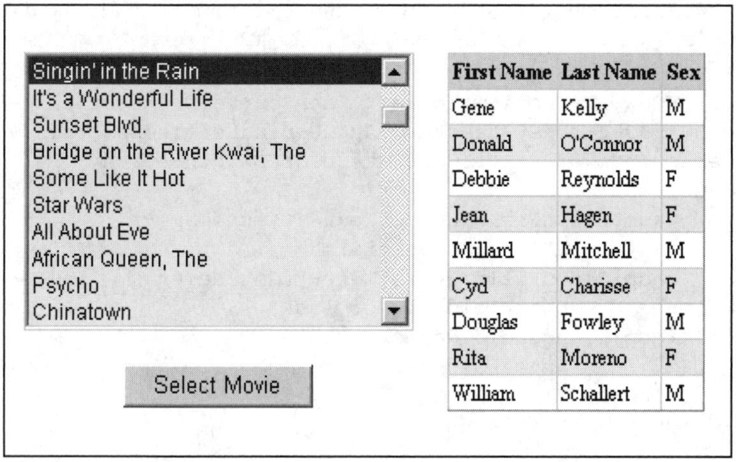

Figure 16-13   Using data source controls to depict a parent-child relationship

The data for the `GridView` also comes from a new data source control. The purpose of this control is to dynamically retrieve a list of actors for any movie selected in the `ListBox`. The challenge is to identify the movie selected and to specify it in the query. Here's how it's done.

The query assigned to the SelectCommand property contains a parameter (@movieID) that serves as a placeholder for the actual movie ID. Within the data source control is another control, ControlParameter, that has the same name as the parameter in our query. It links the data source control to the ListBox via two properties: ControlID, which specifies the ListBox ID, and PropertyName, which specifies the value to assign to the query parameter. When an item in the ListBox is selected, ASP.NET replaces the parameter with the current SelectedValue of List-BoxMovie (which is a movie ID) and executes the query to retrieve the actor data.

```
<asp:SqlDataSource ID="ActorSource" RunAt="server"
    connectionstring="SERVER=(local);DATABASE=FILMS;
        Integrated Security=SSPI; "
    SelectCommand= "SELECT actor_first, actor_last, actor_sex FROM
        actor_movie LEFT JOIN actors ON actor_movie.actor_ID=
        actors.actor_ID WHERE movie_ID=@movieID">
        <SelectParameters>
            <asp:ControlParameter Name="movieID"
                ControlID="ListBoxMovie"
                PropertyName="SelectedValue">
            </asp:ControlParameter>
        </SelectParameters>
</asp:SqlDataSource>
```

The GridView control contains three columns that are bound to the data source control:

```
<asp:GridView ID="MovieGridView" DataSourceID="ActorSource"
    Width="100%" runat="server" AutoGenerateColumns="false"
    SelectedIndex="0" AutoGenerateSelectButton="true" >
        <Columns>
            <asp:BoundField HeaderText="First Name"
                DataField="actor_first" />
            <asp:BoundField HeaderText="Last Name"
                    DataField="actor_last" />
            <asp:BoundField HeaderText="Sex"
                    DataField="actor_sex" />
        </Columns>
</asp:GridView>
```

Core Note

In addition to the ControlParameter that specifies the control from which a query's parameter value comes, ASP.NET recognizes five other parameter sources: CookieParameter, FormParameter, ProfileParameter, SessionParameter, and QueryStringParameter.

ObjectDataSource Control

The `ObjectDataSource` is used when data is retrieved through a data access layer, rather than directly from the database. To demonstrate, recall the three-tier structure we created earlier by placing the `getMovies` method in a separate assembly. An `ObjectDataSource` control can be declared to access this method by setting its `typename` field to the class containing the method and its `selectmethod` field to the name of the method.

```
<asp:objectdatasource
    id="ObjectDataSource1"
    runat="server"
    typename="myUtil.DataMethods"
    selectmethod="getMovies">
</asp:objectdatasource>
```

This could be used to populate the `ListBox` control in Listing 16-7 by replacing the `SqlDataSource` control with the `ObjectDataSource` control and resetting `DataSourceID` to `ObjectDataSource1` in the `ListBox` declaration.

It is also worth noting that an `ObjectDataSource` can be used to fetch data from a Web Service. Because Web Services (described in Chapter 18) are nothing more than classes that expose remotely accessible methods, the `typename` and `selectmethod` properties can be used to refer to the class and method as if they were in a local assembly.

XmlDataSource Control

The `XmlDataSource` control is likely to be the most popular of the data source controls. It reads XML data from a local file or a stream transmitted across a network. It's particularly useful for handling the XML formats that are becoming standards for exchanging information across the Internet. To illustrate, we'll create an example that uses the control to read data in the increasingly popular RSS format.

RSS, which stands for *Really Simple Syndication*, is an XML formatting standard designed originally for news feeds. However, it is now used as a generic way for Web sites to periodically publish information feeds that can be picked up by RSS readers. It not only provides an easy way to distribute data, but the simple format makes it easy for the recipient to determine when any updates have occurred. Because the data is sent as an XML stream, the `XmlDataSource` control can play the role of a simple RSS reader. As an example, we pair it with a `DataList` control to capture and display a sample RSS feed from the BBC news network (see Figure 16-14).

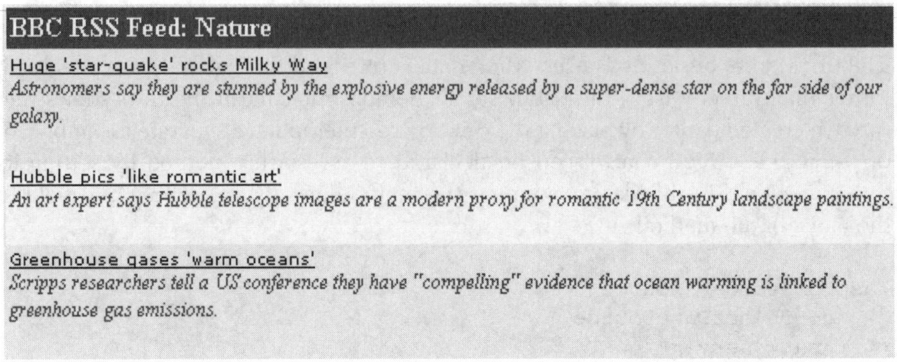

Figure 16-14   Display RSS feed using `XmlDataSource` and `DataList` controls

The underlying XML conforms to the RSS standard (several versions are now in use). At the top level is the `<rss>` element that contains a required version attribute. Subordinate to it is a single `<channel>` element that contains a description of the channel along with its content. The content is supplied by `<item>` elements that have three mandatory subelements: `<title>`, `<link>`, and `<description>`. Their purpose should be clear from the portion of the XML feed shown here:

```
<rss version="0.91">
   <channel>
      <title>BBC News | Science/Nature | World Edition</title>
      <link>
         http://news.bbc.co.uk/go/click/rss/0.91/public/-
            /2/hi/science/nature/default.stm
      </link>
      <description>Updated every minute of every day</description>
      <item>
         <title>Huge 'star-quake' rocks Milky Way</title>
         <description>
            Astronomers say they are stunned by the explosive
            energy released by a super-dense star on the
            far side of our galaxy.
         </description>
      <link>
         http://news.bbc.co.uk/go/click/rss/0.91/public/-
            /2/hi/science/nature/4278005.stm
      </link>
      </item>
      <item>
      ... other items go here
   </channel>
</rss>
```

Listing 16-8 shows how the XML is displayed using only a `DataList` and `Xml-DataSource` control. The `XmlDataSource` control identifies the data source with the `DataFile` property. As mentioned, this can be a file or a URL. The purpose of the `XPath` property is to set a filter for the XML document so that only a subset of the document is returned. In this case, we are interested in only the `<item>` data.

The `DataList` control identifies the data source component it is bound to by setting the `DataSourceID` property to the component's ID—`XmlDataSource1`. The `XPathBinder` object is used to select items or nodes from the XML document. Its `XPath` method returns a single node, whereas the `XPathSelect` method returns an `ArrayList` of matching values. Both take an `XPath` expression (see Chapter 10) to identify the desired item.

```
<%# XPath("xpath-expression"[, "format"]) %>
<%# XPathSelect("xpath-expression") %>
```

Listing 16-8	Displaying RSS Feed with a `DataList` and `XmlDataSource` Control

```
<asp:DataList ID="DataList1" Runat="server"
    RepeatColumns=1
    RepeatDirection="Horizontal"
    GridLines="Horizontal"
    BorderWidth="1px" BackColor="White" CellPadding="2"
    BorderStyle="None" BorderColor="#E7E7FF"
    DataSourceID="XmlDataSource1">
    <ItemTemplate>
        <asp:HyperLink ID="HyperLink1" Runat="server"
            Text=<%# XPath("title") %>
            NavigateUrl=<%# XPath("link") %>
            Target="_blank" Font-Names="Sans-Serif"
            Font-Size="X-Small">
        </asp:HyperLink><br/>
        <i><%# XPath("description")%></i><br /><br />
    </ItemTemplate>
    <AlternatingItemStyle BackColor="#F7F7F7">
    </AlternatingItemStyle>
    <ItemStyle ForeColor="#4A3C8C"
        Font-Size=9pt BackColor="#E7E7FF">
    </ItemStyle>
    <HeaderTemplate>BBC RSS Feed: Nature</HeaderTemplate>
    <HeaderStyle ForeColor="#F7F7F7"
        Font-Bold="True" BackColor="#4A3C8C">
    </HeaderStyle>
</asp:DataList>
```

Listing 16-8	Displaying RSS Feed with a `DataList` and `XmlDataSource` Control *(continued)*

```
<asp:XmlDataSource
    ID="XmlDataSource1"
    Runat="server"
    XPath="rss/channel/item"
    DataFile=
        "http://news.bbc.co.uk/rss/newsonline_world_edition/
        science/nature/rss091.xml">
</asp:XmlDataSource>
```

By binding a data component to a sophisticated visual data control, we are able to create an application in which all data binding is specified through declarations. This can eliminate the need for code to input data, iterate through it, and parse it into a format that can be displayed. In addition, data components have built-in caching features that improve the efficiency of accessing data and eliminate code-managed caching. We look at caching in the next chapter.

16.4 Validation Controls

One of the more frustrating Internet experiences is to fill in a long form, submit it, and—after a lengthy wait—have it rejected due to an invalid field entry. Any well-designed form should attempt to avoid this by including client-side verification to check fields before the form is submitted. Validation is typically used to ensure that a field is not empty, that a field contains a numeric value only, that a phone number or credit card has the correct format, and that an e-mail address contains the @ character. JavaScript is traditionally used for this purpose.

ASP.NET offers *validation controls* as a flexible alternative to implementing your own client-side JavaScript functions. The purpose of these controls is to perform a specific type of validation on an associated control. For example, a `RequiredField-Validator` control checks an input control to ensure it is not empty.

Table 16-5 lists the six built-in validation controls along with their unique properties and values.

Table 16-5 Validation Controls

Control	Properties	Description and Possible Values
RequiredField Validator	**Checks whether input control field contains a value.**	
CompareValidator	**Compares the value of an input control with a constant or other control.**	
	Operator	Has value of: Equal, NotEqual, GreaterThan, Greater-ThanEqual, LessThan, LessThanEqual, DataTypeCheck
	Type	Currency, Date, Double, Integer, String.
	ValueToCompare	Constant value used for comparison.
	ControlToCompare	Other control to compare value with.
RangeValidator	**Checks the value of the input control against a range of values.**	
	MaximumValue	Constant value that represents upper value.
	MinimumValue	Constant value that represents lowest value.
	Type	Currency, Date, Double, Integer, String.
RegularExpression Validator	**Matches the value of the input control against a regular expression.**	
	ValidationExpression	Regex to match input control's value against.
CustomValidator	**Checks a field's value against custom validation logic.**	
	ClientValidation-Function	JavaScript client-side function to perform validation.
	OnServerValidate	Server-side method to perform validation.
ValidationSummary	**Collects and lists all the error messages from the form validation process.**	
	DisplayMode	Format of error messages: BulletList, List, SingleParagraph
	HeaderText	Title for error message summary.
	ShowMessageBox	Display errors in pop-up box: true or false.
	ShowSummary	Display errors on control: true or false.

Only the final control in the table, ValidationSummary, does not perform a validation. Instead, it displays a summary of the errors generated by the other validation controls.

Using Validation Controls

Validation controls are used only with controls that have a single input field type. These include the HTMLInputText, HTMLSelect, TextBox, DropDownList, and ListBox controls. ASP.NET implements the validation function on both the server and client side. To handle the client side, it includes a .js file containing validation code in the response to the browser. Note, however, that if scripting is disabled on the browser, only client-side checking will occur.

To illustrate the mechanics of using a validation control, here is the code to associate a RequiredFieldValidator and RangeValidator control with a TextBox control. The range validator control uses its MaximumValue and MinimumValue properties to ensure that the value entered in the text box is a numeric value from 0 to 12.

```
<td><asp:TextBox Width=30 id=hti maxlength=2
    runat=server></td>

<asp:RequiredFieldValidator id="htivalidator" runat=server
    ControlToValidate="hti"
    ErrorMessage="Must enter height value."
    Display="dynamic">
</asp:RequiredFieldValidator>

<asp:RangeValidator id="htirangevalidator"
    ControlToValidate="hti"
    MaximumValue="12"
    MinimumValue="0"
    Type="Integer"
    Display="dynamic "
    ForeColor="Blue"
    ErrorMessage="Invalid Height."
    runat=server>
</asp:RangeValidator>
```

This example also illustrates useful properties that all validator controls inherit from the BaseValidator class:

- ControlToValidate. Set to the identifier of the control to be validated.
- Display. static, dynamic, or none. This specifies how the error message takes up space on the form: static reserves space and

makes the message visible when it is needed; `dynamic` uses no space on the form until it is displayed; `none` is used when the error message is to be displayed by the `ValidationSummary` control.

- `ForeColor`. Sets the color of the error message text. Red is the default.
- `ErrorMessage`. The message displayed when a validation exception is detected.
- `ValidationGroup`. A `string` value that enables validation controls to be grouped by assigning the same value to this property. When a `Button` control that has its `ValidationGroup` property set to a group value submits a form, only controls with validators in the group are validated. This allows sections of a page to be validated separately. This property is introduced in ASP.NET 2.0.

Of the controls listed in Table 16-4, the `CustomValidator` and `Validation-Summary` exhibit unique behavior that requires further explanation.

CustomValidator Control

There are many common validation patterns that the built-in validation controls do not handle. For example, the contents of one control may be dependent on another, such as when a credit card number format depends on the type of card selected. Another common example is to require that a string entered in a field conform to a minimum and maximum length. Cases such as these are handled with a `CustomValidator` control that points to server-side and/or client-side routines that implement custom validation logic. To demonstrate how this control works, let's use it to validate a field that accepts a password, which must be between 8 and 12 characters in length.

The declaration of the control is similar to that of the other validation controls. The main difference is the `ClientValidationFunction` and `OnServerValidate` fields that specify client and server routines to validate the associated password field.

```
<input type=password id="pw" runat="server" />
<br>
<asp:CustomValidator  id="pwvalidator"
   ControlToValidate="pw"
   ClientValidationFunction="checkPWClient"
   OnServerValidate="checkPW"
   Display=dynamic
   ErrorMessage="A password must be between 8 and 12 characters."
   runat="server"/>
```

The validation routines contain identical logic. The client side is written in Java-Script and the server side in C#. They are contained in separate `<script/>` blocks in the `.aspx` file.

```
<script language=javascript>
<!-
   // Client side function to check field length
   function checkPWClient(source, args)
   {
      var pw = args.Value;
      var ln= pw.length;
      args.IsValid=true;
      if(ln <8 || ln > 12) args.IsValid=false
   }
//-->
</script>
<script Language="C#"  runat="Server">
private void checkPW(object source, ServerValidateEventArgs args){
   if(args.Value.Length<8 || args.Value.Length>12)
        {args.IsValid=false;
   } else{
      args.IsValid=true;
   }
}
</script>
```

Two parameters are passed to the validation routines: source and args. Args is the more important of the two. Its value property exposes the content of the form field being validated. In this example, the length of the field value is checked. If it falls within the bounds, IsValid is set to true; otherwise, it is set to false. A false value triggers the error message defined by the CustomValidator control.

For consistency with the built-in validation controls, include both server- and client-side routines for custom validation. If only one is to be implemented, server side is always preferred.

ValidationSummary Control

This control collects all of the error messages generated by the validation controls and displays them as a list or customizable paragraph. The messages are displayed either within the control (as a <span> element within the HTML) or as a pop-up window by setting the ShowMessageBox to true.

```
<asp:ValidationSummary id=validsumm runat="server"
   ShowMessageBox=true
   DisplayMode=List
   ShowSummary=false>
</asp:ValidationSummary>
```

The most important factor to consider when deciding how to display validation error messages is that the ValidationSummary control displays messages when a form is submitted, and individual validation controls display a message when their associated control loses focus. Thus, displaying the message at a validation control provides immediate feedback to the user. Also note that if the validation control has its `Display` property set to `static` or `dynamic`, the error message is displayed by both the validation control and the `ValidationSummary` control.

16.5 Master and Content Pages

A principal design objective when creating a multi-page Web site is visual and functional consistency. Headers and footers should look the same, and the layout and use of controls should be similar from page to page. One way to achieve this is to drag and drop common controls on to each new Web page; but in many cases, a better approach is to create a template from which new pages can be derived. In Windows Forms programming, a form can be filled with controls and used as a base class to create other interfaces. ASP.NET has a similar feature known as *master pages*. The idea is to create a template, or master page, containing visual elements that will be common to other pages, as well as placeholders that will be filled in with the unique content from other pages. Pages that provide content for the master page are referred to as *content pages*.

The major advantages to this approach are that any changes made to a master page are automatically reflected in the content pages and that the act of creating content pages is limited to providing statements that specify the content to be associated with the placeholders in the master page.

To illustrate the fundamentals of using master pages, we'll create a master page that defines the layout for the Web page shown in Figure 16-15. In addition, we'll create two content pages that correspond to the menu items shown on the left side of the page.

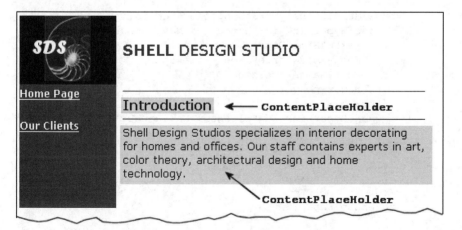

Figure 16-15 Web page derived from a master page

Creating a Master Page

Master pages are so similar to regular .aspx pages that converting an .aspx page to a master page requires only three changes: the file must have the .master extension; the @Page directive is replaced with the @Master directive; and one or more ContentPlaceHolder controls are added to serve as containers that will be filled at runtime with content from content pages.

Listing 16-9 shows the master page used by content pages to create the Web page in Figure 16-15. The two menu items are implemented as HyperLink controls that reference the two content pages. Two ContentPlaceHolder server controls designate the area in the page where a content page's title and main body are placed.

Listing 16-9	Master Page Definition—shell.master

```
<%@ Master  %>
<html>
<head>
   <title>Master Page for Shell Design Studio</title>
</head>
<body bgcolor=#ffffff link=#ffffff alink=#ffffff vlink=#ffffff>
<FORM id="mainform" runat="server">
<table width="500" cellpadding="0" cellspacing="0">
   <tr><td bgcolor=black align=center>
         <img src=./images/sdslogo.gif>
      </td><td>  
      </td><td>
         <font size=4 face=Verdana> <b>SHELL</b> DESIGN STUDIO
      </td></tr>
   <tr>
      <td width=120 height=300 bgcolor=red valign=top>
         <asp:HyperLink id="homepage" NavigateUrl="home.aspx"
            Text="Home Page"
            Font-Bold="true" Font-Size=9pt
            Font-Names="Verdana"
            runat=server />
         <br><br>
         <asp:HyperLink id="clients" NavigateUrl="clients.aspx"
            Text="Our Clients"
            Font-Bold="true" Font-Size=9pt
            Font-Names="Verdana"
            runat=server />
      </td>
      <td>  </td>
```

Listing 16-9 | Master Page Definition—`shell.master` *(continued)*

```
        <td valign=top>
          <hr size=1 color=red>
          <asp:contentplaceholder id="Header" runat="Server">
            <b>Introduction</b>
          </asp:contentplaceholder>
          <hr size=1 color=red>
          <asp:contentplaceholder id="PageBody" runat="Server">
            This is Default Content to be overridden
            by content pages
          </asp:contentplaceholder>
        </td></tr>
  </table>
  </FORM>
  </body>
  </html>
```

Creating a Content Page

A content page is an `.aspx` file containing `<asp:Content>` tags (instances of Content controls) that override corresponding `<asp:contentplaceholder>` tags in the master page. The `ContentPlaceHolderID` property of the content tag matches the `ID` of the placeholder where the content is to be inserted. The `home.aspx` content page in our example illustrates this. It contains two content tags that define the content for the `Header` and `PageBody` placeholders, respectively. The `masterpagefile` attribute specifies the master page from which this page inherits.

```
[home.aspx]
<%@ Page language="C#" masterpagefile=~/shell.master %>
<asp:content id="Header" runat="server"
   contentplaceholderid="Header">
   <font size=3 face=Verdana> <b>Introduction </b>
</asp:content>

<asp:content id="MainBody" runat="server"
   contentplaceholderid="PageBody">
   <font face=Verdana size=2>
   Shell Design Studios specializes in interior decorating for
   homes and offices. Our staff contains experts in art, color
   theory, architectural design and home technology.
</asp:content>
```

The content may consist of any combination of standard HTML markup code, images, managed code, and server controls. In this example, the `MainBody` placeholder is replaced with literal text for the `home.aspx` page and a list of clients—using the `<UL>` tag—for the `clients.aspx` content page.

```
[clients.aspx]
<%@ Page language="C#" masterpagefile=~/shell.master %>
<asp:content id="Header" runat="server"
   contentplaceholderid="Header">
   <font size=3 face=Verdana> <b>Our Clients </b>
</asp:content>

<asp:content id="MainBody" runat="server"
   contentplaceholderid="PageBody">
   <font face=Verdana size=2>
   <ul>
      <li>Swanburg Medical </li>
      <li>Lombard & Gable Law </li>
      <li>Coble Architectural Design</li>
   </ul>
</asp:content>
```

There are only a few commonsense rules to keep in mind when using master/content pages:

- A content page does not have to provide content for all placeholders. When content is not mapped to a placeholder, its default value is used.
- Content may include ASP.NET server controls. However, controls cannot be placed outside of the content tags.
- A placeholder's ID is unique. You cannot, for example, map the same content to two sections in a master page.

Accessing the Master Page from a Content Page

Recall that `.aspx` files are compiled at runtime into (`System.UI.Web`) Page objects. The Page object serves as the naming container for all objects on the page. When a master page is involved, one of the objects included is a `MasterPage` object that, in turn, serves as a container for the `ContentPlaceHolder` and `Content` objects. This hierarchy of objects comprises the Web page that is rendered to the client.

To support master pages, the Page object includes a `Master` property that can be used to reference objects in a master page's control collection. Content pages have access to this property and can thus alter the appearance of the master page template when they are loaded. As an example of how this can be used, consider the menu on our sample Web page (see Figure 16-15). The items have the same appearance no matter which page is loaded. As a rule, Web pages should distinguish the menu item for the currently loaded page from the other items. One popular technique is to highlight it. This requires adding only a few lines of code to our content files:

```
<%@ Import namespace=System.Drawing %>
<script runat="Server">
// Highlight link for home.aspx page
void Page_Load(object sender, EventArgs e)
{
    // Change color of link to indicate current page
    HyperLink h = (HyperLink)Master.FindControl("homepage");
    h.BackColor=Color.Goldenrod;   // highlight menu item
}
</script>
```

The `Master.FindControl` method is used to reference the link pointing to the current page. In this case, the returned object's `BackColor` property is set to highlight the link.

16.6 Building and Using Custom Web Controls

This section provides an overview of how to write and consume a custom Web control. Its objective is twofold: to introduce the fundamentals of implementing a control and, in the process, provide insight into the architecture of the intrinsic .NET controls.

In its simplest form, a custom control is a class that inherits from the `System.Web.UI.Control` class, implements (overrides) a `Render` method, and uses its `HtmlTextWriter` parameter to emit the HTML code that represents the control. Add some public properties to define the control's behavior, and you have a custom control that functions like the built-in ASP.NET controls. More complex controls may require features such as data binding and caching support, which are not covered in this chapter. For a full understanding of those topics, refer to a good ASP.NET book.[1]

---

1. *Essential ASP.NET* by Fritz Onion (Addison-Wesley, 2003) is a good choice.

A Custom Control Example

Listing 16-10 defines a custom control that we will use to illustrate the basics of control creation. The purpose of this control is to display a large or small version of a company logo, along with the company's name. Two properties determine its appearance and behavior: LogoType takes a value of small or large to indicate the size of the image to be displayed, and Link specifies the URL to navigate to when the small logo is clicked.

Listing 16-10   A Custom Control—`logocontrol.cs`

```
using System;
using System.Web;
using System.Web.UI;
namespace CompanyControls
{
   // (1) Inherit from the System.Web.UI.Control class
   public class CompanyLogo : Control
   {
      // Custom control to display large or small company logo
      private string logo_sz;    // "small" or "large"
      // Page to go to when logo is clicked
      private string myLink;
      public string LogoType
      {
         get {return logo_sz;}
         set {logo_sz = value;}
      }
      public string Link
      {
         get {return myLink;}
         set {myLink = value;}
      }
      // (2) Override the Render method
      protected override void Render(HtmlTextWriter output)
      {
         // (3) Emit HTML to the browser
       if (LogoType == "large"){
          output.Write("<a href="+Link+">");
          output.Write("<img src=./images/logo_big.gif
             align=middle border=0>");
          output.WriteLine("</a>");
          output.Write("  ");
          output.Write("<b style=font-style:24;");
```

| Listing 16-10 | A Custom Control—`logocontrol.cs` *(continued)* |

```
            output.Write("font-family:arial;color:#333333;>");
            output.Write("STC Software</b>");
        } else {
            output.Write("<a href="+Link+">");
            output.Write("<img src=./images/logo_small.gif
              align=middle border=0>");
            output.WriteLine("</a>");
            output.Write<br>");
            output.Write("<b style=font-style:12;");
            output.Write("font-family:arial;color:#333333;>");
            output.Write("Shell Design Studio</b>");
        }
    }
  }
}
```

Let's examine the three distinguishing features of a custom control class:

1. Inherits from `System.Web.UI.Control`.

This class provides properties, methods, and events that the custom control requires. The most important of these is the `Render` method that we describe next. Other members include the `Page` events (`Init`, `Load`, `PreRender`, `Unload`) and members for managing child controls.

If you are using Visual Studo.NET for control development, the base class will be `System.Web.UI.WebControls.WebControl`. This class derives from the `Control` class and adds several members, most of which affect appearance.

2. Overrides the `Render` method.

Each control must implement this method to generate the HTML that represents the control to the browser. Note that the `Render` method is not called directly; instead, a call is made to `RenderControl`, which then invokes `Render`. For controls that contain child controls, the `RenderChildren` method is available. This is called automatically by the `Render` method, and an implementation that overrides this method should include a `base.Render()` call if the control contains child controls.

3. Uses `HtmlTextWriter` object to generate HTML code.

This example uses the `HtmlTextWriter.Write` method to generate HTML for the control. This is the simplest approach, but `HtmlTextWriter` offers several other methods that you may prefer. One alternative is to use a set of helper methods that eliminate writing full literal strings.

```
//Following yields: <table border=0>
Output.WriteBeginTag("table")
Output.WriteAttribute("border","0");
Output.WriteEndTag("table")
```

A third approach uses "stack-based" methods to render code. It uses AddAttribute methods to define attributes for a tag that is then created with a RenderBeginTag method call and closed with a RenderEndTag call. Although the approach is verbose, it has the advantage of automatically detecting which version of HTML a browser supports and emitting code for that version.

The following code generates the same HTML as is in Listing 16-7 for the large image. It relies on a mixture of HtmlTextWriter methods and special tag, attribute, and style enumerations. Refer to the documentation of HtmlTextWriter for the lengthy list of methods and enumerations.

```
output.AddAttribute(HtmlTextWriterAttribute.Href,Link);
output.RenderBeginTag(HtmlTextWriterTag.A);   // <a
output.AddAttribute(HtmlTextWriterAttribute.Src,bgImg);
output.AddAttribute(HtmlTextWriterAttribute.Align,"middle");
output.AddAttribute(HtmlTextWriterAttribute.Border,"0");
output.RenderBeginTag(HtmlTextWriterTag.Img);
output.RenderEndTag();
output.RenderEndTag();                          // </a>
output.Write ("   ");
output.AddStyleAttribute(HtmlTextWriterStyle.FontSize,"24");
output.AddStyleAttribute(HtmlTextWriterStyle.FontFamily,"arial");
output.AddStyleAttribute(HtmlTextWriterStyle.Color,"#333333");
output.RenderBeginTag(HtmlTextWriterTag.B);
output.Write("Shell Design Studio");
output.RenderEndTag();
```

Using a Custom Control

The key to using a custom control is the @Register directive, which was discussed in Section 16.1. Its Assembly and Namespace attributes identify the assembly and namespace of the custom control. Its TagPrefix attribute notifies the ASP.NET runtime that any tag containing this prefix value refers to the control specified in the directive. Here is a Web page that includes the custom CompanyLogo control:

```
<%@ Page Language="C#" %>
<%@ Register Namespace="CompanyControls" TagPrefix="logo"
   Assembly="logocontrol"    %>
```

```
<script runat="server">
    protected void SendPage(object src, EventArgs e)
    {
        // Process page here.
    }
</script>
<html>
<body>
    <logo:CompanyLogo runat="server" id="lgc"
        Link="products.aspx"
        LogoType="large"/>
    <hr>
    <font size=2 face=arial color=black><center>
    This page contains ways to contact us
<br>
    <asp:Button runat="server" text="submit"
        OnClick="SendPage" />
</body>
</html>
```

The control that we have created behaves similarly to the built-in Web controls, but lacks one important feature that they all have: the capability to maintain its state during a postback operation.

Control State Management

Let's change the preceding code to set the LogoType property when the page is first loaded, rather than within the body of the code. We use the IsPostBack property for this purpose:

```
protected void Page_Load(object src, EventArgs e)
{
    if (!IsPostBack) {
        lgc.LogoType="large";
    }
}
```

On the initial request, LogoType is set and the page is returned with a large image. However, subsequent postbacks result in the small image being displayed because the value is not retained, and the code defaults to the small image. Recall that state is maintained between postbacks in the hidden _VIEWSTATE field. This field contains the values of the ViewState collection, so the secret to state control is to place values in this collection. It operates like a hash table—accepting name/value pairs—and is accessible by any control. The following code demonstrates how property values are placed in ViewState as a replacement for the simple fields used in Figure 16-7.

```
public class CompanyLogo : Control
{
    // Custom control to display large or small company logo
    public CompanyLogo() {
        ViewState["logo_sz"] = "small";
        ViewState["myLink"] = "";
    }
    public string LogoType
    {
        get {return (string) ViewState["logo_sz"]; }
        set {ViewState["logo_sz"]= value;   }
    }
    public string Link
    {
        get {return (string) ViewState["myLink"]; }
        set {ViewState["myLink"]= value;   }
    }
    // Rest of class code is here...
```

The property values are now maintained in the _VIEWSTATE field and persist between postbacks.

Composite Controls

At the beginning of the chapter, we created a Web page (refer to Figure 16-2) that calculates the Body Mass Index. This calculator consists of text boxes, labels, and a button. To turn this into a custom control, we could take our previous approach and override the Render method with a lengthy list of statements to generate the appropriate HTML. In addition, special code would have to be added to maintain the state of the control during postback operations. A better solution is to create a custom *composite control*.

A composite control is created from existing controls. Its advantage is that these controls, referred to as child controls, are very low maintenance. They render themselves—eliminating the need to override Render—and they maintain their state during postbacks. In addition, they let you program with familiar objects and their members, rather than output statements.

There are two major differences in the code used for the "from scratch" custom class in our preceding example and that of a composite control:

- The composite does not have to override the Control.Render method to display controls. Instead, it must override the Control.CreateChildControls method to add existing controls to the collection of controls making up the composite control.

- The custom control class should inherit from the `INamingContainer` interface. Its purpose is to indicate to ASP.NET that child controls exist and they should be placed in a separate namespace. This prevents name collision problems when a page contains more than one composite control.

Listing 16-11 contains the code to implement the BMI calculator as a composite control. The calculator comprises three text boxes, a label to display the result, and a button to invoke a method to perform the calculation. Most of the code of interest is in the overridden `CreateChildControls` method. It adds the standard controls to the collection, and uses `LiteralControl` to add HTML and descriptive information that helps format the control. To simplify the listing, code validation is included on only one control.

Listing 16-11   A Composite Control—`bmicompos.cs`

```csharp
using System;
using System.Web;
using System.Web.UI;
using System.Web.UI.WebControls;
namespace CompositionControls {
   public class BMIComposition : Control, INamingContainer {
        TextBox htf;
        TextBox hti;
        TextBox wt;
        Label bmi;
   private void getBMI(object sender, System.EventArgs e)
   {
      if (Page.IsValid) {
         decimal f =  Convert.ToDecimal(htf.Text);
         decimal inch = Convert.ToDecimal(hti.Text);
         decimal w = Convert.ToDecimal(wt.Text);
         decimal totinches = f * 12 + inch;
         decimal h2 = totinches * totinches;
         decimal massIndex = (w * 703 * 10/ h2)/10;
         bmi.Text = massIndex.ToString("##.##");
      }
   }
   protected override void CreateChildControls() {
      htf = new TextBox();
      hti = new TextBox();
      wt  = new TextBox();
      bmi = new Label();
```

Listing 16-11   A Composite Control—`bmicompos.cs` *(continued)*

```
        bmi.Width= 50;
        bmi.BorderStyle= BorderStyle.Solid;
        bmi.BorderWidth=2;
        htf.Width= 30;
        hti.Width= 30;
        hti.ID = "hti";
        wt.Width = 40;
        // Display calculator interface
        Controls.Add(new LiteralControl
                ("  <b>BMI Calculator</b>"));
        Controls.Add(new LiteralControl
                ("<br>BMI:   "));
        Controls.Add(bmi);
        Controls.Add(new LiteralControl("<br>Height:  "));
        Controls.Add(htf);
        Controls.Add(new LiteralControl("  "));
        Controls.Add(hti);
        Controls.Add(new LiteralControl(" (feet/inches)"));
        Controls.Add(new LiteralControl("<br>Weight: "));
        Controls.Add(wt);
        Controls.Add(new LiteralControl("<br>"));
        // Validation control for inches accepted
        RangeValidator rv = new RangeValidator();
        rv.ControlToValidate="hti";
        rv.MaximumValue="12";
        rv.MinimumValue="0";
        rv.Type=ValidationDataType.Integer;
        rv.ErrorMessage="Inches must be 1-12";
        Controls.Add(rv);
        // Button to invoke BMI calculation routine
        Button calcBMI = new Button();
        calcBMI.Text = "Submit Form";
        calcBMI.Click += new EventHandler(this.getBMI);
        this.Controls.Add(calcBMI);
        }
    }
}
```

Note that `getBMI` performs the BMI calculation only if the `Page.IsValid` property is `true`. Include this check when validation controls are used, because server-side validation sets the `IsValid` flag to `false` if validation tests fail, but does not prevent code execution.

To make the control available, compile it and place it in the \bin directory of the Web page.

```
csc /t:library bmicompos.cs
```

The control is included in a page using the @Register directive as described earlier:

```
<%@ Register Namespace="CompositionControls" TagPrefix="bmicon"
   Assembly="bmicompos" %>
<HTML>
   <table border=0 color=#cccccc>
   <tr><td>
      <bmicon:BMIComposition runat="server" id="bmic" />
   </td></tr></table>
```

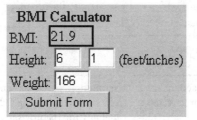

Figure 16-16   BMI composite control

16.7 Selecting a Web Control to Display Data

ASP.NET developers have an overflowing toolbox of controls to choose from—many with overlapping functionality. Table 16-6 offers some recommendations for selecting a control, or combination of controls, to handle frequently encountered Web page tasks. Some of the suggested controls have been introduced in this chapter; but for other important ones, such as the GridView, DetailsView, and FormView, you should refer to an in-depth ASP.NET 2.0 book or reference source.

Table 16-6   Controls Recommended for Typical Web Page Applications

Page Requirement	Controls
Display multiple data records in a spreadsheet or grid format.	GridView. Provides sorting, pagination, and editing. Permits controls to be embedded in cells. Performance can be slow, so use only when these features are required. If displaying data is the only objective, use the DataList or Repeater.
Display multiple data records in a custom format using simple controls.	DataList or Repeater. Use the DataList if editing and event handling is required. Use the Repeater strictly to display data in a repeated format.
Display a parent-child relationship between data.	ListBox or DropDownList and a GridView. See Figure 16-13 on page 779.
Display a hierarchical view, such as a directory or XML elements.	TreeView. Allows nodes to be expanded to display data on lower level.
View, edit, or delete data, one record at a time.	DetailsView or FormView.
Web page with multiple sections or one that steps through a process in multiple steps.	Use multiple panels as containers for simple controls. Panels in ASP.NET 2.0 include a scrolling capability for IE browsers.

16.8 Summary

ASP.NET is a development platform that offers a variety of techniques to overcome the inherent problems that plague client-server interaction over the Internet. These problems include browser incompatibility, the difficulty of retaining an application's state between requests, and a reliance on interpreted script rather than compiled code to implement program logic.

The ASP.NET answer to these problems is server-side based model whose code is written in C# or VB.NET. A Web page is a class deriving from the Page class. Controls are all classes that implement a Render method to generate the HTML code that represents them in the browser. An important design feature of this model is the ability to separate presentation logic from the business logic by placing the latter in a code-behind file.

Controls fall into two categories: HTML server controls and Web controls. The former correspond to traditional HTML tags, but include a runat=server attribute that indicates they are run on the server. Web controls are much richer than HTML controls. They include list controls; data display controls—`DataList` and `Grid-View`—that are usually bound to data sources; and validation controls, which are helper controls that validate the content of other controls. If none of these controls meet an application's need, custom controls can be designed that extend existing controls or present a new interface.

16.9 Test Your Understanding

1. What are the two standard HTTP methods of sending data to a Web host? Which does ASP.NET use as its default?

2. Indicate whether the following statements are true or false.

   a. All controls in ASP.NET are classes.
   b. An `.aspx` page must be compiled before it can respond to a request.
   c. A user must have the .NET runtime installed to take advantage of ASP.NET Web pages.
   d. ASP.NET may render different HTML code for different browsers.
   e. A Web page may contain both HTML Server and Web controls.

3. Which collection class contains the data for List controls?

4. You set up an event handler to be called when the contents of a `Text-Box` change. If the contents are changed, when is the event handler code executed?

5. Which property enables the controls on a master page to be programmatically accessed?

6. Which property must be set and which method executed to bind a control to a data source?

7. Indicate whether the following statements are true or false with regard to a data-bound control.

   a. It can bind directly to a `DataAdapter`.
   b. It can bind directly to a `DataReader`.
   c. The control is populated with data when its `Fill` method is invoked.
   d. Its `DataSource` property can specify a `DataSet` or a data source control.

8. You have a form containing a text box field that is used to input a phone number. Which control would you use to ensure that the phone number includes an area code?

9. Which directive must a Web page include to use a custom control on the page?

    a. `@Page`
    b. `@Import`
    c. `@Register`
    d. `@Assembly`

10. What role does the `HtmlTextWriter` class play in the implementation of a custom control?

11. What are the advantages of creating a composite control versus a non-composite custom control?

THE ASP.NET
APPLICATION
ENVIRONMENT

Topics in This Chapter

- *HTTP Request and Response Objects:* These ASP.NET classes correspond closely to the HTTP request and response specifications, and expose information about a request or response through class properties.

- *Configuration Files:* Configuration files provide an easy way to specify the behavior and performance of a Web application. Focus is on the `web.config` file.

- *ASP.NET Security:* Forms Authentication is a platform-neutral technique that can be used to control who can access a Web page. An example demonstrates the use of Forms Authentication to manage *authentication* and *authorization*.

- *State Management:* Both the `Application` and `Session` classes can be used to maintain information during a Web session or during the life of a Web application.

- *Caching:* Data caching and output caching can be used to improve Web application performance.

- *Accessing Web Resources*: The `WebRequest` and `WebResponse` classes provide a simple way to request and process Web pages for the purpose of extracting page content.

- *HTTP Pipeline:* The HTTP pipeline is the combination of events, HTTP modules, and HTTP handlers that affect how requests and responses are handled as they pass between a client and server.

Chapter 17

Chapter 16, "ASP.NET Web Forms and Controls," dealt with the most visible aspect of ASP.NET—the Web page. It described a Web application in terms of the controls, HTML, and compilable C# code that comprise it. Much of the emphasis was on how to construct the interface presented to a client. This chapter shifts the focus to the underlying details of ASP.NET support for the Hypertext Transfer Protocol (HTTP), which defines how Web requests and responses are transported between client and host.

You'll find that a discussion of the ASP.NET environment is heavily tilted toward those issues that fall under the responsibility of the Web server—as opposed to a Web client. This is only natural because one of the purposes of ASP.NET is to enable developers and architects to manage the difficult side of Web performance, while allowing Web clients to remain blissfully thin and unaffected.

The chapter begins with a little background information on the structure of a response and request—as defined by the HTTP standard. It shows how the `HttpRequest` and `HttpResponse` objects serve as proxies that expose and extend the information you'll find in the standard HTTP message structure. Next, the role of configuration files is discussed—a significant role that allows XML elements to be used to manage the behavior and performance of Web applications at an application, domain, and machine level. Controlling who can gain access to a Web page or resource is the next topic. Included is an overview of the .NET options for user authentication and authorization, as well as a detailed example of forms authentication.

One of the challenges of designing a Web application is determining how to maintain and manage state information. A discussion of how to persist data between Web requests includes examples of using both `Session` and `Application` objects to store information. ASP.NET also offers data and output caching as a way to store state information or to buffer frequently used data or Web pages. When used correctly, caching can greatly improve Web performance. Its advantages and disadvantages are considered.

The client side is not totally abandoned. The penultimate section demonstrates how to access Web resources using the WebRequest and WebResponse classes. An example uses an HttpWebRequest object to retrieve a Web page and glean information about the server.

The final section discusses the HTTP pipeline—a metaphor for the series of internal events that occur along the roundtrip journey that a request and response travel.

17.1 HTTP Request and Response Classes

HTTP specifications[1] concisely define messages as "requests from client to server and responses from server to client." At its most elemental level, the role of ASP.NET is to enable server-based applications to handle HTTP messages. The primary way it does this is through HTTPRequest and HttpResponse classes. The request class contains the HTTP values sent by a client during a Web request; the response class contains the values returned to the client.

HttpRequest Object

An HttpRequest object is available to a Web application via the Page.Request or Context.Request property. The object's properties represent the way that .NET chooses to expose the content to an underlying HTTP request message. Consequently, the best way to understand HttpRequest is to examine the layout of the message it represents.

HTTP Request Message Structure

Figure 17-1 represents the general structure of the HTTP request message as defined by the HTTP/1.1 specifications.

---

1. RFC 2616—Hypertext Transport Protocol—HTTP/1.1.

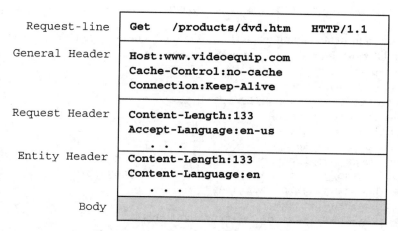

Figure 17-1   Structure of a request message

Unless you are writing a browser, it is not necessary to understand the full details of the standard. However, a general understanding is useful to a developer who needs to extract information from the HttpRequest object. A few observations:

- The Request-Line consists of three parts: the method token, the Request-URI, and the protocol version. Several methods are available, the most common being the POST and GET methods described in Chapter 16. The *Uniform Resource Identifier* (URI) specifies the resource being requested. This most commonly takes the form of a Uniform Resource Locator (URL), but can be a file or other resource. The protocol version closes out the Request-Line.
- The general-header is used to pass fields that apply to both requests and responses. The most important of these is the cache-control field that specifies, among other things, what can be cached and how long it can be cached.
- The request-header is used by the client to pass additional information about the request, as well as the client. Most of the HttpRequest object's properties correspond to values in this header.

Viewing the Request Message

For debugging—or simply out of curiosity—you may want to view the raw contents of the HTTP request. A simple way to do this is to use the SaveAs method of the HttpRequest class to write the request to a file where it can be viewed with a text editor. The method, as shown here, takes two parameters: the name of the output file and a bool type switch that indicates whether HTTP headers are to be included in the output.

```
this.Request.SaveAs("c:\\myrequest.txt",true);
```

Posting a form containing two text boxes to the Web server generates this sample output. Of most interest are the browser description, referring Web page, and text box content values.

```
POST /ideas/panel.aspx HTTP/1.1
Cache-Control: no-cache
Connection: Keep-Alive
Content-Length: 158
Content-Type: application/x-www-form-urlencoded
Accept: image/gif, image/x-xbitmap, image/jpeg, */*
Accept-Encoding: gzip, deflate
Accept-Language: en-us
Cookie: ASP.NET_SessionId=uszrfs45z4f20y45v0wyyp45
Host: localhost
Referer: http://localhost/ideas/panel.aspx
User-Agent: Mozilla/4.0 (compatible; MSIE 6.0; Windows NT 5.0;
.NET CLR 1.0.3705; .NET CLR 1.1.4322; .NET CLR 2.0.40607)

__VIEWSTATE=%2FwEPDwULLTEwODExMTgwOTAPZBYCA ...
    &txtFirstName=joanna&txtLastName=larson&btnSubmit=Submit
```

HttpRequest Class Structure

Table 17-1 summarizes selected properties of the HttpRequest class. Where applicable, it includes the underlying header and message field on which its content is based.

Table 17-1 HttpRequest Properties

HttpRequest Property	Request Message Field	Description
AcceptTypes	—	String array of client-supported MIME accept types.
Browser	(request-header) User-Agent	Identifies software program making request.
ClientCertificate	—	Returns the client's security certificate as an HttpClientCertificate object. Used with SSL when a client is configured with a personal certificate.
ContentEncoding	(entity-header) Content-Type	Character set of the entity body.

Table 17-1   HttpRequest Properties *(continued)*

HttpRequest Property	Request Message Field	Description
ContentLength	(entity-header) Content-Length	Size of client request.
ContentType	(entity-header) Content-Type	MIME content type of request.
Cookies	Not defined in HTTP protocol	Collection of client's cookie variables.
FilePath	Request-Line URI	The virtual path of the currently requested page.
Files	—	Files uploaded by the client.
Form	Body	The collection of form variables including ViewState.
Headers	general and request-header fields	Collection containing content of headers contained in request message.
HttpMethod	Request-Line method	HTTP data transfer method.
IsAuthenticated	(request-header) Authorization	Has user been authenticated. True or False.
IsSecureConnection	Request-Line	True if HTTPS used.
Path	Request-Line URI	Virtual path of current request.
PhysicalPath	—	Physical path of current page.
QueryString	Request-Line URI	Query string arguments.
RawUrl	Request-Line URI	Part of a URL following the domain name.
RequestType	Request-Line method field	HTTP data transfer method (GET, POST).
TotalBytes	(entity-header) Content-Length	Number of bytes in input stream.
Url	Request-Line URI field and Host field of header	URL of current request.

Table 17-1 HttpRequest Properties *(continued)*

HttpRequest Property	Request Message Field	Description
UrlReferrer	(request-header) Referer field	Information about the URL of the client's previous request that linked to the current URL.
UserAgent	(request-header) User-Agent	String containing raw information about the client software used for request—usually a browser.
UserHostAddress	—	IP host address of the remote client.

The built-in features of ASP.NET reduce the amount of direct interaction required between an application and the HttpRequest object. For example, we saw in Section 16.2, "Web Forms Controls," that ASP.NET Web controls generate code that is automatically tailored to the client's browser—eliminating the need for the application code to implement logic to identify the browser. There are, however, some cases where an application must access the object fields directly. Logging Web statistics is one; another is working with *cookies*.

Cookies are used to store information on the computer of a client that has cookies enabled on his browser. The browser is responsible for passing the cookie value as part of the request and handling any cookies returned from the server. The Cookies attribute references the collection of cookies returned by the browser. The following code loops through the collection displaying the name, value, and expiration date of cookies in the collection.

```
// Read cookies returned by browser
foreach(string cookieName in Request.Cookies.AllKeys){
   HttpCookie cookie = Request.Cookies[cookieName];
   Response.Write(cookie.Name+" = "+cookie.Value
             +"<br>Expires: "+cookie.Expires);
}
```

The only cookie in this collection is the ID used by ASP.NET to identify sessions. ASP.NET's use of cookies is discussed further in the next section.

```
.NET_SessionId = avsqkn5501m3u2a41e3o4z55
Expires: 1/1/0001 12:00:00 AM
```

HttpResponse Object

The HttpResponse class contains properties that encapsulate the information returned in a response message. It also provides methods that construct the response and send it to the requestor. As we did with the Request object, let's begin by taking a quick look at the underlying HTTP response message represented by the Response object (see Figure 17-2).

HTTP Response Message Structure

The server responds with a status line that includes the message's protocol version, a success or error code, and a textual description of the error code. This is followed by the general header and the response header that provides information about the server. The entity header provides metainformation about the body contents or the resource requested.

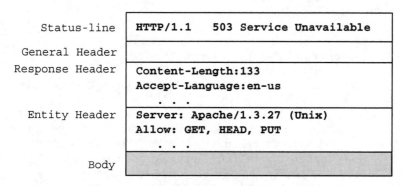

Figure 17-2   Structure of a response message

Viewing an HTTP Response Message

ASP.NET provides the HttpWebRequest and HttpWebResponse classes for working with HTTP requests and responses, respectively. They are discussed in detail later in the chapter, but let's take a preliminary look at how they can be used to display portions of a response message.

Listing 17-1 contains a simple application that sends a request to a user-entered URL, receives the response, and extracts the status code and server description. Run the program from the command line by typing in the program name and domain name you want to contact:

Example:	showserver www.addison-wesley.de/
Output:	Web Host: Microsoft-IIS/5.0
	Response Status: OK

Listing 17-1	Getting Status and Server Information from a Response Message

```
//File: showserver.cs
using System;
using System.Net;
class WebClient
{
   // To run, type in:  showserver <domain name>
   public static void Main(string[] args)
   {
      HttpWebRequest request;
      HttpWebResponse response;
      if(args.Length>0)
      {
         string url="http://"+args[0];
         // Create a request to the URL
         request = (HttpWebRequest) WebRequest.Create(url);
         try
         {
           response = (HttpWebResponse) request.GetResponse();
           Console.WriteLine("Web Host: "+response.Server);
           Console.WriteLine("Response Status: "+
                             response.StatusCode);
         } catch ( Exception ex)
         {
            Console.Write(ex.Message);
         }
      } else
      {
         Console.Write("You must enter a domain name.");
      }
   }
}
```

HttpResponse Class Properties

Table 17-2 lists selected properties of the HttpResponse class. Some of those excluded exist only for ASP compatibility and have been deprecated by newer properties.

Table 17-2 Selected `HttpResponse` Properties

Property	Description
BufferOutput	Set to `true` or `false` to indicate whether output is buffered and sent only when a page has been completely processed. Default is `true`.
Cache	`HttpCachePolicy` object that describes the caching policy features such as expiration time and privacy. Example: `Response.Cache.SetExpires(` `DateTime.Parse("6:00:00PM"));`
CharSet	Gets or sets the character set of the output stream.
ContentEncoding	An `Encoding` object that contains information about the character set of the current response. Encoding type includes ASCII, UTF-7, UTF-8, and others.
ContentType	String value containing MIME type of the output—for example, "text/html".
Cookies	Collection of cookies sent to the client.
Filter	A developer-written `Stream` object that filters all data being sent to the client.
IsClientConnected	Indicates whether client is still connected to the server.
Output	`TextWriter` object that sends text output to the client software. Example: `Response.Output.Write("{0} Years Old", age);`
StatusCode	Status code returned in the response message status line.
StatusDescription	Status code description returned in the response message status line.

Particularly noteworthy is the `Cache` property, which can greatly affect how pages are displayed to a browser. It is used to define a caching policy that dictates if and how long pages are cached. We'll look at this property in Section 17.5, "Caching."

An example that displayed the contents of a cookie was presented in the discussion of the `HttpRequest` class. Let's extend that example by demonstrating how the response object is used to create and return a cookie to the client.

```
// Create a cookie
HttpCookie myCookie = new HttpCookie("userid","007");
// Cookie will live for 10 minutes
// Timespan(days, hours, minutes, seconds)
```

```
myCookie.Expires = DateTime.Now.Add(new TimeSpan(0,0,10,0));
// Add to collection
Response.Cookies.Add(myCookie);
// Later... Read specific cookie
myCookie = Request.Cookies["userid"];
if(myCookie !=null) Response.Write("userid: "+myCookie.Value);
```

Using HttpResponse Methods

The `Response.Write` method, which we have used in numerous examples to emit output into the response stream, is the most commonly used method. Other useful methods include the following:

- `Redirect`. Redirects the client's request to another URL.
- `AppendHeader`. Adds an HTTP header to the response stream.
- `ClearContent`. Clears the contents of the response stream.
- `End`. Stops page execution and sends buffered output to the client.
- `WriteFile`. Places the contents of a file directly into the output stream.

A simple, but useful, example (see Listing 17-2) illustrates how these methods can be used to download a file. The client request for this page includes a query string with the name of a requested file. The page locates the file (or returns an error message) and uses `WriteFile` to send it to the user. The `AppendHeader`, `ClearContent`, and `End` methods prepare and manage the response stream.

Listing 17-2   Using `HttpResponse` to Download a File

```
//File: requestfile.aspx
<%@ Page Language="C#"  %>
<script Language="C#"  runat="Server">
   private void Page_Load(object sender, EventArgs e)
   {
      //http://localserver/ideas/requestfile.aspx?file=notes.txt
      string fileRequest = Request.QueryString["file"];
      if(fileRequest!=null) {
         // File is store in directory of application
         string path = Server.MapPath(fileRequest);
         System.IO.FileInfo fi = new System.IO.FileInfo(path);
         if (fi.Exists) {
            Response.ClearContent(); // Clear the response stream
```

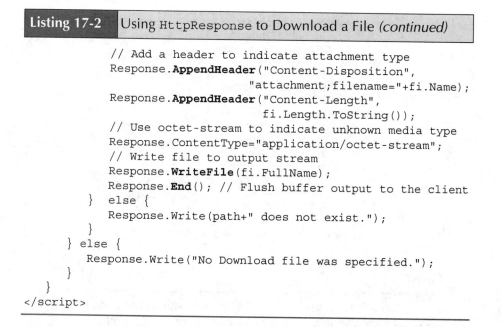

Listing 17-2   Using `HttpResponse` to Download a File *(continued)*

```
              // Add a header to indicate attachment type
              Response.AppendHeader("Content-Disposition",
                             "attachment;filename="+fi.Name);
              Response.AppendHeader("Content-Length",
                              fi.Length.ToString());
              // Use octet-stream to indicate unknown media type
              Response.ContentType="application/octet-stream";
              // Write file to output stream
              Response.WriteFile(fi.FullName);
              Response.End(); // Flush buffer output to the client
          } else {
              Response.Write(path+" does not exist.");
          }
      } else {
          Response.Write("No Download file was specified.");
      }
   }
}
</script>
```

17.2 ASP.NET and Configuration Files

One of the advantages of working with ASP.NET, as a developer or administrator, is the ease of configuring and customizing the settings. The use of XML-based configuration files replaces the previous ASP approach that required shutting down and restarting server software to change a setting or replace DLLs. Now, changes that affect the underlying behavior of a Web page can be made dynamically. The beauty of this approach is that changes can be made using a simple text editor—although an XML editor is preferable—and that ASP.NET automatically detects and applies these changes when they occur.

Configuration information is stored in a required `machine.config` file and optional `web.config` files. The format of these files is the same; the difference is their scope.

As shown in Figure 17-3, configuration files can be placed in a hierarchy on the Web server. Each file lower down in the hierarchy overrides the settings (with a few exceptions) of files above it. The `machine.config` file is at the top of the hierarchy, and its settings apply to all applications running on the machine. `Web.config` files placed in application directories and subdirectories apply their settings to a specific application or pages in an application.

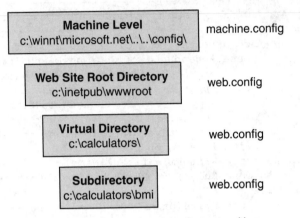

Figure 17-3   Hierarchy of configuration files

Core Note

As an alternative to a text editor, ASP.NET includes a configuration editor with the IIS management console. It is accessed from the Properties menu of a virtual directory.

A Look Inside web.config

The `web.config` file is an XML-formatted text file comprising numerous sections and subsections. Listing 17-3 offers a sampling of sections you're likely to find most useful: `<configSections>`, `<appSettings>`, `<location>`, `<system.web>`, and `<connectionStrings>`. After summarizing key features of these predefined sections, we'll look at how to create a custom configuration section.

Listing 17-3	Sample `web.config` File

```
<configuration>
<!-- (1) Define custom configurations                       -->
   <configSections>
      <section name="RewriterConfig"
         type="RewriteSectionHandler, URLRewriter" />
   </configSections>
   <RewriterConfig>
      <!-- Contents of custom configuration section -->
   </RewriterConfig>
```

Listing 17-3	Sample `web.config` File *(continued)*

```
<!-- (2) Place application data in here      -->
    <appSettings>
        <add key="mainFont" value="arial" />
        <add key="fontSize" value="2" />
    </appSettings>
<!-- (3) Define system.web settings for a directory  -->
    <location path="calculators\bmi">
        <system.web>
            <trace enabled="true"
            pageOutput="true" />
        </system.web>
    </location>
<!-- (4) Main ASP.NET Application settings       -->
    <system.web>
        <sessionState
            cookieless="false"
            timeout=20   />
        ...
    </system.web>
<!-- (5) Connection string for database       -->
    <connectionStrings>
        <!-- connection string description  -->
    </connectionStrings>
</configuration>
```

<appSettings> Configuration Section

This area is used by developers to hold constant data values required by an application. These values typically include preference settings that define the appearance of a Web page. This entry illustrates how font settings are added using an `<add>` element and a key-value pair of attributes:

```
<add key="mainFont" value="arial" />
```

Values are retrieved from the `appSettings` section using the static `AppSettings` property of the `ConfigurationSettings` class:

```
myFont = ConfigurationSettings.AppSettings["mainFont"];
```

<location> Configuration Section

As mentioned previously, `web.config` files can be placed hierarchically within a directory structure, with files at lower levels overriding the settings of files in parent directories. This approach permits you to tailor the actions of ASP.NET down to the application and page level. However, this flexibility brings with it the potential problem of keeping track of the settings in multiple configuration files. As an alternative, ASP.NET provides a way to configure the settings for multiple directories in a single `web.config` file by using `<location>` elements. The `<location>` section operates as a configuration file within a configuration file. The element has a `path` attribute that takes the value of a virtual directory name. The settings within the contained `<system.web>` block apply to the virtual directory.

As an example, suppose that during application development we want to view the trace information as we test our applications. Because we don't want this voluminous output in the final product, we can set up a virtual "test" directory and enable tracing for that directory only.

```
<location path="test">
  <system.web>
    <trace enabled="true" pageOutput="true" />
  </system.web>
</location>
```

This has the same effect as placing a `web.config` file with this trace setting in the physical directory associated with the "test" virtual directory.

<system.web> Configuration Section

This is the area in `web.config` where an administrator can configure just about any aspect of the ASP.NET environment. It can be used to set session time-out length, user authentication and authorization rules, the type of session state management used, and the default culture used for processing requests. Table 17-3 summarizes the more important elements in this section.

Table 17-3   Selected `system.web` Elements

Element	Use
`<compilation>`	Sets default language and debug option.
`<customErrors>`	Defines custom errors and error pages.
`<trace>`	Enables or disables the trace feature for an application.
`<pages>`	Sets default Web page attributes.

Table 17-3 Selected `system.web` Elements *(continued)*

Element	Use
`<globalization>`	Defines response/request encoding and culture-specific setting for Web pages.
`<processModel>`	Used to configure process setting for an IIS Web server.
`<authentication>`	Specifies authentication mode for a client: `Windows`, `Forms`, `Passport`, `None`.
`<authorization>`	Allows or denies access to resources.
`<membership>`	Defines how the Membership class manages user credentials and authentication.
`<identity>`	Specifies whether client impersonation is used on a Web page request.
`<sessionState>`	Configures the session state features of ASP.NET.

Of particular interest are the `authentication`, `authorization`, and `membership` elements that are discussed in Section 17.3, "ASP.NET Application Security." Other useful sections are summarized here.

The <compilation> Section

Use the `debug` attribute to indicate whether debugging symbols will be included in the compiled code. The `defaultLanguage` attribute sets the default language used in a Web page's script blocks. Multiple languages can be selected by using a semicolon to separate them.

```
<compilation  debug="true"  defaultLanguage="C#"  />
```

The <customErrors> Section

The primary use of this section is to redirect errors to custom Web pages. Here is an entry that establishes a default error page, and a page to handle the HTTP 404 status code that arises when a resource cannot be found:

```
<customErrors defaultRedirect = "defaultError.aspx" mode="On" >
   <error statusCode="404" redirect="Error404.aspx" />
</customErrors>
```

The `mode` attribute takes the value `On`, `Off`, or `RemoteOnly`. The latter value, which is also the default, specifies that the default page is called only if the request comes from a machine other than the Web server. This permits local developers to see details of the actual error, whereas clients see only the custom page. Off should be used when a developer is testing pages on a remote machine. Note that multiple <error> elements can be included in the section.

The <trace> Section

The <trace> element is used to enable application-level trace logging. This is in contrast to the trace attribute of the <%@Page> directive that provides only page-level tracing. Here is an example that illustrates the use of the <trace> element and its associated attributes:

```
<trace
    enabled="true"
    pageOutput="false"
    traceMode="SortByTime"
     requestLimit="5",
    localOnly="false"
</trace>
```

Aside from the enabled attribute that turns tracing on or off, the most interesting attributes are pageOutput and localOnly.

- pageOutput specifies whether the trace log is appended to the Web page for display on the client's browser. If set to false, the output can be viewed in the trace.axd page of the application's root. Here is an example:

    Application URL: http://localhost/calculation

    Trace log: http://localhost/calculation/trace.axd

- The requestLimit attribute sets the maximum number of trace logs maintained.
- localOnly indicates whether tracing is enabled for localhost users only or all users. The default is true.

The <sessionState> Section

One of the more powerful features of ASP.NET is the ability to maintain state information for a session; and the <sessionState> element plays a definitive role in selecting how it is implemented. By setting its mode attribute to one of four values, the software architect can specify where the session state information is stored.

- off disables the use of session state management.
- Inproc enables in-process state management (aspnet_state.exe).

- StateServer state is stored by a surrogate process running on a selected server.
- SqlServer state is maintained in a temporary SQL Server table.

These options are described in detail in Section 17.4. Our interest in this section is to understand the elements and attributes that define how ASP.NET manages session state. To illustrate, here are the default settings for the <sessionState> element:

```
<sessionState
    mode="InProc"
    stateConnectString="tcpip=127.0.0.1:42424"
    sqlConnectionString="data
        source=127.0.0.1;Trusted_Connection=yes"
    cookieless="false"
    timeout="15"
/>
```

The timeout attribute specifies the number of minutes the session can be idle before it is abandoned. The cookieless attribute indicates whether the identification of the client session is maintained using a cookie or by mangling the URL (placing encoded session information in the URL line). The other two attributes are dependent upon the mode setting: stateConnectString specifies the IP address of the machine running the Session State Server process, and sqlConnectionString contains the connection string value used to access SQL Server if it is used to maintain state information.

The <connectionStrings> Section

Prior to .NET version 2.0, developers usually resorted to storing connection strings as a key-value pair in the <appSettings> section. ASP.NET 2.0 now provides a predefined <connectionStrings> section for this purpose. As shown in this example, the section takes three attributes: name, connectionString, and providerName.

```
<connectionStrings>
    <add name="movies"
        connectionString=
        "Provider=Microsoft.Jet.OLEDB.4.0;Data Source=/movies.mdb;"
        providerName="System.Data.OleDb"/>
</connectionStrings>
```

The connection string is retrieved using the ConfigurationSettings class, which retrieves the string associated with a specified name attribute. Note that multiple strings may be defined.

```
string cs=
ConfigurationSettings.ConnectionStrings["movies"].ConnectionString;
```

Adding a Custom Configuration Section

The web.config file can be a convenient place to stash information needed by an application. We saw earlier how simple name/value pairs can be stored in the <app-Settings> section. Suppose, however, your application requires data represented by a more complex XML structure. The solution is to add a custom configuration section to web.config. However, it is not as simple as choosing a configuration name and inserting appropriately formatted code into the configuration file. When you try to access a Web application that uses the configuration file, you'll receive an Unrecognized Configuration Section error.

It turns out that each section in web.config has a special handler that parses the section and makes its content available to an application. This handler is a class that implements the System.Configuration.IConfigurationSectionHandler interface and is declared in the <configSections> section of the web.config file.

Core Note

You can view the section handlers for the standard predefined sections, such as <appSections> in the machine.config *file.*

To demonstrate how section handlers work, let's create one for the <Rewriter-Config> section shown in the code that follows. The first thing to note is the <con-figSections> element that contains a definition of the new section. Its type attribute specifies the handler (class) that parses the <RewriterConfig> section. The data section represents URLs that have been changed and need to be replaced with a new URL.

```
<configSections>
   <sectionGroup name="RewriterConfig">
      <section name="RewriterRules"
         type="ConfigRewriter.RulesHandler,RulesConfigHandler" />
   </sectionGroup>
</configSections>

<!--   Custom Configuration Section for URL Rewriting -->
<RewriterConfig>
   <RewriterRules>
      <Rule>
      <OldPath>/ideas/calculator.aspx</OldPath>
      <NewPath>/utilities/calculator.aspx</NewPath>
      </Rule>
      <Rule>
```

```
      <OldPath>/ideas/bmi.aspx</OldPath>
      <NewPath>/utilities/bmi.aspx</NewPath>
    </Rule>
  </RewriterRules>
</RewriterConfig>
```

After the XML data structure is determined, the next step in developing a section handler is to create a class that is populated with the contents of the section and contains members that make the data available to an application. In this example, data is defined by any number of <Rule> elements. Consequently, the class must provide some sort of collection to return multiple values. We'll use a Hashtable for the purpose. The GetNewPath method accepts a string value that it uses as a key to retrieve and return its associated value from the hash table.

```csharp
// File: SectionRules.cs
using System.Collections;
namespace ConfigRewriter
{
    // Class to contain content of configuration section
    public class RulesData
    {
        private Hashtable paths;
        // Constructor accepts hash table as parameter
        public RulesData (Hashtable pathCollection){
            paths = pathCollection;
        }
        // Use old path as key and return hash table value
        public string GetNewPath(string OldUrl)
        {
            return ((string)paths[OldUrl]);
        }
    }
}
```

The final step, shown in Listing 17-4, is to create the section handler code. Its primary function is to implement the Create method. This method is passed an XML-Node parameter that corresponds to the <RewriterRules> node in our section. It is used to parse its child nodes and fill the hash table with its contents. An instance of the RulesData class is instantiated by passing the hash table to its constructor. This object is then available to a Web application.

Listing 17-4   Configuration Section Handler

```
//File: RedirectConfigHandler.cs
using System.Xml;
using System.Configuration;
using System.Collections;
namespace ConfigRewriter
{
    public class RulesHandler: IConfigurationSectionHandler
    {
      public object Create(object parent, object input,
                           XmlNode section)
      {
          Hashtable paths = new Hashtable();
          string oldUrl="";
          XmlElement root = (XmlElement) section;
          foreach (XmlNode node in root.ChildNodes){
             foreach(XmlNode child in node.ChildNodes)
             {
                if(child.Name=="OldPath") oldUrl= child.InnerText;
                if(child.Name=="NewPath")
                {
                   paths[oldUrl]= child.InnerText;
                }
             }
          }
          RulesData urlRules = new RulesData(paths);
          return urlRules;
      }
    }
}
```

After the section has been constructed, accessing its content is trivial: use the `ConfigurationSettings.GetConfig` method to return an instance of the section object, and use its properties to retrieve values.

```
// Retrieve object returned by section handler
// and use it to access content of section
RulesData r;
r = ConfigurationSettings.GetConfig(
     "RewriterConfig/RewriterRules")
     as RulesData;
if(r!=null)
// Pass old path to method and receive redirected path
string newURL = r.GetNewPath("/ideas/bmi.aspx");
```

17.3 ASP.NET Application Security

Web-based applications must address many of the same security issues that are faced by applications situated on a local network. The most important of these—and the subject of this section—is *client authentication*. By this, we mean the capability to identify the user attempting to access a Web resource. Unlike traditional static Web sites that permit anonymous user access, an application that wants to tailor its content for the user, or restrict access based on authorization rights, must first authenticate the user.

ASP.NET offers three forms of client authentication:

- **Windows Authentication.** Relies on the relationship between IIS (Internet Information Server) and the underlying operating system's directory security. Its options include using the native Microsoft Windows login authentication.
- **Microsoft Passport Service.** Microsoft's proprietary "single sign-on" authentication service. Requires subscribing to the Passport network and installing the Passport SDK to link .NET to the service.
- **Forms Authentication.** Allows an application to define user credentials and handle authentication based on it own requirements. This approach relies on .NET classes to create and manage a cookie that maintains user authentication information during the lifetime of a user's session.

The most flexible—and least proprietary—of these techniques is Forms Authentication. It represents the natural evolution from a do-it-yourself approach that requires creating a login screen, writing code to match user credentials against a database or file, and building a cookie to maintain client data during a session. ASP.NET offers substitutes for each of these tasks, which can be easily plugged into a developer's custom solution. The remainder of this section examines this form of authentication.

Forms Authentication

The general framework for implementing Forms Authentication is based on a mixture of configuration files, authentication modules, ASP.NET security classes, and the script (C# code) to work with the methods and properties of these classes. Figure 17-4 illustrates how it works.

A `web.config` file defines a login page to which a user's browser is redirected when it first attempts to access a Web resource. This login page accepts the client's credentials—usually name and password—and determines if they are valid. If so, the user is authenticated and ASP.NET methods are used to create a `FormsAuthenti-cationTicket` that contains the user's security information. The ticket is encrypted and stored as a cookie. The cookie may be configured to expire at the end of the session, or remain on the client's machine so that the user can be automatically identified in future sessions. An optional step in this process is to add authorization information about a client to the ticket. For example, users may be assigned to groups that define their access rights. The code to add this *role* information can be placed in the `global.asax` file to handle the application's `AuthenticateRequest` event.

After these steps are complete and the user is authenticated, control passes to the Web page originally requested. Subsequent session authentication uses information in the authentication cookie and avoids these steps.

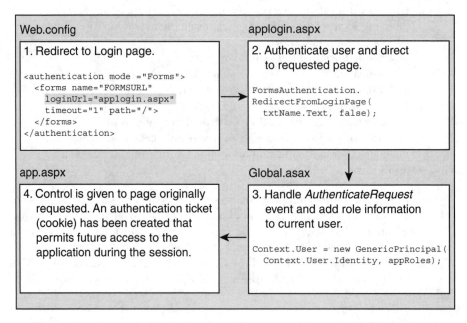

Figure 17-4   Forms Authentication steps that occur when a page is first requested

Security Settings in web.config
for Forms Authentication

The `web.config` file plays an important role in supporting authentication and authorization in ASP.NET security. Listing 17-5 presents many of its elements and optional attribute values that are used to select and implement a security method.

The first thing to note is the mode attribute in the <authentication> element, which specifies the type of authentication being used. Contained in the <authentication> section is a <forms> tag or <passport> tag (not shown) that corresponds to the type of authentication chosen. The <forms> tag, which is used in a later example, contains several key attributes. The loginurl specifies the login page that a user is directed to when she has not been authenticated. The timeout attribute specifies how long a user may wait between requests before the authentication ticket expires. Thus, if the value is set to 5 minutes and the user has not requested a page in that interval, she is forced to log in again at her next request. The protection attribute specifies how, or if, ticket authentication information is processed before it is written to a cookie. You'll normally set this to All.

The <forms> element may contain a <credentials> element that can be used as a mini-database to list each user and his password. The advantage of placing them here, as we see in a later example, is that .NET authentication classes provide methods to automatically perform authentication against these names. To add a measure of security for storing the passwords, the passwordFormat attribute is provided to specify how the passwords are encrypted.

Web.config may also contain an <authorization> section that explicitly allows or denies access to users based on their name or role (think of role as a group the user belongs to). The <allow> and <deny> tags are processed in the order they occur in the file. When the tag's policy can be applied to the user, processing stops. If no allow or deny policy matches the user, the user is authorized to access the resource.

Listing 17-5	Authentication and Authorization Configuration Sections

```
<Configuration>
   <system.web>
      <authentication mode="{Windows|Forms|Passport|None}">
         <forms name="Cookiename"
            loginurl="path to login file"
            timeout="minutes"
            protection="{None|All|Encryption|Validation}"
            path="Cookiepath"  >
         <credentials passwordFormat="Clear|MDS|SHA1}">
            <user name="User Name" password="password" />
         </credentials>
         </forms>
      </authentication>
```

| Listing 17-5 | Authentication and Authorization Configuration Sections *(continued)* |

```
    <authorization>
        <allow users="comma-separated list"
            roles="roles list" />
        <deny  users="comma-separated list"
            roles="roles list />
    </authorization>
    . . .
  </system.web>
  . . .
</configuration>
```

An Example of Forms Authentication

We'll now create a simple Web page that can only be accessed by users who provide a valid name and password. The example is then extended to demonstrate how client *role* information can be incorporated in the authorization process. As you work through the example, the most important things to observe are

- The interrelationship between the web.config file and authentication methods used in the login screen code.
- How roles can be assigned to users by the use of global.asax.
- How to access authentication ticket information through the underlying .NET classes that manage authentication.

Using web.config for Authentication and Authorization

The configuration file segment in this example is used for both user authentication and authorization. The <credentials> element contains the names and passwords of three users who may access the system. The <authorization> element contains rules that deny login access to all anonymous users as well as one individual user. Only users Joanna and Ruth are permitted to access the Web page.

```
<system.web>
    <authentication mode="Forms">
        <forms name="AppCookie"
            loginUrl="applogin.aspx" protection="All"
            timeout="10" path="/"    >
            <credentials passwordFormat="Clear">
                <user name="joanna" password="chicago" />
```

```
                <user name="ruth"    password="raleigh" />
                <user name="kim"     password="newyork" />
           </credentials>
        </forms>
    </authentication>
    <authorization>
        <deny users="?,kim" />
    </authorization>
```

The same authorization rights can be granted by a combination of allow/deny rules:

```
<allow users="joanna,ruth"   />
<deny users="*" />
```

This denies access to all users (the asterisk (*) wildcard selects all users) except for those that are explicitly allowed. When both <allow> and <deny> are present, the order in which they are placed can be important. In this example, placing the <deny> rule first would deny access to all users, and the <allow> rule would be ignored.

The Login Screen—Using the FormsAuthentication Class

The web.config file used in this example redirects the initial request for a Web page to applogin.aspx, which accepts login credentials and performs user authentication. The login part is easy—two text boxes are used to accept a user name and password. The technique for authenticating the user is more interesting.

Traditionally, login screens validate a user-supplied name and password against a database or file containing valid users. You are still free to do this in ASP.NET, but there are other options. These include storing names and passwords in the web.config file, or using the ASP.NET Membership class and its preconfigured database to manage user credentials. For demonstration purposes, this example uses web.config as the data store. Keep in mind that this is not the recommended approach if there are more than a few users, or multiple servers are used, which would require synchronizing the configuration file across machines.

As Listing 17-6 illustrates, the FormsAuthentication class plays the key role in authenticating a user and creating the authentication ticket that identifies the user. This important class provides static properties and methods that are used to manipulate and manage authentication information. Two of its methods are used here: Authenticate accepts a name and password, which it attempts to validate against the data in web.config; RedirectFromLoginPage redirects the user to the page originally requested, and creates an authentication cookie for the user. The second parameter to this method indicates whether the cookie should persist on the user's machine beyond the lifetime of the session.

Listing 17-6   Login Screen Using ASP.NET Authentication

```
<%@ Page Language="C#" %>
<html>
<head>
<title>login</title>
<script  runat="Server">
  void verify_Form(object sender, System.EventArgs e)
  {
    // Code to verify user against a database goes here...
    // or use .NET to verify user using web.config info.
    // Name and password are compared against web.config content
    if( FormsAuthentication.Authenticate(
          txtName.Text,txtPW.Text))
    {
      // Redirect to original form and
      // create authentication ticket
      bool persistCookie=false;
      FormsAuthentication.RedirectFromLoginPage(txtName.Text,
          persistCookie);
    }
    else
    { errmsg.Text="Cannot log in user."; }
  }
</script>
</head>
<body >
<form id=Form1 method=post runat="server">
  <asp:Panel id="pnlName"
        style="Z-INDEX: 101; LEFT: 20px; POSITION: absolute;
        TOP: 64px"
        BackColor = "#efefe4"
        Height="120px" Width="278px"
        runat="server" >
  <TABLE>
    <TR>
      <TD><asp:Label id="lblName" Runat="server"
              text="User ID:"></asp:Label></TD>
      <TD><asp:TextBox id="txtName" Runat="server">
            </asp:TextBox></TD></TR>
    <TR>
      <TD><asp:Label id="lblPW" Runat="server"
              text="Password:"></asp:Label></TD>
      <TD><asp:TextBox id="txtPW" TextMode="Password"
          Runat="server"> </asp:TextBox></TD></TR>
```

| Listing 17-6 | Login Screen Using ASP.NET Authentication *(continued)* |

```
  <TR>
    <TD colspan=2 align=center>
        <asp:Button ID="btnSubmit"
            Text="Submit" Font-Bold="true"
            OnClick="verify_Form" Runat="server" /></TD></TR>
    <TR>
      <TD colspan=2 align=center>
            <asp:Label id=errmsg runat="server" /></TD>
    </TR>
  </TABLE>
</asp:Panel>
</FORM>
</body>
</html>
```

Adding Role-Based Authorization with global.asax

Authentication is often only the first step in permitting a user to access Web resources; the second step is *authorization*—the process of determining what resources the user is authorized to access. If all users have full access, this step can be ignored. However, if a user's access rights, or role, are determined by membership in a group, this group must be identified and associated with the user.

After a user is created in ASP.NET, information about that user is available through the Page.User property. This property returns a *principal* object, so named because it implements the IPrincipal interface. This interface has two important members (see Figure 17-5) that the principal object implements: Identity, which can be used to get the name of the user, and the IsInRole method that is used to check a user's group membership.

The IsInRole method is passed a role name and returns a bool value indicating whether the user is in that role. It is the developer's task to assign the roles to the authenticated user object so that this method will have an internal list to check against. Looking at Figure 17-5, you would expect this list to be part of the GenericPrincipal object—and you would be right. The constructor for this class accepts as one of its parameters a string array of roles to be associated with the user. To assign these roles, the application can take advantage of the AuthenticateRequest event that occurs when the identity of a user is established. A handler for this event is placed in the global.asax file.

Listing 17-7 shows how code in the event handler assigns roles to the current user. It determines the user roles—in this case, calling GetRoles—and places them in a string array. This array, along with the current Identity, is passed to the GenericPrincipal constructor to create a new object that updates the value of the User property.

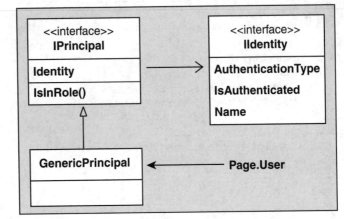

Figure 17-5   User information is encapsulated in a `GenericPrincipal` object

---

Listing 17-7   Using `global.asax` to Add Role Information for a User

```
<%! file:global.asax %>
<%@ Import Namespace="System.Security" %>
<%@ Import Namespace="System.Security.Principal" %>
<%@ Application   %>
<script language = "C#" runat=server>
protected void Application_AuthenticateRequest(
                    object src, EventArgs e)
{
   if (Request.IsAuthenticated)
   {
      string currUser= Context.User.Identity.Name;
      string roles= GetRoles(currUser);
      string[] appRoles = roles.Split(new char[]{'|'});
      // Create GenericPrincipal class and add roles to it
      // GenericPrincipal(IIdentity identity, string[] roles)
      Context.User = new GenericPrincipal(
                       Context.User.Identity, appRoles);
   }
}
private string GetRoles( string username )
{
   // Code here would query database for user's role(s).
   // Return role as delimited string that can split into array.
   return "Administrator|Operator";
}
```

Viewing Authentication Information

After the authentication steps are complete, an application may want to log information or make decisions based on information about the user. The User property exposes all of the members shown in Figure 17-5. Further authentication details, such as when the authentication cookie expires or when it was issued, can be obtained from properties exposed by the authentication ticket. As shown in Listing 17-8, an instance of the cookie is created and then converted to a FormsAuthenticationTicket object by using the Decrypt method of the FormsAuthentication class. The properties of this object are then displayed.

Listing 17-8	Displaying Authentication Details

```
// Display authentication details
Response.Write("Client: "+ User.Identity.Name+"<br>");
if(User.IsInRole("Operator")) Response.Write(
        "Role: Operator<br>");
string cookieName = FormsAuthentication.FormsCookieName;
HttpCookie authCookie = Context.Request.Cookies[cookieName];
if(authCookie !=null)
{
    // Create ticket from cookie and display properties
    FormsAuthenticationTicket authTicket = null;
    authTicket = FormsAuthentication.Decrypt(authCookie.Value);
    Response.Write("Issued: "+authTicket.IssueDate+"<br>");
    Response.Write("Expiration: "+authTicket.Expiration+"<br>");
    Response.Write("Persistent: "+authTicket.IsPersistent);
}
```

17.4 Maintaining State

The standard for the HTTP protocol is contained in a document known as RFC 2616. In printed form, it is more than 120 pages in length. If you search this document, you'll find that not one page, section, or sentence discusses a method for maintaining state information between HTTP requests. The term *cookie* is completely absent. So, unlike human memory where "our thoughts are linked by many a hidden chain" (Alexander Pope), the Internet protocol is designed to be stateless—each request unlinked to the preceding one.

Yet, for Internet applications to flourish, a means has to exist to identify specific users. Online purchasing, surveys, and the need to recognize user preferences depend on it. The first efforts to maintain state information relied on using features defined in the HTTP protocol: hidden fields that could be sent back and forth using the POST method, and a string full of values that could be placed after the ? character in an HTTP URL path. The former technique is used to maintain .NET ViewState information; the latter constitutes a "query string" consisting of name/value pairs.

A third client-side approach to managing state is the use of cookies, a small (4K) text-only string that is stored in browser memory during a session and may be written to disk. Many applications maintain session-related state information, such as a shopping cart's identification, in cookies. ASP.NET identifies each session by creating a cookie containing a unique session ID.

These approaches are plagued by a common weakness: They can be compromised by the client. Query strings and hidden fields can be altered; cookies can be altered or simply turned off on the browser.

To overcome these shortcomings, ASP.NET offers two general types of server-side state management: *session state*, which maintains information for the life of the session; and *application state*, which maintains information across multiple sessions. Although these techniques maintain information on a server—rather than passing it back and forth between requests—they still rely on a cookie, where possible, to uniquely identify a user's session. However, the server-based solution presents another problem: All session activity must be handled by that server possessing the state information. This is incompatible with large Web sites where a server-selection algorithm assigns requests to any machine in a *Web farm*. An ASP.NET solution to this is the use of a central database to store session state information.

Table 17-4 summarizes the client- and server-side state management approaches. Of those listed, this section focuses on the application and session management techniques.

Table 17-4   State Management Techniques for Web Applications

Technique	Web Farm Compatible	Description
Query String	Yes	Data passed as part of URL.
View State	Yes	ASP.NET hidden View_State field used.
Cookie	Yes	Information passed to/from browser in a cookie.
Application	No	An Application object maintains information available to all sessions accessing an application.
Session: In-Process	No	Session state is stored and managed using the Aspnet_wp.exe process.
Session: State Server	Yes	Session state is stored in the Aspnet_state.exe process.
Session: SQL Server	Yes	State information is maintained in a temporary table in a database.

Application State

Application state data is maintained in an instance of the `HttpApplicationState` class—an in-memory dictionary holding key-value objects. The contents of this dictionary object are available to all sessions using that application.

The data is usually loaded within the `global.asax` file when the `Application_Start` event fires.

```
protected void Application_Start(object sender, EventArgs e)
{
    Application["targetBMI"]= 21;
    Application["obeseBMI"] = 26;
}
```

Users of the application then have read and write access to the data without having to regenerate it. This is particularly useful when working with data from a database. It can also be a convenient way to initialize variables used for collecting usage statistics. (See Section 17.2 for background on `global.asax` file.)

Accessing and Updating Application State Data

All sessions using the application may access the `Application` object through the `Application` property of the `System.Web.UI.Page` type. The only thing to note about accessing data is that it must be cast, because the information is stored as an object. Here is a segment that illustrates the primary properties and methods for working with the `Application` object:

```
int target = (int) Application["targetBMI"];
// Change value
Application["targetBMI"] = 22;
// List all HttpApplicationState values
foreach( string s in Application.AllKeys){
      Response.Output.Write("<br>{0} = {1}",s,Application[s]);
}
// Remove Application item
Application.Remove("obeseBMI");
```

Not illustrated are the `Lock` and `UnLock` methods that allow application variables to be updated in a thread-safe manner.

Considerations in Using Application State

The variables contained in application state have two primary uses: as read-only data globally available across all of the application's sessions, and as variables that are updated to keep statistics regarding the application's use. Both of these uses can be handled more efficiently using a different approach.

The ASP.NET data cache provides a more flexible approach for making read-only data available on an application-wide basis. Its contents are as accessible as those in the application object, and it offers the advantage of having its contents automatically refreshed at a specified time interval. (Its use is described in Section 17.5.) As a rule-of-thumb, use application state to preload small amounts of read-only data required by an application; use the data cache when working with large amounts of data.

The problem with maintaining usage data in application state is that the data is available only during the life of the application. When it ends, the data is gone. In addition, if there are multiple servers, the data will apply to only one server. A better approach is store the information in a central database.

Core Note

Application recycling refers to shutting down and restarting an application based on criteria such as time, memory usage, and number of client requests. It is set using the `<processModel>` *tag in the* `web.config` *file. The following setting recycles the application every two hours.*

```
<processModel timeout="120">
```

Session State

When a new client requests an ASP.NET application, ASP.NET creates a cookie containing a unique session ID and returns it to the client's browser. This ID, or session key, is used to identify subsequent requests from the client. State information unique to each session is maintained in an instance of the HttpSessionState object. The contents of this object are available through the Session properties of both the Page and HttpContext class. Note that Session can be used in place of the fully qualified HttpContext.Session. Working with session state is analogous to working with application state. Many applications perform state session initialization in a Session_Start event handler in the global.asax file. This segment initializes variables for an online survey:

```
// global.asax file
protected void Session_Start(object sender, EventArgs e)
{
   Session["Start"]= DateTime.Now;
   Session["QuestionsAnswered"] = 0;
}
```

The variables can be updated in the application with the same syntax used for the `Application` object:

```
int ict= (int)Session["QuestionsAnswered"]+1;
Session["QuestionsAnswered"]=ict;
```

The `HttpSessionState` class contains several members that are useful in manipulating and interrogating the `Session` object. The following code demonstrates their use:

```
// Session ID is unique to each session
Response.Write("<br>Session ID: "+Session.SessionID);
// Mode may be InProc, StateServer, SqlServer, Off
Response.Write("<br>Processing Mode: "+Session.Mode);
// Session times out after 20 minutes (default) of inactivity
Response.Write("<br> Timeout: "+Session.Timeout);
// Number of items in session state
Response.Write("<br>Items: "+Session.Count);
// List key-values in session state
foreach( string key in Session.Keys)
      Response.Output.Write("<br>{0} = {1}",key, Session[key]);
```

The most interesting of these properties, by far, is `Session.Mode`, which indicates where the `Session` object is configured to store its data. Session state information can be stored using one of three methods: `InProc`, `StateServer`, or `SqlServer`. Although the choice does not affect the way information is accessed through the `Session` object, it does affect application performance, manageability, and extensibility. Let's look at the details of using all three backing stores (see Figure 17-6).

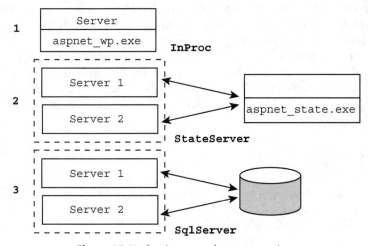

Figure 17-6 Session state data store options

In-Process Session State

By default, ASP.NET stores session state in-process using the `aspnet_wp.exe` process. This means that the information is managed in memory space where the application is running. This has the advantage of providing fast access to the data. The drawbacks are that it must run on a single server—precluding its use with Web farms—and that all session data is lost if the server reboots. Given this, it is recommended for single-server sites that need to maintain moderate amounts of data in state.

To select in-process session state management, set the `mode` attribute to `InProc` in the `<sessionState>` element of the `web.config` file. As shown here, you can also specify a time limit specifying how long the process may be idle before the session data is discarded.

```
<configuration>
  <system.web>
    <sessionState mode="InProc" timeout="30"/>
  </system.web>
</configuration>
```

Out-of-Process Session Using a State Server Process

The concept of out-of-process session state management entails the use of a mechanism outside of the application's process to store state data. ASP.NET provides two such mechanisms: a separate process running on a selected state server and the use of a data server to store state information.

When session state mode is used, session state is stored in the `Aspnet_state.exe` process. This allows an application running on multiple servers to share state information. Because the server running this process is accessed via a network on the Internet, performance is slower than using the in-process approach. Also, the data is susceptible to a server reboot.

To access a state server, make sure the machine selected is running the `Aspnet_state.exe` process. Any server accessing the state server must set the `<sessionState>` element in its `web.config` file to point to the state server. The default port used is 42424. On a Windows-based operating system, this can be changed through the registry.

```
<configuration>
  <system.web>
    <sessionState mode="StateServer"
        stateConnectionString="192.168.1.109:42424"
    />
  </system.web>
</configuration>
```

Out-of-Process Session Using SQL Server

Using a SQL Server database to store session state data also offers the capability of sharing data among machines. In addition, SQL Server security features can be used to selectively provide access to the data; and, of course, the data is not transient because it exists in tables. The disadvantages of this approach are that it only works with Microsoft SQL Server and it is the slowest of the three session state modes.

To prepare a machine running SQL Server to handle session state requires no more than creating the tables that ASP.NET expects. The `InstallPersistSql-State.sql` script takes care of this. By default, the script is located in the `\system-root\Microsoft.NET\Framework\version` folder. It creates a database named `ASPState` that contains the state tables.

`Web.config` is used to tell ASP.NET that session information for the application(s) is stored on a SQL Server. The `<sessionState>` element is set to specify the mode and connection string.

```
<configuration>
  <system.web>
    <sessionState mode="SQLServer"
      sqlConnectionString="datasource=x; user id=sa; password="/>
  </system.web>
</configuration>
```

SQL Server should be considered when there is a need to maintain data beyond the life of the session. For example, sites often persist the content of a shopping cart so it is available when the user logs in again.

Because the use of SQL Server slows Web page performance, it should be used only on those pages in an application that require state data. The `@Page` directive has an `EnableSessionState` attribute that dictates how state is used on the page. It can be set to `false` to disable session state, `true` to enable read and write session state, or `readOnly`.

17.5 Caching

Consider a Web page with a list box containing the names of a thousand movie actors whose movies are displayed when an actor is selected. The first time the page is requested, a query is sent to the database, the list box is populated with the results, and the rendered HTML is returned to the user's browser. This is a relatively slow and expensive process. Multiply it by a thousand user requests and Web server response time will slow measurably.

One solution is to use *caching* to bypass most, or all, of this reprocessing by keeping an HTML page or data in memory. Subsequent requests for the page are handled using the cached information—obviating the need to fetch data from the database. A sound caching strategy can improve Web server response more than any other single factor. This section presents the factors to be weighed in designing a caching strategy and the two broad categories of caching available in ASP.NET: output caching and data (or request) caching.

Page Output Caching

ASP.NET permits a developer to indicate whether all or part of a Web Form should be cached, where it should be cached, and how long it should remain in the cache before it expires and must be refreshed. The key to cache control for a Web Form is the @OutputCache directive:

```
<%@OutputCache Duration="30" Location="Any"
   VaryByParam="none" %>
```

Its attributes declare the specific caching policies in effect for that Web page. Let's look at how these attributes are used.

Core Note

ASP.NET processes the @OutputCache directive by translating its attributes into HTTPCachePolicy method calls.

Specifying Cache Duration

The mandatory Duration attribute specifies the length, in seconds, that the page or control is cached. Setting this to 20 seconds generates the underlying statement:

```
Response.Cache.SetExpires(DateTime.Now.AddSeconds(20));
```

Specifying the Caching Location

The Location attribute specifies where the caching can occur. In general, caching occurs on a server, browser, or somewhere in between, such as on a proxy server. The values of this attribute correspond to these locations: Any, Client, DownStream, Server, ServerAndClient, or None. DownStream refers to a cache-capable device other than the origin server. None disables caching everywhere.

Conditional Caching with VaryByParam, VaryByHeader, and VaryByCustom

In Chapter 16, we developed a BMI calculator Web page in which the user enters a height and weight value and the BMI value is returned. Because there are thousands of combinations of height (htf, hti) and weight (wt) parameters, several slightly different versions of the same page are likely to be created. The VaryByParam attribute is available for cases such as this. Its value indicates the parameter(s) (from a POST or query string) that should be considered when selecting a page to cache. For example, the following statement causes a page to be cached for each unique combination of wt, hti, and htf values:

```
<%@ OutputCache Duration="60"  VaryByParam="wt;hti;htf" %>
```

Figure 17-7 shows four requests that result in three unique pages being cached with their calculated BMI value. Note that we could have also assigned an asterisk (*) to VaryByParam to indicate that each parameter's value affects the cache.

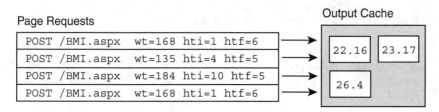

Figure 17-7   Cached page: VaryByParam="wt;hti;htf"

Be aware that you can create some unexpected results if you set VaryByParam incorrectly. If only the wt parameter were specified in this example, requests with a weight of 168 and heights of 5'1" and 6'1" would return the same Web page. The page returned to both would be the one requested earliest.

VaryByHeader caches a different version of a page, based on the value of the Request Header fields (refer to Figure 17-1). This is the most commonly used with the Accept-Language field to ensure that different language versions of a Web page are cached.

The final conditional attribute to be familiar with is VaryByCustom. This is most useful when you have a Web page that is rendered differently depending on the client's browser type and version. To create different page versions by browser type, set the VaryByCustom attribute to "Browser".

```
<%@ OutputCache Duration="60"  VaryByParam="*"
                               VaryByCustom="Browser" %>
```

This attribute also can be set to recognize custom values that your program generates. Please refer to caching documentation for details on this.

Caching a Partial Page (Fragment Caching)

All parts of a Web page are not created equally. Some, such as headers and links, rarely change, whereas other sections, such as the latest stock exchange quotes, change by the minute. A desirable caching strategy is to identify the static objects on the page and cache only those. This can be done in ASP.NET by creating custom controls (.ascx files) for the sections of the Web page to be cached. Custom controls have their own OutputCache directive that determines how they are cached, irrespective of the form containing them.

To illustrate the concept, let's create a simple control to be embedded within a Web page (see Figure 17-8). This segment simply contains a couple of links to other Web sites.

```
<!-- File: CacheFrag.ascx  -->
<%@ OutputCache Duration="30" VaryByParam="None" %>
<b>My Links</b><br>
<a href=http://www.moviesites.org>Movies</a><br>
<a href=http://www.imdb.com>Movie Reviews</a>
<br>
```

The application Web page to hold this control displays a title and date. Note that its caching is turned off by setting Location to None. The result is that only the control is cached.

```
<!-- File: CacheMain  -->
<%@ Page Language="C#"  %>
<%@ OutputCache Location="None" VaryByParam="*" %>
<%@ Register TagPrefix="frag" TagName="fraglinks"
              Src="CacheFrag.ascx" %>
<HTML>
   <HEAD><TITLE>Sample Web Site</TITLE>
   <body>
      <center> <b>Fragment Sample</b>
      <br>
      <% Response.Output.Write(DateTime.Now.ToString("f")); %>
      </center>
      <frag:fraglinks id="fragmentlink" runat="server" />
   </body>
</html>
```

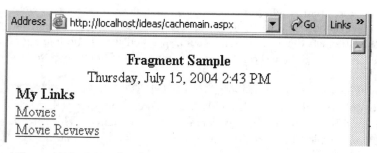

Figure 17-8   Example of custom control with its own caching policy

Data Caching

Data caching, sometimes referred to as request caching, is often an alternative to
using application state or `ViewState` to store read-only data. It is as easy to use as
the `Application` object, and adds the flexibility of assigning expiration and priority
values to the stored data.

Adding Items to a Data Cache

The simplest way to add data to a data cache is to use the key-value syntax of the
`Cache` property of the `Page` class:

```
Cache["userid"] = "rigoletto";
```

The `Cache.Insert` method is often a better approach since it takes full advantage of the fact that each cache entry is actually an instance of the `CacheEntry` class.
This class contains many useful properties that are set by passing parameters to the
`Insert` method:

Syntax:	Example:

<pre>public void Insert(
   string key,
   object value,
   CacheDependency dependencies,
   DateTime absoluteExpiration,
   TimeSpan slidingExpiration,
   CacheItemPriority priority,
   CacheItemRemovedCallBack cb
);</pre>
	<pre>Cache.Insert (
	   "userid",
	   "rigoletto",
	   null,
	   DateTime.Now.AddMinutes(20),
	   TimeSpan.Zero,
	   CacheItemPriority.Normal,
	      null
	);</pre>

Either the absoluteExpiration or slidingExpiration parameter can be used to determine when the cached data expires. The former sets a specific date and time; the latter sets the expiration to occur a specified amount of time after the value is last accessed. To disable sliding expiration, assign the value Cache.NoSlidingExpiration.

The dependencies parameter allows cached data to be tied to files, directories, or other objects in the cache. Establishing this dependency causes the cached data to be removed when the object it is dependent upon changes. Thus, if cached data comes from a file and the file contents are modified, the data in the cache is removed.

```
string filename = "actors";
CacheDependency dep = new CacheDependency(fileName);
cache.Insert("key", "value", dep);
```

The priority parameter makes sense when you understand that data in a cache is not guaranteed to remain there. Because there is no limit on what can be placed in the cache, ASP.NET periodically invokes a *resource scavenging* process to remove less important data from the cache. The determination of what is important is based on the priority of the resource. By setting this priority to a CacheItemPriority enum value, you can reduce, or increase, its likelihood of being removed through scavenging. Enum values may be set to AboveNormal, BelowNormal, Default, High, Low, Normal, and NotRemovable.

Retrieving Items from the Data Cache

To retrieve data from the cache, simply specify the key (case is ignored) of the desired data:

```
String user = (string) Cache["userid"];
```

Because the data is stored as an object, it is necessary to cast the result. If no data exists for the key, a null value is returned.

Data Caching as a Substitute for ViewState

The true value of data caching comes into play when large amounts of data need to be saved to restore a page's state. As was explained in the previous chapter, ViewState automatically saves data and state information for Web controls on a page as long as the page posts to itself. Figure 17-9 illustrates this. In it, we have Web page A containing a list box populated with several hundred items from a database. In steps 1 and 2, a user performs some action that results in a modified version of the same page being returned to the client. State is retained automatically because the contents of the page's list box—and any other fields—are passed in the ViewState field.

Suppose the user selects an item in the list box on page A that requires loading page B to show more details about the item. The server constructs the description as page B and returns it to the browser, discarding page A. After viewing this page, the user now wants to return to A. In the absence of caching, page A must be reconstructed by retrieving data from the database. To avoid this, the contents of the list box can be cached prior to navigating to page B (step 3):

```
// Step 3: Save listbox data before making server request
Cache["listbox"]= actors.Items;
```

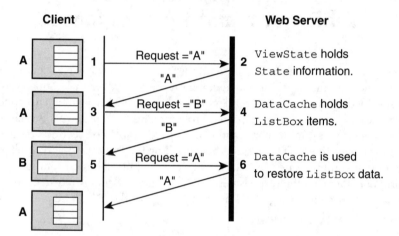

Figure 17-9 Use a data cache to preserve information between separate pages

In step 6, page A is constructed using data from the cache to restore the list box.

```
// Step 6: Fill list box from cache
if(Cache["listbox"] !=null){
   ListItemCollection li= (ListItemCollection)Cache["listbox"];
   for(int i=0;i< li.Count; i++){
      ListItem a= li[i];
      actor.Items.Add(a);
   }
}
Cache["listbox"] = null;   // Clear cache
```

The cache is cleared after the page is restored; otherwise, both the cache and view state will contain the contents of the ListBox. It is worth noting that another option is to turn view state off for the ListBox (EnableViewState=false) and rely on caching to maintain its content.

Core Note

Data caching should be considered as a substitute for ViewState when data is read-only, or there is a large amount of it, or its update frequency is in minutes or hours rather than seconds, or when the data is not unique to individual users.

17.6 Creating a Web Client with WebRequest and WebResponse

As you would expect in a chapter on ASP.NET, the role of the Web client does not receive much attention. It's usually assumed to be a browser that requests a Web page specified by the user, and renders the returned HTML content. Despite the evolution of browser features, its primary role remains to display what it receives. It is of less use if you want to parse and extract portions of the received content—or want to examine the HTTP message headers. For this, you need a Web client—a program that communicates with an HTTP server and includes custom methods to perform operations on the response object. This section demonstrates how easy it is to write a Web client using .NET classes to handle the HTTP request/response duties.

WebRequest and WebResponse Classes

The System.Net namespace contains classes that are intended for applications involved with network communications. Included in these are the abstract WebRequest and WebResponse classes that contain generic properties to upload and download data given a specific Uniform Resource Identifier (URI). These classes are designed to support the response/request model—not a specific protocol. The details of that are left to descendant classes. To handle the HTTP protocol, we call on the HttpWebRequest and HttpWebResponse classes. Note that other classes are available to support the file:// URI scheme and FTP operations.

Web Client Example

This example accepts a URL, sends a request for its Web page, and uses the response object to display the server description, IP address(es) of the server, and source code for the requested Web page. Figure 17-10 shows the interface for the application.

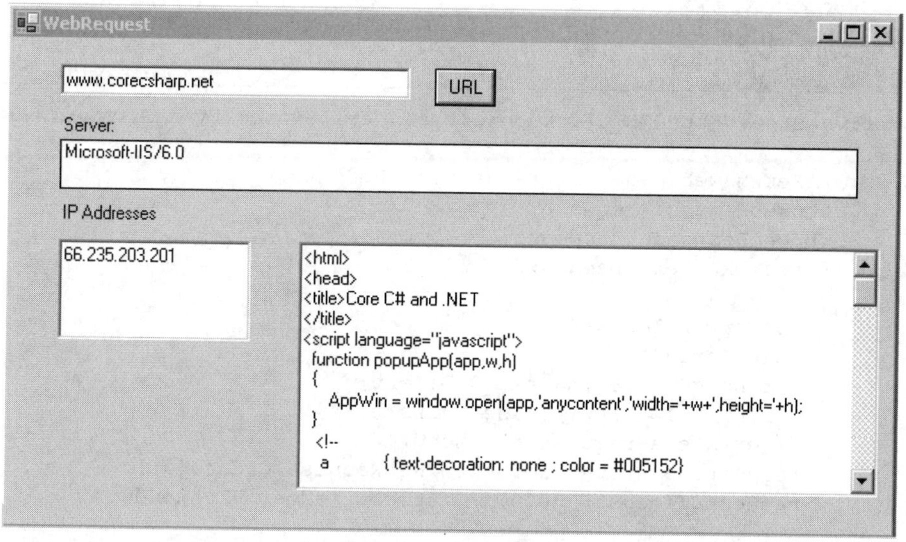

Figure 17-10 Example using `HttpWebRequest` and `HttpWebResponse` classes

The basic steps for communicating synchronously with the HTTP server are quite simple:

1. Create an `HttpWebRequest` object that identifies the URL using the `Create` method:

   ```
   request = (HttpWebRequest) WebRequest.Create(url);
   ```

2. Get a response from the Internet resource using the `WebRequest.GetResponse` method:

   ```
   response = (HttpWebResponse) request.GetResponse();
   ```

3. Get the `Stream` used to read the body of the response and read its contents.

   ```
   Stream s = response.GetResponseStream();
   string strContents = new StreamReader(s).ReadToEnd();
   ```

Note that request and response are cast to `HttpWebRequest` and `HttpWebResponse` types, respectively. As mentioned, these subclasses deal specifically with the HTTP protocol (see Listing 17-9).

Listing 17-9	Using `WebRequest` and `WebResponse` to Scrape a Web Page

```
private void btnURL_Click(object sender, System.EventArgs e)
{
    // Fetch web page for requested URL
    HttpWebRequest request;
    HttpWebResponse response;
    if(txt_URL.Text.Length>0)
    {
        lblServer.Text="";
        tbIP.Text="";
        string serverPath= txt_URL.Text;
        string url="http://"+serverPath;
        // create a request to the url
        request = (HttpWebRequest) WebRequest.Create(url);
        request.Timeout= 7000; // timeout after 7 seconds
        try
        {
            response = (HttpWebResponse)
                    request.GetResponse();
            lblServer.Text= response.Server;
            // Get a stream to send the web page source
            Stream s = response.GetResponseStream();
            string strContents = new
                    StreamReader(s).ReadToEnd();
            // Place Web page source in text box
            HTMLViewer.Text= strContents;
            s.Close();
            ListIP(serverPath);    // List IP address(es)
        }
        catch ( Exception ex)
        {
            lblServer.Text= ex.Message;
        }
    }
    else
    {
        lblServer.Text= "Please enter a domain name.";
    }
}
private void ListIP(string uri)
{
    // List IP addresses for this domain
```

Listing 17-9	Using `WebRequest` and `WebResponse` to Scrape a Web Page *(continued)*

```
   // Use only server name part of URI for IP resolution
   int ndx= uri.IndexOf("/");
   if(ndx>0) uri= uri.Substring(0,ndx);
   string ips="";
   // Get a list of IP addresses for the URI
   // Dns contacts the Internet Domain Name System
   IPHostEntry IPHost = Dns.GetHostByName(uri);
   foreach(IPAddress addr in IPHost.AddressList)
   ips+= addr.ToString()+"\r\n";
   tbIP.Text= ips;
}
```

You may encounter Web pages that check the `UserAgent` property of the request object and do not allow their pages to be downloaded unless they can identify the browser. You can assign a legitimate browser value to overcome this.

17.7 HTTP Pipeline

The purpose of this section is to provide background information about the components and classes that come into play between the time a Web server receives a request and the time it finishes crafting a response. An understanding of this HTTP pipeline can be crucial to improving Web application performance, because it enables a developer to create components that affect how ASP.NET responds to requests. The references to HTTP modules and handler factories can make the subject appear daunting, but underneath there is a simple logic at work that is rooted in event handling.

Processing a Request in the Pipeline

As a request makes its way to a server, several events occur. ASP.NET permits a developer to interact with the request or response at the point of these events—through special code referred to as an HTTP module or by script in a `global.asax` file. Both the module and file function as event handlers, and the nature of what goes on in these event handlers is the topic of this section. Figure 17-11 depicts how a request flows from the beginning of the HTTP pipeline to the endpoint, where a handler provides a response.

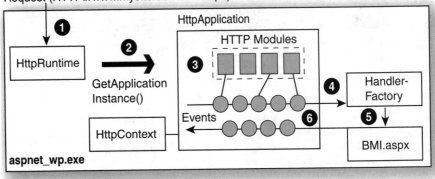

Figure 17-11   Handling a request within the HTTP pipeline

Let's take a simplified look at the sequence of events that occur.

1. **Request is received by Web server.** The HTTP request for the
    `bmi.aspx` resource is passed to the ASP.NET Worker Process
    (`aspnet_wp.exe`). It creates an instance of the `HttpRuntime` class,
    which initiates processing of the request.

    The processing begins with the creation of an `HttpContext`
    object. You can think of this as the central repository of all information
    pertaining to the request. When another class needs information
    about the request, it can find it in an `HttpContext` field or property.
    In addition to the `HttpRequest` and `HttpResponse` fields, the class
    also exposes state information through `HttpSessionState` and
    `HttpApplicationState` properties.

2. `HttpApplicationFactory` **provides the** `HttpApplication`
    object to process the request. After the `HttpContext` object is
    created, the `HttpRuntime` calls on the static factory method `Http-
    ApplicationFactory.GetApplicationInstance` to create or
    find an `HttpApplication` object to process the request.

3. `HttpApplication` **is initialized with HTTP modules that filter
    request and response.** HTTP modules are used to process a request
    and response as they pass through the pipeline. Predefined ASP.NET
    modules provide authentication, caching, and session state services.

4. **Locate handler factory.** After the `HttpApplication` object takes
    over the processing from the `HttpRuntime`, it locates the `Handler-
    Factory` that finds or creates the HTTP handler object. It does this
    by examining the type of request (`.aspx`) and searching the
    `machine.config` file or `web.config` for the name of the handler

that maps to this request type. Different handlers are needed for the different types of resources that may be requested. For example, a request for a Web page is handled differently than one for a text or XML file.

5. **Handler processes request.** In our example, the handler class is the requested .aspx page. It may seem strange that the page is a handler, but the main requirement for a handler is that it implement the IHttpHandler interface—which the .aspx page does via its Page class.

6. **Response is constructed and returned.** The ProcessRequest method of the handler is called to generate the response. This method takes an HttpContext object parameter that gives it access to the requested information needed to complete the processing.

As requests and responses move through the HTTP pipeline, an ordered chain of deterministic events—starting with the HttpApplication.BeginRequest event and concluding with the HttpApplication.EndRequest event—defines each stage of the processing. In addition, random error events can arise at any time from unhandled exceptions.

A developer can greatly improve the robustness and effectiveness of an application by selectively developing handlers for these events. Handlers are typically used to trap error events and direct them to a custom error page, log session lengths and number of users, authenticate users, and adorn pages with common header and footer information. These events can be handled using either a custom application class or custom HTTP modules. We'll look at both, and see how they compare.

A third place to customize the pipeline is at the endpoint, where an HTTP handler processes a resource request. As we will see, different resources, such as .aspx or .soap files, use their own handler components. ASP.NET makes it easy to write your own handler to manage special resources

HttpApplication Class

The HttpApplication object handles most of the duties required to process a request. Its properties expose caching and application/session state information, as well as a collection of predefined HttpModules. Equally important are the set of events it exposes. We can customize an application by including code in a global.asax file to handle these events.

Table 17-5 lists the HttpApplication events in the order that they occur in the HTTP pipeline. The Error event is an exception because it can occur at any time during the process.

Table 17-5 `HttpApplication` Events

Event	Description
BeginRequest	Fires when ASP.NET receives a request. A request can be modified here before it reaches the page.
AuthenticateRequest	The identity of the user has been established.
AuthorizeRequest	User authorization has been verified.
ResolveRequestCache	Fires when ASP.NET determines whether to handle request from a cached page or pass request to a handler.
AcquireRequestState	Acquires the state of the current session.
PreRequestHandlerExecute	Fires before the request is sent to a handler. In the case of a request for an .aspx file, the handler is the page itself.
PostRequestHandlerExecute	Fires after the handler has packaged a response. The response object contains the text returned to the client.
ReleaseRequestState	Fires after all request handlers have been executed and ASP.NET is ready to store session state information.
UpdateRequestCache	Data being sent to client is stored in the cache for future requests.
EndRequest	Occurs when request has been processed.
Error	Occurs in response to unhandled application exception.

Your code can provide a handler for these events by creating a component that uses a delegate to subscribe to the event or define event handlers in the `global.asax` file. We'll demonstrate the former approach when discussing HTTP modules, but first let's look at how to use the `global.asax` file.

global.asax File

This file is stored in the root of the virtual directory containing the application(s) it is to be associated with. Its primary purpose is to hold the handlers that respond to the `Application` object's events. It is similar to an .aspx file in that it is compiled into an assembly when the Web application is first accessed. Unlike the Web page, however, it inherits from the `HttpApplication` class.

Here is a simple `global.asax` file that displays copyright information at the bottom of each page returned by an application in its virtual directory. It does this by implementing a custom handler for the `EndRequest` event. Notice that the format of the event handler for this, and all `Application` events in the `global.asax` file, is `Application_eventname`.

```
<%! file:global.asax %>
<%@ Application Language="C#" %>
<script runat=server>
protected void Application_EndRequest(object sender, EventArgs e)
{
    this.Context.Response.Output.Write(
       "<br>&copy2005 BMI Software");
}
</script>
```

`Global.asax` supports four other important events that are not members of the `HttpApplication` class: `Application_Start`, `Application_End`, `Session_Start`, and `Session_End`. The purpose of these events, which should be clear from their name, is to mark the beginning and end of an application and the sessions using it. They are the most frequently implemented event handlers in the `global.asax` file—performing the bookend operations of state initialization and cleanup. To illustrate this, let's extend the preceding `global.asax` example to keep track of the number of sessions that request an application and display this session number below the copyright.

The session counters are kept in an `HttpApplicationState` object represented by the `Application` property of the `HttpApplication` base class. It acts like a dictionary to hold information during the lifetime of an application (refer to Section 17.4, "Maintaining State").

As shown in Listing 17-10, counters that track the number of sessions and sessions cancelled are initialized to zero when the `Application_Start` event fires. The session counter is incremented when a `Session_Start` occurs, and the counter for terminated sessions is incremented when a `Session_Ends` event occurs.

Listing 17-10   Using `global.asax` to Count Sessions

```
<%! global.asax %>
<%@ Application Language="C#" %>
<script language = "C#" runat=server>
// Can also use Application_OnStart syntax
void Application_Start(Object Sender, EventArgs e)
    {
        // Initialize counters with application scope
        Application["Sessions"] = 0;
        Application["TerminatedSessions"] = 0;
    }
```

Listing 17-10   Using `global.asax` to Count Sessions *(continued)*

```
void Session_Start(Object Sender, EventArgs e)
    {
        Application.Lock();
        Application["Sessions"]=(int) Application["Sessions"] + 1;
        Application.UnLock();
    }
void Session_End(Object Sender, EventArgs e)
    {
        Application.Lock();
        Application["TerminatedSessions"] =
            (int) Application["TerminatedSessions"] + 1;
        Application.UnLock();
    }
protected void Application_EndRequest(object sender,
                                          EventArgs e)
    {
        string sessionCt= "Session #:
            "+Application["Sessions"].ToString();
        // Display copyright and current session number
        this.Context.Response.Output.Write(
            "<br>&copy2005 BMI Software<br>"+sessionCt);
    }
</script>
```

Using a Code-Behind File with global.asax

As with the `.aspx` file, code can be separated from the `global.asax` file and placed in a code-behind file. The code is compiled into a DLL and placed it in the `\bin` subdirectory of the application. The `Inherits` attribute of the `Application` directive points to the class implemented in the DLL.

To convert the preceding example to use a code-behind file, we remove code from the `global.asax` file, leaving only the `Application` directive:

```
<%! file:global.asax %>
<%@ Application  Inherits="sessionctr" %>
```

The code-behind file must be implemented as a class that inherits from `Http-Application`. Here is a segment of the code:

```
// file: sessionctr.cs
using System;
using System.Web;
```

```
public class sessionctr: HttpApplication
{
    void Application_OnStart(Object Sender, EventArgs e)
    {
        Application["Sessions"] = 0;
        Application["TerminatedSessions"] = 0;
    }
    // Remainder of assembly code goes here
}
```

HTTP Modules

An HttpModule is a component that implements the IHttpModule interface. The role of the module is similar to that of the global.asax file: It processes events (refer to Table 17-2) associated with response and request messages in the HTTP pipeline. In many cases, you can implement the same functionality using either the module or global.asax file. We discuss the factors that affect your choice later in this section.

Listing 17-11 shows the predefined modules that ship with ASP.NET. The physical modules (assemblies) are stored in the Global Assembly Cache (GAC) and are made available by listing them in the <httpModules> section of the machine.config file. They perform such diverse tasks as user authentication, caching, and state management. Although you do not work with the modules directly, they should give you an idea of the type of pre- and post-request processing that can be performed.

Listing 17-11 HTTP Modules in machine.config File

```
<httpModules>
    <add name="OutputCache"
        type="System.Web.Caching.OutputCacheModule" />
    <add name="Session"
        type="System.Web.SessionState.SessionStateModule" />
    <add name="WindowsAuthentication"
        type="System.Web.Security.WindowsAuthenticationModule" />
    <add name="FormsAuthentication"
        type="System.Web.Security.FormsAuthenticationModule" />
    <add name="PassportAuthentication"
        type="System.Web.Security.PassportAuthenticationModule" />
    <add name="UrlAuthorization"
        type="System.Web.Security.UrlAuthorizationModule" />
    <add name="FileAuthorization"
        type="System.Web.Security.FileAuthorizationModule" />
```

Listing 17-11	HTTP Modules in `machine.config` File *(continued)*

```
    <add name="ErrorHandlerModule"
       type="System.Web.Mobile.ErrorHandlerModule,
       System.Web.Mobile, Version=1.0.5000.0, Culture=neutral,
       PublicKeyToken=b03f5f7f11d50a3a" />
</httpModules>
```

Implementing a Custom HttpModule

There are two minimal requirements for building a functioning `HttpModule`: It must contain a class that implements the `IHttpModule` interface and it must register an event handler to process one of the `HttpApplication` events. An example of this is shown in Listing 17-12. The code adds copyright information to the bottom of all pages returned by the application—exactly the same function performed by the earlier `global.asax` file.

The `IHttpModule` interface consists of two methods—`Init` and `Dispose`—that must be accounted for. We use `Init` to register the event handler that will be called when the `EndRequest` event occurs. Note that access to the events is provided through the `HttpApplication` object that `Init` receives as a parameter.

Listing 17-12	Module to Append Copyright to Web Pages

```
using System;
using System.Web;
namespace CustomModules{
public class FooterModule: IHttpModule
{
    public void Init(HttpApplication httpApp)
    {
       httpApp.EndRequest += new EventHandler(this.OnEndRequest);
    }
    public void Dispose() {}
    //
    public void OnEndRequest (Object obj, EventArgs e)
    {
       HttpApplication httpApp = (HttpApplication) obj;
       httpApp.Context.Response.Output.Write(
             "<br>&copy2005 BMI Software");
    }
}
}
```

Deploying a Custom HttpModule

To use the module with a Web application, compile it and place it in the \bin subdirectory of the application or in the Global Assembly Cache (GAC). Next, the assembly must be registered in either the web.config or machine.config file. In this example, we use a web.config file, which is placed in the root of the application's virtual directory. A portion of the file is shown here:

```
<configuration>
   <system.web>
      <httpModules>
         <add name="copyright"
         type="CustomModules.FooterModule, footmodule" />
      </httpModules>
   </system.web>
</configuration>
```

The key part is the <add> element that takes the form:

```
<add name=friendly name  type=class name, assembly />
```

This element is enclosed by the <httpModules> elements. Multiple <add> elements can be used to specify multiple modules.

URL Rewriting with a Custom Module

URL rewriting is the process of changing a requested URL so that it is redirected to another resource. This is commonly used to ensure that bookmarked links continue to work when directories and resource names are changed on a Web server.

An HTTP module provides a convenient and easy-to-use approach for rewriting a URL. The implementation logic in the module is straightforward:

1. An HttpApplication event invokes event handler code.
2. The event handler examines the Context.Request.Path property for the requested path.
3. If the path URL needs to be redirected, the Context.RewritePath method is called with the substitute path.

The most important issue to be resolved in developing a rewriter is selecting an event in the request's lifecycle where the URL checking and modification should occur. The three HttpAppliction event candidates are shown in Table 17-6, along with the criteria for selecting them. (Authentication is discussed in Section 17.5.)

In general, if no authentication is being used, place the rewrite logic in an event handler for the BeginRequest event.

Table 17-6   Event Choices for Implementing a URL Rewriter Module

Event	Criteria for Selecting Event
BeginRequest	Use unless forms authentications is also used.
AuthenticateRequest	Use if Windows authentication is used.
AuthorizeRequest	Use if Forms Authentication is used and Windows authentication is not.

Listing 17-13 contains code for a simple rewriter module with the rewriting logic included in the `AuthorizeRequest` event handler. Look closely at this code. It first calls a static method `Rewrites.getRewrites()` that returns a hash table in which the keys are old URLs and the associated value is the replacement URL. The hash table is checked to see if it contains the currently requested path and if it's in the table, a call is made to `Context.RewritePath`. The new URL is passed to it, and the method automatically takes care of details such as including any query string with the new URL.

Listing 17-13   Custom HTTP Module to Rewrite a URL

```
using System;
using System.Web;
using System.Collections;
namespace CustomModules
{
    public class ReWriteModule: IHttpModule
    {
        public void Init(HttpApplication httpApp)
        {
            httpApp.AuthorizeRequest += new
                EventHandler(this.OnAuthorizeRequest);
        }
        public void Dispose() {}
        // Determine if requested URL needs to be rewritten
        public void OnAuthorizeRequest( Object obj, EventArgs e)
        {
            // Get hash table containing old and replacement URLs
            Hashtable urls = Rewrites.getRewrites();
            HttpApplication httpApp = (HttpApplication) obj;
            // Get path of requested URL
            string path = httpApp.Context.Request.Path.ToUpper();
```

Listing 17-13 Custom HTTP Module to Rewrite a URL *(continued)*

```
            // See if path is in hash table
            if(urls.ContainsKey(path))
               path= (string)urls[path];
            httpApp.Context.RewritePath(path);    // Rewrite URL
         }
      }
}
```

The module is registered by placing the following entry in the `web.config` file:

```
<add name="redirector"
        type="CustomModules.ReWriteModule, rewritemodule" />
```

The process of identifying URLs to be rewritten can be implemented in various ways. This example stores the old and replacement URLs in an XML file using the following format:

```
<!-- File: redirector.xml   -->
<RewriterConfig>
   <RewriterRules>
      <Rule>
         <OldPath>/ideas/calculator.aspx</OldPath>
         <NewPath>/utilities/calculator.aspx</NewPath>
      </Rule>
      <Rule>
         <OldPath>/ideas/bmi.aspx</OldPath>
         <NewPath>/utilities/bminew.aspx</NewPath>
      </Rule>
   </RewriterRules>
</RewriterConfig>
```

This information could also be stored in the `web.config` file, although some overhead is required to do this. For details, refer to "Adding a Custom Configuration Section" on page 824.

Choosing Between an HTTP Module and global.asax

In many cases, the functionality you want to add to a Web server environment can be implemented using HTTP modules or the `global.asax` file. As a guide to making the choice, let's review their features:

- Both can contain handlers to service HttpApplication events.
- Global.asax can receive notification of session and application start and end events. An HTTP module cannot service these events.
- Modules are deployed at the machine (machine.config) or virtual directory (web.config) level; global.asax operates at a directory level only.

Either can be used to handle HttpApplication events. If the feature being added applies to all applications on the server, a module is the better choice; if the feature is specific to an application, use a global.asax file.

HTTP Handlers

When a request is made for a resource, ASP.NET directs control to the appropriate handler for that resource. For example, if the request is for an .aspx file, control passes to the PageHandlerFactory component, which returns the requested .aspx page. The default ASP.NET handlers are registered in the machine.config file within the <httpHandlers> section. An extract of that file shows how the resource type is mapped to the class capable of creating a handler for it:

```
<httpHandlers>
    <add verb="*" path="trace.axd"
            type="System.Web.Handlers.TraceHandler" />
    <add verb="*" path="*.aspx"
            type="System.Web.UI.PageHandlerFactory" />
    <add verb="*" path="*.ashx"
            type="System.Web.UI.SimpleHandlerFactory" />
    <add verb="GET,HEAD" path="*"
            type="System.Web.StaticFileHandler" />
    ...
</httpHandlers>
```

An HTTP handler is a component that implements the System.Web.IhttpHandler interface. Unlike an HTTP module, only one handler is called to process a request. ASP.NET maps a request to the target handler based on information in a machine.config or web.config file. The request can be mapped directly to a handler or to a handler factory that creates or retrieves the appropriate handler. As shown in the preceding machine.config file, .aspx requests are handled by a PageHandlerFactory class. We'll look at both techniques.

Implementing a Custom HTTP Handler

ASP.NET provides handlers for .aspx, .soap, .asmx (Web services), and other standard ASP.NET file types. So why create a custom handler? The primary motivation is to support new file extensions or existing file extensions that require added processing features. For example, when a text file (.txt) is requested, ASP.NET simply returns the contents of the file. As an exercise, let's improve this with a handler that accepts a URL with the name of the text file and a query string parameter that specifies a keyword to search for in the file. The output from the handler is a listing of the text file with all instances of the keyword highlighted, as well as a count of the number of times the keyword occurs in the document.

The IHttpHandler interface contains two members that must be implemented in our custom handler class: the ProcessRequest method and the Reuseable property. As shown in Listing 17-14, ProcessRequest contains the code that processes the HTTP request; IsReusable indicates whether the instance of the handler can be reused for other requests. This is applicable only when a handler factory is providing handlers and pools them for reuse.

This handler responds to URL requests that contain a text file and query string containing a keyword to search for in the file:

```
HTTP://www.scilibrary.com/films.txt?kwd=Bogart
```

The context object provides access to the file name through the Request.PhysicalPath property. An attempt is made to open the text file and read it line by line. Each line is searched for the keyword using Regex.Match. If a match is found, the method BoldWord is called to place HTML bold (<b>) tags around the text. This method also increments the word counter.

Listing 17-14   Custom HTTP Handler to Display a Text File

```csharp
// file: txthandler.cs
using System;
using System.Web;
using System.IO;
using System.Text.RegularExpressions;
public class TextHandler: IHttpHandler
{
    static int wordCt=0;
    static string BoldWord(Match m)
    {
        // Get the matched string and place bold tags around it
        string kwd = m.ToString();
        kwd="<b>"+kwd+"</b>";
        wordCt += 1;
        return kwd;
    }
    public void ProcessRequest(HttpContext ctx)
    {
```

| Listing 17-14 | Custom HTTP Handler to Display a Text File *(continued)* |

```
// Get file to be opened
string filePath= ctx.Request.PhysicalPath;
int ndx= filePath.LastIndexOf(@"\");
string fileName = filePath.Substring(ndx+1);
// Keyword to search for in file
string keyWord = ctx.Request["kwd"];
// Create HTML response
ctx.Response.Output.Write("<html><body >");
ctx.Response.Output.Write("File: "+fileName+
        "  Keyword: <b>"+keyWord+"</b><hr size=1>");
string line;
try {
   StreamReader reader= new StreamReader(filePath);
   // Read lines of file and display in response
   while ((line = reader.ReadLine()) != null)
   {
      if (keyWord!= null) {
      // search for keyword and highlight
         string newLine = Regex.Replace(line, keyWord,
            new MatchEvaluator(TextHandler.BoldWord),
                              RegexOptions.IgnoreCase);
         line= newLine;
      }
      ctx.Response.Output.Write("<br>"+line);
   }
   reader.Close();
} catch (Exception e)
{
   ctx.Response.Output.Write("<br>"+e.Message);
}
// Display number of matches
ctx.Response.Output.Write("<br><br>Word Matches: " +
      wordCt.ToString());
ctx.Response.Output.Write("</body></html>");
wordCt=0; // reset since it is static
}
public bool IsReusable
{
   get {return false;}
}
}
```

The final code is compiled and placed in the \bin subdirectory of the application.

Deploying a Custom HTTP Handler

For ASP.NET to be aware of the handler, an entry is made in the `machine.config` or application's `web.config` file. In this example, we place an `<add>` element in the `web.config` file. This element contains three attributes that define the handler and the conditions for using it. `Verb` specifies the type of request to be handled, such as `GET` or `POST`. The `*` is a wildcard character that represents any type request. The `path` attribute indicates the requested resource name that is mapped to the handler; and `type` specifies the handler class or handler factory and its containing assembly.

```
<httpHandlers>
    <add verb="*" path="*.txt" type="TextHandler,txthandler"/>
</httpHandlers>
```

The final step in deployment is to make IIS (Internet Information Service) aware that requests for the `.txt` extension are to be handled by ASP.NET. This is done by using Internet Services Manager to map the file extension to the ISAPI extension DLL (`aspnet_isapi.dll`). Follow these steps:

1. Invoke Internet Services Manager and right-click Default Web Site.
2. Select Properties – Home Directory – Configuration.
3. Click Add and a pop-up window appears.
4. Fill in the Executable field with the path to the `aspnet_isapi.dll` file. This file should be in the version directory of the Framework installation.
5. Fill in the Extension field with ***.txt**.

With these steps completed, `TextHandler` is now called to process all requests for `.txt` files. Figure 17-12 shows output from a sample request.

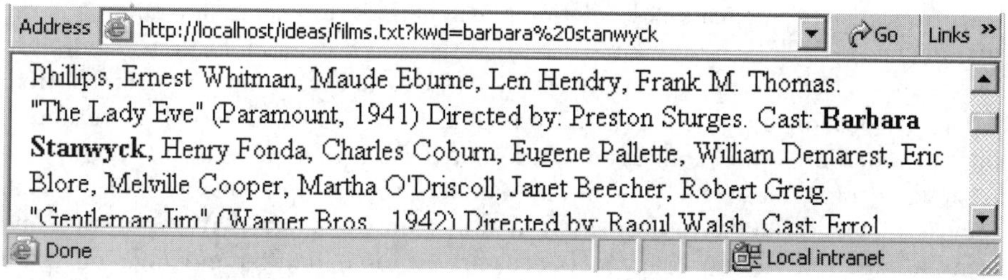

Figure 17-12 Output from HTTP handler that displays text files

Core Note

If an extension used by an HTTP handler is not mapped in IIS to ASP.NET, IIS attempts to return the contents of any file requested having that extension. ASP.NET never sees the request.

17.8 Summary

The ASP.NET environment offers a variety of types and configuration files that enable a developer or software architect to customize how Web requests are handled by a server. Configuration files such as `web.config` provide a flexible and easy way to customize the ASP.NET settings. These files contain sections that enable/disable tracing, specify the default culture of a page, define the way session state information is stored, and define an authentication/authorization security model. The security model enables an application to limit page access to users based on credentials such as their name, password, and role. Credential information may be stored in the `web.config` file, an XML file, or an application's proprietary database.

ASP.NET provides several mechanisms for handling both Application and Session state data. The application data is available to all sessions using that application; session data is limited to the individual session and can be configured to support Web farms and permanent storage in a database. An alternative to using an application state object is data caching. ASP.NET provides an area in memory where `CacheEntry` objects are stored and made available to all sessions. Output caching is also supported to enable an entire Web page or Web page fragment to be stored in a cache on the server, a proxy server, or the browser. This reduces the load on a server by allowing a Web page to be retrieved from memory rather than being recreated on the server.

Advanced Web application development can benefit from an understanding of the underlying ASP.NET architecture that supports HTTP communications. Central to this is the HTTP pipeline through which requests and responses are transported. After a request or response enters this pipeline, it can be parsed, modified, rerouted, or rejected. Both the `global.asax` file and HTTP module can be designed to respond to pipeline events. The event handlers they supply are used to do such things as append standard information to all responses, maintain Web statistics, and transparently reroute requests when necessary. At the end of the pipeline, a handler is responsible for providing the requested resource. Custom handlers can be written to handle specially defined resources or enhance the existing handlers.

17.9 Test Your Understanding

1. True or False: A Web application requires at least one `web.config` file in its directory tree.

2. Name the two places that trace output can be viewed.

3. Regarding ASP.NET security:
   a. List the three types of .NET authentication available.
   b. Where is the authentication type specified?
   c. What is the difference between authentication and authorization?
   d. Which property of the `Page` class provides information about an authenticated user?

4. Which mechanism(s) for storing session state information supports multiple servers?

5. You have a reasonably static Web page that is rendered differently for different browsers and you want to refresh the cached page every three hours. What would be included in your `OutputCache` directive for this page?

6. What factors influence whether state data is maintained in a data cache or an application state variable?

7. What is resource scavenging, and how can a data cache prevent it from occurring?

8. Fill in the blanks:

   As a _____ or _____ passes through the HTTP pipeline, an _____ object fires a series of events that may be handled by a/an _____ or in the _____ file.

XML
WEB SERVICES

Topics in This Chapter

- *Web Service Overview:* The popularity of Web Services stems from the fact that they are implemented using the non-proprietary technologies of HTTP, XML, and SOAP. For them to become truly useful, users must have a way to locate them on the Internet. UDDI offers one such discovery service.

- *Creating a Web Service:* In C#, a Web Service is created by implementing a method that is exposed to clients across the Internet. To indicate a method is available, a `WebService` directive is required on the Web page, and a `WebMethod` attribute is attached to the Web Service method.

- *Building an XML Web Service Client:* The easiest way to create a Web Service client is to build a proxy using the *Web Services Description Language* (WSDL) provided by the Web Service. The proxy handles the physical connection to the Web Service and provides asynchronous and synchronous access.

- *WSDL and SOAP:* WSDL provides the information that describes a Web Service; Simple Object Access Protocol (SOAP) is the format in which the requests and responses are delivered. An understanding of both offers added insight into how Web Services operate.

- *Web Service Examples:* To satisfy real-world business needs, Web Services must deliver more than simple data types. Examples in this section show how to build a service that delivers images and how to build a client to retrieve datasets from the publicly available Amazon Web Services.

Chapter

XML Web Services provide a relatively simple technique for accessing a method on an object that is running on a local or remote computer. Many embrace this lightweight approach to making Remote Procedure Calls (RPC) as technology that will spell the end to much heavier and complex solutions for distributed communications such as DCOM and CORBA. At the root of its appeal is the fact that Web Services are based on standardized technologies such as HTTP and XML that are designed to promote seamless interoperability among different operating systems. Not everyone is sold on them. Critics point out the lack of security standards, the heavy bandwidth requirements of XML, and the lack of notification and transaction services.

The chapter takes a practical look at the pluses and minuses of implementing and consuming Web Services in a .NET environment. It presents Web Services from the perspective of both the server and client. On the server side, the chapter explores how to define a Web Services class, make its methods available to HTTP clients, and access the ASP.NET Application and Session objects. The emphasis on the client side is how to use the Web Services Description Language (WSDL) contract to create a proxy class that implement calls to the Web Service.

HTTP and SOAP—a protocol that codifies how XML is used to package the request and response data that comprise a Web Service operation—are the two cornerstones of Web Services. Other protocols such as GET and POST are available, but the Simple Object Access Protocol (SOAP) has fewer limitations and is used in the majority of real-world applications. This chapter takes a look at the SOAP format as well as several issues related to SOAP, including the handling of complex data types, exception handling, and security.

We begin the exploration of the .NET Web Services architecture by creating a simple Web Service and Web Service consumer. Our first examples are created "by hand" to emphasize the underlying principles. After these are understood, we see how Visual Studio.NET simplifies the development. The chapter also demonstrates how to use the `wsdl.exe` tool and .NET classes that are integral to the development process. Closing out the chapter is a sample application to access the Amazon Web Services.

18.1 Introduction to Web Services

The Web Service architecture is a service-oriented architecture that enables applications to be distributed across a network or the Internet to clients using any language or operating system. As shown in Figure 18-1, Web Service communications are implemented using existing technology and standards that require no proprietary vendor support. This technology either formed the basis of the Internet or evolved from it. HTTP and XML have been discussed in earlier chapters, but let's take a brief look at them—from a Web Services perspective—along with TCP/IP and SOAP:

- **TCP/IP (Transmission Control Protocol/Internet Protocol).** A communications protocol suite that forms the basis of the Internet. It's an open system that governs the flow of data between computers by breaking data into chunks that are easily routed over a network. A Web Service user or developer rarely has direct contact with this layer.
- **HTTP (Hypertext Transfer Protocol).** Technically, this text-based protocol is a Remote Procedure Call (RPC) protocol that supports request/response communications. The .NET Framework as well as most production Web Services use it because it has wide support and generally allows information to sail unimpeded through firewalls. Both the HTTP POST and HTTP GET methods are supported in .NET as a way to call a Web Service. Most applications use POST, because it packages the request inside the request body (in a SOAP envelope), rather than as part of a less secure query string.

Core Note

The rules that describe how a message is carried within or on top of a protocol is referred to as a binding. *The default protocol binding used by .NET for Web Services is* HttpSoap, *which should be used to access Web Services that understand SOAP. It is specified inside the* System.Web *section of the* machine.config *file.*

- **XML (Extended Markup Language).** We have seen in earlier chapters how data can be serialized into XML format for storage or transmission. The fact that it is text based makes it easy to work with. Just about every programming environment supports tools for encoding and decoding XML formatted data. Its inherent flexibility, extensibility, and validity checking make it attractive to Web Services that must deal with simple data types such as strings, as well as more complex data structures. There are currently two XML-based protocols used for delivering Web Services: XML-RPC and SOAP. Because .NET supports SOAP, this chapter focuses on it. After you understand SOAP, you should have no difficulty with XML-RPC if you encounter it.

- **SOAP (Simple Object Access Protocol).** SOAP is defined as "a lightweight protocol for exchange of information in a decentralized, distributed environment."[1] It is not designed specifically for Web Services, nor restricted to HTTP; but its RPC specifications define a model for invoking methods on a specified target machine, passing parameters, handling faults, and receiving a method response. We will look at SOAP in detail later in the chapter. For now, keep in mind that the details of XML and SOAP are typically handled transparently by .NET. The provider code only needs to focus on implementing the method that returns the desired data; the requestor code simply places a method call and processes the returned data.

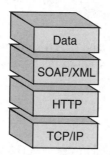

Figure 18-1   Web Service transport

Discovering and Using a Web Service

To use a Web Service, a client must have a description of how to access the service. This information is provided by a Web Services Description Language (WSDL) document that provides the name of the service, the signature of the method(s) that can

---

1. Simple Object Access Protocol (SOAP) 1.1—W3C Note, May 8, 2000.

be called, the address of the service (usually a URL), and binding information that describes how the transport operation will occur. In practical terms, the WSDL information contains the methods that actually call a Web Service. We implement these methods in our client code (as source or a DLL reference) and use them as a proxy to access the service. Section 18.2, "Building an XML Web Service," provides a concrete example of using .NET to retrieve WSDL information and incorporate it into a client application.

Introduction to UDDI

Web sites are identified by a domain name and IP address that are maintained by a distributed network service known as the Domain Name System (DNS). Servers in this network are responsible for controlling e-mail delivery and translating domain names into IP addresses. The combination of DNS and Web search engines enables users to quickly locate Web content. However, neither DNS servers nor search engines provide a formal way of identifying Web Services.

To organize Web Services into a publicly searchable directory, a public consortium (www.uddi.com) comprising hundreds of companies has defined a standard known as *Universal Description Discovery and Integration* (UDDI). This standard defines a SOAP-based interface that can be used to publish a service or inquire about services in a UDDI-compliant registry. The registry has a business-to-business flavor about it—containing information about a company, its services, and interface specifications for any Web Services it offers. Importantly, there is no single UDDI registry. IBM, SAP, and Microsoft maintain the most prominent registries. Users may query each separately by entering a business name or service as a search term. Figure 18-2 provides an overview of the inquiry process.

The dialog between the client and UDDI registry server is conducted using SOAP messages. Overall, UDDI defines approximately 40 SOAP messages for inquiry and publishing.

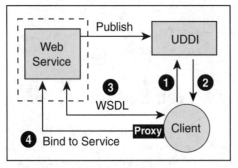

Figure 18-2   Discovering and accessing a Web Service

UDDI Discovery Example

To demonstrate how to use UDDI, we'll look at the SOAP messages sent between client and server as we seek to discover a Web Service that can provide a stock quote. A Web-based UDDI browser (described shortly) sends and receives the messages.

Step 1: Send Discovery Request

For our example, we'll search the UDDI registry provided by Microsoft:

```
http://uddi.microsoft.com/inquire
```

An inquiry may request business information or tModel information. The former contains information about a business, including contact information and a description of services. The tModel structure is much simpler: It consists of a unique key, optional description, and a URL or pointer to a Web page where information for using the service is described. The following message requests a list of tModel keys for companies whose service includes providing a stock quote.

```
<Envelope>
    <Body>
        <find_tModel generic="1.0" maxRows="100">
            <findQualifiers/>
            <name>stock quote</name>
        </find_tModel>
    </Body>
</Envelope>
```

Step 2: Registry Service Responds with List of Services Matching Request

A list of tModel keys is returned. These keys are used for the subsequent query:

```
<soap:Envelope>
    <soap:Body>
        <tModelList generic="1.0" operator="Microsoft Corporation" >
            <tModelInfos>
                <tModelInfo
                    tModelKey="uuid:7aa6f610-5e3c-11d7-bece-000629dc0a53">
                    <name>Stock Quote</name>
                </tModelInfo>
                <tModelInfo
                    tModelKey="uuid:265973ab-31cb-4890-83e0-34d9c1b385e5">
                    <name>Stock Quotes and Information</name>
                </tModelInfo>
            </tModelInfos>
```

```
    </tModelList>
  </soap:Body>
</soap:Envelope>
```

Step 3: Retrieve Overview Document Containing WSDL

Send a request for tModel details for the service with the specified tModelKey:

```
<Envelope>
  <Body>
    <get_tModelDetail generic="1.0">
      <tModelKey>uuid:7aa6f610-5e3c-11d7-bece-000629dc0a53
      </tModelKey>
    </get_tModelDetail>
  </Body>
</Envelope>
```

The response message includes the OverviewURL element that points to a WSDL document. This document contains the information needed to create an application to access the service.

```
<overviewDoc>
  <description xml:lang="en">
    Get Stock quote for a company symbol
  </description>
  <overviewURL>
    http://www.webservicex.net/stockquote.asmx?WSDL
  </overviewURL>
</overviewDoc>
```

You can display the WSDL by pointing your browser to this URL. To invoke the Web Service, remove the query string (?WSDL) from the URL, and navigate to it with your browser.

How to Communicate with a UDDI Service Registry

To interact with a UDDI registry—whether to publish or inquire—you need a way to generate SOAP requests and interpret responses. One option is to write your own application using the Microsoft UDDI 2.0 SDK. It contains excellent C# examples that demonstrate the API and can be run against a test UDDI registry hosted by Microsoft.

For making registry inquires, Web-based UDDI browsers are available. A publicly available one—as well as a wealth of accompanying UDDI information—can be found at

```
http://www.soapclient.com/UDDISearch.html
```

18.2 Building an XML Web Service

In this section, we demonstrate how to build a Web Service by hand and then access it using a browser. We also show how to create the same Web Service using Visual Studio.NET. Although IIS is used, the examples run on any Web server.

Creating a Web Service by Hand

The first step is to select or create a virtual directory under IIS that will hold the Web Service source code file(s). Any physical directory can be mapped to an IIS virtual directory. You can use the Internet Service Manager or simply right-click the directory and select Sharing-Web Sharing. Then, assign it an alias that will be used in its URL. In our example, we will place the service in the \ws subdirectory.

After the directory has been set up, the next step is to use a text editor to create a file in this directory with the .asmx extension to contain the Web Service code. Listing 18-1 contains the code for our simple Web Service. This service exposes a method GetDayBorn that accepts three integer parameters that represent the month, day, and year for birth date. A string value containing the day of the week (Monday, Tuesday, and so on) for this date is returned. The service performs rudimentary error checking and returns an error message if the date is invalid.

Listing 18-1	Web Service to Return a Date's Day of Week— BirthDayWS.asmx

```
<%@ WebService Language="C#" Class="BirthDayWS.BirthDay" %>
using System;
namespace BirthDayWS
{
    public class BirthDay
    {
        [System.Web.Services.WebMethod
        (Description="Return day of week for a date")]
        public string GetDayBorn(int mo, int day, int yr)
        {
            bool err = false;
            string dob;
            if (mo <1 || mo >12) err=true;
            if (day < 1 || day > 31) err=true;
            if (err)
                dob = "Invalid Date";
```

Listing 18-1	Web Service to Return a Date's Day of Week— `BirthDayWS.asmx` *(continued)*

```
        } else {
            DateTime dt = new DateTime(yr,mo,day);
            dob = dt.ToString("dddd"); // Get day
        }
        return(dob);
    }
  }
}
```

The code consists of a single class and a method that is invoked by a client to return the day-of-week value. In addition to the C# code that implements the logic of the service, two other elements are required: a `WebService` directive and a `WebMethod` attribute.

WebService Directive

The `WebService` directive identifies the file as defining a Web Service:

```
<%@ WebService Language="C#" Class="BirthDayWS.BirthDay" %>
```

The directive specifies the class implementing the XML Web Service and the programming language used in the implementation. In this example, the directive and the code for the class are present in the `BirthDayWS.asmx` file. Note, however, that the class can be in a separate assembly. In that case, the separate assembly is placed in a `\bin` directory below the Web application where the Web Service resides. If the class were in `bdAssembly.dll`, the `WebService` directive would look like this:

```
<%@ WebService Language="C#"
     Class="BirthDayWS.BirthDay, bdAssembly" %>
```

This statement would be the only line needed in the `.asmx` file.

WebMethod Attribute

The `WebMethod` attribute identifies a method as being accessible to clients making HTTP requests—that is, as an XML Web Service. Although not required, it is a good practice to include the `Description` property to describe the purpose of the method:

```
[System.Web.Services.WebMethod
     (Description="Return day of week for a date")]
```

The description is added to the WSDL for the service and—as we will see next—is displayed when a Web Service is accessed via a browser. The `WebMethod` attribute has other optional parameters, which are described later in this chapter.

Testing the Web Service

A quick way to test the newly developed Web Service is to point a browser to its location. For this example, we enter the address:

```
http://localhost/ws/BirthDayWS.asmx
```

This brings up a Web page that lists all the services (methods) available through this `.asmx` file as well as a Service Description link that displays WSDL information. For our example, there is only one method, `GetDayBorn`. Clicking it yields the page shown in Figure 18-3. This page contains the name of the class implementing the Web Service, the name of the method to be invoked, a description of the method, and text boxes for entering values to be passed to the Web Service method.

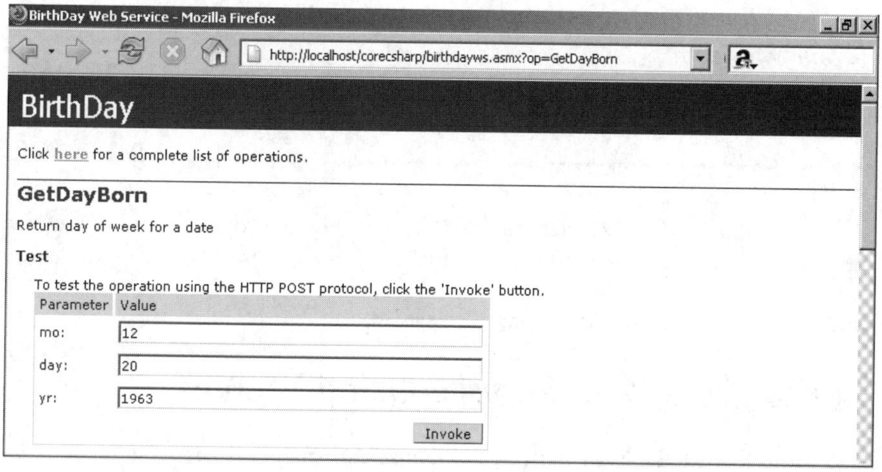

Figure 18-3   Using a browser to access the `BirthDay` Web Service

To use the Web Service, fill in the parameter values and select the Invoke button. This causes the parameters to be sent to the Web Service using the HTTP POST protocol. The output received from the service is an XML document shown in Figure 18-4.

> **Source of: http://localhost/corecsharp/birthdayWS.asmx/GetDayBorn - Mozilla Firefox**
>
> ```
> <?xml version="1.0" encoding="utf-8"?>
> <string xmlns="http://tempuri.org/">Friday</string>
> ```

Figure 18-4 BirthDayWS output

The output from the method is included in the `string` element of the XML wrapper. Fortunately, we do not have to parse the XML to retrieve this value when writing our own SOAP client. The WSDL contract provides information that allows our client to treat the remote Web Service as a method that returns data conforming to the method's type—not as XML.

Core Note

It is unnecessary to compile the `.asmx` *file containing the Web Service in order to deploy it. On a Microsoft Windows server, the ASP.NET runtime automatically compiles the file the first time it is requested and places it in a subdirectory—named after the virtual directory—on the following path:*

```
<%windir%>\Microsoft.NET\Framework\<version>\
Temporary ASP.NET Files\
```

To view the WSDL associated with this Web Service, open your browser and append `?WSDL` to the URL of the `.asmx` file:

```
http://localhost/ws/BirthDayWS.asmx?WSDL
```

Creating a Web Service Using VS.NET

Aside from the usual advantages of IntelliSense and single key compilation (F5), the major advantage of VS.NET over a manual approach is that it automatically creates a new virtual directory under IIS to host the Web Service. This directory takes the same name as the project.

To create a Web Service with VS.NET, open it up and select ASP.NET Web Service as the project type. Assign it a project name (`BirthDayWS`, in this case) that reflects the purpose of the Web Service. When the project opens, select View Code and you will find that the following template class is predefined:

```
namespace BirthDayWS
{
```

```
public class Service1 : System.Web.Services.WebService
{
    public Service1()
    { InitializeComponent(); }
    private IContainer components = null;
    private void InitializeComponent()    {    }
    protected override void Dispose( bool disposing )
    {
        if(disposing && components != null)
        {
            components.Dispose();
        }
        base.Dispose(disposing);
    }
        // --> Place BirthDayWS code here
}
}
```

To implement the service, rename the class to `Birthday` and add the code for the `GetDayBorn` method. Use the browser to test the service by either compiling the code, which automatically invokes the browser, or directly pointing the browser to

```
http://localhost/BirthDayWS/BirthDayWS.asmx
```

The only significant difference between this code and our handcrafted version is that the Web class now inherits from `WebService` rather than the default `System.Object`. The service works either way, but by inheriting from `WebService` it gains the functionality of an ASP.NET application.

System.Web.Services.WebService Class

The `WebService` base class exposes properties to a Web Service that enable it to access the intrinsic ASP.NET objects introduced in Chapter 17, "The ASP.NET Application Environment."

- `Application`. Provides access to an `Application` object that can be used to maintain state information for all sessions accessing the Web Service. For example, it can be used to keep track of how many times the service is called.
- `Session`. Provides access to the `HttpSessionState` object that maintains session state information. It can be used, for example, to track how many times a service is called while the current session is alive. This property is available only if the `EnableSession` property of the `WebMethodAttribute` is set to `true`.

- Context. Exposes the HttpContext class. Recall that this class provides a wealth of information about the current request.
- User. Returns the IPrincipal object that provides user authentication information and can be used to determine whether the request is authorized (see Chapter 17).

To demonstrate the use of state information, let's extend our example to use the Application object to keep track of the number of times the Web Service is called. Our first step is to add the statement in bold to the GetDayBorn method:

```
dob = dt.ToString("dddd"); // extracts day
this.Application["count"] = GetCount()+1;
```

Next, add a method to the class that internally returns the "count" value of the Application object. Finally, add a method, GetVisitors, which allows clients to view the number of calls to the Web Service as a Web Service call:

```
private int GetCount()
{
    object ob = this.Application["count"];
    if (ob == null) {
        return(0);
    } else {
        return((int)ob);
    }
}
[WebMethod(Description="Number of times Web Service called.")]
public int GetVisitors()
{
    return (GetCount());
}
```

Extending the Web Service with the WebService and WebMethod Attributes

The BirthDayWS example demonstrates that a functioning Web Service can be created with a minimal use of .NET classes. However, before releasing a Web Service to the Internet, there are additional features that should be considered. For instance, each XML Web Service should be given a unique namespace rather than relying on the default <http://tempuria.org.>, caching can be implemented to improve performance, and overloaded methods can be implemented using the WebMethod attribute.

The WebService Attribute

The optional `WebService` attribute (not to be confused with the `WebService` directive) is applied to the class implementing the XML Web Service. It has two useful properties: `Description`, which describes the overall Web Service, and `Namespace`, which sets the default XML namespace for the service. In general terms, namespaces are used to avoid naming conflicts among XML elements and attributes. In this case, it is used to make the Web Service name unique.

Let's add a `WebService` attribute containing a namespace and description to the class in our `BirthDayWS` example:

```
[WebService(Namespace="http://www.dateservices.com/ws/",
    Description="<b>Web Service that Provides Date
    Functions.</b>")]
public class BirthDay : System.Web.Services.WebService
```

It is important to note that the namespace is intended to be a unique identifier, and does not need to actually point to anything. Domains are typically used to take advantage of their uniqueness.

Figure 18-5 shows the page that is returned when we call the Web Service that is now updated with the `WebService` attribute and the `GetVisitors` method.

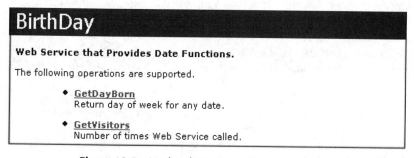

Figure 18-5   Updated `BirthDayWS` Web Service

The WebMethod Attribute

As mentioned previously, the `WebMethod` attribute is required to expose a method as part of a Web Service. Its properties include `Description`, which we have already used, `EnableSession`, `MessageName`, `CacheDuration`, and `TransactionOption`. The latter property applies to applications that call transactional COM+ components—a topic not discussed in this book. The other three properties are useful for developing general Web Services. Let's look at the role of each.

EnableSession: Activate the Use of Session State Information

This property is used with Web Services that inherit from the `WebService` class. Turning it on allows a Web Service method to access session information through `WebService.Session` or `HttpContext.Current.Session`. By default, this is set to `false`, because maintaining session data increases memory consumption and reduces performance.

```
Example: [WebMethod(EnableSession=true)]    // Default is false
```

Be aware that Windows Forms clients do not provide the same support for session state variables that a browser does. Sessions rely on cookies to preserve state data. Unlike browsers, Windows Forms applications do not store cookies. Thus, the service thinks that each request is the first request. There is a work-around, however, which is described in the following section on building a Web Services client.

MessageName: Create Overloaded Web Operations

Suppose we want to add a method to our Web Service that accepts the month as a string rather than an integer. Because the signature is different than the original `GetDayBorn` method, we can give it the same method name and C# will compile it as an overloaded method. However, when we try to access it from a browser, we receive a system exception indicating that the two methods have the same name.

The problem lies in the WSDL, which requires that each Web method in its XML elements be uniquely named, irrespective of its signature. By default, the routine in ASP.NET that generates WSDL code uses the name for both. The solution—aside from renaming the method—is to use the `MessageName` property to indicate a surrogate name.

```
[WebMethod(Description="Return day of week for any date",
     MessageName="GetDayBorn2")]
public string GetDayBorn(string month, int day, int yr){
    // Code to convert string month to int value
    string allMos= "JANFEBMARAPRMAYJUNJULAUGSEPOCTNOVDEC";
    month = month.Substring(0,3).ToUpper();
    int ndx = allMos.IndexOf(month);
    if(ndx <0) err=true; else mo = ndx/3 +1;
    // Remainder of code goes here...
```

CacheDuration: Caching Output from a Web Operation

Just like ASP.NET Web pages, output from a Web method can be cached to obviate executing it each time the method is called. The `CacheDuration` property specifies how long (in seconds) the output is to be cached. For methods that accept arguments, cached output is saved for each unique set of arguments.

```
Example: [WebMethod(CacheDuration=1800)]    // Value is in seconds
```

The only rule to follow when (if) setting up caching is to do it judiciously. Caching greatly improves performance for methods that are requested frequently and implement logic that requires lengthy processing. On the other hand, methods such as GetDayBorn in our example can actually hurt performance because most requests to it will yield unique results.

Using web.config to Configure Web Service Options

.NET Web Services support four protocols: HttpGet, HttpPost, HttpSoap, and HttpLocalHost. Of these, HttpPost and HttpGet are disabled for security reasons. The effect of this is to limit Web Service access to URLs located on http://localhost; an attempt by a remote machine to access a local Web Service results in this message being displayed:

```
The test form is only available for requests from the local
machine
```

To make a Web Service available to remote users, it is necessary to enable the HttpPost and HttpGet protocols. This is easily done by configuring the <protocol> section of the web.config file to "add" the two protocols.

```
<system.web>
    <webServices>
        <protocols>
            <add name="HttpGet"/>
            <add name="HttpPost"/>
        </protocols>
    </webServices>
</system.web>
```

Recall that navigating to a Web Services page with no parameters brings up a help page that describes how to use the service, and provides links to invoke the Web Service methods or display the WSDL. If you do not want to expose this information, you can disable the display of help pages by removing the Documentation protocol. To do so, place the following statement in the <protocols> element of the web.config file:

```
<remove name="Documentation" />
```

18.3 Building an XML Web Service Client

This section describes how to create a client application that consumes a Web Service. The objective is to make the client's call to the remote Web method as simple as calling a method in its own code. Although the actual implementation does not reach quite that level of simplicity, the code is straightforward, and much of it can be generated automatically using .NET tools.

Before delving into details, let's first take a high-level view of how a .NET Web Services client interacts with a Web Service.

The most important thing to observe in Figure 18-6 is that the client does not directly invoke the Web Service method. Instead, it calls a proxy object that performs this task. The proxy class is created from the WSDL information provided by the Web Service. We'll see how to do this shortly. The proxy code is a class that has the same class name and method names as the Web Service class does. It contains the transport logic that allows it to make the actual connection to the Web Service. It may do this either synchronously (without receiving confirmation) or asynchronously. The messages exchanged between the proxy and server are bundled within an HTTP request and transmitted using either the HTTP or the SOAP *wire protocol*.

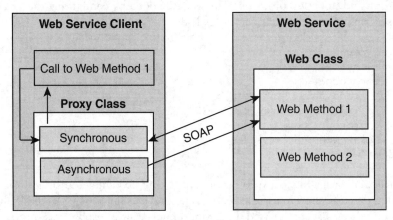

Figure 18-6   Overview of how a client accesses a Web Service

Creating a Simple Client to Access the Web Service Class

To demonstrate the basic principles involved in creating a Web Service client, let's develop a console client application to access the BirthDayWS Web Service (refer to

Figure 18-1). The client passes three arguments to the service and prints the string it returns. Recall that the service consists of the Web class `Birthday` and a single method `GetDayBorn`:

```
public class BirthDay
{
    [System.Web.Services.WebMethod
        (Description="Return day of week for a date")]
public string GetDayBorn(int mo, int day, int yr)
```

Although the Web Service method can reside on a remote machine anywhere on the Internet, we can approach the client design as if we were within the same assembly. Here is the client code contained in the file `bdClient.cs`:

```
using System;
using System.Web.Services;
public class BirthDayClient
{
    static void Main(string[] args)
    {
        BirthDay bd = new BirthDay();
        string dayOfWeek = bd.GetDayBorn(12,20,1963);
        Console.WriteLine(dayOfWeek);
    }
}
```

Compiling this, of course, results in an error stating that `BirthDay` and `bd` cannot be found. We resolve this by creating a proxy class that performs the remote call, yet can be accessed locally by the client. The code for the proxy class is obtained by feeding the WSDL information that defines the Web Service into the .NET `wsdl.exe` utility.

Using wsdl.exe to Create a Proxy

The `wsdl.exe` utility reads the WSDL describing a Web Service and generates the source code for a proxy class to access the service; it can also use the information to create the skeleton code for a Web Service. This latter feature is designed for developers who prefer to design the WSDL as the first step in creating a Web Service. We do not take that approach in this chapter, but you should be aware that there are WSDL editors available for that task.

The `wsdl.exe` utility is run from the command line and has numerous flags or options to govern its execution. Table 18-1 lists those most commonly used.

Table 18-1   `wsdl.exe` Command-Line Options

Option	Description
/appsettingurlkey /urlkey:	Specifies a key within the client's `*.config` file that contains the URL of the Web Service. The default is to hardcode the URL within the proxy class.
/language /l:	Specifies the language to use for generating the proxy class. Choices are: CS (C#), VB (Visual Basic), JS (JScript), and VJS (Visual J#). C# is the default.
/namespace /n:	Specifies the namespace for the proxy.
/out	Specifies file in which the generated proxy code is placed. The default is to use the XML Web Service name with an extension reflecting the language used for the code.
/protocol	The wire protocol to use within the proxy code: `/protocol:SOAP` SOAP 1.1 is generated `/protocol:SOAP12` SOAP 1.2 is generated `/protocol:HttpGet` or `/protocol:HttpPost`
/server	Generates an abstract class for the Web Service. This is used when the WSDL document is used to create a Web Service.
/serverinterface	Generates interfaces—rather than abstract classes—for the Web Service. Available only in 2.0 and later.

The following statement creates a proxy class from the `BirthDayWS.asmx` Web Service and places it in `c:\BDProxy.cs`:

```
wsdl.exe /out:c:\BDProxy.cs http://localhost/ws/
BirthDayWS.asmx?WSDL
```

This proxy source code can be used in two ways: include it in the client's source code, or compile it into a DLL and add a reference to this DLL when compiling the client code. Let's look first at the DLL approach. This command line compiles the source code and links two DLL files containing classes required by the proxy:

```
csc /t:library /r:system.web.services.dll /r:system.xml.dll
        BDProxy.cs
```

We are now ready to compile the client source code into an executable file, `bdClient.exe`:

```
csc /r:BDProxy.dll  bdClient.cs
```

If we add the proxy code directly to the `bdClient.cs` file and compile it, the result is a module that produces the same output as a version that links the proxy as a separate DLL file.

Core Note

When `wsdl.exe` creates proxy code, it checks the associated Web Service for compliance with the WS-I Basic Profile 1.0 standards and emits a warning if the service is noncompliant. For information on this standard, refer to the Web Services Interoperability Organization's Web site at `http://www.ws-i.org`.

Listing 18-2 examines the proxy source code to understand how it converts a client's call into a remote Web Service invocation.

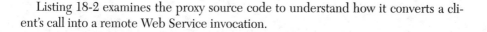

Listing 18-2	Proxy Source Code to Access `BirthDayWS.asmx` Web Service

```
using System;
using System.ComponentModel;
using System.Diagnostics;
using System.Web.Services;
using System.Web.Services.Protocols;
using System.Xml.Serialization;
//
// Auto-generated by wsdl, Version=2.0.40607.16.
[System.Diagnostics.DebuggerStepThroughAttribute()]
[System.ComponentModel.DesignerCategoryAttribute("code")]
[System.Web.Services.WebServiceBindingAttribute(
      Name="BirthDaySoap",
      Namespace="http://tempuri.org/")]
public class BirthDay : SoapHttpClientProtocol {
   private System.Threading.SendOrPostCallback
         GetDayBornOperationCompleted;
   public BirthDay() {
         this.Url = "http://localhost/ws/BirthDayWS.asmx";
   }
   public event GetDayBornCompletedEventHandler
         GetDayBornCompleted;
```

Listing 18-2	Proxy Source Code to Access BirthDayWS.asmx Web Service *(continued)*

```
// (1) Synchronous Call to Web Service
[SoapDocumentMethodAttribute(
    "http://tempuri.org/GetDayBorn",
    RequestNamespace="http://tempuri.org/",
    ResponseNamespace="http://tempuri.org/",
    Use=
    System.Web.Services.Description.SoapBindingUse.Literal,
    ParameterStyle=
    System.Web.Services.Protocols.SoapParameterStyle.Wrapped)]
public string GetDayBorn(int mo, int day, int yr)
{
    object[] results = this.Invoke("GetDayBorn", new object[] {
        mo,
        day,
        yr});
    return ((string)(results[0]));
}
// (2) Asynchronous call to Web Service
public System.IAsyncResult BeginGetDayBorn(int mo, int day,
        int yr, System.AsyncCallback callback,
        object asyncState) {
    return this.BeginInvoke("GetDayBorn", new object[] {
        mo,
        day,
        yr}, callback, asyncState);
}

public string EndGetDayBorn(System.IAsyncResult asyncResult) {
        object[] results = this.EndInvoke(asyncResult);
        return ((string)(results[0]));
}
// (3) Call this for event-based asynchronous handling
public void GetDayBornAsync(int mo, int day, int yr) {
        this.GetDayBornAsync(mo, day, yr, null);
}

public void GetDayBornAsync(int mo, int day, int yr,
        object userState) {
    if ((this.GetDayBornOperationCompleted == null)) {
        this.GetDayBornOperationCompleted = new
        System.Threading.SendOrPostCallback(
            this.OnGetDayBornOperationCompleted);
```

Listing 18-2	Proxy Source Code to Access BirthDayWS.asmx Web Service *(continued)*

```
        }
        this.InvokeAsync("GetDayBorn", new object[] {
            mo,
            day,
            yr}, this.GetDayBornOperationCompleted,
            userState);
    }

    private void OnGetDayBornOperationCompleted(object arg) {
        if ((this.GetDayBornCompleted != null)) {
            InvokeCompletedEventArgs invokeArgs =
                ((InvokeCompletedEventArgs)(arg));
            this.GetDayBornCompleted(this, new
                GetDayBornCompletedEventArgs(invokeArgs.Results,
                invokeArgs.Error, invokeArgs.Cancelled,
                invokeArgs.UserState));
        }
    }
    public new void CancelAsync(object userState) {
        base.CancelAsync(userState);
    }
}
public delegate void GetDayBornCompletedEventHandler(
    object sender, GetDayBornCompletedEventArgs args);
public class
    GetDayBornCompletedEventArgs :AsyncCompletedEventArgs
{
    private object[] results;
    internal GetDayBornCompletedEventArgs(object[] results,
        System.Exception exception, bool cancelled,
        object userState) : base(exception, cancelled, userState) {
            this.results = results;
    }
    // Results are available as a property
    public string Result {
        get {
            this.RaiseExceptionIfNecessary();
            return ((string)(this.results[0]));
        }
    }
}
```

Observe that the proxy class has the same name as the Web Service class (Birth-day) it represents, and implements a method (GetDayBorn) having the same name as the Web Service method. The supporting code is quite different, however. It contains transport logic rather than application logic. This code uses methods provided by the System.Web.Services.Protocols.SoapHttpClientProtocol class from which the proxy class derives. Table 18-2 summarizes of the more useful members of the class.

Table 18-2   Selected Members of SoapHttpClientProtocol

Member	Description
BeginInvoke()	Begins an asynchronous invocation of the Web method.
EndInvoke()	Ends an asynchronous invocation of the Web method.
Invoke()	Invokes the Web method synchronously.
CookieContainer	Gets or sets the collection of cookies. This permits a proxy-based client to accept cookies and allow a server to maintain state information.
Proxy	Gets or sets proxy information needed to make a Web Service call through a firewall.
Timeout	Gets or sets the timeout (in milliseconds) a client waits for a synchronous call to a Web Service to be completed.
Url	Gets or sets the URL used to access the Web server.

Let's look at how these members are used in a proxy class.

Synchronous Calls to a Web Service Method

A proxy provides the capability to invoke a Web Service method synchronously or asynchronously. Recall from Chapter 13, "Asynchronous Programming and Multi-threading," that a synchronous operation uses only one thread, which is blocked until control returns from the called method. An asynchronous call, on the other hand, creates a worker thread that handles the operations of the called method. Control returns immediately to the main thread while a separate thread handles the auxiliary task. The calling routine is notified when the task is completed.

Synchronous communication is implemented with a proxy method that has the same name as the Web method and uses the Invoke method to request the service.

```
public string GetDayBorn(int mo, int day, int yr) {
    object[] results = this.Invoke("GetDayBorn", new object[] {
        mo, day, yr});
    return ((string)(results[0]));
}
```

This is the most intuitive way to access a service because a client can be totally unaware of the proxy and execute a call to the Web Service method, using its actual name. However, because a synchronous call by definition does not require a response, the client code should include a timeout interval and handle any exception that occurs if the interval is exceeded. The following code sets a timeout of four seconds and handles any System.Net.WebException that is thrown.

```
// Must add using System.Net;
BirthDay bd = new BirthDay();
bd.Timeout= 4000;          // Set timeout to 4 seconds
try
{
    string dayOfWeek = bd.GetDayBorn(12,20,1963);
    Console.WriteLine(dayOfWeek);
}
catch (WebException ex)
{
    Console.WriteLine(ex.Message);   // Will report timeout
}
catch (Exception ex)
{
    Console.WriteLine("Unknown error occurred.");
}
```

Core Note

An easy way to test the timeout exception is to add a Thread.Sleep() call within the Web method being called on the Web server. This suspends thread execution for a specified amount of time. For example:

```
System.Threading.Thread.Sleep(3000);   // Sleep 3 seconds
```

Asynchronous Calls to a Web Service Method

Asynchronous communication is performed using the Begin*methodname* and End*methodname* methods supplied by the proxy. Internally, these call the Begin-Invoke and EndInvoke methods, respectively. BeginInvoke queues the method to be run on a separate (worker) thread. It returns an `IAsyncResult` type that is subsequently passed to the `EndInvoke` method to retrieve the results. As shown in the following code, the `IAsyncResult` type is also used to determine if the call has been completed.

```
BirthDay bd = new BirthDay();
// Pass null callback argument since we will poll status
IAsyncResult dayOfWeek =bd.BeginGetDay-
Born(12,20,1963,null,null);
// Perform other operations here while waiting for response
If (dayOfWeek.IsCompleted)
    Console.Write(bd.EndGetDayBorn(dayOfWeek));
```

This "polling" approach can be used to periodically check the status of the request. Another approach is to have the Web Service call a method in the client code when the response is ready. The `AsyncCallback` delegate is used to specify the method that receives the callback.

```
// Create delegate that specifies method to be called back
AsyncCallback wscb = new AsyncCallback(DayReturned);
BirthDay bd = new BirthDay();
IAsyncResult dayOfWeek =
    bd.BeginGetDayBorn(12,20,1963,wscb,null);
// This method is called back when the web method completes
public static void DayReturned(IAsyncResult result)
{
    BirthDay bd = new BirthDay();
    Console.WriteLine(bd.EndGetDayBorn(result));
}
```

As with polling, the method implementing `EndInvoke` (`EndGetDayBorn`, in this example) is called to return the result.

Event-Based Asynchronous Calls

If you take a close look at the proxy code in Listing 18-2, you'll notice that it includes a delegate and corresponding event declaration:

```
public event GetDayBornCompletedEventHandler
    GetDayBornCompleted;

public delegate void GetDayBornCompletedEventHandler(
    object sender, GetDayBornCompletedEventArgs args);
```

These enable client code to treat the Web Service invocation as an event that can be handled by a local event handler. Only a few lines of code are required to hook up an event handler to the event defined in the proxy:

```
Birthday service = new Birthday();
// (1) Associate event handler with event
service.GetDayBornCompleted += new
     GetDayBornCompletedEventHandler(this.ShowOutput);
// (2) Invoke service asynchronously
service.GetDayBornAsync();
// (3) Event handler called when service returns value
private void ShowOutput(object sender,
     GetDayBornCompletedEventArgs args)
{
   Console.WriteLine(args.Result);
}
```

The Web Service is invoked asynchronously by calling the proxy provided method GetDayBornAsync (<web service name>Async). When the Web Service finishes execution, .NET returns the results to the event handler through the args parameter.

Using the CookieContainer Property to Maintain Session State

Setting a Web Service method's EnableSession attribute to true enables the method to maintain state information. However, this is only effective if the client can accept cookies. This is not usually a problem with browsers, but Windows Forms (WinForms) applications do not store cookies by default. The CookieContainer property is a way to permit WinForms clients to accept cookies.

To permit the client to accept cookies, set the CookieContainer property of the proxy class instance to a CookieContainer object. The code shown here permits the Web Service to maintain state information over all queries made by this client.

```
// BirthDay bd = new BirthDay() .. must have class level scope
if (bd.CookieContainer == null)
    bd.CookieContainer = new CookieContainer();
IAsyncResult dayOfWeek =  bd.BeginGetDay-
Born(mo,dy,yr,null,null);
Console.WriteLine(bd.EndGetDayBorn(dayOfWeek));
// List all cookies in CookieContainer collection
// Create a Uniform Resource Identifier object
Uri hostURL = new Uri("http://localhost");
foreach (Cookie ck in bd.CookieContainer.GetCookies(hostURL))
Console.WriteLine(ck.Name+" "+ck.TimeStamp.ToString());
```

Notice that the `CookieContainer` class has a method `GetCookies` that returns a collection of cookies stored in the container. In the example, `foreach` is used to enumerate the collection and list the name of each cookie along with the date it was created.

Creating a Proxy with Visual Studio.NET

We have shown how the proxy code can be generated using `wsdl.exe` and compiled into a DLL or used as source code within the client application. If you use VS.NET to create your Web Service client, you have no need for the `wsdl.exe` utility. Instead, VS.NET lets you select a Web Service for which you want to generate the proxy code. It adds the code to the project, and you can use the techniques described in the preceding examples to access it. Here are the details:

1. Open up .NET and select a Windows application.
2. Select Add Web Reference under the Project menu tab. The subsequent screen contains a text box at the top in which you enter the URL of the Web Service. For example:

    ```
    http://localhost/ws/BirthDayWS.asmx
    ```

3. Press the Enter key and a screen appears that includes a Web Service Help page for the selected service. Click the Add Reference button and the source code containing the proxy is added to the project.
4. The proxy code has its own namespace that should be added to the client code. In this example, `wsdlclient` is the name of the VS.NET project.

    ```
    using wsdlclient.localhost;
    ```

You will see that a `Web References` folder has been added to the directory of the project. To view the proxy source, click the Show All Files buttons in the Solution Explorer and open the `Reference.cs` file beneath the `localhost` node. Notice that in addition to the proxy code, the directory includes the WSDL file from which the proxy was generated. We'll look at this file in detail in the next section to gain an understanding of how WSDL describes a Web Service. In addition, we will look at how SOAP is used to define the format of messages transported between the Web Service consumer and provider.

18.4 Understanding WSDL and SOAP

The purpose of this section is to add some depth to the topic of Web Services—to look underneath at the XML grammar that is used to describe the service (WSDL) and the protocol (SOAP) used for transporting data between the service and client. Be aware that both of these have been submitted to the World Wide Web Consortium (W3C), but neither is an official standard.

Web Services Description Language (WSDL)

WSDL is broadly defined as "an XML format for describing network services as a set of endpoints operating on messages containing either document-oriented or procedure-oriented information."[2] In our case, the endpoints are the client and a Web Service, and WSDL defines how the client interacts with the service.

When developing a Web Service from the ground up, it is good practice to develop the interface definition first—in the form of WSDL—and then map it to the implementation code. Although the sheer complexity of WSDL demands that WSDL editors be used for the task, there is still a need for the developer to have a general understanding of the WSDL structure. The same is true even if you work only on the client side and use wsdl.exe to create source code directly from the WSDL. Problems can arise using utilities and editors that require a familiarity with the format in order to perform troubleshooting. For example, a well-designed WSDL interface is often built from multiple documents tied together by an XML import element. Being familiar with the semantics and existence of the import element goes a long way toward solving import issues—a not uncommon source of WSDL errors.

This section introduces the basic structure of WSDL, which should satisfy the curiosity of the occasional Web Service consumer or developer. Those interested in learning more should refer to the specification that is published by W3C at http://www.w3.org/TR/wsdl.

The WSDL Structure

Specifications for the WSDL grammar define six major elements: definitions, types, message, port type, binding, and service. Let's discuss these within the context of the WSDL file that describes the sample BirthDayWS Web Service.

---

2. Web Services Descriptive Language (WSDL) 1.1—W3C Note, March 15, 2002.

<Definitions>

This is the root element of the WSDL document. It declares multiple namespaces used throughout the document, and contains all of the other elements:

```
<definitions xmlns:http="http://schemas.xmlsoap.org/wsdl/http/"
    xmlns:soap="http://schemas.xmlsoap.org/wsdl/soap/"
    xmlns:s="http://www.w3.org/2001/XMLSchema"
    xmlns:s0="http://tempuri.org/"
    xmlns:soapenc="http://schemas.xmlsoap.org/soap/encoding/"
    xmlns:tm="http://microsoft.com/wsdl/mime/textMatching/"
    xmlns:mime="http://schemas.xmlsoap.org/wsdl/mime/"
    targetNamespace="http://tempuri.org/"
    xmlns="http://schemas.xmlsoap.org/wsdl/">
```

Namespaces are used to distinguish elements because it is possible that elements from different namespaces could have the same name.

<Types>

This element contains an XSD (XML Schema Definition Language) schema that describes the data types publicly exposed by the service: the parameters passed in the Web Service request, and the response:

```
<types>
    <s:schema elementFormDefault="qualified"
        targetNamespace="http://tempuri.org/">
    <s:element name="GetDayBorn">
    <s:complexType>
    <s:sequence>
    <s:element minOccurs="1" maxOccurs="1" name="mo"
        type="s:int" />
    <s:element minOccurs="1" maxOccurs="1" name="day"
        type="s:int" />
    <s:element minOccurs="1" maxOccurs="1" name="yr"
        type="s:int" />
    </s:sequence>
    </s:complexType>
    </s:element>
    <s:element name="GetDayBornResponse">
    <s:complexType>
    <s:sequence>
    <s:element minOccurs="0" maxOccurs="1" name="GetDayBornResult"
        type="s:string" />
    </s:sequence>
    </s:complexType>
    </s:element>
    </s:schema>
</types>
```

<Message>

Defines the data that is exchanged between the Web Service provider and consumer. Each message is assigned a unique name and defines its parameters—if any—in terms of names provided by the `types` element:

```
<message name="GetDayBornSoapIn">
   <part name="parameters" element="s0:GetDayBorn" />
   </message>
   <message name="GetDayBornSoapOut">
   <part name="parameters" element="s0:GetDayBornResponse" />
   </message>
```

<PortType>

Each `<portType>` element defines the `<Message>` elements that belong to a communications transport. The name attribute specifies the name for the transport. The `<portType>` element contains `<operation>` elements that correspond to the methods in the Web Service. The `<input>` and `<output>` elements define the messages associated with the operation. Four types of operations are supported: *one-way*, in which the service receives a message; *request-response*, in which the client sends a request; *solicit-response*, in which the service first sends a message to the client; and *notification*, where the service sends a message to clients.

```
<portType name="BirthDaySoap">
   <operation name="GetDayBorn">
   <documentation>Return day of week for any date</documentation>
   <input message="s0:GetDayBornSoapIn" />
   <output message="s0:GetDayBornSoapOut" />
   </operation>
</portType>
```

<Binding>

A set of rules that describe how the `<portType>` operation is transmitted over the wire. Wire protocols available are HTTP GET, HTTP POST, and SOAP. This example demonstrates how SOAP is specified.

As acknowledgement of the importance of SOAP as a transport protocol, the WSDL 1.1 specification includes extensions for SOAP 1.1. These extension elements include `<binding>`, `<operation>`, and `<body>`.

```
<binding name="BirthDaySoap" type="s0:BirthDaySoap">
   <soap:binding transport=
      "http://schemas.xmlsoap.org/soap/http"
      style="document" />
   <operation name="GetDayBorn">
      <soap:operation soapAction="http://tempuri.org/GetDayBorn"
         style="document" />
```

```
      <input>
        <soap:body use="literal" />
      </input>
      <output>
        <soap:body use="literal" />
      </output>
    </operation>
  </binding>
```

Note that the `<operation>` element specifies the entry point for the Web method that is called on the server. One other thing to be aware of is the `style` attribute in the binding element. This value, which may be `document` or `rpc`, specifies how an operation is formatted. By default, .NET sets this value to `document`. To specify `rpc`, you must apply the `SoapRpcMethodAttribute` to the Web method:

```
[SoapRpcMethod] [WebMethod]
public string GetDayBorn(string month, int day, int yr)
```

Although there is a rather spirited debate among WSDL purists as to which is better, you can safely ignore the histrionics and use the .NET default. However, knowing your options will enable you to easily work with third parties that may have a preference.

<Service>

Identifies the location of the Web Service. Specifically, it lists the name of the Web Service class, the URL, and references the binding for this endpoint.

```
<service name="BirthDay">
  <port name="BirthDaySoap" binding="s0:BirthDaySoap">
    <soap:address location=
    "http://localhost/ws/BirthDayWs.asmx" />
  </port>
</service>
```

Simple Object Access Protocol (SOAP)

SOAP is a platform-neutral protocol for exchanging information. Its cross-platform capabilities are attributable to its use of XML to define the data being passed and support for HTTP as a communications protocol. SOAP is the most popular and flexible protocol for the exchange of information between Web Service consumers and providers. Its format allows it to define complex data structures not supported by the competing HTTP GET and POST protocols.

Our discussion of SOAP follows the same approach used with WSDL: We examine the basic features of SOAP using the request/response messages generated from the BirthDayWS Web Service example. The format of these messages is described on the Web page containing the desired method(s) of the Web Service.

A SOAP Request Message

The header for a SOAP request reveals that the SOAP request is packaged as an HTTP POST request to the server designated by the Host field. The length field specifies the number of characters in the body of the POST, and SOAPAction indicates the namespace and method to be contacted.

```
POST /ws/BirthDayWS.asmx HTTP/1.1
Host: localhost
Content-Type: text/xml; charset=utf-8
Content-Length: length
SOAPAction: "http://tempuri.org/GetDayBorn"
```

Listing 18-3 shows the XML template for the SOAP message that is sent to the server.

Listing 18-3	GetDayBorn SOAP Request Content

```
<?xml version="1.0" encoding="utf-8"?>
<soap:Envelope
xmlns:xsi="http://www.w3.org/2001/XMLSchema-instance"
xmlns:xsd="http://www.w3.org/2001/XMLSchema" xmlns:soap-
enc="http://schemas.xmlsoap.org/soap/encoding/"
xmlns:tns="http://tempuri.org/" xmlns:types="http://tem-
puri.org/encodedTypes" xmlns:soap="http://schemas.xml-
soap.org/soap/envelope/">
    <soap:Body
        soap:encodingStyle=
            "http://schemas.xmlsoap.org/soap/encoding/">
        <tns:GetDayBorn>
            <mo xsi:type="xsd:int">int</mo>
            <day xsi:type="xsd:int">int</day>
            <yr xsi:type="xsd:int">int</yr>
        </tns:GetDayBorn>
    </soap:Body>
</soap:Envelope>
```

The overall structure of a SOAP message is not complex. It is an XML document that has a mandatory root element, <Envelope>, an optional <Header> element, and a mandatory <Body>.

A SOAP envelope, as the name implies, is conceptually a container for the message. The SOAP header represents a way to extend the basic message. It may contain additional information about the message and—as we will see later—can be used to add a measure of security. The SOAP body contains what one would regard as the actual data: the arguments sent to the service and the response. The contents of the `<Body>` element in this example consist of the method name and its three parameters that correspond to the call made within the client code:

```
string dayOfWeek = bd.GetDayBorn(12,20,1963);
```

A SOAP Response Message

The SOAP body of the response includes a `<GetDayBornResult>` element (see Listing 18-4) that contains the response from the Web Service and identifies it as a string type.

Listing 18-4	GetDayBorn SOAP Response Content

```xml
<?xml version="1.0" encoding="utf-8"?>
<soap:Envelope
xmlns:xsi="http://www.w3.org/2001/XMLSchema-instance"
xmlns:xsd="http://www.w3.org/2001/XMLSchema" xmlns:soap-
enc="http://schemas.xmlsoap.org/soap/encoding/"
xmlns:tns="http://tempuri.org/" xmlns:types="http://tem-
puri.org/encodedTypes" xmlns:soap="http://schemas.xml-
soap.org/soap/envelope/">
   <soap:Body
      soap:encodingStyle=
         "http://schemas.xmlsoap.org/soap/encoding/">
      <tns:GetDayBornResponse>
         <GetDayBornResult
            xsi:type="xsd:string">string</GetDayBornResult>
      </tns:GetDayBornResponse>
   </soap:Body>
</soap:Envelope>
```

Using the SOAP Header for User Authentication

The optional SOAP header is available for adding miscellaneous information about its associated SOAP message. One popular use for this header is to include identification information about the user making the request. This enables user authentication to be performed by the methods within the Web Service.

Core Note

A question that arises when a Web Service is being invoked from a Web page is whether Forms Authentication (Chapter 17) can be used. The short answer is yes, but it requires a special implementation. Unlike a regular Web page, a Web Service does not recognize the authentication cookie created by the separate login screen. The solution is to add a login method to the Web Services that creates the authentication cookie. In addition, each service must check user authentication before performing its operation. The coding requirements are comparable to using SOAP header authentication.

Listing 18-5 demonstrates a Web Service that checks the header for an ID and password before making the service available to the requestor. It consists of the code taken from Listing 18-1 and updated to include features required to access a SOAP header.

Listing 18-5	Authenticate Web Service User by Checking SOAP Header

```
using System;
using System.Web.Services;
// Required for SoapException
using System.Web.Services.Protocols;
namespace BirthDayWS
{
// (1) Class to hold data passed in the header
   public class SOAPHeaderContent : SoapHeader
   {
      public string UserName;
      public string PassWord;
   }
   public class BirthDay : System.Web.Services.WebService
   {
      // (2) Member class accessing header data
      public SOAPHeaderContent headerInfo;
      // (3) Add SoapHeader attribute
      [WebMethod(Description="Return day of week for any date"),
         SoapHeader("headerInfo")]
      public string GetDayBorn(int mo, int day, int yr)
      {
```

```
            if (!Verify())
            {
                throw new SoapException(
                    "Valid User info not included.",
                    SoapException.ClientFaultCode);
            } else {
              bool err = false;
              string dob;
              if (mo <1 || mo >12) err=true;
              if (day < 1 || day > 31) err=true;
              if ( ! err)
              {
                 DateTime dt = new DateTime(yr,mo,day);
                 dob = dt.ToString("dddd"); // extracts day
              } else {
                 dob = "Invalid Date";
              }
              return(dob);
            }
        }
        // Method to check password and ID in SOAP header
        private bool Verify()
        {
            // (4) Access data in header
            if (headerInfo.UserName != "Vincent" ||
                headerInfo.PassWord != "arles")
            { return(false);
            } else { return(true);}
        }
    }
}
```

This example illustrates the four steps that are followed to receive and access any SOAP header data:

1. Create a class to represent the data in the header. This class must inherit from the SoapHeader class. SOAPHeaderContent serves the purpose in this code.

2. Add a member to the Web Service class that is the same type as the class created in Step 1. The example uses headerInfo.

3. Apply a `SoapHeader` attribute that references the member created in Step 2. Applying this to a method makes the information in the header available to the method.

4. Process the header data by accessing the members of the class created in Step 1. The `Verify` method contains the simple logic to check `PassWord` and `UserName`. In reality, the comparison information would come from a database rather than being hardcoded.

The proxy for this Web Service includes the class that represents the header contents. The client creates an instance of this class and assigns a password and user name. The class instance is assigned to a field that is now a member of the proxy class representing the Web Service class. In this example, `Birthday` now has a field named `SOAPHeaderContentValue`. As you have probably guessed, .NET creates this field name by appending `Value` to the name of the class that accesses the header info (`SOAPHeader`).

```
using System;
using System.Web.Services;
using system.Web.Services.Protocols;
using System.Text.RegularExpressions;
public class BirthDayClient
{
    static void Main(string[] args)
    {
        SOAPHeaderContent acctInfo = new SOAPHeaderContent();
        acctInfo.UserName = "Vincent";
        acctInfo.PassWord = "arles";
        BirthDay bd = new BirthDay();
        bd.SOAPHeaderContentValue = acctInfo;
        try {
            string dayOfWeek = bd.GetDayBorn(12,20,1963);
            Console.WriteLine(dayOfWeek);
        } catch (SoapException ex)
            {
                // Extract Soap error message
                // Be sure to add:
                // using System.Text.RegularExperssions
                Match errMatch = Regex.Match(ex.Message,":(.*)");
                Console.WriteLine(errMatch.Groups[1]);
            }
    }
}
```

Handling SOAP Exceptions

As shown in Listing 18-5, the Web Service throws an exception if the user name and password cannot be authenticated:

```
throw new SoapException("Valid User info not included.",
    SoapException.ClientFaultCode);
```

The exception is rendered as a `SoapException` object. In this example, its constructor receives a message and a SOAP *fault code* that signifies the type of error. This information is returned to the client as a `<Fault>` element in the SOAP body and is converted by the .NET Framework back to a `SoapException` object that can be processed by the client's code.

The `SoapException` object includes four properties that provide information about the exception:

- `Message`. The error message that explains the reason for the exception.
- `Actor`. The URL of the Web Service that threw the exception.
- `Code`. An `XMLQualifiedName` object that specifies one of four SOAP fault codes that categorize the exception. These fault codes are represented as static fields of the `SoapException` class.
- `Detail`. An `XMLNode` object containing application-specific information about the error.

The `Message` and `Code` properties are used most frequently in processing a SOAP exception. The message is verbose: It consists of the full namespace qualification of the `SoapException` class followed by the actual message and the name of the Web method where the exception occurred. A regex was used in the preceding client code to extract the actual message.

The `SoapException` class contains static fields that can be compared with the `Code` value to broadly classify the exception. These fields include the following:

- `VersionMismatchFaultCode`. The SOAP envelope has an invalid namespace.
- `ClientFaultCode`. The message sent by the client is incorrectly formatted or contains incorrect information.
- `ServerFaultCode`. The error occurs on the server and is not related to the SOAP message. An example would be a network or hardware problem.
- `MustUnderstandFaultCode`. A SOAP element marked with the `MustUnderstand` attribute set to `true` is not processed. This is an attribute that indicates the particular element must be processed.

Here is a code sample that demonstrates using the Code property. It first extracts a message embedded in the Message property and prints it. Then it checks the Code property to classify the excepton.

```
try {
      string dayOfWeek = bd.GetDayBorn(12,20,1963);
      Console.WriteLine(dayOfWeek);
}
catch (SoapException ex)
    {
        Match errMatch = Regex.Match(ex.Message,":(.*)");
        Console.WriteLine(errMatch.Groups[1]);
        // Check various fault codes here
        if(ex.Code == SoapException.ClientFaultCode)
        {
            Console.WriteLine("Problem with Client message.");
        }
        if(ex.Code == SoapException.ServerFaultCode)
        {
            Console.WriteLine("Problem with Server. Try again.");
        }
    }
```

SOAP Security

The preceding example illustrates a lightweight technique for using SOAP headers to authenticate a user. Its main drawback is that the contents of the SOAP headers are passed as cleartext. To overcome this, you can add a layer of encryption by using this technique in conjunction with Secure Sockets Layer (SSL).

As an alternative to this and other ad hoc approaches to SOAP security, there is now a *Web Services Security* (WS-Security) specification[3] that defines enhancements to SOAP messaging. Its objectives are to ensure the following:

- **Authentication.** How a SOAP message expresses the identity of its sender.
- **Integrity.** How to verify that a SOAP message has not been tampered with.
- **Confidentiality.** What protects the contents of a SOAP message from being read by an intermediary.

---

3. http://docs.oasis-open.org/wss/2004/01/
   oasis-200401-wss-soap-message-security-1.0.pdf

In support of this specification, Microsoft provides an add-on to the .NET Framework known as *Web Services Enhancements 2.0* (WSE 2.0). This tool set comprises a .NET class library that can be used to integrate the WS-Security specification into Web Service applications. Note that the use of these enhancements requires .NET on both the client and service provider endpoints, so it's not yet a generic Web Service security solution. See the MSDN Web site, `msdn.microsoft.com/webservices/webservices/building/wse/default.aspx`, for whitepapers and a free download of the enhancements library

18.5 Using Web Services with Complex Data Types

The `BirthDayWS` Web Service used throughout this chapter accepts integers as input and returns a `string` value. This is useful for introducing Web Service principles because HTTP GET, HTTP POST, and SOAP all support it. However, Web Services also have the capability of serving up more complex data types such as data sets, hash tables, images, and custom objects.

Before data can be sent to or from a Web Service, it is serialized using XML serialization. Conversely, it is deserialized on the receiving end so it can be restored to its original type. As we saw in Chapter 4, "Working with Objects in C#," not all data can be serialized. Thus, when designing a Web Service, it is important to understand restrictions that apply to serialization:

- XML serialization can only be used with classes that contain a public parameterless constructor. For example, you may have a Web Service that returns a hash table because it has the constructor `public Hashtable()`. On the other hand, the `Bitmap` class does not have a parameterless constructor and cannot be used as a return type.
- Read-only properties in a class cannot be serialized. The property must have a `get` and `set` accessor and be public.
- Fields must be public to be serialized; private ones are ignored.

In this section, we work with two Web Service examples that illustrate the use of complex data. Our first example creates a Web Service that accepts the name of an image and returns it as a byte stream. The second example creates a client to use the Amazon Web Services provided by Amazon.com, Inc. These services offer a rich—but practical—sampling of accessing multiple Web methods and processing a wide variety of custom classes.

A Web Service to Return Images

Image manipulation usually requires representing an image as a `Bitmap` object. However, because bitmaps cannot be serialized and transferred directly, we must find an indirect way to transport an image. The not-so-difficult solution is to break the image into bytes and return a byte stream to the client, who is responsible for transforming the stream to an image.

The logic on the server side is straightforward: a `FileStream` is opened and associated with the image file. Its contents are read into memory and converted to a byte array using

```
tempStream.ToArray()
```

This byte array is then sent to the Web client (see Listing 18-6).

Listing 18-6   Web Service to Return an Image as a String of Bytes

```csharp
<%@ WebService Language="C#" Class="WSImages" %>
using System;
using System.Web.Services;
using System.IO;
using System.Web.Services.Protocols;
public class WSImages: System.Web.Services.WebService {
    [WebMethod(Description="Request an Image")]
    public byte[] GetImage(string imgName) {
        byte[] imgArray;
        imgArray = getBinaryFile("c:\\"+imgName+".gif");
        if (imgArray.Length <2)
        {
            throw new SoapException(
              "Could not open image on server.",
               SoapException.ServerFaultCode);
        } else
        {
            return(imgArray);
        }
    }
    public byte[] getBinaryFile(string filename)
    {
        if(File.Exists(filename)) {
            try {
                FileStream s = File.OpenRead(filename);
                return ConvertStreamToByteBuffer(s);
            }
```

Listing 18-6   Web Service to Return an Image as a String of Bytes

```
        catch(Exception e)
        {
            return new byte[0];
        }
    } else { return new byte[0]; }
}
// Write image to memory as a stream of bytes
public byte[] ConvertStreamToByteBuffer(Stream imgStream) {
    int imgByte;
    MemoryStream tempStream = new MemoryStream();
    while((imgByte=imgStream.ReadByte())!=-1) {
        tempStream.WriteByte(((byte)imgByte));
    }
    return tempStream.ToArray();   // Convert to array of bytes
}
}
```

Our client code receives the byte stream representing an image and reassembles it into a `Bitmap` object. Because the `Bitmap` constructor accepts a stream type, we convert the byte array to a `MemoryStream` and pass it to the constructor. It can now be manipulated as an image.

```
WSImages myImage = new WSImages();
try {
    // Request an image from the Web Service
    byte[] image = myImage.GetImage("stanwyck");
    MemoryStream memStream = new MemoryStream(image);
    Console.WriteLine(memStream.Length);
    // Convert memory stream to a Bitmap
    Bitmap bm = new Bitmap(memStream);
    // Save image returned to local disk
    bm.Save("c:\\bstanwyck.jpg",
        System.Drawing.Imaging.ImageFormat.Jpeg);
}
catch (WebException ex)
{
    Console.WriteLine(ex.Message);
}
```

Using Amazon Web Services

To use the Amazon E-Commerce Service, you must register for a developer's token, which is required as part of all requests made to the Web Services. In addition, you should download (http://www.amazon.com/webservices) the developer's kit that contains the latest documentation, examples, and—most importantly—a WSDL file defining all the services.

An examination of the WSDL file reveals that AmazonSearchService is the Web Service class that contains the numerous search methods available to clients. These methods provide the ability to search the Amazon product database by keyword, author, artist, ISBN number, manufacturer, actor, and a number of other criteria. Each search method takes a search object as an argument that describes the request to the server and returns a ProductInfo object. For example, a request to search by keywords looks like this:

```
AmazonSearchService amazon = new AmazonSearchService();
KeywordRequest kwRequest = new KeywordRequest();
// Set fields for kwRequest
ProductInfo products = amazon.KeywordSearchRequest(kwRequest);
```

Sending a Request with the AmazonSearchService Class

Table 18-3 contains a sampling of the methods available for searching Amazon products. These methods are for accessing the Web Service synchronously. An asynchronous form of each method is also available that can be accessed using the techniques discussed earlier in this chapter.

Table 18-3   Selected Methods of AmazonSearchService Class

Method	Description
ProductInfo KeyWordSearchRequest (KeywordRequest req)	Method to return items that contain one or more keywords provided in request.
ProductInfo AsinSearchRequest (AsinRequest req)	Method to return a book having a requested Amazon Standard Identification Number (ASIN) that is the same as the book's ISBN. Represented as a 10-digit string.
ProductInfo AuthorSearchRequest (AuthorRequest req)	Method to return names of all books by requested author.

Table 18-3   Selected Methods of `AmazonSearchService` Class *(continued)*

Method	Description
`ProductInfo ActorSearchRequest` `(ActorRequest req)`	Method to return video titles of movies in which a specified actor or actress was a cast member.
`ProductInfo PowerSearchRequest` `(PowerRequest req)`	Method to retrieve book information based on a Boolean query that may include a combination of title, subject, author, keyword, ISBN, publisher, language, and publication date (pubdate).

Each call to a Web method passes an object that describes the search request. This object is different for each method—for example, `AuthorSearchRequest` requires an `AuthorRequest` object, whereas `KeyWordSearchRequest` requires an instance of the `KeywordRequest` class. These classes expose almost identical fields. Each contains a unique string field that represents the search query, five other required fields common to each class, and some optional fields for sorting or specifying a locale. Table 18-4 lists unique and shared fields for each method listed in Table 18-3.

Table 18-4   Selected Fields for Classes That Define a Search Request

Field	Description

`KeywordRequest.Keyword`
`AsinRequest.Asin`
`ActorRequest.Actor`
`AuthorRequest.Author`
`PowerRequest.Power`
	These are string values containing the search value or query. For example:
	
	`PowerRequest pr = new PowerRequest();`
	`    pr.Power = "author:Nabokov and`
	`    keyword:butterfly";`

`string page`	Page of results to display.
`string mode`	Type of products being searched—for example, `"books"`.
`string tag`	Amazon associate's ID. Use `"webservices-20"` as default.
`string type`	`"lite"` or `"heavy"`. Determines how much XML data is returned.
`string devtag`	Developer's token assigned to you by Amazon.

Using the ProductInfo Class to Process the Web Service Response

The Web Service responds to the search request with a `ProductInfo` object containing results from the search. This object exposes three important fields: a `Total-Results` string contains the number of products retrieved by the request, a `TotalPages` string that indicates how many pages these results are displayed in, and the important `Details` array that contains a detailed description of products that constitute one returned page of results. This array is of the `Details` type. Table 18-5 shows the fields that are related to books.

Table 18-5   Selected Fields of the `Details` Class

Field	Description
`string ProductName`	Name of a single product.
`string SalesRank`	Ranking of product based on sales of items of its type.
`string Publisher`	Publisher of book.
`String ListPrice` `string OurPrice`	List and sales price of book.

`Reviews[] Reviews`	The `Reviews` class contains several fields relating to reviews of the book:
	
	`string AvgCustomerRating`
	`string TotalCustomerReviews`
	`CustomerReview CustomerReviews`
	`string Comment`
	`string Rating`

`String[] Authors`	One or more authors for the book.

This is only a small sample of the fields available in the `Details` class. There is a particularly rich set of fields worth exploring that define video products.

Creating a Proxy for the Amazon Web Services

Our first step is to create a proxy class from the Amazon WSDL information. The downloadable kit includes a WSDL file, and it can also be retrieved from the Internet, as we do here. Using the VS.NET command line, we place the proxy source code in the file `AZProxy.cs`.

```
wsdl.exe  /out:c:\client\AZProxy.cs
       http://soap.amazon.com/schema3/AmazonWebServices.wsdl
```

Next, we create an assembly, AZProxy.dll, containing the proxy that will be used by client code. It is linked to assemblies containing .NET Web classes required by the application.

```
csc/t:library /r:system.web.services.dll /r:system.xml.dll
       AZProxy.cs
```

You can make a quick test of the service using this barebones application, azclient.cs:

```
using System;
using System.Web.Services;
namespace webclient.example {
public class AmazonClient
{
    static void Main(string[] args)
    {
        // Search for books matching keyword "butterflies"
        AmazonSearchService amazon = new AmazonSearchService();
        KeywordRequest kwRequest = new KeywordRequest();
        kwRequest.keyword = "butterflies";
        kwRequest.type = "heavy";
        kwRequest.devtag= "*************"; // your developer token
        kwRequest.mode = "books";          // search books only
        kwRequest.tag = "webservices-20";
        kwRequest.page = "1";               // return first page
        ProductInfo products =
            amazon.KeywordSearchRequest(kwRequest);
        Console.WriteLine(products.TotalResults);  // Results count
    }
}
}
```

Compile and execute this from the command line:

```
csc /r:AZProxy.dll azclient.cs
azclient
```

When azclient.exe is executed, it should print the number of matching results.

Building a WinForms Web Service Client

Let's design a Windows Forms application that permits a user to perform searches on books using multiple search options. Open VS.NET and select a Windows application. After this is open, we need to add a reference to the proxy assembly AZProxy.dll. From the menu, select Project – Add Reference – Browse. Click the assembly when it is located and then click OK to add it as a reference. You also need to add a reference to System.Web.Services.dll, which contains the required Web Service namespaces.

The purpose of the application is to permit a user to search the Amazon book database by keyword, author, or title. The search can be on a single field on a combination of fields. Figure 18-7 shows the interface for entering the search values and viewing the results. The Search buttons submit a search request based on the value in their corresponding text box. The Power Search button creates a query that logically "ands" any values in the text boxes and submits it.

A single page of results is displayed in a ListView control. Beneath the control are buttons that can be used to navigate backward and forward through the results pages.

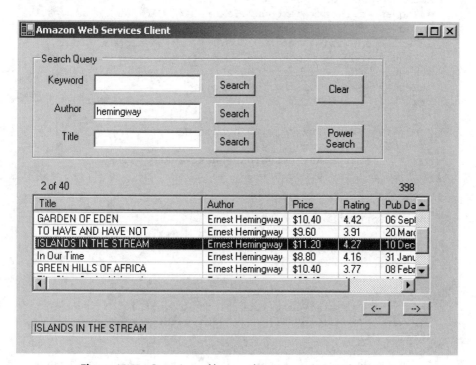

Figure 18-7   Overview of how a client accesses a Web Service

Each Search button has a Click event handler that calls a method to create an appropriate request object and send it to the Amazon Web Service. A successful call returns a ProductInfo object containing information about up to 10 books meeting the search criteria. Listing 18-7 displays code that creates an AuthorRequest object, sends it to the Web Service, and calls FillListView to display the results in the ListView control.

Listing 18-7   Client Code to Display Results of Author Search—
azwsclient.cs

```
// Fields having class-wide scope
int CurrPg;                    // Current page being displayed
string SearchMode = "";        // Current search mode
int MaxPages =1;               // Number of pages available
// This method is called when author Search button is clicked
private bool AuthorReq()
{
   AmazonSearchService amazon = new AmazonSearchService();
   AuthorRequest auRequest = new AuthorRequest();
   auRequest.author = textBox2.Text;     // Get author from GUI
   auRequest.type = "heavy";
   auRequest.devtag= "****KLMJFLGV9";    // Developer token
   auRequest.mode = "books";
   auRequest.tag = "webservices-20";
   auRequest.page = CurrPg.ToString();
   try
   {
       // Call Web Service with author query
       ProductInfo products =
             amazon.AuthorSearchRequest(auRequest);
       FillListView(products);
       return(true);
   }
   catch (SoapException ex)
   {
       MessageBox.Show(ex.Message);
       return(false);
   }
}
private void FillListView(ProductInfo products)
   listView1.Items.Clear();   // Remove current entries
   label6.Text="";            // Clear any title
   label4.Text = products.TotalResults;
   label5.Text = CurrPg.ToString()+" of "+products.TotalPages;
```

Listing 18-7	Client Code to Display Results of Author Search— `azwsclient.cs` *(continued)*

```
{
    MaxPages =  Convert.ToInt32(products.TotalPages);
    ListViewItem rowItem;
    string auth,rev;
    for (int i=0; i< products.Details.Length; i++)
    {
        rowItem = new
            ListViewItem(products.Details[i].ProductName);
        // Add Author. Make sure author exists.
        object ob = products.Details[i].Authors;
        if (ob != null)   auth =
            products.Details[i].Authors[0]; else auth="None";
        rowItem.SubItems.Add(auth);
        // Add Price
        rowItem.SubItems.Add(products.Details[i].OurPrice);
        // Add Average Rating
        ob = products.Details[i].Reviews;
        if (ob != null)   rev =
            products.Details[i].Reviews.AvgCustomerRating;
            else rev="None";
        rowItem.SubItems.Add(rev);
        // Add Date Published
        rowItem.SubItems.Add(
            products.Details[i].ReleaseDate);
        listView1.Items.Add(rowItem);
    }
}
```

The keyword, title, and power searches use an identical approach: Each has a routine comparable to `AuthorReq` that creates its own request object. The only significant difference pertains to the power search that creates a Boolean query from the search field values. The format for this type query is `field:value   AND   field2:value   AND field3:value`. For example:

```
"author:hemingway AND keywords:Kilimanjaro"
```

This application was designed as a Windows Forms application. It could just as easily be set up as Web page under ASP.NET. The code to reference the assembly `AZProxy.dll` is identical. The `ListView` control is not supported on a Web Form, but you could easily substitute a `DataGrid` for it.

18.6 Web Services Performance

The performance of a Web Service from both the client and server side is affected by a variety of factors. Some are .NET related and others are inherent in the technology. The solutions for improving Web Services performance range from shaving a few milliseconds off the way .NET sends a request to simply eschewing Web Services for an alternate protocol when transferring large amounts of data. We'll look at all of these.

Configuring the HTTP Connection

Connections (HTTP) to Internet resources are managed in .NET by the `Service-Point` class. This class includes properties to specify a connection's timeout interval, set its security protocol, and manage the use of server security certificates. It also includes properties that directly affect how much delay is incurred before a Web Service request is transmitted over a network: `UseNagleAlgorithm` and `Expect100-Continue`. Despite the awkward sounding names, setting their properties is as easy as assigning a `true` or `false` value to them. The default for both is `true`.

Expect100Continue

This property determines whether a `POST` request should expect to receive a 100-Continue response from the server to indicate that the data can be posted. If this value is set to `true`, only the request header portion of a request is sent to the server. If the server finds no problem with the header, it returns a 100-Continue response, and the data is then sent. Two trips are required. If the property is set to `false`, the initial request includes the headers and data. If it is rejected by the server, the data has been sent unnecessarily; if it is accepted, a second trip is not necessary.

Because Web Service calls tend to pass small amounts of data, it can be beneficial to turn this property off. Even if a request is rejected, only a small amount of data will have been sent.

The Nagle Algorithm

One way to improve network efficiency is to reduce the number of small data packets sent across a network. To accomplish this, the software layer controlling the underlying TCP (Transmission Control Protocol) connection attempts to accumulate, or buffer, small messages into a larger TCP segment before they are sent. The technique to do this is based on the *Nagle algorithm.*[4]

---

4. RFC 896, "Congestion Control in IP/TCP Internetworks," by John Nagle, 1984.

The crux of the algorithm is that small amounts of data should continue to be collected by TCP until it receives acknowledgment to send the data. .NET institutes a delay of up to 200 milliseconds to collect additional data for a packet. For a typically small Web Service request, there may be no reason to include this delay. It's an option you can experiment with.

To set the `Expect100Continue` and `UseNagleAlgorithm` properties, it is necessary to get a reference to the `ServicePoint` object being used to handle the Web request. This is done in the proxy code on the client side. Refer to Listing 18-2, and you'll see that the proxy code consists of a class derived from the base `SoapHttp-ClientProtocol` class. By overriding the inherited `GetWebRequest` method, you can customize the `WebRequest` object before the request is sent to the Web Service.

Add the following code to override the `GetWebRequest` method. Inside the method, you use the `Uri` object to get the `ServicePoint`. Its properties can then be turned off or on to test performance:

```
// Using System.Net must be added
protected override WebRequest GetWebRequest( Uri uri)
{
    // Locate ServicePoint object used by this application
    ServicePoint sp =
        ServicePointManager.FindServicePoint(uri);
    sp.Expect100Continue = false;
    sp.UseNagleAlgorithm = false;
    return WebRequest.Create(uri);
}
```

Working with Large Amounts of Data

Although the XML format offers a great deal of flexibility in representing data, it can place a potentially large burden on a network because of the large files that can be generated. Moreover, processing XML data can require extensive memory resources on the client and server. Finally, there is the nature of a Web Service: If the transmission fails at any point, the entire response must be resent. This is in contrast to FTP and the HTTP GET verb that allow partial data transmission.

For large amounts of data, consider these options:

- Use FTP or a Web client as described in Section 17.6, "Creating a Web Client with WebRequest and WebResponse."
- Avoid calls as much as possible by caching data rather re-requesting it.
- Look at compression techniques such as HTTP transport compression or the SOAP extensions that can compress part of a Web Service message.

- Wait for new Web Service standards. Of particular note is *Message Transmission Optimization Mechanism* (MTOM), a new W3C recommendation—pushed by Microsoft—that details a method for attaching large binary data to a SOAP message.

18.7 Summary

.NET supports the development of both Web Service provider and Web Service consumer applications. On the server side, a .NET Web Service is easily constructed using a WebService directive to define the Web Service class and a WebMethod attribute to identify methods accessible to HTTP requests. For the Web Service to be used by clients, a description of the service(s) must be made available. This is the purpose of the Web Service Description Language (WSDL) contract. This XML file describes the service, the methods available, and a description of the arguments each method accepts. You can generate the contract by using a browser to navigate to a URL address that consists of the URL of the Web Service with ?WSDL appended to it.

The WSDL information is used on the client side to create a Proxy class that is used to actually communicate with the Web Service. This proxy is created using the wsdl.exe utility or within a Visual Studio.NET project as part of the Add Web Service option. The proxy defines methods that permit the Web Service methods to be accessed synchronously or asynchronously. The latter technique returns control to the application while the request is being processed.

SOAP (Simple Object Access Protocol) describes the XML format that is used to transport information between a Web Service provider and consumer. Its structure consists of an envelope, optional header, and body. The body contains the actual data or message; the header may contain annotation about the message. One such use is to include user authentication information. The main advantage of SOAP over the other two wire protocols—HTTP GET and HTTP POST—is that it supports the transmission of non-text data such as images and objects. We demonstrated this by building a client to access the Amazon Web Services.

18.8 Test Your Understanding

1. Which base class must the Web Service class inherit from for the Web Service to use the ASP.NET Session and Application objects?

2. What is the difference between a WebService attribute and a WebService directive?

3. How can we create a Web Service that exposes two methods having the same name?

4. Which `SoapHttpClientProtocol` member is used to make a synchronous call to a Web method? An asynchronous call?

5. You are using a Web Service that has heavy traffic or is subject to downtime. How can you ensure that your client program waits no longer than 10 seconds for a request?

6. Which WSDL element contains the URL of the target Web Service?
   a. `<Definitions>`
   b. `<Message>`
   c. `<Service>`
   d. `<Binding>`

7. Which attribute must be applied to a Web method for the method to access a SOAP header?

8. What three ways can a proxy be used to make asynchronous calls to a Web Service?

FEATURES SPECIFIC TO .NET 2.0 AND C# 2.0

In This Appendix

Table A-1 provides a shortcut to reference the types and classes described in this book that are supported only in .NET 2.0 and C# 2.0.

Appendix

Table A-1 .NET 2.0 and C# 2.0 Features Index

Chapter. Section	Feature	Description
2.2	`float` type	Now referred to as a `single`.

2.2	`TryParse` method	Has been added to return a Boolean value if a string can be successfully converted into the target type:
		`int iParse =`
		`    Int32.TryParse("100", out  result);`

3.2	Static class	A class containing only static members can be declared.
3.4	Property access modifier	The get and set accessors can now have modifiers: `protected set { name= value; }`
3.7	Anonymous methods	Eliminates the need for a separate event handler for delegates.
3.10	Generics syntax	New syntax that enables collection objects to be made type-safe. An application specifies the type of data a class can hold in a parameter: `myStack<T> = new myStack<T>();`

Table A-1   .NET 2.0 and C# 2.0 Features Index *(continued)*

Chapter. Section	Feature	Description
4.4	Iterators	An easier way to implement enumeration on a custom class.
4.4	`System.Collection.Generic` namespace	Holds a generic version of the collection classes. New classes include `List<>`, `Dictionary<>`, and `Stack<>`.
7.1	`DataGridView` and `MenuStrip` controls	Some new WinForms controls.
7.6	`StatusStrip` and `ToolStripProgressBar` controls	`StatusStrip` control supersedes `StatusBar`. `ToolStripProgressBar` can be displayed on a `StatusStrip`.
10.2	`XmlReaderSettings` class	New class used to define the behavior of the `XmlReader` object. Notably, it allows XML validation to be performed automatically while reading nodes.
10.4	`XmlReader.Create` method	New method that returns an instance of an `XmlReader`.

11.1	`ProviderFactory` class	Used to return connection and command objects from a specified data provider:
		`string pvdr="System.Data.SqlClient";`
		`DBProviderFactory factory;`
		`factory = DBProviderFactories.GetFactory(pvdr);`
		`DbConnection conn = factory.CreateConnection();`

11.4	`DataTable.Load()` method	Accepts a `DataReader` object as a parameter and fills a table based on `DataReader`.
12.3	`DataGridView` class	WinForms class that supersedes the `DataGrid` control. Includes a *virtual mode* that permits the application to dynamically control the contents of the grid
13.2	`GZipStream` class	Class to perform text compression.
13.3	`ParameterizedThreadStart` delegate	Permits data to be passed to a thread.
13.4	`Semaphore` class	A new synchronization class that is used to control the number of threads that can access a resource.
16.1	Partial classes	A code-behind page can now contain a partial class that extends the class in the main Web page.

Table A-1   .NET 2.0 and C# 2.0 Features Index *(continued)*

Chapter. Section	Feature	Description
16.1	`PostBackUrl` property	Permits a Web page to easily post its content to a Web page other than itself.
16.3	`GridView` control	ASP.NET's new control that supersedes the `DataGrid` control.
16.3	`AppendDataBoundItems` property	Indicates whether data bound to a list control should overwrite existing data in the control.
16.3	`DataSource` controls	The logic for accessing a data source can now be encapsulated in controls designed to serve as a bridge to a variety of data sources including SQL and XML.
16.4	`ValidationGroup` property	Allows validation controls to be grouped so that when a page is submitted, only controls whose validators are in a specific group are validated.
16.5	Master pages	Allow a Web page to be created as a template that provides a consistent interface to users. New content pages are created by replacing the placeholders in the template.
17.2	`<connectionStrings>` section	New section in the `web.config` file reserved for connection strings.
18.3	Web Service response handled as event	.NET now includes in a Web proxy a delegate and event that fire when a Web Service returns a response. An application can process the results in its custom event handler.

DataGridView
Events and
Delegates

In This Appendix

This section contains two tables that describe the events and delegates associated with the System.Windows.Forms.DataGridView control. Table B-1 contains a list of the events (first column) and corresponding delegates (second column). Table B-2 contains the parameters for the delegate.

Appendix B

The contents of both tables are generated using reflection to extract all the events in the namespace associated with the DataGridView control and write them to a text file. The output files can be sorted in a text editor and imported into word processor's table format. Alternatively, you can extend the program to create XML or HTML formatted output. Here is the code to create Table B-1. The code used to create Table B-2 follows Table B-1.

```
//  Use reflection to extract DataGridView events
using System;
using System.Reflection;
using System.Collections;
using System.IO;
class MyApp
{
    public static void Main()
    {
        // This DLL is found in the Framework version folder
        // You will need to specify the path
        Assembly myassembly =
              Assembly.LoadFrom("System.windows.forms.dll");
        Type grid  = myassembly.GetType(
              "System.Windows.Forms.DataGridView");
        Hashtable events = new Hashtable();
        StreamWriter sw = new StreamWriter("c:\\events.txt");
        foreach(EventInfo gev in grid.GetEvents())
        {
            events.Add(gev.Name, gev.EventHandlerType);
        }
```

```
    // Tab allows columns to be imported into table
    string mytab= ((char)9).ToString();
    // Write event and delegate info to file
    foreach (DictionaryEntry de in events)
        sw.WriteLine(de.Key+mytab+de.Value);
    sw.Close();
  }
}
```

Table B-1   DataGridView Events and Delegates

Note: System.Windows.Forms has been truncated to Forms in the Delegate description.

DataGridView Event	Delegate
AllowUserToAddRowsChanged	System.EventHandler
AllowUserToDeleteRowsChanged	System.EventHandler
AllowUserToOrderColumnsChanged	System.EventHandler
AlternatingRowsDefaultCellStyle Changed	System.EventHandler
AutoGenerateColumnsChanged	System.EventHandler
AutoSizeChanged	System.EventHandler
AutoSizeColumnCriteriaChanged	Forms.DataGridViewAutoSizeColumnCriteria EventHandler
AutoSizeColumnHeadersEnabledChanged	System.EventHandler
AutoSizeRowHeadersModeChanged	Forms.DataGridViewAutoSizeModeEventHandler
AutoSizeRowsModeChanged	Forms.DataGridViewAutoSizeModeEventHandler
BackColorChanged	System.EventHandler
BackgroundColorChanged	System.EventHandler
BackgroundImageChanged	System.EventHandler
BackgroundImageLayoutChanged	System.EventHandler
BindingContextChanged	System.EventHandler
BorderStyleChanged	System.EventHandler
CancelRowEdit	Forms.QuestionEventHandler
CausesValidationChanged	System.EventHandler

Table B-1 DataGridView Events and Delegates *(continued)*

DataGridView Event	Delegate
CellBeginEdit	Forms.DataGridViewCellCancelEventHandler
CellBorderStyleChanged	System.EventHandler
CellClick	Forms.DataGridViewCellEventHandler
CellContentClick	Forms.DataGridViewCellEventHandler
CellContextMenuStripChanged	Forms.DataGridViewCellEventHandler
CellContextMenuStripNeeded	Forms.DataGridViewCellContextMenuStripNeeded EventHandler
CellEndEdit	Forms.DataGridViewCellEventHandler
CellEnter	Forms.DataGridViewCellEventHandler
CellErrorTextChanged	Forms.DataGridViewCellEventHandler
CellErrorTextNeeded	Forms.DataGridViewCellErrorTextNeededEvent Handler
CellFormatting	Forms.DataGridViewCellFormattingEventHandler
CellLeave	Forms.DataGridViewCellEventHandler
CellMouseClick	Forms.DataGridViewCellMouseEventHandler
CellMouseDoubleClick	Forms.DataGridViewCellMouseEventHandler
CellMouseDown	Forms.DataGridViewCellMouseEventHandler
CellMouseEnter	Forms.DataGridViewCellEventHandler
CellMouseLeave	Forms.DataGridViewCellEventHandler
CellMouseMove	Forms.DataGridViewCellMouseEventHandler
CellMouseUp	Forms.DataGridViewCellMouseEventHandler
CellPainting	Forms.DataGridViewCellPaintingEventHandler
CellParsing	Forms.DataGridViewCellParsingEventHandler
CellStateChanged	Forms.DataGridViewCellStateChangedEventHandler
CellStyleChanged	Forms.DataGridViewCellEventHandler
CellStyleContentChanged	Forms.DataGridViewCellStyleContentChangedEvent Handler

Table B-1   DataGridView Events and Delegates *(continued)*

DataGridView Event	Delegate
CellToolTipTextChanged	Forms.DataGridViewCellEventHandler
CellToolTipTextNeeded	Forms.DataGridViewCellToolTipTextNeededEvent Handler
CellValidated	Forms.DataGridViewCellEventHandler
CellValidating	Forms.DataGridViewCellValidatingEventHandler
CellValueChanged	Forms.DataGridViewCellEventHandler
CellValueNeeded	Forms.DataGridViewCellValueEventHandler
CellValuePushed	Forms.DataGridViewCellValueEventHandler
ChangeUICues	Forms.UICuesEventHandler
Click	System.EventHandler
ColumnContextMenuStripChanged	Forms.DataGridViewColumnEventHandler
ColumnDataPropertyNameChanged	Forms.DataGridViewColumnEventHandler
ColumnDefaultCellStyleChanged	Forms.DataGridViewColumnEventHandler
ColumnDisplayIndexChanged	Forms.DataGridViewColumnEventHandler
ColumnDividerWidthChanged	Forms.DataGridViewColumnEventHandler
ColumnHeaderCellChanged	Forms.DataGridViewColumnEventHandler
ColumnHeaderMouseClick	Forms.DataGridViewCellMouseEventHandler
ColumnHeaderMouseDoubleClick	Forms.DataGridViewCellMouseEventHandler
ColumnHeadersBorderStyleChanged	System.EventHandler
ColumnHeadersDefaultCellStyleChanged	System.EventHandler
ColumnHeadersHeightChanged	System.EventHandler
ColumnMinimumWidthChanged	Forms.DataGridViewColumnEventHandler
ColumnNameChanged	Forms.DataGridViewColumnEventHandler
ColumnSortModeChanged	Forms.DataGridViewColumnEventHandler
ColumnStateChanged	Forms.DataGridViewColumnStateChangedEvent Handler
ColumnToolTipTextChanged	Forms.DataGridViewColumnEventHandler

Table B-1 `DataGridView` Events and Delegates *(continued)*

`DataGridView` Event	Delegate
ColumnWidthChanged	Forms.DataGridViewColumnEventHandler
ContextMenuChanged	System.EventHandler
ContextMenuStripChanged	System.EventHandler
ControlAdded	Forms.ControlEventHandler
ControlRemoved	Forms.ControlEventHandler
CurrentCellChanged	System.EventHandler
CurrentCellDirtyStateChanged	System.EventHandler
CursorChanged	System.EventHandler
DataBindingComplete	Forms.DataGridViewBindingCompleteEventHandler
DataError	Forms.DataGridViewDataErrorEventHandler
DataMemberChanged	System.EventHandler
DataSourceChanged	System.EventHandler
DefaultCellStyleChanged	System.EventHandler
DefaultValuesNeeded	Forms.DataGridViewRowEventHandler
Disposed	System.EventHandler
DockChanged	System.EventHandler
DoubleClick	System.EventHandler
DragDrop	Forms.DragEventHandler
DragEnter	Forms.DragEventHandler
DragLeave	System.EventHandler
DragOver	Forms.DragEventHandler
EditingControlShowing	Forms.DataGridViewEditingControlShowingEvent Handler
EditModeChanged	System.EventHandler
EnabledChanged	System.EventHandler
Enter	System.EventHandler

Table B-1   `DataGridView` Events and Delegates *(continued)*

DataGridView Event	Delegate
FontChanged	System.EventHandler
ForeColorChanged	System.EventHandler
GiveFeedback	Forms.GiveFeedbackEventHandler
GotFocus	System.EventHandler
GridColorChanged	System.EventHandler
HandleCreated	System.EventHandler
HandleDestroyed	System.EventHandler
HelpRequested	Forms.HelpEventHandler
ImeModeChanged	System.EventHandler
Invalidated	Forms.InvalidateEventHandler
KeyDown	Forms.KeyEventHandler
KeyPress	Forms.KeyPressEventHandler
KeyUp	Forms.KeyEventHandler
Layout	Forms.LayoutEventHandler
Leave	System.EventHandler
LocationChanged	System.EventHandler
LostFocus	System.EventHandler
MarginChanged	System.EventHandler
MouseCaptureChanged	System.EventHandler
MouseClick	Forms.MouseEventHandler
MouseDoubleClick	Forms.MouseEventHandler
MouseDown	Forms.MouseEventHandler
MouseEnter	System.EventHandler
MouseHover	System.EventHandler
MouseLeave	System.EventHandler
MouseMove	Forms.MouseEventHandler

Table B-1   DataGridView Events and Delegates *(continued)*

DataGridView Event	Delegate
MouseUp	Forms.MouseEventHandler
MouseWheel	Forms.MouseEventHandler
Move	System.EventHandler
MultiSelectChanged	System.EventHandler
NewRowNeeded	Forms.DataGridViewRowEventHandler
PaddingChanged	System.EventHandler
Paint	Forms.PaintEventHandler
ParentChanged	System.EventHandler
QueryAccessibilityHelp	Forms.QueryAccessibilityHelpEventHandler
QueryContinueDrag	Forms.QueryContinueDragEventHandler
ReadOnlyChanged	System.EventHandler
RegionChanged	System.EventHandler
Resize	System.EventHandler
ResizeBegin	System.EventHandler
ResizeEnd	System.EventHandler
RightToLeftChanged	System.EventHandler
RowContextMenuStripChanged	Forms.DataGridViewRowEventHandler
RowContextMenuStripNeeded	Forms.DataGridViewRowContextMenuStripNeeded EventHandler
RowDefaultCellStyleChanged	Forms.DataGridViewRowEventHandler
RowDirtyStateNeeded	Forms.QuestionEventHandler
RowDividerHeightChanged	Forms.DataGridViewRowEventHandler
RowEnter	Forms.DataGridViewCellEventHandler
RowErrorTextChanged	Forms.DataGridViewRowEventHandler
RowErrorTextNeeded	Forms.DataGridViewRowErrorTextNeededEvent Handler

Table B-1   `DataGridView` Events and Delegates *(continued)*

DataGridView Event	Delegate
RowHeaderCellChanged	Forms.DataGridViewRowEventHandler
RowHeaderMouseClick	Forms.DataGridViewCellMouseEventHandler
RowHeaderMouseDoubleClick	Forms.DataGridViewCellMouseEventHandler
RowHeadersBorderStyleChanged	System.EventHandler
RowHeadersDefaultCellStyleChanged	System.EventHandler
RowHeadersWidthChanged	System.EventHandler
RowHeightChanged	Forms.DataGridViewRowEventHandler
RowHeightInfoNeeded	Forms.DataGridViewRowHeightInfoNeededEvent Handler
RowHeightInfoPushed	Forms.DataGridViewRowHeightInfoPushedEvent Handler
RowLeave	Forms.DataGridViewCellEventHandler
RowMinimumHeightChanged	Forms.DataGridViewRowEventHandler
RowPostPaint	Forms.DataGridViewRowPostPaintEventHandler
RowPrePaint	Forms.DataGridViewRowPrePaintEventHandler
RowStateChanged	Forms.DataGridViewRowStateChangedEventHandler
RowUnshared	Forms.DataGridViewRowEventHandler
RowValidated	Forms.DataGridViewCellEventHandler
RowValidating	Forms.DataGridViewCellCancelEventHandler
RowsAdded	Forms.DataGridViewRowsAddedEventHandler
RowsDefaultCellStyleChanged	System.EventHandler
RowsDeleted	Forms.DataGridViewRowsDeletedEventHandler
Scroll	Forms.ScrollEventHandler
SelectionChanged	System.EventHandler
SizeChanged	System.EventHandler
SortCompare	Forms.DataGridViewSortCompareEventHandler
Sorted	System.EventHandler

Table B-1 DataGridView Events and Delegates *(continued)*

DataGridView Event	Delegate
StyleChanged	System.EventHandler
SystemColorsChanged	System.EventHandler
TabIndexChanged	System.EventHandler
TabStopChanged	System.EventHandler
TextChanged	System.EventHandler
UserAddedRow	Forms.DataGridViewRowEventHandler
UserDeletedRow	Forms.DataGridViewRowEventHandler
UserDeletingRow	Forms.DataGridViewRowCancelEventHandler
Validated	System.EventHandler
Validating	System.ComponentModel.CancelEventHandler
VisibleChanged	System.EventHandler

This code is added to the code for the first table in order to gather information about the delegates' signature. The signatures are stored in a hash table and written to a text file of your choice. The content of the output file can then be loaded into a table with three columns.

```
Hashtable signature = new Hashtable();  // Holds signatures

events.Add(gev.Name, gev.EventHandlerType);
Type deleg = gev.EventHandlerType;
if(!signature.Contains(deleg))
{
   // Get parameters
   MethodInfo invoke = deleg.GetMethod("Invoke");
   ParameterInfo[] pars = invoke.GetParameters();
   string sig = "";
   foreach (ParameterInfo p in pars)
   {
      Console.WriteLine(p.ParameterType);
      sig += mytab +p.ParameterType  ;
   }
   signature.Add(deleg, sig);
}
```

Table B-2 `DataGridView` Delegates and Parameters

Note: The first parameter is always `System.Object`, which is not shown in the table.

Delegate	Parameter 2
`ControlEventHandler`	`Forms.ControlEventArgs`
`DataGridViewAutoSizeColumnCriteria` `EventHandler`	`Forms.DataGridViewAutoSizeColumn` `CriteriaEventArgs`
`DataGridViewAutoSizeModeEventHandler`	`Forms.DataGridViewAutoSizeModeEvent` `Args`
`DataGridViewBindingCompleteEventHandler`	`Forms.DataGridViewBindingCompleteEvent` `Args`
`DataGridViewCellCancelEventHandler`	`Forms.DataGridViewCellCancelEventArgs`
`DataGridViewCellContextMenuStripNeeded` `EventHandler`	`Forms.DataGridViewCellContextMenuStrip` `NeededEventArgs`
`DataGridViewCellErrorTextNeededEvent` `Handler`	`Forms.DataGridViewCellErrorTextNeeded` `EventArgs`
`DataGridViewCellEventHandler`	`Forms.DataGridViewCellEventArgs`
`DataGridViewCellFormattingEventHandler`	`Forms.DataGridViewCellFormattingEvent` `Args`
`DataGridViewCellMouseEventHandler`	`Forms.DataGridViewCellMouseEventArgs`
`DataGridViewCellPaintingEventHandler`	`Forms.DataGridViewCellPaintingEvent` `Args`
`DataGridViewCellParsingEventHandler`	`Forms.DataGridViewCellParsingEventArgs`
`DataGridViewCellStateChangedEventHandler`	`Forms.DataGridViewCellStateChanged` `EventArgs`
`DataGridViewCellStyleContentChangedEvent` `Handler`	`Forms.DataGridViewCellStyleContent` `ChangedEventArgs`
`DataGridViewCellToolTipTextNeededEvent` `Handler`	`Forms.DataGridViewCellToolTipText` `NeededEventArgs`
`DataGridViewCellValidatingEventHandler`	`Forms.DataGridViewCellValidatingEvent` `Args`
`DataGridViewCellValueEventHandler`	`Forms.DataGridViewCellValueEventArgs`
`DataGridViewColumnEventHandler`	`Forms.DataGridViewColumnEventArgs`
`DataGridViewColumnStateChangedEvent` `Handler`	`Forms.DataGridViewColumnStateChanged` `EventArgs`

Table B-2 `DataGridView` Delegates and Parameters *(continued)*

Delegate	Parameter 2
`DataGridViewDataErrorEventHandler`	`Forms.DataGridViewDataErrorEventArgs`
`DataGridViewEditingControlShowingEvent Handler`	`Forms.DataGridViewEditingControl ShowingEventArgs`
`DataGridViewRowCancelEventHandler`	`Forms.DataGridViewRowCancelEventArgs`
`DataGridViewRowContextMenuStripNeeded EventHandler`	`Forms.DataGridViewRowContextMenuStrip NeededEventArgs`
`DataGridViewRowErrorTextNeededEvent Handler`	`Forms.DataGridViewRowErrorTextNeeded EventArgs`
`DataGridViewRowEventHandler`	`Forms.DataGridViewRowEventArgs`
`DataGridViewRowHeightInfoNeededEvent Handler`	`Forms.DataGridViewRowHeightInfoNeeded EventArgs`
`DataGridViewRowHeightInfoPushedEvent Handler`	`Forms.DataGridViewRowHeightInfoPushed EventArgs`
`DataGridViewRowPostPaintEventHandler`	`Forms.DataGridViewRowPostPaintEvent Args`
`DataGridViewRowPrePaintEventHandler`	`Forms.DataGridViewRowPrePaintEventArgs`
`DataGridViewRowStateChangedEventHandler`	`Forms.DataGridViewRowStateChangedEvent Args`
`DataGridViewRowsAddedEventHandler`	`Forms.DataGridViewRowsAddedEventArgs`
`DataGridViewRowsDeletedEventHandler`	`Forms.DataGridViewRowsDeletedEventArgs`
`DataGridViewSortCompareEventHandler`	`Forms.DataGridViewSortCompareEventArgs`
`DragEventHandler`	`Forms.DragEventArgs`
`GiveFeedbackEventHandler`	`Forms.GiveFeedbackEventArgs`
`HelpEventHandler`	`Forms.HelpEventArgs`
`InvalidateEventHandler`	`Forms.InvalidateEventArgs`
`KeyEventHandler`	`Forms.KeyEventArgs`
`KeyPressEventHandler`	`Forms.KeyPressEventArgs`
`LayoutEventHandler`	`Forms.LayoutEventArgs`
`MouseEventHandler`	`Forms.MouseEventArgs`

Table B-2   DataGridView Delegates and Parameters *(continued)*

Delegate	Parameter 2
PaintEventHandler	Forms.PaintEventArgs
QueryAccessibilityHelpEventHandler	Forms.QueryAccessibilityHelpEventArgs
QueryContinueDragEventHandler	Forms.QueryContinueDragEventArgs
QuestionEventHandler	Forms.QuestionEventArgs
ScrollEventHandler	Forms.ScrollEventArgs
System.ComponentModel.CancelEventHandler	System.ComponentModel.CancelEventArgs
System.EventHandler	System.EventArgs
UICuesEventHandler	Forms.UICuesEventArgs

ANSWERS TO CHAPTER EXERCISES

Chapter 1

1. The .NET Framework Redistributable is required by a client to run a .NET application and is available as a free download on the Internet.

2. Managed code is produced by a compiler that meets the Common Type System (CTS) requirements that are necessary before code produced by it can be run by the Common Language Runtime (CLR). Unmanaged code does not meet the CTS standard. The Windows API and COM objects are examples of unmanaged code.

3. The Common Type System defines the types and their members that must be used by compilers that create code to run on the Common Language Runtime. The Common Language Specification provides stricter requirements that ensure interoperability between languages.

4. All .NET compilers generate an Intermediate Language (IL) code. Since IL is compatible, irrespective of its source, the CLR doesn't care which compiler produces it.

5. The Global Assembly Cache (GAC) holds shared assemblies—assemblies that can be used by more than one application. Assemblies in the GAC have a digital signature that uniquely identifies them, even if they have the same file name.

6. A strong name consists of an assembly name, a version, a culture setting, and a public key token that is required by a client to use the assembly.

7. A namespace usually identifies a group of types that provide related services. An assembly may contain one or more namespaces. Also, a namespace may contain types in more than one assembly.

8. CLR—Common Language Runtime
FCL—Framework Class Library
GAC—Global Assembly Cache
IL—Intermediate Language (also, CIL or MSIL)

Chapter 2

1. A C# program must have an entry point defined by the static `Main()` method. It accepts a string array `args` as input.

2. `//` is used for single line comments; `/* */` is used to enclose multi-line comments; and `///` is used to create XML comments that can be exported to a text file.

3. A primitive refers to a simple value type such as an `int` or `byte`.

4. `true`

5. A `do` loop is evaluated at the end of the iteration and thus must execute at least once.

6. A `break` statement causes control to exit the enclosing loop immediately; a `continue` statement continues the same loop by skipping to the beginning of the loop.

7. a does not compile because an `int` cannot be converted to a `char`.
c does not compile because a `string` cannot be converted to a `char`.

8. Each time concatenation occurs, a new string is created in memory. For a large number of concatenations, this wastes memory and also degrades performance. The `StringBuilder` class can be used as an alternative—but only where there are many concatenations. Otherwise, it will not outperform concatenation.

9. All classes inherit from `System.Object`. In addition, value types inherit from `System.ValueType`.

10. 7

Chapter 3

1. A `sealed` class cannot be inherited. A `sealed` class is used primarily when the class contains static members. Note that a `struct` is implicitly sealed.

2. A class can inherit from one class explicitly and inherits from `System.Object` implicitly. It can inherit from any number of interfaces.

3. a. ShowName is static and cannot be referenced from a class instance.

    b. ShowName.ShowMe("My Name is Ishmael");

4. An abstract class may contain both abstract and non-abstract methods.

5. new is used to replace (not override) an inherited method with one of the same name.

6. (a) x=60 y=40. x is passed by reference; y by value.

7. Include a method that performs the same operation as the operator overloading.

8. A class cannot be instantiated if it is abstract or if it has a private constructor.

9. Example event handler:

```
private void PrintSale(object sender, SaleEvArgs e)
{
    decimal prc=   (decimal)e.saleprice;
    DateTime dt =  (DateTime)e.date;
    int itemNum =  (int)e.itemnum;
    // Now print the values
}
```

10. (a) Compilation error indicating that keyword new is required on Child.amethod(int, string) because it hides the inherited method. If new is used, the code prints "Base Constructor".

Chapter 4

1. The advantages of a class factory pattern are that it can control the number of objects created, encapsulates the logic required to create an object, and makes it easier to add new products by isolating the code in the factory.

2. Custom exceptions should inherit from the ApplicationException class. Three constructors should be included: a parameterless one, a constructor accepting a string parameter, and a constructor that accepts a string and Exception object parameter.

3. System.Object.Equals bases equality on objects having the same memory location.

4. A class must implement the IEnumerable and IEnumerator interfaces to support the foreach statement.

5. Generics permit a collection to be type-safe. This means the collection class is restricted to holding and processing objects of one type. Non-generic collections can hold any mixture of objects and require casting to detect their type.

6. The `IDisposable` interface is a convenient way to notify a client that an object's `Dispose` method should be called. The client only needs to check for the existence of the interface.

7. a. `false`
    b. `true`
    c. `false`
    d. `true`

    The `Clone` method creates a copy of an object at a new address.

8. Objects with a `Finalize` method implemented are placed in a special queue so that `Finalize` can be executed before Garbage Collection occurs. This delays the actual Garbage Collection by one cycle.

Chapter 5

1. `CultureInfo` represents information about a culture. Here is an example of its use:

    ```
    CultureInfo ci = new CultureInfo("de-AT");   // German-Austria
    ```

2. `CultureInfo()` with no parameters and `Thread.CurrentThread.Current-Culture` return objects with current culture.

3. a. 2
    b. 3
    c. 1

4. Use the instance method when the expression is used repeatedly, because, unlike the static approach, it does not have to recompile the expression each time.

5. `Equals()` is used to check the memory location. If different, a character-by-character comparison is performed.

6. a. 2
    b. 1
    c. 3

7. a. `FileInfo` is not created from a `FileStream`.

8. a

9. a. `true`
    b. `true`
    c. `false`
    d. `false`

Chapter 6

1. `System.Windows.Forms.Form` is the required base class for a Windows application.

2. Docking attaches a control to an edge of its container; anchoring places a control in a fixed position relative to the edge(s) of a container. As the container is resized, the control remains a fixed distance from the edges.

3. x and y yield the coordinates. The `Button` property is set to a `MouseButtons` enumeration value.

4. The `Form.TransparencyKey` permits part of a form to appear transparent. Any part of the Form have the color assigned to this property becomes transparent. For example, to set the red portion of `myForm` to red, set the `TransparencyKey` as follows:

   ```
   myForm.TransparencyKey = Color.Red;
   ```

5. A modal form maintains focus until it is closed. A modeless form allows the parent form to regain focus.

6. The owned form is always on top, and closing or minimizing the parent also closes or minimizes the owned form.

7. `Minimize` and `Maximize` properties are set to `false`; the `HelpButton` property is set to `true`.

8. A `MouseOver` displays information associated with a control's `ToolTip`. Help text is enabled by pressing F1 or selecting the Help button and clicking a control to show context-sensitive Help.

9. Have the original event handler in the base Form call a virtual method to deal with the event. The inheriting Form then overrides the virtual method.

Chapter 7

1. Only one radio button in a group may be selected at a time. A `GroupBox` provides a way to group radio buttons logically.

2. `SizeMode = PictureBoxSizeMode.StretchImage`

3. To display selected fields of an object in a `ListBox`, override the object's `ToString()` method to display the desired fields.

4. The `SelectedIndexChanged` event is fired. Use the `SelectedIndex` to get the index of the selected item, or `SelectedItem` to get the object selected.

5. Set `View` property to `View.Details`.

6. The `Tag` property can be used to store objects.

7. DragEnter and DragDrop must be supported by a destination control for drag and drop to work.

8. Assign Browsable, Category, and Description attributes.

9. The ResourceManager class is used to access resources. Its GetString (name) method returns the value associated with a name in the text file.

Chapter 8

1. The Graphics object encapsulates the drawing surface and is used to draw; the ClipRectangle represents the area that needs to be redrawn.

2. Control.Invalidate().

3. C

4. b fails because Brush is an abstract class.

5. b is more transparent because its alpha value (200) is less than the value (255) of color a.

6. 100%. The image is scaled to fit the rectangle.

7. Here is one solution:

```
Graphics g = panel1.CreateGraphics();
g.SmoothingMode = SmoothingMode.AntiAlias;
GraphicsPath gp = new GraphicsPath();
gp.AddLine(10, 170, 30, 170);
gp.AddLine(16, 100, 100, 100);
gp.AddLine(100, 100, 190, 180);
gp.AddLine(40, 50, 50, 20);
gp.StartFigure();
gp.AddLine(50, 20, 145, 100);
gp.StartFigure();
gp.AddArc(65, 10, 120, 180, 180, 80);
gp.StartFigure();
gp.AddArc(65, 5, 120, 100, 200, 70);
g.DrawPath(new Pen(Color.Black, 2), gp);
```

8. D

Chapter 9

1. Typeface

2. Point is the default measurement for a font. It is 1/72nd of an inch.

3. Graphics.DrawString method is used. It is passed a StringFormat object that has its Alignment property set to StringAlignment.Far.

4. The third column begins at x coordinate of 310 (usually in $1/100^{ths}$ of an inch). The tab numbers are cumulative.

5. The `BeginPrint` event is fired when `PrintDocument.Print` is executed.

6. The `PrintPageEventArgs` parameter has a `MarginBounds` property that represents the margins.

7. To preview a document on the screen, you must create a `PrintPreviewDialog` object, set its `Document` property to the `PrintDocument`, and then call `ShowDialog` to display the preview:

```
PrintPreviewDialog prvDialog = new PrintPreviewDialog();
PrvDialog.Document = pd;
PrvDialog.ShowDialog();  // Show preview
```

Chapter 10

1. Use its static `Create` method to create an instance.

2. `XmlReaderSettings` defines how an `XmlReader` processes the input stream. It can specify node types to be ignored and a schema to be used for validation.

3. An `XPathDocument` is used for reading only.

4. a. Two movies nodes are retrieved: `Raging Bull` and `Taxi Driver`.
   b. One movies node is retrieved: `Taxi Driver`.
   c. One movies node is retrieved: `Raging Bull`.
   d. Two movie_Title nodes are retrieved: `Raging Bull` and `Taxi Driver`.

5. Two validation techniques were discussed in this chapter. One approach is to use the `XmlReader` class directly by setting the `Schemas` and `XsdValidate` properties to enable validation. The other approach is to use the `XmlValidatingReader` class.

Chapter 11

1. A .NET data provider must supply a connection, command, `DataReader`, and `DataAdapter` object to provide access to its data source.

2. b is the correct choice. a and c are invalid statements.

3. `ExecuteNonQuery()` executes a command but does not return a resultset. `ExecuteReader()` returns a resultset in response to a query. `ExecuteScalar()` returns a single value—or null—if the query generates no value.

4. The `DataReader` remains connected to a data source and returns data in a forward, read-only cursor. A `DataAdapter` is a bridge between a data source and

an internal data store. It typically loads data from a data source into a `DataSet`. It can also update the data source.

5. A `DataSet` object contains one or more `DataTables`.

6. `Rejected` and `Changed` are not valid `DataRowState` values. `Detached`, `Unchanged`, and `Modified` are the other values.

7. A `DataSet` schema can be created (without loading actual XML data) by

    `DataInferXmlSchema(xml file);`

Chapter 12

1. a. False
   b. True
   c. True
   d. False
   e. False
   f. False
   g. True
   h. False
   i. True

2. Simple binding occurs on a control that displays a single value; complex binding associates a control with a collection of data in a data source. In one-way data binding, the control is bound to the source for read-only purposes. Changes to the control's value are not reflected in the data source. Two-way binding permits the data source to be updated by changing the control's value(s).

3. The properties on a custom data source that expose the bound data must be writable, so the object can be updated.

4. `DataGridView.SelectionMode =`
   `DataGridViewSelectionMode.FullRowSelect;`

5. A `ListBox` cannot be included in a `DataGridView` cell. Other controls that can be included are a `Link`, `CheckBox`, and `Image`.

6. To freeze a column, set the column's `Frozen` property to `true`. The column and all to its left remain visible during scrolling.

    `dgv.Columns[1].Frozen=true;`

Chapter 13

1. False. An asynchronous delegate may have a return value.

2. ia is an IAsyncResult object returned by BeginInvoke that is later passed to EndInvoke.

   p1 is a string parameter defined in the delegate's signature.

   p2 is an optional callback method.

   p3 is a value that can be passed to the callback method when the thread ends.

3. Thread Local Storage (TLS) holds state information about a thread. This is required when a thread is swapped out before completion.

4. The default number of threads in a thread pool is 25.

5. ThreadStart and ParameterizedThreadStart delegates are used to create a thread. The latter permits parameters to be passed to a thread.

6. lock (this) {   } expands into an identical construct.

7. a. The message is never printed because the semaphore is created with zero initial threads, and then goes into a wait state.

8. b. It prints "Primary Thread" followed by "Worker Thread".

   The mutex in the main thread is created with ownership. The spawned thread's mutex must wait for the original one to finish before its thread continues processing.

9. There are many solutions. Here is one based on not grabbing a chopstick until both are available:

```
using System;
using System.Threading;
class Stick {
  //Sticks available are designated as true
  bool[] chopStick = {true, true, true, true, true};
  // Attempt to pick up left and right chopstick
  public void GetSticks(int left, int right)
  {
    lock (this)
    {
      // Release lock and wait until both chopsticks are free
      while (!chopStick[left] && !chopStick[right])
        Monitor.Wait(this);
      chopStick[right] = false; chopStick[left] = false;
    }
  }

  // Put chopsticks down
  public void FreeSticks(int left, int right)
  {
    lock(this)
    {
      chopStick[right] = true;
```

```
          chopStick[left]   = true;
          // Signal threads in queue that chopsticks are available
          Monitor.PulseAll(this);
      }
    }
}
class Philosopher
{
    int n;                 // Philosopher number
    int eatDelay;
    int thinkDelay;
    int left, right;
    Stick chopSticks;
    public Philosopher (int n, int thinkTime, int eatTime,
                        Stick sticks)
    {
      this.n = n;
      this.eatDelay   = eatTime;
      this.thinkDelay = thinkTime;
      this.chopSticks = sticks;
      // Fifth philosopher has chopstick 1 on left
      left = n == 5 ? 1 : n+1;
      right = n;
      new Thread(new ThreadStart(Run)).Start();
    }

    public void Run()
    {
      while(true)
      {
        try
        {
          // Philosopher thinks for random amount of time
          Thread.Sleep(thinkDelay);
          chopSticks.GetSticks(left-1, right-1);
          Console.WriteLine("Philosopher {0} is eating for
                            {1} ms ",n, eatDelay);
          Thread.Sleep(eatDelay);
          chopSticks.FreeSticks(left-1, right-1);
        } catch { return; }
      }
    }
}     // End of class Philosopher

public class Diners
{
  public static void Main()
```

```
    {
        Stick sticks = new Stick();
        // Create thread for each philosopher
        // Eat time is random
        Random r = new Random(DateTime.Now.Millisecond);
        new Philosopher(1, 100, r.Next(500), sticks);
        new Philosopher(2, 200, r.Next(500), sticks);
        new Philosopher(3, 300, r.Next(500), sticks);
        new Philosopher(4, 400, r.Next(500), sticks);
        new Philosopher(5, 500, r.Next(500), sticks);
    }
}
```

Chapter 14

1. a. True. A process may contain multiple AppDomains.
    b. True. An AppDomain may contain multiple assemblies.
    c. True. An AppDomain may contain .dll and .exe files.
    d. True. An AppDomain can be unloaded from a process.

2. Three activation modes: client activation, server activation (single call), and server activation (singleton). HTTP or TCP can be used with all.

3. Single call server activation creates a new object on each call; single call singleton creates an object on the first call only. The object is then used for other calls.

4. CurrentLeaseTime—Amount of time until object is available for Garbage Collection.
    InitialLeaseTime—Initial lifetime of a lease.
    RenewalOnCallTime—Amount that CurrentLeaseTime is increased on called object.

5. Set the LeaseManagerPoolTime in a configuration file to specify how frequently the lease manager checks for expirations.

6. Client-activated and server-activated singleton use leases.

7. c. A server-activated singleton object is created when the first call is made to the host object.

8. Channel registration indicates the type of protocol to be used—usually TCP or HTTP—in the remoting and the port number to be used. Type registration specifies the available remote object and the activation mode type.

9. An interface or SoapSuds is used to prevent having to place a full assembly on the remoting client's machine. The assembly provides metadata, but can also expose proprietary code. An interface provides only the metadata a client requires. SoapSuds extracts the metadata and places it in a file that is deployed on the client's machine.

Chapter 15

1. a. False. Only a strongly named assembly may be placed in the GAC—but it does not have to be there.

   b. False. The compiler does not automatically check the GAC for references.

   c. True. The CLR checks the GAC for assembly references.

   d. True. A client must have a valid public key token to use an assembly in the GAC.

2. A `Permission` attribute should be added to the assembly, specifying the permission(s) required by the assembly.

3. A strong name consists of a simple name, version number, culture info, and public key token.

4. Assign version: `[assembly: AssemblyVersion("1.1.0.1")]`

   Assign culture: `[assembly: AssemblyCulture("fr-CA")]`

   The default build number is the number of days since 1/1/2000; the default revision number is the number of seconds past midnight divided by 2.

5. The `IStackWalk` interface defines the `Assert`, `Deny`, and `PermitOnly` methods to modify a stack walk. `Assert` stops the walk; `Deny` specifies permissions that cause the walk to fail; and `PermitOnly` specifies the only permissions that do not cause the stack walk to fail..

6. Delayed signing refers to using a public key to create a digital signature, as opposed to using the private key. When the final assembly is ready, the private key replaces the public key for encryption. This reduces the need to expose the private key during development.

7. A predefined permission is an individual permission class provided by .NET. A named permission set is a predefined set of permission objects. A security zone classifies where an assembly originates: `Internet`, `Intranet`, `MyComputer`, `NoZone`, `Trusted`, `Untrusted`.

8. a. True.

   b. True.

   c. False. `<Binding Redirect />` is used to redirect CLR to newer version.

   d. False.

9. Add to the configuration:

```
<binding Redirect OldVersion="1.0.0.0"
          NewVersion="2.0.0.0" />
```

Chapter 16

1. GET and PUT are used to transfer data from a client to a server. PUT is default for ASP.NET.

2. a. True.
    b. True.
    c. False. ASP.NET returns HTML, therefore a client does not require the .NET runtime.
    d. True.
    e. True.

3. The ListItem class contains a collection for List controls.

4. If the TextBox.AutoPostBack property is set to true, the event handler is called immediately on the server; otherwise, it waits until the next round trip to the server occurs.

5. The .Master property allows access to the MasterPage object.

6. The DataSource property must be set to the data source, and DataBind must be executed to load the data into the control.

7. a. False. You cannot bind directly to a DataAdapter.
    b. True. A control can bind to a DataReader.
    c. False. It is populated when DataBind is executed.
    d. True. A DataSet or data source control can bind to a control.

8. Use a validating control to manage input to a text box.

9. The @Register directive is required to specify a custom control.

10. The HtmlTextWriter class emits HTML that renders a control.

11. The controls in a composite control render themselves and offer the standard properties to work with.

Chapter 17

1. False. A web.config file is not required.

2. pageOutput in the web.config file specifies whether the trace log is appended to the Web page for display on the client's browser. If set to false, the output can be viewed in the trace.axd file in the application's root.

3. a. Windows, Forms, and Microsoft Passport authentication are offered by .NET.
    b. Authentication is specified using the <authentication> element of the web.config file.

    c. Authentication verifies that a user is who he says he is; authorization determines what actions the user may perform or what resources he may access.

    d. The `Page.User` property provides information about a user.

4. *Out-of-Process* Session management supports storing state information on a server on process on another server.

5.
```
<%@ OutputCache Duration="180"  VaryByParam="*"

                                VaryByCustom="Browser"

%>
```

6. A data cache is read-only versus read/write for application state data. However, a data cache is much more flexible: An expiration can be assigned to it, and it can be tied to other objects, causing the cache data to be removed if the objects' value changes.

7. ASP.NET periodically invokes a resource scavenging process that removes less important data from a data cache. Importance is determined by priority. Thus, setting a high priority reduces the chance of the data cache being removed.

8. As a <u>request</u> or <u>response</u> passes through the HTTP pipeline, an `Application` object fires a series of events that may be handled by an <u>HTTP module</u> or in the `global.asax` file.

Chapter 18

1. `System.Web.Services.WebService`

2. `WebService` attribute is applied to a class providing a Web Service. It describes the Web Service. `WebService` directive identifies a file as containing a Web Service.

3. Use the Web Service attribute to specify a namespace to uniquely identify a service.

4. The `Invoke` method is used for a synchronous call; `BeginInvoke` is used for asynchronous.

5. Use the `Timeout` property on the Web Service object to set the timeout in milliseconds.

6. The `<Service>` element contains the target URL for a Web Service.

7. A Web method requires the `SoapHeader` attribute to access the SOAP header info.

8. `BeginInvoke` with polling using the `IsCompleted` property to check for a response. `BeginInvoke` with `EndInvoke` to retrieve results. Call `<web service name>Async` and implement event handler to process response.

Index

A

aborting threads, 611–613
abstract classes, comparing to interfaces, 130
abstract modifiers, 86, 102–103
accessor methods, 93
activating forms, 294
adding
    data bindings, 547
    Help to forms, 308–313
    items
        to data caches, 845–846
        data sources, 560–561
        to list boxes, 336–338
    nodes, 351
        on trees, 491–493
    radio buttons into groups, 326–327
    role-based authorization, 833–834
    rows (`DataGridView` class), 566–568
ADO.NET
    binding, 548–549
    connected models, 502–504, 506–518
    connection classes, 506–510
    data access models, 502–506
    disconnected models, 504–506, 518–533
    overview of, 497–502
    XML, 533–540
algorithms
    DES, 253
    Nagle, 916–917
aligning
    strings, 438–439
    tab stops, 436–437
allocating
    memory, 74–75, 77
    `StringBuilder` class, 220–223
AlphaRGB (ARGB), 400
alpha values, 400
`AmazonSearchService` class, 909–910
Amazon Web services, 909–912
analysis, FxCop tool, 683–686

anchoring controls, 275–276
annotations, `ToolTip` controls, 310
anonymous methods, delegates, 117–118
`AppDomain` class, 640–643
applications
    configuration files, 23
    data binding, 555–563
    deploying, 722–727
    state, 837–838
    Windows, 268–271
`<appSettings>` configuration file section, 819
architecture
    ADO.NET. *See* ADO.NET
    CLI, 7. *See also* CLI
    remoting, 644–648
    Web services, 870. *See also* Web services
ARGB (AlphaRGB), 400
arithmetic operators, 50–51
`ArrayList` class, 179–180
    binding, 558–560
    objects, 69
arrays
    C#, 69–73
    controls (binding), 558–559
    declaring, 70
    `System.Array` class, 71
ASCII, 204, 219
`.asmx` files, 877
ASP.NET
    binding, 772–884
    buttons, 763–764
    caching, 841–848
    client-server Internet interaction, 734–758
    code-behind models, 749–754
    configuration files, 817–826
    content pages, 789–793
    `DataList` controls, 768–772
    HTTP
        pipelines, 851–866
        requests/responses, 808–817
    inline code models, 741–749

master pages, 789–793
Page class, 754–758
panels, 764–765
security, 827–835
state maintenance, 835–841
text boxes, 766
validation controls, 784–789
Web clients, 848–851
Web controls
    customizing, 793–801
    selecting, 801–802
Web Forms controls, 758–772
assemblies, 10
    application domains, 639–640
    clients, 658–660
    configuration file management, 726
    configuring, 29
    deploying, 724–725
    FCL, 19
    FxCop tool, 683–686
    GAC, 16, 723–724
    hosts, 657–658, 665
    interfaces (SAO), 662–664
    managing, 29
    multiple files, 15, 34–35
    .NET, 13–18
    permissions
        granting, 709–710
        requesting, 711–714
    precompiling, 17–18
    private, 16–17
    satellite, 369–376
    servers, 656–657, 665–666
    shared, 16–17
    strongly named, 14, 686–691
    versioning, 690–691, 727
@Assembly directive, 748
asynchronous programming, 595–608
    calls
        event-based, 892–893
        implementing, 599–608
        I/O (Input/Output), 607–608
        to Web service methods, 891–892
    delegate invocation, 596
attributes
    C# classes, 83–85
    conditional, 84–85
    @Page directives, 746–748
    permissions, 695, 698
        applying, 712–713
        declarative security, 721–722
        testing, 713–714
    Synchronization, 622–623
    VaryByCustom, 843–844
    VaryByHeader, 843–844
    VaryByParam, 843–844
    WebMethod, 876–877, 881–883
    WebService, 881
    XML serialization, 465–466
authentication, 827
    forms, 827–835

FormsAuthentication class, 831–833
SOAP, 900–903
viewing, 835
authorization
    role-based, 833–834
    web.config file, 830–831
AutoSizeRows method, 569
availability of interface members, 129–130
avoiding deadlock, 628–630

B

background threads, 593–594
backing store, 245
base classes, 87
BeginInvoke method, 598–599
BeginPrint event, 446–447
BinaryFormatter object, 188
binary serialization, 188–192
binding
    ADO.NET, 548–549
    ArrayList class, 558–560
    ASP.NET, 772–784
    DataReader class, 772–774
    DataSet class, 556–557, 774–776
    DataTables class, 555–557
    lists, 547–548
    managers, 547, 552–554
    policies, 29
<Binding>, 897
BindingManagerBase class, 553–554
Bit Block Transfer, 421–422
bit flags and enumerated types, 69
bitmaps (BMP), 408
blocks
    catch, 151–153
    finally, 153
    try, 151
BMI (Body Mass Index), 648
    calculating, 735–741
BMP (bitmaps), 408
bool type, 47
boxing, 75–77
BreakBar property, 306
Break property, 306
brightness, 400
brushes, 395–400
BufferedStream class, 248–249
buffering images, 413–414
built-in events, 115–116
built-in named permission sets, 694–695
built-in security permissions, 695–697
Button class, 323–324
buttons
    ASP.NET, 763–764
    click events, 271
    controls, 270
    formatting, 323–324
    Help, 311–312
byte type, 48

C

C#
  applications
    case sensitivity, 42
    embedding comments, 43–45
    naming conventions, 42–43
  arrays, 69–73
  classes
    constants, 89–97
    constructors, 106–112
    defining, 82–87
    delegates, 112–123
    fields, 89–97
    generics, 130–133
    interfaces, 126–130
    members, 88–89
    methods, 97–106
    operator overloading, 123–126
    properties, 89–97
    structures, 134–139
  code-behind models (ASP.NET), 749–754
  compiling, 31–35
  enumerated types, 66–69
  features specific to, 920–923
  layouts, 40–45
  loops, 55–59
    do, 56
    for, 56–57
    foreach, 57
    transferring control within, 58–59
    while, 55
  objects
    creating, 145–149
    exception handling, 149–160
    implementing System.Object methods, 160–167
    life cycle management, 192–196
    .NET collection classes and interfaces, 167–187
    serialization, 187–192
  operators, 50
    arithmetic, 50–51
    conditional, 51–52
    equality (==), 65
    relational, 51–52
  preprocessing directives, 59–61
  primitives, 45–50
    bool type, 47
    byte type, 48
    char type, 48
    decimal type, 47
    double type, 49
    int type, 48
    long type, 48
    Parse method, 49–50
    sbyte type, 48
    short type, 48
      single type, 49
      TryParse method, 49–50
    statements
      control flow, 52–53
      if-else, 53–54
      switch, 54–55
    strings, 61–66
    text
      comparing strings, 212–215
      formatting DateTime/numeric values, 223–231
      modifying strings, 216–220
      regular expressions, 232–243
      StringBuilder class, 220–223
      System.IO namespace, 244–263
      System.String class, 209–212
      Unicode, 204–209
CacheDuration property, 882
caching
  ASP.NET, 841–848
  data, 845–848
  deploying, 723–724
  duration of, 842
  fragments, 844–845
  GAC, 16, 689–690
  location of, 842
  output from Web operations, 882
callbacks, 113, 595
  asynchronous calls, 603–605
calls
  asynchronous
    event-based, 892–893
    to Web service methods, 891–892
  synchronous calls to Web service methods, 890–891
CAO (client-activated objects), 649, 650
carriage returns, 334–335
case sensitivity of C# applications, 42
casting, 46
catch block, 151–153
catching exceptions, 149
cells
  formatting, 573–574
  recognizing, 574–575
channels
  naming, 647–648
  remoting, 646–647
characters, 204–208
  carriage returns, 334–335
  dates, 227–228
  encoding schemes, 219–220
  matching, 237
  positional, 237
  repetition, 237
  standards, 205–209
  strings
    escape, 62, 216
  tab stops, 436–437
  XML, 482–484

char type, 48
Char variables, assigning, 205–206
CheckBox class, 324–325
CheckedListBox class, 341–342
Checked property, 306
CIL (Common Intermediate Language), 7
classes
    AmazonSearchService, 909–910
    AppDomain, 640–643
    ArrayList, 179–180
        binding, 558–560
    base, 87
    BindingManagerBase, 553–554
    BufferedStream, 248–249
    built-in permission, 696–697
    Button, 323–324
    C#
        constants, 89–97
        constructors, 106–112
        defining, 82–87
        delegates, 112–123
        fields, 89–97
        generics, 130–133
        interfaces, 126–130
        members, 88–89
        methods, 97–106
        operator overloading, 123–126
        properties, 89–97
        structures, 134–139
    CheckBox, 324–325
    CheckedListBox, 341–342
    ComboBox, 341–342
    connections (ADO.NET), 506–510
    ConnectionStringBuilder, 508
    ContextMenu, 307
    CryptoStream, 252–255
    DataAdapter, 504–506, 525–529
    DataGridView
        configuring master-detail, 576–579
        data binding, 563–584
        delegates, 924–936
        events, 571–576, 924–936
        parameters, 934–936
        properties, 564–571
        virtual mode, 579–584
    DataReader, 503–504, 516–518
        binding, 772–774
    DataRow, 521–523
    DataSet, 504–506, 518–519
        binding, 556–557, 774–776
        defining relationships, 530–532
        loading data into, 523–525
        XML, 534–540
    DataTables, 519–523, 555–557
    DateTimeFormatInfo, 230
    DbCommand, 511
    DbProviderFactories, 500

DefaultPageSettings, 441
Delegate, 597–599
Directory, 256–260
DirectoryInfo, 256–260
DrawImage, 410
events, 118–119
exceptions, 155–157
FCL, 6, 18–22
File, 261–263
FileInfo, 261–263
FileStream, 245–247
FileSystemInfo, 256
Font, 430–433
FontFamily, 428–429
Form, 285–305
FormsAuthentication, 831–833
generics, 132
Graphics
    GDI+, 380–384
    methods, 383–384
GraphicsPath, 390–391
GroupBox, 327
HatchBrush, 396–397
HttpApplication, 853–857
HttpRequest objects, 808–812
HttpResponse
    objects, 813–817
    properties, 814–816
identifiers, 86–87
identity permissions, 698
instances, 92
Label, 330–331
LinearGradientBrush, 397–400
ListBox, 335–341
ListView, 342–349
MemoryStream, 247–248
MenuItem properties, 306
MessageBox, 299–300
Monitor, 623–625
Mutex, 625–626
.NET collections, 167–187
NumberFormatInfo, 230
operators, 123–126
Page (ASP.NET), 754–758
PageSettings, 445–446
Panel, 328–330
Path, 256–260
Pen, 393–395
PictureBox, 331–333
PrintDocument, 439–456
    customizing, 454–456
    events, 440, 446–448
ProductInfo, 911
ProgressBar, 355–358
ProviderFactory, 500
proxy
        Amazon Web services, 911–912

classes, proxy (*continued*)
    creating with Visual Studio.NET, 894
    wsdl.exe utility, 885–890
  Queue, 177–179
  RadioButton, 325–327
  Regex, 232–237
  ResourceManager, 371–372
  ResourceWriter, 371
  ResXResourceReader, 372–373
  ResXResourceWriter, 372
  Semaphore, 627–628
  ShowDialog, 300–301
  Stack, 177–179
  StatusStrip, 355–358
  Stream, 244–245
  StringBuilder, 220–223
  StringFormat, 435
  StringReader, 251–252
  StringWriter, 251–252
  structures, 137–139
  synchronization, 621–622
  System.Array, 71
  System.Collections, 168
    generic namespaces, 184–187
    namespaces, 177
  System.Exception, 150–151
    properties, 150–151
  System.Object
    customizing, 160–167
  System.String, 209–215
  System.Timers.Timer, 618–619
  System.Web.Services.WebService, 879–880
  System.Windows.Forms.Timer, 619
  TextBox, 333–335
  Thread, 592
  Timer, 355–358
  TreeNode, 349–352
  TreeView, 349–355
  WebRequest, 848–851
  WebResponse, 848–851
  Windows.Forms.Form control classes, 271–284
  XmlDataDocument, 491–493
  XmlDocument, 489
  XmlNodeReader, 477–479
  XmlReader, 472–477
  XmlReaderSettings, 489–490
  XmlSerializer, 463–465
  XmlWriter, 482–484
  XPathDocument, 490
  XslTransform, 469–471
click event buttons, 271
CLI (Common Language Infrastructure), 6
  standards, 7–9
client-activated objects. *See* CAO
clients
  ASP.NET, 848–851

assemblies, 658–660, 666–669
remoting, 643–671
servers (Internet interaction), 734–758
UDDI, 872–874
Web services
  building, 884–894
  Windows Forms, 913–915
Clone method, 73
cloning objects, 165
closing forms, 294
CLR (Common Language Runtime), 9–18
  .NET, 10–11
  reference/value type support, 73–77
CLS (Common Language Specification), 12
code
  design, 682–686
  exception handling 151–153
  forms, 296–298
  groups, 692
    creating, 708–709
    testing, 709
  inline code models (ASP.NET), 741–749
  isolation, 638
  libraries, 34
  managed, 10
  .NET, 10–11
  regions, 61
Code Access Security model, 692. *See also* security
CodeBase configuration, 725
code-behind models
  ASP.NET, 749–754
  global.asax files, 856–857
code points (Unicode identifiers), 205
collections, 167–187
  bindings, 547
  enumeration, 172
  members (iterators), 172–174
colors, 400–402
  multi-color gradients, 400
  objects, 401
  viewers, 402–407
  wheels, 400
columns
  DataTable.Columns property, 519–521
  headers, 344–345
  recognizing, 574–575
  tab stops, 436–437
  types, 570–571
  value access, 517–518
ComboBox class, 341–342
CommandBuilder object, 525–526
command line, compiling from the, 32–35
commands
  objects, 511–515
  SQL, 512–513
comments, embedding, 43–45

Common Intermediate Language. *See* CIL
Common Language Infrastructure. *See* CLI
Common Language Runtime. *See* CLR
Common Language Specification. *See* CLS
Common Type System. *See* CTS
Compact Profile, 8
comparing
    abstract classes and interfaces, 130
    classes and structures, 137–139
    strings, 212–213
`<compilation>` configuration file section, 821
compiling
    C#, 31–35
    code (.NET), 10–11
    from the command line, 32–35
    multiple files, 34
    Web pages, 740
complex data types, Web Services, 906–915
components
    `HelpProvider`, 312–313
    services, 623
composite controls, 798–801
compressing files, 607–608
concatenation
    `StringBuilder` class, 222
    strings, 63–64
conditional attributes, 84–85
conditional caching, 843–844
conditional compilation, 60
conditional operators, 51–52
configuration
    application configuration files, 23
    assemblies, 29
configuration files
    ASP.NET, 817–826
    assembly management, 726
    customizing, 824–826
    message servers, 660–662
configuring
    CodeBase configuration, 725
    column headers, 344–345
    `DataGridViews` class, 576–579
    integrated help systems, 308–313
    leasing, 673–674
    .NET Framework Configuration tool security, 704–706
    permissions, 708
    printer resolution, 444
    security, 702–704, 706–711
    strongly named assemblies, 687–688
    Web services (`Web.config` file), 883
connected models
    ADO.NET, 502–504, 506–518
    selecting, 532–533
connections
    classes (ADO.NET), 506–510
    pooling, 510
    strings, 507–509

`ConnectionStringBuilder` class, 508
`<connectionStrings>` configuration file section, 823
constants, C# classes, 89–91
constraints, relationships, 531–532
constructors
    C# classes, 106–112
    `Delegate` class, 598
    `Font` class, 430
    inheritance, 107
    instances, 106–110
    private, 110–111
    static, 111–112
    `StringBuilder` class, 221
content pages (ASP.NET), 789–793
context
    devices, 380
    menus, 307–308
`ContextMenu` class, 307
control flow statements (C#), 52–53
controls. *See also* user controls
    anchoring, 275–276
    arrays, 558–559
    buttons, 270
    classes, 271–284
    composite, 798–801
    `CreateGraphics` method, 381
    `CustomValidator`, 787–788
    data binding, 546–554
    data display, 759
    `DataList`, 768–772
    `DataSource` property, 776–784
    data sources, 551, 760
    docking, 275–276
    dragging and dropping, 363–368
    events, 279–284
    extending, 358–359
    filling, 767–768
    `FlowLayoutPanel`, 328–329
    forms, 319–323
        buttons, 323–331
        `CheckedListBox`, 341–342
        `ComboBox`, 341–342
        customizing, 358–363
        dragging and dropping, 363–368
        group boxes, 323–331
        iterating, 278
        `ListBox`, 335–341
        `ListView`, 342–349
        panels, 323–331
        `PictureBox`, 331–333
        populating, 550
        `ProgressBar`, 355–358
        resources, 369–376
        `StatusStrip`, 355–358
        `TextBox`, 333–335
        `Timer`, 355–358
        `TreeView`, 349–355

controls *(continued)*
    interfaces, 605–606
    lists, 549–550, 759, 766–768
    login, 760
    ObjectDataSource, 781
    positioning, 274–275
    properties, 272–274
    servers (View state), 744–746
    sizing, 274–275
    SqlDataSource, 777–780
    state management, 797–798
    TableLayoutPanel, 329–330
    ToolTip, 309–310
    validating, 760, 784–789
    ValidationSummary, 787–789
    values, 550–551
    Web
        customizing ASP.NET, 793–801
        selecting ASP.NET, 801–802
    Web Forms, 758–772
    Web pages, 802
    XmlDataSource, 781–784
conventions, naming, 42–43
converting
    Char values, 206
    narrowing, 46
    numeric types, 49–50
    resource files, 373
    widening, 46
CookieContainer property, 893–894
copying images, 418
Copy method, 73
CreateGraphics method, 381
creational patterns, 145
cross-page posting, 758
CryptoStream class, 252–255
CTS (Common Type System), 11–13
cultures
    assembly settings, 17
    dates, 230
    strings, 213–215
CurrentThread property, 609
custom Web controls, 796–797
custom date formats, 228–229
<customErrors> configuration file section, 821–822
customizing
    ADO.NET Web controls, 793–801
    class exceptions, 155–157
    configuration files, 824–826
    controls, 358–363
    data sources, 559–560
    events, 118–119
    HTTP
        handlers, 862–864
        modules, 858
    interfaces, 127–129
    list boxes, 339–341
        PrintDocument class, 454–456
        System.Object class, 160–167
CustomValidator control, 787–788

D

DashStyle property, 394
data access models (ADO.NET), 502–506
DataAdapter class, 504–506, 525–529
databases
    SQL, 507. *See also* SQL
    synchronizing, 526–529
    updating, 525–529, 562–563
data binding. *See also* binding
    applications, 555–563
    DataGridView class, 563–584
    overview of, 546–554
DataBindings.Add method, 547
data caching, 845–848
data display controls, 759
DataError event, 575
data error handling, 575–576
DataGridView class
    data binding, 563–584
    delegates, 924–936
    events, 571–576, 924–936
    master-detail, 576–579
    parameters, 934–936
    properties, 564–571
    virtual mode, 579–584
DataList controls, 768–772
data providers
    factories, 500–502
    .NET, 499–502
DataReader class, 503–504, 516–518
    binding, 772–774
DataRow class, 521–523
DataSet class, 504–506, 518–519
    binding, 556–557, 774–776
    defining relationships, 530–532
    loading data into, 523–525
    XML, 534–540
DataSource property controls, 776–784
data sources
    controls, 551, 760
    customizing, 559–560
    items, 560–561
    for reports, 450
DataTable.Columns property, 519–521
DataTables class, 519–523, 555–557
data types
    C# primitive, 45–46
    Web Services, 906–915
dates, 230
DateTime class, formatting, 223–231
DateTimeFormatInfo class, 230
DbCommand class, 511

`DbProviderFactories` class, 500
deactivating forms, 294
deadlock, avoiding, 628–630
`decimal` type, 47
declarative security, 711
    permission attributes, 721–722
decoding, 219. *See also* encoding
`<Definitions>`, 896
delayed signing, 688–689
`Delegate` class, 597–599
delegates
    anonymous methods, 117–118
    asynchronous invocation, 596
    C# classes, 112–123
    `DataGridView` class, 924–936
    events
        defining, 119–120
        handling, 115–123
    `MethodInvoker`, 606–607
    multicasting, 114
deleting
    nodes, 351, 491–493
    subdirectories, 258
deploying
    applications, 722–727
    CAO applications, 669
    custom HTTP handlers, 865
    custom HTTP modules, 859
    GAC, 723–724
    private assemblies, 724–725
    XCOPY, 722–723
derived classes, 87
DES algorithm, 253
devices, context, 380
2-D graphics, 388–393
diagnostic directives, 60–61
dialog boxes, forms, 298–301
Dijkstra, Edsger, 633
directives
    @Assembly, 748
    diagnostic, 60–61
    @Import, 748
    @Page, 746–748
    preprocessing C#, 59–61
    @Register, 748–749
    `WebService`, 876
directories
    members, 257
    `System.IO` namespace, 255–263
`Directory` class, 256–260
`DirectoryInfo` class, 256–260
DISconnected models, selecting, 532–533
disconnected models (ADO.NET), 504–506, 518–533
discovery
    UDDI. *See* UDDI
    Web services, 871–874
`Dispose` method, 195–198, 382

docking controls, 275–276
documenting XML tags, 44
Document Object Model. *See* DOM
documents
    fragments, 474
    printing, 441. *See also* printing
    XML, 463. *See also* XML
`DoDragDrop` method, 363
do loops, 56
domains
    `AppDomain` class, 640–643
    applications, 638–643
    assemblies, 639–640
DOM (Document Object Model), 485
`double` type, 49
downloading files, 816–817
dragging and dropping controls, 363–368
`DrawImage` class, 410
drawing, 380. *See also* GDI+
    multi-line text, 434–435
    rectangles, 417–419
    text strings, 433–439
`DrawRectangle` method, 382
duration of caching, 842

E

ECMA International, 6
embedding comments, 43–45
`Enabled` property, 306
`EnableSession` property, 882
encapsulation, monitoring, 624–625
encoding
    strings, 219–220
    Unicode, 204–208
encryption, 252–255. *See also* security
`EndCap` property, 395
`EndInvoke` method, 599
`EndPrint` event, 447
enumerated types
    bit flags and, 69
    C#, 66–69
enumeration
    collections, 172
    iterators, 173
    `System.Enum` methods, 68
    XML, 476
environments
    IDE, 31
    .NET Framework. *See* .NET Framework
equality (==) operator, 65
`Equals( )` method, 163–165
errors. *See also* troubleshooting
    data error handling, 575–576
    updating, 528
escape characters, 62
escape sequences, 237

events
  asynchronous calls, 892–893
  BeginPrint, 446–447
  binary serialization, 190–191
  built-in, 115–116
  buttons, 271, 324
  controls, 279–284
  customizing, 118–119
  DataError, 575
  DataGridView class, 571–576, 924–936
  declaring, 118
  delegates, 119–120
  dragging and dropping, 365–368
  EndPrint, 447
  handling, 115–123
  keyboard, 282–284
  mouse, 279–282
  overriding, 314–315
  Page_Load, 762–763
  pages, 757–758
  Paint (GDI+), 384–388
  PrintDocument class, 440, 446–448
  PrintPage, 448–449
  propertyChanged, 551
  QueryPageSettingsEvent, 447–448
  servers, 753
Everything permission, 694
evidence, 692, 698–701
exceptions
  classes, 155–157
  handling, 149–160
    guidelines, 159–160
    SEH, 149
    writing code to, 151–153
  SOAP, 904–905
  System.Exception class, 150–151
  unhandled, 157–159
ExecuteReader method, 512, 772
Executexxx methods, 512
executing
  SQL commands, 512–513
  stored procedures, 513–515
Execution permission, 694
Expect100Continue property, 916
Extended Markup Language. See XML
Extended Style Language Transformation. See XSLT
extending
  controls, 358–359
  Web services, 880–883
extracting substrings, 64–65

F

factories
  creational patterns, 145
  data providers, 500–502
  multiple, 148–149

familles of fonts, 428
FCL (Framework Class Library), 6, 18–22
  factory creational patterns, 145
  namespaces, 20–22
fields
  C# classes, 91–93
  initializing, 135
  static read-only, 92
File class, 261–263
FileInfo class, 261–263
files. See also directories
  application configuration, 23
  .asmx, 877
  code-behind models, 856–857
  compressing, 607–608
  configuration
    ASP.NET, 817–826
    customizing, 824–826
    managing assemblies, 726
    message servers, 660–662
  downloading, 816–817
  global.asax, 854–856
  listing files and directories, 259–260
  manifests, 14
  multi-file assemblies, 15
  multiple, 34
  opening files, 261–263
  resources, 369–373
  schemas, 534–536
  System.IO namespace, 255–263
  text
    creating resource strings from, 380–371
    reading from, 250–251
    writing to, 249–250
  web.config, 818–823
    authorization, 830–831
    configuring Web services, 883
    forms authentication, 828–830
  XML, 463. See also XML
FileStream class, 245–247
FileSystemInfo class, 256
finalization, 194–195
Finalize method, 196–198
finally block, 153
F1 keys, invoking help, 311–312
flags, bit and enumerated types, 69
FlowLayoutPanel control, 328–329
Focus and tab order, 277
Font class, 430–433
FontFamily class, 428–429
fonts
  formatting, 430–431
  GDI+, 428–433
  metrics, 431–433
foreach loops, 57
foreground threads, 593–594
foreign keys, 532

`for` loops, 56–57
formatters, remoting, 646
formatting
   `BinaryFormatter` object, 188
   buttons, 323–324
   cells, 573–574
   checkboxes, 325
   content pages, 791–792
   control buttons, 270
   DateTime values, 223–231
   files (XML), 463
   fonts, 430–431
   forms, 270, 293
      appearance, 286–290
      localized, 373–376
      locations, 290–291
      MDI menus, 303–305
   items (`ListView`), 345–346
   master pages, 790–791
   numeric values, 223–231
   objects, 145–149
      colors, 401
      `FontFamily`, 429
   pages for printing, 445–446
   regular expressions, 237–238
   schemas, 534–536
   `String.Format` method, 223
   strings, 209–211, 435
   tab stops, 436–437
   text, 333–335
   Web controls, 760–761
   XML, 917–918
`Form` class, 285–305
forms
   activating, 294
   ASP.NET. *See* ASP.NET
   authentication, 827–835
   closing, 294
   code, 296–298
   controls, 319–323
      buttons, 323–331
      `CheckedListBox`, 341–342
      `ComboBox`, 341–342
      customizing, 358–363
      dragging and dropping, 363–368
      group boxes, 323–331
      iterating, 278
      labels, 323–331
      `ListBox`, 335–341
      `ListView`, 342–349
      panels, 323–331
      `PictureBox`, 331–333
      populating, 550
      `ProgressBar`, 355–358
      resources, 369–376
      `StatusStrip`, 355–358
      `TextBox`, 333–335

      `Timer`, 355–358
      `TreeView`, 349–355
   creating, 270
   deactivating, 294
   dialog boxes, 298–301
   formatting, 286–290, 293
   Help, 308–313
   inheritance, 313–315
   interaction, 294–298
   life cycles, 292–294
   locations, 290–291
   MDI, 301–306
   menus, 306–308
   messages, 298–301
   opacity, 287
   owned, 298–299
   owner, 298–299
   sizing, 290–291
   transparency, 287–290
   viewing, 292, 293
`FormsAuthentication` class, 831–833
fragments, 474, 844–845
Framework Class Library. *See* FCL
Framework Configuration tool, 29–30
frozen columns, 570
`FullTrust` permission, 694
functions (XPath), 488–489
FxCop tool, 683–686

G

GAC (Global Assembly Cache), 16, 689–670
   deploying, 723–724
Garbage Collection (.NET), 192–198
GDI+, 379–423
   fonts, 428–433
   `Graphics` class, 380–384
   `Graphics` object, 388–407
   images, 407–422
   `Paint` events, 384–388
   printing, 439–456
   text, 433–439
   Windows, 421–422
GDI (Graphical Device Interface), 379
generics
   C# classes, 131–133
   classes, 132
   collection class example, 184-187
`GetHashCode` method, overriding, 164–165
GIF (Graphics Interchange Format), 408
`global.asax` files, 854–856
   code-behind models, 856–857
Global Assembly Cache. *See* GAC
gradients, creating, 400
granting permissions, 709–710
Graphical Device Interface. *See* GDI
Graphical User Interface. *See* GUI

graphics. *See also* GDI+; images
  2-D, 388–393
  GDI+, 379. *See also* GDI+
Graphics class
  GDI+, 380–384
  methods, 383–384
Graphics.DrawString method, 433
Graphics Interchange Format (GIF), 408
Graphics object (GDI+), 388–407
GraphicsPath class, 390–391
GroupBox class, 327
guidelines
  code design, 682–686
  connection pooling, 510
  handling exceptions, 159–160
GUI (Graphical User Interface), 267

H

handlers (HTTP), 862–866
handling
  data errors, 575–576
  events, 115–123
    buttons, 324
    on servers, 753
  exceptions, 149–160
    guidelines, 159–160
    SEH, 149
    SOAP, 904–905
    writing code to, 151–153
  keyboard events, 282–284
  mouse events, 279–282
Hashtable
  creating, 182–183
  interfaces, 181-184
  keys, 183, 210
  serialization, 189
  values, 183
HatchBrush class, 396–397
headers
  columns, 344–345
  SOAP, 900–903
heaps, 11, 74
height
  fonts, 431–433
  rows in DataGridView, 569–570
Help, adding forms, 308–313
HelpProvider component, 312–313
hiding IL, 27–28
high surrogates, 205
hit testing shapes, 391–393
hosts, assemblies, 657–658, 665
hot keys, 306
HSB (hue/saturation/brightness), 400
HSL (hue/saturation/luminosity), 400
HTML (Hypertext Markup Language), 734
  code-behind models (ASP.NET), 749–754

inner content, 767
  tags, 752
  XML style sheets, 470–471
HttpApplication class, 853–857
HTTP (Hypertext Transfer Protocol), 734, 870
  ASP.NET, 808–817
  handlers, 862–866
  modules, 857–862
  pipelines, 851–866
HttpRequest class objects, 755–756, 808–812
HttpResponse class
  object, 755–756, 813–817
  properties, 814–816
Hypertext Markup Language. *See* HTML
Hypertext Transfer Protocol. *See* HTTP

I

ICollection interfaces, 169–170
IComparable interfaces, sorting, 175–176
IComparer interfaces, sorting, 175–176
icons, specifying, 345–346
IDbCommand interface, 511–515
IDbConnection interface, 506
IDE (Integrated Development Environment), 31, 267
identifiers, classes, 86–87
identifying updating, 561–562
identity permissions, 697–698
IDictionaryEnumerator interfaces, 182
IDictionary interfaces, 181
IEnumerable interfaces, 170–172
IEnumerator interfaces, 170–172
if-else statements, 53–54
IHashCodeProvider interfaces, 170
Ildasm.exe, 25–28
IL (Intermediate Language), 10
  hiding, 27–28
  viewing, 26
IList interfaces, 179–180
images
  buffering, 413–414
  copying, 418
  creating, 414–421
  GDI+, 407–422
  loading, 408–411
  menus, 415–417
  mirroring, 412–413
  modifying, 411–414, 420–421
  Ngen, 17
  PictureBox class, 331–333
  rectangles, 417–419
  returning, 907–908
  rotating, 412–413
  saving, 408–411
  servers, 664–669
  ToolTip controls, 310
@Import directive, 748

indexers (C# classes), 95–97
IndexOf method, 64
infrastructure (CLI), 6
inheritance
    classes
        C#, 87
        defining, 82
    constructors, 107
    forms, 313–315
    methods, 100–101
    structures, 138
Initialization Vector (IV), 253
initializers, 108–110
initializing
    fields, 135
    interfaces, 762–763
    virtual DataGridView, 581
inline code models (ASP.NET), 741–749
inner HTML content, 767
in-process session state, 840
Input/Output. See I/O
inserting. See adding
instances
    class references, 92
    constructors, 106–110
Integrated Development Environment. See IDE
integrated help systems, configuring, 308–313
interaction, forms, 294–298
interfaces
    abstract classes, 130
    assemblies (SAO), 662–664
    C# classes, 87, 126–130
    controls, 605–606
    customizing, 127–129
    GDI, 379. See also GDI
    GUI, 267
    Hashtable, 181–184
    ICollection, 169–170
    IComparable, 175–176
    IComparer, 175–176
    IDbCommand, 511–515
    IDbConnection, 506
    IDictionary, 181
    IDictionaryEnumerator, 182
    IEnumerable, 170–172
    IEnumerator, 170–172
    IHashCodeProvider, 170
    IList, 179–180
    initializing, 762–763
    MDI, 301–306
    members, 129–130
    methods, 130
    .NET collections, 167–187
    OLE DB, 499
    simple controls, 761–766
Intermediate Language. See IL

Internet client-server interaction, 734–758
Internet permission, 694
interning strings, 209–211
Interop, 8
int type, 48
Invalidate method, 381, 384–385
Invoke method, 598
I/O (Input/Output), asynchronous calls, 607–608
isolation, code, 638
IsPostBack property, 756
items
    data caches
        adding to, 845–846
        retrieving from, 846
    data sources, 560–561
    detecting, 347–348
    iterating, 347
    ListView, 345–346
    selecting, 768
    sorting, 348–349
iterating
    controls on forms, 278
    items, 347
    nodes, 352
iterators, 172–174
IV (Initialization Vector), 253

J

JavaScript, BMI calculators, 736–739
JIT (Just-in-Time), 10
JPEG (Joint Photographics Experts Group), 408
Just-in-Time. See JIT

K

Kernel Profile, 8
keyboard events, handling, 282–284
keys
    F1 (help), 311–312
    foreign, 532
    hashtables, 183, 210
    hot, 306
    primary, 521
    private, 253, 688
    public, 17, 253, 687

L

Label class, 330–331
leasing, 671–675
    objects, 650
libraries
    code, 34
    FCL, 6, 18–22
    forms, 313–314

life cycles
    forms, 292–294
    object management, 192–198
lifetimes of leases, 674–675
LinearGradientBrush class, 397–400
lines
    DrawLine method, 382
    multi-line text, 434–435
linking, 546. *See also* binding
    ASP.NET, 740
ListBox class, 335–341
listing
    files, 259–260
    font families, 429
    Hashtable keys and values, 183
lists
    binding, 547–548
    controls, 549–550, 759, 766–768
    navigating, 553–554
ListView class, 342–349
literals, strings, 61–63
loading
    data
        ADO.NET, 505
        into DataSet class, 523–525
    images, 408–411
LocalIntranet permission, 694
localization
    characters, 206–207
    forms, 373–376
<location> configuration file section, 820
location
    Control property, 272
    form location, 290-291
locking
    deadlock, 628–630
    objects, 624
login
    controls, 760
    FormsAuthentication class, 831–833
long type, 48
loops (C#), 55–59
    do, 56
    for, 56–57
    foreach, 57
    transferring control within, 58–59
    while, 55
low surrogates, 205

M

Main() method, 41
maintenance
    CookieContainer property, 893–894
    state (ASP.NET), 835–841
manifests, 14, 686
marshaling by reference (MBR), 649–650

marshaling by value (MBV), 648–649
master-detail views, configuring, 576–579
master pages (ASP.NET), 789–793
Matches() method, 235–237
matching characters, 237
Match() method, 235–237
MBR (marshaling by reference), 649–650
MBV (marshaling by value), 648–649
MDI (Multiple Document Interface), 301–306
memory
    allocating, 74–75, 77
    intern pools, 209
    releasing, 77
MemoryStream class, 247–248
MenuItem class properties, 306
menus
    buttons (ASP.NET), 763–764
    context, 307–308
    forms, 306–308
    images, 415–417
    MDI forms, 303–305
<Message>, 896
MessageBox class, 299–300
MessageName property, 882
messages
    HTTP response, 813–814
    request, 809–810
metadata, 10, 14
MethodInvoker delegate, 606–607
methods
    accessor, 93
    anonymous, 117–118
    asynchronous, 598–607
    C# classes, 97–106
    ExecuteReader, 512, 772
    inheritance, 100–101
    interfaces, 130
    modifiers, 98–103
    multicasting, 114
    Parse, TryParse, 49–50
    ShowHelp, 312
    structures, 136–137
methods, .NET Framework
    ControlBindingsCollection, 547
    System.Array, 71-73
    System.Char, 206–208
    System.Enum, 68
    System.Drawing.Graphics, 388–391, 433
    System.IO.DirectoryInfo, FileSystem-
        Info, 256-260
    System.Object, 160-167,195-198
    System.RegularExpressions.Regex, 233-237
    System.String, 212-219,223
    System.Text.StringBuilder, 221–222
    System.Web.HttpResponse, 816
    System.Windows.Forms.Control, 381
    System.Xml.XmlWriter, 482-484

`System.Xml.Xsl.XslTransform`, 471
metrics, sizing fonts, 431–433
Microsoft CIL standards, 7
Microsoft Intermediate Language. *See* MSIL
mirroring images, 412–413
MMC (Microsoft Management Console)
    Framework Configuration tool, 29
modeless forms, life cycles of, 292
modifiers
    abstract, 86, 102–103
    access, 85–86, 89
    fields, 91
    methods, 98–103
    override, 100–101
    sealed, 86, 102–103
    stack walk, 719–720
    versioning, 101–102
    virtual, 100–101
modules (HTTP), 857–862
`Monitor` class, 623–625
monitoring encapsulation, 624–625
mouse events, handling, 279–282
moving controls, 363–368
MSIL (Microsoft Intermediate Language), 10
multicasting delegates, 114
multi-color gradients, creating, 400
multi-file assemblies, 15
multi-line text, drawing, 434–435
Multiple Document Interface. *See* MDI
multiple files, compiling, 34
multithreading, 592–595
    applying, 613–617
    user interface controls, 605–606
`Mutex` class, 625–626

N

Nagle algorithm, 916–917
namespaces
    FCL, 20–22
    `System.Collections` class, 177, 184–187
    `System.Drawing.Drawing2D`, 390
    `System.IO`
        directories, 255–263
        files, 255–263
        streams, 244–255
    `System.Web.UI.WebControls`, 759
    using statements, 40
naming
    assemblies, 16
    channels, 647–648
    conventions, 42–43
    identifiers, 86–87
    paths, 260
    permission sets, 694–695
    strongly named assemblies, 686–691
narrowing conversion, 46

Native Image Generator. *See* Ngen
navigating
    lists, 553–554
    XPath, 485
.NET
    ADO.NET. *See* ADO.NET
    ASP.NET. *See* ASP.NET
    assemblies, 13–18
    built-in security permissions, 695–697
    compiling code, 10–11
    CTS, 11–13
    data providers, 499–502
    FCL, 6, 18–22
    features specific to, 920–923
    Framework
        Configuration tool, 704–706
        overview of, 6–9
        SDK, 22–30
        standards, 7–9
        tools, 23–30
        updating, 23
    Garbage Collection, 192–198
    generics, 131–133
    OLE DB providers in, 498–499
    operator overloading, 125
    security policies, 701–704
    Visual Studio.NET. *See* Visual Studio.NET
Ngen (Native Image Generator), 17
nodes
    adding, deleting, iterating `TreeView`, 351-352
    trees
        adding on, 491–493
        deleting on, 491–493
    `XmlNodeReader` class, 477–479
`Nothing` permission, 694
`NumberFormatInfo` class, 230
numeric types, primitives, 49–50
numeric values, formatting, 223–231

O

obfuscation and Ildasm.exe, 27–28
`ObjectDataSource` control, 781
objects
    `ArrayList`, 69
    `BinaryFormatter`, 188
    C#
        creating, 145–149
        exception handling, 149–160
        implementing `System.Object` methods, 160–167
        life cycle management, 192–196
        .NET collection classes and interfaces, 167–187
        serialization, 187–192
    CAO, 649–650, 664–669
    cloning, 165
    `CommandBuilder`, 525–526

objects *(continued)*
  commands, 511–515
  finalization, 194–195
  locking, 624
  polling, 600–603
  SAO, 649–652, 654–664
  SOAP, 643
  synchronization, 600–603
  WKO, 649
OLE DB providers in .NET, 498–499
one-way data binding, 550–551
opacity of forms, 287
opening files, 261–263
OpenType fonts, 428. *See also* fonts
operators
  C#, 50
    arithmetic, 50–51
    conditional, 51–52
    equality (==), 65
    relational, 51–52
  overloading, 123–126
  XPath, 487–489
optimistic concurrency, 526
ordering tabs, 277
out-of-process sessions, 840–841
output caching, pages, 842–845
overloading
  operators, 123–126
  strings, 65–66
override modifiers, 100–101
overriding
  events, 314–315
  GetHashCode method, 164–165
owned and owner forms, 298–299

P

Page class (ASP.NET), 754–758
@Page directives, 746–748
Page_Load event, 762–763
pages. *See also* Web pages
  events, 757–758
  output caching, 842–845
PageSettings class, 445–446
pages to print, selecting, 443–444
Paint events (GDI+), 384–388
Panel class, 328–330
panels
  ASP.NET, 764–765
  images, 420–421
parameters
  commands without stored procedures, 515
  DataGridView class, 934–936
  passing, 103–106
  passing to threads, 610–611
  types, 184
Parse method, 49–50

parsing numbers, 243
partial classes, code-behind with, 753–754
partial pages, caching, 844–845
Path class, 256–260
paths
  naming, 260
  synchronization, 620
patterns
  creational, 145
  custom date formatting, 228–229
  regular expressions, 237–238
Pen class, 393–395
performance
  AppDomain, 639
  View state, 745
  Web services, 916–918
permissions, 693–698
  assembly requests, 711–714
  attributes, 695, 698
    applying, 712–713
    declarative security, 721–722
    testing, 713–714
  built-in security, 695–697
  creating, 708
  granting, 709–710
  identity, 697–698
PictureBox class, 331–333
pipelines (HTTP), 851–866
PNG (Portable Network Graphics), 408
policies
  binding, 29
  default configuration, 705–706
  security, 701–704
polling objects, 600–603
polymorphism, 98
pooling
  connections, 510
  threads, 596, 617–618
populating controls in forms, 550
positioning
  controls, 274–275
  tab stops, 436–437
postbacks, 756
posting, cross-page, 758
precompiling. *See also* compiling
  assemblies, 17–18
preprocessing directives (C#), 59–61
previewing printing, 449–454
primary keys, 521
primary threads, 592
primitives (C#), 45–50
  bool type, 47
  byte type, 48
  char type, 48
  decimal type, 47
  double type, 49
  int type, 48

long type, 48
  Parse method, 49–50
  sbyte type, 48
  short type, 48
  single type, 49
  TryParse method, 49–50
PrintDocument class, 439–456
  customizing, 454–456
  events, 440, 446–448
printers
  resolution, 444
  selecting, 443
PrinterSettings object, 442–444
printing
  GDI+, 439–456
  pages, 443–444
  previewing, 449–454
PrintPage event, 448–449
priority threads, 592
private assemblies, 16–17
  deploying, 724–725
private constructors, 110–111
private keys, 253
  delayed signing, 688
processing HTTP pipeline requests, 851–853
ProductInfo class, 911
profiles
  Compact Profile, 8
  Kernel Profile, 8
programmatic security, 715–722
ProgressBar class, 355–358
properties
  C# classes, 93–95
  controls, 272–274, 546
  DataGridView class, 564–571
  DataSource controls, 776–784
  DataTable.Columns, 519–521
  forms, 285
  HttpRequest class, 810–812
  HttpResponse class, 814–816
  MenuItem class, 306
  Page class, 755
  structures, 136–137
  System.Array class, 71
  System.Exception class, 150–151
  XmlReaderSettings class, 489–490
propertyChanged event, 551
ProviderFactory class, 500
providers. See also data providers
proxy classes
  Amazon Web services, 911–912
  remoting, 645–646
  Visual Studio.NET, 894
  wsdl.exe utility, 885–890
public keys, 253
  tokens, 17, 687

Q

queries (XPath), 486–489
QueryPageSettingsEvent event, 447–448
Queue class, 177–179

R

RadioButton class, 325–327
RadioCheck property, 306
RAD (Rapid Application Development), 15
reading
  resource files, 372–373
  text, 249–251
  XML, 472–482, 537–540
ReadOnly columns, 570
read-only fields, static, 92
rectangles
  drawing, 417–419
  DrawRectangle method, 382
red/green/blue (RGB), 400
references
  instances, 92
  MBR, 649–650
  objects, 165
  support for CLR, 73–77
  types, 11, 138
reflection, 8
  TreeView class, 352–355
Regex class, 232–237
  IsMatch method, 233
  Replace method, 233
  Split method, 234
regions, code, 61
@Register directive, 748–749
registering
  methods, 113
  types, 652–654
registries (UDDI), 874
regular expressions, 232–243
  backreferencing groups, 241–242
  creating regular expressions, 237-238
  repetition characters, 237
relational operators (C#), 51–52
relationships
  constraints, 531–532
  tables
    creating, 521
    defining, 530–532
releasing memory, 77
Remote Procedure Call. See RPC
remoting applications, 643–671
  architecture, 644–648
  CAO, 650, 664–669
  design, 670–671
  real proxies, 645
  registration, 652–654

remoting applications (*continued*)
  SAO, 650–652, 654–664
  types of, 648–650
reports
  code for, 451–454
  data sources for, 450
  previewing printing, 449–454
requests
  Amazon Web services, 909–910
  HTTP, 808–817, 851–853
  permissions, 711–714
  SOAP, 899–900
  UDDI discovery, 873–874
  Web (ASP.NET), 848–851
resolution, configuring printers, 444
`ResourceManager` class, 371–372
resources
  files, 369–373
  forms, 369–376
  localization, 375
  scavenging, 846
`ResourceWriter` class, 371
responses
  HTTP, 808–817
  SOAP, 900
  Web (ASP.NET), 848–851
`ResXResourceReader` class, 372–373
`ResXResourceWriter` class, 372
retrieving items from data caches, 846
reversing text, 242
rewriting URLs, 859
RGB (red/green/blue), 400
role-based authorization, adding, 833–834
rolling back updates, 527
rotating images, 412–413
rows
  `DataGridView` class, 566–568
  `DataRow` class, 521–523
  height, 569–570
  recognizing, 574–575
  updating, 528
RPC (Remote Procedure Call), 870
runtime, localization resources, 375

S

safety threads, 620
SAO (server-activated objects), 649–652
satellite assemblies, 369, 374
  Visual Studio.NET, 375–376
`sbyte` type, 48
schemas
  creating, 534–536
  XML, 480–481
  XSD, 466–468
scraping Web pages, 850
SDK (Software Development Kit), 22–30

sealed modifiers, 86, 102–103
searching. *See also* queries
  strings, 216–217
  substrings, 64–65
  XML with XPath, 484–493
Secure Sockets Layer. *See* SSL
security, 692–722
  AppDomain, 639
  ASP.NET, 827–835
  configuring, 706–711
  `CryptoStream` class, 252–255
  declarative, 711
  evidence, 698–701
  .NET Framework Configuration tool, 704–706
  permissions, 693–698
    attributes, 721–722
    requesting for assemblies, 711–714
  policies, 701–704
  programmatic, 715–722
  SOAP, 905–906
  stack walk, 715–720
  viewing, 29
SEH (structured exception handling), 149
selecting
  ADO.NET access models, 532–533
  ASP.NET Web controls, 801–802
  list boxes, 338–339
  pages to print, 443–444
  printers, 443
semantics values, 134
`Semaphore` class, 627–628
send and forget, 590
sequences, escape, 237
serialization
  attributes, 465–466
  binary, 188–192
  events, 190–191
  objects, 187–192
  XML, 462–466
server-activated objects. *See* SAO
server-activated single calls, 651–652
server-activated singleton, 651
servers
  assemblies, 656–657, 665–666
  clients, 734–758
  configuration files, 660–662
  event handling, 753
  remoting, 643–671
  UDDI, 872–874
`<Service>`, 898
sessions
  `CookieContainer` property, 893–894
  `global.asax` files, 854–856
  state, 838–841
  Web services, 882
`<sessionState>` configuration file section, 822–823
shallow copies, creating, 166–167

shapes
 drawing, 380. *See also* GDI+
 `DrawLine` method, 382
 `DrawRectangle` method, 382
 hit testing, 391–393
shared assemblies, 16–17
short circuit evaluation, 52
`Shortcut` property, 306
`short` type, 48
`ShowDialog` class, 300–301
`ShowHelp` method, 312
signatures, methods, 97
signing, 17
simple controls, 759, 761–766
Simple Object Access Protocol. *See* SOAP
`single` type, 49
sink chains, 644
site evidence, 692
sizing
 arrays, 70
 controls, 274–275
 fonts, 431–433
 forms, 290–291
 rows, 569–570
SOAP (Simple Object Access Protocol), 643, 870–871,
  898–906
Software Development Kit. *See* SDK
sorting
 columns, 570
 `IComparable` interfaces, 175–176
 `IComparer` interfaces, 175–176
 items, 348–349
`Sort` method, 73
source control responsibilities, 365–366
special characters, carriage returns, 334–335
specifications of CLS, 12
sponsorship, 675–677
`SqlDataSource` control, 777–780
SQL (Structured Query Language)
 commands, 512–513
 connection strings, 507–509
 stored procedures, 513–515
SSL (Secure Sockets Layer), 905
`Stack` class, 177–179
stacks
 runtime, 74
 walk, 711, 715–720
standards
 CLI, 7–9
 ECMA International, 6
 .NET Framework, 7–9
`StartCap` property, 395
state, 734
 applications, 837–838
 ASP.NET, 835–841
 `CookieContainer` property, 893–894
 management of controls, 797–798

 sessions, 838–841
 threads, 594–595
 View, 744–746
statements
 C#
  control flow, 52–53
  `if-else`, 53–54
  `switch`, 54–55
  `using`, 40
static constructors, 111–112
static method modifiers, 99–100
static read-only fields, 92
`StatusStrip` class, 355–358
stops, tags, 436–437
stored procedures, executing, 513–515
`Stream` class, 244–245
streams
 members, 245
 `System.IO` namespace, 244–255
`StringBuilder` class, 220–223
`String.Compare` method, 213–215
`String.CompareOrdinal` method, 215
`StringFormat` class, 435
`String.Format` method, 223
`StringReader` class, 251–252
strings
 aligning, 438–439
 C#, 61–66
 comparing, 212–213
 concatenation, 63–64
 connections, 507–509
 creating, 209–211
 encoding, 219–220
 formatting, 435
 interning, 209–211
 literals, 61–63
 methods, 211–212
 modifying, 63–66
 overloading, 65–66
 resources, 370–371
 searching, 216–217
 text, 433–439
 transformations, 212, 217–219
 trimming, 438–439
 wrapping, 438–439
`StringWriter` class, 251–252
strongly named assemblies, 14, 686–691
structured exception handling. *See* SEH
Structured Query Language. *See* SQL
structures
 C# classes, 134–137
 comparing, 137–139
 defining, 134–135
 inheritance, 138
 methods, 136–137
 properties, 136–137
style sheets (XSLT), 468–471

subdirectories. *See also* directories
  creating, 258
  deleting, 258
substrings. *See also* strings
  extracting, 64–65
  searching, 64–65
surrogates
  pairs, 205
  strings, 217
`switch` statements, 54–55
synchronization
  databases, 526–529
  objects, 600–603
  threads, 620–630
`Synchronization` attribute, 622–623
synchronous calls to Web service methods, 890–891
`System.Array` class, 71
`System.Collections` class, 168
  generic namespaces, 184–187
  namespaces, 177
`System.Drawing.Drawing2D` namespace, 390
`System.Enum` methods, 68
`System.Exception` class, 150–151
`System.IO` namespace
  directories, 255–263
  files, 255–263
  streams, 244–255
`System.Object` class, customizing, 160–167
`System.String` class, 209–215
`System.Timers.Timer` class, 618–619
`<system.web>` configuration file section, 820–823
`System.Web.Services.WebService` class, 879–880
`System.Web.UI.WebControls` namespace, 759
`System.Windows.Forms.Timer` class, 619

T

`TableLayoutPanel` control, 329–330
tables
  keys, 210
  master-detail, 577
  relationships
    creating, 521
    defining, 530–532
tabs, ordering, 277
Tag Image File Format (TIFF), 408
tags
  HTML, 752
  XML documentation, 44
target control responsibilities, 366–368
TCP/IP (Transmission Control Protocol/Internet Protocol), 870
text
  boxes, 766
  C#
    comparing strings, 212–215

  formatting DateTime/numeric values, 223–231
  modifying strings, 216–220
  regular expressions, 232–243
  `StringBuilder` class, 220–223
  `System.IO` namespace, 244–263
  `System.String` class, 209–212
  Unicode, 204–209
  files, 380–371
  formatting, 333–335
  GDI+, 433–439
  patterns, 240–242
  printing, 441. *See also* printing
  reading, 249–251
  reversing, 242
  strings, 433–439
  writing, 249–251
`TextBox` class, 333–335
`Thread` class, 592
Thread Local Storage. *See* TLS
threads, 590. *See also* asynchronous programming
  aborting, 611–613
  applying, 609–619
  creating, 606–607, 610–611
  `CurrentThread` property, 609
  multithreading, 592–595
  overview of, 592–595
  parameters, 610–611
  pooling, 596, 617–618
  priority, 592
  safety, 620
  synchronization, 620–630
  timers, 618–619
throwing exceptions, 149
TIFF (Tag Image File Format), 408
time, formatting, 227–231
`Timer` class, 355–358
timer threads, 618–619
time slices, 592
time-to-live (TTL), 671
TLS (Thread Local Storage), 592
tokens, public keys, 17, 687
tools
  FxCop, 683–686
  .NET Framework, 23–25
    Framework Configuration tool, 29–30, 704–706
    Ildasm.exe, 25–28
    wincv.exe, 28
  SDK, 22–30
  `wsdl.exe` utility, 885–890
`ToolTip` controls, 309–310
`ToString( )` method, 161–162
`<trace>` configuration file section, 822
transactions, rolling back updates, 527
transferring control within loops, 58–59
transforming strings, 212, 217–219
Transmission Control Protocol/Internet Protocol. *See* TCP/IP

transparency of forms, 287–290
transparent proxies, 645
transport sinks, 644
TreeNode class, 349–352
tree nodes
    adding on, 491–493
    deleting on, 491–493
TreeView class, 349–355
trimming strings, 438–439
TrueType fonts, 428. *See also* fonts
try block, 151
TryParse method, 49–50
TTL (time-to-live), 671
two-way data binding, 550–551
typefaces. *See* fonts
types
    CLS, 12
    CTS, 11–13
    enumeration (C#), 66–69
    generics, 131–133
    numeric, 49–50
    references, 11
        classes, 138
        support for CLR, 73–77
    registering, 652–654
<Types>, 896

U

UDDI (Universal Description Discovery and Integration), 872
unhandled exceptions, 157–159. *See also* handling exceptions
Unicode standards, 204–208
Uniform Resource Identifier. *See* URI
Uniform Resource Locator. *See* URL
Universal Description Discovery and Integration. *See* UDDI
updating
    application state data, 837
    controls
        data sources, 551
        values, 550–551
    databases, 525–529, 562–563
    errors, 528
    identifying, 561–562
    .NET Framework, 23
URI (Uniform Resource Identifier), 734
URL (Uniform Resource Locator), 859
user controls
    applying, 361–362
    building, 359–361
    at design time, 362–363
user interfaces. *See also* interfaces
    multithreading, 605–606
using statements, namespaces, 40
UTF-8, UTF-16, 219

V

validation
    XML, 480–481
    XSD, 467–468
Validation controls, 784-789
    CustomValidator control, 787-788
    ValidationSummary control, 788–789
Value types
    support for CLR, 73–77
    types, 11
variables
    assigning, 77
    Char, 205–206
VaryByCustom attribute, 843–844
VaryByHeader attribute, 843–844
VaryByParam attribute, 843–844
verbatim strings, 62
versioning
    assemblies, 16, 690–691, 727
    modifiers, 101–102
    serialized objects, 191–192
View state, 744–746
    data caching as substitute for, 846–847
virtual mode, DataGridView class, 579–584
virtual modifiers, 100–101
Visual Studio.NET
    inherited forms
        creating, 315
    MDI menus, 305–306
    proxy classes, 894
    resource localization, 374
    satellite assembles, 375–376
    Web services, 878–880

W

walking the call stack, 693
Web clients, creating, 848–851
web.config file, 818–823
    authorization, 830–831
    forms authentication, 828–830
    Web services, 883
Web controls, customizing, 793–801
Web Form controls, 758–772
WebMethod attribute, 876–877, 881–883
Web pages
    compiling, 740
    controls, 802
    scraping, 850
WebRequest class, 848–851
WebResponse class, 848–851
WebService attribute, 881
WebService directive, 876
Web services
    access, 877
    Amazon, 909–912

Web services *(continued)*
   applying, 871–874
   building, 875–894
   clients (Windows Forms), 913–915
   complex data types, 906–915
   extending, 880–883
   overview of, 870–874
   performance, 916–918
   sessions, 882
   SOAP, 898–906
   testing, 877–878
   Web.config file, 883
Web Services Description Language. *See* WSDL
Web Services Security. *See* WS-Security
well known objects. *See* WKO
while loop, 55
widening conversion, 46
wincv.exe, 28
Windows
   application unhandled exceptions, 158–159
   Bit Block Transfer, 421–422
   Forms, 268–271. *See also* forms
   GDI+, 421–422
Windows Forms
   Web services clients, 913–915
Windows.Forms.Form class, 271–284
WKO (well known objects), 649
wrappers, HelpProvider, 312–313
writing
   resource files, 372
   XML, 482–484
wsdl.exe utility, 885–890
WSDL (Web Services Description Language), 871, 895–898
WS-Security (Web Services Security), 905

X

XCOPY, 722–723
XmlDataDocument class (XPath), 491–493

XmlDataSource control, 781–784
XmlDocument class (XPath), 489
XML (Extended Markup Language)
   ADO.NET, 533–540
   applying, 462–471
   attributes, 465–466
   DataSet class, 534–540
   documentation tags, 44
   enumeration, 476
   formatting, 917–918
   overview of, 461–462
   reading, 472–482, 537–540
   resource files, 369–373
   schemas, 480–481
   searching with XPath, 484–493
   serialization, 462–466
   Web services, 870. *See also* Web services
   writing, 482–484
XmlNodeReader class, 477–479
XmlReader class, 472–477
XmlReaderSettings class, 489–480
XML Schema Definition. *See* XSD
XmlSerializer class, 463–465
XmlWriter class, 482–484
XPath
   functions, 488–489
   navigating, 485
   operators, 487–489
   queries, 486–489
   searching XML with, 484–493
   XmlDataDocument class, 491–493
   XmlDocument class, 489
XPathDocument class, 490
XSD (XML Schema Definition), 466–468
XSLT (Extended Style Language Transformation), 468–471
XslTransform class, 469–471

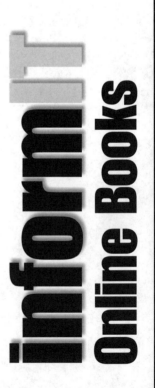

TOMORROW'S SOLUTIONS FOR TODAY'S PROFESSIONALS

Prentice Hall Professional Technical Reference

| Browse | Book Series | What's New | User Groups | Alliances | Special Sales | Contact Us |

Search | Help | Home

Quick Search

PTR Favorites

Find a Bookstore

Book Series

Special Interests

Newsletters

Press Room

International

Best Sellers

Solutions Beyond the Book

Shopping Bag

Keep Up to Date with
PH PTR Online

We strive to stay on the cutting edge of what's happening in professional computer science and engineering. Here's a bit of what you'll find when you stop by **www.phptr.com**:

❗ What's new at PHPTR? We don't just publish books for the professional community, we're a part of it. Check out our convention schedule, keep up with your favorite authors, and get the latest reviews and press releases on topics of interest to you.

@ Special interest areas offering our latest books, book series, features of the month, related links, and other useful information to help you get the job done.

✍ User Groups Prentice Hall Professional Technical Reference's User Group Program helps volunteer, not-for-profit user groups provide their members with training and information about cutting-edge technology.

↔ Companion Websites Our Companion Websites provide valuable solutions beyond the book. Here you can download the source code, get updates and corrections, chat with other users and the author about the book, or discover links to other websites on this topic.

📖 Need to find a bookstore? Chances are, there's a bookseller near you that carries a broad selection of PTR titles. Locate a Magnet bookstore near you at www.phptr.com.

✉ Subscribe today! Join PHPTR's monthly email newsletter! Want to be kept up-to-date on your area of interest? Choose a targeted category on our website, and we'll keep you informed of the latest PHPTR products, author events, reviews and conferences in your interest area.

Visit our mailroom to subscribe today! **http://www.phptr.com/mail_lists**

informIT

THE COUNT OF
MONTE CRISTO

THE COUNT OF MONTE CRISTO

Alexandre Dumas

Supplementary material written by
Margaret Brantley

Series edited by Brantley Johnson

POCKET BOOKS
NEW YORK LONDON TORONTO SYDNEY

This book is a work of fiction. Names, characters, places and incidents are products of the author's imagination or are used fictitiously. Any resemblance to actual events or locales or persons, living or dead, is entirely coincidental.

POCKET BOOKS, a division of Simon & Schuster, Inc.
1230 Avenue of the Americas, New York, NY 10020

Supplementary materials copyright © 2004 by Simon & Schuster, Inc.

ISBN: 0-7434-8755-9

First Pocket Books printing May 2004

10 9 8 7 6 5 4 3 2 1

POCKET and colophon are registered trademarks of Simon & Schuster, Inc.

Cover art by Dan Craig

Manufactured in the United States of America

For information regarding special discounts for bulk purchases, please contact Simon & Schuster Special Sales at 1-800-456-6798 or business@simonandschuster.com

Contents

Introduction	ix
Chronology of Alexandre Dumas's Life and Work	xvii
Historical Context of *The Count of Monte Cristo*	xix

The Count of Monte Cristo

I	Marseilles—The Arrival	1
II	Father and Son	10
III	The Catalans	15
IV	The Betrothal Feast	23
V	The Deputy Procureur du Roi	31
VI	The Examination	36
VII	The Château d'If	45
VIII	Villefort and Mercédès	54
IX	The Little Cabinet of the Tuileries	58
X	The Ogre	64
XI	The Hundred Days	68
XII	Numbers 34 and 27	72
XIII	An Italian Scholar	83

v

XIV	THE TREASURE	100
XV	THE THIRD ATTACK	112
XVI	THE CEMETERY OF THE CHÂTEAU D'IF	118
XVII	THE ISLE OF TIBOULEN	122
XVIII	THE ISLE OF MONTE CRISTO	133
XIX	THE TREASURE CAVE	138
XX	THE STRANGER	145
XXI	THE PONT DU GARD INN	148
XXII	CADEROUSSE'S STORY	154
XXIII	THE PRISON REGISTER	165
XXIV	MORREL AND SON	171
XXV	THE FIFTH OF SEPTEMBER	183
XXVI	ROMAN BANDITS	192
XXVII	THE APPARITION	198
XXVIII	THE CARNIVAL AT ROME	208
XXIX	THE CATACOMBS OF ST SEBASTIAN	221
XXX	THE GUESTS	237
XXXI	THE PRESENTATION	254
XXXII	UNLIMITED CREDIT	263
XXXIII	THE PAIR OF DAPPLED GREYS	271
XXXIV	HAYDEE	279
XXXV	THE MORREL FAMILY	284
XXXVI	TOXICOLOGY	290
XXXVII	THE RISE AND FALL OF STOCKS	300
XXXVIII	PYRAMUS AND THISBE	308
XXXIX	M. NOIRTIER DE VILLEFORT	316
XL	THE WILL	323
XLI	THE TELEGRAPH	331
XLII	THE DINNER	337
XLIII	A CONJUGAL SCENE	348
XLIV	MATRIMONIAL PLANS	355
XLV	A SUMMER BALL	361

XLVI	MME DE SAINT-MÉRAN	377
XLVII	THE PROMISE	383
XLVIII	MINUTES OF THE PROCEEDINGS	402
XLIX	THE PROGRESS OF CAVALCANTI JUNIOR	419
L	HAYDEE'S STORY	426
LI	THE REPORT FROM JANINA	444
LII	THE LEMONADE	452
LIII	THE ACCUSATION	463
LIV	THE TRIAL	468
LV	THE CHALLENGE	479
LVI	THE INSULT	484
LVII	THE NIGHT	491
LVIII	THE DUEL	498
LIX	REVENGE	502
LX	VALENTINE	512
LXI	THE SECRET DOOR	525
LXII	THE APPARITION AGAIN	531
LXIII	THE SERPENT	537
LXIV	MAXIMILIAN	542
LXV	DANGLARS' SIGNATURE	550
LXVI	CONSOLATION	557
LXVII	SEPARATION	568
LXVIII	THE JUDGE	582
LXIX	EXPIATION	591
LXX	THE DEPARTURE	597
LXXI	THE FIFTH OF OCTOBER	611
	NOTES	621
	INTERPRETIVE NOTES	637
	CRITICAL EXCERPTS	647
	QUESTIONS FOR DISCUSSION	661
	SUGGESTIONS FOR THE INTERESTED READER	663

INTRODUCTION

The Count of Monte Cristo:
THE NINETEENTH CENTURY'S
POP CULTURE SUPERHERO

Alexandre Dumas's rise to fame was boosted by changes in France's social fabric. Literacy was surging, newspapers were booming, and the general population was clamoring for something to read. Dumas gave them what they wanted: page-turning thrills and romance. Elitist critics accused him of pandering to the coarse tastes of the common people, but such criticisms went virtually unnoticed. When *The Count of Monte Cristo* appeared in serial form in 1844, it became a sensation. Within months, it had been translated into ten languages and could count the highest intellects of the era among its fans. William Makepeace Thackeray and Robert Louis Stevenson sang its praises unabashedly. Its popularity has hardly dimmed in more than 150 years. Since the dawn of motion pictures and television, it has been adapted no fewer than fifty times.

In eulogies that appeared in the years after his death, critics grudgingly began to give Dumas his due, and the place of *The Count of Monte Cristo* in literary history came into focus. These critics now acknowledged what readers had long known: that the adventure, thrills, and sheer pleasure of reading the book could overcome its historical inaccuracies, plot contrivances, and one-dimensional characters. Dumas's masterful pacing and dialogue hold readers' rapt attention as the Count's mission ignites their imaginations. Finer novels have been written, to be sure, but *The Count of Monte Cristo* remains relevant, beloved, and admired to this day, despite its imperfections.

The Count is Dumas's greatest contribution to literature. He is seemingly superhuman, and his story lunges forward on the steam of injustice, vengefulness, and righteousness. The patron saint of the wronged, he inspires our fantasies like the shadowy heroes of comic books to come—figures like Batman, the Daredevil, and the Crow—who draw strength and stamina from their thirst for justice and desire for revenge.

The Life and Work of Alexandre Dumas

Alexandre Dumas ranks among the most widely read novelists of Romantic literature and may be the most beloved writer France has ever produced. His works are stories of adventure depicting the heroic triumph of human strength and endurance, a legacy he was born to recount.

Dumas's father, Thomas-Alexandre, was born a slave on Santo Domingo (now Haiti) in 1762 to a black slave, Cessette Dumas, and her owner, the Marquis de la Pailleterie, a Frenchman who had come to the Caribbean to seek his fortune as a sugar planter. The marquis sold Thomas and three of his siblings, but bought him back and then took him to France when he was fourteen years old. The young man severed ties with his father, took his mother's name, and joined the army. By thirty-one he was serving as a general under Napoleon Bonaparte. The bravery Thomas-Alexandre exhibited and the injustices he suffered were worthy of one of his son's plot lines. During the Egyptian campaign, he had a falling out with Napoleon, who refused to pay his pension, and died at the age of forty-three, leaving his widow and two children virtually penniless.

Alexandre Dumas was born in Villers-Cotterêts, France,

on July 24, 1802. His early education was provided by family, neighbors, and the local priest, but in 1812 Alexandre's mother was granted a license to sell tobacco, which ultimately gave her enough money to send him to private school. At the age of thirteen, Dumas felt the first stirrings of literary ambition when a friend, Auguste Lafarge, wrote a witty epigram to get back at a girl who had jilted him. Soon the stanza became very popular. Dumas was impressed by the glory of having others speak his friend's name even when he wasn't there, as well as by the power of the pen as an instrument of revenge.

He moved to Paris in 1823, and with his beautiful penmanship found a position as a clerk for the secretary of the Duc d'Orleans—the future King Louis-Philippe. Dumas's son, also called Alexandre, was born in 1824 to his mistress Catherine Lebay. The son would earn his own renown as a writer, most notably of *La Dame aux Camélias*, which would be adapted as the opera *La Traviatta* and later as the classic Greta Garbo film *Camille*. History distinguishes the two Alexandre Dumases as Dumas *père* (the father) and Dumas *fils* (the son).

Dumas *père* spent his early twenties reading, attending the theater, and writing, but it was a season of Shakespeare performed in Paris by an English company in 1827 and 1828 that inspired him and spurred his success. In 1829 his play *Henri III et sa cour (Henry III and His Court)* debuted at the Comedie Française, with the Duc d'Orleans along with some thirty princes and princesses as his guests. The duc led a lengthy, roaring standing ovation, and fame and glory came to Dumas overnight. Another play, *Christine*, was staged in 1830, followed by five more—*Napoléon Bonaparte, Antony, Hernani, Charles VII et ses grands vassaux (Charles VII and the Barons)*, and *Richard Darlington*—in 1831. Now the darling of Parisian literary and social circles, Dumas traveled extensively and turned each of his travels into yet another successful book.

The 1830s brought two social developments in France

that would take Dumas to even greater heights. In 1833, French primary education was reorganized under Guizot's law, and literacy jumped from about 40 percent to almost 100 percent in a generation. Press censorship was also lifted in the 1830s, leading to a proliferation of newspapers. In their fight to gain readers, editors began to publish serial novels that attracted readers of every class, age, and background. Dumas was a master of the form, writing stories of French history with engaging characters and at a lively pace. He was also a master of suspense, always leaving his audience hungry for more.

As a writer, Dumas was extraordinarily prolific: his complete works fill more than three hundred volumes. Though he freely admitted to collaborating with assistants and secretaries, his critics still dismissed him as a plagiarist. His most fruitful creative partnership was with Auguste Maquet, a young historian endowed with a lively imagination. It was through this partnership that Dumas's most remembered novels were produced, including *The Three Musketeers*, *The Count of Monte Cristo*, *Twenty Years After*, and *Queen Margot*. Amazingly, the two best known of these were written at least partly at the same time. *The Three Musketeers* was published serially in *La Siècle* in 1844, while installments of *The Count of Monte Cristo* began running in *La Journal des débats*. With the success of these *romans-feuilletons*, or serial novels, Dumas became known as "the King of Paris." A saying held that "when Dumas snores, Paris turns in its sleep."

In 1840 he married Ida Ferrier, his mistress of eight years, but they separated in 1844. He made fortunes and spent lavishly, including Ida's dowry, claiming never to have denied money to anyone but his creditors. He spent 200,000 francs to build his home, the Château de Monte Cristo, and had six hundred people at the house-warming party in 1847. By 1850 Dumas was nearly bankrupt and was forced to sell the estate for about 30,000 francs. He fled to Belgium in 1851 to avoid his creditors, but returned to Paris

in 1853 and founded a daily paper called *Le Mousquetaire.*
It was followed in 1857 by the literary weekly *Le Monte
Cristo,* and in 1860 by *L'Indipendente,* a political and liter-
ary journal in French and Italian, which he edited from
Naples.

Dumas was a big man with a big imagination and a big
appetite for life. He lived as adventurously as he wrote and
was notorious for having fathered dozens of illegitimate
children—though he acknowledged only three. Alexandre
Dumas died on his son's estate on December 5, 1870. A
statue was erected of him in Paris on the Place Malesherbes
in 1883, and another in Villers-Cotterets commemorates
the town's favorite son, one of the most prolific and loved
writers of the nineteenth century.

Historical and Literary Context of
The Count of Monte Cristo

Power Shifts in Nineteenth-Century France

In less than a century, from 1789 to 1870, France's political
structure was utterly transformed no fewer than a dozen
times. Schemes to overthrow or restore one faction or
another meant each regime guarded its power fiercely, suppressing those who threatened to usurp it, or when a new
authority ascended, punishing those who had suppressed it
under the previous rule.

Until the 1780s France's privileged classes—the clergy
and the nobility—governed the country, while the productive class—the third estate—paid heavy taxes to foot the
bill. Outdated farming methods created food shortages,
while extravagance in the court of King Louis XVI and his
queen, Marie Antoinette, sparked outrage. A bloody revolution began in 1789, and both monarchs were beheaded in
the overthrow of the monarchy. In 1792 the new assembly
declared itself to be the French Republic. Internal power

struggles led to the creation not of a democracy but of a war dictatorship that tried to maintain order by executing everyone it considered a threat. In the span of about a year, from 1793 to 1794, thousands lost their heads to the guillotine in a period known as the Reign of Terror.

The turmoil spread beyond the country's borders. France had declared war on Austria in 1792, and was busy in Europe fighting governments sympathetic to the Austrian monarchy. Seventeen ninety-five saw another new constitution in France, followed in 1797 by another coup. In 1799, General Napoleon Bonaparte, returning home from a military campaign in Egypt, seized control of French leadership and established the Consulate. Five years later, abandoning any charade of a French Republic, he declared himself emperor, and within a decade he had conquered Europe from Spain to the border of Russia. In 1814, after losses at the hands of Britain, Germany, and Spain, Napoleon abdicated and went into exile on the Isle of Elba.

The Bourbon monarchy was restored under King Louis XVIII, but a brief return by Napoleon in 1815 interrupted the king's rule. After Napoleon's second exile, Louis XVIII reassumed the throne, and this second restoration lasted until 1830, when a popular revolution forced the ultra-Royalist Charles X out in favor of the more moderate Duc d'Orleans, or King Louis Philippe. His reign lasted eighteen years, ending when the failure of his elitist government to embrace social progress prompted another revolution and the establishment of the Second Republic in 1848, with Napoleon Bonaparte's nephew, Napoleon III, as president. Though Napoleon III seized power from the parliament in 1851 and declared himself emperor in 1852, he began shifting power back to the legislature in 1860. By 1870, France was again a parliamentary monarchy. Napoleon III's rule collapsed with France's defeat in the Franco-Prussian War, and was replaced by the Third French Republic. It was a rocky government, but consistent enough to remain in power until the German occupation and installation of the Vichy regime during World War II.

The Romantic Movement in Literature

The Romantic movement in literature lasted from the late eighteenth century to the middle of the nineteenth century. It was a rejection of the order, calm, and rationalism of the preceding Enlightenment era in favor of change, chaos, and emotional expression. Romantics were inspired by the idealism behind the French Revolution and the rise of Napoleon Bonaparte, but appalled by the viciousness of the Reign of Terror. Some were optimistic that humankind could create its own utopia, but the reality of events around them made them wary of the darker side of human nature.

Romantic art is marked by an appreciation of the beauty of nature, the importance of self-examination, and the value of the creative spirit. Nationalism, folk culture, the exotic, and the supernatural were also topics of interest. To the Romantic, inspiration, intuition, and imagination were seen as divine sparks that pointed to truth. The literature of the Romantic movement also focused on the faraway, the long-ago, and the lurid; escapism from contemporary problems; and nature as a source of knowledge, refuge, and divinity. To explore these subjects, Romantic writers emphasized emotion and subjectivity, and often expected that their readers suspend their disbelief.

Romantic writers valued individual voices, including those of women and "common people." These voices tended to idealize the pastoral lives of farmers, shepherds, milkmaids, and other rustic people—figures who seemed to them to belong to a simpler, more wholesome, less cynical time when people lived in harmony with nature. The works of poet William Wordsworth—especially his *Lyrical Ballads* (1798)—provide good examples of this idealization. The Romantic sensibility also allowed women authors such as

Ann Radcliffe, Jane Austen, Mary Shelley, and the Brontë sisters to flourish.

Romantic Writers

The "Byronic hero" emerged as a Romantic archetype in the early nineteenth century. Inspired by the poetry of Lord Byron, the Byronic hero is not a particularly virtuous figure. He is larger than life, often an exile of sorts, with a dark past, fierce passions, superior intellect, and brooding nature. Common in Gothic English literature, versions of this persona were found throughout Europe as the nineteenth century progressed. The passions and struggles of exceptional individuals would become the focus of Romantic novels from Goethe, Victor Hugo, and Alexandre Dumas.

. As the dust settled on France's political upheavals, the public earlier content with diverting comedies wanted to see more noble emotions displayed. The Romantic melodrama—featuring elements of comedy, tragedy, and music—gained popularity. These melodramas focused on anti-Classical structure with sensational plots involving a dark villain, an unfortunate heroine, a dashing hero, and a simpleton for comic relief. Virtue always triumphed. The works of Victor Hugo and Alexandre Dumas were paragons of the form. As the stories moved from the stage to the page, they bloomed into historical and adventure novels, where again Hugo and Dumas excelled.

CHRONOLOGY OF ALEXANDRE DUMAS'S LIFE AND WORK

Time Line: Alexandre Dumas

1802: Born on May 1 at Villers-Cotterêts.

1806: General Dumas, Alexandre's father, dies on February 26.

1812: Alexandre's mother is granted a license to sell tobacco, and begins earning enough to send him to private school.

1817: Becomes an office boy for a notary.

1823: Moves to Paris and works as a clerk for the Duc d'Orleans, the future King Louis-Philippe. He meets and falls in love with Marie-Catherine Lebay.

1824: Alexandre Dumas *fils* (the son) is born on July 27 to Alexandre Dumas *père* (the father) and his mistress, Catherine Lebay.

1826: Publishes *Nouvelles contemporaines (Tales of Today),* a small volume of short stories.

1829: *Henri III et sa cour (Henry III and His Court)* opens—a sensation that runs for thirty-seven performances.

1830: *Christine* is staged and is well received. He begins his affair with Belle Krelsamer.

1831: Marie-Alexandrine, his daughter by mistress Belle Krelsamer, is born on March 5. His plays *Napoléon Bonaparte, Antony, Hernani, Charles VII et ses grands vassaux (Charles VII and the Barons),* and *Richard Darlington* debut.

1832: In February an affair begins with the actress Ida Ferrier.

1836: Returns to the theater with the successful *Kean.*

1837: Dumas is made a chevalier (knight) in the French Legion of Honor.

1840: On February 1 marries Ida Ferrier.

1842: His first collaboration with Auguste Maquet, the historical novel *Le Chevalier d'Harmental,* is published.

1843: *Georges,* a tale of vengeance and forerunner to *The Count of Monte Cristo,* is published.

1844: *The Three Musketeers* is published serially in *La Siècle,* while installments of *The Count of Monte Cristo* begin running in *La Journal des débats.* Dumas and Ida separate in October. His son comes to live with him for three years.

1848: Establishes and edits a newspaper, *Le Mois.*

1851: Flees to Belgium to avoid his creditors. Son Henri Bauër is born.

1852: · The first volumes of his memoirs, *Mes Mémoires,* are published. Declares bankruptcy.

1853: Reaches an agreement with his creditors and returns to Paris, where he begins producing the periodical *Le Mousquetaire,* for which he writes most of the copy.

1859: Ex-wife, Ida, dies of cancer. He begins an affair with Emilie Cordier.

1860: Begins editing *L'Indipendente,* a literary and political journal published in French and Italian. Micaëlla Cordier, his daughter by Emilie, is born on December 24.

1870: Suffers a stroke in September and dies at his son's home in December.

HISTORICAL CONTEXT OF
The Count of Monte Cristo

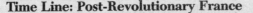

Time Line: Post-Revolutionary France

1789: The storming of the Bastille begins the French Revolution.

1792: War with Austria begins. The French royal family is imprisoned and the First Republic is established.

1793: Louis XVI and Marie Antoinette are executed. The Reign of Terror begins.

1794: Robespierre is executed, ending the Reign of Terror. Capital punishment is abolished.

1796: General Napoleon Bonaparte's first big campaign: a victory over Austria.

1799: Bonaparte seizes power in a coup d'état and declares himself First Consul.

1802: Napoleon becomes First Consul for life.

1804: Napoleon crowns himself emperor and states his intention to conquer England, Spain, and Russia. The Code Napoleon forms the basis of a new French civil and judicial system.

1805: British Admiral Nelson defeats Napoleon in the Battle of Trafalgar.

1806: Napoleon dissolves the Holy Roman Empire and

makes his brothers kings of Naples, Holland, and Westphalia.

1812: Napoleon is forced to withdraw from Russia.

1813: Napoleon's army is defeated by Russia, Prussia, and Austria at the Battle of Leipzig.

1814: The allies then capture Paris in March, and Napoleon abdicates and is exiled to Elba in April. Louis XVIII, the younger brother of Louis XVI, ascends the French throne as a constitutional monarch.

1815: Napoleon escapes from exile and returns to Paris; Louis XVIII flees to Belgium. Napoleon's forces are soundly defeated at Waterloo by British and Prussian armies. Napoleon is exiled to St. Helena and Louis XVIII is restored to the throne.

1824: Charles X becomes king of France after the death of his brother Louis XVIII.

1830: Charles X's repressive policies provoke upheaval. He abdicates in August and is succeeded by the former Duc d'Orleans, now Louis-Philippe I.

1835: An attempt to assassinate Louis-Philippe results in harsh measures and social unrest.

1848: The Second Republic is proclaimed after revolution in Paris. Louis-Philippe abdicates. Napoleon's nephew Louis Napoleon (Napoleon III) is elected president.

1851: Louis Napoleon stages a coup d'état and establishes the Second Empire.

1852: Napoleon III is ratified as emperor by the Legislative Assembly.

Chapter I

MARSEILLES—THE ARRIVAL

✦

On the 24th of February, 1815, the watch-tower of Notre Dame de la Garde signalled the arrival of the three-master *Pharaon*, from Smyrna, Trieste, and Naples.[1]

The usual crowd of curious spectators immediately filled the quay of Fort Saint-Jean, for at Marseilles[2] the arrival of a ship is always a great event, especially when that ship, as was the case with the *Pharaon*, has been built, rigged, and laden in the dockyard of old Phocaea and belongs to a shipowner of their own town.

Meanwhile the vessel drew on, and was approaching the harbour under topsails, jib, and foresail, but so slowly and with such an air of melancholy that the spectators, always ready to sense misfortune, began to ask one another what ill-luck had overtaken those on board. However, those experienced in navigation soon saw that if there had been any ill-luck, the ship had not been the sufferer, for she advanced in perfect condition and under skilful handling; the anchor was ready to be dropped, the bowsprit shrouds loose. Beside the pilot, who was steering the *Pharaon* through the narrow entrance to the port, there stood a young man, quick of gesture and keen of eye, who watched every movement of the ship while repeating each of the pilot's orders.

The vague anxiety that prevailed among the crowd

affected one of the spectators so much that he could not wait until the ship reached the port; jumping into a small boat, he ordered the boatman to row him alongside the *Pharaon*, which he reached opposite the creek of La Réserve.

On seeing this man approach, the young sailor left his post beside the pilot, and, hat in hand, leant over the ship's bulwarks.[3] He was a tall, lithe young man of about twenty years of age, with fine dark eyes and hair as black as ebony; his whole manner bespoke that air of calm resolution peculiar to those who, from their childhood, have been accustomed to face danger.

"Ah, is that you, Dantès!" cried the man in the boat. "You are looking pretty gloomy on board. What has happened?"

"A great misfortune, Monsieur Morrel," replied the young man, "a great misfortune, especially for me! We lost our brave Captain Leclère off Civita Vecchia."[4]

"What happened to him?" asked the shipowner. "What has happened to our worthy captain?"

"He died of brain-fever in dreadful agony. Alas, monsieur, the whole thing was most unexpected. After a long conversation with the harbourmaster, Captain Leclère left Naples in a great state of agitation. In twenty-four hours he was in high fever, and died three days afterwards. We performed the usual burial service. He is now at rest off the Isle of El Giglio,[5] sewn up in his hammock, with a thirty-six-pounder shot at his head and another at his heels. We have brought home his sword and his cross of honour to his widow. But was it worth his while," added the young man, with a sad smile, "to wage war against the English for ten long years only to die in his bed like everybody else?"

"Well, well, Monsieur Edmond," replied the owner, who appeared more comforted with every moment, "we are all mortal, and the old must make way for the young, otherwise there would be no promotion. And the cargo . . . ?"

"Is all safe and sound, Monsieur Morrel, take my word for it. It has been a voyage that will bring you in a good twenty-five thousand francs!"

As they were just past the Round Tower the young man shouted out: "Ready there! Lower topsails, foresail, and jib!"

The order was executed as promptly as on board a man-of-war.

"Lower away! and brail[6] all!"

At this last order, all the sails were lowered and the ship moved on almost imperceptibly.

"And now, Monsieur Morrel," said Dantès, "here is your purser, Monsieur Danglars, coming out of his cabin. If you will step on board he will furnish you with every particular. I must look after the anchoring and dress the ship in mourning."

The owner did not wait to be invited twice. He seized a rope which Dantès flung to him, and, with an agility that would have done credit to a sailor, climbed up the ladder attached to the side of the ship, while the young man, returning to his duty, left the conversation to the individual whom he had announced under the name of Danglars, and who now came toward the owner. He was a man of twenty-five or twenty-six, of unprepossessing countenance, obsequious to his superiors, insolent to his subordinates; and besides the fact that he was the purser—and pursers are always unpopular on board—he was personally as much disliked by the crew as Edmond Dantès was beloved by them.

"Well, Monsieur Morrel," said Danglars, "you have heard of the misfortune that has befallen us?"

"Yes, yes, poor Captain Leclère! He was a brave and honest man!"

"And a first-rate seaman, grown old between sky and ocean, as a man should be who is entrusted with the interests of so important a firm as that of Morrel and Son," replied Danglars.

"But," replied the owner, watching Dantès at his work, "it seems to me that a sailor need not be so old to understand his business; our friend Edmond seems to understand it thoroughly, and to require no instructions from anyone."

"Yes," said Danglars, casting a look of hatred on Dantès, "yes, he is young, and youth is never lacking in self-confidence. The captain was hardly dead when, without consulting anyone, he assumed command of the ship, and was the cause of our losing a day and a half off the Isle of Elba[7] instead of making direct for Marseilles."

"As captain's mate, it was his duty to take command, but he acted wrongly in losing a day and a half off Elba unless the ship was in need of repair."

"The ship was as right as I am and as I hope you are, Monsieur Morrel; it was nothing more than a whim on his part, and a fancy for going ashore, that caused the delay off Elba."

"Dantès," called the owner, turning toward the young man, "just step this way, will you?"

"One moment, monsieur," he replied, "and I shall be with you." Then turning to the crew, he called out: "Let go!"

The anchor was instantly dropped and the chain ran out with a great rattle. In spite of the pilot's presence Dantès remained at his post until this last task was accomplished, and then he added: "Lower the flag and pennant to half-mast and slope the yards!"

"You see," said Danglars, "he already imagines himself captain."

"And so he is," said his companion. "Why should we not give him the post? I know he is young, but he seems to be an able and thoroughly experienced seaman."

A cloud passed over Danglars' brow.

"Your pardon, Monsieur Morrel," said Dantès, approaching. "Now that the boat is anchored, I am at your service. I believe you called me."

Danglars retreated a step or two.

"I wished to know the reason of the delay off Elba."

"I am unaware of the reason, monsieur; I only followed the last instructions of Captain Leclère, who, when dying, gave me a packet for the Maréchal Bertrand."

"And did you see the Maréchal?"

"Yes."

Morrel glanced around him and then drew Dantès on one side.

"How is the Emperor?" he asked eagerly.

"Very well, so far as I could see. He came into the Maréchal's room while I was there."

"Did you speak to him?"

"It was he who spoke to me, monsieur," said Dantès, smiling. "He asked me some questions about the ship, about the time of her departure for Marseilles, the route she had followed, and the cargo she carried. I believe that had she been empty and I the master, he would have bought her; but I told him I was only the mate and that the ship belonged to the firm of Morrel and Son. 'Ah, ah,' said he. 'I know the firm. The Morrels have all been ship-owners for generations, and there was a Morrel who served in the same regiment with me when I was garrisoned at Valance.'"

"Quite true! Quite true!" Monsieur Morrel exclaimed, delighted. "It was Policar Morrel, my uncle, who afterwards became a captain. Dantès, you must tell my uncle that the Emperor still remembers him and you will see tears of joy in the old soldier's eyes. Well, well!" he added, giving Dantès a friendly tap on the shoulder, "you were quite right in carrying out Captain Leclère's instructions and putting in at the Isle of Elba, though if it were known that you delivered a packet to the Maréchal and talked with the Emperor you might get into trouble."

"How so?" said Dantès. "I don't even know what the packet contained, and the Emperor merely made such inquiries as he would of any newcomer. But excuse me, monsieur, for one moment, here are the medical and customs officers coming on board."

As the young man departed Danglars approached.

"Well," said he, "it would seem that he has given you good reasons for dropping anchor off Porto Ferrajo?"

"Most satisfactory ones, dear Monsieur Danglars."

"So much the better," replied the purser, "for it is never pleasant to see a comrade neglect his duty."

"Dantès certainly did his, and there is nothing more to be said on the matter. It was Captain Leclère who ordered him to call at Elba."

"Talking of Captain Leclère, hasn't Dantès given you a letter from him?"

"No, was there one for me?"

"I think that, in addition to the packet, Captain Leclère gave him a letter."

"What packet do you mean, Danglars?"

"The one Dantès delivered at Porto Ferrajo."

"How do you know that he had a packet for Porto Ferrajo?"

Danglars turned red.

"I was passing the captain's door, which was ajar, and saw him give Dantès the packet and the letter."

"He has not mentioned a letter to me, but if he has one I have no doubt he will give it to me."

"Then, Monsieur Morrel, pray don't mention it to Dantès. Perhaps I am mistaken."

Just then the young man returned and Danglars retreated as before.

"Well, Dantès, have you finished now?"

"Yes, monsieur."

"Then you can come and dine with us?"

"I beg you to excuse me, Monsieur Morrel. I owe my first visit to my father. All the same, I greatly appreciate the honour you pay me."

"You are quite right, Dantès. I know you are a good son."

"And do you know if my father is quite well?" he asked with some hesitation.

"Oh, I believe so, my dear Edmond, but I have not seen him lately. At any rate I am sure that he has not wanted for anything during your absence."

Dantès smiled. "My father is proud, monsieur, and even had he been in want of everything, I doubt whether he would have asked anything of anybody except God."

"Well, then, after this first visit has been paid, may we count on you?"

"Once more I must ask you to excuse me, Monsieur Morrel. There is yet another visit which I am most anxious to pay."

"True, Dantès; I had forgotten that there is at the Catalans someone who is awaiting you with as much impatience as your father—the fair Mercédès."

Dantès smiled.

"Well! well!" said the shipowner. "Now I understand why she came to me three times for news of the *Pharaon*. Upon my word, Edmond, you are to be envied: she is a handsome girl. But don't let me keep you any longer. You have looked after my affairs so well that it is but your due that you should now have time to look after your own. Are you in need of money?"

"No, thank you, monsieur, I have all my pay from the voyage; that is nearly three months' salary."

"You are a careful fellow, Edmond."

"Say rather that I have a poor father."

"Yes, yes, I know you are a good son. Off you go to your father. I too have a son, and I should be very angry with anyone who kept him away from me after a three months' voyage."

"I have your leave, monsieur?" said the young man, saluting.

"Yes, if you have nothing more to say to me. By the way, before Captain Leclère died, did he not give you a letter for me?"

"He was unable to write, monsieur. But that reminds me, I shall have to ask you for a fortnight's leave."

"To get married?"

"First of all, and then for a journey to Paris."

"Very well, take what time you need. It will take us quite

six weeks to unload the cargo, and we shall not be ready to put to sea again for another three months. But you must be back in three months, for the *Pharaon* cannot sail without her captain," he added, patting the young sailor on the back.

"Without her captain, did you say?" cried Dantès, his eyes sparkling with joy. "Oh! if you really mean that, monsieur, you are touching on my fondest hopes. Is it really your intention to make me captain of the *Pharaon*?"

"If it depended on me alone, my dear Dantès, I should give you my hand saying, 'It is settled,' but I have a partner, and you know the Italian proverb, *Chi ha compagne ha padrone.*[8] But half the battle is won since you already have my vote. Leave it to me to get my partner's for you. Now, off you go; I shall remain here awhile and go over the accounts with Danglars. By the by, were you satisfied with him on the voyage?"

"That depends on what you mean by that question. If you mean as comrade I must say no, for I do not think he has been my friend ever since the day I was foolish enough to propose to him that we should stop for ten minutes at the Isle of Monte Cristo to settle a little dispute. I never ought to have made the suggestion, and he was quite right in refusing. If you mean as purser I have nothing to say against him, and I think you will be satisfied with the way in which he has discharged his duties."

Thereupon the young sailor jumped into the boat, seated himself in the stern, and ordered the oarsmen to put him ashore at the Cannebière. With a smile on his lips M. Morrel glanced after him till he saw him jump ashore. There he was immediately lost in the motley crowd that, from five o'clock in the morning until nine o'clock in the evening, collects in that famous street of the Cannebière, of which the modern Phocaeans are so proud that they say in all seriousness, and with that peculiar accent which lends so much character to what they say, "If Paris owned the Cannebière she would be a little Marseilles."

On turning round the shipowner saw Danglars standing behind him. The latter, who appeared to be awaiting his orders, was in reality, like him, following the movements of the young sailor. But how different was the expression in the eyes of each of these two men as they gazed after Dantès' retreating figure!

II

FATHER AND SON

Let us leave Danglars struggling with his feeling of hatred and trying to whisper some evil insinuation against his comrade into their master's ear, and let us follow Dantès, who, after having run along the Cannebière, turned down the Rue Noailles. Here he entered a small house situated to the left of the Allées de Meilhan, ran up the four flights of dark stairs, and, trembling with excitement, stopped before a half-open door which revealed the interior of the little room.

It was the room which Dantès' father inhabited.

The news of the *Pharaon*'s arrival had not yet reached the old man, who was mounted on a chair, and, with a hand trembling with old age, was busy staking some nasturtiums that, intermingled with clematis, climbed up the trellis before his window. Suddenly he felt an arm thrown round him, and a well-known voice called out:

"Father, my dear old Dad!"

With a cry of joy the old man turned round and saw his son; pale and visibly trembling he threw his arms round him.

"What ails you, Father?" the young man anxiously inquired. "Are you ill?"

"No, no! my dear Edmond . . . my boy . . . my son . . . not

at all, but I was not expecting you, and the joy at suddenly seeing you again has given me rather a shock."

"Well, calm yourself, Father, it is really I. They say that joy never harms anyone, so I came in without any warning. I have come back and we are going to be happy together."

"That's right, my boy," replied the old man, "but in what way are we going to be happy? You are not going to leave me any more? Come, now, tell me how you have fared."

"May God forgive me that I should rejoice in good fortune brought about by another's death! Goodness knows, I never sought it. It has happened and I have not the strength to regret it. Our good old Captain Leclère is dead, Father, and it is probable that with Monsieur Morrel's assistance I shall take his place. Do you understand, Father? A captain at twenty, with a salary of a hundred louis, besides a share in the profits! Isn't it really more than a poor sailor like me could hope for?"

"Yes, my son, yes, it certainly is," said the old man.

"With my first pay I shall buy you a little house with a garden where you can plant your clematis, your nasturtiums, and your honeysuckle. But, Father, what *is* the matter? You don't look well."

"It is nothing, it will soon pass," said the old man; but his strength failed him and he fell backward.

"This will never do!" exclaimed the youth. "A glass of wine will soon put you right. Tell me where you keep it," he continued, opening one cupboard after another.

"It is useless to look for it," said the old man. "There is no wine."

"What! no wine?" said the young man, turning pale and looking first at the old man's sunken and pallid cheeks and then at the bare cupboards. "No wine? Have you been in want of money, Father?"

"I have not wanted for anything now that you are here," said the old man.

"Yet," stammered Edmond, wiping the perspiration

from his brow, "yet when I went away three months ago I left you two hundred francs."

"True enough, but you forgot a little debt you owed to our neighbour Caderousse. He reminded me of it, and told me that if I did not pay it for you he would go to Monsieur Morrel for the money. Fearing that might do you harm, I paid it for you."

"But," cried Dantès, "I owed Caderousse a hundred and forty francs. Do you mean to say that you paid him that sum out of the two hundred francs I left you?"

The old man nodded.

"So that you have lived for three months on sixty francs?"

"You know that I require very little."

"May God forgive me!" cried Edmond, throwing himself on his knees before his father.

"Nay, nay!" said the old man, with a quiet smile. "Now that you are with me again the past is all forgotten and all is well."

"Yes," said the young man, "here I am with a little money in my pockets and a good future before me. Here, Father, take some money, take some and send for something good to eat and drink." So saying, he emptied the contents of his pockets on to the table—a dozen pieces of gold, five or six crowns, and some smaller coins.

His father's face brightened. "Whose is that?" said he.

"Mine . . . yours . . . ours! Take some, buy some provisions and be happy, for we shall have some more tomorrow."

"Gently, gently," said the old man, smiling. "If you don't mind, I shall spend your money warily. If people see me buying too many things at a time, they will think I have had to wait for your return before buying them. But hush! here comes some one; it is Caderousse, who has no doubt heard of your arrival, and has come to welcome you home."

At that moment Caderousse entered. He was a man of five- or six-and-twenty, with a mass of black hair. He carried in his hand a piece of cloth which, in his capacity of tailor, he was going to turn into a coat-lining.

"So you have come back, Edmond?" he said with a strong Marseilles accent, and with a broad smile that disclosed teeth as white as ivory.

"Yes, as you perceive, neighbour Caderousse, and ready to serve you in any way," Dantès answered, but ill concealing his coldness by these civil words.

"Thank you. Happily I am not in need of anything; it is sometimes others who have need of my assistance." Dantès made a slight movement. "I don't mean that for you, boy; I lent you money and you returned it. That was but a neighbourly action and we are now quits."

"We are never quits with those who oblige us," said Dantès, "when we no longer owe them money we owe them gratitude."

"Why speak of it? What is past is gone and done with. Let us talk of your happy return. It would appear that you have had a stroke of luck and are already well in Monsieur Morrel's good books."

"Monsieur Morrel has always been very kind to me."

"In that case you were wrong to refuse to dine with him."

"What! refuse to dine with him!" exclaimed old Dantès. "So he asked you to dinner, did he?"

"Yes, Father," returned Edmond, with a smile, "because, you know, I wanted to come to you as soon as possible."

"I don't suppose your dear kind Monsieur Morrel was over-pleased at that," said Caderousse, "and of course when a man aims at being captain he mustn't offend his employer. You should butter him up a bit."

"Oh! I hope to be captain without doing that," replied Dantès.

"Capital! That will please your old friends, and I know some one who won't be sorry to hear it."

"Do you mean Mercédès?" said the old man.

"Yes," Edmond replied. "And now that I have seen you, Father, and assured myself that you are well and want for nothing, I will ask your permission to leave you for a time. I am anxious to see Mercédès."

"Go, my son, go," said old Dantès. "And may God bless you in your wife as He has blessed me in my son."

Edmond took leave of his father, nodded to Caderousse, and went out. Caderousse waited a few minutes, and then he also descended the stairs and joined Danglars, who had been waiting for him at the corner of the Rue Senac.

"Well," said Danglars, "did you see him?"

"I have just left him," said Caderousse.

"Did he speak of his hopes of becoming captain?"

"He spoke as if it were quite settled."

"Patience," said Danglars; "it seems to me he is in too much of a hurry."

"But I believe Monsieur Morrel has even promised him the captaincy."

"Pooh!" said Danglars, "he is not captain yet! Is he still in love with the beautiful Catalan?"[1]

"Head over ears! He has just gone to see her, but if I am not greatly mistaken there is a storm brewing in that direction."

"What do you mean?"

"I do not know anything for certain, but I have seen things which make me think that the future captain will not have it all his own way up at the Vieilles-Infirmeries."[2]

"What have you seen?"

"Every time that Mercédès has come to town lately, she has been accompanied by a tall, gay young Catalan with black eyes and red complexion who seems very attentive to her, and whom she addresses as cousin."

"Really! And do you think he is making love to her?"

"I suppose so. What else would a man of twenty-one be doing with a beautiful young girl of seventeen?"

"And you say Dantès has gone to the Catalans?"

"He left before me."

"Let us go in the same direction; we can turn in at La Réserve and await events over a glass of wine."

Chapter III

THE CATALANS

About a hundred paces from the spot where the two friends were sitting sipping their wine the village of the Catalans rose behind a bare hill, exposed to the fierce sun and swept by the biting north-west wind.

One day a mysterious colony set out from Spain and landed on the narrow strip of land which they inhabit to this very day. No one knew whence they came or what tongue they spoke. One of their chiefs who could speak a little Provençal solicited from the commune of Marseilles the bare and barren promontory on which they, like the sailors of ancient times, had run their boats ashore. Their request was granted, and three months later, around the twelve or fifteen boats which had brought these Bohemians from the sea, there arose a little village.

This is the same village that we see to-day constructed in an odd and picturesque fashion, half Moorish and half Spanish, inhabited by the descendants of these people and speaking the language of their fathers. For three or four centuries they remained faithful to the little promontory on which they had settled like a flight of sea-birds. They did not mix with the inhabitants of Marseilles, but intermarried amongst their own folk and preserved the customs and costumes of their original country just as they preserved its language.

We would ask our readers to follow us along the only street of this little hamlet and enter with us one of its tiny houses. A young and beautiful girl, with hair as black as jet and eyes of the velvety softness of the gazelle, was standing leaning against the wall. Three steps away a young man of about twenty years of age was sitting tilting his chair and leaning his elbow on an old worm-eaten piece of furniture. He was looking at the girl with an air which betrayed both vexation and uneasiness; his eyes questioned her, but the girl's firm and steady gaze checked him.

"Mercédès," said the young man, "Easter is nearly round again, and it is just the right time for a wedding. Give me an answer, do!"

"I have answered you a hundred times, Fernand. I really think you must be your own enemy that you should ask me again. I have never encouraged you in your hopes, Fernand; you cannot reproach me with one coquettish look. I have always said to you: 'I am fond of you as a brother, but never ask anything more of me. My heart belongs to another.' Haven't I always told you that, Fernand?"

"Yes, I know, Mercédès. I know that you have always been cruelly frank with me."

"Fernand," Mercédès answered, shaking her head, "a woman becomes a bad housekeeper and cannot even be sure of remaining a good wife when she loves another than her husband. Be satisfied with my friendship, for, I repeat it once more, this is all I can promise you."

Fernand rose from his seat, walked round the room, and returned to Mercédès, standing before her with scowling brows.

"Tell me once more, Mercédès; is this your final answer?"

"I love Edmond Dantès," the girl answered coldly, "and none other shall be my husband."

"You will always love him?"

"As long as I live."

Fernand bowed his head in defeat, heaving a sigh resembling a groan, and then, suddenly raising his head, hissed between his clenched teeth:

"But if he is dead?"

"If he is dead I too shall die."

"But if he forgets you?"

"Mercédès!" cried a gladsome voice outside the door, "Mercédès!"

"Ah!" the girl exclaimed, blushing with joy and love, "you see he has not forgotten me since here he is!"

And she ran toward the door which she opened, calling:

"Here, Edmond, here I am!"

Fernand, pale and trembling, recoiled like a wayfarer at the sight of a snake, and, finding a chair, sat down on it.

Edmond and Mercédès fell into each other's arms. The fierce Marseilles sun which penetrated the room through the open door covered them with a flood of light. At first they saw nothing around them. Their intense happiness isolated them from the rest of the world. Suddenly Edmond became aware of the gloomy countenance of Fernand peering out of the shadows, pale and menacing, and instinctively the young man put his hand to the knife at his belt.

"I beg your pardon," said Dantès, "I did not perceive that there were three of us here." Then, turning to Mercédès, he asked, "Who is this gentleman?"

"He will be your best friend, Dantès, for he is my friend. He is my cousin Fernand, the man whom, after you, I love best in the world. Don't you recognize him?"

"Ah, so it is!" Edmond said, and, still keeping Mercédès' hand clasped in his, he held the other one out in all friendliness to the Catalan. Instead, however, of responding to this show of cordiality Fernand remained mute and motionless as a statue. Edmond cast an inquiring glance at the agitated and trembling Mercédès, and then at Fernand, who stood there gloomy and forbidding.

This glance told him all, and his brow became suffused with anger.

"I did not hasten thus to your side to find an enemy here, Mercédès."

"An enemy?" Mercédès cried, with an angry look at her cousin. "An enemy in my house, did you say, Edmond? You have no enemy here. Fernand, my brother, is not your enemy. He will grasp your hand in token of devoted friendship."

So saying, Mercédès fixed the young Catalan with an imperious look, and, as though mesmerized, he slowly approached Edmond and held out his hand. Like a powerless though furious wave his hatred had broken against the ascendancy which this girl exercised over him.

But no sooner had he touched Dantès' hand than he felt he had done all that was within his power; he turned tail and fled out of the house.

"Oh!" he cried out, running along like one demented and tearing his hair. "How can I get rid of this fellow? Poor, wretched fool that I am!"

"Hey, Fernand, where are you running to?" a voice called out.

The young man suddenly stopped, turned round, and perceived Caderousse seated at a table in an arbour of a tavern with Danglars.

"Why don't you join us?" said Caderousse. "Are you in such a hurry that you cannot wait to pass the time of the day with your friends?"

"Especially when those friends have got a full bottle before them," Danglars added.

Fernand looked at the two men as though dazed, and answered not a word. Then he wiped away the perspiration that was coursing down his face, and slowly entered the arbour. The cool shade of the place seemed to restore him to calmness and brought a feeling of relief to his exhausted body. He uttered a groan that was almost a sob, and let his head fall on to his arms crossed on the table.

"Shall I tell you what you look like, Fernand?" said Caderousse, opening the conversation with that frank brutality which the lower classes show when their curiosity gets the upper hand of them. "You look like a rejected lover!" And he accompanied his little jest with a coarse laugh.

"What are you saying?" said Danglars. "A man of his good looks is never unlucky in love. You've made a bad shot this time, Caderousse!"

"Not at all. Just listen to his sighs. Come, Fernand, raise your head and give us an answer. It is not polite to give no reply when friends inquire about your health."

"I am quite well," said Fernand, without raising his head.

"Ah, you see, Danglars," Caderousse said, winking at his friend. "This is how the land lies. Fernand, whom you see here and who is one of the bravest and best of the Catalans, to say nothing of being one of the best fishermen in Marseilles, is in love with a pretty girl called Mercédès; unfortunately, however, this fair damsel appears to be in love with the mate of the *Pharaon*, and as the *Pharaon* put into port to-day . . . well, you understand."

"No, I don't understand."

"Poor Fernand has been given his *congé*,[3] that's all."

"And what about it?" said Fernand, raising his head and looking at Caderousse as if he would vent his anger on him. "Mercédès is tied to no man, and is free to love anyone she likes, isn't she?"

"Of course, if you take it like that, it is quite a different matter, but I thought you were a Catalan and I have always been told that a Catalan is not a man to be supplanted by a rival; it has even been said that Fernand is terrible in his vengeance."

"Poor fellow!" Danglars exclaimed, pretending to feel a great pity for the young man. "You see, he did not expect Dantès to return in this way without giving any warning. Perhaps he thought him dead or even faithless."

"When is the wedding to take place?" asked Caderousse,

on whom the fumes of the wine were beginning to take effect.

"The date is not yet fixed," Fernand mumbled.

"No, but it will be, as surely as Dantès will be captain of the *Pharaon*, eh, Danglars?"

Danglars started at this unexpected attack, and, turning toward Caderousse, scrutinized his face to try to detect whether this blow had been premeditated; he could read nothing, however, but envy on that drink-besotted face.

"Ah, well," said he, filling the glasses, "let us drink to Captain Edmond Dantès, husband of the beautiful Catalan!"

Caderousse raised his glass to his mouth with a trembling hand and emptied it at one gulp. Fernand took his glass and dashed it to the ground.

"Look there!" hiccoughed Caderousse. "What do I see on the top of the hill yonder near the Catalans? You have better sight than I, Fernand, come and look. I believe my sight is beginning to fail me, and you know wine is treacherous. I seem to see two lovers walking side by side and clasping hands. Heaven forgive us! They have no idea we can see them, for they are actually kissing!"

Danglars did not lose one agonized expression on Fernand's face.

"Do you know them, Monsieur Fernand?" he asked.

"Yes," the latter answered in a husky voice. "It is Monsieur Edmond and Mademoiselle Mercédès."

"You don't mean to say so!" said Caderousse. "Fancy my not recognizing them! Hallo, Dantès! hello, fair damsel! Come here and tell us when the wedding is to be, for Monsieur Fernand is so obstinate that he won't say a word."

"Be quiet!" said Danglars, pretending to restrain Caderousse, who, with the tenacity of a drunkard, was leaning out of the arbour. "Try to stand up straight and leave the lovers to their love-making. Now, look at Fernand, he at any rate has got some sense."

Danglars looked first at the one and then at the other of

the two men: the one intoxicated with drink, the other mad with love.

"I shall not get any further with these two fools," he murmured. "Dantès will certainly carry the day; he will marry that fair damsel, become captain, and have the laugh over us, unless . . ."—a livid smile was seen to pass over his lips— "unless I set to work."

"Hallo," Caderousse continued to call out, half out of his seat and banging on the table, "hi, there! Edmond, don't you recognize your friends, or are you too proud to speak to them?"

"No, my dear fellow, I am not proud, but I am in love, and I believe love is more apt to make one blind than pride is."

"Bravo! a good excuse!" Caderousse said. "Good day, Madame Dantès!"

Mercédès curtsied gravely and said: "That is not yet my name, and in my country it is looked upon as bringing bad luck when a girl is given her sweetheart's name before he has become her husband. Call me Mercédès, if you please."

"I suppose your wedding will take place at once, Monsieur Dantès?" said Danglars, bowing to the young couple.

"As soon as possible, Monsieur Danglars. All the preliminaries will be arranged with my father to-day, and to-morrow or the day after at the latest we shall give the betrothal feast at La Réserve here, at which we hope to see all our friends. You are invited, Monsieur Danglars, as also you, Caderousse, and you of course, Fernand."

Fernand opened his mouth in answer, but his voice died in his throat and he could not say a single word.

"The preliminaries to-day . . . to-morrow the betrothal feast . . . to be sure, you are in a great hurry, captain."

"Danglars," Edmond said smiling, "I repeat what Mercédès said to Caderousse just now. Do not give me the title that does not yet belong to me. It brings bad luck."

"I beg your pardon. I simply said that you seemed to be

in a great hurry. Why, there's plenty of time. The *Pharaon* won't put out to sea for another three months."

"One is always in a hurry to be happy, Monsieur Danglars, for when one has been suffering for a long time it is difficult to believe in one's good fortune. But it is not self-ishness alone that prompts me to press this matter. I have to go to Paris."

"You are going on business?"

"Not on my own account. I have a last commission of Captain Leclère's to execute. You understand, Danglars, it is sacred. But you can put your mind at rest. I shall go straight there and back again."

"Yes, yes, I understand," said Danglars aloud. Then to himself he said: "To Paris? No doubt to deliver the letter the Maréchal gave him. Better and better! This letter has given me an excellent idea. Ah, Dantès, my friend, you are not yet entered in the *Pharaon's* log book as number one." Then, turning to Edmond, who was moving away, he called out, "*Bon voyage!*"

"Thank you," Edmond replied, turning round and giving him a friendly nod.

Then the two lovers went on their way, peaceful and happy, like two of the elect on their way to Heaven, while the three men continued their interesting conversation.

Chapter IV

THE BETROTHAL FEAST

The next day was gloriously fine. The sun rose red and resplendent, its first rays tinting the fleecy clouds with many delicate and brilliant hues. The festive board had been prepared in a large room at La Réserve, with whose arbour we are already acquainted. Although the meal was fixed for noon, the tavern had been filled with impatient guests since eleven o'clock. They consisted chiefly of some of the favoured sailors of the *Pharaon*, and several soldier friends of Dantès'. In order to do honour to the happy couple they had all donned their finest clothes. To crown all, M. Morrel had determined to favour the occasion with his presence, and on his arrival he was greeted with hearty cheers from the sailors of the *Pharaon*. Their owner's presence was to them a confirmation of the report that Dantès was to be their captain, and, as he was popular with them all, they wished to show their owner, by this means, their appreciation of the fact that by a stroke of good luck his choice coincided with their wishes on the subject. Danglars and Caderousse were immediately dispatched to inform the bridegroom of the arrival of this important personage whose entrance had caused such a sensation, and to bid him make haste.

They had barely gone a hundred yards when they perceived the small bridal party approaching. It was composed of the betrothed pair, four maids in attendance on the bride, and Dantès' father, who walked beside Mercédès. Fernand walked behind, wearing an evil smile.

Neither Edmond nor Mercédès noticed this evil smile. They were so happy that they had eyes only for each other, and for the beautiful blue sky whence they hoped would come a blessing on their union.

Having acquitted themselves of their errand, the two ambassadors shook hands amicably with Edmond; and while Danglars took his place beside Fernand, Caderousse joined old Dantès, who was the object of general attention as he walked along, supporting himself on his curiously carved stick. He was attired in his best black suit, adorned with large steel buttons beautifully cut in facets. His thin but still vigorous legs were arrayed in a pair of beautifully embroidered stockings, which had obviously been smuggled from England. Long blue and white streamers flowed from his three-cornered hat.

Dantès himself was simply clad. As he belonged to the mercantile marine his uniform was half military and half civilian, and, with his good-looking face radiant with joy and happiness, a more perfect specimen of manly beauty could scarcely be imagined.

As the bridal party came in sight of La Réserve, M. Morrel advanced to meet them, followed by the soldiers and sailors and other guests. Dantès at once withdrew his arm from that of his betrothed and placed Mercédès' arm respectfully in that of his patron. The shipowner and the blushing girl then led the way up the wooden steps to the room where the feast was prepared. For fully five minutes the boards creaked and groaned under the unwonted pressure of the many steps.

No sooner were they seated than the dishes were handed round. Arles sausages, brown of meat and piquant of flavour, lobsters and prawns in brilliant red shells, sea-urchins whose prickly exteriors resemble chestnuts just fallen from the trees, cockles esteemed by the epicure of the South as surpassing the oyster of the North, in fact every delicacy which the sea washes up on to the sandy beach, and which the fishermen call sea-fruit.

"What a silent party!" old Dantès remarked as he caught a whiff of the fragrant yellow wine that old Pamphile himself had just put before Mercédès. "Who would think there are thirty light-hearted and merry people assembled here!"

"A husband is not always light-hearted," Caderousse replied.

"The fact is," said Dantès, "at the present moment I am too happy to be gay. If that is what you mean by your remark, neighbour Caderousse, you are quite right. Joy has that peculiar effect that at times it oppresses us just as much as grief."

Danglars looked at Fernand, whose impressionable nature was keenly alive to every emotion.

"Well, I never!" said he; "are you anticipating trouble? It seems to me you have everything you can desire."

"That is just what alarms me," said Dantès. "I cannot help thinking it is not man's lot to attain happiness so easily. Good fortune is like the palaces of the enchanted isles, the gates of which were guarded by dragons. Happiness could only be obtained by overcoming these dragons, and I, I know not how I have deserved the honour of becoming Mercédès' husband."

"Husband?" said Caderousse, laughing. "Nay, captain, not yet. Act toward her as if you were husband, and you will see how she will like it."

Mercédès blushed, but made no reply. Fernand grew very restless: he started at every sound, and from time to time wiped away the perspiration that gathered on his brow like large drops of rain, the precursors of a storm.

"Upon my word, neighbour Caderousse, it is hardly worth while taking notice of such a little slip on my part," Dantès said. " 'Tis true that Mercédès is not yet my wife, but . . ." here he pulled out his watch— "she will be in an hour and a half. Yes, my friends, thanks to the influence of Monsieur Morrel, to whom, after my father, I owe all I possess, every difficulty has been removed. We have got a special licence, and at half-past two the Mayor of Marseilles will be awaiting us at the Hôtel de Ville. As it has just struck a quarter-past one I think I am quite right in saying that in another hour and thirty minutes Mercédès will have changed her name to Madame Dantès."

Fernand closed his eyes, for they gave him a burning pain; he leant against the table to save himself from falling, but in spite of his effort he could not restrain a groan, which, however, was lost amid the noisy congratulations of the company.

"This feast, then, is not in honour of your betrothal, as we supposed, but is your wedding breakfast?"

"Not at all," said Dantès. "I leave for Paris to-morrow morning. Four days to go, four days to return, one day to execute my commission, and I shall be back again on the first of March. We will have our real wedding breakfast the very next day."

At this moment Danglars noticed that Fernand, on whom he had kept an observant eye and who was seated at the window overlooking the street, suddenly opened his haggard eyes, rose with a convulsive movement, and staggered back on to his seat. Almost at the same moment a confused noise was heard on the stairs. The tread of heavy steps and the hubbub of many voices, together with the clanking of swords and military accoutrements drowned the merry voices of the bridal party. The laughter died away. An ominous silence fell on all as the noise drew nearer, and when three peremptory knocks resounded on the door, they looked at each other with uneasy glances.

"Open in the name of the law!" cried a peremptory voice. There was no answer.

The door opened, and a police commissary entered, followed by four armed soldiers and a corporal.

"What is all this about?" the shipowner asked, advancing toward the commissary, whom he knew. "I fear there must be some mistake."

"If there is a mistake, Monsieur Morrel," the commissary replied, "you may rest assured that it will be promptly put right. In the meantime I am the bearer of a warrant for arrest, and, though I regret the task assigned me, it must nevertheless be carried out. Which of you gentlemen answers to the name of Edmond Dantès?"

Every eye was turned on the young man as he stepped forward, obviously agitated, but with great dignity of bearing, and said:

"I do, monsieur. What do you want of me?"

"Edmond Dantès, I arrest you in the name of the law."

"You arrest me?" said Dantès, changing colour. "Why, I pray?"

"I know not, monsieur. Your first examination will give you all information on that score."

Resistance was useless, but old Dantès did not comprehend this. There are certain things the heart of a father or a mother will never understand. He threw himself at the officer's feet and begged and implored, but his tears and supplications were of no avail.

"There is no call for alarm, monsieur," the commissary said at last, touched by the old man's despair. "Perhaps your son has but neglected to carry out some customs formality or health regulation, in which case he will probably be released as soon as he has given the desired information."

In the meantime Dantès, with a smile on his face, had shaken hands with all his friends and had surrendered himself to the officer, saying:

"Do not be alarmed. You may depend on it there is some mistake which will probably be cleared up even before I reach the prison."

"To be sure. I am ready to vouch for your innocence," Danglars said as he joined the group round the prisoner.

Dantès descended the stairs preceded by the police

officer and surrounded by soldiers. A carriage stood at the door. He got in, followed by two soldiers and the commissary. The door was shut, and the carriage took the road back to Marseilles.

"Good-bye, Edmond, oh, my Edmond! Good-bye!" Mercédès called out, leaning over the balcony.

The prisoner heard these last words sobbed from his sweetheart's breast, and, putting his head out of the window, simply called out: "*Au revoir*, my Mercédès!"

The carriage then disappeared round the corner of Fort Saint-Nicholas.

"Await me here," M. Morrel said to the rest of the party. "I shall take the first carriage I can find to take me to Marseilles, and shall bring you back news."

"Yes, do go," they all cried out. "Go, and come back with all possible speed."

The guests, who had been making merry but a short time before, now gave way to a feeling of terror. They feverishly discussed the arrest from every point of view. Danglars was loud in his assertion that it was merely a trifling case of suspected smuggling: the customs officials had been aboard the *Pharaon* during their absence and something had aroused their suspicion: M. the purser was sure of it. But Mercédès felt, rather than knew, that the arrest had some deeper significance. She suddenly gave way to a wild fit of sobbing.

"Come, come, my child, do not give up hope," said old Dantès, hardly knowing what he was saying.

"Hope!" repeated Danglars.

Fernand also tried to repeat this word of comfort, but it seemed to choke him; his lips moved but no word came from them.

"A carriage! A carriage!" cried one of the guests, who had stayed on the balcony on the look-out. "It is Monsieur Morrel. Cheer up! He is no doubt bringing us good news."

Mercédès and the old father rushed out to the door to meet the shipowner. The latter entered, looking very grave.

"My friends," he said, with a gloomy shake of the head, "it is a far more serious matter than we supposed."

"Oh, Monsieur Morrel," Mercédès exclaimed. "I know he is innocent!"

"I also believe in his innocence," replied the shipowner, "but he is accused of being an agent of the Bonapartist faction!"[1]

Those of my readers who are well acquainted with the period of my story must be aware of the gravity of such an announcement. Consternation and dismay were written on the faces of the assembled guests as the party silently and sadly broke up.

Fernand, who had now become the horror-stricken girl's only protector, led her home, while some of Edmond's friends took charge of the brokenhearted father; and it was soon rumoured in the town that Dantès had been arrested as a Bonapartist agent.

"Would you have believed it, Danglars?" M. Morrel asked as he hastened to the town with his purser and Caderousse in the hopes of receiving direct news of Edmond through his acquaintance, M. de Villefort, the Deputy of the Procureur du Roi.[2]

"Why, monsieur, you may perhaps remember I told you that Dantès anchored off the Isle of Elba without any apparent reason. I had my suspicions at the time."

"Did you mention these suspicions to anyone but myself?"

"God forbid," exclaimed Danglars; and then in a low whisper he added: "You know, monsieur, that on account of your uncle who served under the old Government and does not attempt to hide his feelings, you are also suspected of sympathizing with Napoleon; so if I mentioned my suspicions, I should be afraid of injuring not only Edmond, but you also. There are certain things it is the duty of a subordinate to tell his master, but to conceal from everyone else."

"Quite right, Danglars. You are a good fellow. I had

not forgotten your interests in the event of poor Dantès becoming captain."

"In what respect, monsieur?"

"I asked Dantès to give me his opinion of you and to say whether he would have any objection to your retaining your post, for it seemed to me that I had noticed a certain coolness between you two of late."

"What answer did he give you?"

"He merely referred to some personal grievance he had against you, but said that any person who enjoyed his master's confidence was also sure of his."

"The hypocrite!" Danglars muttered.

"Poor Dantès!" said Caderousse. "He's the right sort, and that's a fact."

"Quite agreed," said M. Morrel, "but in the meantime the *Pharaon* is captainless."

"We cannot put to sea for another three months," Danglars added, "and it is to be hoped that Dantès will be released before then."

"No doubt, but in the meantime . . . ?"

"I am at your service. You know that I am as capable of managing a ship as the most experienced captain. Then when Dantès comes out of prison, he can take his post and I will resume mine."

"Thanks, Danglars, that would be a way out of the difficulty. I therefore authorize you to assume command of the *Pharaon* and superintend the loading of the cargo. No matter what misfortune befalls any one of us, we cannot let business suffer." So saying, he proceeded in the direction of the law courts.

"So far everything is succeeding wonderfully," Danglars said to himself. "I am already temporary captain, and if that fool of a Caderousse can be persuaded to hold his tongue, I shall soon have the job for good and all."

Chapter V

THE DEPUTY PROCUREUR DU ROI

✦

In one of the old mansions built by Puget[1] in the Rue du Grand Cours, opposite the fountain of the Medusa, another betrothal feast was being celebrated on the same day, and at the same hour, as that which took place in the humble inn. There was, however, a great difference in the company present. Instead of members of the working class and soldiers and sailors, there was to be seen the flower of Marseilles society: former magistrates who had resigned their office under the usurper's[2] reign, old officers who had deserted their posts to join Condé's[3] army, young men in whom their families had kindled a hatred for the man whom five years of exile were to convert into a martyr and fifteen years of restoration into a demi-god.

The guests were still at table. Their heated and excitable conversation betrayed the passions of the period, passions which in the South had been so much more terrible and unrestrained during the past five years, since religious hatred had been added to political hatred. The Emperor, king of the Isle of Elba after having held sovereign sway over one half of the world, now reigning over five or six thousand souls after having heard "Long live Napoleon" uttered by a hundred and twenty million subjects, and in ten different languages—the Emperor was regarded as a man that was lost to the throne of France for ever. The magistrates recounted political blunders, the military officers discussed Moscow and Leipzig, the ladies aired their views on his divorce from Josephine. It was not in the downfall of the man that these Royalists rejoiced and gloried, but rather in the annihilation of the principle, for it seemed to them that they were awakening from a dreadful nightmare and were about to enter upon a new life.

An old man, the Marquis of Saint-Méran, wearing the cross of Saint-Louis,[4] rose and proposed the health of King Louis XVIII.

The toast, recalling the exiled but peace-loving King of France, elicited an enthusiastic and almost poetic response; glasses were raised after the English fashion, and the ladies, taking their bouquets from their dresses, strewed the table with flowers.

"Ah," said the Marquise de Saint-Mèran, a woman with a forbidding eye, thin lips, and an aristocratic and elegant bearing despite her fifty years, "if those revolutionists were here who drove us out of our old castles, which they bought for a mere song, and in which we left them to conspire against each other during the Reign of Terror, they would have to own that true devotion was on our side. We attached ourselves to a crumbling monarchy; they, on the contrary, worshipped the rising sun and made their fortunes, while we lost all we possessed. They would be compelled to own that our king was truly Louis the Well-beloved to us, while their usurper has never been more to them than Napoleon the Accursed! Don't you agree with me, de Villefort?"

"What did you say, madame? I must crave your pardon. I was not listening to the conversation."

"Leave the young people alone," interposed the old gentleman who had proposed the toast. "They are thinking of their approaching wedding, and naturally they have more interesting subjects of conversation than politics."

"I am sorry, Mother," said a beautiful, fair-haired girl

with eyes of velvet floating in a pool of mother-o'-pearl. "I will give up Monsieur de Villefort to you, for I have been monopolizing him for some few minutes. Monsieur de Villefort, my mother is speaking to you."

"I am at your service, madame, if you would be kind enough to repeat your question," M. de Villefort said.

"You are forgiven, Renée," said the Marquise with a smile of tenderness that one hardly expected to see on that dry hard face. "I was saying, Villefort, that the Bonapartists had neither our conviction, nor our enthusiasm, nor our devotion."

"No, madame, but they had fanaticism to take the place of all those other virtues. Napoleon is the Mahomet[5] of the West to all those plebeian[6] but highly ambitious people; he is not only a legislator and a master, he is a type, the personification of equality."

"Equality?" exclaimed the Marquise. "Napoleon the personification of equality! Do you know, Villefort, that what you say has a very strong revolutionary flavour? But I excuse you; one cannot expect the son of a Girondin[7] to be quite free from a spice of the old leaven."

A deep crimson suffused the countenance of Villefort.

"It is true that my father was a Girondin, madame, but he did not vote for the King's death. My father was an equal sufferer with yourself during the Reign of Terror, and he well-nigh lost his head on the same scaffold which saw your father's head fall."

"True," said the Marquise, "but they would have mounted the scaffold for reasons diametrically opposed, the proof being that whereas my family have all adhered to the exiled princes, your father lost no time in rallying to the new government, and that after Citizen Noirtier had been a Girondin, Count Noirtier became a senator."

"Mother," said Renée, "you know we agreed not to discuss such painful reminiscences any more."

"I quite agree with Mademoiselle de Saint-Méran," de Villefort replied. "For my own part, I have discarded not only the views, but also the name of my father. My father has been, and possibly still is, a Bonapartist and bears the name of Noirtier. I am a Royalist and style myself de Villefort."

"Well said, Villefort!" the Marquis replied. "I have always urged the Marquise to forget the past, but I have never been able to prevail upon her to do so. I hope you will be more fortunate than I."

"Very well, then," the Marquise rejoined. "Let it be agreed that we forget the past. But, Villefort, should a conspirator fall into your hands, remember that there will be so many more eyes watching you since it is known that you come of a family which is perhaps in league with the conspirators."

"Alas, madame," Villefort replied, "my profession and especially the times in which we live compel me to be severe. I have already had several political prosecutions which have given me the opportunity of proving my convictions. Unfortunately we have not yet done with such offenders."

"Don't you think so?" the Marquise inquired.

"I am afraid not. Napoleon on the Isle of Elba is very near to France; his presence there, almost in view of our coasts, stimulates the hopes of his partisans."

At this moment a servant entered and whispered something into his ear. Villefort, excusing himself, left the table, returning a few minutes later.

"Renée," he said, as he looked tenderly on his betrothed, "who would have a lawyer for her husband? I have no moment to call my own. I am even called away from my betrothal feast."

"Why are you called away?" the girl asked anxiously.

"Alas! if I am to believe what they tell me, I have to deal with a grave charge which may very well lead to the scaffold."

"How dreadful!" cried Renée, turning pale.

"It appears that a little Bonapartist plot has been discovered," Villefort continued. "Here is the letter of denunciation," and he read as follows:

> "The Procureur du Roi is hereby informed by a friend to the throne and to religion that a certain Edmond Dantès, mate on the *Pharaon*, which arrived this morning from Smyrna after having touched at Naples and Porto Ferrajo, has been entrusted by Murat[8] with a letter for the usurper, and by the usurper with a letter for the Bonapartist party in Paris. Corroboration of this crime can be found on arresting him, for the said letter will be found either on him, or at his father's house, or in his cabin on board the *Pharaon*."

"But," Renée said, "this letter is addressed to the Procureur du Roi and not to you, and is, moreover, anonymous."

"You are right, but the Procureur du Roi is absent, so the letter has been handed to his secretary, who has been instructed to open all correspondence. On opening this one, he sent for me and, not finding me, gave orders for the man's arrest."

"Then the culprit is already arrested?" the Marquise said.

"You mean the accused person," Renée made answer. Then, turning to Villefort, "Where is the unfortunate man?"

"He is at my house."

"Then away, my dear boy," said the Marquis, "do not neglect your duty in order to stay with us. Go where the King's service calls you."

Chapter VI

THE EXAMINATION

Villefort had no sooner left the room than he discarded his jaunty manner and assumed the grave air of a man called upon to decide upon the life of his fellow-man. In reality, however, apart from the line of politics which his father had adopted, and which might influence his future if he did not separate himself altogether from him, Gérard de Villefort was at this moment as happy as it is given to any man to be. Already rich, and, although only twenty-seven years of age, occupying a high position on the bench, he was about to marry a young and beautiful girl, whom he loved, not passionately, it is true, but with calculation as befits a future Procureur du Roi; for in addition to her beauty, which was remarkable, Mademoiselle de Saint-Méran, his betrothed, belonged to one of the most influential families of the period, and furthermore had a dowry of fifty thousand crowns, besides the prospect of inheriting another half-million.

At the door he met the commissary of police, who was waiting for him. The sight of this man brought him from his seventh Heaven down to earth; he composed his face and, advancing toward the officer, said: "Here I am, monsieur. I have read the letter. You were quite right in arresting this man. Now give me all the information you have discovered about him and the conspiracy."

"As yet we know nothing about the conspiracy, monsieur; all the papers found on the man have been sealed and placed on your desk. You have seen by the letter denouncing him that the prisoner is a certain Edmond Dantès, first mate of the three-master *Pharaon*, trading in cotton with Alexandria and Smyrna, and belonging to Morrel and Son of Marseilles."

"Did he serve in the navy before he joined the mercantile marine?"

"Oh, no, monsieur, he is too young. He is only nineteen or twenty at the most."

At this moment, just as Villefort had arrived at the corner of the Rue des Conseils, a man, who seemed to be waiting for him, approached. It was M. Morrel.

"Ah, Monsieur de Villefort," he cried, "I am very fortunate in meeting you. A most extraordinary and unaccountable mistake has been made: the mate of my ship, a certain Edmond Dantès, has just been arrested."

"I know," Villefort made answer, "and I am on my way to examine him."

"Oh, monsieur!" M. Morrel continued, carried away by his friendship for the young man, "you do not know the accused, but I do. He is the gentlest and most trustworthy man imaginable, and I don't hesitate to say he is the best seaman in the whole mercantile service. Oh, Monsieur de Villefort, with all my heart I commend him to your kindly consideration."

"You may rest assured, monsieur, that you will not have appealed to me in vain if the prisoner is innocent, but if, on the contrary, he is guilty—we live in a difficult age, monsieur, when it would be a fatal thing to be lenient—in that case I shall be compelled to do my duty."

As he had just arrived at his own house beside the law courts, he entered with a lordly air, after having saluted with icy politeness the unhappy shipowner who stood petrified on the spot where Villefort had left him.

The antechamber was full of gendarmes[1] and policemen, and in their midst stood the prisoner, carefully guarded.

Villefort crossed the room, threw a glance at Dantès, and, after taking a packet of papers from one of the gendarmes, disappeared. His first impression of the young man was favourable, but he had been warned so often against trusting first impulses that he applied the maxim to the term impression, forgetting the difference between the two words. He therefore stifled the feelings of pity that were uppermost in his heart, assumed the expression which he reserved for important occasions, and sat down at his desk with a frown on his brow.

"Bring in the prisoner."

An instant later Dantès was before him. Saluting his judge with an easy politeness, he looked round for a seat as if he were in M. Morrel's drawing-room.

"Who are you, and what is your name?" asked Villefort, as he fingered the papers which he received from the police officer on his entry.

"My name is Edmond Dantès," replied the young man calmly. "I am mate of the *Pharaon*, owned by Messrs. Morrel and Son."

"Your age?" continued Villlefort.

"Nineteen."

"What were you doing when you were arrested?"

"I was at my betrothal breakfast, monsieur," the young man said, and his voice trembled slightly as he thought of the contrast between those happy moments and the painful ordeal he was now undergoing.

"You were at your betrothal feast?" the Deputy said, shuddering in spite of himself.

"Yes, monsieur, I am about to marry a woman I have loved for three years."

Villefort, impassive though he usually was, was struck with this coincidence; and the passionate voice of Dantès, who had been seized in the midst of his happiness, touched a sympathetic chord in his own heart. He also was about to be married, he also was happy, and his happiness had been interrupted in order that he might kill the happiness of another.

"Now I want all the information in your possession," he said. "Have you served under the usurper?"

"I was about to be drafted into the marines when he fell."

"I have been told you have extreme political views," said Villefort, who had never been told anything of the kind but was not sorry to put forward the statement in the form of an accusation.

"Extreme political views, monsieur? Alas! I am almost ashamed to say it, but I have never had what one calls a view; I am barely nineteen years of age, as I have already had the honour to tell you. I know nothing, for I am not destined to play any great *rôle*[2] in life. The little I am and ever shall be, if I am given the position I desire, I owe to Monsieur Morrel. My opinions, I do not say political, but private, are limited to these three sentiments: I love my father, I respect Monsieur Morrel, and I adore Mercédès. That, monsieur, is all I have to tell you. You see for yourself that it is not very interesting."

As Dantès spoke, Villefort looked at his genial and frank countenance, and, with his experience of crime and criminals, he recognized that every word Dantès spoke convinced him of his innocence. In spite of Villefort's severity, Edmond had not once expressed in his looks, his words, or his gestures anything but kindness and respect for his interrogator.

"This is indeed a charming young man," Villefort said to himself, but aloud he said: "Have you any enemies?"

"Enemies, monsieur? My position is happily not important enough to make me any enemies. As regards my character, I am perhaps too hasty, but I always try to curb my temper in my dealings with my subordinates. I have ten or twelve sailors under me: if you ask them, monsieur, you will find that they love and respect me, not as a father, for I am too young, but as an elder brother."

"Perhaps you have no enemies, but you may have

aroused feelings of jealousy. At the early age of nineteen you are about to receive a captaincy, you are going to marry a beautiful girl who loves you; these two pieces of good fortune may have been the cause of envy."

"You are right. No doubt you understand men better than I do, and possibly it is so, but if any of my friends cherish any such envious feelings toward me, I would rather not know lest my friendship should turn into hatred."

"You are wrong, you should always strive to see clearly around you, and indeed, you seem such a worthy young man that I am going to depart from the ordinary rule by showing you the denunciation which has brought you before me. Here is the paper. Do you recognize the writing?"

So saying, Villefort took the letter from his pocket and handed it to Dantès. Dantès looked at it and read it. His brow darkened as he said:

"No, monsieur, I do not know this writing. It is disguised and yet it is very plainly written. At any rate it is a clever hand that wrote it. I am very lucky," he continued, looking at Villefort with an expression of gratitude, "in having you to examine me, for there can be no doubt that this envious person is indeed my enemy."

And the light that shone in the young man's eyes as he said this revealed to Villefort how much energy and deep feeling lay concealed beneath his apparent gentleness.

"Very well, then," said the Deputy, "answer me quite frankly, not as a prisoner before his judge, but as a man in a false position to another man who has his interest at heart. What truth is there in this anonymous accusation?"

"It is partly true and partly false, monsieur. Here is the plain truth. I swear it by my honour as a sailor, by my love for Mercédès, and by my father's life! When we left Naples, Captain Leclère fell ill of brain-fever; as we had no doctor on board and as he would not put in at any port, since he was very anxious to reach Elba, he became so very ill that toward the end of the third day, feeling that he was dying, he called me to him. 'My dear Dantès,' he said, 'swear to me on your honour that you will do what I bid you, for it is a matter of the utmost importance.'

" 'I swear it, captain,' I said.

" 'After my death the command of the ship devolves upon you as mate; take command, head for the Isle of Elba, go ashore at Porto Ferrajo, ask for the Maréchal, and give him this letter. You may be given another letter and be entrusted with a mission. That mission was to have been mine, Dantès, but you will carry it out in my stead and get all the glory of it.'

" 'I shall carry out your instructions, captain, but perhaps I shall not be admitted into the Maréchal's presence as easily as you think.'

" 'Here is a ring which will give you admittance and remove all difficulties.'

"He then gave me a ring. It was only just in time. Two hours later he was delirious and the next day he died."

"What did you do then?"

"What I was bound to do, and what everyone would have done in my place. In any circumstances the requests of a dying man are sacred, but with a sailor a superior's request is an order that has to be carried out. So I headed for Elba, where I arrived the next day. I gave orders for everybody to remain on board while I went ashore alone. The ring gained admittance for me to the Maréchal's presence. He asked me about poor Captain Leclère's death and gave me a letter which he charged me to deliver in person at an address in Paris. I gave him my promise in accordance with the last request of my captain. I landed here, rapidly settled all the ship's business, and hastened to my betrothed, whom I found more beautiful and loving than ever. Finally, monsieur, I was partaking of my betrothal breakfast, was to have been married in an hour, and was counting on going to Paris to-morrow, when owing to this denunciation, which you seem to treat as lightly as I do, I was arrested."

"I believe you have told me the truth," was Villefort's

answer, "and if you have been guilty it is through imprudence, an imprudence justified by your captain's orders.
Hand me the letter that was given you at Elba, give me your
word of honour that you will appear directly if you are summoned to do so, and you may rejoin your friends."

"I am free, monsieur!" Dantès cried out, overcome with
joy.

"Certainly, but first give me the letter."

"It must be in front of you, monsieur. It was taken along
with my other papers, and I recognize some of them in that
bundle."

"Wait a moment," the Deputy said as Dantès was taking
his hat and gloves. "To whom was it addressed?"

"To Monsieur Noirtier, Rue Coq Héron, Paris."

These words fell on Villefort's ears with the rapidity and
unexpectedness of a thunderbolt. He sank into his chair
from which he had risen to reach the packet of letters, drew
the fatal letter from the bundle, and glanced over it with a
look of inexpressible terror.

"Monsieur Noirtier, Rue Coq Héron, number thirteen,"
he murmured, growing paler and paler. "Have you shown
this letter to anyone?"

"To no one, monsieur, on my honour!"

Villefort's brow darkened more and more. When he had
finished reading the letter his head fell into his hands, and
he remained thus for a moment quite overcome. After a
while he composed himself and said:

"You say you do not know the contents of this letter?"

"On my honour, monsieur, I am in complete ignorance
of its contents."

Dantès waited for the next question, but no question
came. Villefort again sank into his chair, passed his hand
over his brow dripping with perspiration, and read the letter
for the third time.

"Oh! if he should know the contents of this letter!" he
murmured, "and if he ever gets to know that Noirtier is the
father of Villefort, I am lost, lost for ever!"

Villefort made a violent effort to pull himself together, and said in as steady a voice as possible:

"I cannot set you at liberty at once as I had hoped. I must first consult the Juge d'Instruction.[3] You see how I have tried to help you, but I must detain you a prisoner for some time longer. I will make that time as short as possible. The principal charge against you has to do with this letter, and you see————" Villefort went to the fire, threw the letter into the flames, and remained watching it until it was reduced to ashes.

"You see," he continued, "I have destroyed it."

"Oh, monsieur," Dantès exclaimed, "you are more than just, you are kindness itself!"

"But listen," Villefort went on, "after what I have done you feel you can have confidence in me, don't you? I only wish to advise you. I shall keep you here until this evening. Possibly someone else will come to examine you: in that event, repeat all that you have told me, but say not a word about this letter."

"I promise, monsieur."

"You understand," he continued, "the letter is destroyed, and you and I alone know of its existence; should you be questioned about it, firmly deny all knowledge of it, and you are saved."

Villefort rang and the commissary[4] entered. The Deputy whispered a few words into his ear, and the officer nodded in answer.

"Follow the commissary!" Villefort said to Dantès.

Dantès bowed, cast a look of gratitude at Villefort, and did as he was bid.

The door was hardly closed when Villefort's strength failed him, and he sank half fainting into his chair.

After a few moments he muttered to himself: "Alas! alas! if the Procureur du Roi had been here, if the Juge d' Instruction had been called instead of me, I should have been lost! This little bit of paper would have spelt my ruin. Oh! Father, Father, will you always stand in the way of my happiness in this world, and must I eternally fight against your past!"

Suddenly an unexpected light appeared to flash across his mind, illuminating his whole face; a smile played around his drawn mouth, and his haggard eyes became fixed as though arrested by a thought.

"The very thing!" he said. "Yes, this letter which was to have spelt my ruin will probably make my fortune. Quick to work, Villefort!"

And after having assured himself that the prisoner had left the antechamber, the Deputy hastened to the house of his betrothed.

Chapter VII

THE CHÂTEAU D'IF

***

As he passed through the antechamber, the commissary of police made a sign to two gendarmes, who instantly placed themselves on either side of Dantès; a door communicating with the law courts was opened; they passed down one of those long, dark passages which make all those who enter them give an involuntary shudder.

In the same way as Villefort's chambers communicated with the law courts, the law courts communicated with the prison, that sombre edifice overlooking the clocktower of the Accoules.[1] They wound their way along the passage and at last they came to a door; the commissary knocked on it thrice with an iron knocker, and it seemed to Dantès as if each blow had been aimed at his heart. The door was opened, the gendarmes gave their hesitating prisoner a push forward, Dantès crossed the formidable threshold, and the door closed behind him with a loud bang. He now breathed a different air, a thick and mephitic[2] air. He was in a prison.

His cell was clean enough, though it was barred and bolted, and its appearance did not fill him with any dread. Why should it? The words of the Deputy, who seemed to show so much interest in him, rang in his ears like a sweet promise of hope.

It was four o'clock when Dantès was taken to his cell, and, as it was the first of March, the prisoner soon found himself in utter darkness. With loss of sight, his hearing became more acute: at the least sound he rose quickly and advanced toward the door in the firm conviction that they had come to set him free; but the noise died away in another direction and Dantès sank back on to his stool.

At last, about ten o'clock, when Dantès was beginning to lose all hope, he heard steps approaching his door. A key was turned in the lock, the bolts creaked, the massive oak door swung open, and a dazzling light from two torches flooded the cell.

By the light of these torches, Dantès saw the glittering swords and carbines of four gendarmes.

"Have you come to fetch me?" Dantès asked.

"Yes," was the answer of one of the men.

"By order of the Deputy?"

"I should say so!"

"Very well," said Dantès, "I am ready to follow you."

In the belief that they came at the Deputy's orders, Dantès, relieved of all apprehension, calmly stepped forward and placed himself in their midst. A police van was waiting at the door, the coachman was on the box, and a police officer was seated beside him. The door of the carriage was opened and Dantès was pushed in. He had neither the power nor the intention to resist and he found himself in an instant seated between two gendarmes, the other two taking their places opposite, and the heavy van lumbered away.

The prisoner glanced at the windows: they were grated. He had but changed his prison; only this one moved and was conveying him he knew not whither. Through the grating, the bars of which were so close that there was barely a hand's-breadth between them, Dantès recognized the Rue Casserie, and saw that they were passing along the Rue Saint-Laurent and the Rue Taramis toward the quay.[3] Soon he saw the lights of the Consigne before him. The van stopped, the officer got down from the box, and opened the locked door with his key; whereupon Dantès stepped out and was immediately surrounded by the four gendarmes, who led him along a path lined with soldiers to a boat which a customs-house officer held by a chain near the quay. The soldiers looked at Dantès with vacant curiosity. He was given a place in the stern of the boat and was again surrounded by the four gendarmes, whilst the officer stationed himself at the bows. The boat was shoved off, four oarsmen plied their oars vigorously, and soon Dantès found himself in what they call the Frioul, that is, outside the harbour.

His first feeling on finding himself once more in the open air was one of joy, for did it not mean freedom? But the whole proceeding was incomprehensible to him.

"Whither are you taking me?" he asked.

"You will know soon enough."

"But . . ."

"We are forbidden to give you any explanation."

Dantès knew from experience that it was useless to question a subordinate who had been forbidden to answer any questions, and he remained silent.

As he sat there, the most fantastic thoughts passed through his mind. It was not possible to undertake a long voyage in such a small boat, so perhaps they were going to take him a short distance from the coast and tell him he was free; they had not attempted to handcuff him, which he considered a good augury;[4] besides, had not the Deputy, who had been so kind to him, told him that, provided he did not mention the fatal name of Noirtier, he had nothing to fear? Had not de Villefort destroyed the dangerous letter in his presence, the letter which was the only evidence they had against him?

He waited in silence and deep in thought. With that faraway look in his eyes peculiar to sailors, he tried to pierce the depths of the night. Leaving Ratonneau Island with its lighthouse on their right, and keeping close to the coast, they arrived opposite the Catalan creek. It was here that

Mercédès lived, and now and then he imagined he saw the indistinct and vague form of a woman outlined on the dark shore.

Why did a presentiment not warn her that the man she loved was but a hundred yards away from her? If he gave a shout, she could hear him. A false shame restrained him, however. What would these men say if he called out like a madman?

In spite of the repugnance he felt at putting fresh questions to the gendarmes, he turned to the one nearest him and said:

"Comrade, I adjure[5] you on your honour as a soldier to have pity on me and answer! I am Captain Dantès, an honest and loyal Frenchman, though accused of treason. Whither are you taking me? Tell me, and on my honour as a sailor, I will submit to my fate."

The gendarme scratched his ear and looked at his comrade. The latter made a motion with his head which seemed to say: "I can't see any harm in telling him now"; and the gendarme, turning to Dantès, replied:

"You are a native of Marseilles and a sailor, and yet you ask us where we are heading for?"

"Yes, for on my honour I do not know."

"Have you no idea?"

"None at all."

"Impossible!"

"I swear it by all that I hold most sacred! Tell me, I entreat you!"

"Unless you are blind or have never been outside the port of Marseilles, you must know. Look round you."

Dantès got up and quite naturally looked in the direction the boat was moving. Before him, at a distance of a hundred fathoms, rose the black, steep rock on which stood the frowning Château d'If.

This strange pile, this prison whose very name spelt terror, this fortress around which Marseilles had woven its legends for the past three hundred years, rising up so suddenly before Dantès, had the effect on him that the sight of a scaffold must have on a condemned man.

"My God!" he cried, "the Château d'If! Why are we going there?"

The gendarme smiled.

"You cannot be taking me there to imprison me?" Dantès went on. "The Château d'If is a State prison, and is only used for important political offenders. I have committed no crime. Are there any judges or magistrates at the Château d'If?"

"As far as I know there are a governor, some gaolers,[6] a garrison, and some good thick walls."

"Are you trying to make out that I am to be imprisoned there? What about Monsieur Villefort's promise?"

"I don't know anything about Monsieur Villefort's promise; all I know is that we are going to the Château d'If."

Quick as lightning Dantès sprang to his feet and tried to hurl himself into the sea, but four stout arms caught him before even his feet left the bottom boards of the boat. With a howl of rage he fell back. The next moment a sudden impact shook the boat from stem to stern and Dantès realized that they had arrived. His guardians forced him to land, and dragged him to the steps that led to the gate of the fortress, the police officer following him with fixed bayonet.

Dantès made no useless resistance; his slow movements were caused by inertia rather than opposition—he was dazed, and reeled like a drunken man. He saw more soldiers stationed along the slope, he felt the steps which forced him to raise his feet, he perceived that he passed under a door, and that this door closed behind him, but all his actions were mechanical and he saw as through a mist; he could distinguish nothing. He did not even see the ocean, that cause of heart-breaking despair to the prisoners who look on that wide expanse of water with an awful conviction that they are powerless to cross it.

There was a moment's halt, during which he tried to collect his thoughts. He looked around him; he was in a square

courtyard enclosed by four high walls; the slow and measured tread of the sentinels was heard, and each time they
passed before the light which shone from within the
château he saw the gleam of their musket-barrels.

They waited here about ten minutes, evidently for
orders. At last a voice called out:

"Where is the prisoner?"

"Here," one of the gendarmes replied.

"Let him follow me. I will take him to his cell."

"Go!" said the gendarme, giving Dantès a push.

The prisoner followed his guide, who led him into a subterranean room whose bare and reeking walls seemed as
though impregnated with tears. A sort of lamp, standing on
a stool, the wick swimming in fetid oil, illuminated the shiny
walls of this terrible abode, and revealed to Dantès the features of his guide, an under-gaoler, ill-clad and of a low type.

"Here is your cell for to-night," he said. "It is late and the
governor is in bed. To-morrow, when he has read the
instructions regarding you, he may change your cell. In the
meantime here is some bread, there is some water in the
pitcher over there and some straw in the corner yonder.
That is all a prisoner requires. Good night."

Before Dantès could think of an answer, before he had
noticed where the gaoler had placed the bread and the
pitcher of water, or looked at the corner where lay the straw
for his bed, the fellow had taken the lamp and locked the
door behind him, leaving his prisoner to the darkness and
silence of the gaol.[7]

When the first rays of the sun had brought some light
into the den, the gaoler returned with the information that
Dantès was not to change his cell. An iron hand seemed to
have nailed him to the spot where he stood the night
before; he was motionless with his eyes fixed on the ground.
Thus he had stood the whole night long without sleep. The
gaoler advanced; Dantès did not appear to see him. He
tapped him on the shoulder; Dantès shuddered and shook
his head.

"Have you not slept?" asked the gaoler.

"I do not know," was Dantès' reply.

The gaoler stared at him in astonishment.

"Are you not hungry?"

"I do not know," Dantès still made answer.

"Do you want anything?"

"I want to see the governor."

The gaoler shrugged his shoulders and went out.

Dantès gazed after him, stretched out his hands toward the half-open door, but the door was closed upon him.

Then his whole frame was shaken with one mighty sob. The tears which choked him streamed down his cheeks; he beat his forehead against the ground; he remained a long time in prayer, and, while reviewing his past life, asked himself what crime he had committed at his tender age to merit such a cruel punishment.

The day passed thus. He scarcely touched his bread or water. At times he would sit absorbed in thought, at other times he would walk round and round his cell like a wild animal in a cage.

The next morning the gaoler again made his appearance.

"Well," he said, "are you more reasonable to-day than you were yesterday?"

Dantès made no reply.

"Come, now, don't lose heart! Is there anything I can do for you?"

"I want to speak to the governor."

"I have already told you that is impossible," the gaoler answered impatiently.

"Why is it impossible?"

"Because the rules of the prison do not allow it."

"Then what is allowed here?"

"Better food if you pay for it, a walk in the courtyard, and sometimes books."

"I don't want any books, neither do I want to walk in the courtyard, and I find my food good enough. I only desire one thing and that is to see the governor."

"If you keep on bothering me with that every time I come, I shall not bring you any more food."

"Well, then," said Dantès, "I shall die of starvation, that's all about it."

"Now, look here!" said the gaoler, "don't go on brooding over the impossible in this way, or you will go mad before the end of a fortnight."

"Do you think so?" was the reply.

"I am sure of it. Madness always begins like that. We have an instance of it here. There was an abbé in this cell before you came: it was through his unceasingly offering a million francs to the governor if he would set him free that his brain was turned."

"Listen, I am not an abbé, neither am I mad, though I may be before long; unforunately I am at present in full possession of my senses. Now I too have a proposal to make. I can't offer you a million francs for the simple reason that I have not so much to give you, but I offer you a hundred crowns if, the next time you go to Marseilles, you will go to the Catalans and give a letter to a girl named Mercédès . . . not even a letter, just a couple of lines."

"If I were to take that letter and were found out I should lose my place which is worth a thousand francs a year in addition to my food, so you see I should be a fool to risk a thousand francs for three hundred."

"Very well," said Dantès, "but remember this. If you refuse to take my letter to Mercédès or at least to tell her that I am here, I shall one day hide behind the door and, as you enter, break your head with this stool."

"Threats!" the gaoler called out, retreating a step and placing himself on the defensive. "You are certainly going mad. The abbé commenced like that. In three days you will be raving mad. Luckily we have dungeons at the Château d'If."

Dantès picked up the stool and swung it round his head.

"That's enough! that's enough!" the gaoler exclaimed. "Since you insist on it, I will go and tell the governor."

"That's something like!" said Dantès, putting the stool down and sitting on it with bent head and haggard eyes as though he were really losing his senses.

The gaoler went out and returned a few minutes later with four soldiers and a corporal.

"The governor's orders are that the prisoner shall be taken to the dungeon. We must put madmen with madmen."

The four soldiers seized Dantès, who fell into a kind of coma and followed them without resistance. He descended fifteen steps, the door of a dungeon was opened, and he entered mumbling, "He is right, they must put madmen with madmen."

Chapter VIII

VILLEFORT AND MERCÉDÈS

⚓

As we have said, Villefort hastened back to the Rue du Grand Cours, and on entering the house of Madame de Saint-Méran found the guests he had left at table seated in the salon at their coffee. Renée with the rest of the company was anxiously awaiting him, and he was received with a universal fire of exclamations.

"Hallo, decapitator, guardian of the State, Brutus," said one. "Tell us your news!"

"Are we threatened with a new Reign of Terror?" asked another.

"Has the Corsican Ogre[1] broken loose?" cried a third.

"Marquise," Villefort said, advancing toward his future mother-in-law. "I have come to ask you kindly to excuse my abrupt departure . . . Monsieur le Marquis, would you honour me with a few moments' private conversation?"

"Is it really so serious as all that?" the Marquise asked, noticing the dark cloud that had gathered on Villefort's brow.

"It is so serious that I must take leave of you for a few days."

"You are going away?" Renée cried, unable to conceal the emotion she felt at this unexpected news.

"Alas! mademoiselle, I am obliged to do so."

"Where are you going?" the Marquise asked.

"That is a State secret, madame, but if you have any commissions for Paris a friend of mine is going there to-night."

Everyone looked at him.

"You wish to speak to me," asked the Marquis.

"Yes, let us go into your study."

The Marquis took Villefort's arm and they left the room together.

"Well, and what has happened?"

"An affair which I consider to be of a very grave nature and which necessitates my immediate departure for Paris. Will you give me a letter to the King?"

"To the King? But I dare not take upon myself to write to His Majesty."

"I do not ask you to write the letter. I want you to ask Monsieur de Salvieux to do so. He must give me a letter which will enable me to gain His Majesty's presence without all the formalities attendant on the request for an audience which would only lose precious time."

"If it is so urgent, my dear Villefort, go and pack your things and I will make de Salvieux write the letter."

"Do not lose any time, I must start in a quarter of an hour."

So saying, Villefort ran out, but at the door he bethought himself that the sight of the Deputy of the Procureur du Roi running through the streets would be enough to disturb the general peace of the town, so he resumed his ordinary magisterial pace.

At his door he perceived in the shadow a white spectre waiting for him, erect and motionless. It was Mercédès. Having no news of Edmond, she had come in person to inquire the reason of her lover's arrest.

As Villefort drew near, she moved from the wall against which she had been leaning and barred his way. Dantès had spoken to the Deputy of his betrothed and he now recognized her at once. He was astonished at her beauty and dignity, and when she asked him what had become of him whom she loved he felt as though he were the culprit and she his judge.

"The man you speak of," he said abruptly, "is a criminal, and I can do nothing for him."

A great sob escaped Mercédès' lips, and when Villefort tried to pass by she again stopped him.

"But tell me at least where he is," she said, "so that I may learn whether he is alive or dead."

"I know not," was the answer, "he has passed out of my hands."

Embarrassed by the straight look she gave him, as also by her entreaties, he pushed by her and entered his house, locking the door after him as though to shut out all sadness. But sadness is not banished so easily. Like the wounded hero of Virgil[2] he carried the arrow in his wound. He had no sooner entered his room than his legs gave way under him; he heaved a deep sigh, which was more like a sob, and sank into his chair. For a moment the man was in doubt. He had often passed sentence of death, but the condemned men who owed their execution to his crushing eloquence had not caused him the slightest compunction, for they had been guilty, or at all events Villefort had believed them to be so. But if at this moment the fair Mercédès had entered and had said to him: "In the name of Almighty God, Who watches over us and is our judge, give me back my lover," he would have given way and, in spite of the risk to himself, his icy-cold hand would have signed the order for Dantès' release. But no voice broke the stillness, the door opened only to admit Villefort's valet, who came to tell him that his carriage was at the door.

Poor Mercédès had returned to the Catalans followed by Fernand. Grief-stricken and desperate, she threw herself on her bed. Fernand, kneeling by her side, took her hand, which she did not attempt to withdraw, and covered it with kisses: but she was oblivious to it all.

So passed the night. The lamp went out when the oil was

consumed. Mercédès was no more aware of the darkness than she had been of the light. Day broke but she heeded it not. Grief had made her blind to all but Edmond.

M. Morrel did not give up hope: he had learnt of Dantès' imprisonment and had gone to all his friends and all the influential men of the town, but it was already reported that Dantès had been arrested as a Bonapartist, and since even the most sanguine[3] looked upon any attempt of Napoleon's to remount the throne as impossible he met with nothing but coldness, fear, or refusals, and returned home in despair.

Caderousse was restless and uneasy, but instead of trying to do something to help Dantès he had shut himself up in his house with two bottles of wine.

Danglars alone felt no pang of remorse or restlessness: he was even happy, for had he not avenged himself on an enemy and assured for himself the position on board the *Pharaon* he was in danger of losing? He was one of those calculating men who are born with a pen behind their ears and an ink pot in place of a heart. He went to bed at the usual hour and slept peacefully.

Chapter IX

THE LITTLE CABINET OF THE TUILERIES

⚜

We will now leave Villefort travelling with all speed to Paris and pass into the little cabinet of the Tuileries[1] with its arched windows, which is so well known as being the favourite cabinet of Napoleon, Louis XVIII, and Louis-Philippe.

There, seated at a walnut table which he had brought from Hartwell, and to which he was greatly attached, King Louis XVIII was listlessly listening to a grey-haired, well-groomed, aristocratic-looking man of fifty or fifty-two years of age, and was at the same time making notes on the margin of a volume of Gryphius' edition of *Horace*, an edition full of inaccuracies but nevertheless much valued, from which His Majesty drew many of his wise, philosophical observations.

"What did you say?" the King inquired.

"That I am somewhat harassed, Sire."

"Really? What carking[2] care is on your mind, my dear Blacas?"

"Sire, I have every reason to believe that a storm is brewing in the South."

"Well, my dear Duke," Louis XVIII replied, "I believe that you are misinformed, for I know for certain that the weather is very fine in that quarter."

Intellectual as he was, Louis XVIII was very fond of a pleasant jest.

"Sire," M. de Blacas continued, "if only to ease the mind of a faithful servant, could Your Majesty not send to Languedoc, Provence, and Dauphiné some trustworthy men who would report on the feeling in these three provinces?"

"*Canimus surdis,*"[3] answered the King, continuing his annotations.

"Sire," the courtier laughingly replied, "as you appear to understand the hemistich of the poet of Venusia,[4] it is only fitting that Your Majesty should believe in the good feeling of France; nevertheless I do not think I am quite wrong in fearing some desperate attempt."

"By whom?"

"By Bonaparte, or at any rate his party."

"My dear Blacas," replied the King, "your alarms prevent me from working."

"And your feeling of security, Sire, prevents me from sleeping."

"Wait, my dear Duke, wait a moment. I have a happy note on *pastor quum traheret;*[5] you can continue afterwards."

There was a moment's silence during which Louis XVIII wrote in as minute a handwriting as possible a note on the margin of his *Horace*, which having finished, he said, rising with the satisfied air of a man who thinks he has an idea of his own because he has commented on the idea of another, "Continue, my dear Duke, I am listening."

"Sire," Blacas said, for one moment hoping to use Villefort to his own advantage, "I must tell you that these are not mere meaningless rumours and idle tales that disquiet me. A man of strong common sense, meriting all my confidence and charged by me to watch over the South"— the Duke uttered these last words hesitatingly—"has arrived in all haste to bring me the news that a great danger threatens the King. I came without delay to you, Sire."

"*Mala ducis avi domum,*"[6] Louis XVIII continued, still

making his notes. "Ah, here is Monsieur Dandré. You did say Monsieur Dandré?" he asked of the chamberlain, who had just announced the Minister of Police.

"Yes, Sire, Baron Dandré."

"You have just come at the right moment," said Louis. "Come in, Baron, and tell the Duke your latest news of Monsieur Bonaparte. Do not conceal anything, no matter how serious. Is the Isle of Elba a volcano from which will issue a bloody, death-bringing war? *Bella, horrida bella?*"[7]

M. Dandré balanced himself gracefully on the back of a chair on which he was leaning his hands, and said:

"Has Your Majesty been pleased to peruse yesterday's report?"

"Yes, yes, but give the Duke the contents of the report; tell him exactly what the usurper is doing on his island."

"Monsieur," said the Baron to the Duke, "all His Majesty's faithful servants have good reason to rejoice at the latest news that has reached us from Elba. Bonaparte . . ."

M. Dandré looked at Louis, who, busily engaged in writing a note, did not even raise his head.

"Bonaparte is bored to distraction," continued the Baron. "He spends whole days watching his miners at work at Porto Longone. Moreover, we have ascertained that it will not be very long before the usurper is quite insane. His brain is giving way. One moment he is weeping bitterly, the next laughing boisterously. At other times he will spend hours on the shore throwing pebbles into the water, and if he succeeds in making five or six ducks and drakes he is as pleased with himself as if he had won another Marengo or a second Austerlitz.[8] You must agree with me that these are sure signs of insanity."

"Or else signs of wisdom, monsieur," smiled Louis. "The great captains of olden times amused themselves by casting pebbles into the sea; see Plutarch's *Life of Scipio Africanus.* Well, Blacas," the King continued triumphantly, "what do you say to that?"

"I say, Sire, that either the Minister of Police is mistaken or else I am; but as this would be impossible for a Minister of Police who has the safe custody of Your Majesty in his keeping, it is probably I who am under a wrong impression. Nevertheless, Sire, I would question before Your Majesty the gentleman of whom I spoke just now; in fact, I beg Your Majesty to do him this honour."

"Most willingly, Duke. Under your auspices, I will receive whom you will, but I must receive him armed to the teeth. Have you a later report than this one, Dandré? This one is dated February the twentieth and to-day is March the third."

"No, Sire, I am expecting one hourly. I have been out since early morning and it is possible that one has arrived during my absence."

"Then hie[9] you to your office and do not forget that I am waiting for you."

"I go, Sire, and shall be gone but ten minutes."

"In the meantime, Sire," said Monsieur de Blacas, "I will fetch my messenger. He has covered two hundred and twenty leagues in barely three days."

"Why all this unnecessary fatigue and anxiety when we have the telegraph which takes but three or four hours!"

"Ah, Sire, that is poor recompense for Monsieur de Villefort, who has come all that distance with such haste to communicate to Your Majesty some valuable information."

"Monsieur de Villefort?" exclaimed the King. "Is that the messenger's name?"

"Yes, Sire. I thought the name was unknown to Your Majesty."

"Not at all, not at all, Blacas. He is a serious-minded and intellectual young man, and above all he's ambitious. Added to that his father's name is Noirtier!"

"Noirtier the Girondin? Noirtier the Senator?"

"The very same."

"And Your Majesty has employed the son of such a man?"

"Blacas, my dear friend, you are very slow of understanding. I told you that Villefort was ambitious; he would sacrifice everything to gain his end, even his father. Go and fetch him."

When Blacas returned with Villefort, the King said:

"The Duke of Blacas tells me you have some important information. Give me full details, if you please, and above all begin at the beginning. I like order in all things."

"Sire," Villefort answered, "I will give Your Majesty a faithful report. I have come to Paris with all speed to inform Your Majesty that, in the exercise of my duties, I have discovered a conspiracy; not one of those everyday, meaningless, vulgar plots of the lower classes of our people, but a veritable tempest which threatens Your Majesty's very throne. Sire, the usurper has manned three vessels; he meditates some attack, senseless perhaps, yet it may have terrible consequences. By this time he will have left Elba, bound for I know not whither. He will most probably attempt to land either at Naples or on the coast of Tuscany, or even in France. Your Majesty is aware that the lord of the Isle of Elba has maintained relations with Italy and France?"

"Yes, monsieur, I know," replied the King, greatly agitated, "and lately we have been informed of Bonapartist meetings in the Rue Saint-Jacques. Whence have you your details?"

"Sire, I have them from a man whom I have been watching for some time past, and for whose arrest I gave orders the day before my departure from Marseilles. He is a turbulent sailor whom I suspected of Bonapartism, and he has been secretly to Elba. There he saw the Grand Maréchal, who entrusted him with a verbal mission to a Bonapartist in Paris, whose name he would not disclose; the nature of the mission was to prepare the adherents of Bonaparte for a return—note, Sire, these are the man's very words—for a return which must take place very shortly."

"Where is this man?"

"In prison, Sire."

"Do you think the thing is serious?"

"Sire, I fear it is more than a mere plot, it is a conspiracy."

"In these days it is easy to plan a conspiracy," the King answered, smiling, "but it is difficult to carry it out for the simple reason that, being recently re-established on the throne of our ancestors, we have our eyes at once on the past, the present, and the future. If Bonaparte landed at Naples, the whole coalition would be at his heels before he reached Piombino; if he landed in Tuscany, he would be in a hostile country; whereas if he landed in France he would have but a handful of men and we should soon overpower him."

At this moment the Minister of Police entered, pale and trembling and with a scared look.

Chapter X

The Ogre

O n perceiving the Minister's agitated demeanour, Louis violently pushed back the table at which he had been sitting.

"Why, Baron," he cried, "what is your trouble? You appear completely upset! Is your agitation in any way connected with the report given by Monsieur Blacas and confirmed by Monsieur de Villefort?"

"Sire . . ." stammered the Baron.

"Well . . . go on," replied Louis.

The Minister of Police was about to throw himself in despair at the King's feet, but the latter drew back a step and knitting his brows, said:

"Well, are you going to speak? I command you to give me your news!"

"Sire, the usurper left Elba on February the twenty-eighth and disembarked on March the first in France, at a little port near Antibes in the Gulf of Juan."

"The usurper disembarked in France near Antibes in the Gulf of Juan, two hundred and fifty leagues from Paris on March the first and you only report it to me on March the third?"

Louis XVIII made a movement of indescribable anger

and alarm and drew himself up straight as if a sudden blow had struck him both mentally and physically.

"In France!" he cried. "The usurper in France! Is he marching on Paris?"

"Sire, I know not. The dispatch only states that he has landed and the route he has taken," was the Police Minister's answer.

"How did you get the dispatch?"

The Minister bowed his head while a deep colour suffused his cheeks.

"By telegraph, Sire."

Louis XVIII took a step forward and crossed his arms as Napoleon would have done.

"So," he said, turning pale with anger, "seven allied armies overthrew that man; a miracle of God placed me on the throne of my fathers after an exile of twenty-five years, during which time I studied, probed, analysed the men and affairs of this France that was promised me, so that when I had attained my desires the power I held in my hand should burst and break me! What our enemies say of us is only too true. We have learnt nothing and forgotten nothing! If I had been betrayed like him, some consolation would be left to me; but to be surrounded by men whom I have raised to high dignities, who were to watch over me with more care than over themselves, who before my time were nothing, and who, when I have gone, will again be nothing and will probably perish through their own inability and ineptitude! Oh, cruel fate! Oh, I would sooner mount the scaffold of my brother Louis the Sixteenth than thus be forced down the steps of the Tuileries by ridicule! You do not know what ridicule is in France, yet you ought to know. And now, messieurs," he continued, turning toward M. de Blacas and the Police Minister, "I have no further need of you. The War Minister alone can help now." Then suddenly turning to Baron Dandré, he asked: "What further news have you in regard to the Rue Saint-Jacques affair?"

"Sire," the Minister of Police replied, "I was about to

give Your Majesty the latest information on the matter
when Your Majesty's attention was attracted toward this
other terrible catastrophe; now these facts will not interest
Your Majesty."

"On the contrary, monsieur, on the contrary. It seems to
me that this affair may have some direct connexion with the
other, and the death of General Quesnel will perhaps put us
on the direct track of a great internal conspiracy."

Villefort shuddered at the name of General Quesnel.

"In fact, Sire," the Minister of Police continued, "everything goes to show that his death was not due to suicide as
was at first believed, but was the work of some assassin.
Apparently General Quesnel left the precincts of a
Bonapartist Club and disappeared. An unknown man had
called on him in the morning and arranged a meeting in the
Rue Saint-Jacques."

While the Minister was telling his story, Villefort, who
seemed to hang on his very words, turned alternately red
and pale.

The King turned to him. "Do you not share my opinion,
Monsieur de Villefort, that Quesnel, who was believed to be
attached to the usurper though he was in reality entirely
loyal to me, was the victim of a Bonapartist trap?"

"It is very probable, Sire, but have you no further information?"

"We are on the track of the man who made the appointment with him. We have his description. He is a man of fifty
to fifty-two years of age, has brown hair, dark eyes with
bushy eyebrows, and wears a moustache. He was dressed in
a blue coat, and in his buttonhole wore the rosette of an
Officer of the Legion of Honour. Yesterday a man answering
to this description was followed but was lost sight of at the
corner of the Rue de la Jussienne and the Rue Coq Héron."

Villefort leaned against the back of a chair; his legs
seemed to be giving way under him, but when he heard that
the unknown man had escaped his pursuers he breathed
again.

"Seek this man out!" said the King to the Police Minister, "for if, as everything leads me to suppose, General Quesnel, who would have been so useful to us now, has been the victim of a murder, I will have his assassins severely punished, be they Bonapartists or not. I will not detain you longer, Baron. Monsieur de Villefort, you must be fatigued after your long journey; go and rest. You are putting up at your father's house, no doubt?"

Villefort seemed on the point of fainting.

"No, Your Majesty," he said, "I am staying at the Hôtel de Madrid, in the Rue de Tournon."

"But you will see him?"

"I think not, Sire."

"Ah! Of course," said Louis XVIII, smiling in a manner which showed that all these questions had been put to him with a motive. "I was forgetting that you are not on good terms with Monsieur Noirtier. Another sacrifice to the royal cause, for which you shall be recompensed." The King detached the cross of the Legion of Honour which he usually wore on his blue coat and giving it to Villefort said: "In the meantime take this cross."

Villefort's eyes filled with tears of joy and pride. He took the cross and kissed it.

Chapter XI

THE HUNDRED DAYS

✦

Events followed one another very rapidly. Everyone knows the history of the famous return from Elba,[1] a return which, unexampled as it was in the past, will probably remain unimitated in the future.

Louis XVIII made but a feeble attempt to parry the blow. The monarchy which he had but ill reconstructed trembled on its insecure foundation, and a wave of the Emperor's hand brought down with a crash the whole edifice that was naught but an unsightly mass of ancient prejudices and new ideas. Villefort therefore gained nothing from the King but a gratitude which was not only useless but dangerous at the present time, and the cross of the Legion of Honour, which he had the prudence not to display.

Napoleon would, doubtless, have dismissed Villefort but for the protection of Noirtier, who was all-powerful at the Court of the Hundred Days; the Procureur du Roi alone was deprived of his office, being under suspicion of lukewarm support of Bonaparte.

Meanwhile the imperial power had hardly been reestablished, the Emperor had hardly re-entered the Tuileries and issued his numerous and divergent orders from that little cabinet into which we have introduced our readers, and on the table of which he found Louis XVIII's snuff-box, still open and half full, when the flames of civil war, always smouldering in the South, began to light up in Marseilles, and the populace seemed like to indulge in acts of violence against the Royalists of the town in place of the shouts and insults with which they hitherto had greeted them whenever they ventured abroad.

Villefort retained his post, but his marriage was postponed until happier times. If the Emperor remained on the throne, Gérard would require a different alliance and his father undertook to find this for him; if, on the contrary, a second Restoration brought back Louis XVIII, the influence of M. de Saint-Méran and himself would be strengthened and the marriage would be more suitable than ever.

As for Dantès, he remained a prisoner; hidden away in the depths of his dungeon he was ignorant of the downfall of Louis XVIII's throne and the re-establishment of Napoleon.

Twice during this short revival of the Empire, which was called the Hundred Days, had M. Morrel renewed his appeal for the liberation of Dantès, and each time Villefort had quietened him with promises and hopes. Finally there was Waterloo.[2] Morrel did not present himself before Villefort any more; he realized he had done all that was humanly possible for his young friend and that to make any further attempts under this second restoration would be to compromise himself unnecessarily.

When Louis XVIII remounted the throne, Villefort successfully petitioned for the post of Procureur du Roi at Toulouse, and a fortnight later he married Mademoiselle de Saint-Méran.

When Napoleon returned to France, Danglars understood the full significance of the blow he had struck at Dantès; his denunciation had been given some sort of justification and he called this extraordinary coincidence the Hand of Providence. But when Napoleon reached Paris and his voice was once more heard, imperious and powerful,

Danglars grew afraid. Dantès might return any day with full information on the cause of his arrest and eager for vengeance. He, therefore, informed M. Morrel of his desire to leave the merchant service and obtained a recommendation from him to a Spanish merchant. He went to Madrid and was heard of no more for a long time.

Fernand, on the other hand, could not understand anything. Dantès was absent and that was all he cared about. What had happened to him? He did not know, neither did he care.

In the meantime the Empire made a last appeal to her soldiers, and every man, capable of bearing arms, rushed to obey the far-reaching voice of his Emperor. Fernand left Mercédès and joined up with the others, but the gloomy and terrible thought preyed upon his mind that Dantès might return now that his back was turned and marry her whom he loved. His devotion to Mercédès, the pity he pretended to have for her in her sorrow, the care with which he anticipated her least desire, had produced the effect that outward signs of devotion always produce on generous hearts: Mercédès had always been fond of him as a friend and this affection was now increased by a feeling of gratitude.

Fernand therefore went off to the army with hope in his heart, and Mercédès was now left alone. She could be seen, bathed in tears, wandering incessantly round the little village of the Catalans: at times she would stand under the fierce midday sun as motionless and dumb as a statue, with her eyes fixed on Marseilles; at other times she would sit on the beach listening to the moaning of the sea, as eternal as her grief, and ask herself whether it would not be better to leap down into the abyss below than to suffer this cruel alternative of a hopeless suspense. She did not lack the courage to do this deed; it was her religion that came to her aid and saved her from suicide.

As for old Dantès, he had now lost all hope. Five months after he had been separated from his son, and almost at the very hour at which he had been arrested, the old man breathed his last in Mercédès' arms. M. Morrel paid the expenses of the funeral and the small debts the old man had incurred during his last illness. It required more than benevolence to do this, it required courage. The South was aflame, and to help the father of a Bonapartist as dangerous as Dantès, even though he were on his deathbed, was a crime.

Chapter XII

NUMBERS 34 AND 27

⚓

Dantès passed through all the various stages of misery that affect a forgotten and forsaken prisoner in his cell. First there was pride born of hope and a consciousness of his innocence; next he was so reduced that he began to doubt his innocence; finally his pride gave way to entreaty, yet it was not God he prayed to, for that is the last resource, but man. The wretched and miserable should turn to their Saviour first, yet they do not hope in Him until all other hope is exhausted.

Dantès begged to be taken from his dungeon and placed in another one, even though that were deeper and darker. Even a change for the worse would be welcome and would give him a few days' distraction. He entreated his gaolers to let him go for a walk, to give him books, anything to while away the time. One day he entreated his gaoler to ask for a companion for him. The gaoler passed the request of prisoner No. 34 to the proper quarter, but the governor, being as prudent as a politician, imagined that Dantès would stir up the prisoners to mutiny, weave some plot, or make an attempt to escape, so he refused.

Dantès had now exhausted all human resources and turned toward God. All the pious thoughts which are sown broadcast in the human field and which are gleaned by the victims of a cruel fate came to comfort him; he recalled the prayers taught him by his mother and discovered in them a hidden meaning hitherto unknown to him. To the happy and prosperous man, prayer is but a meaningless jumble of words until grief comes to explain to the unfortunate wretch the sublime language which is our means of communication with God.

In spite of his prayers, however, Dantès still remained a prisoner.

His gloom gave way to wrath. He began to roar out blasphemies which made even his gaoler recoil with horror, and dashed himself in a paroxysm of fury against the walls of the prison. Then there recurred to his mind the informer's letter which Villefort had shown him. Each line of it was reflected on the walls in fiery letters. He told himself it was the hatred of men and not the vengeance of God that had thrust him into this dark abyss. He doomed these unknown men to the most cruel torments his fiery imagination was capable of conjuring up, but, even so, the most awful of these torments seemed to him too mild and too short for them, for after the torment would come death, and in death they would find, if not repose, at all events that insensibility which so nearly resembles repose.

Sometimes he said to himself: "When I was still a man, strong and free, commanding other men, I have seen the heavens open, the sea rage and foam, the storm rise in a patch of sky and like a gigantic eagle beat the two horizons with its wings. Then I felt that my ship was but a weak refuge from the tempest, for did it not shiver and shake like a feather in the hand of a giant? Soon the sight of the sharp rocks, coupled with the frightful noise of the waves, announced to me that death was near, and death terrified me. I exerted all my efforts to escape it, and I combined all my man's strength with all my sailor's skill in that terrible fight against God! For to me life was happy then, and to escape from the jaws of death was to return to happiness. I had no use for death; I loathed the thought of sleeping my last sleep on a bed of hard rocks and seaweed, or of serving after my death as food for gulls and vultures, I who was made in the image of God! Now, however, it is quite a different matter. I have lost all that bound me to life; now death smiles on me as a nurse smiles on the child she is about to rock to sleep; now welcome death!"

No sooner had this idea taken possession of the unhappy young man than he became more calm and resigned; he felt more contented with his hard bed and black bread, ate less, slept not at all, and almost found his miserable existence supportable, for could he not cast it off at will as one casts off old clothes?

There were two ways of dying open to him. One was quite simple; it was only a question of tying his handkerchief to a bar of the window and hanging himself. The other way was by starving himself. Hanging seemed to him a disgraceful thing, so he decided upon the second course.

Nearly four years had passed since he had taken this resolution; at the end of the second year he ceased to count the days.

Dantès had said to himself, "I will die," and had chosen his mode of death; he had weighed the matter well, but, being afraid he might go back on his resolution, he had sworn to himself that he would starve himself to death. "When the gaoler brings me my food in the morning and evening," he said to himself, "I shall throw it through the window and he will think I have eaten it." He kept his word. At first he threw it away with pleasure, then with deliberation, and finally with regret. It was only the remembrance of his oath that gave him the strength to carry out this dreadful purpose. The food which he had once loathed, hunger now made pleasant to the eye and delicious to the smell. At times he would hold his plate in his hand for an hour, his eyes fixed on the morsel of putrid meat or tainted fish and the black and mouldy bread. It was the last instincts of life struggling within him and breaking down his resolution. At length came the day when he had no longer the strength to raise himself to throw his supper away. The next day he could no longer see and scarcely hear; the gaoler thought he was seriously ill. All at once, toward nine in the evening, just as he was hoping that death would come soon, Dantès heard a dull sound on the wall against which he was lying.

So many loathsome animals had made their noises in his cell that little by little he had grown accustomed to them and did not let them disturb his sleep. This time, however, whether it was that his senses had become intensified by his long abstinence or that the noise was louder or more significant than usual, Edmond raised his head to hear better. And what he heard was an even scraping noise as though caused by an enormous claw, a powerful tooth, or the pressure of some sharp instrument on the stone. Though weakened, the young man's brain seized on the idea that is ever present to the mind of a prisoner: liberty. The noise lasted for about three hours, then Edmond heard the sound of something crumbling away and all was silence again.

Some hours later the scraping was continued again, but this time louder and nearer. Edmond's interest was aroused, and the noise seemed almost like a companion to him. "As it continues even in daylight," he thought to himself, "it must be some unfortunate prisoner trying to escape. Oh, if I were only near and could help him! But I must ascertain this. I have only to knock on the wall and if it is an ordinary workman, he will instantly cease working and will endeavour to discover who it is that knocks, and why he knocks; and then, as his work is lawful, he will soon resume it. If, on the contrary, it is a prisoner, the noise I make will alarm him; he will be afraid of being discovered; he will cease his work and only resume it at night when he believes every one to be in bed and asleep."

Edmond went to a corner of the cell, detached a stone that had become loosened with the damp, and knocked three times on the wall, just where the sound had been loudest. At the first knock the noise stopped as if by magic. Edmond listened intently all through that day but there was complete silence. "It is a prisoner," Dantès said with inexpressible joy.

Three days—seventy-two deadly hours—passed without a repetition of the noise. One evening, however, after the gaoler had paid his last visit, Dantès, who had his ear to the wall, thought he heard an almost imperceptible sound. He moved away, paced round the cell several times to calm himself, and then returned to the same spot. There could be no doubt about it: something was happening on the other side of the wall. The prisoner had recognized the danger of his previous tactics and had substituted the crowbar for the chisel.

Encouraged by this discovery, Edmond resolved to help the untiring worker. He looked round for some object he could use as a tool, but could discover nothing. He had no knife or sharp instrument; the only iron in the cell was that at the windows, and he had already proved the impossibility of moving the bars.

He had but one resource, and this was to break his pitcher and use one of the jagged fragments. Accordingly he dashed the pitcher to the ground, and, choosing two or three of the sharp, broken bits, hid them under his bed; the others he left scattered about the floor. The breaking of the jug was such a natural accident that it would cause no suspicion.

He had the whole night to work in, but, groping about in the dark, he did not make much headway, and he soon found that he blunted his instrument against the hard stone. He laid down his tool and waited for the morning. Hope had given him patience.

All night long he listened to the unknown miner at his subterranean work. Day came, the gaoler entered. Dantès told him the pitcher had fallen from his hands as he was drinking out of it the previous evening. The gaoler went grumbling to fetch another one without even taking the trouble to pick up the bits of the old one.

The grinding of the lock in the door which had always caused Dantès a pang now gave him inexpressible joy. He listened for the last of the dying footsteps and then, hastily moving his bed away, he saw by the faint ray of light that penetrated his cell how useless had been his work of the previous night in attacking the hard stone instead of the plaster surrounding it.

The damp had rendered the plaster friable,[1] and Dantès' heart beat with joy when he saw it break off in little bits: they were but tiny atoms, it is true, but within half an hour he had scraped away nearly a handful. A mathematician would have calculated that if he worked like that for about two years, and if he did not encounter a rock, he might succeed in excavating a passage two feet square and twenty feet deep.

In three days he managed, with untold precautions, to lay bare a stone. The wall was made of ashlars, for the greater solidity of which a freestone had been placed at intervals. It was one of these freestones which Dantès had now laid bare, and which he must now dislodge. He used his nails, but they were useless tools; the fragments of the pitcher broke whenever he tried to make them do the duty of a crowbar. After an hour of useless toil, he paused, his forehead bathed in perspiration. Was he to be thus stopped at the beginning, and must he wait, inert and useless, while his neighbour, who was perhaps growing weary, should accomplish all?

Suddenly an idea occurred to him. He stood up smiling; the perspiration on his forehead dried.

The gaoler always brought him his soup in a tin saucepan with an iron handle. It was this iron handle he longed for, and he would have given ten years of his life to get it. The contents of the saucepan were always poured into Dantès' plate; this he ate with his wooden spoon and washed his plate in readiness for the next day.

On the evening in question Dantès placed his plate on the floor, half-way between the door and the table. When the gaoler entered, he stepped on it and broke it to pieces. This time the gaoler could not blame Dantès; it is true he should not have left his plate on the floor, but then, the gaoler should have looked where he was going. He contented himself with grumbling and looked around for some other vessel for Dantès' soup.

"Leave the saucepan," the prisoner said, "you can take it again when you bring me my breakfast in the morning."

This advice suited the gaoler as it spared him the necessity of going up and down the many steps again. He left the saucepan.

Dantès was trembling with delight. He ate his soup and meat hastily, and then, after waiting an hour to make sure the gaoler would not change his mind, he set himself to the task of dislodging the freestone, using the saucepan handle as a lever. At the end of an hour he had extricated the stone, leaving a hole of more than a foot and a half in diameter. Dantès collected all the plaster very carefully, carried it into the corners of the cell, and, with a piece of broken earthenware, scraped some of the grey earth from the floor and strewed it over the plaster.

He continued to work all night and at dawn of day replaced the stone, pushed the bed up against the wall, and lay down to sleep.

His breakfast consisted of a piece of bread which the gaoler placed on the table.

"Aren't you going to bring me another plate?" Dantès asked.

"No, you break everything. First of all there was your pitcher, then you made me break your plate. You can keep the saucepan now and your soup will be poured into that."

Dantès lifted up his eyes to Heaven, joined his hands under the coverlet, and said a prayer of thanks. The piece of iron which had been left him created in him a feeling of gratitude toward God stronger than any he had felt for the greatest blessings in past years.

He worked all day unremittingly; thanks to his new instrument he had scraped out more than ten handfuls of broken stone, plaster, and cement by the end of the day. He continued working all through the night, but after two or three hours he encountered an obstacle. The iron did not grip any more, it simply slid off a smooth surface. He touched the obstacle with his hand and soon recognized it as a beam. It crossed, or rather blocked, the hole that Dantès had commenced. It now meant that he had to dig either above or below it.

"Oh, my God! my God!" he cried, "I prayed so fervently that I hoped Thou hadst heard my prayer. My God! after having deprived me of my liberty! after having deprived me of the peace of death, oh, my God! and after calling me back to existence, have pity on me, oh, my God! and let me not die of despair!"

"Who speaks of God and of despair in the same breath?" said a voice that seemed to come from under the ground and sounded sepulchral to the young man. His hair stood on end and he drew back.

"Ah," he murmured, "I hear a man's voice!"

Edmond had not heard any man's voice but that of his gaoler for the past four or five years, and to a prisoner a gaoler is not a man; he is but a living door added to his oaken door; he is but a bar of flesh added to his bar of iron.

"In Heaven's name," Dantès cried out, "speak once more, though the sound of your voice frightened me. Who are you?"

"And who are you?" the voice asked.

"An unhappy prisoner," replied Dantès, who had no difficulty in answering this question.

"What nationality?"

"French."

"Your name?"

"Edmond Dantès."

"Your profession?"

"A sailor."

"How long have you been here?"

"Since February twenty-eighth, eighteen-fifteen."

"Your crime?"

"I am innocent of any crime."

"But what are you accused of?"

"Of having conspired in favour of the Emperor's return."

"What? The Emperor's return? Is the Emperor, then, no longer on the throne?"

"He abdicated at Fontainebleau in eighteen-fourteen and was banished to the Isle of Elba. How long have you been here that you do not know this?"

"Since eighteen-eleven."

Edmond shuddered. This man had been in prison four years longer than himself.

"Dig no more," the voice continued, speaking quicker, "tell me only at what height your hole is."

"On a level with the floor."

"How is it concealed?"

"It is behind my bed."

"Where does your room lead to?"

"To the passage."

"And the passage?"

"To the courtyard."

"Alas! alas!" muttered the voice.

"Oh, my God! What is the matter?" Dantès cried out.

"Only that I have made a mistake, that the inaccuracy of my plans has misled me, that the lack of a compass has ruined all, that one wrong line on my plan is equivalent to fifteen feet, and that what I believed to be the wall of the fortress is the wall you have been digging!"

"But in any case the fortress would only give you access to the sea."

"That is what I desired."

"And if you had succeeded?"

"I should have thrown myself into the sea, swum to one of the islands round the Château d'If, or even to the shore, and then I should have been saved. Now all is lost. Fill in your hole again very carefully, work no more, and wait till you hear from me again."

"Tell me at least who you are."

"I am—I am number twenty-seven."

"Ah! you surely mistrust me," cried Dantès. "I swear by the living God that I will not betray you. Do not forsake me! You will not leave me alone any more, will you? Come to me or else let me come to you. We will escape together, and if we cannot escape we will talk together, you of those you love, and I of those I love. You must love someone."

"I am all alone in the world."

"Then you will learn to love me. If you are young, I shall be your companion: if you are old, I shall be your son. I have a father who must be seventy years of age if he is still alive. I love but him and a girl named Mercédès. I know that my father has not forgotten me, but who knows whether she still thinks of me! I will love you as I loved my father."

"So be it," said the prisoner. "Farewell till to-morrow."

From this moment Dantès' happiness knew no bounds; he was not going to be alone any more, and perhaps he might even gain his freedom; anyway, even if he remained a prisoner, he would have a companion, and captivity shared with another is but half captivity. He walked up and down his cell all day long, his heart beating wildly with joy. At moments it almost seemed to choke him. At the least sound he heard he sprang to the door. Once or twice he was seized with the fear that they would separate him from this man whom he knew not, but whom he already loved as a friend.

Night came. Dantès thought his neighbour would take advantage of the silence and the darkness to renew conversation with him, but he was mistaken; the night passed without a single sound breaking in upon his feverish waiting. But the next morning, after the gaoler had been, he heard three knocks at equal intervals. He threw himself upon his knees:

"Is that you?" he said. "Here I am."

"Has your gaoler gone?" inquired the voice.

"Yes," replied Dantès, "and he will not come again till this evening, so we have got twelve full hours of freedom."

"I can set to work, then?"

"Oh, yes, yes, without delay. This very instant, I beg of you."

The piece of earth on which Dantès was leaning suddenly gave way; he threw himself back, and a mass of earth and loose stones crumbled into a hole which opened up just beneath the aperture he himself had made; then from the bottom of this hole, of which he could not gauge the depth, he saw a head appear, then a pair of shoulders, and finally the body of a man who crept with great agility out of the hole just made.

Chapter XIII

AN ITALIAN SCHOLAR

Dantès threw himself into the arms of his new friend, for whom he had waited so impatiently and so long, and drew him toward the window that the little light that penetrated into his cell might reveal his features.

His new-found friend was short, with hair blanched with suffering rather than with age. His keen, penetrating eyes were almost hidden beneath thick grey eyebrows, and his beard, which was still black, reached down to his chest. His thin face, furrowed with deep lines, and the bold outlines of his characteristic features revealed a man who was more accustomed to exercise his mental faculties than his physical strength. Large drops of perspiration stood on his brow, and as for his garments, it was impossible to distinguish their original form, for they were in rags.

He appeared at least sixty-five years of age, but the agility of his movements seemed to imply that this aged appearance was due to long captivity. He received the young man's enthusiastic outbursts with a certain pleasure; his icy soul seemed to gather warmth for an instant and to melt in the contact with this ardent youth. He thanked him with much feeling for his cordiality, though his disappointment had been very bitter at finding another dungeon where he had hoped to find liberty.

"Now let us see whether we can conceal from the eyes of your gaolers all traces of my entrance," said the newcomer; and, stooping down to the aperture, he lifted the stone with the greatest ease, in spite of its weight, and fitted it into the hole.

"This stone has been removed very carelessly," he said, shaking his head. "Hadn't you any tools?"

"Have you any?" Dantès asked with astonishment.

"I made some. With the exception of a file, I have all I need: chisel, pincers, crow-bar."

"Oh, I should like to see these products of your patience and industry."

"Well, to begin with, here is my chisel."

And he showed Dantès a sharp, strong blade with a handle of beech-wood.

"How did you make that?" asked Dantès.

"Out of one of the clamps of my bed. I have hollowed out the passage, a distance of about fifty feet, with this instrument. To think that all my work has been in vain! There is now no means of escape. God's will be done!"

Dantès looked with astonishment mingled with admiration at this man, who renounced with such philosophy a hope cherished for so long.

"Now," Dantès said, "will you tell me who you are?"

"Yes, if it interests you." Then he continued sadly: "I am the Abbé Faria,[1] a prisoner in the Château d'If since eighteen-eleven, and previously imprisoned in the fortress of Fenestrella for three years. In the year eighteen-eleven I was transferred from Piedmont to France. It was then that I learned that the god of destiny, who at that time seemed subservient to Napoleon's every wish, had given him a son, and that while still in its cradle the child had been named King of Rome. Little did I think then that this superman would be overthrown."

"But why are you here at all?"

"Because in eighteen-seven I meditated the very scheme that Napoleon tried to realize in eighteen-eleven;[2] because like Machiavelli[3] I desired Italy to be one great, strong, and compact empire, instead of a nest of petty principalities each with its weak and despotic ruler; because I thought I had found my Caesar Borgia[4] in a crowned fool, who pretended to share my views so as the better to betray me. It was the scheme of Alexander the Sixth and Clement the Seventh; it will never materialize now, for their attempt was fruitless, and not even Napoleon has accomplished it. There is no doubt, Italy is an accursed country."

For a moment Dantès stood motionless and mute.

"Then you abandon all hope of escaping?" he said at last.

"I realize that it is impossible, and that it is tantamount to revolting against God to attempt what is contrary to His designs."

"Why despair? Why not start afresh?"

"Start afresh! Ah! you little know how I have toiled. Do you know that it took me four years to make my tools? Do you know that for the past two years I have been scraping and digging out earth as hard as granite? I have had to move stones that I once thought it impossible to loosen. I have spent whole days in these titanic efforts, and there were times when I was overjoyed if by nighttime I had scraped away a square inch of the cement that age had made as hard as the stones themselves. I have had to pierce the wall of a staircase so that I could deposit all my stones and earth in its well. And I thought I had almost finished my task, and felt I had just enough strength left to accomplish it, when I found that all my plans were frustrated. I assure you, I have known very few successful attempts to escape. Only those have been crowned with success which were planned and worked out with infinite patience. We shall do best now to wait till some unforeseen occurrence gives us the opportunity of making our escape. When such an opportunity occurs, we will seize it."

"You could well wait," Dantès said with a sigh. "Your work occupied every minute of your time, and when you could not work, you had your hope in a brighter future to console you."

"I accomplished other things besides all this."

"What did you do?"

"I wrote or studied."

"Who gave you paper, pens, and ink?"

"No one," said the abbé, "I made them myself."

Dantès looked at the man with admiration; only he could scarcely credit all he told him. Faria noticed this shade of doubt on the young man's face and said:

"When you come to my cell, I will show you an entire volume entitled *Treatise on the Possibility of a General Monarchy in Italy*, which is the result of the thoughts, reflections, and researches of my whole life; ideas which I have worked out in the shadow of the Colosseum at Rome, at the foot of Saint Mark's Column at Venice, or on the banks of the Arno at Florence."

"Do you mean to say you have written it?"

"On two shirts. I have invented a preparation by means of which linen is rendered as smooth and glossy as parchment. I also made some excellent quills which everyone would prefer to the ordinary ones if once they were known. I made them from the cartilage of the head of those enormous whiting they sometimes give us on fast-days. Formerly there must have been a fireplace in my cell which was doubtless closed up some time before I came. It must have been used for very many years, for the interior was coated with soot. I dissolved some soot in a portion of the wine they bring me every Sunday, and my ink was made. For notes to which I wished to draw special attention, I pricked my fingers and wrote with my blood."

"When can I see all this?" Dantès asked.

"As soon as you like."

"Let it be at once, then!" the young man exclaimed.

"Then follow me."

So saying the abbé re-entered the subterranean passage and disappeared. Dantès followed and found himself at the far end of the passage, into which the abbé's door opened. Here the passage became narrower; indeed there was scarcely room for a man to crawl through on his hands and knees. The abbé's room was paved; it had been by raising one of the flag-stones in the darkest corner of the room that he had commenced the laborious task of which Dantès witnessed the completion.

As soon as he entered the cell, the young man examined it very carefully, but at first sight it presented nothing out of the ordinary.

"And now I am very anxious to see your treasures," Dantès said.

The abbé went toward the fireplace, removed a stone which was formerly the hearthstone, and which hid a fairly deep cavity.

"What do you wish to see first?"

"Show me your work on the Monarchy of Italy."

Faria took from his cupboard three or four rolls of linen four inches wide and eighteen long which were folded like papyrus leaves. These strips of linen were numbered and covered with writing.

"Here you have the whole of it," he said, "I put the word *finis* at the bottom of the seventy-eighth strip just a week ago. I have used for it two of my shirts and all the handkerchiefs I had. If ever I gain my liberty and can find a publisher in Italy who will publish it, my reputation is made."

He then showed Dantès the quills he had made; the penknife of which he was particularly proud and which he had made out of an old iron candlestick; the ink; the matches, the sulphur for which he had obtained by feigning a skin disease; the rope-ladder, the material for which he had obtained by unravelling the ends of his sheets; and finally the needle. On seeing these ingenious products of an intelligent and highly developed brain, Dantès became thoughtful, and it occurred to him that the man might be able to clear up the mystery surrounding his own misfortune, which he himself had been unable to fathom.

"What are you thinking of?" the abbé asked with a smile, seeing his companion's pensiveness, and attributing it to inexpressible admiration.

"I was thinking that though you have related to me the events of your life, yet you know nothing of mine."

"Your life, young man, is far too short to contain anything of importance."

"Nevertheless it contains a very great misfortune," said Dantès, "a misfortune that I do not deserve, and I would rather attribute the authorship of it to mankind and no longer blaspheme God as I have hitherto done."

"Tell me your story, then."

Dantès then related what he called the story of his life, consisting of a voyage to India, two or three voyages to the East, and finally his last voyage, the death of Captain Leclère, the package confided to him for the Grand Maréchal, the letter given him by the latter addressed to a certain M. Noirtier. Then he went on to tell his friend of his arrival at Marseilles, his interview with his father, his love for Mercédès, his betrothal feast, his arrest, his examination, his temporary imprisonment in the Law Courts, and finally his permanent imprisonment in the Château d'If. After this he knew nothing more, not even how long he had been a prisoner.

When Dantès had finished his story, the abbé sat silent, deep in thought. After a time he said: "There is a maxim with a very deep meaning which says: 'If you wish to discover the author of a crime, endeavour to find out in the first place who would derive advantage from the crime committed.' You were about to be nominated captain and also to marry a beautiful girl, were you not?"

"That is true."

"Was it to anyone's interest that you should not be appointed captain of the *Pharaon*? And again, was it to anyone's interest that you should not marry Mercédès? Answer the first question first; order is the key to all problems."

"I was very popular on board. If the sailors could have

chosen their chief, I am sure they would have chosen me. There was only one person who had any reason to wish me ill; I quarrelled with him some time ago and challenged him to a duel, but he refused."

"Now we are coming to the point. What was this man's name?"

"Danglars, the purser of the ship."

"Had you been appointed captain, would you have retained him as such?"

"Not if it had depended on me, for I thought I had noticed some inaccuracies in his accounts."

"Good. Now who was present at your last conversation with Captain Leclère?"

"No one; we were alone."

"Could anyone have overheard your conversation?"

"Yes, the door was open, and . . . wait . . . yes, it is true, Danglars passed at the very moment Captain Leclère was handing me the package for the Grand Maréchal."

"Better still. Now we are on the right track. Did you take anyone ashore when you put in at the Isle of Elba?"

"No one at all."

"What did you do with the letter the Grand Maréchal gave you?"

"I put it in my portfolio."

"Had you your portfolio with you then? How could a portfolio large enough to contain an official letter find room in a sailor's pocket?"

"My portfolio was on board."

"So you did not put the letter into the portfolio until you returned to the ship?"

"No."

"What did you do with the letter from the time you left Porto Ferrajo till you reached the ship?"

"I carried it in my hand."

"So that when you went on board, everyone could see that you carried a letter?"

"Yes."

"Danglars as well?"

"Yes; Danglars as well as the others."

"Now listen to me and try to recall all the incidents. Do you remember how the denunciation was phrased?"

"Oh, yes, I read it over three times and each word is engraved on my memory." And he repeated it word for word.

The abbé shrugged his shoulders. "It is as clear as daylight," he said. "You must have a very noble heart and simple mind that you had not your suspicions from the very outset."

"Do you really think so?" Dantès exclaimed. "Such infamy is not possible!"

"How did Danglars usually write?"

"He had a good, round hand."

"How was the anonymous letter written?"

"With a backward slant."

The abbé smiled. "I suppose it was a disguised hand?"

"It was too bold to be disguised."

The abbé took one of his quills and wrote the first two or three lines of the denunciation on a piece of prepared linen. Dantès stood aghast and looked at the abbé in terror, and exclaimed: "How extraordinarily alike the two writings are!"

"The simple explanation is that the denunciation was written with the left hand. I have noticed that whereas handwritings written with the right hand vary, those written with the left hand are nearly always like. Now let us pass to the second question. Was it to anyone's interest that you should not marry Mercédès?"

"Yes, there was a young man who loved her, a young Catalan named Fernand."

"Do you think he would be capable of writing the letter?"

"No, he would rather have stuck his knife into me. Besides, he was ignorant of the details stated in the denunciation. I had not mentioned them to anyone."

"Stay a moment. Did Danglars know Fernand?"

"No. Oh, yes, I remember now. On the eve of my betrothal, I saw them together in old Pamphile's tavern.

Danglars was friendly and jocular, but Fernand looked pale and agitated. A tailor, named Caderousse, whom I know very well, was with them. He was quite drunk, though."

"Do you want to know something else?" asked the abbé, laughing.

"Yes, since you seem to be able to fathom every mystery. Tell me why I was only submitted to one examination, and why I was condemned without trial."

"This is a more serious matter," was the reply. "What we have just done for your two friends is mere child's play by comparison. You must give me the most precise details. Who examined you?"

"The Deputy."

"Did you tell him everything?"

"Yes, everything."

"Did his manner toward you change at all in the course of the examination?"

"He certainly did appear disturbed when he read the compromising letter. He seemed quite upset at my misfortune."

"Are you quite sure he was so perturbed on your account?"

"At any rate he gave me one great proof of his sympathy. He burnt the letter, my one incriminating document, before my very eyes."

"Ah! This man may have been a greater scoundrel than you imagine. The Deputy's conduct was too sublime to be natural. To whom was the letter addressed?"

"To Monsieur Noirtier, thirteen, Rue Coq Héron, Paris."

"Can you think of any selfish motive the Deputy might have had in destroying the letter?"

"I do not know of any, but he may have had some reason, for he made me promise two or three times that, in my own interest, I would not speak to anyone of the letter, and he made me swear that I would not utter the name of the person to whom it was addressed."

"Noirtier?" the abbé repeated. "Noirtier? . . . I knew a

Noirtier at the Court of the old Queen of Etruria, a man who was a Girondist during the Revolution. What was the Deputy's name?"

"De Villefort."

The abbé burst into loud laughter. Dantès looked at him in stupefaction. "What is the matter?" he said.

"Only that I have a clear and complete understanding of everything now. Poor blind young man! This Noirtier was no other than the Deputy's father."

"His father?" Dantès cried out.

"Yes, his father, who styles himself Noirtier de Villefort," the abbé replied.

Dantès now began to see clearly, and many details which had been incomprehensible to him up to this moment now began to assume their real significance. Villefort's change of demeanour during the examination, the burning of the letter, the exacted oath, the magistrate's almost supplicating voice which seemed to implore rather than to threaten, all passed through his mind. A cry broke from his lips and he staggered like a drunken man; then, rushing toward the opening which led to his cell, he called out: "I must be alone to think this over."

Reaching his cell he fell on his bed, and here the turnkey found him in the evening, motionless, his eyes staring into space, his features drawn.

During these hours of meditation, which had passed like so many seconds, he had formed a terrible resolution and taken a fearful oath.

At length a voice roused him from his reverie; it was the voice of Faria, who had come to invite Dantès to have his supper with him. The young man followed him. His face had lost that drawn look it had worn, and instead there was a determined, almost radiant expression which clearly denoted that he had taken a resolution. The abbé looked at him attentively.

"I almost regret having helped you in your researches and having told you what I did," he said.

"Why?"

"Because I have instilled into your heart a feeling that previously held no place there—vengeance."

Dantès smiled and said: "Let us speak of something else."

The abbé looked at him again and shook his head sadly; but he did what his companion asked him and spoke of other matters.

Dantès listened to his words with admiring attention. At first he spoke of things and ideas of which the young man had no comprehension until later on; like the aurora borealis[5] which lights the navigator of the northern seas on his way, he showed the young man new landscapes and horizons illuminated by fantastic lights, and Dantès realized what happiness it would bring to an intelligent being to follow this exalted mind to those moral, philosophical, or social heights to which he was wont to soar.

"You must impart to me a little of your knowledge," Dantès said, "otherwise an ignoramus like myself will only be a bore to you. I am sure that you must prefer solitude to a companion without education such as I am. If you do what I ask, I promise to speak no more of escaping."

"Alas, my good friend," said the abbé, smiling, "human knowledge is very limited, and when I have taught you mathematics, physics, history, and the three or four living languages I speak, you will know all that I know. It will not take more than two years to give you the knowledge I possess."

"Two years?" exclaimed Dantès. "Do you really think you can teach me all these things in two years? What will you teach first? I am anxious to begin. I am thirsting for knowledge."

That selfsame evening the two prisoners drew up a plan for the younger man's education and began to put it into execution the next day. Dantès had a prodigious memory and a great facility for assimilation. The mathematical turn of his mind gave him aptitude for all kinds of calculation, while the sense of poetry that is in every sailor gave life to dryness of figures and severity of lines.

Whether it was that the distraction afforded him by his study had taken the place of liberty, or because he adhered strictly to the promise given to the abbé, he made no further reference to escaping, and the days passed rapidly, each day adding to his store of knowledge. At the end of the year he was a different man. Dantès noticed, however, that in spite of his companionship, the Abbé Faria seemed to lose some of his animation with each succeeding day. It seemed as though there was something on his mind. At times he would become wrapt in thought, sigh unconsciously, then suddenly rise and, with his arms crossed over his breast, gloomily pace his cell. One day, all at once, he ceased his incessant wandering and exclaimed: "If only there were no sentry!"

"Have you found a means of escape then?" asked Dantès excitedly.

"Yes, provided that the sentry in the gallery is both deaf and blind."

"He shall be deaf and he shall be blind," answered the young man in such a determined way that it frightened the abbé.

"No! No!" he cried out. "I will have no bloodshed."

Dantès wanted to pursue the subject, but the abbé shook his head and refused to answer any more questions. Three months passed.

"Are you strong?" the abbé one day asked Dantès.

Without replying Dantès picked up the chisel, bent it into the shape of a horse-shoe, and straightened it out again.

"Will you promise not to kill the sentry except as a last resort?"

"Yes, on my honour."

"Then we may accomplish our task," was the reply.

"How long will it be before we can accomplish it?"

"At least a year."

"Shall we begin at once?"

"Without any delay. Here is my plan."

The abbé showed Dantès a drawing he had made. It was a plan of his own cell, that of Dantès, and the passage joining them. In the middle of this passage they would bore a tunnel, like those used in mines. This tunnel would lead the prisoners under the gallery where the sentry was on duty; arrived there, a large excavation would be made by loosening one of the flag-stones with which the floor of the gallery was paved; at a given moment the stone would give way under the soldier's weight and he would disappear into the excavation below. Dantès would throw himself upon him before he had recovered from the shock of the fall and while he was still unable to defend himself. He would gag and blindfold him, and then the two prisoners would jump through one of the windows, climb down the outside wall by means of the rope-ladder the abbé had made, and they would be saved!

Dantès clapped his hands, and his eyes shone with joy. It was such a simple plan that it was bound to succeed.

That same day the two miners commenced operations with renewed vigour after their long rest.

At the end of fifteen months the hole was made, the excavation was completed under the gallery, and the two prisoners could distinctly hear the measured tread of the sentry. They were obliged to wait for a dark, moonless night for the success of their plans, and their one fear was that the flag-stone might give way under the soldier's heavy tread sooner than they desired. To guard against this, they decided to prop the stone up with a kind of beam they had found in the foundations. Dantès was busy putting it into position when he suddenly heard the abbé cry out in pain. He rushed to him and found him standing in the middle of the room, his face ghastly pale, his hands clenched, and the perspiration streaming down his forehead.

"Good heavens!" cried Dantès. "Whatever has happened? What ails you?"

"Quick! quick!" the abbé replied. "Listen to me!"

Dantès looked at Faria's livid face. His eyes had deep lines under them, his lips were white, and his very hair seemed to stand on end.

"Oh! What is the matter with you?" Dantès cried terror-stricken.

"All is over with me! A terrible disease, it may even be mortal, is about to attack me. I feel it coming. I was seized with it the year before my imprisonment. There is only one remedy for it. Run quickly to my cell and raise the foot of my bed. It is hollow, and you will find in it a little glass bottle half filled with a red liquid. Bring it to me. No, I might be found here; help me back to my cell while I still have the strength. Who knows what may happen while the attack lasts?"

In a flash Dantès realized that his hopes of escape were now dashed to the ground; nevertheless he did not lose his head. He crept into the tunnel dragging his luckless companion after him, and with infinite trouble helped him to his cell and placed him on the bed.

"Thank you," the abbé said, trembling in every limb as though he had just stepped out of freezing water. "I am seized with a cataleptic fit.[6] It may be that I shall not move or make a sound; on the other hand, I may stiffen, foam at the mouth, and shriek. Try not to let them hear me, for if they do, they might change my cell and we should be separated for ever. When you see me motionless, cold, and to all appearances dead, then and not until then force my teeth apart with the knife, and pour eight to ten drops of the liquid down my throat and I shall perhaps revive."

"Perhaps?" exclaimed Dantès grief-stricken.

"Help! Help!" the abbé cried. "I am . . . I am dy—"

The attack was so sudden and so violent that the unfortunate prisoner was unable to finish the word. His features became distorted, his eyes dilated, his mouth twisted, his cheeks took on a purple hue; he struggled, foamed at the mouth, moaned and groaned. This lasted for two hours, then stretching himself out in a last convulsion, he became livid and lay as inert as a block of wood, whiter and colder than marble, more crushed than a reed trampled underfoot.

Edmond waited until life seemed to have departed from the abbé's body and he apparently lay cold in death; then, taking the knife, with great difficulty he forced the blade between the clenched teeth. He carefully poured ten drops of the red liquid down his friend's throat and waited.

An hour elapsed and still the abbé made not the slightest movement. Dantès began to fear he had waited too long before administering the remedy, and stood anxiously gazing at him. At last a faint colour spread over his cheeks, his eyes which had remained open in a fixed stare, now began to see, a slight sigh escaped his lips, and he began to move.

"He is saved! he is saved!" Dantès exclaimed.

The abbé could not yet speak, but he pointed with visible anxiety toward the door. Dantès listened and heard the gaoler's footsteps. He jumped up, darted toward the opening, which he entered, replacing the flag-stone after him, and regained his cell.

An instant later the gaoler entered and, as usual, found his prisoner sitting on his bed.

Scarcely had he turned his back, scarcely had the sound of his footsteps in the passage outside died away, when Dantès, too anxious to eat anything, hastened back to the abbé's cell by the same way he had come a few seconds before. Faria had regained consciousness, but he was still lying stretched on his bed helpless and inert.

"I little thought I should see you again," he said.

"Why?" asked the young man. "Did you think you were going to die?"

"No, but everything is ready for your flight, and I thought you would go."

"Without you?" he exclaimed. "Did you really think I was capable of such a base action?"

"I see now that I was mistaken. But, alas! I feel very weak and worn."

"Take courage, your strength will return," said Dantès,

seating himself on the bedside and taking the abbé's hands.

Faria shook his head.

"My first fit lasted but half an hour, leaving only a feeling of hunger; I could even get up alone. To-day, I can move neither my right leg nor my arm; my head feels heavy, which proves a rush of blood to the brain. The third attack will leave me entirely paralysed or else it will kill me."

"No, no, I assure you, you will not die. When you have your third attack, if you have one, you will be at liberty."

"My friend," the old man said, "you are mistaken. The attack I have just had has condemned me to perpetual imprisonment. Before fleeing, one must be able to walk."

"Well then, we will wait a week, a month, two months if necessary; during that time you will regain your strength. All is ready for our escape, we have but to choose the day and hour. The day you feel strong enough to swim, we will put our plan into execution."

"I shall swim no more," Faria said. "My arm is paralysed not for one day only, but for ever. Raise it yourself and you will soon know by the weight of it."

The young man did as he was bid and the arm fell back heavy and lifeless.

"You are convinced now, I expect," Faria said. "Believe me, I know what I am saying; I have thought about it unceasingly ever since I had the first attack. I have been expecting this, for it runs in the family. My father, as well as my grandfather, died after the third attack. The physician who prepared this medicine for me has predicted the same fate for me."

"The physician has made a mistake," Dantès cried out. "As for your paralysis, that will not trouble me in the least. I shall swim the sea with you on my shoulders."

"My son," the abbé said, "you are a sailor and a swimmer, and should therefore know that a man could not possibly make more than fifty strokes with such a load on his back. I shall stay here till the hour of my deliverance has struck, the hour of my death. But you, my son, flee, escape! You are young, lithe, strong; trouble not about me . . . I give you back your word!"

"Very well," said Dantès, "in that case I shall stay here too!" Rising and solemnly stretching one hand over the old man, he said: "By all that I deem most holy, I swear that I shall not leave you till death takes one of us!"

Faria looked up at this noble-minded, simple young man, and read in the expression on his face, now animated by a feeling of pure devotion, the sincerity of his affection and the loyalty of his oath.

"So be it," said the sick man, "I accept. Thank you." Then holding out to him his hand, he said: "It may be that you will be rewarded for this unselfish devotion, but as I cannot leave, and you will not, we must fill in the tunnel under the gallery. The soldier might notice that that particular spot is hollow and call the inspector's attention to it. We should then be found out and separated. Go and do it at once; unfortunately I cannot help you. Spend the whole night on the task if necessary, and come to me again in the morning after the gaoler has made his visit. I shall have something important to tell you."

Dantès took the abbé's hand and was rewarded with a smile. With a feeling of deep respect, the young man then left his old friend in obedience to his wishes.

Chapter XIV

THE TREASURE

⚓

The next morning when Dantès entered the cell of his friend in captivity, he found him sitting up with a resigned expression on his face. In the ray of light which entered his cell by the narrow window, he held in his left hand, the only one he could use now, a piece of paper which, from being continuously rolled up very tightly, had taken on a cylindrical shape. Without saying a word, he showed it to Dantès.

"What is this?" the young man asked.

"Look at it well," the abbé said, smiling. "This paper, my friend—I can tell you everything now for I have tried you—this piece of paper is my treasure, half of which belongs to you from this day forward."

"Your treasure?" Dantès stammered.

Faria smiled.

"Yes," he said. "You are a noble-hearted lad, Dantès, but I know by the way you shuddered and turned pale what is passing in your mind. This treasure really exists, and though it has not been my lot to possess it, you will one day be the owner of it all."

"My friend, your attack has tired you, will you not rest a little?" said Dantès. "If you wish, I will listen to your story

100

to-morrow; to-day I only want to nurse you back to health, nothing more. Besides," he continued, "a treasure is not a very pressing matter for us just now, is it?"

"Very pressing indeed," replied the old man. "How do we know that I shall not be seized with the third attack to-morrow or the day after? Remember that then all will be over. Yes, it is true. I have often thought with bitter joy of these riches, which are vast enough to make the fortunes of ten families, and which my persecutors will never enjoy. This has been my vengeance, and in the despair of my captivity I have lived on it during the long nights spent in my dungeon. But now that I have forgiven them all, for love of you, now that I see you full of youth and with a bright future before you, now that I think of all the happiness which will result to you from this disclosure, I tremble at any delay in securing to one so worthy as you the possession of such an enormous buried treasure."

Edmond turned away with a deep sigh.

"You persist in your incredulity, Edmond," Faria continued. "I see you must have proofs. Well, then, read this paper which I have not shown to anyone until now."

"I will not vex him," Dantès said to himself, and, taking the paper, half of which was missing, having, no doubt, been burnt by accident, he read:

This treasure which may amount to two . . .
Roman crowns in the farthest cor . . .
of the secret opening which . . .
declare belongs to him as . . .
heir . . .
    April 25, 1498

"Well?" said Faria when the young man had finished reading.

"I see nothing here but broken lines and disjointed words; fire has made it unintelligible."

"That may be so to you who are reading it for the first

time, but not to me who have toiled over it for many a long night, and reconstructed each phrase and completed each thought."

"Do you think you have discovered the whole meaning?"

"I am sure of it, but you shall judge for yourself presently. First of all let me relate the story of the piece of paper."

"Hush!" exclaimed Dantès, "I hear footsteps . . . someone is coming . . . I am going . . . Good-bye."

Dantès was very glad thus to escape a story and explanation which would only confirm his fear that the attack of catalepsy had deprived his friend of his reason. He stayed in his room all day in order to postpone the terrible moment when he would be quite satisfied that the abbé was mad. But when evening drew on and Dantès still did not make his appearance, not even after the gaoler had paid his customary visit, Faria tried to cover the space between his cell and that of his friend. Edmond shuddered when he heard the painful efforts he made to drag himself along; his leg was lifeless and he could no longer use his arm. Edmond was compelled to assist him, for alone he would never have been able to get through the narrow opening that led to Dantès' cell.

"Here I am, obstinately resolved on pursuing you," he said with a kindly smile. "You thought to escape my munificence, but it is useless. Now listen to me."

Edmond realized that he had to comply, so he placed the old man on the bed while he seated himself on the stool.

"You know already," the abbé began, "that I was the secretary and intimate friend of Cardinal Spada, the last prince of that name. It is to this worthy lord that I owe all the happiness of my life. He was not rich, although the riches of his family were proverbial, and he lived on the reputation of his wealth. His palace was my paradise. I taught his nephews but they died, and when he was alone in the world, I made some return for all he had done for me during ten years by absolute devotion to his every wish.

"The Cardinal's house held no secrets for me. I often saw Monsignor examining some old books and eagerly searching among family manuscripts. One day when I reproached him with the uselessness of working thus for whole nights together, which alone could account for his low spirits, he looked at me and, smiling bitterly, opened a book which was a history of Rome. There in the twentieth chapter of the *Life of Pope Alexander the Sixth*, I read the following lines which I shall never forget:

" 'The great wars of the Romagna were ended. Caesar Borgia, who had made his conquest, had need of money with which to buy the whole of Italy. The Pope too had need of money to rid himself of Louis the Twelfth, King of France, who was still a formidable foe in spite of his recent defeats. It was necessary, therefore, to make some profitable speculation, which was no easy matter in Italy at that time owing to her impoverished and exhausted condition.'

"His Holiness had an idea. He decided to create two new cardinals. By choosing two of the greatest and, above all, richest personages in Rome he would make a very profitable speculation. First of all he could hold up for sale the splendid appointments and offices these two Cardinals already held, and besides, he expected to realize a large sum by the sale of the two hats.

"There was still a third factor which we shall come to presently.

"The Pope and Caesar Borgia found the desired prospective cardinals, in John Rospigliosi, who alone held four of the highest titles of the Holy See,[1] and Caesar Spada, one of the noblest and richest Romans. They both appreciated such high favour from the Pope for they were both ambitious. Caesar soon found purchasers for their appointments. The result was that Rospigliosi and Spada paid for the honour of being made cardinals, and eight other persons paid for the honour of holding the late appointments of the newly created cardinals. Eight hundred thousand crowns passed into the coffers of the speculators.

"It is now time we touched upon the third part of the speculation. The Pope having overwhelmed Rospigliosi and Spada with favours, having conferred on them the insignia of a cardinalate and feeling sure that they must have realized their fortunes to enable them to pay their very material debt of gratitude and to establish themselves at Rome, he and Caesar Borgia invited the two Cardinals to dinner.

"There now arose a dispute between the Holy Father and his son. Caesar Borgia thought that use might be made of one of those expedients which were always at the disposal of his intimate friends. There was first of all the famous key with which certain people were asked to open a particular cupboard. The key was furnished with a small iron point, due to negligence on the part of the maker. When bringing pressure to bear on this key, for the lock was a difficult one, the person would prick himself with this point and the next day he would die. Then there was the ring with the lion's head which Caesar placed on his finger when he shook hands with certain people. The lion bit the favoured hand and at the end of twenty-four hours this bite proved mortal.

"Caesar proposed to his father that they should send the Cardinals to open the cupboard or else shake each one heartily by the hand; but Alexander the Sixth replied:

" 'Do not let us begrudge these two worthy Cardinals a dinner. Something tells me we shall get our money back. Besides, you forget that an attack of indigestion declares itself immediately, whereas the results of a prick or bite do not manifest themselves for a day or two.'

"Caesar gave way to this reasoning and the two Cardinals were invited to dinner. The table was laid in a vineyard belonging to the Pope near San Pietro in Vincoli, a charming residence of which the Cardinals had often heard.

"Rospigliosi, overwhelmed with his new dignity, made all preparations for this new favour. Spada, being a prudent man who only loved his nephew, a hopeful young captain, took paper and pen and wrote his will. He then sent a message to his nephew to meet him near the vineyard, but apparently the messenger did not find him.

"Spada left for the vineyard near San Pietro in Vincoli at about two o'clock; the Pope was awaiting him. The first person Spada saw was his nephew, in full dress, the recipient of marked attentions from Caesar Borgia. Spada turned pale as Caesar cast on him a look full of irony, which seemed to say that he had foreseen everything and had seen to it that the trap was well laid.

"They went in to dinner. Spada had only been able to ask his nephew whether he had received his message. The nephew answered that he had not. He understood what was meant by this question but it was too late. He had just drunk a glass of excellent wine which the Pope's butler had set aside for him. Spada was liberally supplied from another bottle, and an hour later the physician declared they had both been poisoned through eating mushrooms. Spada died on the threshold of the vineyard, his nephew expired at his door while making a sign to his wife which she did not understand.

"Caesar and the Pope hastened to lay their hands on the heritage on the pretext that they were seeking for the dead man's papers. But the sole heritage was a piece of paper on which were written the words:

" 'I bequeath to my dearly beloved nephew my coffers and my books, amongst which he will find my gold-cornered breviary, and I desire him to keep them in memory of his affectionate uncle.'

"Spada's would-be heirs searched everywhere, admired the breviary, laid hands on the furniture, and were filled with astonishment that Spada, the rich man, was in reality the most worthless of uncles: there were no treasures unless one reckoned the works of science in the library and the laboratories. There was nothing more. Caesar and his father searched and examined, rummaged amongst the papers, investigated everything, but nothing could they find, or at any rate very little: about a thousand crowns' worth of plate[55] and about the same value in ready money. Yet, before dying, the nephew had had time to say to his wife:

" 'Look among my uncle's papers; there is a will.'

"She searched even more energetically than the august heirs had done but all was in vain. There was nothing more than two palaces and a vineyard; and as at that period real property was of very little value, palaces and vineyards remained in the family as unworthy of the rapacity of the Pope and his son.

"Months and years rolled on. Alexander the Sixth was poisoned; Caesar was poisoned at the same time, but escaped death by shedding his skin like a snake, assuming a new cuticle on which the poison left spots like those on a tiger's skin. Compelled to leave Rome, he was killed in a nocturnal brawl almost forgotten by history.

"After the death of the Pope and the exile of the son, it was generally supposed that the Spada family would resume their splendour of the Cardinal's time, but it was not the case. They continued to live in doubtful comfort, and a mystery veiled the whole affair. It was noised abroad that Caesar, who was more politic than his father, had taken the fortunes of the two Cardinals from under his father's nose.

"Do you find my story very stupid?" Faria suddenly asked his companion with a smile.

"Oh, no, my friend," returned Dantès, "on the contrary. It is as though I were reading a most interesting narrative. Pray continue."

"I will. Spada's family accustomed themselves to living in obscurity and the years rolled on. Some of the descendants were soldiers, others diplomats, some entered the church, others became bankers. Some of them grew rich, while others lost all their fortunes. I come now to the last of the family, the Count Spada to whom I acted as secretary.

"I felt sure that neither the Cardinal's relations nor Borgia had profited by his fortune, and that it had remained ownerless in the bowels of the earth guarded by some genie. I searched and ransacked everything and everywhere; thousands of times did I add up the income and expenditure of the family for the past three hundred years, but it was all in vain. I remained ignorant and Count Spada remained poor.

"My patron died. He bequeathed to me his library, composed of five thousand books, his breviary, which had remained in the family and had been handed down from father to son, and in addition a thousand Roman crowns with the request that I should have anniversary masses said for the repose of his soul, draw up a genealogical tree, and write a history of his family. All this I carried out most scrupulously.

"In eighteen-seven, a month before my arrest, and fifteen days after Count Spada's death, on December the twenty-fifth—you will understand presently why the date of this memorable day became fixed in my memory—I was reading for the thousandth time the papers I was putting in order, for the palace had been sold to a stranger and I was leaving Rome to settle at Florence, taking with me what money I possessed, my library, and the famous breviary, when, tired with my assiduous study and rendered drowsy by the heavy dinner I had partaken of, my head fell in my hands and I dropped off to sleep. This was at three o'clock in the afternoon.

"I awoke as the clock was striking six to find that I was in complete darkness. I rang for a servant to bring me a light, but as no one came I resolved to help myself. Taking the candle in one hand, I groped about with the other for a piece of paper which I intended to light at the last flame flickering in the hearth. However, fearing that in the dark I might take a valuable piece of paper, I hesitated, but suddenly recollected that I had seen in the famous breviary which lay on the table beside me an old piece of paper, yellow with age, which had probably served as a bookmark and had been kept in the same place for centuries by the different owners. I found this useless piece of paper and, putting it into the dying flame, lighted it.

"But as the flames devoured the paper I held between my fingers, I saw yellowish characters appear, as if by magic; an unholy terror seized me. I crushed the paper in my hand and choked the flame. Then I lighted the candle and with inexpressible emotion opened out the crumpled paper. I recognized that a mysterious, sympathetic ink had traced these characters which could only become apparent when placed in contact with heat. A little more than one-third of the paper had been consumed by the flames. It was the very paper you read this morning; read it again, Dantès, and then I will give you the missing words to make the sense complete."

So saying, Faria gave Dantès the paper, and he read this time with great eagerness the following words which had been written with an ink of the colour of rust:

This 25th day of April 1498, be . . .
Alexander VI, and fearing that, not . . .
he may desire to become my heir, and re . . .
and Bentiviglio, who were poisoned, . . .
my sole heir, that I have bu . . .
and has visited with me—that is, in . . .
isle of Monte Cristo—all I pos . . .
els, diamonds, gems; that alone . . .
may amount to about two mil . . .
will find on raising the twentieth ro . . .
creek to the East in a straight line. Two open . . .
in these caves; the treasure is in the farthest cor . . .
which treasure I bequeath to him and leave en . . .
sole heir.

CAES . . .

April 25, 1498

"Now," continued the abbé, "read this other paper." And

he gave Dantès a second piece containing the other half of the broken sentences.

                    . . . ing invited to dinner by His Holiness
                       . . . content to make me pay for my hat
                . . . serve for me the fate of Cardinals Crapara
                    . . . I declare to my nephew, Guido Spada,
                            . . . ried in a spot he knows
                              . . . the caves of the small
                       . . . sess in ingots, gold, money, jew-
            . . . I know the existence of this treasure, which
                . . . lion Roman crowns, and which he
                              . . . ck from the small
                              . . . ings have been made
                              . . . ner of the second,
                              . . . tire to him as my
                              . . . AR † SPADA

Faria watched him attentively.

When he saw that Dantès had read the last line, he said: "Now place the two fragments together and judge for yourself."

Dantès obeyed and read as follows:

This 25th day of April 1498, being invited to dinner by His Holiness Alexander VI, and fearing that, not content to make me pay for my hat, he may desire to become my heir, and reserve for me the fate of Cardinals Crapara and Bentiviglio, who were poisoned, I declare to my nephew, Guido Spada, my sole heir, that I have buried in a spot he knows and has visited with me—that is, in the caves of the small isle of Monte Cristo—all I possess in ingots, gold, money, jewels, diamonds, gems; that alone I know the existence of this treasure, which may amount to about two million Roman crowns and which he will find on raising the twentieth rock from the small creek to the East in a straight line. Two openings have been made in these caves; the treasure is in the farthest corner of the second, which treasure I bequeath to him and leave entire to him as my sole heir.

CAESAR † SPADA

April 25, 1498

"Well! Do you understand it now?" Faria asked.

"Then it is the declaration of Cardinal Spada and the will so long sought for?" Dantès asked with incredulity.

"Yes, and a thousand times yes."

"Who reconstructed it in this way?"

"I did. With the assistance of the half of the will I had rescued, I worked out the rest by measuring the length of the lines with that of the paper, and by fathoming the missing words by means of those already in my possession, just as in a vault one is guided by a ray of light that enters from above."

"And what did you do when you thought you had solved the mysterious script?"

"I made up my mind to leave Rome at once, which I did, taking with me the beginning of my big work on the unity of the Kingdom of Italy. The imperial police, however, had been watching me for some time past, and my sudden departure aroused their suspicions. I was arrested just as I was about to embark at Piombino.

"Now, my dear friend," Faria continued, looking at Dantès with an almost paternal expression, "you know as much as I do; if we ever escape together half of my treasure is yours; if I die here and you escape alone, the whole of it belongs to you."

"But is there not a more legitimate owner to this treasure than ourselves?" asked Dantès hesitatingly.

"No, none whatever. You can make your mind easy on that score. The family is completely extinct and, besides, the last Count Spada made me his heir; in bequeathing the breviary to me, he bequeathed to me all that it contained. No, if we lay our hands on this fortune, we can enjoy it without any compunction."

"And you say this treasure consists of . . ."

"Two million Roman crowns and about thirteen millions of money in French coin."

Edmond thought he was dreaming: he wavered between incredulity and joy.

"I have kept this a secret from you for so long," Faria continued, "simply because I wanted to give you proofs, and also because I thought to give you a surprise. Had we escaped before my attack, I should have taken you to Monte Cristo, but now," he added with a sigh, "it will be you who will take me. Well, Dantès, are you not going to thank me?"

"This treasure belongs to you alone, my friend, and I have no right to it," Dantès replied. "I am not even related to you."

"You are my son, Dantès," exclaimed the old man. "You are the child of my captivity. My profession condemned me to celibacy, but God has sent you to console the man who could not be a father, and the prisoner who could not be a free man."

Faria held out his one remaining arm to the young man, who threw himself round his neck and burst into tears.

Chapter XV

THE THIRD ATTACK

———✦———

Now that this treasure, which had been the object of the abbé's meditations for so long, could give future happiness to him whom he truly loved as a son, it had redoubled its value in his eyes; daily would he expatiate on the amount, holding forth to Dantès on the good a man could do to his friends in modern times with a fortune of thirteen or fourteen millions. Dantès' face would darken, for the oath of vengeance he had taken would come into his mind, and he was occupied with the thought of how much harm a man could do to his enemies in modern times with a fortune of thirteen or fourteen millions.

The abbé did not know the Isle of Monte Cristo, which was situated twenty-five miles from Pianosa between Corsica and Elba, but Dantès had often passed it and had once landed there. He drew a plan of the island and Faria advised him as to the best means to adopt to recover the treasure. He had kept silent about it for all these many long years, but now it became a daily topic of conversation between the two. Fearing that the will might one day be mislaid or lost, he made Dantès learn it by heart until he knew it word for word. Then he destroyed the second part in the firm conviction that, even if the first part were discovered and seized, nobody could understand its meaning. Sometimes Faria would spend whole hours giving Dantès instructions what to do against the time he should be a free man. Once free he was not to lose an hour, not even a minute, before setting out for Monte Cristo; he was to remain alone on the island under some pretext or other, and as soon as he was alone endeavour to discover the marvellous caves and search the spot designated in the will.

In the meantime the hours passed, if not rapidly, at least not unendurably. One night Edmond woke suddenly and thought he heard someone calling him. He opened his eyes and tried to penetrate the darkness. He heard his name, or rather a plaintive voice trying to articulate his name. He raised himself in his bed and listened, his anxiety bringing great beads of perspiration to his forehead. There could be no doubt, the voice came from his companion's cell.

"Great God!" he murmured. "Could it be?"

He moved his bed, drew the stone away, and rushed to his friend's cell. There by the flickering light of the lamp he beheld the old man clinging to the bedside. His features were drawn with the horrible symptoms which Edmond already knew, and which had filled him with such terror the first time he saw them.

"Ah! my friend," Faria said resignedly, "you understand, don't you? There is no need to explain anything. Think only of yourself now, think only how to make your captivity supportable and your escape possible. It would take you years to achieve unaided what I have done here. In any case, you need have no fear that my cell will remain empty for any length of time; another unfortunate wretch will soon take my place and you will be to him an angel of salvation. He may be young, strong, and patient like yourself, and may even help you to escape, whereas I have only been an obstacle. You will no longer have a half-dead body fettered to you to paralyse your every movement. God is decidedly doing you a good turn at last. He is giving you more than He is taking away, and it is quite time for me to die."

Edmond could only wring his hands and exclaim: "Oh, my friend, my dearest friend, don't talk like that any more! I saved you once and I will save you a second time." And raising the foot of the bed, he took the phial, which was still one-third full of the red liquid.

"See," he said, "there is still some of this saving draught. Tell me quickly what I am to do this time. Have you any fresh instructions? Speak, my friend, I am all attention."

"There is no hope," Faria replied, shaking his head.

"Oh, yes, yes!" exclaimed Dantès. "I tell you, I shall save you!"

"Try then if you like! Do as you did the first time, but do not wait so long. If I do not revive after you have administered twelve drops, pour the remaining contents of the phial down my throat. Now, carry me to my bed. I can no longer stand."

Edmond took the old man in his arms and placed him on his bed.

"And now, my dear boy," said Faria, "sole consolation of my miserable life, whom Heaven sent to me somewhat late in life, yet sent me an invaluable gift for which I am most thankful, at this moment when I must leave you, I wish you all the happiness and prosperity you desire. My son, I give you my blessing."

A violent shock checked the old man's speech. Dantès raised his head; he saw his friend's eyes all flecked with crimson as though a flow of blood had surged up from his chest to his forehead.

"Farewell! farewell!!" the old man murmured, clasping the young man's hand convulsively. "Farewell! Forget not Monte Cristo!"

And with these words he fell back on to his bed.

The attack was terrible: convulsed limbs, swollen eyelids, foam mingled with blood, a rigid body, was all that remained on this bed of agony in place of the intelligent being that had been there but an instant before.

Dantès took the lamp, placed it on a ledge formed by a

stone at the head of the bed, whence its flickering light cast a strange and weird reflection on the contorted features and inert, stiff body. With staring eyes, he anxiously awaited the propitious moment for administering the saving draught. When he thought the moment had come, he took the knife, forced apart the teeth, which offered less resistance than on the previous occasion, counted ten drops one after the other, and waited: the phial still contained double that quantity.

He waited ten minutes, a quarter of an hour, half an hour, and still there was no sign of movement. Trembling in every limb, his hair on end, his forehead bathed in perspiration, he counted the seconds by the beatings of his heart. Then he thought it was time to make the last desperate attempt. He placed the phial to Faria's purple lips—his jaws had remained wide apart—and poured the rest of the liquid down his throat. A violent trembling seized the old man's limbs, his eyes opened and were frightful to behold, he heaved a sigh that sounded like a scream, and then his trembling body gradually reverted to its former rigidity. The face assumed a livid hue, and the light faded out of the wide-open eyes.

It was six o'clock in the morning; day began to dawn and its yet feeble gleam invaded the cell, putting to shame the dying light of the lamp. Weird reflections were cast over the face of the corpse, giving it from time to time a lifelike appearance. As long as this struggle between night and day lasted, Dantès still doubted, but as soon as the day held its own, he knew that he was alone with a corpse.

Then an overmastering terror seized him; he dared press no more the hand that hung down from the bed: he dared look no more on those vacant and staring eyes which he endeavoured in vain to close several times, for they opened again each time. He extinguished the lamp, hid it carefully, and fled from the cell, replacing the stone behind him as carefully as he could.

It was time he went too, for the gaoler was coming. Dantès was seized with an indescribable impatience to know what would happen in his unfortunate friend's cell; he, therefore, went into the subterranean passage, where he arrived in time to hear the turnkey calling for assistance.

Other turnkeys soon arrived; then was heard the tread of soldiers, heavy and measured even when off duty; behind them came the governor.

Edmond heard the bed creaking; he heard too the voice of the governor, who ordered water to be thrown on the face of the dead man, and then, as this did not revive him, sent to summon the doctor.

The governor left the cell, and some words of compassion, mingled with coarse jokes and laughter, reached Dantès' ears.

"Perhaps," said one, "as he is a man of the church, they will go to some expense on his account."

"Then he will have the honour of the sack," said another.

Edmond listened and did not lose a word of the conversation, though he could not comprehend very much of it. Soon the voices ceased and it seemed to him they had all left the cell. Still he dared not yet go back; it was possible they had left some turnkeys to watch by the dead man.

At the end of an hour or so he heard a faint noise which gradually increased. It was the governor coming back with the doctor and several officials.

The doctor declared the prisoner dead and diagnosed the cause of death. There was more coming and going, and, a few seconds later, a sound like the rubbing together of sacking[1] reached Dantès' ears. The bed creaked, a heavy step like that of a man lifting a weight resounded on the floor, then the bed creaked again under the weight placed on it.

"To-night, then," Dantès heard the governor say.

"Will there be a Mass?" asked one of the officials.

"That is impossible," replied the governor, "the chaplain asked me yesterday for leave to go to Hyères for a week. The poor abbé should not have been in such a hurry, and then he would have had his requiem."

In the meantime the body was being laid out.

"At what o'clock to-night?" asked one of the turnkeys.

"Between ten and eleven."

"Shall we watch by the corpse?"

"Whatever for? Lock the door as though he were alive; nothing more is needed."

The footsteps died away, the voices became gradually less distinct, the grating noise of the lock and the creaking of the bolts were heard, and then a silence more penetrating than solitude, the silence of death, prevailed, striking its icy chill through the young man's whole frame.

Then he slowly raised the stone with his head and cast a swift glance round the room. It was empty. Dantès entered.

Chapter XVI

THE CEMETERY OF THE CHÂTEAU D'IF

On the bed, at full length, faintly lighted by a dim ray that entered through the window, Dantès saw a sack of coarse cloth, under the ample folds of which he could distinctly discern a long, stiff form: it was Faria's shroud. All was over then. Dantès was separated from his old friend. Faria, the helpful, kind companion, to whom he had become so attached, to whom he owed so much, existed now but in his memory. He sat on the edge of the bed and became a prey to deep and bitter melancholy.

Alone! He was quite alone once more! Alone! No longer to see, to hear the voice of, the only human being that attached him to life! Would it not be better to seek his Maker, as Faria had done, to learn the mystery of life even at the risk of passing through the dismal gates of suffering?

The idea of suicide, which had been dispelled by his friend and which he himself had forgotten in his presence, rose again before him like a phantom beside Faria's corpse.

"If I could only die," he said, "I should go where he has gone. But how am I to die? It is quite simple," said he with a smile. "I will stay here, throw myself on the first one who enters, strangle him, and then I shall be guillotined."

Dantès, however, recoiled from such an infamous death,

and swiftly passed from despair to an ardent desire for life and liberty. "Die? Oh, no!" he cried out, "it would hardly have been worth while to live, to suffer so much and then to die now. No, I desire to live, to fight to the end. I wish to reconquer the happiness that has been taken from me. Before I die, I have my executioners to punish, and possibly also some friends to recompense. Yet they will forget me here and I shall only leave this dungeon in the same way that Faria has done."

As he uttered these words, Edmond stood stock-still, with eyes fixed like a man struck by a sudden and terrifying idea.

"Oh, who has given me this thought?" he murmured. "My God, comes this from Thee? Since it is only the dead who go free from here, I must take the place of the dead!"

Without giving himself time to reconsider his decision, and as though he would not give reflection time to destroy his desperate resolution, he leaned over the hideous sack, slit it open with the knife Faria had made, took the dead body out, carried it to his own cell, and placed it on his bed, put round the head the piece of rag he always wore, covered it with the bed-clothes, kissed for the last time the ice-cold forehead, endeavoured to shut the rebellious eyes, which were still open, and stared so horribly, and turned the head to the wall so that, when the gaoler brought his evening meal, he would think he had gone to bed as he often did. Then he returned to the other cell, took the needle and thread from the cupboard, flung off his rags that the men might feel naked flesh under the sacking, slipped into the sack, placed himself in the same position as the corpse, and sewed the sack up again from the inside. If, by any chance, the gaolers had entered then, they would have heard the beating of his heart.

Now this is what Dantès intended doing. If the grave-diggers discovered that they were carrying a live body instead of a dead one, he would give them no time for thought. He would slit the sack open with his knife from top to bottom, jump out, and taking advantage of their terror, escape; if they tried to stop him, he would use his knife. If they took him to the cemetery and placed him in a grave, he would allow himself to be covered with earth; then, as it was night, as soon as the grave-diggers had turned their backs, he would cut his way through the soft earth and escape; he hoped the weight would not be too heavy for him to raise.

He had eaten nothing since the previous evening, but he had not thought of his hunger in the morning, neither did he think of it now. His position was much too precarious to allow him time for any thought but that of flight.

At last, toward the time appointed by the governor, he heard footsteps on the staircase. He realized that the moment had come, he summoned all his courage, and held his breath.

The door was opened, a subdued light reached his eyes. Through the sacking that covered him he saw two shadows approach the bed. There was a third one at the door holding a lantern in his hand. Each of the two men who had approached the bed took the sack by one of its two extremities.

"He is very heavy for such a thin old man," said one of them as he raised the head.

"They say that each year adds half a pound to the weight of one's bones," said the other, taking the feet.

They carried away the sham corpse on the bier. Edmond made himself rigid. The procession, lighted by the man with the lantern, descended the stairs. All at once Dantès felt the cold, fresh night air and the sharp north-west wind, and the sensation filled him at once with joy and with anguish.

The men went about twenty yards, then stopped and dropped the bier on to the ground. One of them went away, and Dantès heard his footsteps on the stones.

"Where am I?" he asked himself.

"He is by no means a light load, you know," said the man who had remained behind, seating himself on the edge of the bier.

Dantès' impulse was to make his escape, but, fortunately, he did not attempt it. He heard one of the men draw near and drop a heavy object on the ground; at the same moment a cord was tied round his feet, cutting into his flesh.

"Well, have you made the knot?" one of the men asked.

"Yes, and it is well made. I can answer for that."

"Let's on, then."

The bier was lifted once more, and the procession proceeded. The noise of the waves breaking against the rocks on which the Château is built sounded more distinctly to Dantès with each step they took.

"Wretched weather!" said one of the men, "the sea will not be very inviting to-night."

"Yes, the abbé runs a great risk of getting wet," said the other, and they burst out laughing.

Dantès could not understand the jest; nevertheless his hair began to stand on end.

"Here we are at last!"

"No, farther on, farther on! You know the last one was dashed on the rocks and the next day the governor called us a couple of lazy rascals."

They went another five yards, and then Dantès felt them take him by the head and feet and swing him to and fro.

"One! Two! Three!"

With the last word, Dantès felt himself flung into space. He passed through the air like a wounded bird falling, falling, ever falling with a rapidity which turned his heart to ice. At last—though it seemed to him like an eternity of time—there came a terrific splash; and as he dropped like an arrow into the icy cold water he uttered a scream which was immediately choked by his immersion.

Dantès had been flung into the sea, into whose depths he was being dragged down by a cannon-ball tied to his feet.

The sea is the cemetery of the Château d'If.

Chapter XVII

THE ISLE OF TIBOULEN

Though stunned and almost suffocated, Dantès had yet the presence of mind to hold his breath and, as he grasped the open knife in his right hand ready for any emergency, he rapidly ripped open the sack, extricated his arm and then his head; but in spite of his efforts to raise the cannon ball, he still felt himself being dragged down and down. He bent his back into an arch in his endeavour to reach the cord that bound his legs, and, after a desperate struggle, he severed it at the very moment when he felt that suffocation was getting the upper hand of him. He kicked out vigorously and rose unhampered to the surface, while the cannon-ball dragged to the unknown depths the sacking which had so nearly become his shroud.

Dantès merely paused to take a deep breath and then he dived again to avoid being seen. When he rose the second time, he was already fifty yards from the spot where he had been thrown into the sea. He saw above him a black and tempestuous sky; before him was the vast expanse of dark, surging waters; while behind him, more gloomy than the sea and more sombre than the sky, rose the granite giant like some menacing phantom, whose dark summit appeared to Dantès like an arm stretched out to seize its prey. He had always been reckoned the best swimmer in Marseilles, and he was now anxious to rise to the surface to try his strength against the waves. To his joy he found that his enforced inaction had not in any way impaired his strength and agility, and he felt he could still master the element·in which he had so often sported when a boy.

An hour passed. Exalted by the feeling of liberty, Dantès continued to cleave the waves in what he reckoned should be a direct line for the Isle of Tiboulen. Suddenly it seemed to him that the sky, which was already black, was becoming blacker than ever, and that a thick heavy cloud was rolling down on him. At the same time he felt a violent pain in his knee. With the incalculable rapidity of imagination, he thought it was a shot that had struck him, and he expected every moment to hear the report. But there was no sound. He stretched out his hand and encountered an obstacle; he drew his leg up and felt land; he then saw what it was he had mistaken for a cloud. Twenty yards from him rose a mass of strangely formed rocks looking like an immense fire petrified at the moment of its most violent combustion: it was the Isle of Tiboulen.

Dantès rose, advanced a few steps, and, with a prayer of gratitude on his lips, stretched himself out on the jagged rocks which seemed to him more restful and comfortable than the softest bed he had ever slept on. Then, in spite of the wind and storm, in spite of the rain that began to fall, worn out with fatigue as he was, he fell into the delicious sleep of a man whose body becomes torpid but whose mind remains alert in the consciousness of unexpected happiness.

For an hour he slept thus, and was awakened by the roar of a tremendous clap of thunder. A flash of lightning that seemed to open the heavens to the very throne of God illuminated all around, and by its light he saw about a quarter of a mile away, between the Isle of Lemaire and Cap Croisille, a small fishing boat borne along by the wind, and riding like a phantom on the top of a wave only to disappear in the abyss below. A second later it appeared on the crest of another wave advancing with terrifying rapidity. By the light of another flash, he saw four men clinging to the masts and rigging; a fifth was clinging to the broken rudder. Then he heard a terrific crash followed by agonizing cries. As he clung to his rock like a limpet, another flash revealed to him the little boat smashed to pieces and, amongst the wreckage, heads with despairing faces, and arms stretched heavenward. Then all was dark again. There was nothing left but tempest.

By degrees the wind abated; the huge grey clouds rolled toward the west. Shortly afterward a long, reddish streak was seen along the horizon; the waves leaped and frolicked, and a sudden light played their foamy crests, turning them into golden plumes. Daylight had come.

It must have been five o'clock in the morning; the sea continued to grow calm. "In two or three hours," Dantès said to himself, "the turnkeys will enter my cell, and find the dead body of my poor friend, recognize him, seek me in vain, and give the alarm. Then they will find the aperture and the passage; they will question the men who flung me into the sea and who must have heard the cry I uttered. Boats filled with armed soldiers will immediately give chase to the wretched fugitive, who, they know, cannot be far off. The cannon will warn the whole coast that no one shall give shelter to a naked, famished wanderer. The spies and police of Marseilles will be notified, and they will beat the coast while the Governor of the Château d'If beats the sea. And what will become of me pursued by land and by sea? I am hungry and cold and have even lost my knife. I am at the mercy of the first peasant who cares to hand me over to the police for the reward of twenty francs. Oh God! my God! Thou knowest I have suffered to excess; help me now that I cannot help myself!"

As Dantès finished this fervent prayer that was torn from his exhausted and anguished heart, he saw appearing on the horizon what he recognized as a Genoese *tartan*[1] coming from Marseilles.

"To think that I could join this vessel in half an hour if it were not for the fear of being questioned, recognized as a fugitive, and taken back to Marseilles," said Dantès to himself. "What am I to do? What can I say? What story can I invent which might sound credible? I might pass as one of the sailors wrecked last night." So saying he turned his gaze toward the wreck and gave a sudden start. There, caught on a point of rock, he perceived the cap of one of the shipwrecked sailors, and close by still floated some of the planks of the unfortunate vessel.

Dantès soon thought out a plan and as quickly put it into action. He dived into the sea, swam toward the cap, placed it on his head, seized one of the timbers, and turning back, struck out in a direction which would cut the course the vessel must take.

The boat changed her course, steering toward him, and Dantès saw that they made ready to lower a boat. He summoned all his strength to swim toward it, but his arms began to stiffen, his legs lost their flexibility, and his movements became heavy and difficult. Breath was failing him. A wave that he had not the strength to surmount passed over his head, covering him with foam. Then he saw and heard nothing more.

When he opened his eyes again, Dantès found himself on the deck of the *tartan*; a sailor was rubbing his limbs with a woollen cloth, another was holding a gourd to his mouth, and a third, who was the master of the vessel, was looking at him with that feeling of pity which is uppermost in the hearts of most people when face to face with a misfortune which they escaped yesterday, and of which they may be the victim to-morrow.

"Who are you?" the skipper asked in bad French.

"I am a Maltese sailor," replied Dantès in equally bad Italian. "We were coming from Syracuse laden with wine and grain. We were caught in a storm last night off Cape Morgion and we were wrecked on the rocks you see yonder."

"Where have you come from?"

"From those rocks over there. Fortunately for me I was able to cling to them, but our poor captain and my three companions were drowned. I believe I am the sole survivor. I saw your ship, and I risked swimming toward you. Thank you," he continued, "you have saved my life. I was lost when one of your sailors caught hold of my hair."

"It was I," said a sailor with a frank and open face, encircled by long black whiskers. "It was time too, for you were sinking."

"Yes," said Dantès, holding out his hand to him. "I know, and I thank you once more."

"Lord! but you nearly frightened me," the sailor replied. "You looked more like a brigand than an honest man, with your beard six inches long and your hair a foot in length."

Dantès suddenly recollected that neither his hair nor his beard had been cut all the time that he had been at the Château d'If.

"Once when I was in danger," he said, "I made a vow to the Madonna of Piedigrotta not to cut my hair or beard for ten years. The time is up this very day, and I nearly celebrated the event by being drowned."

"Now, what are we going to do with you?" asked the skipper.

"Alas! do with me what you will," replied Dantès. "The bark I sailed in is lost, my captain is dead, and I nearly shared the same fate. Fortunately I am a good sailor. Leave me at the first port you touch at, and I shall be sure to find employment in some merchantman."

"Take the helm and let us see how you frame."

The young man did as he was bid. Ascertaining by a slight pressure that the vessel answered to the rudder, he saw that, without being a first-rate sailer, she was yet tolerably obedient.

"Man the lee-braces,"[2] he cried.

The four seamen, who composed the crew, obeyed, whilst the skipper looked on.

"Haul away!"

They obeyed.

"Belay!"

This order was also executed, and, instead of tacking about, the vessel made straight for the Isle of Rion, leaving it about twenty fathoms to starboard.

"Bravo!" said the captain.

"Bravo!" repeated the sailors.

And they all regarded with astonishment this man whose eye had recovered an intelligence and his body a vigour they were far from suspecting him to possess.

"You see," said Dantès, handing over the tiller to the helmsman, "I shall be of some use to you, at any rate during the voyage. If you do not want me at Leghorn, you can leave me there and with the first wages I earn, I will pay you for my food and for the clothes you lend me."

"Very well," said the captain. "We can fix things up if you are not too exacting."

"Give me what you give the others," returned Dantès.

"Hallo! What's the matter at the Château d'If?" exclaimed the captain.

A small white cloud crowned the summit of the bastion of the Château d'If. At the same moment, the faint report of a gun was heard. The sailors all looked at one another.

"A prisoner has escaped from the Château d'If, and they are firing the alarm gun," said Dantès calmly.

"What is the day of the month?" he presently asked of Jacopo, the sailor who had saved him and who now sat beside him.

"The twenty-eighth of February."

"What year?"

"Have you forgotten, that you ask such a question?"

"I was so frightened last night," replied Dantès, with a smile, "that I have almost lost my memory. What year is it?"

"The year eighteen-twenty-nine," returned Jacopo.

It was fourteen years to the very day since Dantès' arrest. He was nineteen when he entered the Château d'If; he was thirty-three when he escaped.

A sad smile passed over his lips. He wondered what had become of Mercédès, who must now believe him dead. Then his eyes flashed with hatred as he thought of the three men to whom he owed so long and cruel a captivity. Against Danglars, Fernand, and Villefort he renewed the oath of implacable vengeance which he had vowed in his dungeon.

This oath was no longer a vain threat, for the fastest sailer in the Mediterranean could never have overhauled the little *tartan*, which, with all sails set, was scudding before the wind in the direction of Leghorn.

Dantès had not been a day on board before he realized who the people were with whom he was sailing. With his experience of the ways of seafaring men it was not difficult to guess that the *Jeune Amélie*—for such was the name of the Genoese *tartan*—was a smuggler. The skipper had received Dantès on board with a certain amount of misgiving. He was well known to all the customs officers of the coast, and as there was between these worthies and himself an interchange of the most cunning stratagems, he had at first thought that Dantès might be an emissary of the excise authorities who had employed this ingenious means of penetrating some of the secrets of his trade. The skilful manner in which Dantès had manoeuvred the little bark, however, had entirely reassured him, and when he saw the light smoke floating like a plume above the bastion of the Château d'If and heard the distant report, it occurred to him for an instant that he had on board his vessel one for whom; as for the arrivals and departures of kings, they accord a salute of guns. This made him less uneasy, it must be owned, than if the newcomer had been a custom-house officer, but even this latter supposition disappeared like the first, when he beheld the perfect tranquillity of his recruit.

Edmond thus had the advantage of knowing what the skipper was, without the skipper knowing what he was; and, however much the old sailor and his crew tried to pump him, they extracted nothing more from him: he gave accurate descriptions of Naples and Malta, which he knew equally as well as Marseilles, and persisted stoutly in his first statement. Thus, subtle as he was, the Genoese was duped by Edmond, whose gentle demeanour, nautical skill, and admirable dissimulation stood him in good stead. Moreover, it is possible that the Genoese was one of those shrewd persons who know nothing but what they should know, and believe nothing but what it suits them to believe. Such was the position when they reached Leghorn.

As Dantès had landed at Leghorn very many times before, he knew a barber in the Via San Fernando and went straight there to have his hair and beard cut, for his comrades believed his vow was now fulfilled.

When the operation was concluded and Edmond's chin was smooth and his hair reduced to the fashionable length, he asked for a mirror. He was now, as we have said, thirty-three years of age, and the fourteen years' imprisonment had worked a great change in his features.

When he first went to the Château d'If his face was the round, smiting, cheerful face of a happy young man whose early years had passed smoothly, and who looked forward to his future in the light of his past. All this was now changed.

His oval face had lengthened; his smiling mouth had assumed the firm and determined lines indicative of resolution; his eyebrows had become arched beneath a single pensive wrinkle; his eyes had a look of deep sadness in them, and at times gloomy fires of misanthropy and hatred would sparkle in their depths; his skin, hidden from the light of day and the rays of the sun for so long, had assumed the pale and soft colour which, when the face is encircled with black hair, makes the aristocratic beauty of the North. The deep learning he had acquired was reflected on his face in an expression of intelligent self-confidence; in addition, though naturally tall, he had acquired the healthy vigour of a body continuously concentrating all its force within itself.

The elegance of his wiry, slender form had given way to the solidity of a round, muscular figure. His voice too had undergone a change. The continuous prayers, sobs, and imprecations had given it at times a strangely soft intonation, while at others it was gruff and almost hoarse. Moreover, his eyes, having been accustomed to twilight and darkness, had acquired the peculiar faculty of distinguishing objects in the dark, like those of the hyena and the wolf.

Edmond smiled when he saw himself: it was impossible that even his best friend, if he had any friends left, would recognize him: he did not even recognize himself.

The skipper of the *Jeune Amélie*, who was most anxious to keep amongst his crew such a valuable man as Dantès, offered to re-engage him, but Dantès had other plans in view, and would only accept for three months.

The *Jeune Amélie* had a very active crew ready to obey their master's orders, and he was accustomed to losing no time. He had barely been at Leghorn a week when the rounded sides of his vessel were stacked with printed muslins and prohibited cottons, English powders, and tobacco, on which the excise authorities had forgotten to affix their seal. He had to get all this out of Leghorn free of duty and land it on the shores of Corsica, whence certain speculators undertook to transmit the cargo to France.

They put off, and Dantès was once more sailing the blue ocean, which he had seen so often in his dreams while in confinement.

The next morning when the captain went on deck, which he always did at a very early hour, he found Dantès leaning over the bulwarks and gazing with a strange expression on his face at a pile of granite rocks that the rising sun had tinged a rosy hue: it was the Isle of Monte Cristo. The *Jeune Amélie* left it about three-quarters of a league to starboard and kept to her course for Corsica.

Fortunately Dantès had learnt to wait: he had waited fourteen years for his liberty. Now that he was free he could easily wait six months or a year for his treasure. Besides, was not this treasure chimerical?[3] Born in the diseased brain of poor Abbé Faria, had it not died with him? It is true Cardinal Spada's letter was singularly convincing, and

Dantès repeated it word for word from beginning to end: he had not forgotten a single syllable of it.

Two months and a half passed in similar trips, and he had become as skilful a coaster as he had been a hardy sailor. He had struck up an acquaintance with all the smugglers on the coast, and had learned all the masonic signs by which these semi-pirates recognize each other. He had passed and repassed his Isle of Monte Cristo twenty times, but had never once found an opportunity of going ashore. He therefore made up his mind that immediately after the termination of his engagement with the skipper of the *Jeune Amélie*, he would hire a small bark on his own account (he was able to do so for he had picked up a hundred piastres or so on his different voyages), and under some pretext or other make for the Isle of Monte Cristo.

Once there he would be free to make his researches, perhaps not entirely free, for he was fully aware that he would be spied upon by those who accompanied him. But in this world one must risk something.

Dantès was trying to solve the problem when one evening the skipper, who placed great confidence in him and was very anxious to keep him in his service, took him by his arm and led him to a tavern in the Via del Oglio, where the aristocrats of the Leghorn smugglers were wont to congregate.

It was here they discussed the affairs of the coast. This time a matter of great importance was debated: it concerned a ship laden with Turkish carpets, materials from the Levant, and cashmere shawls. They would have to find some neutral ground where an exchange could be made, and then endeavour to land the goods on the coast of France. The prize-money would be enormous, and if they succeeded it would mean fifty or sixty piastres for each one of the crew. The skipper proposed the Isle of Monte Cristo as a suitable place for discharging the cargo. Trembling with joy, Dantès got up to hide his emotion and paced round the smoky tavern where all the known languages of the world are mixed into a lingua franca.[4] When he joined the skipper again, it was already decided that they should touch at Monte Cristo, and that they should start on the expedition the following evening. When Edmond was consulted, he gave it as his opinion that the island afforded every possible security, and that if enterprises were to succeed, they should be carried out quickly.

Nothing was changed in the program: they were to weigh anchor the next morning and, given a good sea and a favourable wind, they hoped to be in the waters of the neutral island by the evening of the following day.

Chapter XVIII

THE ISLE OF MONTE CRISTO

A t seven o'clock the next evening all was ready, at ten
minutes past seven they rounded the lighthouse just as
the beacon was kindled. The sea was calm with a fresh wind
blowing from the south-east; they sailed under a sky of
azure where God was also lighting up his lanterns, each one
of which is a world.

The vessel skimmed merrily over the water under full
sail: there was not a rag of cloth that was not bellied in the
wind.

The Isle of Monte Cristo loomed large on the horizon.

Toward five o'clock they saw a complete view of the
island. They could see the smallest objects, thanks to the
clearness of atmosphere peculiar to the light that is shed by
the rays of the sun at sunset. Edmond gazed and gazed on
this mass of rocks, which was tinged with all the colours of
twilight, from bright pink to deep blue; at times his face
would become a deep red, and a blue mist passed before his
eyes. Never did a gamester, whose whole fortune was
staked on one throw of the dice, experience the anguish
that Dantès felt.

Night came. They landed at ten o'clock. The *Jeune
Amélie* was first at the rendezvous. Notwithstanding his

usual self-restraint, Dantès could control himself no longer:
he jumped on to the shore and, like Brutus, he would have
kissed the earth if he had dared. It was already dark night,
but at eleven o'clock the moon rose over the ocean, silver-
ing every little ripple, and, as she ascended, began to play
on the mass of rocks casting white cascades of light on this
second Pelion.

Dantès' every thought was concentrated on finding
Spada's grotto. It was useless to search for it during the
night, so he put off all investigations until the next day.
Besides, a signal hoisted half a league out at sea, to which
the *Jeune Amélie* immediately answered with a similar signal, indicating that it was time to set to work.

The late-comer, reassured by the signal that all was well,
soon came in sight, silent and pale as a phantom, and cast
anchor within a cable's length of the shore. Then the work
of unloading began. While working, Dantès continually
reflected upon the shout of joy which one word of his would
draw from the throats of all these men if he were to express
aloud the thought that was incessantly in his mind. But far
from revealing his precious secret, he feared he had already
said too much, and that he had, by his comings and goings
and his repeated questions, minute observations, and continual preoccupation, aroused suspicion.

This was not the case, however, and when he took a gun
and some powder and shot the next day, and manifested a
desire to go and shoot some of the numerous wild kids they
could see jumping from rock to rock, they attributed his
proposed excursion to nothing more than a love of sport or
a desire for solitude.

Thus Dantès, who, three months previously, had desired
nothing more than liberty, was now no longer satisfied with
that alone and aspired after riches. He started forth. Lost to
view between two walls of rock, he followed a path hollowed out by continuous torrents and which, in all probability, no human foot had ever trodden before. He approached
the spot where he supposed the grottos to be situated.

Following the coast and examining the most minute objects with serious attention, he thought he noticed on several rocks incisions that had been made by man.

Time, which casts its mantle of moss on all things material, and its mantle of oblivion on all things mortal, seemed to have respected these marks, which were made with a certain regularity, no doubt to indicate some trail; now and then, however, they disappeared beneath tufts of myrtle which grew in large clusters laden with flowers, and beneath parasitical lichen. Then Edmond was obliged to raise the branches or remove the moss to find the marks which were to lead him to this labyrinth. The marks had filled him with new hope. Surely it must have been the Cardinal who had traced them, so that in the event of a catastrophe, which even he had not foreseen would be so complete, they would serve as a guide to his nephew. This isolated spot was a most appropriate place for burying a treasure. But had these unfaithful signs not already attracted the attention of other eyes than those for which they were meant? Or had the isle of gloomy marvels faithfully kept its precious secret?

About sixty yards from the harbour, it seemed to Dantès, who was still hidden from his companions by the inequalities of the ground, that the incisions ceased. There was no grotto! A large round rock, perched on a solid base, seemed the only goal to which they led. He thought that, instead of having arrived at the end, he was perhaps only at the beginning, so he turned round and retraced his steps.

In the meantime his companions were preparing breakfast and when it was ready they fired a shot as a signal. Edmond at once came running toward them. Just as they were all watching him jumping like a chamois[1] from rock to rock, his foot gave way under him. They saw him stagger at the edge of a rock and disappear. They all rushed toward him with one bound, for, in spite of his superiority, they all loved him. They found him lying bleeding and half conscious. They forced some rum down his throat, and this remedy, which had been so beneficial to him before, had the same good effect on him now. Edmond opened his eyes, complained of a sharp pain in his knee, a feeling of heaviness in his head, and unbearable pain in his back. They wanted to carry him to the beach, but directly they touched him, he declared, with groans, that he had not the strength. The old skipper urged Dantès to rise, for he was obliged to leave in the morning to deposit his cargo on the frontiers of Piedmont and France, between Nice and Fréjus. Edmond made a superhuman effort to comply with his wishes, but, turning very white, he fell back each time with a moan.

"He has broken his back," the skipper said in a low voice. "No matter, we will not forsake him. Let us carry him on board."

But Dantès declared that he would sooner die where he was than bear the agonizing pain that the slightest movement caused him.

"Very well," said the skipper, "come what may, it shall not be said that we have deserted such a good shipmate as you. We will not leave till this evening."

This proposal was a cause of great astonishment to the sailors though no one opposed it. Dantès, however, would not allow such a serious violation of the rules of discipline on his behalf. "No," he said, "I have been clumsy and it is only right that I should pay the penalty. Leave me a supply of biscuit, a gun, some powder and shot for killing some kids or maybe to use in my own defence, also a pickaxe so that I can make myself some sort of shelter in case you should be delayed in returning to fetch me."

"But you will die of hunger," replied the skipper. "We cannot leave you like this, and on the other hand we cannot stay."

"Leave me! Go!" Dantès cried out.

Nothing could shake Dantès' determination to remain and to remain alone. The smugglers gave him all he had asked for and left him. He dragged himself cautiously to the top of a rock which afforded him full view of the sea, whence he watched the *tartan* making ready to sail; he saw her weigh anchor and, balancing herself as gracefully as a gull ere it takes wing, put out to sea.

At the end of an hour she had completely disappeared from his view, and rising, more agile and light of limb than the kids jumping about these rugged rocks among myrtle- and mastic-trees, Dantès took his gun in one hand, the pick-axe in the other, and ran toward the rock on which the incisions terminated.

"Now," he exclaimed, thinking of the story of the Arabian fisherman which Faria had related to him. "Now, open, Sesame!"

Chapter XIX

THE TREASURE CAVE

❧

The sun had run about a third of his course, sending his warm and invigorating rays full on the rocks which seemed almost insensible to their warmth. The monotonous and continuous chirp of thousands of grasshoppers invisible in the heath could be heard; the leaves of the myrtles and olive-trees waved and shook in the wind, sending forth an almost metallic sound. With every step Edmond took on the warm granite, he sent scurrying away numerous lizards bright as emeralds. In the distance wild goats were to be seen jumping from crag to crag. In a word, the island was inhabited and very much alive. Yet Dantès felt quite alone under God's blue sky. He felt an indescribable sensation akin to fear; a distrust of daylight which, even in the desert, gives us the feeling that inquisitive eyes are following us. The feeling was so strong in him that no sooner had he commenced his task than he stopped, laid down his pickaxe, picked up his gun, and, climbing to the top of the highest rock, gazed all around him. But he could see neither man nor ship; nothing but the blue sky overhead and the azure sea below. Reassured, he descended rapidly, but at the same time cautiously, fearing an accident similar to the one he had so cleverly simulated.

138

As we have already said, Dantès traced the marks on the rocks back the other way, and found that they led to a kind of small creek hidden away like the bath of a nymph of ancient days; the creek was wide enough at its mouth and deep enough in the centre to allow a small ship to enter and lie concealed there. Then, as he followed the clue that had been so skilfully handled by Faria to guide him through the labyrinth of probabilities, he came to the conclusion that Cardinal Spada, in order to avoid being seen, must first have landed in this little creek, where he hid his small bark, followed the path indicated by the incisions, and finally buried his treasure at the extreme end.

This supposition had brought Dantès to the circular rock. There was only one thing that perplexed him and upset his whole theory. How could this rock, at least several tons in weight, have been hoisted on to its base without the employment of considerable force?

Suddenly an idea occurred to Dantès. "Instead of having been lifted," thought he, "it has been lowered." And he jumped on to the rock to find its original resting place. He soon perceived that a slope had been formed; the rock had slid along until it stopped in its present position, another medium-sized rock serving as a wedge. Stones and pebbles had been carefully placed to conceal every sign of an orifice. This piece of masonry had been covered with earth, grass, and moss which had taken seed there, myrtle- and mastic-bushes had taken root, and the old rock appeared fixed to the ground.

Dantès raised the earth carefully, and detected, or thought he did, the whole of this ingenious artifice. But, he reflected, the rock was too firmly wedged and too heavy for any one man to move, were he Hercules himself. What means could he employ? He looked around for something, and his eye suddenly lighted upon the powderhorn his friends had left him. He smiled: this infernal invention would serve his purpose.

By means of his pickaxe, Dantès then cut an opening

between the upper and the lower rocks and filled it with powder. Then he shredded his handkerchief, rubbed it in the powder, and thus had a match. Directly he had set a light to it, he withdrew.

The explosion was instantaneous. The upper rock was lifted from its base by the terrific force, while the lower one was blown to pieces. Thousands of trembling insects scuttled away and a long snake, the guardian of this mysterious cave, crawled away on its blue belly and disappeared.

Dantès returned to the spot. The upper rock was hanging with scarcely any support over the cliff. The intrepid treasure-hunter walked round it, chose the loosest spot, and inserting his lever into one of the crevices, like Sisyphus,[1] he strained every muscle in his attack on the huge mass.

The rock, already shaken by the explosion, tottered; Dantès redoubled his efforts. He looked like one of the Titans uprooting the mountains in their war against the father of the gods. At last the rock yielded and rolled headlong into the sea. It had uncovered a circular place revealing an iron ring set in the middle of a square-shaped flagstone. Dantès uttered a cry of joy and astonishment. Never had a first attempt been crowned with such splendid success. He would fain[2] have continued his task, but his legs trembled so uncontrollably, his heart beat so violently, and his eyes became so dim, that he was compelled to pause awhile. He did not wait long, however. Passing his lever through the ring, he lifted with all his might; the flag-stone yielded and revealed a kind of staircase which went deeper and deeper into an increasingly dark grotto.

Dantès descended, murmuring the supreme word of human philosophy: "Perhaps." But, instead of the darkness and the thick and mephitic air he had expected to find, he saw a soft and bluish light. The air and light filtered not only through the aperture just made but also through some cracks in the rocks which were invisible from without, while from the inside Dantès could see the blue of the sky.

After having been for a few seconds in the cave, the

atmosphere of which was warm rather than damp, fragrant rather than fetid, Dantès' eyes, accustomed as they were to the dark, could penetrate into its furthermost corners; it was of granite, the facets of which sparkled like diamonds.

"Alas!" said Dantès with a smile, "these are no doubt the only treasures the Cardinal has left!"

Suddenly he thought of the words of the will which he knew by heart: "In the farthest corner of the second cave." He had only gained admittance to the first cave and must now find the entrance to the second one, which must naturally penetrate farther into the interior of the island. He examined the stones and sounded the wall where he supposed the opening would be—no doubt disguised for precaution's sake. The pickaxe resounded for an instant with a thick echo which caused the perspiration to stand in great beads on Dantès' forehead; but at length it appeared to the persevering miner that one portion of the granite wall gave forth a hollower and deeper sound. He scanned this part eagerly and recognized with a perception that probably no one but a prisoner possesses, that there must be an opening there. He struck it again with more vigour. This time he noticed something peculiar. As he struck the wall, a sort of stucco fell to the ground laying bare soft white stone. The opening in the rock had been closed with stones of a different kind; these had been covered with stucco, and on this the colour and sparkle of the granite had been imitated.

Dantès struck into the wall with the sharp end of his pick, which penetrated about an inch. Here then was the spot where he must dig.

As yet he had had no food, but this was not the moment to eat. He swallowed a mouthful of rum and again attacked his work somewhat strengthened. He took up his pickaxe, and after several strokes with it he perceived that the stones were not cemented, but simply placed one on top of the other and covered with stucco. He pushed the point of his pick into one of the interstices, pressed on the handle, and to his joy one of the stones fell at his feet. The opening thus made was large enough to admit him, and so he was able to pass from the first grotto into the second. It was lower, darker, and more uncanny than the first: the air, which only entered by the aperture he had just made, had that fetid smell Dantès had expected to find in the first. He gave the exterior air time to replace this foul air and then he entered.

To the left of the aperture there was a dark and gloomy corner. As we have already mentioned, however, there was no darkness for the eyes of Dantès. He looked round the second grotto; like the first one it was empty! The treasure, if it existed, was buried in the dark corner yonder. Dantès' hour of anguish had arrived. To dig through two feet of earth was all that remained to him between supreme joy and bottomless despair. He approached the corner and, as though seized by a sudden resolution, set to work on the soil with all his might. At the fifth or sixth stroke it sounded as though the pickaxe had encountered some iron substance. Never did funeral knell or alarm bell produce such an effect on its hearer. Had Dantès found nothing, he could not have become more deadly pale. He plunged his pick into the earth a little to one side of this spot and encountered resistance but not the same sound.

"It is a wooden chest bound with iron," he said.

In a very short time he had cleared a space about three feet long and two wide, and, by the light of the torch he had improvised, he recognized an oak chest bound with wrought iron. In the middle of the lid on a silver plate which the earth had left untarnished were engraved the arms of the Spada family, namely, a sword on an oval shield like that of the Italians, and surmounted by a cardinal's hat. Dantès easily recognized them. Faria had drawn them for him time and again. There could now be no doubt that the treasure was there; no one would have taken such precautions for an empty chest.

Edmond laid bare the chest in very little time and saw appearing bit by bit the centre lock placed between two padlocks and the handles at each end, all carved as things were carved at that period when art lent beauty to the basest of metals.

Dantès took the chest by the handles and tried to lift it, but that was quite impossible. He tried to open it: it was locked. He inserted the sharp end of his pickaxe between the chest and the lid and burst it open. The chest was uncovered!

The chest was divided into three compartments. In the first shone bright red gold crown pieces. In the second unpolished ingots arranged in order, their only attraction being their weight and value. In the third compartment, which was but half full, Dantès took up whole handfuls of diamonds, pearls, and rubies, which as they fell through his fingers in a sparkling cascade gave forth the sound of hail beating against the windowpanes.

After he had touched, fingered, buried his trembling hands in the gold and precious stones, Edmond rose and rushed through the caves like a man seized with a frenzy. He leapt on to a rock whence he could behold the sea. He was alone, quite alone with these incalculable, unheard-of, fabulous riches which all belonged to him! Was he awake or was it all a dream? Could he possibly be face to face with reality? He wanted to see his gold, yet he felt he had not the strength to look at it. For a moment he pressed his head in his hands as though to prevent his senses from leaving him; then he rushed wildly about the island, terrifying the wild goats and scaring the seagulls with his shouts and gesticulations. Finally he returned, still with doubt in his mind, rushed from the first grotto into the second, and found himself in the presence of his mine of gold and diamonds.

This time he fell on his knees, murmuring a prayer that was intelligible to God alone. He soon became calmer and happier, and began to believe in his good fortune. He began to count his treasures; there were a thousand ingots of gold, each weighing two or three pounds; he piled up twenty-five thousand gold crowns, each one of which he valued at twenty-four francs of the present currency, and which bore the effigy of Pope Alexander VI or his predecessors: yet this did not constitute one-half of the contents of the compartment. He measured out ten handfuls of pearls, precious stones, and diamonds, many of which were mounted by the best goldsmiths of the period and were valuable on account of their remarkable workmanship in addition to their intrinsic worth.

This night was for Edmond one of those delicious yet terrible nights, of which this man of astounding emotions had already spent two or three in his lifetime.

Chapter XX

THE STRANGER

Day broke. Dantès had long been waiting for it with wide-open eyes. He rose with the first streak of daylight, climbed the highest peak of the island, as on the previous evening, and explored his surroundings. As on the previous evening also silence reigned supreme.

Edmond descended, raised the stone, filled his pockets with precious stones, replaced the lid on the chest, covered it with earth which he carefully stamped down, and sprinkled some sand over it so as to make this spot look like the rest of the ground. Then he left the cave, replacing the stone after him, and effaced all traces of his steps for some distance round the grotto. He now longed with impatience for his companions' return, for in truth he could not waste his time in Monte Cristo looking at his gold and diamonds like a dragon guarding a useless treasure. He must return into the world and take the rank, influence, and power in society bestowed by riches only, the first and greatest force at man's disposal.

The smugglers returned on the sixth day. Dantès recognized the *Jeune Amélie* from a distance and dragged himself to the port. When his comrades landed, he assured them that he was better, though still suffering, and listened to an account of their adventures.

He displayed the most admirable self-possession; he did not even smile at the enumeration of the gains he would have derived had he been able to leave the island. As the *Jeune Amélie* had only come to Monte Cristo to fetch him, he embarked the same evening and went with the skipper to Leghorn. Arrived at Leghorn, he sought out a Jew to whom he sold four of his smallest diamonds for five thousand francs each. The Jew might have wondered how it came about that a sailor was in possession of such valuable jewels, but he asked no questions and made a profit of one thousand francs on each one of them.

The next day Dantès bought a small, fully equipped bark for one of his comrades, on condition that he should set out at once for Marseilles for news of Mercédès and old Dantès and rejoin him at Monte Cristo. He accounted for his sudden wealth by saying that on his arrival at Leghorn he found that a very rich uncle had died, leaving him sole heir to the whole of his fortune. Dantès' superior education made this story plausible, and no one doubted his word.

As the period of his engagement on board the *Jeune Amélie* had now expired, Dantès took leave of the captain, who tried in vain to retain him in his service, and of his comrades, giving each one of them a handsome present. He then set sail for Genoa.

Here he bought a small yacht. It had been built for an Englishman for forty thousand francs; Dantès offered sixty thousand on condition that it should be delivered to him at once. He ordered a secret cupboard containing three secret compartments to be made in the cabin at the head of his bunk. This was finished the next day, and two hours later a crowd of curious sightseers was speculating on the destination of a vessel which put out from Genoa with a crew of one man, who said he preferred to sail alone. His destination, of course, was the Isle of Monte Cristo, where he arrived at the end of the second day. His yacht was an excellent sailer and had done the distance in thirty-eight hours. Instead of landing at the customary landingplace, Dantès cast anchor in the little creek.

The island was deserted; no one seemed to have been on it since he left. He made straight for his treasure, and found everything just as he had left it. The next day he carried his enormous fortune to his yacht and locked it up in the three compartments of his secret cupboard.

He had to wait eight weary days before his comrade returned from Marseilles, which time he spent in sailing his yacht round the island. When his comrade arrived, he had a sad reply to each of the two questions put to him. His father was dead and Mercédès had disappeared.

Edmond heard these tidings with apparent calm, though he expressed a desire to be left alone and sprang on shore. Two hours later he reappeared and set sail for Marseilles. He had quite expected to hear of his father's death, but what had become of Mercédès?

A glance at himself in a mirror at Leghorn had reassured him that he ran no risk of being recognized; besides, he had now at his disposal every means of disguising himself. One fine morning, therefore, he boldly entered the port of Marseilles and stopped opposite the spot where, on that memorable, fatal evening, he had set out for the Château d'If.

It was not without a tremor that he saw a gendarme accompanied by the quarantine officer come on board, but with the perfect self-command he had acquired, Dantès presented an English passport which he had bought at Leghorn, and, this permit being more respected in France than any other, he was allowed to land without let or hindrance. That same evening he stepped forth on to the Cannebière alone, unknown, as it were a stranger in a strange land.

Chapter XXI

THE PONT DU GARD INN

Such of my readers as have, like me, made a walking tour through the south of France, may perchance have noticed midway between the town of Beaucaire and the village of Bellegarde a small roadside inn, in front of which hung, creaking and flapping in the wind, an iron shield bearing a grotesque representation of the Pont du Gard.

The little inn had been occupied for the last seven or eight years by no other than Dantès' old acquaintance Gaspard Caderousse. He was standing, as was his wont, at his place of observation before the door, his eyes wandering listlessly from a small patch of grass, where some hens were scratching for food, to the deserted road leading from north to south, when suddenly he descried the dim outline of a man on horseback approaching from Bellegarde at that easy amble which betokens the best of understanding between horse and rider. The rider was a priest robed in black and wearing a three-cornered hat in spite of the scorching sun, which was then at its zenith.

Arrived at the door of the inn, he halted. It would have been difficult to say whether it was the horse that stopped the man or the man that stopped the horse. In any case the man dismounted, and, dragging the animal after him by the bridle, tied it to a dilapidated shutter.

Caderousse advanced, all bows and smiles.

"Are you not Monsieur Caderousse?" asked the priest in a strong Italian accent.

"Yes, monsieur," replied the innkeeper. "That is my name. Gaspard Caderousse, at your service. Can I not offer you some refreshment, Monsieur l'Abbé?"

"Certainly, give me a bottle of your best wine and afterward, with your permission, we will resume our conversation."

When mine host reappeared after a few minutes' absence he found the abbé sitting on a stool with his elbows on the table; he placed a bottle of wine and a glass before him.

"Are we alone?" asked the abbé.

"Oh, yes, all alone or nearly so, for my wife doesn't count as she is always ailing."

"First of all I must convince myself that you are really he whom I seek. In the year eighteen-fourteen or fifteen did you know a sailor named Dantès?"

"Dantès? I should think I did! Poor Edmond! Why, he was one of my best friends," exclaimed Caderousse. "What has become of poor Edmond, monsieur? Do you know him? Is he still living? Is he free? Is he happy?"

"He died a prisoner, more wretched and more miserable than any prisoner lying in chains in the prison at Toulon."

The deep red of Caderousse's face gave way to a ghastly paleness. He turned aside, and the abbé saw him wipe away a tear with a corner of the handkerchief tied round his head.

"Poor fellow!" Caderousse murmured.

"You seem to have been very fond of this boy?"

"I was indeed," answered Caderousse, "though I have it on my conscience that at one time I envied him his happiness. But I swear to you, Monsieur l'Abbé, I swear it on my honour, that since then I have deeply deplored his lot."

There was a moment's silence during which the abbé's

fixed gaze did not cease to examine the agitated features of the innkeeper.

"Did you know the poor lad?" continued Caderousse.

"I was called to his bedside to administer to him the last consolation of his religion. What is so very strange about it all," the abbé continued, "is that on his deathbed, Dantès swore by the crucifix that he was entirely ignorant of the cause of his imprisonment. He besought me, therefore, to clear up the mystery of his misfortune, which he had never been able to explain himself and, if his memory had been sullied, to remove the tarnish from his name."

The abbé's eyes were fixed on Caderousse's countenance and seemed to penetrate to his very soul.

"A rich Englishman," countinued the abbé, "his companion in misfortune for a time, but released at the Second Restoration, owned a diamond of very great value. On leaving the prison he wished to give his companion a token of his gratitude for the kind and brotherly way he had nursed him through an illness, and gave him the diamond. When on his deathbed, Dantès said to me: 'I had three good friends and a sweetheart, and I am sure they have deeply regretted my misfortune. One of these good friends was named Caderousse.' "

Caderousse could not repress a shudder.

" 'Another one,' " the abbé went on without appearing to notice Caderousse's emotion, " 'was named Danglars: the third one,' he said, 'also loved me though he was my rival, and his name was Fernand; the name of my betrothed was . . . ' I do not remember the name of his betrothed."

"Mercédès," said Caderousse.

"Oh, yes, that was it," replied the abbé with a repressed sigh. "Mercédès it was. 'Go to Marseilles,' Dantès said, 'and sell this diamond. The money obtained for it divide into five parts and give an equal share to each of these good friends, the only beings on earth who have loved me.' "

"Why into five parts?" exclaimed Caderousse. "You only named four persons."

"Because I hear that the fifth person is dead. The fifth share was for Dantès' father."

"Alas! it is only too true!" said Caderousse, deeply moved by the contending passions that were aroused in him. "The old man died less than a year after his son disappeared."

"What did he die of?"

"I believe the doctors called his disease gastric enteritis, but those who knew him say that he died of grief, and I, who practically saw him die, say that he died of . . ."

Caderousse hesitated.

"Died of what?" the priest asked anxiously.

"Why, of hunger . . ."

"Of hunger?" the abbé cried, jumping up. "Do you say of hunger? Why, the vilest animals are not allowed to starve. The dogs wandering about the streets find a compassionate hand to throw them a piece of bread, and a man, a Christian, has died of hunger amidst men who also call themselves Christians! Is it possible? No, it cannot be!"

"It is as I have said," replied Caderousse.

"But," continued the priest, "was the unhappy old man so completely forsaken by everyone that he died such a death?"

"It was not because Mercédès or Monsieur Morrel had forsaken him," replied Caderousse. "The poor old man took a strong dislike to this same Fernand whom Dantès named as one of his friends," he added with an ironical smile.

"Was he not a friend then?" asked the abbé.

"Can a man be a friend to him whose wife he covets? Dantès was so large-hearted that he called them all his friends. Poor Edmond!"

"Do you know in what way Fernand wronged Dantès?"

"No one better than I."

"Will you not tell me?"

"What good would it do?"

"Then you would prefer me to give these men who, you say, are false and faithless friends a reward intended for faithful friendship?"

"You are right," said Caderousse. "Besides, what would poor Edmond's legacy be to them now? No more than a drop of water in the mighty ocean!"

"How so, have they become rich and mighty?"

"Then you do not know their history?"

"No, tell it to me."

Caderousse appeared to reflect for an instant. "No," he said. "It would take too long."

"You may please yourself, my friend," said the abbé with an air of complete indifference. "I respect your scruples and admire your sentiment. We will let the matter drop. I will sell the diamond."

So saying he took the diamond out of his pocket and let the light play on it right in front of Caderousse.

"Oh, what a magnificent diamond!" exclaimed the latter in a voice almost hoarse with emotion. "It must be worth at least fifty thousand francs."

"Remember it is your wish that I divide the money amongst all four of you," the abbé said calmly, replacing the diamond in the pocket of his cassock. "Now, be kind enough to give me the addresses of Edmond's friends, so that I may carry out his last wishes."

The perspiration stood out in big drops on Caderousse's forehead; he saw the abbé rise and go toward the door as if he wished to ascertain that his horse was all right; afterward he returned and asked:

"Well, what have you decided to do?"

"To tell you everything," was the innkeeper's reply.

"I really believe that is the best thing you can do," replied the priest, "not because I am anxious to know what you wish to conceal from me, but simply because it will be much better if you can help me to distribute the legacy as the testator would have desired. Begin; I am all attention."

Caderousse went to the door and closed it, and, by way of greater precaution, shot the bolt. The priest chose a seat in a corner where he could listen at his ease and where he would have his back to the light while the narrator would have the light full on his face. There he sat, his head bent, his hands joined, or rather clenched, ready to listen with all attention. Caderousse took a stool and sat in front of him and began his story.

Chapter XXII

CADEROUSSE'S STORY

"It is a very sad story, monsieur," said Caderousse, shaking his head. "I dare say you already know the beginning."

"Yes, Edmond told me everything up to the moment of his arrest. He himself knew nothing except what touched him personally, for he never again set eyes on any of the five people I mentioned just now, nor did he ever hear their names mentioned."

"Well, directly after Dantès' arrest in the middle of his betrothal feast Monsieur Morrel left to obtain further information. The news he brought us was very sad. The old father returned to the house alone, and, with tears streaming from his eyes, folded up his wedding clothes. He spent the whole night pacing up and down his room and did not go to bed at all, for my room was beneath his, and I heard him walking about the whole night long. I must say, I did not sleep either; I was too upset at the old man's grief, and every step he took caused me as much pain as if he had actually trampled on me.

"The next day Mercédès went to Marseilles to implore Monsieur de Villefort's protection, but in vain. She paid the old man a visit at the same time. When she saw him so miserable and grief-stricken, she wanted to take him with her to her cottage to look after him, but the old man refused.

" 'No,' said he, 'I will not leave the house. My poor son loves me more than anyone else, and, if he is let out of prison, he will come to see me first of all. What would he say if I were not there to welcome him?'

"I was at the window listening to all this, for I was very anxious that Mercédès should persuade the old man to go with her; the sound of his footsteps overhead gave me not a second's rest."

"Didn't you go to the old man yourself and try to console him?" the priest asked.

"Ah! monsieur! One can only console those who will let themselves be consoled, and he would not," was Caderousse's reply. "He became more and more lonely with each succeeding day. Mercédès and Monsieur Morrel often came to see him, but they always found his door shut, and, though I knew he was at home, he never opened it to them. One day, contrary to custom, he received Mercédès, and when the poor girl, herself desperate and hopeless, tried to comfort him, he said:

" 'Believe me, my daughter, he is dead. Instead of our waiting for him, it is he who awaits us. I am very glad that I am the elder, as I shall therefore be the first to see him again.'

"However good and kind-hearted one may be, you can quite understand that one soon ceases to visit those that depress one, and thus it came about that poor old Dantès was left entirely alone. Now I only saw strangers go to his room from time to time, and these came out with suspicious-looking bundles: little by little he was selling all he possessed to eke out his miserable existence. At length he had nothing left but his few clothes.

"During the next three days I heard the old man pacing the floor as usual, but on the fourth day, there wasn't a sound to be heard. I ventured to go up to him. The door was locked, but I peeped through the keyhole and saw him so pale and haggard-looking that I felt sure he must be very ill.

I sent word to Monsieur Morrel and myself ran for Mercédès. Neither of them wasted any time in coming. Monsieur Morrel brought with him a doctor, who diagnosed gastric enteritis and put his patient on diet.

"Mercédès came again and saw such a change in the old man that, as before, she wanted to have him moved to her own cottage. Monsieur Morrel was also of the opinion that this would be best, and wanted to move him by force, but he protested so violently that they were afraid to do so. Mercédès remained at the bedside. Monsieur Morrel went away, making a sign to Mercédès that he had left a purse on the mantelshelf. Nevertheless, taking advantage of the doctor's instructions, the old man would eat nothing. Finally after nine days' despair and wasting, the old man died, cursing those who had caused all his misery. His last words to Mercédès were: 'If you see my Edmond again, tell him I died blessing him.' "

The abbé rose, and twice paced round the room, pressing his trembling hand to his parched throat.

"And you believe that he died of . . ."

"Of hunger, monsieur, pure starvation," said Caderousse. "I am as certain of it as that we two are Christians."

"A sad, sad tragedy!" said the priest, and his voice was hoarse with emotion.

"All the more sad," said Caderousse, "because it was none of God's doing but the work of those men."

"Let me know about those men," said the abbé, "and remember you have bound yourself to tell me everything. Who are the men who caused the son to die of despair and the father of hunger?"

"Two men who were jealous of him, the one through love and the other through ambition. Their names are Fernand and Danglars."

"In what way did they show this jealousy?"

"They denounced Edmond as a Bonapartist agent."

"Which of the two denounced him? Who was the real culprit?"

"Both were guilty. The letter was written on the day before the betrothal feast. It was Danglars who wrote it with his left hand, it was Fernand who posted it."

"And yet you did not protest against such infamy?" said the abbé. "Then you are their accomplice."

"They both made me drink so excessively, monsieur, that I was no longer responsible for my actions. I only saw through a mist. I said all that a man is capable of saying when in such a state, but they both told me that they were only playing a harmless joke which would carry no consequences with it."

"But the next day you saw what consequences it had, yet you said nothing, though you were present when he was arrested."

"Yes, monsieur, I was there and I tried to speak. I wanted to say all I knew, but Danglars prevented me. I will own that I stood in fear of the political state of things at that time, and I let myself be overruled. I kept silence. It was cowardly, I know, but it was not criminal."

"I understand. You just let things take their course."

"Yes, monsieur," was Caderousse's rejoinder, "and I regret it night and day. I often ask pardon of God for it, I assure you, especially as this action, the only one I have to reproach myself with during the whole of my lifetime, is no doubt the cause of my adversity. I am paying the penalty for one moment's selfishness."

With these words Caderousse bowed his head with all the signs of a true penitent. There followed a short silence; the abbé got up and paced the room in deep thought. At length he returned to his place and sat down, saying: "You have mentioned a Monsieur Morrel two or three times. Who was he?"

"He was the owner of the *Pharaon*."

"What part did he play in this sad affair?"

"The part of an honest, courageous, and affectionate man, monsieur. Twenty times did he intercede for Dantès. When the Emperor returned, he wrote, entreated, and threatened, with the result that during the Second Restoration, he was persecuted as a Bonapartist. As I told you before, he came again and again to Dantès' father to persuade him to live with him in his house, and, as I also mentioned, the day before the old man's death, he left on the mantelshelf a purse which contained sufficient money to pay off his debts and to defray the expenses of the funeral. Thus the poor old man was enabled to die as he had lived, without doing wrong to anyone. I have still got the purse; it is a red silk one."

"If Monsieur Morrel is still alive, he must be enjoying God's blessing: he must be rich and happy."

Caderousse smiled bitterly. "Yes, as happy as I am," was the answer. "He stands on the brink of poverty, and, what is more, of dishonour. After twenty-five years' work, after having gained the most honoured place in the business world of Marseilles, Monsieur Morrel is utterly ruined. He has lost five ships during the last two years, has had to bear the brunt of the bankruptcy of three large firms, and his only hope is now in the *Pharaon*, the very ship that poor Dantès commanded, which is expected from the Indies with a cargo of cochineal and indigo. If this ship goes down like the others, all is lost."

"Has the unfortunate man a wife and children?"

"Yes, he has a wife who is behaving like a saint through all this trouble; he has a daughter who was to have married the man she loves, but his family will not allow him to marry the daughter of a bankrupt; and he has a son, a lieutenant in the army. But you may well understand that this only increases the wretched man's grief instead of alleviating it. If he were alone, he would blow out his brains and there would be an end to it."

"It is terrible," murmured the priest.

"It is thus that God rewards virtue, monsieur. Just look at me. I have never done a wrong action apart from the one I related to you a moment ago, yet I live in poverty, while Fernand and Danglars are rolling in wealth. Everything they have touched has turned into gold, whereas everything I have done has gone all wrong."

"Danglars was the more guilty of the two, the instigator, was he not? What has become of him?"

"He left Marseilles and, upon the recommendation of Monsieur Morrel, who was unaware of his crime, he became cashier in a Spanish bank. During the war with Spain, he was employed in the commissariat of the French army and made a fortune. Then he speculated with his money and quadrupled his capital. He married his banker's daughter and was left a widower after a short time; then he married a widow, the daughter of the chamberlain who is in great favour at Court. He became a millionaire and was made a Baron. Thus he is now Baron Danglars, owns a large house in the Rue du Mont Blanc, has ten horses in his stable, six footmen in his antechamber, and I don't know how many millions in his coffers."

"But how could Fernand, a poor fisherman, make a fortune? He had neither resources nor education. I must own this surpasses my comprehension."

"It is beyond the comprehension of every one. There must be some strange secret in his life of which we are all ignorant. It is all very mysterious. A few days before the Restoration, Fernand was called up for conscription. The Bourbons left him in peace at the Catalans, but when Napoleon returned, an extraordinary muster was decreed and Fernand was compelled to join up. I also joined up, but as I was older and had just married, I was only sent to the coast. Fernand was enrolled in a fighting unit, reached the frontier, and took part in the battle of Ligny.[1]

"The night following the battle, he was on sentry duty outside the door of a general who was in secret communication with the enemy and who intended going over to the English that very night. He suggested that Fernand should accompany him. To this Fernand agreed, and, deserting his post, followed the general.

"This would have meant a court-martial for Fernand if

Napoleon had remained on the throne, but to the Bourbons it only served him as a recommendation. He returned to France with the epaulette[2] of a sublieutenant and, as he still enjoyed the protection of the general, who stood in high favour, he was promoted captain during the Spanish war in eighteen-twenty-three; that is to say, at the time when Danglars was first launching forth in speculation. Fernand was a Spaniard, so he was sent to Madrid to inquire into the feeling existing among his compatriots. While there he met Danglars, who became very friendly with him, promised his general support amongst the Royalists of the capital and the provinces, obtained promises for himself, and on his side made pledges. He led his regiment along paths known only to himself in gorges guarded by Royalists, and in short rendered such services during that short campaign that after the fall of Trocadero, he was promoted colonel and received the cross of an Officer of the Legion of Honour."

"Fate! Fate!" murmured the abbé.

"Yes, but that is not all. When the Spanish war was ended, Fernand's career was checked by the long period of peace which seemed likely to prevail throughout Europe. Greece alone had risen against Turkey and had just commenced her war of independence. All eyes were turned toward Athens, and it became the fashion to pity and support the Greeks. Fernand sought and obtained permission to serve in Greece, but his name was still retained on the army list.

"Some time later it was stated that the Count of Morcerf, which was the name he now bore, had entered the service of Ali Pasha with the rank of instructor-general. Ali Pasha was killed, as you know, but before he died, he recompensed Fernand for his services by leaving him a considerable sum of money. Fernand returned to France, where his rank of lieutenant-general was confirmed, and to-day he owns a magnificent house at Paris in the Rue du Helder, number twenty-seven."

The abbé opened his mouth as though to speak, hesitated for a moment, then, with a great effort, said: "What about Mercédès? They tell me she has disappeared."

"Disappeared?" said Caderousse. "Yes, as the sun disappears only to rise with more splendour the next day."

"Has she also made her fortune then?" asked the abbé with an ironical smile.

"Mercédès is at present one of the grandest ladies in Paris. At first she was utterly overcome by the blow which had robbed her of her Edmond. I have already told you how she importuned Villefort with entreaties, and have also touched upon her devoted care for Dantès' father. In the midst of her despair she was assailed by another trouble, the departure of Fernand, of whose crime she was unaware and whom she regarded as a brother.

"Mercédès was alone and uncared for. She spent three months weeping and sorrowing. No news of Edmond and none of Fernand, with nothing to distract her but an old man dying of despair.

"One evening after she had been sitting all day at the crossroads leading to Marseilles and the Catalans, as was her wont, she returned home more depressed than ever. Neither her lover nor her friend had returned along either of these two roads, neither had she any news of them.

"Suddenly she seemed to recognize a step behind her and turned round anxiously. The door opened, and Fernand entered in the uniform of a sublieutenant. It was only the half of what she was grieving for, but it was a portion of her past life restored to her. She seized Fernand's hands in an ecstasy of joy. This he took for love, whereas it was nothing more than joy at being no longer alone in the world, and at seeing a friend again after so many long hours of solitary sadness. Then you must remember she had never hated Fernand, she simply did not love him. Another one owned Mercédès' heart, and he was absent . . . he had disappeared . . . perhaps he was dead. At this last thought, Mercédès always burst into tears and wrung her hands in anguish; but, whereas she had always rejected the idea when suggested by someone else, the same thought now began to prey on her mind, and old Dantès incessantly said to her: 'Our Edmond is dead, for, if he were not, he would have come back to us.'

"The old man died. Had he lived, in all probability Mercédès would never have become the wife of another; he would have been there to reproach her with her infidelity. Fernand realized that fact. As soon as he heard that the old man was dead, he returned. This time he was a lieutenant. The first time he returned he had not spoken of love; the second time he reminded her that he loved her. Mercédès asked for six months in which to await and bewail Edmond."

"Well, that made eighteen months in all," said the abbé with a bitter smile. "What more could the most adored lover ask?" Then he murmured the words of the English poet:[3] " 'Frailty, thy name is woman!' "

"Six months later," continued Caderousse, "the wedding took place in the Church des Accoules."

"The very church in which she was to have married Edmond," murmured the abbé. "The bridegroom was changed, that was all."

"So Mercédès was married," continued Caderousse, "but although to all appearances she was calm, she was neverthe-less well nigh fainting when she passed La Réserve, where, eighteen months previously, she had celebrated her betrothal with him whom she still loved, which she would have realized herself had she dared to probe to the depths of her heart."

"Did you see Mercédès again?" asked the priest.

"Yes, during the Spanish war at Perpignan, where Fernand had left her; she was attending to the education of her son."

The abbé started. "Her son, did you say?"

"Yes," was Caderousse's reply, "little Albert's education."

"But I am sure Edmond told me she was the daughter of a simple fisherman and that, though she was beautiful, she was uneducated. Had she taken a course of instruction that she was able to teach her son?"

"Oh!" exclaimed Caderousse. "Did he know his sweetheart so little? If crowns were bestowed upon beauty and intelligence, Mercédès would now be a queen. Her fortune was growing, and she grew with it. She learnt drawing, music, everything. Personally I think she did all this simply to distract her mind, to help her to forget; she crammed so much knowledge into her head to alleviate the weight in her heart. I must tell you everything as it is," continued Caderousse. "Her fortune and honours have no doubt afforded her some consolation; she is rich, she is a Countess, and yet . . ." Caderousse hesitated.

"Yet what?" asked the abbé.

"Yet I am sure she is not happy."

"Do you know what has happened to Monsieur de Villefort and what part he played in Edmond's misfortune?"

"No, I only know that some time after he had him arrested he married Mademoiselle de Saint-Méran and shortly afterwards left Marseilles. No doubt Dame Fortune has smiled upon him too, no doubt like Danglars he is rich, and like Fernand covered with honours, while I alone, you understand, have remained poor, miserable, and forsaken by all."

"You are mistaken, my friend," said the abbé. "There are times when God's justice tarries for a while and it appears to us that we are forgotten by Him, but the time always comes when we find it is not so, and here is the proof."

With these words the abbé took the diamond from his pocket and handed it to Caderousse.

"Here, my friend," he said. "Take this, it is yours."

"What! For me alone!" exclaimed Caderousse. "Ah, monsieur, do not jest with me!"

"The diamond was to be divided amongst Edmond's friends. He had but one friend, therefore it cannot be divided. Take the diamond and sell it; it is worth fifty thousand francs, a sum which will, I trust, suffice to relieve you of your poverty."

"Oh, monsieur, do not play with the happiness or despair of a man!" said Caderousse, putting out one hand timidly, while with the other he wiped away the perspiration that gathered in big drops on his forehead.

"I know what happiness means as I also know what despair means, and I should never play with either of these feelings. Take the diamond, but in exchange . . ."

Caderousse already had his hand on the diamond, but at these last words he hastily withdrew it.

The abbé smiled.

"In exchange," continued he, "give me the red silk purse Monsieur Morrel left on the mantelshelf in old Dantès' room."

More and more astonished, Caderousse went to a large oak cupboard, opened it, and, taking out a long purse of faded red silk on two copper rings, once gilt, he handed it to the priest.

The abbé took it and gave the diamond in exchange.

"You are verily a man of God, monsieur!" exclaimed Caderousse. "No one knew Dantès gave you the diamond, and you could easily have kept it."

The abbé rose and took his hat and gloves, unbarred the door, mounted his horse, and, saying good-bye to Caderousse, who was most effusive in his farewells, started off by the road he had come.

Chapter XXIII

THE PRISON REGISTER

T he day following the events just recorded, a man of
about thirty or thirty-two years of age, clad in a bright
blue coat, nankeen trousers, and a white waistcoat, and having both the appearance and the accent of an Englishman,
presented himself before the Mayor of Marseilles.

"Monsieur," said he, "I am head clerk of the firm of
Thomson and French, of Rome. We have had business connexions with Morrel and Son, of Marseilles, for the last ten
years involving a hundred thousand francs or so of our
money. As reports are current that the firm is faced with
ruin, we are beginning to feel somewhat anxious, so I have
come from Rome for the sole purpose of obtaining some
information from you in regard to the firm."

"I know well enough, monsieur, that misfortune seems to
have dogged Monsieur Morrel for the past four or five
years," replied the Mayor. "He has lost five ships one after
the other, and has suffered badly through the bankruptcy of
three or four firms, but though I am his creditor to the
extent of some ten thousand francs, it is not my place to give
you any information of the state of his finances. If you ask
me in my capacity as Mayor what I think of Monsieur
Morrel, I can but answer that he is as honest as it is possible

for a man to be, and that up to the present he has fulfilled his engagements with absolute punctuality. That is all I can tell you, monsieur. If you wish to know more, apply to Monsieur de Boville, Inspector of Prisons, Rue de Noailles, number fifteen. I believe he has two hundred thousand francs invested with the firm, and if there are really any grounds for apprehension you will doubtless find him better informed on the subject than I am."

The Englishman appeared to appreciate this great delicacy on the part of the Mayor, bade him good morning, and, with that gait peculiar to the sons of Great Britain, set off for the street mentioned.

M. de Boville was in his office. With the coolness of his race, the Englishman put almost the same question to him as he had put to the Mayor.

"Unfortunately your fears are only too well founded, monsieur," exclaimed M. de Boville, "and you see before you a ruined man. I have two hundred thousand francs in that firm and they were to constitute the dowry of my daughter, who is to be married in a fortnight. One hundred thousand francs of this sum was redeemable on the fifteenth of this month, and another hundred thousand francs on the fifteenth of next month. I notified Monsieur Morrel of the fact that I desired to have the payment punctually made, and here he comes hardly an hour back and tells me that if his ship, the *Pharaon*, does not return by the fifteenth, he will find it impossible to effect the payment. It looks very much like bankruptcy."

"Then, monsieur, you fear for your money?"

"I consider it as good as lost."

"Well, then, I will buy it from you."

"You will? But at an enormous discount, I presume."

"No, for two hundred thousand francs. Our firm does not conduct business in that way," he added with a smile. "What is more, I will pay you cash down."

The Englishman took from his pocket a bundle of banknotes amounting to about double the sum M. de Boville was fearful of losing. An expression of joy lit up M. de Boville's face, but he restrained his feelings and said: "I must warn you, monsieur, that in all probability, you will not get six percent of that sum."

"That has nothing to do with me," was the reply. "It is the affair of Thomson and French, for whom I am acting. It may be that it is to their interest to hasten the ruin of a rival firm. What I do know, monsieur, is that I am ready to hand over this sum in exchange for a deed of assignment;[1] all I require of you is a commission."

"That is but just, monsieur!" exclaimed M. de Boville. "The commission is generally one and a half. Do you want two . . . three . . . five . . . percent, or even more? You have only to say the word."

"I am like my firm, monsieur," replied the Englishman with a smile. "I do not conduct business on those lines. My commission is something entirely different. You are the Inspector of Prisons, are you not?"

"I have been for the last fourteen years and more."

"Do you keep a register of entrances and dismissals?"

"Of course."

"Are there any notes in the register pertaining to the different prisoners?"

"Each prisoner has his dossier."

"Well, monsieur, I was educated at Rome by a poor old abbé who suddenly disappeared. Later I learned that he had been detained in the Château d'If, and I should like to have some details in regard to his death."

"What was his name?"

"The Abbé Faria."

"Oh, yes, I remember him perfectly. He died last February."

"You have a good memory, monsieur."

"I remember this case because the poor fellow's death was accompanied by a very peculiar circumstance. The abbé's dungeon was about forty-five or fifty feet from that of a Bonapartist agent, one of those who had greatly contributed to the return of the usurper in eighteen-fifteen. He was a very determined and dangerous man."

"Really?" said the Englishman.

"Yes," was the reply. "I had an opportunity of seeing this man myself in eighteen-sixteen or seventeen. We could only go down to his dungeon accompanied by a file of soldiers. He made a deep impression on me, and I shall never forget his face."

The Englishman gave the ghost of a smile.

"Edmond Dantès was the man's name," continued the inspector, "and he must have either procured some tools or else made some, for a passage was found by means of which the two prisoners communicated with one another."

"The passage was doubtless made with a view to escape?"

"Exactly, but unfortunately for the prisoners, the abbé was seized with an attack of epilepsy and died."

"I understand; that must have put an end to their plans."

"As far as the dead man was concerned, it certainly did, but not for the one who lived. On the contrary, Dantès saw a means of effecting his escape more easily. He doubtless thought that the prisoners who die in the Château d'If are buried in an ordinary cemetery, so he carried the corpse into his own cell and took its place in the sack in which it had been sewn up, and waited for the burial. The Château d'If has no cemetery, however. The dead are simply thrown into the sea with a cannon-ball attached to their feet."

"Is that really so?" exclaimed the Englishman.

"Yes, monsieur," continued the inspector. "You may imagine the fugitive's astonishment when he felt himself being hurled down the rocks. I should like to have seen his face at that moment."

"That would have been somewhat difficult."

"Never mind," said M. de Boville, whom the certainty of getting his two hundred thousand francs had put into a good humour. "Never mind, I can imagine it." And he burst out laughing.

"I can also imagine it," said the Englishman, with a forced laugh. "So I suppose the fugitive was drowned. But if he was, no doubt some official report must have been made on the occurrence."

"Oh, yes, a death certificate was made out. You see, his relatives, if he had any, might be interested to know whether he was dead or alive. Would you like to see what documents we have relating to the poor abbé?"

"It would give me great pleasure," replied his companion.

"Let us go to my office then."

And they both passed into the office of M. de Boville. Everything was in perfect order; each register had its number, each dossier had its file. The inspector gave the Englishman his easy-chair, set before him the register and the dossier relating to the Château d'If, and let him look through them at his leisure, while he himself sat in a corner of the room and read his paper.

The Englishman had no difficulty in finding the dossier relating to the Abbé Faria. It appeared as though the story which the inspector had related greatly interested him, for, after having perused the first documents, he turned over the leaves until he reached the deposition respecting Edmond Dantès. There he found everything arranged in due order—the denunciation, the examination, Morrel's petition, Monsieur de Villefort's marginal notes. He folded up the denunciation noiselessly and put it into his pocket, read the examination, and noted that the name of Noirtier was not mentioned in it; perused too the application dated the 10th of April, 1815, in which Morrel, on the Deputy's advice, exaggerated with the best intentions (for Napoleon was then on the throne) the services Dantès had rendered to the imperial cause—services which Villefort's certificate rendered incontestable. Then he saw through it all. The petition to Napoleon, kept back by Villefort, had become under the Second Restoration a terrible weapon against him in the hands of the Procureur du Roi. On searching further he was no longer astonished to find in the register the following remarks placed in brackets against his name:

EDMOND DANTÈS {
> An inveterate Bonapartist; took an active part in the return from the Isle of Elba.
> To be kept in solitary confinement and under strict supervision.

He compared the writing of the bracketed remarks with that of the certificate placed beneath Morrel's petition and felt convinced that they were both in the same handwriting: they were both written by Villefort.

"Thanks!" said the Englishman, closing the register with much noise. "I have all I want; now it is my turn to perform my promise. Give me a simple assignment of your credit; acknowledge therein receipt of the cash, and I will hand you over the money."

He rose, gave his seat at the desk to M. de Boville, who took it without ceremony and drew up the required assignment, while the Englishman counted out the banknotes on the ledge of the filing-cabinet.

Chapter XXIV

MORREL AND SON

Anyone who had left Marseilles a few years back knowing the interior workings of the firm of Morrel and Son and returned at this period would have noted a great change. Instead of the animation, comfort, and happiness that seem to radiate from a prosperous house, instead of the merry faces seen from behind the window curtains, of the busy clerks hurrying to and fro with their pens behind their ears, instead of the yard filled with bales of goods and echoing with the shouts and laughter of the porters, he would at once have perceived a certain sadness and a gloomy listlessness. The corridor was deserted and the yard empty; of the numerous employees who formerly filled the office two only remained; the one a young man of twenty-three or twenty-four, named Emmanuel, who was in love with Morrel's daughter and had stayed with the firm in spite of his relatives' efforts to get him to resign; the other an old one-eyed cashier, called Coclès,[68] a nickname which had been given him by the young people who used to throng this buzzing hive, now almost uninhabited, and which had so completely taken the place of his real name that in all probability he would now not have answered to the latter.

Coclès had remained in M. Morrel's service, and a singular change had been effected in his position. He had been raised to the rank of cashier, and at the same time lowered to that of servant. Nevertheless, it was the same good patient Coclès, inflexible where arithmetic was concerned, the only point on which he would stand his ground against the whole world; if need be, even against M. Morrel himself.

Nothing had yet occurred to shake Coclès' belief in the firm; last month's payments had been effected with rigorous punctuality. Coclès had detected an error of seventy centimes made by M. Morrel to his own disadvantage, and the same day he had brought the money to his chief, who took it and, with a sad smile, dropped it into the almost empty drawer saying: "Thanks, Coclès, you are a pearl among cashiers."

No man could have been happier than Coclès was at hearing his master speak thus, for praise from M. Morrel, the pearl of all honest men of Marseilles, counted more with Coclès than a gift of fifty crowns.

M. Morrel had spent many a cruel hour since the end of the month. To enable him to meet his liabilities he had been obliged to gather in all his resources, and, fearing lest a rumour of his difficulties should be spread about the town of Marseilles when it was known that he had had recourse to such extremities, he had himself gone to the Fair at Beaucaire to sell some of his wife's and daughter's jewellery and some of his silverware. By means of this sacrifice the honour of the firm had been preserved, but funds were now exhausted. Following the reports that had been noised abroad, credit was no longer to be had, and M. Morrel's only hope of meeting the payment of a hundred thousand francs, due to M. Boville on the 15th of that month and the hundred thousand due on the 15th of the following month, lay in the return of the *Pharaon*. He had had news of her departure from another ship that had weighed anchor at the same time and had arrived safely in port. This was more than a fortnight ago, and yet there was still no further news of the *Pharaon*.

Such was the state of affairs when the representative of

Thomson and French of Rome called on M. Morrel. Emmanuel received him. Every fresh face was a new cause of alarm to the young man, for it suggested yet one more anxious creditor come to question the head of the firm, and he was ever desirous of sparing his employer an embarrassing interview. He now questioned the newcomer, but the stranger would have nothing to do with M. Emmanuel and wished to see M. Morrel in person. Emmanuel rose with a sigh, and, summoning Coclès, bade him conduct the stranger to M. Morrel.

Coclès walked in front and the stranger followed. On the staircase they met a pretty girl of sixteen or seventeen who looked at the stranger with an uneasy expression.

"Is Monsieur Morrel in his office, Mademoiselle Julie?" asked the cashier.

"Yes, at least I think so," answered the girl hesitatingly. "Go first and see whether my father is there, Coclès, and announce the gentleman."

"It would be useless to announce me, mademoiselle," replied the Englishman; "Monsieur Morrel does not know my name. All that this good man can say is that I am the head clerk of Messrs Thomson and French of Rome, with whom your father has business connexions."

The girl turned pale, and passed downstairs, while Coclès and the Englishman went up.

On seeing the stranger enter his office, M. Morrel closed the ledger he had before him, rose, and offered him a chair. Fourteen years had worked a great change in the worthy merchant, who, but thirty-six at the beginning of this story, was now nearing fifty. His hair had turned white, anxiety and worry had ploughed deep furrows on his brow, and the look in his eyes, once so firm and staunch, had now become vague and irresolute.

The Englishman looked at him with a feeling of curiosity mingled with interest.

"You wished to speak with me, monsieur?" said Morrel, becoming embarrassed under the stranger's steady gaze.

"Yes, monsieur. Messrs Thomson and French of Rome have to pay three or four hundred thousand francs in France during the course of the present month and the next, and, knowing your strict promptitude in regard to payments, they have collected all the bills bearing your signature and have charged me to collect the money from you as it falls due, and to make appropriate use of the money."

M. Morrel heaved a deep sigh, and passed his hand over his sweat-bedewed forehead.

"You hold bills signed by me, monsieur?" asked Morrel.

"Yes, monsieur, for a considerable sum. But first of all," he continued, taking a bundle of papers from his pocket, "I have here an assignment for two hundred thousand francs, made over to our firm by Monsieur de Boville, the Inspector of Prisons. Do you acknowledge this debt?"

"Yes, monsieur. He invested the money with me at four and a half per cent nearly five years ago, half of it being redeemable on the fifteenth of the present month, and the other half on the fifteenth of the coming month."

"Just so; then I have here thirty-two thousand five hundred francs payable at the end of the month; these are bills signed by you and assigned to our firm by the holders."

"I recognize them," said Morrel, whose face became red with shame at the thought that for the first time in his life he would in all probability not be able to honour his signature. "Is that all?"

"No, monsieur. I have these bills for the end of the month assigned to us by Pascal and Wild and Turner of Marseilles—about fifty-five thousand francs in all, making a total of two hundred and eighty-seven thousand five hundred francs."

What M. Morrel suffered during this enumeration is impossible to describe.

"Two hundred and eighty-seven thousand five hundred francs," he repeated automatically.

"Yes, monsieur," replied the Englishman. "But," he

continued after a moment's silence, "I will not conceal from you, Monsieur Morrel, that though I am fully aware of your blameless probity up to the present, public report is rife in Marseilles that you are not in a position to meet your obligations."

At this almost brutal frankness Morrel turned pale.

"Up to the present, monsieur," said he, "and it is more than twenty-four years since I took over the directorship of the firm from my father, who had himself managed it for thirty-five years—until now not one bill signed by Morrel and Son has ever been presented for payment that has not been duly honoured."

"I am fully aware of that," replied the Englishman, "but as one man of honour to another, tell me quite frankly, shall you pay these with the same exactitude?"

Morrel started and looked at this man who spoke to him with more assurance than he had hitherto shown.

"To questions put with such frankness," said he, "a straight-forward answer must be given. Yes, monsieur, I shall pay if, as I hope, my ship arrives safely, for its arrival will restore to me the credit which one stroke of ill-fortune after another has deprived me of. But should, by some ill-chance, this, my last resource, the *Pharaon*, fail me, I fear, monsieur, I shall be compelled to suspend payment."

"The *Pharaon* is your last hope, then?"

"Absolutely the last. And," he continued, "her delay is not natural. She left Calcutta on February the fifth and should have been here more than a month ago."

"What is that?" exclaimed the Englishman, listening intently. "What is the meaning of this noise?"

"Oh, heavens!" cried Morrel, turning a ghastly colour. "What fresh disaster is this?"

In truth, there was much noise on the staircase. People were running hither and thither, and now and then a cry of distress was heard. Morrel rose to open the door, but his strength failed him and he sank into his chair.

The two men sat facing each other: Morrel was trembling in every limb, while the stranger was looking at him with an expression of profound pity. The noise ceased, but, nevertheless, it was apparent that Morrel was simply awaiting events; the hubbub was not without reason and would naturally have its sequel.

The stranger thought he heard several people come up the stairs quietly and stop on the landing. A key was inserted in the lock of the first door, which creaked on its hinges. Julie entered, her cheeks bathed with tears. Supporting himself on the arm of his chair, Morrel rose unsteadily. He wanted to speak, but his voice failed him.

"Oh, Father! Father!" exclaimed the girl, clasping her hands. "Forgive your daughter for being the bearer of bad news. Father, be brave!"

Morrel turned deadly pale. "So the *Pharaon* is lost?" he asked in a choked voice.

The girl made no answer, but she nodded her head and fell into his arms.

"And the crew?"

"Saved!" said the young girl. "Saved by the Bordeaux vessel that has just entered the port."

"Thank God!" said he. "At least Thou strikest me alone!"

Scarcely had he uttered these words when Mme Morrel came in sobbing, followed by Emmanuel. Standing in the background were to be seen the stalwart forms of seven or eight half-naked sailors. The Englishman started at sight of these men; he took a step toward them, but then restrained himself and withdrew to the farthest and darkest corner of the room.

Mme Morrel seated herself in a chair and took her husband's hand in hers, whilst Julie still lay with her head on her father's shoulder. Emmanuel remained in the middle of the room like a link between the Morrel family and the sailors at the door.

"How did it happen?" asked Morrel.

"Draw nearer, Penelon," said the young man, "and relate all that happened."

An old sailor, bronzed by tropical suns, advanced, twirling the remains of a hat in his hand.

"Good day, my friend," said the shipowner, unable to refrain from smiling through his tears. "What has become of your captain?"

"The captain, monsieur, has stayed behind sick at Palma, but there is nothing serious the matter, and, God willing you will see him here in a few days as well as you or I."

"I am glad of that. Now, Penelon, say what you have to say."

Penelon rolled his quid of tobacco from his left to his right cheek, put his hand before his mouth, turned round, and shot a long jet of dark saliva into the antechamber; then he drew nearer and, with arms akimbo, said:

"Well, then, Monsieur Morrel, we were somewhere between Cape Blanc and Cape Boyador, sailing along with a good south-south-westerly breeze, after dawdling along under eight days' calm, when Captain Gaumard comes up to me—I must explain that I was at the helm—and says: 'Daddy Penelon, what do you make of those clouds rising on the horizon?'

"I was just looking at them myself. 'What do I make of them, captain? I think they are rising faster than they have any business to do, and they are too black for clouds that mean no mischief.'

" 'I think so too,' says the captain, 'and I am going to be prepared. We have too much canvas for the gale we shall have in a very short time.'

" 'A gale,' says I. 'He who bets that what we are going to have is a gale will get more than he bargained for. We are in for a downright good hurricane, or I know nothing about it.'

"You could see the wind coming just as you can see the dust at Montredon; luckily, it had someone to deal with it who had met it before.

" 'All hands take in two reefs in the topsails,' bawls the captain. 'Let go the bowlines, brace to, lower the top-gallant sails, haul out the reef-tackles on the yards!'

"Well, after being tossed about for twelve hours, we sprung a leak. 'Penelon,' says the captain to me, 'I believe we are sinking. Give me the helm and go down to the hold.'

"I gave him the helm and went down. We had already shipped three feet of water. I came up again, crying out: 'To the pumps! To the pumps!' But it was too late. We all set to work, but the faster we pumped, the more water she seemed to take.

" 'Well, since we are sinking,' says I, 'let us sink. One can die but once!'

" 'Is that the example you set, Master Penelon?' says the captain. 'Just wait a bit!'

"He went to his cabin and fetched a brace of pistols.

" 'I will blow the brains out of the first man who leaves the pumps!' he bellows out.

"There is nothing like common sense to put courage into a man," continued the sailor, "especially as by that tune the wind had abated and the sea gone down. Still the water continued to rise, not much it is true, about two inches an hour. Nevertheless it rose. Two inches an hour does not seem much, but in twelve hours that is no less than twenty-four inches, and twenty-four inches are two feet. Two feet added to the three we had before made five. When a ship has got five feet of water inside her, she is as much good as a man with the dropsy.[2]

" 'Come along now,' says the captain. 'We have had enough of this. We have done what we could to save the ship, now we must try to save ourselves. To the boats, boys, as quick as you can!'

"You see, Monsieur Morrel," continued Penelon, "we loved the *Pharaon* well enough, but, much as a sailor may love his ship, he loves his life more. We required no second telling, especially as the boat seemed to moan and call out to us: 'Get along, save your lives!' And the poor *Pharaon* told no lie, we literally felt her sink under our feet. We had the boat out in a trice, with eight of us in it.

"The captain was the last to leave the ship, or rather he

would not leave her, so I takes hold of him and throws him down to my comrades, and then I jumps down after him. We were only just in time, for I had no sooner jumped into the boat than the deck burst with a noise like the broadside of a man-of-war. Ten minutes later she pitched forward, then she pitched the other way, and finally began to spin round like a dog after its tail. Then it was good-bye to the *Pharaon*!

"As for us, we were three days without food or drink. We had already spoken about drawing lots as to which of us should serve as food for the others, when we sighted the *Gironde*. We made signals to her, she sighted us, made toward us, put out her boat, and took us on board. There now, Monsieur Morrel, that is exactly how it all happened, on my word of honour as a sailor. Speak up, you others, and say whether it is the truth."

A general murmur of assent indicated that the narrator had their votes as to the verity of the subject and the picturesqueness of the details.

"Well done, my friends," said M. Morrel; "you are good fellows. I felt sure I had nothing to blame for what has happened but my own bad luck. It is God's will and not man's doing! Let us submit to the will of God. Now, what pay is due to you?"

"Oh, don't let us speak of that, Monsieur Morrel."

"On the contrary, we must," said the shipowner with a sad smile.

"Well, then, there is three-months' pay due to us."

"Coclès, pay each of these good men two hundred francs. At another time," continued M. Morrel, "I should have added: 'Give each one an extra two hundred!' But times are hard, my friends, and the little bit of money I have left does not belong to me. Excuse me, therefore, and don't think any the worse of me for that."

Penelon was visibly and deeply moved, and, turning toward his comrades, he exchanged a few words with them.

"As far as that goes, Monsieur Morrel," said he, rolling

his quid to the other side of his mouth and shooting a second jet of saliva into the antechamber, "as far as that goes, my shipmates and I say that for the time being fifty francs is quite enough for us, and that we will wait for the rest."

"Thank you, my friends, thank you," M. Morrel exclaimed, deeply touched. "You are dear, good fellows. Take the money though, and if you find another employer, enter his service. You are free to do so. I have no more ships and therefore have no further use for sailors."

"You have no more ships?" said Penelon. "Well, then, you will build some, and we will wait. A spell of short commons³ won't hurt us, thank Heaven!"

"I have no money to build other ships, Penelon," said the shipowner with a sad smile, "so I cannot accept your offer, much as I appreciate it."

"If you have no money, you surely shall not pay us; like the *Pharaon*, we can go under bare poles."

"Enough, enough, my friends!" said Morrel, choking with emotion. "Leave me, I beg you. We will see each other again at a happier time. Emmanuel," he continued, "accompany them and see to it that my wishes are carried out."

He made a sign to Coclès, who went on in front, followed by the sailors and finally by Emmanuel.

"Now," said the shipowner to his wife and daughter, "leave me awhile, I wish to speak with this gentleman."

The two ladies looked at the stranger, whom they had entirely forgotten, and withdrew. When going out, however, the girl cast an entreating look on the Englishman, to which he responded with a smile, such as one would hardly expect to see on those stern features. The two men were left alone.

"Well, monsieur," said Morrel, sinking into his chair. "You have seen and heard all. I have nothing further to tell you."

"Yes, monsieur, I have learnt that you are the victim of fresh misfortune, as unmerited as the rest. This has only confirmed my desire to render you a service. I am one of your principal creditors, am I not?"

"In any case, you are in possession of the bills that will fall due first."

"Would you like the date of payment prolonged?"

"It would certainly save my honour and consequently my life."

"How long do you ask?"

Morrel hesitated a moment and then he said: "Three months. But do you think Messrs Thomson and French . . ."

"Do not worry about that. I will take all responsibility upon myself. Today is the fifth of June. Renew these bills up to the fifth of September, and at eleven o'clock" (at that moment the clock struck eleven) "on the fifth of September, I shall present myself."

"I shall await you, monsieur," said Morrel, "and you will be paid or else I shall be dead."

These last words were said in such a low voice that the stranger did not hear them.

The bills were renewed and the old ones destroyed so that the unfortunate shipowner was given another three months in which to gather together his last resources.

The Englishman received his thanks with the coldness peculiar to his race and bade farewell to Morrel, who, calling down blessings on him, accompanied him to the door.

On the stairs he met Julie. She pretended to be going down, but in reality she was waiting for him.

"Oh, monsieur!" she exclaimed, clasping her hands.

"Mademoiselle," said the stranger, "one day you will receive a letter signed Sindbad the Sailor. Do exactly what the letter bids you to do, no matter how extraordinary the instructions may appear. Will you promise me to do this?"

"I promise."

"Very good, then. Farewell, mademoiselle, always remain as good and virtuous as you are now, and I am sure God will reward you by giving you Emmanuel as your husband."

Julie uttered a faint exclamation and blushed like a rose, while the stranger nodded a farewell and went on his way.

In the yard he met Penelon, who had a roll of a hundred francs in each hand, and seemed as though he could not make up his mind to keep them.

"Come along with me, my friend," the Englishman said to him. "I should like to have a word with you."

Chapter XXV

THE FIFTH OF SEPTEMBER

The extension of time granted by Messrs Thomson and French's agent, at a time when Morrel least expected it, seemed to the poor shipowner like one of those returns to good fortune which announce to man that fate has at last become weary of spending her fury on him. The same day he related to his daughter, his wife, and Emmanuel all that had occurred, and a ray of hope, one might almost say of peace, once more entered their hearts.

Unfortunately, however, Morrel had other engagements than those with Thomson and French, who had shown themselves so considerate toward him, and, as he has said, one had correspondents only in business, and not friends. Any bill signed by Morrel was presented with the most scrupulous exactitude, and, thanks to the extension granted by the Englishman, each one was paid by Coclès at sight.

Coclès therefore maintained his prophetic calmness and his hope in a better future. Morrel alone realized with terror that if he had to repay 100,000 francs to de Boville on the 15th as also the 32,500 francs which would fall due on the 30th, he would be a ruined man. He spent the next three months in strenuous efforts to gather in all his outstanding resources.

Thomson and French's agent had been seen no more at Marseilles. He disappeared a couple of days after his visit to M. Morrel, and, as he had had nothing to do with anyone except the Mayor, the Inspector of Prisons, and M. Morrel, his sojourn there had left no other trace than the different memories these three people had retained of him.

August rolled by in untiring and unsuccessful attempts on the part of Morrel to renew his old credit or to open up fresh ones. Then he remembered Danglars, who was now a millionaire and could save Morrel without taking a penny from his pocket by guaranteeing a loan; but there are times when one feels a repugnance one cannot master, and Morrel had delayed as long as possible before having recourse to this. His feeling of repugnance was justified, for he returned from Paris borne down by the humiliation of a refusal. Yet he uttered no complaint and spoke no harsh word. He embraced his weeping wife and daughter, shook hands with Emmanuel, and closeted himself in his office with Coclès.

When he appeared for dinner, he was outwardly quite calm. This apparent calmness, however, alarmed his wife and daughter more than the deepest dejection would have done. Emmanuel tried to reassure them, but his eloquence failed him. He was too well acquainted with the business of the firm not to realize that a terrible catastrophe was pending for the Morrel family.

Night came. The two women watched, hoping that when Morrel left his office he would rejoin them, but they heard him pass by their door, stepping very lightly, no doubt lest they should hear and call him. They heard him go to his room and lock the door.

Mme Morrel sent her daughter to bed, and an hour later, taking off her shoes, she crept down the landing and peeped through the keyhole to see what her husband was doing. She saw a retreating figure on the landing. It was Julie, who, being anxious, had anticipated her mother.

"He is writing," she said to her mother. They understood

each other without speaking. Mme Morrel stooped down to the keyhole. Morrel was indeed writing. The terrible idea flashed across her mind that he was making his will. It made her shudder, yet she had strength enough to say nothing.

Two days passed. On the morning of the 5th of September Morrel came down, calm as usual, but the agitation of the previous days had left its mark on his pale and careworn face. He was more affectionate toward his wife and daughter than he had ever been; he gazed fondly on the poor child and embraced her again and again. When he left the room Julie made as if to accompany him; but he pushed her back gently, saying:

"Stay with your mother."

Julie tried to insist.

"I wish it!" said Morrel.

It was the first time Morrel had ever said "I wish it" to his daughter, but he said it in a tone of such paternal fondness that Julie dared not advance a step. She remained rooted to the spot, and spake never a word.

An instant later the door opened again. Julie felt two strong arms about her and a mouth pressing a kiss on her forehead. She looked up with an exclamation of joy: "Maximilian! my brother!"

At these words Mme Morrel sprang up, and, running toward her son, threw herself in his arms.

"Mother, what has happened?" said the young man, looking alternately at Mme Morrel and her daughter. "Your letter made me feel very anxious, so I hastened to you."

"Julie, go and tell your father that Maximilian has come," said Mme Morrel, making a sign to the young man.

The girl hastened to obey, but, on the first stair, she met a young man with a letter in his hand.

"Are you not Mademoiselle Julie Morrel?" he said with a very pronounced Italian accent.

"Yes, monsieur," stammered Julie. "What do you wish of me? I do not know you."

"Read this letter," said the man, handing her a note.

The girl snatched the note from his hands, opened it hastily, and read:

> Go this moment to No. 15 Allées de Meilhan, ask the porter for the key to the room on the fifth floor. Enter the room, take a red silk purse that is on the corner of the mantelshelf, and give it to your father. It is important that he should have it before eleven o'clock. You promised me blind obedience, and I now remind you of that promise.
>
> SINDBAD THE SAILOR

Julie uttered an exclamation of joy, yet even in her joy she felt a certain uneasiness. Was there nothing to fear? Was this not all a trap that had been laid for her? She hesitated and decided to ask advice, but a strange feeling urged her to apply to Emmanuel rather than to her brother or her mother. She told him all that had happened the day Thomson and French's agent came to see her father, repeated the promise she had made, and showed him the letter.

"You must go, mademoiselle," Emmanuel said, "and I shall go with you."

"Then it is your opinion, Emmanuel," said the girl with some misgiving, "that I should carry out these instructions?"

"Listen," he said. "Today is the fifth of September, and at eleven o'clock your father must pay out nearly three hundred thousand francs, whereas he does not possess fifteen thousand."

"What will happen then?"

"If your father has not found someone to come to his aid by eleven o'clock, he will be obliged by twelve o'clock to declare himself bankrupt."

"Come along then, come!" cried Julie, pulling Emmanuel after her.

In the meantime Mme Morrel had told her son everything. He knew that after his father's successive misfortunes all expenditure in the house had been rigidly cut down, but he was unaware that matters had come to such a pass. He was horror-struck.

Then he suddenly rushed out of the room and ran upstairs, expecting to find his father in the office, but he received no answer to his repeated knocks. As he was waiting at the door, however, his father came from his bedroom. He uttered a cry of surprise on seeing Maximilian; he did not know of his arrival. He stood where he was, pressing with his left hand something he was trying to conceal under his coat. Maximilian ran down the stairs quickly and threw himself round his father's neck. Suddenly he drew back, and stood there as pale as death.

"Father," said he, "why have you a brace of pistols under your coat?"

"Ah, I feared as much," murmured Morrel.

"Father! Father!" cried the young man. "In God's name, why have you got those weapons?"

"Maximilian, you are a man and a man of honour," replied Morrel, looking at his son with a fixed stare. "Come with me and I will tell you."

With a firm step Morrel went up to his office followed by Maximilian in great agitation. Morrel closed the door behind his son, then crossing the antechamber, went to his desk, placed the pistols on a corner of the table, and pointed to an open ledger. This ledger gave an exact statement of his affairs.

"Read that," said Morrel.

The young man read, and for a moment was quite overcome. Morrel did not speak. What could he have said in the face of the damning figures?

"In half an hour, then," said Maximilian in a grim voice, "our name will be dishonoured."

"Blood washes out dishonour!" said Morrel.

"You are right, Father. I understand."

Morrel was about to throw himself on his knees before his son, but Maximilian caught him in his arms and for a moment these two noble hearts beat one against the other.

"You know it is not my fault?" said Morrel.

Maximilian smiled. "I know, Father, that you are the most honourable man I have ever known!"

"Good, my son; enough is said. Now go and rejoin your mother and sister."

"Father," said the young man, kneeling down, "bless me!"

Morrel seized his son's head between his two hands and, pressing his lips to it again and again, said: "Yes, yes, I bless you in my own name and in the name of three generations of irreproachable men. See to it, my son, that our name shall not be dishonoured. Work, fight zealously and courageously; see that you, your mother, and sister expend only what is strictly necessary so that the sacred trust I leave to you of repaying my debts of honour may be speedily fulfilled. Think how glorious the day will be, how grand and solemn, when you can restore all, and when, sitting at this same desk, you will say: 'My father died because he could not do what I am doing to-day, but he died in peace and at rest because he knew he could put his faith in me.'"

"Oh, Father, Father!" cried the young man. "If only you could live!"

"I should be looked upon as a man who has broken his word and failed in his engagements. If I lived you would be ashamed of my name. When I am dead, you will raise your head and say 'I am the son of him who killed himself because, for the first time in his life, he was unable to keep his word.' Now," continued Morrel, "leave me alone and keep your mother away. Once more farewell. Go, go, I need to be alone. You will find my will in the desk in my room."

When his son had gone Morrel sank into his chair and looked up at the clock. He had only seven minutes left and the hand seemed to move round with incredible rapidity. The pistols were loaded; stretching out his hand, he seized one, murmuring his daughter's name. Putting the weapon down again, he took up his pen to write a few words. It occurred to him he might have been more affectionate in his farewell to his beloved daughter.

Then he turned to the clock again; he no longer counted by minutes, but by seconds. Taking the weapon once more, he opened his mouth with his eyes on the clock. The noise he made in cocking the pistol sent a shiver through him: a cold perspiration broke out on his forehead and he was seized by a mortal anguish.

He heard the outer door creak on its hinges. The inner door opened. The clock was about to strike eleven. Morrel did not turn round.

He put the pistol to his mouth . . . Suddenly he heard a cry . . . It was his daughter's voice. He turned round and saw Julie. The pistol dropped from his hands.

"Father!" cried the girl out of breath and overcome with joy. "You are saved! You are saved!"

She threw herself into his arms, at the same time holding out to him a red silk purse.

"Saved, my child?" said he. "What do you mean?"

"Yes, saved! See here!"

Morrel started at sight of the purse, for he had a faint recollection that it had once belonged to him. He took it in his hand. At one end it held the receipted bill for 287,500 francs, at the other a diamond as big as a nut, with these two words written on a piece of parchment attached to it:

JULIE'S DOWRY

Morrel passed his hand across his brow: he thought he must be dreaming. At the same moment the clock struck eleven.

"Explain, my child," said he. "Where did you find this purse?"

"On the corner of the mantelshelf of a miserable little room on the fifth floor of number fifteen, Allées de Meilhan."

"But this purse is not yours!"

Julie showed her father the letter she had received that morning.

Just then Emmanuel came rushing in full of excitement and joy.

"The *Pharaon*!" cried he. "The *Pharaon*!"

"What? The *Pharaon*? Are you mad, Emmanuel? You know quite well she is lost."

Then in came Maximilian. "Father, how could you say the *Pharaon* was lost? The look-out has just signalled her, and she is putting into port."

"If that is the case, my friends," said his father, "it must be a miracle. Let us go and see, but God have pity on us if it is a false report."

They all went out and on the stairs met Mme Morrel, who had not dared to go into the office. They were soon on the Cannebière, where a large crowd was gathered. All made way for Morrel, and every voice was calling out: "The *Pharaon*! The *Pharaon*!"

True enough, though wonderful to relate, there, in front of the St Jean tower, was a ship with the words "*Pharaon* (Morrel and Son, Marseilles)" in white letters on her stern; she was the exact counterpart of the other *Pharaon*, and also carried a cargo of indigo and cochineal. She was casting her anchor with all sails brailed. On the deck Captain Gaumard was issuing orders.

As Morrel and his son were embracing each other on the quay-side amid the applause of the onlookers, a man whose face was half hidden by a black beard and who had been watching the scene from behind a sentry-box, muttered to himself: "Be happy, noble heart. May you be blessed for all the good you have done and will do hereafter!" And with a smile of joy he left his hiding-place without being observed, descended the steps to the water, and called out three times: "Jacopo! Jacopo! Jacopo!"

A shallop came alongside, took him on board, and conveyed him to a beautifully rigged yacht. He jumped on deck with the nimbleness of a sailor, and from thence once more gazed on the happy scene on the quay.

"Now, farewell to kindness, humanity, gratitude," said he. "Farewell to all the sentiments which rejoice the heart. I have played the part of Providence in recompensing the good, may the god of vengeance now permit me to punish the wicked!"

Muttering these words, he made a sign, and the yacht immediately put out to sea.

Chapter XXVI

ROMAN BANDITS

Toward the beginning of the year 1838 two young men belonging to the best society of Paris were staying at Florence: one was Viscount Albert de Morcerf and the other Baron Franz d'Épinay. They had decided to spend the Carnival together at Rome, and Franz, who had lived in Italy for more than four years, was to be his friend's cicerone.[1]

As it is no small matter to spend the Carnival at Rome, especially when you have no great desire to sleep in the Piazza del Popolo or the Campo Vaccino,[2] they wrote to Signor Pastrini, the proprietor of the Hôtel de Londres, to ask him to reserve a comfortable suite for them.

On the Saturday evening before the Carnival they arrived in Rome. The suite reserved for them consisted of two small bedrooms and a sitting-room. The bedrooms overlooked the street, a fact which Pastrini commented upon as a priceless advantage. The remaining rooms on that floor were let to an immensely rich gentleman who was supposed to be either a Sicilian or a Maltese, the proprietor was not quite sure which.

"That is all very well, Pastrini," said Franz, "but we want some supper at once, and also a carriage for tomorrow and the following days."

"You shall have supper instantly, signore, but as for the carriage . . . we will do all we can to procure one for you, and that is all I can say."

"Then we shall harness the horses to mine; it is a little the worse for the journey but that doesn't matter."

"You will not find any horses," said Pastrini.

Albert looked at Franz with the expression of a man who has been given an incomprehensible answer.

"Do you understand that, Franz? No horses! Then surely we can have post horses?"

"They were hired out a month ago, and there are now none left but those absolutely necessary for the postal service."

"What do you say to that?" asked Franz.

"What I say is that when a thing surpasses my comprehension, I cease to think about it at all. Supper ready, Pastrini?"

"Yes, Excellency."

"Well, then, let us go and have it."

"But what about the carriage and horses?"

"Make your mind easy about that, my friend, they will come by themselves. It is only a question of price."

And with that admirable philosophy which believes nothing impossible to a full purse and a well-lined pocketbook, Morcerf supped, went to bed, and dreamed he was racing all over Rome in a carriage and six.

The next morning Franz was the first to wake and immediately rang the bell. The tinkling had not yet ceased when mine host appeared.

"Well, Excellency," said he triumphantly, "I was quite right not to promise you anything yesterday. You are too late; there is not a single carriage to be had in Rome, in any case not for the last three days of the Carnival."

"Well, I don't think much of your Eternal City!"

"That is to say, Excellency, there are no more carriages to be had from Sunday morning till Tuesday evening, but until Sunday you can have fifty if you wish," replied Pastrini, anxious to preserve the dignity of the capital of the Christian world in the eyes of his guests.

"Ah, that is something," said Albert. "To-day is Thursday. Who knows what good things will come our way by Sunday?"

"Ten to twelve thousand trippers to make it more difficult than ever!" was Franz's reply.

"My friend, let us enjoy the present and give no thought to the evils of the future."

"I presume we can at least have a window?" asked Franz. "Where?"

"Overlooking the Corso, naturally!"

"Impossible! Absolutely out of the question!" exclaimed Pastrini. "There was only one left on the fifth floor of the Doria Palace and that has been taken by a Russian Prince for twenty sequins a day."

The two friends looked at each other astounded.

"In that case," said Franz to Albert, "we had better go to Venice for the Carnival. Even if we don't find a carriage there, we shall be sure to find a gondola."

"No fear," cried Albert, "I have made up my mind to see the Carnival at Rome, and see it I will, even if I have to go about on stilts."

"Do Your Excellencies still wish for a carriage until Sunday?"

"What do you think?" said Albert. "Do you imagine we are going to run about the streets of Rome on foot like lawyers' clerks?"

"I will hasten to execute Your Excellencies' orders," said Pastrini. "I will do my best, and I hope you may be satisfied. At what time do you wish the carriage?"

"In an hour."

"Very well, Excellency. In an hour it shall be at the door."

When Albert and Franz descended an hour later, the carriage was there.

"Where do Your Excellencies wish to go?" asked the cicerone.

"To St Peter's, of course, and then on to the Colosseum," said Albert.

Albert did not know, however, that it takes a day to see St Peter's and a month to study it. Suddenly the two friends noticed that the day was drawing to a close. Franz took out his watch—it was half-past four.

They immediately returned to the hotel. At the door Franz ordered the coachman to be ready again at eight. He wanted to show Albert the Colosseum by moonlight, as he had seen St Peter's by daylight. They were to leave by the Porta del Popolo, follow the outer walls, and return by the Porta San Giovanni.

When they had finished their dinner the innkeeper appeared before them.

"I hear," he said, "that you have ordered the carriage for nine o'clock and that you propose visiting the Colosseum?"

"You have heard aright."

"Is it also true that you intend to start from the Porta del Popolo, then to follow the outer walls, and to return by the Porta San Giovanni?"

"Those were my very words."

"Your itinerary is impossible, or to say the least very dangerous."

"Dangerous! Why?"

"Because of the bandit, Luigi Vampa."

"Prick up your ears, Albert! Here's a bandit for you at last!"

"Well, and what has that to do with my orders to the coachman to leave by the Porta del Popolo and return by the Porta San Giovanni?"

"Simply that you may leave by the one, but I very much doubt whether you will return by the other, and because, as soon as night falls, one is not safe fifty yards from the gates."

"Here's a great adventure for us, old man," said Albert, turning to Franz. "We will fill our carriage with pistols, blunderbusses,[3] and double-barrelled guns. Instead of Luigi Vampa holding us up, we will hold him up. We will take him to Rome and present him to His Holiness the Pope, who will ask us what recompense we desire for such great service. We shall merely ask for a carriage and pair. Then we shall have a carriage for the Carnival and, what is more, the Roman people will in all probability give expression to their gratitude by crowning us in the Capitol and proclaiming us the saviours of their country."

"Your Excellency knows that it is not customary to defend oneself when attacked by bandits."

"What!" cried Albert, whose courage revolted at the idea of letting himself be robbed without making any resistance. "It is not customary, did you say?"

"No, for it would be useless. What would you do against a dozen bandits suddenly springing out at you from a ditch, a rum, or an aqueduct, with their guns levelled at your head?"

Albert poured himself out a glass of Lachryma Christi,[4] which he drank in sips, muttering unintelligibly to himself all the time.

"Well, Signor Pastrini," said Franz, "now that my companion has cooled down and you can appreciate our peaceful intentions, tell us who this Luigi Vampa is. Is he a shepherd or a nobleman? Is he young or old? Tall or short? Describe him to us, so that if by any chance we should meet him we shall recognize him."

"I knew Luigi Vampa when he was a mere boy. He was a shepherd on a farm belonging to the Count de San Felice. He is now about twenty-two years of age and is of medium height. When hardly more than a youth, he killed the captain of a gang of bandits and himself became their captain. I fell into his hands once when going from Ferentino to Alatri. Luckily for me he remembered me and not only set me free without making me pay a ransom, but also made me a present of a beautiful watch."

"What do you think of Luigi Vampa now, old man?" said Franz, turning to his friend.

"I say that he is a myth and that he has never existed."

"Do you say he still carries on his business in the outskirts of Rome?"

"Yes, and with a boldness unequalled by any before him."

"What is his procedure in regard to foreigners?"

"Oh, that is quite simple. According to the distance from the town he gives them eight, twelve, or twenty-four hours wherein to pay their ransom; after this time has elapsed, he grants an hour's grace. If he has not received the money by the sixtieth minute of that hour, he blows out his prisoner's brains with one shot, or thrusts a dagger into his heart, and the matter is ended."

"What do you think about it?" Franz asked his companion. "Are you still inclined to go to the Colosseum by the outer Boulevards?"

"Certainly, if the route is picturesque," was the reply.

Nine o'clock struck and the door opened to admit the coachman. "Excellencies," said he, "your carriage is waiting."

"To the Colosseum then!" said Franz.

"By the Porta del Popolo, Your Excellencies, or through the streets?"

"Through the streets; most certainly through the streets!" cried Franz.

"Really, my dear friend, I thought you were braver than that," said Albert, rising and lighting his third cigar.

The two young men went down the stairs and entered the carriage.

Chapter XXVII

THE APPARITION

Franz arranged the route in such a way that Albert might reach the Colosseum without passing a single ancient ruin, so that nothing should attract his eye till the Colosseum itself burst upon him in all its gigantic proportions. They therefore followed the Via Sistina, cut across in front of Santa Maria Maggiore, and drove along the Via Urbana and by San Pietro in Vincoli until they came to the Via del Colosseo.

When they arrived at the sombre-looking and gigantic Colosseum the long, pale rays of the moon were pouring through the gaping apertures in its massive walls.

The carriage stopped a few yards from the Meta Sudans. The coachman opened the door of the carriage, whereupon the two young men leapt out and found themselves face to face with a cicerone who seemed to have sprung from nowhere.

Franz had already visited the Colosseum some ten times. His companion, however, had never set foot in it before, and it must be said to his credit that, in spite of the ignorant prattle of his guide, he was deeply impressed. And, indeed, no one who has not beheld it can have any idea of the majesty of a ruin such as this, with its proportions magnified by the mysterious clearness of a Southern moon which darts forth rays that are like the phantasy of an Eastern twilight.

Scarcely had Franz, the pensive one, gone a hundred yards under the inner portals, however, when he left Albert to his guide, who would not renounce his prescriptive right to show him all around the Lions' Den, the Loggia of the Gladiators, the Podium of the Caesars. Ascending a half-dilapidated staircase, Franz seated himself in the shadow of a column facing a niche which gave him an all-embracing view of the gigantic dimensions of this majestic ruin.

He had been sitting thus for about a quarter of an hour when he seemed to hear a stone rolling down the staircase opposite the one by which he had ascended. It was no strange matter for a stone, loosened by age, to break away, but it seemed to Franz that this stone had been displaced by the pressure of a human foot, and that the sound of a muffled footstep reached his ears.

He was not mistaken; a moment later a man appeared, and from the hesitating manner in which he came up the last few steps and stopped at the top, apparently listening, it was obvious he had come for some particular purpose and was expecting to meet someone.

Instinctively Franz withdrew behind his column.

The individual whose mysterious arrival had attracted his attention stood partly in the shadow of the ruins, so that Franz was unable to distinguish his features, although the details of his dress were plainly discernible. He wore a large, dark-brown cloak, one end of which was thrown over his left shoulder in such a way as to hide the lower part of his face, while a broad-brimmed hat concealed the upper part.

He had been standing there for some minutes and began to show visible signs of impatience, when another man appeared.

"I crave your pardon for keeping you waiting, Excellency," said he with a Roman accent. "I am, however, but a few minutes late; it has just struck ten by the clock on

Saint John Lateran. I have just come from the Castle of Saint Angelo and had great difficulty in seeing Beppo."

"Who is Beppo?"

"Beppo is employed in the prison, and I pay him a small fee every year for information as to what is going on in His Holiness' Palace."

"Ha ha! I see you are a prudent man."

"Why, just so, Excellency! One never knows what may happen. One day I may be entrapped like poor Peppino and shall also be in need of a rat to gnaw the cords that keep me a prisoner."

"To come to the point, what news did you glean?"

"There will be two executions on Tuesday at two o'clock, as is customary in Rome at the commencement of all great festivals. One of the condemned men will be *mazzolato*.[1] He is a worthless wretch who has murdered the priest that brought him up and therefore deserves no pity. The other one will be *decapitato*,[2] and he, Your Excellency, is no other than poor Peppino."

"What can you expect, my dear friend? You have struck such terror into the pontifical government and the neighbouring kingdoms that they are going to make an example of him."

"But Peppino does not even belong to my gang. He is a poor shepherd whose only crime consisted in supplying us with provisions."

"Which certainly made him your accomplice. But mark the consideration that is being shown him. Instead of clubbing him to death, as they will do to you if they ever get hold of you, they content themselves with merely guillotining him."

"I am in the mood to do anything and everything to prevent the execution of this poor wretch who has got himself into trouble by doing me a service. *Per la Madonna!* I should be a coward if I did not do something for the poor fellow!"

"What do you intend doing?"

"I shall place a score of men round the scaffold and the moment they bring him out I shall give the signal, and, with daggers drawn, my men and I will throw ourselves on the guard and carry off their prisoner."

"That seems to me very risky. I veritably believe my plan is better than yours."

"What is your plan, Excellency?"

"I shall give ten thousand piastres to a friend of mine who will arrange to have Peppino's execution delayed until next year. In the course of the year I shall give another ten thousand piastres to someone else I know, by which means his escape from prison shall be effected."

"Are you sure of success?"

"I shall do more with my gold than you and your people will do with all your daggers, pistols, carbines, and blunderbusses. Leave it to me."

"Splendid! We will, however, keep ourselves in readiness in case your plan should fail."

"Certainly do so if you like, but you can count on the reprieve."

"How shall we know whether you have been successful?"

"That is easily arranged. I have hired the three last windows of the Café Ruspoli. If I obtain the reprieve, the two corner windows will be draped in yellow damask, while the centre one will be hung with white damask, having a large red cross marked upon it."

"Excellent! But who will bring the reprieve?"

"Send me one of your men disguised as a friar, and I will give it to him. His dress will give him access to the foot of the scaffold. There he can give the bull[3] to the officer in charge, who will hand it to the executioner. In the meantime, however, I would advise you to let Peppino know lest he should die of fright or go mad, which would mean that we had gone to unnecessary expenditure on his behalf."

"If you save Peppino, Excellency, you may count not only on my devotion to you but on my absolute obedience."

"Be careful what you say, my friend. I may remind you of that one day! Sh . . . I hear a noise. It is unnecessary for us to be seen together. All these guides are spies and they might recognize you, and, though I appreciate your friendship, I fear my reputation would suffer if they knew we were on such a friendly footing."

"Farewell, then, Excellency, I rely on you as you may rely on me."

With these words the last speaker disappeared down the stairs, while the other, covering himself more closely with his cloak, almost touched Franz as he descended to the arena by the outer steps.

Just then Franz heard his name echoing through the vaults. It was Albert calling him. Ten minutes later the two were rumbling along toward the hotel, and Franz was listening in a very indifferent and distracted manner to the learned dissertations Albert made, in the style of Pliny and Calpurnius,[4] on the iron-pointed nets used to prevent the ferocious beasts from springing on the spectators. He let him talk on without interruption; he wanted to be alone to think undisturbed over what had happened.

The next day Franz had several letters to write and left Albert to his own devices. Albert made the most of his time; he took his letters of introduction to their addresses, and received invitations for every evening. He also achieved the great feat of seeing all Rome in one day, and spent the evening at the opera. Moreover, by the time he reached his hotel he had solved the carriage question. When the two friends were smoking their last cigar in their sitting-room before retiring for the night, Albert suddenly said:

"I have arranged a little surprise for you. You know how impossible it is to procure a carriage. Well, I have a wonderful idea."

Franz looked at his friend as though he had no great confidence in his imagination.

"We cannot get a carriage and horses, but what about a wagon and a pair of oxen?"

Franz stared, and a smile of amused interest played about his lips.

"Yes, a wagon and a yoke of oxen. We will have the wagon decorated and we will dress ourselves up as Neapolitan harvesters, and represent a living picture after the magnificent painting by Leopold Robert."[5]

"Bravo!" exclaimed Franz. "For once you have hit upon a capital idea. Have you told anyone about it?"

"I have told our host. When I came in, I sent for him and explained to him all that I should require. He assured me that it would be quite easy to obtain everything. I wanted to have the oxen's horns decorated, but he told me it would take three days to do it, so we must do without this superfluity."

"Where is our host now?"

"Gone out in search of our things."

As he spoke, the door opened, and their landlord put his head in.

"*Permesso?*"[6] said he.

"Certainly," Franz replied.

"Well, have you found the wagon and oxen for us?" said Albert.

"I have done better than that," he replied in a very self-satisfied manner. "Your Excellencies are aware that the Count of Monte Cristo is on the same floor as yourselves. Hearing of the dilemma in which you are placed, he offers you two seats in his carriage and two seats at his window in the Palazzo Ruspoli."

Albert and Franz exchanged looks.

"But can we accept this offer from a stranger, a man we do not even know?" asked Albert.

"It seems to me," said Franz to Albert, "that if this man is as well-mannered as our host says he is, he would have conveyed his invitation to us in some other way, either in writing or—"

At this instant there was a knock at the door.

"Come in," said Franz.

A servant wearing a very smart livery made his appearance.

"From the Count of Monte Cristo to Monsieur Franz d'Épinay and the Viscount Albert de Morcerf," said he, handing two cards to the host, who gave them to the young men.

"The Count of Monte Cristo asks permission to call upon you to-morrow morning," continued the servant. "He will be honoured to know what hour is convenient to you."

"Upon my word, there is nothing to find fault with here," said Albert to Franz. "Everything is as it should be."

"Tell the Count that, on the contrary, we shall do ourselves the honour of calling upon him."

The servant withdrew.

"That is what I should call assaulting us with politeness," said Albert. "Signor Pastrini, your Count of Monte Cristo is a very gentlemanly fellow."

"You accept his offer then?"

"Of course we do," replied Albert. "Nevertheless, I must own that I regret the wagon and the harvesters, and if it were not for the window at the Palazzo Ruspoli to compensate us for our loss, I think I should revert to my first idea. What about you, Franz?"

"The window in the Palazzo Ruspoli is the deciding point with me too."

In truth, the offer of two seats in the Palazzo Ruspoli reminded Franz of the conversation he had overheard in the ruins of the Colosseum, when the man in the cloak undertook to obtain the condemned man's reprieve. Were he and the Count one and the same person? He would doubtless recognize him, and then nothing would deter him from satisfying his curiosity regarding him.

The next morning Franz woke up at eight o'clock, and, as soon as he was dressed, sent for the landlord, who presented himself with his usual obsequiousness.

"Signor Pastrini," said Franz, "is there not an execution to-day?"

"There is, Your Excellency; but if you ask me because you wish to have a window, it is too late."

"No, that is not the reason," replied Franz. "What I want to know is how many condemned men there are, their names, and the nature of their punishment."

"What a bit of good luck, Your Excellency! They have just brought me the *tavolette*."

"What are the *tavolette*?"

"They are wooden tablets put up at the corners of the streets on the evening before an execution, giving the names of the condemned men, the reason of their condemnation, and the nature of their punishment. The purpose of the notice is to invite the faithful to pray to God that He may grant the culprits sincere repentance."

"I should like to read one of the *tavolette*," said Franz.

"Nothing could be easier," said the landlord, opening the door, "I have had one put on the landing." Taking the *tavolette* from the wall, he handed it to Franz. A literal translation of the wording on the tablet is as follows:

It is hereby made known to all that the following will be executed in the Piazza del Popolo by order of the Rota Tribunal on Tuesday, the 22nd of February, the first day of Carnival: Andrea Rondolo, accused of the murder of the highly honoured and venerable priest Don Cesare Terlini, canon at the church of St. John Lateran, and Peppino, alias Rocca Priori, accused of complicity with the detestable bandit Luigi Vampa and other members of his gang.

The first-named shall be *mazzolato*, the latter shall be *decapitato*.

All charitable souls are hereby entreated to pray God to grant these two unfortunates the grace of sincere repentance.

This was exactly what Franz had heard the previous evening in the ruins of the Colosseum.

Time was passing, however; it was nine o'clock, and Franz was just going to waken Albert when, to his great astonishment, he came out of his room fully dressed.

"Well, now that we are ready, do you think we could go and pay our respects to the Count of Monte Cristo?" Franz inquired of his host.

"Certainly," was the reply. "The Count of Monte Cristo is an early riser and I feel sure he has been up these two hours."

"Then you do not think we shall be committing an act of indiscretion if we call on him now?"

"I am sure we should not."

"Then, Albert, if you are ready, let us go and thank our neighbour for his courtesy."

They had only to cross the landing; the landlord preceded them and rang the bell. A servant opened the door.

"*I signori francesi,*"[7] said the landlord.

The servant bowed and invited them to enter.

They were conducted through two rooms, more luxuriously furnished than they had thought possible in Pastrini's hotel, and were then shown into a very elegant sitting-room. A Turkey carpet covered the parquet floor, and the most comfortably upholstered settees and chairs seemed to invite one to their soft, well-sprung seats and slanting backs. Magnificent paintings intermingled with glorious war trophies decorated the walls, while rich tapestried curtains hung before the door.

"If Your Excellencies will take a seat," said the servant, "I will let the Count know you are here." And he disappeared through one of the doors.

As the door opened, the sound of a *guzla* reached the ears of the two friends but was immediately lost; the door, being closed almost as soon as it was opened, merely permitted one swell of harmony to penetrate the room.

Franz and Albert looked at one another and then at the furniture, pictures, and trophies. On closer inspection it all appeared to them even more magnificent than at first.

"Well, what do you think of it all?" Franz asked his friend.

"Upon my word, I think our neighbour must be some stockbroker who has speculated on the fall of Spanish funds; or else some prince travelling incognito."

"Hush! hush! that is what we are now going to find out, for here he comes."

As he finished speaking, the sound of a door turning on its bulges was heard, and almost immediately the tapestry was drawn aside to admit the owner of all these riches.

Albert advanced toward him, but Franz remained glued to his seat. He who entered was no other than the cloaked man of the Colosseum.

Chapter XXVIII

THE CARNIVAL AT ROME

❦

"Messieurs," said the Count of Monte Cristo as he entered, "pray accept my excuses for allowing myself to be forestalled, but I feared I might disturb you if I called on you at an early hour. Besides, you advised me you were coming, and I held myself at your disposal."

"Franz and I owe you a thousand thanks, Count," said Albert. "You have truly extricated us from a great dilemma."

"Indeed!" returned the Count, motioning the two young men to be seated on a settee, "it is only that idiot Pastrini's fault that you were not relieved of your anxiety sooner. As soon as I learnt that I could be of use to you, I eagerly seized the opportunity of paying you my respects."

The two young men bowed. Franz had not yet found anything to say; he was still undecided whether this was the same man he had seen at the Colosseum. He determined, therefore, to turn the conversation to a subject which might possibly throw light on the situation.

"You have offered us seats in your carriage, Count," said he, "as well as at your window in the Palazzo Ruspoli! Could you now tell us where we can obtain a view of the Piazza del Popolo?"

"Yes, I believe there is to be an execution in the Piazza

del Popolo, is there not?" said the Count in a casual tone.

"That is so," replied Franz, delighted to see that the Count was at last coming to the point he wished.

"Just one moment, I believe I told my steward to attend to this yesterday. Perhaps I can be of service to you in this matter also."

He put out his hand toward the bell-rope and pulled it three times. The Count's steward immediately appeared.

"Signor Bertuccio," said the Count, "have you procured a window overlooking the Piazza del Popolo, as I instructed you to do?"

"Yes, Excellency," replied the steward, "but it was very late."

"What!" said the Count frowning, "did I not tell you that I wanted one?"

"And Your Excellency has one, the one which had been let to Prince Lobanieff, but I had to pay a hundred . . ."

"That will do, that will do, Signor Bertuccio! Spare these gentlemen such domestic details. You have procured a window and that is all I want to know. Give the coachman the address and hold yourself in readiness on the staircase to conduct us thither. You may go."

The steward bowed and was about to retire when the Count said: "Ah! be good enough to ask Signor Pastrini if he has received the *tavolette* and if he will send me the program of the execution."

"It is unnecessary," said Franz, taking his notebook from his pocket, "I have seen the tablets and copied them here."

"Very well. In that case I require nothing more; you can retire. Let me know when breakfast is ready." Then turning to Albert and Franz he said: "You will, I hope, do me the honour of staying to breakfast with me."

"Nay, Count, that would really be abusing your hospitality," replied Albert.

"Not at all. On the contrary, you will give me great pleasure, and perhaps one of you, or even both, will return the compliment one day in Paris. Signor Bertuccio, have covers laid for three."

He took the notebook out of Franz's hand.

"We were saying," he continued in the same tone in which he would have read a gossipy newspaper paragraph, "that 'the following will be executed on the Piazza del Popolo by order of the Rota Tribunal on Tuesday, the twenty-second of February, the first day of the Carnival; Andrea Rondolo, accused of the murder of the highly honoured and venerable priest Don Cesare Terlini, Canon of the Church of Saint John Lateran, and Peppino, alias Rocca Priori, accused of complicity with the detestable bandit Luigi Vampa and the other members of his gang.

" 'The first-named shall be *mazzolato*, the latter shall be *decapitato*.

" 'All charitable souls are hereby entreated to pray God to grant these two unfortunates the grace of sincere repentance.' Hm! 'The first-named shall be *mazzolato*, the latter shall be *decapitato*.' Quite right," continued the Count, "this is how it was arranged first, but since yesterday, I think, some change has been made in the order of the ceremony."

"Really!" said Franz.

"Yes, I spent yesterday evening with Cardinal Rospigliosi, and there was a question of one of the two condemned men being reprieved."

"Andrea Rondolo?" asked Franz.

"No," the Count answered carelessly, "the other one" (he glanced at the notebook as if to recall the name), "Peppino, alias Rocca Priori. It will deprive you of seeing a man guillotined, but there is still the *mazzolata*, which is an extraordinary and interesting form of punishment when you see it for the first time, and even for the second time. You asked me for a seat at my window. Well, you shall have it. But let us first sit down to table, for they are just coming to inform us that breakfast is ready."

And in truth a servant opened one of the four doors saying, "*Al suo commodo.*"

They all rose and passed into the dining-room.

At the end of the breakfast Franz took out his watch.

"Well," said the Count, "what are you doing?"

"Excuse us, Count," said Franz, "but we have a thousand and one things to attend to."

"What things?"

"We have no disguises, and they cannot be dispensed with to-day."

"Do not concern yourselves about that. As far as I know, we have a private room in the Piazza del Popolo; I will have any costumes you desire sent there, and we can change into our disguises on the spot."

"After the execution?" said Franz.

"After, during, or before, just as you like."

"In front of the scaffold?"

"The scaffold is part of the festival."

"Count, upon reflection, I shall content myself with accepting a seat in your carriage and in the window of the Palazzo Ruspoli, but I leave you free to dispose of my seat in the window of the Piazza del Popolo, though I appreciate your courtesy."

"But I warn you, you will miss a very curious sight," was the Count's reply.

"You will tell me all about it," replied Franz, "and I am convinced that the recital from your lips will make almost as great an impression on me as the sight itself. More than once have I wished to witness an execution, but have never been able to make up my mind to it. I should very much like to pass through the Corso," continued he. "Would that be possible?"

"It would on foot, but not in a carriage."

"Well, then, I shall go on foot."

"Is it necessary for you to go down the Corso?"

"Yes, I want to see something."

"In that case the carriage can wait for us at the Piazza del Popolo. I shall be quite pleased to go along the Corso myself to see whether some orders I have given have executed."

"Excellency," said the servant, opening the door, "a man in the habit of a friar wishes to speak with you."

"Ah, yes, I know what he wants," said the Count. "If you will go into the salon, you will find some excellent Havana cigars on the centre table. I will rejoin you in a minute."

The two young men arose and went out by one door while the Count, after renewing his apologies, left by the other.

"Well, what do you think of the Count of Monte Cristo?" asked Franz of his friend.

"What do I think of him?" said Albert, obviously astonished that his companion should ask him such a question. "I think he is a charming man who does the honours of his table to perfection; a man who has seen much, studied much, and thought much; who, like Brutus, belongs to the school of the Stoics,[1] and who possesses most excellent cigars," he added appreciatively, sending out a whiff of smoke which rose to the ceiling in spirals.

That was Albert's opinion of the Count, and as Franz knew that he prided himself on forming an opinion of men and things only after mature reflection, he did not attempt to change his own opinion of him.

"But did you notice how attentively he looked at you?"

"At me?"

"Yes."

Albert thought for a moment.

"Ah, that is not surprising," he said with a sigh. "I have been away from Paris for nearly a year, and my clothes must have become old-fashioned. The Count probably thinks I come from the provinces; undeceive him, old man, and the first opportunity you have, tell him that this is not the case."

Franz smiled, and an instant later the Count returned.

"Here I am, messieurs," he said, "and entirely at your service. I have given the necessary orders; the carriage will go to the Piazza del Popolo, and we shall go down the Corso if you really wish to. Take some of those cigars, Monsieur de Morcerf."

"By Jove, I shall be delighted," said Albert, "for your Italian cigars are awful. When you come to Paris, I shall return all this hospitality."

"I will not refuse; I hope to go there some day and, with your permission, I shall pay you a visit. Come along, messieurs, we have no time to lose; it is half-past twelve. Let us be off."

All three went out together and, passing the Piazza di Spagna, went along the Via Frattina, which led them straight to the Fiano and Ruspoli Palaces. Franz's whole attention was directed to the windows of the Palazzo Ruspoli; he had not forgotten the signal agreed upon by the cloaked man and his mysterious companion.

"Which are your windows?" he asked the Count as naturally as he could.

"The last three," replied the Count with a carelessness which was quite unaffected, for he could not guess the reason of the question.

Franz rapidly looked up at the three windows. The side windows were draped with yellow damask and the centre one with white damask having a red cross on it. The man in the cloak had kept his word, and there was no doubt that the cloaked man and the Count were one and the same person.

By this time the Carnival had begun in real earnest. Picture the wide and beautiful Corso lined from end to end with tall palaces with their balconies tapestried and the windows draped, and at these windows and balconies three hundred thousand spectators, Romans, Italians, and strangers from every part of the world: aristocrats by birth side by side with the aristocrats by wealth and genius; charming women who, succumbing to the influence of the spectacle, bent over the balconies or leaned out of the windows showering confetti on the carriages and catching bouquets hurled up at them in return; the air thickened with sweetmeats thrown down and flowers thrown up; in the streets a gay, untiring, mad crowd in fantastic costumes:

gigantic cabbages walking about, buffalo heads bellowing on human bodies, dogs walking on their hind legs. In the midst of all this a mask is raised revealing, as in Callot's dream of the temptation of St Antony,[2] a beautiful face that one follows only to be separated from it by these troops of demons such as one meets in one's dreams; picture all this to yourself, and you have a faint idea of the Carnival at Rome.

When they had driven round for the second time, the Count stopped the carriage and asked his companions' permission to quit them, leaving his carriage at their disposal. Franz looked up; they were opposite the Palazzo Ruspoli. At the centre window, the one hung with white damask with a red cross, was a blue domino.

"Messieurs," said the Count, jumping out, "when you are tired of being actors and wish to become spectators, you know you have seats at my windows. In the meantime, my coachman, my window, and my servants are at your disposal."

Franz thanked the Count for his kind offer; Albert, however, was busy coquetting with a carriageful of Roman peasants who had taken their stand near the Count's carriage, and was throwing bouquets at them.

Unfortunately for him the line of carriages drove on, and while he went toward the Piazza del Popolo, the carriage that had attracted his attention moved on toward the Palazzo di Venezia.

In spite of Albert's hopes he could boast of no other adventure that day than that he had passed the carriage with the Roman peasants two or three times. Once, whether by accident or intentionally, his mask fell off. He took his remaining bouquets and threw them into the carriage.

One of the charming ladies whom Albert suspected to be disguised in the coquettish peasant's costume was doubtless touched by this gallantry, for, when the friends' carriage passed the next time, she threw him a bouquet of violets. Albert seized it and put it victoriously into his buttonhole, while the carriage continued its triumphant course.

"Well!" said Franz, "here is the beginning of an adventure."

"Laugh as much as you like," said Albert. "I think you are right though, anyway I shall not let this bouquet go!"

"I should think not indeed, it is a token of gratitude."

The Count of Monte Cristo had given definite orders that his carriage should be at their disposal for the remaining days of the Carnival, and they were to make use of it without fear of trespassing too much on his kindness. The young men decided to take advantage of the Count's courtesy, and the next afternoon, having replaced their costume of the previous evening, which was somewhat the worse for the numerous combats they had engaged in, by a Roman peasant's attire, they gave orders for the horses to be harnessed. With a sentimental touch, Albert slipped the bouquet of faded violets in his buttonhole. They started forth and hastened toward the Corso by the Via Vittoria.

When they were going round the Corso for the second time, a bouquet of fresh violets was thrown into their carriage from one filled with pierrettes,[3] from which it was quite clear to Albert that the *contadine*[4] of the previous evening had also changed their costumes, and that, whether by chance or whether both parties had been prompted by a similar sentiment, he was now wearing their costume and they were wearing his.

Albert put the fresh flowers into his buttonhole, but kept the faded ones in his hand, and when he again met the carriage he put it amorously to his lips, which appeared to afford great amusement, not only to the one who had thrown it but also to her gay companions.

The day was no less animated than the previous evening; it is even probable that a keen observer would have noted more noise and gaiety. Once the two friends saw the Count at his window, but when they next passed he had disappeared. Needless to say, the flirtation between Albert and the pierrette with the violets lasted the whole day.

When they returned home in the evening Franz found a letter awaiting him from the Ambassador informing him

that he would have the honour of being received by His
Holiness on the morrow. At each previous visit to Rome he
had solicited and had been granted the same honour, and,
moved by a religious feeling as much as by gratitude, he did
not wish to leave the capital of the Christian world without
paying his respectful homage at the feet of one of the suc-
cessors of St Peter, who has been such a rare example of all
virtues. There was, therefore, no question of the Carnival
for him that day; for, in spite of his simplicity and kindness,
the grandeur of the noble and holy old man whom they
called Gregory XVI was such that one was always filled with
awe and respectful emotion at the thought of kneeling
before him.

On leaving the Vatican Franz went straight to the hotel,
carefully avoiding the Corso. He had brought away with
him a treasure of pious thoughts, and he felt it would be
profanation to go near the mad gaiety of the *mascherata*⁵ for
some little time.

At ten minutes past five Albert entered overjoyed. The
pierrette had reassumed her peasant's costume, and, as she
passed his carriage, had raised her mask. She was charming
to behold.

Franz congratulated Albert, who received his congratulations with the air of a man conscious that they were merited. He had recognized, by certain unmistakable signs, that
his fair incognita belonged to the aristocracy, and had made
up his mind to write to her the next day.

Though given no details, Franz noticed that Albert had
something to ask him, but hesitated to formulate the
request. He insisted upon it, however, declaring beforehand
that he was willing to make any sacrifice for his pleasure.
Albert's reluctance to tell his friend his secret lasted just as
long as politeness demanded, and then he confessed to
Franz that he would do him a great favour by permitting
him to go in the carriage alone the next day, for he attributed to Franz's absence the extreme kindness of the fair
contadina in raising her mask.

Franz was not so selfish as to stand in Albert's way in the case of an adventure that promised to prove so agreeable to his curiosity and so flattering to his vanity. He felt assured that his friend would duly blurt out to him all that happened; and as a similar piece of good fortune had never fallen to his share during the three years that he had travelled in Italy, Franz was by no means sorry to learn what was the proper thing to do on such an occasion. He therefore promised Albert that he would be quite pleased to witness the Carnival on the morrow from the windows of the Ruspoli Palace.

The next morning he saw Albert pass and repass. He held an enormous bouquet, which he, doubtless, meant to make the bearer of his amorous epistle. This probability was changed into certainty when Franz saw the bouquet, a beautiful bunch of white camellias, in the hands of a charming pierrette dressed in rose-coloured satin.

The evening was no longer joy but ecstasy. Albert did not doubt that the fair unknown would reply in the same manner; nor was he mistaken, for the next evening saw him enter, triumphantly waving a folded paper he held by the corner.

"Well," said he, "what did I tell you?"

"She has answered you?" asked Franz.

"Read!"

Franz took the letter and read:

At seven o'clock on Tuesday evening, descend from your carriage opposite the Via dei Pontefici, and follow the Roman peasant who snatches your *moccoletto*[6] from you. When you arrive at the first step of the church of St Giacomo, be sure to fasten a knot of rose-coloured ribbons to the shoulder of your pierrot's[7] costume so that you will be recognized. Until then you will not see me. Constancy and discretion.

"Well?" asked he, when Franz had finished reading. "What do you think of that?"

"I think that the adventure is looking decidedly interesting."

"If my unknown be as amiable as she is beautiful," said Albert, "I shall stay at Rome for at least six weeks. I adore Rome and I have always had a great taste for archaeology."

"Yes, to be sure, two or three more such adventures and I do not despair of seeing you a member of the Academy!"

At length Tuesday, the last and most tumultuous day of the Carnival, arrived; the day on which the theatres open at ten o'clock in the morning and Lent begins at eight in the evening; the day when all those who, through lack of money or enthusiasm, have not taken part in the Carnival before, let themselves be drawn into the orgy and gaiety and contribute to the general noise and excitement. From two o'clock till five, Franz and Albert followed in the line of carriages, exchanging handfuls of confetti with other carriages and pedestrians, who crowded about the horses' feet and the carriage-wheels without a single accident, a single dispute, or a single fight.

Albert was triumphant in his pierrot costume with a knot of rose-coloured ribbons falling from his shoulder almost to the ground.

As the day advanced, the tumult became greater. On the pavement, in the carriages, at the windows, there was not one silent tongue, not one idle hand. It was in truth a human storm composed of a thunder of shouts and a hail of sweetmeats, flowers, eggs, oranges, and nosegays. At three o'clock the sound of rockets let off in the Piazza del Popolo and at the Palazzo di Venezia (heard but dimly amid the din and confusion) announced that the races were about to begin. Like the *moccoli*, the races are one of the episodes peculiar to the last days of Carnival. At the sound of the rockets, the carriages instantly broke the ranks and retired by the nearest by-streets.

The pedestrians ranged themselves against the walls; the trampling of horses and the clashing of steel was heard. A detachment of carabineers, fifteen abreast, galloped up the

Corso to clear it for *barberi*.[8] Almost instantly, in the midst of a tremendous and general outcry, seven or eight horses, excited by the shouts of three thousand spectators, passed by with lightning speed. Then three cannons were fired to indicate that number three had won, whereupon the carriages moved on again toward the Corso, surging down all the streets, like torrents which, pent up for a while, flow back more rapidly than ever into the parent river; and the immense stream again continued its course between its two granite banks.

A new source of noise and movement was given to the crowd when the *moccoletti* appeared on the scene. These are candles which vary in size from the pascal taper to the rushlight, and which awaken in the actors of the great scene which terminates the Carnival two opposed ideas—the first is how to keep their own *moccoletti* alight, and the second how to extinguish those of the others.

Night was rapidly approaching, and already at the cry of "Moccoletti!" repeated by the shrill voices of a thousand vendors, two or three stars began to twinkle amidst the crowd. It was a signal. At the end of ten minutes fifty thousand lights were glittering. It seemed like a dance of Jack-o'-lanterns. It is impossible to form any idea of it without having seen it. Imagine all the stars come down from the sky and mingling in a wild dance on the face of the earth, the whole accompanied by cries never heard in any other part of the world! Irrespective of class, the mad revellers blow, extinguish, relight. Had old Aeolus[9] appeared at this moment, he would have been proclaimed king of the *moccoli*, and Aquilo[10] the heir presumptive to the crown.

This flaming frolic continued for two hours; the Corso was light as day; the features of the spectators on the third and fourth storeys were visible. Every five minutes Albert took out his watch; at length it pointed to seven. The two friends were at that moment in the Via dei Pontefici. Albert sprang out of the carriage, *moccoletto* in hand. Two or three masks strove to tear it from him or extinguish it, but, being a neat boxer, Albert sent them sprawling one after the other, and continued his course toward the church of St Giacomo. The steps were crowded with curious and masked revellers striving to snatch the torches from each other's hands. Franz watched Albert's progress and saw him put his foot on the first step; a masked lady wearing the well-known peasant's costume instantly stretched out her hand and, without meeting with any resistance, snatched the *moccoletto* from him.

Franz was too far away to hear the words that passed between them, but they must have been friendly, for he saw them go away together arm in arm. He watched them for some time making their way through the crowd, but lost sight of them in the Via Macello. Suddenly the bell sounded signalling the close of Carnival, and at the same moment all the *moccoletti* were extinguished as if by magic. It was just as though one tremendous gust of wind had risen, carrying everything before it, and Franz found himself in complete darkness.

The shouts ceased just as suddenly, as though the strong wind had not only blown out the lights, but had also carried all the noise with it. No sound was heard save the rolling of carriages taking the revellers to their homes; no lights were to be seen save those at a few isolated windows. The Carnival was over.

Chapter XXIX

The Catacombs of St Sebastian

In his whole life Franz had never experienced such a sudden change of impressions, such a swift transition from jollity to sadness as at that moment. It was as though Rome had been changed by the magic breath of some demon of darkness into a vast tomb. It so chanced too that the moon was on the wane and would not rise until about eleven o'clock, which added to the intensity of the darkness. The streets the young man traversed were, therefore, plunged into blackest obscurity. He had not far to go, however, and at the end of ten minutes his carriage, or rather the Count's, stopped before the Hôtel de Londres.

Dinner was waiting, but as Albert had said he did not expect to be in so soon, Franz sat down to table without him.

At eleven o'clock Albert had not come back. Franz put on his coat and went out, telling his host that he was spending the evening at the Duke of Bracciano's.

The Duke of Bracciano's house was at that time one of the most charming in Rome; his wife, who was one of the last descendants of the Colonnas,[1] did the honours in the most perfect style, and the parties she gave attained European celebrity. Franz and Albert had brought letters of introduction to them, and the Duke's first question was as to what had become of Albert. Franz replied that he had left him when they were extinguishing the *moccoletti* and had lost sight of him in the Via Macello.

"Do you know where he went to?" asked the Duke.

"Not exactly, but I believe there was some question of a rendezvous."

"Good heavens!" cried the Duke. "It is a bad day, or rather night, to be out late. You know Rome better than he does and should not have let him go."

"I should just as easily have stopped number three of the *barberi* that won the race to-day. Besides, what could happen to him?"

"Who knows! It is a very dark night and the Tiber is very close to the Via Macello."

Franz felt a shudder run down his back when he observed that the Duke was as uneasy in his mind as he himself was.

"I left word at the hotel that I had the honour of spending the evening with you, Duke," he said, "and that they were to inform me directly he returned."

"Wait a moment; I believe one of my servants is looking for you."

The Duke was not mistaken; on observing Franz, the servant came up to him.

"Excellency," said he, "the proprietor of the Hôtel de Londres has sent to inform you that a man is waiting for you there with a letter from Viscount Morcerf."

"A letter from the Viscount!" cried Franz. "Where is the messenger?"

"He went away directly he saw me come into the ball-room to find you."

Franz took his hat and hastened away. As he neared the hotel, he saw a man standing in the middle of the road and did not doubt he was Albert's messenger. He went up to him, and said:

"Have you not brought me a letter from Viscount Morcerf?"

"What is Your Excellency's name?"

"Baron Franz d'Épinay."

"Then the letter is addressed to Your Excellency."

"Is there an answer?" asked Franz, taking the letter.

"Your friend hopes so!"

Franz went in and, as soon as his candle was lit, unfolded the paper. The letter was written in Albert's handwriting and signed by him. Franz read it twice before he could comprehend the contents, which were as follows:

DEAR FRANZ,

Directly you receive this, be good enough to take my letter of credit from my portfolio in the drawer of the writing-desk and add yours to it should it not be enough. Hasten to Torlonia's and draw out at once four thousand piastres, which give to bearer. It is urgent that this sum of money should be sent to me without delay.

I will say no more, for I count on you as you would count on me.

Yours ever,
ALBERT DE MORCERF

P. S.—I now believe in Italian bandits.

Beneath these lines the following words were written in a strange hand:

Se alle sei della mattina le quattro mile piastre non sono nelle mie mani, alle sette il conte Alberto avrà cessato di vivere.°

LUIGI VAMPA

This second signature explained all to Franz. Albert had fallen into the hands of the famous chief of *banditti* in whose existence he had for so long refused to believe.

°If the four thousand piastres are not in my hands by six in the morning Count Albert will have ceased to exist at seven o'clock.

There was no time to lose. He hastened to the desk, opened it, found the portfolio in the drawer, and in the portfolio the letter of credit: it was made out for six thousand piastres, but Albert had already spent three thousand. Franz had no letter of credit; as he lived at Florence and had come to Rome for but seven or eight days, he had only taken a hundred louis with him, and of these he had not more than fifty left.

Seven or eight hundred piastres were therefore lacking to make up the requisite sum, but in such circumstances Franz could always be sure that Messrs Torlonia would oblige him. He was about to return to the Bracciano Palace without loss of time, when a bright idea occurred to him; he would appeal to the Count of Monte Cristo.

The Count was in a small room which was surrounded by divans which Franz had not yet seen.

"Well, what good wind blows you here at this hour?" said he. "Have you come to ask me to supper? That would indeed be very kind of you."

"No, I have come to speak to you of a very serious matter. Are we alone?"

The Count went to the door and returned. "Quite alone," said he.

Franz gave him Albert's letter. "Read that," said he.

The Count read it.

"What do you say to that?" asked Franz.

"Have you the money he demands?"

"Yes, all but eight hundred piastres."

The Count went to his desk, opened a drawer filled with gold, and said:

"I hope you will not offend me by applying to anyone but me."

"You see that, on the contrary, I have come straight to you."

"Thank you. Take what you please."

"Is it absolutely necessary to send the money to Luigi Vampa?" asked the young man, looking fixedly at the Count.

"Judge for yourself. The postscript is explicit."

"I have an idea that if you took the trouble to reflect, you would find an easier way out of it," said Franz.

"How so?" returned the Count with surprise.

"I am sure that if we went together to Luigi Vampa, he would not refuse you Albert's freedom."

"What influence can I possibly have over a bandit?"

"Have you not just rendered him one of those services that are never forgotten?"

"What is that?"

"Have you not saved Peppino's life?"

"Who told you that?"

"No matter. I know it."

The Count knit his brows and remained silent a moment.

"And if I were to seek Vampa, would you accompany me?"

"If my society would not be disagreeable."

"Very well, then. It is a lovely night, and a drive in the outskirts of Rome will do us both good. Where is the man who brought this letter?"

"In the street."

"We must learn where we are going to. I will call him in."

The Count went to the window and whistled in a particular manner. The man left the cover of the wall and advanced into the centre of the street.

"*Salife!*" said the Count in the same tone in which he would have given an order to a servant. The messenger obeyed without the least hesitation, with alacrity rather, and, coming up the steps at a bound, entered the hotel; five seconds later he was at the door.

"Ah! it is you, Peppino," said the Count.

Instead of answering, Peppino threw himself on his knees and, seizing the Count's hands, covered them with kisses.

"You have not forgotten that I saved your life then!"

"No, Excellency, and I shall never forget it!" returned Peppino in a tone of profound gratitude.

"Never? That is a long time; but it is something that you believe so. Rise and answer me."

Peppino glanced anxiously at Franz.

"Oh, you may speak before His Excellency," said the Count, "he is one of my friends—permit me to give you this title," continued the Count in French, "it is necessary so as to give this man confidence."

"Good," returned Peppino, "I am ready to answer any questions Your Excellency may address to me."

"How did Viscount Albert fall into Luigi's hands?"

"Excellency, the Frenchman's carriage several times passed the one in which Teresa was driving. The Frenchman threw her a bouquet; Teresa returned the compliment; of course with the consent of the chief, who was in the carriage."

"What!" cried Franz. "Was Luigi Vampa in the carriage with the Roman peasants?"

"It was he who drove, disguised as a coachman. The Frenchman took off his mask, and Teresa, with the chief's consent, did the same. The Frenchman asked for a rendezvous; Teresa gave him one, but instead of Teresa it was Beppo on the steps of the church of San Giacomo."

"What?" exclaimed Franz. "The peasant girl who snatched his *moccoletto* from him . . . ?"

"Was a lad of fifteen," replied Peppino. "But it was no shame on your friend to have been deceived. Beppo has taken in many more."

"And Beppo led him outside the walls?" asked the Count.

"Exactly so. A carriage was waiting at the end of Via Macello. Beppo got in and invited the Frenchman to follow him, and he did not wait to be asked twice. Beppo told him he was going to take him to a villa a league from Rome; the Frenchman assured him he would follow him to the ends of the world. When they were about two hundred yards outside the gates, the Frenchman became somewhat too familiar, so Beppo put a brace of pistols to his head; the coachman pulled up and did likewise. At the same time four of the band, who were concealed on the banks of the Almo, dashed up to the carriage doors. The Frenchman tried to defend himself and indeed nearly strangled Beppo, but he was powerless against five armed men and was forced to give in. They made him get out and walk along the bank of the river, and thus brought him to Teresa and Luigi, who were waiting for him in the catacombs of Saint Sebastian."

"Well, this seems quite a likely story," said the Count, turning to Franz. "What do you say to it?"

"Why, that I should think it very funny if it had happened to anyone but Albert."

"He is in a very picturesque spot. Do you know the catacombs of Saint Sebastian?"

"I have never been there, though I have often wanted to go."

"Well, here is an opportunity ready to hand, and it would be difficult to find a better one."

The Count rang, and a footman appeared.

"Order out the carriage," he said, "and remove the pistols which are in the holsters. You need not awaken the coachman. Ali will drive."

In a very short time the noise of wheels was heard and the carriage stopped at the door. The Count took out his watch. "Half-past twelve," he said. "If we started at five o'clock, we should be in time, but the delay might cause your friend an uneasy night, so we had better go with all speed to rescue him from the hands of the brigands. Are you still resolved to accompany me?"

"More determined than ever."

"Well then, come along."

Franz and the Count went downstairs accompanied by Peppino and found the carriage at the door with Ali on the box. Franz and the Count got in, Peppino placed himself beside Ali, and they set off at a rapid pace. At the St Sebastian gate the porter raised objections, but the Count of Monte Cristo produced an authorization from the

Governor of Rome to leave or enter the city at any hour of the day or night; the portcullis[2] was therefore raised, the porter had a louis for his trouble, and they went on their way. The road which the carriage now traversed was the ancient Appian Way, with its border of tombs. By the light of the moon which was now rising, Franz imagined from time to time that he saw a sentry emerge from behind a ruin and at a sign from Peppino disappear again.

A short time before they reached the Circus of Caracalla the carriage stopped; Peppino opened the door, and the Count and Franz alighted.

"We shall be there in about ten minutes," said the Count to his companion.

Taking Peppino aside, he gave him some instructions in a low voice, and Peppino went away, taking with him a torch they had brought with them in the well of the carriage.

Five minutes elapsed, during which time Franz saw a shepherd advance along a narrow path in between the irregularities of the ground and then disappear in the tall red grass that looked like the bristling mane of some gigantic lion.

"Now, let us follow him," said the Count. They went along the same path which, after about a hundred yards, led them down a sharp incline to the bottom of a little valley. There they perceived two men talking together in a sheltered nook. One of these men was Peppino, the other was a man on sentry-duty. Franz and the Count advanced, and the bandit saluted.

"Excellency," said Peppino, addressing the Count, "have the goodness to follow me; the opening to the catacombs is but two yards from here."

"Very well," said the Count, "lead the way."

And there behind a clump of bushes in the midst of several rocks an opening presented itself which was hardly large enough for a man to pass through. Peppino was the first to creep through the crack, but had not gone many steps before the subterranean passage suddenly widened.

He stopped, lighted his torch, and looked round to ascertain whether the others were following him. Franz and the Count were still compelled to stoop, and there was only just sufficient width to allow them to walk two abreast. They had proceeded about fifty yards in this manner when the cry "Who goes there?" brought them to a standstill. At the same time, they saw the light of their torch reflected on the barrel of a carbine in the darkness beyond.

"A friend," said Peppino, and, advancing alone, he said a few words in an undertone to the sentry, who, like the first, saluted and signed to the nocturnal visitors to continue on their way.

Behind the sentry there were some twenty steps. Franz and the Count went down them and found themselves in front of the cross-roads of a burial place. Five roads diverged like the rays of a star, and the sides of the walls, hollowed out into niches in the shape of coffins, indicated that they had at last come to the catacombs. In one of these cavities, of which it was impossible to discover the size, some rays of light were visible. The Count placed his hand on Franz's shoulder and said: "Would you like to see a bandit camp at rest?"

"I should indeed," was Franz's reply.

"Come with me, then; Peppino, put out the torch!"

Peppino obeyed, and they were in complete darkness. They proceeded in silence, the Count guiding Franz as if he possessed the peculiar faculty of seeing in the dark. Three arches confronted them, the centre one forming a door. On one side these arches opened on to the corridor in which Franz and the Count were standing, and on the other into a large square room entirely surrounded by niches similar to those already mentioned. In the centre of this room were four stones, which had formerly served as an altar, as was evident from the cross which still surmounted them. A lamp, placed at the base of a pillar, lighted with a pale and flickering flame the singular scene which presented itself to the eyes of the two visitors concealed in the shadow. A man was seated reading, with his elbow on the column and his back to the arches, through which the newcomers watched him. This was the chief of the band, Luigi Vampa. Around him, grouped according to fancy, could be seen some twenty brigands lying on their mantles or with their backs against one of the stone seats which ran all around the Columbarium;[3] each one had his carbine within reach. Down below, silent, scarcely visible, and like a shadow, was a sentry, who was walking up and down before a kind of opening. When the Count thought Franz had gazed long enough on this picturesque tableau, he raised his finger to his lips to warn him to be quiet, and, ascending the three steps which led from the corridor to the Columbarium, entered the room by the centre arch, and advanced toward Vampa, who was so intent on the book before him that he did not hear the sound of his footsteps.

"Who goes there?" cried the sentry, who was on the alert and saw by the light of the lamp a growing shadow approaching his chief.

At this cry Vampa rose quickly, at the same time taking a pistol from his belt. In a moment twenty bandits were on their feet with their carbines levelled at the Count.

"Well," said he in a perfectly calm voice, and without moving a muscle, "well, my dear Vampa, it appears to me that you receive your friends with a great deal of ceremony!"

"Ground arms!" shouted the chief with a commanding sweep of one hand, whilst with the other he respectfully took off his hat. Then, turning to the singular person who was watching this scene, he said: "Excuse me, Count, but I was far from expecting the honour of a visit from you and did not recognize you."

"It seems that your memory is equally short in everything, Vampa," said the Count, "and that, not only do you forget people's faces, but also the conditions you make with them."

"What conditions have I forgotten, Count?" inquired the bandit with the air of a man who, having committed an error, is anxious to repair it.

"Was it not agreed," asked the Count, "that not only my person but that of my friends should be respected by you?"

"And how have I broken faith, Your Excellency?"

"You have this evening carried off and conveyed hither the Viscount Albert de Morcerf. Well," continued the Count, in a tone which made Franz shudder, "this young gentleman is one of my friends, this young gentleman is staying in the same hotel as myself, this young gentleman has done the Corso for a week in my carriage, and yet, I repeat to you, you have carried him off and conveyed him hither, and," added the Count, taking a letter from his pocket, "you have set a ransom on him as if he were just anybody."

"Why didn't some of you tell me all this?" inquired the brigand chief, turning toward his men, who all retreated before his look. "Why have you allowed me to fail thus in my word toward a gentleman like the Count who has all our lives in his hands? By heavens! if I thought that one of you knew that the gentleman was a friend of His Excellency's, I would blow his brains out with my own hand!"

"You see," said the Count, turning toward Franz, "I told you there was some mistake."

"Are you not alone?" asked Vampa with uneasiness.

"I am with the person to whom this letter was addressed, and to whom I desired to prove that Luigi Vampa was a man of his word. Come, Your Excellency, here is Luigi Vampa, who will himself express to you his regret at the mistake he has made."

Franz approached; the chief advanced several steps toward him.

"Your Excellency is right welcome," he said to him. "You heard what the Count just said and also my reply; let me add that I would not have had such a thing happen, not even for the four thousand piastres at which I had fixed your friend's ransom."

"But where is the Viscount?" said Franz, looking round anxiously.

"Nothing has happened to him, I hope?" asked the Count, with a frown.

"The prisoner is there," replied Vampa, pointing to the recess in front of which the bandit sentry was on guard, "and I will go myself and tell him he is free."

The chief went toward the place he had pointed out as Albert's prison, and Franz and the Count followed. Vampa drew back a bolt and pushed open a door.

By the gleam of a lamp Albert was seen wrapped up in a cloak which one of the bandits had lent him, lying in a corner of the room in profound slumber.

"Well, I never!" said the Count, smiling in his own peculiar way. "That is not so bad for a man who is to be shot at seven o'clock to-morrow morning!"

Vampa looked at Albert in admiration. "You are right, Count," he said, "this must be one of your friends."

Then, going up to Albert, he touched him on the shoulder, saying: "Will Your Excellency please to awaken?"

Albert stretched out his arms, rubbed his eyes, and said: "Ah, is that you, captain? Well, you might have let me sleep. I was having such a delightful dream. I was dancing the galop at the Duke's with the Countess G———"

Then he drew from his pocket his watch, which he had kept by him that he might see how the time sped.

"Half-past one only!" said he. "Why the devil do you . rouse me at this hour?"

"To tell you that you are free, Excellency! A gentleman to whom I can refuse nothing has come to demand your liberty."

"Come here?"

"Yes, here."

"Really, that's very kind of him!"

Albert looked round and perceived Franz.

"What! is it you, Franz, who have been so friendly . . . ?"

"No, not I, but our friend the Count of Monte Cristo."

"You, Count?" said Albert gaily, the while arranging his neck-band and cuffs. "You are really a most valuable friend, and I hope you will consider me as eternally obliged to you, in the first place for the carriage and now for this service!" And he put out his hand; the Count shuddered as he gave his own, but he gave it nevertheless.

The bandit gazed on this scene with amazement; he was evidently accustomed to see his prisoners grovel before him, yet here was one whose gay spirits never faltered, even for one moment. As for Franz, he was delighted at the way in which Albert had maintained the honour of his country, even in the presence of death.

"If you make haste, Albert," he said, "we shall still have time to finish the night at the Duke's. You can continue your interrupted galop, so that you will owe no ill-will to Signor Luigi, who has, indeed, acted like a gentleman throughout this whole affair."

"Quite right, we may reach the Palazzo by two o'clock. Signor Luigi," continued Albert, "is there any formality to fulfil before I take leave of Your Excellency?"

"None, signore," replied the bandit. "You are as free as the air."

"Well, then, a happy and merry life to you! Come, messieurs, come! Ah! excuse me! May I?" And he lighted a cigar at a torch which one of the bandits was holding. "Now, Count," he continued, "let us make all possible speed. I are most anxious to finish my evening at the Duke of Bracciano's."

They found the carriage where they had left it. The Count said a word to Ali, and the horses went off at a great speed.

It was just two o'clock by Albert's watch when the two friends entered the ball-room.

Their return made quite a stir, but, as they entered together, all uneasiness on Albert's account was instantly dispelled.

"Madame, you were kind enough to promise me a galop," said Viscount Morcerf, advancing toward the Countess. "I am rather late in claiming this gracious promise, but my friend here, whose truthful character you well know, will assure you the delay was through no fault of mine."

At this moment the music struck up for a waltz, and Albert put his arm round the Countess' waist and disappeared with her in the whirl of dancers. Franz in the meanwhile was pondering over the peculiar shudder that shook the Count of Monte Cristo's whole frame when he had been, in some sort, compelled to give his hand to Albert.

On rising the next morning, Albert's first thought was to pay a visit to the Count. He had thanked him in the evening, it is true, but it seemed to him it was not too much to thank a man twice for a service such as the Count had rendered him.

The Count of Monte Cristo attracted Franz, yet filled him with terror, and he would not let Albert go alone. They were shown into the salon, where the Count joined them five minutes later.

Albert advanced toward him, saying: "Permit me, Count, to say to you this morning what I expressed so badly yesterday evening. Never shall I forget the way in which you came to my assistance, nor the fact that I practically owe you my life."

"My dear fellow," replied the Count, smiling, "you are exaggerating your obligations toward me. You are indebted to me for a small economy of some twenty thousand francs in your travelling budget, and that is all; it is scarcely worth mentioning. On the other hand," he added, "permit me to congratulate you on your admirable coolness and indifference in the face of danger."

"Oh! tut, tut!" said Albert. "I tried to imagine I had had a quarrel resulting in a duel, and I wanted to show these bandits that though duels are fought in nearly every country of the world, it is only the French who fight with a smile on their lips. This, however, in no way lessens my obligations toward you, and I have come to ask you whether I, my friends, or my acquaintances cannot serve you in any way.

My father, the Count of Morcerf, who is of Spanish origin, holds a high position both in France and in Spain, and he and all who love me will be only too pleased to be of any service to you."

"I will own that I expected your offer, Monsieur de Morcerf," said the Count, "and I accept it wholeheartedly. I had already decided to ask you a great favour. I have never yet been to Paris. I do not know it at all. I should probably have undertaken this indispensable journey long ago, had I known someone to introduce me into Paris society. Your offer has decided me. When I go to France, my dear Monsieur de Morcerf" (the Count accompanied these words with a peculiar smile), "will you undertake to introduce me to the society of the capital, where I shall be as complete a stranger as though I came from Huron or Cochin China?"

"It would give me great pleasure to do so," replied Albert. "You can depend on me and mine to do all in our power for you."

"I accept your offer," said the Count, "for I assure you I have only been waiting for just such an opportunity to realize a hope I have had in view for some time past."

"When do you propose going?"

"When shall you be there yourself?"

"Oh, I shall be there in a fortnight or three weeks at the latest."

"Very well," said the Count, "I will give you three months, which would be allowing a wide margin." Then, examining a calendar that was hanging near the mirror, he continued: "To-day is the twenty-first of February. Will it suit you if I call on you on the twenty-first of May at half-past ten in the morning?"

"Splendid!" said Albert, "breakfast will be ready."

"Where do you live?"

"Rue du Helder, number twenty-seven."

"Very well," said the Count. He took his notebook from his pocket and wrote: "Rue du Helder, number twenty-seven, May the twenty-first at 10.30 A.M. And now," said he, replacing his notebook, "you may rely on me. The hand of your timepiece will not be more accurate than I shall be."

"Shall I see you again before I leave?" Albert asked.

"That depends upon when you leave."

"I leave at five o'clock to-morrow evening."

"In that case I must bid you farewell. I have to go to Naples on business, and shall not be back until Saturday or Sunday. What about you, Baron?" the Count asked Franz. "Are you leaving Rome too?"

"Yes, I am going to Venice. I intend staying in Italy for another year or two."

"We shall not see you in Paris, then?"

"I regret that I shall not have that pleasure."

"Well then, I wish you a safe journey, messieurs," said the Count to the two friends, shaking hands with them both.

It was the first time Franz had touched this man's hand, and he felt a shudder go through him, for his hand was as cold as a corpse.

"It is quite understood then," said Albert, "that on your honour, you will visit me at number twenty-seven, Rue du Helder, at ten-thirty on the morning of the twenty-first of May, is it not?"

"At ten-thirty on the morning of the twenty-first of May," repeated the Count.

Upon this the two young men took their leave of the Count and went to their own quarters.

"What is the matter with you?" Albert asked Franz. "You have a somewhat worried look!"

"I must own," said Franz, "that the Count is a peculiar man, and I feel very uneasy about the appointment he has made with you in Paris."

"Uneasy about our appointment! Really, my dear Franz, you must be mad!" exclaimed Albert.

"Whether I am mad or not, that's what I feel about it," said Franz.

Chapter XXX

THE GUESTS

In the house in the Rue du Helder to which Albert de Morcerf had invited the Count of Monte Cristo, great preparations were being made on the morning of the twenty-first of May to do honour to the guest.

Albert de Morcerf's house was at the corner of a large courtyard opposite another building set apart for the servants' quarters. Only two of the windows faced the street; three others overlooked the courtyard, and two at the back overlooked the garden. Between the court and the garden was the spacious and fashionable residence of the Count and Countess of Morcerf, built in the unsightly Imperial style. A high wall ran the whole length of the property facing the street, and was surmounted at intervals by vases, and divided in the middle by a large wrought-iron gate, with gilt scrollings, which served as a carriage entrance; while pedestrians passed in and out of the building through a small door next to the porter's lodge.

In the choice of a house for Albert it was easy to discern the delicate foresight of a mother, who, while not wishing to be separated from her son, realized that a young man of the Viscount's age needed entire liberty. On the other hand, the intelligent egotism of a young man enchanted with the free and easy life of an only son who had been thoroughly pampered could also be recognized.

On the morning of the appointed day the young man was sitting in a small salon on the ground floor. A valet entered. He had in one hand a bundle of newspapers, which he deposited on a table, and in the other a packet of letters, which he gave to his young master.

Albert glanced carelessly at the different missives, selected two perfumed envelopes which were written in a small, neat handwriting, opened them, and perused their contents with a certain amount of attention.

"How did these letters come?" he asked.

"The one came by post, and the other one was brought by Madame Danglars' valet."

"Inform Madame Danglars that I accept the seat she offers me in her box. Wait a moment . . . some time during the day tell Rosa that when I leave the Opera, I will sup with her as she asks. Take her six bottles of assorted wines, Cyprus, sherry, and Malaga, and a barrel of Ostend oysters; get the oysters from Borel's, and be sure to tell him they are for me."

"What time do you wish breakfast, monsieur?"

"What time is it now?"

"A quarter to ten."

"Very well, have it ready punctually by half-past. By the way, is the Countess up yet?"

"If the Viscount wishes, I will inquire."

"Do—and ask her for one of her liqueur cellarets, mine is incomplete; tell her also that I shall have the honour of calling on her at about three o'clock, and that I ask permission to introduce someone to her."

The valet left the room. Albert threw himself on the divan, opened two or three newspapers, looked at the theatre page, turned up his nose on perceiving that an opera and not a ballet was to be given, looked in vain amongst the advertisements for a toothpowder of which he had heard, and finally threw down one after the other of the three leading papers of Paris, muttering between his yawns: "Really these newspapers become more and more boring every day!"

Just then a carriage drew up at the door, and a moment later the valet announced M. Lucien Debray. A tall, fair young man with a pale face, clear grey eyes, and thin, compressed lips, wearing a blue suit with chased gold buttons, a white necktie, and tortoise-shell eyeglasses on a fine silk cord, entered the room with a semi-official air, without a smile and without saying a word.

"Good morning, Lucien! Good morning!" said Albert. "What punctuality! Did I say punctuality? Why, I expected you last, and you have arrived at five minutes to ten, whereas the time fixed was half-past ten. It is really marvellous!"

"Monsieur Beauchamp," announced the servant.

"Come in, come in! you wielder of the terrible pen!" said Albert, rising and advancing to meet the young man. "Here is Debray, who detests you and will not read your works. Anyhow, that is what he says."

"Quite right too, for I criticize his works without even knowing what he does," said Beauchamp. "Good morning." Then, turning to Albert, he asked: "What sort of people are you expecting for breakfast?"

"A gentleman and a diplomat," was the reply.

"That means waiting another two hours for the gentleman and about three hours for the diplomat."

"Nonsense, Beauchamp," said Albert, "we shall sit down to breakfast punctually at half-past ten. In the meantime, follow Debray's good example and taste my sherry and biscuits."

"Well, then, I will stay. I must do something to distract my thoughts this morning."

"Monsieur de Château-Renaud! Monsieur Maximilian Morrel!" said the valet, announcing two fresh guests.

"Now we are all here and can go in to breakfast," said Beauchamp. "If I remember rightly, you only expected two more guests."

"Morrel?" Albert murmured, surprised. "Morrel? Who is that?"

But before he had finished speaking, Monsieur de Château-Renaud, a handsome young man of thirty, and a gentleman to his fingertips, took Albert by the arm, saying:

"Allow me to introduce to you Monsieur Maximilian Morrel, Captain of Spahis, my friend, and, what is more, my saviour. Salute my hero, Viscount!"

So saying, he stepped to one side and disclosed to the view of all present the tall and noble-looking young man with the wide brow, penetrating eyes, and black moustache, whom our readers will remember having seen at Marseilles in circumstances sufficiently dramatic to prevent his being forgotten. A handsome uniform, partly French and partly Oriental, set off to perfection his broad chest decorated with the cross of the Legion of Honour, and showed up his graceful and stalwart figure. The young officer bowed with easy politeness. Being strong, he was graceful in his every movement.

"The Baron of Château-Renaud knew what pleasure it would give me, monsieur, to make your acquaintance," said Albert courteously. "You are his friend, be mine too."

"Well said!" remarked Château-Renaud, "and I hope that, given the occasion, he will do as much for you, Viscount, as he has done for me."

"What has he done for you?"

"Oh, nothing worth mentioning!" said Morrel. "My friend is exaggerating."

"What? Not worth mentioning!" said Château-Renaud. "Is life, then, not worth mentioning? Upon my word, that is rather too philosophical, my dear Morrel."

"It is evident from all this that Captain Morrel saved your life. Tell us all about it," said Beauchamp.

"Beauchamp, old fellow, you know I am dying of hunger," said Debray. "Don't begin any of your stories now."

"Well, that won't prevent us from sitting down to table,"

replied Beauchamp. "Château-Renaud can tell us the story while we are at breakfast."

"Messieurs," said Albert, "it is not yet a quarter-past ten, and you know I am expecting another guest."

"Well, then, as we cannot yet go in to breakfast," said Debray, "pour yourself out a glass of sherry as we have done, and tell us what took place."

"You all know that I had a fancy for a trip to Africa," began Château-Renaud. "Being unwilling to let such talents as mine lie dormant, I decided to try upon the Arabs some new pistols that had been given me. I therefore embarked for Oran,[1] whence I reached Constantine,[2] arriving in time to witness the raising of the siege. I retreated with the others, and withstood the rain during the day and the snow at night fairly well for forty-eight hours. On the morning of the third day, my horse died of the cold, poor beast! My horse now being dead, I was compelled to make my retreat on foot. Six Arabs rushed upon me at a gallop to cut off my head. I dropped two of them with two shots of my gun and two more with my pistol; but there were still two more, and I was disarmed. One of the Arabs caught hold of me by the hair—that is why I now wear it short, for one never knows what may happen—the other one put his yataghan[3] to my throat, and I already felt the cold point of the steel when this gentleman, whom you see here, charged down upon them, killed with a shot of his pistol the one who held me by the hair, and with his sword severed the head of the other who was making ready to cut my throat. He had set himself the task of saving a man on that particular day, and chance chose me to be that man. When I am rich, I shall have a statue of Chance made by Klagmann[4] or Marochetti."[5]

"It was the fifth of September," said Morrell, smiling, "the anniversary of the day on which my father was miraculously saved. Every year I celebrate the day as far as possible by some action——"

"The story Monsieur Morrel is alluding to is a most interesting one," continued Château-Renaud, "and he will tell it you when he knows you better. To-day let us fill our stomachs and not our memories. What time are you having breakfast, Albert?"

"At half-past ten."

"To the minute?" asked Debray, taking out his watch.

"You must give me five minutes' grace," said Morcerf, "for I am expecting a saviour too."

"Whose saviour?"

"Mine, to be sure," replied Morcerf. "Do you think I cannot be saved too, and that it is only Arabs who cut off heads? Our breakfast is a philanthropic one, and we shall have at table two benefactors of humanity, at least I hope so."

"Do you think he is likely to be punctual?" asked Debray.

"Everything is possible with him."

"Well, with the five minutes' grace, we have only ten left."

"I will profit by them to tell you something about my guest. I was at Rome last Carnival."

"We know that," said Beauchamp.

"Yes, but what you don't know is that I was carried off by bandits."

"There are no bandits!" exclaimed Debray.

"Indeed there are, and ugly fellows too, or rather I should say fine ones, for I found them frightfully handsome. To continue, the brigands carried me off to a very gloomy spot called the Catacombs of Saint Sebastian. I was told I was their prisoner subject to a ransom, a mere trifle of four thousand Roman crowns. Unfortunately I had no more than one thousand five hundred. I was at the end of my journey and my credit was exhausted, so I wrote to Franz. Oh, yes, Franz was there too; and you can ask him whether I am telling you the absolute truth or not. Well, I wrote to Franz that if he did not come with the four thousand crowns by six o'clock, I should have gone to join the blessed saints and glorious martyrs by ten minutes past. And I can assure you that Monsieur Luigi Vampa (that is the name of the chief of the bandits) would have kept most scrupulously to his word."

"But Franz did arrive with the four thousand crowns?" said Château-Renaud. "A man bearing the name of Franz d'Épinay or Albert de Morcerf is certainly not at a loss for a sum of that amount!"

"No, he simply came accompanied by the guest whom I hope to introduce to you in a few minutes. He said two words in the chief's ear, and I was free!"

"I suppose they even apologized for having kidnapped you?" said Beauchamp.

"Just so," was the reply.

"Why this man is a second Ariosto!"[6]

"No, he is nothing more nor less than the Count of Monte Cristo!"

"There is no Count of Monte Cristo!" said Debray.

"I do not think there is," added Château-Renaud with the air of a man who has got the whole of European nobility at his fingertips. "Does anyone know of a Count of Monte Cristo anywhere?"

"Perhaps he comes from the Holy Land," said Beauchamp. "One of his ancestors most likely owned Calvary just as the Mortemart owned the Dead Sea."

"Pardon me, messieurs, but I think I can help you out of the dilemma," said Maximilian. "Monte Cristo is a small island I have often heard mentioned by my father's old sailors. It is a grain of sand in the middle of the Mediterranean, an atom in the infinite."

"You are quite right," said Albert, "and the man I speak of is lord and master of this grain of sand, this atom. He has doubtless purchased his title of Count somewhere in Tuscany."

"There is no Count of Monte Cristo," exclaimed Debray. "There is half-past ten striking!"

"Confess that you have had a nightmare, and let's go in to breakfast."

The sound of the clock had hardly died away, however, when the door opened and the valet announced:

"His Excellency the Count of Monte Cristo!"

All those present started involuntarily, thus showing the impression Albert's recital had made on them. Albert himself was seized with a sudden emotion. They had not heard the carriage in the street nor any steps in the antechamber; even the door had been opened noiselessly.

The Count appeared on the threshold dressed with the utmost simplicity, yet the most exacting dandy[7] could not have found fault with his attire. He advanced smiling into the centre of the room and went straight up to Albert, who shook his hand warmly.

"Punctuality is the politeness of kings," said Monte Cristo, "at any rate according to one of our sovereigns, but in spite of their good will, travellers cannot always achieve it. I trust, however, that you will accept my good will, Count, and pardon me the two or three seconds by which I have failed in keeping our appointment. Five hundred leagues are not made without some trouble, especially in France, where it is apparently forbidden to beat the postilions."[8]

"I was just announcing your visit to some of my friends whom I have invited to do honour to the promise you were good enough to make me, and whom I now have the pleasure of introducing to you. They are the Count of Château-Renaud, who traces his nobility back to the twelve peers and whose ancestors had a seat at the Round Table; Monsieur Lucien Debray, private secretary to the Minister of the Interior; Monsieur Beauchamp, a formidable journalist and the terror of the French Government; and Monsieur Maximilian Morrel, Captain of Spahis."

On hearing this latter name the Count, who had till now bowed courteously, but almost with the proverbial coldness and formality of the English, involuntarily took a step forward, and a slight tinge of red spread over his pale cheek.

"You wear the uniform of the new conquerors, monsieur," he said. "It is a handsome uniform."

One could not have said what caused the Count's voice to vibrate so deeply or why his eye, usually so calm and limpid, now shone as though against his will.

"Have you never seen our Africans, Count?" Albert asked.

"Never!" replied the Count, who had gained complete possession over himself once more.

"Beneath this uniform beats one of the bravest and noblest hearts of the army."

"Oh, Monsieur de Morcerf!" interrupted Morrel.

"Let me speak, Captain. We have just heard tell of such an heroic action on his part," continued Albert, "that though I see him to-day for the first time, I ask his permission to introduce him to you as my friend."

At these words there was again discernible in Monte Cristo that strange fixed stare, that furtive flush, and that slight trembling of the eyelids which in him denoted emotion.

"You have a noble heart!" said he.

"Messieurs," said Albert, "breakfast is ready. Count, permit me to show you the way."

They passed into the dining-room in silence.

The Count was, it soon became apparent, a most moderate eater and drinker. Albert remarked this and expressed his fear that at the outset Parisian life might be distasteful to the traveller in the most material, but at the same time the most essential, point.

"If you knew me better," said the Count, smiling, "you would not worry about such an almost humiliating matter in regard to a traveller like myself, who has lived successively on macaroni at Naples, polenta at Madrid, olla podrida at Valencia, pilau at Constantinople, karrick in India, and swallows' nests in China. Cooking does not enter into the calculations of a cosmopolitan like myself. I eat whatever is set before me, only I eat very little. To-day, however, when you reproach me with moderation, I have a good appetite, for I have not eaten since yesterday morning."

"Not since yesterday morning?" the guests exclaimed. "You have not eaten for twenty-four hours?"

"No, I was compelled to deviate from my route to get some information at Nîmes, which made me a little late, so I would not wait for anything."

"So you ate in your carriage?" said Morcerf.

"No, I slept as I always do when I am bored and have not the courage to amuse myself, or when I am hungry and have not the desire to eat."

"Can you then command sleep at will?" asked Morrel.

"More or less. I have an infallible recipe."

"That would be an excellent thing for us Africans, who have not always enough to eat and rarely enough to drink," said Morrel.

"That may be," said Monte Cristo. "Unfortunately, however, my recipe, which is excellent for a man like myself who leads an exceptional life, would be very dangerous when administered to an army, which might not wake when it was needed."

"But do you always carry this drug about with you?" asked Beauchamp, who, being a journalist, was very incredulous.

"Always," replied Monte Cristo.

"Would you mind if I asked to see one of these precious pills?" continued Beauchamp, hoping to take him at a disadvantage.

"Not at all," replied the Count, and he took from his pocket a wonderful *bonbonnière*[9] scooped out of a single emerald and closed by means of a gold screw, which, being turned, gave passage to a small round object of a greenish colour and about the size of a pea. The pill had an acrid and penetrating odour. There were four or five of them in the emerald, which was large enough to contain a dozen.

The *bonbonnière* passed from one guest to another, but it was to examine the wonderful emerald rather than to see the pills.

"It is a magnificent emerald, and the largest I have ever seen, though my mother has some remarkable family jewels," said Château-Renaud.

"I had three like that one," returned Monte Cristo. "I gave one of them to the Grand Seigneur, who has had it mounted on his sword, and the second to His Holiness the

Pope, who has had it set in his tiara opposite one that is very similar, but not quite so magnificent, which was given to his predecessor, Pius the Seventh, by the Emperor Napoleon. I have kept the third one for myself and have had it hollowed out. This has certainly reduced its value by one-half, but has made it more adapted to the use I wished to make of it."

Everyone looked at Monte Cristo in astonishment. He spoke so simply that it was evident he either was telling the truth or was mad.

"What did the two sovereigns give you in exchange for your magnificent gift?" asked Debray.

"The Grand Seigneur gave me a woman's freedom; His Holiness the life of a man."

"Was it not Peppino you saved?" exclaimed Morcerf. "Was it not in his favour that you made use of your right to a pardon?"

"Perhaps," said Monte Cristo, smiling.

"You have no idea, Count, what pleasure it gives me to hear you talk thus," said Morcerf. "I had spoken of you to my friends as a fabulous man, a magician out of the *Arabian Nights*, a sorcerer of the Middle Ages, but Parisians are so subtle in paradoxes that they think the most incontestable truths are but flights of the imagination when such truths do not enter into their daily routine. For instance, they contest the existence of the bandits of the Roman Campagna or the Pontine Marshes. Pray tell them yourself, Count, that I was kidnapped by these bandits and that in all probability, without your generous intervention, I should to-day be awaiting the eternal resurrection in the Catacombs of Saint Sebastian instead of inviting them to breakfast in my humble little house in the Rue du Helder."

"Tut, tut! You promised me never to speak of that trifle," said Monte Cristo.

"If I relate all that I know," said Morcerf, "will you promise to tell what I do not know?"

"That is only fair," replied Monte Cristo.

"Well, then, I will relate my story, though my pride must

inevitably suffer thereby," began Albert. "For three days I thought I was the object of the attentions of a masked lady whom I took to be the descendant of Tullia or Poppaea,[10] whereas I was but being lured on by the coquetry of a *contadina*; you will note I say *contadina* to avoid using the word peasant. All I know is that, fool that I was, I mistook for this *contadina* a young bandit of fifteen or sixteen with a beardless chin and slim figure. Just as I was taking the liberty of imprinting a kiss on his chaste shoulder, he put his pistol to my throat and with the aid of seven or eight of his companions, led or rather dragged me to the depths of the Catacombs of Saint Sebastian. Here I was informed that if by six o'clock the next morning I had not produced a ransom of four thousand crowns, I should have ceased to exist by a quarter-past six. The letter is still to be seen and is in Franz's possession, signed by me, and with a postscript by Luigi Vampa. If you doubt my word, I will write to Franz, who will have the signature legalized. That is all I know. What I do not know, Count, is how you contrived to instil such great respect into the Roman bandits, who have respect for so little. I will own that both Franz and I were lost in admiration."

"I have known this famous Vampa for more than ten years," said the Count. "When he was quite young and still a shepherd, I once gave him a gold coin for showing me my way. To be under no obligation to me, he gave me a poniard carved by himself which you must have seen in my collection of arms. Later on, whether it was that he had forgotten this little exchange of presents which should have sealed our friendship, or whether it was that he did not recognize me, I know not, but he tried to kidnap me. I, however, captured him together with twelve of his men. I could have delivered him up to Roman justice, which is somewhat expeditious, but I did not do so. I set him and his men free."

"On condition that he should sin no more!" said the journalist, laughing. "It delights me to see that they have kept their word so conscientiously."

"No, Monsieur Beauchamp, on the simple condition that they should always respect me and mine. And," continued the Count, "I will appeal to these gentlemen, how could I have left my host in the hands of these terrible bandits, as you are pleased to call them? Besides, you know I had a motive in saving you. I thought you might be useful in introducing me into Parisian society when I visited France. No doubt you thought this but a vague plan on my part, but to-day you see you are faced with the stern reality and must submit to it under pain of breaking your word."

"And I shall keep my word," said Morcerf, "but I fear you will be greatly disillusioned, accustomed as you are to mountains, picturesque surroundings, and fantastic horizons, whereas France is such a prosaic country and Paris such a civilized city. There is but one service I can render you, my dear Count, and in regard to that, I place myself entirely at your disposal. I can introduce you myself or get my friends to introduce you everywhere. You have really no need of anyone though. With your name, your fortune, and your talented mind"—Monte Cristo bowed with a somewhat ironical smile—"you can present yourself everywhere and will be well received. I can, therefore, only serve you in one way. If my knowledge of Parisian customs, of what is comfortable, and if our shops can be of any use to you, I can assist you in finding a suitable establishment. I will not offer to share my apartments with you, as I shared yours at Rome, for, except for myself, you would not see a shadow here, unless it were the shadow of a woman."

"Ah, the reservation of a family man! May I congratulate you on your coming happiness?"

"It is nothing more than a project, Count."

"And he who says project means accomplishment," retorted Debray.

"Not at all!" said Morcerf. "My father is anxious it should be so, and I hope soon to introduce to you, if not my wife, at least my future wife, Mademoiselle Eugénie Danglars."

"Eugénie Danglars!" exclaimed Monte Cristo. "One moment . . . Is not her father Baron Danglars?"

"Yes, a newly created Baron."

"What does that matter so long as he has rendered a service to the State which merits such a distinction?" was Monte Cristo's reply.

"He has rendered the State very signal services," said Beauchamp. "Though a Liberal in opinions, in eighteen-twenty-nine he effected a loan of six millions for King Charles the Tenth, who made him a Baron and Commander of the Legion of Honour. Now he wears the ribbon, not in his waistcoat pocket as one would imagine, but in full view in the buttonhole of his coat."

"Oh, Beauchamp, Beauchamp," said Morcerf, smiling. "Keep that for the *Corsaire* and the *Charivari*, but spare my future father-in-law in my presence." Then, turning to Monte Cristo, he said: "You mentioned the Baron's name just now as though you knew him?"

"I do not know him," said Monte Cristo, carelessly, "but in all probability I shall not be long in making his acquaintance, since I have a credit opened with him through Richard and Blount of London, Arstein and Eskeles of Vienna, and Thomson and French of Rome."

As he pronounced these last two names, Monte Cristo stole a glance at Maximilian Morrel, and if he expected to startle him, he was not disappointed. The young man started as though he had had an electric shock.

"Thomson and French?" said he. "Do you know that firm?"

"They are my bankers in Rome," said the Count calmly. "Can I exert my influence with them on your behalf?"

"You might, perhaps, be able to help us in inquiries which have up to the present been ineffective. Some years back, these bankers rendered a great service to our firm, and for some reason have always denied having done so."

"I am at your orders," replied Monte Cristo.

"But in speaking of Monsieur Danglars, we have altogether strayed from the subject of our conversation," said Maximilian. "We were talking about a suitable house for the Count of Monte Cristo. I should like to offer him a suite in a charming little house in the Pompadour style which my sister has taken in the Rue Meslay."

"You have a sister?" asked Monte Cristo.

"Yes, and an excellent one."

"Married?"

"For the past nine years."

"Happy?"

"As happy as it is permitted to a human creature to be," replied Maximilian. "She is married to a man she loves, who remained faithful to us in our bad fortune, Emmanuel Herbault. I live with them when I am on furlough," continued Maximilian, "and my brother-in-law, Emmanuel, and I will be only too pleased to place ourselves at your disposal, Count."

"Thank you, Monsieur Morrel, thank you very much. I shall be most happy if you will introduce me to your brother-in-law and your sister, but I cannot accept your kind offer of a suite in your sister's house as my accommodation is already provided for."

"What? Are you going to put up at an hotel?" exclaimed Morcerf. "You will not be very comfortable."

"I have decided to have my own house at Paris. I sent my valet on in advance, and he will have bought a house and furnished it ere this. He arrived here a week ago, and will have scoured the town with the instinct a sporting dog alone possesses. He knows all my whims, my likes, and my needs, and will have arranged everything to my liking. He knew I was to arrive at ten o'clock this morning, and was waiting for me at the Barrière de Fontainebleau from nine o'clock, and gave me this piece of paper. It is my new address. Read it for yourself."

So saying, Monte Cristo passed Albert a piece of paper.

"Number thirty, Champs Élysées," read Morcerf.

The young men stared at one another. They did not

know whether Monte Cristo was joking; there was such an air of simplicity about every word he uttered in spite of its originality that it was impossible to believe he was not speaking the truth. Besides, why should he lie?

"We must content ourselves with doing the Count any little service within our power," said Beauchamp. "In my capacity of journalist, I will give him access to all the theatres of Paris."

"Thank you, monsieur," said the Count, smiling, "I have already instructed my steward to take a box for me at every theatre. You know my steward, Monsieur de Morcerf?"

"Is it by any chance that worthy Signor Bertuccio, who understands the hiring of windows so well?"

"The very same; you saw him the day you honoured me by breakfasting with me. He is a very good man and has been a soldier and a smuggler, and in fact has tried his hand at everything possible. I would not even say that he has not been mixed up with the police for some trifling stabbing affair."

"Then you have your household complete," said Château-Renaud, "you have a house in the Champs Élysées, servants, and stewards. All you want now is a mistress."

"I have something better than that. I have a slave. You take your mistresses from the Opera House, the Vaudeville, the Music Halls, but I bought mine at Constantinople. She cost me dear, but I have nothing to fear so far as she is concerned."

"But you forget that we are 'Franks by name and frank by nature'? as King Charles said, and that the moment she steps on French soil your slave becomes free," said Debray.

"Who will tell her that?" asked Monte Cristo.

"Why, the first person who sees her."

"She speaks nothing but Romaic."

"That is a different matter, but shall we not at least see her? Or have you eunuchs as well as mutes?"

"Oh, dear no," said Monte Cristo. "I do not carry Orientalism so far as that. Everybody around me is at liberty to leave me, and on leaving me will have no further need of me or anyone else. It may be that is the reason why they do not leave me."

They had long since passed to dessert and cigars.

"My dear Albert, it is half-past twelve," said Debray, rising. "Your guest is charming, but you know the best of friends must part. I must return to my office. Are you coming, Morrel?"

"As soon as I have handed the Count my card. He has promised to pay us a visit at fourteen Rue Meslay."

"Rest assured that I shall not forget," said the Count with a bow.

Maximilian Morrel left with the Baron of Château-Renaud, leaving Monte Cristo alone with Morcerf.

Chapter XXXI

THE PRESENTATION

When Albert was alone with Monte Cristo, he said: "Permit me to commence my office of cicerone by showing you my bachelor quarters. Accustomed as you are to the palaces of Italy, it will be interesting for you to note in what a small space a young man of Paris can live, and not feel that he is too badly off in regard to accommodation."

Albert conducted the Count to his study, which was his favourite room.

Monte Cristo was a worthy appreciator of all things Albert had collected here: old cabinets, Japanese porcelain, Oriental stuffs, Venetian glass, weapons of all countries of the world; everything was familiar to him, and he recognized at a glance their date and country of origin. Morcerf had expected to be the guide, whereas it was he who, under the Count's guidance, followed a course of archaeology, mineralogy, and natural history. He led his guest into the salon, which was filled with works of modern artists; there were landscapes by Dupré, Arabian horsemen by Delacroix, water colours by Boulanger, paintings by Diaz, drawings by Decamps—in a word, all that modern art can give in exchange and as recompense for the art lost and gone with ages long since past.

Albert expected to have something new to show the traveller this time at least, but, to his surprise, without looking for the signatures, many of which were only initials, the Count at once named the author of every picture in such a manner that it was easy to see that each man was not only known to him, but that each style had been appreciated and studied.

From the salon they passed into the bed-chamber. It was a model of good taste and simple elegance. One portrait only, signed Leopold Robert, loomed forth from an unpolished gilt frame.

It was this portrait that first of all attracted the Count's attention, for he took three rapid steps across the room and suddenly stopped in front of it. It was the portrait of a young woman of about five- or six-and-twenty, with a dark complexion, eyes which glowed beneath languishing eyelids. She wore the picturesque costume of a Catalan fisherwoman, a red and black bodice, and had golden pins stuck in her hair. She was looking at the sea, and her beautiful profile was outlined against the two-fold azure of sky and ocean.

"This is a beautiful woman you have here, Viscount," said Monte Cristo in a perfectly calm voice, "and her dress, doubtless a ball dress, suits her charmingly."

"That," said Albert, "is my mother's portrait. She had it painted six or eight years ago, during the Count's absence. Doubtless she thought to give him a pleasant surprise upon his return, but, strange to say, he did not like the portrait, and could never get over his antipathy to it. Between ourselves, I must tell you that Monsieur de Morcerf is one of the most hard working peers at the Luxembourg, and as a general is renowned for theory, but is an indifferent connoisseur of works of art. It is not so with my mother, who paints remarkably well, and who, esteeming such a work too good to part with altogether, gave it to me to hang up in my room, where it would be less exposed to Monsieur de Morcerf's displeasure. Forgive my talking so much on fam-

ily matters, but as I shall have the honour of introducing you
to the Count, I tell you this lest you should praise this portrait before him. The portrait seems to have a malign influence, for my mother rarely comes to the room without looking at it, and still more rarely does she look at it without
weeping. The appearance of this portrait in the house is,
however, the only contention between my mother and
father, who are still as united to-day, after more than twenty
years of married life, as they were on their wedding day.
And now that you have seen all my treasures, will you
accompany me to Monsieur de Morcerf, to whom I wrote
from Rome giving an account of the service you rendered
me and announcing your visit? I may say that both the
Count and the Countess are anxious to tender you their
thanks. Look upon this visit as an initiation into Paris life, a
life of formalities, visits, and introductions."

Monte Cristo bowed without replying. He accepted the
proposal without enthusiasm and without regret as one of
those society conventions which every gentleman looks
upon as a duty. Albert called his valet and ordered him to
announce to M. and Mme de Morcerf the arrival of the
Count of Monte Cristo. On entering the salon they found
themselves face to face with Monsieur de Morcerf himself.

He was a man of forty to forty-five years of age, but he
appeared at least fifty, and his black moustache and eyebrows contrasted strangely with his almost white hair which
was cut short in the military fashion. He was dressed in
civilian clothes and wore in his buttonhole the ribbons indicating the different orders to which he belonged.

"Father," said the young man, "I have the honour to
introduce to you the Count of Monte Cristo, the generous
friend I had the good fortune to meet in the difficult circumstances with which you are acquainted."

"You are welcome amongst us," said the Count of
Morcerf with a smile. "In preserving the life of our only
heir, you have rendered our house a service which solicits
our eternal gratitude."

So saying, the Count of Morcerf gave Monte Cristo an armchair, while he seated himself opposite the window.

In taking the chair indicated to him, Monte Cristo arranged himself in such a manner as to be hidden in the shadow of the large velvet curtains whence he could read on the careworn features of the Count a whole history of secret griefs in each one of the wrinkles time had imprinted there.

"The Countess was at her toilet when your visit was announced," said Morcerf, "she will join us here in ten minutes or so."

"It is a great honour for me," said Monte Cristo, "that on the very day of my arrival at Paris I should be brought into contact with a man whose merits equal his reputation, and on whom Dame Fortune, acting with equity for once, has never ceased to smile. But has she not on the Mitidja Plains[1] or the Atlas Mountains[2] still the baton of a marshal to offer you?"

"I have left the service, monsieur," said Morcerf, turning somewhat red. "Created a peer at the Restoration, I served during the first campaign under Maréchal de Bourmont; I was therefore entitled to a higher rank, and who knows what would have happened had the elder branch remained on the throne! But the July revolution was apparently glorious enough to permit of ingratitude; and it was, indeed, inappreciative of any service that did not date from the imperial period. I, therefore, tendered my resignation. I have hung up my sword and have flung myself into politics. I devote myself to industry and study the useful arts. I was anxious to do so during the twenty years I was in the army, but had not the time."

"Such are the ideas that render your nation superior to all others," replied Monte Cristo. "A gentleman of high birth, in possession of a large fortune, you were content to gain your promotion as an obscure soldier. Then after becoming a general, a peer of France, a commander of the Legion of Honour, you are willing to go through another apprenticeship with no other prospects, no other reward than that one day you will serve your fellow-creatures. Really, Count, this is most praiseworthy; it is even more than that, it is sublime."

"If I were not afraid of wearying you, Count," continued the General, obviously charmed with Monte Cristo's manners, "I would have taken you to the Chamber with me; to-day's debate will be very interesting to such as do not know our modern senators."

"I should be most grateful to you, Count, if you would renew this invitation another time. I have been flattered with the hope of an introduction to the Countess to-day, and I will wait for her."

"Ah, here is my mother!" exclaimed Albert.

And in truth, as Monte Cristo turned round, he saw Mme de Morcerf, pale and motionless, on the threshold of the door. As Monte Cristo turned toward her, she let fall her arm which, for some reason, she had been resting against the gilt door-post. She had been standing there for some seconds, and had overheard the last words of the conversation.

Monte Cristo rose and bowed low to the Countess, who curtsied ceremoniously without saying a word.

"Whatever ails you, madam?" said the Count. "Perhaps the heat of this room is too much for you?"

"Are you ill, Mother?" exclaimed the Viscount, rushing toward Mercédès.

She thanked them both with a smile. "No," said she. "It has upset me a little to see for the first time him without whose intervention we should now be in tears and mourning. Monsieur, it is to you that I owe my son's life," she continued, advancing with queenly majesty, "and I bless you for this kindness. I am also grateful to you for giving me the opportunity of thanking you as I have blessed you, that is from the bottom of my heart."

"Madame, the Count and yourself reward me too generously for a very simple action. To save a man and thereby to spare a father's agony and a mother's feelings is not to do a noble deed, it is but an act of humanity."

These words were uttered with the most exquisite softness and politeness.

"It is very fortunate for my son, Count, that he has found such a friend," replied Madame de Morcerf, "and I thank God that it is so." And Mercédès raised her beautiful eyes to Heaven with an expression of such infinite gratitude that the Count fancied he saw two tears trembling in them.

M. de Morcerf went up to her. "Madame, I have already made my excuses to the Count," said he. "The session opened at two o'clock; it is now three, and I have to speak."

"Go along, then, I will try to make up to the Count for your absence," said the Countess in the same tone of deep feeling. "Will you do us the honour, Count, of spending the rest of the day with us?" she continued, turning to Monte Cristo.

"Believe me, Countess, no one could appreciate your kind offer more than I do, but I stepped out of my travelling-carriage at your door this morning and know not yet where or how my residence is provided for. I know it is but a slight cause for uneasiness, yet it is quite appreciable."

"Then we shall have this pleasure another time. Promise us that at least."

Monte Cristo bowed without replying, but his gesture might well have been taken for assent.

"Then I will not detain you longer," said the Countess. "I would not have my gratitude become indiscreet or importunate."

Monte Cristo bowed once more and took his leave. A carriage was waiting for him at the door.

The illustrious traveller sprang into it, the door was closed behind him, and the horses went off at a gallop, yet not so quickly that the Count did not notice an almost imperceptible movement which fluttered the curtain in the salon where he had just left Madame de Morcerf.

When Albert returned to his mother he found her reclining in a deep velvet armchair in her boudoir.

"What is this name Monte Cristo?" asked the Countess when the servant had gone out. "Is it a family name, the name of an estate, or simply a title?"

"I think it is nothing more than a title. The Count has bought an island in the Tuscan Archipelago. Otherwise he lays no claim to nobility and calls himself a 'Count of Chance,' though the general opinion in Rome is that he is a very great lord."

"He has excellent manners," said the Countess, "at least so far as I could judge during the few moments he was here."

The Countess was pensive for a moment, then after a short pause, she said: "I am addressing a question to you, Albert, as your mother. You have seen Monsieur de Monte Cristo at home. You are perspicacious,[3] know the ways of the world, and are more tactful than most men of your age. Do you think the Count is really what he appears to be?"

"And what is that?"

"You said it yourself a minute ago, a great lord."

"I told you, Mother, that he was considered as such."

"But what do you think of him yourself, Albert?"

"I must own, I do not quite know what to make of him; I believe he is a Maltese."

"I am not questioning you about his origin but about himself."

"Ah! that is a totally different matter. I have seen so many strange traits in him that if you wish me to say what I think, I must say that I consider him as a man whom misfortune has branded; a derelict, as it were, of some old family, who, disinherited of his patrimony, has found one by dint of his own venturesome genius which places him above the rules of society. Monte Cristo is an island in the middle of the Mediterranean, without inhabitants or garrison, the resort of smugglers of every nationality and of pirates from every country. Who knows whether these worthy industrialists do not pay their lord for his protection?"

"Possibly," said the Countess, deep in thought.

"What does it matter," replied the young man, "whether he be a smuggler or not? Now that you have seen him, Mother, you must agree that the Count of Monte Cristo is a remarkable man who will create quite a sensation in Paris."

"Has this man any friendship for you, Albert?" she asked with a nervous shudder.

"I believe so, Mother."

"And you . . . are you fond of him?"

"I like him in spite of Franz d'Épinay, who always tries to convince me that he is a being returned from the other world."

There was a strange terror in the Countess' voice as she said:

"Albert, I have always put you on your guard against new acquaintances. Now you are a man and capable of giving me advice. Nevertheless, I repeat to you: be prudent, Albert."

"Yet, if this advice is to be profitable, Mother, I must know in advance what I am to guard against. The Count does not gamble, he drinks nothing but water coloured with a little Spanish wine; he is said to be so rich that, without making himself a laughing-stock, he could not borrow money from me. What, then, have I to fear from him?"

"You are right," said the Countess, "my fears are stupid; especially when directed against a man who has saved your life. By the way, did your father receive him nicely, Albert? It is important that we should not receive him like a mere stranger. Your father is sometimes preoccupied, his business worries him, and it may be that unintentionally . . ."

"My father was perfect, Mother," Albert broke in, "what is more, he seemed greatly flattered by two or three clever and appropriate compliments the Count paid him with such ease that he might have known him for thirty years. They parted the best of friends."

The Countess did not answer. She was so deeply absorbed in her own thoughts that her eyes gradually closed. The young man stood before her, looking down on her with filial affection, which is more tender and loving in children whose mother is still young and beautiful; then, seeing her close her eyes, he listened for a moment to her peaceful breathing and tiptoed out of the room.

Chapter XXXII

UNLIMITED CREDIT

The next day, toward two o'clock in the afternoon, a carriage drawn by two magnificent English horses drew up before Monte Cristo's door. In it sat a man dressed in a blue coat with silk buttons of the same colour, a white waistcoat over which passed a heavy gold chain, and brown trousers; his hair was jet black, and descended so far over his forehead that it hardly looked natural, for it formed too great a contrast with the deep furrows left uncovered. In short, he was a man of some fifty to fifty-five years of age who tried to appear forty. He put his head through the door of the carriage, on which a coronet was painted, and sent the groom to ask whether the Count of Monte Cristo was at home.

The groom tapped at the porter's window and asked: "Does the Count of Monte Cristo live here?"

"His Excellency does live here, but he is engaged," replied the porter.

"In that case, here is the card of my master, Baron Danglars. Hand it to the Count of Monte Cristo and tell him that my master stopped on his way to the Chamber in order to have the honour of seeing the Count."

"I never speak to His Excellency," replied the porter. "The valet will deliver the message."

The groom returned to the carriage, and, somewhat crestfallen at the rebuke he had just received, gave his master the porter's answer.

"Oh, the man whom they call Excellency is a prince then, to whom only the valet has the right to speak. Never mind! Since he has a credit on my bank, I shall see him when he wants money."

Then throwing himself back in his carriage, he called out to his coachman in a voice that could be heard at the other side of the street:

"To the Chamber of Deputies!"

The Count had been informed of this visit, and had had time to examine the Baron from behind a window-blind.

"He's decidedly an ugly brute," he said with a gesture of disgust. "At the very first sight of the man anyone can recognize in him the snake by his flat forehead, the vulture by his protruding cranium, and the buzzard by his sharp beak!

"Ali!" he cried, striking once on the copper gong. Ali appeared. "Call Bertuccio!" said he. Bertuccio instantly made his appearance.

"Your Excellency sent for me?" said the steward.

"Yes!" said the Count. "Did you see the horses that just now drew up before my door?"

"Certainly, Excellency, and very beautiful they were too."

"How comes it," said Monte Cristo, frowning, "that when I instructed you to obtain for me the best horses to be had in Paris there are in the town two other horses outside my stables as good as mine?"

"The horses you mention were not for sale, Count," said Bertuccio.

Monte Cristo shrugged his shoulders.

"Do you not know, steward, that everything is for sale to him who cares to pay the price?"

"Monsieur Danglars paid sixteen thousand francs for them, Count!"

"Well, then offer him thirty-two thousand; he is a banker,

and a banker never loses the opportunity of doubling his capital."

"Do you mean that seriously?" asked Bertuccio.

Monte Cristo looked at the steward as one astonished that he should dare to ask such a question.

"I have a call to make this evening," said he. "I wish to have these horses harnessed to my carriage."

Bertuccio retired bowing. He stopped near the door and said: "At what time does Your Excellency propose paying this call?"

"At five o'clock," replied the Count.

"May I point out to Your Excellency that it is now two o'clock," the steward ventured to remark.

"I know," was Monte Cristo's sole reply.

At five o'clock the Count sounded his gong three times. One stroke summoned Ali, two Baptistin, and three strokes Bertuccio. The steward entered.

"My horses!" said the Count.

"They've been put in, Excellency," was Bertuccio's reply.

The Count went down and saw the much-coveted horses of Danglars harnessed to his own carriage.

"They are really beautiful," he said. "You did well to buy them, though you were late in doing so."

"Excellency, I had considerable difficulty in getting them," said Bertuccio. "They have cost a great deal of money."

"Are the horses less beautiful for that?" asked the Count, shrugging his shoulders.

"If Your Excellency is satisfied, all is well," said Bertuccio. "Where is Your Excellency going?"

"To Baron Danglars', Rue de la Chaussée d'Antin."

Arrived at the Baron's residence the Count was ushered into that nobleman's presence.

"Have I the honour of addressing Monsieur de Monte Cristo?"

"And I of addressing Baron Danglars, Chevalier of the Legion of Honour and member of the Chamber of Deputies?" said the Count.

Monte Cristo repeated all the titles he had read on the Baron's card.

Danglars felt the thrust and bit his lips.

"I have received a letter of advice from Messrs Thomson and French," he said.

"I am delighted to hear it, Baron; I am delighted. It will not be necessary to introduce myself, which is always embarrassing. You say you have received a letter of advice?"

"Yes, but I must confess I do not quite understand its meaning," said Danglars. "This letter . . . I have it with me I think . . ." He searched in his pocket. "Yes, here it is. This letter opened credit on my bank to the Count of Monte Cristo for an unlimited sum."

"Well, Baron, what is there incomprehensible in that?"

"Nothing, monsieur, but the word unlimited."

"And is that word unknown in France?"

"Oh, no, monsieur, it is quite all right in regard to syntax, but not quite so from a banker's point of view."

"Is the banking firm of Thomson and French not sound, do you think, Baron?" asked Monte Cristo as naïvely as possible. "That would be a nice thing, to be sure. I have some property deposited with them."

"Oh, they are perfectly sound," replied Danglars with an almost mocking smile, "but the meaning of the word unlimited in connexion with finances is so vague . . . And what is vague is doubtful, and in doubt, says the wise man, there is danger."

"In other words," replied Monte Cristo, "if Thomson and French are inclined to commit a folly, Danglars' bank is not going to follow suit. No doubt Messrs Thomson and French do not need to consider figures in their operations, but Monsieur Danglars has a limit to his. As he said just now, he is a wise man."

"No one has ever questioned my capital, monsieur," replied the banker proudly.

"Then obviously I am the first one to do so."

"How so?"

"The explanations you demand of me, monsieur, which certainly appear to imply hesitation . . ."

"Why, then, monsieur, I will try to make myself clear by asking you to name the amount for which you expect to draw on me," continued Danglars after a moment's silence.

"But I have asked for unlimited credit because I am uncertain of the amount I shall require," replied Monte Cristo, determined not to lose an inch of ground.

The banker thought the moment had come for him to take the upper hand; he flung himself back in the armchair and with a slow, arrogant smile on his lips, said: "Do not fear to ask, monsieur; you will then be convinced that the resources of the firm of Danglars, limited though they may be, are sufficient to meet the highest demands, even though you asked for a million . . ."

"What did you say?"

"I said a million," repeated Danglars with the audacity of stupidity.

"What should I do with a million?" said the Count. "Good heavens! I should not have opened an account for such a trifling sum. Why, I always carry a million in my pocket-book or my suitcase." And he took from his small card-case two Treasury bills of five hundred thousand francs each.

A man of Danglars' type requires to be overwhelmed, not merely pinpricked, and this blow had its effect. The banker was simply stunned. He stared at Monte Cristo in a stupefied manner, his eyes starting out of his head.

"Come, now, own that you mistrust Messrs Thomson and French. I expected this, and, though I am not very businesslike, I came forearmed. Here are two other letters of credit similar to the one addressed to you; one is from Arstein and Eskeles of Vienna on Baron Rothschild, the other is from Baring Bros. of London on Monsieur Lafitte. You have only to say the word, and I will relieve you of all anxiety by presenting my letter of credit to one or the other of these two firms."

That was enough; Danglars was vanquished. Trembling visibly, he took the letters from London and Germany that the Count held out to him, opened them, verified the authenticity of the signatures with a care that would have been insulting to Monte Cristo had they not served to mislead the banker.

"Here are three signatures which are worth many millions," said Danglars, rising as though to pay homage to the power of gold personified in the man before him. "Three unlimited credits on our banking firms. Excuse me, Count, though I am no longer mistrustful, I cannot help being astonished."

"But nothing can astonish a banking establishment like yours," said Monte Cristo with a great show of politeness. "You can send me some money, then, I suppose?"

"Speak, Count, I am at your service."

"Well, since we understand each other and you no longer mistrust me . . . I am not presuming too much in saying this, am I? Let us fix on a general sum for the first year; six millions for example."

"Very well, let it be six millions," replied Danglars hoarsely.

"If I require more," said Monte Cristo carelessly, "we can add to it, but I do not expect to stay in Paris more than a year and I don't suppose I shall exceed that sum in a year. Anyway we shall see. To begin with, will you please send me to-morrow five hundred thousand francs, half in gold and half in notes? I shall be at home until noon, but should I have to go out, I will leave the receipt with my steward."

"You shall have the money at ten o'clock in the morning, Count."

The Count rose.

"I must confess to you, Count," said Danglars, "I thought I was well informed on all the large fortunes of Europe, and yet I must own that though yours appears to be very considerable I had no knowledge of it. Is it of recent date?"

"No, monsieur; on the contrary, it is of very long standing," replied Monte Cristo. "It is a kind of family treasure which it was forbidden to touch. The interest has gone on accumulating and has trebled[1] the capital. The period fixed by the testator expired only a few years ago, so your ignorance of the matter was quite natural. You will know more about it, though, in a short time."

The Count accompanied his words with one of those pale smiles that struck such terror into the heart of Franz d'Épinay.

"If you would allow me, Count, I should like to introduce you to Baroness Danglars. Excuse my haste, but a client like you almost forms part of the family."

Monte Cristo bowed as a sign that he accepted the preferred honour. The financier rang the bell, and a footman in a brilliant livery appeared.

"Is the Baroness at home?" asked Danglars.

"Yes, Monsieur le Baron," replied the footman.

"Is she alone?"

"No, Monsieur le Baron, Monsieur Debray is with her."

Danglars nodded his head, then turning to the Count, he said: "Monsieur Debray is an old friend of ours and private secretary to the Minister of the Interior. As for my wife, she belongs to an ancient family and lowered herself in marrying me. She was Mademoiselle de Sevières, and when I married her she was a widow after the death of her first husband, Colonel the Marquis de Nargonne."

"I have not the honour of knowing Madame Danglars, but I have already met Monsieur Lucien Debray."

"Really? Where?"

"At the house of Monsieur de Morcerf."

"Ah, you know the little Viscount then?"

"We were together at Rome during the Carnival."

"It is true," said Danglars. "Have I not heard something about a strange adventure with bandits in the ruins? He had a most miraculous escape! I believe he told my daughter and wife something about it when he returned from Italy."

"The Baroness awaits your pleasure, messieurs!" said the footman, who had been to inquire of his mistress whether she would receive visitors.

"I will go on in front to show you the way," said Danglars, bowing.

"And I will follow you!"

Chapter XXXIII

THE PAIR OF DAPPLED GREYS

Mme Danglars, whose beauty was quite remarkable in spite of her thirty-six years, was at the piano, a little masterpiece of inlay, while Lucien Debray was seated at a work-table turning over the pages of an album. Before the Count's arrival, Lucien had had time to relate many particulars regarding him to Mme Danglars, and her curiosity, being aroused by the old stories related by Morcerf, was brought to its highest pitch by the details told her by Lucien. In consequence she received the Baron with a smile, which was not her custom, while the Count received a ceremonious but at the same time graceful curtsey in acknowledgment of his bow.

"Baroness, permit me to present to you the Count of Monte Cristo, who has been most warmly recommended to me by my correspondents at Rome," said Danglars. "I will only add one fact which will make him a favourite among the ladies: he intends staying in Paris for a year, and during that time he proposes spending six millions; that sounds promising for a series of balls, dinners, and supper parties, and I hope the Count will not forget us, as we shall not forget him in the small parties we give."

Though the introduction was so vulgar in its flattery, it is such a rare event that a man comes to Paris to spend a princely fortune that Mme Danglars gave the Count a look which was not devoid of interest.

"You have come at a very bad season," said she. "Paris is detestable in summer. There are no more balls, receptions, or parties. The Italian opera is at London, the French opera is everywhere except at Paris; there remain for our sole entertainment a third-rate race-meeting or two on the Champs de Mars or at Satory."

At this moment Baroness Danglars' confidential maid entered and, approaching her mistress, whispered something into her ear.

Madame Danglars turned pale.

"Impossible!" said she.

"It is nevertheless the truth, madame," replied the maid.

Madame turned to her husband: "Is this true, monsieur, what my maid tells me?"

"What has she told you, madame?" asked Danglars, visibly agitated.

"She tells me that when my coachman went to put my horses to the carriage, they were gone from the stables. What does this signify, may I ask?"

"Madame, listen to me," said Danglars.

"I will certainly listen to you, for I am curious to know what you have to tell me. I will ask these gentlemen to be our judge. Messieurs," continued she, "Danglars has ten horses in his stables; two of these, the handsomest in Paris, belong to me. You know my dappled greys, Monsieur Debray. I have promised to lend Madame de Villefort my carriage to go to the Bois to-morrow, and now my horses are gone! I suppose monsieur has found some means of making a few thousands of francs on them and has sold them. What a money-grasping lot speculators are!"

Just then Debray, who was looking out of the window, suddenly exclaimed: "By Jove! surely those are your very horses in the Count's carriage!"

"My dappled greys?" cried out Madame Danglars, rushing to the window. "Yes, those are mine indeed!"

Danglars was astounded.

"Is it possible?" said Monte Cristo, affecting astonishment.

"It is incredible!" said the banker.

Danglars looked so pale and discomfited that the Count almost had pity on him. The banker foresaw a disastrous scene in the near future; the Baroness' frowning brow predicted a storm. Debray saw the gathering clouds and, on pretext of an appointment, took his leave, while Monte Cristo, not wishing to mar the advantages he hoped he had gained by staying any longer, bowed to Mme Danglars and withdrew, leaving the Baron to his wife's anger.

"All is well!" thought Monte Cristo. "I have achieved my object. The domestic peace of this family is now in my hands, and with one action I am going to win the gratitude of both the Baron and the Baroness. What a stroke of luck! But with all this," he added, "I have not been introduced to Mademoiselle Eugénie, whose acquaintance I am very anxious to make. Never mind," he continued with that peculiar smile of his, "I am in Paris with plenty of time before me . . . That can be left for a later date." With this reflection, he stepped into his carriage and returned to his house.

Two hours later Mme Danglars received a charming letter from the Count of Monte Cristo, in which he wrote that he did not wish to make his entrance into Paris society by causing annoyance to a beautiful woman, and entreated her to take back her horses. The horses were sent back wearing the same harness as in the morning, but in the centre of each rosette which adorned the sides of their heads, there was a diamond. Danglars also received a letter. The Count asked his permission to satisfy a millionaire's whim, and requested him to excuse the Eastern fashion adopted in returning the horses.

In the evening Monte Cristo went to his country-house at Auteuil accompanied by Ali.

Toward three o'clock the next day, Ali, summoned by a stroke of the gong, entered the Count's study.

"Ali, you have often spoken to me of your skill in throwing the lasso," said the Count.

Ali drew himself up proudly and nodded assent.

"Good! You could stop a bull with your lasso?"

Ali nodded assent.

"A tiger?"

Another nod.

"A lion?"

Ali pretended to throw the lasso and imitated the choked roar of a lion.

"I understand," said Monte Cristo. "You have hunted lions."

Ali nodded his head proudly.

"But could you stop two runaway horses?"

Ali smiled.

"Well, then, listen," said Monte Cristo. "In a few minutes a carriage will come along drawn by two runaway horses, the same dappled greys that I had yesterday. Even at the risk of being run over, you must stop these horses before my door."

Ali went out into the street and traced a line on the pavement before the door. Then the Nubian seated himself on the stone that formed the angle of the house and the road and began smoking his chibouque,[1] while Monte Cristo returned to his study.

Toward five o'clock, however, when the Count expected the arrival of the carriage, he began to manifest distinct signs of impatience; he paced a room overlooking the road, stopped at intervals to listen, and from time to time approached the window through which he could see Ali blowing out puffs of smoke with a regularity which indicated that he was quite absorbed in his important occupation.

Suddenly a distant rumbling was heard which drew nearer with lightning rapidity; then a carriage appeared, the coachman vainly striving to restrain the wild, infuriated horses who were bounding along at a mad speed.

In the carriage a young lady and a child of seven or eight years were lying in each other's embrace; their terror had deprived them of all power to utter a sound. A stone under the wheel or any other impediment would have sufficed to upset the creaking carriage. It kept to the middle of the road, and the cries of the terrified spectators could be heard as it flew along.

Suddenly Ali laid down his chibouque, took the lasso from his pocket and threw it, catching the forelegs of the near horse in a triple coil; he suffered himself to be dragged along three or four yards, by which time the tightening of the lasso so hampered the horse that it fell on to the pole which it snapped, thus paralysing the efforts the other horse made to pursue its mad course. The coachman took advantage of this short respite to jump down from his box, but Ali had already seized the nostrils of the other horse in his iron grip, and the animal, snorting with pain, sank down beside its companion.

All this took no more time than it takes a bullet to hit its mark. It was nevertheless sufficient for a man, followed by several servants, to rush out from the house opposite which the accident had happened. As soon as the coachman opened the door of the carriage, he lifted out the lady who was clinging to the cushion with one hand, while with the other she pressed to her bosom her fainting son. Monte Cristo carried them both into the salon and, placing them on a sofa, said:

"You have nothing more to fear, madame, you are safe!"

The lady soon came round, and pointed to her son with a look which was more eloquent than all entreaties. The child, indeed, was still unconscious.

"I understand, madame," said the Count, examining the child, "but you need not be alarmed, the child has received no injury. It is only fear that has rendered him unconscious."

"Are you only telling me this to still my anxiety? Look

how pale he is. My son! My child! My Edward! Answer your mother! Oh, monsieur, send for a doctor! I will give my fortune to him who restores my son to me!"

Monte Cristo opened a casket and took out a flagon of Bohemian glass incrusted with gold, containing a blood-red liquid, a single drop of which he placed on the child's lips. Though still pale, the child immediately opened his eyes. On seeing this, the mother was beside herself with joy.

"Where am I?" she cried out, "and to whom do I owe so much happiness after such a cruel trial?"

"Madame, you are under the roof of a man who esteems himself most fortunate at having been able to spare you any pain," said Monte Cristo.

"It is all the fault of my wretched inquisitiveness!" said the lady. "All Paris talked of Madame Danglars' magnificent horses, and I was foolish enough to want to try them."

"Is it possible?" exclaimed the Count with admirably feigned surprise. "Do these horses belong to the Baroness?"

"Yes, monsieur, do you know her?"

"I have that honour, and I feel a double joy at having been the means of saving you from the danger that threatened you, for you might have attributed the accident to me. I bought these horses from the Baron yesterday, but the Baroness appeared to regret their loss so deeply that I sent them back with the request that she would accept them from me."

"Then you must be the Count of Monte Cristo of whom Hermine spoke so much yesterday."

"That is so, madame."

"And I, monsieur, am Madame Héloïse de Villefort."

The Count bowed as though he heard a name completely unknown to him.

"How grateful Monsieur de Villefort will be," continued Héloïse. "He owes both our lives to you; you have restored to him his wife and his son. If it had not been for your brave servant, this dear child and myself would certainly have been killed."

"Alas, madame, I still shudder at the thought of your danger!"

"I hope you will permit me to give your servant the just reward for his devotion."

"Madame, I beg of you not to spoil Ali either by praise or by reward," replied the Count. "Ali is my slave; in saving your life, he served me, and it is his duty to serve me."

"But he risked his life!" said Madame de Villefort, who was strangely impressed by the Count's masterful tone.

"I saved his life, madame, consequently it belongs to me," replied Monte Cristo.

Madame de Villefort made no reply. Perhaps she was thinking about this man who made such a strong impression on everybody who set eyes on him.

During this momentary silence, the Count had leisure to examine the child whom his mother was covering with kisses. He was small and slender; his skin was of that whiteness generally found with auburn-haired children, yet a mass of rebellious black hair covered his rounded forehead. It fell on to his shoulders, encircling his face and redoubling the vivacity of his eyes which were so expressive of sly malice and childish naughtiness. His mouth was large, and his lips, which had scarcely regained their colour, were thin; the features of this child of eight were those of a boy of twelve or more. His first movement was to wriggle himself free from his mother's arms, and to open the casket from which the Count had taken the phial of elixir. With the air of a child accustomed to satisfy his every whim and without asking anyone's permission, he began to unstopper the phials.

"Don't touch anything there, sonny," said the Count sharply. "Some of those liquids are dangerous, not only to taste but even to inhale."

Madame de Villefort turned pale and, seizing her son's arm, drew him toward her. Her fears calmed, she immediately cast on the casket a fleeting but expressive glance, which did not escape the Count's notice.

"Do you reside here?" Madame de Villefort inquired as she rose to take her leave.

"No, madame," replied the Count. "This is only a little country house I have just bought. I reside at number thirty Champs Élysées. But I see that you have quite recovered and are desirous of returning home. I have just given orders for the same horses to be put to my carriage, and Ali will have the honour of driving you home, while your coachman stays here to repair the damage."

"I dare not go with the same horses!" said Madame de Villefort.

"Oh, you will see, madame, that in Ali's hands they will be as gentle as lambs," was Monte Cristo's reply.

Indeed, Ali had already tackled the horses that had only with difficulty been set on their legs again. He held in his hand a sponge soaked in aromatic vinegar with which he rubbed away the sweat and foam that covered their heads and nostrils. Almost immediately they began to breathe loudly and to tremble violently; this lasted several seconds. Then, in the midst of a large crowd which the news of the accident had gathered before the house, Ali harnessed the horses to the Count's brougham, took the reins, mounted the box, and to the utter astonishment of those spectators who had beheld these same horses bolting like a whirlwind, he was compelled to use his whip vigorously to make them move. Even then they went at such a slow trot that it took nearly two hours to reach the Faubourg Saint-Honoré, where Madame de Villefort lived.

Chapter XXXIV

HAYDEE

My readers will remember that the new, or rather old, acquaintances of the Count of Monte Cristo were Maximilian, Julie, and Emmanuel. He had promised Maximilian that he would call at the house in the Rue Meslay, and the day had now come. Anticipation of the visit he was about to make, of the few happy moments he was about to spend, of the fleeting glimpse of paradise in the hell to which he had voluntarily engaged himself, brought a charming expression of serenity to Monte Cristo's countenance, and his face was radiant with a joy rarely depicted there.

It was midday and the Count had set apart one hour to be spent with Haydee. It seemed as though he sensed that his crushed spirit needed to be prepared for gentle emotions as other spirits have to be prepared for violent ones.

The young Greek occupied a suite separated from the Count's. It was furnished entirely in the Oriental style; the floors were covered with thick Turkish carpets, rich brocades hung suspended from the walls, and in each room there was a large and spacious divan with piles of cushions, which could be placed according to the fancy of those that used them.

The Greek girl was in the room at the far end of her suite. She was reclining on the floor on cushions of blue satin with her back against the divan; one softly rounded arm encircled her head, and between her lips she had the coral tube in which was set the flexible pipe of a narghile.[1] Her dress was that of a woman of Epirus:[2] white satin trousers embroidered with pink roses displayed two small childlike feet, which might have been taken for Parian marble[3] had they not been playing with two little slippers with curling toes embroidered with gold and pearls, a long white-and-blue-striped vest with long sleeves ornamented with loops of silver and buttons of pearl, and on her head was a small gold cap embroidered with pearls which she wore tilted to one side; from under the cap, on the side where it was tilted up, fell a beautiful natural rose of a deep crimson hue mingling with her hair, which was of such a deep black that it appeared almost blue.

The beauty of her face was of the perfect Grecian type, with large black eyes of the softness of velvet, straight nose, coral lips, and pearly teeth. To complete the picture she had all the charm and freshness of young womanhood, for Haydee had seen no more than nineteen or twenty summers.

When Monte Cristo entered, she raised herself on her elbow and, welcoming him with a smile, held out her hand to him.

"Why do you ask permission to see me?" she said in the sonorous language of the daughters of Sparta and Athens. "Are you my master no longer? Have I ceased to be your slave?"

Monte Cristo smiled as he replied: "Haydee, we are in France, you know, so you are free!"

"Free to do what?" asked the girl.

"Free to leave me!"

"To leave you! Why should I leave you?"

"How do I know? We shall see people . . ."

"I do not wish to see anyone."

"Should you meet amongst the handsome young men one who pleases you, I should not be so unjust . . ."

"I have never yet seen a man more handsome than you, and I have never loved anyone but my father and you."

"Poor child!" said Monte Cristo. "That is only because you have scarcely spoken to anyone but your father and me."

"What need have I to converse with others? My father called me his joy, you call me your love, and both of you have called me your child."

"Do you remember your father, Haydee?"

The girl smiled. "He is here and here," pointing to her eyes and her heart.

"And where am I?" Monte Cristo asked with a smile.

"You? Why, you are everywhere!"

Monte Cristo took her hand to kiss it, but the simple child withdrew it and offered her cheek.

"Listen to me, Haydee," said the Count. "You know that you are free. You are your own mistress. You may still wear your national costume or discard it according to your inclination; you may stay here if and when you wish, and go out if and when you wish. There will always be a carriage in readiness for you. Ali and Myrta will accompany you everywhere and will be at your command. There is but one thing I ask of you."

"Speak!"

"Disclose not the secret of your birth, say not a word in regard to your past; on no occasion mention the name of your illustrious father or of your poor mother."

"I have already told you, my lord, that I will not see anyone."

"Listen, Haydee, it may be that this seclusion, which is customary in the East, will be impossible in Paris. Continue to learn all you can of our Northern countries as you did at Rome, Florence, and Madrid; such knowledge will always stand you in good stead whether you continue to live here or return to the East."

The slave girl raised her large tear-bedewed eyes to the Count and said: "You mean to say whether *we* return to the East, do you not, my lord?"

"Yes, child, you know I shall never leave you. The tree does not forsake the flower, it is the flower that forsakes the tree."

"My lord, I shall never leave you," said Haydee. "I could not live without you."

"Poor child! I shall be old in ten years, and you will still be young."

"My father had a long white beard but that did not prevent my loving him. My father was sixty years of age, but to me he was more handsome than all the young men I saw."

"Do you think you will be able to settle down here?"

"Shall I see you?"

"Every day."

"Then what do you fear for me?"

"I fear you may grow weary."

"That cannot be, my lord, for in the morning I shall be occupied with the thought that you will be coming to see me, and in the evening I shall dwell on the memories of your visit. Besides, when I am alone, I have much to occupy my mind. I summon up mighty pictures of the past, vast horizons with Pindus and Olympia[4] in the distance. Then again, my heart is filled with three great sentiments—sadness, love, and gratitude—and with these as companions it is impossible to grow weary."

"You are a worthy daughter of Epirus, Haydee, full of grace and poetry. It is easily seen that you are descended from that family of goddesses born in your own country. Rest assured, my daughter, I will not permit your youth to be lost, for if you love me as a father, I love you as my child."

"You are mistaken, my lord, I did not love my father as I love you. The love I bear you is quite different. My father is dead, yet I am not dead; whereas if you die I die."

With a smile of exquisite tenderness the Count held out his hand to her; she pressed her lips to it as she always did.

The Count was now fully prepared for his interview with Morrel and his family, and took his leave of Haydee, murmuring these lines of Pindar:

Youth is the flower of which love is the fruit; Happy the gatherer who picks it after watching it slowly mature.

In accordance with his orders the carriage was ready. He stepped in and sped along at his usual high speed.

Chapter XXXV

THE MORREL FAMILY

The Count arrived at no. 14 Rue Meslay in a very few minutes. Coclès opened the door, and Baptistin, springing from the box, asked if M. and Mme Herbault and M. Maximilian Morrel were at home to the Count of Monte Cristo.

"To the Count of Monte Cristo!" cried Maximilian, throwing away his cigar and hastening toward his visitor. "I should think we are at home to him! A thousand thanks, Count, for having kept your promise."

The young officer shook the Count's hand so cordially that there could be no doubt as to the sincerity of his feelings.

"Come along," said Maximilian, "I will announce you myself. My sister is in the garden plucking the dead roses; my brother is within five yards of her reading his two papers, for wherever Madame Herbault is, Monsieur Herbault will be found within a radius of four yards and vice versa."

At the sound of their steps, a young woman of twenty to twenty-five, dressed in a morning gown, raised her head from the rose-bush which she was carefully trimming.

It was no other than Julie, who, as Thomson and French's representative had predicted, had become Mme

Emmanuel Herbault. She uttered a cry of surprise on seeing the stranger. Maximilian began to laugh. "Don't upset
yourself, Julie," said he. "The Count has only been in Paris
two or three days, and knows what a householder of the
Marais has to do, and if he does not, you will show him."

"It is most unkind of my brother to bring you thus, but
he never has any regard for his poor sister's vanity. Penelon!
Penelon! . . ."

An old man who was digging a bed of Bengal roses stuck
his spade into the ground and approached, cap in hand, the
while striving to hide a quid of tobacco he had just put into
his mouth. A few silvery strands mingled with his thick hair,
while his bronzed face and bold keen eye betrayed the old
sailor, tanned by tropical suns and many a tempestuous sea.

"I believe you hailed me, Mademoiselle Julie," he said.
Penelon had retained the habit of calling his master's
daughter "Mademoiselle Julie," and could never accustom
himself to addressing her as "Madame Herbault."

"Penelon, go and inform Monsieur Emmanuel of this
gentleman's arrival."

Then, turning to Monte Cristo, she said:

"You will permit me to leave you for a few minutes? In
the meantime Maximilian will take you into the salon."

Without waiting for a reply she disappeared behind a
clump of trees, and regained the house by a side entrance.

The salon was impregnated with the scent of sweet-
smelling flowers massed together in a huge Japanese vase.
Julie, appropriately dressed and her hair coquettishly
arranged (she had accomplished this feat in ten minutes),
was waiting to receive the Count.

The birds could be heard chirping in a neighbouring
aviary; the laburnum and acacia trees spread their branches
so close to the window that the clusters of bloom almost
formed a border to the blue velvet curtains. Everything in
this little retreat breathed peaceful tranquillity, from the song
of the birds to the smiles of its owners. From the moment the
Count entered, he sensed the atmosphere of happiness; he

stood silent and pensive, forgetting that the others were waiting for him to continue the conversation which had been interrupted during the exchange of salutations.

He suddenly became aware of this almost embarrassing silence and, tearing himself away from his dreams with a great effort, he said:

"Pray excuse my emotion, madame. It must astonish you who are accustomed to the peace and happiness I find here, but it is so unusual for me to find contentment expressed on a human face that I cannot grow weary of looking at you and your husband."

"We are very happy, monsieur," replied Julie, "but we have gone through long and bitter suffering, and there are few people who have bought their happiness at such a high price."

The Count's face manifested great curiosity.

"It is a family history, Count," said Maximilian. "The humble little picture would have no interest for you who are accustomed to the misfortunes of the illustrious and the jobs of the rich. We have known bitter suffering."

"And did God send you consolation in your sorrow as He does to all?" asked Monte Cristo.

"Yes, Count, we can truly say that He did," replied Julie. "He did for us what He only does for His elect: He sent us one of His angels."

The Count's cheeks became scarlet, and he coughed in order to have an excuse for hiding his emotion behind his handkerchief.

"Those who are born in a gilt cradle and have never wanted for anything, do not know what happiness life contains," said Emmanuel, "just as they do not appreciate to the full a clear sky who have never entrusted their lives to the mercy of four planks on a raging sea."

Monte Cristo got up and, without replying, for he feared the tremulousness of his voice would betray his emotion, began to pace round the room.

"Our magnificence makes you smile!" said Maximilian, who was watching Monte Cristo.

"Not at all," replied Monte Cristo, deathly pale and pressing one hand to his heart to still its throbbings, while with the other he pointed to a glass case under which lay a silk purse carefully placed on a black velvet cushion. "I was only wondering what could be the use of this purse containing what looks like a piece of paper at one end and a fairly valuable diamond at the other."

"That is the most precious of our family treasures, Count."

"The diamond is, indeed, quite a good one."

"My brother was not alluding to the value of the stone, though it has been estimated at a hundred thousand francs; what he meant was that the articles contained in that purse are the relics of the angel I mentioned just now."

"Forgive me, madame, I did not mean to be indiscreet. I could not understand the meaning of the purse, and will ask for no explanation."

"Indiscreet, did you say? On the contrary, we are grateful to you for giving us an opportunity to open our hearts on the subject. If we wished to make a secret of the noble action which that purse reminds us of, we should not expose it thus to view. We would rather make it known to everyone, so that our benefactor may be compelled to betray his presence by his emotion."

"Really!" said Monte Cristo in a stifled voice.

"This has touched the hand of a man who saved my father from death, all of us from ruin, and our name from dishonour," said Maximilian, raising the glass case and devoutly kissing the silk purse. "It has touched the hand of one whose merit it is that, though we were doomed to misery and mourning, others now express their wonder at our happiness. This letter," continued Maximilian, taking the piece of paper from the purse and handing it to the Count, "this letter was written by him on a day when my father had taken a desperate resolution, and the diamond was given by our unknown benefactor to my sister as her dowry."

Monte Cristo opened the letter and read it with an indescribably happy expression. As our readers will know, it was the note addressed to Julie and signed "Sindbad the Sailor."

"I have not given up hope of one day kissing that hand as I kiss the purse it has touched," said Julie. "Four years ago, Penelon, the gallant tar you saw in the garden with a spade, was at Trieste; on the quay he saw an Englishman on the point of boarding a yacht; he recognized him as the man who came to see my father on the fifth of June, eighteen-twenty-nine, and who wrote this note on the fifth of September. He assures me it was he, but he dared not speak to him."

"An Englishman?" asked Monte Cristo, deep in thought and feeling most uneasy every time Julie looked at him. "An Englishman, did you say?"

"Yes," replied Morrel, "an Englishman who introduced himself to us as the representative of Messrs Thomson and French of Rome. That is why you saw me start the other day when you mentioned that they were your bankers. As we have said, all this happened in eighteen-twenty-nine. For pity's sake, Count, tell us, do you know this Englishman?"

"What was his name?" asked Monte Cristo.

"He left no name but the one he signed at the bottom of the letter, 'Sindbad the Sailor,' " said Julie, looking at the Count very closely.

"Which is evidently only a pseudonym," said Monte Cristo. Then, remarking that Julie was eyeing him more closely than ever and was trying to detect some resemblance in his voice, he continued: "Was this man not about my height, perhaps a little taller, and somewhat thinner; his neck imprisoned in a high cravat; his coat closely buttoned up; and hadn't he the habit of constantly taking out his pencil?"

"You know him then?" exclaimed Julie, her eyes sparkling with joy.

"No, I am only guessing," said Monte Cristo. "I knew a Lord Wilmore who was continually doing things of this kind."

"Sister, sister, remember what father so often told us,"

interposed Morrel. "He always said it was not an Englishman who had done us this good turn."

Monte Cristo started. "What did your father tell you?" he asked.

"My father regarded the deed as a miracle. He believed that a benefactor had come from his tomb to help us. It was a touching superstition, Count, and, though I could not credit it myself, I would not destroy his faith in it. How often in his dreams did he not mutter the name of a dear friend who was lost to him for ever! On his deathbed, when his mind had been given that lucidity that the near approach of death brings with it, this thought which had till then only been a superstition became a conviction. The last words he spoke were: 'Maximilian, it was Edmond Dantès!' "

At these words, the Count, who had been gradually changing colour, became alarmingly pale. The blood rushed from his head, and he could not speak for a few seconds. He took out his watch as though he had forgotten the time, picked up his hat, took a hurried and embarrassed leave of Mme Herbault, and, pressing the hands of Emmanuel and Maximilian, said: "Permit me to renew my visit from time to time, madame. I have spent a happy hour with you and am very grateful for the kind way in which you have received me. This is the first time for many years that I have given way to my feelings." With that he strode rapidly out of the room.

"What a peculiar man this Count of Monte Cristo is," said Emmanuel.

"He certainly is," replied Maximilian, "but I believe he is very noble-hearted, and I am sure he likes us."

"As for me," said Julie, "his voice went to my heart, and two or three times it occurred to me that I had heard it before."

Chapter XXXVI

TOXICOLOGY

The Count of Monte Cristo had arrived at Mme de Villefort's door, and the mere mention of his name had set the whole house in confusion.

Mme de Villefort was in the salon when the Count was announced, and immediately sent for her son to come and renew his thanks to the Count. Edward had heard of nothing but this great personage for the last two days, and hastened to obey the summons, not through obedience to his mother, nor yet because he wanted to thank the Count, but from sheer curiosity and in the hope that he might fire off one of his saucy jokes which always elicited from his mother the remark: "The bad boy! but I must really overlook it, he is so clever!"

After the first formalities were exchanged, the Count inquired after M. de Villefort.

"My husband is dining with the Chancellor," replied Mme de Villefort. "He has only just left, and I am sure he will greatly regret that he has been deprived of the pleasure of seeing you. Where is your sister Valentine?" said Mme de Villefort, turning to Edward. "Send someone for her, so that I may introduce her to the Count."

"You have also a daughter, madame?" asked the Count. "She must be quite a young child."

"It is Monsieur de Villefort's daughter by his first marriage, and a pretty, well-grown girl she is too."

"But melancholy," interrupted Edward, who, wishing to have a plume for his hat, was pulling feathers out of the tail of a parrot that screeched with pain.

Mme de Villefort merely said: "Be quiet, Edward! This young madcap is quite right, nevertheless, and is only repeating what he has, unfortunately, often heard me say. In spite of all we do to distract her, Mademoiselle Villefort is of a melancholy and taciturn disposition, which often mars her beauty. Why is she not coming, Edward? Go and see what is keeping her so long."

"They are looking for her where she is not to be found."

"Where are they looking for her?"

"In Grandpa Noirtier's room."

"Where is she, then? If you know, tell me."

"She is under the large chestnut-tree," continued the mischievous boy as, notwithstanding his mother's expostulations, he presented live flies to the parrot, who appeared to relish them.

Mme de Villefort stretched out her hand to ring for the maid to tell her where Valentine was to be found when the girl herself entered. She certainly looked sad, and on closer inspection the traces of tears were to be seen in her eyes. She was a tall, slim girl of nineteen, with bright chestnut hair and deep blue eyes; her whole deportment was languid but stamped with the elegance which had characterized her mother. Her white and slender hands, her pearly neck and blushing cheek, gave her at first sight the aspect of one of those beautiful Englishwomen who have been rather poetically compared to swans admiring themselves.

On seeing beside her mother the stranger of whom she had already heard so much, she curtsied with such grace that the Count was more struck with her than ever. He stood up at once.

"My stepdaughter, Mademoiselle de Villefort," said Mme de Villefort.

"And the Count of Monte Cristo, King of China, Emperor of Cochin China," said the young imp, casting a sly look at his sister.

"Have I not had the honour of seeing both you and mademoiselle somewhere?" asked the Count, looking first at Madame de Villefort and then at Valentine. "It occurred to me just now that I had, and when I saw mademoiselle enter, her face seemed to throw some light on the confused remembrance, if you will excuse the remark."

"It is hardly likely, Count. Mademoiselle de Villefort does not like society, and we rarely go out."

"It is not in society that I have met you, mademoiselle, and the charming little rogue. I shall remember in a moment, stay . . ."

The Count put his hand to his forehead as though to concentrate his thoughts.

"No . . . it was abroad. It was . . . I do not quite know where, but it seems to me that this recollection is connected with a beautiful sunny sky and some religious feast . . . mademoiselle had some flowers in her hand, and the boy was chasing a peacock, while you, madame, were under a vine-arbour . . . Help me out, madame, does nothing I have told you bring back anything to your mind?"

"No, nothing," replied Mme de Villefort, "and it seems to me, Count, that if I had met you anywhere, I should not have forgotten you."

"Perhaps the Count saw us in Italy," said Valentine timidly.

"That, indeed, is possible," said Monte Cristo. "Have you travelled in Italy, mademoiselle?"

"My stepmother and I went there two years ago. The doctor feared for my chest and prescribed Naples air for me. We stayed at Bologna, Perugia, and Rome."

"You are right, mademoiselle," exclaimed Monte Cristo as though this simple indication had sufficed to freshen his memory. "It was at Perugia on the Feast of Corpus Christi in a garden of the Hôtel de la Poste that we chanced to meet, you, madame; mademoiselle, the boy, and myself. Yes, I remember having had the pleasure of seeing you there."

"I remember Perugia perfectly, also the Hôtel de la Poste and the feast you mention," said Mme de Villefort, "but though I have taxed my memory, I am ashamed to say, I do not recollect having seen you."

"Strangely enough, I do not recollect it either," remarked Valentine, raising her beautiful eyes to the Count.

"I remember," said Edward.

"I will assist you, madame," resumed the Count. "It was a baking hot day; you were waiting for your carriage, which had been delayed in consequence of the feast-day celebrations, mademoiselle went down to the garden while your son was chasing the bird; you stayed in the arbour. Do you not remember sitting on a stone bench there, talking for a long time with someone?"

"It is true," said the lady, turning a deep red. "I recollect now. I was conversing with a gentleman in a long woollen mantle . . . I believe he was a doctor."

"Exactly so. I was that man. I had been staying at that hotel for the past fortnight and had cured my valet of a fever and my host of the jaundice, so that I was looked upon as a great doctor. We talked for a long time on different topics. I do not recollect all the details of our conversation, but I do remember that, sharing the general erroneous opinion about me, you consulted me about your daughter's health."

At this moment the clock struck six.

"It is six o'clock," said Mme de Villefort, obviously agitated. "Will you go and see whether your grandfather is ready for his dinner, Valentine?"

Valentine rose and, bowing to the Count, left the room without saying a word.

"Was it on my account that you sent Mademoiselle Valentine away?" asked the Count when Valentine had gone.

"Not at all," was the quick reply. "It is the hour when we

give Monsieur de Noirtier the miserable repast which supports his wretched existence. You are aware, monsieur, of the deplorable condition of Monsieur de Villefort's father?"

"Yes, madame. He is paralysed, I think?"

"He is, alas! The poor man has lost all power of movement; his mind alone is active in this poor human machine, and even that is weak and flickering like a lamp waiting to be extinguished. Excuse me for worrying you with our domestic troubles. I interrupted you when you were telling me that you were a skilful doctor."

"I did not say that, madam," replied the Count with a smile. "Quite the contrary. I have studied chemistry because, having decided to live chiefly in the East, I wished to follow the example of King Mithridates."[1]

"Mithridates, rex Ponticus," said the young scamp, cutting up some illustrations in a magnificent album; "that was the one who breakfasted every morning off a cup of poison with cream."

"Edward, you naughty child!" Mme de Villefort cried out, snatching the mutilated book from her son's hands. "You are unbearable and only make yourself a nuisance. Leave us and go along to your sister in your grandfather's room."

"The album!" said Edward.

"What do you mean?"

"I want the album!"

"Why have you cut up the drawings?"

"Because it amused me!"

"Leave us! Go!"

"I shan't go until you have given me the album!" said the child, settling himself down in a big armchair, true to his habit of never yielding.

"Here it is! Now leave us in peace!" said Mme de Villefort.

She gave Edward the book, and he went out.

"Allow me to observe, madame," said the Count goodnaturedly, "that you are very severe with your mischievous child."

"It is sometimes necessary," replied Mme de Villefort with all the firmness of a mother.

"He was reciting his Cornelius Nepos[2] when he spoke of King Mithridates," said the Count, "and you interrupted a quotation which proves that his tutor has not lost time with him; in fact that your son is advanced for his age."

"The fact is, Count," replied the mother, pleasantly flattered, "that he is very quick, and can learn all he wants to. He has only one fault: he is very self-willed. But do you really think Mithridates took such precautions and that they were efficacious?"

"I believe it so firmly that I myself have taken these precautions so as not to be poisoned at Naples, Palermo, and Smyrna, that is to say, in the three cases when without these precautions I should have lost my life."

"Did you find this means successful?"

"Perfectly."

"It is true. I recollect that you told me something about it at Perugia."

"Really?" said the Count with well-feigned surprise. "I do not remember."

"I asked you whether poisons acted with the same force with Northerners as with Southerners, and you informed me that the cold, lymphatic temperament of the Northerners did not offer the same aptitude as the rich and energetic nature of the Southerners."

"It is true," said Monte Cristo, "I have seen Russians devour vegetable substances without being in the least indisposed, which would have infallibly killed a Neapolitan or an Arab."

"Then do you think the result would be more certain with us than in the East, and that, in the midst of our fog and rain, a man would become more easily accustomed to this progressive absorption of poison than he would do in a warm climate?"

"Certainly. It must be understood, however, that he

would only become immune from the particular poison to which he had accustomed himself."

"I quite understand that. But tell me, how would you accustom yourself, or rather how did you accustom yourself?"

"It is quite easy. Supposing you knew beforehand what poison was going to be administered to you, supposing this poison were brucine, for instance——"

"Brucine is extracted from the *Brucea ferruginea*, is it not?" inquired Mme de Villefort.

"Just so. Well, then, supposing the poison were brucine," resumed the Count, "and that you took a milligram the first day, two milligrams the second day, and so on progressively. Well, at the end of ten days you would have taken a centigram; at the end of twenty days, by increasing this by another milligram, you would have taken another three centigrams; that is to say, a dose you would absorb without suffering inconvenience, but which would be extremely dangerous for any other person who had not taken the same precautions as yourself. Well, then, at the end of a month you would have killed the person who drank the water out of the same carafe as yourself; yet, except for a slight indisposition, you would have no other indication that there was poisonous substance mixed with the water."

"Do you know of any other antidote?"

"I do not."

Mme de Villefort sat pensive. After a short silence she said:

"It is very fortunate that such substances can only be prepared by chemists, otherwise one-half of the world would be poisoning the other."

"By chemists or those who dabble in chemistry," replied Monte Cristo carelessly.

"And then no matter how scientifically planned a crime may be, it is still a crime," said Mme de Villefort, tearing herself from her thoughts with an effort, "and though it may escape human investigation, it cannot escape the eye of

God. Yes, there is conscience to grapple with," continued Mme de Villefort in a voice broken with emotion and stifling a sigh.

"It is fortunate that we still have some conscience left, otherwise we should be very unhappy," said Monte Cristo. "After any vigorous action it is conscience that saves us, for it furnishes us with a thousand and one excuses of which we alone are judges, and however excellent these reasons may be to lull us to sleep, before a tribunal they would most likely avail us little in preserving our lives. Take, for instance, Lady Macbeth. She found an excellent servant in her conscience, for she wanted a throne, not for her husband but for her son. Ah, maternal love is a great virtue and such a powerful motive that it excuses much. But for her conscience, Lady Macbeth would have been very unhappy after Duncan's death."

"Do you know, Count, that you are a terrible reasoner," said Mme de Villefort after a moment's silence, "and that you view the world through very dark spectacles! Is it by regarding humanity through alembics[3] and retorts that you have formed your opinion? You are right; you are a great chemist, and the elixir you administered to my son which brought him back to life so rapidly . . ."

"Oh! madame," said Monte Cristo, "one drop of the elixir sufficed to call the dying child back to life, but three drops would have forced the blood to his lungs in such a manner as to produce palpitations of the heart; six would have arrested respiration and caused a much more serious syncope; ten would have killed him! You may remember, madame, how eagerly I snatched from him the phials that he so imprudently touched."

"Is it such a terrible poison then?"

"Good gracious, no! First of all let us admit that the word poison does not exist, since poisons are used in medicines and, according to the manner in which they are administered, become health-giving remedies."

"What is your elixir then?"

"A scientific preparation of my friend, the Abbé Adelmonte, who taught me the use of it."

"It must be an excellent antispasmodic," observed Mme de Villefort.

"A perfect one, madame. You saw for yourself. I frequently make use of it; with all possible prudence, of course," he added with a laugh.

"I should think so," replied Mme de Villefort in the same tone. "As for me, who am so nervous and prone to fainting, I need a Doctor Adelmonte to invent for me some means of breathing freely to relieve me of my fear that I shall suffocate one of these days. In the meantime, as it is difficult to obtain it in France, and as your abbé will not feel inclined to make a journey to Paris on my account, I must content myself with Monsieur Planche's antispasmodics."

"But I have the pleasure of offering it to you," said Monte Cristo, rising.

"Oh, Count!"

"Only remember one thing. In small doses it is a remedy, in large doses it is a poison! One drop will restore life as you have witnessed, five or six will inevitably kill and all the more terribly that, even when diluted in a glass of wine, it in no way changes the flavour. But I will say no more, madame. It is almost as if I were advising you."

The clock struck half-past six, and a friend of Mme de Villefort's, who was dining with her, was announced.

"If I had the pleasure of seeing you for the third or fourth time, Count, instead of the second, if I had the honour of being your friend instead of simply having the pleasure of being under an obligation to you, I should insist on keeping you for dinner, and I should not let myself be daunted by a first refusal."

"A thousand thanks, madame," replied Monte Cristo, "but I have an engagement which I cannot avoid. I have promised to take to the Opera a Grecian princess of my acquaintance, who has never yet seen Grand Opera and is relying on me to escort her."

"I will not detain you then, but do not forget my recipe."

"Most assuredly not, madame, for that would mean forgetting the hour's conversation I have just had with you, and that would be impossible."

Monte Cristo bowed and went out.

Mme de Villefort remained standing, wrapt in thought.

"He is a strange man," said she, "and I could almost believe his baptismal name is Adelmonte."

As for Monte Cristo, the results had far surpassed all expectations. "Here is fruitful soil," said he to himself as he went away. "I am convinced that the seed I have sown has not fallen on barren ground."

Next morning, faithful to his promise, he sent the prescription Mme de Villefort had requested.

Chapter XXXVII

The Rise and Fall of Stocks

⚓

Some days later, Albert de Morcerf called on the Count of Monte Cristo at his house in the Champs Élysées, which had already assumed that palacelike appearance that the Count, thanks to his immense fortune, always gave even to his temporary residences.

Albert was accompanied by Lucien Debray. The Count attributed this visit to a twofold sentiment of curiosity, the larger share of which emanated from the Rue de la Chaussée d'Antin. It was obvious that Mme Danglars, being unable to view with her own eyes the home of the man who gave away horses worth thirty thousand francs, and who went to the Opera accompanied by a slave wearing a million's worth of diamonds, had sent her deputy to gather what information he could. Notwithstanding, the Count did not appear to suspect the slightest connexion between Lucien's visit and the Baroness' curiosity.

"You are in constant communication with Baron Danglars?" he inquired of Albert de Morcerf.

"Oh, yes, you know what I told you."

"It still holds good then?"

"It is quite a settled affair," interposed Lucien, and, doubtless thinking that this remark was all he was called upon to make, he put his tortoise-shell lorgnette[1] to his eye and, with the gold top of his stick in his mouth, began to pace round the room examining the different pictures and weapons.

"Is Mademoiselle Eugénie pretty?" asked Monte Cristo. "I seem to remember that is her name."

"Very pretty, or rather beautiful," replied Albert. "But it is a beauty I do not appreciate. I am an undeserving fellow! Mademoiselle Danglars is too rich for me. Her riches frighten me."

"That's a fine reason to give!" said Monte Cristo. "Are you not rich yourself?"

"My father has an income of some fifty thousand francs, and will probably give me ten or twelve thousand when I marry. But there is something besides that."

"I must own I can hardly understand your objections to such a beautiful and rich young woman," replied the Count.

"Even if there are any objections, they are not all on my side."

"Who raises objections then? I think you told me your father was in favour of the marriage."

"My mother objects to it, and she has a very prudent and penetrating eye. She does not smile on this union; for some reason she has a prejudice against the Danglars family."

"Ah, that is quite comprehensible," said the Count in a somewhat strained tone of voice. "The Countess of Morcerf, who is distinction, aristocracy, and refinement personified, is somewhat disinclined to touch the thick, clumsy hand of a plebeian; that is only natural."

"I really do not know whether that is the reason," said Albert. "What I do know is that, if this marriage is concluded, it will make her unhappy. It would be too great a disappointment to my father if I did not marry Mademoiselle Danglars. And yet I would rather quarrel with the Count than cause my mother pain."

Monte Cristo turned away, apparently agitated.

"What are you doing there?" said he to Debray, who was

seated in a deep armchair at the other end of the room with a pencil in one hand and a notebook in the other. "Are you making a sketch of that Poussin?"

"I?" said he calmly; "a sketch! No, I am doing something very different. I am doing some arithmetic."

"Arithmetic?"

"Yes, and it concerns you indirectly, Morcerf. I was reckoning what the firm of Danglars have gained by the last rise in Hayti[2] stock; they have risen from two hundred and six to four hundred and nine in three days, and the wise banker bought a large amount at two hundred and six. He must have gained three hundred thousand francs."

"That is not his best deal," said Morcerf. "Didn't he make a million this year with his Spanish bonds?"

"Yes, but the Haytis are quite a different matter. Yesterday Monsieur Danglars sold them at four hundred and six and pocketed three hundred thousand francs; had he waited until to-day when the bonds fell to two hundred and five, he would have lost twenty-five thousand francs instead of making three hundred thousand."

"But why have the bonds fallen from four hundred and nine to two hundred and five?" asked Monte Cristo. "Pardon my question, but I am very ignorant of all these tricks on the Exchange."

"Because one piece of news follows the other and there is great dissimilarity between them," replied Albert with a laugh.

"What? Does Monsieur Danglars speculate at the risk of losing or gaining three hundred thousand francs a day? He must be enormously rich!"

"It is not he who speculates," exclaimed Lucien energetically. "It is Madame Danglars. She is very daring."

"But you should stop her," said Morcerf with a smile. "You have common sense enough to know how little one can rely on communiqués, for you are at their very source."

"How should I be able to stop her when her husband has not yet succeeded in doing so? You know the Baroness. No one has any influence over her. She does just what she pleases."

"If I were in your place, I should cure her," said Albert. "You would be doing a kind action to her future son-in-law."

"How would you set about it?"

"It would be perfectly easy. I should teach her a lesson. Your position as Minister's secretary gives you great power over telegraphic dispatches. You never open your mouth to speak but stockbrokers take down every word you say. Make her lose a hundred thousand francs and she will soon be more careful."

"I don't understand," stammered Lucien.

"Nevertheless it is quite comprehensible," replied the young man simply. "One fine morning tell her something stupendous, a telegraphic communication that you alone could know, for example, that Henry the Fourth was seen yesterday at Gabrielle's. That would cause the bonds to rise, she would speculate, and would certainly lose when Beauchamp wrote in his journal the following day: 'The news circulated by some well-informed person that King Henry the Fourth was seen at Gabrielle's the day before yesterday is absolutely without foundation; King Henry the Fourth has not left the Pont Neuf.'"

Lucien gave a forced laugh. Monte Cristo, to all appearances quite indifferent to the conversation, had not lost one word of it, and his quick perception had detected a hidden secret in the private secretary's embarrassment.

In fact Lucien was so embarrassed, though Albert did not perceive it, that he cut short his visit. He evidently felt ill at ease. When the Count accompanied him to the door, he said something to him in a low voice to which he replied: "I accept with pleasure, Count."

The Count returned to young Morcerf and said: "Do you not think that, on reflection, you were wrong to speak as you did of your mother-in-law before Monsieur Debray?"

"Not so fast, Count," said Morcerf. "I pray, do not give her that title so prematurely."

"Without any exaggeration, is your mother really so greatly opposed to this marriage?"

"To such an extent that the Baroness rarely comes to the house, and so far as I know, my mother has not visited Madame Danglars twice in her whole life."

"Then I am emboldened to speak openly to you," said the Count. "Monsieur Danglars is my banker; Monsieur de Villefort has overwhelmed me with politeness in return for a service which a casual piece of good fortune enabled me to render him. I predict from this an avalanche of dinners and parties. Now, in order to forestall them, and if it be agreeable to you, I propose inviting Monsieur and Madame Danglars and Monsieur and Madame de Villefort to my country house at Auteuil. If I were to invite you and the Count and Countess of Morcerf to this dinner, it would give it the air of a matrimonial rendezvous, or at least, Madame de Morcerf would look upon it in that light, especially if Baron Danglars did me the honour of bringing his daughter. In that case I should incur your mother's displeasure, and that I do not wish; on the contrary (pray tell her this whenever the occasion arises), I desire to occupy a prominent place in her esteem."

"I thank you sincerely for having been so candid with me, Count, and I gratefully accept the exclusion you propose. You say you desire my mother's good opinion of you; I assure you it is already yours to a very large extent."

"Do you think so?" said Monte Cristo interestedly.

"I am sure of it; we talked of you for an hour after you left us the other day. But to return to what we were saying. If my mother knew of this consideration on your part, and I will venture to tell her, I am sure she would be most grateful to you; it is true that my father will be equally furious."

The Count laughed.

"But I think your father will not be the only angry one," he said to Morcerf. "Monsieur and Madame Danglars will think me a very ill-mannered person. They know that I am on an intimate footing with you, that you are in fact one of my oldest Paris acquaintances, yet they will not find you at my house. They will certainly ask me why I did not invite you. Be sure to provide yourself with some prior engagement with a semblance of probability, and communicate the fact to me in writing. You know that with bankers nothing but a written document is valid."

"I will do better than that," said Albert. "My mother is anxious to go to the seaside. For which day is your dinner fixed?"

"Saturday."

"This is Tuesday. Well, we will leave to-morrow evening, and the day after we shall be at Tréport. Do you know, Count, you have a charming way of setting people at their ease."

"Indeed, you give me credit for more than I deserve; I only wish to do what would be agreeable to you."

"That is settled, then. Now will you show yourself a true friend and come and dine with me? We shall be a small party, only yourself, my mother, and I. You have scarcely seen my mother; you will have an opportunity of making her closer acquaintance. She is a remarkable woman, and I only regret there does not exist another about twenty years younger like her. In that case I assure you there would very soon be a Countess and a Viscountess of Morcerf."

"A thousand thanks," said the Count. "Your invitation is most kind, and I regret exceedingly that it is not in my power to accept it. I am not so free as you suppose; on the contrary, I have a most important engagement."

"Take care! You showed me just now how one could creditably refuse an unwelcome invitation. I require proofs. I am not a banker like Monsieur Danglars, but, I assure you, I am as incredulous as he."

"I will give you a proof," said the Count as he rang the bell.

"Humph!" said Morcerf. "This is the second time you have refused to dine with my mother; it is evidently done deliberately."

Monte Cristo started. "You do not mean that," said he. "Besides, here comes my proof."

Baptistin entered and remained standing at the door.

"Baptistin," said the Count, "what did I tell you this morning when I called you into my study?"

"To close the door against visitors as soon as the clock struck five," replied the valet.

"What then?"

"You further told me to admit no one but Major Bartolomeo Cavalcanti and his son."

"You hear: Major Cavalcanti, a man who ranks amongst the most ancient nobility of Italy, whose name Dante has celebrated in the tenth canto of the *Inferno*; you remember it, don't you? Then there is his son, a charming young man of about your own age, Viscount, and bearing the same title as yourself, who is making his début into Paris society aided by his father's millions. The Major will bring his son, the *contino*, as we say in Italy, with him this evening; he wishes to confide him to my care. If he prove himself worthy of it, I will do what I can for him; you will assist me, will you not?"

"Most certainly. This Major Cavalcanti is an old friend of yours?"

"By no means. I met him several times at Florence, Bologna, and Lucca, and he has now communicated to me that he has arrived here. I shall give him a good dinner; he will confide his son to my care; I shall promise to watch over him; I shall let him follow in whatever path his folly may lead him, and then I shall have done my part."

"Splendid! I see you are a valuable mentor," said Albert. "Good-bye. We shall be back on Sunday. By the way, I have received news of Franz."

"Have you? Is he still enjoying himself in Italy?"

"I believe so, and he greatly regrets your absence. He says you were the sun of Rome, and that without you all appears dark and cloudy; I am not sure that he does not go so far as to say that it rains."

"He is a charming young man," said Monte Cristo, "and I have always felt a lively interest in him. He is the son of General d'Épinay, I think."

"Yes, he is."

"The same who was ao shamefully assassinated in eighteen-fifteen?"

"By the Bonapartists."

"That's it. Really, I like him extremely. Is there not a matrimonial engagement contemplated for him too?"

"Yes, he is to marry Mademoiselle de Villefort."

"Indeed!"

"And you know I am to marry Mademoiselle Danglars," said Albert, laughing.

"You smile? Why?"

"I smile because there seems to be as much sympathy for that marriage as there is for my own. But really, my dear Count, we are talking as much of women as they do of us; it is unpardonable."

Albert rose.

"Give my compliments to your illustrious visitor, Cavalcanti," he continued, "and if by any chance he should be desirous of finding a wife for his son who is very rich, of very noble birth on her mother's side, and a Baroness in right of her father, I will help you to find one."

And with a laugh Albert departed.

Chapter XXXVIII

PYRAMUS AND THISBE

Our readers must permit us to conduct them to the enclosure surrounding Monsieur de Villefort's house, and, behind the gate half hidden by widespreading chestnut-trees, we shall find some persons of our acquaintance.

Maximilian was the first to arrive. With his eyes close to the fence he was watching for a shadow among the trees at the bottom of the garden, and listening for a footfall on the gravel paths.

At length the desired sound was heard, but instead of one shadow there were two. Valentine had been delayed by a visit from Mme Danglars and Eugénie which had lasted longer than she had anticipated; but that she might not fail to keep her appointment with Maximilian, she had proposed to Mlle Danglars that they should take a walk in the garden, which would enable her to show Maximilian that the delay was not caused by any fault of hers.

With the intuitive perception of a lover, the young man understood the circumstances and was greatly relieved. Besides, without coming within speaking distance, Valentine led her companion where Maximilian could see her go by, and each time she passed near him a look, unperceived by her companion, said to him: "Have patience, my friend, you see it is none of my doing."

And Maximilian was patient and spent his time appreciating the contrast between the two young girls: the one fair-haired, with languid eyes and a tall figure, slightly bent like a beautiful weeping willow; the other dark-haired, with fiery eyes and a figure as upright as a poplar. Needless to say, the comparison between these two opposed natures was all in Valentine's favour, at least in the opinion of the young man.

At the end of half an hour, the girls disappeared, and an instant later Valentine returned alone. She ran up to the gate.

"Good evening, Valentine," said a voice.

"Good evening, Maximilian. I have kept you waiting, but you saw the reason."

"Yes, I recognized Mademoiselle Danglars. I did not know you were so intimate with her."

"Who told you we were intimate?"

"No one, but the manner in which you walked and talked rather suggested it. You looked like two schoolgirls exchanging confidences."

"We were in fact exchanging confidences," returned Valentine. "She was telling me how repugnant to her was the idea of a marriage with Monsieur de Morcerf, and I confessed to her how unhappy I was at the thought of marrying Monsieur d'Épinay. In speaking of the man I cannot love, I thought of the man I love. She told me that she detests the idea of marriage, that her greatest joy would be to lead a free and independent life, and that she almost wished her father would lose his fortune so that she could become an artist like her friend, Mademoiselle Louise d'Armilly. But let us talk of ourselves and not of her, for we have not more than ten minutes together."

"Why, what has happened, Valentine, that you must leave me so soon?"

"I do not know. Madame de Villefort told me to go to her room as she had something to communicate to me which influences a part of my fortune. Ah, well! let them take the whole of my fortune, I am too rich. When they have taken it, perhaps they will leave me in peace. You would love me just as much if I were poor, would you not, Maximilian?"

"I shall always love you. What should I care about wealth or poverty as long as my Valentine was near me, and I was sure no one could take her from me! But do you not fear the communication may be in connexion with your approaching marriage?"

"I do not think so."

"In any case, listen to me, Valentine, and do not be afraid, for as long as I live, I will never belong to another."

"Do you think you make me happy by telling me that, Maximilian?"

"Forgive me, dear, for being such a churl. What I wanted to tell you is that the other day I met Monsieur de Morcerf, who, as you know, is Monsieur Franz's friend. He had received a letter from him intimating his early return."

Valentine turned pale and leaned against the gate for support.

"Can it be that?" she cried. "But no, such a communication would not come from Madame de Villefort."

"Why not?"

"Because . . . I scarcely know why . . . but though she does not oppose my proposed marriage openly, Madame de Villefort seems to be against it."

"Is that so? Then I think I almost love Madame de Villefort!"

"Do not be in such a hurry, Maximilian," said Valentine with a sad smile.

"If she is averse to this marriage, let the engagement be broken off, and then perhaps she would lend her ear to some other proposal."

"Do not lay any hopes on that, Maximilian, it is not the husband my stepmother objects to, it is marriage itself."

"You don't mean to say so! But if she has such a strong aversion to marriage, why did she herself marry?"

"You do not understand. A year ago, when I spoke of entering a convent, though she felt it her duty to make certain comments, she accepted my proposal with joy. Even my father consented—at her instigation, I am sure. It was my poor grandfather kept me back! Maximilian, you can have no idea of the expression in the eyes of the old man, who loves no one but me, and (may God forgive me if I am wrong) who is loved by no one but me. If you knew how he looked at me when he heard of my resolution! What reproach there was in those dear eyes and despair in the uncomplaining tears that chased each other down his lifeless cheeks! Oh, Maximilian, I felt such remorse that I threw myself at his feet exclaiming: 'Forgive me. Oh, forgive me, Grandfather! Let them do with me what they will, I will never leave you!' He just raised his eyes to Heaven! I can suffer much! That look recompensed me in advance for all I shall suffer."

"Dearest Valentine! You are an angel, and I am sure I do not know in what way I have merited your love. But tell me, how could it be to Madame de Villefort's interest that you should not marry?"

"Did I not tell you just now that I was rich, too rich? I have an income of nearly fifty thousand francs from my father; my grandfather and grandmother, the Marquis and Marquise of Saint-Méran, will leave me a similar amount; Monsieur Noirtier obviously intends to make me his sole heir. By comparison with me, therefore, my brother, Edward, who will inherit no fortune from his mother, is poor. Madame de Villefort's love for this child amounts to adoration, and if I had taken the veil, all my fortune would have descended to my father, and would ultimately have reverted to her son."

"How strange that such a young and beautiful woman should be so avaricious!"

"It is not for herself she wants the money; it is for her son, and what you consider a vice is almost a virtue from the point of view of maternal love."

"But why not give up part of your fortune to her son?"

"How could I propose such a thing, especially to a woman who continually speaks of her disinterestedness?"

"Valentine, my love is sacred to me, and, this being so, I have covered it with the veil of respect and locked the door to my heart. No one knows of its existence there, for I have confided in no one. Will you permit me to speak of this love to a friend?"

Valentine started. "To a friend?" said she. "Oh, to hear you speak thus makes me shudder. Who is this friend?"

"Valentine, have you never felt for anyone an irresistible sympathy so that, though you meet this person for the first time, you feel you have known him long since?"

"I have."

"Well, then, this is the feeling I had the first time I saw this extraordinary man, who has, I hear, the power to prophesy."

"Then," said the girl sadly, "let me know him that I may learn from him whether I shall be loved sufficiently to compensate me for all I have suffered."

"Poor girl! You know him already. It is he who saved the life of your stepmother and her son."

"The Count of Monte Cristo!"

"It is he."

"Oh, he can never be my friend!" exclaimed Valentine. "He is too much the friend of Madame de Villefort ever to be mine."

"The Count is your stepmother's friend, Valentine? That cannot be! I am sure you must be mistaken."

"If you but knew! It is no longer Edward who rules in the house, it is the Count. Courted by my stepmother, who sees in him the essence of human knowledge; admired, mark well, Maximilian, admired by my father, who says he has never heard the most elevated ideas expressed so eloquently; idolized by Edward, who, despite his fear of the Count's large black eyes, runs to him as soon as he arrives and forces his hand open, where he always finds some fascinating toy. Monte Cristo is not in my father's or my stepmother's house, he is in his own house."

"Valentine, you are mistaken, I assure you!"

"If it were otherwise, he would have honoured me at least with one of those smiles, of which you think so much. On the contrary, he sees me unhappy, but he realizes that I can be of no use to him, so he does not pay any attention to me. Quite frankly, I am not a woman to be treated with contempt in this manner without any reason for it. You yourself have told me as much. Forgive me, Maximilian," she continued on seeing the impression her words were producing on Maximilian. "I am a wicked girl, and am saying things about this man that I did not know existed in my heart. Alas, I see that I have pained you! If only I could take your hand to ask your forgiveness! I desire nothing better than to be convinced. Tell me, what has this Count done for you?"

"I must confess that question rather embarrasses me. He has done nothing that I can definitely mention. My friendship for him is as unaccountable as his is for me. A secret voice warns me that there is something more than chance in this unlooked-for reciprocity of friendship. You will laugh at me, I know, but ever since I have known him the absurd idea possesses me that everything good that befalls me comes from him! Yet I have lived for thirty years without feeling the need of this friendship. I will give you an example of his consideration for me. He has invited me to dinner on Saturday, which is quite natural in view of our present relations. But what have I learned since? Your mother and father are also invited. I shall meet them, and who knows what will be the issue of such a meeting? In appearance this is a perfectly simple circumstance, I know; nevertheless I see in it something that astonishes me and fills me with a strange hope. I cannot help thinking that this extraordinary man, who divines all things, has arranged this meeting with some aim in view. I assure you there are times when I try to read in his eyes whether he has not even guessed my love for you."

"My dear," said Valentine, "I should take you for a visionary, and should really fear for your reason if I were to listen to many more such arguments from you. No, no, believe me, apart from you, there is no one in this world to whom I can turn for help and support but my grandfather, who is not much more than alive, and my poor mother, of whom there is nothing left but a shadow."

"I feel that you are right, Valentine, from a logical point of view, but your sweet voice, which at other times possesses so much power over me, cannot convince me to-day."

"Neither can you convince me," said Valentine, "and I will confess that if you have no other proofs to give me . . ."

"But I have," interrupted Maximilian, "though I am compelled to own that it sounds even more absurd than the first one. Look through the palings[1] and you will see tied to that tree yonder the horse that brought me here."

"What a beautiful animal!" exclaimed Valentine. "Why did you not bring him up to the gate? I should have spoken to him, and he would have understood me!"

"As you see, it is really a very valuable animal," Maximilian continued. "You also know that my income is limited, and I am what one would call a careful man. I went to a horsedealer's and saw this magnificent animal that I have called Médéah. On asking the price, I was told four thousand five hundred francs. As you can imagine I admired it no longer but, I must confess, I left with a heavy heart. I had a few friends at my house that evening, and they proposed a game of *bouillotte*.[2] As we were seating ourselves at the table, the Count of Monte Cristo arrived. He took his seat, we played, and I won. I hardly dare tell you how much: it was five thousand francs! We parted at midnight. I could contain myself no longer; I took a cab and drove to the horsedealer's and, filled with feverish excitement, rang the bell. The man who opened the door to me must have taken me for a madman. I rushed through to the stable. Oh, joy! There was Médéah calmly eating his hay. I took a saddle and bridle and put them on him; then, placing the four thousand five hundred francs in the astonished dealer's hand, I leapt on to Médéah's back and spent the night riding in the Champs Elysées. I saw a light in the Count's window, and I seemed to see his shadow behind the curtain. Now, I am perfectly certain the Count knew how badly I wanted that horse, and that he intentionally lost at cards so that I might win."

"Dearest Maximilian, you are becoming so fanciful that I verily believe you will not love me any more. A man who lives in such a world of poetry will grow weary of a monotonous passion such as ours. But listen, they are calling me. Do you hear?"

"Oh, Valentine, give me your little finger through the gate that I may kiss it!"

"Maximilian, we said we would be to each other as two voices, two shadows."

"As you wish, Valentine."

"Will it make you happy if I do what you ask?"

"Oh, yes!"

Valentine jumped on to a bench and passed her whole hand, not her little finger, through the grating.

Maximilian uttered a cry of joy and, springing forward, seized the beloved hand and imprinted on it a long and impassioned kiss; but the little hand slipped out of his almost immediately, and the young man heard his beloved running toward the house, frightened perhaps at her own sensations.

Chapter XXXIX

M. NOIRTIER DE VILLEFORT

This is what happened in the house of the Procureur du Roi after the departure of Mme Danglars and her daughter, and while the foregoing conversation was taking place.

M. de Villefort entered his father's room followed by Mme de Villefort. After saluting the old man and dismissing Barrois, his old servant, they seated themselves on either side of the old gentleman.

M. Noirtier was sitting in his wheel-chair, to which he was carried every morning and left there until the evening. Sight and hearing were the only two senses that, like two solitary sparks, animated this poor human body that was so near the grave. His hair was white and long, reaching down to his shoulders, while his eyes were black, overshadowed by black eyebrows, and, as is generally the case when one organ is used to the exclusion of the others, in these eyes were concentrated all the activity, skill, strength, and intelligence which had formerly characterized his whole body and mind. It is true that the gesture of the arm, the sound of the voice, the attitude of the body were now lacking, but his masterful eye supplied their place. He commanded with his eyes and thanked with his eyes; he was a corpse with living eyes, and nothing was more terrifying than when, in this face of marble, they were lit up in fiery anger or sparkled with joy. There were only three persons who understood the language of the poor paralytic—Villefort, Valentine, and the old servant. As Villefort rarely saw his father, however, and even then did not take any pains to understand him, all the old man's happiness centred upon his granddaughter, and by force of devotion, love, and patience, she had learned to read all his thoughts by his look. To this dumb language, unintelligible to all others, she replied by throwing her whole soul into her voice and the expression of her countenance. In this manner animated dialogues took place between the granddaughter and this mere lump of clay, now nearly turned to dust, which constituted the body of a man still in possession of an immense fund of knowledge and most extraordinary perception, together with a will as powerful as it is possible for a mind to possess which is encumbered by a body over which it has lost the power of compelling obedience.

His servant had been with him for twenty-five years and was so perfectly acquainted with his master's habits that Noirtier rarely had to ask for anything.

"Do not be astonished, monsieur," Villefort began, "that Valentine is not with us or that I have dismissed Barrois, for our interview is one which could not take place before a young girl or a servant. Madame de Villefort and I have a communication to make which we feel sure will be agreeable to you. We are going to marry Valentine."

A wax figure could not have evinced more indifference on hearing this intelligence than did M. Noirtier.

"The marriage will take place within three months," continued Villefort.

The old man's eyes were still expressionless.

Mme de Villefort then took her part in the conversation, and added: "We thought this news would be of interest to you, monsieur, for Valentine has always appeared to be the object of your affection. It now only remains for us to tell you the name of the young man for whom she is destined. It is one of the most desirable connexions Valentine could aspire to; he has a fortune, a good name, and her future happiness is guaranteed by the good qualities and tastes of him for whom we have destined her. His name is not unknown to you, for the young man in question is Monsieur Franz de Quesnel, Baron d'Épinay."

During his wife's discourse, Villefort fixed his eyes upon the old man with greater attention than ever. When the name of Franz d'Épinay was uttered Noirtier's eyes, whose every expression was comprehensible to his son, quivered like lips trying to speak, and sent forth a lightning dart. The Procureur du Roi was well aware of the reports formerly current of public enmity between his own father and Franz's father, and he understood Noirtier's agitation and anger. Feigning not to perceive either, however, he resumed the conversation where his wife had left off.

"It is important, monsieur," he said, "that Valentine, who is about to enter upon her nineteenth year, should finally be settled in life. Nevertheless, we have not forgotten you in our discussions on the matter and have ascertained that the future husband of Valentine will consent not to live with you, as that might be embarrassing for a young couple, but that you live with them. In this way you and Valentine, who are so greatly attached to one another, will not be separated, and you will not need to make any change in your mode of living. The only difference will be that you will have two children to take care of you instead of one."

Noirtier's look was one of fury. It was evident that something desperate was passing through the old man's mind and that there rose to his throat a cry of anger and grief which, being unable to find vent in utterance, was choking him, for his face became purple and his lips blue.

"This marriage," continued Mme de Villefort, "is acceptable to Monsieur d'Épinay and his family, which, by the way, only consists of an uncle and aunt. His mother died in giving him birth, and his father was assassinated in eighteen-fifteen, that is to say, when the child was barely two years of age. He has, therefore, only his own wishes to consult."

"That assassination was most mysterious," continued Villefort, "and the perpetrators are still unknown, although suspicion has fallen on many."

Noirtier made such an effort to speak that his lips expanded into a weird kind of smile.

"Now the real criminals," continued Villefort, "those who are conscious of having committed the crime and upon whose heads the justice of man may fall during their lifetime and the justice of God after their death, would be only too happy if they had, like us, a daughter to offer to Monsieur Franz d'Épinay to allay all appearances of suspicion."

Noirtier composed his feelings with a mastery one would not have supposed existed in that shattered frame.

"I understand," his look said to Villefort, and this look expressed at once a feeling of profound contempt and intelligent anger. Villefort read in it all that it contained, but merely shrugged his shoulders in reply, and made a sign to his wife to take her leave.

"I will leave you now," she said. "May I send Edward to pay his respects to you?"

It had been arranged that the old man should express assent by closing his eyes, refusal by blinking several times, a desire for something by casting a look heavenward. If he wanted Valentine, he only closed his right eye, if Barrois the left.

At Mme de Villefort's proposal he bunked vigorously. Vexed at this refusal, Mme de Villefort bit her lips as she said: "Would you like me to send Valentine then?"

"Yes," signed the old man, shutting his right eye tightly.

M. and Mme de Villefort bowed and left the room, giving orders for Valentine to be summoned. She had, however, already been warned that her presence would be required in her grandfather's room during the day. Still flushed with emotion, she entered as soon as her parents had left. One glance at her grandfather told her how much he was suffering, and that he had a great deal to communicate to her.

"Grandpapa, dear, what has happened?" she exclaimed. "Have they vexed you? Are you angry?"

"Yes," said he, closing his eyes.

"With whom are you angry? Is it with my father? No. With Madame de Villefort? No. With me?"

The old man made a sign of assent.

"With me?" repeated Valentine, astonished. "What have I done, dear Grandpapa? I have not seen you the whole day. Has anyone been speaking against me?"

"Yes," said the old man, closing his eyes with emphasis.

"Let me think. I assure you, Grandpapa . . . Ah! Monsieur and Madame de Villefort have been here. They must have said something to annoy you? What is it? How you frighten me! Oh, dear, what can they have said?" She thought for a moment. "I have it," she said, lowering her voice and drawing closer to the old man. "Did they perhaps speak of my marriage?"

"Yes," replied the angry look.

"I understand. Are you afraid I shall forsake you and that my marriage will make me forgetful of you?"

"No," was the answer.

"Did they tell you that Monsieur d'Épinay agrees that we shall all live together?"

"Yes."

"Then why are you angry?"

The old man's eyes beamed with an expression of gentle affection.

"I understand," said Valentine. "It is because you love me."

The old man made a sign of assent.

"Are you afraid I shall be unhappy?"

"Yes."

"Do you not like Franz?"

His eyes repeated three or four times: "No, no, no."

"Then you are very grieved?"

"Yes."

"Well, listen," said Valentine, throwing herself on her knees and putting her arms round his neck. "I am grieved too, for I do not love Monsieur Franz d'Épinay. If only you could help me! If only we could frustrate their plans! But you are powerless against them, though your mind is so active and your will so firm."

As she said these words, there was such a look of deep cunning in Noirtier's eyes that the girl thought she read these words therein: "You are mistaken, I can still do much for you."

Noirtier raised his eyes heavenward. It was the sign agreed upon between Valentine and himself whenever he wanted anything.

"What do you wish, Grandpapa?" She then recited all the letters of the alphabet until she came to N, all the while watching his eyes with a smile on her face. When she came to N he signalled assent.

"Then what you desire begins with the letter N. Now, let me see what you can want that begins with the letter N. Na . . . ne . . . ni . . . no . . ."

"Yes, yes, yes," said the old man's eyes.

Valentine fetched a dictionary, which she placed on a desk before Noirtier. She opened it, and, as soon as she saw that his eyes were fixed on its pages, she ran her fingers quickly up and down the columns. All the practice she had had during the six years since M. Noirtier first fell into this pitiable state had made her expert at detecting his wishes in this manner, and she guessed his thoughts as quickly as though he himself had been able to seek for what he wanted.

At the word notary the old man made a sign for her to stop.

"You wish me to send for a notary?" asked Valentine.

"Yes."

"Do you wish to have the notary at once?"

"Yes."

"Then he shall be sent for immediately."

Valentine rang the bell, and told the servant to request M. and Mme de Villefort to come to M. Noirtier.

"Are you satisfied now?" Valentine asked. "Yes, I am sure you are. But it was not easy to discover what you wanted, was it?"

And the maiden smiled at her grandfather as though he were a child.

Chapter XL

THE WILL

Three-quarters of an hour later, Barrois returned bringing the notary with him.

"You were sent for by Monsieur Noirtier, whom you see here," said Villefort after the first salutations were over. "He is paralysed and has lost the use of his voice and limbs, and we ourselves have great difficulty in understanding his thoughts."

Noirtier cast on Valentine an appealing look which was at once so earnest and imperative that she answered immediately: "Monsieur, I understand all that my grandfather wishes to say."

"That is true, absolutely true," said Barrois, "and it is what I told the gentleman as we walked along."

"Permit me," said the notary, turning first to Villefort and then to Valentine, "permit me to state that the case in question is just one of those in which a public official like myself cannot proceed to act without due consideration, as he might incur serious responsibility. The first thing necessary to render a document valid is that the notary is absolutely convinced that he has faithfully interpreted the wishes of the person dictating them. Now, I cannot be sure of the approbation or disapprobation of a client who cannot speak,

323

and, as owing to his loss of speech the object of his desire or repugnance cannot be clearly proved to me, my services here would be more than useless and cannot be exercised legally."

The notary prepared to retire. An almost imperceptible smile of triumph was expressed on Villefort's lips, but Noirtier looked at Valentine with such an expression of grief that she arrested the departure of the notary.

"The language I speak with my grandfather, monsieur," said she, "is easily learnt, and in a very few minutes I can teach you to understand it almost as well as I do myself. By the help of two signs, you can be absolutely certain that my grandfather is still in full possession of all his mental faculties. Being deprived of power of speech and motion, Monsieur Noirtier closes his eyes when he wishes to signify yes and blinks when he means no. You now know quite enough to enable you to converse with Monsieur Noirtier; try."

Noirtier gave Valentine such a look of love and gratitude that it was comprehended by the notary himself.

"Have you heard and understood what your granddaughter was telling me, monsieur?" the notary asked.

Noirtier closed his eyes gently and after a second opened them again.

"And you approve of what she said—that is, that the signs she mentioned are really those by means of which you are accustomed to convey your thoughts to others?"

"Yes."

"It was you who sent for me?"

"Yes."

"And you do not wish me to go away without carrying out your original intention?"

The old man blinked violently.

"Well, monsieur," said Valentine, "do you understand now? Will your conscience be at rest in regard to this matter? I can discover and explain to you my grandfather's thoughts so completely as to put an end to any doubts and fears you may have. I have now been six years with Monsieur Noirtier, and let him tell you if, during that time, he has ever entertained a thought which he was unable to make me understand."

"No," signalled the old man.

"Let us try what we can do then," said the notary. "Do you accept this young lady as your interpreter, Monsieur Noirtier?"

"Yes."

"What do you require of me, monsieur? What document do you wish me to draw up?"

Valentine named all the letters of the alphabet until she came to W. At this letter Noirtier's eloquent eyes notified that she was to stop.

"It is very evident that it is the letter W Monsieur Noirtier wants," the notary said.

"Wait," said Valentine, and, turning to her grandfather, she repeated: "Wa . . . we . . . wi . . ."

Her grandfather stopped her at the last syllable.

Valentine then took the dictionary, and the notary watched her whilst she turned over the pages. She passed her finger slowly down the columns, and when she came to the word will Monsieur Noirtier's eyes bade her stop.

"Will!" cried the notary. "It is very evident that monsieur desires to make his will."

"Yes, yes, yes!" motioned the invalid.

"Really, monsieur," interposed Villefort, "you must allow that this is most extraordinary; for I cannot see how the will is to be drawn up without Valentine's intervention and she may, perhaps, be considered as too much interested in its contents to allow of her being a suitable interpreter of the obscure and ill-defined wishes of her grandfather."

"No, no, no!" replied the eyes of the paralytic.

"What! Do you mean to say that Valentine is not interested in your will?" said Villefort.

"No."

"What appeared to me so impossible an hour ago has

now become quite easy and practicable," said the notary, whose interest had been greatly excited. "This will be a perfectly valid will, provided it be read in the presence of seven witnesses approved by the testator, and sealed by the notary in the presence of the witnesses. In order to make the instrument incontestable, I shall give it the greatest possible authenticity. One of my colleagues will help me, and, contrary to custom, will assist in the dictation of the instrument. Are you satisfied, monsieur?" continued the notary, addressing M. Noirtier.

"Yes," looked the invalid, his eyes beaming with delight that his meaning had been so well understood.

"What is he going to do?" thought Villefort, whose position demanded so much reserve, though he was longing to know what were his father's intentions. He left the room to give orders to send for another notary, but Barrois, who had heard all that passed, had guessed his master's wishes and had already gone to fetch one. The Procureur du Roi called his wife up.

In the course of a quarter of an hour everyone had assembled in the paralytic's room, and the second notary had also arrived. A few words sufficed for a mutual understanding between the two officers of the law. They read to Noirtier the formal copy of a will in order to give him an idea of the terms in which such documents are generally couched; then, to test the intelligence of the testator, the first notary, turning toward him, said:

"When an individual makes his will, it is generally in favour or in prejudice of some person."

"Yes."

"Have you an exact idea of the amount of your fortune?"

"Yes."

"Your fortune exceeds three hundred thousand francs, does it not?"

Noirtier made a sign that it did.

"Do you possess four hundred thousand francs?" inquired the notary.

Noirtier's eyes remained unmoved.

"Five hundred thousand?"

There was still no movement.

"Six hundred—seven hundred—nine hundred thousand?"

Noirtier stopped him at the last-mentioned sum.

"You are then in possession of nine hundred thousand francs?" asked the notary.

"Yes."

"In scrip?"

"Yes."

"The scrip is in your own hands?"

The look which Noirtier cast on Barrois sent the old servant out of the room, and he presently returned, bringing a small casket.

"Do you permit us to open the casket?" asked the notary. Noirtier gave his assent.

They opened it and found nine hundred thousand francs in bank scrip.

The first notary examined each note and handed them all to his colleague. The total amount was found to be as M. Noirtier stated.

"It is all as he said; it is very evident that his mind has retained its full force and vigour." Then, turning toward the paralytic, he said: "You possess nine hundred thousand francs of capital, which, according to the manner in which you have invested it, should bring in an income of forty thousand francs?"

"Yes."

"Is it, then, to Mademoiselle Valentine de Villefort that you leave these nine hundred thousand francs?" demanded the notary, thinking that he had but to insert this clause, though he must first wait for Noirtier's assent, which needed to be given before all the witnesses of this singular scene.

Valentine had stepped back with eyes cast down and was weeping silently. The old man looked at her for a moment with an expression of the deepest tenderness; then, turning toward the notary, he blinked in a most emphatic manner.

"What!" said the notary. "Do you not intend making Mademoiselle Valentine de Villefort your residuary legatee?"

"No."

"You are not making any mistake, are you?" said the notary. "You really mean to say no?"

"No, no."

Valentine raised her head; she was astonished not so much at the fact that she was disinherited as that she should have provoked the feeling which generally dictates such actions. Noirtier, however, looked at her so lovingly that she exclaimed:

"Oh, Grandpapa! I see now that it is only your fortune of which you deprive me; you still leave me your love."

The old man's declaration that Valentine was not the destined inheritor of his fortune had raised hopes in Mme de Villefort; she approached the invalid and said:

"Then, doubtless, dear Monsieur Noirtier, you desire to leave your fortune to your grandson, Edward de Villefort?"

The blinking of the eyes was terrible in its vigour and expressed a feeling almost amounting to hatred.

"No!" said the notary. "Then perhaps to your son, Monsieur de Villefort?"

"No."

The two notaries looked at each other in mute astonishment and inquiry. Villefort and his wife both flushed a deep crimson, the one from shame, the other from anger.

"What have we all done, then, dear Grandpapa?" said Valentine. "Do you not love us any more?"

Noirtier fixed his intelligent eyes on Valentine's hand.

"My hand?" said she. "Ah, I understand, I understand. It is my marriage you mean, is it not, dear Grandpapa?"

"Yes, yes, yes!" the paralytic repeated three times, and each time he raised his eyelids his eyes gleamed angrily.

"You are angry with us all on account of this marriage, are you not?"

"Yes."

"Really this is too absurd!" exclaimed Villefort.

"Excuse me, monsieur," said the notary, "but it is, on the contrary, very logical and I quite follow his train of thought."

"You do not wish me to marry Monsieur Franz d'Épinay?" observed Valentine.

"I do not wish it!" said her grandfather's eyes.

"And you disinherit your granddaughter," continued the notary, "because she has contracted an engagement contrary to your wishes?"

"Yes."

There was profound silence. The two notaries entered into consultation; Valentine, her hands clasped, looked at her grandfather with a smile of intense gratitude, and Villefort bit his thin lips in suppressed anger, whilst Mme de Villefort could not succeed in repressing an inward feeling of joy which, in spite of herself, was depicted on her whole countenance.

"But I consider that I am the best judge of the propriety of the marriage in question," said Villefort, who was the first to break the silence. "I alone possess the right to dispose of my daughter's hand. It is my wish that she should marry Monsieur Franz d'Épinay—and marry him she shall!"

Valentine sank into a chair, weeping.

"How do you intend disposing of your fortune, monsieur, in the event of Mademoiselle de Villefort marrying Monsieur Franz?" said the notary. "You will, of course, dispose of it in some way or other?"

"Yes."

"In favour of some member of your family?"

"No."

"Do you intend devoting it to charitable purposes, then?"

"Yes."

"But you are aware that the law does not allow a son to be entirely deprived of his patrimony?" said the notary.

"Yes."

"Then you only intend to dispose of that part of your fortune which the law allows you to subtract from your son's inheritance?"

Noirtier made no answer.

"Do you still wish to dispose of all?"

"Yes."

"But they will contest the will after your death!"

"No."

"My father knows me," replied Villefort. "He is quite sure that his wishes will be held sacred by me; besides, he understands that, in my position, I cannot plead against the poor."

Noirtier's eyes beamed triumphantly.

"What have you decided on, monsieur?" asked the notary of Villefort.

"Nothing; it is a resolution which my father has taken, and I know he never changes his mind. I am quite resigned. These nine hundred thousand francs will pass from the family to enrich some hospital; but I shall not yield to the whims of an old man, and I shall therefore act according to the dictates of my conscience."

Having said this, Villefort quitted the room with his wife, leaving his father at liberty to do what he pleased.

The same day the will was drawn up, the witnesses were brought forward, it was approved by the old man, sealed in the presence of all, and given into the charge of M. Deschamps, the family notary.

Chapter XLI

THE TELEGRAPH

O n returning to their own apartments, M. and Mme de
Villefort learned that the Count of Monte Cristo, who
had come to pay them a visit, had, during their absence,
been shown into the salon where he was awaiting them.
Mme de Villefort was too agitated to see him at once and
retired to her bedroom, while her husband, being more
self-possessed, went straight into the salon. But though he
was able to master his feelings and compose his features, he
could not dispel the cloud that shadowed his brow, and the
Count, who received him with a radiant smile, noticed his
gloomy and preoccupied manner.

"What on earth is the matter, Monsieur de Villefort?"
said Monte Cristo after the first compliments were
exchanged. "Have you just been drawing up some capital
indictment?"

"No, Count," said he, trying to smile, "this time I am the
victim. It is I who have lost my case, and fate, obstinacy, and
madness have been the counsel for the prosecution."

"What do you mean?" asked the Count, with well-
feigned interest. "Have you really met with some serious
misfortune?"

"Oh, it is not worth mentioning," said he with a calmness

331

that betokened bitterness. "It is nothing, only a loss of money."

"Loss of money is, indeed, somewhat insignificant to a man with a fortune such as you possess, and to a mind as elevated and philosophical as yours is."

"It is, however, not the loss of the money that grieves me, though after all nine hundred thousand francs is worthy of regret, and annoyance at its loss is quite comprehensible. What hurts me is the ill-will manifested by fate, chance, fatality, or whatever the designation of the power may be that has dealt this blow. My hopes of a fortune are dashed to the ground, and perhaps even my daughter's future blasted by the whims of an old man who has sunk into second childhood."

"Nine hundred thousand francs, did you say?" exclaimed the Count. "That is certainly a sum of money that even a philosopher might regret. Who has caused you this annoyance?"

"My father, of whom I spoke to you."

"My dear," said Mme de Villefort, who had just entered the room, "perhaps you are exaggerating the evil."

"Madame," said the Count, bowing.

Mme de Villefort acknowledged the salutation with one of her most gracious smiles.

"What is this Monsieur de Villefort has just been telling me?" asked Monte Cristo. "What an incomprehensible misfortune!"

"Incomprehensible! That is the very word," exclaimed Villefort, shrugging his shoulders. "A whim born of old age!"

"Is there no means of making him revoke his decision?"

"There is," was Mme de Villefort's reply. "It is even in my husband's power to have the will changed in Valentine's favour instead of its being to her prejudice."

"My dear," said Villefort in answer to his wife, "it is distasteful to me to play the patriarch in my own house; I have never believed that the fate of the universe depended upon a word from my lips. Nevertheless my opinions must be respected in my family, and the insanity of an old man and the caprices of a child shall not be allowed to frustrate a project I have entertained for so many years. The Baron d'Épinay was my friend, as you know, and an alliance with his son is most desirable and appropriate."

"Notwithstanding your father's wishes?" asked Madame de Villefort, opening a new line of attack. "That is a very serious matter."

Though pretending not to listen, the Count did not lose a word of the conversation.

"I may say that I have always entertained the highest respect for my father, madame. To-day, however, I must refuse to acknowledge intelligence in an old man who vents his anger on a son because of his hatred for the father. I shall continue to entertain the highest respect for Monsieur Noirtier. I shall submit uncomplainingly to the pecuniary loss, but I shall remain adamant in my determination. I shall, therefore, bestow my daughter's hand on Baron Franz d'Épinay because in my opinion this marriage is appropriate and honourable and, finally, because I shall marry my daughter to whom I choose."

"But it seems to me," said Monte Cristo after a moment's silence, "and I crave your pardon for what I am about to say, it seems to me that if Monsieur Noirtier disinherits Mademoiselle de Villefort because she wishes to marry a young man whose father he detested, he cannot have the same cause for complaint against this dear child Edward."

"You are right, Count. Is it not atrociously unjust?" cried Mme de Villefort in tones impossible to describe. "Poor Edward is just as much Monsieur Noirtier's grandchild as Valentine is, and yet if she were not going to marry Monsieur Franz she would inherit all his riches. Edward bears the family name, yet, even though she be disinherited by her grandfather, she will be three times as rich as he!"

Having thrust his dart, the Count merely listened and said nothing.

"We will not entertain you longer with our family troubles, Count," said M. de Villefort. "It is quite true that my patrimony will swell the coffers of the poor, who are the truly rich. My father has frustrated my legitimate hope, without any reason whatsoever; nevertheless I have acted as a man of intelligence and feeling. I have promised Monsieur d'Épinay the income accruing from this sum, and he shall have it, though I have to suffer the cruellest privations in consequence."

When M. de Villefort had finished speaking, the Count rose to depart.

"Are you leaving us, Count?" said Mme de Villefort.

"I am obliged to, madame. I only came to remind you of your promise for Saturday. You will come?"

"Did you think we should forget it?"

"You are too kind, madame. Now you must allow me to take leave of you. I am going, merely as a looker-on, you understand, to see something that has given me food for many long hours' thought."

"What is that?"

"The telegraph. There, my secret is out!"

"The telegraph!" repeated Mme de Villefort.

"Yes, indeed. On a hillock at the end of the road I have sometimes seen these black, accommodating arms shining in the sun like so many spiders' legs, and I assure you they have always filled me with deep emotion, for I thought of the strange signs cleaving the air with such precision, conveying the unknown thoughts of one man seated at his table three hundred leagues distant to another man at another table at the other end of the line; that these signs sped through the grey clouds or blue sky solely at the will of the all-powerful operator. Then I began to think of genii, sylphs, gnomes; in short, of occult powers until I laughed aloud. Nevertheless I never felt any desire to see at close quarters these fat, white-bellied insects with their long, slender legs, for I feared I might find under their stone-like wings some stiff and pedantic little human genius puffed out with science or sorcery. One fine morning, however, I discovered that the operator of every telegraph was a poor wretch earning a miserable pittance of twelve thousand francs, who spent his whole day not in observing the sky as the astronomer does, not in watching the water as the fisherman does, nor yet in studying the landscape as the dreamer does, but in watching that other white-bellied blacklegged insect, his correspondent, placed at some four or five leagues from him. Then I was seized with a strange desire to see this living chrysalis at close quarters, and to be present at the little comedy he plays for the benefit of his fellow chrysalis by pulling one piece of tape after another. I will tell you my impressions on Saturday."

The Count of Monte Cristo hereupon took his departure. That same evening the following telegram was read in the *Messenger*:

King Don Carlos has escaped the vigilance exercised over him at Burgos and has returned to Spain across the Catalonian frontier. Barcelona has risen in his favour.

All that evening nothing was talked about but Danglars' foresight in selling his shares, and his luck as a speculator in having lost but five hundred thousand francs by the deal.

The next day the following paragraph was read in the *Moniteur*:

The report published in yesterday's *Messenger* of the flight of Don Carlos and the revolt of Barcelona is devoid of all foundation. King Don Carlos has not left Burgos, and perfect peace reigns in the Peninsula. A telegraphic sign improperly interpreted owing to the fog gave rise to this error.

Shares rose to double the price to which they had fallen, so that, with what he had actually lost and what he had failed to gain, it meant a difference of a million francs to Danglars.

Chapter XLII

THE DINNER

A t first sight the exterior of Monte Cristo's house at Auteuil presented nothing magnificent, nothing of what one would have expected of a house chosen for such a grand personage as the Count of Monte Cristo. But no sooner was the door opened than the scene changed. Monsieur Bertuccio had certainly surpassed himself in the taste he had displayed in furnishing the house and in the rapidity with which the work had been executed. Just as formerly the Duke of Antin in one single night had an avenue of trees hewn down which obstructed Louis XIV's view, so M. Bertuccio in three days had an entirely bare yard planted with beautiful poplars and sycamores which gave shade to the whole of the house. Instead of the flag-stones, overgrown with grass, there extended a lawn which had only been laid down that morning and now looked like a vast carpet, upon which still glistened the water with which it had been sprinkled.

But then the Count himself had given all instructions; he had drawn up for Bertuccio a plan indicating the number and position of the trees to be planted, and the shape and extent of the lawn that was to succeed the flag-stones.

That which best manifested the ability of the steward

and the profound science of the master, the one in serving
and the other in being served, was that this house, which
had been deserted for twenty years and had appeared sad
and gloomy on the previous evening, impregnated as it was
with the insipid smell of decay, had with its return to life
become permeated with its master's favourite perfumes and
had been given the system of lighting especially favoured by
him. Directly he arrived the Count had his books and
weapons at hand; his eyes rested upon his favourite pictures; in the hall he was welcomed by his dogs, whose
caresses he loved, and his birds, in whose songs he rejoiced;
throughout the whole house, suddenly awakened from its
long sleep like the Sleeping Beauty's castle in the wood,
there burst forth life, song, and gaiety.

Servants were merrily moving hither and thither across
the fine courtyard; those belonging to the kitchen were
skipping down the staircase, but yesterday repaired, as
though they had always inhabited the house; others filled
the coach-houses, where the carriages were each numbered
and each one had its allotted place, as though they had been
installed there for the last fifty years; in the stables the
horses at the mangers were whinnying to the grooms, who
spoke to them with considerably more respect than many a
servant does to his master.

The library was divided into two parts and contained
about two thousand books; one complete section was
devoted to modern novels, and even the one that had only
been published the day before was to be seen in its place,
proudly displaying its red and gold binding.

On the other side of the house, and matching the library,
was a conservatory with exotic plants displayed in large
Japanese pots, which were at once wonderful to behold and
most pleasing in perfume, and in the middle of the conservatory there was a billiard-table which looked as if it had
been abandoned but an hour ago by players who had left
the balls on the cloth.

At five precisely the Count arrived, followed by Ali.

Bertuccio was awaiting his arrival with impatience mingled with anxiety; he hoped for praise, yet he feared frowns.

Monte Cristo alighted from his carriage in the courtyard, went over the whole house, and strolled through the garden in silence, and without giving the least sign of approval or disapproval. When he came to his bedroom, however, he pointed to a little piece of furniture in rosewood, saying: "The only use you can make of that is for my gloves."

"If Your Excellency will open the drawer, he will find gloves in it," said Bertuccio, delighted.

In the various cupboards and drawers about the room the Count found everything for his personal use: bottles of all kinds, cigars, jewellery.

"Good!" said he, and so real was the influence of this man on all around him that M. Bertuccio withdrew greatly elated.

At six o'clock sharp a horse was heard pawing the ground before the front door. It was our friend the Captain's horse, Médéah. Monte Cristo awaited Morrel on the steps, a smile on his lips.

"I am the first, I know," Morrel called to him. "I have done it on purpose so as to have you to myself for a minute before the others come. Julie and Emmanuel sent you all kinds of messages. It is truly magnificent here! But are you sure your servants will take good care of my horse?"

"You need not worry about that, my dear Maximilian. They understand horses."

"He will want rubbing down. If you knew at what a pace I came—like the wind!"

"I should say so too, with a horse that cost five thousand francs!" said Monte Cristo in the tone that a father might adopt toward his son.

"Do you regret it?" said Morrel with his frank smile.

"Good gracious, no!" replied the Count. "I should only regret it if the horse were no good."

"He is so good that I have outdistanced Monsieur de Château-Renaud, the greatest expert in France, and

Monsieur Debray, who rides the Minister's Arabs; at their heels are Baroness Danglars' horses which always do their six leagues an hour."

"They are following you then?" asked the Count.

"See, here they are!"

Indeed at that moment a carriage drawn by a sweating pair of bays and two gentlemen on winded horses arrived at the gate, which opened before them. The carriage drove round and stopped at the steps, followed by the two riders. Debray instantly dismounted and opened the carriage door. He offered his hand to the Baroness, who, in alighting, made a sign to Debray which passed unnoticed by all except Monte Cristo. Nothing ever escaped the Count's eye, and he perceived a note slipped almost imperceptibly, and with an ease indicating practice, from the Baroness' hand into that of the Minister's secretary.

The Baroness was followed by the banker, looking as pale as though he had issued from the grave instead of his carriage. Madame Danglars threw a rapid and inquiring glance around her, embracing in her view the courtyard, the peristyle, and the front of the house. Monte Cristo showed her two immense Chinese porcelain jars on which was intertwined marine vegetation, the size and beauty of which denoted that it could but be the work of nature herself. The Baroness expressed great admiration.

"Why, that would hold a chestnut-tree from the Tuileries," she said. "How did they manage to bake such enormous jars?"

"Oh, madame, that is a question we manufacturers of statuettes and fine glass cannot answer. It is the work of another age, that of the genii of the earth and sea."

"What do you mean by that? To what period do these jars belong?"

"I know not; I have heard it said, however, that the Emperor of China had an oven built for the purpose. In this oven twelve jars were baked, one after the other, like the one you see here. Two were broken by the fierceness of the fire, the other ten were sunk three hundred fathoms deep into the sea. As though it knew what was demanded of it, the sea threw over them its weeds, encircled them with coral, and encrusted them with shells: the whole being cemented by two hundred years' submersion in the depths; for the Emperor who made this experiment was carried away by a revolution, and left nothing but a document stating that the jars had been baked and let down into the sea. At the end of two hundred years this document was found, and it was decided to raise the vases. Special diving apparatus was made, and divers descended into the depths of the bay where they had been cast. Of the ten, however, but three were recovered; the others had been shattered and scattered by the waves. I like these vases, and at times my mind conjures up the unshapely, terrifying, and mysterious monsters, such as have been seen by divers only, which have cast their dull, cold, wondering gaze into the depths of the jars, wherein myriads of fish have slept finding refuge there from the pursuit of their enemies."

In the meantime Danglars, caring little for curiosities, had been mechanically plucking one blossom after another from a magnificent orange-tree; when tired of that tree, he turned his attention to a cactus which, being of a less easygoing character, pricked him outrageously. He rubbed his eyes with a shudder as though awakening from a dream.

"Major Bartolomeo Cavalcanti! The Viscount Andrea Cavalcanti!" announced Baptistin.

A black satin stock, fresh from the maker's hands, a well-trimmed beard and grey moustache, a bold eye, a major's uniform decorated with three stars and five crosses, in short the irreproachable bearing of an old soldier, such was the appearance of Bartolomeo Cavalcanti, the tender father. Close beside him, in brand-new clothes, and with a smile upon his lips, came Viscount Andrea Cavalcanti, the respectful son.

The three young men chatted together; their eyes wandered from the father to the son and from the very nature of things rested longer on the latter, whom they began criticizing.

"Cavalcanti!" said Debray.

"A fine name, to be sure," said Morrel.

"You are right," said Château-Renaud. "These Italians have a fine name, but they are badly dressed."

"You are difficult to please," added Debray. "Their clothes are very well cut and are quite new."

"That is precisely where they are at fault. This gentleman looks as though he were dressed for the first time in his life."

"Who are they?" Danglars inquired of Monte Cristo.

"You heard . . . the Cavalcantis."

"That tells me their name, but nothing further."

"I had forgotten that you do not know Italian nobility: to speak of the Cavalcantis is the same as speaking of a princely race."

"Any fortune?" asked the banker.

"A fabulous one."

"What do they do?"

"They try to get through their fortune, but cannot succeed. From what they told me when they called on me the other day, I gather that they intend opening a credit account with your bank. I have invited them today on your account. I will introduce you to them."

"They appear to speak very good French."

"The son was educated at a college in the South, at Marseilles or somewhere in that district, I believe. You will find him most enthusiastic."

"On what subject?" inquired the Baroness.

"On the subject of French women, madame. He is quite decided to find a wife for himself in Paris."

"That is a fine idea," said Danglars, shrugging his shoulders.

"The Baron is very grim to-day," said Monte Cristo to Mme Danglars. "Do they by any chance wish to make him a Minister?"

"Not so far as I know. I am more inclined to think he has been speculating and has lost money; now he does not know whom to blame for it."

"Monsieur and Madame de Villefort!" announced Baptistin.

Five minutes later the two doors of the salon opened; Bertuccio appeared and announced in a loud voice:

"Dinner is served, Your Excellency!"

Monte Cristo offered his arm to Mme de Villefort.

"Monsieur de Villefort," said he, "will you escort Baroness Danglars?"

Villefort did as he was requested, and they all passed into the dining-room.

The repast was magnificent. Monte Cristo had endeavoured to deviate from the uniformity observed at all such Paris dinners, and his object was to satisfy the curiosity rather than the appetites of his guests. It was an Oriental feast he offered them, but such as one would attribute to Arabian fairies. Every kind of delicious fruit that the four quarters of the globe can send to fill Europe's cornucopia was piled pyramid-like in Chinese vases and Japanese bowls. Rare birds in all their brilliant plumage, monstrous fish on silver dishes, every wine of the Archipelago, Asia Minor, and the Cape, in decanters of every weird shape, the sight of which seemed to add to the flavour, passed like one of Apicius'[1] reviews before his guests.

Monte Cristo noticed the general amazement and began to laugh and jest about it.

"My friends, you will no doubt admit," said he, "that, arrived at a certain degree of fortune, the superfluous takes the place of the necessary, and, as you ladies will admit, arrived at a certain degree of exaltation, the ideal takes the place of the real. Now to continue this argument, what is marvellous? That which we do not comprehend. What is truly desirable? That which we cannot have. Now to see things I cannot understand, to procure things impossible of possession, such is the plan of my life. I can realize it by two means: money and will. For instance, I expend as much perseverance in the pursuit of a whim as you, Monsieur Danglars, would expend in constructing a new railway line, as you, Monsieur de Villefort, in condemning a man to death, as you, Monsieur Debray, in pacifying a kingdom, as you, Monsieur de Château-Renaud, in pleasing a lady, and you, Morrel, in taming a horse that no one can ride. Thus, for example, you see these two fish. One was born fifty leagues from St Petersburg, the other five leagues from Naples. Do you not find it amusing to unite them on the same table?"

"What are these two fish?" asked Danglars.

"Monsieur de Château-Renaud, who has lived in Russia, will tell you the name of the one, and Major Cavalcanti, who is an Italian, will tell you the name of the other," said Monte Cristo.

"This one is a sterlet, I believe," said Château-Renaud.

"Capital!"

"And if I mistake not," said Cavalcanti, "this one is a lamprey."

"Just so. Now, Monsieur Danglars, ask these two gentlemen where these fish are found."

"Sterlets are found only in the Volga," said Château-Renaud.

"And I know that the Lake of Fusaro alone supplies lampreys of this size."

"Exactly so. One comes from the Volga, the other from the Lake of Fusaro."

"Impossible!" the guests exclaimed unanimously.

"You see, this is precisely what affords me amusement. I am like Nero: *cupitor impossibilium.*[2] At the present moment it is amusing you too, and the reason why these fish, which, I dare say, are in reality not such good eating as a perch or a salmon, seem exquisite is that in your opinion it was impossible to procure them. Yet here they are."

"How did you have them brought to Paris?"

"Nothing simpler. They were each brought in a large

cask, the one lined with reeds and river weeds, the other with rushes and other lake plants: these were placed in a wagon built specially for them. Here the sterlet lived twelve days and the lamprey eight. Both of them were alive when my cook took them out of the casks to kill them, the former in milk and the latter in wine. You do not believe me, Monsieur Danglars?"

"At any rate I doubt it," replied Danglars, with a heavy smile.

"Baptistin, send for the other sterlet and lamprey," said Monte Cristo. "You know, those that came in the other casks and are still alive."

Danglars opened his eyes in amazement; the rest of the company clapped their hands.

Four servants brought in two casks decorated with marine plants, in each of which was panting a fish similar to those on the table.

"But why are there two of each kind?" asked Danglars.

"Because one of them might have died," replied Monte Cristo simply.

"You are really a wonderful man," said Danglars. "Philosophers may well say it is superb to be rich."

"Above all to have ideas," said Mme Danglars.

"Oh, do not give me credit for this one, madame. It is an idea that was much esteemed by the Romans, and Pliny relates that they sent relays of slaves from Ostia to Rome who carried on their heads fish of the species he calls *mullus*, which, from the description he gives, is probably the goldfish. It was considered a luxury to have them alive, and an amusing sight to see them die; when dying they changed colour two or three times and, like the fading rainbow, they passed through all the prismatic shades; then they were sent to the kitchens. Their agony formed part of their merit. If they were not seen alive, they were despised when dead."

"Yes, but it is only seven or eight leagues from Ostia to Rome!"

"Quite true," said Monte Cristo. "But where would be

the merit of living eighteen hundred years after Lucullus if we did not go one better than he?"

The two Cavalcantis opened their enormous eyes wide, but they had the good sense not to say a word.

"This is all very amusing," said Château-Renaud, "but I must confess that what I admire most is the wonderful promptitude with which you are served. Is it not true, Count, that you bought this house only five or six days ago?"

"Certainly no longer."

"Well, I am sure it has undergone complete transformation in a week, for, if I mistake not, it had quite a different entrance and the yard was paved and empty, whereas what formerly was the yard is to-day a magnificent lawn bordered by trees which look a hundred years old."

"Why not? I like grass and shade," said Monte Cristo.

"In four days!" said Morrel. "It is marvellous!"

The evening wore on. Mme de Villefort expressed her desire to return to Paris, which Mme Danglars did not dare to do notwithstanding her obvious uneasiness.

At his wife's request M. de Villefort was the first to give the signal for departure, and offered Mme Danglars a seat in his landau. As for M. Danglars, he was so absorbed in a most interesting conversation on industry with M. Cavalcanti that he did not pay any attention to what was going on around him. More and more delighted with the Major, he offered him a seat in his carriage.

Andrea Cavalcanti found his tilbury[3] awaiting him at the gate, and the groom, fitted out in an exaggeration of the prevailing English fashion, was standing on the tips of his high boots holding the head of the enormous iron-grey horse.

Andrea had not spoken much during dinner, but afterward he had been seized upon by M. Danglars, who, after a rapid glance at the stiff-necked old Major and his timid son, and taking into consideration the hospitality of the Count, had come to the conclusion that he was face to face with some nabob[4] come to Paris to put the final polish on his society education.

He had noticed with indescribable satisfaction the enormous diamond which shone on the Major's little finger, and after dinner, of course on pretext of business and travels, he questioned the father and son on their mode of living, and both the father and the son had been most charming and affable.

He was, therefore, greatly pleased when Cavalcanti said: "To-morrow, monsieur, I shall have the honour of calling on you on business matters."

"And I shall be happy to receive you," was Danglars' reply, and he further proposed that he should accompany him to his hotel if it would not be depriving him too much of his son's company.

Cavalcanti replied that for some time past his son had been accustomed to living independently of him; he had his own horses and carriages, and, as they had not come to the Count's house together, it would offer them no difficulty to leave separately. The Major had already seated himself in Danglars' carriage, and the banker took his place beside him, more and more charmed with the ideas of order and economy of this man who, notwithstanding, gave his son fifty thousand francs a year, which meant an income of five or six hundred thousand francs.

As for Andrea, in order to look grand, he began by reprimanding his groom because instead of driving up to the steps he had waited at the gate, thus giving him the fatigue of walking thirty yards to reach his tilbury. The groom received the scolding with humility, and, taking the bit in his left hand to keep back the impatient horse that was pawing the ground, with his right hand he gave the reins to Andrea.

Chapter XLIII

A CONJUGAL SCENE

✦

At the Place Louis XV the three young men separated.
Debray drove on till he reached the house of M.
Danglars, arriving there just as M. de Villefort's landau
drove up to the door with Mme Danglars. Debray was the
first to enter the courtyard, and, with the air of a man on a
familiar footing at the house, he threw the bridle to a footman and handed the Baroness from the carriage and into
the house.

At the door of her room, the Baroness met Mlle
Cornélie, her confidential maid. "What is my daughter
doing?" she asked her.

"She practised the whole evening and then went to bed,"
replied Mlle Cornélie.

"I seem to hear her at the piano now."

"That is Mademoiselle Louise d'Armilly, who is playing
to Mademoiselle Danglars while she is in bed."

"Very well," said Mme Danglars, "come and undress me."

They entered the bedroom. Debray stretched himself
out on a large settee, and Mme Danglars went into her
dressing-room with Mlle Cornélie.

"My dear Monsieur Lucien," said Mme Danglars
through the door, "you are always complaining that Eugénie

does not do you the honour of addressing a word to you."

"I am not the only one to make such complaints, madame," said Lucien, playing with the Baroness' little dog, which, recognizing him as a friend of the house, was making a great fuss of him. "I believe I heard Morcerf tell you the other day that he could not get a single word out of his betrothed."

"It is true," said Mme Danglars, "but I think all that will change, and one of these days you will see Eugénie at your office."

"At my office?"

"That is to say, at the Minister's office."

"What for?"

"To ask for an engagement at the Opera House. Really, I have never known such an infatuation for music: it is ridiculous in a society girl."

Debray smiled as he said: "Well, let her come with your consent and the Baron's, and we will try to give her an engagement in accordance with her merits."

"You may go, Cornélie," said Mme Danglars, "I do not need you any more."

Cornélie disappeared, and an instant later Mme Danglars emerged from her dressing-room and seated herself beside Debray. She began to caress the little spaniel in a thoughtful mood. Lucien looked at her for a moment in silence.

"Tell me frankly, Hermine," he said presently, "what it is that is annoying you?"

"Nothing," replied the Baroness.

Suddenly the door opened and M. Danglars entered. "Good evening, madame," said he. "Good evening, Monsieur Debray!"

The Baroness no doubt thought that this unexpected visit signified a desire to repair the sharp words he had uttered during the day. Assuming a dignified air, she turned to Lucien and, without answering her husband, said: "Read something to me, Monsieur Debray."

"Excuse me," said the Baron. "You will tire yourself if you stay up so late, Baroness; it is eleven o'clock and Monsieur has far to go."

Debray was dumbfounded, for, though Danglars' tone was perfectly calm and polite, he seemed to detect in it a certain determination to do his own will that evening and not his wife's. The Baroness was equally surprised and showed it by a look which would no doubt have given her husband food for thought if he had not been busy reading the closing prices of shares in the paper. The haughty look was entirely lost on him.

"Monsieur Lucien," said the Baroness, "I assure you I have not the least inclination for sleep. I have much to tell you this evening, and you shall listen to me though you go to sleep standing."

"At your service, madame," replied Lucien phlegmatically.

"My dear Monsieur Debray, don't ruin a good night's rest by staying here and listening to Madame Danglars' follies to-night," said M. Danglars; "you can hear them just as well to-morrow. Besides, I claim to-night for myself, and, with your permission I propose to talk over some important business matters with my wife."

This time the blow was struck with such directness that Lucien and the Baroness were staggered. They exchanged looks as though each was asking the other for help in the face of such intrusion, but the irresistible power of the master of the house prevailed and he gained the ascendancy.

"Don't think I am turning you out my dear Debray," continued Danglars. "Not in the least! Unforeseen circumstances oblige me to demand this interview of madame to-night; it is such an unusual occurrence that I am sure you will bear me no ill-will."

Debray stammered out a few words, bowed, and left the room.

"Do you know, monsieur," said the Baroness when

Lucien had gone, "you are really making progress? As a rule you are merely churlish, to-night you are brutal."

"That is because I am in a worse temper to-night than usual," replied Danglars.

"What is your bad temper to me?" replied the Baroness, irritated at her husband's impassiveness. "What have I to do with it?"

"I have just lost seven hundred thousand francs in the Spanish loan."

"And do you wish to make me responsible for your losses?" asked the Baroness with a sneer. "Is it my fault that you have lost seven hundred thousand francs?"

"In any case it is not mine."

"Once and for all, monsieur, I will not have you talk money with me," returned the Baroness sharply. "It is a language I learnt neither with my parents nor in my first husband's house. The jingling of crowns being counted and recounted is odious to me, and there is nothing but the sound of your voice that I dislike more."

"That is really strange!" replied Danglars. "I always thought you took the greatest interest in my affairs!"

"I should like you to show me on what occasion."

"Oh! that's easily done. Last February you were the first to tell me of the Hayti bonds. You dreamt that a ship had entered the harbour at Havre, bringing the news that a payment which had been looked on as lost was about to be effected. I know how clear-sighted your dreams are. On the quiet I bought up all the bonds of the Hayti debt I could lay my hands on, and made four hundred thousand francs, of which I conscientiously paid you one hundred thousand. You spent it as you wished, but that was your affair.

"In March there was talk of a railway concession. Three companies presented themselves, each offering equal securities. You told me that your instinct—and though you pretend to know nothing about speculation I consider, on the contrary, that you have a very clear comprehension of certain affairs—well, you said your instinct told you that the privilege would be given to a so-called Southern Company. I instantly subscribed two-thirds of the company's shares and made a million out of the deal. I gave you two hundred and fifty thousand francs for pin-money. What have you done with it?"

"But what are you driving at, monsieur?" cried the Baroness, trembling with anger and impatience.

"Have patience, madame, I am coming to it. In April you dined with the Minister. The conversation turned upon Spain and you heard some secret information. There was talk of the expulsion of Don Carlos. I bought some Spanish bonds. Your information was correct, and I made six hundred thousand francs the day Charles the Fifth crossed the Bidassoa. Of these six hundred thousand francs you had fifty thousand crowns. They were yours, and you disposed of them according to your fancy. I do not ask you to account for the money, but it is none the less true that you have received five hundred thousand francs this year.

"Then three days ago you talked politics with Monsieur Debray, and you gathered from his words that Don Carlos had returned to Spain. I sold out, the news was spread, and a panic ensued. I did not sell the bonds, I gave them away. The next day it transpired that the news was false, but it cost me seven hundred thousand francs."

"Well?"

"Well, since I give you a quarter of my profits, it is only right you should give me a quarter of what I lose. The quarter of seven hundred thousand francs is one hundred and seventy-five thousand francs!"

"That is ridiculous, and really I do not see why you should bring Debray's name into this affair."

"Simply because if you don't happen to have the hundred and seventy-five thousand francs I claim, you have lent it to your friends, and Monsieur Debray is one of them!"

"For shame!"

"No gesticulations, screams, or modern drama, if you please, madame, otherwise I shall be compelled to tell you that I can see Monsieur Debray having the laugh of you over the five hundred thousand francs you have handed to him this year, and priding himself on the fact that he has finally found that which the most skilful gamblers have never discovered, that is, a game in which he wins without risking a stake and is no loser when he loses."

The Baroness was boiling with rage.

"You wretch!" said she. "You are worse than despicable!"

"But I note with pleasure, madame, that you are not far behind me in that respect."

"You would insult me now?"

"You are right: let us look facts in the face and reason coolly. I have never interfered in your affairs, except for your good; treat me in the same way. You suggest that my cash-box is no concern of yours. Be it so. Do as you like with your own, but do not fill or empty mine. Besides, how do I know that this is not a political trick, that the Minister, enraged at seeing me in the Opposition and jealous of the popular sympathy I enjoy, is not conspiring with Monsieur Debray to ruin me?"

"As though that were likely!"

"Why not? Whoever has heard before of such an almost impossible thing as false telegraphic news? Yet in the last two telegrams, some signs were interpreted quite differently. It was done on purpose for me, I am sure of it. Monsieur Debray has made me lose seven hundred thousand francs; let him bear his share of the loss and we will continue business together; otherwise, let him declare himself bankrupt for the hundred and seventy-five thousand francs and then do what all bankrupts do—disappear. He is quite a charming man, I know, when his news is correct, but when it is not, there are fifty others in the world better than he."

Mme Danglars was simply overwhelmed, but she made a supreme effort to reply to this last attack. She sank into a chair, thinking of the strange chain of misfortunes that had befallen them one after another. Danglars did not even look at her, though she did her best to faint. Without saying another word, he opened the door and went into his room; when Mme Danglars recovered from her semi-faint she thought she must have had a bad dream.

Chapter XLIV

Matrimonial Plans

The day following this scene, M. Debray's carriage did not make its appearance at the customary hour to pay a little visit to Mme Danglars on his way to the office. She, therefore, ordered her carriage to be brought round and went out. This was only what Danglars expected. He gave instructions that he should be informed directly Madame returned, but when two o'clock struck and she was not yet back, he went to the Chamber and put his name down to speak against the Budget.

From midday until two o'clock Danglars stayed in his office deciphering telegrams and heaping figure upon figure till he became increasingly depressed. Among other visits, he received one from Major Cavalcanti, who, as stiff and exact as ever, presented himself precisely at the hour named the previous evening to transact his business with the banker. On leaving the Chamber, where he had shown marked signs of agitation during the sitting and had been more bitter than usual against the Ministry, Danglars once more entered his carriage and told the coachman to drive him to no. 30 Avenue des Champs Élysées.

Monte Cristo was at home, but he was engaged with some one and asked Danglars to wait a moment in the salon. While the banker was waiting, the door opened, and a man in priest's garb entered. He was evidently more familiar with the house than the Baron, for, instead of waiting, he merely bowed and passing into the other room disappeared. A minute later the door through which the priest had entered reopened, and Monte Cristo made his appearance.

"Pray, excuse me, Baron," said he, "but one of my good friends, Abbè Busoni, whom you may have seen pass by, has just arrived in Paris. It is a long time since we saw each other, and I could not make up my mind to leave him at once. I trust you will find the motive good enough to forgive my keeping you waiting. But what ails you, Baron? You look quite careworn; really, you alarm me. A careworn capitalist is like a comet, he presages some great misfortune to the world."

"Ill-luck has been dogging my steps for the last few days," said Danglars, "and I receive nothing but bad news."

"Did you really lose by that affair in Spain?"

"Assuredly. Seven hundred thousand francs out of my pocket, that is all!"

"How could an old hand like you make such a mistake?"

"Oh, it was all my wife's fault. She dreamed Don Carlos had returned to Spain, and she believes in dreams. She says it is magnetism and assures me that what she dreams is bound to come true. But do you mean to say you have not heard of this affair? It created such a stir."

"I certainly heard something about it, but I was ignorant of the details. I know so little about the Exchange."

"You do not speculate then?"

"How could I? It gives me quite enough to do to regulate my income, and if I were to speculate I should be compelled to employ an agent and cashier in addition to my steward. But in regard to this Spanish affair, I believe it was not only the Baroness who dreamed of Don Carlos' return. Did not the newspapers say something about it?"

"Do you believe all the newspapers say?"

"Oh, dear, no. But I thought that the *Messenger* was an

exceptionally reliable paper, and that the news it published was telegraphic and therefore true."

"That is just what is so inexplicable."

"So you have lost about seventeen hundred thousand francs this month?"

"About that."

"Have you ever reflected on the fact that seven times seventeen hundred thousand francs makes about twelve millions? Be careful, my dear Monsieur Danglars! Be on your guard!"

"What a bad calculator you are!" exclaimed Danglars, calling to his assistance all his philosophy and art of dissimulation. "Money has flowed into my coffers from other successful speculations. I have lost a battle here and there, but my Indian navy will have taken some galleons, my Mexican pioneers will have discovered some mine."

"Very good, very good! The wound is still there, however, and will reopen at the first loss."

"No, it will not, for I tread on sure ground," continued Danglars in the idle language of the mountebank crying out his wares. "Three governments must fall before I am involved in difficulties."

Then turning the conversation into other channels he added: "Tell me what I am to do for Monsieur Cavalcanti."

"Give him money, of course, if he has a letter of credit and you think the signature good."

"The signature is good enough. He came to me this morning with a bill for forty thousand francs payable at sight, signed by Busoni, and sent by you to me with your endorsement. Naturally I immediately counted him out the forty banknotes."

Monte Cristo nodded in token of approval.

"But that is not all," continued Danglars. "He has also opened a credit account for his son."

"May I ask how much he allows the young man?"

"Five thousand francs a month."

"Sixty thousand francs a year! I thought as much," said

Monte Cristo, shrugging his shoulders. "How niggardly these Cavalcantis are! What does he expect a young man to do with five thousand francs a month?"

"But of course if the young man needs a few thousand more . . ."

"Do not advance anything. His father will never pay you. You do not know what misers these ultra-millionaires are! Keep to the terms of the letter."

"Do you mistrust this Cavalcanti then?"

"I? I would give him ten millions on his signature."

"Yet how simple he is! I should have taken him for nothing more than a Major. The young man is better, though."

"Yes, a little nervous perhaps, but on the whole quite presentable. He has apparently been travelling with a very severe tutor and has never been to Paris before."

"All Italians of high standing marry amongst themselves, do they not?" asked Danglars carelessly. "They like to unite their fortunes, I believe."

"I believe they do as a rule, but Cavalcanti is an eccentric man who never does as others do. I am convinced he has sent his son to France to choose a wife."

"Do you really think so?"

"I am sure of it."

"The boy is sure to marry a Bavarian or a Peruvian princess; he will want a crown or an Eldorado."

"No, the great lords from beyond the Alps frequently marry into plain families. Are you thinking of finding a wife for Andrea, my dear Monsieur Danglars, that you ask so many questions?"

"It would not be a bad speculation, I fancy, and after all I am a speculator."

"You are not thinking of Mademoiselle Danglars, I presume? I thought she was engaged to Albert."

"Monsieur Morcerf and I have certainly discussed this marriage, but Madame de Morcerf and Albert . . ."

"You are not going to tell me it would not be a good match?"

"Oh, I think Mademoiselle Danglars is as good as Monsieur de Morcerf."

"Mademoiselle will have a good dowry, no doubt, especially if the telegraph does not play any more tricks. But then Albert has a good name."

"I like mine as well!" said Danglars.

"Your name is certainly popular, and it gives distinction to the title that was intended to distinguish it. At the same time you have too much intelligence not to realize that according to prejudices, which are too deeply rooted to be exterminated, a patent of nobility which dates back five centuries confers greater lustre than that which only dates back twenty years."

"That is precisely the reason why I should prefer Monsieur Cavalcanti to Monsieur Albert de Morcerf," responded Danglars with a smile he attempted to make sardonic.

"Still, I should not think the Morcerfs would yield preference to the Cavalcantis," said Monte Cristo.

"The Morcerfs . . . See here, Count, you are a gentleman, are you not?"

"I hope so."

"And you understand something about heraldry?"

"A little."

"Well, look at my coat-of-arms; it is worth more than Morcerfs, for, though I may not be a Baron by birth, I do at least keep to my own name, whereas Morcerf is not his name at all."

"Do you really mean that?"

"I have been made a Baron, so I actually am one; he has given himself the title of Count, therefore he is not one at all."

"Impossible!"

"Monsieur de Morcerf and I have been friends or rather acquaintances for the last thirty years. As you know, I make good use of my coat-of-arms, and I do so for the simple reason that I never forget whence I sprang."

"Which shows either great pride or great humility," said Monte Cristo.

"When I was a clerk, Morcerf was but a simple fisherman."

"What was his name?"

"Fernand Mondego."

"Are you sure of that?"

"Good gracious, he has sold me enough fish for me to know his name."

"Then why are you letting his son marry your daughter?"

"Because as Fernand and Danglars are both upstarts, have both been given a title of nobility and become rich, there is a great similarity between them except for one thing that has been said about him which has never been said about me."

"What is that?"

"Nothing."

"I understand! What you have just told me has brought back to my mind that I have heard his name in Greece."

"In connexion with the Ali Pasha affair?"

"Just so."

"That is a mystery I would give much to discover," replied Danglars.

"It would not be difficult. No doubt you have correspondents in Greece, perhaps at Janina?"

"I have them everywhere."

"Why not write to your correspondent at Janina and ask him what part a certain Frenchman named Fernand played in the Ali Tebelin affair?"

"You are right!" exclaimed Danglars, rising quickly. "I will write this very day."

"And if you receive any scandalous news . . ."

"I will let you know."

"I should be much obliged."

Danglars rushed out of the room and leaped into his carriage.

Chapter XLV

A SUMMER BALL

Scarcely had M. Danglars left the Count of Monte Cristo to write in all haste to his correspondent at Janina when Albert de Morcerf was announced. The Count received him with his habitual smile. It was a strange thing, but nobody ever seemed to advance a step in that man's favour. Those who attempted to force a way into his heart encountered an impassable wall.

Morcerf ran toward him with open arms, but as soon as he drew near, he dropped them in spite of the Count's friendly smile, and did no more than put out his hand. The Count merely touched the tips of his fingers as he always did.

"Here I am, Count. What is the news?"

"News! You ask that question of me, a stranger?"

"Of course. I mean, have you done anything for me?"

"Did you ask me to do anything for you?" asked the Count, feigning uneasiness.

"Oh, nonsense!" said Albert. "Don't pretend to be so indifferent. They say that one mind can communicate with another through space. When I was at Tréport I felt that you were either working for me or thinking of me."

"That is possible," said Monte Cristo. "As a matter of

fact I have been thinking of you. Monsieur Danglars dined with me."

"I know that. Was it not to avoid meeting him that my mother and I left town for a few days?"

"But Monsieur Cavalcanti also dined with me."

"Your Italian prince?"

"That is an exaggeration. Monsieur Andrea only styles himself Viscount."

"Styles himself, do you say?"

"Yes, I said styles himself."

"Is he not a viscount then?"

"How do I know? He gives himself the title, I give it him, everybody does, which is the same as if he actually was a viscount."

"What a strange man you are! So Monsieur Danglars dined here with your Viscount Andrea Cavalcanti?"

"With Viscount Andrea Cavalcanti, the Marquis his father, Madame Danglars, Monsieur and Madame de Villefort, all charming people, then Monsieur Debray, Maximilian Morrel, and . . . let me see . . . oh yes, and Monsieur de Château-Renaud."

"Did they speak of me?"

"Not a word."

"More's the pity."

"Why? It seems to me you would prefer them to forget you."

"My dear Count, if they did not speak of me, it only means that they thought all the more of me. Truly, I am an unlucky fellow."

"What does that matter since Mademoiselle Danglars was not amongst the number? Ah, it is true enough, she might have been thinking of you at home."

"I have no fear of that; at any rate, if she was, it was in the same way in which I think of her."

"What touching sympathy! Do you really hate each other?"

"I think Mademoiselle Danglars would make a charming mistress, but as a wife . . . !"

"Is that the way you think of your future spouse?" said Monte Cristo, laughing.

"It is a little unkind, perhaps, but true none the less. Since this dream cannot be realized, I shrink from the idea of Mademoiselle Danglars becoming my wife; that is to say, living with me, thinking, singing in my company, composing her verses and music by my side, my whole life long! One can always leave a mistress, but a wife . . . Deuce take it! that is a different matter, you must live with her perpetually."

"You are difficult to please, Viscount."

"I am, for I so often crave for the impossible."

"What is that?"

"To find a wife such as my father found."

"So your father was one of the few fortunate ones?" said he.

"You know my opinion of my mother. She is an angel sent from Heaven. She is still beautiful, quick-witted, sweeter than ever. I have just been to Tréport with her. Most sons would look upon that as an irksome filial duty or an act of condescension on their part, but I assure you, Count, the four days I spent alone with my mother were more restful, more peaceful, and more poetic than if I had been accompanied by Queen Mab or Titania."[1]

"That is perfection indeed! Anyone hearing you speak thus will take the vow of celibacy!"

"The reason I do not care about marrying Mademoiselle Danglars is that I know a perfect woman. This is the reason why my joy will be indescribable the day she realizes that I am but a piteous atom with scarcely as many hundred thousand francs as she has millions!"

"Let things take their course. Perhaps everything will come as you wish. But tell me, do you seriously wish to break off your engagement?"

"I would give a hundred thousand francs to do so."

"Then make yourself quite happy. Monsieur Danglars would give twice that much to attain the same end."

"That is too good to be true," replied Albert. Yet as he

spoke an almost imperceptible cloud passed over his brow, and he asked: "Has Monsieur Danglars any reason?"

"Ah, here comes your proud and selfish nature to the fore! Well, well, I have once again found a man ready to hack at another's self-respect with a hatchet, but who cries out when his own is pricked with a pin."

"Not at all, but I think Monsieur Danglars . . ."

"Should be charmed with you! Well, Monsieur Danglars has such execrably bad taste that he is still more charmed with someone else."

"With whom?"

"How should I know? Look around you, judge for yourself, and profit by the inferences you draw."

"All right. I think I understand. Listen, my mother . . . no, not my mother, my father is thinking of giving a ball."

"At this time of the year?"

"Summer balls are fashionable. You see, those who remain in Paris in the month of July are the real Parisians. Will you convey our invitation to the Messieurs Cavalcanti?"

"When is the ball to take place?"

"On Saturday."

"Monsieur Cavalcanti Senior will have left Paris by then."

"But Monsieur Cavalcanti Junior will be here. Will you bring him along with you?"

"I do not know him. I never saw him till two or three days ago, and cannot hold myself responsible for him."

"But you receive him at your house."

"That is quite a different matter. He was recommended to me by a worthy abbé who may himself be mistaken in him. Invite him yourself, if you like, but do not ask me to introduce him. If he marries Mademoiselle Danglars later on, you will accuse me of interfering and challenge me to a duel. Besides, I do not know whether I shall go to your ball myself."

"Why not?"

"In the first place because you have not yet invited me."

"I have come for that express purpose."

"That is very kind of you. I may, however, still be compelled to refuse."

"When I tell you that my mother especially asks you to come, I am sure you will brush aside all obstacles."

"The Countess of Morcerf asks me?" inquired Monte Cristo with a start.

"I can assure you, Count, Madame de Morcerf speaks freely to me, and if you have not been stirred by a sympathetic impulse during the last four days, it must be that you have no response in you, for we have talked incessantly of you. May we expect you on Saturday?"

"You may, since Madame de Morcerf expressly invites me."

"You are very kind."

"Will Monsieur Danglars be there?"

"Oh, yes, he has been invited. My father has seen to that. We shall also try to persuade Monsieur de Villefort to come, but have not much hope of success. Do you dance, Count?"

"No, I do not, but I enjoy watching others. Does your mother dance?"

"No, never. You can entertain her. She is very anxious to have a talk with you."

"Really?"

"On my word of honour. Do you know, you are the first person in whom my mother has manifested such curiosity."

Albert rose and took his hat; the Count accompanied him to the door.

"I have to reproach myself with having been somewhat indiscreet," he said, stopping at the top of the steps. "I should not have spoken to you about Monsieur Danglars."

"On the contrary, continue speaking about him, now and always, so long as it is in the same strain."

"That's all right then. By the way, when does Monsieur d'Épinay arrive?"

"In five or six days at the latest."

"And when is he to be married?"

"As soon as Monsieur and Madame de Saint-Méran arrive."

"Bring him to see me when he comes. Though you always say I do not like him, I shall be very glad to see him."

"Your orders shall be obeyed, Count."

"Good-bye!"

"Until Saturday. That is quite certain?"

"I have given you my promise."

It was in the warmest days of June when, in due course of time, the Saturday arrived on which M. de Morcerf's ball was to take place. It was ten o'clock in the evening. From the rooms on the ground floor might be heard the sounds of music and the whirl of the waltz and galop, while brilliant light streamed through the interstices of the Venetian blinds. At that moment the garden was occupied only by some ten servants, who were preparing the supper-tables. The paths had already been illuminated by brilliant coloured lanterns, and a mass of choice flowers and numberless candles helped to decorate the sumptuous supper-tables.

No sooner had the Countess returned to the salon after giving her final orders than the guests began to arrive, drawn thither by the charming hospitality of the Countess more than by the distinguished position of the Count. Mme Danglars came, not only beautiful in person, but radiantly splendid. Albert went up to her and, paying her well-merited compliments on her toilette, offered her his arm and conducted her to a seat. Albert looked around him.

"You are looking for my daughter?" said the Baroness with a smile.

"I confess I am," responded Albert. "Could you have been so cruel as not to bring her?"

"Now don't get excited; she met Mademoiselle de Villefort and will be here presently. Look, there they come, both of them wearing white, one with a bouquet of roses and the other with myosotis. But tell me . . ."

"What do you wish to know, madame?"

"Is the Count of Monte Cristo not coming this evening?"

"Seventeen!" said Albert.

"What do you mean?"

"Only that you are the seventeenth person who has put that same question to me," replied Albert, laughing. "He is doing well . . . I congratulate him."

"Have you answered everyone as you have answered me?"

"Oh, to be sure, I have not yet replied to your question. Do not fear, madame, we shall have the privilege of enjoying the company of the lion of the day."

"Were you at the Opera yesterday? He was there."

"No, I did not go. Did the eccentric man do anything original?"

"Does he ever do anything else? Elssler was dancing in *le Diable Boiteux*,[2] and the Greek Princess was in raptures. After the *cachucha*,[3] he threw the dancer a bouquet in between the flowers of which there was a magnificent ring; when she appeared again in the third act, she did honour to the gift by wearing it on her little finger. But leave me here now and go and pay your respects to Madame de Villefort. I can see she is longing to have a talk with you."

Albert bowed and went toward Mme de Villefort, who was about to say something when Albert interrupted her.

"I am sure I know what you are going to ask me," he said.

"What is it?"

"Whether the Count of Monte Cristo is coming."

"Not at all. I was not even thinking of him just then. I wanted to ask you whether you had received news of Franz."

"I had a letter from him yesterday. He was then leaving for Paris."

"That's good. Now what about the Count?"

"The Count is coming right enough."

Just then a handsome young man with keen eyes, black hair, and a glossy moustache bowed respectfully to Mme de Villefort. Albert held out his hand to him.

"Madame, I have the honour of presenting to you Monsieur Maximilian Morrel, Captain of Spahis, one of our best and bravest officers."

"I had the pleasure of meeting this gentleman at Auteuil, at the Count of Monte Cristo's," replied Mme de Villefort, turning away with marked coldness.

This remark, and above all the tone in which it was said, chilled the heart of poor Morrel. There was a recompense in store for him, however. Turning round he perceived near the door a beautiful figure all in white, whose large blue eyes were fixed on him without any apparent expression, whilst the bouquet of myosotis slowly rose to her lips.

Morrel understood the salutation so well that, with the same expressionless look in his eyes, he raised his handkerchief to his mouth. These two living statues, whose hearts beat so violently under their apparently marblelike forms yet were separated from one another by the whole length of the room, forgot themselves for a moment, or rather for a moment forgot everybody and everything in their mute contemplation of one another. They might have remained lost in one another much longer without anyone noticing their obliviousness to all things around them had not the Count of Monte Cristo just entered. As we have already remarked, the Count seemed to exercise a fascination, whether artificial or natural, which attracted general attention wherever he went; it was certainly not his black coat, irreproachable in cut but perfectly plain and devoid of all trimmings, that attracted attention; nor was it his white unembroidered waistcoat, nor his trousers displaying a perfectly shaped foot. It was rather his pale face and black wavy hair, his calm and serene expression, his deep-set, melancholy eyes, and his delicately chiselled mouth, which so easily expressed excessive disdain, that drew all eyes toward him.

There may have been men who were more handsome than he, but there were certainly none who were more significant, if we may use the expression. Everything about the

Count seemed to have its meaning and value, for the habit of profitable thinking had given an incomparable ease and firmness to his features, to the expression of his face, and to his slightest gesture. Yet the world is so strange that all this would have been passed by unheeded, if it had not been complemented by a mysterious story gilded over by an immense fortune.

However that may be, the Count was the cynosure[4] of every eye as he advanced, exchanging bows on his way, to where Mme de Morcerf was standing before a flower-laden mantelshelf. She had seen his entrance in a mirror placed opposite the door and was prepared to receive him. She turned toward him with a serene smile just as he was bowing to her. No doubt she thought the Count would speak to her, while he on the other hand thought she was about to address him. They both remained silent, therefore, apparently feeling that banalities were out of place between them, so after exchanging salutations, Monte Cristo went in search of Albert.

"Have you seen my mother?" was Albert's first remark.

"I have just had the pleasure," said the Count, "but I have not yet seen your father."

"He is talking politics with a small group of great celebrities."

Just then the Count felt his arm pressed; he turned round to find himself face to face with Danglars.

"Ah, it is you, Baron," said he.

"Why do you call me Baron?" returned Danglars. "You know quite well I care nothing for my title. I am not like you in that respect, Viscount; you lay great value on your title, do you not?"

"Certainly I do," replied Albert, "for if I were not a viscount, I should be nothing at all, whereas, while sacrificing your title of Baron, you would still be a millionaire."

"Which appears to me the finest title in existence," replied Danglars.

"Unfortunately," said Monte Cristo, "the title of millionaire does not always last one's lifetime as does that of Baron, Peer of France, or Academician: as a proof you have only to consider the case of the millionaires Francke and Poulmann, of Frankfort, who have just become bankrupt."

"Is that really the case?" asked Danglars, turning pale.

"Indeed it is. I received the news this evening by courier. I had about a million deposited with them, but, having been warned in time, I demanded its withdrawal some four weeks ago."

"Good heavens! They have drawn on me for two hundred thousand francs!"

"Well, you are warned."

"But the warning has come too late," said Danglars. "I have honoured their signature."

"Ah, well," said the Count, "that's another two hundred thousand francs gone to join . . ."

"Hush, do not mention such things before Monsieur Cavalcanti," added the banker, turning his head toward the young man with a smile.

In the meantime the heat in the room had become excessive. Footmen went round with trays laden with fruit and ices. Monte Cristo wiped with his handkerchief the perspiration that had gathered on his forehead; nevertheless he stepped back when the tray passed before him and would not take refreshment.

Mme de Morcerf did not lose sight of Monte Cristo. She saw him refuse to take anything from the tray and even noticed his movement as he withdrew from it.

"Albert," said she, "have you noticed that the Count will not accept an invitation to dine with your father?"

"But he breakfasted with me," said Albert, "in fact it was at that breakfast that he was first introduced into our society."

"That is not your father's house. I have been watching him to-night, he has not taken anything."

"The Count is very temperate."

Mercédès smiled sadly.

"Go to him, Albert," said she, "and, the next time a waiter goes round, persuade him to take something."

"Why, Mother?"

"Because I ask you, Albert."

Albert kissed his mother's hand, and went to do her bidding. Another tray was handed round; Mercédès saw how Albert tried to persuade the Count, how he himself took an ice from the tray and presented it to him, only to meet with an obstinate refusal.

Albert rejoined his mother; she was very pale.

"Well, you see he refused?" said she.

"Yes, but why need that worry you?"

"You know, women are singular creatures, Albert. It would give me pleasure to see him take something, even though it were nothing more than a bit of pomegranate. It may be that he is not yet reconciled to the French way of living or that he would prefer something else."

"Oh dear, no, I have seen him eat of everything in Italy. No doubt he does not feel inclined this evening."

"Then again, he may not feel the heat as much as we do, since he has always lived in hot climates."

"I do not think that is so," said Albert, "he complained just now of feeling almost suffocated, and asked why the Venetian blinds were not opened as well as the windows."

"Ah! It will give me the means of ascertaining whether or not his abstinence is deliberate."

She left the room, and an instant later the Venetian blinds were opened, permitting a view through the jasmine and clematis that overhung the windows of the lantern-illuminated garden. Dancers, players, and talkers all uttered an exclamation of joy; everybody inhaled with delight the air that flowed in.

At the same moment Mercédès returned, even paler than before, but with a determined look on her face which was characteristic of her in certain circumstances. She went straight up to the group of gentlemen round her husband, and said: "Do not detain these gentlemen here; if they are not playing I have no doubt they would prefer to take the fresh air in the garden rather than stay in this suffocating room."

"But, madame, we will not go into the garden alone!" said a gallant old general.

"Very well, I will set the example," said Mercédès, and turning to Monte Cristo, she added: "Will you give me your arm, Count!"

The Count was staggered at these simple words; he looked at Mercédès. It was but a momentary glance, but the Count put so many thoughts into that one look that it seemed to Mercédès it lasted a century. He offered the Countess his arm; she laid her delicate hand gently on it, and together they went into the garden, followed by some twenty of the guests. With her companion, Mme de Morcerf passed under an archway of lime-trees leading to a conservatory.

"Did you not find it too hot in the room?" said she.

"Yes, madame, but it was an excellent idea of yours to open the windows and Venetian blinds."

As he said the last words he felt Mercédès' arm tremble.

"Maybe you feel cold, though, in that thin dress with no other wrap than a thin gauze scarf?" said he.

"Do you know whither I am taking you?" said Mercédès without answering Monte Cristo's question.

"No, madame, but, as you see, I make no resistance."

"To the conservatory at the end of this path."

The Count looked at Mercédès as if he were about to ask her a question, but she went on her way without saying another word, and the Count also remained silent.

They reached the building resplendent with magnificent fruit of every kind. The Countess left the Count's side, and went over to a vine-stock to pluck a bunch of Muscatel grapes. "Take these, Count," said she with such a sad smile that one could almost see the tears springing up into her eyes. "I know our French grapes cannot compare with yours of Sicily and Cyprus, but you must make allowances for our poor Northern sun."

The Count bowed and drew back a step.

"Do you refuse?" said Mercédès in a tremulous voice.

"I must ask you to excuse me, madame, I never eat Muscatel grapes."

With a sigh Mercédès dropped the grapes. A magnificent peach, warmed by the artificial heat of the conservatory, was hanging against an adjoining wall. Mercédès plucked it.

"Take this peach, then."

The Count again refused.

"What, again!" she exclaimed in so plaintive a tone that one felt she was stifling a sob. "Really, Count, you pain me."

A long silence ensued; like the grapes, the peach rolled to the ground.

"There is a touching Arabian custom, Count," Mercédès said at last, looking at Monte Cristo supplicatingly, "which makes eternal friends of those who share bread and salt under the same roof."

"I know it, madame, but we are in France and not in Arabia, and in France eternal friendships are as rare as the beautiful custom you just mentioned."

"But we are friends, are we not?" said the Countess breathlessly, with her eyes fixed on Monte Cristo, whose arm she convulsively clasped between her two hands.

"Certainly we are friends, madame," he replied, "in any case, why should we not be?"

His tone was so different from what Mercédès desired that she turned away to give vent to a sigh resembling a groan.

"Thank you!" was all she said; she began to walk on, and they went all round the garden without uttering another word. After about ten minutes' silence, she suddenly said: "Is it true that you have seen much, travelled far, and suffered deeply?"

"I have suffered deeply, madame," answered Monte Cristo.

"But now you are happy?"

"Doubtless," replied the Count, "since no one hears me complain."

"And has your present happiness softened your heart?"

"My present happiness equals my past misery," said the Count.

"Are you not married?" asked the Countess.

"I, married!" exclaimed Monte Cristo, shuddering, "who could have told you that?"

"No one told me you were, but you have frequently been seen at the Opera with a young and lovely person."

"She is a slave whom I bought at Constantinople, madame, the daughter of a prince. Having no one else to love in the world, I have adopted her as my daughter."

"You live alone, then?"

"I do."

"You have no sister, no son, no father?"

"I have no one."

"How can you live thus, with no one to attach you to life?"

"It is not my fault, madame. At Malta, I loved a young girl, and was on the point of marrying her when war came and carried me away, as in a whirlpool. I thought she loved me well enough to wait for me, even to remain faithful to my memory. When I returned she was married. Most men who have passed thirty have the same tale to tell, but perhaps my heart was weaker than that of others, and in consequence I suffered more than they would have done in my place. That's all."

The Countess stopped for a moment, as if gasping for breath. "Yes," she said, "and you have still preserved this love in your heart—one can only love once—and have you ever seen her again?"

"Never!"

"Never?"

"I have never returned to the country where she lived."

"At Malta?"

"Yes, at Malta."

"She is now at Malta, then?"

"I think so."

"And have you forgiven her for all she has made you suffer?"

"Yes, I have forgiven her."

"But only her. Do you still hate those who separated you?"

The Countess placed herself before Monte Cristo, still holding in her hand a portion of the fragrant grapes.

"Take some," she said.

"I never eat Muscatel grapes, madame," replied Monte Cristo as if the subject had not been mentioned before.

The Countess flung the grapes into the nearest thicket, with a gesture of despair.

"Inflexible man!" she murmured.

Monte Cristo remained as unmoved as if the reproach had not been addressed to him. At this moment Albert ran up to them.

"Oh, Mother!" he exclaimed, "such a misfortune has happened!"

"What has happened?" asked the Countess, as though awaking from a dream to the realities of life. "A misfortune, did you say? Indeed, it is little more than I should expect!"

"Monsieur de Villefort has come to fetch his wife and daughter."

"Why?"

"Madame de Saint-Méran has just arrived in Paris, bringing the news of Monsieur de Saint-Méran's death, which occurred at the first stage after he left Marseilles. Madame de Villefort was in very good spirits when her husband came, and could neither understand nor believe in such misfortune. At the first words, however, Mademoiselle Valentine guessed the whole truth, notwithstanding all her father's precautions; the blow struck her like a thunderbolt, and she fell down senseless."

"How was Monsieur de Saint-Méran related to Mademoiselle Valentine?" asked the Count.

"He was her maternal grandfather. He was coming here to hasten her marriage with Franz."

"Indeed!"

"Franz is reprieved then! Why is Monsieur de Saint-Méran not grandfather to Mademoiselle Danglars too?"

"Albert! Albert!" said Mme de Morcerf, in a tone of mild reproof, "what are you saying? Ah! Count, he esteems you so highly, tell him he has spoken amiss."

So saying she took two or three steps forward. Monte Cristo glanced after her with such a pensive expression, at the same time so full of affectionate admiration, that she retraced her steps. Taking his hand and that of her son, she joined them together, saying: "We are friends, are we not?"

"Oh, madame, I do not presume to call myself your friend, but at all times I am your most respectful servant."

Chapter XLVI

MME DE SAINT-MÉRAN

✦

Valentine found her grandmother in bed; silent caresses, heartrending sobs, broken sighs, and burning tears were the sole recountable details of the distressing interview, at which Mme de Villefort was present, leaning on her husband's arm, and manifesting, outwardly at least, great sympathy for the poor widow.

After a few moments she whispered to her husband: "I think it would be better for me to retire, for the sight of me still appears to distress your mother-in-law."

Mme de Saint-Méran heard her and whispered to Valentine: "Yes, yes, let her go, but do you stay with me."

Mme de Villefort went out and Valentine remained alone with her grandmother, for the Procureur du Roi, dismayed at the sudden death, had followed his wife.

At last, worn out with grief, Mme de Saint-Méran succumbed to her fatigue and fell into a feverish sleep. Valentine placed a small table within her reach and on it a decanter of orangeade, her usual beverage, and, leaving her bedside went to see old Noirtier. She went up to the old man and kissed him. He looked at her with such tenderness that she again burst into tears.

"Yes, yes, I understand," she said. "You wish to convey to me that I have still a good grandfather, do you not?"

He intimated that such was his meaning.

"Happily I have," returned Valentine. "Otherwise what would become of me?"

It was one o'clock in the morning. Barrois, who wished to go to bed himself, remarked that after such a distressing evening everyone had need of rest. M. Noirtier would have liked to say that all the repose he needed was to be found in his granddaughter's presence, but he bade her good-night, for grief and fatigue had made her look quite ill.

When Valentine went to see her grandmother the next day she found her still in bed; the fever had not abated; on the contrary, the old Marquise's eyes were lit up with a dull fire and she was prone to great nervous irritability.

"Oh, Grandmama, are you feeling worse?" exclaimed Valentine on perceiving all these symptoms.

"No, child, but I was impatiently waiting for you to fetch your father to me."

"My father?" inquired Valentine uneasily.

"Yes, I wish to speak to him."

Valentine did not dare oppose her grandmother's wish, and an instant later Villefort entered.

"You wrote me, monsieur, concerning this child's marriage," said Mme de Saint-Méran, coming straight to the point as though afraid she had not much time left.

"Yes, madame," replied Villefort. "The matter has already been settled."

"Is not the name of your future son-in-law Monsieur Franz d'Épinay?"

"Yes, madame."

"Is he the son of General d'Épinay, who belonged to our party and was assassinated a few days before the usurper returned from Elba?"

"The very same."

"Is he not opposed to this alliance with the granddaughter of a Jacobin?"

"Our civil dissensions are now happily dispelled," said

Villefort. "Monsieur d'Épinay was little more than a child when his father died. He hardly knows Monsieur Noirtier and will greet him, if not with pleasure, at least with unconcern."

"Is it a desirable match?"

"In every respect. He is one of the most gentlemanly young men I know."

Valentine remained silent throughout this conversation.

"Then, monsieur, you must hasten on the marriage, for I have not much longer to live," said Mme de Saint-Méran after a few seconds' reflection.

"You, madame?" "You, Grandmama?" cried Monsieur de Villefort and Valentine simultaneously.

"I know what I am saying," returned the Marquise. "You must hasten on the arrangements so that the poor mother-less child may at least have a grandmother to bless her marriage. I am all that is left to her of dear Renée, whom you appear so soon to have forgotten."

"But, Grandmama, consider decorum—our recent mourning. Would you have me begin my married life under such sad auspices?"

"Nay, I tell you I am going to die, and before dying I wish to see your husband. I wish to bid him make my child happy, to read in his eyes whether he intends to obey me. In short, I must know him," continued the grandmother with a terrifying expression in her eyes, "so that I may arise from the depths of my grave to seek him out if he is not all he should be."

"Madame, you must dispel such feverish ideas that are almost akin to madness," said Villefort. "When once the dead are laid in their graves, they remain there never to rise again."

"And I tell you, monsieur, it is not as you think. Last night my sleep was sorely troubled. It seemed as though my soul were already hovering over my body; my eyes, which I tried to open, closed against my will; and, what will appear impossible, above all to you, monsieur, with my eyes shut I saw in yonder dark corner, where there is a door leading to Madame de Villefort's dressing-room, I tell you I saw a white figure enter noiselessly."

Valentine screamed.

"It was the fever acting on you, madame," said Villefort.

"Doubt my word if it pleases you, but I am sure of what I say. I saw a white figure, and, as if God feared I should discredit the testimony of my senses, I heard my tumbler move—the same one that is now on the table."

"But it was a dream, Grandmama!"

"So far was it from being a dream that I stretched out my hand toward the bell, but as I did so the shadow disappeared and my maid entered with a light. Phantoms are visible only to those who are intended to see them. It was my husband's spirit. If my husband's spirit can come to me, why should not mine appear to guard my granddaughter? It seems to me there is an even stronger tie between us."

"Madame, do not give way to such gloomy thoughts," said Villefort, deeply affected in spite of himself. "You will live long with us, happy, loved, and honoured, and we will help you to forget . . ."

"Never, never, never!" said the Marquise. "When does Monsieur d'Épinay return?"

"We expect him any moment."

"It is well; as soon as he arrives, let me know. We must lose no time. Then I also wish to see a notary that I may be assured that all our property reverts to Valentine."

"Ah, my Grandmother!" murmured Valentine, pressing her lips to her grandmother's burning brow, "do you wish to kill me? Oh, how feverish you are! It is a doctor we must send for, not a notary."

"A doctor?" she said, shrugging her shoulders, "I am not ill; I am thirsty—nothing more."

"What are you drinking, Grandmama?"

"The same as usual, my dear, orangeade. Give me my glass, Valentine."

Valentine poured the orangeade into a glass and gave it to her grandmother, though not without a feeling of dread, for it was the same glass she declared the shadow had touched. The Marquise drained the glass at a single draught, and then, turning over on her pillow, repeated: "The notary! the notary!"

M. de Villefort left the room, and Valentine seated herself at her grandmother's bedside.

Two hours passed thus, during which Mme de Saint-Méran was in a restless, feverish sleep. At last the notary arrived. He was announced in a very low voice; nevertheless Mme de Saint-Méran heard and raised herself on her pillows.

"Go, Valentine, go," she said, "and leave me alone with this gentleman."

Valentine kissed her grandmother and left the room with her handkerchief to her eyes. At the door she met the valet, who told her the doctor was waiting in the salon. She instantly went down.

"Oh! dear Monsieur d'Avrigny, we have been waiting for you with such impatience."

"Who is ill, dear child?" said he. "Not your father or Madame de Villefort?"

"It is my grandmother who needs your services. You know the calamity that has befallen us?"

"I know nothing," said M. d'Avrigny.

"Alas!" said Valentine, choking back her tears, "my grandfather is dead."

"Monsieur de Saint-Méran?"

"Yes."

"Suddenly?

"From an apoplectic stroke."

"An apoplectic stroke?" repeated the doctor.

"Yes! and my poor grandmother fancies that her husband, whom she never left, is calling her, and that she must go and join him. Oh! Monsieur d'Avrigny, I beseech you, do something for her!"

"Where is she?"

"In her room with the notary."

"And Monsieur Noirtier?"

"Just as he was, perfectly clear in his mind but still incapable of moving or speaking."

"And the same love for you—eh, my dear child!"

"Yes," said Valentine, "he is very fond of me."

"Who does not love you?"

Valentine smiled sadly.

"What are your grandmother's symptoms?"

"An extremely nervous excitement and an unnatural restlessness. This morning, in her sleep, she fancied that her soul was hovering over her body, which she saw asleep. It must have been delirium! She fancies too that she saw a phantom enter her chamber, and even heard the noise it made in touching her glass."

"It is singular," said the doctor. "I was not aware that Madame de Saint-Méran was subject to such hallucinations."

"It is the first time I ever saw her thus," said Valentine, "and this morning she frightened me so that I thought she was mad and even my father, who you know is a strong-minded man, appeared deeply impressed."

"We will go and see," said the doctor. "What you tell me seems very strange."

The notary came downstairs, and Valentine was informed her grandmother was alone.

"Go upstairs," she said to the doctor.

"And you?"

"Oh, I dare not. She forbade my sending for you, and I am agitated, feverish, unwell. I will go and take a turn in the garden to compose myself."

The doctor pressed Valentine's hand, and, while he visited her grandmother, she went into the garden. We need not say which was her favourite walk. After remaining for a short time in the flower garden surrounding the house, and gathering a rose to place in her waist or hair, she turned into the dark avenue which led to the bench, from thence to the gate. As she advanced she fancied she heard a voice pronounce her name. She stopped astonished, then the voice reached her ear more distinctly, and she recognized it to be the voice of Maximilian.

Chapter XLVII

THE PROMISE

❧

It was indeed Maximilian Morrel. He had been in despair since the previous day. With the instinct of a lover he had divined that with the arrival of Mme de Saint-Méran and the death of the Marquis, some change would take place in the Villefort household which would touch his love for Valentine.

Valentine had not expected to see Morrel, for it was not his usual hour, and it was only pure chance or, better still, a happy sympathy that took her into the garden. When she appeared, Morrel called her, and she ran to the gate.

"You here, at this hour!" she said.

"Yes, my poor dear," replied Morrel. "I have come to bring and to hear bad tidings."

"This is indeed a house of mourning," said Valentine. "Speak, Maximilian, yet in truth my cup of sorrow seems full to overflowing."

"Dear Valentine, listen, I entreat you," said Morrel, endeavouring to conceal his emotion. "I have something grave to tell you. When are you to be married?"

"I will conceal nothing from you, Maximilian," said Valentine. "This morning the subject was introduced and my grandmother, in whom I had hoped to find a sure support, not only declares herself favourable to the marriage, but is so anxious for it that the day after Monsieur d'Épinay arrives the contract will be signed."

A sob of anguish was wrung from the young man's breast, and he looked long and mournfully at his beloved.

"Alas!" he whispered, "it is terrible thus to hear the woman you love calmly say: 'The time of your execution is fixed, and will take place in a few hours; it had to be, and I will do nothing to prevent it!' Monsieur d'Épinay arrived this morning!"

Valentine uttered a cry.

"And now, Valentine, answer me, and remember that my life or death depends on your answer. What do you intend doing?"

Valentine hung her head; she was overwhelmed.

"This is not the first time we have reflected on our present grave and critical position. It is not now the moment to give way to useless sorrow: leave that to those who delight in suffering, and wallow in their grief. There are such people, but those who feel in themselves the desire to fight against their bitter lot must not lose one precious moment. Are you prepared to fight against our ill-fortune, Valentine? Tell me, for this is what I have come to ask you."

Valentine trembled visibly, and stared at Maximilian with wide-open eyes. The idea of opposing her grandmother, her father, in short her whole family, had never occurred to her.

"What is this you bid me do, Maximilian?" asked Valentine. "How could I oppose my father's orders and my dying grandmother's wish! It is impossible!"

Morrel started.

"You are too noble-hearted not to understand me, and your very silence is proof that you do. I fight! God preserve me from it! No, I need all my strength to hold back my tears. Never could I grieve my father or disturb the last moments of my grandmother!"

"You are right," said Morrel phlegmatically.

"How can you say that?" cried Valentine in a hurt voice.

"I speak as one full of admiration for you, mademoiselle."

"Mademoiselle!" exclaimed Valentine. "Mademoiselle?—how selfish! He sees me in despair and pretends he cannot understand my point of view!"

"On the contrary, I understand you perfectly. You do not wish to thwart your father or disobey the Marquise, so you will sign the contract to-morrow which will bind you to your husband."

"How can I do otherwise?"

"It is no good appealing to me, mademoiselle, for I am not a competent judge. My selfishness will blind me," Morrel continued, and his toneless voice and clenched hands showed his increasing exasperation.

"What would you have proposed, had you found me willing to comply with your wishes? Ah! Maximilian, tell me what you advise!"

"Do you mean that seriously?"

"Certainly I do, and, if your advice is good, I shall follow it. You know how I love you."

"Valentine, give me your hand in token that you forgive me my anger," said Morrel. "I am utterly distraught, and for the past hour the most extravagant ideas have been running through my head. Follow me, Valentine. I will take you to my sister, who is worthy to be your sister also. We will embark for Algiers . . . England . . . America . . . Or if you prefer, we can go together to some province until our friends have persuaded your family to a reconciliation."

Valentine shook her head.

"Then you will submit to your fate whatever it may be, without even attempting to oppose it?"

"Even if it spelt death!"

"I repeat once more, Valentine, you are quite right. Indeed, it is I who am mad and you are but giving me a proof that passion blinds the most balanced minds. Fortunate are you that you can reason dispassionately. It is, therefore, an understood thing that to-morrow you will be irrevocably promised to Franz d'Épinay, not by the theatrical formality invented to bind a couple together which is called the signing of the contract, but by your own free will."

Morrel said these words with perfect calmness. Valentine looked at him for a moment with her large searching eyes, at the same time endeavouring to conceal from him the grief that struggled in her heart.

"And what are you going to do?" she asked.

"I shall have the honour of bidding you farewell, mademoiselle, calling on God to make your life so happy and contented that there may be no place for me even in your memory. He will hear my prayers for He sees to the bottom of my heart. Farewell, Valentine, farewell!" continued he, bowing.

"Where are you going?" cried the distracted girl, thrusting her hand through the gate and seizing Maximilian's coat. Her own agitated feelings told her that her lover's calmness could not be real. "Where are you going?"

The young man gave a sad smile.

"Oh! speak, speak! I entreat you!" said Valentine.

"Has your resolution changed, Valentine?"

"It cannot change, unhappy man! You know it cannot!" cried she.

"Then farewell, Valentine!"

Valentine shook the gate with a strength she had not thought herself capable of, and as Morrel was going away pushed her two hands through, and, clasping them, called out:

"Maximilian, come here; I wish it."

Maximilian drew near with his sweet smile, and had it not been for his pallor, one would have thought that nothing unusual had taken place.

"Listen to me, my dear, my adored Valentine," said he in a solemn voice. "People like us who have never harboured a thought for which we had reason to blush before the world, our parents, or God, people like ourselves can read one another's heart like an open book. I have never been romantic, and I shall not be a melancholy hero. However, without words, protestations, or vows, I have laid my life in your hands. You fail me, and, I repeat once more, you are quite right in acting thus; nevertheless in losing you I lose part of my life. The moment you part from me, Valentine, I am alone in the world. My sister is happy with her husband; her husband is only my brother-in-law, that is to say a man who is attached to me solely by social laws; no one on earth has any further need of my useless existence. This is what I shall do: I shall wait until you are actually married, for I win not lose the smallest of one of those unexpected chances fate sometimes holds in store for us. After all, Monsieur Franz might die, a thunderbolt might fall on the altar as you approach it; everything appears possible to the condemned man, to whom a miracle becomes an everyday occurrence when it is a question of saving his life. I shall therefore wait until the very last moment, and when my fate is sealed, and my misery beyond all hope and remedy, I shall write a confidential letter to my brother-in-law, another one to the prefect of police, to notify him of my design; then, in a corner of some wood, in a ditch, or on the bank of some river, I shall blow out my brains, as certainly as I am the son of the most honest man who ever breathed in France."

A convulsive trembling shook Valentine in every limb; she relaxed her hold of the gate, her arms fell to her sides, and two large tears rolled down her cheeks.

The young man stood before her, gloomy and resolute.

"Oh! my God . . . ! Promise me, Maximilian, that you will not take your life!" she cried.

"I promise you I will not," said Maximilian. "But what does that matter to you? You will have done your duty and your conscience will be at rest."

Valentine fell on her knees, pressing her hand to her breaking heart.

"Maximilian, my friend, my brother on earth, my real husband before Heaven," she cried, "I entreat you, do as I am going to do—live in suffering; one day, perhaps, we shall be united."

"Farewell!" repeated Morrel.

"My God," said Valentine, raising her two hands to Heaven with a sublime expression on her face. "Thou seest I have done my utmost to remain a dutiful daughter. I have begged, entreated, implored. He has heeded neither my entreaties, nor my supplications, nor my tears . . . I would rather die of shame than of remorse," she continued, wiping away her tears and resuming her air of determination. "You shall live, Maximilian, and I shall belong to no other than you! When shall it be? At once? Speak, command, I will obey."

Morrel had already gone several steps; he returned on hearing these words, and pale with joy, his heart beating tumultuously, he held his two hands through the gate to Valentine, and said:

"Valentine, my beloved, you must not speak to me thus; better let me die. Why should I win you by force if you love me as I love you? Is it for pity that you compel me to live? Then I would rather die!"

" 'Tis too true!" murmured Valentine to herself, "who but he loves me? Who but he has consoled me in all my sorrow? In whom but in him do my hopes lie, and to whom but to him can I fly when in trouble? He is my all! Yes, you are right, Maximilian, I will follow you. I will leave my father's home, leave all! Ungrateful girl that I am!" she cried, sobbing. "Yes, I will leave all, even my grandfather, whom I had nearly forgotten!"

"No, you shall not leave him," said Maximilian. "You say that your grandfather likes me. Very well, then, before you flee, tell him all; his consent will be your justification before God. As soon as we are married, he shall come to us: instead of one child, he will have two children. Oh, Valentine, instead of our present hopelessness, nought but happiness is in store for you and me. But if they disregard your entreaties, Valentine," he continued, "if your father and

Madame de Saint-Méran insist on sending for Monsieur d'Épinay to-morrow to sign the contract . . ."

"You have my word, Maximilian."

"Instead of signing . . ."

"I shall flee with you, but until then, Morrel, let us not tempt Providence. We will see each other no more: it is a marvel, almost a miracle one might say, that we have not been discovered before. If it were found out, and if they learned how we see each other, our last resource would be gone. In the meantime I will write to you. I hate this marriage, Maximilian, as much as you do."

"Thank you, my beloved Valentine," Morrel replied. "Then all is settled. As soon as I know the time, I will hasten here. You will climb the wall with my help and then all will be easy. A carriage will be awaiting us at the gate which will take us to my sister's."

"So be it! Good-bye!" said Valentine, tearing herself away. "*Au revoir!*"

"You will be sure to write to me?"

"Yes."

"Thank you, my beloved wife. *Au revoir!*"

Morrel stayed, listening, till the sound of her footsteps on the gravel had died away, then he raised his eyes heavenward with an ineffable smile of gratitude that such supreme love should be given him.

The young man returned home and waited the whole of that evening and the next day without receiving any news. Toward ten o'clock of the third day, however, he received by post a note which he knew was from Valentine, although he had never before seen her handwriting. The note read as follows:

Tears, supplications, entreaties have been of no avail. I went to the church of St Philip du Roule yesterday and for two hours prayed most fervently. But God appears as unfeeling as man is and the signing of the contract is fixed for this evening at nine o'clock. I have but one heart and can give my hand to one person only: both my hand and my heart are yours, Maximilian.

I shall see you this evening at the gate at a quarter to nine.

Your wife,
VALENTINE DE VILLEFORT

P.S.—I think they are keeping it a secret from Grandpapa Noirtier that the contract is to be signed to-morrow.

Not satisfied with the information Valentine had given him, Morrel went in search of the notary, who confirmed the fact that the signing of the contract had been fixed for nine o'clock that evening.

Maximilian had made all arrangements for the elopement. Two ladders were hidden in the clover near the garden; a cabriolet, which was to take Maximilian to the gate, was in readiness. No servants would accompany him, and the lanterns would not be lit till they reached the first bend of the road.

From time to time a shudder passed through Morrel's whole frame as he thought of the moment when he would assist Valentine in her descent from the top of the wall, and when he would clasp in his arms the trembling form of her whose fingertips he had as yet hardly ventured to kiss.

In the afternoon, when the hour drew near, Morrel felt the necessity of being alone. He shut himself up in his room and attempted to read, but his eyes passed over the pages without understanding what he was reading, and in the end he flung the book from him. At last the hour arrived. The horse and cabriolet were concealed behind some ruins where Maximilian was accustomed to hide.

The day gradually drew to its close, and the bushes in the garden became nothing but indistinct masses. Morrel came out of his hiding-place, and, with beating heart, looked through the hole in the paling. There was no one to be seen. The clock struck nine . . . half-past nine . . . ten! In the darkness he searched in vain for the white dress, in the stillness he waited in vain for the sound of footsteps. Then one idea took possession of his mind: she had been coming to him, but her strength had failed her and she had fallen in a faint on one of the garden paths. He ventured to call her name, and he seemed to hear an inarticulate moan in response. He scaled the wall and jumped down on the other side. Distracted and half mad with anxiety, he decided to risk everything and anything in order to ascertain if and what misfortune had befallen Valentine. He reached the outskirts of the clump of trees and was just about to cross the open flower-garden with all possible speed when a distant voice, borne upon the wind, reached his ear.

He retreated a step and stood motionless, concealed, hidden among the trees. He made up his mind that if Valentine was alone, he would warn her of his presence; if she was accompanied, he would at least see her and know whether she was safe and well.

Just then the moon escaped from behind a cloud and by its light Morrel saw Villefort on the steps followed by a man in black garb. They descended the steps and approached the clump of trees where Morrel was hiding, and he soon recognized the other gentleman as Doctor d'Avrigny. After a short time, their footsteps ceased to crunch the gravel, and the following conversation reached his ears:

"Oh, Doctor, the hand of God is heavy upon us! What a terrible death! What a blow! Seek not to console me, for alas, the wound is too deep and too fresh. Dead! dead!"

A cold perspiration broke out on Maximilian's forehead, and his teeth chattered. Who was dead in that house that Villefort himself called accursed?

"I have not brought you here to console you, quite the contrary," said the doctor, in a voice that added to the young man's terror.

"What do you mean?" asked the Procureur du Roi, alarmed.

"What I mean is that behind the misfortune that has just befallen you, there is perhaps a much greater one. Are we quite alone?"

"Yes, quite alone. But why such precautions?"

"I have a terrible secret to confide in you," said the doctor. "Let us sit down."

Villefort sank on to a bench. The doctor stood in front of him, one hand on his shoulder. Petrified with fear, Morrel put one hand to his head, and pressed the other to his heart to stop the beatings lest they should be heard.

"Speak, Doctor, I am listening," said Villefort. "Strike your blow. I am prepared for all."

"Madame de Saint-Méran had attained a great age, it is true, but she was in excellent health."

Morrel began to breathe freely again.

"Grief has killed her," said Villefort, "yes, Doctor, grief! After living with the Marquis for more than forty years!"

"It is not grief, my dear Villefort," said the doctor. "Grief does kill, though very rarely, but not in a day, not in an hour, nor yet in ten minutes."

Villefort made no reply; he just raised his bowed head, and looked at the doctor with staring eyes.

"Were you present during the death agony?" asked Doctor d'Avrigny.

"Certainly," replied the Procureur du Roi, "you yourself whispered to me not to go away."

"Did you note the symptoms of the disease to which Madame de Saint-Méran succumbed?"

"Perfectly. Madame de Saint-Méran had three successive attacks at intervals of a few minutes, each one worse than the other. When you arrived, she had been gasping for breath for some few minutes; then she had a fit which I took for a simple nervous attack. I did not actually become alarmed till I saw her raise herself on her bed, and her limbs and neck stiffen. Then I saw by your face that it was more serious than I had supposed. When the attack was over, I sought your eyes, but you did not look at me. You were feeling her pulse, counting her respirations, and the second attack seized her before you had turned round. This was more terrible than the first, the same twitching of the nerves, the mouth contracted and purple in colour. At the end of the third attack she died. At the very first attack I saw signs of tetanus; you confirmed my opinion."

"Yes, in the hearing of everybody," replied the doctor, "but now we are alone."

"My God! What are you going to tell me?"

"That the symptoms of tetanus and poisoning by vegetable matter are absolutely identical!"

M. de Villefort sprang up, then after a moment sank on to the bench again.

"My God! Doctor," said he, "do you realize what you are telling me?"

Morrel knew not whether he was awake or dreaming.

"I know both the significance of my statement and the character of the man to whom I make it."

"Do you speak to me as magistrate or as friend?" asked Villefort.

"At this moment as friend only; the similarity of tetanus and poisoning by vegetable matter is so great that I should hesitate to sign the statement I have just made. I therefore repeat once more, I speak not to the magistrate but to the friend, and to the friend I declare that during the three-quarters of an hour the agony lasted, I watched the convulsions and the death struggle of Madame de Saint-Méran, and my firm conviction is that she died of poisoning, and what is more, I can name the poison that killed her."

"Oh, Doctor! Doctor!"

"All the symptoms were there; sleep disturbed by nervous tremors, excitement of the brain followed by torpor. Madame de Saint-Méran has succumbed to a large dose of brucine or strychnine, which has doubtless been administered to her by mistake."

Villefort seized the doctor's hands.

"It is impossible!" he said. "Am I dreaming? Surely I must be. It is terrible to hear such things from a man like you! For pity's sake, Doctor, tell me you have been mistaken!"

"Did anyone see Madame de Saint-Méran besides myself?"

"No one."

"Has any prescription been made up at the chemist's that has not been shown me?"

"None."

"Had Madame de Saint-Méran any enemies?"

"I do not know of any."

"Would her death be to anyone's interest?"

"No, no, surely not! My daughter is her sole heiress, Valentine alone . . . Oh, if such a thought came into my heart, I should stab that heart to punish it for having harboured such a thought if only for one moment."

"God forbid that I should accuse anyone," exclaimed M. d'Avrigny. "I speak of an accident, a mistake, you understand. But whether accident or mistake, the fact remains and is appealing to my conscience, which compels me to speak to you. Make inquiries."

"Of whom? How? About what?"

"Is it not possible that Barrois, the old servant, has made a mistake and given Madame de Saint-Méran a potion prepared for his master?"

"But how could a potion prepared for my father kill Madame de Saint-Méran?"

"Nothing more simple. You know that in the case of certain diseases poison becomes a remedy. Paralysis is one of these cases. I have been giving Monsieur Noirtier brucine for the past three months, and in his last prescription I ordered six grains, a quantity that would be perfectly safe for one whose paralysed organs have gradually become accustomed to it, whereas it would be sufficient to kill anyone else."

"But there is no communication between Monsieur Noirtier's room and that of Madame de Saint-Méran, and Barrois never went near my mother-in-law."

"It is through carelessness that this has happened; watch your servants; if it is the work of hatred, watch your enemies. In the meantime let us bury this terrible secret in the depths of our hearts. Keep constant watch, for it may be that it will not end here. Make active investigations and seek out the culprit, and if you should find him, I shall say to you: 'You are a magistrate, do as you will.' "

"Oh, thank you, Doctor, thank you!" said Villefort with indescribable joy. "Never have I had a better friend than you."

Fearing lest d'Avrigny might think better of his decision, he rose and ran into the house. The doctor also went away.

As though he had need of air, Morrel immediately put his head out of the bushes, and the moon shining on his face gave him the appearance of a ghost.

"I have been protected in a wonderful yet terrible way," said he. "Valentine, my poor Valentine! how will she bear so much sorrow!"

As though in answer, he seemed to hear a sob coming from one of the open windows of the house, and he thought he heard his name called by a shadow at the window. He rushed out of his hiding-place, and, at the risk of being seen and of frightening Valentine, and thus causing some exclamation to escape her lips which would lead to discovery, he crossed the flower-garden, which looked like a large white lake in the moonlight, reached the steps, ran up them quickly, and pushed open the door, which offered no resistance. The description of the house Valentine had given him now stood him in good stead, and the thick carpets deadened his tread. He reached the top of the stairs without any accident; a half-open door, from which issued a stream of light, and the sound of a sob indicated to him which direction to take. Pushing open the door, he entered the room.

In an alcove, under a white sheet, lay the corpse, more terrifying than ever to Morrel since chance had revealed to him the secret concerning the dead woman. Beside the bed knelt Valentine, her hands stretched out in front of her and her whole frame shaking with sobs. The moon shining through the open blinds made pale the light of the lamp, and cast a sepulchral hue over this picture of desolation. Morrel was not of a pious or impressionable nature, but to see Valentine suffering and weeping was almost more than he could endure in silence. With a deep sigh he murmured her name, and the tear-stained face buried in the velvet of the armchair was slowly raised and turned toward him. Valentine manifested no astonishment at seeing him.

"How came you here?" she asked. "Alas! I should say you are welcome, but that Death has opened the doors of this house to you!"

"Valentine, I have been waiting there since half-past eight," said Morrel in a trembling voice. "Such anxiety was tearing at my heart when you did not come that I scaled the wall and . . ."

"But we shall be lost if you are found here!" said Valentine in a voice devoid of all fear or anger.

"Forgive me," replied Morrel in the same tone. "I will go at once."

"No, you cannot go out either by the front door or the garden gate. There is only one safe way open to you and that is through my grandfather's room. Follow me!"

"Have you thought what that means?"

"I have thought long since. He is the only friend I have in the world and we both have need of him. Come!"

Valentine crossed the corridor and went down a small staircase which led to Noirtier's room. She entered; Morrel followed her on tiptoe.

Still in his chair, Noirtier was listening for the least sound. He had been informed by his old servant of all that had happened and was now watching the door with eager eyes. He saw Valentine, and his eyes brightened. There was something grave and solemn about the girl's whole attitude which struck the old man, and his eyes looked on her questioningly.

"Dear Grandpapa," she said, "you know that Grandmama Saint-Méran died an hour ago, and now I have no one but you in the whole world to love me."

An expression of infinite tenderness shone in the old man's eyes.

"Thus to you alone can I confide all my sorrows and hopes."

The old man made a sign of assent.

Valentine took Maximilian by the hand. "Then look well at this gentleman," said she.

Somewhat astonished, the paralytic fixed his scrutinizing gaze on Morrel.

"This is Maximilian Morrel," said she, "the son of an honest merchant at Marseilles, of whom you have doubtless heard."

"Yes," was the answer.

"It is an irreproachable name, and Maximilian is in a fair way to making it a glorious one, for, though but thirty years of age, he is Captain of Spahis and an Officer of the Legion of Honour."

The old man made a sign that he recollected him.

Valentine threw herself on her knees before the old man saying: "Grandpapa, I love him and will belong to no other. If they force me to marry another, I shall die or kill myself."

The paralytic's eyes expressed a wealth of tumultuous thoughts.

"You like Monsieur Maximilian Morrel, do you not, Grandfather?" asked Valentine.

"Yes," was the old man's motionless reply.

"Will you protect us, then, who are your children, against my father's will?"

Noirtier fixed his intelligent gaze on Morrel as though to say: "That depends."

Maximilian understood him.

"Mademoiselle, you have a sacred duty to fulfil in your grandmother's room. Will you permit me to have a few minutes' conversation with Monsieur Noirtier?"

"Yes, yes, that is right," said the old man's eyes. Then he looked at Valentine with an expression of anxiety.

"You wonder how he will understand you, Grandpapa? Have no fear; we have spoken of you so often that he knows quite well how I converse with you." Then turning to Maximilian with a smile that was adorable, though overshadowed by great sadness, she said: "He knows all that I know."

Valentine rose and kissed her grandfather tenderly, and, taking leave of Morrel, sorrowfully left the two men together.

Then, to show that he was in Valentine's confidence and knew all their secrets, Morrel took the dictionary, a pen, and some paper and placed them on the table near the lamp.

"First of all, monsieur," said he, "permit me to tell you who I am, how deeply I love Valentine, and what plans I entertain in regard to her."

"I am listening," said Noirtier's eyes.

It was an imposing sight to behold this old man, to all appearances a useless mass, now become the sole protector and support of two young handsome lovers just entering upon life. Imprinted on his face was a noble and remarkably austere expression which filled Morrel with awe. He related how he had become acquainted with Valentine, how he had learned to love her, and how in her unhappiness and solitude Valentine had welcomed his offer of devotion; he gave full information regarding his birth and position, and more than once when he questioned the paralytic's eye, it said to him: "That is well! Continue!"

Then Morrel related to him how they had intended to flee together that very night. When he had finished speaking, Noirtier closed and opened his eyes several times which, as we know, was his manner of expressing negation.

"No?" said Morrel. "You disapprove of my plan?"

"Yes, I do disapprove of it."

"But then, what am I to do?" asked Morrel. "Madame de Saint-Méran's last words were to the effect that her grand-child's marriage should not be delayed. Am I to allow it to take place?"

Noirtier remained motionless.

"I understand you," said Morrel. "I am to wait. But we shall be lost if we delay. Alone Valentine is powerless, and she will be compelled to submit like a child. It was little short of miraculous the way I gained admittance to this house to learn what was happening, and was permitted to enter your room; but I cannot reasonably expect the fates to be so kind to me again. Believe me, there is no other course for me to take. Do you give Mademoiselle Valentine permission to entrust herself to my honour?"

"No!" looked the old man.

"Whence will help come to us then; are we to seek it in chance?"

"No."

"In you?"

"Yes."

"Do you fully comprehend what I ask, monsieur? Forgive my importunity, but my life depends upon your answer. Is our salvation to come from you?"

"Yes."

"You are sure?"

"Yes."

"You can answer for it?"

"Yes."

There was so much determination in the look that gave this answer that it was impossible to doubt his will, even if one could not credit his power.

"Oh, thank you, thank you a hundred times. But unless a miracle restore to you your speech and power of movement, how can you, chained to your chair, mute and motionless, how can you prevent this marriage?"

A smile illumined the old man's face—a weird smile in the eyes alone, while the rest of his face was impassive.

"You say I must wait?" asked the young man.

"Yes."

"But the contract?"

Again the same smile.

"Do you mean to say that it will not be signed?"

"I do," said Noirtier.

"The contract will not be signed!" exclaimed Morrel. "Forgive me, but I cannot help doubting such happiness. Will the contract really not be signed?"

"No," said the paralytic.

Whether it was that Noirtier understood the young man's decision, or whether he had not complete confidence in his docility, he looked steadily at him.

"What do you wish, monsieur?" asked Morrel. "Do you wish me to renew my promise to do nothing?"

Noirtier's eyes remained on him in a fixed and firm stare, as though he wished to say that a promise was not sufficient; then they wandered from the face to the hand.

"Do you wish me to swear it?" asked Maximilian.

"Yes," motioned the old man with great solemnity.

Morrel understood that the old man attached great importance to an oath. He held up his hand: "On my honour," said he, "I swear to await your decision before acting in any way against Monsieur d'Épinay."

"That is right," said the old man with his eyes.

"Do you wish me to retire now, monsieur?" asked Morrel.

"Yes."

"Without seeing Mademoiselle Valentine again?"

"Yes."

Morrel made a sign that he was ready to obey. "Now, monsieur, will you permit your grandson to embrace you as your granddaughter did just now?" There was no mistaking the expression in Noirtier's eyes.

The young man pressed his lips to the old man's forehead, on the same spot where the girl had imprinted her kiss. Then he bowed again and retired.

He found the old servant waiting for him on the landing. Valentine had given him all instructions. He took Morrel along a dark corridor which led to a small door opening on to the garden. Once in the garden, Morrel soon scaled the wall, and by means of his ladder reached the field where his cabriolet was waiting for him. He jumped in, and worn out by so many emotions, though feeling more at peace, he reached his home toward midnight, threw himself on his bed, and fell into a deep, dreamless sleep.

Chapter XLVIII

MINUTES OF THE PROCEEDINGS

N o sooner were the Marquis and Marquise laid to rest together in the family vault than M. de Villefort thought about putting into execution the Marquise's last wishes. He sent a message to Valentine to request her to be in the salon in half an hour, as he was expecting M. d'Épinay, his two witnesses, and the notary.

This unexpected news created a great stir throughout the house. Mme de Villefort could scarcely believe it, and Valentine was thunderstruck. She looked round her, as though seeking for help, and would have gone to her grandfather, but on the stairs she met M. de Villefort, who, taking her arm, conducted her to the salon. In the hall she met Barrois, and threw him a despairing look. A moment later Mme de Villefort with her son, Edward, joined them. It was evident the young woman shared the family grief, for she was pallid, and looked terribly fatigued.

She sat down with Edward on her knees, and from time to time convulsively caught him to her breast. Soon the rumbling of two carriages was heard. The notary alighted from one, and Franz and his friends from the other.

Everyone was now united in the salon. Valentine was so

pale that one could trace the blue veins round her eyes and down her cheeks.

After arranging his papers on the table in true lawyer-like fashion, the notary seated himself in an armchair, and taking off his eyeglasses turned to Franz. "Are you Monsieur Franz de Quesnel, Baron d'Épinay?" he asked, though he knew perfectly well that he was.

"Yes, monsieur," replied Franz.

The notary bowed. "I must warn you, monsieur," he continued, "on Monsieur de Villefort's behalf, that your projected marriage with mademoiselle has effected a change in Monsieur Noirtier's designs toward his granddaughter, and that he has disinherited her entirely. I will add, however, that the testator has no right to will away the whole of his fortune. In doing so he has made the will contestable and liable to be declared null and void."

"That is right," said Villefort, "but I should like to warn Monsieur d'Épinay that never in my lifetime shall the will be contested, for my position does not permit of the slightest scandal."

"I greatly regret that this point should have been raised in Mademoiselle Valentine's presence," said Franz. "I have never asked the amount of her fortune, which, reduced though it may be, is still considerably larger than mine. What my family seeks in this alliance with Mademoiselle de Villefort is prestige, what I seek is happiness."

Valentine made a slight movement in acknowledgment, while two large tears rolled down her cheeks.

"Apart from the disappointment to your hopes, which is due solely to Monsieur Noirtier's weakness of mind," said Villefort, addressing his future son-in-law, "this unexpected will contains nothing that adversely affects you. What displeases my father is not that Mademoiselle de Villefort is about to marry you, but that she marries at all; a union with any other would have caused him the same grief. Old age is selfish, monsieur. Mademoiselle de Villefort has been a faithful companion to Monsieur de Noirtier: this will be impossible once she is Baroness d'Épinay.

"My father's sad condition prevents our speaking to him of serious affairs, which the weakness of his mind would not permit him to understand, and I am perfectly convinced that while grasping the fact that his granddaughter is to be married, Monsieur Noirtier has even forgotten the name of the man who is to be his grandson."

Scarcely had M. de Villefort finished these words, which Franz acknowledged with a bow, when the door opened and Barrois appeared.

"Messieurs," said he, in a voice strangely firm for a servant speaking to his masters on such a solemn occasion, "messieurs, Monsieur Noirtier de Villefort desires to have speech with Monsieur Franz de Quesnel, Baron d'Épinay, immediately."

That there might be no mistake made in the person, he also, like the notary, gave Franz his full title.

Villefort started; Mme de Villefort let her son slip from her knees; Valentine rose as white and silent as a statue. The notary looked at Villefort.

"It is impossible!" said the Procureur du Roi. "Monsieur d'Épinay cannot leave the room for the moment. Tell Monsieur Noirtier that what he asks cannot be."

"In that case Monsieur Noirtier warns you, messieurs, that he will have himself carried into the salon," replied Barrois.

Astonishment knew no bounds. A smile appeared on Mme de Villefort's face. Valentine instinctively raised her eyes to the ceiling to thank her God in Heaven.

"Valentine, please go and see what this new whim of your grandfather's is," said Villefort.

Valentine jumped up to obey, but M. de Villefort changed his mind.

"Wait," said he, "I will accompany you."

"Excuse me, monsieur," spoke Franz, "it seems to me that since Monsieur Noirtier has sent for me it is only right that I should do as he desires; besides, I shall be happy to pay him my respects, as I have not yet had the opportunity of doing so."

"I beg you, monsieur, do not give yourself so much trouble," said Villefort with visible uneasiness.

"Pardon me, monsieur," said Franz in a determined tone, "I will not miss this opportunity of showing Monsieur Noirtier that he does wrong to harbour bad feeling toward me, and that I am decided to overcome it by my devotedness."

With these words he rose and followed Valentine, who was running downstairs with the joy of a shipwrecked mariner who has touched a rock. M. de Villefort followed them.

Noirtier was waiting, dressed in black, and seated in his chair. When the three persons he expected to see had entered his room, he looked at the door, and his valet immediately closed it.

Villefort went up to Noirtier.

"Here is Monsieur Franz d'Épinay," said he, "you sent for him; he has granted your wish. We have long desired this interview, and I hope it will prove to you that your opposition to this marriage is ill-founded."

Noirtier's sole answer was a look which made the blood run cold in Villefort's veins. He made a sign to Valentine to approach.

With her usual alertness in conversing with her grandfather, she very quickly understood him to signify the word key. Then she consulted the paralytic's eyes, which were fixed on the drawer of a little chest placed between the windows. She opened it, and found therein a key.

The paralytic made a sign that that was what he wanted, and then his eyes rested on a writing-desk which had been forgotten for years and which was believed to contain nothing but useless papers.

"Do you wish me to open the desk?" asked Valentine.

"Yes," signalled the old man.

"Do you wish me to open the drawers?"

"Yes."

"The middle one?"

"Yes."

Valentine opened it and took out a bundle of papers.

"Is this what you want, Grandpapa?" said she.

"No."

She took out all the papers, one after the other, till there were no more left in the drawer.

"The drawer is empty now," said she.

Noirtier's eyes were fixed on the dictionary.

"Very well," said Valentine, "I understand you," and she repeated the letters of the alphabet; at S, Noirtier stopped her. She opened the dictionary and found the word secret. Noirtier looked at the door by which his servant had gone out.

"Do you wish me to call Barrois?" Valentine said.

"Yes."

She did as he bade her.

Villefort was becoming more and more impatient during this conversation, and Franz was stupefied with amazement.

The old servant entered.

"Barrois," began Valentine, "my grandfather desired me to take a key from this chest and open his desk. There is a secret drawer which you apparently understand; open it."

Barrois looked at his master.

"Obey!" said Noirtier's intelligent eyes.

Barrois obeyed and took out the false bottom, revealing a bundle of papers tied together with a black ribbon.

"Is this what you wish, monsieur?" asked Barrois.

"Yes."

"Shall I give the papers to Monsieur de Villefort?"

"No."

"To Monsieur Franz d'Épinay?"

"Yes."

Amazed, Franz advanced a step and took the papers from Barrois. Casting a glance over the envelope, he read:

"To be given, after my death, to General Durand;
who shall bequeath the packet to his son with an
injunction to preserve it as containing a paper of the
utmost importance."

"And what do you wish me to do with this paper, monsieur?" asked Franz.

"He doubtless wishes you to keep it, sealed as it is," said
the Procureur du Roi.

"No, no!" replied Noirtier vigorously.

"Perhaps you wish Monsieur Franz to read it?" said
Valentine.

"Yes," was the reply.

"Then let us be seated," said Villefort impatiently, "for it
will take some time."

Villefort sat down, but Valentine remained standing
beside her grandfather, leaning against his chair, while
Franz stood before him. He held the mysterious document
in his hand; he unsealed the envelope, and complete silence
reigned in the room as he read:

"Extract from the Minutes of a Sitting of the
Bonapartist Club in Rue Saint-Jacques, held on
February the fifth, eighteen-fifteen.

"The undersigned, Louis-Jacques Beaurcepaire,
Lieutenant-Colonel of Artillery, Étienne Duchampy,
Brigadier-General, and Claude Lecharpal, Director
of Waterways and Forests, hereby declare that on
February the fourth, eighteen-fifteen, a letter arrived
from the Isle of Elba recommending to the goodwill
and confidence of the members of the Bonapartist
Club one General Flavien de Quesnel who, having
served the Emperor from eighteen-four to eighteen-
fifteen, was supposed to be most devoted to the
Napoleonic dynasty notwithstanding the title of
Baron that Louis the Eighteenth had conferred on
him, together with his estate of Épinay.

"In consequence thereof, a note was dispatched to General de Quesnel inviting him to attend the meeting the next day, the fifth. The note gave neither the name of the road nor the number of the house where the meeting was to be held, neither did it bear any signature, but it informed the General that, if he were ready at nine o'clock, some one would call for him.

"The meeting lasted from nine o'clock in the evening until midnight.

"At nine o'clock the President of the club presented himself. The General was ready. The President told him that one of the conditions of his introduction into the club was that he should be for ever ignorant of the place of the meeting and that he should allow himself to be blindfolded, at the same time swearing on oath that he would not attempt to raise the bandage.

"General de Quesnel accepted these conditions, and gave his word of honour not to attempt to see whither he was being conducted.

"The General ordered his carriage, but the President told him it was impossible to use it as it would not be worth while blindfolding the master if the coachman was permitted to know through which streets they passed.

" 'What shall we do then?' asked the General.

" 'I have my own carriage,' said the President.

" 'Are you so sure of your coachman that you can trust him with a secret you cannot confide in mine?'

" 'Our coachman is a member of the club,' said the President, 'we shall be driven by a State Councillor.'

" 'Then we run the risk of being upset,' said the General, laughing.

"We record this joke as a proof that the General was in no way forced to attend the meeting, but on the contrary came of his own free will.

"As soon as they were in the carriage, the

President reminded the General of his promise to suffer himself to be blindfolded and he made no objection to this act of formality. On the way, the President thought he saw the General endeavour to see under his bandage and reminded him of his oath.

" 'Ah! just so,' said the General.

"The carriage drew up at a passage leading to the Rue Saint-Jacques. The General alighted, leaning on the arm of the President, whom he took for an ordinary member of the club. They crossed the passage, went up some stairs, and entered the conference room. The sitting was in progress. The members of the club, apprised of the introduction that was to take place, were in full complement. The General was invited to remove his bandage, which he instantly did, and appeared extremely astonished to find such a large number of acquaintances in a society of whose existence he had had no idea. They questioned him as to his sentiments, but he merely answered that the letters from the Isle of Elba must have given them full information on that score."

Franz stopped short, saying: "My father was a Royalist; it was unnecessary to question him regarding his views, they were well known."

"Hence my acquaintance with your father, dear Monsieur Franz," said Monsieur Villefort. "A similarity of views soon draws people together."

"Read on," said the old man's eyes.

Franz continued:

"The President then requested the General to express himself more explicitly. Monsieur de Quesnel replied that he first of all wished to know what they wanted of him. He was made acquainted with the contents of the letter from the Isle of Elba which recommended him to the members of the club as a man on whose assistance they might rely. One paragraph was entirely devoted to the probable return of Napoleon from Elba and gave promise of another letter with further details upon the arrival of the *Pharaon,* a ship belonging to Morrel of Marseilles, whose captain was a loyal adherent of the Emperor's. While the letter was being read, the General, on whom they thought they could rely as on a brother, gave visible signs of discontent and repugnance. When they had finished, he stood silent with knit brows.

" 'Well, what have you to say to this letter, General?' the President asked.

" 'What I say is, that the vows of fealty made to Louis the Eighteenth are still too fresh to be violated in favour of the ex-Emperor.'

"This answer was too plain to permit of any doubt as to his views.

" 'General,' said the President, 'for us there is no King Louis the Eighteenth any more than there is an ex-Emperor. For us there is but His Majesty the Emperor and King, who was driven out of France, his kingdom, ten months ago by violence and treason!'

" 'Pardon, messieurs,' returned the General, 'maybe there is no King Louis the Eighteenth for you, but there is for me; it was he who created me Baron and Maréchal, and I shall never forget that I owe these two titles to his happy return to France.'

" 'Be careful what you say, monsieur,' said the President in a very grave tone as he rose from his seat. 'Your words clearly denote that they were mistaken about you in the Isle of Elba and that they have also misled us. The communication made to you was inspired by the confidence they placed in you, a sentiment which does you honour. We have been acting under a misapprehension; for the sake of promotion and a title, you have thrown in your lot with the new

Government, a Government we would overthrow. We will not force you to give us your assistance; we do not enroll anyone against his will or conscience, but we would compel you to act like a man of honour, even though you do not feel that way disposed.'

" 'What you call acting like a man of honour is presumably knowing of your conspiracy and not revealing it. I call that being your accomplice. You see, I am more frank than you are.' "

"Poor father!" Franz broke in again. "Now I understand why they assassinated you!"

Valentine subconsciously looked at Franz; the young man was actually beautiful in his filial enthusiasm. Villefort paced up and down behind him. Noirtier watched the expression on each face, while he himself preserved his dignified and severe attitude.

Franz took up the manuscript and continued:

" 'You were not brought by force into the midst of our assembly, monsieur,' continued the President, 'you were invited; it was suggested you should be blindfolded, and you accepted. When you acceded to these two requests, you knew perfectly well we were not interested in securing the throne to Louis the Eighteenth, otherwise we should not have taken such precautions. Now, you understand, it would be too convenient for you to put on a mask to aid you in learning the secret of others and then have nothing further to do than remove the mask to ruin those who put their trust in you. No, no, you must tell us quite frankly whether you stand for the king of the moment who is now reigning, or for His Majesty the Emperor.'

" 'I am a Royalist,' was the General's reply. 'I have taken the oath of allegiance to Louis the Eighteenth, and I shall abide by my oath.'

"These words were followed by a general murmur,

and it was evident that a large number of the members of the club were discussing the propriety of making Monsieur d'Épinay repent of his foolish words.

"The President stood up, and, calling for silence, said: 'You are too serious-minded and too sensible, monsieur, not to understand the consequences of our present position. Your candour dictates to us what conditions to make. You will swear on your honour to reveal nothing of what you have heard.'

"The General put his hand to his sword and cried out: 'If you speak of honour, begin by not ignoring its laws and impose nothing by violence.'

" 'And I would advise you, General, not to touch your sword,' continued the President with a calmness that was perhaps more terrible than the General's anger.

"The General glanced round him, and the look in his eyes betrayed signs of uneasiness. Nevertheless, summoning all his courage, he said without flinching: 'I will not swear.'

" 'Then, monsieur, you shall die!' replied the President calmly.

"Monsieur d'Épinay turned very pale; he looked round him once more and perceived that several of the members were whispering together and getting their arms from under their cloaks.

" 'You need fear nothing as yet, General,' said the President. 'You are amongst men of honour who will employ every means to convince you before having recourse to the last extremity. At the same time, however, as you yourself said, you are amongst conspirators. You are in possession of their secret and must restore it to them.'

"An ominous silence ensued, and, as the General still made no reply, the President called out to the doorkeeper: 'Shut the doors!'

"Again there was a deathlike silence. Then the

General advanced and, making a violent effort, said: 'I have a son and must think of him when surrounded by assassins.'

" 'One man always has the right to offer insult to fifty, General, it is the privilege of weakness,' said the head of the assembly gallantly; 'nevertheless, you act wrongly in using this privilege. It were best to take the oath instead of heaping insults upon our members.'

"Once more dominated by the superiority of the President, the General hesitated an instant; finally he advanced to the presidential desk and asked: 'What is the formula?'

" 'The formula is this: I swear on my honour never to reveal to anyone what I have seen and heard between nine and ten o'clock of the evening of February the fifth, eighteen-fifteen, and I hereby declare that, if I violate my oath, it is only just that my life pay forfeit.'

"The General was so affected by a nervous shivering for a few seconds that he was unable to reply. Finally overcoming his obvious repugnance, he took the oath demanded of him, but in such a low and inaudible voice that several of the members insisted that it should be repeated louder and more distinctly. This the General did.

" 'Now I should like to retire,' said the General. 'Am I at liberty to do so?'

"The President rose, appointed three members of the assembly to accompany him, and after having blindfolded the General stepped into the carriage with him. In addition to the three members was the coachman who had driven them before. The other members of the club dispersed in silence.

" 'Where would you like us to take you?' asked the President.

" 'Anywhere, so long as it is out of your presence,' responded d'Épinay.

" 'Have a care, monsieur,' responded the President, 'you are no longer in the midst of an assembly, you have now only individuals before you. Do not insult them, or you may he held responsible for such insults.'

"Instead of taking this warning to heart, Monsieur d'Épinay said: 'You are as brave in your carriage as in your club, monsieur, and with good reason, for four men are always stronger than one.'

"The President stopped the carriage. They had just reached the entrance to the Quai des Ormes, where steps lead down to the river.

" 'Why do you stop here?' Monsieur d'Épinay asked.

" 'Because you have insulted a man, monsieur,' said the President, 'and that man refuses to go a step farther without honourable reparation.'

" 'A different form of assassination,' said the General, shrugging his shoulders.

" 'No fuss, if you please, monsieur,' replied the President, 'unless you wish me to regard you as one of those you designated just now as cowards, using their weakness as a shield. You are alone, and one only shall answer you. You have a sword at your side, and I have one in my cane. You have no second, but one of these gentlemen is at your service. If these arrangements meet with your approval, you may now remove the bandage.'

" 'The General instantly tore the kerchief from his eyes, saying: 'At last I shall know with whom I have to deal!'

" 'The carriage door was opened and the four men alighted."

Franz stopped once more and wiped away the cold sweat that stood out on his brow. There was something awe-inspiring in hearing the pale and trembling son read aloud the hitherto unknown details of his father's death.

Valentine clasped her hands as though in prayer; Noirtier looked at Villefort with an almost sublime expression of contempt and pride.

Franz continued:

"It was, as we have said, the fifth of February. For three days there had been five or six degrees of frost and the steps were covered with ice. The General was tall and stout, so the President offered him the side with the railing. The two seconds followed at their heels.

"It was a dark night, and the ground from the steps to the river was slippery with snow and hoar-frost;[1] the river looked black and deep, and was covered with drifting ice. One of the seconds fetched a lantern from a coal barge, and by its light the weapons were examined. The President's sword, which, as he had said, was simply one he carried in his cane, was shorter than his adversary's and had no guard. General d'Épinay suggested they should draw lots for the swords, but the President replied that he was the one who had challenged and in so doing had presumed that each one should use his own weapon. The seconds attempted to insist, but the President ordered them to silence.

"The lanterns were placed on the ground; the two adversaries stood opposite one another; the duel started. In the weird light the two swords had the appearance of flashes of lightning, while the men were scarcely visible in the darkness.

"The General had the reputation of being one of the best swordsmen in the army, but he was pressed so closely from the outset that before long he fell from sheer exhaustion. The seconds thought he was dead, but his adversary, who knew he had not hit him, offered him his arm to assist him to rise. Instead of calming the General, this circumstance only irritated him and he again rushed upon his opponent. The latter, however, did not budge an inch and received him on his sword. Finding himself too closely pressed, the General recoiled three times only to renew the attack, and the third time he fell once more. At first they thought he had slipped as before, but when the seconds saw that he did not move they went to him and tried to raise him: in so doing the one that put his arm round his body felt something warm and damp. It was blood.

"The General, who had almost fainted, revived a little and said: 'Ah, they have sent some ruffian, some fencing-master, to fight me.'

"Without replying the President went up to the second who had the lantern and, drawing back his sleeve, showed where his arm had twice been pierced with the sword; then, opening his coat, he unbuttoned his waistcoat, and there in his side was a third wound where his adversary's sword had pierced him. Yet he had not even uttered a sigh.

"General d'Épinay died five minutes later."

Franz read these last words in such a choked voice that they could scarcely be heard, then he stopped and passed his hand across his eyes as if to disperse a cloud. After a moment's silence, he continued:

"After replacing his sword in his cane, the President went up the steps, leaving traces of blood in the snow. He had not reached the top step when he heard a heavy splash in the water. After ascertaining that the General was dead, the seconds had thrown his body into the river.

"Thus the General fell in an honourable duel and not in ambush, as will probably be reported.

"In witness whereof we hereby sign this document to establish the truth of the facts, lest the time should arrive when one of the actors of the terrible scene should be accused of premeditated murder, or of violation of the laws of honour.

"SIGNED: BEAUREPAIRE, DUCHAMPY,
AND LECHARPAL"

When Franz had finished reading this report, truly a terrible ordeal for a son—when Valentine, pale with emotion, had wiped away her tears, and Villefort, trembling in a corner, had attempted to calm the storm by sending appealing looks at the implacable old man, he turned to Noirtier with the following words:

"Since you know this terrible story in all its details, monsieur, and have had it witnessed by honourable signatures; since you seem to take some interest in me, although, until now, that interest has brought me nothing but grief, do not refuse me the satisfaction of making known to me the name of the President of the club, so that I may at least learn who killed my poor father."

Dazed and bewildered, Villefort reached for the door handle. Valentine knew what her grandfather's answer must be, for she had often seen the scars of two sword wounds on his arm, and she drew back a few steps.

"For Heaven's sake, mademoiselle," said Franz, turning to his betrothed, "unite your efforts with mine, so that I may know the name of the man who made me an orphan at two years of age."

Valentine remained silent and motionless.

"I pray you, do not prolong this horrible scene," said Villefort. "The names have been concealed intentionally. My father does not know the President, and, even if he did, he would not know how to communicate his name to you; proper names are not to be found in the dictionary."

"Woe is me!" cried Franz, "the only hope that sustained me throughout this report, and gave me the strength to finish reading it, was that I should at least learn the name of him who killed my father." Then turning to Noirtier: "Oh! I entreat you, in the name of all that is holy, do what you can to indicate to me, to make me understand."

"Yes," was Noirtier's reply.

"Oh! mademoiselle, mademoiselle," cried Franz, "your grandfather has made a sign that he can indicate to me the name of this man. Help me . . . you understand him . . . give me your aid."

Noirtier looked at the dictionary. Franz took it, trembling nervously, and repeated the letters of the alphabet till he came to M, when the old man made a sign for him to stop.

The young man's finger glided over the words, but at each one Noirtier made a sign in the negative.

Finally he came to the word myself.

"Yes," motioned the old man.

"You?" cried Franz, his hair standing on end. "You, Monsieur Noirtier? It was you who killed my father?"

"Yes," replied Noirtier, with a majestic look at the young man.

Franz sank lifeless into a chair.

Villefort opened the door and fled, for he was seized with the impulse to choke out of the old man the little life that remained to him.

Chapter XLIX

THE PROGRESS OF CAVALCANTI JUNIOR

<hr/>

A short time after the events just recorded, Monte Cristo called one evening on M. Danglars. The banker was out, but Mme Danglars would be pleased to receive him.

When the Count entered the boudoir, the Baroness was glancing at some drawings which her daughter had passed to her, after she and M. Cavalcanti Junior had looked at them together. His presence produced its usual effect, and the Baroness received him with a smile though she had been somewhat discomforted when his name was announced.

Monte Cristo took in the whole scene at a glance. The Baroness was reclining on a settee, and seated beside her was Eugénie, while Cavalcanti stood in front of them. The latter, clad in black, like one of Goethe's heroes, with patent-leather shoes and white silk open-work stockings, passed his white and manicured hand through his fair hair, thus displaying a sparkling diamond which the vain young man could not resist wearing on his finger. This gesture was accompanied by killing glances at Mlle Danglars and sighs meant for that same lady.

Mlle Danglars was still the same—cold, scornful, and beautiful. Not one of Andrea's looks or sighs escaped her. She greeted the Count coldly, and took advantage of the first opportunity to escape to her studio. Soon two laughing, noisy voices were mingled with a piano, which told Monte Cristo that Mlle Danglars preferred the society of her singing-mistress, Mlle Louise d'Armilly, to either his or M. Cavalcanti's.

While conversing with Mme Danglars, and appearing absorbed by the charm of the conversation, the Count watched M. Andrea's solicitude; how he listened to the music at the door he dared not pass, and how he manifested his admiration.

The Baron soon came in. His first glance was for Monte Cristo, it is true, but the second was for Andrea.

"Have the young ladies not invited you to join them at the piano?" Danglars asked Andrea.

"I am sorry to say they have not," replied Andrea with a deeper sigh than ever.

Danglars went to the communicating door and opened it. "Well! Are we all to be excluded?" he asked his daughter.

Then he took the young man into the room, and, whether by chance or dexterity, the door was closed behind Andrea in such a way that from where they were sitting, the Baroness and Monte Cristo could not see into the room, but, as the banker had followed Andrea, Mme Danglars did not appear to notice this circumstance.

Shortly afterward, the Count heard Andrea's voice singing a Corsican song to the accompaniment of the piano.

In the meantime, Mme Danglars began boasting to Monte Cristo of the strength of character of her husband, who, that very morning, had lost three or four hundred thousand francs by a business failure in Milan. The praise was certainly well merited, for, if the Count had not known of this fresh piece of ill-luck from the Baroness, or perhaps by one of the means he had of learning everything, the Baron's face would have told him nothing.

"Ha!" thought he, "he is already beginning to hide his losses: a month ago he boasted of them." Then aloud he said:

"But Monsieur Danglars has so much experience on the Exchange that what he has lost in one way, he will soon make up in another."

"I see you are under a misapprehension, along with everyone else. Monsieur Danglars never speculates."

"Oh, yes, that's true. I remember now, Monsieur Debray told me . . . By the way, what has become of Monsieur Debray? I have not seen him for three or four days."

"Neither have I," said Madame Danglars, with miraculous self-possession. "But you commenced a sentence you did not finish."

"Oh, yes. I was saying Monsieur Debray told me it was you who had made sacrifices to the demon of speculation."

"I will own that I was fond of speculating at one time," replied Mme Danglars, "but I do not care for it any more. But we have talked enough about the Exchange, let us change the conversation to the Villeforts. Have you heard how fate is pursuing them? After losing Monsieur de Saint-Méran within three or four days of his departure for Paris, the Marquise died a few days after her arrival. But that is not all. You know their daughter was going to marry Monsieur Franz d'Épinay?"

"Do you mean to say their engagement is broken off?"

"Franz declined the honour yesterday morning."

"Really! Is the reason known?"

"No."

"That is strange. How does Monsieur de Villefort take all this misfortune?"

"As always, quite philosophically."

Just then Danglars re-entered the room alone.

"Well, have you left Monsieur Cavalcanti with your daughter?" asked the Baroness.

"And Mademoiselle d'Armilly," said the banker. "Is she no one?" Turning to Monte Cristo he said: "Prince Cavalcanti is a charming young man, is he not? Is he really a prince, though?"

"I cannot answer for that," said Monte Cristo.

"Do you realize what you are risking?" said the Baroness. "If Monsieur de Morcerf should happen to come, he will find Monsieur Cavalcanti in a room where he, Eugénie's intended, has never had permission to enter."

"Oh, he will not do us the honour of being jealous of his betrothed. He does not care enough for her. Besides, what do I mind if he is vexed or not."

"The Viscount of Morcerf," announced the valet.

The Baroness rose quickly. She was going to tell her daughter when Danglars stopped her.

"Let her be!" he said.

She looked at him in astonishment.

Monte Cristo pretended he had not seen this little comedy.

Albert entered, looking handsome and very cheerful. He greeted the Baroness with ease, Danglars with familiarity, and Monte Cristo with affection; then turning toward the Baroness he said: "May I ask how mademoiselle is?"

"Very well," replied Danglars hastily; "at the present moment she is at the piano with Monsieur Cavalcanti."

Albert remained calm and indifferent; perhaps he felt some annoyance, but he knew that Monte Cristo's eye was on him.

"The fact is, the Prince and my daughter get on very well together. They were the object of general admiration yesterday. How was it we did not see you, Monsieur de Morcerf?"

"What Prince?" asked Albert.

"Prince Cavalcanti," replied Danglars, who persisted in giving the young man this title.

"Oh, pardon, I was unaware that he was a Prince. I was unable to accept your invitation, as I was compelled to accompany Madame de Morcerf to a German concert given by the Countess of Château-Renaud."

After a moment's silence he asked: "May I be permitted to pay my respects to Mademoiselle Danglars?"

"Just one moment, please," said the banker, stopping the

young man. "Do you hear that delightful Cavatina? *Ta, ti, ta, ti, ta, ti, ta, ta,* it is charming. It will be finished in a second! Splendid! Bravo! Bravo!"

With these words the banker began applauding enthusiastically.

"Yes, indeed, it is charming," said Albert. "No one could understand the music of his country better than Cavalcanti does. You did say Prince, did you not? In any case, if he is not a Prince now, they will make him one. It is a very easy matter in Italy. But to return to the charming musicians. You should ask them to give us the pleasure of another song, without letting them know there is a stranger here."

This time it was Danglars who was vexed by the young man's indifference. He took Monte Cristo aside.

"What do you think of our lover now?"

"He is decidedly very cool. But what can you do? You have given your word."

"I have certainly given my word to bestow my daughter on a man who loves her, but not on a man who does not love her. Look at this one, as cold as marble, as proud as his father; if he were rich, if he had a fortune like the Cavalcantis, one would overlook it. I have not consulted my daughter, but, do you know, if I thought she cared . . ."

"I do not know whether it is my friendship that blinds me," said Monte Cristo, "but I assure you, I find Monsieur de Morcerf a charming young man. He should make your daughter happy and sooner or later he will achieve much, for his father has an excellent position."

"Humph!" was Danglars' reply.

"Why do you doubt?"

"I am thinking of his past . . . his mysterious past."

"But the father's past has nothing to do with the son. You cannot break off the engagement thus. The Morcerfs look upon this marriage as certain."

"Well, then, let them explain themselves. You might give the father a hint to that effect. Count, you are on such an intimate footing there."

"Certainly, if you wish it."

A servant came up to Danglars and said something to him in a low voice.

"I shall be back in a minute," said the banker to Monte Cristo. "Wait for me, I may have something interesting to tell you."

Indeed not many minutes had elapsed before Monsieur Danglars returned visibly agitated.

"Well," said he, "my courier has returned from Greece!"

"And how is King Otto?" asked Albert in a playful tone.

Danglars looked at him slyly without answering; Monte Cristo turned away his head to hide the momentary expression of pity that had found its way to his face.

"Shall we go together?" said Albert to the Count.

"Yes, if you like," replied the latter.

Albert could not understand the banker's look and, turning to Monte Cristo, who understood only too well, he said:

"Did you notice how he looked at me?"

"Yes," replied the Count. "Do you think he meant anything by that look?"

"I am sure of it. What can he have meant by his news from Greece?"

"How can you expect me to know."

"I thought perhaps you had some correspondents in the country."

Monte Cristo smiled in the way one always does when trying to avoid giving an answer.

"Here he is coming toward you," said Albert. "I will go and compliment Mademoiselle Danglars upon her performance, and in the meanwhile you will have an opportunity of speaking to her father."

Albert went up to Eugénie with a smile on his lips. Danglars whispered into the Count's ear: "You gave me excellent advice. There is a long and terrible history connected with the two words Fernand and Janina."

"Nonsense," was Monte Cristo's reply.

"Yes, there is. I will tell you about it. But now take the

young man away. It is too embarrassing for me to be together with him at this moment."

"That is just what I was going to do. Do you still wish me to send his father to you?"

"More than ever."

The Count made a sign to Albert. They took their leave of the ladies and went away, and M. Cavalcanti remained master of the field.

Chapter L

HAYDEE'S STORY

❧

Scarcely had the horses turned the corner of the boulevard when Albert looked at the Count and burst into a loud fit of laughter, so loud that it was obviously forced.

"Well," said he, "I will ask you the same question King Charles put to Catherine de' Medici after the massacre of St Bartholomew.[1] How do you think I played my part?"

"In what respect?" asked Monte Cristo.

"Why, with regard to the reception of my rival and your protégé, Monsieur Andrea Cavalcanti, in the bosom of the Danglars family."

"None of your poor jokes, Viscount! Monsieur Andrea is no protégé of mine, at any rate not so far as Monsieur Danglars is concerned."

"That is just what I should reproach you with if the young man had any need of protection. Happily for me, he can dispense with it."

"What, do you think he is paying her attentions?"

"I am sure of it. He makes eyes at her, sighs, and speaks to her in amorous tones. He aspires to the hand of the proud Eugénie!"

"What does that matter so long as they favour you?"

"Don't say that, Count. I am being repulsed from two

426

sides: Mademoiselle Eugénie scarcely answered me today, while Mademoiselle d'Armilly, her confidante, did not answer me at all. As to the father, I will warrant that within a week he will shut the door in my face."

"You are quite mistaken, my dear Viscount."

"Have you proofs?"

"Do you want one?"

"Yes."

"Well, then, I have been requested to ask the Count of Morcerf to come to some definite arrangement with the Baron."

"Who requested you?"

"The Baron himself."

"Oh, you surely will not do that, will you?" said Albert coaxingly.

"Oh, yes, I shall since I have promised to."

"Come, now," said Albert with a sigh. "You are absolutely determined to make me marry."

"I only wish to be on good terms with every one."

The carriage stopped.

"Here we are," said Monte Cristo. "It is only half-past ten. Will you come in with me?"

"With pleasure."

They both entered the house. The salon was lit up.

"Give us some tea, Baptistin," said the Count.

Baptistin went out without saying a word. Two minutes later he reappeared with a tray laden with all his master's requirements as though, like the supper-tables in fairy plays, it had sprung up from the earth.

"Really, Count," said Morcerf, "what I admire in you is not your wealth, for there are perhaps others richer than you; it is not your wit—Beaumarchais had no more, but he had as much as you; no, what I admire is your way of being served without a question, to the minute, to the second, as though your servants guessed what you desired by your manner of sounding the gong, and as though everything were ready and waiting upon your desire."

"What you say is more or less true. My servants know my habits. I will give you an instance. Is there nothing you would like to have with your tea?"

"Indeed there is, I should dearly love a smoke."

Monte Cristo went up to the gong and sounded it once. Within a second a private door opened, and Ali appeared with two chibouques filled with excellent Latakia.

"It is wonderful," said Morcerf.

"Oh, no, it is quite simple," said Monte Cristo. "Ali knows that I generally smoke when I am drinking tea or coffee; he knows I have asked for tea, also that you came in with me. On hearing the gong he guessed my desire, and, coming from a country where the chibouque plays an essential part in hospitality, he brings in two of them."

"That is certainly quite a simple explanation, but it is nevertheless true that you alone . . . Ah, but what is that I hear!" he added, bending his ear toward a door through which sounds were issuing similar to those of a guitar.

"You are doomed to have music this evening, Viscount. You have only just escaped from Mademoiselle Danglars' piano and must now submit to Haydee's *guzla*."

"Haydee! What a charming name. Are there really women elsewhere than in Byron's poems with the name of Haydee?"

"Certainly. It may be an uncommon name in France, but it is common enough in Albania and Epirus; it is as though you said, for instance, Chastity, Modesty, Innocence: it is a baptismal name, as you Parisians call it."

"How very charming! How I should like to hear our French girls called Mademoiselle Goodness, Mademoiselle Silence, Mademoiselle Christian Charity. I say, supposing Mademoiselle Claire Marie Eugénie Danglars were called Mademoiselle Chastity Modesty Innocence Danglars, what a fine effect it would have when the banns of marriage were published!"

"You are mad," said the Count. "Do not joke so loud, Haydee might hear you."

"Would she be annoyed?"

"Certainly not," said the Count. "A slave has no right to be annoyed with her master."

"Now it is you who are joking. There are no slaves now!"

"Since Haydee is my slave there must be."

"Really, Count, you have nothing and do nothing like other people. Monte Cristo's slave! What a position in France! To judge from the lavish way in which you spend your money, it must be worth a hundred thousand crowns a year."

"A hundred thousand crowns! The poor child possesses a great deal more than that. She came into the world to a cradle lined with treasures compared with which those in *A Thousand and One Nights* are as nought."

"Is she a real princess then?"

"She is; one of the greatest in her country."

"I thought as much. But tell me, how did such a princess become your slave?"

"You are one of my friends and will not chatter. Do you promise to keep a secret?"

"On my word of honour."

"Do you know the history of the Pasha of Janina?"

"Of Ali Tebelin? Surely, since my father made his fortune in his service."

"True, I had forgotten that."

"Well, what has Haydee to do with Ali Tebelin?"

"She is merely his daughter!"

"What! The daughter of Ali Pasha your slave!"

"Oh, dear me, yes."

"But how comes it?"

"Simply that I was passing through the market at Constantinople one fine day and bought her."

"Wonderful! With you, Count, life becomes a dream. Now, listen, I am going to ask you something very indiscreet."

"Say on."

"Since you go out with her and take her to the Opera . . ."

"Well?"

"Will you introduce me to your princess?"

"With pleasure, but on two conditions."

"I accept them in advance."

"The first is that you never tell anyone of this introduction; the second is that you do not tell her that your father served under her father."

"Very well." Morcerf held up his hand. "I swear I will not."

The Count again struck the gong, whereupon Ali appeared and Monte Cristo said to him: "Inform your mistress that I am coming to take my coffee with her, and give her to understand that I ask permission to introduce one of my friends to her."

Ali bowed and retired.

"Then it is understood that you will not ask her any direct questions. If you wish to know anything, tell me and I will ask her."

"Agreed!"

Ali reappeared for the third time and held up the door curtain as an indication to his master and Albert that they were welcome.

"Let us go," said Monte Cristo.

Albert passed his hand through his hair and curled his moustache, while the Count took his hat, put on his gloves, and preceded Albert into the room, which was guarded by Ali as advance guard, and defended by three French maids under his command.

Haydee was awaiting them in her salon, her eyes wide-open with surprise. This was the first time that any other man than Monte Cristo had found his way to her room. She was seated in a corner of a sofa with her legs crossed under her, thus making, as it were, a nest of the richly embroidered striped Eastern material that fell in soft folds around her. Beside her was the instrument whose sounds had revealed her presence. Altogether she made a charming picture.

"Whom do you bring me?" the girl asked of Monte Cristo in Romaic. "A brother, a friend, a simple acquaintance, or an enemy?"

"A friend," replied Monte Cristo in the same language.

"His name?"

"Count Albert. It is he whom I delivered from the hands of the bandits at Rome."

"In what tongue do you wish me to speak to him?"

Monte Cristo turned toward Albert with the question: "Do you speak modern Greek?"

"Alas! not even ancient Greek," said Albert. "Never have Homer and Plato had a more unworthy, I might almost say contemptuous, scholar than myself."

"Then I shall use the French or Italian tongue if my lord wishes me to speak at all," responded Haydee, showing by this remark that she had understood the Count's question and Albert's answer.

Monte Cristo thought for a moment. "You will speak in Italian," said he at last. Then turning toward Albert: "It is a pity you do not speak either modern or ancient Greek. Haydee speaks both to perfection, and the poor girl may give you a wrong impression of herself by being forced to speak in Italian."

He made a sign to Haydee.

"Welcome, my friend, who have come hither with my lord and master," said the girl in excellent Tuscan with the soft Roman accent which makes the language of Dante as sonorous as that of Homer. "Ali, bring coffee and pipes," she then added.

Ali went to execute his young mistress' order, while Monte Cristo and Albert drew their seats up to a table which contained a narghile as its centrepiece, and on which were arranged flowers, drawings, and music albums. Ali returned with the coffee and chibouques, but Albert refused the pipe the Nubian offered him.

"Take it, take it," said Monte Cristo, "Haydee is almost as civilized as a Parisian. Havanas are distasteful to her because she does not like their strong odour, but Eastern tobacco is a perfume, you must know."

Haydee put out her hand and, encircling the cup of Japanese china with her dainty pink fingers, carried it to her lips with the simple pleasure of a child drinking or eating something it likes.

At the same time two women entered carrying trays laden with ices and sherbet, which they placed on two small tables intended for that purpose.

"Pray excuse my amazement," said Albert in Italian. "I am quite bewildered, and it could not well be otherwise. But a few moments ago I heard the rumbling of the omnibuses and the tinkling of the lemonade-sellers' bells, yet here I am transported to the East, the true East, not as I have seen it, unfortunately, but as I have pictured it to myself in the dreams I have dreamt in the heart of Paris. Oh, signora! if only I could speak Greek, your conversation, coupled with these fairylike surroundings, would afford an evening that would ever remain in my memory!"

"I speak Italian well enough to converse with you, monsieur," said Haydee calmly. "If you love the East, I will do my best to bring its atmosphere to you."

Albert turned toward Haydee, saying: "At what age did you leave Greece, signora?"

"When I was five years old," responded Haydee.

"Do you remember your country?"

"When I close my eyes, I seem to see once more all that I have ever seen. We have a twofold power of vision, that of the body and that of the mind. Whereas the body may sometimes forget the impressions it has received, the mind never does."

"How far back does your memory go?"

"To the time when I could scarcely walk."

"How old were you at the time?"

"Three years," said Haydee.

"Do you then remember everything that happened around you from the time you were three years of age?"

"Everything."

"Count," said Morcerf to Monte Cristo, "you should let the signora tell us something of her sad history. You have forbidden me to mention my father to her, but perhaps she may speak of him herself, and you have no idea what happiness it would give me to hear his name pronounced by those beautiful lips."

Monte Cristo turned toward Haydee and, making a sign to her to pay great attention to the injunction he was about to impose on her, said in Greek: "Tell us your father's fate, but mention not the treason nor the name of the traitor."

Haydee sighed deeply, and a dark cloud passed over her beautiful brow.

"You are still young, signora," said Albert, taking refuge in banality in spite of himself, "what sufferings can you have experienced?"

Haydee looked at Monte Cristo, who made an almost imperceptible sign to her, murmuring: "Tell it all!"

"Nothing makes such a deep impression on our minds as our earliest memories, and all those of my childhood are mingled with sadness. Do you really wish me to relate them?"

"I implore you to tell them!" said Albert.

"Well, I was four years old when I was awakened one evening by my mother. We were at the palace at Janina. She snatched me up with the cushions on which I was lying, and when I opened my eyes I perceived that hers were filled with big tears. She carried me away without a word. On seeing her weeping, I began to cry too. 'Be quiet, child!' she said.

"At any other time, no matter what my mother might do to console me, or what threats she held out to me, I should have continued to cry, but this time there was such a note of terror in her voice that I stopped instantly. She bore me rapidly away. Then I perceived that we were going down a wide staircase and rushing on in front of us were my mother's women, carrying trunks, bags, clothing, jewellery, and purses filled with gold. Behind the women came a guard of twenty men armed with long rifles and pistols and clad in the uniform which must be familiar to you in France now that Greece has once more become independent. Believe me," continued Haydee, shaking her head and turning pale at the thought of the scene, "there was something ominous in this long line of slaves and women all heavy with sleep, or at least I thought they were, though perhaps it may only have been that as I was only half awake myself, I imagined they were still as sleepy as I. Gigantic shadows thrown by the flickering light of the pine torches chased each other along the walls of the staircase and descended to the very vaults.

" 'Quickly, quickly!' said a voice from the end of the gallery, and every one bent forward like a field of corn bowed down by the passing wind. It was my father's voice. He marched in the rearmost, clad in his most splendid robes and holding in his hand the carbine your Emperor gave him. Leaning on his favourite Selim, he drove us on before him as a shepherd drives his straggling flock. My father," continued Haydee, raising her head, "was an illustrious man known in Europe under the name of Ali Tebelin, Pasha of Janina, before whom all Turkey trembled."

Without any apparent reason, Albert shuddered on hearing these words uttered with such unspeakable pride and dignity. There seemed to be something terrifying and sombre lurking in the maiden's eyes.

"Soon we came to a halt; we had reached the bottom of the staircase and were on the borders of a lake. My mother pressed me to her heaving bosom, and two paces from us I saw my father looking anxiously round him. Before us were four marble steps, at the bottom of which was a small boat. In the middle of the lake a black object was discernible; it was the kiosk to which we were going. It looked to me to be very far away, but that was probably owing to the darkness of the night.

"We stepped into the boat. I remember noticing that there was no sound as the oars skimmed the water, and I leaned over to look for the cause: they were muffled with the sashes of our Palikars. Besides the oarsmen there was no one in the boat but some women, my father, my mother, Selim, and myself. The Palikars had remained on the edge of the lake to protect us in case of pursuit. Our bark sped like the wind.

" 'Why is our boat going so fast?' I asked my mother.

"'Hush, child, hush!' she said. 'It is because we are fleeing.'

"I did not understand. Why should my father, the all-powerful one, flee? He before whom others were accustomed to flee? He who had taken as his device: 'They hate me, therefore they fear me.'

"My father was indeed fleeing across the lake. He told me later that the garrison of the Janina Castle, tired of long service . . ."

Here Haydee cast a questioning look at Monte Cristo, who had never taken his eyes off her. She then continued slowly as though inventing or suppressing some part of her narrative.

"You were saying, signora," returned Albert, who was paying the utmost attention to the recital, "that the garrison of Janina, tired of long service . . ."

"Had treated with the Seraskier Kourschid sent by the Sultan to seize my father. Upon learning this Ali Tebelin sent to the Sultan a French officer in whom he placed entire confidence, and then resolved to retire to the place of retreat he had since long prepared for himself, to which he had given the name of *kataphygion*, which means his refuge."

"Do you recollect the officer's name, signora?" Albert asked.

Monte Cristo exchanged a lightninglike glance with the girl which was unobserved by Morcerf.

"No, I do not recollect his name," she said, "but it may come to my mind later on."

Albert was about to mention his father's name when Monte Cristo quietly held up his finger enjoining silence, and, remembering his oath, the young man obeyed.

"It was toward this kiosk that we were making our way. From the outside the kiosk appeared to consist of nothing more than a ground floor ornamented with arabesques[2] with a terrace leading down to the water, and another story overlooking the lake. Under the ground floor, however, was a vast subterranean cave extending the whole length of the island, whither my mother and myself together with our womenfolk were taken, and where sixty thousand bags and two hundred casks were piled up in a heap. The bags contained twenty-five millions in gold, and the casks were filled with thirty thousand pounds of powder.

"Near these casks stood Selim, my father's favourite slave, whom I mentioned just now. Night and day he stood on guard, holding a lance at the tip of which was a lighted match. His orders were that directly my father gave him the signal, he was to blow up everything, kiosk, guards, women, gold, and the Pasha himself. I still see before me the pale-faced, black-eyed young soldier, and when the angel of Death comes to fetch me I am sure I shall recognize Selim.

"I cannot tell you how long we remained thus, for at that period I was ignorant of the meaning of time. Sometimes, though rarely, my father would summon my mother and me to the terrace of the palace. Those were hours of real pleasure for me, for in the cave I heard nothing but the wailing of the slaves, and saw nothing but Selim's fiery lance. Seated before a large aperture my father would try to pierce the black horizon; he examined every tiny speck that appeared in the lake, whilst my mother reclined at his side with her head upon his shoulder and I played at his feet.

"One morning my father sent for us; we found him quite calm but paler than usual.

" 'Have courage, Vasiliki,' he said to my mother. 'Today my lord's firman arrives, and my fate will be decided. If I am pardoned, we shall return to Janina in triumph, but if the news is bad, we shall flee to-night.'

" 'But what if they do not let us flee?'

" 'Set your mind at rest on that score,' replied Ali with a smile. 'Selim and his fiery lance will settle them. They want my death, but they will not want to die with me.'

"My mother's sighs were her only answer to this poor consolation. She prepared some iced water which he drank incessantly, for since his retreat to the kiosk he had been the victim of a burning fever; then she anointed his beard and lighted his chibouque. Sometimes he would sit for hours together pulling at his chibouque abstractedly, and watching the smoke ascend and dwindle into nothingness.

"All of a sudden, he started up abruptly. Without taking his eyes from the object which was attracting his attention, he asked for his telescope, and my mother, whiter than the stucco against which she was leaning, gave it to him. I saw my father's hands trembling.

" 'A ship . . . ! two . . . ! three . . . ! four!' he murmured.

"With that he rose, and as I sit here I can still see him priming his pistols.

" 'Vasiliki,' he said to my mother, visibly trembling, 'the time has now come when our fate will be decided, for in half an hour we shall learn the Sublime Sultan's answer. Go to the cave with Haydee.'

" 'I will not leave you,' said Vasiliki. If you die, my master, I will die with you.'

" 'Go and stay with Selim!' cried my father.

" 'Farewell, my lord!' murmured my mother, obedient to the end and bowed down by the near approach of death.

" 'Take Vasiliki away,' he said to one of the Palikars.

"But I, whom they had forgotten, ran up to him and held out my arms to him. He saw me, and, bending down, pressed his lips to my forehead.

"All this time twenty Palikars, hidden by the carved woodwork, were seated at my father's feet watching with bloodshot eyes the arrival of the boats. Their long guns, inlaid with mother-of-pearl and silver, were ready to hand and a large number of cartridges were strewn about the floor. My father looked at his watch and began pacing up and down with a look of anguish on his face. This was the scene which impressed itself on my mind when I left my father after he had given me that last kiss.

"My mother and I went down to the cave. Selim was still at his post and gave us a sad smile. We fetched some cushions from the other side of the cave and seated ourselves beside him. Devoted hearts seek one another in time of danger, and, child though I was, I instinctively sensed that some great danger was hanging over our heads."

These sad reminiscences appeared for a single instant to have deprived Haydee of the power of speech. Her head fell into her hands like a flower bowed down by the force of the storm, and her eyes gazed into vacancy as though she were conjuring up before her mind the verdant summit of Pindus and the blue waters of the Lake of Janina, which reflected like a magic mirror the grim picture she was sketching.

Monte Cristo looked at her with an indefinable expression of interest and pity.

"Continue, my child," he said to her in Romaic.

Haydee raised her head as though the sonorous words uttered by Monte Cristo had awakened her from a dream, and she resumed her narrative.

"It was four o'clock in the afternoon, but whereas the day was brilliant and bright outside, we in the cave were plunged in darkness. One single light shone in our cave like a solitary star twinkling in a dark and cloud-covered sky; it was Selim's match.

"From time to time Selim repeated the sacred words: 'Allah is great!' My mother was a Christian, and she prayed incessantly, but she still had a ray of hope. When she was leaving the terrace she had thought she recognized the Frenchman who had been sent to Constantinople and in whom my father placed implicit confidence, for he well knew that the soldiers of the French King are generally noble and generous. She advanced toward the staircase and listened. 'They are drawing near,' she said. 'If only they bring life and peace to us!'

" 'What do you fear, Vasiliki?' replied Selim in a voice so gentle and at the same time so proud. 'If they do not bring peace, we will give them death.' And he revived the flame of his lance.

"But I, who was only an unsophisticated child, was frightened by this courage, which appeared to me both ferocious and insensate, and I was filled with alarm by the atmosphere of death I seemed to feel all round me and to see in Selim's flame. My mother must have had the same impression for I felt her shudder.

" 'Oh, Mama, Mama!' I cried, 'are we going to die?'

" 'May God preserve you, my child, from ever desiring the death you fear to-day!' said my mother. Then in a low voice to Selim: 'What are my master's orders?'

" 'If he sends me his poniard, it signifies that the Sultan has refused his pardon, and I am to apply the match; if he sends me his ring, it means that the Sultan pardons him and I am to hand over the powder.'

" 'Friend,' said my mother, 'when the master's order arrives and if it be the poniard he sends, we will both bare our throats to you and do you kill us with the same poniard instead of dispatching us by that terrible death we both fear.'

" 'I will, Vasiliki,' was Selim's calm reply.

"All of a sudden we heard loud shouts. We listened. They were shouts of joy. The name of the French officer who had been sent to Constantinople burst from the throats of the Palikars on all sides. It was evident he had brought the Sultan's answer and that the answer was a favourable one."

"Do you not recollect the name?" said Morcerf, ready to aid the narrator's memory.

Monte Cristo made a sign to her.

"I do not remember it," responded Haydee. "The noise increased; there was the sound of approaching footsteps; they were descending the steps to the cave. Selim made ready his lance. Soon a figure appeared in the grey twilight created by the rays of day which penetrated to the entrance of the cave.

" 'Who goes there?' cried Selim. 'Whosoever it may be, advance no farther!'

" 'Glory be to the Sultan!' said the figure. 'He has granted full pardon to the Vizier Ali and not only grants him his life, but restores to him his fortune and all his possessions.'

"My mother uttered a cry of joy and pressed me to her heart.

" 'Stop!' cried Selim on perceiving that she was about to rush out of the cave. 'You know I must have the ring.'

" 'You are right,' replied my mother, and she fell on her knees holding me up toward Heaven as though, while praying to God for me, she wished to lift me up toward Him!"

For the second tune Haydee paused, overcome by an emotion which made the perspiration break out in drops upon her forehead and her words choke in her parched throat. Monte Cristo poured a little iced water into a glass and handed it to her, saying with a tenderness in which was mingled a suspicion of command: "Take courage, my child!"

Haydee wiped her eyes and forehead and continued:

"By this time our eyes had become accustomed to the darkness and we recognized the Pasha's envoy: he was a friend. Selim too recognized him, but the brave young man had one duty to fulfil—that was, to obey.

" 'In whose name do you come?' said he.

" 'I come in the name of our master, Ali Tebelin.'

" 'If you come in the name of Ali, do you know what you have to hand me?'

" 'Yes,' said the messenger. 'I bring the ring.'

"So saying he held his hand above his head, but from where we were it was too dark and he too far away for Selim to distinguish and recognize the object he held up.

" 'I see not what you have there,' said Selim.

" 'Come nearer, or if you so wish, I will come nearer to you,' replied the messenger.

" 'Neither the one nor the other,' replied the young soldier. 'On the spot where you now stand, so that the rays of this light may fall on it, set down the object you wish to show me and retire till I have seen it.'

" 'It shall be done,' answered the messenger. Placing the symbol on the spot indicated, he withdrew.

"Our hearts beat fast, for the object was actually a ring, but was it my father's ring? Still holding in his hand the lighted match, Selim went to the entrance, bent down, and picked up the token. 'The master's ring!' he exclaimed, kissing it. 'All is well!' Throwing the match on the ground, he trampled on it till it was extinguished.

"The messenger uttered a cry of joy and clapped his hands. At this signal, four of the Seraskier Kourschid's soldiers rushed in, and Selim fell pierced by the dagger of each of the men. Intoxicated by their crime, though still pale with fear, they then rushed into the cave and made for the bags of gold.

"By this time my mother had seized me in her arms and running nimbly along windings known only to ourselves, reached some secret stairs, where reigned a frightful tumult and confusion. The lower halls were filled with the armed ruffians of Kourschid, our enemies. My mother glued her eyes to a chink in the boards; there happened to be an aperture in front of me, and I looked through it.

" 'What do you want?' we heard my father saying to some men who held in their hands a piece of paper inscribed with letters of gold.

" 'We wish to communicate to you the will of His Highness. Do you see this firman?'[3]

" 'I do,' was my father's reply.

" 'Well, read it. It demands your head.'

"My father burst into laughter, more terrible to hear than the wildest threats, and he had not ceased when two pistol shots rang out and the two men were dead.

"The Palikars, who were lying face downward all round my father, rose and began firing. The room became filled with noise, flames, and smoke. At the same time firing started on the other side of the hall, and the boards all around us were soon riddled with shot.

"Oh, how handsome, how noble was the Vizier Ali Tebelin, my father, as he stood there in the midst of the shot, his scimitar in his hand, his face black with powder! How his enemies fled before him!

" 'Selim! Selim!' cried he. 'Guardian of the fire, do your duty!'

" 'Selim is dead,' replied a voice which seemed to come from the depths of the kiosk, 'and you, my lord Ali, are lost!'

At the same moment a dull report was heard, and the flooring was shattered to atoms all around my father.

"Twenty shots were fired from underneath through the gap thus created, and flames rushed up as from the crater of a volcano and, gaining the hangings, quickly devoured them.

"In the midst of this frightful tumult two reports more distinct than the others, and two cries more heartrending than all the rest, petrified me with terror. These two shots had mortally wounded my father, and it was he who had uttered the two cries. Nevertheless he would not fall but stood clinging to a window. My mother shook the door in her efforts to force it open to go and die beside him, but the door was locked from the inside. All round him the Palikars were writhing in agony; two or three who were only slightly or not at all wounded leaped through the windows. The floor gave way entirely. My father fell on one knee; instantly twenty hands were stretched out and twenty blows were dealt simultaneously at one man. My father disappeared in a blaze of fire stirred by these roaring demons as though hell had opened under his feet. I felt myself roll to the ground: my mother had fainted."

Haydee's arms fell to her side, and, uttering a groan, she looked at the Count as though to ask him whether he was satisfied with her obedience. Monte Cristo went up to her, and taking her hand said to her in Romaic: "Calm yourself, dear child, and console yourself in the thought that there is a God who punishes traitors."

"It is a frightful story, Count," said Albert, alarmed at Haydee's paleness, "and I reproach myself with having been so cruelly indiscreet."

"It is nothing," replied Monte Cristo. Then, placing his hand on the maiden's shoulder, he continued: "Haydee is a courageous girl and she sometimes finds solace in recounting her troubles."

"Because my sufferings remind me of your kindness, my lord," was the girl's eager response.

Albert looked at her with curiosity, for she had not yet told him what he was most anxious to know, namely, how she had become the Count's slave. She saw this desire expressed both in the Count's and in Albert's eyes and continued:

"When my mother recovered consciousness we were before the Seraskier. 'Kill me,' she said to him, 'but preserve the honour of Ali's widow.'

" 'It is not to me that you have to address yourself,' Kourschid said.

" 'Then to whom?'

" 'To your new master.'

" 'Who is my new master?'

" 'Here he is,' said Kourschid, pointing to one of those who had most contributed to my father's death."

"Then you became that man's property?" asked Albert.

"No," responded Haydee. "He did not dare keep us; he sold us to some slave merchants who were going to Constantinople. We crossed over Greece and arrived at the imperial gates in a dying condition surrounded by a curious crowd, who made way for us to pass. My mother followed the direction of their eyes and with a cry suddenly fell to the ground, pointing to a head on a spike of the gate. Above this head were written the words:

"THIS THE HEAD OF ALI TEBELIN, PASHA OF JANINA."

"Weeping, I tried to raise my mother. She was dead!

"I was taken to the bazaar; a rich American bought me, had me educated, and, when I was thirteen years of age, he sold me to the Sultan Mahommed."

"From whom I bought her, as I told you, Albert, for an emerald similar to the one in which I keep my hashish pills," said the Count.

"You are good, you are great, my lord," said Haydee, kissing Monte Cristo's hand. "I am very happy to belong to you."

Albert was quite bewildered by all he had heard.

"Finish your coffee," said the Count. "The story is ended."

Chapter LI

THE REPORT FROM JANINA

Franz left Noirtier's room so distraught that even Valentine felt pity for him. Villefort only muttered some incoherent words and took refuge in his study. Two hours later he received the following letter:

> "After all that has been disclosed this morning, Monsieur Noirtier de Villefort will appreciate the impossibility of an alliance between his family and that of Monsieur Franz d'Épinay. Monsieur Franz d'Épinay is sorry to think that Monsieur de Villefort, who appeared to be cognizant of the incidents related, should not have anticipated him in the expression of this view."

This outspoken letter from a young man who had always shown so much respect toward him was a deadly blow to the pride of a man like Villefort. He had not been in his study long when his wife entered. The fact that Franz had been called away by M. Noirtier at such a moment had caused so much amazement that Mme de Villefort's position, left alone with the lawyer and the witnesses, had become most embarrassing. At length she determined to stay no longer and she too took her leave, saying she was going to make inquiries as to the cause of the interruption.

M. de Villefort merely told her that as the result of an explanation between M. Noirtier, M. d'Épinay, and himself, Valentine's engagement was broken off. This was a very awkward answer to have to give to those awaiting her return, so she contented herself with saying that M. Noirtier had been taken with a slight fit of apoplexy at the beginning of their discussion, in consequence of which the signing of the contract would be postponed for a few days. This news, false though it was, came so singularly in the train of the two other similar misfortunes, that her auditors looked at each other in amazement and withdrew without saying a word.

In the meantime Valentine, happy though at the same time terrified at all she had heard, embraced the feeble old man in loving gratitude for having broken a tie she had considered indissoluble, and asked his permission to go to her room for a while to recover her composure. Instead of going to her room, however, Valentine went into the garden. Maximilian was waiting in his customary place ready for any emergency, and convinced that Valentine would run to him the first moment she was free to do so.

He was not mistaken. With his eyes glued to the cracks in the palings he saw her running toward him and throwing her usual precaution to the winds. The first word she uttered filled his heart with joy.

"Saved!" she cried.

"Saved?" repeated Morrel, unable to believe such happiness. "Who has saved us?"

"My grandfather. You should really love him, Morrel!"

Morrel swore to love him with his whole heart; the oath cost him nothing, for at that moment he felt it was not sufficient to love him as a father or a friend, he almost adored him as a god.

"How did he manage it?" he asked. "What means did he use?"

Valentine was about to recount everything when she

remembered that at the root of all was a secret which did not belong wholly to her grandfather.

"I will tell you all about it later," she said.

"When?"

"When I am your wife."

The turn the conversation was taking was so pleasing to Morrel that he was quite content to leave the matter at that and be satisfied with the one all-important piece of news for that day. He would not leave her, however, till she had given her promise that she would see him the next evening. This Valentine was ready to do. Her outlook had undergone a complete change and it was certainly less difficult for her now to believe that she would marry Maximilian than it was for her to believe an hour back that she would not marry Franz.

In the meantime Mme de Villefort went up to Noirtier's room, where she was received with the habitual cold and forbidding look.

"There is no need for me to tell you, monsieur," said she, "that Valentine's engagement is broken off since it is here that the rupture took place; but what you do not know is that I have always been opposed to this marriage and that it was being contracted against my will."

Noirtier looked at his daughter-in-law as though demanding an explanation.

"Now that this marriage, which I know did not meet with your approval, has been stopped, I have come to speak to you of something which neither Monsieur de Villefort nor Valentine could mention."

Noirtier's eyes bade her proceed.

"As the only one disinterested and therefore the only one who has the right to speak on the matter," she continued, "I come to ask you to restore not your love, for that she has always had, but your fortune to your grandchild."

For an instant Noirtier's eyes hesitated; evidently he was trying to find a motive for this request, but was unable to do so.

"May I hope, monsieur," said Mme de Villefort, "that your intentions coincide with my request?"

"Yes," signalled Noirtier.

"In that case, I leave you a grateful and happy woman, monsieur," she said, and, bowing to Noirtier, she withdrew.

True to his word, M. Noirtier sent for the notary the next day: the first will was torn up and a new one made in which he left the whole of his fortune to Valentine on condition that she should not separate herself from him.

It was then noised abroad that Mlle de Villefort, the heiress of the Marquis and Marquise de Saint-Méran, had been restored to her grandfather's good graces, and that one day she would have an income of over three hundred thousand francs.

While the events recorded above were taking place in the house of Monsieur de Villefort, the Count of Morcerf had received Monte Cristo's visit, ordered his carriage, and driven to the Rue de la Chaussée d'Antin. Danglars was making his monthly balance, and it was certainly not the best time to find him in a good humour; as a matter of fact, it had not been so for the past few months. On seeing his old friend, he assumed his most commanding air and seated himself squarely in his chair. Morcerf, on the other hand, laid aside his habitual stiffness of manner and was almost jovial and affable. Feeling sure that his overtures would be well received, he lost no time in coming to the point.

"Well, here I am, Baron. We have made no headway in our plans since our former conversation."

"What plans, Count?" Danglars asked as though vainly trying to discover some explanation of the General's words.

"Since you are such a stickler, my dear Baron, and since you desire to remind me that the ceremony is to be carried out in all due form, I will comply with your wishes." With a forced smile he rose, made a deep bow to Danglars, and said: "I have the honour, Baron, to ask the hand of Mademoiselle Eugénie Danglars, your daughter, for my son the Viscount Albert de Morcerf."

But instead of welcoming these words as Morcerf had every right to expect, Danglars knit his brows and, without even inviting the Count to take a seat, replied:

"Before giving you an answer, Count, I must think the matter over."

"Think the matter over?" exclaimed Morcerf, more and more astonished. "Have you not had time enough for reflection during the eight years that have elapsed since we first spoke of this marriage?"

"Every day things happen, Count, which call for reconsideration of questions which we believed to be exhaustively considered," was Danglars' reply.

"What do you mean?" asked Morcerf. "I do not understand you."

"What I mean is that during the last fortnight unforeseen circumstances . . ."

"Excuse me, but is this a play we are acting?"

"A play?"

"Yes. Pray let us be more explicit."

"I should be delighted."

"Have you seen the Count of Monte Cristo lately?"

"I see him very often. He is a friend of mine."

"When you saw him the other day did you not tell him that I appeared to you to be irresolute and forgetful in regard to this marriage? You see that I am neither the one nor the other since I have come to bid you keep your promise."

Danglars made no reply.

"Have you changed your mind so soon?" continued Morcerf. "Or have you but egged me on to make this proposal in order to see me humiliated?"

Danglars understood that if he continued the conversation in the same strain as that in which he had begun it, he might be taken at a disadvantage, so he said: "I quite comprehend that you are amazed at my reserve, Count. Believe me, I am the first one to regret that painful circumstances compel me to act thus."

"These are but so many empty words," replied the Count. "They might perhaps satisfy an ordinary man, but not the Count of Morcerf. When a man of his position comes to another man to remind him of his plighted word, and that man breaks his word, he is at least justified in demanding from him a good reason for his conduct."

Danglars was a coward but did not wish to appear one; besides he was annoyed at the tone Morcerf had adopted.

"I do not break my word without good reason," he retorted.

"What do you mean by that?"

"That my reason is good enough, but it is not an easy one to tell."

"You must understand, however, that I cannot be put off by such cryptic remarks. In any case, it is quite clear that you reject my proposal."

"Not altogether," replied Danglars, "I merely suspend my decision."

"But surely you do not presume to think that I am going to submit to your whims, and wait patiently and humbly until such time as I shall be restored to your favour again?"

"Then, Count, if you will not wait, we must consider our plan as null and void."

The Count bit his lips till they bled in his effort to suppress the outburst which was so natural to his proud and irritable temper. He realized, however, that in this case, a scene would only make him look ridiculous, and had reached the door when he changed his mind and turned back. A cloud had gathered on his brow, which showed that his pride had given way to uneasiness.

"Come now, my dear Danglars," said he, "we have known each other for many long years and should, therefore, have some consideration for one another. You owe me an explanation, and the least you can do is to inform me what unfortunate occurrence has deprived my son of your favour."

"I bear the Viscount personally no ill-will, that is all I can tell you, monsieur," replied Danglars, adopting his insolent attitude once more now that the Count had become calmer.

"Then against whom is your ill-will directed?" asked Morcerf, his uneasiness showing itself in his changed voice and pale face.

Danglars did not let any of these symptoms escape him, and, fixing a look of greater assurance on the Count than was his wont, said: "You may be thankful I do not give a more detailed explanation."

A nervous trembling caused by repressed anger shook Morcerf's whole frame, but pulling himself together with a violent effort, he said: "I have the right to insist on an explanation. Have you anything against Madame de Morcerf? Is my fortune too small for you? Is it because my opinions differ from yours?"

"Nothing of the kind, monsieur," said Danglars. "If it were so, I should be at fault, for I was fully informed on these matters at the time of the engagement. Seek no more for a reason, I pray. I am really quite ashamed to see you indulging in such self-examination. Let us leave the matter as it stands and agree to a postponement. Surely, monsieur, there is no hurry. My daughter is but seventeen and your son twenty-one. In the meanwhile, time follows its course carrying events with it; what is obscure one evening is often revealed the next, and the vilest calumnies ofttimes die in one day."

"Calumnies,[1] did you say?" exclaimed Morcerf, turning livid. "Can anyone be slandering me?"

"As I already said, monsieur, we will not go into details. I assure you this is more painful for me than for you, for I had reckoned on the honour of an alliance with you, and the breaking off of a marriage proposal always injures the lady more than the gentleman."

"Enough, monsieur, we will drop the subject," said Morcerf, as, crumpling his gloves up in his rage, he left the room.

Danglars noticed that not once had Morcerf dared to ask

whether it was on his own account that he, Danglars, had broken his word.

That same evening the banker had a long conference with several friends, and M. Cavalcanti, who had remained in the salon with the ladies, was the last to leave the house.

As soon as he awoke the next morning, Danglars asked for the newspapers. He flung three or four on one side till he came to the *Impartial*, of which Beauchamp was the chief editor. He nastily tore off the wrapper and opened it nervously. Disdainfully passing over the leading article, he came to the miscellaneous news column, and, with a malicious smile, stopped at a paragraph which read as follows:

A correspondent at Janina writes: A fact hitherto unknown, or at any rate unpublished, has just come to my knowledge. The castles defending this town were given up to the Turks by a French officer in whom the Vizier Ali Tebelin had placed entire confidence. This French officer who was in the service of Ali, Pasha of Janina, and who not only surrendered the Castle of Janina, but also sold his benefactor to the Turks, at that time was called Fernand, but he has since added to his Christian name a title of nobility and a family name. He is now styled the Count of Morcerf and ranks among the peers.

"Good!" Danglars observed after having read the paragraph; "here is a nice little article on Colonel Fernand which will, methinks, relieve me of the necessity of giving any explanation to the Count of Morcerf."

Chapter LII

THE LEMONADE

✦

Morrel was, indeed, very happy. M. Noirtier had sent for him, and he was in such haste to learn the reason that, trusting to his own two legs more than to the four legs of a cab-horse, he started off from the Rue Meslay at a rapid pace and ran all the way to the Faubourg Saint-Honoré, while Barrois followed as well he might. Morrel was thirty-one years of age and was urged on by love; Barrois was sixty and parched with the heat. On arriving at the house, Morrel was not even out of breath, for love lends wings; but Barrois had not been in love for many long years and was bathed in perspiration.

The old servant let Morrel in by a private door, and before long the rustling of a dress on the parquet floor announced the arrival of Valentine. She looked adorable in her mourning, in fact so charming that Morrel could almost have dispensed with his interview with Noirtier; but the old man's chair was soon heard being wheeled along to the room in which they were awaiting him.

Noirtier acknowledged with a kind look Morrel's effusive thanks for his marvellous intervention which had saved Valentine and himself from despair. Then, in view of the new favour accorded him, Maximilian sought Valentine's eyes; she was sitting in the far corner timidly waiting till she was forced to speak. Noirtier fixed his eyes on her.

"Am I to say what you told me?" she asked.

"Yes," was Noirtier's reply.

"Grandpapa Noirtier had a great many things to say to you, Monsieur Morrel," said Valentine to the young man, who was devouring her with his eyes. "These he told me three days ago, and he has sent for you to-day that I may repeat them all to you. Since he has chosen me as his interpreter, I will repeat everything in the light of his intentions."

"I am listening with the greatest impatience," replied the young man. "Pray speak, mademoiselle."

"My grandfather wishes to leave this house," she continued. "Barrois is now looking for a suitable flat for him."

"But what will become of you, mademoiselle, who are so dear and so necessary to Monsieur Noirtier?"

"Me?" replied Valentine. "It is quite agreed that I shall not leave my grandfather. I shall live with him. Then I shall be free and have an independent income, and with my grandfather's consent I shall keep the promise I made you."

Valentine said these last words in such a low voice that nothing but Morrel's great interest in them made them audible to him.

"When I am with my grandfather," continued Valentine, "Monsieur Morrel can come and see me in the presence of my good and worthy protector, and if we still feel that our future happiness lies in a union with each other, he can come and claim me. I shall be waiting for him."

"Oh!" cried Morrel. "What have I done to deserve such happiness?"

Noirtier looked at the lovers with ineffable tenderness. Barrois, before whom there were no secrets, had remained at the far end of the room and smiled happily as he wiped away the last drops of perspiration that were rolling down his bald forehead.

"How hot poor old Barrois is!" said Valentine.

"That is because I have been running fast, mademoiselle,

but I must give Monsieur Morrel the credit for running still faster."

Noirtier indicated by a look a tray on which were standing a decanter of lemonade and a tumbler. Noirtier himself had drunk some of the lemonade half an hour before.

"Have some of this lemonade, Barrois," the girl said. "I can see you are looking at it with envious eyes."

"The fact is, mademoiselle, I am dying of thirst, and I shall be only too glad to drink your health in a glass of lemonade."

Barrois took the tray and was hardly outside the door, which he had forgotten to close, when they saw him throw back his head to empty the tumbler Valentine had filled for him. Valentine and Morrel were bidding each other goodbye; they heard a bell ringing on Villefort's staircase. It was the signal that a visitor had called. Valentine looked at the clock.

"It is noon," said she, "and as it is Saturday, it is doubtless the doctor. He will come here, so Monsieur Morrel had better go, do you not think so, Grandpapa?"

"Yes," replied the old man.

"Barrois!" called Valentine, "Barrois, come!"

The voice of the old servant was heard to reply: "I am coming, mademoiselle."

"Barrois will conduct you to the door," Valentine said to Morrel. "And now, remember, Monsieur l'Officier, Grandpapa does not wish us to risk anything that might compromise our happiness."

"I have promised to wait, and wait I shall," said Morrel.

At that moment Barrois entered.

"Who rang?" asked Valentine.

"Doctor d'Avrigny," said Barrois, staggering.

"What is the matter, Barrois?" Valentine asked him.

The servant did not answer; he looked at his master with wildly staring eyes, while his cramped hand groped for some support to prevent himself from falling.

"He is going to fall!" cried Morrel.

In fact, the trembling fit which had come over Barrois gradually increased, and the twitching of his facial muscles announced a very grave nervous attack. Seeing his old servant in this state, Noirtier looked at him affectionately, and in those intelligent eyes was expressed every emotion that moves the human heart.

Barrois went a few steps toward his master.

"Oh, my God! My God! Lord have pity on me!" he cried. "What is the matter with me? I am ill. I cannot see. A thousand darts of fire are piercing my brain. Oh, don't touch me! Don't touch me!"

His haggard eyes started out of their sockets, his head fell back, and the rest of his body stiffened. Valentine uttered a cry of horror, and Morrel took her in his arms as though to defend her against some unknown danger.

"Monsieur d'Avrigny! Monsieur d'Avrigny!" the girl called out in a choking voice. "Help! help!"

Barrois turned round, walked a few steps, stumbled, and fell at his master's feet with his hand on his knee, and cried out: "My master! my good master!"

Attracted by the screams, Villefort rushed into the room. Morrel instantly relaxed his hold of Valentine, who was now in a half-fainting condition, and going to a far corner of the room, hid behind a curtain. As pale as if he had seen a snake start up to attack him, he gazed in horror on the agonized sufferer. Noirtier was burning with impatience and terror, his soul went out to help the poor old man who was his friend rather than his servant. The terrible struggle between life and death that was going on within him made his veins stand out and the few remaining live muscles round his eyes contract.

With convulsed features, bloodshot eyes, and head thrown back, Barrois lay beating the floor with his hands, whilst his legs had become so stiff that they looked more ready to break than to bend. He was foaming at the mouth and his breathing was laboured. Stupefied, Villefort stood still for an instant, gazing on the spectacle which had met his eyes directly he entered the room. He had not seen Morrel. After a second's dumb contemplation of the scene, during which his face had turned deathly pale and his hair appeared to stand on end, he rushed to the door crying out: "Doctor! Doctor! Come! come!"

"Madame de Villefort, come! Oh, come quickly, and bring your smelling-salts!" Valentine called, running up the stairs.

"What is the matter?" Mme de Villefort asked in a metallic and constrained voice.

"Oh, come quickly."

"But where is the doctor?" cried Villefort. "Where can he have gone?"

The stairs were heard to creak as Mme de Villefort slowly came down them, holding in one hand a handkerchief, with which she was wiping her face, and in the other a bottle of smelling-salts. When she entered the room, her first glance was for Noirtier, who, save for the emotion he naturally felt in the circumstances, appeared to be in his usual state of health; then her eyes fell on the dying man. She turned pale as she saw him, and her eyes, as it were, leaped from the servant to his master.

"For pity's sake, where is the doctor, madame?" exclaimed Valentine. "He went into your room. Barrois has an attack of apoplexy, as you see, and he may be saved if he is bled."

"Has he eaten anything lately?" asked Mme de Villefort, evading the question.

"He has not yet had his breakfast," replied Valentine, "but he was running very fast this morning on an errand for my grandfather, and when he came back he drank a glass of lemonade."

"Why did he not have some wine? Lemonade is very bad."

"The lemonade was near at hand in Grandpapa's decanter. Poor Barrois was thirsty, and he drank what he could get."

Mme de Villefort started; M. Noirtier watched her with the closest scrutiny.

"He has such a short neck!" said she.

"I ask you once more, madame, where is the doctor?" said Villefort. "For Heaven's sake, answer!"

"He is with Edward, who is poorly," replied Mme de Villefort, seeing she could no longer evade the question.

Villefort rushed up the stairs to fetch him.

"Here," said the young woman, giving the smelling-salts to Valentine. "The doctor will doubtless bleed him, so I will return to my room. I cannot bear the sight of blood."

With which she followed her husband.

Morrel emerged from his dark corner, where he had remained unseen throughout the general consternation.

"Go quickly, Maximilian, and wait till I call you," said Valentine to him.

Morrel cast a questioning glance at Noirtier, and the old man, who had not lost his composure, made a sign of approval. The young man pressed Valentine's hand to his heart, and left by the deserted landing just as Villefort and the doctor came in together by the opposite door.

Barrois was returning to consciousness; the attack had passed. He began to groan and raised himself on one knee. D'Avrigny and Villefort carried him on to a sofa.

"What do you prescribe, Doctor?" asked Villefort.

"Get me some water and ether, and send for some oil of turpentine and tartaric acid. And now let every one retire."

"Must I go too?" Valentine asked timidly.

"Yes, mademoiselle, you particularly," said the doctor abruptly.

Valentine looked at d'Avrigny in astonishment, but, after kissing her grandfather, left the room. The doctor shut the door behind her with a look of grim determination.

"See, Doctor, he is coming round. It was only a slight attack after all."

M. d'Avrigny smiled grimly.

"How do you feel?" he asked Barrois.

"A little better, Doctor."

"Can you drink this glass of ether and water?"

"I will try, but do not touch me."

"Why not?"

"I feel that if you touch me, if only with the tip of your fingers, the attack will return."

Barrois took the glass, put it to his lips, and drank about half of its contents.

"Where have you pain?" the doctor asked.

"Everywhere. It is as though I had frightful cramp everywhere."

"What have you eaten to-day?"

"Nothing at all. All I have taken is a glass of my master's lemonade," Barrois replied, making a sign with his head toward Noirtier, who was sitting motionless in his chair, contemplating this dreadful scene without letting a movement or a word escape him.

"Where is the lemonade?" asked the doctor eagerly.

"In the decanter in the kitchen."

"Shall I fetch it, Doctor?" Villefort asked.

"No, stay here and try to make the patient drink the rest of this ether and water."

"But the lemonade . . ."

"I will fetch it myself."

D'Avrigny bounded toward the door, and, rushing down the servants' staircase, nearly knocked over Mme de Villefort, who was also going into the kitchen. She screamed, but the doctor did not even take any notice of her. Obsessed with the one idea, he jumped down the last three or four stairs and flew into the kitchen. Seeing the decanter three parts empty, he pounced upon it like an eagle upon its prey, and with it returned to the sickroom out of breath. Mme de Villefort was slowly going up the stairs leading to her room.

"Is this the decanter?" Monsieur d'Avrigny asked Barrois.

"Yes, Doctor."

"Is this some of the same lemonade you drank?"

"I believe so."

"What did it taste like?"

"It had a bitter taste."

The doctor poured several drops of the lemonade into the palm of his hand, sucked it up with his lips, and, after rinsing his mouth with it as one does when tasting wine, he spat it out into the fireplace.

"It is the same right enough," he said. "Did you drink some too, Noirtier?"

"Yes," looked the old man.

"Did you notice the bitter taste?"

"Yes."

"Oh, Doctor, the fit is coming on again! Oh, God, have pity on me!"

The doctor ran to his patient.

"The tartar emetic, Villefort, see if it has come!"

Villefort rushed out shouting: "The emetic! Has it not been brought yet?"

"If I had some means of injecting air into his lungs," said d'Avrigny, looking around him, "I might possibly be able to prevent asphyxiation. But there is nothing, nothing!"

"Are you going to let me die without help, Doctor? Oh, I am dying! Have pity on me, I am dying!"

Barrois was seized with a nervous attack which was more acute than the first one. He had slipped from the sofa on to the floor and lay stretched stiff and rolling in pain. The doctor left him, for he could do nothing to help him. Going over to Noirtier, he asked him in a low voice:

"How do you feel? Well?"

"Yes."

"Does your stomach feel light or heavy? Light?"

"Yes."

"The same as when you have taken the pills I ordered you to take every Sunday?"

"Yes."

"Did Barrois make the lemonade?"

"Yes."

"Did you invite him to drink it?"

"No."

"Monsieur de Villefort?"

"No."

"Madame de Villefort?"

"No."

"It was Valentine, then?"

"Yes."

A sigh from Barrois, and a yawn which made his jaw-bones crack, attracted the attention of d'Avrigny, who hastened to his side.

"Can you speak, Barrois?"

Barrois uttered a few inaudible words.

"Make an effort, my friend."

Barrois opened his bloodshot eyes.

"Who made the lemonade?"

"I did."

"Did you take it to your master as soon as it was made?"

"No."

"Did you leave it somewhere, then?"

"In the pantry, because I was called away."

"Who brought it into this room?"

"Mademoiselle Valentine."

"Oh, again!" exclaimed d'Avrigny, striking his forehead.

"Doctor! Doctor!" cried Barrois, who felt a third attack approaching.

"Are they never going to bring the emetic?" cried the doctor.

"Here is a glass with one already prepared by the chemist himself, who has come back with me," said Villefort.

"Drink!" said the doctor to Barrois.

"Impossible, Doctor. It is too late. My throat is closing up. I am suffocating. Oh, my heart! My head! Oh, what agony! Am I going to suffer like this for long?"

"No, no, my friend," said the doctor. "You will soon be suffering no more."

"Oh, I understand," said the poor wretch. "My God, have pity on me." With a cry he fell back as though struck by lightning. D'Avrigny placed his hand to his heart and put a mirror to his mouth.

"Well?" said Villefort.

"Go to the kitchen quickly and ask for some syrup of violets." Villefort went immediately.

"Do not be alarmed, Monsieur Noirtier," said the doctor. "I am taking my patient into another room to bleed him; such an attack is truly ghastly to behold."

Taking Barrois under the arms, he dragged him into an adjoining room, but returned at once for the remainder of the lemonade.

Noirtier closed his right eye.

"You want Valentine? I will have her sent to you."

Villefort came back with the syrup of violets and met d'Avrigny on the landing.

"Come with me," said the doctor, taking him into the room where the dead man lay.

"Is he still unconscious?" asked Villefort.

"He is dead."

Villefort started back, clasped his hands to his head, and looking at the dead man, exclaimed in tones of infinite pity, "Dead so soon!"

"Yes, it was very quick, was it not?" said d'Avrigny, "but that should not astonish you. Monsieur and Madame de Saint-Méran died just as suddenly. Death makes a very sudden appearance in your house, Monsieur de Villefort."

"What!" cried the magistrate in a tone of horror and consternation, "are you still harping on that terrible idea?"

"I am, monsieur, and the thought has not left me for one instant," said d'Avrigny solemnly. "Furthermore, that you may be convinced that I have made no mistake this time, listen to what I have to say."

Villefort trembled convulsively.

"There is a poison which destroys life without leaving any traces after it. I know the poison well. I have made a deep study of it. I recognize the presence of this poison in poor Barrois just as I did in Madame de Saint-Méran. There is one means of detecting its presence. It restores the blue colour of litmus paper which has been dyed red by an acid, and it turns syrup of violets green. We have no litmus paper, but we have syrup of violets. If the lemonade is pure and inoffensive, the syrup will retain its colour; on the other hand, if it contains poison, the syrup will turn green. Watch closely!"

The doctor slowly poured a few drops of lemonade into the cup, and a cloudy sediment was immediately formed at the bottom. First of all this sediment took on a blue hue, then it changed from sapphire to the colour of opal, and again to emerald—to change no more. The experiment left no room for doubt.

"The unfortunate Barrois has been poisoned," said d'Avrigny, "and I am ready to answer for this statement before God and man."

Villefort made no reply; he raised his arms heavenward, opened wide his haggard eyes, and sank back into a chair horror-stricken.

Chapter LIII

THE ACCUSATION

M. d'Avrigny soon brought the magistrate round, though he still looked like another corpse in this chamber of death.

"Death is in my house!" he exclaimed.

"Say rather crime," replied the doctor, "for the time has now come when we must act. We must put an end to these incessant deaths. So far as I am concerned, I feel I can no longer conscientiously hold such secrets unless I have the hope of soon seeing the victims, and through them society, avenged."

Villefort cast a melancholy look around him. "Do you, then, suspect anyone?"

"I do not suspect anyone. Death knocks at your door—it enters and goes not blindly, but with circumspection, from room to room. Ah, well! I follow its track, I know its passage and adopt the wisdom of the ancients; I grope about in the dark, for my respect for you and my friendship for your family are like two bandages before my eyes."

"Speak, Doctor, speak. I have courage."

"Well, then, you have in your house, perhaps in the midst of your family, one of those terrible phenomena every century produces."

463

Villefort wrung his hands and cast a pleading look on the doctor, but the latter continued pitilessly:

"An axiom of jurisprudence says: 'Seek whom the crime would profit!'"

"Alas! Doctor, how many times has not justice been deceived by those fatal words!" exclaimed Villefort. "I know not why, but I think this crime . . ."

"Ah, you admit at last that it is a crime?"

"Yes, I acknowledge it. What else can I do? But let me continue. It seems to me this crime is directed against me alone and not against the victims. I sense some calamity for myself at the root of all these strange disasters."

"Oh, Man," muttered d'Avrigny. "The most selfish of all creatures, who believes that the earth turns, the sun shines, and the scythe of death reaps for him alone. And have those who have lost their lives lost nothing? Monsieur de Saint-Méran, Madame de Saint-Méran, Monsieur Noirtier . . ."

"Monsieur Noirtier?"

"Certainly. Do you think it was the unfortunate servant's life they wanted? No, no, like Shakespeare's Polonius, he died for another. Noirtier was intended to drink the lemonade; the other one only drank it by accident."

"How was it my father did not succumb?"

"As I told you one evening in the garden after the death of Madame de Saint-Méran, his system has become accustomed to this very poison; no one, not even the murderer himself, knows that for the past year I have been treating Monsieur Noirtier with brucine for his paralysis, whereas the murderer knows, and has proved by experience, that brucine is a virulent poison."

"Stop! For Heaven's sake, have pity on me!" cried Villefort, wringing his hands.

"Let us follow the criminal's course. He kills Monsieur de Saint-Méran, then Madame de Saint-Méran; a double inheritance to look forward to."

Villefort wiped away the perspiration that was streaming down his forehead.

"Listen! Monsieur Noirtier willed his fortune away from you and your family," continued M. d'Avrigny pitilessly, "so he is spared. But he has no sooner destroyed his first will and made a second one than he becomes the victim, no doubt lest he should make a third will. This will was made the day before yesterday, I believe. You see there was no time lost."

"Have mercy, Doctor!"

"No mercy, monsieur! A doctor has a sacred mission on earth, and to fulfil it he has to start at the source of life and descend to the mysterious darkness of the tomb. When a crime has been committed, and God, doubtless horrified, turns away His head, it is for the doctor to say: 'Here is the culprit!' "

"Have mercy on my daughter!" murmured Villefort.

"You see it is you yourself who have named her, you, her father!"

"Have mercy on Valentine. I say, it is impossible! I would sooner accuse myself. Valentine, who is pure as a lily and whose heart is of gold!"

"No mercy! It is a flagrant crime. Mademoiselle de Villefort herself packed the medicines that were sent to Monsieur de Saint-Méran, and he is dead. She prepared the cooling draughts for Madame de Saint-Méran, and she is dead. Mademoiselle de Villefort took from Barrois, who was sent out, the decanter with the lemonade her grandfather generally drinks in the morning, and he escapes but by a miracle. Mademoiselle de Villefort is the guilty one! She is the poisoner, and I denounce her as such. Now, do your duty, Monsieur le Procureur du Roi!"

"Doctor, I can hold out no longer. I no longer defend myself. I believe you. But for pity's sake, spare my life, my honour!"

"Monsieur de Villefort, there are times when I overstep the limits of foolish human circumspection," said the doctor with increasing vehemence, "if your daughter had only committed one crime and I saw her meditating a second one, I should say to you: 'Warn her, punish her. Send her to some convent to pass the rest of her days in weeping and praying.' If she had committed two, I should say: 'Monsieur de Villefort, this is a poison for which there is no known antidote; its action is as quick as thought, as rapid as lightning, and as deadly as a thunderbolt. Recommend her soul to God and give her this poison; thus only will you save your honour and your life, for you are her target. I see her coming toward your pillow with her hypocritical smiles and her sweet exhortations! Woe to you if you do not strike first!' This is what I should have said had she killed two persons, but she has witnessed three death agonies, she has watched three people die, she has knelt by three corpses! To the scaffold with the prisoner! To the scaffold!"

Villefort fell on his knees.

"Listen to me!" he cried. "Pity me, help me! No, my daughter is not guilty. You may drag us before a tribunal, but I shall still say: 'My daughter is not guilty. There is no crime in this house,' . . . Do you understand, I will have no crime in this house, for, like death, crime comes not alone. What does it signify to you if I am murdered? Are you my friend? Are you a man? No, you are a physician . . . Well, then, I say to you: 'I will not drag my daughter into the hands of the executioner.' Ah, the very thought of it would drive me mad! I should tear my heart out with my fingernails. And if you were mistaken, Doctor? If it were another than my daughter? If I came to you one day like a ghost and said to you: 'Murderer! you have killed my daughter!' If that were to happen, Monsieur d'Avrigny, Christian though I am, I should take my life!"

"Very well," said the doctor after a moment's silence. "I will wait."

Villefort looked at him as though he still doubted his words.

"But remember this," continued M. d'Avrigny solemnly and slowly. "If someone falls ill in your house, if you yourself are stricken, do not send for me—I shall not come. I will share this terrible secret with you, but I will not let shame and remorse eat into my conscience like a worm, just as misfortune and crime will undermine the foundations of your house."

"Do you forsake me then, Doctor?"

"Yes, for I can follow you no further, and I will only stop at the foot of the scaffold. Another revelation will be made which will bring this terrible tragedy to a close. Good-bye!"

That evening all Villefort's servants, who had assembled in the kitchen to discuss the matter, came in a body to M. de Villefort to give notice. No entreaties, no promises of higher wages could persuade them to stay. To everything they said: "We wish to go, because death is in your house." And in spite of all persuasions, they left, expressing their regret at leaving such a good master and mistress, above all Mademoiselle Valentine, who was so good, so kind-hearted, so gentle.

On hearing what the servants said, Villefort looked at Valentine. She was weeping, and the sight of her tears filled him with a deep emotion. He looked at Mme de Villefort too, and, strange to say, he seemed to see a fleeting but grim smile pass over her lips like a meteor passing ominously between two clouds in a stormy sky.

Chapter LIV

THE TRIAL

The paragraph which appeared in the papers regarding the part Morcerf had played in the surrender of Janina caused great excitement in the Chamber of Peers among the usually calm groups of that high assembly. That day almost every member had arrived before the usual hour to discuss with his compeers the sinister event that was to fix public attention on one of the best-known names in that illustrious body.

Some were reading the article in a subdued voice, others making comments or exchanging reminiscences which substantiated the charges still more. The Count of Morcerf was not popular with his colleagues. In order to maintain his position, he had, like all upstarts, adopted a very haughty manner. The aristocrat smiled at him, the man of talent disclaimed him, and the justly proud instinctively despised him.

The Count of Morcerf alone was ignorant of the news. He did not receive the newspaper containing the defamatory information and had spent the morning writing letters and trying a new horse. He arrived at the Chamber at his usual hour, and with proud step and haughty mien alighted from his carriage and passed along the corridors into the hall without remarking the hesitation of the doorkeepers, or the coldness of his colleagues. The sitting had been in progress about half an hour when he entered.

Everyone had the accusing paper before him, and it was evident that all were aching to start the debate, but, as is generally the case, no one wished to take upon himself the responsibility of opening the attack. At length, one of the peers, an open enemy of Morcerf's, ascended the tribune with such solemnity that all felt that desired moment had arrived.

There was an awe-inspiring silence. Morcerf alone was ignorant of the cause of the deep attention given to an orator they were accustomed to hear with indifference. The Count paid little heed to the preamble in which the speaker announced that he was about to touch upon a subject so grave, so sacred, and at the same time of such vital importance to the Senate that he demanded the undivided attention of all his colleagues. When Janina and Colonel Fernand were mentioned, the Count of Morcerf turned so horribly pale that a shudder went through the whole assembly and all eyes were turned toward him.

The article was read during this painful silence, and then the speaker declared his reluctance to open the subject, and the difficulty of his task, but it was the honour of M. de Morcerf and of the whole Chamber he proposed to defend by introducing a debate on these personal and ever-pressing questions. He concluded by demanding a speedy inquiry into the matter before the calumny had time to spread, so that M. de Morcerf might be reinstated in the position in public opinion he had so long held.

Morcerf was so completely overwhelmed by this enormous and unexpected attack that it was almost more than he could do to stammer a few words in reply, staring the while at his colleagues with wide-open eyes. This nervousness, which might have been due to the astonishment of innocence as much as to shame of guilt, evoked some sympathy in his favour. An inquiry was voted for, and the Count was asked what time he required to prepare his defence. On realizing that this terrible blow had still left him alive, Morcerf's courage returned to him.

"My brother peers," he replied, "it is not with time that one repulses an attack of this kind that has been made on me by some unknown enemies. I must answer this flash of lightning, which for a moment overpowered me, by a thunderbolt. Instead of defending myself in this way, would that I could shed my blood to prove to my colleagues that I am worthy to be their equal!"

These words made a favourable impression.

"I therefore request that the inquiry be instituted as soon as possible," he continued, "and I undertake to furnish the Chamber with all the necessary evidence."

"Is the Chamber of opinion that the inquiry should take place this very day?" asked the President.

"Yes!" was the unanimous reply.

A Committee of twelve members was appointed to examine the evidence supplied by Morcerf, and the first session was fixed for eight o'clock that evening in the committee room. This decision arrived at, Morcerf asked permission to retire; he had to collect the evidence he had long since prepared against such a storm, which his cunning and indomitable character had foreseen.

The evening arrived; all Paris was agog with expectation. Many believed that Morcerf had only to show himself to overthrow the charge; on the other hand some asserted he would not make an appearance. There were a few who said they had seen him leave for Brussels, and one or two even went to the police station to inquire whether it was true that he had taken out a passport.

Every one arrived punctually at eight o'clock. M. de Morcerf entered the hall at the last stroke of the clock. In his hand he carried some papers. He was carefully but simply dressed, and, according to the ancient military custom, wore his coat buttoned up to the chin. Outwardly he was calm, and, contrary to habit, walked with an unaffected gait.

His presence produced a most favourable effect, and the

Committee was far from being ill-disposed toward him. Several of the members went forward to shake hands with him. One of the doorkeepers handed a letter to the President.

"You are now at liberty to speak," said the President, unsealing his letter.

The Count commenced his defence in a most eloquent and skilful manner. He produced evidence to show that the Vizier of Janina had honoured him with entire confidence up to his last hour, the best proof being that he had entrusted him with a mission to the Sultan himself, the result of which meant life or death to him. He showed the ring with which Ali Pasha generally sealed his letters, and which he had given him as a token of authority so that upon his return he might gain access to him at any hour of the day or night. He said his mission had unfortunately failed, and, when he returned to defend his benefactor, he found him dead. So great was Ali Pasha's confidence in him, however, that before he died he had entrusted his favourite wife and his daughter to his care.

In the meantime, the President carelessly glanced at the letter that had been given him, but the very first lines aroused his attention; he read the missive again and again, then, fixing his eyes on Morcerf, said:

"You say, Count, that the Vizier of Janina confided his wife and daughter to your care."

"Yes, Monsieur le President," replied Morcerf. "But in that, as in all else, misfortune dogged my steps. Upon my return, Vasiliki and her daughter, Haydee, had disappeared."

"Do you know them?"

"Thanks to my intimacy with the Pasha and his great confidence in me, I saw them more than twenty times."

"Have you any idea what has become of them?"

"I have been told that they succumbed to their grief, and maybe to their privation. I was not rich, my life was in constant danger, and, much to my regret, I could not go in search of them."

The President frowned almost imperceptibly as he said:

"Messieurs, you have heard Monsieur de Morcerf's defence. Now, Count, can you produce any witnesses to support the truth of what you say?"

"Alas, I cannot," replied the Count. "All those who were at the Pasha's Court and who knew me there are either scattered or dead. I believe I am the only one of my compatriots who survived that terrible war. I have only Ali Tebelin's letters, which I have laid before you, and the ring, the token of his goodwill. The most convincing evidence I can put forward is the complete absence of testimony against my honour, and the clean record of my military career."

A murmur of approbation went through the assembly, and at this moment, M. Morcerf's cause was gained; it only needed to be put to the vote when the President rose and said: "Messieurs, you and the Count will, I presume, not be averse to hearing a witness who claims to hold important evidence and has come forward of his own accord. He is doubtless come to prove the perfect innocence of our colleague. Here is the letter I have just received on the matter." The President read as follows:

"Monsieur le Président,
    "I can furnish the Committee of Inquiry appointed to examine the conduct in Epirus and Macedonia of a certain Lieutenant-General the Count of Morcerf with important facts."

The President made a short pause. The Count of Morcerf turned deathly pale, and the tightly clenched papers that he held in his hand audibly crackled.

The President resumed:

"I was present at Ali Pasha's death and know what became of Vasiliki and Haydee. I hold myself at the disposal of the Committee, and even claim the honour of being heard. I shall be waiting in the corridor when this note is handed to you."

"Who is this witness, or rather enemy?" said the Count, in a very changed voice.

"We shall learn in a moment, monsieur. Is the Committee agreed to hear this witness?"

"Yes, yes," was the unanimous reply.

The President called the doorkeeper, and inquired of him whether anyone was waiting in the corridors.

"A woman, accompanied by her attendant," said the doorkeeper.

The members looked at each other in amazement.

"Let this woman enter," said the President.

All eyes were turned toward the door, and five minutes later the doorkeeper reappeared. Behind him came a woman enveloped in a large veil which completely covered her, but the form outlined, and the perfume which exhaled from her, denoted that she was a young and elegant woman. The President requested her to lay aside her veil, and it was seen that she was dressed in Grecian attire and was a remarkably beautiful woman.

M. de Morcerf looked at her in amazement mingled with terror, for this woman held his life in her hands. To the rest of the assembly, however, it was a turn of events so strange and interesting that Morcerf's welfare became but a secondary consideration.

The President offered the young woman a seat, but she made a sign that she would rather stand. The Count, on the other hand, had sunk into his chair, for his legs refused to support him.

"Madame," began the President. "You state in your letter to the Committee that you have important information on the Janina affair, and that you were an eyewitness of the events. Permit me to remark that you must have been very young then."

"I was four years old, but as the events so peculiarly concerned me, not a detail has escaped my memory."

"How did these events so concern you? Who are you that this tragedy should have made so deep an impression on you?"

"My name is Haydee," replied the young woman. "I am the daughter of Ali Tebelin, Pasha of Janina, and of Vasiliki, his much-beloved wife."

The modest and at the same time proud blush that suffused the young woman's cheeks, the fire in her eye, and the majestic way in which she revealed her identity, made an indescribable impression on the assembly. The Count, on the other hand, could not have been more abashed if a thunderbolt had fallen and opened a chasm at his feet.

"Madame," resumed the President, making a respectful bow, "permit me a simple question. Can you prove the authenticity of what you say?"

"I can, monsieur," said Haydee, taking a perfumed satin bag from under her veil. "Here is my birth certificate, drawn up by my father and signed by his principal officers, also my certificate of baptism, my father having allowed me to be brought up in my mother's religion. This latter bears the seal of the Grand Primate of Macedonia and Epirus. Lastly, and this is perhaps the most important, I have the document pertaining to the sale of my person and that of my mother to an Armenian merchant, named El Kobbir, effected by the French officer who, in his infamous treaty with the Porte, had reserved for his share of the booty the wife and daughter of his benefactor. These he sold for the sum of four hundred thousand francs."

A ghastly pallor spread over the Count's cheeks and his eyes became bloodshot when he heard these terrible imputations, which were received by the assembly in grim silence.

Haydee, still calm, but more dangerous in her very calmness than another would have been in anger, handed to the President the record of her sale, drawn up in the Arab tongue.

As it was thought likely that a testimony might be forthcoming in the Arabic, Romaic, or Turkish language, the interpreter of the Chamber had been advised that his presence might be needed, and he was now summoned.

One of the peers, to whom the Arabic tongue was familiar, followed closely the original text as the translator read:

"I, El Kobbir, slave merchant and purveyor to the harem of His Highness, acknowledge having received for transmission to the Sublime Sultan from the Count of Monte Cristo an emerald valued at eight hundred thousand francs as purchase money for a young Christian slave, aged eleven years, of the name of Haydee, a recognized daughter of the late Ali Tebelin, Pasha of Janina, and of Vasiliki, his favourite, she having been sold to me seven years ago together with her mother, who died on her arrival at Constantinople, by a French Colonel in the service of the Vizier Ali Tebelin of the name of Fernand Mondego.

"The aforesaid purchase was made on behalf of His Highness, whose mandate I had, for the sum of four hundred thousand francs.

"Given at Constantinople with the authorization of His Highness in the year twelve-forty-seven of the Hegira.

"Signed: EL KOBBIR"

"In order to give this document due credence and authority, it will be vested with the imperial seal, which the vendor consents to have affixed."

Beside the merchant's signature was the seal of the Sublime Sultan.

A dreadful silence followed. The Count was speechless; his eyes instinctively sought Haydee, and he fixed her with a frenzied stare.

"Is it permitted, madame, to interrogate the Count of Monte Cristo, who, I believe, is staying in Paris just now?" asked the President.

"The Count of Monte Cristo, my second father, has been in Normandy for the past three days, monsieur."

"Then who advised you to take this step, for which this Committee is indebted to you, and which was the natural proceeding in view of your birth and misfortunes?"

"This step was urged upon me by my grief and respect. May God forgive me! Though I am a Christian, my one thought has always been to avenge my illustrious father's death. Therefore as soon as I set foot in France and learned that the traitor lived in Paris, I have ever watched for this opportunity. I live a retired life in my noble protector's house; I wish it so because I like retirement and silence, so that I may live in the thoughts and memories of the past. The Count of Monte Cristo surrounds me with every paternal care, and in the silence of my apartments I receive each day all newspapers and periodicals. From them I glean all information concerning what is going on in the world; from them I learned what transpired in the Chamber this morning and what was to take place this evening."

"Then the Count of Monte Cristo knows nothing of this action on your part?" asked the President.

"He is in absolute ignorance of it, monsieur, and my only fear is that he may disapprove of what I have done. Nevertheless, this is a glorious day for me," continued the young woman, raising her eager eyes heavenward, "the day when I at last have the opportunity of avenging my father."

During all this time the Count had not uttered a single word; his colleagues looked it him, no doubt commiserating with him on this calamity which had been wrought on him by a woman. The ever-increasing lines and wrinkles on his face betrayed his misery.

"Monsieur de Morcerf, do you recognize this lady as the daughter of Ali Tebelin, Pasha of Janina?"

"No," said Morcerf, making an effort to rise. "This is nothing but a plot woven against me by my enemies."

Haydee was looking at the door as though she expected someone, and at these words she turned round sharply, and, seeing the Count standing there, uttered a fearful cry.

"You do not recognize me!" she cried. "Fortunately I recognize you! You are Fernand Mondego, the French officer who instructed my father's troops. It was you who surrendered the castle of Janina! It was you who, having been sent to Constantinople by my father to treat directly with the Sultan for the life or death of your benefactor, brought back a falsified firman granting full pardon! It was you who obtained with this same firman the Pasha's ring which would secure for you the obedience of Selim, the guardian of the fire! It was you who stabbed Selim! It was you who sold my mother and myself to El Kobbir! Murderer! Murderer! Your master's blood is still on your brow! Look at him, all of you!"

These words were spoken with such vehemence and with such force of truth that everyone looked at the Count's forehead, and he himself put his hand up as though he felt Ali's blood still warm upon his forehead.

"You positively recognize Monsieur de Morcerf as this same officer, Fernand Mondego?"

"Do I recognize him?" cried Haydee. "Oh, Mother! You said to me: 'You are free. You had a father whom you loved; you were destined to be almost a queen. Look well at this man who has made you a slave; it is he who has placed your father's head on the pike, it is he who has sold us, it is he who has betrayed us! Look at his right hand with its large scar. If you forget his face, you will recognize this hand into which El Kobbir's gold fell, piece by piece!' Oh, yes, I know him! Let him tell you himself whether he does not recognize me now!"

Each word cut Morcerf like a knife, and broke down his determination. At the last words he instinctively hid his hand in his bosom, for as a matter of fact it bore the mark of a wound, and once more he sank back into his chair.

This scene had set the opinions of the assembly in a veritable turmoil, like leaves torn from their branches by the violence of a north wind.

"Do not lose courage, Count," said the President. "The justice of this court, like that of God, is supreme and equal to all; it will not permit you to be crushed by your enemies without giving you the means of defending yourself. Do you wish to have further investigations made? Do you wish me to send two members of the Chamber to Janina? Speak!"

Morcerf made no reply.

All the members of the Committee looked at one another in horror. They knew the Count's energetic and violent temper, and realized it must have needed a terrible blow to break down this man's defence; they could but think that this sleeplike silence would be followed by an awakening resembling thunder in its force.

"What have you decided?" the President asked.

"Nothing," said the Count, in a toneless voice.

"Then Ali Tebelin's daughter has spoken the truth? She is indeed the dreaded witness in face of whose evidence the guilty one dares not answer: 'Not guilty'? You have actually committed the crimes of which she accuses you?"

The Count cast around him a look of despair such as would have elicited mercy from a tiger, but it could not disarm his judges; then he raised his eyes toward the roof but instantly turned them away again, as though fearful lest it should open and he should find himself before that other tribunal they call Heaven, and face to face with that other judge whom they call God. He tore at the buttons that fastened the coat which was choking him and walked out of the room like one demented. For an instant his weary steps echoed dolefully, but the sound was soon followed by the rattling of his carriage wheels as he was borne away at a gallop.

"Messieurs," said the President when silence was restored, "is the Count of Morcerf guilty of felony, treason, and dishonour?"

"Yes," was the unanimous reply of all the members.

Haydee was present to the end of the meeting; she heard the verdict passed on the Count, but neither pity nor joy was depicted on her features. Covering her face with her veil, she bowed to the councillors and left the room with queenly tread.

Chapter LV

THE CHALLENGE

$\bigwedge$

Albert was resolved to kill the unknown person who had struck this blow at his father. He had discovered that Danglars was making inquiries through his correspondents concerning the surrender of the castle of Janina, and he now proposed to his friend Beauchamp to accompany him to an interview with the banker, since, in his view, it was unfitting that such a solemn occasion should be unmarked by the presence of a witness.

When they reached Danglars' house they perceived the phaeton and the servant of M. Andrea Cavalcanti at the door.

"Ah, that is all the better," said Albert grimly. "If Monsieur Danglars will not fight with me, I will kill his son-in-law. A Cavalcanti should not shirk a duel."

The young man was announced, but, on hearing Albert's name, the banker, cognizant of what had taken place the previous evening, refused to see him. It was too late, however; he had followed the footman, and, hearing the instructions given, pushed open the door and entered the room, followed by Beauchamp.

"Pray, monsieur, is one not at liberty to receive whom one chooses?" cried the banker. "You appear to have forgotten yourself sadly."

"No, monsieur," said Albert coldly; "there are certain circumstances, such as the present one, when one is compelled to be at home to certain persons, at least if one is not a coward—I offer you that refuge."

"Then what do you want of me?"

"All I want of you," said Albert, going up to him and pretending not to notice Cavalcanti, who was standing with his back to the fireplace, "is to propose a meeting in some secluded spot where we shall not be disturbed for ten minutes; where, of the two men who meet, one will be left under the leaves."

Danglars turned pale. Cavalcanti took a step forward. Albert turned round to the young man and said:

"Oh, certainly! Come too, if you wish, Count. You have a right to be present since you are almost one of the family. I am willing to give this kind of appointment to as many as will accept."

Cavalcanti looked with a stupefied air at Danglars, who rose with an effort and stepped between the two men. This attack on Cavalcanti led him to hope that Albert's visit was due to a different reason from the one he had at first supposed.

"If you have come here, monsieur," said he to Albert, "to pick a quarrel with this gentleman because I preferred him to you, I shall bring the matter before the court."

"You are under a misapprehension, monsieur," said Morcerf with a grim smile. "The appointment I ask for has nothing at all to do with matrimony. I merely addressed Monsieur Cavalcanti because, for a moment, he appeared inclined to interfere in our discussion."

"I warn you, monsieur, that when I have the misfortune to meet a mad dog, I kill it," said Danglars, white with fear and rage, "and far from thinking myself guilty of a crime, I should consider I had rendered a service to society. Therefore, if you are mad and try to bite me, I shall kill you without mercy. Is it my fault that your father is dishonoured?"

"Yes, it is your fault, you scoundrel," replied Morcerf.

"My fault! Mine?" cried Danglars. "You are mad! Do I know anything about the history of Greece? Have I travelled in those parts? Was it upon my advice that your father sold the castle of Janina and betrayed . . ."

"Silence!" roared Albert. "You did not bring this calamity on us directly, but you hypocritically led up to it. Who wrote to Janina for information concerning my father?"

"It seems to me that anyone and every one can write to Janina."

"Nevertheless, only one person wrote, and you were that person."

"I certainly wrote. If a man's daughter is about to marry a young man, it is surely permissible for him to make inquiries about the young man's family. It is not only a right, it is a duty."

"You wrote knowing full well what answer you would receive," said Albert.

"I assure you," cried Danglars with a confidence and security which emanated perhaps less from fear than from his feeling for the unhappy young man. "I solemnly declare that I should never have thought of writing to Janina. What do I know of Ali Pasha's adversities?"

"Then some one persuaded you to write?"

"Certainly. I was speaking about your father's past history to someone and mentioned that the source of his wealth was still a mystery. He asked where your father had made his fortune. I replied: 'In Greece.' So he said: 'Well, write to Janina.' "

"Who gave you this advice?"

"Why, none other than your friend, the Count of Monte Cristo. Would you like to see the correspondence? I can show it you."

"Does the Count of Monte Cristo know what answer you received?"

"Yes, I showed it him."

"Did he know that my father's Christian name was Fernand, and his family name Mondego?"

"Yes, I told him a long time ago. After all, I have not done more than anyone else would have done in my place, perhaps less. The day after I received the answer, your father, acting on Monte Cristo's advice, asked me officially for my daughter's hand for you. I refused him definitely, but without giving any reason. In what way does the honour or dishonour of Monsieur de Morcerf concern me?"

Albert felt the flush rise to his cheeks. There was no doubt that Danglars was defending himself with the baseness, but at the same time with the assurance, of a man speaking at any rate the partial truth, not for conscience's sake, it is true, but through fear. Besides, what did Morcerf seek? It certainly was not to know whether Danglars or Monte Cristo was more to blame. What he sought was a man who would acknowledge the charge, whether venial or grave, a man who would fight, and it was evident that Danglars would not do so.

Then many a detail forgotten or unobserved presented itself to his mind. Monte Cristo knew all since he had bought Ali Pasha's daughter, yet, knowing all, he had advised Danglars to write to Janina. After the answer had been received he had yielded to Albert's desire to be introduced to Haydee; he had allowed the conversation to turn on the death of Ali, and had not opposed the recital of her story (doubtless after giving her instructions in the few Romaic sentences he spoke not to let Morcerf recognize his father); besides, had he not begged Morcerf not to mention his father's name before Haydee? There could be no doubt that it was all a premeditated plan, that Monte Cristo was in league with his father's enemies.

Albert took Beauchamp aside and expounded these views to him.

"You are right," his friend said. "In all that has happened Monsieur Danglars has only done the duty work. You must demand satisfaction of Monsieur de Monte Cristo."

Albert turned to Danglars with the words: "You must understand, monsieur, I am not taking definite leave of you.

I must first ascertain from the Count of Monte Cristo that your accusations against him are justified."

Bowing to the banker, he went out with Beauchamp, without taking any further notice of Cavalcanti. Danglars accompanied them to the door, renewing his assurance that he had not been actuated by any motive of personal hatred against the Count of Morcerf.

Chapter LVI

THE INSULT

They drove to no 30. Avenue des Champs-Élysées, but the Count was in his bath and could not see anyone. Albert ascertained from Baptistin, however, that he would be going to the Opera that evening.

Retracing his steps, he said to Beauchamp: "If you have anything to do, Beauchamp, do it at once. I count upon you to go to the Opera with me this evening and if you can bring Château-Renaud with you, do so."

On his return home, Albert sent a message to Franz, Debray, and Morrel that he would like to see them at the Opera that evening. Then he went to his mother, who, since the events of the previous evening, had kept her room and refused to see anyone. He found her in bed overwhelmed at their public humiliation. On seeing Albert, she clasped his hand and burst into tears. For a moment he stood silently looking on. It was evident from his pale face and knit brows that his determination for revenge was gaining in force.

"Mother, do you know whether Monsieur de Morcerf has any enemies?" Albert asked.

Mercédès started; she noticed the young man did not say my father.

"My son," she replied, "people in the Count's position

always have many secret enemies. Furthermore, the enemies one is cognizant of are not always the most dangerous."

"I know that, and for that reason, I appeal to your perspicacity. You are so observant that nothing escapes you. You remarked, for instance, that at the ball we gave Monsieur de Monte Cristo refused to partake of anything in our house."

Mercédès raised herself on her arm. "What has Monte Cristo to do with the question you asked me?"

"You know, Mother, Monsieur de Monte Cristo is almost an Oriental, and in order to reserve for themselves the liberty of revenge, Orientals never eat or drink in the house of an enemy."

"Do you wish to imply that Monte Cristo is our enemy, Albert?" cried Mercédès. "Who told you so? Why, you are mad, Albert! Monsieur de Monte Cristo has shown us only kindness. He saved your life and you yourself presented him to us. Oh, I entreat you, my son, if you entertain such an idea, dispel it, and I advise you, nay I beg of you, to keep on good terms with him."

"Mother, you have some reason for wishing me to be friendly with this man," replied the young man with a black look.

"I?" said Mercédès.

"Yes, you," replied the young man. "Is it because he has the power to do us some harm?"

Mercédès shuddered, and, casting on him a searching glance, said: "You speak strangely and appear to have singular prejudices. What has the Count done to you?"

An ironical smile passed over Albert's lips. Mercédès saw it with the double instinct of a woman and a mother and guessed all, but, being prudent and strong, she hid both her sorrows and her fears.

Albert dropped the conversation, but after a moment or two the Countess resumed:

"You inquired just now after my health. I will tell you frankly that I do not feel at all well. Stay with me and keep me company. I do not wish to be alone."

"Mother, you know how happy I should be to comply with your wishes, but important and urgent business compels me to be away from you the whole evening."

"Very well," replied Mercédès, with a sigh. "Go, Albert. I will not make you a slave to your filial affection."

Albert feigned not to hear; he took leave of his mother and went to his room to dress. At ten minutes to eight Beauchamp appeared; he had seen Château-Renaud, who promised to be at the Opera before the curtain rose. The two men got into Albert's brougham, and, having no reason to hide whither he was going, Albert said in a loud voice: "To the Opera!"

It was not until the end of the second act that Albert sought Monte Cristo in his box. The Count, whose companion was Maximilian Morrel, had been watching the young man all the evening, so that when he turned round on hearing his door open, he was quite prepared to see Albert before him, accompanied by Beauchamp and Château-Renaud.

"A welcome visit!" said the Count, with that cordiality which distinguished his form of salutation from the ordinary civilities of the social world. "So you have reached your goal at last! Good evening, Monsieur de Morcerf."

"We have not come here to exchange banalities or to make false professions of friendship," returned Albert. "We have come to demand an explanation of you, Count."

The quivering voice of the young man was scarcely louder than a whisper.

"An explanation at the Opera?" said the Count, with the calm tone and penetrating look which characterize the man who has complete confidence in himself. "Unfamiliar as I am with the customs of Paris, I should not have thought this was the place to demand an explanation."

"Nevertheless, when people shut themselves up and will not be seen on the pretext that they are in the bath, we must not miss the opportunity when we happen to meet them elsewhere."

"I am not difficult of access, monsieur," said Monte Cristo. "If I mistake not, it was but yesterday that you saw me in my house."

"Yesterday I was at your house, monsieur, because I knew not who you were."

Albert had raised his voice to such a pitch when saying these last words that every one in the adjoining boxes and in the corridors heard him.

"Where have you come from, monsieur?" said Monte Cristo, outwardly quite calm. "You do not appear to be in your right senses."

"So long as I understand your perfidies[1] and make you realize that I will be revenged, I am reasonable enough," said Albert in a fury.

"I do not understand you, and even if I did, there is no reason for you to speak in such a loud voice. I am at home here, and I alone have the right to raise my voice. Leave the box, Monsieur de Morcerf!" said the Count of Monte Cristo, as he pointed toward the door with an admirable gesture of command.

Albert understood the allusion to his name in a moment, and was about to throw his glove in the Count's face when Morrel seized his hand. Leaning forward in his chair, Monte Cristo stretched out his hand and took the young man's glove, saying in a terrible voice:

"I consider your glove as having been thrown, monsieur, and I will return it wrapt round a bullet. Now leave me, or I shall call my servants to throw you out!"

Utterly beside himself with anger, and with wild and bloodshot eyes, Albert stepped back; Morrel seized the opportunity to shut the door. Monte Cristo took up his glasses again as though nothing out of the ordinary had happened. The man had, indeed, a heart of iron and a face of marble.

"How have you offended him?" whispered Morrel.

"I? I have not offended him—at least not personally."

"But there must be some reason for this strange scene."

"The Count of Morcerf's adventures have exasperated the young man."

"What shall you do about it?"

"What shall I do? As true as you are here I shall have killed him before the clock strikes ten to-morrow morning. That is what I shall do."

Morrel took the Count's hands in his; they were so cold and steady that they sent a shudder through him.

"Ah, Count," said he, "his father loves him so."

"Tell me not such things!" cried Monte Cristo, with the first signs of anger that he had yet shown. "I would make him suffer!"

Morrel let Monte Cristo's hand fall in amazement.

"Count! Count!" said he.

"My dear Maximilian," interrupted the Count, "listen to the charming manner in which Duprez sings this line:

"Matilda! idol of my heart!"

"I was the first to discover Duprez at Naples and the first to applaud him. Bravo! Bravo!"

Morrel saw it was useless to say anything more. The curtain which had been raised at the conclusion of the scene with Albert was dropped once more, and a knock was heard at the door.

"Come in," said Monte Cristo, in a voice devoid of all emotion.

Beauchamp entered.

"Good evening, Monsieur Beauchamp," said Monte Cristo as though this were the first time he had seen the journalist that evening. "Pray be seated."

Beauchamp bowed, and, taking a seat, said: "As you saw, monsieur, I accompanied Monsieur de Morcerf just now."

"Which in all probability means that you had dined together," replied Monte Cristo, laughing. "I am glad to see you are more sober than he was."

"I will own that Albert was wrong in losing his temper,

monsieur," said Beauchamp, "and I have come on my own account to apologize for him. Now that I have made my apologies, mine, you understand, I should like to add that I consider you too gentlemanly to refuse me some explanation on the subject of your connexion with the people of Janina; then Count . . ."

"Monsieur Beauchamp," interrupted this extraordinary man, "the Count of Monte Cristo is responsible only to the Count of Monte Cristo. Therefore not a word on this subject, if you please. I do as I please, Monsieur Beauchamp, and believe me, what I do is always well done."

"Honest men are not to be paid with such coin, Count. You must give honourable guarantees."

"I am a living guarantee, monsieur," replied the Count, unmoved, but with a threatening look in his eyes. "Both of us have blood in our veins that we are anxious to shed, and that is our mutual guarantee. Deliver this answer to the Viscount, and tell him that before ten o'clock tomorrow I shall have seen the colour of his blood."

"Then all that remains for me to do is to make the necessary arrangements for the duel," said Beauchamp.

"I am quite indifferent on that score," replied the Count of Monte Cristo. "It was unnecessary to disturb me in the middle of an opera for such a trifling matter. Tell the Viscount that although I am the one insulted, I will give him the choice of arms and will accept everything without discussion or dispute. Do you understand me? Everything, even combat by drawing lots, which is always very stupid. With me it is different, I am sure of winning."

"Sure of winning?" said Beauchamp, looking at the Count in amazement.

"Certainly," said the Count, slightly shrugging his shoulders. "Otherwise I should not fight with Monsieur de Morcerf. I shall kill him; I cannot help myself. Send me word this evening to my house, indicating the weapon and the hour. I do not like to be kept waiting."

"Pistols the weapon, eight o'clock the hour in the Bois de

Vincennes," said Beauchamp somewhat disconcerted, for he could not make up his mind whether he had to deal with an arrogant braggadocio or a supernatural being.

"Very well," said Monte Cristo. "Now that all is arranged, pray let me listen to the opera and tell your friend Albert not to return this evening. Tell him to go home and sleep."

Beauchamp left the box perfectly amazed.

"Now," said Monte Cristo, turning toward Morrel, "I may reckon on you, may I not? The young man is acting blindfolded and knows not the true cause of this duel, which is known only to God and to me; but I give you my word, Morrel, that God, Who knows it, will be on our side."

"Enough," said Morrel. "Who is your second witness?"

"I do not know anyone in Paris on whom I could confer the honour except you, Morrel, and your brother-in-law. Do you think Emmanuel will render me this service?"

"I can answer for him as for myself, Count."

"Very well, that is all I require. You will be with me at seven o'clock in the morning?"

"We shall be there."

"Hush! the curtain is rising. Let us listen. I would not lose a note of this opera; the music of *Wilhelm Tell* is charming!"

Chapter LVII

THE NIGHT

❧

Monte Cristo waited, as he usually did, until Duprez had sung his famous *Follow me,* then he rose and went out, followed by Morrel, who left him at the door, renewing his promise to be at his house, together with Emmanuel, at seven o'clock the next morning. Still calm and smiling, the Count entered the brougham and was at home in five minutes. On entering the house, he said to Ali: "Ali, my pistols inlaid with ivory!" and no one who knew him could have mistaken the tone in which he said it.

Ali brought the box to his master, who was beginning to examine them when the study door opened to admit Baptistin. Before the latter could say a word, a veiled woman who was following behind him, and who through the open door caught sight of a pistol in the Count's hand and two swords on the table, rushed into the room. Baptistin cast a bewildered look on his master, but upon a sign from the Count, he went out, shutting the door behind him.

"Who are you, madame?" the Count asked of the veiled woman.

The stranger looked round her to make sure they were alone, then, throwing herself on to one knee and clasping her hands, she cried out in a voice of despair:

"Edmond, you will not kill my son!"

The Count started, and, dropping the weapon he held in his hand, uttered a feeble cry.

"What name did you pronounce then, Madame de Morcerf?" said he.

"Yours!" she cried, throwing back her veil. "Your name which I alone, perhaps, have not forgotten. Edmond, it is not Madame de Morcerf who has come to you. It is Mercédès."

"Mercédès is dead, madame. I know no one now of that name."

"Mercédès lives, and not only lives, but remembers. She alone recognized you when she saw you, and even without seeing you, Edmond, she knew you by the very tone of your voice. From that moment she has followed your every step, watched you, feared you. She has no need to seek the hand that has dealt Monsieur de Morcerf this blow."

"Fernand, you mean, madame," returned Monte Cristo, with bitter irony. "Since we are recalling names, let us remember them all."

He pronounced the name of Fernand with such an expression of venomous hatred that Mercédès was stricken with fear.

"You see, Edmond, I am not mistaken. I have every reason to say: 'Spare my son!' "

"Who told you, madame, that I have evil designs against your son?"

"No one, but alas! a mother is gifted with double sight. I have guessed everything. I followed him to the Opera this evening, and, hiding in another box, I saw all that occurred."

"If you saw everything, madame, you also saw that Fernand's son insulted me in public," said Monte Cristo with terrible calmness. "You must also have seen," he continued, "that he would have thrown his glove in my face but that one of my friends held back his arm."

"Listen to me. My son has discovered your identity; he attributes all his father's misfortunes to you."

"Madame, you are under a misapprehension. His father

is suffering no misfortune; it is a punishment, and it is not inflicted by me, it is the work of Providence."

"Why should you take the place of Providence? Why should you remember when He forgets? In what way do Janina and the Vizier concern you, Edmond? What wrong has Fernand Mondego done you by betraying Ali Tebelin?"

"As you infer, madame, that is all a matter as between the French officer and Vasiliki's daughter and does not concern me. But if I have sworn to take revenge, it is not on the French officer or on the Count of Morcerf; it is on Fernand, the fisherman, the husband of Mercédès the Catalan."

"What terrible vengeance for a fault for which fate alone is responsible! I am the guilty one, Edmond, and if you take revenge on some one, it should be on me, who lacked the strength to bear your absence and my solitude."

"But do you know why I was absent? Do you know why you were left solitary and alone?"

"Because you were arrested and imprisoned, Edmond."

"Why was I arrested? Why was I imprisoned?"

"I know not," said Mercédès.

" 'Tis true, you do not know; at least, I hope you do not. Well then, I will tell you. I was arrested and imprisoned because on the eve of the very day on which I was to be married, a man named Danglars wrote this letter in the arbour of La Réserve, and Fernand, the fisherman, posted it."

Going to a writing-desk, Monte Cristo opened a drawer and took out a discoloured piece of paper and laid it before Mercédès. It was Danglars' letter to the Procureur du Roi which the Count of Monte Cristo had taken from the dossier of Edmond Dantès the day he, disguised as an agent of Messrs Thomson and French, paid M. de Boville the sum of two hundred thousand francs.

Filled with dismay, Mercédès read the following lines:

"The Procureur du Roi is herewith informed by a friend to the throne and to religion that a certain Edmond Dantès, mate on the *Pharaon*, which arrived this morning from Smyrna after having touched at Naples and Porto Ferrajo, has been entrusted by Murat with a letter for the usurper and by the usurper with a letter for the Bonapartist party in Paris. Corroboration of this crime can be found either on him, or at his father's house, or in his cabin on board the *Pharaon.*"

"Good God!" exclaimed Mercédès, passing her hand across her forehead wet with perspiration. "This letter . . ."

"I bought it for two hundred thousand francs, Madame," said Monte Cristo. "But it is cheap at the price since it to-day enables me to justify myself in your eyes."

"What was the result of this letter?"

"You know it, Madame. It led to my arrest. But what you do not know is how long my imprisonment lasted. You do not know that I lay in a dungeon of the Château d'If, but a quarter of a league from you, for fourteen long years. On each day of those fourteen years, I renewed the vow of vengeance I had taken the first day, though I was unaware that you had married Fernand, and that my father had died of hunger."

"Merciful heavens!" cried Mercédès, utterly crushed.

"That is what I learned on leaving my prison fourteen years after I had been taken there. I have sworn to revenge myself on Fernand because of the living Mercédès, and my deceased father, and revenge myself I will!"

"Are you sure this unhappy Fernand did what you say?"

"On my oath it is so. In any case it is not much more odi-ous than that, being a Frenchman by adoption, he passed over to the English; a Spaniard by birth, he fought against the Spanish; a hireling of Ali's, he betrayed and assassinated Ali. In the face of all this, what is that letter you have just read? The French have not avenged themselves on the trai-tor, the Spaniards have not shot him, and Ali in his tomb has let him go unpunished; but I, betrayed, assassinated, cast into a tomb, have risen from that tomb by the grace of God, and it is my duty to God to punish this man. He has sent me for that purpose and here I am."

"Then take your revenge, Edmond," cried the heartbroken mother, falling on her knees, "but let your vengeance fall on the culprits, on him, on me, but not on my son!"

"I must have my revenge, Mercédès! For fourteen years have I suffered, for fourteen years wept and cursed, and now I must avenge myself."

"Edmond," continued Mercédès, her arms stretched out toward the Count, "ever since I knew you, I have adored your name, have respected your memory. Oh, my friend, do not compel me to tarnish the noble and pure image that is ever reflected in my heart! If you knew how I have prayed for you, both when I thought you living and later when I believed you dead. Yes, dead, alas! I imagined that your dead body had been laid in its shroud in the depths of some gloomy tower or hurled into the bottom of an abyss where gaolers fling their dead prisoners, and I wept. What else could I do, Edmond, but weep and pray? Every night for ten long years I dreamed the same dream. It was reported you had endeavoured to escape, that you had taken the place of another prisoner; that you had slipped into the winding-sheet of a dead man, that your living body had been flung from the top of the Château d'If, and that the scream you gave as you were dashed against the rocks first revealed to the men, now become your murderers, what had taken place. Well, Edmond, I swear to you by the son for whose life I now plead, that every night for ten years I have seen these men swinging a shapeless and indistinguishable object on the top of a rock; every night for ten years have I heard a terrible scream that has awakened me trembling and cold. Oh, believe me, Edmond, guilty as I am, I too have suffered much!"

"Have you seen your father die in your absence?" cried Monte Cristo, thrusting his hands into his hair. "Have you seen the woman you loved give her hand to your rival while you were pining away in the depths of a dungeon? . . ."

"No, but I have seen him whom I loved about to become my son's murderer!"

Mercédès said these words with such infinite sadness and in such tones of despair that they wrung a sob from the Count's throat. The lion was tamed, the avenger was overcome!

"What do you ask of me?" he said. "Your son's life? Well then, he shall live!"

Mercédès uttered a cry which forced two tears into Monte Cristo's eyes, but they disappeared again immediately; doubtless God had sent some angel to collect them, for they were far more precious in his eyes than the richest pearls of Guzerat or Ophir.

"Oh, Edmond, I thank you!" cried Mercédès, taking the Count's hand and pressing it to her lips. "Now you are the man of my dreams, the man I have always loved! I can own it now."

"It is just as well, for poor Edmond will not have long to enjoy your love," replied Monte Cristo. "Death will return to its tomb, the phantom to darkness!"

"What is that you say, Edmond?"

"I say that since you so command me, I must die!"

"Die! Who said that? Who told you to die? Whence come these strange ideas of death?"

"You cannot suppose I have the least desire to live after I have been publicly insulted, before a theatre full of people, in the presence of your friends and those of your son, challenged by a mere child who will glory in my pardon as in a victory? What I have loved most after you, Mercédès, has been myself, that means to say, my dignity, the force that made me superior to all others. This force was life to me. You have broken it, and I must die!"

"But the duel will not take place, Edmond, since you pardon my son."

"It will take place," said Monte Cristo solemnly, "but it will be my blood instead of your son's that will stain the ground."

Mercédès screamed and rushed up to Monte Cristo, but suddenly she came to a halt.

"Edmond," said she, "I know there is a God above, for you still live and I have seen you. I put my whole trust in Him to help me, and in the meantime I depend upon your word. You said my son would live and you mean it, do you not?"

"Yes, madame, he shall live," said Monte Cristo.

Mercédès held out her hand to him, her eyes filling with tears as she said: "Edmond, how noble it is of you, how great, how sublime to have taken pity on a poor woman who appealed to you without daring to hope for mercy. Alas! I have grown old through sorrow rather than years, and I cannot remind my Edmond by a smile or a look of the Mercédès who has been so many years in his thoughts. Believe me, Edmond, I too have suffered as I said before. Ah, it is sad to see one's life pass without having a single joy to recall, without preserving a single hope. I repeat once more, Edmond, it is noble, beautiful, sublime, to forgive as you have done."

"You say that now, Mercédès, but what would you say if you knew how great is the sacrifice I have made?"

· Mercédès looked at the Count with eyes full of admiration and gratitude. Without answering his question she said:

"You see that, though my cheeks have become pale and my eyes dull and I have lost all my beauty, that, though Mercédès is no longer like her former self, her heart has remained the same. Farewell, Edmond, I have nothing more to ask of Heaven; I have seen you, and you are as noble and as great as in the days long past. Farewell, Edmond, farewell, and thank you."

The Count made no reply. Mercédès opened the door, and had disappeared before he had woken from his painful and deep reverie into which his thwarted vengeance had plunged him. The clock on the Invalides struck one as the rumbling of the carriage which bore Mme de Morcerf away brought the Count of Monte Cristo back to realities.

"Fool that I am," said he, "that I did not tear out my heart the day I resolved to revenge myself!"

Chapter LVIII

THE DUEL

✦

The night wore on. The Count of Monte Cristo knew not how the hours passed, for his mental tortures could only be compared to those he had suffered when, as Edmond Dantès, he had lain in the dungeon of the Château d'If. History was repeating itself once more, only the external circumstances were changed. Then his plans were frustrated at the eleventh hour through no action on his part; now, just as his schemes for revenge were materializing, he must relinquish them for ever, solely because he had not reckoned with one factor—his love for Mercédès!

At length as the clock struck six he roused himself from his dismal meditations, and made his final preparations before going out to meet his voluntary death. When Morrel and Emmanuel called to accompany him to the ground, he was quite ready, and, outwardly at least, calm. They were the first to arrive, but Franz and Debray soon followed. It was not until ten minutes past eight, however, that they saw Albert coming along on horseback at full gallop, followed by a servant.

"How imprudent to come on horseback when about to fight with pistols! And after all the instructions I gave him!" said Château-Renaud.

"And just look at his collar and tie, his open coat and white waistcoat!" said Beauchamp. "He might just as well have marked the exact position of his heart—it would have been simpler and would have ensured a speedier ending."

In the meantime, Albert had arrived within ten paces of the group of five young men; he pulled up his horse, jumped down, and, throwing the bridle to the servant, walked up to the others. He was pale and his eyes red and swollen; it was easily seen he had not slept all night. There was about his whole demeanour an unaccustomed sadness.

"Thank you, messieurs, for having granted my request!" he said. "Believe me, I am most grateful for this token of friendship." Noticing that Morrel had stepped back as he approached, he continued: "Draw nearer, Monsieur Morrel, to you especially are my thanks due!"

"I think you must be unaware that I am Monsieur de Monte Cristo's second," replied Morrel.

"I was not certain, but I thought you were. All the better; the more honourable men there are here, the better pleased shall I be."

"Monsieur Morrel, you may inform the Count of Monte Cristo that Monsieur de Morcerf has arrived," said Château-Renaud. "We are at his service."

"Wait, messieurs, I should like a few words with the Count of Monte Cristo," said Albert.

"In private?" Morrel asked.

"No, before every one."

Albert's seconds looked at one another in surprise. Franz and Debray began whispering to one another, while Morrel, overjoyed at this unexpected incident, went in search of the Count, who was walking with Emmanuel a short distance away.

"What does he want?" asked Monte Cristo.

"I only know that he wishes to speak to you."

"I hope he is not going to tempt me with fresh insults?"

"I do not think that is his intention," was Morrel's reply.

The Count approached, accompanied by Maximilian and

Emmanuel, his calm and serene mien forming a strange contrast with the grief-stricken face of Albert, who also advanced toward his adversary. When three paces from each other they stopped.

"Messieurs, come nearer," Albert said. "I do not want you to lose a word of what I have to say to the Count of Monte Cristo, for strange as it may seem to you, you must repeat it to all who will listen to you."

"I am all attention, monsieur," said the Count.

"I reproached you, monsieur, with having made known Monsieur de Morcerf's conduct in Epirus," began Albert in a tremulous voice, which became firmer as he went on. "I did not consider you had the right to punish him, however guilty he might be. Yet to-day I know better. It is not Fernand Mondego's treachery toward Ali Pasha that makes me so ready to forgive you, it is the treachery of Fernand the fisherman toward you, and the untold sufferings his conduct has caused you. I therefore say to you and proclaim it aloud that you were justified in revenging yourself on my father, and I, his son, thank you for not having done more."

Had a thunderbolt fallen in the midst of his listeners, it would not have astonished them more than did Albert's declaration. Monte Cristo slowly raised his eyes to Heaven with an expression of gratitude; he could not comprehend how Albert's proud nature could have submitted to this sudden humiliation. He recognized in it Mercédès' influence, and understood now why the noble woman had not refused the sacrifice which she knew would not be necessary.

"Now, Monsieur," continued Albert, "if you consider this apology sufficient, give me your hand. In my opinion the quality of recognizing one's faults ranks next to the rare one of infallibility, which you appear to possess. But this confession concerns me alone. I have acted well in the eyes of man, but you have acted well in the eyes of God. An angel alone could have saved one of us from death, and that angel has appeared, not to make us friends, perhaps, but at least to make us esteem one another."

With moistened eyes and heaving bosom, Monte Cristo extended his hand to Albert, who pressed it with respectful awe as he said: "Messieurs! Monsieur de Monte Cristo accepts my apology. I was guilty of a rash act, but have now made reparation for my fault. I trust the world will not look upon me as a coward because I have followed the dictates of my conscience."

"What has happened?" Beauchamp asked Château-Renaud. "Methinks we make a very sorry figure here."

"In truth, Albert's action is either most despicable or else very noble," replied the Baron.

"What does all this mean?" Debray asked Franz. "The Count of Monte Cristo brings dishonour on Monsieur de Morcerf, and his son acknowledges that he is justified in doing so. In his place, I should consider myself bound to fight at least ten duels."

As for Monte Cristo, his head was bowed, his arms hung listless. He was crushed under the weight of twenty-four years' memories. He was not thinking of Albert, Beauchamp, or Château-Renaud, nor yet of anyone around him; he was thinking of the courageous woman who had come to him to crave her son's life. He had offered her his, and now she had saved it by confessing a terrible family secret, capable of killing for ever the young man's love for her.

Chapter LIX

REVENGE

The Count of Monte Cristo bowed to the five young men with a sad smile, and, getting into his carriage, drove away with Maximilian and Emmanuel. Albert stood wrapt in deep and melancholy thought for a few moments, then suddenly loosing his horse from the tree around which his servant had tied the bridle, he sprang lightly into the saddle and returned to Paris at a gallop. A quarter of an hour later he entered his house in the Rue du Helder. As he dismounted from his horse, he thought he saw his father's pale face peeping from behind the curtain of his bedroom. Albert turned away his head with a sigh and went to his own apartments. Once there, he cast a last lingering look at all the luxuries that had made his life so easy and happy from his childhood. He looked once more at the pictures; the faces seemed to smile at him and the landscapes to be animated with brighter colours. Taking from its oak frame the portrait of his mother, he rolled it up, leaving empty and bare the gilt frame that had surrounded it. Then he put all his precious knickknacks in order; went to the cupboards and placed the key in each door; threw into a drawer of his writing-desk all the money he had about him; gathered together all the countless pieces of jewellery that were lying about in cups, in jewel-cases, and on brackets, and made an exact inventory of all, placing it in a conspicuous place on a table from which he first removed all the books and papers which encumbered it.

While he was in the midst of this work and in spite of the instructions Albert had given that he was not to be disturbed, his servant entered.

"What do you want?" Morcerf asked him in a sad, rather than an annoyed, tone of voice.

"Excuse me, Monsieur," said the valet, "I know you forbade me to disturb you, but the Count of Morcerf has sent for me."

"Well?"

"I did not wish to go to him before I had received your instructions."

"Why?"

"Because the Count doubtless knows that I accompanied you to the Bois de Vincennes."

"No doubt."

"And if he asks me what happened, what reply shall I make?"

"Tell the truth."

"Then I am to say that the duel did not take place?"

"Say that I apologized to the Count of Monte Cristo. Go!"

The valet bowed and went out, and Albert returned to his inventory. When he had finished, his thoughts turned to his mother, and as no one was there to announce him, he went straight to her bedroom, but, distressed by what he saw and still more by what he guessed, he paused on the threshold.

As though one mind animated these two beings, Mercédès was doing in her room what Albert had been doing in his. Everything was in disorder; lace, clothing, jewellery, money, all was carefully placed in the drawers, and the Countess was just collecting the keys. Albert saw all these preparations and understood; calling out "Mother!"

he threw his arms around her neck. The painter who could have caught the expression on those two faces just then would certainly have made a beautiful picture!

All these signs of a firm decision which gave him no cause for fear where he himself was concerned alarmed him for his mother.

"What are you doing, Mother dear?" he asked.

"What have you been doing?" was her reply.

"Oh, Mother!" cried Albert, almost too overwhelmed to speak. "It does not affect you as it does me. No, you surely cannot have taken the same resolutions as I have! I am come to inform you that I am leaving this house . . . and you?"

"I am leaving it too, Albert," replied Mercédès. "I must confess, I had reckoned on being accompanied by my son. Was I mistaken?"

"Mother, I cannot let you share the life I have chosen. I must live henceforth without name and without fortune; to start my apprenticeship, I must borrow from a friend my daily bread till I can earn it myself. So I am going from here, Mother, to Franz, to ask him to lend me the small sum of money I think will be necessary."

"You are going to suffer hunger, poverty, my son?" exclaimed Mercédès. "Oh, say not so or you will break all my resolution."

"But not mine, Mother dear," replied Albert. "I am young and strong and I think I am brave, and I have also learned since yesterday what force of will means. Alas! Mother, there are those who have suffered so much and yet have not succumbed to their sufferings, but instead have built up a new fortune on the ruins of their former happiness. I have learnt this, Mother, and I have seen such men; I know that they have risen with such vigour and glory from the abyss into which their enemies had cast them that they have overthrown their former conquerors. No, Mother, from to-day I have done with the past, and I will accept nothing from it, not even my name, for you understand, do you not, Mother, that your son could not bear the name of a man who should blush before every other man?"

"Albert, my son, had I been stronger, that is the advice I should have given you," said Mercédès. "Your conscience has spoken to you when my enfeebled voice was still; follow its dictates, my son. You had friends, Albert; break with them, but, for your mother's sake, do not despair. Life still has its charms at your age, for you can barely count twenty-two summers, and as a noble character such as yours must carry with it a name without blemish, take my father's. It was Herrara. Whatever career you pursue, you will soon make this name illustrious. When you have accomplished this, my son, make your appearance again in a world rendered more beautiful by your past sufferings. But, even though the golden future I foresee for you should not come to pass, let me at least cherish the hope. I have nothing else left to me; for me there is no future, and when I leave this house, I go toward my tomb."

"I shall do as you wish, Mother," the young man said. "Your hopes are mine. God's anger cannot follow us, you who are so noble and I who am so innocent. But since we have taken our resolution, let us act with all speed. Monsieur de Morcerf left the house about an hour ago. The opportunity is therefore propitious, and we shall be relieved of the necessity of giving any explanations."

"I am ready," said Mercédès.

Albert ran into the boulevard for a cab to take them away. He thought of a nice little furnished house in the Rue des Saints-Pères where his mother would find a humble but comfortable lodging. As the cab drew up at the door and Albert alighted, a man approached and handed him a letter. Albert recognized the Count of Monte Cristo's steward.

"From the Count," said Bertuccio.

Albert took the letter and read it; then, with tears in his eyes and his breast heaving with emotion, he went in to find Mercédès and handed it to her without a word.

Mercédès read:

ALBERT

While showing you that I have discovered the plans you are contemplating, I hope to prove to you also that I have a sense of what is right. You are free, you are leaving the Count's house, taking with you your mother. But remember, Albert, you owe her more than your poor noble heart can give her. Keep the struggle to yourself, bear all the suffering alone, and save her the misery that must inevitably accompany your first efforts, for she has not deserved even one fraction of the misfortune that has this day befallen her.

I know you are both leaving the Rue du Helder without taking anything with you. Do not try to discover how I know it; it is enough that I do know it.

Listen, Albert, to what I have to say. Twenty-four years ago, I returned to my country a proud and happy man. I had a sweetheart, Albert, a noble young girl whom I adored, and I was bringing to her a hundred and fifty louis which I had painfully amassed by ceaseless toil. This money was for her, and, knowing how treacherous the sea is, I buried the treasure in the little garden behind the house in Marseilles which your mother knows so well.

Recently I passed through Marseilles on my way from Paris. I went to see this house of sad memories. In the evening I took a spade and dug in the corner where I had buried my treasure. The iron chest was still in the same place: no one had touched it. It is in the corner that is shaded by a beautiful fig tree my father planted on the day of my birth.

By a strange and sad coincidence this money, which was to have contributed to the comfort of the woman I adored, will to-day serve the same purpose. Oh! understand well my meaning. You are a generous man, Albert, but maybe you are blinded by pride or resentment. If you refuse me, if you ask another for what I have the right to offer you, I can but say it is ungenerous of you to refuse what is offered to your mother by one whose father was made to suffer the horrors of hunger and despair by your father.

Albert waited in silence for his mother's decision after she had finished reading the letter.

"I accept," said she. "He has the right to pay the dowry I shall take with me to the convent."

Placing the letter against her heart, she took her son's arm and went down the stairs with a step that surprised her by its firmness.

Meanwhile Monte Cristo had also returned to town with Emmanuel and Maximilian, and was sitting wrapt in thought when the door suddenly opened. The Count frowned.

"Monsieur le Comte de Morcerf," announced Baptistin, as though this name was excuse enough for his admittance.

"Ask Monsieur de Morcerf into the salon."

When Monte Cristo joined the General, he was pacing the length of the floor for the third time.

"Ah, it is really you, Monsieur de Morcerf," said Monte Cristo calmly. "I thought I had not heard aright."

"Yes, it is I," said the Count, with a frightful contraction of the lips which prevented him from articulating clearly.

"I only require to know now to what I owe the pleasure of seeing the Count of Morcerf at such an early hour," continued Monte Cristo.

"You had a meeting with my son this morning, monsieur?"

"You knew about it?"

"I also know that my son had very good reason to fight you and to do his utmost to kill you."

"He had, but you see that, notwithstanding these reasons, he did not kill me; in fact he did not fight."

"Yet he looked upon you as the cause of his father's dishonour and the terrible calamity that has now befallen my house."

"That is true, monsieur," said Monte Cristo, with dreadful calmness; "the secondary cause, but not the principal one."

"No doubt you made some sort of apology or gave some explanation?"

"I gave him no explanation, and it was he who apologized."

"But to what do you attribute such conduct?"

"To conviction; probably he discovered there was one more guilty than I."

"Who is that man?"

"His father!"

"That may be," said the Count, "but you know the guilty do not like to hear themselves convicted of their guilt."

"I know, and I expected all this."

"You expected my son to be a coward?" cried the Count.

"Monsieur Albert de Morcerf is not a coward!" said Monte Cristo.

"A man who holds a sword in his hand, with an enemy within reach of it, is a coward if he does not strike. Ah, that he were here that I might tell him so!"

"I presume you have not come here to tell me your little family affairs," replied Monte Cristo coldly. "Go and say that to Monsieur Albert, perhaps he will know what answer to give you."

"No, no, I have not come for that!" replied the General, with a smile which disappeared immediately. "I came to tell you that I too look upon you as my enemy. I have come to tell you that I instinctively hate you, that I seem to have known and hated you always! As the young men of this generation no longer fight, it is for us to do so. Are you of this opinion?"

"Certainly. But let me tell you that when I said I was expecting this, I was referring to your visit."

"All the better. Your preparations are made?"

"I am always ready, monsieur."

"You understand that we shall fight till one of us drops?" said the General, clenching his teeth in rage.

"Till one of us drops," repeated the Count of Monte Cristo, slowly nodding his head.

"Let us go, then; we have no need of seconds."

"Indeed, it were useless," replied Monte Cristo. "We know each other so well."

"On the contrary, it is because we do not know each other."

"Bah!" said Monte Cristo, with the same exasperating coolness. "Are you not the soldier Fernand who deserted on the eve of the battle of Waterloo? Are you not the Lieutenant Fernand who served the French army as guide and spy in Spain? Are you not the Colonel Fernand who betrayed, sold, and assassinated his benefactor, Ali? And have not all these Fernands combined made Lieutenant-General Count of Morcerf, Peer of France?"

"Villain! to reproach me with my shame when you are perhaps about to kill me!" cried the General, as though struck by a red-hot iron. "I did not say I was unknown to you. I know well that, demon that you are, you have penetrated the obscurity of my past and have read, by the light of what torch I know not, every page of my life. But perhaps there is more honour in my shame than in all your outward pomp. No, no, I am known to you, but I do not know you, adventurer sewn up in gold and precious stones! In Paris you call yourself the Count of Monte Cristo, in Italy Sindbad the Sailor, in Malta—who knows? I have forgotten. It is your real name I now ask and wish to know, so that I may pronounce it in the field when I plunge my sword into your heart."

The Count of Monte Cristo turned a ghastly colour; his wild eyes were burning with a devouring flame; he bounded into the adjoining room, and, within a second, tearing off his tie, his coat, and his waistcoat, had put on a small sailor's blouse and a sailor's hat, from under which his long black hair flowed.

He returned thus attired, and, with his arms crossed, walked up to the General, who had wondered at his sudden disappearance. On seeing him again his teeth chattered, his legs gave way under him, and he stepped back until he found a table against which to lay his clenched hand for support.

"Fernand!" cried Monte Cristo, "I need but mention one of my many names to strike terror into your heart. But you guess this name, or rather you remember it, do you not? For, in spite of all my grief and tortures, I show you to-day a face made young by the joy of vengeance, a face that you must often have seen in your dreams since your marriage with—Mercédès."

With head thrown back and hands stretched out, the General stared at this terrible apparition in silence; then, leaning against the wall for support, he glided slowly along it to the door through which he went out backward, uttering but the one distressing and piercing cry: "Edmond Dantès!"

With a moan that can be compared with no human sound, he dragged himself to the yard, staggering like a drunken man, and fell into his valet's arms. "Home! home!" he muttered.

The fresh air and the shame he felt at having given way before his servant made him pull himself together, but the drive was a short one, and the nearer he got to his house the greater was his anguish.

A few paces from his door, the carriage stopped, and the Count alighted. The door of the house was wide open; a cab, whose driver looked surprised at being called to this magnificent residence, was stationed in the middle of the yard. The Count looked at it in terror, and, not daring to question anyone, fled to his room.

Two people were coming down the staircase, and he had only just time to hide himself in a room near by. It was Mercédès, leaning on her son's arm. They were both leaving the house. They passed quite close to the unhappy man, who, hidden behind a door-curtain, felt Mercédès' silk dress brush past him and the warm breath of his son on his face, as he said:

"Have courage, Mother! Come away, this is no longer our home."

The words died away and the steps were lost in the distance. The General drew himself up, clinging to the curtains with clenched hands, and the most terrible sob escaped him that ever came from the bosom of a father abandoned at the same time by his wife and his son.

Soon he heard the door of the cab closed and the voice of the coachman, followed by the rumbling of the lumbersome vehicle as it shook the windowpanes. He rushed into his bedroom to see once more all that he had loved on earth; the cab passed, and neither Mercédès nor Albert's heads appeared at the door to take a last farewell of the deserted house, or to cast on the abandoned husband and father a last look of farewell and regret.

At the very moment when the wheels of that cab passed under the arched gate, a report was heard, and dark smoke issued through the glass of the bedroom window, which had been broken by the force of the explosion.

Chapter LX

VALENTINE

On leaving Monte Cristo, Morrel walked slowly toward Villefort's house. Noirtier and Valentine had allowed him two visits a week, and he was now going to take advantage of his rights.

Valentine was waiting for him. Almost beside herself with anxiety, she seized his hand and led him to her grandfather. She had heard of the affair at the Opera and its consequences, and, with her woman's instinct, had guessed that Morrel would be Monte Cristo's second, and, knowing the young man's courage and his affection for the Count, she feared he would not be satisfied with the impassive part assigned to him.

One can understand with what eagerness all details were asked, given, and received, and the expression of indescribable joy that appeared in Valentine's eyes when she learned the happy issue of the terrible affair.

"Now, let us speak of our own affairs," said Valentine, making a sign to Morrel to take a seat beside her grandfather while she sat on a hassock at his feet. "You know Grandpapa wants to leave this house? Do you know what reason he has given?"

Noirtier looked at his granddaughter to impose silence

on her, but she was not looking at him; her eyes and smiles were all for Morrel.

"Whatever the reason may be that Monsieur Noirtier has given, I am sure it is a good one!" exclaimed Maximilian.

"He pretends that the air of the Faubourg Saint-Honoré does not suit me!"

"Monsieur Noirtier may be right too," said Morrel. "You have not looked at all well for the past fortnight."

"Perhaps not," replied Valentine, "but my grandfather has become my physician, and, as he knows everything, I have the greatest confidence that he will soon cure me."

"Then you are really ill, Valentine?" Morrel asked anxiously.

"Oh, not really ill; I only feel a little unwell, nothing more."

Noirtier did not let one of Valentine's words escape him.

"What treatment are you following for this strange illness?"

"A very simple one," said Valentine. "Every morning I take a spoonful of my grandfather's medicine; that is, I commenced with one spoonful, but now I take four. Grandfather says it is a panacea."

Valentine smiled, yet her smile was a sad one. Maximilian looked at her in silence, but his eyes looked his love. She was very beautiful, but her paleness had become more marked, her eyes shone more brilliantly than usual, and her hands, which were generally of the whiteness of mother-of-pearl, now resembled wax turned yellow with age.

"But I thought this medicine was made up especially for Monsieur Noirtier?" said Morrel.

"I know it is, and it is very bitter," replied Valentine. "Everything I drink afterwards seems to have the same taste."

Noirtier looked at his granddaughter questioningly.

"Yes, Grandpapa, it is so," she replied. "Just now before coming to you I drank some sugared water; it tasted so bitter that I left half of it."

Noirtier made a sign that he wished to say something. Valentine at once got up to fetch the dictionary, her grandfather following her all the while with visible anguish. As a matter of fact, the blood was rushing to the girl's head, and her cheeks became red.

"Well, this is singular," she said, without losing any of her gaiety. "I have become giddy again. It is the sun shining in my eyes." And she leaned against the window.

"There is no sun," replied Morrel, more concerned by the expression on Noirtier's face than by Valentine's indisposition. He ran toward her.

"Do not be alarmed," she said with a smile. "It is nothing and has already passed. But listen! Do I not hear a carriage in the courtyard?" She opened Noirtier's door, ran to a window in the passage, and returned quickly.

"Yes," she said. "It is Madame Danglars and her daughter, who have come to call on us. Good-bye, I must run away, otherwise they will come to look for me here. Stay with Grandpapa, Max. I promise you to come back very soon."

With that she ran out, but she had scarcely gone down three stairs when a cloud passed before her eyes, her legs became stiff, her hands lost the power of holding the baluster, and she rolled down to the bottom.

Morrel started up, and, opening the door, found Valentine stretched out on the landing. Quick as lightning he picked her up in his arms, and, carrying her back into the room, seated her on a chair. Valentine opened her eyes and looked round her. She saw the deepest terror depicted on her grandfather's features, and, trying to smile, said: "Do not be alarmed, Grandpapa. It is nothing at all. I only went giddy."

"Giddy again!" exclaimed Morrel, alarmed. "I beg of you, Valentine, take care of yourself."

"But it has passed now, and I am quite myself again. Now let me give you some news. Eugénie Danglars is going to be married in a week, and in three days her mother is going to give a sort of betrothal festival. We are all invited, my father, Madame de Villefort, and myself—at least I understand so."

"When will it be our turn to think of these things? Oh, Valentine, you can do so much with your grandfather. Try to persuade him to say it will be soon! Do something quickly. So long as you are not really mine, I am always afraid I may lose you."

"Really, Maximilian, you are too timid for an officer, a soldier who, they say, knows not what fear is," said Valentine with a spasmodic movement of pain, and she burst into harsh, painful laughter. Her arms stiffened, her head fell back on her chair, and she remained motionless.

The cry of terror which was imprisoned in Noirtier's throat found expression in his eyes. Morrel understood he was to call for help. The young man pulled at the bell; the maid, who was in Valentine's room, and the servant who had taken Barrois' place came rushing in immediately.

Valentine was so cold, pale, and inanimate that the fear that prevailed in this accursed house took possession of them, and they flew out of the room shouting for help. At the same moment, Villefort's voice was heard calling from his study: "What is the matter?"

Morrel looked questioningly at Noirtier, who had now regained his composure, and indicated by a look the little room where Morrel had already taken refuge on a similar occasion. He was only just in time, for Villefort's footsteps were heard approaching. He rushed into the room, ran up to Valentine, and took her in his arms for an instant, calling out the while: "A doctor! Monsieur d'Avrigny! No, I will go for him myself," and he flew out of the room.

Morrel went out by the other door. A dreadful recollection chilled his heart; the conversation between Villefort and the doctor which he had overheard the night Mme de Saint-Méran died came back to his mind. These were the same symptoms, though less acute, that had preceded Barrois' death. On the other hand Monte Cristo's words seemed to resound in his ears: "If you have need of anything, Morrel, come to me. I can do much," and, quicker than thought, he sped from the Faubourg Saint-Honoré to the Champs Élysées.

In the meantime, Villefort arrived at the doctor's house in a hired cabriolet, and rang the bell so violently that the porter became quite alarmed and hastened to open the door. Without saying a word, Villefort ran up the stairs. The porter knew him and let him pass, calling after him: "In his study, monsieur, in his study!" Villefort pushed open the door.

"Doctor," cried Villefort, shutting the door behind him, "there is a curse on my house!"

"What!" cried d'Avrigny, outwardly calm though inwardly deeply moved. "Is there someone ill again?"

"Yes, Doctor," said Villefort, clutching at his hair.

D'Avrigny's look said: "I told you so," but his lips slowly articulated the words: "Who is dying in your house now? What new victim is going to accuse us of weakness before God?"

A painful sob broke from Villefort's lips. He went up to the doctor and, seizing his arm, said: "Valentine! It is Valentine's turn!"

"Your daughter!" cried the doctor with grief and surprise.

"You see you were mistaken," said the magistrate. "Come and see her on her bed of torture and ask her forgiveness for having harboured suspicion against her."

"Each time you have summoned me, it has been too late," said d'Avrigny. "No matter, I will come. But let us hasten. You have no time to lose in fighting against your enemies."

"Oh, this time you shall not reproach me with weakness, Doctor. This time I shall seek out the murderer and give him his desserts."

"Let us try to save the victim before thinking of vengeance," said d'Avrigny. The cabriolet which had brought Villefort took them both back at a gallop just as Morrel knocked at the Count of Monte Cristo's door.

The Count was in his study, and, with a worried look, was reading a note Bertuccio had just brought him. On hearing Morrel, who had left him barely two hours before, announced, he raised his head. Doubtless the last two hours had held much for him as well as for the Count, for, whereas he had left him with a smile on his face, he now returned with a troubled mien.

"What is the matter, Maximilian?" the Count asked. "You are quite white, and the perspiration is rolling down your forehead."

"I need your help, or rather, fool that I am, I thought you could help me where God alone can help!"

"In any case tell me what it is."

"I really do not know whether I should reveal this secret to any human ears, Count, but misfortune urges me to it, necessity constrains me to do so."

Morrel hesitated a moment.

"Do you believe in my affection for you?" said Monte Cristo, taking the young man's hands affectionately in his.

"There, you give me courage, and something tells me here"—Morrel laid his hand on his heart—"that I must withhold no secrets from you."

"You are right, Morrel. God speaks to your heart and your heart speaks to you. Tell me what it says."

"Count, will you allow me to send Baptistin to inquire after someone you know?"

"I have placed myself at your service and with me my servants."

"I could not live if I did not know she was better!"

Morrel went out, and, calling Baptistin, said a few words to him in a low voice, whereupon the valet ran to do the young man's errand.

"Well, have you sent him?" said Monte Cristo, when he made his appearance again.

"Yes, and I shall be a little calmer now."

"I am all attention," said the Count, smiling.

"Well, then, I will begin. One evening I was in a certain

garden. I was hidden behind a clump of trees so that no one was aware of my presence. Two people passed close to me—allow me to conceal their names for the present. They were talking in a low voice, but I was so interested in all they said that I did not lose a word of their conversation. Someone had just died in the house to which this garden belonged. One of the two persons thus conversing was the owner of the garden, the other was the doctor. The former was confiding his fears and troubles to the latter, for it was the second time in a month that death had dealt such a sudden and unexpected blow in this house."

"What reply did the doctor make?" asked Monte Cristo.

"He replied . . . he replied that it was not a natural death, and that it could only be attributed to . . ."

"To what?"

"To poison."

"Really!" said Monte Cristo with a slight cough, "did you really hear that?"

"Yes, I did, and the doctor added that if a similar case occurred again, he would be compelled to appeal to justice. Well, death knocked a third time, yet neither the master of the house nor the doctor said anything. In all probability it is going to knock for the fourth time. In what way do you think the possession of this secret obliges me to act?"

"My dear friend," said Monte Cristo, "you are telling me something that every one of us knows by heart. Look at me; I have not overheard any confidence, but I know it all as well as you do, and yet I have no scruples. If God's justice has fallen on this house, turn away your face, Maximilian, and let His hand hold sway. God has condemned them, and they must submit to their sentence. Three months ago it was Monsieur de Saint-Méran, two months ago it was Madame de Saint-Méran, to-day it is old Noirtier or young Valentine."

"You knew about it then?" cried Morrel in a paroxysm of terror that made Monte Cristo shudder. "You knew it and said nothing?"

"What is it to me?" replied Monte Cristo, shrugging his shoulders. "Do I know these people? Must I lose the one to save the other? Indeed not, for I have no preference between the guilty one and the victim."

"But I . . . I love her!" cried Morrel piteously.

"You love whom?" exclaimed Monte Cristo, jumping on to his feet and seizing Morrel's hands.

"I love her dearly, madly; I love her so much that I would shed all my blood to save her one tear. I love Valentine de Villefort, whom they are killing, do you hear? I love her, and I beseech you to tell me how I can save her."

Monte Cristo uttered a wild cry, which only those can conceive who have heard the roar of a wounded lion.

Never had Morrel beheld such an expression; never had such a dreadful eye flashed before his face, never had the genius of terror, which he had so often seen either on the field of battle or in the murder-infested nights of Algeria, shed round him such sinister fires! He shrunk back in terror. As for Monte Cristo, he closed his eyes for a moment after this outburst, and, during these few seconds, he restrained the tempestuous heaving of his breast as turbulent and foamy waves sink after a shower under the influence of the sun.

This silence and inward struggle lasted about twenty seconds, and then the Count raised his pale face.

"Behold, my dear friend, how God punishes the most boastful and unfeeling for their indifference in the face of terrible disasters," he said. "I looked on unmoved and curious. I watched this grim tragedy developing, and, like one of those fallen angels, laughed at the evil committed by men under the screen of secrecy. And now my turn has come, and I am bitten by the serpent whose tortuous course I have been watching—bitten to the core."

A groan escaped Morrel's lips.

"Come, come, lamenting will not help us. Be a man, be strong and full of hope, for I am here, I am watching over you. I tell you to hope! Know once and for all that I never lie and never make a mistake. It is but midday and you can be grateful, Morrel, that you have come to me now instead of this evening or to-morrow morning. Listen to what I am going to tell you. It is midday, and, if Valentine is not dead now, she will not die!"

"How can you say that when I left her dying!"

Monte Cristo pressed his hand to his forehead. What was passing through that mind heavy with terrible secrets? What was the angel of light, or the angel of darkness, saying to that implacable human mind? God alone knows.

Monte Cristo raised his head once more, and this time his face was as calm as that of a sleeping child.

"Maximilian, return quietly to your home," he said. "I command you to do nothing, to take no steps, to let no shadow of sorrow be seen on your face. I will send you tidings. Go!"

"Count, you frighten me with your calm. Have you any power over death? Are you more than man? Are you an angel?"

The young man who would shrink from no danger now shrank from Monte Cristo in unutterable terror. Monte Cristo only looked at him with a smile mingled with sadness which brought the tears to Morrel's eyes.

"I can do much, my friend," replied the Count. "Go, I need to be alone . . ."

Conquered by the prodigious ascendancy Monte Cristo exercised on all around him, Morrel did not even attempt to resist. He shook the Count's hand and went out, but waited at the door for Baptistin, whom he saw running toward him.

In the meantime Villefort and d'Avrigny had made all possible haste. When they returned Valentine was still unconscious, and the doctor examined her with the care called for by the circumstances and in the light of the secret he had discovered. Villefort awaited the result of the examination, watching every movement of the doctor's eyes and lips. Noirtier, more eager for a verdict than Villefort himself, was also waiting, and all in him became alert and sensitive.

At last d'Avrigny slowly said: "She still lives!"

"Still!" cried Villefort. "Oh, Doctor, what a terrible word."

"Yes," said the doctor. "I repeat my words; she is still living, and I am surprised to find it is so."

"She is saved?" asked the father.

"Since she still lives, she is."

At this moment d'Avrigny met Noirtier's eyes, which sparkled with such extraordinary joy that he was startled and stood for a moment motionless, looking at the old man, who, on his part, seemed to anticipate and commend all he did.

The doctor laid the girl back on her chair; her lips were so pale and bloodless that they were scarcely outlined against the rest of her pallid face.

"Call Mademoiselle de Villefort's maid, if you please," he said to Villefort.

Villefort left his daughter's side and himself went in search of the maid. Directly the door was shut behind him, the doctor approached Noirtier.

"You have something to say to me?" he asked.

The old man blinked expressively.

"To me alone?"

"Yes."

"Very well, I will stay with you."

Villefort returned, followed by the maid, and after them came Mme de Villefort.

"What ails the dear child?" she exclaimed with tears in her eyes, and affecting every proof of maternal love as she went up to Valentine and took her hand.

D'Avrigny continued to watch Noirtier; he saw the eyes of the old man dilate and grow large, his cheeks turn pale, and the perspiration break out on his forehead.

"Ah," said he involuntarily as he followed the direction of Noirtier's eyes and fixed his own gaze on Mme de Villefort, who said: "The poor child would be better in bed. Come and help me, Fanny."

M. d'Avrigny saw an opportunity of being alone with M.
Noirtier and nodded his assent, but forbade anyone to give
her to eat or drink except what he prescribed. Valentine had
returned to consciousness, but her whole frame was so shattered by the attack that she was unable to move and scarcely
able to speak. She had the strength, however, to throw a
farewell glance to her grandfather, and it seemed almost as
though in carrying her away, they were taking away part of
himself. D'Avrigny followed the invalid, wrote his prescriptions, and told Villefort to take a cab and go himself to the
chemist's, have the prescriptions made up before his eyes,
and wait for him in the girl's room. After renewing his
instructions that Valentine was not to partake of anything,
he returned to Noirtier and carefully closed the doors.
Ascertaining that no one was listening, he said: "Come now,
you know something about your granddaughter's illness."

"Yes," motioned the old man.

"We have no time to lose. I will question you, and you
will answer."

Noirtier made a sign that he agreed.

"Did you anticipate the accident that has occurred to
Valentine to-day?"

"Yes."

D'Avrigny thought for a moment, then, drawing closer to
Noirtier, said: "Forgive me what I am going to say, but no
stone must be left unturned in this terrible predicament.
You saw Barrois die. Do you know what he died of?"

"Yes," was the reply.

"Do you think he died a natural death?"

Something like a smile showed itself on Noirtier's
immovable lips.

"Then the idea occurred to you that Barrois had been
poisoned?"

"Yes."

"Do you think the poison was intended for him?"

"No."

"Now do you think that the same hand that struck

Barrois in mistake for someone else has to-day struck Valentine?"

"Yes."

"Then she will also succumb to it?" d'Avrigny asked, looking attentively at Noirtier to mark the effect these words would have on him.

"No," he replied with an air of triumph which would have bewildered the cleverest of diviners.

"You hope, then? What do you hope?" said the doctor with surprise.

The old man gave him to understand that he could not answer.

"Ah, yes, it is true," murmured d'Avrigny, and turning to Noirtier again: "You hope that the murderer will grow weary of his attempts?"

"No."

"Then do you hope that the poison will not take effect on Valentine?"

"Yes."

"Then in what way do you think Valentine will escape?"

Noirtier fixed his gaze obstinately on one spot; d'Avrigny followed the direction of his eyes and saw that they were fixed on a bottle containing his medicine.

"Ha, ha," said d'Avrigny, struck by a sudden thought. "You conceived the idea of preparing her system against this poison?"

"Yes."

"By accustoming her to it little by little?"

"Yes, yes, yes!" replied Noirtier, delighted at being understood.

"In fact, you heard me say there was brucine in your medicine, and wished to neutralize the effects of the poison by getting her system accustomed to it?"

Noirtier showed the same triumphant joy.

"And you have achieved it too!" exclaimed the doctor. "Without this precaution Valentine would have died this day, and no one could have helped her. As it is her system has suffered a violent shock, but this time, at any rate, she will not die."

A supernatural joy shone in the old man's eyes as he raised them to Heaven with an expression of infinite gratitude. Just then Villefort returned.

"Here is what you asked for, Doctor," said he.

"Was this medicine made up before you? It has not left your hands?"

"Just so."

D'Avrigny took the bottle, poured a few drops of its contents into the palm of his hand, and swallowed them.

"It is all right," said he. "Now let us go to Valentine. I shall give my instructions to every one, and you must see that no one disregards them."

At the time that d'Avrigny returned to Valentine's room, accompanied by Villefort, an Italian priest, with dignified gait and a calm but decided manner, rented for his use the house adjoining that inhabited by M. de Villefort. It is not known what was done to induce the former occupiers to move out of it, but it was reported that the foundations were unsafe; however, this did not prevent the new tenant from moving in with his humble furniture at about five o'clock in the afternoon of the same day. The new tenant's name was Signer Giacomo Busoni.

Workmen were summoned at once, and the same night the few passers-by were astonished to find carpenters and masons at work repairing the foundations of this tottering house.

Chapter LXI

THE SECRET DOOR

Valentine was confined to her bed; she was very weak and completely exhausted by the severe attack. During the night her sick brain wove vague and strange ideas and fleeting phantoms, while confused forms passed before her eyes, but in the day-time she was brought back to normal reality by her grandfather's presence. The old man had himself carried into his granddaughter's room every morning and watched over her with paternal care. Villefort would spend an hour or two with his father and child when he returned from the Law Courts. At six o'clock Villefort retired to his study, and at eight o'clock Monsieur d'Avrigny arrived, bringing with him the night draught for his young patient. Then Noirtier was taken back to his room, and a nurse, of the doctor's choice, succeeded them. She did not leave the bedside until ten or eleven o'clock, when Valentine had dropped off to sleep, and gave the keys of the room to M. de Villefort, so that no one could enter the room except through that occupied by Mme de Villefort and little Edward.

Morrel called on Noirtier every morning for news of Valentine, and, extraordinary as it seemed, each day found him less anxious. For one thing, though she showed signs of great nervous excitement, Valentine's improvement was more marked each day; then, again, had not Monte Cristo already told him that if she was not dead in two hours, she would be saved? Four days had elapsed, and she still lived!

The nervous excitement we mentioned even pursued Valentine in her sleep, or rather in that state of somnolence which succeeded her waking hours. It was in the silence of the night, when the darkness of the room was relieved by a night-light burning in its alabaster receptacle on the chimney-piece, that she saw the shadows pass which come to the rooms of the sick, fanning their fever with their quivering wings. At one time she would see her stepmother threatening her, at another time Morrel was holding his arms out to her, or again she was visited by beings who were almost strangers to her, such as the Count of Monte Cristo; during these moments of delirium even the furniture appeared to become animated. This lasted until about two or three o'clock, when she fell into a deep sleep from which she did not wake until the morning.

One evening after Villefort, d'Avrigny, and Noirtier had successively left her room, and the nurse, after placing within her reach the draught the doctor had prepared for her, had also retired, carefully locking the door after her, an unexpected incident occurred.

Ten minutes had elapsed since the nurse left. For the past hour Valentine had been a prey to the fever which returned every night, and she gave herself up to the active and monotonous workings of her unruly brain, which repeatedly reproduced the same thoughts and conjured up the same images. The night-light threw out countless rays, each one assuming some weird shape. All at once Valentine dimly saw the door of the library, which was beside the fireplace in a hollow of the wall, slowly open without making the least sound. At any other time she would have seized the bell-pull to call for help, but nothing astonished her in her present state. She was aware that all the visions that surrounded her were the children of her delirium, for in the morning there was no trace of all these phantoms of the night.

A human figure emerged from behind the door. Valentine had become too familiar with such apparitions to be alarmed; she simply stared, hoping to see Morrel. The figure continued to approach her bed, then it stopped and appeared to listen with great attention. Just then a reflection from the night-light played on the face of her nocturnal visitor. "It is not he," she murmured, and waited, convinced that she was dreaming and that the man would disappear or turn into some other person. She noticed the rapid beating of her pulse, and remembered that the best means of dispelling these importunate visions was to take a drink of the draught which had been prescribed by the doctor to calm these agitations. It was so refreshing that, while allaying the fever, it seemed to cause a reaction of the brain and for a moment she suffered less. She, therefore, reached out her hand for the glass, but as she did so the apparition made two big strides to her bed and came so close to her that she thought she heard his breathing and felt the pressure of his hand. This time the illusion, or rather the reality, surpassed anything she had yet experienced. She began to believe herself fully awake and alive, and the knowledge that she was in full possession of her senses made her shudder.

Then the figure, from whom she could not divert her eyes and who appeared desirous of protecting rather than threatening her, took the glass, went over to the light, and looked at the draught as though wishing to test its transparency and purity. But this elementary test did not satisfy him, and the man, or rather phantom, for he trod so gently that the carpet deadened the sound of his steps, took a spoonful of the beverage and swallowed it. Valentine watched all this with a feeling of stupefaction. She felt that it must all disappear to give place to another picture, but, instead of vanishing like a shadow, the man came alongside the bed, and, holding the glass to her, he said in an agitated voice: "Now drink!"

Valentine started. It was the first time any of her visions

had spoken to her in a living voice. She opened her mouth to scream: the man put his finger to his lips.

"The Count of Monte Cristo!" she murmured.

"Do not call anyone and do not be alarmed," said the Count. "You need not have the slightest shadow of suspicion or uneasiness in your mind. The man you see before you (for you are right this time, Valentine, it is not an illusion) is as tender a father and as respectful a friend as could ever appear to you in your dreams. Listen to me," he went on, "or rather, look at me. Do you see my red-rimmed eyes and my pale face, paler than usual? That is because I have not closed my eyes for an instant during the last four nights; for the last four nights have I been watching over you to protect and preserve you for our friend Maximilian."

The sick girl's cheeks flushed with joy. "Maximilian," she repeated, for the sound of the name was very sweet to her. "Maximilian! He has told you all then!"

"Everything. He has told me that you are his, and I have promised him that you shall live."

"You have promised him that I shall live? Are you a doctor then?"

"Yes, and believe me, the best one Heaven could send just now."

"You say you have been watching over me?" Valentine asked uneasily. "Where? I have not seen you."

"I have been hidden behind that door," he said. "It leads to an adjoining house which I have rented."

Valentine bashfully turned her eyes away and said with some indignation: "I think you have been guilty of an unparalleled indiscretion, and what you call protection I look upon as an insult."

"Valentine, during this long vigil over you," the Count said, "all that I have seen has been what people have come to visit you, what food was prepared for you, and what was given you to drink. When I thought there was danger in the drink served to you, I entered as I have done now and emptied your glass, substituting a health-giving potion for the poison. Instead of producing death, as was intended, this drink made the blood circulate in your veins."

"Poison! Death!" cried Valentine, believing that she was again under the influence of some feverish hallucination. "What is that you say?"

"Hush, my child," said Monte Cristo, placing his finger to his lips. "I said poison and I also said death, but drink this." The Count took from his pocket a phial containing a red liquid, of which he poured a few drops into a glass. "When you have drunk that, take nothing more to-night."

Valentine put out her hand but immediately drew it back in fear. Monte Cristo took the glass, drank half of its contents, and handed it back to Valentine, who smiled at him and swallowed the rest.

"Oh, yes," said she, "I recognize the flavour of my nightly drinks—the liquid which refreshed and calmed me. Thank you."

"This has saved your life during the last four nights, Valentine," said the Count. "But how have I lived? Oh, the horrible nights I have gone through! The terrible tortures I have suffered when I saw the deadly poison poured into your glass and feared you would drink it before I could pour it away!"

"You say you suffered tortures when you saw the deadly poison poured into my glass?" replied Valentine, terror-stricken. "If you saw the poison poured into my glass, you must have seen the person who poured it?"

"Yes, I did."

Valentine sat up, pulling over her snow-white bosom the embroidered sheet still moist with the dews of fever, to which were now added those of terror.

"Oh, horrible! You are trying to make me believe that something diabolical is taking place; that they are continuing their attempts to murder me in my father's house; on my bed of sickness even! Oh, no, it cannot be, it is impossible!"

"Are you the first one this hand has struck, Valentine? Have you not seen Monsieur de Saint-Méran, Madame de

Saint-Méran, and Barrois fall under this blow? Would not
Monsieur Noirtier have been another victim but for the
treatment they have been giving him for nearly three years
which has accustomed his system to this poison?"

"Then that is why Grandpapa has been making me share
all his beverages for the past month?"

"Had they a bitter flavour, like half-dried orange-peel?"

"Oh, yes, they had."

"That explains all," said Monte Cristo. "He also knows
there is someone administering poison here, perhaps he
even knows who the person is. He has been protecting you,
his beloved child, against this evil. That is why you are still
alive after having partaken of this poison, which is as a rule
unmerciful."

"But who is this . . . this murderer?"

"Have you never seen anyone enter your room at night?"

"Indeed I have. I have frequently seen shadows pass
close to me and then disappear, and even when you came in
just now I believed for a long time that I was either delirious
or dreaming."

"Then you do not know who is aiming at your life?"

"No. Why should anyone desire my death?"

"You will see this person," said Monte Cristo, listening.

"How?" asked Valentine, looking round her in terror.

"Because you are not delirious or feverish to-night, you
are wide awake. Midnight is just striking; this is the hour
murderers choose. Summon all your courage to your assistance; still the beatings of your heart; let no sound escape
your lips, feign sleep, and you will see, you will see!"

Valentine seized the Count's hand. "I hear a noise," said
she. "Go quickly."

"Au revoir," replied the Count, as with a sad smile he tiptoed to the door of the library. Before closing the door, he
turned round once more and said: "Not a movement, not a
word, pretend you are asleep." With this fearful injunction,
the Count disappeared behind the door, which he closed
noiselessly after him.

Chapter LXII

THE APPARITION AGAIN

✦

Valentine was alone. Except for the rumbling of distant carriages, all was still. Valentine's attention was concentrated on the clock in the room, which marked the seconds, and noticed that they were twice as slow as the beating of her heart. Yet she was in a maze of doubt. She, who never did harm to anyone, could not imagine that anyone should desire her death. Why? To what purpose? What harm had she done that she should have an enemy? There was no fear of her falling asleep. A terrible thought kept her mind alert: there existed a person in the world who had attempted to murder her, and was going to make another attempt. What if the Count had not the time to run to her help! What if her last moment were approaching, and she would see Morrel no more!

This train of thought nearly compelled her to ring the bell for help, but she fancied she saw the Count's eye peering through the door, and at the thought of it her mind was overwhelmed with such shame that she did not know whether her feeling of gratitude toward him could be large enough to efface the painful effect of his indiscreet attention.

Thirty minutes, which seemed like an eternity, passed thus, and at length the clock struck the half-hour; at the

same moment a slight scratching of fingernails on the door
of the library apprised Valentine that the Count was still
watching.

Then Valentine seemed to hear the floor creaking on the
opposite side, that is to say, in Edward's room. She listened
with bated breath; the latch grated, and the door swung on
its hinges. Valentine had raised herself up on her elbow, and
she only just had time to lay herself down again and cover
her eyes with her arms. Then trembling, agitated, and her
heart heavy with indescribable terror, she waited.

Someone approached her bed and touched the curtains.
Valentine summoned all her strength and breathed with the
regular respiration which proclaims tranquil sleep.

"Valentine," said a low voice.

A shudder went through the girl's whole frame, but she
made no reply.

"Valentine," the same voice repeated.

The same silence: Valentine had promised not to waken.
Then all was still except for the almost noiseless sound of
liquid being poured into the tumbler she had just emptied.
Then from the vantage ground of her arm she risked opening her eyes a little and saw a woman in a white dressing-
gown emptying some liquid from a phial into her tumbler.
Perhaps Valentine held her breath for an instant, or made a
slight movement, for the woman became uneasy, paused in
her devilish work, and leaned over the bed to see if
Valentine was really asleep. It was Mme de Villefort!

When Valentine recognized her stepmother she trembled so violently that the whole bed shook. Mme de
Villefort instantly stepped back close to the wall, and from
there, herself hidden behind the bed-hangings, watched
attentively and silently for the slightest movement on
Valentine's part. Summoning all her will power to her assistance, the sick girl forced herself to close her eyes, but so
strong was the feeling of curiosity which prompted her to
keep her eyes open and learn the truth that this function of
the most delicate of our organs, which is generally such a

simple action, became almost impossible of achievement at that moment.

However, hearing Valentine's even breathing once more and reassured thereby that she was asleep, Mme de Villefort stretched out her arm once more, and, hidden as she was behind the curtains at the head of the bed, emptied the contents of the phial into Valentine's tumbler. Then she withdrew, but so quietly that not the least sound told Valentine that she was gone.

It is impossible to describe what Valentine went through during the minute and a half that Mme de Villefort was in the room. The scratching of the fingernails on the library door roused the poor girl from the stupor into which she had fallen, and she raised her head with an effort. The door noiselessly turned on its hinges, and the Count of Monte Cristo appeared again.

"Well," he asked, "do you still doubt?"

"Alas!"

"Did you recognize her?"

Valentine groaned as she answered: "I did, but I still cannot believe it! What am I to do? Can I not leave the house? . . . Can I not escape?"

"Valentine, the hand that pursues you now will follow you everywhere; your servants will be seduced with gold, and death will face you disguised in every shape and form; in the water you drink from the well, in the fruit you pluck from the tree."

"But did you not say my grandfather's precautions had made me immune from poisoning?"

"From one kind of poisoning, but, even then, not large doses. The poison will be changed or the dose increased."

He took the tumbler and put his lips to it.

"You see, it has already been done. She is no longer trying to poison you with brucine but with a simple narcotic. I can recognize the taste of the alcohol in which it has been dissolved. If you had drunk what Mme de Villefort has just poured into this tumbler, you would have been lost."

"Oh, dear!" cried the young girl. "Why does she pursue me thus? I cannot understand. I have never done her any harm!"

"But you are rich, Valentine; you have an income of two hundred thousand francs; what is more, you are keeping her son from getting this money."

"Edward? Poor child! Is it for his sake that all these crimes are committed?"

"Ah, you understand at last."

"Heaven grant that he may not suffer for this!"

"You are an angel, Valentine."

"But why is my grandfather allowed to live?"

"Because she thought that once you were dead, the money would naturally revert to your brother; unless, of course, he were disinherited, and that after all it would be running a useless risk to commit this crime."

"Has such a plan really been conceived in the mind of a woman? 'Tis too horrible!"

"Do you remember the vine arbour of the Hôtel de la Poste at Perugia and the man in the brown mantle whom your mother questioned about *aqua tofana*? Well, this infernal plan has been maturing in her brain ever since that period!"

"Then if it is so, I see that I am doomed to die!" cried the girl, bursting into tears.

"No, Valentine, for I have foreseen all her plots, and so your enemy is beaten. You will live, Valentine, you will live to love and be loved; you will live to be happy and make a noble heart happy. But to attain this, you must have confidence in me. You must take blindly what I give you. You must trust no one, not even your father."

"My father is not a party to this frightful plot, is he?" cried Valentine, wringing her hands.

"No, and yet your father, who is accustomed to juridical accusations, must know that all these people who have died in your house have not died natural deaths. Your father should have watched over you; he should be where I am now; he should have emptied this tumbler, and he should have risen up against this murderer."

"I shall do all I can to live, for there are two persons in the world who love me so much that my death would mean their death—my grandfather and Maximilian."

"I shall watch over them as I have watched over you," said Monte Cristo. Then he went on: "Whatever happens to you, Valentine, do not be alarmed. Though you suffer and lose your sight and hearing, do not be afraid; though you awaken and know not where you are, fear not; even though on awakening you find yourself in some sepulchral vault or coffin, collect your thoughts quickly and say to yourself: 'At this moment a friend is watching over me, a father, a man who desires our happiness, mine and Maximilian's.' "

"Alas! alas! To think that I have to go through all that!"

"Valentine, would you prefer to denounce your step-mother?"

"I would sooner die a hundred times."

"No, you shall not die, but promise me that whatever happens, you will not complain or lose hope?"

"I shall think of Maximilian."

"You are my darling child, Valentine! I alone can save you, and save you I will! My daughter, believe in my devotion to you, as you believe in the goodness of God and in Maximilian's love for you," said the Count with an affectionate smile.

Valentine gave him a grateful look and became submissive as a little child. Then the Count took from his waistcoat pocket the little emerald box, and, taking off the lid, put into Valentine's right hand a pill about the size of a pea. Valentine took it into her other hand and looked earnestly at the Count. There was a look of grandeur almost divine in the features of her sure protector. He answered her mute inquiry with a nod of assent.

She placed the pill in her mouth and swallowed it.

"Now good-bye, my child," said he. "I shall try to gain a little sleep, for you are saved!"

Monte Cristo looked long at the dear child as she gradually dropped off to sleep, overcome by the powerful narcotic he had given her. Taking the tumbler, he emptied three-quarters of its contents into the fireplace, so that it might be believed Valentine had drunk it, and replaced it on the table. Then, regaining the door of his retreat he disappeared after casting one more look on Valentine, who was sleeping with the confidence and innocence of an angel at the feet of the Lord.

Chapter LXIII

THE SERPENT

The night-light continued to burn on the mantelpiece; all noise in the streets had ceased and the silence of the room was oppressive. The door of Edward's room opened, and a head we have already seen appeared in the mirror opposite: it was Mme de Villefort, who had come to see the effects of her draught. She paused on the threshold and listened; then she slowly approached the night-table to see whether Valentine's tumbler was empty.

It was still a quarter full, as we know. Mme de Villefort took it and emptied the rest of the draught on to the embers, which she disturbed to facilitate the absorption of the liquid; then she carefully washed the tumbler, and drying it with her handkerchief, placed it on the table. Anyone looking into the room at that moment would have observed Mme de Villefort's reluctance to turn her eyes toward Valentine, or to go up to the bed. The dim light, the silence, and the heaviness of the night no doubt combined with the frightful heaviness of her conscience; the poisoner stood in fear of her work!

At length she gained courage, drew aside the curtain, and, leaning over the head of the bed, looked at Valentine. The girl breathed no more; her white lips had ceased to quiver, her eyes appeared to float in a bluish vapour, and her long black eyelashes veiled a cheek as white as wax. Mme de Villefort contemplated this face with an expression eloquent in its impassivity. Lowering the quilt, she ventured to place her hand on the young girl's heart. It was still and cold. The only pulsation she felt was that in her own hand. She withdrew her hand with a shudder.

One of Valentine's arms was hanging out of bed. It was a beautiful arm, but the forearm was slightly contorted, and the delicately shaped wrist was resting with fingers outspread on the mahogany woodwork of the bed. The nails were turning blue. Mme de Villefort could not doubt that all was over. This terrible work was done; the poisoner had nothing more to do in the room. She retired with great precaution, fearing even to hear the sound of her own footsteps.

The hours passed, until a wan light began to filter through the blinds. It gradually grew brighter and brighter, till at length every object in the room was distinguishable. About this time the nurse's cough was heard on the staircase, and she entered the room with a cup in her hand.

One glance would have sufficed to convince a father or a lover that Valentine was dead, but this mercenary woman thought she slept.

"That is good," she said, going up to the night-table; "she has drunk some of her draught, the tumbler is three-quarters empty." Then she went to the fireplace, rekindled the fire, made herself comfortable in an armchair, and, though she had but just left her bed, took advantage of the opportunity to snatch a few minutes' sleep.

She was awakened by the clock striking eight. Astonished to find the girl still asleep, and alarmed at seeing her arm still hanging out of bed, she drew nearer. It was not until then that she noticed the cold lips and still bosom. She tried to place the arm alongside the body, and its terrible stiffness could not deceive a nurse. With a horrified scream, she rushed to the door, crying out: "Help! help!"

"Help? For whom?" asked the doctor from the bottom of the stairs, it being the hour he usually called.

"What is the matter?" cried Villefort, rushing out of his room. "Do you not hear the cry for help, Doctor?"

"Yes, let us go quickly to Valentine," replied d'Avrigny.

But before the father and doctor could reach the room, all the servants who were on the same story had rushed in, and, seeing Valentine pale and motionless on the bed, raised their hands heavenward and stood rooted to the spot with terror.

"Call Mme de Villefort! Wake Mme de Villefort!" shouted the Procureur du Roi from the door, for he seemed almost afraid to enter the room. But, instead of obeying, the servants simply stared at d'Avrigny, who had run to Valentine and taken her in his arms.

"This one too!" he murmured, letting her fall back on to the pillow again. "My God! My God! When will it cease!"

Villefort rushed in. "What do you say, Doctor?" he called out. "Oh, Doctor . . . Doctor . . ."

"I say that Valentine is dead!" replied d'Avrigny in a voice that was terrible in its gravity.

M. de Villefort staggered as though his legs had given way under him, and he fell with his head on Valentine's bed.

On hearing the doctor's words and the father's cries, the servants fled terrified, muttering imprecations as they went. They were heard running down the stairs and the passages, there was a great stir in the courtyards, and all was silence again. The servants had, one and all, deserted the accursed house!

Just then Mme de Villefort, with her dressing-gown half on, appeared. For a moment she stood on the threshold and seemed to be interrogating those present, at the same time endeavouring to summon up a few rebellious tears. Suddenly she stepped, or rather bounded, toward the table, with outstretched hands. She had seen d'Avrigny bend curiously over the table and take the tumbler she was sure she had emptied during the night. The tumbler was one-quarter full, just as it had been when she threw its contents on to the embers. Had Valentine's ghost suddenly confronted her, she would not have been more alarmed. The liquid was actually of the same colour as that which she had poured into the tumbler and which the girl had drunk; it was certainly the poison, and it could not deceive M. d'Avrigny, who was now examining it closely. It must have been a miracle worked by the Almighty that, notwithstanding all her precautions, there should be some trace left, some proof to denounce the crime.

While Mme de Villefort remained as though rooted to the spot, looking like a statue of terror, and Villefort lay with his head hidden in the bedclothes oblivious to everything, d'Avrigny went to the window in order to examine more closely the contents of the tumbler. Dipping his finger into it, he tasted it.

"Ah!" he murmured, "it is no longer brucine, let me see what it is!"

He went to one of the cupboards, which was used as a medicine-chest, and, taking some nitric acid, poured a few drops into the liquid, which instantly turned blood-red.

"Ah!" said d'Avrigny in a tone which combined the horror of a judge to whom the truth has been revealed and the joy of the student who has solved a problem.

For an instant Mme de Villefort was beside herself; her eyes flared up and then dulled again; she staggered toward the door and disappeared. An instant later the distant thud was heard of a body falling. Nobody paid any attention to it, however. The nurse was intent on watching the chemical analysis, and Villefort was still prostrate. Only M. d'Avrigny had watched her and had noticed her departure. He raised the door-curtain, and, looking through Edward's room, perceived her stretched unconscious on the floor of her own room.

"Go and attend to Madame de Villefort, she is not well," he said to the nurse.

"But Mademoiselle de Villefort?" stammered the nurse.

"Mademoiselle de Villefort has no further need of help: she is dead!"

"Dead! dead!" moaned Villefort in a paroxysm of grief which the novelty of such a feeling in this heart of stone made all the more terrible.

"Dead, did you say?" cried a third voice. "Who says that Valentine is dead?"

The two men turned round and perceived Morrel standing at the door, pale and terrible in his grief.

This is what had happened. Morrel had called at his usual hour to obtain tidings of Valentine. Contrary to custom, he found the side door open, and, having no occasion to ring, entered. He waited in the hall for a moment, calling a servant to announce him to M. de Noirtier, but there was no answer, for, as we know, the servants had all fled. Morrel had no particular reason for anxiety that day; he had Monte Cristo's promise that Valentine should live, and so far this promise had held good. The Count had given him a good report each evening which was confirmed by Noirtier the next day. There was something strange about this silence, however; he called a second and a third time, but still there was no sound. In a turmoil of doubt and fear he flew up the stairs and through several deserted rooms until he reached Valentine's chamber. The door was open, and the first sound he heard was a sob. As through a mist, he saw a black figure on his knees and lost in a mass of white drapery. Fear, a terrible fear, rooted him to the spot.

It was at this moment that he heard a voice say: "She is dead!" and a second voice repeat like an echo: "Dead! dead!"

Chapter LXIV

MAXIMILIAN

Villefort rose, almost ashamed at being surprised in such a paroxysm of grief. The terrible office he had held for twenty-five years had placed him far outside the range of any human feeling. He looked at Morrel in a half-dazed manner.

"Who are you," said he, "that you are unaware that one does not enter a house where death reigns? Go, go!"

Morrel stood still; he could not take his eyes from the disordered bed and the pale figure lying on it.

"Do you hear me, go!" cried Villefort, while d'Avrigny advanced toward Morrel to persuade him to leave.

Dazed, the young man looked at the corpse, the two men, and the room; then he hesitated for a moment and opened his mouth to reply, but could not give utterance to any of the thoughts that crowded in his brain; he thrust his hand in his hair and turned on his heels. D'Avrigny and Villefort, distracted for a moment from their morbid thoughts, looked at one another as though to say: "He is mad."

But in less than five minutes they heard the stairs creaking under a heavy weight and perceived Morrel carrying Noirtier in his chair up the stairs with almost superhuman strength. Arrived at the top, Morrel set the chair down and wheeled it rapidly into Valentine's room. Noirtier's face was dreadful to behold as Morrel pushed him toward the bed: all the resources at the disposal of his intelligence were displayed therein, and all his power was concentrated in his eyes, which had to do duty for the other faculties. This pale face with its glaring eyes seemed to Villefort like a terrible apparition. Every time he had come in contact with his father something disastrous had happened.

"Look what they have done!" cried Morrel, resting one hand on the arm of the chair he had just wheeled up to the bedside, and with the other one pointing to Valentine. "Look, Father, look!"

Villefort started back and looked with amazement on this young man, almost unknown to him, who called M. Noirtier Father.

In response to Morrel's words, the old man's whole soul seemed to show itself in his eyes, which became bloodshot; the veins of his throat swelled, and his neck, cheeks, and temples assumed a bluish hue. Nothing, indeed, was needed to put the finishing touch to this internal ebullition[1] in his whole being but the utterance of a cry. And in truth a mute cry issued from him, if we may use the expression, which was terrifying and heartrending because of its very silence. D'Avrigny rushed up to the old man and made him inhale a strong restorative.

"They ask me who I am, monsieur, and what right I have to be here!" cried Morrel, seizing the inert hand of the paralytic. "Oh, you know! Tell them! Tell them!" And the young man's voice was choked with sobs. "Tell them that I was betrothed to her; tell them she was my darling, the only one I love on earth." And looking like the personification of broken strength, he fell heavily on his knees before the bed which his hands grasped convulsively. His grief was such that d'Avrigny turned his head away to hide his emotion, and Villefort, attracted by the magnetism which draws us toward such as have loved those we mourn, gave his hand to the young man without asking any further explanations.

For some time nothing was heard in the room but sobs, imprecations, and prayers. Yet one sound gained the mastery over all the rest; it was the harsh and heartrending breathing of Noirtier. With each intake it seemed as though his very lungs must burst asunder. At length Villefort, who had, so to say, yielded his place to Morrel and was now the most composed of them all, said to Maximilian: "You say that you loved Valentine and that you were betrothed to her. I was unaware of your love for her, as also of your engagement. Yet I, her father, forgive you, for I see that your grief is deep and true. Besides, my own grief is too great for anger to find a place in my heart. But, as you see, the angel you hoped to possess has left us. Take your farewell of her sad remains: Valentine has now no further need of anyone but the priest and the doctor."

"You are mistaken, monsieur," cried Morrel, rising on to one knee, and his heart was pierced with a pang sharper than any he had yet felt. "You are quite wrong. Valentine, as I judge from the manner of her death, not only needs a priest but also an avenger. Send for the priest, Monsieur de Villefort; I will be her avenger!"

"What do you mean, monsieur?" murmured Villefort, trembling before this new idea of Morrel's.

"What I mean is that there are two personalities in you: the father has done enough weeping, it is now time that the magistrate bethought him of his duty."

Noirtier's eyes gleamed, and d'Avrigny drew nearer.

"I know what I am saying," continued Morrel, reading the thoughts that were revealed on the faces of those present, "and you all know as well as I do what I am going to say. Valentine has been murdered!"

Villefort hung his head; d'Avrigny advanced a step farther, and Noirtier made a sign of assent.

"You know, monsieur," continued Morrel, "that nowadays a girl does not suddenly disappear without inquiries being made as to her disappearance, even though she be not so young, beautiful, and adorable as Valentine was.

Show no mercy, Monsieur le Procureur!" he cried with increasing vehemence. "I denounce the crime; it is now your duty to find the murderer."

"You are mistaken, monsieur," replied Villefort. "No crimes are committed in my house. Fate is against me, God is trying me. It is a horrible thought, but no one has been murdered."

"I tell you that murder has been committed here!" cried the young man, lowering his voice but speaking in a very decided tone. "This is the fourth victim during the past four months. I declare that they attempted to poison Valentine four days ago but failed owing to Monsieur Noirtier's precautions. I declare that the dose has now been doubled or else the poison changed, so that their dastardly work has succeeded. You know all this as well as I do, for this gentleman warned you, both as a friend and a doctor."

"You are raving, monsieur," said Villefort, vainly endeavouring to escape from the trap into which he felt he had fallen.

"I raving!" cried Morrel. "Well, then, I appeal to Monsieur d'Avrigny himself. Ask him, Doctor, whether he remembers his words to you in your garden on the evening of Madame de Saint-Méran's death when you and he thought you were alone! You were conversing about her tragic death, and, as now, you unjustly blamed fate, but the only blame that can attach to fate is that by her decree the murderer was created who has poisoned Valentine. Yes, yes," he continued, "recall those words that you thought were spoken in silence and solitude, whereas every one of them fell on my ear. On seeing Monsieur de Villefort's culpable indifference toward his relatives that evening, I certainly ought to have revealed everything to the authorities. Then I should not have been an accomplice to your death, Valentine, my darling Valentine! But the accomplice shall become the avenger. I swear to you, Valentine, that if your father forsakes you, I, yes I, shall pursue the murderer!"

And then it was d'Avrigny's turn.

"I too join Monsieur Morrel in demanding justice for the crime," said he. "My blood boils at the thought that my cowardly indifference has encouraged the murderer."

"Have mercy! Oh, my God, have mercy!" murmured Villefort, beside himself.

Morrel raised his head, and, seeing that Noirtier's eyes were shining with an almost supernatural light, he said: "Wait a moment, Monsieur Noirtier wishes to speak. Do you know the murderer?" he continued, turning to the old man.

"Yes," replied Noirtier.

"And you will help us to find him?" cried the young man. "Listen, Monsieur d'Avrigny, listen!"

Noirtier threw the unhappy Morrel a sad smile, one of those smiles expressed in his eyes which had so often made Valentine happy, and demanded his attention. Then having, so to say, riveted his questioner's eyes on his own, he looked toward the door.

"Do you wish me to leave the room?" asked Morrel sadly.

"Yes," looked Noirtier.

"Alas! Alas! Have pity on me!"

The old man's eyes remained relentlessly fixed on the door.

"May I at least come back again?"

"Yes."

"Am I to go alone?"

"No."

"Whom shall I take with me? The doctor?"

"Yes."

"But will Monsieur de Villefort understand you?"

"Yes."

"Have no fear, I understand my father very well," said Villefort, overjoyed that the inquiries between him and his father were to be made privately.

D'Avrigny took the young man's arm and led him into the adjoining room. At length, after a quarter of an hour had elapsed, a faltering footstep was heard, and Villefort appeared on the threshold. "Come," said he, leading them back to Noirtier.

Morrel looked fixedly at Villefort. His face was livid; large drops of perspiration rolled down his face; between his teeth was a pen twisted out of shape and bitten to half its natural length.

"Messieurs," said he in a voice choked with emotion, turning to d'Avrigny and Morrel. "Give me your word of honour that this terrible secret shall remain buried for ever amongst ourselves."

The two men stirred uneasily.

"I entreat you! . . ." continued Villefort.

"But the culprit! . . . the murderer! . . ." cried Morrel.

"Fear not, justice shall be done," said Villefort. "My father has revealed to me the name of the culprit, and, though he is as anxious for revenge as you are, he entreats you even as I do to keep the crime a secret. Oh! if my father makes this request, it is only because he knows that Valentine will be terribly avenged. He knows me, and I have given him my word. I only ask three days. Within three days the vengeance I shall have taken for the murder of my child will be such as to make the most indifferent of men shudder." As he said these words, he ground his teeth and grasped the lifeless hand of his old father.

"Will this promise be fulfilled, Monsieur Noirtier?" Morrel asked, while d'Avrigny questioned him with his eyes.

"Yes," signalled Noirtier with a look of sinister joy.

"Then swear," said Villefort, joining d'Avrigny's and Morrel's hands, "swear that you will spare the honour of my house and leave it to me to avenge my child!"

D'Avrigny turned round and gave a faint "Yes" in reply, but Morrel pulled his hand away and rushed toward the bed. Pressing his lips to Valentine's mouth, he fled out of the room with a long groan of despair.

As we have said, all the servants had disappeared. M. de Villefort was therefore obliged to request M. d'Avrigny to take charge of the numerous arrangements consequent upon a death, above all upon a death of such a suspicious nature. This he consented to do, and went in search of the official registrar.

The registrar duly gave the death certificate without having the least suspicion of the real cause of death, and, when he had gone, d'Avrigny asked Villefort whether he desired any particular priest to pray over Valentine.

"No," was Villefort's reply. "Fetch the nearest one."

"The nearest one is an Italian priest who lives in the house next to your own," replied the doctor. "Shall I summon him?"

"Pray do so."

"Do you wish to speak to him?"

"All I desire is to be left alone. Make my excuse to him. Being a priest, he will understand my grief."

D'Avrigny found the priest standing at his door and went up to him saying: "Would you be good enough to render a great service to an unhappy father who has lost his daughter? I mean Monsieur de Villefort, the Procureur du Roi."

"Ah, yes, I know that death is rife in that house," replied the priest in a very pronounced Italian accent.

"Then I need not tell you what service it is that he ventures to ask of you?"

"I was just coming to offer myself, monsieur," said the priest. "It is our mission to forestall our duties."

"It is a young girl who has died."

"Yes, I know, I learnt that from the servants whom I saw fleeing from the house. I know that she was called Valentine, and I have already prayed for her."

"Thank you, monsieur, thank you," said d'Avrigny. "Since you have commenced your sacred office, continue it. Come and watch beside the dead girl, and all her mourning relatives will be grateful to you."

"I am coming, monsieur," replied the priest, "and I venture to say that no prayers will be more fervent than mine."

D'Avrigny led the priest into Valentine's room without

meeting M. de Villefort, who was closeted in his study. As soon as they entered the room Noirtier's eyes met those of the priest, and no doubt something particular attracted him, for his gaze never left him. D'Avrigny recommended the living as well as the dead to the priest's care, and he promised to devote his prayers to Valentine and his attentions to Noirtier.

The abbé set to his task in all seriousness, and as soon as d'Avrigny had left the room, he not only bolted the door through which the doctor had passed, but also the one leading to Mme de Villefort's room—doubtless that he might not be disturbed in his prayers or Noirtier in his grief.

The Abbé Busoni watched by the corpse until daylight, when he returned to his house without disturbing anyone. When M. de Villefort and the doctor went to see how M. Noirtier had spent the night, they were greatly amazed to find him sitting in his big armchair, which served him as a bed, in a peaceful sleep, with something approaching a smile on his face.

Chapter LXV

DANGLARS' SIGNATURE

Before paying his last respects to Valentine, Monte Cristo called on Danglars. From his window the banker saw the Count's carriage enter the courtyard, and went to meet him with a sad though affable smile.

"Well, Count," said he, holding out his hand. "Have you come to offer me your condolence? Ill-fortune is certainly dogging my steps. I was beginning to ask myself whether I had not wished bad luck to those poor Morcerfs, thus proving the truth of the proverb: "He who wishes harm to others shall himself suffer misfortune." But, on my word, I have wished no harm to Morcerf. He was perhaps a little proud, considering he was a man who had risen from nothing, like myself, and, like myself, owed everything he had to his own wits. But we all have our faults. Have you noticed, Count, that people of our generation—pardon me, you are not of our generation, for you are still young—people of my generation are not lucky this year. For example, look at our puritan, the Procureur du Roi, whose whole family are dying in a most mysterious fashion, the latest victim being his daughter. Then again there is Morcerf, who is dishonoured and killed by his own hand, while I not only am covered with ridicule by that scoundrel Cavalcanti, but have lost my daughter as well."

"Your daughter?"

"Yes, she has gone away with her mother, and, knowing her as I do, I am sure she will never return to France again. She could not endure the shame brought on her by that impostor. Ah! he played his part well! To think that we had been entertaining a murderer, a thief, and an impostor; and that he so nearly became my daughter's husband! The only piece of good fortune in the whole affair was that he was arrested before the contract was signed."

"Still, my dear Baron," said Monte Cristo, "such family griefs, which would crush a poor man whose child was his only fortune, are endurable to a millionaire. Philosophers may say what they like, a practical man will always give them the lie: money compensates for a great deal, and if you recognize the sovereignty of this sovereign balm you should be easily consoled, you who are the king of finance."

Danglars looked at the Count out of the corner of his eye; he wondered whether he was mocking him or whether he meant it seriously. "Yes," he said, "it is a fact; if wealth brings consolation, I should be consoled, for I am certainly rich."

"So rich, my dear Baron, that your wealth is like the Pyramids; if you wanted to demolish them, you would not dare, and if you dared, you would not be able to do so."

Danglars smiled at this good-natured pleasantry of the Count's.

"That reminds me," said he, "when you came in, I was drawing up five little bills; I have already signed two, will you excuse me while I sign the other three?"

"Certainly, Baron."

There was a moment's silence broken only by the scratching of the banker's pen.

"Are they Spanish, Hayti, or Neapolitan bonds?" said Monte Cristo.

"Neither the one nor the other," replied Danglars with a self-satisfied smile. "They are bearer bonds on the Bank of France. Look there," he added, "if I am the king, you are the emperor of finance, but have you seen many scraps of paper this size each worth a million?"

The Count took the scraps of paper which the banker proudly handed him and read:

> To the Governor of the Bank of France.
>
> Please pay to my order from the deposit placed by me with you the sum of one million in present currency.
>
> BARON DANGLARS

"One, two, three, four, five!" counted Monte Cristo. "Five millions! Why, you are a regular Croesus![1] It is marvellous, especially if, as I suppose, the amount is paid in cash."

"It will be."

"It is truly a fine thing to have such credit and could only happen in France. Five scraps of paper worth five millions: it must be seen to be believed."

"Do you discredit it?"

"No."

"You say it in such a tone . . . But wait, if it gives you pleasure, accompany my clerk to the bank, and you will see him leave with treasury bills to that amount."

"No," said Monte Cristo, folding the five notes, "indeed not. It is so interesting that I will make the experiment myself. My credit with you amounted to six millions: I have had nine hundred thousand, so that I still have a balance of five million, one hundred thousand francs. I will accept the five scraps of paper that I now hold as bonds, on the strength of your signature alone; here is a general receipt for six millions which will settle our account. I made it out beforehand because, I must confess, I am greatly in need of money to-day."

With one hand Monte Cristo put the notes into his pocket, and with the other presented the receipt to the banker.

Danglars was terror-stricken.

"What!" he stammered. "Do you intend taking that money, Count? Excuse me, it is a deposit I hold for the hospitals, and I promised to pay it this morning."

"That is a different matter," said Monte Cristo. "I do not care particularly about these five notes. Pay me in some other way. It was only to satisfy my curiosity that I took these, so that I might tell everyone that, without any advice or even asking for five minutes' grace, Danglars' bank had paid me five millions in cash. It would have been so remarkable! Here are your bonds, however. Now give me bills of some other sort."

He held out the five bonds to Danglars, who, livid to the lips, stretched out his hand as the vulture stretches out its claw through the bars of its cage to seize the piece of meat that is being snatched from it. All of a sudden he changed his mind, and with a great effort restrained himself. A smile passed over his face and gradually his countenance became serene.

"Just as you like," he said, "your receipt is money."

"Oh, dear, yes; if you were at Rome, Messrs Thomson and French would make no more difficulty about paying you on my receipt than you have done yourself. I can keep this money, then?"

"Yes," said Danglars, wiping his forehead. "Yes, yes."

Monte Cristo put the five bills into his pocket again,

"Yes," said Danglars. "Certainly keep my signatures. But you know no one sticks to formalities more than a financier does, and as I had destined that money for the hospitals it appeared to me, for a moment, that I should be robbing them by not giving them just those five bonds: as though one franc were not as good as another." And he began to laugh, loudly but nervously. "But there is still a sum of one thousand francs?"

"Oh, that is a mere trifle. The commission must come to nearly that much. Keep it and we shall be quits."

"Are you speaking seriously, Count?" asked Danglars.

"I never joke with bankers," replied Monte Cristo with

such a serious air that it was tantamount to impertinence, and he turned toward the door just as the footman announced M. de Boville, Treasurer General of Hospitals.

"Upon my word," said Monte Cristo, "it appears I was only just in time for your signatures—another minute and I should have had a rival claimant."

The Count of Monte Cristo exchanged a ceremonious bow with M. de Boville, who was standing in the waiting-room and was at once shown into M. Danglars' room. The Count's stern face was illuminated by a fleeting smile as he caught sight of the portfolio the Treasurer General carried in his hand. He found his carriage at the door and drove to the bank.

In the meantime the banker advanced to meet the Treasurer General with a forced smile on his lips.

"Good morning, my dear creditor," he said, "for I am sure it is the creditor."

"You are quite right, Baron," said M. de Boville. "I come in the name of the hospitals; through me the widows and orphans have come to ask you for an alms of five millions!"

"Yet they say orphans are to be pitied!" said Danglars, gaining time by joking. "Poor children!"

"Well, I have come in their name," said M. de Boville. "Did you receive my letter yesterday?"

"Yes."

"Here is my receipt."

"My dear Monsieur de Boville," began Danglars, "if you so permit, your widows and orphans will be good enough to wait twenty-four hours, as Monsieur de Monte Cristo, who has just left me . . . You saw him, I think, did you not?"

"I did. Well?"

"Well, Monsieur de Monte Cristo took with him their five millions."

"How is that?"

"The Count had unlimited credit upon me opened by Messrs Thomson and French of Rome. He came to ask me for five millions right away, and I gave him cheques on the bank. You can well understand that if I draw ten millions on one and the same day, the Governor will think it rather strange. Two separate days will be quite a different matter," he added with a smile.

"What!" cried M. de Boville in an incredulous tone. "You paid five millions to the gentleman who just left the house! Five millions!"

"Yes, here is his receipt."

M. de Boville took the paper Danglars handed him and read:

> Received from Baron Danglars the sum of five million francs, which he will redeem at will from Messrs Thomson and French of Rome.

"It is really true then," he said. "Why, this Count of Monte Cristo must be a nabob! I must call on him, and get a pious grant from him."

"You have as good as received it. His alms alone amount to more than twenty thousand francs a month."

"How magnificent! I shall set before him the example of Madame de Morcerf and her son."

"What is that?"

"They have given their whole fortune to the hospitals. They say they do not want money obtained by unclean means."

"What are they to live on?"

"The mother has retired to the provinces, and the son is going to enlist. I registered the deed of gift yesterday."

"How much did they possess?"

"Oh, not very much. Twelve to thirteen thousand francs. But let us return to our millions."

"Willingly," said Danglars, as naturally as possible. "Do you require this money urgently?"

"Yes, our accounts are to be audited to-morrow."

"To-morrow? Why did you not tell me so at once? Tomorow is a long time hence. At what time does the auditing take place?"

"At two o'clock."

"Send round at midday, then," said Danglars with a smile.

"I will come myself."

"Better still, as it will give me the pleasure of seeing you again." With which they shook hands.

"By the way," said M. de Boville, "are you not going to the funeral of poor Mademoiselle de Villefort, which I met on the way here?"

"No," said the banker, "that Cavalcanti affair has made me look rather ridiculous, and when one bears a name as irreproachable as mine, one is rather sensitive. I shall keep out of sight for a while."

M. de Boville left expressing great sympathy with the banker in his trouble. He was no sooner outside than Danglars called after him with great force, "Fool!" Then, putting Monte Cristo's receipt into his pocket, he added: "Yes, yes, come at noon; I shall be far from here."

Then he double-locked the door, emptied all the cash drawers, collected about fifty thousand francs in banknotes, burnt several papers, placed others in conspicuous parts of the room, and finally wrote a letter which he sealed and addressed to Baroness Danglars.

Taking a passport from his drawer, he looked at it, muttering: "Good! It is valid for another two months!"

Chapter LXVI

CONSOLATION

M. de Boville had indeed met the funeral procession which was accompanying Valentine to her last resting-place in the cemetery of Père-Lachaise. As the cortège was leaving Paris, a carriage drawn by four horses came along at full speed and suddenly stopped. Monte Cristo alighted and mingled in the crowd who were following the hearse on foot. When Château-Renaud and Beauchamp perceived him, they also alighted from their carriages and joined him. The Count's eager eyes searched the crowd; it was obvious that he was looking for someone. At length he could restrain himself no longer.

"Where is Morrel?" he asked. "Do either of you gentlemen know?"

"We have already asked ourselves that question. No one seems to have seen him."

The Count remained silent but continued to look around him.

They arrived at the cemetery. Monte Cristo peered into every clump of yew and pine, and was at length relieved of all anxiety: he saw a shadow glide along the dark bushes and recognized him whom he sought. This shadow crossed rapidly but unseen to the hearse and walked beside the coffin-bearers to the spot selected for the grave. Everyone's attention was occupied, but Monte Cristo saw only the shadow, which was otherwise unobserved by all around him. Twice did the Count leave the ranks to see whether the man had not some weapon hidden under his clothes. When the procession stopped, the shadow was recognized as Morrel. His coat was buttoned up to his chin, his cheeks were hollow and livid, and he nervously clasped and unclasped his hands. He took his place against a tree on a hillock overlooking the grave, so that he might not miss one detail of the service.

Everything was conducted in the usual manner, though Monte Cristo heard and saw nothing; or rather, he saw nothing but Morrel, whose calmness and motionlessness were alarming to him, who could read what was passing through the young man's mind.

The funeral over, the guests returned to Paris. When everyone had gone, Maximilian left his place against the tree and spent a few minutes in silent prayer beside Valentine's grave; then he got up, and, without looking back once, turned down the Rue de la Roquette. Monte Cristo had been hiding behind a large tomb, watching Morrel's every movement. Dismissing his carriage, he now followed the young man on foot as he crossed the canal and entered the Rue Meslay by the boulevards.

Five minutes after the door had been closed on Morrel, it was opened again for Monte Cristo. Julie was in the garden watching Penelon, who, taking his position as gardener very seriously, was grafting some Bengal roses.

"Ah, is that you, Count!" she cried with the delight each member of the family generally manifested every time he made his appearance there.

"Maximilian has just come in, has he not?" asked the Count.

"I think I saw him come in," replied the young woman, "but pray call Emmanuel."

"Excuse me a minute, madame, I must go up to

Maximilian at once. I have something of the greatest importance to tell him."

"Go along, then," she said, giving him a charming smile.

Monte Cristo soon ran up the two flights of stairs that separated Maximilian's room from the ground floor; he stood on the landing for a moment and listened; there was not a sound. As is the case in most old houses, the door of the chamber was panelled with glass. Maximilian had shut himself inside, and it was impossible to see through the glass what was happening in the room, as a red silk curtain was drawn across. The Count's anxiety was manifested by his high colour, an unusual sign of emotion in this impassive man.

"What am I to do?" he murmured, as he reflected for a moment. "Shall I ring? Oh, no, the sound of a bell announcing a visitor often hastens the resolution of those in the position in which Maximilian must now be; then the tinkling of the bell will be accompanied by another sound." He was trembling from head to foot, and, with his usual lightning-like rapidity in coming to a decision, he suddenly pushed his elbow through one of the panes of the door, which broke into a thousand pieces. Raising the curtain, he saw Morrel at his desk with a pen in his hand. He started up with a jump when he heard the noise made by the broken glass.

"I am so sorry," said the Count. "It is nothing; I slipped, and in doing so pushed my elbow through your door. However, I will now take the opportunity of paying you a visit. Pray, do not let me disturb you." Putting his hand through the broken glass, he opened the door.

Obviously annoyed, Morrel came forward to meet the Count, not so much with the intention of welcoming him as of barring his way.

"It is your servant's fault," said Monte Cristo, rubbing his elbow. "Your floors are as slippery as glass."

"Have you cut yourself?" Morrel asked coldly.

"I do not know. But what were you doing? Were you writing with those ink-stained fingers?"

"Yes, I was writing," replied Morrel. "I do sometimes, though I am a soldier."

Monte Cristo went farther into the room, and Morrel was compelled to let him pass.

"You were writing?" inquired Monte Cristo, with an annoyingly searching look.

"I have already had the honour of telling you that I was."

The Count looked around him.

"Your pistols on your desk beside you?" said he, pointing to the two weapons.

"I am going on a journey."

"My friend!" said Monte Cristo with infinite tenderness, "my good friend, make no hasty resolution, I beg of you!"

"I make a hasty resolution!" exclaimed Morrel. "In what way can a journey be deemed a hasty resolution?"

"Maximilian," resumed Monte Cristo, "let us lay aside our masks. You can no more deceive me with your exterior calmness than I can mislead you with my frivolous solicitude. You no doubt understand that to have acted as I have done, to have broken a pane of glass, intruded on the privacy of a friend, I must have been actuated by a terrible conviction. Morrel, you intend to take your life!"

Morrel started. "Whence do you get that idea, Count?" he said.

"I declare that you intend taking your life. Here is my proof!" said Monte Cristo, in the same tone of voice; going to the desk, he removed the blank piece of paper with which the young man had covered a half-finished letter and picked it up. Morrel reached forward to wrest it from him, but Monte Cristo had anticipated this and forestalled him by seizing his wrist.

"You must confess that you intended to kill yourself, for it is written here," said the Count.

"Well, and if I have decided to turn this pistol against myself, who shall prevent me?" cried Morrel, passing from his momentary appearance of calmness to an expression of violence. "When I say that all my hopes are frustrated, my heart broken, and my life worthless, since the world holds no more charms for me, nothing but grief and mourning; when I say that it would be a mercy to let me die, for, if you do not, I shall lose my reason and become mad; when I tell you all this with tears of heartfelt anguish, who can say to me: 'You are wrong?' Who would prevent me from putting an end to such a miserable existence? Tell me, Count, would you have the courage?"

"Yes, Morrel," said Monte Cristo, in a voice which contrasted strangely with the young man's excitement. "Yes, I would."

"You!" cried Morrel with an angry and reproachful expression. "You who deceived me with absurd hopes! You who cheered me, solaced, and soothed me with vain promises when I could have saved her life by some swift and drastic step, or at least could have seen her die in my arms! You who pretended to have all the resources of science at your disposal and all power over matter, yet could not administer an antidote to a poisoned girl! In truth, Count, if it were not that you inspire me with horror, I should feel pity for you!"

"Morrel . . . !"

"You told me to lay aside my mask, and rest assured I will do so. When you followed me here, I allowed you to enter, for I am soft-hearted, but since you abuse my confidence and defy me in my own room, where I had enclosed myself as in my tomb, since you bring me new tortures when I thought all were exhausted, then, Count of Monte Cristo, my false benefactor, the universal saviour, be satisfied, you shall see your friend die . . ."

With a maniacal laugh, he rushed toward the pistols again. Pale as a ghost, his eyes darting fire, Monte Cristo put his hand over the weapons saying: "And I repeat once more that you shall not take your life!"

"And who are you that you should take upon yourself such an authority over a free and rational being?"

"Who am I?" repeated Monte Cristo. "I will tell you. I

am the only man who has the right to say to you: 'Morrel, I do not wish your father's son to die to-day!' "

Morrel, involuntarily acknowledging the Count's ascendancy over him, gave way a step.

"Why do you speak of my father?" he stammered. "Why bring my father's memory into what I am going to do to-day?"

"Because I am the man who saved your father's life when he wanted to take it as you do to-day! Because I am the man who sent the purse to your sister and the *Pharaon* to old Monsieur Morrel! Because I am Edmond Dantès!"

Morrel staggered, choking and crushed; his strength failed him, and with a cry he fell prostrate at Monte Cristo's feet. Then all of a sudden his true nature completely reasserted itself; he rose and flew out of the room, calling out at the top of his voice:

"Julie! Julie! Emmanuel! Emmanuel!"

Monte Cristo also attempted to rush out, but Maximilian would sooner have let himself be killed than let go of the handle of the door, which he shut against him. Upon hearing Maximilian's shouts, Julie, Emmanuel, Penelon, and several servants came running up the stairs in alarm. Morrel seized Julie by the hand, and, opening the door, called out in a voice stifled with sobs: "On your knees! on your knees! This is our benefactor, this is the man who saved our father, this is . . ." He was going to say "Edmond Dantès," but the Count restrained him. Julie threw herself into the Count's arms, Emmanuel embraced him, and Morrel once more fell on to his knees. Then this man of iron felt his heart swelling within him, a burning flame seemed to rise in his throat, and from thence rush to his eyes; he bowed his head and wept. For a while nothing was heard in the room but weeping and sobbing; a sound that must have been sweet to the angels in Heaven!

Julie had scarcely recovered from the deep emotion that had overcome her when she rushed down to the salon and, with a childlike joy, raised the glass case that protected the purse given by the unknown man of the Allés de Meilhan.

Meanwhile, Emmanuel said to the Count in a broken voice:

"Oh, Count, when you heard us speak so often of our unknown benefactor and perceived with what gratitude and homage we clothed his memory, how could you wait until to-day to make yourself known to us? It was cruel to us, and, I almost venture to say, to yourself too, Count!"

"Listen, my friend," said the Count. "I may call you thus, for, without knowing it, you have been my friend for eleven years. The discovery of this secret has been torn from me by a great event of which you must ever remain in ignorance. God is my witness that I intended to bury it for ever in the depths of my heart, but your brother, Maximilian, has wrested it from me by a violence which, I am sure, he now regrets." Then, seeing that Maximilian had thrown himself on to a chair apart from the others, he added in a low voice: "Watch over him."

"Why?" asked the young man, amazed.

"I cannot give you the reason, but watch over him."

Emmanuel looked round the room and caught sight of the pistols. With a frightened look, he slowly raised his hand and pointed to them. Monte Cristo nodded his head. Emmanuel went to take the pistols.

"Leave them!" said the Count, and, going to Maximilian, took his hand. The tumultuous emotions that had for a moment shaken the young man's heart had now given way to profound stupor.

Julie returned, holding in her hand the red silk purse; two bright tears of joy coursed down her cheeks like two drops of morning dew.

"Here is the relic," she said, "but do not imagine it will be less dear to us because our benefactor has been revealed to us."

"Permit me to take back that purse," responded Monte Cristo, turning a deep red. "Since you know the features of my face, I only wish to be remembered by the affection I ask you to give me."

"Oh, no! no!" said Julie, pressing the purse to her heart. "I entreat you not to take it away, for unfortunately you might be leaving us one day. Is that not so?"

"You have guessed rightly," replied Monte Cristo with a smile. "In a week I shall have left this country where so many people who merit the vengeance of Heaven live happily, whilst my father died of grief and hunger."

Then, realizing that he must make one final struggle against his friend's grief, he took Julie's and Emmanuel's hands in his, and said to them with the gentle authority of a father: "My good friends, I pray you, leave me alone with Maximilian."

Julie saw a means of carrying away her precious relic, which Monte Cristo had forgotten to mention again, so she drew her husband away, saying: "Let us leave them."

The Count stayed behind with Morrel, who remained as still as a statue.

"Come, come!" said the Count, tapping him on the shoulder with his burning fingers. "Are you going to be a man again?"

"Yes, since I am again beginning to suffer."

The Count's forehead wrinkled in apparent indecision. "Maximilian! Maximilian," said he. "The ideas to which you are giving way are unworthy of a Christian."

"Oh, do not be afraid!" said Morrel, raising his head and smiling at the Count with a smile of ineffable sadness. "I shall make no attempt on my life."

"Then we shall have no more weapons and no more despair!"

"No, for I have a better remedy for my grief than a bullet or the point of a knife."

"You poor, foolish fellow! What is this remedy?"

"My grief itself will kill me!"

"Listen to me, my friend," said Monte Cristo. "One day, in a moment of despair as deep as yours, since it evoked a similar resolution, I, like you, wished to take my life; one day your father, equally desperate, wanted to kill himself. If anyone had said to your father at the moment when he put the muzzle of the pistol to his forehead—if anyone had said to me when I pushed from me the prison bread I had not tasted for three days—if anyone had said to us both at those critical moments: 'Live! The day will come when you will be happy and will bless your life!'—no matter whence the voice had come, we should have welcomed it with a doubtful smile or with agonizing incredulity. Yet how many times has your father not blessed his life when he embraced you—how many times have I myself . . ."

"Ah! you only lost your liberty," interrupted Morrel. "My father had only lost his fortune, but I have lost Valentine!"

"Look at me, Morrel," said Monte Cristo with that air of solemnity which, on certain occasions, made him so grand and persuasive. "I have neither tears in my eyes nor fever in my veins, yet I see you suffer, Maximilian, you whom I love as a son! Does that not tell you that in grief as in life there is always a hidden future? And if I entreat, nay, command you to live, Morrel, it is because I am convinced that the day will come when you will thank me for having saved your life!"

"Good God!" cried the young man. "What are you telling me, Count? Take care. But perhaps you have never loved?"

"Child!" was the sole reply.

"I mean as I love. You see I have been a soldier ever since I was a boy, and was twenty-nine before I fell in love, for none of the feelings I experienced before that time were worthy of the name of love. Well, when I was twenty-nine years of age, I met Valentine, and have loved her for the past two years, and during that time I have observed in her all the virtues that make a true daughter and wife. To have possessed Valentine, Count, would have been an infinite and immense happiness, too complete and divine for this world. Since this happiness has been denied me, there is nothing left for me on earth but despair and desolation."

"I tell you to hope, Morrel," repeated the Count.

"Ah! you are trying to persuade me, you are trying to inspire me with the belief that I shall see Valentine again."

The Count smiled.

"My friend, my father!" cried Morrel excitedly. "The ascendancy you hold over me alarms me. Weigh your words carefully, for my eyes lighten up again and my heart takes on a fresh lease of life. I should obey you though you commanded me to raise the stone which once more covers the sepulchre of the daughter of Jairus;[1] I should walk upon the waves like the apostle if you made a sign to me to do so; so have a care, I should obey in all."

"Hope, my dear friend!" repeated the Count.

"Ah, you are playing with me," said Morrel, falling from the heights of exaltation to the abyss of despair. "You are doing the same as those good, or rather selfish, mothers who calm their children's sorrow with honeyed words because their cries annoy them. No, my friend. I will bury my grief so deep down in my heart and shall guard it so carefully from the eyes of man that you will need have no sympathy for me. Good-bye, my friend, good-bye!"

"On the contrary," said the Count. "From now onward, you will live with me and not leave me. In a week we shall have left France behind us."

"Do you still bid me hope?"

"I do, for I know of a remedy for you."

"You are only prolonging my agony, Count!"

"Are you so feeble-hearted that you cannot give your friend a few days' trial? I have great faith in my promise, so let me make the experiment. Do you know what the Count of Monte Cristo is capable of? Do you know that he has faith enough in God to obtain miracles from Him who said that with faith one would remove mountains? Well, wait for the miracle for which I hope, or . . ."

"Or . . ." repeated Morrel.

"Or take care, Morrel, lest I call you ungrateful."

"Have pity on me, Count!"

"I feel so much pity for you that if I do not cure you in a month to the very day, mark my words, Morrel, I myself will place before you two loaded pistols and a cup of the deadliest poison—a poison which is more potent and prompt of action than that which killed Valentine."

"Do you promise me this?"

"I not only promise it, I swear it," said Monte Cristo, giving him his hand.

"Then on your word of honour, if I am not consoled in a month, you leave me free to take my life, and, whatever I may do, you will not call me ungrateful?"

"In a month to the day, and it is a date that is sacred to us. I do not know whether you remember that to-day is the fifth of September? It is ten years ago to-day that I saved your father when he wanted to take his life."

Morrel seized the Count's hands and kissed them, and the Count suffered him to do it, for he felt that this homage was due to him.

"In a month," continued Monte Cristo, "you will have before you on the table at which we shall both be seated two trusty weapons and a gentle death-giving potion, but in return you must promise me to wait until then and live."

"I swear it!" exclaimed Morrel.

Monte Cristo drew the young man toward him and held him for a few minutes in close embrace.

"Well, then, from to-day you will live with me; you can occupy Haydee's rooms, and my daughter will be replaced by my son."

"Haydee?" said Morrel. "What has happened to Haydee?"

"She left last night."

"To leave you for ever?"

"To wait for me . . . Make ready to join me at Rue des Champs Élysées and now let me out without anyone seeing me."

Chapter LXVII

SEPARATION

In the house in the Rue Saint-Germain-des-Prés that Albert de Morcerf had chosen for his mother, the first floor was let to a very mysterious person. The porter himself had never seen this man's face, for in the winter he buried his chin in one of those red kerchiefs worn by coachmen of the nobility, and in the summer he always blew his nose when he passed the porter's lodge. Contrary to custom, he was not watched, and it was reported that he was a man of high standing with a great deal of influence, so that his incognito was respected. His visits were generally regular. At four o'clock, winter and summer, he would arrive, and twenty minutes later a carriage drew up at the house. A woman dressed in black or dark blue, and always thickly veiled, would alight, and, passing by the lodge like a shadow, run up the stairs so gently that not a stair creaked under the pressure of her light foot. No one ever asked her whither she was going, and no one ever saw her face. Needless to say, she never went higher than the first floor. She tapped at the door in a peculiar way; it was opened to her and then fastened again. They left the house in the same way; the woman went first and was followed twenty minutes later by the unknown man.

The day after that on which the Count of Monte Cristo had called on M. Danglars, the day of Valentine's funeral, the mysterious tenant entered his flat at ten o'clock in the morning, instead of his usual hour. Almost immediately afterward, without the usual interval, a hired cab arrived, and the veiled lady quickly ran up the stairs. The door was opened, and before it could be closed again, she called out, "Oh, Lucien, oh, my dear!"

In this way the porter who had overheard the exclamation learned for the first time that his tenant was named Lucien, but as he was a model porter he decided not even to tell his wife.

"Well, what is the matter, dear?" asked he whose name either trouble or eagerness had forced from the veiled lady's lips. "Tell me quickly."

"Can I depend upon you?"

"You know you can. But what is the matter? Your note of this morning, so hastily and untidily written, has made me feel very anxious."

"A great event has happened," said the lady. "Monsieur Danglars left last night."

"Left! Monsieur Danglars left! Where has he gone to?"

"I do not know."

"How do you mean, you do not know? Has he gone away for good?"

"No doubt. At ten o'clock last night his horses took him to the Charenton gate, where he found a post-chaise[1] waiting for him. He stepped into it with his valet, telling his coachman that he was going to Fontainebleau. He left me a letter."

"A letter?"

"Yes, read it." And the Baroness took from her pocket an unsealed letter, which she handed to Debray.

Before reading it he hesitated a moment as though trying to guess its contents, or rather, as though knowing its contents, he was making up his mind what action to take. He had no doubt come to a decision after a second or two, for he read the note which had caused Mme Danglars so much anxiety and which ran as follows:

MADAME AND MOST FAITHFUL WIFE . . .

Debray involuntarily paused and looked at the Baroness, who blushed to the roots of her hair.

"Read," she said; and Debray continued:

When you receive this letter, you will no longer have a husband. Oh, you need not be alarmed, you will only have lost him in the same way in which you have lost your daughter, that is to say, I shall be travelling along one of the thirty or forty roads which lead out of France.

I owe you an explanation, and, as you are a woman of quick comprehension, I will give it to you. A bill of five million francs was unexpectedly presented to me for repayment this morning, which I effected. This was immediately followed by another bill for the same amount; I postponed this payment until to-morrow, and I am going away in order to escape that to-morrow, which would be too unpleasant for me to endure. You understand me, do you not, my most precious wife? I say you understand because you are as conversant with my business affairs as I am myself, in fact more so, for if I had to say what had become of a good half of my fortune, which until recently was quite a considerable one, I should be unable to do so, whereas I am certain that you, on the contrary, would be able to give a very fair answer. Women have infallible instincts, and, by means of an algebra unknown to man, they can explain the most marvellous things. I only understand my figures: from the day these figures fail me, I know nothing.

I am leaving you, madame and most prudent wife, and my conscience does not reproach me in the least at doing so. You have your friends, and, to complete your happiness, the liberty I hasten to restore to you.

There is one more observation I should like to make. As long as I hoped you were working for the good of our firm and the fortune of our daughter, I philosophically closed my eyes to all, but since you have brought about the ruin of our firm, I do not wish to serve as a foundation for another's fortune. You were rich when I married you, though little respected. Pardon me for speaking with such frankness, but as this is in all likelihood only between ourselves, I do not see why I should choose my words.

I augmented our fortune, and it continued to increase for fifteen years until unexpected and incomprehensible disasters overtook me, and, through no fault of my own, I find myself a ruined man. You, madame, have only sought to increase your own fortune, and I am convinced you have been successful.

I leave you then as you were when I married you, rich, though with little honour. Farewell! From to-day I also shall work for myself. Accept my gratitude for the example which you have set me and which I intend following.

> Your very devoted husband,
> BARON DANGLARS

The Baroness watched Debray as he read this long and painful letter, and saw that in spite of his self-command the young man had changed colour once or twice. When he had finished reading the letter, he folded it up slowly and reassumed his pensive attitude.

"Well?" asked Mme Danglars, with very comprehensible anxiety.

"Well, madame?" repeated Debray mechanically.

"What do you think of that letter?"

"It is quite simple, madame. Monsieur Danglars has gone away full of suspicion."

"Undoubtedly. But is that all you have to say to me?"

"I do not understand you," said Debray, with freezing coolness.

"He has gone! Gone, never to return."

"Oh, do not believe that, Baroness."

"I tell you he will never return. Had he thought I should be useful to him, he would have taken me with him. He has left me at Paris because our separation would serve his purpose. It is therefore irrevocable, and I am free for ever," added Madame Danglars, with the same tone of entreaty.

But, instead of replying, Debray left her in suspense.

"What!" she said at last. "You have no answer?"

"I have but one question to put to you. What do you intend to do?"

"That is what I was going to ask you," replied the Baroness, with wildly beating heart. "I ask you to advise me."

"Then I advise you to travel," replied the young man coldly.

"To travel!" murmured Mme Danglars.

"Certainly. As Monsieur Danglars says, you are rich and perfectly free. It is absolutely necessary for you to leave Paris, at least I think so, after the double scandal of your daughter's rejected marriage and your husband's disappearance. The world must be led to think that you are poor, for opulence in a bankrupt's wife is an unforgivable sin. You have only to remain in Paris for a fortnight, telling everyone that you have been deserted; relate to your best friends how it all happened, and they will soon spread it abroad. Then you can quit your home, leaving your jewels behind you, and giving up your jointure, and then everyone will be singing your praises because of your disinterestedness. It will be known that your husband has deserted you, and it will be thought that you are poor. I alone know your financial position, and am ready to render you an account as an honest partner."

Pale with amazement, the Baroness listened to this discourse with as much despair and terror as Debray had manifested indifference in pronouncing it.

"Deserted!" she repeated. "Ah, yes, utterly deserted. You are right, monsieur, everyone will know that."

"But you are rich, nay, very rich," continued Debray, taking from his pocket-book some papers which he spread on the table. Mme Danglars suffered him to give her the details of their joint financial transactions, but she did not heed his words. She was fully occupied in stilling the turbulent beating of her heart and in keeping back the tears which she felt rising to the surface. At length her dignity conquered, and, though she may not have succeeded in restraining her heart, she at least prevented the fall of a single tear. It was with indifference that she listened as he recounted how he had multiplied their money, for all she wanted was a tender word to console her for being so rich. But she waited in vain for that word.

"Now, madame," Debray continued, "your share amounts to one million three hundred and forty thousand francs, so that you have a fine income, something like sixty thousand francs, which is enormous for a woman who cannot keep up an appearance of wealth, at least not for a year or so. Nevertheless, if this should prove insufficient for your needs, for the sake of the past, I am disposed to offer you the loan of all I possess, that is, one million sixty thousand francs."

"Thank you," replied the Baroness. "You have already handed over to me far more than is required by a poor woman who intends to live in retirement for some time to come."

Debray was astonished for a moment, but he quickly recovered himself and made a gesture which in the most polite manner possible seemed to imply: "Just as you please."

Until that moment, Mme Danglars had hoped for something more; but when she saw Debray's gesture of indifference and the sidelong glance which accompanied it, as well as the profound and significant silence which followed it, she raised her head, opened the door, and calmly and unhesitatingly descended the stairs without even a farewell look at one who could let her leave him in this manner.

Debray quietly waited until Mme Danglars had been gone twenty minutes before he made up his mind to leave, and during all this interval he occupied himself with calculations, his watch by his side.

Above the room where Debray had been dividing his two and a half million francs with Mme Danglars, there was another room in which we shall find friends who have played important parts in the incidents related, friends whose reappearance will cause us pleasure. Mercédès and Albert were there. Mercédès was very much changed in the last few days, not that even in the height of her fortune she had ever dressed with that display of ostentatious magnificence which renders a woman unrecognizable as soon as she appears in simple attire; not that she had lapsed into that state of depression in which one feels constrained to put on again the garments of poverty; no, Mercédès had changed because her eyes had lost their sparkle, her mouth its smile, and to complete all, abashment and perplexity ever arrested on her lips that flow of speech which had issued so easily in former days from her ever-ready wit. Poverty had not broken her spirit, and want of courage had not made her poverty appear unendurable to her. Descended from the high position in which she had been living, lost in the new sphere she had chosen like someone passing suddenly from a brilliantly lighted room to utter darkness, Mercédès was like a queen who had stepped from her palace into a hut and could not accustom herself to the earthenware vessels she was obliged to place on the table herself, nor the pallet which had succeeded her bed.

In truth, the beautiful Catalan and noble Countess had lost her proud look and her charming smile, for her eyes saw nothing but what was distasteful and distressing to her. The walls of her room were hung with a dull grey paper chosen by economical landlords because it would not show the dirt; the floor was uncarpeted; the furniture attracted attention by its poor attempt at magnificence; in fact, everything was so gaudy that it was a continual eyesore to anyone accustomed to refinement and elegance. Mme de Morcerf had lived here ever since she left her magnificent house. The perpetual silence oppressed her, but she knew that Albert was secretly watching her to discover the state of her mind, and this forced her lips into the appearance of an empty smile, which, deprived of the warmth infused into it by her eyes, appeared only like a simple ray of light, that is to say, light without heat.

Albert too was very moody and ill at ease. The results of a luxurious life hampered him in his present position. When he wanted to go out without gloves, his hands appeared too white; when he wished to go about the town on foot, his boots appeared too elegant. Yet these two noble and intelligent beings, united by the indissoluble ties of maternal and filial love, had succeeded in tacitly understanding one another. Thus they could face bitter facts without their being preceded by softening words. Albert had been able to say: "Mother, we have no more money," without evoking any visible agitation.

Mercédès had never known what real want was; in her youth she had often spoken of poverty, but it is not the same thing, for between want and necessity there is a wide gulf. When she was at the Catalans, Mercédès wanted a number of things, but she was never in need of the necessaries of life. As long as the nets were good, they caught fish, and as long as they sold fish, they could mend their nets. Devoid of all friendship and having but one great affection which did not enter into her material life, she thought of no one but herself and of nothing but herself. She had managed very well on the little she had, but to-day there were two to manage for and she had nothing with which to do it.

Winter approached. Mercédès, who had been accustomed to a house heated from the hall to her boudoir, had no fire in her cold, bare room; she whose house had been one conservatory of costly exotic plants had not one humble little flower! But she had her son!

Hitherto the excitement of fulfilling a duty, an exaggerated one perhaps, had sustained them, but their enthusiasm had worn off, and they had been compelled to descend from their world of dreams to face stern realities.

"Mother, let us count our wealth, if you please," Albert was saying at the precise moment that Mme Danglars was descending the staircase. "I must know what it totals before I make my plans."

"Total: nothing," said Mercédès with a sad smile.

"Oh, yes it is, Mother! Total: three thousand francs to begin with, and I dare to hope that with this amount we two shall have a very happy time."

"Child!" said Mercédès.

"Alas, Mother," said the young man, "I have unfortunately spent too much of your money not to know the value of it. Look you, three thousand francs is an enormous sum, and with it I have planned a secure and wonderful future."

"You may well say that, my son, but in the first place are we going to accept this money?" said Mercédès, blushing.

"But I thought we had agreed to that," said Albert, in a firm tone. "We will accept it all the more readily since we have not got it, for as you know it is buried in the little garden in the Allées de Meilhan at Marseilles. Two hundred francs will take the two of us to Marseilles."

"Two hundred francs? Have you thought it out, Albert?"

"Oh, yes, I have made inquiries with regard to diligences and steamboats, and have made all my calculations. An inside seat in the diligence to Chalon will cost you thirty-five francs. You see, Mother, I am treating you like a queen!"

Albert took his pen and wrote:

Diligence to Chalon . . . . 35 francs
From Chalon to Lyons by steamboat . . . . 6 "
From Lyons to Avignon by steamboat . . . . 16 "
From Avignon to Marseilles . . . . 7 "
Incidental expenses 50
                                                    114

"Let us say a hundred and twenty," added Albert, smiling. "Am I not generous, Mother?"

"But what about you, my son?"

"Don't you see that I have reserved eighty francs for myself? A young man does not need too much comfort; besides, I am used to travelling."

"Do as you like. But where are the two hundred francs coming from?"

"Here they are, and two hundred more as well. I have sold my watch for a hundred francs and the seals for three hundred. How fortunate that the seals fetched more than the watch! The same story of superfluities again! See how rich we are! Instead of the necessary hundred and fourteen francs for the journey you have two hundred and fifty."

"But we owe something here."

"Thirty francs, which I shall pay out of my hundred and fifty. With care I shall only need eighty francs for my journey, so you see I am wallowing in riches. And it does not end with this. What do you think of this, Mother?"

He took out a small pocket-book with gold clasps and from it a note for one thousand francs.

"What is that?" asked Mercédès.

"A thousand francs, Mother! Oh, it is perfectly genuine."

"But whence have you obtained them?"

"Listen to what I have to say, Mother, and do not get too agitated." He went up to his mother and kissed her on both cheeks, then he paused a moment to look at her.

"You have no idea how beautiful you are to me!" said the young man with deep feelings of filial love. "You are truly the most beautiful and the noblest woman I have ever seen!"

"And I shall never be unhappy so long as I have my son," replied Mercédès, vainly endeavouring to keep back the tears which would rise to her eyes.

"Just so, but this is where our trial begins," said Albert. "Mother, do you know what we have decided?"

"Have we decided anything?"

"Yes, we have agreed that you shall live at Marseilles while I go to Africa, where I shall win the right to the name I have adopted in the place of the one I have cast aside. I joined the Spahis yesterday, or rather, I thought that as my body was my own, I could sell it. Yesterday I took the place of another. And I sold myself for more than I thought I was worth," he continued, trying to smile, "that is to say, for two thousand francs."

"So these thousand francs . . . ?" inquired Mercédès, trembling.

"It is half the amount, Mother. I shall receive the other half in a year."

Mercédès raised her eyes to Heaven with an expression which it would be impossible to describe, and the tears lurking in her eyes overflowed with the power of her emotion and silently ran down her cheeks.

"The price of his blood!" she murmured.

"Yes, if I am killed, Mother," said he, laughing. "But I assure you I shall sell my life dearly, for never has it been so precious to me as now. Besides, why should I be killed? Has Lamouricière[2] been killed? Or Changarnier?[3] Or yet again, Morrel, whom we know? Think of your joy, Mother, when I come back dressed in my embroidered uniform! I must own that I shall look splendid in it, and that I chose this regiment from pure vanity!"

Though Mercédès attempted to smile she could not repress a sigh. This devoted mother felt it was wrong of her to let the whole weight of the sacrifice fall upon her son.

"Well, Mother, you understand that this means that you have a sure four thousand francs," continued Albert, "and you can live on that for two years at least."

"Do you think so?" said Mercédès mechanically, but in tones of such deep sorrow that the real sense of the words did not escape Albert; he felt his heart grow heavy, and, taking his mother's hand, he said tenderly: "Oh, yes, you will live!"

"Then you must not leave me, my son."

"Mother, I must go," said Albert, in a calm but firm voice. "You love me too much to let me stay idle and useless with you. Besides, I have signed the agreement."

"Do as you will, my son. I shall do God's will."

"It is not as I will, Mother, but according to the dictates of common sense and necessity. We are two despairing creatures, are we not? What is life to you to-day? Nothing! What is it to me? Worth very little without you. Mother, I assure you. But I will live if you promise not to give up hope, and in permitting me to care for your fixture you give me double strength. Out there in Algeria, I shall go to the Governor, who is a noble-hearted man and essentially a soldier, and shall tell him my story and entreat him to interest himself in me. Then, Mother, I shall either be an officer within six months or else dead. If I am an officer, your future is assured, for I shall have money enough for you and for me, and in addition a name of which we shall both be proud, for it will be your own name. If I am killed . . . then, Mother dear, you also will die, and our misfortunes and sorrows will have an end."

"As you wish," replied Mercédès, with a noble and eloquent glance.

"But you must have no morbid thoughts, Mother," exclaimed the young man. "I assure you we can be very happy. Then it is settled that we separate? We can even begin from to-day; I will go and procure your ticket."

"But what about yours?"

"I must stay on here two or three days longer. It will accustom us to our separation, and I have to gather some information on Africa, and also, I want some introductions before I join you at Marseilles."

"Well, then, let us go!" said Mercédès, wrapping round her the only shawl she had taken away with her, which happened to be a valuable black cashmere one. "Let us go."

Albert quickly gathered up his papers, rang for the proprietor, and paid him the thirty francs owing. Then he gave his arm to his mother, and they descended the stairs.

Someone was going down in front of them, who, on hearing the rustling of a silk dress against the balustrade, turned round.

"Debray!" murmured Albert.

"You, Morcerf!" replied the minister's secretary, standing still. Then, noticing in the semi-darkness the veiled and still youthful figure of Mme de Morcerf: "Oh, pardon," he said with a smile. "I will leave you, Albert."

Albert understood his thoughts.

"Mother," said he, turning toward Mercédès, "this is Monsieur Debray, secretary to the Minister of the Interior, and a former friend of mine."

"Former?" stammered Debray. "Why do you say that?"

"I say that, Monsieur Debray, because to-day I have no more friends and must not have any," replied Albert. "I thank you, monsieur, for having acknowledged me."

Debray went up two stairs and cordially shook Albert's hand as he said with all the feeling of which he was capable: "Believe me, I have felt deep sympathy with you in the misfortune that has befallen you, and if I can serve you in any way, pray call on me to do so."

"Thank you, monsieur," said Albert, smiling, "but in the midst of our misfortune we are still rich enough to require no outside help. We are leaving Paris, and, after our travelling expenses are paid, we shall still have five thousand francs."

The colour rose to Debray's cheeks at the thought of the million francs he had in his pocket-book, and, unimaginative though he was, he could not help reflecting that a few minutes back there were in that house two women: the one, justly dishonoured, had left with 1,500,000 francs under her cloak, while the other one, unjustly smitten, yet superb in her misfortune, considered herself rich with a few francs. This parallel disturbed his usual politeness, the philosophy of the example overwhelmed him; he stammered a few words of general courtesy and quickly ran down the stairs. The minister's clerks, his subordinates, had to suffer from his ill-humour the rest of the day. In the evening, however, he consoled himself by becoming the owner of a splendid house in the Boulevard de la Madeleine, yielding an income of fifty thousand francs.

About five o'clock the next evening, at the very moment when Debray was signing the agreement, Mme de Morcerf entered the diligence after tenderly kissing her son and being as tenderly embraced by him, and was driven away.

A man was hidden behind an arched window of Laffitte's offices. He saw Mercédès enter the diligence, watched the conveyance drive away, and saw Albert turn back. Then he passed his hand across his wrinkled forehead, saying to himself: "Alas! by what means can I restore to these two innocent beings the happiness I have snatched from them? God will help me."

Chapter LXVIII

THE JUDGE

✦

It will be remembered that the Abbé Busoni stayed alone with Noirtier in the chamber of death. Perhaps it was the Abbé's Christian exhortations, perhaps his tender compassion, or, maybe, his persuasive words that gave Noirtier courage; whatever it may have been, certain it is that ever since the day on which he had conversed with the priest, his despair had given way to complete resignation, to the great astonishment of all who knew his deep affection for Valentine.

M. de Villefort had not seen his father since the morning of the tragedy. The whole household had undergone a complete change; another valet had been engaged for himself, a new servant for Noirtier; two women had entered the service of Mme de Villefort: everywhere there were new faces.

The assizes[1] were to be opened in three days, and Villefort spent most of his day closeted in his study preparing his cases, which afforded him the only distraction from his sorrow. Once only had he seen his father. Harassed and fatigued, he had gone into the garden and, deep in gloomy thought, he paced the avenues, lopping off with his cane the long, withering stalks of the hollyhocks, which stood on either side of the path like the ghosts of the brilliantly coloured flowers that had bloomed in the season just passed. More than once had he reached the bottom of the garden where the famous paling separated it from the deserted enclosure, but he always returned by the selfsame path, and at the same pace. All of a sudden his eyes were involuntarily attracted toward the house, where he heard the noisy play of Edward, who had come home from school to spend the Sunday and Monday with his mother. At the same time he perceived Noirtier at one of the open windows, to which he had had his chair wheeled so that he might enjoy the last warm rays of the sun as they took leave of the red leaves of the Virginia creeper round the balcony.

The old man's eyes were riveted on a spot which Villefort could only imperfectly distinguish, but their expression was so full of hatred, venom, and impatience that the Procureur du Roi, ever quick to read the impressions on that face that he knew so well, turned out of his path to discover the object of that dark look. He saw Mme de Villefort seated under a clump of lime-trees nearly divested of their foliage. She had a book in her hand which she laid aside from time to time to smile at her son or to return to him his ball, which he persisted in throwing into the garden from the salon. Villefort turned pale, for he understood what was passing through his father's mind. Noirtier continued to look at the same object, but suddenly his eyes were turned from the wife to the husband, and Villefort himself had to submit to the gaze of those piercing eyes, which, while changing their objective, had also changed their language, but without losing their menacing expression.

Drawn by an irresistible attraction, as a bird is attracted by a snake, Villefort approached the house. Noirtier's eyes followed him all the while, and the fire they emitted was so fierce that it seemed to pierce him to the very core. Indeed, the look held a deep reproach, and at the same time a terrible menace. He raised his eyes to Heaven as though reminding his son of an unfulfilled promise.

"Yes, yes!" Villefort replied from below. "Have patience for one day more; what I have said shall be done!"

These words seemed to calm Noirtier, for he turned away his eyes. Villefort, on the other hand, tore open his coat, for it was choking him, and, passing his hand over his brow, returned to his study.

The night was cold and calm; everybody in the house had gone to bed as usual, only Villefort once more remained up and worked till five o'clock in the morning. The first sitting of the assizes was to take place the next day, which was a Monday. Villefort saw that day dawn pale and gloomy. He dropped off to sleep for a moment or two when the lamp was at its last flicker; its flickering awakened him, and he found his fingers damp and red as though they had been dipped in blood.

He opened his window; a red streak traversed the sky in the distance, and seemed to cut in two the slender poplars which stood out in black relief against the horizon. In the lucerne-field beyond the chestnut-trees, a lark rose to the sky, pouring out its clear morning song. The dews bathed Villefort's head and refreshed his memory. "To-day," said he with an effort, "the man who wields the knife of justice must strike wherever there is guilt!"

Involuntarily his glance fell on the window where he had seen Noirtier the previous evening. The curtains were drawn, yet his father's image was so vividly impressed on his mind that he addressed himself to the closed window, as though it were open and he still beheld the menacing old man.

"Yes," he muttered, "yes, it shall be done!"

His head dropped upon his chest, and, with his head thus bowed, he paced his room several times till at last he threw himself on a settee, not so much because he wanted to sleep as to rest his tired and cold limbs. By degrees everybody in the house began to stir. From his room Villefort heard all the noises that constitute the life of a house: the opening and shutting of doors, the tinkle of Mme de Villefort's bell summoning her maid, and the shouts of his boy, who woke fully alive to the enjoyments of life, as children at that age generally do.

Villefort rang his bell. His new valet entered, bringing the newspapers, and with them a cup of chocolate.

"What have you there?" asked Villefort.

"A cup of chocolate, monsieur."

"I did not ask for it. Who has so kindly sent it me?"

"Madame; she said you would doubtless have to do much speaking at the assizes to-day and needed to fortify yourself," said the valet, as he placed the cup on the paper-bestrewn table near the sofa. Then he went out.

For a moment Villefort looked at the cup with a gloomy expression, then he suddenly seized it in a nervous grasp and swallowed the whole of its contents at a single draught. It appeared almost as though he hoped that the beverage was poisoned, and that he sought death to deliver him from a duty which demanded of him something which was more difficult of accomplishment than it would be to die. He rose and began walking up and down the room with a smile which would have been terrible to behold, if anyone had been there to see it. The chocolate was harmless, and M. de Villefort felt no ill effects from it.

The breakfast-hour arrived, but M. de Villefort did not make his appearance. The valet entered his room.

"Madame desires me to remind you that it has struck eleven o'clock, monsieur, and that the sitting begins at noon," he said.

"Well, what else?"

"Madame is ready to accompany you, Monsieur."

"Whither?"

"To the Law Courts."

"Does she really wish to go?" said Villefort in terrifying tones.

The servant started back.

"If you wish to go alone, monsieur, I will inform madame."

For a moment Villefort remained silent, digging his fingernails into his cheek, the paleness of which was accentuated by his ebony black hair.

"Tell madame that I wish to speak to her," he said at length, "and that I request her to wait for me in her room. Then come and shave me."

"Yes, monsieur."

The valet returned almost immediately, and, after having shaved Villefort, helped him into a sombre black suit. When he had finished, he said: "Madame said she would expect you, monsieur, as soon as you were dressed."

"I am going to her."

With his papers under his arm and his hat in his hand, he went to his wife's room. He paused outside for a moment to wipe his clammy forehead. Then he pushed open the door.

Mme de Villefort was sitting on an ottoman, impatiently turning over the leaves of a newspaper which Edward, by way of amusing himself, was tearing to pieces before his mother had time to finish reading it. She was dressed ready to go out; her hat was lying on a chair, her gloves were on her hands.

"Ah, here you are," she said, with a calm and natural voice. "But you are very pale! Have you been working all through the night again? Why did you not come and breakfast with us? Well, are you going to take me or shall I go alone with Edward?"

Mme de Villefort had asked one question after another in order to elicit one single answer, but to all her inquiries M. de Villefort remained as cold and mute as a statue.

"Edward, go and play in the Salon," he said, looking sternly at the child. "I wish to speak to your mother."

Mme de Villefort trembled as she beheld his cold countenance and heard his resolute tone, which presaged some new disaster. Edward raised his head and looked at his mother, and, seeing she did not confirm his father's orders, proceeded to cut off the heads of his lead soldiers.

"Edward, do you hear me? Go!" cried M. de Villefort, so harshly that the child jumped.

Unaccustomed to such treatment, he rose, pale and trembling, but whether from fear or anger it were difficult to say. His father went up to him, took him in his arms, and, kissing him, said: "Go, my child, go!"

Edward went out, and M. de Villefort locked the door behind him.

"Oh, heavens! what is the matter?" cried the young woman, endeavouring to read her husband's inmost thoughts, and forcing a smile which froze M. de Villefort's impassibility.

"Madame, where do you keep the poison you generally use?" the magistrate said slowly without any preamble, as he placed himself between his wife and the door.

Madame's feelings were those of the lark when it sees the kite over its head making ready to swoop down upon it. A harsh, stifled sound, which was neither a cry nor a sigh, escaped from her lips, and she turned deathly white.

"I . . . I do not understand," she said, sinking back on to her cushions.

"I asked you," continued Villefort in a perfectly calm voice, "where you hide the poison by means of which you have killed my father-in-law, my mother-in-law, Barrois, and my daughter, Valentine."

"Whatever are you saying?" cried Mme de Villefort, clasping her hands.

"It is not for you to question, but to answer."

"My husband or the judge?" stammered Mme de Villefort.

"The judge, madame, the judge."

The pallor of the woman, the anguish in her look, and the trembling of her whole frame, were frightful to behold.

"You do not answer, madame?" cried her terrible examiner. Then, with a smile which was more terrifying than his anger, he added: "It must be true since you do not deny it."

She made a movement.

"And you cannot deny it," added Villefort, extending his hand toward her as though to arrest her in the name of the law. "You have accomplished these crimes with impudent skill; nevertheless, you have only been able to deceive those who were blinded by their affection for you. Ever since the death of Madame de Saint-Méran have I known that there was a poisoner in my house— Monsieur d'Avrigny warned me of it. After the death of Barrois—may God forgive me!—my suspicions fell on someone, an angel, for I am ever suspicious, even where there is no crime. But since the death of Valentine there has been no doubt in my mind, madame, or in that of others. Thus your crime, known by two persons and suspected by many, will be made public. Moreover, as I told you just now, I do not speak to you as your husband, but as your judge!"

The young woman hid her face in her hands.

"Oh, I beg of you, do not trust to appearances," she stammered.

"Are you a coward?" cried Villefort in a contemptuous tone. "Indeed, I have always remarked that poisoners are cowards. Is it possible, though, that you are a coward, you who have had the awful courage to watch the death agony of three old people and a young girl, your victims? Is it possible that you are a coward, you who have counted the minutes while four people were slowly done to death? Is it possible that you, who were able to lay your plans so admirably, forgot to reckon on one thing, namely, where the discovery of your crimes would lead you? No, it is impossible! You must have kept some poison, more potent, subtle, and deadly than all the rest, to save you from the punishment you deserve! At all events I hope so!"

Mme de Villefort wrung her hands and fell on her knees.

"I understand, oh yes! I understand that you own your guilt," he continued. "But a confession made to your judges at the eleventh hour when it is impossible to deny the crime in no way diminishes the punishment they inflict on the guilty one."

"Punishment!" cried Mme de Villefort. "Punishment! Twice have you said that word!"

"Yes, twice. Did you think you would escape because you had been guilty four times? Did you think that because you were the wife of him who demands retribution it would be withheld you? No, madame, no! The poisoner shall go to the scaffold whoever she may be, unless, as I said just now, she was cautious enough to keep for herself a few drops of the deadliest poison."

Mme de Villefort uttered a wild scream, and a hideous and invincible terror laid hold of her distorted features.

"Oh, do not fear the scaffold, madame," resumed the magistrate. "I do not wish to dishonour you, for in doing so, I should bring dishonour on myself. On the contrary, if you have heard me correctly, you must understand that you are not to die on the scaffold!"

"No, I do not understand. What do you mean?" stammered the unhappy woman, completely overwhelmed.

"I mean that the wife of the first magistrate will not, by her infamy, sully an unblemished name and, with one blow, bring dishonour on her husband and her child."

"No . . . Oh, no . . . !"

"Well, madame, it will be a kind action on your part, and I thank you for it."

"You thank me? For what?"

"For what you have just told me."

"What did I say? My head is in a whirl, and I can understand nothing. Oh, my God! My God!"

She rose from her seat, foaming at the mouth and her hair all dishevelled.

"You have not answered the question that I put to you when I came in, madame. Where is the poison you generally use, madame?"

She raised her arms to Heaven, and wringing her hands in despair, exclaimed: "No, no! You could not wish that!"

"What I do not wish, madame, is that you should perish on the scaffold, do you understand?" replied Villefort.

"Have mercy!"

"What I demand, madame, is that justice shall be done.

My mission on earth is to punish," he added with a fierce look in his eyes. "I should send the executioner to any other woman were she the Queen herself, but to you I am merciful! To you I say: 'Madame, have you not put aside a few drops of the most potent, the swiftest, and deadliest poison?'"

"Oh, forgive me! Let me live! Remember that I am your wife!"

"You are a poisoner."

"For heaven's sake . . . ! for the sake of the love you once bore me! for our child's sake! Oh, let me live for our child's sake!"

"No! no! no! I tell you. If I let you live, you will perhaps kill him like the rest."

"I kill my son!" cried the desperate mother, throwing herself upon Villefort. "I kill my Edward! Ha! ha!" She finished the sentence with a frightful laugh, a mad, demoniacal laugh, which ended in a terrible rattle. She had fallen at her husband's feet! Villefort bent down to her.

"Remember, madame," he said, "if justice has not been done when I return, I shall denounce you with my own lips and arrest you with my own hands!"

She listened panting, overwhelmed, crushed; only her eyes had any life in them, and they glared horribly.

"Remember what I say," said Villefort. "I am going to the Courts to pass sentence of death upon a murderer . . . If I find you alive upon my return, you will spend the night in a prison cell."

Mme de Villefort groaned, her nerves relaxed, and she sank upon the floor exhausted.

For a moment the magistrate appeared to feel pity for her; he looked at her less sternly, and, slightly bending toward her, he said: "Good-bye, madame, good-bye!"

This farewell fell upon Mme de Villefort like the knife of an executioner, and she fainted.

The judge went out and double-locked the door behind him.

Chapter LXIX

EXPIATION

The Court had risen, and as the Procureur du Roi drove home through the crowded streets, the tumultuous thoughts of the morning surged through and through his weary brain. His wife a murderess! Doubtless she was at this moment recalling all her crimes to her memory and imploring God's mercy; perhaps she was writing a letter asking her virtuous husband's forgiveness. Suddenly he said to himself: "That woman must live. She must repent and bring up my son, my poor son, the sole survivor of my unfortunate family except the indestructible old man. She loved him. It was for him that she committed the crimes. One must never despair of the heart of a mother who loves her child. She will repent, and no one shall know of her guilt. She shall take her son and her treasures far away from here, and she will be happy, for all her happiness is centred round her love for her son, and her son will never leave her. I shall have done a good deed, and that will ease my mind."

The carriage stopped in the yard. He stepped out and ran into the house. When passing Noirtier's door, which was half open, he saw two men, but he did not trouble himself about who was with his father, his thoughts were elsewhere. He went into the salon—it was empty!

He rushed up to her bedroom. The door was locked. A shudder went through him, and he stood still.

"Héloïse!" he cried, and he thought he heard some furniture move.

"Héloïse!" he repeated.

"Who is there?" asked a voice.

"Open quickly!" called Villefort. "It is I."

But, notwithstanding the request and the tones of anguish in which it was made, the door remained closed, and he broke it open with a violent kick.

Mme de Villefort was standing at the entrance to the room which led to her boudoir. She was pale and her face was contracted; she looked at him with a terrifying glare.

"Héloïse! Héloïse!" he cried. "What ails you? Speak!"

The young woman stretched out her stiff and lifeless hand.

"It is done, monsieur," she said with a rattling which seemed to tear her very throat. "What more do you want?" And with that she fell her full length on the carpet. Villefort ran up to her and seized her hand, which held in a convulsive grasp a glass bottle with a gold stopper. Mme de Villefort was dead!

Frantic with horror, Villefort started back to the door and contemplated the corpse.

"My son!" he called out. "Where is my son? Edward! Edward!"

He rushed out of the room calling out "Edward! Edward!" in tones of such anguish that the servants came crowding round him in alarm.

"My son—where is my son?" asked Villefort. "Send him out of the house! Do not let him see . . ."

"Monsieur Edward is not downstairs, monsieur," said the valet.

"He is probably playing in the garden. Go and see quickly."

"Madame called her son in nearly half an hour ago, monsieur. Monsieur Edward came to madame and has not been down since."

A cold sweat broke out on Villefort's forehead; his legs gave way under him, and thoughts began to chase each other across his mind like the uncontrollable wheels of a broken clock.

"He came into Madame de Villefort's room?" he murmured, as he slowly retraced his steps, wiping his forehead with one hand and supporting himself against the wall with the other.

"Edward! Edward!" he muttered. There was no answer. Villefort went farther. Mme de Villefort's body was lying across the doorway leading to the boudoir in which Edward must be; the corpse seemed to guard the threshold with wide staring eyes, while the lips held an expression of terrible and mysterious irony. Behind the body the raised curtain permitted one to see into part of the boudoir: an upright piano and the end of a blue satin sofa. Villefort advanced two or three steps, and on this sofa—no doubt asleep—he perceived his child lying. The unhappy man had a feeling of inexpressible joy; a ray of pure light descended into the depths in which he was struggling. All he had to do was to step across the dead body, take the child in his arms, and flee far, far away.

He was no longer the exquisite degenerate typified by the man of modern civilization; he had become like a tiger wounded unto death. It was not prejudice he now feared, but phantoms. He jumped over his wife's body as though it were a yawning furnace of red-hot coals. Taking the boy in his arms, he pressed him to his heart, called him, shook him, but the child made no response. He pressed his eager lips to the child's cheeks—they were cold and livid; he felt the stiffened limbs; he placed his hand over his heart—it beat no more. The child was dead.

Terror-stricken, Villefort dropped upon his knees; the child fell from his arms and rolled beside his mother. A folded paper fell from his breast; Villefort picked it up and recognized his wife's handwriting, and eagerly read the following:

> You know that I have been a good mother, since it was for my son's sake that I became a criminal. A good mother never leaves her son!

Villefort could not believe his eyes, and thought he must

be losing his reason. He dragged himself toward Edward's body, examined it once more with the careful attention of a lioness contemplating its cub.

Then a heartrending cry escaped his breast. "God!" he murmured. "It is the hand of God!"

Villefort rose from his knees, his head bowed under the weight of grief. He, who had never felt compassion for anyone, decided to go to his father so that in his weakness he would have someone to whom he could relate his sufferings, someone with whom he could weep. He descended the little stairs with which we are acquainted, and entered Noirtier's room.

As he entered, Noirtier appeared to be listening attentively, and as affectionately as his paralysed body would permit, to Abbé Busoni, who was as calm and cold as usual. On seeing the abbé, Villefort drew his hand across his forehead. The past all came back to him, and he recollected the visit the abbé had paid him on the day of Valentine's death.

"You here?" he said. "Do you never appear except hand in hand with Death?"

Busoni started up. "I came to pray over the body of your daughter," replied Busoni.

"And why have you come to-day?"

"I have come to-day to tell you that you have made abundant retribution to me and from to-day I shall pray God to forgive you."

"Good heavens!" cried Villefort, starting back with a look of terror in his eyes. "That is not Abbé Busoni's voice!"

"No," said the abbé, and as he tore off his false tonsure his long black hair fell around his manly face.

"That is the face of Monte Cristo!" cried Villefort, a haggard look in his eyes.

"You are not right yet. You must go still further back."

"That voice! That voice! Where have I heard it before?"

"You first heard it at Marseilles twenty-three years ago, on the day of your betrothal to Mademoiselle de Saint-Méran."

"You are not Busoni? Nor yet Monte Cristo? My God! you are my secret, implacable, mortal enemy. I must have wronged you in some way at Marseilles. Ah! woe is me!"

"You are right, it is so," said the Count, crossing his arms over his broad chest. "Think! Think!"

"But what did I do to you?" cried Villefort, whose mind was struggling on the borders between reason and insanity and had sunk into that state which is neither dreaming nor reality. "What have I done? Tell me! Speak!"

"You condemned me to a slow and hideous death; you killed my father; you robbed me of liberty, love, and happiness!"

"Who are you then? Who can you be?"

"I am the ghost of an unhappy wretch you buried in the dungeons of the Château d'If. At length this ghost left his tomb under the disguise of the Count of Monte Cristo, and loaded himself with gold and diamonds that you might not recognize him until to-day."

"Ah! I recognize you! I recognize you!" cried the Procureur du Roi. "You are . . ."

"I am Edmond Dantès!"

"You are Edmond Dantès!" cried the magistrate, seizing the Count by the wrist. "Then come with me!" He dragged him up the stairs, and the astonished Monte Cristo followed him, not knowing where he was leading him, though he had a presentiment of some fresh disaster.

"Look, Edmond Dantès!" said Villefort, pointing to the dead bodies of his wife and son. "Are you satisfied with your vengeance?"

Monte Cristo turned pale at the frightful sight. Realizing that he had passed beyond the bounds of vengeance, he felt he could no longer say: "God is for me and with me." With an expression of indescribable anguish, he threw himself on the child's body, opened his eyes, felt his pulse, and, rushing with him into Valentine's room, locked the door.

"My child!" de Villefort called out. "He has taken the body of my dead child! Oh, curse you! Curses on you in life and death!"

He wanted to run after Monte Cristo, but his feet seemed

rooted to the spot, and his eyes looked ready to start out of their sockets; he dug his nails into his chest until his fingers were covered with blood; the veins of his temples swelled and seemed about to burst through their narrow limits and flood his brain with a deluge of boiling fire. Then with a shrill cry followed by a loud burst of laughter, he ran down the stairs.

A quarter of an hour later the door of Valentine's room opened, and the Count of Monte Cristo reappeared. Pale, sad of eye, and heavy of heart, all the noble features of that usually calm face were distorted with grief. He held in his arms the child whom no skill had been able to recall to life. Bending his knee, he reverently placed him beside his mother with his head upon her breast. Then, rising, he went out of the room and, meeting a servant on the staircase, asked: "Where is Monsieur de Villefort?"

Instead of replying, the servant pointed to the garden. Monte Cristo went down the steps, and, approaching the spot indicated, saw Villefort in the midst of his servants with a spade in his hand digging the earth in a fury and widely calling out: "Oh, I shall find him. You may pretend he is not here, but I shall find him, even if I have to dig until the day of the Last Judgment."

Monte Cristo recoiled in terror. "He is mad!" he cried.

And as though fearing that the walls of the accursed house would fall and crush him, he rushed into the street, doubting for the first time whether he had the right to do what he had done.

"Oh, enough, enough of all this!" he said. "Let me save the last one!"

On arriving home he met Morrel, who was wandering about the house in the Champs Élysées like a ghost waiting for its appointed time to enter the tomb.

"Get yourself ready, Maximilian," he said to him with a smile. "We leave Paris to-morrow."

"Have you nothing more to do here?" asked Morrel.

"No," replied Monte Cristo, "and God grant that I have not already done too much!"

Chapter LXX

THE DEPARTURE

✦

The events just recorded were the talk of all Paris. Emmanuel and his wife were recounting them with very natural astonishment in their little salon in the Rue Meslay, and comparing the three sudden and unexpected calamities that had overtaken Morcerf, Danglars, and de Villefort. Morrel, who had come to pay them a visit, listened to them, or rather was present in his usual state of apathy.

"Really, Emmanuel," said Julie, "one could almost imagine that when all these rich people, who were so happy but yesterday, laid the foundations of their wealth, happiness, and prestige, they forgot the part played by their evil genius; and like the wicked fairy of our childhood days who had not received an invitation to some christening or wedding, this genius has suddenly appeared to take his vengeance for the neglect."

"What disasters!" said Emmanuel, thinking of Morcerf and Danglars.

"What suffering!" said Julie, whose sympathy turned toward Valentine but whose name she, with her womanly delicacy of feeling, would not mention before her brother.

"If it is God's hand that has overtaken them," continued Emmanuel, "it must be that He Who is goodness itself has found nothing in the past life of these people which merited mitigation of their suffering."

"Is that not a very rash judgment, Emmanuel?" said Julie. "If anyone had said 'This man deserves his punishment' when my father held his pistol to his head, would that person not have been mistaken?"

"Yes, but God did not permit him to die just as He did not permit Abraham to sacrifice his son. To the patriarch and to us He sent an angel at the last moment to stay the hand of Death."

He had scarcely finished speaking when the bell rang, and almost at the same moment the door opened to admit Monte Cristo. There was a cry of joy from the two young people, but Maximilian only raised his head to let it drop again.

"Maximilian, I have come to fetch you," said the Count, without appearing to notice the different impressions his presence had produced on his hosts.

"To fetch me?" said Morrel, as though waking from a dream.

"Yes," said Monte Cristo. "Is it not agreed that I should take you away? And did I not tell you to be ready?"

"I am quite ready. I have come to bid them farewell."

"Whither are you going, Count?" asked Julie.

"In the first instance to Marseilles, and I am taking your brother with me."

"Oh, Count, bring him back to us cured of his melancholy!" said Julie.

"Have you then noticed that he is unhappy?" said the Count.

"Yes, and I am afraid he finds it very dull with us."

"I shall divert him," said the Count.

"I am ready," said Maximilian. "Good-bye, Emmanuel! Good-bye, Julie!"

"What! Good-bye?" cried Julie. "You are not going away without any preparations and without a passport?"

"Delays only double grief when one has to part," said

Monte Cristo, "and I am sure Maximilian has provided himself with everything; at all events I asked him to do so."

"I have my passports, and my trunks are packed," said Morrel in a lifeless tone of voice. "Good-bye, sister! Good-bye, Emmanuel!"

"Let us be off," said the Count.

"Before you go, Count, permit me to tell you what the other day . . ."

"Madame," replied the Count, taking her two hands, "all that you can tell me in words can never express what I read in your eyes, or the feelings awakened in your heart, as also in mine. Like the benefactors of romances, I would have left without revealing myself to you, but this virtue was beyond me, because I am but a weak and vain man, and because I feel a better man for seeing a look of gratitude, joy, and affection in the eyes of my fellow beings. I will leave you now, and I carry my egoism so far as to say: 'Do not forget me, my friends, for you will probably never see me again!'"

"Never see you again!" exclaimed Emmanuel, while the tears rolled down Julie's cheeks.

He pressed his lips to Julie's hand and tore himself away from this home where happiness was the host; he made a sign to Morrel, who followed him with all the indifference he had manifested since Valentine's death.

"Restore my brother to happiness again," Julie whispered to Monte Cristo.

He pressed her hand as he had done eleven years ago on the staircase leading to Morrel's study.

"Do you still trust Sindbad the Sailor?" he asked with a smile.

"Oh, yes."

"Well, then, sleep in the peace and confidence of the Lord."

The post-chaise was waiting; four vigorous horses were shaking their manes and pawing the ground in their impatience. Ali was waiting at the bottom of the steps, his face bathed in perspiration as though he had been running.

"Well, did you see the old gentleman?" the Count asked him in Arabic.

Ali made a sign in the affirmative.

"And did you unfold the letter before him as I instructed you to do?"

The slave again made a sign in the affirmative.

"What did he say to you, or rather, what did he do?"

Ali placed himself under the light so that his master might see him, and in his intelligent manner he imitated the expression on the old man's face when he closed his eyes in token of assent.

"It is well, he accepts," said Monte Cristo. "Let us start!"

Half an hour passed, and the carriage suddenly stopped; the Count had pulled the silken cord that was attached to Ali's finger. The Nubian alighted and opened the door.

It was a lovely starlit night. They were on top of the Villejuif hill, when Paris appeared like a dark sea, and her millions of lights like phosphorescent waves; waves which were more clamorous, more passionate, more greedy than those of the tempestuous ocean; waves which are ever raging, foaming, and ever ready to devour what comes in their way.

At a sign from the Count, the carriage went on, leaving him alone. Then, with arms crossed, he contemplated for a long time this modern Babylon which inspires the poet, the religious enthusiast, and the materialist alike. Bowing his head and joining his hands as though in prayer, he murmured:

"Oh, great city! In thy palpitating bosom have I found what I sought; like a patient miner have I dug out thy very entrails to root out the evil. My work is accomplished, my mission ended, and now thou canst hold neither pleasure nor pain for me. Farewell, Paris! Farewell!"

His eyes wandered over the vast plain like that of a genius of the night; then passing his hand across his brow, he once more entered his carriage, which disappeared over the hill in a cloud of dust.

They travelled thus for ten leagues in complete silence, Morrel wrapt in dreams and Monte Cristo watching him dream.

"Morrel," said the Count at length, "do you regret having come with me?"

"No, Count, but in leaving Paris . . ."

"If I had thought your happiness was to be found in Paris, I should have left you there."

"Valentine is laid at rest in Paris, and I feel as though I were losing her for a second time."

"Maximilian, the friends we have lost do not repose under the ground," said the Count; "they are buried deep in our hearts. It has been thus ordained that they may always accompany us. I have two such friends. The one is he who gave me being, and the other is he who brought my intelligence to life. Their spirits are ever with me. When in doubt I consult them, and if I ever do anything that is good, I owe it to them. Consult the voice of your heart, Morrel, and ask it whether you should continue this behaviour toward me."

"The voice of my heart is a very sad one," said Maximilian, "and promises nothing but unhappiness."

The journey was made with extraordinary rapidity; villages fled past them like shadows; trees, shaken by the first autumn winds, seemed like dishevelled giants rushing up only to flee as soon as they had reached them. They arrived at Chalon the next morning, where the Count's steamboat awaited them. Without loss of time the two travellers embarked, and their carriage was taken aboard.

The boat was almost like an Indian canoe, and was especially built for racing. Her two paddle-wheels were like two wings with which she skimmed the water like a bird. Even Morrel seemed intoxicated with the rapidity of their motion, and at times it almost seemed as though the wind, in blowing his hair back from his forehead, also momentarily dispelled the dark clouds that were gathered there. Marseilles was soon reached. As they stood on the Cannebière a boat was leaving for Algiers. Passengers were crowded on the decks, relatives and friends were bidding farewell, some weeping silently, others crying aloud in their grief. It was a touching sight even to those accustomed to witnessing it every day, yet it had not the power to distract Morrel from the one thought that had occupied his mind ever since he set foot on the broad stones of the quay.

"Here is the very spot where my father stood when the *Pharaon* entered the port," he said to the Count. "It was here that the honest man whom you saved from death and dishonour threw himself into my arms; I still feel his tears on my face."

Monte Cristo smiled. "I was there," he said, pointing to a corner of the street. As he spoke, a heartrending sob was heard issuing from the very spot indicated by the Count, and they saw a woman making signs to a passenger on the departing boat. The woman was veiled. Monte Cristo watched her with an emotion which must have been evident to Morrel had his eyes not been fixed on the boat.

"Good heavens!" cried Morrel. "Surely I am not mistaken. That young man waving his hand, the one in uniform, is Albert de Morcerf."

"Yes," said Monte Cristo. "I recognized him."

"How can you have done? You were looking the other way."

The Count smiled in the way he had when he did not wish to answer. His eyes turned again to the veiled woman, who soon disappeared round the corner of the street. Then, turning to Maximilian, he said: "Have you nothing to do in the town?"

"Yes, I wish to pay a visit to my father's grave," replied Morrel in a lifeless voice.

"Very well, go and wait for me; I will join you there."

"You are leaving me?"

"Yes . . . I have also a visit of devotion to make."

Morrel let his hand fall into the one the Count held out to him; then, with an inexpressibly melancholy nod of the head, he took his leave of the Count and directed his steps toward the east of the town.

Monte Cristo stayed where he was until Maximilian was out of sight, then he wended his way to the Allées de Meilhan in search of a little house that was made familiar to our readers at the beginning of this story.

In spite of its age the little house, once inhabited by Dantès' father, still looked charming and not even its obvious poverty could deprive it of its cheerful aspect. It was to this little house that the veiled woman repaired when Monte Cristo saw her leaving the departing ship. She was just closing the gate when he turned the corner of the street, so that she disappeared from his vision almost as soon as he had found her again. The worn steps were old acquaintances of his; he knew better than anyone how to open the old gate with its large-headed nail, which raised the latch from the inside.

He entered without knocking or announcing himself in any way. At the end of a paved path was a little garden that caught all the sunshine and light, and its trees could be seen from the front door. It was here Mercédès had found, in the spot indicated, the sum of money which the Count's delicacy of feeling had led him to say had been deposited in this little garden for twenty-four years.

Monte Cristo heard a deep sigh and, looking in the direction whence it came, he beheld Mercédès sitting in an arbour covered with jasmine with thick foliage and slender purple flowers; her head was bowed, and she was weeping bitterly. She had partly raised her veil and, being alone, was giving full vent to the sighs and sobs which had so long been repressed by the presence of her son.

Monte Cristo advanced a few steps, crunching the gravel under his feet as he trod. Mercédès raised her head and gave a cry of fear at seeing a man before her.

"Madame, it is no longer in my power to bring you happiness," said the Count, "but I offer you consolation. Will you deign to accept it from a friend?"

"In truth I am a most unhappy woman, and all alone in the world," replied Mercédès. "My son was all I had, and he too has left me."

"He has acted rightly, madame," replied the Count. "He is a noble-hearted soul who realizes that every man owes a tribute to his country; some their talents, others their industry, others their blood. Had he remained beside you, he would have led a useless life. In struggling against adversity, he will become great and powerful and will change his adversity into prosperity. Let him remake a future for himself and for you, madame, and I venture to say you are leaving it in safe hands."

"I shall never enjoy the prosperity of which you speak," said the poor woman, shaking her head sadly, "but from the bottom of my heart I pray God to grant it to my son. There has been so much sorrow in my life that I feel my grave is not far distant. You have done well, Count, in bringing me back to the spot where I was once so happy. One should wait for death there, where one has found happiness."

"Alas!" said Monte Cristo, "your words fall heavily on my heart, and they are all the more bitter and cutting since you have every reason to hate me. It is I who am the cause of all your misfortunes; why do you pity me instead of reproaching me?"

"Hate you! Reproach you, Edmond! Hate and reproach the man who saved my son's life, for I know it was your intention to kill the son of whom Monsieur de Morcerf was so proud, was it not? Look at me and you will see whether I bear the semblance of a reproach against you."

The Count looked up and fixed his gaze on Mercédès, who, half rising from her seat, stretched her hands toward him.

"Oh, look at me," she continued in tones of deep melancholy. "My eyes are no longer bright, as in the days when I smiled upon Edmond Dantès, who was waiting for me at the window of this garret where his father lived. Since then many sorrowful days have passed and made a gulf between that time and now. Reproach you! Hate you, Edmond! my friend! No, it is myself that I hate and reproach!" she cried, wringing her hands and raising her eyes to Heaven. "Ah, but I have been sorely punished . . . I had faith, innocence, and love—everything that makes for supreme happiness, yet, unhappy wretch that I am, I doubted God's goodness!"

Monte Cristo silently took her hand.

"No, my friend, do not touch me," she said, gently withdrawing it. "You have spared me, yet of all I am the most to blame. All the others were prompted by hatred, cupidity,[1] or selfishness, but cowardice was at the root of all my actions. No, do not take my hand, Edmond; you wish to say some kind and affectionate words, I know, but keep them for someone else. I am not worthy of them. See—see how misfortune has silvered my hair. I have shed so many tears that dark rings encircle my eyes; my forehead is covered with wrinkles. You, on the contrary, are still young, Edmond; you are still handsome and dignified. That is because you have preserved your faith and your strength: you trusted in God, and He has sustained you. I was a coward; I denied Him, and He has forsaken me."

Mercédès burst into tears; her woman's heart was breaking in the clash of her memories. Monte Cristo took her hand and kissed it respectfully, but she knew that it was a kiss without feeling, such as he would have imprinted on the marble statue of a saint.

"No, Mercédès," said he, "you must form a better opinion of yourself. You are a good and noble woman, and you disarmed me by your sorrow; but behind me there was concealed an invisible and offended God, Whose agent I was and Who did not choose to withhold the blow I had aimed. I call God to witness, at Whose feet I have prostrated myself every day for the last ten years, that I have offered the sacrifice of my life and my lifelong projects to you. But, and I say it with pride, Mercédès, God had need of me and my life was spared. The first part of my life passed away amid terrible misfortunes, cruel sufferings, desertion on the part of those who loved me, persecution by those who did not know me. Then after captivity, solitude, and tribulation, I was suddenly restored to fresh air and liberty, and I became the possessor of a large fortune, so dazzling and fabulous that I could only conclude that God had sent it me for some great purpose. I looked upon His wealth as a sacred charge. From that time I did not experience a single hour's peace: I felt myself pushed onward like a cloud of fire sent from Heaven to burn the cities of the wicked. I habituated my body to the most violent exercise, and my spirit to the severest trials. I taught my arm to slay, my eyes to behold suffering, my lips to smile at the most terrible sights. From being a kind and confiding nature, I made myself into a vindictive, treacherous, and wicked man. Then I set forth on the path that was opened up to me; I conquered space and I have reached my goal: woe to those I encountered on my way!"

"Enough, Edmond, enough," said Mercédès. "Now bid me farewell, Edmond. We must part."

"Before I leave you, Mercédès, is there nothing I can do for you?" asked Monte Cristo.

"I have but one desire, Edmond—my son's happiness."

"Pray to God, Who alone disposes over life and death, to spare his life, and I will do the rest. And for yourself, Mercédès?"

"I need nothing for myself. I live, as it were, between two graves. The one is that of Edmond Dantès, who died many years ago. Ah! how I loved him! The other grave belongs to the man Edmond Dantès killed; I approve of the deed, but I must pray for the dead man."

"Your son shall be happy, madame," the count repeated.

"Then I also shall be as happy as it is possible for me to be."

"But . . . what are you going to do?"

"All I am fit for now is to pray. I do not need to work; I have the little treasure you buried and which has been found in the spot you indicated. There will be much gossip as to who I am, what I do, and how I subsist, but what does that matter? Those are questions which concern but God, you, and me."

"Mercédès," said the Count, "I do not wish to reproach you, but you have taken an exaggerated view as to your sacrifice of the fortune amassed by Monsieur de Morcerf. By rights half of it was yours in virtue of your vigilance and economy."

"I know what you are going to propose. I cannot accept it, Edmond; my son would not permit it."

"I will not do anything without Albert's approval. I will make myself acquainted with his intentions and shall submit to them. But if he agrees to what I propose, will you follow his example?"

"You know, Edmond, that I have no longer any reasoning powers, and no will, unless it be the will not to take any decision. My will has been swept away by the storms that have raged over my head. I am as helpless in God's hands as a sparrow in the talons of an eagle. Since He does not wish me to die, I live; if He sends me help, it is because He so desires, and I shall accept it."

Monte Cristo bowed his head under the vehemence of her grief. "Will you not say *au revoir*² to me?" he said, holding out his hand.

"On the contrary, I do say *au revoir*," Mercédès replied, solemnly pointing to Heaven, "and that is a proof that I still hope."

She touched the Count's hand with her own trembling fingers, ran up the stairs, and disappeared from his sight. Monte Cristo left the house with heavy steps. But Mercédès did not see him; her eyes were searching in the far distance for the ship that was carrying her son toward the vast ocean. Nevertheless her voice almost involuntarily murmured softly: "Edmond! Edmond!"

The Count went with a heavy heart from the house where he had taken leave of Mercédès, in all probability never to see her again, and turned his steps toward the cemetery where Morrel was awaiting him.

Ten years previously, he had also sought piously for a grave in this same cemetery, but he had sought in vain. He who had returned to France with millions of money had been unable to find the grave of his father, who had died of hunger. Morrel had had a cross erected, but it had fallen down, and the sexton had burnt it with the rubbish. The worthy merchant had been more fortunate. He had died in the arms of his children, and by them had been laid beside his wife, who had preceded him into eternity by two years.

Two large marble slabs, on which were engraved their names, were standing side by side in a little railed-in enclosure shaded by four cypresses.

Maximilian was leaning against one of these trees staring at the two graves with unseeing eyes. He was obviously deeply affected.

"Maximilian, it is not on those graves you should look, but there!" said the Count, pointing to the sky.

"The dead are everywhere," said Morrel. "Did you not tell me so yourself when you made me leave Paris?"

"On the journey, Maximilian, you asked me to let you stay a few days at Marseilles. Is that still your wish?"

"I have no longer any wishes, Count, but I think the time of waiting would pass less painfully here than anywhere."

"All the better, Maximilian, for I must leave you, but I have your word, have I not?"

"I shall forget it, Count, I know I shall."

"No, you will not forget it, for you are, above all things, a man of honour, Morrel; you have sworn to wait and will now renew your oath."

"Have pity on me, Count, I am so unhappy!"

"I have known a man unhappier than you, Morrel."

"What man is there unhappier than he who has lost the only being he loved on earth?"

"Listen, Morrel, and fix your whole mind on what I am going to tell you. I once knew a man who, like you, had set all his hopes of happiness upon a woman. He was young; he had an old father whom he loved, and a sweetheart whom he adored. He was about to marry her, when suddenly he was overtaken by one of those caprices of fate which would make us doubt in the goodness of God, if He did not reveal Himself later by showing us that all is but a means to an end. This man was deprived of his liberty, of the woman he loved, of the future of which he had dreamed and which he believed was his, and plunged into the depths of a dungeon. He stayed there fourteen years, Morrel. Fourteen years!" repeated the Count. "And during those fourteen years he suffered many an hour of despair. Like you, Morrel, he also thought he was the unhappiest of men, and sought to take his life."

"Well?" asked Morrel.

"Well, when he was at the height of his despair, God revealed Himself to him through another human being. It takes a long time for eyes that are swollen with weeping to see clearly, and at first, perhaps, he did not comprehend this infinite mercy, but at length he took patience and waited. One day he miraculously left his tomb, transfigured, rich, and powerful. His first cry was for his father, but his father was dead! When his son sought his grave, ten years after his death, even that had disappeared, and no one could say to him: 'There rests in the Lord the father who so dearly loved you!' That man, therefore, was unhappier than you, for he did not even know where to look for his father's grave."

"But then he still had the woman he loved."

"You are wrong, Morrel. This woman was faithless. She married one of the persecutors of her betrothed. You see, Morrel, that in this again he was unhappier than you."

"And did this man find consolation?"

"At all events he found peace."

"Is it possible for this man ever to be happy again?"

"He hopes so."

The young man bowed his head, and after a moment's silence he gave Monte Cristo his hand, saying: "You have my promise, Count, but remember . . ."

"I shall expect you on the Isle of Monte Cristo on the fifth of October, Morrel. On the fourth, a yacht named the *Eurus* will be waiting for you in the Port of Bastia. Give your name to the captain, and he will bring you to me. That is quite definite, is it not?"

"It is, Count, and I shall do as you say. You are leaving me?"

"Yes, I have business in Italy. I am leaving you alone with your grief."

"When are you going?"

"At once. The steamboat is waiting for me, and in an hour I shall be far from you. Will you go with me as far as the harbour?"

"I am entirely at your service."

Morrel accompanied the Count to the harbour. The smoke was already issuing from the black funnel like an immense plume. The boat got under way, and an hour later, as Monte Cristo had said, the same feather of white smoke was scarcely discernible on the horizon as it mingled with the first mists of the night.

Chapter LXXI

THE FIFTH OF OCTOBER

✣

It was about six o'clock in the evening; an opalescent light through which the autumn sun shed a golden ray descended on the sea. The heat of the day had gradually diminished into that delicious freshness which seems like nature's breathing after the burning siesta of the afternoon, and a light breeze was bringing to the shores of the Mediterranean the sweet perfume of trees and plants mingled with the salt smell of the sea.

A small yacht, elegant in shape, was drifting in the evening air over this immense lake, like some swan opening its wings to the wind and gliding through the water. It advanced rapidly, although there seemed hardly sufficient wind to ruffle the curls of a young maiden.

Standing on the prow, a tall dark man was watching the approach of land, a cone-shaped mass, which appeared to rise out of the water like a huge Catalan hat.

"Is that Monte Cristo?" he asked of the skipper in a voice full of sadness.

"Yes, Your Excellency," replied the latter. "We are there."

Ten minutes later, with sails furled, they anchored a hundred feet from the little harbour. The cutter was ready with four oarsmen and the pilot. The eight oars dipped together without a splash, and the boat glided rapidly onward. A moment later they found themselves in a small natural creek and ran aground on fine sand.

"If Your Excellency will get on to the shoulders of two of our men they will carry you to dry land," said the pilot. The young man's answer was a shrug of complete indifference as he swung himself out of the boat into the water.

"Ah, Excellency!" cried the pilot. "That is wrong of you! The master will scold us."

The young man continued to follow the two sailors, and after about thirty steps reached the shore, where he stood and peered into the darkness. Then he felt a hand on his shoulder, and a voice startled him by saying: "Good evening, Maximilian. You are very punctual."

"It is you, Count!" cried the young man, delightedly pressing Monte Cristo's two hands in his.

"Yes, and, as you see, as punctual as you are. But you are drenched, my friend; come, there is a house prepared for you, where you will forget cold and fatigue."

The sailors were dismissed, and the two friends proceeded on their way. They walked for some time in silence, each busy with his own thoughts. Presently Morrel, with a sigh, turned to his companion: "I am come," said he, "to say to you as the gladiator would say to the Roman Emperor: 'He who is about to die salutes you.'"

"You have not found consolation then?" Monte Cristo asked, with a strange look.

"Did you really think I could?" Morrel said with great bitterness. "Listen to me, Count, as to one whose spirit lives in Heaven while his body still walks the earth. I am come to die in the arms of a friend. It is true there are those I love, my sister and her husband, Emmanuel, but I have need of strong arms and one who will smile on me during my last moments. I have your word, Count. You will conduct me to the gates of death by pleasant paths, will you not? Oh, Count, how peacefully and contentedly I shall sleep in the arms of death!"

Morrel said the last words with such determination that the Count trembled.

Seeing that Monte Cristo was silent, Morrel continued: "My friend, you named the fifth of October as the day on which my trial should end. It is to-day the fifth of October . . . I have but a short while to live."

"So be it," said Monte Cristo. "Come with me."

Morrel followed the Count mechanically, and they had entered the grotto before he perceived it. There was a carpet under his feet; a door opened, exhaling fragrant perfumes, and a bright light dazzled his eyes. Morrel paused, not venturing to advance. He mistrusted the enervating delights that surrounded him. Monte Cristo gently drew him in.

He sat down, and Morrel took a seat opposite him.

They were in a wonderful dining-room, where the marble statues bore baskets on their heads laden with flowers and fruit. Morrel looked at everything in a vague way, though it is even possible he did not see anything.

"Count, you are the essence of all human knowledge," he resumed, "and you make me think you have descended from a more advanced and wiser world than ours. Tell me, is it painful to die?"

Monte Cristo looked at Morrel with indescribable tenderness. "Yes, it is undoubtedly painful when you violently break this mortal coil that obstinately demands to live. According as we have lived, death is either a friend who rocks us as gently as a nurse, or an enemy who violently tears the soul from the body."

"I understand now why you have brought me here to this deserted isle in the middle of an ocean; to this subterranean palace, which is a sepulchre such as would awaken envy in the heart of a Pharaoh. It is because you love me, is it not, Count? Because you love me well enough to give me a death without agony; a death which will permit me to glide away, holding your hand and murmuring the name of Valentine."

"Yes, yes, you have guessed aright, Morrel," said the Count simply. "That is what I intended. Now," he said to himself, "I must bring this young man back to happiness; he has passed through enough sorrow to merit happiness at last." Then aloud he added: "Listen to me, Morrel; I see that your grief is overwhelming. As you know, I have no one in the world to call my own. I have learned to regard you as my son, and to save that son I would sacrifice my life, nay, even my fortune."

"What do you mean?"

"I mean that you wish to leave this world because you do not know all the pleasures a large fortune can give. Morrel, I have nearly a hundred millions; I give them to you. With such a fortune nothing is denied you. Have you ambitions? Every career is opened to you. Turn the world upside down, change its character, let no mad scheme be too mad for you, become a criminal if it is necessary—but live!"

"I have your word, Count," said Morrel coldly. Taking out his watch, he added: "It is half-past eleven."

"Morrel, consider. You would do this thing before my eyes? In my house?"

"Then let me go hence," replied Maximilian gloomily. "Otherwise I shall think that you do not love me for myself but for yourself."

"It is well," said the Count, whose face had brightened at these words. "You wish it, and you are firmly resolved on death. You are certainly most unhappy, and, as you say, a miracle alone could save you. Sit down and wait."

Morrel obeyed. Monte Cristo rose and went to a cupboard, and unlocking it with a key which he wore on a gold chain, took out a small silver casket wonderfully carved; the corners represented four bending women symbolical of angels aspiring to Heaven.

He placed the casket on the table, and, opening it, took out a small gold box, the lid of which opened by the pressure of a secret spring. This box contained an unctuous, half-solid substance of an indefinable colour. It was like an iridescence of blue, purple, and gold.

The Count took a small quantity of this substance with a gold spoon and offered it to Morrel while fixing a long and steadfast glance upon him. It was then seen that the substance was of a greenish hue.

"This is what you asked for and what I promised to give you," said the Count.

Taking the spoon from the Count's hand, the young man said: "I thank you from the bottom of my heart. Farewell, my noble and generous friend. I am going to Valentine and shall tell her all that you have done for me."

Slowly, but without any hesitation, and waiting only to press the Count's hand, Morrel swallowed, or rather tasted, the mysterious substance the Count offered him.

The lamps gradually became dim in the hands of the marble statues that held them, and the perfumes seemed to become less potent. Seated opposite to Morrel, Monte Cristo watched him in the shadow, and Morrel saw nothing but the Count's bright eyes. An immense sadness overtook the young man.

"My friend, I feel that I am dying."

Then he seemed to see Monte Cristo smile, no longer the strange, frightening smile that had several times revealed to him the mysteries of that profound mind, but with the benevolent compassion of a father toward an unreasonable child. At the same time the Count appeared to increase in stature. Nearly double his height he was outlined against the red hangings, and, as he stood there erect and proud, he looked like one of those angels with which the wicked are threatened on the Day of Judgment. Depressed and overcome, Morrel threw himself back in his chair, and a delicious torpor crept into his veins; he seemed to be entering upon the vague delirium that precedes the unknown thing they call death. He endeavoured once more to give his hand to the Count, but it would not move; he wished to articulate a last farewell, but his tongue lay heavy in his mouth like a stone at the mouth of a sepulchre. His languid eyes involuntarily closed, yet through his closed eyelids he perceived a form moving which he recognized in spite of the darkness that seemed to envelop him.

It was the Count, who was opening a door. Immediately a brilliant light from the adjoining room inundated the one where Morrel was gently passing into oblivion. Then he saw a woman of marvellous beauty standing on the threshold. She seemed like a pale and sweetly smiling angel of mercy come to conjure the angel of vengeance.

"Is Heaven opening before me?" the dying man thought to himself. "This angel resembles the one I have lost!"

Monte Cristo pointed to the sofa where Morrel was reclining. The young woman advanced toward it with clasped hands and a smile on her lips.

"Valentine! Valentine!" Morrel's soul went out to her, but he uttered no sound; only a sigh escaped his lips and he closed his eyes.

Valentine ran up to him, and his lips opened as though in speech.

"He is calling you," said the Count. "He is calling you in his sleep, he to whom you have entrusted your life is calling you. Death would have separated you, but by good fortune I was near and I have overcome death! Valentine, henceforth you must never leave him, for, in order to rejoin you, he courted death. Without me you would both have died; I give you to one another. May God give me credit for the two lives I have saved!"

Valentine seized Monte Cristo's hand, and in a transport of irresistible joy carried it to her lips.

"Oh, yes, yes, I do thank you, and with all my heart," said she. "If you doubt the sincerity of my gratitude, ask Haydee, ask my dear sister Haydee, who, since our departure from France, has helped me to await this happy day that has dawned for me."

"Do you love Haydee?" asked Monte Cristo, vainly endeavouring to hide his agitation.

"With my whole heart."

"Well, then, I have a favour to ask of you, Valentine," said the Count.

"Of me? Are you really giving me that happiness?"

"Yes, you called Haydee your sister; be a real sister to her, Valentine; give to her all that you believe you owe to me. Protect her, both Morrel and you, for henceforth she will be alone in the world."

"Alone in the world?" repeated a voice behind the Count. "Why?"

Monte Cristo turned round.

Haydee was standing there pale and motionless, looking at the Count in mortal dread.

"To-morrow you will be free, my daughter," answered the Count. "You will then assume your proper place in society; I do not wish my fate to overcloud yours. Daughter of a prince! I bestow on you the wealth and the name of your father!"

Haydee turned pale, and, in a voice choking with emotion, she said: "Then you are leaving me, my lord?"

"Haydee! Haydee! You are young and beautiful. Forget even my name and be happy!"

"So be it!" said Haydee. "Your orders shall be obeyed, my lord. I shall even forget your name and be happy!" and stepping back she sought to retire.

The Count shuddered as he caught the tones of her voice which penetrated to the inmost recesses of his heart. His eyes encountered the maiden's, and he could not bear their brilliancy.

"My God!" cried he. "Is it possible that my suspicions are correct? Haydee, would you be happy never to leave me again?"

"I am young," she replied. "I love the life you made so sweet to me, and I should regret to die!"

"Does that mean to say that if I were to leave you . . . ?"

"I should die? Yes, my lord."

"Do you love me then?"

"Oh, Valentine, he asks me whether I love him! Valentine, tell him whether you love Maximilian!"

The Count felt his heart swelling within him; he opened his arms, and Haydee threw herself into them with a cry.

"Oh, yes, I love you!" she said. "I love you as one loves a father, a brother, a husband! I love you as I love my life, for to me you are the noblest, the best, and the greatest of all created beings!"

"Let it be as you wish, my sweet angel," said the Count. "God has sustained me against my enemies and I see now He does not wish me to end my triumph with repentance. I intended punishing myself, but God has pardoned me! Love me, Haydee! Who knows? Perhaps your love will help me to forget all I do not wish to remember!"

"What do you mean, my lord?" asked she.

"What I mean is that one word from you, Haydee, has enlightened me more than twenty years of bitter experience. I have but you in the world, Haydee. Through you I come back to life, through you I can suffer, and through you I can be happy."

"Do you hear him, Valentine?" Haydee cried out. "He says he can suffer through me! Through me, who would give my life for him!"

The Count reflected for a moment.

"Have I caught a glimpse of the truth?" he said. "But, whether it be for recompense or punishment, I accept this fate. Come, Haydee!"

Throwing his arms round the young girl, he shook Valentine by the hand and disappeared.

An hour or so elapsed, and Valentine still stood beside Morrel breathless, voiceless, with her eyes fixed on him. At length she felt his heart beat, his lips parted to emit a slight breath, and the shudder which announces a return to life ran through his whole frame. Finally his eyes opened, though with an expressionless stare at first; then his vision returned and with it the power of feeling and grief.

"Oh, I still live!" he cried in accents of despair. "The Count has deceived me!" Extending his hand toward the table, he seized a knife.

"My dear one!" said Valentine with her sweet smile. "Awake and look at me!"

With a loud cry, frantic, doubting, and dazzled as by a celestial vision, Morrel fell upon his knees.

At daybreak the next day Morrel and Valentine were walking arm in arm along the seashore, while Valentine related how Monte Cristo had appeared in her room, how he had disclosed everything and pointed to the crime, and finally how he had miraculously saved her from death by making believe that she was dead.

They had found the door of the grotto open and had gone out whilst the last stars of the night were still shining in the morning sky. After a time, Morrel perceived a man standing amongst the rocks waiting for permission to advance, and pointed him out to Valentine.

"It is Jacopo, the captain of the yacht!" she said, making signs for him to approach.

"Have you something to tell us?" Morrel asked.

"I have a letter from the Count for you."

"From the Count!" they exclaimed together.

"Yes, read it."

Morrel opened the letter and read:

My dear Maximilian,

There is a felucca waiting for you. Jacopo will take you to Leghorn, where Monsieur Noirtier is awaiting his granddaughter to give her his blessing before you conduct her to the altar. All that is in the grotto, my house in the Champs Élysées, and my little chateau at Tréport are the wedding present of Edmond Dantès to the son of his old master, Morrel. Ask Mademoiselle de Villefort to accept one-half, for I beseech her to give to the poor of Paris all the money which she inherits from her father, who is now insane, as also from her brother, who died last September with her stepmother.

Tell the angel who is going to watch over you, Morrel, to pray for a man who, like Satan, believed for one moment he was the equal of God, but who now acknowledges in all Christian humility that in God alone is supreme power and infinite wisdom. Her prayers will perhaps soothe the remorse in the depths of his heart.

Live and be happy, beloved children of my heart, and never forget that, until the day comes when God will deign to reveal the future to man, all human wisdom is contained in these words: Wait and hope!

Your friend,
EDMOND DANTÈS, COUNT OF MONTE CRISTO

During the perusal of this letter, which informed Valentine for the first time of the fate of her father and her brother, she turned pale, a painful sigh escaped from her bosom, and silent tears coursed down her cheeks; her happiness had cost her dear.

Morrel looked around him uneasily.

"Where is the Count, my friend?" said he. "Take me to him."

Jacopo raised his hand toward the horizon.

"What do you mean?" asked Valentine. "Where is the Count? Where is Haydee?"

"Look!" said Jacopo.

The eyes of the two young people followed the direction of the sailor's hand, and there, on the blue horizon separating the sky from the Mediterranean, they perceived a sail, which loomed large and white like a seagull.

"Gone!" cried Morrel. "Farewell, my friend, my father!"

"Gone!" murmured Valentine. "Good-bye, my friend, my sister!"

"Who knows whether we shall ever see them again," said Morrel, wiping away a tear.

"My dear," replied Valentine, "has not the Count just told us that all human wisdom is contained in the words Wait and hope!"

NOTES

A

Chapter I

1. **Smyrna, Trieste, and Naples:** Seaport trading towns: Smyrna is on the coast of the Aegean Sea in modern Turkey, Trieste is at Italy's easternmost point on the Adriatic Sea, and Naples is on Italy's west coast about one hundred miles south of Rome.
2. **Marseilles:** A seaport city on France's Mediterranean coast.
3. **bulwarks:** Bulwarks are the part of a ship's sides that rise above the upper decks.
4. **Civita Vecchia:** A port town on Italy's west coast, north of Rome.
5. **Isle of El Giglio:** An island in the Tuscan Archipelago, off of Italy's northwestern coast.
6. **brail:** A rope attached to a ship's sail used for drawing the sail in or up.
7. **Isle of Elba:** Elba is the largest island in the

Tuscan chain. Napoleon Bonaparte was exiled there from France as Emperor of Elba from May 1814 until February 1815.

8. *Chi ha compagne ha padrone:* He who has partners has masters.

Chapter II

1. **Catalan:** A native of Catalonia, a region of northeast Spain bordering France on the Mediterranean Sea.

2. **Vieilles-Infirmeries:** Old infirmaries.

Chapter III

1. *congé:* Leave.

Chapter IV

1. **Bonapartist faction:** Supporters of Napoleon's return to power.

2. *Procureur du Roi:* Director of public prosecutions.

Chapter V

1. **Puget:** Pierre Puget (1622–1694) was a painter, sculptor, architect, and naval constructor from Marseilles who worked in Italy and southern France.

2. **the usurper:** Napoleon, to Royalists.

3. **Condé:** Louis Joseph de Bourbon, prince de Condé (1736–1818), fought with distinction for

France in the Seven Years War. At the beginning of the French Revolution he emigrated and fomented counterrevolutionary action. He formed a corps known as the army of Condé, which he allied with the Austrians.

4. **cross of Saint-Louis:** A military award created in 1693 and abolished in 1792 during the French Revolution.

5. **Mahomet:** Mohammed.

6. **plebeian:** A member of the lower classes.

7. **Girondin:** A member of a faction of moderate bourgeois revolutionaries during the French Revolution.

8. **Murat:** Joachim Murat (1767–1815), Napoleon's brother-in-law, Maréchal de France, and King of Naples (1808–1815).

Chapter VI

1. *gendarmes:* The French national police organization constituting a branch of the armed forces with responsibility for general law enforcement.

2. *rôle:* Role.

3. **Juge d'Instruction:** A French judge of inquiry; a magistrate responsible for conducting the investigative hearing before a criminal trial.

4. **commissary:** A deputy.

Chapter VII

1. **Accoules:** One of the oldest churches in Marseilles.

2: **mephitic:** Foul-smelling.

3. **quay:** A wharf.
4. **augury:** A sign of something to come.
5. **adjure:** To entreat earnestly.
6. **gaolers:** Jailers.
7. **gaol:** Jail.

Chapter VIII

1. **Corsican Ogre:** Napoleon.
2. **wounded hero of Virgil:** Aeneas, the subject of *The Aeneid,* Virgil's epic about the founding of Rome.
3. **sanguine:** Optimistic.

Chapter IX

1. **cabinet of the Tuileries:** A room in the Tuileries, a palace of the French monarchs, as well as Emperor Napoleon's official residence.
2. **carking:** Worrying.
3. *Canimus surdis:* "We sing to those who have no ears," misquoted from Virgil's Eclogue X. It should read, "Non canimus surdis."
4. **poet of Venusia:** Horace (65–68 B.C.), the Latin lyric poet and satirist.
5. *pastor quum traheret:* "The shepherd who was leading," from Horace's *Odes,* Book I, Ode XV.
6. *Mala ducis avi domum:* "You bring home dark portents," from Horace's *Odes,* Book I, Ode XV.
7. *Bella, horrida bella:* "War, horrible war," a quote from Virgil's *Aeneid,* Book VI, Line LXXXVI.
8. **another Marengo or a second Austerlitz:** The Battle of Marengo (June 14, 1800) was a crucial

victory for Napoleon's army over the Austrians. The Battle of Austerlitz (December 2, 1805), in which he defeated the Russian and Austrian armies, is considered Napoleon's greatest victory.

9. **hie:** Go quickly.

Chapter XI

1. **history of the famous return from Elba:** Napoleon's return is known as the Hundred Days, lasting from his entry into Paris on March 20, 1815, until his defeat at Waterloo on June 18 and his second abdication on June 22.

2. **Waterloo:** On June 18, 1815, fought against British and Prussian forces, the Battle of Waterloo marked Napoleon's final defeat and the end of his power.

Chapter XII

1. **friable:** Brittle and readily crumbled.

Chapter XIII

1. **abbé:** The title for the superior of a monastery in a French-speaking area.

2. **scheme that Napoleon tried to realize in eighteen-eleven:** By 1809 Italy was split into three main zones: areas absorbed into the French Empire, the Kingdom of Italy ruled by a French viceroy, and the Kingdom of Naples under Murat. The French attempted to re-unify the three zones into one country and impose administrative struc-

ture. The attempt failed in 1814 when Italian kings and princes returned.

3. **Machiavelli:** Niccolò Machiavelli (1469–1527) was the first great political philosopher of the Renaissance. His famous treatise, *The Prince,* focuses on the practical problems a monarch faces in staying in power.

4. **Caesar Borgia:** Cesare Borgia (1476–1507) was an Italian soldier and politician, the younger son of Pope Alexander VI, and is considered the prototype of Niccolò Machiavelli's *Prince*—intelligent, cruel, treacherous, and ruthlessly opportunistic.

5. **aurora borealis:** A luminous atmospheric phenomenon appearing as bands of light, best viewed from the earth's northern regions. Also called northern lights.

6. **cataleptic fit:** A seizure.

Chapter XIV

1. **Holy See:** The Roman Catholic Church.
2. **plate:** Domestic vessels and utensils, such as plates and cups, wrought in precious metal.

Chapter XV

1. **sacking:** A coarse cloth, such as burlap or gunny, used for making sacks.

Chapter XVII

1. **tartan:** A single-masted vessel used mainly for commercial purposes in the Mediterranean.

2. **lee-braces:** Ropes by which yards are swung and secured on square-rigged ships.
3. **chimerical:** Highly improbable.
4. **lingua franca:** A mixture of the languages of the people of a given region or of foreign traders.

Chapter XVIII

1. **chamois:** An extremely agile goat antelope of the mountainous regions of Europe.

Chapter XIX

1. **Sisyphus:** A figure in ancient mythology condemned to forever roll a block of stone against a steep hill, which tumbles back down when he reaches the top.
2. **fain:** Gladly.

Chapter XXII

1. **battle of Ligny:** On June 16, 1815, against the Prussians and British, the battle of Ligny was Napoleon's last victory.
2. **epaulette:** A shoulder ornament, particularly one bearing a soldier's rank.
3. **English poet:** William Shakespeare. The line appears in *Hamlet,* Act I, Scene II.

Chapter XXIII

1. **deed of assignment:** A written transfer of debt.

Chapter XXIV

1. *Coclès:* Cockeye.
2. **dropsy:** Edema; swelling from excessive accumulation of fluid in bodily tissue.
3. **spell of short commons:** To have little food for a time.

Chapter XXVI

1. **cicerone:** Guide of sightseers.
2. **Piazza del Popolo or the Campo Vaccino:** The people's square or the cow field.
3. **blunderbusses:** Short muskets with wide barrels and flaring muzzles, used to scatter shot at close range.
4. *Lachryma Christi:* Literally "Tears of Christ;" an Italian wine.

Chapter XXVII

1. *mazzolato:* Beaten to death with clubs.
2. *decapitato:* Decapitated.
3. **bull:** An official document issued by the pope.
4. **Pliny and Calpurnius:** Gaius Plinius Secundus, better known as Pliny the Elder, was an author and scientist who wrote *Naturalis Historia* and is generally regarded as the greatest naturalist of antiquity. Gaius Calpurnius Piso was a Roman statesman, orator, and patron of literature. Both lived in the first century A.D.
5. **Leopold Robert:** Louis-Leopold Robert (1794–1835) was a Swiss Neoclassical painter.

6. *Permesso:* May I have your permission?
7. *I signori francesi:* The French gentlemen.

Chapter XXVIII

1. **school of the Stoics:** A school of philosophy, founded by Zeno in about 308 B.C., advocating the calm acceptance of all occurrences as the unavoidable result of either divine will or the natural order.
2. **Callot's . . . temptation of St Antony:** Jacques Callot (1592–1635) was a painter and engraver admired by Romantic artists for the grotesque realism with which he portrayed suffering.
3. *pierrettes:* Characters in French pantomime, dressed in floppy white outfits.
4. *contadine:* Peasant.
5. *mascherata:* Masquerade.
6. *moccoletto:* A candle.
7. *pierrot:* Singular form of "pierrettes."
8. *barberi:* A popular event at the Roman carnival was the Barbary Race, run by Barbary horses, held at dusk on each day of the carnival. Barbaries are a North African breed, low and muscular.
9. **Aeolus:** The keeper of the winds in Greek mythology.
10. **Aquilo:** The god of the north wind in Greek mythology.

Chapter XXIX

1. **Colonnas:** A celebrated family that played an important role in Italy during medieval and Renaissance times.

2. **portcullis:** A grating of iron or wooden bars or slats suspended in the gateway of a fortified place and lowered to block passage.

3. **Columbarium:** A sepulchral chamber with niches for holding the ashes of the dead.

Chapter XXX

1. **Oran:** A city northwest of Algeria on the Gulf of Oran.

2. **Constantine:** A city in northeast Algeria east of Algiers.

3. **yataghan:** A Turkish sword or scimitar having a double-curved blade and an eared pommel, and without a handle guard.

4. **Klagmann:** Jean-Baptiste Klagmann (1810–1867) was a sculptor who worked on the decoration of the Théâtre historique, founded by Dumas in 1847.

5. **Marochetti:** Charles Marochetti (1805–62) was one of the most noted sculptors of his day.

6. **Ariosto:** An Italian writer known primarily for his comic epic poem *Orlando Furioso* (1532).

7. **dandy:** A man who affects extreme elegance in clothing and manners.

8. **postilions:** Riders of post-horses; swift messengers.

9. ***bonbonnière:*** Pillbox.

10. **Tullia or Poppaea:** Tullia d'Aragona (ca.1510–1556) was a courtesan and poet who wrote in praise of passionate love. Poppaea Sabina (d. A.D. 65) was the second wife of the Roman Emperor Nero, over whom she was said to have great influence. Nero is believed to have kicked her to death in a fit of temper.

Chapter XXXI

1. **Mitidja Plains:** A plain west of Algeria.
2. **Atlas Mountains:** A system of ranges and plateaus of northwest Africa extending from southwest Morocco to northern Tunisia and between the Sahara Desert and the Mediterranean Sea.
3. **perspicacious:** Shrewd.

Chapter XXXII

1. **trebled:** Tripled.

Chapter XXXIII

1. **chibouque:** Turkish tobacco pipe with a long stem and a red clay bowl.

Chapter XXXIV

1. **narghile:** Hookah.
2. **Epirus:** An ancient country on the Ionian Sea encompassing what is now northwest Greece and southern Albania. It flourished in the third century B.C. and was later a Roman province. Once again an independent state after 1204, Epirus was conquered by the Turks in the 1600s.
3. **Parian marble:** Marble quarried on the Greek island of Páros; highly valued in ancient times for use in sculptures.
4. **Pindus and Olympia:** Mount Pindus and Mount Olympus, two mountains in northern Greece.

Chapter XXXVI

1. **King Mithridates:** Mithridates VI Eupator "the Great," King of Pontus (123–63 B.C.). In addition to speaking twenty-two languages, he was said to be an expert on poisons.
2. **Cornelius Nepos:** A Roman historian from the first century B.C. known for the biographies he authored.
3. **alembics:** Devices for distillation.

Chapter XXXVII

1. **lorgnette:** A pair of eyeglasses with a single short handle.
2. **Hayti:** Haiti.

Chapter XXXVIII

1. **palings:** Pickets; pointed sticks used to make a fence.
2. ***bouillotte:*** A card game.

Chapter XLII

1. **Apicius:** Parcus Gabius Apicius was a first-century Roman known as a lavish host.
2. ***cupitor impossibilium***: He who desires the impossible.
3. **tilbury:** A light, two-wheeled open carriage for two people.
4. **nabob:** A wealthy and prominent person.

Chapter XLV

1. **Queen Mab or Titania:** Fairy queens who appear in Shakespeare. Mab is mentioned in *Romeo and Juliet*, and Titania is a character in *A Midsummer Night's Dream*. Queen Mab is also the subject of a poem by Romantic poet Percy Bysshe Shelley, and Titania appears in the work of fellow Romantic William Blake.

2. *le Diable Boiteux: The Lame Devil*, a ballet that debuted in 1836.

3. *cachucha:* A Spanish solo dance, performed in *le Diable Boiteux*.

4. **cynosure:** The focal point of attention and admiration.

Chapter XLVIII

1. **hoar-frost:** Frozen dew.

Chapter L

1. **King Charles . . . Catherine de' Medici . . . St Bartholomew:** The powerful Catherine de' Medici was Queen Regent during the reign of her son, King Charles IX of France. Charles fell under the influence of the French Huguenot leader Gaspard de Coligny. To regain control, Catherine orchestrated the massacre of St Bartholomew's Day, in which Coligny and thousands of other Huguenots were murdered.

2. **arabesques:** A complex, ornate design of intertwined floral, foliate, and geometric figures.

5. **firman:** In some Eastern countries, a firman is a decree or mandate issued by the sovereign.

Chapter LI

1. **calumnies:** Utterances of slander.

Chapter LVI

1. **perfidies:** Acts of treachery.

Chapter LXIV

1. **ebullition:** Boiling.

Chapter LXV

1. **Croesus:** From Greek mythology, King Croesus of Lydia was known for his wealth and the prosperity of his kingdom.

Chapter LXVI

1. **daughter of Jairus:** In Luke 8:40-56, Jesus raises the daughter of the rabbi Jairus from the dead, saying she was not dead but only sleeping.

Chapter LXVII

1. **post-chaise:** A closed, four-wheeled, horse-drawn carriage used to carry both mail and passengers.
2. **Lamouricière:** Christophe Leon Louis Juchault de Lamorcière (1806–1865) was a general who

played a critical role in the French conquest of Algeria.

3. **Changarnier:** Nicolas Changarnier (1793–1877) was a general and politician who served briefly as governor of Algeria.

Chapter LXVIII

1. **assizes:** Court sessions.

Chapter LXX

1. **cupidity:** Excessive desire or greed.
2. *au revoir:* Good-bye.

INTERPRETIVE NOTES

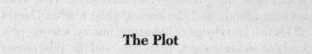

The Plot

The adventure begins with the young sailor Edmond Dantès returning home to Marseilles from a journey aboard the *Pharaon*. Dantès's boss, M. Morrel, plans to make Dantès the *Pharaon*'s next captain. While home between voyages, Dantès and his love, Mercédès, plan to marry.

All Dantès's success has earned him some jealous enemies. The purser of his ship, Danglars, wants to become the captain of the *Pharaon;* Fernand Mondego is in love with Dantès's fiancée; his neighbor Caderousse is simply envious that Dantès is so much luckier in life than he has been. Together, these three men write a letter accusing Dantès of treason. They say Dantès is at present carrying a letter from Napoleon to a group of Bonapartist sympathizers in Paris, which he means to deliver to fulfill the dying wish of the

Pharaon's captain. On what is to be his wedding day, Dantès is arrested.

The public prosecutor, Villefort, sees that Dantès is being framed and is prepared to set him free, but changes his mind when he learns the letter is meant for his own father, a Bonapartist. Rather than risk having rumors of his father's treason circulating, Villefort sends Dantès to prison for life.

Morrel makes several unsuccessful attempts to have Dantes freed. While in prison, Dantès meets a fellow prisoner, the aged Abbé Faria. After hearing his young counterpart's story, the abbé is able to deduce who is responsible for Dantès's incarceration. The two become friends, and the learned abbé teaches Dantès all his vast knowledge of literature, history, science, philosophy, and languages. Years pass, and the abbé comes to think of Dantès as a son, and reveals to him the location of an immense treasure. When Faria dies, Dantès hides in the abbé's death shroud, and is carried out as a presumed corpse fourteen years after his arrest. He finds the treasure on the Isle of Monte Cristo and begins to formulate his revenge.

Disguised as an Italian priest, Dantès returns to Marseilles and calls on Caderousse, now a struggling innkeeper. Caderousse provides the details of the plot to frame Dantès, as well as of the fates of his loved ones and enemies. His father has starved to death, and Mercédès has married Fernand Mondego; Danglars and Mondego have both become rich and powerful and now live in Paris.

Before undertaking his revenge, Dantès rewards the one family that remained true to him. He saves the Morrel firm from financial disaster by anonymously repaying debts, replacing a lost ship and its cargo, and providing a valuable diamond as a dowry for Morrel's daughter.

Ten years later, Dantès emerges in Rome as the Count of Monte Cristo, a rich, eccentric, powerful, mysterious man. He befriends Albert de Morcerf, the son of Fernand Mondego and Mercédès, and intervenes to save him from ransom-seeking bandits. Albert welcomes the Count warmly three months later in Paris, where Albert is happy to introduce his exotic friend into Parisian society. There, the Count meets his old cohorts Danglars, Mondego, and Villefort, and easily enters their lives.

With his obsessive thirst for vengeance, knowledge about his enemies' weaknesses, along with his limitless resources, the Count sets about orchestrating each man's downfall.

Characters

Edmond Dantès/Count of Monte Cristo. Dantès begins as a successful, fortunate young sailor from Marseilles. Jealous rivals get him imprisoned on grounds that he is a threat to the crown. While in prison for fourteen years, he receives the education of an aristocrat from a fellow prisoner, the Abbé Faria. His years in prison also allow him to obsess about avenging himself upon those who wronged him. The means to effect his revenge come from the abbé himself, who shares with Dantès the location of the treasure of Monte Cristo. After Dantès escapes, he dedicates himself to rewarding those who were faithful to him and destroying those responsible for his misery. He believes in the divine righteousness of his cause, and pursues it as the Count of Monte Cristo.

Mercédès Herrara/Countess de Morcerf. Dantès's fiancée at the beginning of the novel, she is part of the reason for the betrayal. Her cousin Fernand is in love with her and wants to remove the competition from Dantès. She marries Fernand and bears his son, Albert.

Abbé Faria. He is Dantès's fellow political prisoner and friend at the Château d'If, becoming like a second father to him. He transforms Dantès into the Count by teaching him everything he knows and by revealing the location of the treasure of Monte Cristo.

Fernand Mondego/Count de Morcerf. He is the cousin of Mercédès, later her husband and the father of Albert de Morcerf. Jealousy over Mercédès's preference for Dantès prompts him to conspire with Danglars to incriminate Dantès. Known publicly as a military hero, he has actually earned his fortune by betraying the Pasha of Janina, Haydee's father.

Monsieur Danglars/Baron Danglars. Originally the purser on the same ship as Dantès, he is led by professional envy to convince Fernand to help get rid of their rival. He becomes a well-known, respected, and extremely wealthy banker and baron in Paris. His daughter is Eugénie.

Caderousse. Dantès's neighbor in Marseilles, he is an inadvertent accomplice in Dantès's betrayal by Fernand and Danglars.

Monsieur de Villefort. The ambitious public prosecutor of Marseilles, he sends Dantès to prison to protect his own name and advance his career. Later living in Paris, he has a daughter, Valentine, by his first wife, and a son, Edward, by his second wife.

Monsieur Morrel. He is initially Dantès's employer, and his only supporter after his arrest. His children are Julie and Maximilian.

Louis Dantès. Dantès's father, he is a proud, honorable man who starves to death soon after his son is imprisoned.

Maximilian Morrel. M. Morrel's son, he is in love with Valentine de Villefort.

Albert de Morcerf. He is the son of Mercédès and Fernand, who brings the Count into Paris society after having met him in Rome. He is initially engaged to marry Eugénie Danglars.

Valentine de Villefort. Villefort's daughter by his first wife, she is engaged to Franz d'Epinay but secretly in love with Maximilian Morrel.

Monsieur de Noirtier. Villefort's father, a senator, and a staunch Bonapartist, he has suffered a stroke that leaves him paralyzed and unable to speak, yet he is his granddaughter Valentine's protector and advocate.

Haydee. This teenage girl is the Count's slave and ultimately his love. He has bought her as a weapon against the Count de Morcerf, who betrayed her father, Ali Tebelin, the Pasha of Janina, and sold her into slavery. She is wholly devoted to the Count, and refuses to leave him even after he has freed her.

Madame Héloise de Villefort. Villefort's second wife is the mother of Edward, their young son.

Doctor d'Avrigny. Villefort's physician.

Julie Morrel. Maximilian's sister and Emmanuel Herbault's wife.

Emmanuel Herbault. Julie's husband, a former clerk for M. Morrel.

Madame Danglars. Baron Danglars's wife and Eugénie's mother.

Eugénie Danglars. The daughter of Baron and Mme Danglars, she is initially engaged to marry Albert, but then becomes engaged to Benedetto/Andrea Cavalcanti.

Louise d'Armilly. Eugénie Danglars's music teacher and constant companion.

Benedetto/Andrea Cavalcanti. He is presented as a wealthy young nobleman and becomes engaged to Eugénie Danglars.

Lucien Debray. The private secretary to the French Minister of the Interior, he is also Mme Danglars's lover.

Ali. The Count's mute Nubian slave, he is an expert with all sorts of weapons.

Bertuccio. The Count of Monte Cristo's Corsican steward.

Luigi Vampa. An Italian bandit, indebted to the Count of Monte Cristo.

Major Cavalcanti. An adventurer styled as a phony Italian nobleman.

Edward de Villefort. Villefort's spoiled young son, by his second wife.

Franz d'Épinay. The son of General Quesnel, he is Albert's friend and traveling companion in Italy as well as Valentine's initial fiancé.

Marquis and Marquise de Saint-Méran. The parents of Villefort's first wife, both of whom are murdered.

Jacopo. The smuggler who rescues Dantès from the sea after he escapes from prison, he later becomes the captain of Monte Cristo's yacht.

Themes, Motifs, and Symbols

The main theme of *The Count of Monte Cristo* is that of divine retribution. When Dantès escapes from prison and finds his treasure, he sees it as a sign that God has opened for him the door of revenge. He ultimately realizes that his vengeance is destroying the innocent as well as the guilty. In his final letter to Maximilian, he asks him to ". . . pray for a man who, like Satan, believed for one moment he was the equal of God, but who now acknowledges in all Christian humility that in God alone is supreme power and infinite wisdom" (pp. 619–20).

Names: In *The Count of Monte Cristo,* many characters go by more than one name, with their aliases signifying changes in the characters themselves. Dantès has one identity for benevolence and another for revenge, and both are his own creations. Villefort changes his name to distance himself from his father, and Fernand and Danglars both adopt titles as their power grows.

Suicide: Dantès, M. Morrel, Maximilian Morrel, Haydee, Fernand Mondego, and Mme de Villefort all consider, or actually perform, an act of suicide during the course of the narrative. Suicide is presented as an honorable and reasonable response to any devastating situation.

Politics: Key plot elements in *The Count of Monte Cristo* are provided by real political events. The characters' political beliefs tell the reader about their true identities. Aristocratic royalists, such as Morcerf and Villefort, are unsympathetic, while the sympathetic characters, like Noirtier and Maximilian, have connections to Bonapartists and democracy.

The Sea: When Dantès escapes from prison, he is thrown into the ocean. It is a baptism of sorts, signifying the end of the innocent Edmond Dantès and the birth of the vengeful Count.

The Red Silk Purse: First used by Morrel in his attempt to save Dantès's father, Dantès later uses the purse when he saves Morrel. The red silk purse is the physical connection between good deeds and reward. Julie Morrel later emphasizes the symbolic power of the purse by keeping it on display as an emblem of her family's salvation.

CRITICAL EXCERPTS

"Works of Alexandre Dumas." *North American Review* 61, no. 118, January 1843, pp. 109–37.

A review of the four-volume *Œuvres d'Alexandre Dumas*, written before *The Three Musketeers* and *The Count of Monte Cristo* were published. It is an indictment of all literature written for mass appeal as much as of Dumas himself, a stance unlikely to have changed after reading the author's masterworks, which appeared soon afterward.

"Our present subject is not equally attractive (as George Sand), for Dumas falls far short of Madame Dudevant in inventive genius and mastery of style. But his plays and novels show much talent, and afford very striking illustrations of the extraordinary *bouleversement*[1] of taste and opinion, which is now exhibited by the reading public of France. The fertility of his pen, and the variety of subjects which he has treated, show a very ready and productive mind,

---

[1] upheaval

stimulated by the public demand, and bent on reaping a present harvest from his popularity, rather than establishing a permanent reputation. . . . A literature created for the people, if not by them, must always be characterized by greater energy and simplicity, by more excitement and a broader license, and by less polish and refinement, than one which is destined for a learned and aristocratic class. . . .

". . . (Dumas's novels) belong to the mass of indifferent fictions, which the press of France, England, and America is now sending forth in vast profusion, adapted for a great multitude of uninstructed readers, who seem to find nothing better than the perusal of such trash for the amusement of their leisure hours."

"Historical Romance—Alexandre Dumas." *British Quarterly Review* 7, no. 13, February 1848, pp. 181–204.

A discussion of the historical romance, and how Dumas's background, personality, and writing style made him the king of the genre.

"Style he has none; but he has an easy, agreeable, off-hand manner, destitute of pretension, and possessing in an extraordinary degree the excellent union of minute detail with rapidity. His dialogue, unless when the passions are called into play, or when the more ideal characteristics of man are touched on, is always very life-like, gay, sparkling, and rapid. His characters are always happily presented, though never deeply conceived, or minutely analysed. They have somewhat the merit of Scott's portraits, only more superficial. Passion he has none; nor has he much humour; but considerable gaiety and a good eye for the picturesque. . . . But his great art lies in the power of minutely yet vividly painting a long scene of adventure or of intrigue, so that it stands before you with almost unrivalled precision.

"Probability is a thing he utterly sets at naught; and this is the great deficit and drawback of *Monte Christo*, where the *incredulus odi*[2] rises in the reader's mind at every chapter. This improbability is the more unpardonable as it is accomplished with great power of accurate delineation of the situations this improbability brought about; but when we reflect upon the rapidity with which he writes, and on the gross indifference of his multitude of readers to anything beyond the sensation of the moment, we are not to wonder at this defect."

Haywood, Adam. "Alexandre Dumas." *Quarterly Review* 131, no. 261, July 1871, pp. 189–229.

A review of *Mémoires d'Alexandre Dumas*, Dumas's autobiography. This review was written shortly after Dumas's death, and considers his body of work and the legacy he has earned.

"A title to fame, like a chain of proofs, may be cumulative. It may rest on the multiplicity and universality of production and capacity. Voltaire, for example, who symbolizes an age, produced no one work in poetry or prose that approximates to first rate in its kind, if we except 'Candide' and 'Zadig;' and their kind is not the first. Dumas must be judged by the same standard; as one who was at everything in the

---

[2]"Being incredulous, I cannot endure it."

ring, whose foot was ever in the stirrup, whose lance was ever in the rest, who infused new life into the acting drama, indefinitely extended the domain of fiction, and (in his 'Impressions de Voyage') invented a new literature of the road. So judged—as he will be, when French criticism shall raise its drooping head and have time to look about it—he will certainly rank as one of the three or four most popular, influential, and gifted writers that the France of the nineteenth century has produced."

Oliphant, Margaret. "Alexandre Dumas." *Blackwood's Edinburgh Magazine* 114, no. 693, July 1873, pp. 111–30.

Oliphant writes in praise of Dumas's life and work, in response to the unflattering *Life and Adventures of Alexandre Dumas*, published in London in 1873 by Percy Fitzgerald.

"The Count de Monte Christo, however, is not so delightful as Edmond Dantes; and though there is the same wild charm of rapid incident and sensation, the same breathless brilliancy of dialogue and interest of situation, the narrative of Monte Christo's vengeance has nothing like the delightful novelty and wholesome stir and bustle of the 'Trois Mousquetaires.' . . . we feel that Monte Christo himself is very poor and petty in many of his expedients, cruel without dignity, and spiteful rather than terrible. . . . We find no feature in him of the Edmond Dantes whose wrongs we felt as if they were our own, and to whom we could accord the right of punishing his enemies. On the contrary, it is altogether a new being, a stranger to us, who steps on to the stage like a magician, and whom we cannot identify. This is the great mistake of the book, a greater mistake than the fact that Monte Christo goes much too far, that his vengeance is diabolical, and his heart unnaturally hard, which was no doubt according to the author's intentions—who meant to show us not only the pleasure and satisfactoriness, but at the same time the unsuccess and evil tendencies of revenge."

Saintsbury, George. *A Short History of French Literature*. Oxford: Clarendon Press, 1901, pp. 508–11.
An overview of French literature from medieval times through the end of the nineteenth century.

"Dumas' dramatic work is of but late value as literature properly so called. His forte is the already mentioned playwright's instinct, as it may be termed, which made him almost invariably choose and conduct his action in a manner so interesting and absorbing to the audience that they had no time to think of the merits of the style, propriety of the morals, the congruity of the sentiments. His plays, in short, are meant to be acted, not to be read. Of his novels many are disfigured by long passages of the inferior work to be expected by mere hack assistants, by unskillful insertions of passages from his authorities, and sometimes by plagiarisms so audacious and flagrant that the reader takes them as little less than an insult. . . . The style is not more remarkable as such than that of the dramas; there is not always, or often, a well-defined plot, and the characters are drawn only in the broadest outline. But the cunning admixture of inci-

dent and dialogue by which Dumas carries on the
interest of his gigantic narrations without wearying
the reader is a secret of his own, and has never been
thoroughly mastered by anyone else."

Bradford, Gamaliel. "Alexandre Dumas." *A Naturalist
of Souls.* Cambridge: Riverside Press, 1926.

Bradford uses Dumas as one of many studies in psy-
chography, "the condensed, essential, artistic presentation of character."

"Even in Hugo, in Balzac, in Flaubert, in Zola, one
has an uneasy feeling that melodrama is not too far
away. In Dumas it is frankly present always. The situation—something that shall tear the nerves, make
the heart leap and the breath stop—for Dumas there
lies the true art of dramatist and novelist. And what
situations! No one ever had more than he the two
great dramatic gifts, which perhaps are only one, the
gift of preparation and the gift of climax. . . .

"Dumas's style has been much abused, and in
some ways deserves it. Mr. Saintsbury considers that
the plays have 'but little value as literature properly
so-called,' and that 'the style of the novels is not
more remarkable as such than that of the dramas.'
But how far more discerning and sympathetic is
Stevenson's characterization of it: 'Light as a
whipped trifle, strong as silk; wordy like a village
tale; pat like a general's dispatch; with every fault,
yet never tedious; with no merit, yet inimitably
right.'"

Reed, F. W. *A Bibliography of Alexandre Dumas Père.*
Middlesex, England: J. A. Neuhuys, 1933, p. 174.

An annotated bibliography of the complete works of Alexandre Dumas.

"[*The Count of Monte Cristo*] is perhaps the outstanding work of fiction to reveal the futility of human vengeance, even when it attains its utmost completeness. Maurice Baring calls it the most popular book in the world (presumably meaning in literature as such).

"Dumas commenced with the Roman episodes, with intent that all the earlier portion dealing with the imprisonment, the treasure and the escape should be narrated by one of the characters. It was Maquet who, by strenuous insistence, persuaded him to alter this and make the story begin as it now does at Marseilles. Maquet was undoubtedly the collaborator, for Dumas states that they talked the plan over together, and moreover Maquet helped with at least the latter portions; and with the first volumes, which are said to have been written at lightning speed at Trouville."

Bell, A. Craig. "1844—Annus Mirabilis." *Alexandre Dumas: A Biography and Study*. London: Cassell & Co. Ltd., 1950.

A history and analysis of the life and works of Alexandre Dumas.

"On the completion of the second volume [of *The Count of Monte Cristo*] Dumas began sending his [manuscript] to the *Débats*, and on June 28, while *Les Trois Mousquetaires* was running in its last installments in the *Siécle*, the first issue of *Le Comte de Monte-Cristo* appeared.

"The result has passed into legend. The Musketeers, even, were eclipsed. Instalments [*sic*] were followed and devoured by a breathless France. Long queues waited for each fresh number of the journal. In the provinces the arrival of the stage coach that carried it was the occasion for the gathering of small crowds at the posting-houses. Readers, unable to wait, wrote for solutions in advance. If an installment were delayed, France cried out. The highest intellects and most omnivorous readers alike came under its spell. Villemessant, one of the most celebrated journalists of his time, confessed that he woke his wife in the early hours to tell her that Dantès had escaped."

Butler, Kathleen T. "The Romantic Drama." *A History of French Literature*. London: Methuen & Co. Ltd., 1966.

In volume II of her history, Butler explores French literature from the revolution through the early twentieth century, with extensive attention to the Romantic movement in philosophy, poetry, drama, fiction, history, and criticism.

"Most French literary historians either disregard Dumas' novels altogether, or dismiss them with a few contemptuous remarks as being unworthy of the name of literature. It is true that he was neither a stylist nor a psychologist, that he had little historical imagination, and that, as he himself puts it, he only used history as a nail on which to hang his pictures. Yet a better story-teller never existed. From the first page to the last he knows how to arouse and hold his readers' interests, and to carry them along in the spirit of high adventure. His dialogue is lively and dramatic, and like Scott, he introduces it as no mere *hors d'œuvre,* but as a means of carrying forward the story."

Kunitz, Stanley, and Vineta Colby, eds. *European Authors: 1000–1900.* New York: The H. W. Wilson Company, 1967.

A dictionary of European literature covering nearly a thousand writers over the course of nine centuries.

"Dumas has been reproached by some critics for careless writing, absurd situations and lack of taste, but all have valued his abounding imagination and portrayal of action. Lamartine declared, 'You are superhuman.' Anatole France wrote to the son, 'Your father amused me!': this, after all, was the declared intention of that father. Michelet wrote to him, 'Monsieur, I love you and admire you, because you are one of the forces of nature.'"

Stowe, Richard S. *Alexandre Dumas (père).* Boston: G. K. Hall & Co., 1976.

A biography of Dumas from the Twayne's World Authors series.

"*Le Comte de Monte-Cristo,* we are frequently reminded, is not a historical novel but a *roman de moeurs*—a novel of manners. The story Dumas tells here was not remote from the first audience to which it was addressed; quite the contrary, the bulk of its action was placed squarely in contemporary time and in the city where most of its first readers lived. . . .

"The most immediately obvious realism is in its settings. From the opening scene on, especially in parts one and three, places are identified and identifiable. All the landmarks of the harbor at Marseilles are named as the *Pharaon* approaches the port and passes them one by one, then streets and squares of the city as Dantès hastens first to see his father, then to the Catalan village to find Mercédès. . . .

"Dumas's realism goes beyond geography, however; it extends to characters, events and milieux as well. Other real persons besides *maître* Pastrini figure in the novel in imagined roles or by way of allusion: the imaginary Haydée, for example, is the daughter of the real Ali Pasha of Janina and is received in the Luxembourg palace by a real *Président de la Chambre des Paris*. . . .

"Maquet's notes reveal with what meticulous care the relationships and psychology of the characters were prepared so that this aspect of the book too would be convincing. Behavior is always believable without being predictable. . . .

"A final realistic element—though it may not at first seem to be one—is the plot, which is drawn, as we have seen, from a true story. . . .

"If the reader believes in this reality of setting and situations, if he finds the characters and motives human and credible, then he will be much more ready to accept the impossible as possible. At every point it is clear that Dumas is working from this assumption."

McDermott, Emily A. "Classical Allusion in *The Count of Monte Cristo.*" *Classical and Modern Literature: A Quarterly* 8, no. 2, Winter 1988, pp. 93–103.

An analysis of references to classical literature in Dumas's *The Count of Monte Cristo*.

"[A]lthough the majority of classical allusions in *The Count of Monte Cristo* are casual, aimed at display of authorial learning and replication of the kind of wittily erudite conversation which, one must assume, was de rigueur among the French upper class of Dumas's time, others are used in subtler and more thematically significant ways. The comparison of Villefort's executionary ruminations to those of Tarquinius Superbus colors the chapter in which several protagonists' doom is prepared, heightening the reader's sense of the disaster to come. Two early allusions (the first Brutus analogy and the reference to the *Aeneid*) prefigure Villefort's peripeteia from the heights of control and success to the nadir of defeated insanity. Conversely, the apparent prefiguring contained within the Pyramus/Thisbe analogy—which proves to be false, in that the foreshadowed doom does not actually befall Maximilian and Valentine—serves not only to heighten the suspense felt by the reader in anticipation of the outcome of events, but also subtly to call into question the moral premise upon which the Count's course of vengeance is based. All in all, Dumas's use of classical allusion suggests that, beyond being no mean reader of the classics, he exhibits in his writing an artful knack for turning the old to new and interesting use."

Levi, Anthony. *Guide to French Literature: 1789 to the Present*. Chicago: St. James Press, 1992, pp. 202–13.

An encyclopedia of French writers since the French Revolution.

"Literacy was on the upswing and rose from 40 per cent in 1820 to almost universal literacy of a sort by 1865, as a result of the Guizot and Falloux acts from 1833–35. Dumas was not writing on the whole for literary reviews, but needed to help Girardin, Véron, and Perrée, who took over *Le Siècle* from Dutacq in 1840, to penetrate to the lowest levels of literacy. Véron rescued *Le Constitutionnel* without fighting Girardin and Perrée on their price cuts, by printing Eugène Sue. He increased the circulation from 3,600 in 1844 to nearly 25,000 in 1846, well behind *Le Siècle*, which had a circulation of 33,000, but ahead of *La Presse* with 22,000, an untypical four fifths of whom lived outside Paris. At the same date the circulation of the *Journal des débats* was 9,300, about two thirds from outside Paris. . . . France's literary artists, like Flaubert, had to move on and write for a small, reflective, upper middle-class elite. Its mass producers, like Dumas, had to become more concerned with entrepreneurial contracts, commercialized publishing, machine-made paper, and mechanical inking."

France, Peter, ed. *The New Oxford Companion to Literature in French*. Oxford: Clarendon Press, 1995.

An encyclopedia of writers, writings, cultural movements, and popular culture from not just France but also the entire French-speaking world, including Africa, Haiti, Quebec, and Belgium.

"*Le Comte de Monte-Cristo* had an immense success and marked a high point of the fashion for the *roman-feuilleton*.[3] As with many of his other novels, it was written in collaboration with Auguste Maquet, who provided Dumas with chapter plans and historical and factual material. . . . Dumas drew on his own previous revenge novel *Georges* (1843) and on the *cause célèbre* of François Picaud, who, wrongfully imprisoned under the Empire, returned after 1814 to exact violent retribution on his accusers. . . . [Edmond Dantès's] campaign of revenge becomes an epic conflict between good and evil, as Dantès, the agent of Providence, destroys high-society schemers and crooks. . . . Dantès is a Byronic hero and sweet revenge is complicated by a gnawing sense of guilt."

Kaplan, Justin. "Treasure and Vengeance." *American Scholar* 72, no. 2, Spring 2003, pp. 140–42.

This essay is a Pulitzer Prize winner's reflection on how *The Count of Monte Cristo,* which he discovered and cherished in his teens, has remained relevant and important to him as he has matured.

"Without much of a stretch, Freud and Jung could have gone to town with the components of this story, not excluding its Oedipal drama. I saw that, like a father, the aged Abbé Faria imparts to Edmond—his sole heir—knowledge, power, pride, manhood, and the secret that will transform him. Edmond assists at his father's death and literally displaces him from his shroud. Edmond's education is itself a rebirth, one of the most prepotent of archetypes. You could see the

3serial romance

burlap sack as a womb—even an amniotic sack, given the watery medium for Edmond's escape. Slitting the burial sack, Edmond delivers himself, like a surgeon doing a Caesarean, and rises to the surface, reborn and baptized a free man, with a new identity and the world is his to conquer . . .

"One other adult resonance for me: Dumas is careful to point out that when Edmond makes his escape he is thirty-three years old, a canonical age for starting over."

QUESTIONS FOR DISCUSSION

Is the Count of Monte Cristo like the vigilante heroes of modern movies and television? How is he different? How is his quest for revenge different?

In what sense is Abbé Faria Dantès's second father? Why do you think Faria emphasized the ways a man could use the treasure to help his friends?

Do you think the Count arranged Albert's kidnapping in Rome? Did the kidnapping further his revenge?

Why do you think the Count does not make any efforts to win back Mercédès once he is free? What effect on the Count does Haydee's love have?

Describe how *The Count of Monte Cristo* plays upon the nineteenth-century French obsession with exotic things. How is the Count of Monte Cristo's adoption of

Eastern culture and society reflected in his treatment of his friends and enemies?

Edmond Dantès takes on a number of aliases during the course of the novel, and many other characters have a variety of names as well. What do you consider to be the significance of names in *The Count of Monte Cristo*? Can you speculate on the meaning of each of Edmond Dantès's assumed names?

Madame Danglars and Mercédès are peers in the story. In what ways are they similar? Do their behaviors contrast? What roles do they play in the revenge on their husbands?

Monte Cristo tells Mercédès, "The sins of the fathers shall fall upon their children." Does he adhere to that philosophy in taking his revenge?

Consider Edmond's personal character at the novel's beginning and at its end. What has he lost? What has he gained? Is he satisfied with what he has done?

The last words that Monte Cristo utters to Maximilian are "Wait and hope." What does he mean? What is the significance of this statement?

SUGGESTIONS FOR THE INTERESTED READER

If you like *The Count of Monte Cristo,* you might also be interested in the following:

The Count of Monte Cristo (DVD, VHS, 1999). A French miniseries production of the novel starring Gerard Depardieu. It is very faithful to the novel, unlike most productions.

The Three Musketeers, by Alexandre Dumas (1844). This equally famous novel by Dumas is full of swashbuckling fun.

Napoleon's Road to Glory, by J. David Markham (2003). This fast-paced biography is an enjoyable introduction to the life of one of the most important figures of the nineteenth century.

BESTSELLING ENRICHED CLASSICS

JANE EYRE
Charlotte Brontë
0-671-01479-X
$5.99

WUTHERING HEIGHTS
Emily Brontë
0-7434-8764-8
$4.95

THE GOOD EARTH
Pearl S. Buck
0-671-51012-6
$6.99

**THE AWAKENING AND
SELECTED STORIES**
Kate Chopin
0-7434-8767-2
$4.95

**HEART OF DARKNESS
AND *THE SECRET SHARER***
Joseph Conrad
0-7434-8765-6
$4.95

GREAT EXPECTATIONS
Charles Dickens
0-7434-8761-3
$4.95

A TALE OF TWO CITIES
Charles Dickens
0-7434-8760-5
$4.95

**THE COUNT OF
MONTE CRISTO**
Alexandre Dumas
0-7434-8755-9
$6.50

10210 (1 of 2)

Introducing the Enriched Classics Books-for-Schools Program*

Get your school involved!

The Enriched Classics Books-for-Schools Program is a great way for teachers, students, and other school representatives to earn **FREE** books for the school library or for classroom use.

How does the Enriched Classics Books-for-Schools Program work?

1. Collect five Enriched Classics proof-of-purchase symbols like the one found at the bottom of this page.
2. Download the Enriched Classics Books-for-Schools official request form from simonsays.com by typing the ISBN for this book (found on the back cover) into the search function and clicking "go." Click on the Enriched Classics book cover that appears. When the next screen appears, click on the link for the official request form. Print out the official request form.
3. Fully complete the official request form.
4. Mail the fully completed official request form plus your five Enriched Classics proof-of-purchase symbols to:

Enriched Classics Books-for-Schools Program
Simon & Schuster, 1230 Avenue of the Americas, New York, NY 10020

...and Simon & Schuster will send your school the Enriched Classics book of your choice—**FREE!**

*All Enriched Classics titles published in 2004 feature this special offer.

Get a free copy of an Enriched Classics book when you submit five proof-of-purchase symbols for previously purchased Enriched Classics books and a fully completed Enriched Classics Books-for-Schools official request form. This offer is only open to schools through their representatives (i.e., a student representative or administrator on behalf of the school) or school employees. Please submit all five proof-of-purchase symbols at one time. Please allow 10-12 weeks for delivery. Delivery cannot be guaranteed unless you include your zip code on the official request form. The Books-for-Schools Program is valid in the U.S., Canada (void in Quebec), and Puerto Rico while supplies last. Enriched Classics proof-of-purchase symbols may not be reproduced.

Void where prohibited or otherwise restricted by law. All submissions become the property of Simon & Schuster and will not be returned. Simon & Schuster is not responsible for lost, late, illegible, incomplete, postage-due, or misdirected forms or mail. Requests not complying with all offer requirements will not be honored. Approximate retail value of Enriched Classics book is $3.95.

Offer may not be combined with any other offer.
Offer ends the earlier of April 30, 2005 or while supplies last.

ENRICHED
CLASSICS
Proof of Purchase

09745